Admiralty Record®

Volume 8

PUBLISHED ADMIRALTY OPINIONS OF
THE SUPREME COURT OF THE UNITED STATES AND
THE UNITED STATES COURTS OF APPEALS ISSUED DURING
THE CALENDAR YEAR

2020

Cite as: 8 Adm. R. _____

REPORTED BY KIRK N. AURANDT, ESQ.
MEMBER OF THE BAR IN LOUISIANA AND PENNSYLVANIA

ADMIRALTY RECORD PUBLISHING COMPANY, L.L.C.
MANDEVILLE, LOUISIANA, U.S.A.

ISSN 2334-5411
ISBN 978-1-7337790-4-3

Admiralty record: published admiralty opinions of the Supreme Court of the United States and the United States Courts of Appeals issued during the calendar year ... Mandeville, Louisiana, U.S.A.: Admiralty Record Publishing Company, LLC, 2014-

KF1104.A75
ISSN: 2334-5411

https://lccn.loc.gov/2014200303

PREFACE

Volume 8—the eighth annual edition of the Admiralty Record®—reports the published admiralty opinions of the Supreme Court of the United States and the United States Courts of Appeals that were issued during the calendar year 2020. The opinions reported are the original majority, concurring, and dissenting opinions of the Court, with only minor changes in formatting to better suit a dual-column presentation. The pagination found in the Court's original opinion is indicated by the number contained inside of black brackets, *see, e.g.*, **[—15—]**. The pagination found in the official Reporter is indicated by the number contained inside of black braces, *see, e.g.*, **{–15–}**. Also, where applicable, I have added parallel citations to opinions reported in this Volume and in prior Volumes of the Admiralty Record®.

The decision to select an opinion to appear in Volume 8 of the Admiralty Record® was made solely by me following an examination of those opinions that each of the above-named courts designated for publication in 2020. Every effort has been made to ensure inclusion of all 2020 federal appellate court admiralty opinions that were designated for publication; however, to the extent that a relevant admiralty opinion has been inadvertently overlooked or otherwise mistakenly omitted, the error is regretted and is solely my own. A few opinions from appeals in civil cases that technically may not have fallen under a federal district court's admiralty or maritime jurisdiction have been reported if they touched upon admiralty matters, or were otherwise deemed to be of potential interest to the admiralty practitioner. Additionally, several opinions from criminal cases involving maritime crimes and civil cases arising under the Federal Employers' Liability Act have been included.

To assist the reader in locating those opinions from 2020 involving subject matters of interest, I have prepared an Index to the opinions. I have also prepared Tables of Authority, which supply page references to the cases, statutes, and rules cited in each opinion. Prior to relying upon any of the opinions reported herein, the reader is reminded to verify the current status of any particular case as valid precedent by checking the case with a reliable citator.

Additional copies of the Admiralty Record® may be ordered at www.admiraltyrecord.com. I hope that the Admiralty Record® will continue to be a valuable and ready reference source for not only the admiralty practitioner, but for anyone who is interested in reading the published admiralty opinions of the federal appellate courts.

KIRK N. AURANDT, ESQ.

This page intentionally left blank

Table of Contents

(Cases arranged chronologically by Court)

This page intentionally left blank

Supreme Court of the United States

Supreme Court of the United States

No. 18-565

CITGO ASPHALT REFINING CO.
VS.
FRESCATI SHIPPING CO.

On Writ of Certiorari to the United States Court of Appeals for the Third Circuit

Decided: March 30, 2020

Citation: 589 U.S. ____, 140 S.Ct. 1081, 8 Adm. R. 2 (2020).

SOTOMAYOR, J., delivered the opinion of the Court, in which **ROBERTS, C.J.,** and **GINSBURG, BREYER, KAGAN, GORSUCH,** and **KAVANAUGH, JJ.,** joined. **THOMAS, J.,** filed a dissenting opinion, in which **ALITO, J.,** joined.

[—1—] {–1084–} SOTOMAYOR, J.: {–1085–}

In 2004, the M/T *Athos I*, a 748-foot oil tanker, allided[1] with a nine-ton anchor abandoned on the bed of the Delaware River. The anchor punctured the tanker's hull, causing 264,000 gallons of heavy crude oil to spill into the river. As required by federal statute, respondents Frescati Shipping Company—the *Athos I*'s owner—and the United States covered the costs of cleanup. They then sought to reclaim those costs from petitioners CITGO Asphalt Refining Company and others (collectively CARCO), which had chartered the *Athos I* for the voyage that occasioned the oil spill. According to Frescati and the United States, CARCO had breached a contractual "safe-berth clause" obligating CARCO **{–1086–}** to select a "safe" berth that would allow the *Athos I* to come and go "always safely afloat."

The question before us is whether the safe-berth clause is a warranty of safety, imposing liability for an unsafe berth **[—2—]** regardless of CARCO's diligence in selecting the berth. We hold that it is.

[1] An allision is "[t]he contact of a vessel with a stationary object such as an anchored vessel or a pier." Black's Law Dictionary 94 (11th ed. 2019).

I

A

During the relevant period, the *Athos I* was the subject of a series of contracts involving three parties: Frescati, Star Tankers, and CARCO. Frescati owned the *Athos I*. Star Tankers, an operator of tanker vessels, contracted with Frescati to charter the *Athos I* for a period of time. CARCO then contracted with Star Tankers to subcharter the *Athos I* for the inauspicious voyage resulting in the oil spill.

Pertinent here is the subcharter agreement between Star Tankers and CARCO. In admiralty, such contracts to charter a vessel are termed "charter parties." Like many modern charter parties, the agreement between Star Tankers and CARCO was based on a standard industry form contract. It drew essentially verbatim from a widely used template known as the ASBATANKVOY form, named after the Association of Ship Brokers & Agents (USA) Inc. (ASBA) trade association that publishes it.

At the core of the parties' dispute is a clause in the charter party requiring the charterer, CARCO, to designate a safe berth at which the vessel may load and discharge cargo. This provision, a standard feature of many charter parties, is customarily known as a safe-berth clause. The safe-berth clause here provides, as relevant, that "[t]he vessel shall load and discharge at any safe place or wharf, . . . which shall be designated and procured by the Charterer, provided the Vessel can proceed thereto, lie at, and depart therefrom always safely afloat, any lighterage being at the expense, risk and peril of the Charterer." Addendum to **[—3—]** Brief for Petitioners 8a.[2]

[2] The parties agree that the safe-berth clause also encompasses what is often referred to as a "safe-port clause." The safe-port clause here provides that "[t]he vessel . . . shall, with all convenient dispatch, proceed as ordered to Loading Port(s) named . . . , or so near thereunto as she may safely get (always afloat), . . . and being so loaded shall forthwith proceed, . . . direct to the Discharging Port[s], or so near thereunto as she may safely get (always afloat), and deliver said

The charter party separately requires CARCO to direct the *Athos I* to a "safe por[t]" along the Atlantic seaboard of the United States. *Id.*, at 24a.

Pursuant to the charter party, CARCO designated as the berth of discharge its asphalt refinery in Paulsboro, New Jersey, on the shore of the Delaware River. In November 2004, the *Athos I* set out on a 1,900-mile journey from Puerto Miranda, Venezuela, to Paulsboro, New Jersey, carrying a load of heavy crude oil. The vessel was in the final 900-foot stretch of its journey when an abandoned ship anchor in the Delaware River pierced two holes in the vessel's hull. Much of the *Athos I*'s freight drained into the river.

B

After the Exxon-Valdez oil spill in 1989, Congress passed the Oil Pollution Act of 1990 (OPA), 104 Stat. 484, 33 U. S. C. §2701 *et seq.*, to promote the prompt cleanup of oil spills. To that end, OPA deems certain entities responsible for the costs of oil-spill cleanups, regardless of fault. §2702(a). It then limits the liability **{–1087–}** of such "responsible part[ies]" if they (among other things) timely assist with cleanup efforts. §2704. Responsible parties that comply with the statutory conditions receive a reimbursement from the Oil Spill Liability Trust Fund (Fund), operated by the Federal Government, for any cleanup costs exceeding a statutory limit. §2708; see also §2704.

Although a statutorily responsible party must pay cleanup costs without regard to fault, it may pursue legal **[—4—]** claims against any entity allegedly at fault for an oil spill. §§2710, 2751(e). So may the Fund: By reimbursing a responsible party, the Fund becomes subrogated to the responsible party's rights (up to the amount reimbursed to the responsible party) against any third party allegedly at fault for the incident. §§2712(f), 2715(a).

As owner of the *Athos I*, Frescati was deemed a "responsible party" for the oil spill under OPA. Frescati worked with the U. S. Coast Guard in cleanup efforts and covered the costs of the cleanup. As a result, Frescati's liability was statutorily limited to $45 million, and the Fund reimbursed Frescati for an additional $88 million that Frescati paid in cleanup costs.

C

Following the cleanup, Frescati and the United States each sought recovery against CARCO: Frescati sought to recover the cleanup costs not reimbursed by the Fund, while the United States sought to recover the amount disbursed by the Fund. As relevant here, both Frescati and the United States claimed that CARCO had breached the safe-berth clause by failing to designate a safe berth, and thus was at fault for the spill.

After a complicated series of proceedings—including a 41-day trial, a subsequent 31-day evidentiary hearing, and two appeals—the Court of Appeals for the Third Circuit found for Frescati and the United States. The court first concluded that Frescati was an implied third-party beneficiary of the safe-berth clause in the charter party between CARCO and Star Tankers, thereby allowing the breach-of-contract claims by Frescati and the United States to proceed against CARCO. *In re Frescati Shipping Co.*, 718 F. 3d 184, 200, 1 Adm. R. 80, 89 (2013). The court then held that the safe-berth clause embodied an express warranty of safety "made without regard to the amount of diligence taken by the charterer," and that CARCO was liable to Frescati and the **[—5—]** United States for breaching that warranty. *Id.*, at 203, 1 Adm. R. at 92; *In re Frescati Shipping Co.*, 886 F. 3d 291, 300, 315, 6 Adm. R. 98, 102, 115 (2018) (case below).

We granted certiorari, 587 U. S. ___ (2019), to resolve whether the safe-berth clause at issue here merely imposes a duty of diligence, as the Fifth Circuit has held in a similar case, or establishes a warranty of safety, as the Second Circuit has held in other analogous cases. Compare *Orduna S. A.* v. *Zen-Noh*

---

cargo." Addendum to Brief for Petitioners 4a. The parties do not dispute that the two clauses should be read in conjunction.

Grain Corp., 913 F. 2d 1149 (CA5 1990), with, *e.g.*, *Paragon Oil Co.* v. *Republic Tankers, S. A.*, 310 F. 2d 169 (CA2 1962). The former interpretation allows a charterer to avoid liability by exercising due diligence in selecting a berth; the latter imposes liability for an unsafe berth without regard to the care taken by the charterer. Because we find it plain from the language of the safe-berth clause that CARCO warranted the safety of the berth it designated, we affirm the judgment of the Third Circuit.

II

Maritime contracts "must be construed like any other contracts: by their terms and consistent with the intent of the parties." **{–1088–}** *Norfolk Southern R. Co.* v. *James N. Kirby, Pty Ltd.*, 543 U. S. 14, 31 (2004); see also 2 T. Schoenbaum, Admiralty & Maritime Law §11:2, p. 7 (6th ed. 2018) ("[F]ederal maritime law includes general principles of contract law"). "'Where the words of a contract in writing are clear and unambiguous, its meaning is to be ascertained in accordance with its plainly expressed intent.'" *M&G Polymers USA, LLC* v. *Tackett*, 574 U. S. 427, 435 (2015) (quoting 11 R. Lord, Williston on Contracts §30:6, p. 108 (4th ed. 2012) (Williston)). In such circumstances, the parties' intent "can be determined from the face of the agreement" and "the language that they used to memorialize [that] agreement." 11 Williston §30:6, at 97–98, 112–113. But "[w]hen a written contract is ambiguous, its meaning is a question **[—6—]** of fact, requiring a determination of the intent of [the] parties in entering the contract"; that may involve examining "relevant extrinsic evidence of the parties' intent and the meaning of the words that they used." *Id.*, §30:7, at 116–119, 124 (footnote omitted).

A

Our analysis starts and ends with the language of the safe-berth clause. That clause provides, as relevant, that the charterer "shall . . . designat[e] and procur[e]" a "safe place or wharf," "provided [that] the Vessel can proceed thereto, lie at, and depart therefrom always safely afloat." Addendum to Brief for Petitioners 8a. As even CARCO acknowledges, the clause plainly imposes on the charterer at least some "duty to select a 'safe' berth." Brief for Petitioners 21. Given the unqualified language of the safe-berth clause, it is similarly plain that this acknowledged duty is absolute. The clause requires the charterer to designate a "safe" berth: That means a berth "free from harm or risk." Webster's Collegiate Dictionary 1030 (10th ed. 1994); see also New Oxford American Dictionary 1500 (E. Jewell & F. Abate eds. 2001) ("safe" means "protected from or not exposed to danger or risk"). And the berth must allow the vessel to come and go "always" safely afloat: That means afloat "at all times" and "in any event." Webster's Collegiate Dictionary, at 35; see also New Oxford American Dictionary, at 47 ("always" means "at all times; on all occasions"). Selecting a berth that does not satisfy those conditions constitutes a breach. The safe-berth clause, in other words, binds the charterer to a warranty of safety.[3] **[—7—]**

No matter that the safe-berth clause does not expressly invoke the term "warranty." It is well settled as a matter of maritime contracts that "[s]tatements of fact contained in a charter party agreement relating to some material matter are called warranties," regardless of the label ascribed in the charter party. 22 Williston §58.11, at 40–41 (2017);

---

[3] The central pillar of the dissent is that the safe-berth clause merely bestows upon the charterer "the *right* to 'designat[e]' the place of discharge," and thus apparently creates no duty to select a safe berth (much less a warranty of safety). *Post*, at 2 (opinion of THOMAS, J.) (quoting Addendum to Brief for Petitioners 8a; emphasis added); see also *post*, at **[—7—]** 3 ("the charterer has a right of selection"). That sidesteps the safe-berth clause's plain terms, which prescribe that the charterer "*shall* . . . designat[e] and procur[e]" a "safe place or wharf." Addendum to Brief for Petitioners 8a (emphasis added). As we have said before, "the word 'shall' usually connotes a requirement." *Kingdomware Technologies, Inc.* v. *United States*, 579 U. S. ___, ___ (2016) (slip op., at 9); see also, *e.g.*, *Lexecon Inc.* v. *Milberg Weiss Bershad Hynes & Lerach*, 523 U. S. 26, 35 (1998). The text thus forecloses the dissent's permissive view that the charterer merely has an elective "right" to select a berth of discharge but no duty to do so. And even CARCO disclaims that atextual position. See Brief for Petitioners 21.

see also **{–1089–}** *Davison* v. *Von Lingen*, 113 U. S. 40, 49–50 (1885) (a stipulation going to "substantive" and "material" parts of a charter party forms "a warranty"); *Behn* v. *Burness*, 3 B. & S. 751, 122 Eng. Rep. 281 (K. B. 1863) ("With respect to statements in a [charter party] descriptive of . . . some material incident . . . , if the descriptive statement was intended to be a substantive part of the [charter party], it is to be regarded as a warranty"). What matters, then, is that the safe-berth clause contains a statement of material fact regarding the condition of the berth selected by the charterer.

Here, the safety of the selected berth is the entire root of the safe-berth clause: It is the very reason for the clause's inclusion in the charter party. And crucially, the charterer's assurance of safety is not subject to qualifications or conditions. Under any conception of materiality and any view of the parties' intent, the charterer's assurance surely counts as material. That leaves no doubt that the safe- **[—8—]** berth clause establishes a warranty of safety, on equal footing with any other provision of the charter party that invokes express warranty language.[4]

CARCO resists this plain reading of the safe-berth clause, arguing instead that the clause contains an implicit limitation: The clause does not impose "strict liability," says CARCO, or "liability without regard to fault." Brief for Petitioners 23, 25. In effect, CARCO interprets the safe-berth clause as imposing a mere duty of due diligence in the selection of the berth. See Tr. of Oral Arg. 19–20 (arguing that "[CARCO] did [its] due diligence" in "selecting the port or the berth"); *id.*, at 28 (suggesting that the safe-berth clause is constrained "as a matter of due diligence in tort concepts"); Reply Brief 5, n. 3 (asserting that a charterer's liability under the safe-berth clause "should be addressed through . . . sources of la[w] such as tort law"). But as a general rule, due diligence and fault-based concepts of tort liability have no place in the contract analysis required here. Under elemental precepts of contract law, an obligor is "liable in damages for breach of contract even if he is without fault." Restatement (Second) of Contracts, p. 309 (1979) (Restatement (Second)). To put that default contract-law principle in tort-law terms, "Contract liability *is* **[—9—]** strict liability." *Ibid.* (emphasis added); see also 23 Williston §63:8, at 499 (2018) ("Liability for a breach of contract is, prima facie, strict liability"). What CARCO thus protests is the straightforward application of contract liability to a breach of contract.

Although contract law generally does not, by its own force, limit liability based on tort concepts of fault, parties are of course free to contract for such limitations. See Restatement (Second), at 309 (obligor who wishes to avoid strict liability for breach may "limi[t] his obligation by **{–1090–}** agreement"). Here, however, the safe-berth clause is clear that the parties contracted for no such thing. CARCO does not identify—nor can we discern—any language in the clause hinting at "due diligence" or related concepts of "fault." That omission is particularly notable in context: Where the parties intended to limit obligations based on due diligence elsewhere in the charter party, they did so expressly. See Addendum to Brief for Petitioners 4a (providing that the vessel "b[e] seaworthy, and hav[e] all pipes, pumps and heater coils in good working order, . . . so far as the foregoing conditions can be attained by the exercise of due diligence"); *id.*, at 13a (relieving vessel

[4] Because the materiality of the charterer's assurance of safety is plain on the face of the charter party, the specific materiality issue here raises no question of fact for a jury to resolve. That is not to say that the materiality of a statement in a charter party is always a question of law. Nor does the materiality analysis here bear on wholly different materiality inquiries. For not all questions of materiality are alike: Sometimes materiality is a question of law. See, *e.g.*, 30 Williston §75:30, at 108 (whether an alteration of a contract is material). Other times, it involves factual determinations uniquely suited for a jury. See, *e.g.*, *TSC Industries, Inc.* v. *Northway, Inc.*, 426 U. S. 438, 450 (1976) (whether a company's misstatements to the public are material for securities-fraud purposes). The dissent's insistence that materiality is a question of fact " 'in other contexts'"—such as securities fraud—thus is inapposite. *Post*, at 8 (quoting *United States* v. *Gaudin*, 515 U. S. 506, 512 (1995)).

owner of responsibility for certain consequences of any "unseaworthiness existing . . . at the inception of the voyage [that] was discoverable by the exercise of due diligence"); *id.*, at 41a (requiring vessel owner to "exercise due diligence to ensure that [a drug and alcohol] policy [onboard the vessel] is complied with").[5] That the parties did not do so in the safe-berth **[—10—]** clause specifically is further proof that they did not intend for such a liability limitation to inhere impliedly.[6]

Unable to identify any liability-limiting language in the safe-berth clause, CARCO points to a separate "general exceptions clause" in the charter party that exempts a charterer from liability for losses due to "perils of the seas." *Id.*, at 14a. According to CARCO, the "general exceptions clause" demonstrates that the parties did not intend the safe-berth clause to impose liability for a "peri[l] of the seas" like an abandoned anchor. That argument founders on a critical component of the "general exceptions clause": By its terms, it does not apply when liability is "otherwise . . . expressly provided" in the charter party. *Ibid.* The safe-berth clause, as explained above, expressly provides for liability stemming from the designation of an unsafe berth. The catchall "general exceptions clause" neither supersedes nor overlays it.[7]

Likewise immaterial is another clause of the charter **[—11—]** party that requires Star Tankers to obtain oil-pollution insurance. According to CARCO, that clause evidences the parties' intent to relieve CARCO of oil-spill liability under the safe-berth **{-1091-}** clause. But the oil-pollution insurance that Star Tankers must obtain covers risks beyond simply those attendant to the selection of an unsafe berth. And CARCO's reading of the insurance clause (as relieving CARCO of oil-spill liability) does not square with its reading of the safe-berth clause (as imposing such liability when CARCO fails to exercise due diligence).

Finally, CARCO offers an alternative interpretation of the safe-berth clause that focuses on the vessel master's right instead of the charterer's duty. This alternative interpretation proceeds from the subclause specifying that the selected berth be one that the vessel may "proceed thereto, lie at, and depart therefrom always safely afloat, any lighterage [*i.e.*, transfer of goods between vessels] being at the expense, risk and peril of the Charterer." *Id.*, at 8a. On CARCO's reading, that subclause means that the vessel master has a right to refuse entry into a berth that the master perceives to be unsafe, and the charterer must pay any expenses resulting from the refusal. We have, to be sure, recognized that similarly worded safe-berth clauses may implicitly denote a vessel master's right to refuse entry and the charterer's resultant obligation to bear the costs of that refusal. See *Mencke* v. *Cargo of*

[5] It also bears mention that many other industry form charter parties—not selected by CARCO and Star Tankers—explicitly limit the liability that may flow from a charterer's selection of a berth. See, *e.g.*, 2E J. Force & L. Lambert, Benedict on Admiralty, ch. XXVII, §27–567 (rev. 7th ed. 2019) (INTERTANKVOY form specifies that "[c]harterers shall exercise due diligence to ascertain that any places to which they order the vessel are safe for the vessel and that she will lie there always **[—10—]** afloat").

[6] After all, language that limits liability is necessary to overcome the default rule of strict liability for contractual breach. *Supra*, at 8–9. That stands in contrast to the established principle that charter parties can, at least in the circumstances here, create warranties without invoking express warranty language. *Supra*, at 7–8. The dissent overlooks this distinction when it claims that the absence of express warranty language in the safe-berth clause and the presence of it elsewhere in the charter party imply that no warranty may be found here. *Post*, at 4.

[7] At oral argument, CARCO urged that the abandoned anchor was not only "a peril of the sea" but also "an abnormal occurrence." Tr. of Oral Arg. 28–29. CARCO's "abnormal occurrence" argument appears to rest on a recent decision by the Supreme Court of the United Kingdom interpreting a safe-berth clause not to impose liability if an "abnormal occurrence" rendered the selected berth unsafe. See *Gard Marine & Energy Ltd.* v. *China Nat. Chartering Co.*, [2017] UKSC 35 (*The Ocean Victory*). In its opening brief to this Court, however, CARCO did not cite *The Ocean Victory* or argue that the abandoned anchor here constituted an "abnormal occurrence."

Java Sugar, 187 U. S. 248 (1902); *The Gazelle and Cargo*, 128 U. S. 474 (1888). But that a charterer may be liable for expenses when a vessel master justifiably refuses to enter an unsafe berth in no way abates the scope of the charterer's liability when a vessel in fact enters an unsafe berth. And a tacit recognition of a vessel master's right of refusal does not overwrite the safe-berth clause's express prescription of a warranty of safety.

The dissent, too, offers an alternative interpretation. It claims that if the safe-berth clause binds the charterer to a **[—12—]** warranty of safety, the clause must bind the vessel master to effectively the same warranty—due to the clause's statement that "'[t]he vessel shall load and discharge at [a] safe place or wharf.'" *Post*, at 6 (quoting Addendum to Brief for Petitioners 8a). Because that would "creat[e] contradictory warranties of safety," the dissent continues, the safe-berth clause must not bind the charterer to a warranty of safety (or, apparently, impose an obligation on the charterer at all). *Post*, at 7. This conclusion does not follow because the conflict diagnosed by the dissent does not exist.

The safe-berth clause says that "[t]he vessel shall load and discharge at any safe place or wharf, . . . which shall be designated and procured by the Charterer." Addendum to Brief for Petitioners 8a. Plainly, that means that the "safe place or wharf . . . shall be designated and procured by the Charterer." *Ibid*. The vessel master's duty is only to "load and discharge" at the chosen safe berth. *Ibid*. (Not, as the dissent urges, at any safe berth the vessel master so desires regardless of the charterer's contractually required selection. *Post*, at 6, n. 4.) On its face, the vessel master's duty creates no tension with the charterer's duty. And it strains common sense to insist (as the dissent does) that the vessel master implicitly has a separate, dueling obligation regarding the safety of the berth, when the clause explicitly assigns that responsibility to the charterer. *Post*, at 6–7. Perhaps the dissent says it best: We must "reject [this] interpretation that . . . 'se[ts] up . . . two clauses in conflict with one another.'" *Post*, at 6 (quoting *Mastrobuono* v. *Shearson Lehman Hutton, Inc.*, 514 U. S. 52, 64 (1995)). **{-1092-}**

We instead take the safe-berth clause at face value. It requires the charterer to select a safe berth, and that requirement here amounts to a warranty of safety.

B

CARCO's remaining arguments point to authorities that have purportedly construed safe-berth clauses to contain **[—13—]** limitations on liability. These arguments find no foothold in the language of the charter party at issue here. And none is otherwise convincing.

CARCO asserts, for instance, that a leading admiralty treatise has urged that safe-berth clauses ought not be interpreted as establishing a warranty. See G. Gilmore & C. Black, Law of Admiralty §4–4, p. 205 (2d ed. 1975) (Gilmore& Black). Gilmore and Black's position, however, stemmed from their belief that vessel masters or vessel owners are generally better positioned than charterers to bear the liability of an unsafe berth. See *ibid*. (reasoning that charterers "may know nothing of the safety of ports and berths, and [are] much less certain to be insured against" liability for losses stemming from an unsafe berth).[8] Gilmore and Black also acknowledged

[8] The dissent's claim that Gilmore and Black looked to " 'the very words of the usual clauses,' " *post*, at 3, n. 1 (quoting Gilmore & Black §4–4, at 204), relies on a discussion not of the charterer's obligation under the safe-berth clause but of the vessel master's lack of such obligation, Gilmore & Black §4–4, at 204–205. At most, Gilmore and Black "suggested" that interpreting safe-berth clauses to relieve vessel masters of any obligation to enter an unsafe berth "might easily be read to contradict" any "affirmative liability" on the part of the charterer "in case of mishap." See *id*., §4–4, at 205. But that supposition is at odds with the language of the safe-berth clause here, which (as even CARCO acknowledges) plainly contemplates at least some liability for the charterer's designation of an unsafe berth. *Supra*, at 6–7, and n. 3, 8. And as explained, a vessel master's ability to refuse entry into an unsafe berth does not logically or textually diminish a charterer's liability when the

that, as of 1975, many courts had not interpreted safe-berth clauses in the manner that they proposed. See *id.*, at 204, and n. 34a, 206, and n. 36. Whatever Gilmore and Black sought to prevail upon courts to adopt as a prescriptive matter does not alter the plain meaning of the safe-berth clause here.

CARCO next contends that in *Atkins* v. *Disintegrating Co.*, 18 Wall. 272 (1874), this Court acknowledged that safe-berth clauses do not embody a warranty of safety. That **[—14—]** greatly overreads *Atkins*. In that case, this Court affirmed a District Court's ruling that, although the berth selected by the charterer was not safe, the vessel master had "waived" the protection of the safe-berth clause. *Atkins* v. *Fibre Disintegrating Co.*, 2 F. Cas. 78, 79 (EDNY 1868); see *Atkins*, 18 Wall., at 299. No one posits that the District Court's waiver holding has any significance in this case. CARCO, however, points to language in the District Court's opinion observing that the "safe" berth referenced in the charter party "impl[ied one] which th[e] vessel could enter and depart from without legal restraint, and without incurring more than the ordinary perils of the seas." *Atkins*, 2 F. Cas., at 79. But the District Court's remark—that a berth may be safe even if certain perils lurk within—did not bear on its finding that the berth in question was *un*safe or its holding that the vessel master had "waived" the protection of the safe-berth clause. When this Court approved of the District Court's "views" and "conclusions," *Atkins*, 18 Wall., at 299, it did not adopt as controlling precedent—for all safe-berth clauses going forward—an observation **{–1093–}** that was not controlling even for the District Court.

Also misplaced is CARCO's reliance on *Orduna S. A.*, 913 F. 2d 1149. True, the Fifth Circuit there held that a similarly unqualified safe-berth clause imposed a duty of due diligence. *Id.*, at 1157. But in so holding, the court did not purport to interpret the language of the safe-berth clause at issue in that case. *Id.*, at 1156–1157. Instead, it looked principally to tort law and policy considerations. See, *e.g.*, *id.*, at 1156 ("requiring negligence as a predicate for the charterer's liability does not increase the risk that the vessel will be exposed to an unsafe berth"); *id.*, at 1157 ("no legitimate legal or social policy is furthered by making the charterer warrant the safety of the berth it selects"). Neither tort principles nor policy objectives, however, override the safe-berth clause's unambiguous meaning.

More consistent with traditional contract analysis is the **[—15—]** Second Circuit's long line of decisions interpreting the language of unqualified safe-berth clauses to embody an express warranty of safety. See, *e.g.*, *Paragon Oil Co.*, 310 F. 2d, at 172–173 ("the express terms of [the] contract" established a "warranty" obliging the charterer "to furnish, not only a place which he believes to be safe, but a place where the chartered vessel can discharge 'always afloat'" (some internal quotation marks omitted)); *Park S. S. Co.* v. *Cities Serv. Oil Co.*, 188 F. 2d 804, 805–806 (CA2 1951) ("the natural meaning of 'safe place' is a place entirely safe, not an area only part of which is safe," and "the charter party was an express assurance that the berth was safe"); *Cities Serv. Transp. Co.* v. *Gulf Refining Co.*, 79 F. 2d 521 (CA2 1935) (*per curiam*) (the "charter party was itself an express assurance . . . that at the berth 'indicated' the ship would be able to lie 'always afloat' "). Those decisions, which focused on the controlling contract language, all point in the same direction: When the language of a safe-berth clause obliges a charterer to select a safe berth without qualifying the charterer's duty or the assurance of safety that language establishes a warranty. That aligns with our decision today.[9]

III

We conclude that the language of the safe-berth clause here unambiguously establishes

vessel master in fact enters an unsafe berth selected by the charterer. *Supra*, at 11.

[9] The parties also dispute whether the prevailing industry usage of safe-berth clauses supports reading the safe-berth clause here as a warranty or as a promise of due diligence. Because the express language of the safe-berth clause is susceptible to only one meaning, we need not address these arguments.

a warranty of safety, and that CARCO has identified "no reason to contravene the clause's obvious meaning." *Kirby*, 543 U. S., at 31–32. We emphasize, however, that our decision today "does no more than provide a legal backdrop against which future [charter parties] will be negotiated." *Id.*, at 36. Charterers remain **[—16—]** free to contract around unqualified language that would otherwise establish a warranty of safety, by expressly limiting the extent of their obligations or liability.

* * *

For the foregoing reasons, we conclude that the plain language of the safe-berth clause establishes a warranty of safety and therefore affirm the judgment of the Third Circuit.

It is so ordered.

(Reporter's Note: Dissenting Opinion follows on p. 10).

[—1—] **{–1093–}** THOMAS, J., with whom ALITO, J., joins, dissenting:

The majority concludes that the safe-berth clause in the contract at issue unambiguously **{–1094–}** created a warranty of safety by the charterer. Although this interpretation provides a clear background rule for the maritime industry to contract against, it is the wrong rule and finds no basis in the contract's plain text. I would hold that the plain language of the safe-berth clause contains no warranty of safety and remand for factfinding on whether industry custom and usage establish such a warranty in this case. Accordingly, I respectfully dissent.

I

In 2001, Star Tankers Inc. (Star) entered into a voyage charter party with CITGO Asphalt Refining Company (CARCO). That contract included a safe-berth clause that provided:

> "SAFE BERTHING — SHIFTING. The vessel shall load and discharge at any safe place or wharf, or alongside vessels or lighters reachable on her arrival, which shall be designated and procured by the Charterer, provided the Vessel can proceed thereto, lie at, and depart therefrom always safely afloat, any lighterage being at **[—2—]** the expense, risk and peril of the Charterer." Addendum to Brief for Petitioners 8a.

I agree with the majority that we must interpret the safe-berth clause "by [its] terms and consistent with the intent of the parties." *Norfolk Southern R. Co.* v. *James N. Kirby, Pty Ltd.*, 543 U. S. 14, 31 (2004). Unlike the majority, however, I conclude that the plain meaning of the safe-berth clause does not include a warranty of safety.

A

The safe-berth clause sets out the rights and obligations of the vessel master and the charterer. The clause requires the vessel master to "load and discharge at [a] safe place or wharf," but it also gives the master the right to refuse to proceed if the vessel cannot "lie at, and depart therefrom always safely afloat." Addendum to Brief for Petitioners 8a. The charterer has the right to "designat[e]" a "safe place or wharf" for discharge. *Ibid.* That right, however, must be exercised by the charterer, see *ibid.* (using mandatory language), and the act of designation must be made in good faith, see Restatement (Second) of Contracts §205 (1979). The right to designate is limited to places that the vessel can reach, with the charterer bearing the "expense, risk and peril" of any "lighterage" (*i.e.*, transfer of cargo by means of another vessel) resulting from its selection. Addendum to Brief for Petitioners 8a. As the leading admiralty treatise succinctly explains, the safe-berth clause provides that "if the port or the berth is unsafe, the master is excused from taking his ship in, and the charterer must bear the extra expense . . . entailed by [a proper] refusal" of its selected place of discharge. G. Gilmore & C. Black, Law of Admiralty §4–4, p. 204 (2d ed. 1975).[1] **[—3—]**

This reading is consistent with this Court's prior decisions. The Court has interpreted safe-berth clauses as providing a limit on the "right to select a dock." **{–1095–}** *Mencke* v. *Cargo of Java Sugar*, 187 U. S. 248, 253 (1902); see also *The Gazelle and Cargo*, 128 U. S. 474, 485–486 (1888) (holding that the right of selection is limited by the terms of the contract). And it has concluded that, if a charterer selects a place of discharge that cannot be safely reached, the charterer is

[1] The majority states that the views of Gilmore and Black "stemmed from their belief that vessel masters or vessel owners are generally better positioned than charterers to bear the liability of an unsafe berth." *Ante*, at 13. While the treatise does contain policy-based arguments, it **[—3—]** also looks to "the very words of the usual clauses" to conclude that the master's clear textual right to refuse to enter an unsafe port "might easily be read to contradict" an interpretation of a safe-berth clause that "creat[es] an affirmative liability of charterer to ship, in case of mishap." Gilmore & Black, Law of Admiralty §4–4, at 204–205. Gilmore and Black's review of safe-berth clauses contains just as much, if not more, analysis of the text than the conclusory assertions of the majority. See *ante*, at 6.

liable for lighterage expenses. *Mencke*, 187 U. S., at 253–254.

Thus, under the plain language of the safe-berth clause, the vessel master has a duty of discharge and right of refusal, while the charterer has a right of selection and duty to pay for lighterage.

B

The majority does not disagree that the safe-berth clause confers these duties and rights. Quite the opposite. It recognizes our precedents as embracing this understanding. *Ante*, at 11. The majority concludes, however, that in addition to the rights of selection and refusal, the language of the safe-berth clause "unambiguously" establishes a warranty of safety by the charterer. *Ante*, at 15. With this, I cannot agree.

1

The majority first concludes that the safe-berth clause contains an "express prescription of a warranty of safety." **[—4—]** *Ante*, at 11; see also *ante*, at 6. This assertion finds no support whatsoever in the plain language of the clause.

First of all, the contract between Star and CARCO contains no express warranty of safety by the charterer, though the parties repeatedly used express language to create warranties elsewhere in the contract. See Addendum to Brief for Petitioners 26a ("Charterer's warrant . . ."), 30a ("Owners warrant . . ."), *ibid.* ("Owner warrants . . ."), 31a ("Owner warrants . . ."), 41a ("Owner warrants . . ."), 42a ("Owner warrants . . ."), 43a ("Owner warrants . . ."), 44a ("Owner warrants . . ."), 45a ("Owner warrants . . ."). In contrast, they did not state that the charterer "warrants" the safety of the place of discharge in the safe-berth clause. As the majority obliquely recognizes—when trying to rebut a different argument—"[t]hat omission is particularly notable in context: Where the parties intended to [create warranties] elsewhere in the charter party, they did so expressly." *Ante*, at 9. "That the parties did not do so in the safe-berth clause specifically is . . . proof that they did not intend for such a . . . limitation to inhere impliedly." *Ante*, at 9–10.[2]

But even setting aside this evidence of the parties' intent (as the majority does), the safe-berth clause contains no language that can be construed to create a warranty of safety. Nor does the clause so much as suggest that the charterer **[—5—]** is liable for all damages arising out of unsafe port conditions. In fact, the trade association that promulgated the ASBATANKVOY form used in this case specifically acknowledged that the language of "the clause *does not specify* whether the charterer absolutely **{-1096-}** warrants the safety of the berth." Brief for Maritime Law Association of the United States and the Association of Ship Brokers & Agents (USA) Inc. as *Amici Curiae* on Pet. for Cert. 19 (emphasis added).

Notwithstanding this, the majority states that the clause "requires the charterer to designate a 'safe' berth" and that requirement "binds the charterer to a warranty of safety." *Ante*, at 6. But certainly not every obligation in a contract is a warranty. See *Brooks, Tarlton, Gilbert, Douglas & Kressler* v. *United States Fire Ins. Co.*, 832 F. 2d 1358, 1375, n. 14 (CA5 1987). Parties often agree to obligations that govern only their conduct without making any assurances as to an ultimate result. For example, "[a] promise to repair parts of [a] powertrain for six years is a promise that the manufacturer will behave in a certain way, not a warranty that the vehicle will behave in a certain way." *Cosman* v. *Ford*

[2] Attempting to avoid the inconsistent application of its own principle, the majority claims there is a distinction between language limiting liability and language creating liability. *Ante*, at 10, n. 6. In the majority's view, express language is "necessary" to limit liability, but the parties can create warranty liability in numerous ways. *Ibid.* Even assuming that is correct, it does not negate the proof of the parties' intent here. The majority can point to no example of the parties "creat[ing] warranties without invoking express warranty language" in this contract. *Ibid.* By contrast, the contract contains no fewer than nine clauses using express language to create a warranty. The commonsense conclusion is that, when the parties intended to create a warranty, they used express language to do so.

Motor Co., 285 Ill. App. 3d 250, 257, 674 N. E. 2d 61, 66 (1996). The majority does not confront, or even acknowledge, this distinction. Instead, it indifferently conflates a duty to take a certain action—"designat[e]" a wharf understood to be safe—with a warranty guaranteeing a certain result—the ultimate safety of the berth.[3]

By conflating an action with an outcome, the majority converts every obligation tangentially related to safety into a warranty of safety. Consider the contract in this case, for example. If the language stating that the charterer "shall **[—6—]** . . . designat[e] and procur[e]" a "safe place or wharf " creates a warranty of safety, then so does the language stating that "[t]he vessel shall load and discharge at [a] safe place or wharf." Addendum to Brief for Petitioners 8a. There is no textual reason that an obligation to "designat[e]" is any different from an obligation to "discharge." *Ibid.* And policy-based rationalizations cannot justify a distinction because "[n]either tort principles nor policy objectives . . . override the safe-berth clause's unambiguous meaning." *Ante*, at 14. Thus, employing the majority's approach, the safe-berth clause contains two competing warranties of safety—one from the charterer and one from the vessel master—that could impose conflicting obligations.[4] Courts typically avoid construing contracts in such a manner. See *Mastrobuono* v. *Shearson Lehman Hutton, Inc.*, 514 U. S. 52, 64 (1995) (rejecting an interpretation that the Court believed "se[t] up . . . two clauses in conflict with one another"); *United States* v. *Pielago*, 135 F. 3d 703, 710 (CA11 1998) ("It is a **{-1097-}** cardinal principle of contract law that no term of a contract should be construed to be in conflict with another unless no other reasonable construction is possible"). **[—7—]** Setting aside this contract, the majority makes no attempt to limit its expansive interpretive approach or provide the barest of explanation as to why all obligations that involve the word "safe" should not be construed as warranties of safety.

In a contract replete with express language creating warranties, I would not construe the plain language of the safe-berth clause as indirectly creating contradictory warranties of safety. And I certainly cannot agree with the majority's conclusion that the safe-berth clause "unambiguously" establishes a warranty of safety by the charterer. *Ante*, at 15.

2

Perhaps recognizing the weakness of its assertion that the safe-berth clause contains a duty or warranty of safety, the majority pivots to an independent legal theory. It claims that the safe-berth clause constitutes a material statement of fact and therefore creates a warranty. *Ante*, at 7. The majority's invocation of this theory is puzzling, to say the least.

As an initial matter, this issue was not preserved in the Court of Appeals, which, understandably, did not address the question. *In re Frescati Shipping Co., Ltd.*, 718 F. 3d 184, 200–203, 1 Adm. R. 80, 89–93 (CA3 2013). Nor was the issue developed before this Court. All we have before us is one conclusory paragraph in the United States' brief. See

---

[3] I am skeptical that the phrase "place or wharf" can be read to include the entire berth. But CARCO failed to develop any argument related to the scope of this phrase, so I do not address the issue.

[4] To support its assertion that no conflict exists, the majority rewrites the text of the safe-berth clause. The majority asserts that "[t]he vessel master's duty is only to 'load and discharge' *at the chosen safe berth.*" *Ante*, at 12 (emphasis added). But that is not what the clause says. The safe-berth clause states: "The vessel shall load and *discharge at any safe place or wharf.*" Addendum to Brief for Petitioners 8a (emphasis added). And, by requiring the charterer to pay for lighterage expenses resulting from the designation of an unsafe port, the clause specifically contemplates the vessel master declining to discharge at a place or wharf that is not safe. *Ibid.*; see also *Mencke* v. *Cargo of Java Sugar*, 187 U. S. 248, 253 (1902) (requiring the charterer to pay lighterage expenses where vessel discharged at a location other than the chosen berth). The "which" clause in the provision—"which shall be designated and procured by the Charterer"—modifies "place or wharf," creating a separate obligation for the charterer. Addendum to Brief for Petitioners 8a. That separate obligation, however, does not negate the express obligation imposed on the vessel. *Ibid.* (emphasis added).

Brief for United States 25. Accordingly, I would decline to address this unpreserved and undeveloped issue.

Even setting aside forfeiture, the majority's analysis is questionable in multiple respects. First, the majority asserts that "the safe-berth clause contains a statement of material fact regarding the condition of the berth selected by the charterer." *Ante*, at 7. Not so. The safe-berth clause says nothing about the safety of the port actually selected by CARCO (the Paulsboro berth), or any specific berth for **[—8—]** that matter. It states only that the charter "shall . . . designat[e]" a place or wharf. The majority infers from CARCO's selection of the Paulsboro berth that CARCO believed the place or wharf was safe. But that is not a statement of fact; it is an inference. I hesitate to equate the two without briefing on the issue, or even a single example of a court adopting this approach.

Second, even assuming the safe-berth clause contains a statement of fact, it is not clear that the Court is in a position to decide whether that statement of fact is "material." Many jurisdictions appear to treat materiality as a question of fact when determining whether a statement creates a warranty. *Royal Bus. Machines, Inc.* v. *Lorraine Corp.*, 633 F. 2d 34, 43 (CA7 1980) ("Whether a seller affirmed a fact or made a promise amounting to a warranty is a question of fact reserved for the trier of fact"); *McDonnell Douglas Corp.* v. *Thiokol Corp.*, 124 F. 3d 1173, 1176 (CA9 1997) ("Whether the seller's representations formed part of the basis of the parties' bargain is a question of fact"); *Crothers* v. *Cohen*, 384 N. W. 2d 562, 563 (Minn. App. 1986) ("Whether a given representation constitutes a warranty is ordinarily a question of fact for the jury"); *General Supply & Equip. Co.* v. *Phillips*, 490 S. W. 2d 913, 917 (Tex. Civ. App. 1972) (citing cases from Illinois, Iowa, Alabama, and Ohio). And "our cases have recognized in other contexts that the materiality inquiry, involving as it does 'delicate assessments of the inferences a "reasonable [decisionmaker]" would draw from a given set of facts and the significance of those inferences to him, . . . [is] peculiarly on[e] for the trier of fact.'" **{-1098-}** *United States* v. *Gaudin*, 515 U. S. 506, 512 (1995). Although this Court has relied on factual findings to support a materiality conclusion, *Davison* v. *Von Lingen*, 113 U. S. 40, 50 (1885), I am not aware of a case in which this Court has treated the materiality inquiry as a pure question of law without relying on any factual findings whatsoever. Again, without briefing on **[—9—]** this issue, I would hesitate to depart, without explanation, from the approach taken by many courts throughout the country.

Third, assuming the contract contains a statement of fact regarding the safety of the berth and further assuming that materiality is a question of law, I am unpersuaded by the majority's materiality analysis. Materiality must turn at least in part on a statement's "tendency to induce the making of the contract." 22 R. Lord, Williston on Contracts §58.11, p. 41 (4th ed. 2017). The majority's opinion says nothing about that (likely fact-driven) question. It first states that the safety of the selected berth is "the entire root of the safe-berth clause" and "the very reason for the clause's inclusion." *Ante*, at 7. Even accepting the majority's interpretation, merely proving that a statement is included in a contract does not mean that it is material. If that were the law, then every statement in a contract would be material and therefore constitute a warranty. That cannot be right. The majority next concludes that "[u]nder any conception of materiality and any view of the parties' intent, the charterer's assurance [of safety with no conditions] surely counts as material." *Ibid.* But what is the basis for this conclusion? The majority's experience negotiating maritime contracts? It defies reality to assert that a standard provision in a form contract—which has been subject to different interpretations for nearly three decades—induced *every single vessel master* using that form contract to enter into the agreement. We should recognize this for what it is: an unsupported judicial pronouncement on a question of fact.

The majority's attempt to shore up its analysis with its alternative statement-of-fact theory makes no difference to the outcome of this case, because the majority erroneously holds that the safe-berth clause contains an absolute duty that was breached. See *ante*, at 6; *supra*, at 3–7. But its unreasoned dicta will undoubtedly cause problems for **[—10—]** lower courts and parties in the future.

II

The lack of unambiguous language creating a warranty of safety in the safe-berth clause does not end our inquiry. "'In this endeavor, as with any other contract, the parties' intentions control.'" *M&G Polymers USA, LLC* v. *Tackett*, 574 U. S. 427, 435 (2015) (quoting *Stolt-Nielsen S. A.* v. *Animal Feeds Int'l Corp.*, 559 U. S. 662, 682 (2010)); see also *ante*, at 5–6. The vessel's owner and the United States argue that, setting aside the plain meaning of the contract's text, longstanding industry custom supports interpreting the safe-berth clause as a warranty of safety. I would remand for factfinding on this issue.

Under both "general maritime law" and ordinary principles of contract interpretation, evidence of an established "custom and usage" can be used as an aid to "determin[e] the parties' intent" and the meaning of the language included in the contract. *Stolt-Nielsen*, 559 U. S., at 674, n. 6 (internal quotation marks omitted); see also U. C. C. §1–303 Comment 3 (2017); Restatement (Second) of Contracts §220. But "the existence and scope of a particular usage is usually a question of fact." **{-1099-}** *Sun Oil Co.* v. *Wortman*, 486 U. S. 717, 732, n. 4 (1988); see also U. C. C. §1–303(c); Restatement (Second) of Contracts §219, Comment *a*; §222(2). Here, we have no factual findings from the District Court to support a custom-or-usage argument. Such findings seem particularly necessary in this case: "A trade usage can of course be confined to a particular geographical area," 5 M. Kniffin, Corbin on Contracts §24.13, p. 110 (J. Perillo ed., rev. 1998), and different areas of the country appeared to have different understandings of the safe-berth clause at the time of contracting. See *ante*, at 5 (recognizing Circuit split); Brief for North American Export Grain Association as *Amicus Curiae* 9 (stating that in "New Orleans . . . safe- **[—11—]** berth clauses are understood to impose due diligence obligations"). Accordingly, I would remand for factual findings on the question whether the parties entered into the charter party with knowledge of an established custom or usage.

* * *

I appreciate the majority's desire to interpret the safe-berth clause in a manner that provides clarity to the maritime industry. The plain meaning of the contract's text, however, does not support the majority's interpretation. Fortunately, the majority's opinion applies only to this specific contract, and its assertions regarding a material statement of fact are but dicta. Because I would reverse the judgment of the Court of Appeals and remand for further proceedings, I respectfully dissent.

United States Court of Appeals for the First Circuit

United States Court of Appeals
for the First Circuit

No. 18-2118

PORTLAND PIPE LINE CORP.
vs.
CITY OF S. PORTLAND

Appeal from the United States District Court for the District of Maine

Decided: January 10, 2020

Citation: 947 F.3d 11, 8 Adm. R. 16 (1st Cir. 2020).

Before **TORRUELLA, THOMPSON,** and **BARRON,** Circuit Judges.

[—3—] {–12–} PER CURIAM:

This case involves a clash between Portland Pipe Line Corporation ("PPLC"), a Maine corporation engaged in the international transportation of oil, and the City of South Portland (the "City"), which enacted a municipal zoning ordinance prohibiting the bulk loading of crude oil onto vessels in the City's harbor. The practical effect of the ordinance at issue, known as the Clear Skies Ordinance (the "Ordinance"), is to prevent PPLC from using its infrastructure to transport oil from Montréal, Québec, Canada to South Portland, Maine via a system of underground pipelines. On appeal, PPLC and the American Waterways Operators, a national trade organization whose industry members employ thousands of seamen (and women) who would be negatively impacted by the loss of port traffic associated with PPLC's pipeline **{–13–}** system, argue, in part, that the Ordinance is preempted by Maine's Coastal Conveyance Act ("CCA") and runs afoul of federal constitutional law.

In accordance with well-settled constitutional avoidance doctrine, *see Vaquería Tres Monjitas, Inc. v. Pagan*, 748 F.3d 21, 26 (1st Cir. 2014), we sidestep the federal quagmire for the moment. This dispute raises important questions of state law preemption doctrine and statutory interpretation that (in our view) are unresolved and may prove dispositive. We therefore certify three questions to the Maine Law Court. *See Fortin v. Titcomb*, 671 F.3d 63, 64 (1st Cir. 2012) (certifying questions to **[—4—]** the Law Court where there were "no clear controlling [state law] precedents" (quoting Me. Rev. Stat. tit. 4, § 57)). Some context for those questions, along with the questions themselves, follow.

I. Background

We begin by reciting the undisputed facts and procedural background germane to the issues of state law presented herein. PPLC and its parent company, Montreal Pipe Line Limited, operate the Portland-Montreal Pipe Line, a mostly underground pipeline system that primarily transports oil from South Portland, Maine, through three states, across the Canadian border, to the system's northern terminus in Montréal, Québec. In connection with this work, PPLC has for years obtained the state and federal regulatory approvals necessary to unload crude oil from tanker vessels in the City's harbor to be held in above-ground storage facilities pending transport to Canada via the pipeline system.

Beginning in or around 2007, to accommodate purported changes in demand, PPLC made efforts to reverse the flow of oil along the pipeline system such that oil would flow southbound from Montréal to South Portland, where it would then be loaded onto tankers in the City's harbor for distribution in the United States. Over the next few years, PPLC requested and received permission to proceed with the reversal project from federal, state, and municipal agencies. On July 18, 2008, for example, the U.S. Department of State approved the reversal project after concluding **[—5—]** it did not represent a substantial deviation from the work previously approved by the federal government pursuant to a Presidential Permit issued to PPLC in 1999.[1] Less than a year later, on August 25, 2009, PPLC obtained an air emissions license from Maine's Department of Environmental Protection ("MDEP"), the agency charged with enforcing the state's

[1] The State Department followed up with PPLC on August 13, 2013, instructing PPLC to provide more information about the changes in advance of implementing the flow reversal.

environmental laws. Additionally, as is relevant to the certification questions presented here, on December 20, 2010, MDEP renewed PPLC's existing oil terminal facility license under the authority granted to MDEP by the CCA.[2] The license application summary, criteria for renewal, findings of fact, and formal approval of the renewal license are memorialized in an MDEP document titled "Department Order," which acknowledges and approves PPLC's plans to "reverse one of its underground pipe lines" and "store[] [oil] in . . . above ground tanks prior to being loaded onto vessels at the South Portland pier for transport to refineries **{-14-}** and terminals outside the state of Maine."[3] At the local level, PPLC sought and received **[—6—]** zoning approval from the City's Planning Board. Despite receiving these and other necessary regulatory approvals, PPLC halted its plans prior to implementation, choosing instead to wait out the economic decline precipitated by the Great Recession.

As economic conditions improved in 2012 and 2013, PPLC revived the pipeline reversal project. Around the same time, however, environmental interest groups began lobbying for a municipal referendum that would (among other things) bar a key component of the project: the transportation of Canadian oil sands (or, as environmentalists call it, "tar sands") via pipeline to South Portland, where PPLC planned to load the same onto vessels in the City's harbor. City residents voted against this citizen-initiated referendum on November 5, 2013. But South Portland's City Council subsequently created a draft ordinance committee to consider changes to City code that, according to the City, would "protect the public health and welfare from adverse or incompatible land uses, or adverse impacts to local air, water, aesthetic, recreational, natural, or marine resources" caused by the loading of unrefined petroleum products, like Canadian oil sands, onto marine tank vessels docking in South Portland's harbor. After a months-long drafting and review process conducted by the draft ordinance committee, the City Council passed Ordinance No. 1-14/15, the Clear Skies Ordinance, on July 21, 2014. The Ordinance prohibits the "bulk loading of crude oil onto any marine tank **[—7—]** vessel," South Portland, ME, Ordinance #1-14/15, nipping PPLC's reversal project in the bud.

According to PPLC (and as disputed by the City), if it cannot move forward with the reversal project, it likely cannot survive as a business.[4] As PPLC tells it, one of the system's two pipelines has been completely idle as a result of insufficient demand for northbound shipping and the Ordinance's impediment to southbound shipping. The other pipeline, while still active, transports what amounts to a "trickle" of oil.

Deprived of the means and method by which it intended to transport oil from Canada into the United States as part of the reversal project, PPLC filed suit against the City and the City's code enforcer in U.S. District Court for the District of Maine on February 6, 2015. Count IX of PPLC's nine-count complaint alleges the Ordinance is preempted by the CCA and, in particular, a provision of the statute that prohibits municipal activity which directly conflicts with a MDEP rule or order, including (as PPLC views it) the 2010 MDEP renewal license authorizing PPLC's reversal project in a document titled "Department Order." The complaint's **[—8—]** remaining claims primarily concern the Ordinance's alleged violation of various federal laws and federal preemption doctrine.[5] **{-15-}**

---

[2] As explained in more detail later, the CCA imbues MDEP with authority to issue licenses to oil terminal facilities and to adopt rules and regulations concerning their operations. *See* Me. Rev. Stat. tit. 38, §§ 544, 546.

[3] MDEP renewed PPLC's license pursuant to a second document titled "Department Order," dated September 11, 2015.

[4] PPLC contends that the flow reversal project is a necessary response to the recent increase in the production of Canadian oil sands, which has reduced demand for northward flow on PPLC's pipelines.

[5] PPLC's federal claims are as follows: (Count I: Preemption - Pipeline Safety Act, 49 U.S.C. §§ 60101 *et seq.*); (Count II: Preemption - Foreign Affairs Doctrine, U.S. Const., art. 2, §§ 2, 3); (Count III: Preemption - The Ports and Waterways Safety Act, 33 U.S.C. §§ 1225(a)(1), 1225(a)(2)(A)); (Count

The City filed a motion to dismiss, which was denied on February 11, 2016. The parties subsequently filed cross-motions for summary judgment, which culminated with the district court dismissing all but one of PPLC's claims on December 29, 2017. In dispensing with PPLC's state law preemption claim, in particular, the district court concluded the 2010 MDEP renewal license document titled "Department Order" is not an "order" with preemptive effect under the CCA and, even if it is, the Ordinance does not directly conflict with the CCA to the extent the statute leaves room for local zoning restrictions like the Ordinance. PPLC's remaining **[—9—]** claim after summary judgment was dismissed on August 27, 2018, following a four-day bench trial.[6]

PPLC timely appealed to this Court on November 7, 2018. The Court heard oral argument on July 23, 2019. We then invited the parties and the State of Maine, which (along with other amici) had filed an amicus brief on behalf of the City, to file supplemental briefs on the following questions that (if answered in the affirmative) would resolve the state law preemption claim and this matter as a whole: (1) whether the 2010 MDEP renewal license is an order with preemptive effect under the CCA; and (2), if the renewal license is an order, whether the Ordinance directly conflicts with the same. Even after careful review of the parties' proffers, we believe the case lacks controlling precedent and presents "close and difficult legal issue[s]" that warrant certification to the Law Court. *In re Engage, Inc.*, 544 F.3d 50, 53 (1st Cir. 2008). We have recognized that certification may be an appropriate option even where, as here, the parties have not requested it. *See Me. Drilling & Blasting, Inc. v. Ins. Co. of N. Am.*, 34 F.3d 1, 3 (1st Cir. 1994) (noting that the Court on occasion certifies "questions to a state's highest court upon our own motion"). **[—10—]**

II. The Issues

With the relevant facts and procedural background covered, we turn to the state law questions for which we seek certification. We begin our discussion with a review of the relevant provisions of the CCA.

A. The Coastal Conveyance Act

In enacting the CCA, the Maine legislature declared that the "highest and best" uses of the state's seacoast include public and private recreation, fishing, lobstering, and "gathering other marine life used and useful in food production and other commercial activities." Me. Rev. Stat. tit. 38, § 541. To preserve the integrity of Maine's coastline for such uses, state lawmakers, through the enactment of the CCA, conferred upon MDEP "the power to deal with the hazards and threats of danger and damage" posed by transfers of oil, petroleum products, and their by-products between vessels and onshore oil facilities in state waters. *Id.* The CCA imposes a licensure requirement on anyone who wishes to perform oil transfers in or around state waters, *see id.* § 545 (prohibiting the "operat[ion]" of any "oil terminal **{-16-}** facility . . . without a license"), and vests MDEP with the authority to issue such licenses, *id.* § 544(2). The CCA also grants MDEP the "power to adopt rules and regulations" for "[o]perating and inspection requirements for facilities, vessels, personnel and other matters relating to licensee operations." *Id.* **[—11—]** § 546(4). MDEP, in turn, has developed regulations governing marine oil terminals and oil transfers.

Although the CCA acknowledges the potential for municipal activity within the sphere of the CCA's (and, by extension, MDEP's) authority, it includes the following

IV: Preemption - Maritime Law, U.S. Const., art. 3, § 2); (Count V: Commerce Clause Violation, U.S. Const., art. 1, § 18); (Count VI: Due Process and Equal Protection Clause Violations, U.S. Const., amend. XIV, § 1); and (Count VII: Civil Rights Act Violation, 42 U.S.C. § 1983).

We should also note the complaint alleges as Count VIII that the Ordinance is inconsistent with the City's Comprehensive Plan enacted and amended under the authority granted municipalities pursuant to Me. Rev. Stat. tit. 30-A, § 4352. Because PPLC does not press this claim in earnest on appeal, we do not seek analysis of the same from the Law Court.

[6] On October 10, 2018, the district court entered an amended judgment clarifying that Count VII of the complaint was dismissed without prejudice.

limitation in the case of conflict between the two:

> Nothing in this subchapter may be construed to deny any municipality, by ordinance or by law, from exercising police powers under any general or special Act; provided that ordinances and bylaws in furtherance of the intent of this subchapter and promoting the general welfare, public health and public safety are valid unless in direct conflict with this subchapter or any *rule or order* of the board or commissioner adopted under authority of this subchapter.

Id. § 556 (emphasis added).

With this regulatory framework in mind, we turn to the state law questions, covering whether MDEP's December 2010 renewal license constitutes an "order" with preemptive effect and then discussing whether the Ordinance is preempted by the text of § 556 and whether, independent of any express preemption powers set forth in § 556, preemption may be otherwise implied by the CCA.

1. Whether the MDEP License Is an Order.

PPLC's license renewal application sought authorization to reverse the flow of one of PPLC's underground pipelines and to store oil in above-ground tanks prior to being loaded onto vessels in the City's harbor. After concluding that PPLC's operations satisfied statutory and regulatory criteria, MDEP's Acting **[—12—]** Commissioner approved the application and issued PPLC a license in a document titled "Department Order." Notwithstanding MDEP's review and approval of PPLC's reversal operations, the City enacted the Ordinance, which serves as a blanket prohibition on all unrefined oil-loading activity in the harbor.

PPLC has argued that MDEP licenses issued pursuant to the CCA are considered orders with preemptive effect. According to PPLC, to decide otherwise would render meaningless certain MDEP enforcement powers outlined in the CCA. PPLC argues, for example, that distinguishing orders from licenses could subject MDEP's licensure decisions to procedural delays that would impede the department's ability to quickly respond to potentially dangerous activity. *See* Me. Rev. Stat. tit. 38, § 557 (explaining that MDEP "orders" cannot be stayed pending appeal, which PPLC cites for the proposition that MDEP's licensure decisions would not be entitled to procedural safeguards against delay if the Court determines such licenses are distinct from orders). The City and the State of Maine, on the other hand, argue that nothing in the text of the MDEP renewal license at issue suggests that it is an order with preemptive effect, and the use of the letterhead "Department Order," without more, does not bestow upon a license the power of preemption. Neither appeal to plain language wins the day in our view. The parties' attempts to define the term "order" by cherry-picking relevant provisions of the CCA are similarly unavailing. **[—13—]**

We therefore seek clarification from the Law Court. In so doing, we respectfully ask the Law Court to consider, as the district court did, whether interpreting **{–17–}** "order" to include MDEP licenses infringes upon "home rule" authority reserved for the state's municipalities. *See Portland Pipe Line Corp. v. City of S. Portland*, 288 F. Supp. 3d 321, 457 (D. Me. 2017) (explaining that "[t]here is no indication in the [CCA] that the State intended to remove local home rule authority over facility siting and use prohibitions through these [M]DEP licenses"); *id.* at 458 (observing that "[i]f the licenses had the preemptive effect PPLC claims, there is virtually no room for local regulation in this realm at all, since every single transfer facility must have a license"); *see also* Me. Rev. Stat. tit. 30-A, § 3001 (implementing home rule authority, which reserves for municipalities power that is "not denied either expressly or by clear implication").

2. Whether the Ordinance Is Expressly or Impliedly Preempted.

Next up, we welcome analysis from the Law Court on whether the CCA expressly or by implication preempts the Ordinance. First, assuming the 2010 MDEP renewal license is an "order" under § 556, we seek guidance regarding whether § 556 of the CCA expressly preempts the Ordinance. As mentioned, the parties disagree as to whether the license is an order such that § 556 applies here. The parties also disagree about whether, even if the license is an order, the terms of § 556 are such that the **[—14—]** Ordinance is expressly preempted. In support of their arguments, the parties offer competing interpretations of "in furtherance of the intent of this subchapter" and "direct conflict," as those terms appear in the text of § 556.

Second, even if the text of § 556 does not require express preemption here, the question remains whether the CCA, independent of any express preemption that it effects in consequence of § 556, impliedly preempts the Ordinance. Under Maine law, ordinances are preempted by implication only where "state law is interpreted to create a comprehensive and exclusive regulatory scheme inconsistent with the local action" or where "the municipal ordinance prevents the efficient accomplishment of a defined state purpose." *Dubois Livestock, Inc.*, 103 A.3d at 561 (citations omitted) (first quoting *Sawyer Envtl. Recovery Facilities, Inc. v. Town of Hampden*, 760 A.2d 257, 264 (Me. 2000) and then quoting *E. Perry Iron & Metal Co. v. City of Portland*, 941 A.2d 457, 462 (Me. 2008)). According to the City and the State of Maine, the Ordinance is not inconsistent with a "comprehensive and exclusive regulatory scheme," because the CCA -- in § 556 -- expressly contemplates local regulation. The City and the State also argue the Ordinance does not "prevent[] the efficient accomplishment of a defined state purpose," but they diverge as to why. PPLC, by contrast, argues both that the Ordinance intrudes into the CCA's comprehensive and exclusive regulatory scheme and that, because **[—15—]** the Ordinance's blanket prohibition on loading crude oil restricts the transfer of the same, the Ordinance prevents the efficient accomplishment of the CCA.

The district court and the parties rely primarily on the Law Court's implied preemption analysis in *Sawyer*, 760 A.2d 257 (Me. 2000) and *Smith v. Town of Pittston*, 820 A.2d 1200 (Me. 2003). In *Sawyer*, a municipal zoning ordinance prohibited the expansion of a solid waste facility after the expansion was approved by MDEP pursuant to state waste management laws. *Sawyer*, 760 A.2d at 265–66. Specifically, the ordinance was found to be preempted because its "absolute prohibition of the expansion prevent[ed] the 'efficient accomplishment' of the 'defined state purpose'" of Maine's Hazardous Waste, Septage and Solid Waste Management Act ("WMA"), **{–18–}** Me. Rev. Stat. tit. 38, §§ 1301-1319. *Id.* at 265. In *Smith*, the Law Court considered whether a municipal septage ordinance was preempted by an MDEP-issued septage spreading permit that the plaintiff received shortly after the ordinance at issue was enacted. *See Smith*, 820 A.2d at 1208-09. In concluding there was no preemption, the Law Court found that the ordinance did not frustrate the purpose of the WMA since it prohibited only one method of septage disposal while leaving other methods authorized by the WMA intact. *Id.* at 1208. Indeed, the Law Court explicitly recognized that "[i]f the Town's ordinance prohibited all methods of septage disposal, [the plaintiff] would have a stronger argument **[—16—]** that the purposes of [the WMA] are frustrated." *Id.* The district court nevertheless let *Smith*, rather than *Sawyer*, guide its application of the Law Court's state law preemption analysis. *See Portland Pipe Line Corp.*, 288 F. Supp. 3d at 458 ("As in *Smith*, this statute contemplates local zoning prohibitions and neither the statute nor [M]DEP review process involves the kind of local land use and impact considerations typically left to localities.").

We need not necessarily opine on the soundness of the district court's reasoning right now because the assertedly preemptive state statute at issue in *Smith* and *Sawyer* was the WMA, not the CCA, and thus those cases are not on all fours with the matter currently before us. In addition to serving a purpose distinct from that set forth in the CCA, the WMA includes an express ceiling on local regulation that would interfere with an activity authorized under the statute. *See* Me. Rev. Stat. tit. 38, § 1310-U (prohibiting municipalities "from enacting stricter standards than those [in the WMA] governing the hydrogeological criteria for siting or designing solid waste disposal facilities" and giving municipalities a limited role in the state licensing process). The CCA is not similarly expressive in outlining the contours of permissible municipal action. *See* Me. Rev. Stat. tit. 38, § 556 (providing that "ordinances and bylaws in furtherance of the intent of this subchapter . . . are valid unless in direct **[—17—]** conflict with this subchapter or any rule or order of the [MDEP]"). Thus, the Law Court's preemption analysis in *Smith* and *Sawyer* is not controlling here, where we must consider the scope of the CCA's regulatory regime to determine whether and to what extent it leaves room for municipal conduct. We are not aware of any decision of the Law Court that resolves whether the CCA preempts (either expressly or by implication) the Ordinance at issue here. Because there are no clear controlling precedents, the state law preemption questions (as set forth below) require certification.

The uniquely local policy interests at stake here also support certification. This is "not a case in which the 'policy arguments line up solely behind one solution.'" *In re Engage*, 544 F.3d at 57 (quoting *Boston Gas Co. v. Century Indem.*, 529 F.3d 8, 14 (1st Cir. 2008)). This case will impact the day-to-day licensure procedures of a state agency, the future of a local business that has been operating in the area for the better part of seventy-five years, and the City's authority to protect against perceived environmental threats to its coastline. The Law Court is better suited for the challenge of balancing these interests to the extent allowed by applicable state law preemption doctrine. **[—18—]**

III. Certification

For the reasons set forth herein, we certify the following three questions to the Maine Law Court:

(1) Is PPLC's license an "order," as that term is used in Me. Rev. Stat. tit. 38, § 556?

(2) If PPLC's license is an order, is the City of South Portland's Clear Skies Ordinance **{–19–}** preempted by Me. Rev. Stat. tit. 38, § 556 of Maine's Coastal Conveyance Act?

(3) Independent of Me. Rev. Stat. tit. 38, § 556, is there any basis for finding that Maine's Coastal Conveyance Act impliedly preempts the City of South Portland's Clear Skies Ordinance?

We would welcome further guidance from the Law Court on any other relevant aspect of Maine law that it believes would aid in the proper resolution of the issues before us.

The Clerk of this Court is directed to forward to the Maine Supreme Judicial Court, under the official seal of this Court, a copy of the certified questions, along with the merits briefs and appendices filed by the parties and the State of Maine as amici, as well as the supplemental briefs filed by the parties and the State of Maine pursuant to this Court's order dated September 23, 2019.

United States Court of Appeals
for the First Circuit

No. 15-2337

UNITED STATES
vs.
AYBAR-ULLOA

Petition for Rehearing En Banc

Entered: January 17, 2020

Citation: 947 F.3d 121, 8 Adm. R. 22 (1st Cir. 2020) (Mem.).

Before **HOWARD,** Chief Judge, and **TORRUELLA, LYNCH, THOMPSON, KAYATTA** and **BARRON,** Circuit Judges.

[—1—] {-121-} HAMILTON, Clerk:

ORDER OF COURT

A majority of the active judges who are not disqualified have voted to hear this case en banc. Accordingly, the petition for rehearing en banc is granted. In accordance with customary practice, the panel opinion and the dissent released on January 9, 2019 are withdrawn, and the judgment entered the same date is vacated. *See* 1st Cir. I.O.P. X(D).

The en banc court will have copies of the parties' previously filed briefs. The parties are also directed to file supplemental briefs addressing the following questions, in addition to any other questions the parties may wish to address.

1. Under Article I, section 8, clause 10 of the Constitution, "The Congress shall have Power . . . to define and punish Piracies and Felonies committed on the high Seas, and Offences against the Law of Nations." Does international law circumscribe Congress's power under this clause to define and to punish "Felonies committed on the high Seas" and exercise jurisdiction over persons who commit them? If so, under what circumstances would there be such a circumscription, what are the limitations on any such circumscription, and are those limits applicable in this case? **[—2—]**

2. Under the protective principle of international law "a nation is permitted to 'assert jurisdiction over a person whose conduct outside the nation's territory threatens the nation's security.'" *United States v. Cardales*, 168 F.3d 548, 553 (1st Cir. 1999) (quoting *United States v. Robinson*, 843 F.2d 1, 3 (1st Cir. 1988)). Does the protective principle allow a nation to prosecute all drug trafficking on the high seas that takes place on stateless vessels? What is the effect on this question of Congress's finding that "trafficking in controlled substances aboard vessels . . . presents a specific threat to the security . . . of the United States," 46 U.S.C. § 70501, on the scope of Congress's power?

3. For the purpose of determining whether Congress has the power under Article I to enact the MDLEA pursuant to the protective principle of international law, or any other constitutional provision, what is the significance, if any, of the fact that the MDLEA authorizes the United States to prosecute individuals engaged in drug trafficking abroad without regard to any geographic or other nexus to the United States? **{-122-}**

4. "International law . . . allows any state to extend its authority over a stateless ship." *United States v. Smith*, 680 F.2d 255, 258 (1st Cir. 1982). In *United States v. Victoria*, 876 F.2d 1009 (1st Cir. 1989), this court relied on that statement in *Smith* in stating that "the United States, as a matter of international law, may prosecute drug offenders on stateless ships found on the high seas." 876 F.2d at 1010 (citing *Smith*, 680 F.2d at 258). Does international law recognize a distinction between a state's authority to exercise juris-

diction over a stateless vessel, as this court recognized in *Smith*, and a state's authority to exercise domestic criminal jurisdiction over a foreign national found on a stateless vessel, as this court recognized in *Victoria*? If so, is our statement in *Victoria* relying on *Smith* nonetheless within the constitutional allocation of powers to the Congress to make?

5. To the extent that international law recognizes that a state has some authority to prosecute a foreign national found on a stateless vessel for a domestic criminal offense, what international law limits exist, if any, on such prosecutorial authority?

6. What is the effect of the doctrines of stare decisis and law of the circuit as to this Circuit's decisions in *Victoria*, *Cardales*, and *Robinson* with respect to questions one, two, three, four, and five?

The supplemental briefs should be filed simultaneously on, or before, February 18, 2020, and shall comply with applicable rules concerning format, service, and other requirements. Any reply supplemental briefs must be filed no later than 14 days after the principal supplemental briefs are filed. Seventeen paper copies of all briefs filed should be provided to the Clerk's Office no later than one business day after the electronic brief is filed. Amici are welcome to submit amicus briefs addressing the aforementioned questions.

The en banc hearing will be scheduled for Tuesday, May 5, 2020, at 9:30 a.m., En Banc Courtroom, 7th Floor, John Joseph Moakley Courthouse, Boston, Massachusetts. **[—3—]**

By the Court:

Maria R. Hamilton, Clerk

United States Court of Appeals
for the First Circuit

No. 18-2087

DANTZLER, INC.
VS.
S2 SERVS. P.R., LLC

Appeals from the United States District Court for the District of Puerto Rico

Decided: May 1, 2020

Citation: 958 F.3d 38, 8 Adm. R. 24 (1st Cir. 2020).

Before **TORRUELLA, DYK,*** and **THOMPSON,** Circuit Judges.

* Of the Federal Circuit, sitting by designation.

[—4—] {-42-} TORRUELLA, Circuit Judge:

These appeals concern a suit brought by a putative class of shippers (collectively, "Dantzler") who use the services of ocean freight carriers to import goods into Puerto Rico through the maritime port of San Juan. Their claims stem from a cargo scanning program implemented by the Puerto Rico Ports Authority ("PRPA") in an effort to improve the safety of the port. Pursuant to that program, PRPA contracted with Rapiscan Systems, Inc. ("Rapiscan")—which later assigned its rights and obligations to its wholly-owned subsidiary S2 Services Puerto Rico LLC ("S2")—to provide the technology and services needed to scan all containerized inbound cargo. To offset the costs of the program, PRPA charged the ocean freight carriers a fee for their use of the scanning facilities in the Port of San Juan. Dantzler alleges that, in response to that fee, ocean freight carriers were "forced" to be "collection agents" that collected fees from the shipper entities. Consequently, Dantzler brought a **{-43-}** Section 1983 lawsuit against PRPA, Rapiscan, and S2 together, seeking money damages and requesting that the United States District Court for the District of Puerto Rico declare and enjoin the collection of the additional fee as violative of the United States Constitution and Puerto Rico law. The defendants filed motions to dismiss the complaint, which the district court **[—5—]** granted in part and denied in part. They now appeal the partial denial of those motions.

In the end, their appeals reduce to a question of standing over which we have jurisdiction in these appeals from the denial of immunity. *See Asociación De Subscripción Conjunta Del Seguro De Responsabilidad Obligatorio v. Flores Galarza*, 484 F.3d 1, 20 n.22 (1st Cir. 2007). For the following reasons, we find that Dantzler has failed to establish its constitutional standing to sue PRPA, Rapiscan, and S2, and thus we vacate the district court's order and remand for dismissal on jurisdictional grounds.

I. *Background*

Because these appeals follow from a decision on motions to dismiss, we draw the facts from Dantzler's amended complaint and any documents incorporated by reference therein. *See Katz v. Pershing, LLC*, 672 F.3d 64, 69 (1st Cir. 2012).

A. Factual Background

On February 18, 2008, the Puerto Rico legislature enacted Act No. 12 of 2008 ("Act 12"), which called for improved safety procedures in Puerto Rico's ports. P.R. Laws Ann. tit. 23, §§ 3221-3223. Prior to this law, port security "was predominantly limited to random and manual searches of cargo." *Industria y Distribución de Alimentos v. Trailer Bridge*, 797 F.3d 141, 143, 3 Adm. R. 56, 56 (1st Cir. 2015). **[—6—]**

As a result of Act 12, on December 17, 2009, PRPA contracted Rapiscan to provide cargo scanning services for the scanning of containerized inbound cargo at the Port of San Juan on behalf of PRPA. On August 6, 2010, with PRPA's consent, Rapiscan assigned its rights and obligations under the contract to its wholly-owned subsidiary, S2.

On February 16, 2011, PRPA and the Puerto Rico Treasury Department executed a "Memorandum of Understanding" ("MOU") in which PRPA acknowledged that "it [was] not the government instrumentality with the proper legal jurisdiction and authority to intervene as of right" in the "well known" practice of concealing items in cargo containers "to avoid—among other reasons—paying the applicable excise or other related taxes." The authority to inspect cargo containers upon their arrival in Puerto Rico inhered in the Puerto Rico Treasury Department "as one of its powers in furtherance of its goal to collect taxes." However, the MOU recalled that on August 2, 2007, PRPA and the Treasury Department had signed a multi-party agreement with other Puerto Rico agencies and instrumentalities whereby they "agreed to cooperate in order to implement Puerto Rico's tax laws."[1] Because **[—7—]** of "the important public policy interest involved and in the spirit of interagency cooperation," PRPA and the Puerto Rico Treasury Department agreed that PRPA, via S2, would assist in the scanning of cargo that arrived at the Port of San Juan.

Subsequently, on September 2, 2011, PRPA approved Regulation 8067,[2] which **{-44-}** enabled PRPA to "implement a fast[-]track method of inspecting inbound [c]argo [c]ontainers which will detect undisclosed taxable goods, as well as increase port security in the Port of San Juan, while preserving a free flow of commerce and the efficient movement of cargo." To recover the heightened costs associated with the scanning program incurred by PRPA, Regulation 8067 established a system of "Enhanced Security Fees" ("ESFs"), which were assessed by PRPA on ocean freight carriers or their agents arriving and unloading cargo in the Port of San Juan (in addition to existing fees already charged for use of the port).[3] Dantzler alleges, without any substantiation, that the defendants "forced ocean carriers . . . into becoming [d]efendants' [ESF] **[—8—]** collection agents" that "collected [ESFs] from shippers like [Dantzler]."

On October 16, 2013, a federal court found the ESFs unconstitutional "as applied to shipping operators that neither use nor have the privilege of using PRPA scanning facilities," because the imposition of such fees on those entities violated the Commerce Clause. *Cámara de Mercadeo, Industria, y Distribución de Alimentos v. Vázquez*, No. 11-1978, 2013 WL 5652076, at *12, *14 (D.P.R. Oct. 16, 2013). The court also enjoined PRPA from collecting ESFs from "shipping operators [whose cargo is] not being scanned pursuant to Regulation No. 8067." *Id.* at *15.[4] We upheld these rulings as well as the constitutionality of PRPA's scanning program as applied to shipping operators who have access to the scanning service. *See Trailer Bridge*, 797 F.3d at 143, 145, 3 Adm. R. at 57–58. PRPA, through S2 and Rapiscan, allegedly continued to assess ESFs on shippers that imported cargo that was not containerized, on shippers which did not have access to scanning stations, and on shippers whose cargo was not scanned at all.

Pursuant to Regulation 8067, the authorization for using the scanning program would end on June 30, 2014, "unless [the] **[—9—]** term was extended, modified[,] or amended prior [to] its expiration." Although PRPA never modified, extended, or amended such term prior to June 30, 2014, it nevertheless "continued to implement the cargo scanning program despite and beyond its expiration." On October 28, 2016, the Puerto Rico Court of Appeals issued a judgment ordering PRPA to cease and desist from continuing to implement the program because Regulation 8067 had expired. *See Cámara de Mercadeo, Industria y Distribución de Alimentos v. Autoridad de los Puertos*, No. 2015-002, 2016 WL 7046805, at *8 (P.R. Ct.

[1] Act 12 adopted the purpose, findings, and policy objectives of the August 2007 multi-party agreement. *See* P.R. Laws Ann. tit. 23, §§ 3221-3223.

[2] Regulation 8067 is titled "Regulation for Implementing the Necessary Means to Guarantee an Efficient Flow of Commercial Traffic in the Scanning of Inbound Cargo Containers, to Improve Security and Safety at the Port Facilities, and/or to Otherwise Implement the Public Policy of the Commonwealth of Puerto Rico Delegated upon the Ports Authority."

[3] The amount of the ESF varied based on the weight and type of cargo.

[4] The court found that "[o]nly three shipping operators' terminals [were] . . . equipped with PRPA scanning facilities," and that bulk cargo was not scanned. *Vázquez*, No. 11-1978, 2013 WL 5652076, at *5.

App. Oct. 28, 2016). Nevertheless, PRPA, Rapiscan, and S2 allegedly continued to assess and collect ESFs in connection with the scanning program.

PRPA, Rapiscan, and S2 have jointly "collected and derived economic benefit from the [ESFs]," which has caused Dantzler to "sustain[] substantial and continuing economic losses in total amounts . . . reasonably believed to be in excess of $150,000,000.00."

B. Procedural History

On April 5, 2017, Dantzler sued PRPA, Rapiscan, and S2 in the United States **{-45-}** District Court for the District of Puerto Rico "seeking disgorgement of unlawfully collected scanning fees on shipments imported through the maritime port of San Juan." Subsequently, on August 30, 2017, it amended its complaint, seeking **[—10—]** relief pursuant to 42 U.S.C. § 1983 for PRPA, Rapiscan, and S2's alleged violation of Dantzler's constitutional rights under the Fifth and Fourteenth Amendments and the Commerce Clause of the United States Constitution. Dantzler alleged that the fees it and other similarly-situated shipper entities paid for the scanning of cargo imported through the Port of San Juan "were illegally collected by Defendants under color of law and authority." The amended complaint also asserted causes of action for unjust enrichment and restitution against all three defendants pursuant to Articles 7 and 1795 of the Puerto Rico Civil Code, respectively. Additionally, Dantzler sought a declaration that S2 was the alter ego of Rapiscan, an injunction of PRPA, Rapiscan, and S2's "unlawful conduct," and the reimbursement "for any monies paid pursuant to [that] unlawful conduct."

On December 19, 2017, Rapiscan and S2 filed a motion to dismiss the amended complaint for lack of subject-matter jurisdiction and failure to state a claim under Fed. R. Civ. P. 12(b)(1) and (12)(b)(6). They argued that (1) Dantzler lacked standing to challenge the ESFs because it was the ocean freight carriers who paid those fees, not Dantzler; (2) the amended complaint failed to state a claim under 42 U.S.C. § 1983 "because it [did] not allege that Rapiscan or S2 individually caused any violation of [Dantzler's] alleged constitutional rights"; **[—11—]** (3) Rapiscan and S2 were entitled to qualified immunity "as a former and current government contractor"; and (4) the amended complaint "fail[ed] to state claims for unjust enrichment and undue collection under Puerto Rico law because it d[id] not allege that Rapiscan or S2 received compensation for their services without cause."

On May 23, 2018, PRPA also moved to dismiss the amended complaint for lack of subject-matter jurisdiction, failure to state a claim, and failure to join a required party under Fed. R. Civ. P. 12(b)(1), 12(b)(6), and 12(b)(7), respectively. PRPA, like Rapiscan and S2, asserted that Dantzler lacked constitutional standing to bring its claims because they were "improperly anchored on [the] [ocean freight] carrier's independent decisions to charge operating fees." PRPA also maintained that, in any event, (1) it was "cloaked with sovereign immunity" because it was "an arm of the state for purposes of the cargo scanning program"; (2) Dantzler's Section 1983 claims were mostly time barred; (3) the amended complaint failed to state a cause of action for unjust enrichment or undue collection; (4) Dantzler's claims grounded on PRPA's alleged ultra vires conduct were inapposite; and (5) Dantzler failed to include the ocean freight carriers, "who [were] indispensable to any litigation challenging the collection of ESFs." **[—12—]**

On September 26, 2018, the district court partially granted Rapiscan, S2, and PRPA's motions to dismiss. *Dantzler, Inc. v. P.R. Ports Auth.*, 335 F. Supp. 3d 226 (D.P.R. 2018). It dismissed Dantzler's Fifth and Fourteenth Amendment claims brought under Section 1983, but it denied the motions as to the Commerce Clause and Puerto Rico law claims. *Id.* at 239. We recount the court's rationale regarding the issues relevant on appeal.

First, the district court rejected PRPA, Rapiscan, and S2's standing argument, concluding that Dantzler had successfully established that it met the constitutional requirements for standing. *Id.* at 242. Specifically, the court found that, while the ESFs were imposed on ocean freight carriers, **{–46–}** the carriers "collected those fees" from Dantzler, and thus, Dantzler was, "[a]t [a] minimum, . . . allegedly injured indirectly by the government regulation," and that injury was "fairly traceable" to PRPA, Rapiscan, and S2. *Id.* at 241-42.

Next, the district court also found that PRPA was not entitled to sovereign immunity because it was not "an arm of the state." *Id.* at 243. It concluded that, although the structural indicators used to determine whether Puerto Rico intended PRPA to be an arm of the state "point[ed] in different directions," *id.*, because PRPA failed to demonstrate that Puerto Rico "would be liable for a judgment against PRPA in this case," or that "the **[—13—]** Puerto Rico Department of Treasury would pay for the damages in this action," *id.* at 244, PRPA was not entitled to immunity, *id.* at 245.

Finally, the district court determined that Rapiscan and S2 were not entitled to qualified immunity because they were "not individual people, and therefore [were] not government 'officials'" for purposes of the qualified immunity analysis. *Id.* at 253. In making its determination, the court adopted the Sixth Circuit Court of Appeals's position that "private corporations are not public officials" and cannot be entitled to qualified immunity. *Id.* at 252 (citing *Hammons v. Norfolk S. Corp.*, 156 F.3d 701, 706 n.9 (6th Cir. 1998)).

On October 19, 2018, Rapiscan and S2 timely appealed the partial denial of their motion to dismiss based on standing and qualified immunity. PRPA similarly filed a notice of appeal seeking review of the district court's denial based on standing and sovereign immunity.

II. *Discussion*

PRPA, Rapiscan, and S2 have a threshold argument in common: they assert that Dantzler's claims must be dismissed for lack of subject matter jurisdiction because Dantzler fails to satisfy the standing requirements of Article III of the United States Constitution to challenge the ESFs. "[B]ecause standing **[—14—]** is a prerequisite to a federal court's subject matter jurisdiction," *Hochendoner v. Genzyme Corp.*, 823 F.3d 724, 730 (1st Cir. 2016), and we must "assure ourselves of our jurisdiction under the federal Constitution" before we proceed to the merits of a case, *Pérez-Kudzma v. United States*, 940 F.3d 142, 144, 7 Adm. R. 88, 89 (1st Cir. 2019), we begin (and end) by addressing the appellants' standing arguments.

A. Article III Standing Principles

"[N]o principle is more fundamental to the judiciary's proper role in our system of government than the constitutional limitation of federal-court jurisdiction to actual cases or controversies." *Massachusetts v. U.S. Dep't of Health & Human Servs.*, 923 F.3d 209, 221 (1st Cir. 2019) (alteration in original) (quoting *DaimlerChrysler Corp. v. Cuno*, 547 U.S. 332, 341 (2006)). To "assure[] respect" for this limitation, *Hochendoner*, 823 F.3d at 731, "plaintiffs must 'establish that they have standing to sue,'" *U.S. Dep't of Health & Human Servs.*, 923 F.3d at 221 (quoting *Raines v. Byrd*, 521 U.S. 811, 818 (1997)).

"The existence vel non of standing is a legal question and, therefore, engenders de novo review." *Me. People's All. & Nat. Res. Def. Council v. Mallinckrodt, Inc.*, 471 F.3d 277, 283 (1st Cir. 2006); *see also ITyX Solutions AG v. Kodak Alaris, Inc.*, 952 F.3d 1, 9 (1st Cir. 2020). PRPA, Rapiscan, and S2's challenge **[—15—]** of Dantzler's standing arises in the pleading stage, so this Court takes all well-pleaded facts in the complaint as true and "indulge[s] all reasonable inferences" in Dantzler's favor **{–47–}** to determine whether it plausibly pleaded facts necessary to demonstrate standing to bring the action. *Hochendoner*, 823 F.3d at 730; *see also Lujan v. Defs. of Wildlife*, 504 U.S. 555, 561 (1992) ("Since [the elements of standing] are not mere pleading requirements but rather an indispensable part of the plaintiff's case, each element must be supported . . . with the manner and degree of evidence required at the successive stages of the litigation."). Conclusory assertions or unfounded speculation will not suffice. *See Hochendoner*, 823 F.3d at 731.

Furthermore, the "irreducible constitutional minimum" of standing entails three elements. *Spokeo, Inc. v. Robins*, 136 S. Ct. 1540, 1547 (2016); *Pérez-Kudzma*, 940 F.3d at 144-45, 7 Adm. R. at 89. A plaintiff must establish "(1) an injury in fact which is 'concrete and particularized' and 'actual or imminent, not conjectural or hypothetical,' (2) that the injury is 'fairly traceable to the challenged action,' and (3) that it is 'likely . . . that the injury will be redressed by a favorable decision.'" *U.S. Dep't of Health & Human Servs.*, 923 F.3d at 221-22 (quoting *Lujan*, 504 U.S. at 560). **[—16—]**

An injury is "concrete" if it is real, and not abstract. *Spokeo, Inc.*, 136 S. Ct. at 1548. To be particularized, the plaintiff must have been affected "'in a personal and individual way' by the injurious conduct," *Hochendoner*, 823 F.3d at 731 (quoting *Spokeo, Inc.*, 136 S. Ct. at 1548), and must allege "that he, himself, is among the persons injured by that conduct," *id.* at 732. The injury must either have happened or there must be a sufficient threat of it occurring to be actual or imminent. *Katz*, 672 F.3d at 71.

The "traceability" or causation element "requires the plaintiff to show a sufficiently direct causal connection between the challenged action and the identified harm." *Id.* That connection "cannot be overly attenuated." *Id.* (quoting *Donahue v. City of Bos.*, 304 F.3d 110, 115 (1st Cir. 2002)). "[C]ausation is absent if the injury stems from the independent action of a third party," *id.* at 71-72, so long as the injury is not the product of that third party's "coercive effect," *Wine & Spirits Retailers, Inc. v. Rhode Island*, 418 F.3d 36, 45 (1st Cir. 2005) (quoting *Bennett v. Spear*, 520 U.S. 154, 169 (1997)).

Finally, the redressability element of standing requires that the plaintiff allege "that a favorable resolution of [its] claim would likely redress the professed injury." *Katz*, 672 F.3d at 72. This means that it cannot be merely speculative that, if **[—17—]** a court grants the requested relief, the injury will be redressed. *See Simon v. E. Ky. Welfare Rights Org.*, 426 U.S. 26, 42-43 (1976).

Against this background, we now consider whether Dantzler has standing to bring its claims against PRPA, Rapiscan, and S2.

B. Article III Standing for Claims Against PRPA

Dantzler posits that it has constitutional standing because it was among the "class of clearly foreseeable shippers" who were "harmed in their individual capacities by improper charges" and it satisfies all the requirements for standing. Specifically, Dantzler argues that (1) its injury does not deal with the regulation of ocean freight carriers but instead with the direct losses it suffered as a result of paying the ESFs, which caused an economic harm of approximately $150 million; (2) it has shown that PRPA's conduct "was a substantial factor in producing" its injury, and even an attenuated causal chain may satisfy Article III's standing requirements; and (3) its injury is redressable through a monetary award. **{-48-}**

We are unconvinced by Dantzler's argument and instead agree with PRPA that Dantzler has failed to set forth allegations in its complaint that are sufficient to establish its Article III standing. **[—18—]**

Dantzler's amended complaint alleges that PRPA's "negligent, reckless[,] and illegal act[]" of collecting ESFs in connection with the cargo scanning program has caused it and "other similarly situated shippers" to "sustain[] substantial and continuing economic losses in total amounts which are unknown at this time, but reasonably believed to be in excess of $150,000,000.00." While PRPA disputes the accuracy of these allegations, we must take them as true at this stage and determine whether they are sufficient to allege an injury-in-fact. *See Hochendoner*, 823 F.3d at 730. "It is a bedrock proposition that 'a relatively small economic loss—even an "identifiable trifle"—is enough to confer standing.'" *Katz*, 672 F.3d at 76 (quoting *Adams v. Watson*, 10 F.3d 915, 924 (1st Cir. 1993)). Thus, Dantzler's allegation of economic harm satisfies the injury-in-fact requirement. *See id.* Nevertheless, it stumbles over the remaining two requirements of Article III standing—causation and redressability.

Dantzler fails to plausibly allege that PRPA's assessment and collection of ESFs from third parties not before the court—*i.e.*, the ocean freight carriers—directly caused its injury. *See id.* at 77–78. The Supreme Court has cautioned against courts finding that a plaintiff's injury is fairly traceable to a defendant's conduct where the plaintiff alleges a **[—19—]** causal chain dependent on actions of third parties. *See Allen v. Wright*, 468 U.S. 737, 757-59 (1984) (finding the "links in the chain of causation" between the challenged conduct and the alleged injury "far too weak for the chain as a whole to sustain . . . standing" where the chain involved "numerous third parties" whose independent actions had an uncertain and speculative effect); *Simon*, 426 U.S. at 42-45 (finding that decisions by a third party were too uncertain, which broke the chain of causation between the injury and the challenged actions). The injury Dantzler alleges it suffered depended on the actions of the ocean freight carriers, the entities that were required to pay the ESFs to PRPA. Dantzler did not directly pay the ESFs to PRPA, nor did PRPA assess the ESFs on Dantzler; rather, Dantzler alleges, without elaboration, that the ocean freight carriers collected ESFs from their customers—*i.e.*, the shipper entities like Dantzler. As the injury here is indirect, Dantzler has a much more difficult job proving a causal chain. *See Lujan*, 504 U.S. at 562; *Simon*, 426 U.S. at 44-45.

Dantzler alleged in its amended complaint the following:

> According to Regulation 8067, the ocean carriers or their agents[] must pay PRPA the [ESFs] to recover the costs incurred by PRPA in the scanning program. Ocean carriers and their agents, in turn, collected [ESFs] from shippers like named Plaintiffs and putative class members who import cargo through the maritime ports of San Juan. Thus, in furtherance of their scheme, Defendants, Rapiscan, S2 Services and **[—20—]** [] PRPA purposely forced ocean carriers and their agents into becoming Defendants' [ESF] collection agents.

But Dantzler's allegation "is nothing more than a bare hypothesis that [ocean freight carriers] possibly might push this aspect of [their] operational costs onto [Dantzler]." *Katz*, 672 F.3d at 77. Under the regulation, ocean freight carriers had to pay PRPA the ESFs, but neither the regulation nor PRPA controlled the ocean freight carriers' **{–49–}** relationships with their customers, such as Dantzler. Dantzler does not otherwise plausibly allege that ocean freight carriers were forced by PRPA (or Rapiscan and S2) to collect the ESFs from Dantzler (or anyone else). *See Ashcroft v. Iqbal*, 556 U.S. 662, 678 (2009). Nor does Dantzler plausibly allege that PRPA coerced the ocean freight carriers to collect the ESFs from Dantzler. *See Wine & Spirits Retailers, Inc.*, 418 F.3d at 45.

The complaint does not describe Dantzler's injury "in terms specific enough to indicate that it will result from" PRPA's imposition of ESFs on ocean freight carriers rather than from a "multitude of other factors." *Pérez-Kudzma*, 940 F.3d at 145, 7 Adm. R. at 90. As a result, Dantzler fails to demonstrate how PRPA imposing ESFs on a third party caused the injury of which it complains. This case is therefore very similar to *Ammex, Inc. v. United States*, 367 F.3d 530 (6th Cir. 2004), which held that a gas station did not **[—21—]** have standing to challenge gas taxes paid by suppliers from which the station purchased gasoline. *Id.* at 534. Moreover, Dantzler has not provided sufficient "factual matter," *Iqbal*, 556 U.S. at 677, in its complaint to support its theory that the ocean freight carriers were "forced" into being the defendants' "collection agent." Dantzler thus fails to satisfy the causation requirement for Article III standing.

While this is dispositive of Dantzler's standing argument, we also address the redressability requirement, as these two elements "hinge on the response" of the ocean freight carriers—the party charged the ESFs. *See Lujan*, 504 U.S. at 562 (finding that "causation and redressability ordinarily hinge on the response of the regulated (or regulable) third party to the government action or inaction").

For much the same reason there is no causation, Dantzler fails to successfully allege redressability. Although Dantzler need not demonstrate that its entire injury will be redressed by a favorable judgment, it must show that the court can fashion a remedy that will at least lessen its injury. *Antilles Cement Corp. v. Fortuño*, 670 F.3d 310, 318 (1st Cir. 2012); *see also Simon*, 426 U.S. at 43-46 (requiring that plaintiffs show it is likely, rather than speculative, that their injury will be redressed). The complaint in this case seeks predominantly **[—22—]** injunctive and declaratory relief. Because redressing Dantzler's injury depends in large part, if not in total, on the conduct of the ocean freight carriers—namely, what they decide to charge (disguised as ESF-related costs or otherwise) to their customers—it is far from certain that enjoining PRPA from collecting ESFs from the ocean freight carriers, or declaring ESFs unconstitutional, will guarantee that those carriers lower the costs they charge Dantzler. *See Lujan*, 504 U.S. at 568; *Simon*, 426 U.S. at 45-46. The ocean freight carriers, who were not made parties to the case, would not be bound to treat Dantzler differently in the event of an injunction or declaration of unconstitutionality. Thus, Dantzler has not demonstrated that its injury would be alleviated by the relief the district court could have provided in this case[5] and has thus failed to show redressability. **{-50-}**

Accordingly, Dantzler has failed to satisfy the constitutional standing requirements with respect to its Commerce Clause and Puerto Rico law claims against PRPA.[6] **[—23—]**

C. Article III Standing for Claims Against Rapiscan and S2

For substantially the same reasons as we find that Dantzler lacked standing to assert its claims against PRPA, we hold that Dantzler similarly fails to set forth allegations in its complaint that are sufficient to establish its constitutional standing to sue Rapiscan and S2. Additionally, we emphasize the limited role that Rapiscan and S2 play in the alleged scheme. Rapiscan and S2 simply provide the scanning services for containerized cargo that arrives at the Port of San Juan pursuant to a contract with PRPA. Rapiscan and S2 are not involved in the assessment or collection of the ESFs. Indeed, the complaint alleges that ocean freight carriers paid those fees exclusively to PRPA.

Consequently, Dantzler does not plausibly allege that its injury resulted from Rapiscan and S2's actual scanning of cargo or from accepting payment from PRPA for its scanning services, **[—24—]** which to some extent was derived from PRPA's collection of ESFs from the ocean freight carriers. It follows, thus, that the causal chain in this scenario is even more attenuated (if not completely broken) than it is in the scenario above with respect to PRPA, as Rapiscan and S2 were not engaged in either the assessment or collection of the ESFs that allegedly injured Dantzler. Therefore, neither the assessment nor the collection of the ESFs is "fairly traceable" to Rapiscan and S2. *Pérez-Kudzma*, 940 F3d at 145, 7 Adm. R. at 89; *see Katz*, 672 F.3d at 71 (finding that "the opposing party must be the source of the harm").

---

[5] We acknowledge that Dantzler satisfies the redressability requirement insofar as it seeks money damages to redress its economic injury. *See Donahue v. City of Bos.*, 304 F.3d 110, 116 (1st Cir. 2002) (requiring that courts examine whether a plaintiff has standing for each form of relief sought). However, as we already explained, it still fails to establish causation, which is fatal to the standing inquiry.

[6] While our conclusion makes it unnecessary to reach PRPA's **[—23—]** argument that it is entitled to sovereign immunity, we note that given the analytical framework set forth in *Grajales v. P.R. Ports Auth.*, 831 F.3d 11 (1st Cir. 2016), combined with the fact that the cargo scanning program was implemented to further the governmental purposes of improving national security and ensuring proper tax collection, we find it difficult to see how PRPA cannot be cloaked with sovereign immunity here in its performance of an inspection function that is governmental in nature. *See id.* at 20 n.9; *see also Thacker v. Tenn. Valley Auth.*, 139 S. Ct. 1435, 7 Adm. R. 31 (2019). We view this, thus, as an alternative ground supporting our ultimate conclusion vacating and remanding the district court's order and partial judgment.

Likewise, with respect to Dantzler's claims against Rapiscan and S2, redressability not only depends on the conduct of the ocean freight carriers who are not parties to this case, but the injunctive and declaratory relief Dantzler seeks, if granted against Rapiscan and S2, would have absolutely no effect to remedy the alleged injury because it is PRPA who imposes the fees Dantzler alleges are being collected from it.[7] And since "a federal court [can] act only to redress injury that fairly can be traced to the challenged action of the defendant, and not injury that results from the independent action of some third party not before the **[—25—]** court," Dantzler has not met the redressability requirement as to its claim for damages. *See Simon*, 426 U.S. at 41-42. Thus, Dantzler has not demonstrated that its injury would be lessened by the relief it requests from the court with respect to Rapiscan and S2, and thus fails to show redressability. Accordingly, Dantzler **{-51-}** lacks Article III standing to assert its claims against Rapiscan and S2.

We need not go further. We agree with PRPA, Rapiscan, and S2 that Dantzler has failed to set forth allegations in its complaint that are sufficient to establish its Article III standing. We therefore conclude that Dantzler cannot assert its claims against the defendants.

III. *Conclusion*

For the foregoing reasons, we vacate the district court's order and partial judgment and remand for dismissal on jurisdictional grounds. The parties shall bear their own costs.

Vacated and Remanded.

---

[7] We do not interpret Dantzler's claims to challenge the actual scanning service performed by Rapiscan and S2 but the assessment of ESFs by PRPA as a consequence of the costs incurred by the scanning program.

United States Court of Appeals
for the First Circuit

No. 17-2213

RIJO
VS.
UNITED STATES

Appeal from the United States District Court for the District of Puerto Rico

Decided: December 3, 2020

Citation: 982 F.3d 13, 8 Adm. R. 32 (1st Cir. 2020).

Before **HOWARD,** Chief Judge, and **THOMPSON** and **KAYATTA,** Circuit Judges.

[—2—] **{-13-}** **KAYATTA,** Circuit Judge: **{-14-}**

Sandri Rijo was found guilty after trial of conspiring to possess with intent to distribute five kilograms of cocaine and of aiding and abetting others to do so as well. On direct appeal, we affirmed his conviction and sentence. *See United States v. Cruz-Feliciano*, 786 F.3d 78, 92, 3 Adm. R. 39, 47 (1st Cir. 2015).

Rijo thereafter timely filed a habeas petition under 28 U.S.C. § 2255. On the papers, the district court dismissed Rijo's section 2255 petition. We then granted a certificate of appealability under 28 U.S.C. § 2253(c)(2), allowing this appeal on a single issue: whether defense counsel rendered ineffective assistance in deciding not to call two witnesses and introduce certain documents. For the following reasons, we now affirm the dismissal of Rijo's petition.

I.

In January 2012, law enforcement apprehended a group of men, including Rijo, after observing them in the process of smuggling a substantial amount of cocaine by motorboat. *See Cruz-Feliciano*, 786 F.3d at 82–83, 3 Adm. R. at 39–40. A later prepared DEA Report of Investigation stated that, according to cooperating witness Freddy Altagracia-Medina, Rijo was on board the motorboat that brought the drugs to shore. *See id.* at 85, 3 Adm. R. at 42. This statement conflicted with Altagracia's testimony at trial that Rijo was on the shore to receive the drugs while his co-defendants Gary Brito-González and **[—3—]** Sandy Navarro were on the boat. *See id.* at 86, 3 Adm. R. at 42. The rough notes of the DEA agent who prepared the report revealed that the agent had apparently confused "Sandy (Navarro)" with "Sandri (Rijo)" in reducing Altagracia's oral statement to rough notes and then to a report. *See id.* at 85-86, 3 Adm. R. at 42.

Rijo's defense counsel at trial opted not to try to exploit this error. In a nutshell, he regarded the inconsistency as a dead end, given that it was so easily explained as the agent's mistake, and he feared that the foray would simply re-run the prosecution's narrative. Rijo now argues that the decision not to introduce the DEA report and the agent's notes and not to cross-examine Altagracia on the inconsistency between the report and his testimony violated Rijo's right to effective assistance of counsel under the Sixth Amendment. *See, e.g., Strickland v. Washington*, 466 U.S. 668, 686 (1984). Success in making such an argument requires a showing that counsel's performance was "outside the wide range of professionally competent assistance," *id.* at 690, and that there is a "reasonable probability" that the trial would have ended more favorably to the defendant but for counsel's errors, *id.* at 694.

For the reasons well stated by the district court, we find it unlikely that counsel's trial strategy decision was so unreasonable as to constitute deficient performance under *Strickland*. But even if counsel's performance was deficient, **[—4—]** Rijo's ineffective assistance claim still fails because there is no reasonable probability that the results of the trial would have differed had counsel done what Rijo now argues he should have done. Law enforcement surveilled the unloading as it occurred and then stopped the smuggler's vehicles as they left the scene, finding Rijo in one of them. *See Cruz-Feliciano*, 786 F.3d at 82–83, 3 Adm. R. at 39–40. Moreover, government witnesses other than Altagracia also testified that Rijo was involved in the smuggling. *See id.*, 3 Adm. R. at 40. Given Rijo's immediate **{-15-}** apprehension at the scene and the government witnesses' testimony, we find it highly unlikely that any jurors would have been persuaded by an effort to exploit the easily explained error in the DEA reports about whether Rijo was on the boat or on the shore unloading drugs from the boat.

II.

For the foregoing reasons, we *affirm.*

This page intentionally left blank

United States Court of Appeals for the Second Circuit

United States Court of Appeals
for the Second Circuit

No. 19-1140

POWER AUTH. OF THE STATE OF N.Y.
vs.
M/V ELLEN S. BOUCHARD[1]

Appeal from the United States District Court for the Southern District of New York

Decided: July 30, 2020

Citation: 968 F.3d 165, 8 Adm. R. 36 (2d Cir. 2020).

Before **LIVINGSTON**, **LOHIER**, and **NARDINI**, Circuit Judges.

[—3—] {-166-} **NARDINI**, Circuit Judge:

This appeal arises from the discharge of several thousand gallons of oil into Long Island Sound from a "submarine cable"—that is, an underwater system that transmits electricity, and through which dielectric fluid is pumped as a lubricant and coolant. The plaintiff-appellant, the Power Authority of the State of New York ("the Authority"), alleges that the dropped anchor of the Barge B. No. 280, which was being towed by the tugboat M/V *Ellen S. Bouchard*, ruptured the cable, which the Authority owns and operates. Following the containment and remediation of the oil discharge, the Authority sought compensation for its expenditures by suing the defendants-appellees: the two vessels and their corporate owners **[—4—]** (collectively, "Bouchard"). The Authority brought claims pursuant to the federal Oil Pollution Act ("OPA"), 33 U.S.C. § 2701 *et seq.*, and the New York Oil Spill Law ("NYOSL"), N.Y. Nav. Law § 170 *et seq.* The corporate defendants-appellees, meanwhile, initiated parallel proceedings pursuant to the Limitation of Liability Act ("Limitation Act"), 46 U.S.C. §§ 30505, 30511.

The Authority now appeals from an order and judgment of the United States District Court for the Southern District of New York (Crotty, *J.*), which determined that the OPA's statutory definition of a "facility," 33 U.S.C. § 2702(9), did not encompass the submarine cable because it was not "used for" any of the "purposes" enumerated in the definition. As a result, the Authority did not have a viable claim under the OPA to recover its costs related to the discharge. The district court entered partial summary judgment in favor of Bouchard on the OPA claims, denied the Authority's cross-motion for summary **[—5—]** judgment, and transferred the Authority's **{-167-}** remaining state-law claims to the parallel Limitation Act proceeding.

We hold that the submarine cable is indeed "used for" one of the enumerated "purposes" in the statute's definition of "facility." It was therefore error for the district court to dismiss the Authority's OPA claims and to conclude that the Authority's NYOSL claims had to be brought in the parallel proceeding on that basis. Accordingly, we vacate the order of the district court and remand for further proceedings consistent with this opinion.

I. Background[2]

A. The Submarine Cables

The Authority owns and operates the Y-49 Cable System, a power transmission cable system that spans Long Island Sound. The cable system runs from the Sprain Brook Substation in Westchester **[—6—]** County, which Consolidated Edison ("Con Edison") operates, to the East Garden City Substation in Nassau County, which the Long Island Power Authority operates.

There are four submarine cables spanning Long Island Sound, with two self-contained fluid-filled ("SCFF") pressurization plants located at the two ends of the cables. The four submarine cables are high-voltage transmission cables consisting of multiple layers, including the electrical conductor and a layer of "fluid-impregnated paper insulation." Joint App'x 479. Additionally, a central duct in each cable is filled with dielectric fluid, which is a "hydrocarbon,

[1] The Clerk of Court is respectfully directed to amend the caption as set forth above.

[2] Except as otherwise noted, these facts are not in dispute.

petroleum-based oil" that "acts as a coolant and lubricant to the electrical components of the submerged cables." *Id.* at 603–04. The four cables combined hold approximately 10,000 gallons of the dielectric fluid at any given time.

The SCFF pressurization plants, meanwhile, are comprised of storage tanks holding reserve dielectric fluid, as well as equipment to **[—7—]** monitor and regulate the pressure in the submarine cables. The plants are required to keep a constant static pressure in the cables to ensure the cables function properly. To do that, the plants increase or decrease the volume of dielectric fluid stored in the cables. Because the maintenance of constant pressure requires differing amounts of fluid depending on, among other things, the temperature of the water surrounding the cables, the dielectric fluid regularly flows through the plants and cables.

B. The Discharge

On January 6, 2014, the defendant Barge B. No. 280, in the course of being towed by the M/V *Ellen S. Bouchard* through Long Island Sound, dropped anchor. Shortly thereafter, Submarine Cable No. 3 experienced an electrical fault; at the same time, the system's monitors reported a sudden pressure drop in the cable, which indicated a leak of dielectric fluid was underway. The Authority alerted local and federal authorities, while also working with Con **[—8—]** Edison and the Long Island Power Authority to initiate a response. Over the next several weeks, these entities, along with the Authority's environmental response contractor, Miller Environmental Group, took efforts to contain and then clean up the spill, in consultation with the U.S. Coast Guard and New York officials. Among the required containment steps was the continued pumping of dielectric fluid into Cable No. 3, to maintain pressure and prevent water from entering the cable and potentially destroying it. Because of this ongoing need to pump fluid into the cable, the total discharge from Cable No. 3 was well above the cable's **{-168-}** capacity of 2500 gallons. On February 27, 2014, the cable was finally capped and set back on to the sea floor. The Authority claims that it paid $9,848,087.12 for the costs of the remediation.

C. Statutory Framework

Congress enacted the OPA in 1990 in the aftermath of the Exxon *Valdez* disaster, with an aim to unify and supplement the then-existing **[—9—]** patchwork of federal regulations governing oil pollution. *See* Pub. L. No. 101-380, 104 Stat. 484 (codified at 33 U.S.C. § 2701 *et seq.*); *see also* S. Rep. No. 101-94, at 2–3 (1989), *reprinted in* 1990 U.S.C.C.A.N. 722, 723–24 (discussing the need for comprehensive federal legislation in light of the "unreasonably slow, confused, and inadequate response by industry and government that failed miserably in containing the [*Valdez*] spill and preventing damage"). Among its provisions, the OPA establishes a framework of liability and compensation for the costs of remediating oil spills. 33 U.S.C. §§ 2702–2712. Under this framework, "each responsible party for a vessel or a facility from which oil is discharged . . . into or upon the navigable waters or adjoining shorelines or the exclusive economic zone is liable for the removal costs and damages . . . that result from such incident." *Id.* § 2702. The responsible party is defined by reference to the source of the oil discharge in question (*e.g.*, a vessel, an onshore facility, or an offshore facility). *See id.* § 2701(32). However, the OPA also provides **[—10—]** a mechanism for shifting liability to third parties: If the responsible party can establish that the discharge and resulting liability "were caused solely by an act or omission of one or more third parties," then those parties become the responsible parties for purposes of OPA liability. *Id.* § 2702(d)(1)(A).

Of central importance to this appeal, the OPA defines a "facility" as follows:

> [A]ny structure, group of structures, equipment, or device (other than a vessel) which is used for one or more of the following purposes: exploring for, drilling for, producing, storing, handling, transferring, processing, or transporting oil. This term includes any

motor vehicle, rolling stock, or pipeline used for one or more of these purposes.

Id. § 2701(9). The OPA also provides separate definitions for an "offshore facility" and an "onshore facility." *See id.* § 2701(22), (24).[3] **[—11—]**

Finally, the OPA contains a savings clause, which governs the effect of the statutory scheme on state law. *See id.* § 2718. The clause states:

> Nothing in this Act or the Act of March 3, 1851 [the Limitation Act] shall . . . affect, or be construed or interpreted as preempting, the authority of any State or political subdivision thereof from imposing any additional liability or requirements with respect to . . . (A) the discharge of oil or other pollution by oil within such State; or (B) any removal activities in connection with such a discharge.

Id. § 2718(a).

The Limitation Act effectively caps the liability of vessel owners for claims for certain damages caused by their vessels, limiting recovery to the value of the vessel **{-169-}** in question and its freight. *See* 46 **[—12—]** U.S.C. § 30505.[4] To enforce this cap, vessel owners may launch proceedings under the Limitation Act, in which all prospective claimants must bring their claims. Once such proceedings are initiated, the Limitation Act provides that any other proceedings to recover from the vessel owner "related to the matter in question shall cease." *Id.* § 30511.

II. Procedural History

Shortly after the rupture, on February 26, 2014, the corporate defendants in this case[5] started a Limitation Act proceeding in the United States District Court for the Southern District of New York. **[—13—]** *See In re Bouchard Transp. Co.*, No. 14-cv-01262-PAC. The Authority and its insurers filed claims in the Limitation Act proceeding in April 2014 but expressly reserved the right (and expressed the intent) to separately bring claims against Bouchard under the OPA and the NYOSL. In June 2014, the Authority did just that, bringing this action against Bouchard.

After discovery, the parties filed cross-motions for summary judgment. Bouchard sought summary judgment on the Authority's OPA claims, as well as dismissal without prejudice of the remaining state-law claims with an order directing the Authority to pursue those claims in the Limitation Act proceeding.

On March 27, 2019, the district court granted Bouchard's motion for summary judgment and denied the Authority's cross-motion. *See Power Auth. of N.Y. v. Tug M/V Ellen S. Bouchard*, 377 F. Supp. 3d 230, 239 (S.D.N.Y. 2019). Acknowledging that there was "virtually no applicable case law elaborating" on the scope of the **[—14—]** OPA's "facility" definition, the district court concluded that the submarine cables did not come within that definition. *Id.* at 236. In so concluding, the district court first determined that its analysis was limited to the submarine

---

[3] An offshore facility is "any facility of any kind located in, on, or under any of the navigable waters of the United States, and any facility of any kind which is subject to the jurisdiction of the United States and is located in, on, or under any other waters, other than a vessel or a public vessel." 33 U.S.C. § 2701(22). An **[—11—]** onshore facility is "any facility (including, but not limited to, motor vehicles and rolling stock) of any kind located in, on, or under, any land within the United States other than submerged land." *Id.* § 2701(24).

[4] Specifically, § 30505(a) states in relevant part that "the liability of the owner of a vessel for any claim, debt, or liability described in subsection (b) shall not exceed the value of the vessel and pending freight." And § 30505(b) states that, barring exclusion by another provision of law, those claims subject to limitation "are those arising from any embezzlement, loss, or destruction of any property, goods, or merchandise shipped or put on board the vessel, any loss, damage, or injury by collision, or any act, matter, or thing, loss, damage, or forfeiture, done, occasioned, or incurred, without the privity or knowledge of the owner."

[5] That is, Bouchard Transportation Company, Inc., Motor Tug Ellen S. Bouchard, Inc., and B No. 280 Corporation.

cables themselves, excluding the pressurization plants. *Id.* The district court determined that the cables were not "used for" any of the enumerated purposes in the definition, meaning that they were not a "facility." It thus held that the discharge did not come within the OPA's scope. Lastly, because the Authority did not have a valid OPA claim, the district court concluded that the OPA's savings clause did not preempt the Limitation Act, so that the Authority could pursue its NYOSL claim only in the parallel proceeding.

III. Discussion

The Authority appeals from the district court's order and judgment, challenging its conclusion that the submarine cables were not a "facility" within the meaning of the OPA because the cables **[—15—]** were not "used for" one of the purposes that the OPA enumerates. In the alternative, the Authority challenges the district court's determination that the OPA's savings clause did not allow the remaining state-law **{-170-}** claims to be brought outside of the Limitation Act proceeding.

As explained below, we agree with the Authority that the submarine cables are "used for" at least one purpose enumerated in the OPA's definition of "facility." We therefore hold that the district court erred in granting Bouchard summary judgment on the OPA claims and transferring the state-law claims to the Limitation Act proceeding on that basis.

A. Standard of Review

We review a grant of summary judgment *de novo*; specifically, where the "disposition presents only a legal issue of statutory interpretation," as here, "we review *de novo* whether the district court correctly interpreted the statute." *Hayward v. IBI Armored Servs., Inc.*, **[—16—]** 954 F.3d 573, 575 (2d Cir. 2020) (quoting *City of Syracuse v. Onondaga Cty.*, 464 F.3d 297, 310 (2d Cir. 2006)).

B. Analysis

The district court's decision was premised on the determination that the submarine cable was not a "facility" within the meaning of the OPA. We disagree. Even assuming *arguendo* that the relevant unit of inquiry here is limited to the cables themselves and does not include the pressurization plants, as the district court held, we conclude that the cables are "used for" an enumerated purpose within the OPA's "facility" definition.

In interpreting a statutory provision, our analysis begins with "the plain meaning of [the] law's text, and, absent ambiguity, will generally end there." *United States v. Balde*, 943 F.3d 73, 81 (2d Cir. 2019) (internal quotation marks omitted); *see also Artis v. District of Columbia*, 138 S. Ct. 594, 603 (2018) ("In determining the meaning of a statutory provision, we look first to its language, giving the words **[—17—]** used their ordinary meaning." (internal quotation marks omitted)). Only if the text is ambiguous do we "turn to canons of statutory construction for assistance in interpreting the statute." *Greathouse v. JHS Sec. Inc.*, 784 F.3d 105, 111 (2d Cir. 2015).

Here, we find that the plain meaning of the OPA's definition of "facility" encompasses at least one of the purposes for which the submarine transmission cables are used. To recall, the OPA defines a "facility" as follows:

> [A]ny structure, group of structures, equipment, or device (other than a vessel) which is used for one or more of the following purposes: exploring for, drilling for, producing, storing, handling, transferring, processing, or transporting oil. This term includes any motor vehicle, rolling stock, or pipeline used for one or more of these purposes.

33 U.S.C. § 2701(9). The cables clearly fit within the first portion of the definition, in that they are a structure or equipment. Neither party disputes that. Moreover, the record shows that the cables have the capability of, at least, "transferring" the dielectric fluid, which for purposes of this

appeal we assume to be an oil within the meaning of **[—18—]** the OPA.[6] *See Transfer, Webster's* **{-171-}** *Ninth New Collegiate Dictionary* (1990) (defining "transfer" as, among other things, "to convey from one person, place, or situation to another"); *Transfer, American Heritage Dictionary* (2d ed. 1990) (in relevant part, defining "transfer" as "to convey or shift from one person or place to another").

The crux of the question, then, is whether the utilization of this capability suffices for the cables to be considered "used for" that "purpose[]." 33 U.S.C. § 2701(9). We hold that it does. The definition's language requires nothing more than that the cables be employed to transfer the dielectric fluid. And it is clear from the undisputed facts in the record that the cables are regularly used to, among other purposes, convey dielectric fluid along the length of the **[—19—]** cables and between the cables and the pressurization plants, as the system calibrates and adjusts the volume of fluid required to maintain proper pressure in light of external conditions. Indeed, the record establishes that this movement of dielectric fluid—that is, its transfer in and out of the cables—is vitally important for the system to function properly.[7]

Bouchard urges—and the district court adopted—a more restrictive reading of this language, but Bouchard's proffered limitations would narrow the scope of the OPA beyond what the words of the statute support. First, Bouchard's assertion that the cables are "primarily" or "substantially" used for power transmission, and only incidentally for one of the statutorily enumerated purposes, is beside the point. The definition contains no **[—20—]** primacy requirement. To the contrary, the law expressly provides that equipment may serve multiple purposes and still count as a "facility": a facility may be "used for one *or more of*" the enumerated purposes. *Id.* § 2701(9) (emphasis added). Further, Congress is fully capable of drafting statutes requiring that a given use be primary or substantial.[8] Its choice to not do so here undermines Bouchard's argument that we should construe the OPA more narrowly than its text would suggest.

Similarly, we are not persuaded by Bouchard's argument that the OPA is "aimed at facilities that are engaged in oil exploration, production and transportation[,] as opposed to facilities that merely **[—21—]** use oil incidental to other industrial uses." Appellant's Br. at 16. Even if the Exxon *Valdez* oil spill prompted Congress to enact the OPA, and that many incidents triggering the OPA will relate to commercial oil exploration, production, and transportation, Congress did not write such a limitation into its definition of "facility." To the contrary, other portions of the OPA demonstrate that the term "facility" is more encompassing than that. For example, the definition of "oil" coming within the OPA's scope is indisputably broad, with the statute **{-172-}** referencing animal- and vegetable-based oils in addition to

---

[6] The OPA defines "oil" broadly, stating in relevant part that an oil covered by the statute includes "oil of any kind or in any form, including petroleum, fuel oil, sludge, oil refuse, and oil mixed with wastes other than dredged spoil." 33 U.S.C. § 2701(23). For purposes of its summary judgment motion below, Bouchard assumed without conceding that the dielectric fluid was an "oil" within the OPA's definition, and the district court made a similar assumption without deciding the issue. We likewise need not answer that question in the first instance to adjudicate this appeal, but it is an issue that will need to be resolved on remand.

[7] Because our conclusion that the cables were used for the purpose of transferring the dielectric fluid is sufficient to determine that the district court erred in concluding they were not a "facility" within the meaning of the OPA on that basis, we need not address whether they were also used for additional qualifying purposes, such as storing or handling the fluid.

[8] The U.S. Code features a number of instances of the phrases "used primarily for," "primarily used for," or "used substantially for," including in Title 33 itself. *See* 33 U.S.C. § 1362(25) (defining recreational vessels in part as those "used primarily for pleasure"); *see also, e.g.*, 40 U.S.C. § 8902 (for purposes of statute on monuments, defining "commemorative works" as excluding those "located within the interior of a structure or a structure which is primarily used for other purposes" beyond those enumerated); 47 U.S.C. § 395(b)(4) (requiring that "facilities and equipment" to be purchased using certain grants be "used substantially for" enumerated activities).

petroleum. *See* 33 U.S.C. § 2701(23) (defining oil as "oil of any kind or any form," and restricting that definition only by excluding substances deemed "hazardous" pursuant to a separate statutory authority); *see also id.* § 2720(a) (requiring that any promulgated oil-related regulations differentiate between varying types of oils, including vegetable- and animal-based oils as well as petroleum). Moreover, the OPA elsewhere *does* limit its reach to the oil exploration **[—22—]** or production industries, limiting its definition of "foreign offshore unit" in just such a manner. *See id.* § 2701(10) (defining "foreign offshore unit" as "a facility which is located, in whole or in part, in the territorial sea or on the continental shelf of a foreign country and which is or was used for one or more of the following purposes: exploring for, drilling for, producing, storing, handling, transferring, processing, or transporting *oil produced from the seabed beneath the foreign country's territorial sea or from the foreign country's continental shelf*" (emphasis added)). In sum, the plain language of the OPA's "facility" definition includes at least one of the purposes for which the cables here are used, and statutory context confirms that reading.[9] **[—23—]**

Because we hold that these cables are used for at least one of the purposes specified in the OPA's definition of "facility," the district court's conclusion that the Authority did not have a viable OPA claim was error.[10] Further, the district court's decision to transfer the Authority's NYOSL claims to the Limitation Act proceeding, predicated as it was on the finding that the Authority did not have a viable OPA claim, was error as well.[11] **[—24—]**

IV. Conclusion

To summarize, we hold as follows:

The submarine cables here are used at least for the purpose of transferring dielectric fluid within the meaning of the OPA's definition of "facility" because they are used to transfer dielectric fluid along the length of the cables and between the cables and the pressurization plants. As a result, the district court erred in concluding that the cables were not a "facility" on the basis that they were not used for any such purpose, and that the Authority thus did not have a viable claim under the OPA. **{-173-}**

We accordingly **VACATE** the order and judgment of the district court and **REMAND** for further proceedings consistent with this opinion.

---

[9] We are similarly unpersuaded by Bouchard's argument that its narrower reading of the OPA is supported by how the Clean Water Act ("CWA") and the OPA respectively define "facility." The CWA, like the OPA, includes separate definitions for "onshore facility" and "offshore facility," *see* 33 U.S.C. § 1321(a)(10), (11); however, only the OPA contains a standalone definition of "facility" as well. Though the district court rightly noted that this "added language means something," *Bouchard*, 377 F. Supp. 3d at 238, we disagree that the language narrows the OPA's definition in such a way as to exclude the cables. Instead, the language merely limits what purposes the relevant structure or equipment must **[—23—]** be used for in order to comprise a facility under the OPA. Nothing in the language, even when contrasted with the CWA, suggests a conclusion that to be a facility, a given object must be used primarily for one of the enumerated purposes or be associated with the oil exploration or production industries in some way.

[10] As noted above, we do not reach the question of whether the dielectric fluid is an "oil" for purposes of the OPA, as would be required to definitively conclude the cables are a "facility." That is a question for the district court to answer, in the first instance.

[11] Because we conclude that the district court erred in evaluating the Authority's OPA claim, we need not reach the question of whether the OPA's savings clause would have preempted the Limitation Act for purposes of the Authority's NYOSL claim if the Authority did not have a viable OPA claim.

United States Court of Appeals
for the Second Circuit

No. 18-671

UNITED STATES
vs.
ALARCON SANCHEZ[1]

Appeal from the United States District Court for the Southern District of New York

Decided: August 27, 2020

Citation: 972 F.3d 156, 8 Adm. R. 42 (2d Cir. 2020).

Before **WINTER, POOLER,** and **RAGGI,** Circuit Judges.

[—4—] {–159–} POOLER, Circuit Judge:

Appeal from the United States District Court for the Southern District of New York (Paul G. Gardephe, *J.*), convicting defendants, after a plea of guilty, of conspiring to engage in drug trafficking activity in violation of the Maritime Drug Law Enforcement Act (the "MDLEA"), 46 U.S.C. § 70501 *et seq.*

Defendants challenge the adequacy of their unconditional guilty pleas on the basis that the government has failed to establish as a factual matter that it complied with the MDLEA's jurisdictional provision requiring that the interdicted vessel in this case be "stateless." Despite having entered unconditional guilty pleas, defendants may assert what is concededly an unusual sufficiency challenge on appeal because we have previously held that the government's failure to establish statelessness renders a defendant's underlying plea to MDLEA charges defective under Rule 11. *See United States v. Prado*, 933 F.3d 121, 153, 7 Adm. R. 92, 115 (2d Cir. 2019) (vacating convictions and guilty pleas where "the government was unable to demonstrate" statelessness and "there was no mention of . . . statelessness during the plea proceedings"). Defendants additionally advance various constitutional challenges to the MDLEA and to its **[—5—]** application to land-based conspirators who have never set foot on the vessel during the scope of the conspiracy.

We hold that the government has met its evidentiary burden in establishing that defendants' boat, the *El Vacan*, was a stateless vessel and thus subject to the jurisdiction of the United States. We also hold that Section 70506(b) of the MDLEA encompasses land-based conspiratorial conduct, which Congress is authorized to proscribe under the Necessary and Proper Clause. Although due process requires a sufficient nexus with the United States for those not on board a stateless vessel to be prosecuted under the MDLEA, we conclude that in this instance, defendants' prosecutions satisfy due process. Finally, we hold that Congress did not exceed its legislative authority in enacting the MDLEA pursuant to the Define and Punish Clause.

BACKGROUND

I. Factual Background

In early 2015, special agents from the Department of Homeland Security undertook **{–160–}** an investigation of a suspicious money transfer from a Colombian drug cartel to a bank account in New York City. That investigation eventually **[—6—]** turned up information about a planned shipment of cocaine from Colombia to Australia scheduled for April 14, 2015.

The investigation also revealed that defendants-appellants Carlos Alberto Salinas Diaz and Daniel German Alarcon Sanchez, along with Luis Fernando Uribe Franco, were working with the cartel and a cooperating source to coordinate the shipment. The cooperating source was introduced to Salinas Diaz and Alarcon Sanchez through a Colombian informant who told Salinas Diaz that the source could help launder cartel money. In February 2015, at a restaurant in Bogota, Colombia, the source met with Salinas Diaz and Alarcon Sanchez where they formally asked for his help. The source told them he had connections with a shipping company that could provide the necessary

[1] The Clerk of Court is directed to amend the caption as above.

logistical assistance for the narcotics transport.

At the direction of Homeland Security, the cooperating source agreed to arrange for a vessel. Salinas Diaz and Alarcon Sanchez gave him three passports of cartel associates who would accompany the drugs at sea. On February 13, 2015, the source told Salinas Diaz that he had secured the use of a U.S.-registered vessel. The men agreed that, on April 14, Salinas Diaz would bring the cocaine on two speedboats to an agreed-upon location in the Pacific Ocean where it **[—7—]** would be loaded onto the cooperating source's vessel for shipment to Australia. Unbeknownst to Salinas Diaz and Alarcon Sanchez, the two operators of the U.S.-registered vessel were undercover agents. On April 6, Salinas Diaz discussed the time, date, and location of the planned cocaine transfer with the undercover agents.

On April 7, Salinas Diaz and the cooperating source discussed having Uribe Franco meet the source in New York City to deliver $3,000 in exchange for Australian visas. Uribe Franco sent his son to make the payment in person.

On April 14, a U.S. Navy helicopter assigned to the frigate U.S.S. Kaufmann was patrolling an area approximately 135 nautical miles off the coast of Costa Rica. Navy personnel in the helicopter eventually spotted one of the two speedboats—the *El Vacan*—a vessel colloquially known as a "go-fast." They observed bales on the vessel's deck, some of which the crew members began throwing overboard. The helicopter ordered the *El Vacan* to halt. The go-fast ignored the order. Naval personnel then fired warning shots, and the *El Vacan* stopped. The frigate dispatched a small boat of U.S. Navy and U.S. Coast Guard personnel to fetch the jettisoned packages and prepared a boarding team. In all, nearly 550 kilograms of cocaine were recovered from the water and the vessel. **[—8—]** Meanwhile, the boarding team wrested control of the vessel where they found four crewmembers: Alexander Catano Aragon, Biojo Torres Robinson Gabriel, Jorge Caveza Valencia, and Jhon Carlos Hurtado Rendon.

The boarding team reported that there was no visible registration number on the vessel, but there was a small Ecuadorian flag—either painted or a decal—by the engine. The crewmembers claimed to be Colombian citizens. At the Navy personnel's request, Rendon, the self-identified captain, told the boarding team that the *El Vacan* was an Ecuadorian vessel with a home port of Puerto Manta, Ecuador.

Pursuant to a treaty between the United States and Ecuador, the U.S. Coast Guard contacted Ecuadorian authorities and requested confirmation or denial as to the nationality of the *El Vacan*. The United **{–161–}** States told Ecuadorian officials, in relevant part: (1) the vessel was named the *El Vacan;* (2) the vessel lacked registration markings; (3) that the *El Vacan* was spotted by helicopter; (4) that the master claimed it was of Ecuadorian nationality with a home port of Puerto Manta, Ecuador; (5) that it was a 9.6 meters-long "panga," the local word for a go-fast; (6) its coordinates; (7) its color and that it was made of fiberglass; (8) that it was on a route consistent with drug smuggling operations; (9) information **[—9—]** about the vessel's master, Rendon, including his nationality (Colombian), date of birth, and passport number; (10) the number of people on board as well as their nationality (Colombian); (11) that the crewmembers claimed that the purpose of their voyage was a search and rescue of a friend at sea; (12) that the master had little knowledge of fishing; (13) that the vessel was on an erratic course when approached; (14) that crewmembers were seen jettisoning bales that testified positive for cocaine; (15) that the crewmembers were the subject of an ongoing criminal investigation by the United States; and (16) that the crewmembers claimed they departed from Puerto Esmeraldas, Ecuador, on April 12, 2015, and planned to return on April 14, 2015.

The Ecuadorian Coast Guard acknowledged receipt of the request, stating that it would provide a Form 3[2] within thirty

[2] A "Form 3" is a "Response to Action Request." Country officials use the form to confirm or deny whether a vessel suspected of narcotics trafficking is registered to that country or is of that country's

minutes. The Ecuadorian authorities requested photographs of the *El Vacan* and the names and identification documents of its crew because there were other boats registered with the same name. The United States did not send the requested information. **[—10—]** About an hour after the United States made its request, the Ecuadorian Coast Guard sent Form 3, indicating that the *El Vacan*'s claim to Ecuadorian nationality could neither be confirmed nor denied and asking again for photographs.

Based on that response, the U.S. government concluded that the vessel was without nationality, subjecting it to the jurisdiction of the United States pursuant to the MDLEA. The U.S. boarding team arrested the four men who were on board and sank the *El Vacan* as a navigational hazard.

II. Procedural History

On May 18, 2016, Alarcon Sanchez and Salinas Diaz were charged with violating and conspiring to violate the narcotics trafficking provisions of the MDLEA. Alarcon Sanchez and Salinas Diaz were subsequently extradited to the United States from Colombia on July 11, 2016, and September 1, 2016, respectively. Alarcon Sanchez, Salinas Diaz, and several other defendants moved to dismiss the superseding indictment, principally on the grounds that the MDLEA's jurisdiction over land-based conspirators violated the U.S. Constitution and the MDLEA's text and, in any event, the *El Vacan* was not a stateless vessel under the statute. The district court denied the motions. *United States v. Aragon*, No. 15-Cr-292, 2017 WL 2889499 (S.D.N.Y. July 5, 2017). **[—11—]**

On November 17, 2017, Alarcon Sanchez pled guilty pursuant to a plea agreement, and on February 28, 2018, the district court sentenced him to five years' imprisonment, four years' supervised release, and a $100 special assessment.

On December 5, 2017, Salinas Diaz pled guilty pursuant to a plea agreement, and on April 10, 2018, the district court sentenced **{-162-}** him to six years' imprisonment, four years' supervised release, and a $100 special assessment.

This appeal followed.

DISCUSSION

Alarcon Sanchez argues on appeal that the district court erred by denying his motion to dismiss the indictment because (1) the government presented insufficient evidence that the *El Vacan* was a stateless vessel subject to the jurisdiction of the United States under the MDLEA; (2) the text of the MDLEA does not reach foreign land-based conspirators; (3) construing the MDLEA to reach foreign land-based conspirators compels the conclusion that Congress exceeded its legislative authority under the Constitution's Define and Punish Clause, *see* U.S. Const., art. I, sec. 8, cl. 10; and (4) his conduct lacked the nexus to the United States that due process requires. **[—12—]**

Salinas Diaz argues that the district court erred in failing to dismiss the superseding indictment because (1) Congress exceeded its legislative authority under the Define and Punish Clause in enacting the MDLEA and (2) the *El Vacan* was not on the high seas when the U.S. Navy interdicted it.

In reviewing the denial of a motion to dismiss an indictment, we review the district court's findings of fact for clear error and its conclusions of law de novo. *United States v. Bout*, 731 F.3d 233, 238 (2d Cir. 2013). Where, as here, defendants challenge convictions based on unconditional guilty pleas, we understand them to have "admit[ted] all of the elements" of their claims and to have "waive[d] all challenges to the prosecution except those going to the court's jurisdiction." *United States v. Yousef*, 750 F.3d 254, 258 (2d Cir. 2014) (internal quotation marks omitted).

---

nationality. *See United States v. Aragon*, No. 15-Cr-292, 2017 WL 2889499, at *3 (S.D.N.Y. July 5, 2017).

I. Evidence of Statelessness

Defendants attack the adequacy of their guilty pleas on the basis that the government failed to establish that the *El Vacan* was a stateless vessel subject to the jurisdiction of the United States. **[—13—]**

A. The MDLEA's Requirements

The MDLEA prohibits specified drug trafficking activity "[w]hile on board a covered vessel." 46 U.S.C. § 70503(a). A "covered vessel" means, as relevant here, "a vessel subject to the jurisdiction of the United States." *Id.* § 70503(e)(1). A vessel may be subject to the jurisdiction of the United States if it is "a vessel without nationality." *Id.* § 70502(c)(1)(A). A vessel is considered without nationality if "the master or individual in charge makes a claim of registry that is denied by the nation whose registry is claimed," *id.* § 70502(d)(1)(A), or "the claimed nation of registry does not affirmatively and unequivocally assert that the vessel is of its nationality," *id.* § 70502(d)(1)(C). A claim of registry may be made in one of three ways: "(1) possession on board the vessel and production of documents evidencing the vessel's nationality . . . ; (2) flying its nation's ensign or flag; or (3) a verbal claim of nationality or registry by the master or individual in charge of the vessel." *Id.* § 70502(e). "The response of a foreign nation to a claim of registry . . . is proved conclusively by certification of the Secretary of State or the Secretary's designee." *Id.* § 70502(d)(2).

"Jurisdiction of the United States with respect to a vessel subject to [the MDLEA] is not an element of an offense." *Id.* § 70504(a). Rather, "[j]urisdictional **[—14—]** issues" that arise under the MDLEA "are preliminary questions of law to be determined solely by the trial judge." *Id.* We recently held that the MDLEA's jurisdictional language functions "not to confer **{-163-}** subject matter jurisdiction on the federal courts, but rather to specify the reach of the statute beyond the customary borders of the United States." *Prado*, 933 F.3d at 132, 7 Adm. R. at 98. In *United States v. Van Der End*, 943 F.3d 98, 7 Adm. R. 123 (2019), this Court observed that,

> where there is no factual basis to find that the vessel on which a defendant was apprehended was a vessel subject to the jurisdiction of the United States, the defendant may still be permitted to raise that issue on appeal even after pleading guilty. That is because "a defective guilty plea will not necessarily be deemed to waive all objections to a conviction."

Id. at 103, 7 Adm. R. at 125 (quoting *Prado*, 933 F.3d at 151, 7 Adm. R. at 114). This Court went on to explain, "when the government's proof that a vessel was subject to the jurisdiction of the United States is lacking," the defendant's guilty plea is invalid. *Id.* at 103, 7 Adm. R. at 125 (internal quotation marks omitted).

Here, defendants did not challenge the validity of their guilty pleas in their initial appellate briefs, although they did so in supplemental briefing following our decision in *Van Der End*. The challenge fails because the government satisfactorily proved United States jurisdiction over the *El Vacan*. **[—15—]**

B. Vessel without nationality

The district court found that the government established that the *El Vacan* was a vessel without nationality because (1) there were insufficient markings and other identifying information on the vessel to put a reasonable official on notice that Ecuador's interests might be affected by the vessel's interdiction, and (2) Ecuadorian authorities responded that they could neither confirm nor deny the vessel's nationality.

The first ground, by itself, would not support a statelessness finding because, in *Prado*, this Court held that in "the absence of indicia of registration such as flying a nation's flag, presenting registration papers, or a volunteered assertion of national registration by the master," the burden is on the boarding party to inquire as to the vessel's nationality. *Prado*, 933 F.3d at 131, 7 Adm. R. at 96. But here the boarding party made the required inquiry and, upon observing a small flag decal or painting near the engine and being told by the purported captain that the *El Vacan* was of Ecuadorian nationality with its home port in Puerto Manta, Ecuador, U.S. officials sought verification from authorities in Ecuador, the "claimed nation of registry." 46 U.S.C. § 70502(d)(1)(C). This comported with MDLEA statutory procedures. *Cf. Prado*, 933 F.3d at 132, 7 Adm. R. at 96 (warning that boarding **[—16—]** party's inattention to MDLEA's statutory procedures can "virtually doom[] the prosecution to failure at the investigation stage"). Those procedures also state that the claimed nation of registry, in delivering its response, must communicate to U.S. officials "by radio, telephone, or similar oral or electronic means," *see id.* § 70502(d)(2), and its failure to "affirmatively and unequivocally assert" that the vessel is registered conclusively establishes statelessness under the statute, *see id.* § 70502(d)(1)(C).

Alarcon Sanchez argues, as did the defendant in *Prado*, that the government failed to adhere to the prescribed procedures. He argues that the government presented insufficient evidence to demonstrate statelessness because the United States cut off the process prematurely, depriving Ecuadorian officials the chance to affirmatively and unequivocally assert anything about the *El Vacan* without considering the additional information it requested—namely, photographs of the vessel taken by U.S. officials. **{-164-}**

The government argues that defendants lack standing to challenge the adequacy of the interchange between the United States and Ecuador because the relevant procedures, though now codified in United States law, derive from an international treaty between sovereign nations. **[—17—]**

We need not conclusively decide this question any more than we need decide the exact quantum of information that U.S. officials must provide to the claimed nation of registry, or whether they have an obligation to act in good faith in seeking verification. We are satisfied that the information the government provided Ecuadorian authorities about the *El Vacan* was sufficient to satisfy the MDLEA and, specifically, 46 U.S.C. § 70502(d)(1)(C). Indeed, the U.S. Coast Guard furnished all of the information that would have otherwise been captured in a photograph of the *El Vacan*, *see supra*, a point all but conceded by Alarcon Sanchez during oral argument.

The Ecuadorian Coast Guard responded to the verification request by indicating that it could neither confirm nor deny the *El Vacan*'s claim to Ecuadorian nationality. And, under the MDLEA, that response patently does not qualify as an affirmative and unequivocal assertion that the *El Vacan* was of Ecuadorian nationality. On this record, we conclude that the government satisfied its burden to prove that the *El Vacan* was a "vessel without nationality" as defined in 46 U.S.C. § 70502(d)(1)(C). **[—18—]**

II. MDLEA and land-based conspirators

Alarcon Sanchez argues that the application of the MDLEA to his foreign land-based conspiratorial conduct violates the Constitution's Define and Punish Clause and Due Process Clause. Before reaching these constitutional issues, we briefly explain why the MDLEA's text, structure, and purpose supports such extraterritorial application.

The MDLEA prohibits specified drug trafficking activity by individuals "[w]hile on board a covered vessel." 46 U.S.C. § 70503(a). The MDLEA explicitly provides that this substantive prohibition applies extraterritorially. *See id.* § 70503(b). The MDLEA also imposes criminal liability on those "attempting or conspiring to violate section 70503"—that is, attempting to engage in prohibited drug trafficking activity on board a covered vessel or conspiring with others to do so—and makes such persons "subject to the same penalties as provided for violating section 70503." *Id.* § 70506(b) (the "attempt-and-conspiracy provision").

Alarcon Sanchez argues that when read together, these provisions allow a person to be convicted of MDLEA conspiracy only when the person himself is found on board a covered vessel, and not when his conduct is entirely land- **[—19—]** based. In support, he cites both the presumption against extraterritoriality and the statutory text. Neither supports his argument.

The presumption against extraterritoriality is a canon of construction instructing that "[w]hen a statute gives no clear indication of an extraterritorial application, it has none." *Morrison v. Nat'l Aust. Bank Ltd.*, 561 U.S. 247, 255 (2010). Even "when a statute provides for some extraterritorial application, the presumption against extraterritoriality operates to limit that provision to its terms." *Id.* at 265. But in the context of ancillary crimes such as aiding and abetting and conspiracy, it is "generally" recognized that "the extraterritorial reach of [the] ancillary offense . . . is coterminous with that of the underlying criminal statute." *United States v. Ballestas,* 795 F.3d 138, 144, 3 Adm. R. 698, 700 (D.C. Cir. 2015) (internal quotation **{-165-}** marks omitted) (alterations in original); *cf. United States v. Hoskins,* 902 F.3d 69, 96–97 (2d Cir. 2018) (stating general rule but concluding it did not apply to certain conspiracies in violation of Foreign Corrupt Practices Act given specific statutory limitations).

Thus, Alarcon Sanchez concedes, as he must, that the extraterritorial application of the MDLEA's substantive provision extends to its conspiracy provision. Nevertheless, he argues that the extraterritorial reach of both **[—20—]** provisions is somehow restricted by the locational limitation of "on board a covered vessel" found in the substantive provision. Because the statement of extraterritorial application is limited to the substantive offense, he argues, "[t]he text and structure are most easily and naturally read as limiting the reach of the statute to crimes," whether substantive or conspiratorial, committed by individuals "while on board covered vessels." Appellant's Br. at 14. In his view, "Section 70506(b) merely fills a gap that would be left if someone on board a vessel conspired with others on board but committed no substantive narcotics crime," Appellant's Br. at 17, rather than sweep up "ordinary drug smugglers who never left home and never compassed any harm to Americans or American interests." Appellant's Br. at 8.

We do not read the MDLEA so narrowly. Most obviously, the attempt-and-conspiracy provision does not mention covered vessels at all. It requires only that the object of the conspiracy encapsulate conduct that violates one of the specified narcotics trafficking prohibitions on a covered vessel. Persons who knowingly and intentionally join in such a conspiracy need not themselves be on board the covered vessel to be guilty under Section 70506. This construction is supported by the D.C. Circuit's decision *United States v. Ballestas,* 795 F.3d 138, 3 Adm. R. 698, on **[—21—]** which the district court relied. In *Ballestas,* the court rejected the same interpretation here urged by Alarcon Sanchez because it would make the MDLEA's conspiracy-and-attempt provision merely redundant of its substantive provision. *Id.* at 146, 3 Adm. R. at 701–02. The court explained that if a person on a covered vessel possessed the requisite intent to violate Section 70503, he would likely be guilty of the underlying substantive offense—either through constructive possession, *see United States v. Tinoco,* 304 F.3d 1088, 1123 (11th Cir. 2002), or aiding and abetting, *see* 18 U.S.C. § 2(a). A court will not construe a statutory provision to render it "insignificant, if not wholly superfluous." *Duncan v. Walker*, 533 U.S. 167, 174 (2001); *see generally United States v. Epskamp,* 832 F.3d 154, 164 (2d Cir. 2016) (rejecting narrow construction of extra-territoriality provision in 21 U.S.C. § 959 because it would cause "redundancy within the federal statutory framework").

And, as the government points out, construing the MDLEA's attempt-and-conspiracy provision to reach conspirators who remain onshore is consistent with traditional notions of conspirator liability. It is a well-settled rule "in the law of conspiracy [that] the overt act of one partner in crime is attributable to all." *Pinkerton v. United States,* 328 U.S. 640, 647 (1946). So, even if the MDLEA **[—22—]** does require an overt act of the conspiracy to take place on board a covered vessel, the acts of the on-board co-conspirator are nonetheless attributable to the land-based co-conspirator. It is not necessary that all conspirators be on board a covered vessel for each to be guilty of conspiring to violate Section 70503. *See Ballestas*, 795 F.3d at 146, 3 Adm. R. at 702.

Our construction also comports with the MDLEA's underlying purpose. **{–166–}** Congress specifically recognized that "trafficking in controlled substances aboard vessels is a serious international problem, is universally condemned, and presents a specific threat to the security and societal well-being of the United States." 46 U.S.C. § 70501. In 1980, Congress enacted the MDLEA's predecessor statute to close a loophole that had hampered the prosecution of drug smugglers apprehended on the high seas absent difficult-to-obtain evidence that the drugs were destined for the United States. S. Rep. No. 96-855, at 1–2 (1980). As the Senate Report explains:

> In most cases, evidence to prove importation or conspiracy beyond a reasonable doubt is impossible to obtain. Thus, in most cases the Coast Guard is able to seize and confiscate the ship and the illegal drugs, but the government is not able to prosecute the crew *or others involved in the smuggling operation.* Such actions have little deterrent effect on the crews or *the trafficking* **[—23—]** *organizations.* In the highly lucrative trade in illegal drugs, such occasional seizures are considered a part of the cost of doing business.

Id. (emphasis added).

Alarcon Sanchez's reading of the attempt-and-conspiracy provision would immunize many persons "involved" in MDLEA-precluded smuggling operations, among them, those decisionmakers who are central to the conspiracy but who never physically step foot on a vessel. He posits that Congress added the MDLEA's inchoate violations to reach the vessel "engineer that was responsible for maintaining the tanks containing cocaine," Appellant's Br. at 17, rather than the higher-ups that engineered the shipment in the first place. This undercuts Congress's findings on the scope and gravity of the threat posed by drug trafficking aboard vessels. *See e.g., United States v. Ali*, 718 F.3d 929, 940 (D.C. Cir. 2013) ("[I]t is self-defeating to prosecute those [persons] desperate enough to do the dirty work but immunize the planners, organizers, and negotiators who remain ashore."). Like the D.C. Circuit, we decline to construe Section 70506 so narrowly as to allow "[d]rug kingpins and other conspirators who facilitate and assist in carrying out [MDLEA] trafficking schemes [to] fall **[—24—]** beyond the reach of the statute, compromising the overriding intent of Congress in enacting it." *Ballestas*, 795 F.3d at 145, 3 Adm. R. at 701.

In sum, based on the MDLEA's purpose, Congress's decision to apply the MDLEA's substantive provisions "outside the territorial jurisdiction of the United States," and the nature of a MDLEA conspiracy offense relative to its substantive objective, we hold that Section 70506(b) encompasses conspiratorial conduct on shore in a foreign country.

III. Define and Punish Clause

Alarcon Sanchez also argues that the MDLEA is unconstitutional as applied to his conduct because he never set foot on the *El Vacan* during the charged conspiracy.[3] Article I, section 8, clause 10 of the U.S. Constitution states: "The Congress shall have Power . . . To define and punish Piracies and *Felonies committed on the high Seas*, and Offences against the Law of Nations." U.S. Const. art I, § 8, cl. 10 (emphasis added). Alarcon Sanchez does not dispute that the **[—25—]** "Felonies" part of the **{–167–}** Define and Punish Clause supports Congress's enactment of the MDLEA. *See United States v. Matos-Luchi*, 627 F.3d 1, 3 (1st Cir. 2010) (recognizing Congress to have invoked its constitutional power under Define and Punish Clause to enact MDLEA). Instead, he argues that, like

[3] In *Class v. United States*, 138 S. Ct. 798, 805 (2018), the Supreme Court held that a criminal defendant who enters an unconditional guilty plea may still appeal his conviction on the ground that the statute of conviction is unconstitutional. Pursuant to the holding in *Class*, defendants have a right to raise on appeal both as-applied and facial constitutional challenges to the MDLEA.

the MDLEA, the Define and Punish Clause contains locational language: the high seas. Because Alarcon Sanchez was never on the high seas in connection with the charged conspiracy, he argues that the MDLEA cannot constitutionally be construed to reach his conduct.

The government offers two arguments in response. First, it contends that "settled principles of conspiracy law" impute the conduct of the four conspirators on the high seas to the other conspirators on land. Appellee's Br. at 29–30. Second, it argues that the Constitution's Necessary and Proper Clause supports the MDLEA's application to Alarcon Sanchez because Congress's regulation of drug trafficking on the high seas would be undermined if it could not reach conspiratorial conduct in a foreign territory that is integral to that trafficking. Because we agree with the government's second argument, we do not address its first. **[—26—]**

The Necessary and Proper Clause provides that "Congress shall have Power . . . To make all Laws which shall be necessary and proper for carrying into Execution the foregoing Powers, and all other Powers vested by this Constitution in the Government of the United States, or in any Department or Officer thereof." U.S. Const. art. I, § 8, cl. 18. "[T]he Necessary and Proper Clause makes clear that the Constitution's grants of specific federal legislative authority are accompanied by broad power to enact laws that are convenient, or useful or conducive to the authority's beneficial exercise." *United States v. Comstock*, 560 U.S. 126, 133-34 (2010) (internal quotation marks and citations omitted). "[T]he word necessary does not mean absolutely necessary." *Id.* at 134 (internal quotation marks and citation omitted). Rather, "in determining whether the Necessary and Proper Clause grants Congress the legislative authority to enact a particular federal statute, we look to see whether the statute constitutes a means that is rationally related to the implementation of a constitutionally enumerated power." *Id.* "The relevant question is simply whether the means chosen are reasonably adapted to the attainment of a legitimate end under the [relevant enumerated power]." *Gonzales v. Raich*, 545 U.S. 1, 37 (2005) (Scalia, *J.*, concurring in the judgment) (internal quotation marks omitted). **[—27—]**

We agree with the government that prosecuting MDLEA conspirators who are not on the high seas is a means that is rationally related to the legitimate end of prosecuting MDLEA conspirators who are on the high seas. *See* 46 U.S.C. § 70501 (congressional findings that "trafficking in controlled substances aboard vessels is a serious international problem, [and] is universally condemned"). Our conclusion is reinforced by recognition that the conspirators most likely to control, direct, finance, and profit from such drug trafficking are more apt to remain on land than to venture on the seas. *See Ballestas*, 795 F.3d at 145, 3 Adm. R. at 701; *cf. Ali*, 718 F.3d at 940. In order reasonably to address the serious problem of drug trafficking on the high seas, it is, therefore, necessary and proper for Congress to confer federal jurisdiction over all conspirators, both those who go on the seas and those who remain on land.

In any event, our task is not to decide whether punishing on-land conspirators actually advances Congress's legitimate objective of punishing drug traffickers **{-168-}** on the high seas, because "the choice of means to that end presents a question primarily addressed to the judgment of Congress." *See Burroughs v. United States*, 290 U.S. 534, 547 (1934). "If it can be seen that the means adopted are really calculated to attain the end, the degree of their necessity, the extent to **[—28—]** which they conduce to the end, the closeness of the relationship between the means adopted, and the end to be attained, are matters for congressional determination alone." *Id.* at 547–48. In light of this deference, we are satisfied that Congress has not exceeded its authority under the Necessary and Proper Clause in extending the MDLEA to cover the conduct of land-based conspirators.

IV. Due Process

Alarcon Sanchez argues that the Due Process Clause requires some nexus or connection between the defendant and the United States in order for the MDLEA to cover land-based conspirators.[4] As a general rule the extraterritorial application of federal criminal law requires such a nexus so that a statute's application is not arbitrary or fundamentally unfair. *See Epskamp*, 832 F.3d at 168. However, we also held in *Van Der End* that no such nexus is required when MDLEA violations occur on stateless vessels because "MDLEA prosecutions involving stateless vessels do not present the same concerns that are present in **[—29—]** the extraterritorial application of typical criminal statutes." 943 F.3d at 105, 7 Adm. R. at 127. As we further explained:

> That is because stateless vessels are international pariahs that subject themselves to the jurisdiction of all nations *solely* as a consequence of the vessel's status as stateless. Because stateless vessels do not fall within the veil of another sovereign's territorial protection, all nations can treat them as their own territory and subject them to their laws. Thus, when a vessel is subject to the jurisdiction of another nation, a person trafficking drugs on board would have a legitimate expectation that because he has subjected himself to the laws of one nation, other nations will not be entitled to exercise jurisdiction without some nexus. The same is not true when a defendant attempts to avoid the law of *all* nations by travelling on a stateless vessel.

Id. at 105-06, 7 Adm. R. at 127 (internal quotation marks and citations omitted).

In reaching this conclusion, we held that United States prosecution of persons on stateless vessels was neither arbitrary nor unfair. Not arbitrary, because any nation can exercise jurisdiction over such vessels. And not unfair, because persons who traffic drugs do so with the imputed knowledge that they are risking prosecution—"somewhere." *Id.* at 106, 7 Adm. R. at 127.

The government maintains that *Van Der End* controls, and no nexus to the United States is required because the *El Vacan* was a stateless vessel. But this case is not on all fours with *Van Der End*. First, in *Van Der End* we specifically **[—30—]** declined to decide "what the Due Process Clause may require before persons *who are not on board a vessel without nationality*" can be prosecuted under the MDLEA. *Id.* at 105 n.4, 7 Adm. R. at 127 n.4 (emphasis added). Second, in *Van Der End* we said that a nexus was not required for those on stateless vessels because the seafaring defendants had forfeited their **{-169-}** protections under international law and were therefore fair game for any nation to "subject them to their laws." *Id.* at 105, 7 Adm. R. at 127 (internal quotation marks and citation omitted). The same cannot be said about these defendants, who were obviously subject to Colombia's jurisdiction and laws—indeed, the United States relied on the Colombian government in their apprehension and extradition. But even if we assume that land-based conspirators who are not physically on board a stateless vessel can raise a nexus challenge to a MDLEA prosecution, that does not help defendants here.

Our precedent stresses that it is a heavy burden for defendants to demonstrate a due process violation in the application of a statute like the MDLEA, which indisputably applies extraterritorially. *Epskamp*, 832 F.3d at 168. Defendants cannot carry that heavy burden here. The due process requirement that there be a nexus between the defendant and the United States ensures that application of any such statute to that defendant "would not be arbitrary or **[—31—]** fundamentally unfair." *Id.*; *see United States v. Al Kassar,* 660 F.3d 108, 118–19 (2d Cir.

[4] We noted in *Van Der End* that this type of Due Process challenge to MDLEA prosecutions "is a purely legal question on which the government's constitutional power to prosecute [the defendant] turns," 943 F.3d at 105, 7 Adm. R. at 127, and therefore, we may consider the argument in spite of a defendant's unconditional guilty plea.

2011). "For non-citizens acting entirely abroad, a jurisdictional nexus exists when the aim of that activity is to cause harm inside the United States or to U.S. citizens or interests." *Epskamp*, 832 F.3d at 168 (internal quotation marks omitted). And, as we noted in *Van Der End*, "[f]air warning does not require that the defendants understand that they could be subject to criminal prosecution *in the United States* so long as they would reasonably understand that their conduct was criminal and would subject them to prosecution somewhere." *Van Der End,* 943 F.3d at 106, 7 Adm. R. at 127 (internal quotation marks and citation omitted).

Applying these principles to the facts here, we conclude that Alarcon Sanchez's MDLEA prosecution was neither arbitrary nor fundamentally unfair. By conspiring with an international drug-trafficking organization to ship over 500 kilograms of cocaine on the high seas, using a U.S.-registered vessel and procuring false visas in the United States, Alarcon Sanchez "cause[d] harm" to the very U.S. interests animating the MDLEA: curtailing international drug trafficking on the high seas, which Congress found to be "a specific threat to the security and societal well-being of the United States." 46 U.S.C. § 70501. There can be no doubt that Alarcon Sanchez and his co-conspirators were aware that **[—32—]** their scheme to transport cocaine on the high seas was illegal and could result in their criminal prosecution "somewhere." *Al Kassar,* 660 F.3d at 119 ("The defendants were not ensnared by a trap laid for the unwary."). Accordingly, in light of the conspiracy's nexus to United States interests in eliminating drug trafficking on the high seas, and the fair warning we ascribe to those that participate in such conspiracies, we conclude that due process was not offended by defendants' MDLEA prosecutions.

V. Remaining arguments

Salinas Diaz argues that the MDLEA is facially unconstitutional because Congress exceeded its legislative authority in its enactment and that the statute is unconstitutional as applied to defendants because the *El Vacan* was not on the high seas when the U.S. Navy interdicted it.

A. Congress's authority to enact the MDLEA

Congress has the authority "[t]o define and punish Piracies and Felonies committed on the high Seas." U.S. Const. art, I, § 8, cl. 10. "The clause encompasses three distinct powers: (i) to define and punish piracy; (ii) to define and punish **{–170–}** felonies committed on the high seas; and (iii) to define and punish offenses against the Law of Nations." *Ballestas,* 795 F.3d at 146-47, 3 Adm. R. at 702. Salinas Diaz **[—33—]** argues that the MDLEA is unconstitutional on its face because Congress lacked the constitutional power to enact it. But he has failed to specify any authority supporting his position. In the MDLEA, Congress punishes specified drug-trafficking activity on the high seas, which falls squarely within its constitutional power to punish felonies on the high seas. *See, e.g., United States v. Estupinan,* 453 F.3d 1336, 1338–39 (11th Cir. 2006); *United States v. Moreno-Morillo,* 334 F.3d 819, 824 (9th Cir. 2003); *United States v. Ledesma-Cuesta,* 347 F.3d 527, 531-32 (3d Cir. 2003). Salinas Diaz's facial challenge is meritless.

B. High Seas

Finally, Salinas Diaz argues, in substance, that applying the MDLEA to a prosecution in connection with the *El Vacan* is unconstitutional because the vessel was not on the "high seas" when the U.S. Navy stopped it. We have previously considered that term as it appears in the Death on the High Seas Act, now codified at 46 U.S.C. § 30301 *et seq. See In re Air Crash Off Long Island, N.Y., on July 17, 1996,* 209 F.3d 200, 205-15 (2d Cir. 2000). We concluded then that "high seas" means those beyond a nation's territorial waters. *Id.* at 205. Under current international law, a nation's territorial waters may extend "up to a limit not exceeding 12 nautical miles." U.N. Convention on the Law of the Sea art. 3, **[—34—]** *opened for signature* Dec. 10, 1982, 1833 U.N.T.S. 397. At the founding, the United States's territorial waters extended "roughly three miles." *In re Air Crash,* 209

F.3d at 205. Here, the *El Vacan* was 132 nautical miles off the coast of Costa Rica. That distance is comfortably beyond Costa Rica's territorial waters as the framers would have understood the term and under current international law. Accordingly, Salinas Diaz's argument fails.

CONCLUSION

For the foregoing reasons, we AFFIRM the judgment of the district court.

United States Court of Appeals for the Second Circuit

No. 19-2471

G4S INT'L EMPLOYMENT SERVS. (JERSEY), LTD.
vs.
NEWTON-SEALEY

On Petition for Review from the United States Department of Labor Benefits Review Board

Decided: September 17, 2020

Citation: 975 F.3d 182, 8 Adm. R. 53 (2d Cir. 2020).

Before **WINTER, CALABRESI,** and **CHIN,** Circuit Judges.

[—2—] {-184-} PER CURIAM:

Petitioners G4S International Employment Services (Jersey), Ltd. ("G4S Jersey"), as successor-in-interest to ArmorGroup Services (Jersey), Ltd. ("AG Jersey"), and Continental Insurance Company, as successor-by-merger to **[—3—]** Fidelity & Casualty Company of New York, seek review of a decision and order of the Department of Labor Benefits Review Board (the "Board") issued June 28, 2019 affirming the decision and order on second remand of the Administrative Law Judge (the "ALJ") awarding respondent David Newton-Sealey disability benefits under the Defense Base Act, 42 U.S.C. §§ 1651-54 (the "DBA"), which extends workers' compensation benefits under the Longshore and Harbor Workers' Compensation Act, 33 U.S.C. § 901 *et seq.* (the "LHWCA"), to certain employees of U.S. government contractors working overseas. On appeal, petitioners argue that the Board erred in affirming the award of benefits to Newton-Sealey. For the reasons set forth below, the petition for review is denied.

BACKGROUND

In 2003, Newton-Sealey, a British citizen, was hired by AG Jersey to provide security in Iraq for engineers working for Bechtel, a U.S. engineering and construction company. On March 23, 2004 Newton-Sealey was seriously injured while on the job when the vehicle he was driving was struck by an apparently hostile Iraqi vehicle. Following the incident, petitioners began providing Newton-Sealey compensation and medical benefits. On May 3, 2007, Newton- **[—4—]** Sealey timely filed a claim for benefits with the United States Department of Labor, Office of Workers' Compensation Programs (the "OWCP"). **{-185-}**

On April 30, 2007, Newton-Sealey filed suit in the United Kingdom against AG Jersey, ArmorGroup Services Ltd. ("AG UK"), and ArmorGroup International plc ("AG PLC").[1] On December 16, 2009, Newton-Sealey entered into a settlement with AG Jersey, AG UK, and AG PLC for an amount less than he would be entitled to under the DBA. Newton-Sealey did not obtain the written permission of "the employer and the employer's carrier" prior to entering into the settlement. *See* 33 U.S.C. 933(g)(1) (providing that "[i]f the [employee] enters into a settlement with a third person . . . the employer shall be liable for compensation . . . only if written approval of the settlement is obtained from the employer and the employer's carrier[] before the settlement is executed"). On August 25, 2010, petitioners informed the OWCP that, as a result of the U.K. settlement, § 933(g) of the LHWCA barred Newton-Sealey from receiving further benefits. Newton-Sealey contested this assertion, and the matter was submitted to the ALJ. **[—5—]**

On May 1, 2012, the ALJ found that while both AG UK and AG Jersey were employers within the meaning of § 933(g), AG PLC was a third party and thus Newton-Sealey was barred from receiving further benefits under the Act. Newton-Sealey appealed to the Board, and on May 29, 2013 the Board vacated the ALJ's decision "because . . . [the] analysis of the facts of this case in terms of the employer-employee relationship tests is vague and, therefore, unreviewable," and remanded for the ALJ to consider which employment relationship test best applied and then to

[1] In May 2008, because of a corporate acquisition, AG Jersey became G4S Jersey, AG UK became G4S Risk Management ("G4S RM"), and AG PLC became G4S plc ("G4S PLC"). To avoid confusion, we will use the parties' original names throughout.

apply that test. S. App'x at 139-40. On April 29, 2014, the ALJ again concluded that AG PLC was a third party and that Newton-Sealey's claim was barred under § 933(g).

Newton-Sealey once again appealed to the Board, and, on May 6, 2015 the Board determined that because § 933(g) is an affirmative defense, AG Jersey bore the burden of proving that AG UK and AG PLC were third parties and that it had failed to do so. The matter returned to the ALJ, who concluded on October 23, 2018 that it had "no real alternative but to interpret the Board's order as finding as a matter of law that Section [933(g)] does not apply to this case," and entered an order in favor of Newton-Sealey. S. App'x at 35-36. Petitioners moved for reconsideration, arguing that the Board did not intend to **[—6—]** find as a matter of law that § 933(g) did not apply, and the ALJ denied the motion on November 15, 2018. On June 28, 2019, on further review, the Board concluded that it had resolved the applicability of § 933(g) in its May 6, 2015 decision and affirmed the ALJ's October 23, 2018 decision and order and the award of benefits to Newton-Sealey.

Petitioners petitioned this Court for review, with the principal issue on review being whether, because Newton-Sealey reached a settlement with AG Jersey, AG UK, and AG PLC in the U.K. proceeding, his claim under the DBA is barred by § 933(g).[2]

DISCUSSION

Our review of decisions of the Board is "limited to whether the Board **{-186-}** made any errors of law and whether the findings of fact of the ALJ are supported by substantial evidence." *Barscz v. Office of Workers' Comp. Programs*, 486 F.3d 744, 749 (2d Cir. 2007). We review questions of law *de novo*, *id.*, and a decision of the ALJ that is "supported by substantial evidence, is not irrational, **[—7—]** and is in accordance with the law . . . must be affirmed," *Rainey v. Office of Workers' Comp. Programs*, 517 F.3d 632, 634 (2d Cir. 2008). "Substantial evidence is such evidence as a reasonable mind might accept as adequate to support a conclusion." *Serv. Emps. Int'l., Inc., v. Office of Workers' Comp. Programs*, 595 F.3d 447, 455 (2d Cir. 2010) (internal quotation marks omitted).

The "basic purpose" of the LHWCA is to "provid[e] prompt relief for employees, and limited and predictable liability for employers." *Fisher v. Halliburton*, 667 F.3d 602, 619 (5th Cir. 2012).[3] The DBA "extends workers' compensation coverage under the [LHWCA] to employees of American contractors engaged in construction related to military bases in foreign countries . . . [and] establishes a uniform, federal compensation scheme for civilian contractors and their employees for injuries sustained while providing functions **[—8—]** under contracts with the United States outside its borders." *Id.* at 609-10 (internal quotation marks omitted).

Employees injured under the LHWCA who may also have a cause of action against a third party as a consequence of sustaining that injury are not required to elect one remedy over another. *See* 33 U.S.C. § 933(a). If the employee, however, seeks damages from a third party, the LHWCA protects the derivative rights of the employer and the carrier. *See id.* Specifically, § 933(g) provides that:

---

[2] The parties stipulated that Newton-Sealey is a person entitled to compensation and that the settlement was for less than the amount he would be entitled to under § 933(g); accordingly, the only disputed element is whether he settled his claim with a "third person." *See* 33 U.S.C. § 933(g).

[3] Generally speaking, the LHWCA is an employer's exclusive liability such that if an employee's injury is covered by the LHWCA, he is typically precluded from pursuing a tort claim against his employer to recover for the same injury. *See Fisher v. Haliburton*, 667 F.3d 602, 610 (5th Cir. 2012). Here, however, Newton-Sealey is a British citizen who sought recourse under U.K. law, rather than seeking enforcement of a foreign law in a U.S. court. U.K. law, unlike U.S. law, permits claimants to pursue both a workers' compensation claim and a tort remedy. *See* Richard Lewis, Employers' Liability and Worker's Compensation: England and Wales (Oct. 20, 2010), https://papers.ssrn.com/sol3/papers.cfm?abstract_id=1695088.

(1) If the person entitled to compensation . . . enters into a settlement with a third person . . . for an amount less than the compensation to which the person . . . would be entitled under this chapter, the employer shall be liable for compensation . . . only if written approval of the settlement is obtained from the employer and the employer's carrier, before the settlement is executed, and by the person entitled to compensation.

(2) If no written approval of the settlement is obtained and filed as required by paragraph (1), or if the employee fails to notify the employer of any settlement obtained from or judgment rendered against a third person, all rights to compensation and medical benefits under this chapter shall be terminated, regardless of whether the employer or the employer's insurer has **[—9—]** made payments or acknowledged entitlement to benefits under this chapter.

Id.

Further, § 920(a) of the LHWCA provides that "[i]n any proceeding for the enforcement of a claim for compensation under this chapter it shall be presumed, in the absence of substantial evidence to the contrary -- . . . [t]hat the claim comes within the provisions of this chapter." *Id.* at § 920(a). A *prima facie* claim for compensation **{-187-}** requires that the employee allege an injury or death that arose out of and in the course of his employment. *See U.S. Indus./Fed. Sheet Metal, Inc. v. Office of Workers' Comp. Programs*, 455 U.S. 608, 615-16 (1982).

Finally, § 933(g) provides an affirmative defense. *See Bundens v. J.E. Brenneman Co.*, 46 F.3d 292, 303 (3d Cir. 1995); *Flanagan v. McAllister Bros., Inc.*, 33 Ben. Rev. Bd. Serv. 209, *3 (1999) ("[T]he applicability of Section 33(g) is an affirmative defense."). "It is well-established that a defendant . . . bears the burden of proving its affirmative defense." *Leopold v. Baccarat, Inc.*, 239 F.3d 243, 245 (2d Cir. 2001); *see also Hardaway v. Hartford Pub. Works Dep't.*, 879 F.3d 486, 490 (2d Cir. 2018). This burden has been interpreted as requiring the employer to demonstrate that named defendants are not employers. *See Fisher v. Halliburton*, 703 F. Supp. 2d 639, 664 (S.D. Texas 2010), *vacated on other grounds*, **[—10—]** 667 F.3d 602 (5th Cir. 2010) ("[T]he court presumes that all named defendants are employers under the [DBA]" as the DBA "must be liberally construed in conformance with its purpose, and in a way which avoids harsh and incongruous results. . . . [Accordingly,] the employer bears the burden to show that it is *not* an employer under the [DBA], thereby avoiding paying compensation.").

Here, Newton-Sealey alleged that his injuries arose out of and in the course of his employment, thereby establishing a *prima facie* case for benefits under the Act. *See* 33 U.S.C. § 920(a); *U.S. Indus./Fed. Sheet Metal, Inc.*, 455 U.S. at 615-16 (1982). Because § 933(g) sets forth an affirmative defense, *see Bundens*, 46 F.3d at 303, petitioners bore the burden of proving that the named defendants in the U.K. proceedings were not employers for the purposes of the Act, *see Fisher*, 703 F. Supp. 2d at 664. Reviewing the record available to the ALJ, the Board concluded that petitioners had not met this burden, *see Serv. Emps. Int'l., Inc.*, 595 F.3d at 455, noting that although at the time of the settlement the AG companies had been acquired by G4S, most of the testimony in the record predated the acquisition and so "shed[] very little light on the structure of, and relationship **[—11—]** among, the G4S companies after the acquisition." S. App'x at 32.[4] The record thus supports the Board's conclusion that

[4] Petitioners' argument that several depositions conducted some two years after the relevant Board decision provide "uncontroverted evidence" that the named defendants were not employers is unpersuasive. Appellant's Br. at 58. As the Board observed, its 2015 decision resolved "the issue of the application of § 33(g) . . . and is the law of the case." S. App'x at 13. The ALJ was bound to follow this finding of the Board. *See FCC v. Pottsville Broad. Co.*, 309 U.S. 134, 140 (1940) (noting the "familiar doctrine that a lower court is bound to respect the mandate of an appellate tribunal and cannot reconsider questions which the mandate has laid to rest").

petitioner failed to present sufficient evidence to prove that the named defendants were not employers. *See Barscz,* 486 F.3d at 749. Accordingly, we conclude that the Board did not err when it affirmed the ALJ's finding that Newton-Sealey's claims were not barred under § 933(g).

CONCLUSION

For the foregoing reasons, the petition for review is **DENIED**.

United States Court of Appeals
for the Second Circuit

No. 19-118

PANJIVA, INC.
vs.
UNITED STATES CUSTOMS AND BORDER PROTECTION

Appeal from the United States District Court for the Southern District of New York

Decided: September 17, 2020

Citation: 975 F.3d 171, 8 Adm. R. 57 (2d Cir. 2020).

Before **SACK, PARKER,** and **CHIN,** Circuit Judges.

[—2—] {-172-} SACK, Circuit Judge:

BACKGROUND

The Smoot-Hawley Tariff Act of 1930 is known principally for the tariffs it raised on imports to the United States and their alleged exacerbation of the Great Depression. *See* Robert Whaples, *Where Is There Economic Consensus Among* **[—3—]** *American Economic Historians? The Results of a Survey on Forty Propositions*, 55 J. Econ. Hist. 139, 151 (1995). This appeal involves a lesser-known component of the Act— **{-173-}** section 431—which required all "vessel[s] arriving in the United States" to maintain a "manifest" on which is recorded information about the just-completed voyage and an account of what is "on board." Pub. L. No. 71-361, § 431, 46 Stat. 590, 710 (1930). Through a series of amendments over its long life, including one that apparently contained a drafting error and is the focus of the case at bar, section 431 has come to comprise, as the district court put it in its decision in this case, "an amalgamation of language from incompatible statutes." *Panjiva, Inc. v. U.S. Customs & Border Prot.*, 342 F. Supp. 3d 481, 490 (S.D.N.Y. 2018).

The plaintiffs-appellants, Panjiva, Inc., a New York Corporation ("Panjiva"), and Trade Data Services, Inc., dba ImportGenius, an Arizona Corporation ("ImportGenius") (collectively the "plaintiffs") brought a lawsuit in the United States District Court for the Southern District of New York against the defendants-appellees, United States Customs and Border Protection ("CBP") and the United States Department of Treasury (collectively, the "government"), asserting, among other things, that somewhere within section 431's text is a requirement that aircraft entering the United States also make available for public disclosure specified **[—4—]** contents of manifests they have maintained detailing each journey and the cargo carried on that journey. The government disagreed, asserting that the statute requires that only waterborne vessels—and not aircraft—publicly disclose such information. The district court (J. Paul Oetken, *Judge*) agreed with the government and therefore dismissed the part of the plaintiffs-appellants' complaint at issue here. (The plaintiffs voluntarily dismissed the remainder of the complaint.) We agree with the government's interpretation of the statute largely for the reasons articulated by the district court. We therefore affirm its judgment.

Statutory Background

In the spring of 1930, early in America's descent into the Great Depression, Congress enacted the Smoot-Hawley Tariff Act. In addition to the controversial tariffs, the Act imposed on imports to the United States, section 431 required "[t]he master of every vessel arriving in the United States" to "have on board his vessel a manifest" "contain[ing]" specified information concerning the vessel's voyage and cargo. Pub. L. No. 71-361, § 431, 46 Stat. at 710. The Act defined "vessel" as "includ[ing] every description of water craft or other contrivance used, or capable of being used, as a means of transportation *in water*, but . . . *not* . . . *aircraft*." *Id.*, § 401(a), 46 Stat. at 708 (emphasis added). **[—5—]**

In 1984, fifty-four years after the statute was enacted, Congress passed a Trade and Tariff Act which, among other things, amended the Smoot-Hawley Act by adding a new subsection, (c)(1), to section 431. Pub. L. No. 98-573, Title II, § 203, 98 Stat. 2948, 2949 (1984). Paragraphs (A) through (G) of subsection (c)(1) specified "information [which], when contained in [the] manifest [required by the Smoot-Hawley Act], shall be available for public disclosure," *id.*, 98 Stat. at 2974:

(A) The name and address of each importer or consignee and the name and address of the shipper to such importer or consignee, unless the importer or consignee has made a biennial certification, in accordance with procedures adopted by the Secretary of the Treasury, claiming confidential treatment of such information.

(B) The general character of the cargo.

(C) The number of packages and gross weight.

(D) The name of the vessel or carrier.

(E) The port of loading.

(F) The port of discharge. **{-174-}**

(G) The country or origin of the shipment.

Id.

The subsection that followed, 431(c)(2), set forth exceptions that the Secretary of the Treasury could invoke to withhold from the public the information otherwise required to be disclosed by subsection (c)(1). *Id.* **[—6—]**

Congress again addressed section 431 some twelve years later, in July 1996. As part of the Anti-Counterfeiting Consumer Protection Act ("ACPA"), Congress amended subsection 431(c)(1) "by inserting the phrase 'vessel or aircraft' before 'manifest.'" Pub. L. No. 104-153, § 11(1), 110 Stat. 1386, 1389 (July 2, 1996). As of early July 1996, therefore, the clause of subsection 431(c)(1) requiring public disclosure of information contained in manifests provided that certain specified "information, when contained in [the] vessel *or aircraft* manifest [required to be kept by the master], shall be available for public disclosure." *See id.*, 110 Stat. at 1389 (emphasis added).

The ACPA also amended section 431(c)(1)(D), (E), and (F), quoted above, requiring that the information to be made available for public disclosure include not only "the name of the vessel or carrier," but "the name of the vessel, *aircraft*, or carrier"; and not only the "port" of loading or discharge, but the "*sea*port *or airport*" of loading and discharge. *See id.*, 110 Stat. at 1389 (emphases added).

Just three months later, in October 1996, though, Congress amended section 431(c)(1) again, this time in what it named the Miscellaneous Trade and Technical Corrections Act (the "Corrections Act"). Pub. L. No. 104-295, § 3(a)(3), 110 Stat. 3514, 3515 (October 11, 1996). In a subsection entitled "Manifests," the Corrections **[—7—]** Act provided that the operative clause of subsection 431(c)(1) was to be "amended . . . by striking 'such manifest' and inserting 'a vessel manifest.'" *Id.*, 110 Stat. at 3515. The Corrections Act did not amend paragraphs (c)(1)(A) through (G). The references to "aircraft" and "airport" remain. Congress has not amended any portion of section 431(c)(1) since.

The Corrections Act contained an obvious mistake: For three months and several days following July 2, 1996, the clause of section 431(c)(1) requiring public disclosure did not contain the phrase "such manifest." Rather, it stated, as noted above, that "information, when contained in *such vessel or aircraft manifest*, shall be available for public disclosure." *See* Pub. L. No. 104-153, § 11(1), 110 Stat. at 1389 (emphasis added). The phrase "such manifest," therefore, was not there to be "stri[cken]," as the Corrections Act purported to require.

Applying the law thus presents a challenge: It is not apparent what the statute in its current incarnation says.

The House of Representatives' Office of Law Revision Council engages in drafting the provision of the U.S. Code corresponding to enacted statutes.[1] In editing 19 U.S.C. § 1431(c)(1)—the provision of the U.S. Code that corresponds to **[—8—]** section 431(c)(1) of the Smoot-Hawley Act—in an effort to reflect the changes effected by the Corrections Act, it added a new subsection (c)(1), to section 431. The relevant part of 19 U.S.C. § 1431(c)(1) read (as it continues to read today): "Except as provided in subparagraph (2), the following information, when contained in a *vessel vessel* or aircraft manifest, shall be available for public disclosure." 19 U.S.C. § 1431(c)(1) (emphasis added). The Code includes a footnote concerning the repeated **{-175-}** use of the word "vessel": "So in original." 19 U.S.C. § 1431 n.1.

Factual Background

Plaintiffs are businesses that seek to service the "global trade community" by "aggregat[ing]" and analyzing "data," "including customs data," from the United States. Joint Appendix ("JA") at 10, 12.

As discussed above, pursuant to section 431 of the Smoot-Hawley Tariff Act, presently codified at 19 U.S.C. § 1431, "Every vessel required to make entry [into the United States] shall have a manifest that complies with the requirements prescribed under subsection (d) [of the statute]." 19 U.S.C. § 1431(a). Subsection (c) of section 1431 requires that some of that information "shall be available for public disclosure." 19 U.S.C. § 1431(c). Subsection (d) sets forth regulations **[—9—]** governing such manifests and their treatment, including the role to be played by the Secretary of the Treasury and the "Customs Service." 19 U.S.C. § 1431(d).

The plaintiffs wish to use, for business purposes, information that is contained in the manifests of aircraft entering the United States. To that end, in January 2015, ImportGenius submitted a request to CBP under the Freedom of Information Act ("FOIA") that sought "access to and copies of the portions of ALL aircraft manifests for inbound shipments f[ro]m January 1, 2014 to July 31, 2014 that have been designated for public disclosure by 19 U.S.C. § 1431(c)." JA at 17. In October 2016, CBP denied the request. ImportGenius appealed CBP's denial in December 2016; CBP denied the appeal in September 2017.

In January 2017, Panjiva submitted a similar FOIA request to CBP seeking "access to and copies of the portions of ALL aircraft manifests for inbound shipments from December 5, 2016 to December 9, 2016 that have been designated for public disclosure by 19 U.S.C. § 1431(c)." JA at 21.

Procedural History

On October 26, 2017, before CBP responded to Panjiva's FOIA request, the plaintiffs filed an action against the government in the United States District Court for the Southern District of New York. The complaint contained eight "counts": **[—10—]** Counts one through five alleged that the government had failed to comply with various requirements of FOIA; counts five[2] and eight alleged that the government's lack of FOIA compliance also violated the Administrative Procedure Act ("APA"); and counts six and seven alleged in essence that the government had violated the Smoot-Hawley Tariff Act of 1930 and the APA by failing upon request to disclose information from aircraft manifests and by failing to promulgate regulations to facilitate public access to aircraft manifest information.

On January 12, 2018, the government filed a motion pursuant to Federal Rule of Civil Procedure 12(b)(6) to dismiss the complaint's Smoot-Hawley Tariff Act (counts 6 and 7) and APA/FOIA (counts 5 and 8) claims. On September 24, 2018, the district court granted the motion.

The court's opinion began by addressing the Smoot-Hawley Tariff Act claims. *See Panjiva*, 342 F. Supp. 3d at 486-94. Those claims, the parties agree, turned on a pure—if challenging—question of statutory interpretation: whether section 431(c)(1) of the

[1] How regularly it does so is not clear from the record.

[2] Count Five contained an allegation under FOIA and an allegation under the APA.

act requires public disclosure of water-vessel manifests only (that is, disclosure of manifests maintained by water craft entering the country only) or of aircraft manifests too. The court concluded that only **[—11—]** information with respect **{–176–}** to water-vessel manifests is covered. It therefore dismissed counts six and seven of the complaint.

The court then addressed the complaint's APA/FOIA claims, *see Panjiva*, 342 F. Supp. 3d at 494-96, concluding that they were duplicative of the Smoot-Hawley Tariff Act claims and therefore should be dismissed too.

On November 13, 2018, the plaintiffs voluntarily dismissed the complaint's remaining FOIA claims. This appeal followed.

DISCUSSION

On appeal, the plaintiffs raise a single argument: that the district court adopted an incorrect interpretation of section 431(c)(1) of the Smoot-Hawley Tariff Act by failing to recognize that it now requires public disclosure of information in aircraft manifests, and therefore erred in its dismissal of the plaintiffs' claims brought under that statute.

Analysis

"We review a district court's grant of a motion to dismiss under Rule 12(b)(6) *de novo*." *Edwards v. Sequoia Fund, Inc.*, 938 F.3d 8, 12 (2d Cir. 2019).

"When interpreting the meaning of a statute," in this case, the Smoot-Hawley Tariff Act, "the starting point of inquiry is of course the language of the **[—12—]** statute itself." *In re Edelman*, 295 F.3d 171, 177 (2d Cir. 2002). "If the statutory terms are unambiguous, we construe the statute according to the plain meaning of its words." *Nwozuzu v. Holder*, 726 F.3d 323, 327 (2d Cir. 2013). In other words, "[i]f the meaning is plain, the inquiry ends there." *United States v. Rowland*, 826 F.3d 100, 108 (2d Cir. 2016). "If, however, the terms are ambiguous or unclear, we may consider legislative history and other tools of statutory interpretation." *Nwozuzu*, 726 F.3d at 327.

1. *Ambiguity*

The government and the plaintiffs disagree at the threshold as to whether section 431(c)(1)'s language is unambiguous. The government contends that the provision's language is ambiguous and tells us that we can and therefore should look to other "tools," including the statute's legislative history, to interpret it. The plaintiffs assert to the contrary that the provision's text is clear and express, and that it therefore would be "inappropriate" for us to "resort to collateral interpretive tools such as legislative history." Pls. Br. at 11.

Determining the clarity of section 431(c)(1)'s text plainly requires us to first determine what the text of section 431(c)(1) is. Although determining the text of a **[—13—]** statute is usually a matter of routine, in the case at bar, it presents a substantial challenge.

As discussed above, the relevant provision was clear throughout most of the long life of the Smoot-Hawley Tariff Act. As enacted in 1930, section 431 provided that "every vessel," which the statute defined to include all "water craft" and "not . . . aircraft," Pub. L. No. 71-361, § 401(a), 46 Stat. at 708 (1930), that "arriv[ed] in the United States" was required to "have on board . . . a manifest" containing information specified in the statute. *Id.*, § 431, 46 Stat. at 710.

In 1984, Congress added a subsection, (c)(1), to section 431 that required statutorily enumerated "information . . . contained in such manifest" to be made "available for public disclosure . . ." Pub. L. No. 98-573, § 203, 98 Stat. at 2974 (1984). So far so good: Section 431 required all vessels (water craft) entering the United States to maintain a manifest, and section 431(c)(1) required specific information to **{–177–}** be both included in "such" manifests and made "available for public disclosure."

In 1996, the combination of two amendments to the statute muddied the statutory waters. **[—14—]**

To repeat, first, in July of that year, Congress passed the ACPA, which amended section 431(c)(1) "by inserting 'vessel or aircraft' before 'manifest.'" Pub. L. No 104-153, § 11(1), 110 Stat. at 1389 (July 2, 1996).[3] As of that point, the clause of section 431(c)(1) covering public disclosure read:

> Except as provided in subparagraph (2), the following information, when contained in such vessel or aircraft manifest, shall be available for public disclosure.

See id., 110 Stat. at 1389. The list of each type of information to be disclosed followed, including the reference to "the name of the vessel, *aircraft*, or carrier," and the "*sea*port *or airport*" of loading and discharge. *See id.*, 110 Stat. at 1389 (emphasis added).

About three months later, in October 1996, Congress enacted the Corrections Act, which amended section 431(c)(1) yet again. *See* Pub. L. No. 104-295, § 3(a)(3), 110 Stat. at 3515 (October 11, 1996). In relevant part, the Corrections Act provided that "Section 431(c)(1) of the Tariff Act . . . is amended . . . by striking 'such manifest' and inserting 'a vessel manifest.'" *Id.*, 110 Stat. at 3515. **[—15—]**

The problem, though, is that the phrase "such manifest" no longer appeared in section 431(c)(1), because the ACPA had replaced "such manifest" with "such vessel or aircraft manifest." It could not simply be amended. If one were to try to do what the statute seems to require—that is, if one were to remove the two words "such" and "manifest" separately—the language that remained would describe "information, when contained in . . . vessel or aircraft . . . ." This reading makes no sense, let alone results in statutory text that is "clear."

Other subsections of section 431 manage, if anything, to add to the lack of clarity. Congress has never changed section 431's core instruction that it is only "vessel[s]"—which are explicitly defined as "not includ[ing] aircraft"—that must "have . . . manifest[s]" when entering the United States. 46 Stat. at 708, 710. To this day, the corresponding section of the U.S. Code, 19 U.S.C. § 1431(a), continues to read: "Every vessel required to make entry . . . shall have a manifest that complies with [the statutory requirements]." The definition of "vessel" contained in the "definitions" section of the Tariff Act, 19 U.S.C. § 1401, also states that "[t]he word 'vessel' includes every description of water craft or other contrivance used, or capable of being used, as a means of transportation in water, **[—16—]** but *does not include aircraft*." (emphasis added). Thus, aside from the question of whether section 431(c)(1) requires the *public disclosure* of "aircraft manifests," it is not even clear whether section 431 requires aircraft to possess and maintain manifests in the first place. We think, therefore, that because we are permitted to "consider . . . other tools of statutory interpretation" when attempting to understand "terms" that are merely "ambiguous [and] unclear," *Nowzuzu*, 726 F.3d at 327, so too can we use those tools in odd circumstances such as these, to attempt to determine what the text of section 431(c)(1) now says, and then what those words mean. **{-178-}**

2. *Tools of Statutory Interpretation*

a. *Canon Against Superfluity*

In addition to their argument that our analysis ought go no further than a plain reading of section 431's text, the plaintiffs also appear to assert that if we do go beyond the statute's plain meaning, their interpretation of the statute is aided by the so-called "canon against superfluity," *see Microsoft Corp. v. i4i Ltd. P'ship*, 564 U.S. 91, 106 (2011), also known as the "canon against surplusage," *see, e.g.*, *Marx v. Gen. Revenue Corp.*, 568 U.S. 371, 385 (2013). It has been referred to as "a cardinal principle of statutory construction" which requires courts to "give effect, if **[—17—]** possible, to every clause and word of a statute." *Williams v. Taylor*, 529 U.S. 362, 404 (2000) (internal quotation marks omitted).

[3] As described more fully above, the ACPA also amended the list of information that must be contained in a manifest to include references to "airports" and "aircraft." Pub. L. No. 104-153, § 11(2)-(4), 110 Stat. at 1389.

The plaintiffs rely on the canon to attack the government's interpretation of section 431, which, as described above, reads the statute as requiring only waterborne vessels—and not aircraft—to publicly disclose information maintained in their manifests. The plaintiffs' contention is straightforward: The government's interpretation of section 431 fails to "give effect" to words in both (1) the provision's clause requiring public disclosure and (2) paragraphs (D), (E), and (F) of the provision, which identify the specific types of information in manifests that must be publicly disclosed.

The plaintiffs assert first that the government's interpretation of section 431(c)(1)'s operative clause fails to give effect to the term "aircraft manifest," which was added to the clause by the ACPA; the term "aircraft manifest," the plaintiffs argue, is thereby rendered surplusage and thus the government's reading violates the canon. As the district court recognized, though, this argument relies on the plaintiffs' assumption that after the ACPA was enacted, the Corrections Act "did not remove" the term "aircraft manifest" from section 431(c)(1), Pls. Br. at 16, thereby leaving it in section 431(c)(1) as surplus. But whether the Corrections Act **[—18—]** removed the allegedly surplus term "aircraft manifest" from the text of section 431(c)(1) is, as the district court put it, the "fundamental question" before us. *Panjiva*, 342 F. Supp. 3d at 490. In other words, the Corrections Act's effect on section 431(c)(1) is precisely what we must determine in order to resolve the issue of "what the text [of]" section 431(c)(1) now says and means. *Id.* Thus, because the plaintiffs assume the answer to this question, and because we on our own see little reason why the Corrections Act should be assumed not to have removed "aircraft manifest" from section 431(c)(1), the plaintiffs' contention is not persuasive.[4]

The plaintiffs' second attack on the government's interpretation is that it does not give effect to the references to "airports" and "aircraft" in paragraphs (D), (E), and (F) of the subsection as amended by the **{-179-}** ACPA. Quoted above, they continue to require manifests to contain:

> (D) The name of the vessel, *aircraft*, or carrier.
> (E) The seaport *or airport* of loading. [and] **[—19—]**
> (F) The seaport *or airport* of discharge.

19 U.S.C. §§ 1431(c)(1)(D), (E), (F). (emphases added).

This assertion, unlike the plaintiffs' first contention, assumes nothing about the effect of the Corrections Act. The Corrections Act did not address subparagraphs (D), (E), and (F) of section 431(c)(1), and it is thus indisputable that the text of those paragraphs continues to refer to airports and aircraft. The plaintiffs are thus correct insofar as the government's interpretation of section 431(c)(1) renders the airport and aircraft references superfluous—if aircraft are not covered by section 431(c)(1), for example, what is the word "aircraft" doing in paragraph (E) as a covered place of loading?

The Supreme Court has made clear, though, that "[t]he canon against surplusage is not an absolute rule," *Marx*, 568 U.S. at 385, and it "assists only where a competing interpretation gives effect 'to every clause and word of a statute.'" *Microsoft Corp.*, 564 U.S. at 106 (quoting *Duncan v. Walker*, 533 U.S. 167, 174 (2001)). And however powerful this attack against the government's interpretation of the provision may be, it cannot aid the plaintiffs' contrary reading of section 431(c)(1) inasmuch as the plaintiffs do

[4] The plaintiffs attempt to support their argument by pointing to a decision by the United States District Court for the District of Minnesota, *Grupo Petrotemex, S.A. De C.V. v. Polymetrix AG*, No. 16-cv-2401, 2018 WL 5307823 (D. Minn. Oct. 26, 2018), which, contrary to the district court in this case, concluded that the reading of section 431 proposed by the government essentially ignores the "plain language" of the provision that requires public disclosure of information in "aircraft manifests," *id.* at *6 n.6. We are of course not bound by that decision; but in any event we disagree with its conclusion because, like the plaintiffs' argument here, it is based on an assumption as to what effect the Corrections Act had on the text of section 431(c)(1).

not even tell us what the words of section 431(c)(1) *are* post-Corrections Act, let alone give effect to every one of them. The closest the **[—20—]** plaintiffs come to offering a suggestion as to how section 431(c)(1)'s text now reads is by quoting 19 U.S.C. § 1431(c)(1), which, as we have noted, the House Office of Law Revision Council decided was: "the following information, when contained in a *vessel vessel* or *aircraft* manifest, shall be available for public disclosure." (emphasis added). Thus, although they attempt to dismiss it as "a minor syntactical issue," Pls. Br. at 6, the plaintiffs' understanding of the text of section 431(c)(1) to contain the phrase "vessel vessel" makes it obvious that their reading of the statute also contains a superfluous term.

In addition, the plaintiffs' interpretation of section 431(c)(1) fails to give effect to *any* clause or word in the Corrections Act amendment because their interpretation of section 431(c)(1) is only possible if the Corrections Act is understood to have had no effect on section 431(c)(1) at all. In other words, the parties agree that in the period after Congress enacted the ACPA in July 1996 and before it enacted the Corrections Act in October 1996, section 431(c)(1) explicitly required the government to publicly disclose manifests of both vessels and aircraft.[5] Because the plaintiffs thus understand section 431(c)(1) to continue to **[—21—]** impose the same requirements as it did before the Corrections Act was enacted, as the district court observed, their interpretation "render[s] the Corrections Act amendment entirely superfluous." *Panjiva*, 342 F. Supp. 3d at 491.

We conclude, therefore, that the canon against surplusage offers little to our analysis: Both the plaintiffs' interpretation and the government's interpretation of section 431(c)(1) leave different portions of the statute without effect. We must therefore turn to other tools of statutory interpretation in our analysis. **{-180-}**

b. *Implied Repeal*

The plaintiffs argue also that their interpretation of section 431(c)(1), which, to reiterate, requires public disclosure of manifests maintained by both vessel and aircraft manifests, is superior to the government's interpretation, which requires public disclosure of vessel manifests only, because the government's interpretation runs counter to the rule against implied repeals.

The Supreme Court has instructed that "repeals [of statutes] by implication are strongly disfavored" and that "it can be strongly presumed that Congress will specifically address language on the statute books that it wishes to change." *United States v. Fausto*, 484 U.S. 439, 452-53 (1988). According to the plaintiffs, the government's interpretation of section 431(c)(1) runs counter to this presumption **[—22—]** inasmuch as its understanding of the statute treats the Corrections Act as having deleted the phrase "aircraft manifests" from section 431(c)(1), and thus having repealed the portion of the ACPA that introduced that phrase into section 431(c)(1) several months previously, by silent implication.

To be sure, the government's interpretation of section 431(c)(1) does treat the Corrections Act as having removed the word "aircraft" from section 431(c)(1)'s operative clause. It is also true that the government asserts that the Corrections Act did so without specifically addressing the term "aircraft." But it does not follow that the government's interpretation relies on understanding the Corrections Act to have repealed the relevant portion of the ACPA by implication. Instead, the government's view of section 431(c)(1) treats the Corrections Act not as having overlooked the phrase "aircraft manifests," or as having silently repealed the relevant portion of the ACPA, but instead as having attempted to remove the word "aircraft" from section 431(c)(1)'s operative clause explicitly, if sloppily. In other words, under the government's reading, the Corrections Act is "an affirmative showing of [Congress'] intention to repeal," *Auburn Hous. Auth. v. Martinez*, 277 F.3d 138, 145 (2d Cir. 2002), a

---

[5] This assumes that section 431 requires an aircraft entering the country to have a manifest in the first place, which, as discussed above, is itself not clear.

specific provision (the ACPA) through an equally specific amendment (the Corrections **[—23—]** Act) that continues to suffer from a drafting error. Therefore, because the government does not contend that that Corrections Act repealed the ACPA by implication, the presumption against implied repeals does not apply and thus favors neither the plaintiffs' nor the government's interpretation of section 431(c)(1).

c. *Legislative History*

Having been pointed to nothing better to aid our interpretation, and with the meaning of section 431(c)(1)'s text still uncertain, we turn to the provision's legislative history. *See Puello v. Bureau of Citizenship & Immigration Servs.*, 511 F.3d 324, 327 (2d Cir. 2007) ("If the meaning of a statute is ambiguous, the court may resort to legislative history to determine the statute's meaning.") "[I]n so doing, we must 'construct an interpretation that comports with [the statute's] primary purpose and does not lead to anomalous or unreasonable results.'" *Id.* (quoting *Conn. ex rel. Blumenthal v. U.S. Dep't of the Interior*, 228 F.3d 82, 89 (2d Cir. 2000)). **[—24—]**

The plaintiffs, as noted above, urge us to ignore the statute's legislative history based on their view that the text of section 431(c)(1) is clear and resort to legislative history therefore improper.[6] **{-181-}**

The government disagrees, identifying legislative history that it contends helps make sense of section 431(c)(1)'s ambiguous text. It cites a report on the Corrections Act by the Senate Finance Committee that states that the act "amends section 431(c)(1) of the Tariff Act of 1930 to clarify that the references in the section is to vessel manifests and not to other types of manifests." S. Rep. No. 104-393, at 3 (1996). The report also includes a graphical representation of the changes the committee intended the Corrections Act to make to section 431, with the words to be removed indicated in brackets: **[—25—]**

Part II—Report, Entry, and Unlading of Vessels and Vehicles

* * * * * * *

SEC. 431. MANIFEST—REQUIREMENT, FORM, AND CONTENTS.

(a) * * *

* * * * * * *

(c)(1) Except as provided in subparagraph (2), the following information, when contained in [such manifest], *a vessel manifest* shall be available to public disclosure:

* * * * * * *

Id. at 43. We agree with the district court that this report is "clear evidence that the Corrections Act amendment was enacted to restrict the scope of § 431(c)(1)" by limiting it to vessels, which means waterborne transport only, and that the committee "understood that the version of § 431(c)(1) that would exist after [the Corrections Act] would cover [such] vessel manifests only, and that [the Corrections Act] would omit any reference to aircraft manifests from the operative clause of § 431(c)(1)." *Panjiva*, 342 F. Supp. 3d at 492.

One might wonder why Congress changed its mind so dramatically and so quickly between July and October of 1996. If the distinction between vessel and aircraft manifests was "unwarranted and out-of-date," S. Rep. No. 104-177, at 11 (1995), when the ACPA was passed in July 1996, one might guess that it would also be "unwarranted and out-of-date" three months later when the Corrections Act was passed. But Congress is permitted a U-turn. This legislative history suggests that it took one. And, critically, this reading allows for both 1996 amendments (*i.e.*, the ACPA and the Corrections Act) to

[6] Before the district court, but not on appeal, the plaintiffs argued that their reading of section 431(c)(1) was bolstered by a report by the Senate Judiciary Committee that expressly states the ACPA "amends section 431(c)(1) of the Tariff Act to permit public disclosure of aircraft manifests under the same terms currently allowed for sea shipments" because the "distinction between information required about goods shipped by sea as compared to goods shipped by air" is "unwarranted and out-of-date." S. Rep. No. 104-177, at 11 (1995). Be that as it may, the report provides little more than what is offered by the text of the ACPA, which, by inserting "vessel or aircraft before manifest" in section 431(c)(1), makes it clear that Congress intended (at least for a short period of time) that section 431(c)(1) require the disclosure of aircraft manifests in addition to vessel manifests. This point does not appear to be disputed by the government. But crucially, the report leaves unanswered what the text of section 431(c)(1) should be read to mean post enactment of the Corrections Act.

carry meaning: **[—26—]** Congress intended the ACPA to add aircraft manifests to section 431(c)(1)'s public disclosure requirement, and (soon thereafter) intended the Corrections Act to remove aircraft manifests from the public disclosure requirement. **{-182-}**

Moreover, if, as all appear to agree, the ACPA was meant to expand section 431(c)(1) to require the public disclosure of both vessel and aircraft manifests, and, as the plaintiffs contend, section 431(c)(1) should be understood to continue that requirement, then the Corrections Act was essentially a nullity. Congress should not be understood to have intended an amendment to be ineffective. Faced with two less than perfect readings of the statute, we conclude that the government's interpretation of section 431(c)(1) more persuasively reflects Congressional intent.[7] **[—27—]**

For the foregoing reasons, we conclude that section 431(c)(1) of the Smoot-Hawley Tariff Act of 1930, presently codified at 19 U.S.C. § 1431(c)(1), continues to require the government to make available for public disclosure manifests only of vessels, meaning "water craft or other contrivance used, or capable of being used, as a means of transportation in water, but . . . not . . . aircraft." *See* 19 U.S.C. § 1401.

[7] The government also relies on "subsequent legislative history," *i.e.*, legislative history from the time since the Corrections Act was passed, to support its interpretation of section 431(c)(1). The argument is discussed at some length in the district court's opinion. *See Panjiva*, 342 F. Supp. 3d at 493-94. But the Supreme Court has warned (as the district court noted, *see id.*) that subsequent legislative history is "a particularly dangerous ground on which to rest an interpretation of a prior statute," inasmuch as "[a] bill can be proposed for any number of reasons, and it can be rejected for just as many others." *Solid Waste Agency of N. Cook Cty. v. Army Corps of Eng'rs*, 531 U.S. 159, 169-70 (2001) (internal quotation marks omitted). The district court concluded that subsequent legislative history "further supports the [g]overnment's reading of the statute." *Panjiva*, 342 F. Supp. 3d at 492. Under the circumstances, though, we need not and therefore do not rely on subsequent legislative history to reach our conclusion.

CONCLUSION

We have considered the plaintiffs' remaining arguments on appeal and conclude that they are without merit. We therefore AFFIRM the judgment of the district court.

United States Court of Appeals
for the Second Circuit

No. 17-3633

MANGOURAS
VS.
SQUIRE PATTON BOGGS

Appeal from the United States District Court for the Southern District of New York

Decided: November 9, 2020

Citation: 980 F.3d 88, 8 Adm. R. 66 (2d Cir. 2020).

Before **LIVINGSTON**, Chief Judge, **LEVAL** and **WESLEY**, Circuit Judges.

[—2—] {–91–} LIVINGSTON, Chief Judge:

The 2002 sinking of the oil tanker *Prestige* off the coast of Spain spawned a complex web of litigation, including a civil action brought by Spain in the U.S. District Court for the Southern District of New York against the vessel classification society that certified the ship (the "New York Action") and a criminal trial of the ship's captain, Petitioner-Appellee-Cross-Appellant Apostolos Mangouras ("Mangouras"), conducted in Spain. At issue in this case is an **[—3—]** application for discovery in aid of foreign proceedings under 28 U.S.C. § 1782 filed by Mangouras in 2017, which sought documents for a proceeding Mangouras sought to institute before the European Court of Human Rights ("ECtHR") stemming from the criminal trial, as well as for potential privately-instituted criminal actions in Spain against three witnesses in the earlier proceedings. Mangouras sought the discovery from Respondents-Appellees-Cross-Appellants, including attorney Brian D. Starer ("Starer") and his law firm, Squire Patton Boggs, who represented Spain in the New York Action (the "Squire Respondents"),[1] as well as from naval architects Charles R. Cushing and his firm, C.R. Cushing & Co., who had inspected the wreckage of the *Prestige* and served as expert witnesses in both proceedings (the "Cushing Respondents") (together, "Respondents").

On appeal, Respondents challenge the October 30, 2017 memorandum and order of the district court (Castel, *J.*) granting discovery, as well as the court's December 10, 2018 entry of final judgment following additional proceedings addressing open issues of privilege. Mangouras cross-appeals, arguing that the district court erred by entering final judgment rather than maintaining the case on **[—4—]** its active docket to facilitate the use of the discovery in future foreign proceedings. For the reasons stated below, we conclude that Mangouras's **{–92–}** cross-appeal, unlike Respondents' appeal, no longer presents a live case or controversy and is therefore moot. We further conclude that the district court erred by failing to conduct a choice-of-law analysis with respect to applicable privileges and in analyzing whether one of the proceedings cited by Mangouras as a basis for his application was within reasonable contemplation, necessitating vacatur and remand of the judgment below. Accordingly, we DISMISS Mangouras's cross-appeal as moot, VACATE the judgment of the district court, and REMAND for further proceedings consistent with this opinion.

BACKGROUND

I

In November 2002, amid severe weather, the *Prestige* sank off the coast of Spain, releasing its cargo of approximately 76,972 metric tons of fuel into coastal waters. The resulting environmental damage was severe, with an economic and industrial impact estimated at over 4.4 billion Euros. Whether the *Prestige* had structural defects at the time of the incident, and whether Mangouras, as the **[—5—]** vessel's captain, had knowledge of any such defects, has remained hotly in dispute.

"[L]ong and tortuous litigation" has ensued ever since. *Mare Shipping Inc. v. Squire Sanders (US) LLP*, 574 F. App'x 6, 7 (2d Cir. 2014). In 2003, Spain, represented by the Squire Respondents, initiated the New York

[1] Starer's prior law firm, Holland & Knight LLP, was also named as a respondent in Mangouras's application, but is not a participant in this appeal.

Action, bringing suit in the U.S. District Court for the Southern District of New York against the American Bureau of Shipping ("ABS"), the classification society that had certified the *Prestige*, on the basis that ABS acted recklessly in evaluating the vessel's seaworthiness. The Squire Respondents hired the Cushing Respondents to prepare a report on the cause of the ship's sinking, with Charles Cushing serving as an expert witness in the litigation. The district court (Swain, *J.*) ultimately granted summary judgment in favor of ABS, and this Court affirmed. *See Reino de España v. Am. Bureau of Shipping, Inc.*, 691 F.3d 461, 476 (2d Cir. 2012).

In 2012, following a ten-year investigation, Mangouras faced criminal charges in a nine-month trial in La Coruña, Spain (the "Spanish Action"). The Cushing Respondents reprised their role as experts, and three witnesses who had provided sworn declarations or expert testimony in the New York Action provided live testimony in the Spanish Action: the ship's former captain, **[—6—]** Efstratios Kostazos ("Kostazos"); a Danish pilot who had guided the Prestige through Danish straits in October 2002, Jens Jørgen Thuesen ("Thuesen"); and George Alevizos ("Alevizos"), who had been retained as an expert in the New York Action and whose former employer was involved in the management of the *Prestige*. The criminal trial culminated in a November 2013 decision by the Court of First Instance that acquitted Mangouras of all major charges and found guilt only as to one count of "serious disobedience to authority." Joint App'x at 403. In January 2016, however, the Spanish Supreme Court reversed, finding Mangouras guilty of gross negligence. Mangouras's subsequent appeals were rejected.

II

In 2013, while the Spanish Action was underway, Mangouras made his first attempt at obtaining discovery in aid of a foreign proceeding under 28 U.S.C. § 1782. Together with Mare Shipping, Inc., which owned the *Prestige*, Mangouras filed an application seeking materials from the Squire Appellants relating to the testimony of Kostazos, Thuesen, and Alevizos for **{–93–}** use in the then-ongoing criminal trial[2] as well as in one of several possible future proceedings such as an appeal of **[—7—]** the Spanish Action; a privately-instituted criminal proceeding in Spain known as a "Querella Criminal"; and/or a submission to the ECtHR. *See Mare Shipping*, 574 F. App'x at 7. The U.S. District Court for the Southern District of New York (Castel, *J.*) found the statutory requirements of § 1782 to be satisfied, but denied the application in its discretion due to Mangouras's "failure . . . to seek the requested material through Spanish proof[] mechanisms" in the Spanish Action. *In re Mare Shipping Inc.*, No. 13-mc-238, 2013 WL 5761104, at *5 (S.D.N.Y. Oct. 23, 2013). This Court affirmed, but noted that because "the various foreign actions cited by plaintiffs as potential avenues for using the sought discovery are continually in flux," Mangouras would be free to renew his application should "appropriate circumstances arise in the future." *Mare Shipping*, 574 F. App'x at 8.[3] **[—8—]**

III

In May and June 2017, seemingly having determined that such "appropriate circumstances" had arisen, Mangouras filed the § 1782 applications at issue in this appeal: one seeking the same discovery from the Squire Respondents that was the subject of the rejected 2013 application, and another seeking materials from the Cushing Respondents with respect to their inspection of the wreckage of the *Prestige*, which had been conducted in the course of preparing their expert report in the New York Action. Echoing his 2013 application, Mangouras

[2] Notably, the public hearing component of the Spanish Action concluded two **[—7—]** days after Mangouras filed his initial § 1782 application.

[3] In order to ensure Mangouras's ability to bring a renewed § 1782 application should suitable circumstances arise, this Court ordered respondents "not [to] destroy any records, documents, or materials that may reasonably be considered to be subject to discovery under the § 1782 request . . . for a period of five years from the date of the entry of this Order." *Mare Shipping*, 574 F. App'x at 8–9.

stated that the discovery from the Squire Appellants was intended for use in potential Querella Criminal proceedings against Kostazos, Thuesen, and Alevizos based on their having allegedly provided false testimony in the prior proceedings, as well as in a submission before the ECtHR that would argue, *inter alia*, that Mangouras had been deprived of due process in the Spanish Action. The discovery sought from the Cushing Respondents, meanwhile, was intended for use solely in the ECtHR.

The applications were consolidated into a single action and once again came before Judge Castel. On October 30, 2017, the district court issued a memorandum and order in which it reasoned that the statutory requirements of § 1782 had been satisfied and that, in light of the procedural posture of the new **[—9—]** application, the discretionary factors now weighed in Mangouras's favor. Accordingly, the court granted the requested discovery, but stated that it would "continue to preside over th[e] action" to address open issues, including those concerning the scope of document production. Special App'x at 18.

Respondents filed a notice of appeal on November 3, 2017. On December 7, 2017, this Court denied a stay pending appeal and noted the ongoing proceedings in the district court, directing the parties to address "the effect of those open issues on the finality of the order as it relates to this Court's jurisdiction." 2d Cir. Dkt. 17-3633, Doc. No. 60. Upon the denial of the stay, Respondents began turning over documents **{–94–}** to Mangouras, with production completed in May 2018. In the meantime, Judge Castel continued to rule on discovery disputes, including ordering expedited production in light of the impending statute of limitations for a Querella Criminal against Thuesen, as well as conducting *in camera* review of subsets of documents and issuing decisions in December 2017 and March 2018 regarding Respondents' assertion of work product doctrine protection.

IV

This Court heard oral argument on September 25, 2018. After directing further briefing regarding the state of ongoing proceedings in the district court, **[—10—]** we issued a summary order on October 31, 2018. *See Mangouras v. Squire Patton Boggs*, 740 F. App'x 757 (2d Cir. 2018). In light of the arguably non-final nature of portions of the district court's October 30, 2017 order, we determined that "additional information" was necessary in order to ensure our jurisdiction over the case. *Id.* at 758. Accordingly, we remanded to the district court pursuant to the procedure set out in *United States v. Jacobson*, 15 F.3d 19, 21–22 (2d Cir. 1994), directing the court "either to complete the discovery proceedings before entry of a final judgment, or to enter an order certifying . . . a partial final judgment pursuant to Rule 54(b)," 740 F. App'x at 758.

On December 7, 2018, the district court issued an order stating that all proceedings related to privilege and work product had concluded. The court further determined that there was no longer a "live controversy on the present applications under section 1782 because the proceedings for which the applications were directed have either been terminated or will not occur." Second Special App'x at 31. The court rejected Mangouras's request to withhold the entry of final judgment in order to facilitate the use of the discovery in a newly filed proceeding before the United Nations Human Rights Committee ("UNHRC"), reasoning that such an action had not been referenced in his prior **[—11—]** applications and that Mangouras could file a new § 1782 application to obtain discovery for use in the UNHRC. Accordingly, over Mangouras's objection, the court directed the entry of final judgment, which issued on December 10, 2018.

On January 4, 2019, Respondents filed an amended notice of appeal, incorporating the district court's December 7, 2018 order and December 10, 2018 judgment. Mangouras followed suit on January 16, 2019 with a notice of cross-appeal from the final judgment.

On February 6, 2019, the original appeal, Respondents' amended appeal, and Mangouras's cross-appeal were consolidated before this Court, and jurisdiction was restored to this panel pursuant to the procedures outlined in *Jacobson*. *See* 15 F.3d at 22. In light of the district court's suggestion that the case no longer presented a live controversy, we directed briefing as to whether the appeals were moot.

The parties' letter briefs apprised the Court of several new developments in the proceedings that had formed the basis for Mangouras's application. As had been previously established in the parties' initial round of briefing, Querella Criminal proceedings against Kostazos, Thuesen, and Alevizos were time-barred as of May 2018, and Mangouras acknowledged that no such proceedings had **[—12—]** ultimately been filed. As for the ECtHR proceeding, it was revealed for the first time before this Court that Mangouras had been informed on January 18, 2018 that his complaint before the ECtHR had been dismissed as "manifestly ill-founded." Feb. 20, 2019 Letter Br. of Respondents at 3; *see also* Suppl. App'x at **{-95-}** 74. Despite the fact that the ECtHR's decision made clear that it was "final and . . . not subject to appeal," Suppl. App'x at 73, Mangouras sought reconsideration of the dismissal on the basis of obvious mistake or bias because the judge who ruled on the dismissal was "from Andorra, a small Principality located at the frontier between Spain and France and with strong political and financial ties with both countries," Feb. 20, 2019 Letter Br. of Pet'r at 1. Mangouras was informed by letter that the decision was not appealable. Nevertheless, Mangouras once again sought reconsideration. After waiting six months without a response, Mangouras filed a new complaint against Spain in the UNHRC in November 2018.

Mangouras was silent as to the termination of the ECtHR proceeding until November 13, 2018, when he informed the district court of that development in the course of arguing against the entry of final judgment following this Court's October 2018 summary order. Until that filing, Mangouras had continued to invoke the long-terminated ECtHR proceedings as a basis for discovery in his **[—13—]** briefing before this Court and in the district court to secure *in camera* review and production of documents that Respondents had designated as work product.

Following the parties' submissions as to mootness, this Court set a schedule for full briefing, which was completed on August 16, 2019. Now that the finality question has been resolved by the district court's December 10, 2018 entry of final judgment, we address the arguments raised by the parties with respect to the district court's original grant of the § 1782 application on October 30, 2017 and its subsequent ruling on December 7, 2018.

DISCUSSION

Respondents argue that the district court erred in granting the § 1782 application because, *inter alia*, the materials are absolutely privileged under Spanish law and because Mangouras failed to establish that the discovery was for use in a foreign proceeding under the statute. Mangouras, meanwhile, contends that the district court erred by entering final judgment rather than maintaining the case on its active docket to facilitate the use of the materials in the new UNHRC proceeding.

For the reasons stated below, we conclude as an initial matter that Mangouras's cross-appeal, unlike Respondents' appeal, is moot because the **[—14—]** proceedings cited by Mangouras in his § 1782 application have been terminated or will not occur. With respect to Respondents' appeal, we further conclude that the district court erred by failing to conduct a threshold choice-of-law analysis to determine which country's privilege laws applied to Mangouras's § 1782 application. The court likewise erred in its analysis of whether the Querella Criminal proceedings were within reasonable contemplation as required by § 1782; notwithstanding the court's separate findings as to the ECtHR proceedings, this error necessitates clarification of the court's analysis of the discretionary factors, which relied in part on the Querella Criminal as one of the bases for the application. Accordingly, we vacate and remand the district court's judgment.[4]

I

In light of the now-defunct status of the foreign proceedings that formed the basis for Mangouras's § 1782 application, **{-96-}** we must first "assure ourselves of our jurisdiction in light of changed circumstances" by addressing whether the appeals before us are moot. *In re Accent Delight Int'l Ltd.*, 869 F.3d 121, 128 (2d Cir. 2017). "A case becomes moot—and therefore no longer a 'Case' or 'Controversy' for **[—15—]** purposes of Article III [of the Constitution]—'when the issues presented are no longer "live" or the parties lack a legally cognizable interest in the outcome.'" *Already, LLC v. Nike, Inc.*, 568 U.S. 85, 91 (2013) (quoting *Murphy v. Hunt*, 455 U.S. 478, 481 (1982) (per curiam)).

Respondents' appeal challenges the validity of the district court's original grant of the § 1782 application and seeks the return or destruction of the documents in the event this Court determines the district court erred in granting the application. Accordingly, if the discovery was improvidently granted, this Court is positioned to grant meaningful relief by ordering that the documents be returned or destroyed. *See Church of Scientology of Cal. v. United States*, 506 U.S. 9, 13 (1992) (holding that owners of documents produced pursuant to what was later determined to be an "unlawful summons" held "an obvious possessory interest in their records," and that a court could "effectuate relief by ordering the . . . return [of] the records"). By contrast, if the discovery was "lawfully . . . obtained," Mangouras is free to retain the documents, absent an order from the district court to the contrary. *In re Accent Delight*, 869 F.3d at 135. Because the outcome of Respondents' appeal thus implicates the parties' respective rights to possess the documents, the parties plainly retain a "legally cognizable interest in the outcome" **[—16—]** of the case, and the appeal is not moot. *Already, LLC*, 568 U.S. at 91 (quoting *Murphy*, 455 U.S. at 481).

Mangouras's cross-appeal, on the other hand, seeks only to reinstate the application as an open case on the district court's docket and is therefore premised on viewing the § 1782 application itself as a live case. Yet a § 1782 application is moot when there are "no foreign proceedings, within the meaning of the statute, in which the discovery could be used." *Euromepa, S.A. v. R. Esmerian, Inc.* (*Euromepa II*), 154 F.3d 24, 29 (2d Cir. 1998). Here, the parties do not dispute that the foreign proceedings relied upon by Mangouras in his application—a proceeding before the ECtHR and potential Querella Criminal proceedings against the three witnesses in the New York and Spanish Actions—have permanently concluded or will not take place, respectively. In arguing that his appeal is not moot, Mangouras points to his new filing before the UNHRC. Mangouras relies on this Court's decision in *In re Accent Delight*, where this Court held that "[§] 1782 does not prevent an applicant who lawfully has obtained discovery under the statute with respect to one foreign proceeding from using the discovery elsewhere unless the district court orders otherwise," 869 F.3d at 135, and further determined that although the district court in that case had evaluated the § 1782 requirements **[—17—]** with respect to a proceeding in Monaco, a "pending French proceeding save[d] th[e] appeal from mootness," *id.* at 128.

Mangouras's reliance is misplaced. Under his reading of *In re Accent Delight*, a § 1782 application would *never* be moot, as applicants could always resurrect otherwise-moot applications by continually concocting novel proceedings in which the disputed discovery could theoretically be used. We reject this interpretation. Rather, **{-97-}** the French proceeding in *In re Accent Delight* saved that case from mootness because, while the district court had analyzed the requirements of § 1782 only with respect to the Monégasque proceeding, the French proceeding was included in the original application and the district court had affirmatively granted the applicant the right to use the materials in

[4] Respondents also challenge the district court's rulings on work product protection for certain subsets of documents. In light of our vacatur and remand of the district court's grant of discovery, we do not reach the work product issue.

that proceeding. *See id.* at 125, 133. Here, by contrast, the UNHRC was not mentioned anywhere in Mangouras's application or at any point before the district court until November 2018, after this Court's remand of Respondents' original appeal, and the district court never issued a protective order explicitly granting Mangouras the right to use the discovery in that proceeding. While it would have been convenient for Mangouras had the district court previously granted him the right to use the discovery in alternate proceedings and thereafter agreed to **[—18—]** maintain the case on its active docket to facilitate such future uses, the court was under no affirmative obligation to do so, and Mangouras therefore has no "legally cognizable interest in the outcome" of his appeal. *Already, LLC*, 568 U.S. at 91 (quoting *Murphy*, 455 U.S. at 481). Unlike Respondents' appeal, which presents a live controversy requiring this court to evaluate whether the original grant of discovery was proper in order to determine whether documents must be returned to Respondents or remain in Mangouras's possession, Mangouras's appeal is therefore moot.

II

We next turn to the merits of Respondents' arguments on appeal asserting that the district court erred in granting the § 1782 application. Under § 1782, applicants must meet several statutory requirements, including that "(1) the person from whom discovery is sought resides (or is found) in the district of the district court to which the application is made, (2) the discovery is for use in a foreign proceeding before a foreign [or international] tribunal, and (3) the application is made by a foreign or international tribunal or any interested person." *Mees v. Buiter*, 793 F.3d 291, 297 (2d Cir. 2015) (quoting *Brandi-Dohrn v. IKB Deutsche Industriebank AG*, 673 F.3d 76, 80 (2d Cir. 2012)). Additionally, the **[—19—]** statute requires that the discovery not be "in violation of any legally applicable privilege." 28 U.S.C. § 1782(a); *see also In re Guo*, 965 F.3d 96, 102 n.3 (2d Cir. 2020) (noting that "[w]hile our case law has often focused on the[] three elements" stated above in delineating the statutory requirements of § 1782, "the statute also imposes other requirements, including that the discovery not be 'in violation of any legally applicable privilege'" (citation omitted)).

Once a court has determined that the mandatory requirements of the statute have been satisfied, the court may grant the application in its discretion, which is "not boundless" but rather "must be exercised 'in light of the twin aims of the statute: providing efficient means of assistance to participants in international litigation in our federal courts and encouraging foreign countries by example to provide similar means of assistance to our courts.'" *Mees*, 793 F.3d at 297–98 (quoting *Schmitz v. Bernstein Liebhard & Lifshitz, LLP*, 376 F.3d 79, 84 (2d Cir. 2004)). The Supreme Court has identified four factors guiding this exercise of discretion, including: "(1) whether 'the person from whom discovery is sought is a participant in the foreign proceeding,' in which case 'the need for § 1782(a) aid generally is not as apparent'; (2) 'the nature of the foreign tribunal, the character of the proceedings underway abroad, and the receptivity of the foreign **[—20—]** government or the **{-98-}** court or agency abroad to U.S. federal-court judicial assistance'; (3) 'whether the . . . request conceals an attempt to circumvent foreign proof-gathering restrictions or other policies of a foreign country or the United States'; and (4) whether the request is 'unduly intrusive or burdensome.'" *Id.* at 298 (quoting *Intel Corp. v. Advanced Micro Devices, Inc.*, 542 U.S. 241, 264–65 (2004)).

"We review de novo a district court's ruling that a petition satisfies [§] 1782's jurisdictional [i.e. statutory] requirements," *Kiobel by Samkalden v. Cravath, Swaine & Moore LLP*, 895 F.3d 238, 243 (2d Cir. 2018), and review for abuse of discretion a district court's application of the discretionary *Intel* factors, *see Brandi-Dohrn*, 673 F.3d at 79-80.

With respect to the district court's analysis of the mandatory factors, we agree with the district court's determination that Respondents can be found in this district, *see Kiobel*, 895 F.3d at 244, and that Mangouras is an "interested person" within the meaning of the statute. We disagree, however, with the district court's approach to the "legally applicable privilege" issue and with its analysis of which proceedings were in reasonable contemplation at the time of the application for purposes of the "for use" requirement. **[—21—]**

A

Before the district court, Respondents argued that all the documents sought by Mangouras were shielded under Spanish privilege law. The district court did not directly address the statute's requirement that discovery not be barred by a "legally applicable privilege" or consider whether Spanish privilege law qualified as "legally applicable." Rather, the court considered Respondents' assertion of the privilege solely in the context of its analysis of the "for use" statutory requirement and the "nature of the foreign proceedings" discretionary factor, and rejected the argument on the basis that the parties' conflicting representations and the absence of "authoritative proof" that Spanish privilege barred the discovery, *see* Special App'x at 14 (quoting *Euromepa S.A. v. R. Esmerian, Inc.*, 51 F.3d 1095, 1100 (2d Cir. 1995)), would require a "speculative foray[] into legal territories unfamiliar to federal judges," Special App'x at 11 (quoting *Mees*, 793 F.3d at 299), which was proscribed by this Court's decision in *Euromepa*, 51 F.3d at 1099.

However, in circumstances where the parties dispute which nation's privilege law furnishes the "legally applicable privilege," and those competing national laws provide different results, courts should first conduct a choice-of-law analysis to determine which body of privilege law applies. The statute specifies **[—22—]** that "[a] person may not be compelled to give his testimony or statement or to produce a document or other thing in violation of any legally applicable privilege." 28 U.S.C. § 1782(a). As we have previously recognized, the "legislative history [of § 1782] makes clear that . . . [the 'legally applicable privilege' language] 'provides for the recognition of all privileges to which the person may be entitled, including privileges recognized by foreign law.'" *In re Erato*, 2 F.3d 11, 14 (2d Cir. 1993) (quoting S. Rep. No. 1580 (1964), *reprinted in* 1964 U.S.C.C.A.N. 3782, 3790).

This Court has yet to articulate an approach for giving effect to the term "legally applicable" as used in the statute. Filling that gap, district courts within this Circuit have applied the "touch base" test, a "traditional choice-of-law 'contacts' analysis to determine the law that applies to claims of privilege involving foreign documents." **{-99-}** *Astra Aktiebolag v. Andrx Pharms., Inc.*, 208 F.R.D. 92, 98 (S.D.N.Y. 2002); *see, e.g., In re financialright GmbH*, No. 17-mc-105 (DAB), 2017 WL 2879696 (S.D.N.Y. June 22, 2017); *In re Berlamont*, No. 14-mc-190 (JSR), 2014 WL 3893953 (S.D.N.Y. Aug. 4, 2014), *aff'd sub nom. In re Application for an Order Pursuant to 28 U.S.C. 1782 to Conduct Discovery for Use in Foreign Proceedings*, 773 F.3d 456, 459 (2d Cir. 2014); *In re Okean BV*, No. 12-mc-104 (PAE) (S.D.N.Y. July 16, 2013) **[—23—]** (Dist. Ct. Dkt. No. 63 at 11–12); *In re Christensen*, No. M19-138 (JFK), 2006 WL 278169 (S.D.N.Y. Feb. 3, 2006). This common law approach derives from Federal Rule of Evidence 501, which provides that claims of privilege in a federal question case are "govern[ed]" by the principles of "common law . . . as interpreted by United States courts in the light of reason and experience." Fed. R. Evid. 501; *see also Golden Trade, S.r.L. v. Lee Apparel Co.*, 143 F.R.D. 514, 519 (S.D.N.Y. 1992) (observing that the federal common law referenced in Rule 501 encompasses questions regarding choice of law).

We now hold that, consistent with the traditional approach, the "touch base" test is the proper choice-of-law test for purposes of determining which privileges are "legally applicable" in the § 1782 context. Under the touch base test, a court applies "the law of the country that has the 'predominant' or 'the most direct and compelling interest' in whether . . . communications should remain confidential, unless that foreign law is contrary to the public policy of this forum." *Astra*, 208 F.R.D. at 98 (quoting *Golden Trade*, 143 F.R.D. at 521–22). The country with the predominant interest is either "the place where the allegedly privileged relationship was entered into," or "the place in which that relationship was centered at the time the communication was sent." *Id.* (citations omitted). Thus, **[—24—]** "communications relating to legal proceedings in the United States, or that reflect the provision of advice regarding American law, 'touch base' with the United States and, therefore, are governed by American law, even though the communication may involve foreign attorneys or a foreign proceeding." *Gucci America, Inc. v. Guess?, Inc.*, 271 F.R.D. 58, 65 (S.D.N.Y. 2010). For example, where documents sought by a § 1782 application were "located in New York, were created and produced in the context of a case pending in New York, and [were] being sought from United States lawyers in a court in New York pursuant to a United States statute," a district court properly determined that U.S., rather than Swiss, privilege law was applicable. *In re Berlamont*, 2014 WL 3893953, at *2; *see also In re Application*, 773 F.3d at 459 (affirming *In re Berlamont* in relevant part "for substantially the reasons outlined in [the district court's] well-reasoned memorandum order").

Respondents insist that the application of the "touch base" test is tantamount to "[c]ompelling discovery over assertions of foreign privileges," with the effect of "encourag[ing] reciprocal infringements of U.S. privileges," Reply Br. at 14, thereby "undercut[ting] the goal of § 1782 of 'encouraging foreign countries by example to provide similar means of assistance to our courts,'" *id.* (quoting **[—25—]** *Intel*, 542 U.S. at 252). We are unpersuaded. Because a foreign jurisdiction retains the ability to refuse to consider any documents it deems privileged under its own law, we conclude that the application of the traditional choice-of-law approach in this context does not offend principles of international comity.

We also note that, while the parties have extensively briefed the issue of the degree of deference due to the submissions made **{-100-}** on behalf of the Spanish government in this case, Spain cannot short-circuit our choice-of-law analysis via submissions asserting that Spanish privilege is applicable, even if those submissions constitute "authoritative proof" within the meaning of *Euromepa*, 51 F.3d at 1100, and *In re Application of Metallgesellschaft AG*, 121 F.3d 77, 80 (2d Cir. 1997). If the "touch base" test points to the application of American, rather than Spanish, privilege law, Spain's submissions are irrelevant on the privilege question, though they may remain probative at other stages of the analysis, including the "for use" prong. *See Euromepa II*, 154 F.3d at 28.

Having now clarified that the "touch base" test is the applicable choice-of-law test for questions of privilege in the § 1782 context, we remand for the district court to apply this test in the course of determining whether Mangouras's application was properly granted. **[—26—]**

B

We turn next to the district court's analysis of whether, as required by the statute, the requested discovery was "for use in a foreign proceeding before a foreign [or international] tribunal." *Mees*, 793 F.3d at 297 (quoting *Brandi-Dohrn*, 673 F.3d at 80). As the Supreme Court clarified in *Intel*, in order to qualify as a "foreign proceeding" within the meaning of the statute, the proceeding in question need not be "pending" or "imminent"; rather, it is necessary only that "a dispositive ruling" be "within reasonable contemplation." *Intel*, 542 U.S. at 259.

This requirement that a proceeding be within "reasonable contemplation" forms an outer limit on which proceedings may constitute the basis of a § 1782 application. Expounding upon that limit, we have clarified that to demonstrate that an action is within reasonable contemplation, "the applicant must have more than a subjective intent to undertake some legal action, and instead must provide some objective indicium that the action is being contemplated." *Certain Funds, Accts., and/or Inv. Vehicles v. KPMG, L.L.P.*, 798 F.3d 113, 123 (2d Cir. 2015). Moreover, we have reasoned that "it suffices to observe that the Supreme Court's inclusion of the word 'reasonable' in the 'within reasonable contemplation' formulation indicates that the proceedings cannot be merely speculative. At a **[—27—]** minimum, a § 1782 applicant must present to the district court some concrete basis from which it can determine that the contemplated proceeding is more than just a twinkle in counsel's eye." *Id.* at 123–24. We have accordingly rejected § 1782 applications where it was "apparent that all that the [applicants] alleged before the district court was that they had retained counsel and were discussing the *possibility* of initiating litigation," such that "at the time the evidence was sought in th[e] case, the [applicants] had done little to make an objective showing that the planned proceedings were within reasonable contemplation." *Id.* at 124.

When Mangouras first filed his applications in May and June 2017, neither of the relied-upon proceedings—the action in the ECtHR or the Querella Criminal proceedings against the three witnesses on the basis that they knowingly provided false testimony—had been initiated. In determining whether Mangouras made the necessary showing with respect to these proceedings, "we assess the indicia of whether the contemplated proceedings were within reasonable contemplation at the time the § 1782 application was filed" and briefed before the district court, and therefore must disregard the post-remand revelations regarding the state of the proceedings. **{-101-}** *Id.* We agree with the district court that Mangouras made a sufficient showing with respect to his ECtHR submission, which had been filed **[—28—]** prior to the district court's ruling on the application. With respect to the Querella Criminal proceedings, however, we conclude that the district court erred in determining that Mangouras had satisfied the requirements of § 1782.

Mangouras failed to provide sufficient "objective indici[a]" that the Querella Criminal proceedings were, at any point, more than merely speculative. *Certain Funds*, 798 F.3d at 123. Mangouras stated that he intended to use the discovery he would obtain through the § 1782 application to draft a Querella Criminal complaint for submission in Spain. His proffered basis for the anticipated Querella Criminal proceedings was that three witnesses—Kostazos, Alevizos, and Thuesen—provided false testimony. However, Mangouras's submissions did not provide the legal theory supporting such a proceeding, nor did he clearly lay out either the content of his claims or even a sufficiently concrete basis for Mangouras's belief that the witnesses gave false testimony in Spain.[5] **[—29—]** Further, unlike cases where we and other courts have concluded that § 1782 applicants showed the anticipated proceedings were reasonably contemplated, *see, e.g., In re Hornbeam Corp.*, 722 F. App'x 7, 9 (2d Cir. 2018), Mangouras did not provide sufficiently "reliable indications of the likelihood that proceedings will be instituted within a reasonable time," *Certain Funds*, 798 F.3d at 123 (quoting *Application of Consorcio Ecuatoriano de Telecomunicaciones S.A. v. JAS Forwarding (USA), Inc.*, 747 F.3d 1262, 1270 (11th Cir. 2014)). Instead, counsel's representations at oral argument before the district court indicated that the Querella Criminal claims were at best speculative. *See* Joint App'x at 1475 ("[Mangouras] is proceeding with the Querella Criminal, and he is going to proceed with the Querella Criminal *depending on what the evidence shows* or he will use it in the European Court of Human Rights." (emphasis added)); *see also id.* at 1479–80 ("The third party discovery is going to help us determine *whether or not* these individuals knew what they were testifying to was false . . . . *If* [the witness] testified falsely knowing he was testifying falsely or recklessly testifying about it, *then* we have a Querella Criminal

[5] We note that Mangouras also stated that he sought the discovery to determine if the witnesses *knowingly* or *recklessly* gave false testimony. *See* Joint App'x at 1479–80 ("The third party discovery is going to help us determine whether or not these individuals *knew* what they were testifying to was false . . . . If [the witness] testified falsely *knowing* he was testifying falsely or *recklessly* testifying about it, then we have a Querella Criminal against him." (emphasis added)). Because Mangouras did not provide a sufficiently concrete basis to believe that the witnesses provided false testimony in Spain, we need not reach the separate issue whether Mangouras could have used the § 1782 application to determine if the witnesses knowingly or recklessly gave false testimony.

against him." (emphases added)).[6] And the **[—30—]** submission of Mangouras's Spanish counsel, Maria Docampo, in support of the application only underscored the tentativeness of the Querella Criminal proceedings. *See id.* at 1074 ("In order to properly pursue the Querella Criminal, the evidence sought in the . . . Application is necessary to establish *whether* the witnesses, each of which provided false evidence, provided false evidence **{-102-}** in New York or in Spain, or *possibly* in both jurisdictions." (emphasis added)). To be clear, given the fact-specific nature of the inquiry, we need not decide here "what precisely an applicant must show to establish" that a proceeding is more than speculative. *Certain Funds*, 798 F.3d at 123. But for the reasons given, under the facts of this case, we conclude that the district court erred in finding that the Querella Criminal proceedings were reasonably contemplated.

To be sure, the Querella Criminal proceeding was not the district court's sole basis for concluding that the statutory requirements of § 1782 were satisfied; Mangouras also relied on his application before the ECtHR, which, as noted above, had already been filed at the time of the district court's ruling. Indeed, the discovery sought from the Cushing Respondents was intended *solely* for use in the **[—31—]** ECtHR. Nevertheless, having consolidated the applications, the district court considered both proceedings together in weighing the discretionary factors and relied heavily on the Querella Criminal proceeding as a valid basis for the application in the course of its discretionary analysis. Accordingly, the court's ultimate decision to grant the application was predicated at least in part on its erroneous reasoning as to the Querella Criminal, requiring vacatur and remand for clarification.

* * *

On remand, the district court must deny the § 1782 application as moot in light of the fact that the ECtHR and Querella Criminal proceedings have either terminated or will not occur. As discussed above, however, there remains a live controversy as to whether the documents were improperly ordered to be produced, such that they should be returned to Respondents. Accordingly, on remand, the district court should determine whether, after applying the touch base test and reevaluating the discretionary factors absent consideration of the Querella Criminal, the § 1782 application was properly granted. While this analysis must necessarily be conducted with reference to the proceeding in the ECtHR as it stood **[—32—]** at the time of the district court's initial ruling, the district court is free to consider the entire course of the litigation in re-weighing the discretionary factors.

Finally, we note that Mangouras has expressed an intent to pursue future § 1782 applications seeking the materials at issue in this case for purposes of his UNHRC submission. To that end, we grant his request to extend until July 30, 2021 our prior directive ordering Respondents, now including the Cushing Respondents, to refrain from destroying, altering, or removing from the territorial limits of the United States any of the records at issue unless otherwise directed by an order of a United States court. *See Mare Shipping*, 574 F. App'x at 8–9.

CONCLUSION

For the foregoing reasons, we DISMISS Mangouras's cross-appeal as moot, VACATE the judgment of the district court, and REMAND for further proceedings consistent with this opinion. Respondents are hereby ORDERED to refrain from destroying or altering any records, materials, or documents that may reasonably be considered to be subject to discovery pursuant to the § 1782 applications at issue in this case until July 30, 2021, unless otherwise directed by an order of a United States court.

---

[6] In his first round of briefing before this Court, Mangouras made the same admission. *See* Br. of Pet'r-Appellee-Cross-Appellant at 16 ("*If* the evidence sought from the [Squire] Respondents show[s] that Kostazos, Alevizos and/or Thuesen knowingly **[—30—]** testified falsely, *then* Capt. Mangouras will pursue a Querella Criminal against them in Spain." (emphasis added)).

This page intentionally left blank

United States Court of Appeals for the Third Circuit

United States Court of Appeals for the Third Circuit

No. 19-1903

CHARTIS PROPERTY CAS. CO.
vs.
INGANAMORT

Appeal from the United States District Court for the District of New Jersey

Decided: March 24, 2020

Citation: 953 F.3d 231, 8 Adm. R. 78 (3d Cir. 2020).

Before **JORDAN, GREENAWAY,** and **KRAUSE,** Circuit Judges.

[—2—] {-232-} JORDAN, Circuit Judge:

Poems and books get written, songs sung, and movies made about sinking ships.[1] But there's nothing stirring or awe-inspiring about a yacht that partially sinks in calm waters while docked. That, sadly, is the event at the center of this case. In the insurance dispute that followed, the District Court granted summary judgment in favor of the insurance company because the yacht's owners, Mr. and Mrs. Inganamort, did not carry their burden of proving that the loss was a matter of chance— **[—3—]** "fortuitous," in the argot of insurance—which is a requirement for coverage under the all-risk insurance policy the Inganamorts had. Because we agree that an insured bears the burden of proving fortuity, and that the Inganamorts did not meet that burden here, we will affirm.

I. BACKGROUND

John and Joan Inganamort left their 65-foot fishing vessel, *Three Times a Lady*, docked behind their part-time residence in **{-233-}** Boca Raton, Florida. In September 2011, when they were at their home in New Jersey, the Inganamorts received the sad news that *Three Times a Lady* had come to the end of her rainbow,[2] sinking enough to sustain serious damage. They reported the loss to their insurance company, Chartis Property Casualty Company, with whom they had an all-risk policy.[3] Chartis sent a claims specialist to conduct a preliminary survey of the vessel on October 24, 2011. The specialist reported three inches of standing water in the starboard forward cabin bilge and multiple potential sources of **[—4—]** water ingress, including a hole in the hull the size of a screw. He also found that the electrical breakers were "severely rust-stained and blackened from an electrical failure[,]" and subsequent testing "revealed obvious water intrusion[.]" (App. at 171.) The final review of the vessel, completed June 28, 2012, confirmed the claim specialist's initial findings and also identified that the ship's battery charger was not working, and without a source of power, the ship's bilge pumps had ceased functioning. Despite that state of disrepair, the Inganamorts pressed Chartis for payment on their insurance policy.

To settle the question of coverage, Chartis filed a complaint in the United States District Court for the District of New Jersey, setting forth three counts: a plea for declaratory judgment that Chartis was not liable for the damage to *Three Times a Lady*, a claim that the Inganamorts were liable for material misrepresentations and rescission of contract, and a reservation of rights to assert additional grounds for declaratory judgment, misrepresentation and rescission. No one disputes that an insurance policy was in place at the time of the loss, so the question was, and remains, whether the vessel's partial sub-

[1] *See, e.g.*, Henry Wadsworth Longfellow, *The Wreck of the Hesperus, in* Ballads and Other Poems (John Owen ed., 1842); Gordon Lightfoot, *The Wreck of the Edmund Fitzgerald, on* Summertime Dream (Reprise Records 1976); Sebastian Junger, *The Perfect Storm* (1997); *The Perfect Storm* (Warner Bros. 2000).

[2] Hat tip to Lionel Richie, The Commodores, *Three Times a Lady, on* Natural High (Motown Records 1978).

[3] An all-risk insurance policy is one "that covers every kind of insurable loss except what is specifically excluded." *Insurance*, Black's Law Dictionary (11th ed. 2019). In marine insurance, all-risk policies are "construed as covering all losses that are 'fortuitous.'" *Goodman v. Fireman's Fund Ins. Co.*, 600 F.2d 1040, 1042 (4th Cir. 1979); *see also Ingersoll Milling Mach. Co. v. M/V Bodena*, 829 F.2d 293, 307 (2d Cir. 1987) ("All risk coverage covers all losses which are fortuitous ....").

mersion was a loss of the kind covered by an all-risk policy, specifically, whether it was a fortuitous loss.

After prolonged discovery, the parties filed cross-motions for summary judgment. The District Court's Local Rule 56.1 requires parties to file a statement of undisputed facts with a motion for summary judgment, and it also requires parties responding to a motion for summary judgment to respond to the moving party's Rule 56.1 Statement. In the absence of a response, the local rules declare that the facts in the movant's Rule 56.1 Statement will be deemed undisputed. Chartis sought summary judgment only on its declaratory **[—5—]** judgment claim, while the Inganamorts did not specify which of the counts in Chartis's complaint they thought warranted summary judgment in their favor. They neither filed a statement of undisputed facts nor opposed Chartis's statement of undisputed facts. The District Court thus treated Chartis's statement of facts as being undisputed. In further consequence, the Court granted summary judgment for Chartis because the Inganamorts "ha[d] no evidence to demonstrate a fortuitous loss[.]" (App. at 19.)

The Inganamorts have timely appealed. **{-234-}**

II. DISCUSSION[4]

We address a simple question of federal maritime law: Who bears the burden of proving a fortuitous loss? Every circuit to decide the issue has determined that the insured bears that burden, and we agree. The Inganamorts did not carry it, so we will affirm the decision of the District Court.[5] **[—6—]**

As already noted, when *Three Times a Lady* sank, it was covered by an all-risk insurance policy, which protects against fortuitous losses, meaning losses that are unexplainable or "dependent on chance." *Intermetal Mexicana, S.A. v. Ins. Co. of N. Am.*, 866 F.2d 71, 77 (3d Cir. 1989) (citation omitted). All-risk policies "arose for the very purpose of protecting the insured in those cases where difficulties of logical explanation or some mystery surround the (loss of or damage to) property." *Morrison Grain Co., Inc. v. Utica Mut. Ins. Co.*, 632 F.2d 424, 430 (5th Cir. 1980) (citation omitted). But just because an insured need not "show the precise cause of loss to demonstrate fortuity[,]" *id.* at 430, that does not mean an all-risk policy covers all damage.[6] "'All-risk' is not synonymous with 'all **[—7—]** loss.'" *Intermetal Mexicana*, 866 F.2d at 75. Despite the Inganamorts' argument, an insured must do more than prove that there was a loss. To enjoy coverage, the insured must prove that the loss was indeed fortuitous.

---

[4] The District Court had jurisdiction under 28 U.S.C. § 1333. We have jurisdiction under 28 U.S.C. § 1291. We review a motion for summary judgment *de novo*, applying the same standard the district court applied. *Blunt v. Lower Merion Sch. Dist.*, 767 F.3d 247, 265 (3d Cir. 2014). Under that standard, we will affirm a grant of summary judgment only if there is no dispute as to any material fact and the moving party is entitled to judgment as a matter of law. *Id.*

[5] Chartis also argued in its Answering Brief that, if we were to decide that the Inganamorts did carry their burden of proving the loss was fortuitous, we should still affirm because several exceptions to coverage apply. Since we conclude that **[—6—]** the Inganamorts did not carry the burden of proving fortuitous loss, we need not address those exceptions.

[6] The Inganamorts have misread *Morrison Grain* to mean that an insured need only show that a loss occurred while the policy was in effect. But that case did not dispense with the insured's burden to establish fortuity; rather, it concluded the insured had impliedly met that burden by demonstrating the ship's cargo was in "good condition when the policy attached and in damaged condition when unloaded from the vessel," *id.* at 432, leaving "no indication" that the loss was caused by "anything but fortuitous circumstances." *Id.* at 430. Likewise, where cargo has simply disappeared without explanation from ships' hulls, courts have sometimes observed that all the "insured need show is that the loss occurred." *See, e.g.*, *Atlantic Lines Ltd. v. American Motorists Ins. Co.*, 547 F.2d 11, 13 (2d Cir. 1976) (citing *Balogh v. Jewelers Mut. Ins. Co.*, 167 F. Supp. 763, 769 (S.D. Fla. 1958), aff'd, 272 F.2d 889 **[—7—]** (5th Cir. 1959)). Again, however, where the record reflected the cargo was previously present, those observations merely reflect that it is unlikely "the average insured would not equate a mysterious disappearance with a fortuitous loss" in those circumstances. *Id.*

The First, Second, Fifth, and Eleventh Circuits have all held that, for marine insurance policies, the insured bears the burden of proving that the loss was fortuitous. *See Banco Nacional de Nicaragua v. Argonaut Ins. Co.*, 681 F.2d 1337, 1340 (11th Cir. 1982) ("The [insured] in a suit under an all-risks insurance policy must show a relevant loss in order to invoke the policy, and proof that the loss occurred within the policy period is part and parcel of that showing of a loss."); *Morrison Grain*, 632 F.2d at 429 ("[T]he burden of proof generally is upon the insured to show that a loss arose from a covered peril."); **{-235-}** *Atlantic Lines Ltd. v. American Motorists Ins. Co.*, 547 F.2d 11, 12 (2d Cir. 1976) ("[F]or recovery under an all risks policy, an insured need demonstrate only that a fortuitous loss has occurred."); *Boston Ins. Co. v. Dehydrating Process Co.*, 204 F.2d 441, 443 (1st Cir. 1953) ("Undoubtedly ... the owner of the barge and its cargo has the burden of establishing ... that its loss was caused by a risk insured against[.]"). In the non-maritime context, we too have held that an insured with an all-risk policy bears the burden of proving that a loss was fortuitous and therefore covered by the policy. *See Intermetal Mexicana*, 866 F.2d at 76-77 (describing what the insurer showed to prove the event was fortuitous). We now **[—8—]** join our sister circuits in saying that, under a maritime all-risk policy, the insured bears the burden of proving that a loss was fortuitous.

That burden is not heavy, but it is more than negligible. *See id.* at 77 ("[T]he 'burden of demonstrating fortuity is not a particularly onerous one[.]'" (quoting *Morrison Grain*, 632 F.2d at 430)); *see also PECO Energy Co. v. Boden*, 64 F.3d 852, 858 (3d Cir. 1995) ("Proving fortuity is not particularly difficult."). Since the nature of a fortuitous loss is that it may not be easily explained, the insured need not point to an exact cause of the loss. *In re Balfour*, 85 F.3d at 77 ("The insured ... need not prove the cause of the loss."); *Morrison Grain*, 632 F.2d at 431 ("[C]ourts which have considered the question have rejected the notion that the insured must show the precise cause of loss to demonstrate fortuity."). When a vessel sinks in calm waters, for example, an insured may create a presumption of fortuitous loss by establishing that the vessel was seaworthy before sinking. *See Ins. Co. of N. Am. v. Lanasa Shrimp Co.*, 726 F.2d 688, 690 (11th Cir. 1984); *Reisman v. New Hampshire Fire Ins. Co.*, 312 F.2d 17, 20 (5th Cir. 1963); *Boston Ins. Co.*, 204 F.2d at 443. There must, in short, be some showing that the loss occurred by chance.

Here, the Inganamorts' primary argument was that they were not required to prove fortuity, which, as the weight of authority just cited proves, is incorrect as a matter of law.[7] **[—9—]** Secondarily, they attempted to show fortuity by asserting that the loss was due to heavy rainfall. But Chartis's statement of undisputed facts notes that there is "no data to support [the] theory that [*Three Times a Lady*] was subject to 'heavy rains' on any date." (App. at 172.) Even if we were tempted to look beyond the statement of undisputed facts, the evidence elsewhere in the record does not support the assertion that the loss was due to heavy rainfall. Not even the Inganamorts' own expert could say with assurance that there was heavy rainfall in the area at the relevant time.[8] Finally, while the Inganamorts had initially claimed that the ship was seaworthy prior to September 15th, they made no effort to present renewed evidence of seaworthiness after the loss was backdated to September 5th or 6th; nor did they press this argument before **{-236-}** the District Court or on appeal. Because there is nothing in the record to support the argument that the loss was due to heavy rainfall and

---

[7] Counsel for the Inganamorts eventually admitted as much at oral argument. *See* Oral Argument at 1:26-1:44, https://www2.ca3.uscourts.gov/oralargument/audio/19-1903ChartisPropertyCasualtyCov.Inganamortetal.mp3.

[8] The expert said that "[i]t had been reported in September [2011] that two (2) or possibl[y] three (3 coastal) events of heavy rains, lightning, and heavy thunderstorms did drench South Florida with 5" to up to 15" of rain." (App. at 217.) But he later backpedaled, saying he had looked at rainfall for September 15th, the day the loss was reported, not September 5th or 6th, the revised date of loss, and that, "you know, weather records are extremely difficult to determine the exact flow ...[.]" (App. at 204.)

there is no other indication of fortuity, the Inganamorts did not carry their burden of proving a fortuitous loss.[9] **[—10—] [—11—]**

III. CONCLUSION

The Inganamorts having failed to carry their burden of proof, we will affirm the District Court's grant of summary judgment against them.

[9] At oral argument, there was some discussion about whether a loss resulting from negligent behavior, or negligently failing to maintain a vessel, would qualify as a **[—10—]** fortuitous loss. *See* Oral Argument at 20:25-27:32 https://www2.ca3.uscourts.gov/oralargument/audio/19-1903ChartisPropertyCasualtyCov.Inganamortetal.mp3. Losses that result from negligent behavior can be considered fortuitous, but losses caused by wear and tear typically cannot. *See Goodman*, 600 F.2d at 1042 ("A loss is not considered fortuitous if it results ... from ordinary wear and tear .... However, loss due to the negligence of the insured or his agents has generally been held to be fortuitous and, absent express exclusion, is covered by an all risks policy."); *see also Youell v. Exxon Corp.*, 48 F.3d 105, 110 (2d Cir. 1995) ("The fortuity rule excludes from coverage losses that arise from ... wear and tear ...; losses that arise from ... the insured's negligence[ ] are covered." (*vacated on other grounds*, 516 U.S. 801 (1995)). We question the suggestion that a loss caused by negligently allowing a vessel to fall into disrepair would be considered fortuitous, as it would seem to create perverse incentives if damage resulting from failure to maintain a vessel were considered as such. Indeed, this would effectively convert all-risk insurance policies into general maintenance contracts or "warrant[ies] of soundness," leaving the insurer liable for all maintenance costs except for those expressly excluded. *Mellon v. Federal Ins. Co.*, 14 F.2d 997, 1002 (S.D.N.Y. 1926). For that reason, courts that have taken that tack and expanded fortuity to include losses caused by the premature failure of a ship's mechanical components have been criticized. *See* Michael I. Goldman, *The Fortuity Rule of Federal Maritime Law: The Scope of "All Risk" Coverage Under Policies of Marine Insurance and the New Decision of the Eleventh Circuit Court of Appeals*, 46 J. Maritime L. & Com. 171 (2015). Expanding fortuity to include losses caused by negligently allowing a vessel to fall into disrepair would appear **[—11—]** equally ill-advised. But because neither party raised the issue in briefing nor addressed it more than in passing at argument, we do not need to decide the question.

United States Court of Appeals
for the Third Circuit

No. 19-2458

WATERFRONT COMM'N OF N.Y. HARBOR
VS.
GOVERNOR OF N.J.

Appeal from the United States District Court for the District of New Jersey

Decided: June 5, 2020

Citation: 961 F.3d 234, 8 Adm. R. 82 (3d Cir. 2020).

Before **SMITH**, Chief Judge, **HARDIMAN**, and **KRAUSE**, Circuit Judges.

[—5—] {-235-} **SMITH**, Chief Judge: **{-236-}**

The States of New Jersey and New York agreed more than half a century ago to enter into the Waterfront Commission Compact. More recently, New Jersey enacted legislation to withdraw from the Compact. To prevent this unilateral termination, the Waterfront Commission sued the Governor of New Jersey in federal court. But because New Jersey is the real, substantial party in interest, its immunity should have barred the District Court from exercising subject-matter jurisdiction. Accordingly, this case must be dismissed.

I

A

By the mid-twentieth century, New York Harbor was rife with corruption, particularly in waterfront hiring practices. *See De Veau v. Braisted*, 363 U.S. 144, 147–48 (1960) (plurality opinion); *N.Y. Shipping Ass'n v. Waterfront Comm'n of N.Y. Harbor*, 835 F.3d 344, 348– **[—6—]** 49, 4 Adm. R. 145, 145–47 (3d Cir. 2016). After studying the problems created by corrupt practices, representatives of New Jersey and New York prepared remedial legislation, which each State enacted in 1953. *See* N.J. Stat. Ann. § 32:23-1 *et seq.* (repealed 2018); N.Y. Unconsol. Law § 9801 *et seq.* Because the reciprocal statutes collectively function as an agreement between the States, Congress consented to the formation of the Waterfront Commission Compact, consistent with the Compacts Clause in Article I, § 10, of the U.S. Constitution.[1] Act of Aug. 12, 1953, Pub. L. No. 83-252, 67 Stat. 541, 541.

The Compact reformed waterfront hiring practices by, *inter alia*, introducing registration and licensing requirements and channeling hiring through designated centers. *E.g.*, N.Y. Unconsol. Law §§ 9812, 9827, 9853. To implement such reforms, the Compact also established the Waterfront Commission of New York Harbor, §§ 9807, 9810, and authorized the Commission to fund its operations by levying assessments on employers, § 9858.[2] **[—7—]**

B

As the decades passed, most of the Harbor workforce shifted from New York to New Jersey, where deepwater berths better accommodated the modern trend toward containerized shipping. Such developments redounded to the benefit of New Jersey's economy. Eventually, the New Jersey legislature came to see the Commission as "over-regulat[ing] the businesses at the port in an effort to justify its existence," which made the Commission "an impediment to future job growth and prosperity at the port." N.J. Stat. Ann. § 32:23-229.

New Jersey repeatedly tried to cabin the Commission's powers, and even to withdraw from the Compact entirely. Those efforts came to fruition at the end of **{-237-}** Governor Chris Christie's term in office, when he signed into law Chapter 324. Act of Jan. 16, 2018, 2017 N.J. Sess. Law Serv. ch. 324 (codified at,

---

[1] Article I, § 10, cl. 3, provides in pertinent part that "[n]o State shall, without the Consent of Congress, . . . enter into any Agreement or Compact with another State."

[2] Although the States could designate funding for the Commission (and the Commission may receive financial support from "federal grants or otherwise"), the Compact contemplates that the bulk of the budget would come from **[—7—]** employer assessments. N.Y. Unconsol. Law §§ 9856, 9858. In fact, the Commission's funding allegedly consists entirely of such assessments.

e.g., N.J. Stat. Ann. §§ 32:23-229 to -230). That chapter immediately repealed the New Jersey legislation that had contributed to the formation of the Compact. Ch. 324, §§ 33–34 (citing N.J. Stat. Ann. § 32:23-1 *et seq.*). **[—8—]**

But Chapter 324 set out additional steps intended to further the State's withdrawal from the Compact. It required the New Jersey Governor to notify Congress, the Governor of New York, and the Commission of the "intention to withdraw." § 2.a. That notification would initiate a ninety-day countdown to the "transfer date" when the Compact and the Commission would be "dissolved." §§ 3, 31. Thereafter, the New Jersey Division of State Police would assume the Commission's law enforcement functions on the New Jersey side of the Harbor. *See* §§ 1.d, 4.b, 34.

C

The day after the outgoing Governor signed Chapter 324, the Commission filed suit in federal district court against New Jersey Governor Philip Murphy in his official capacity.[3] The one-count Complaint sought two forms of relief: a declaration that Chapter 324 violated the Compact and the Supremacy Clause of the U.S. Constitution, and an injunction against its enforcement. The District Court permitted the New Jersey Senate, Senate President, General Assembly, and Assembly Speaker (collectively, the "Legislature") to intervene in defense of Chapter 324. **[—9—]**

The Commission filed a motion for a preliminary injunction to prevent the Governor from effectuating withdrawal, while the Governor and Legislature moved for dismissal. The District Court denied dismissal and granted the injunction. Nearly a year later, the Court granted the Commission's motion for summary judgment and denied the separate motions of the Governor and the Legislature.

In these consolidated appeals, the Governor and Legislature challenge the District Court's orders denying dismissal, granting an injunction, denying them summary judgment, and granting summary judgment to the Commission.[4] Briefing included amicus curiae filings by the New York Shipping Association (NYSA) in support of the Governor and Legislature, and the Columbia River Gorge Commission in support of the Waterfront Commission.

II [—10—]

The District Court had federal-question jurisdiction over this dispute because the Complaint invoked the Supremacy Clause and the Compact. *See* 28 U.S.C. § 1331; *Waterfront Comm'n of N.Y. Harbor v. Elizabeth-Newark Shipping, Inc.*, 164 F.3d 177, 180 (3d Cir. 1998) (observing that Congressional consent enshrined the Compact in federal law). But that jurisdiction does not extend to any claim barred by state sovereign immunity. *Pennhurst State Sch. & Hosp. v. Halderman*, 465 U.S. 89, 98, 119–21 (1984).

In denying the Governor's motion to dismiss, the District Court rejected the "suggest[ion]" that sovereign immunity applied to the Governor in this case. **{-238-}** *Waterfront Comm'n of N.Y. Harbor v. Murphy*, No. 18-650 (SDW) (LDW), 2018 WL 2455927, at *4 (D.N.J. June 1, 2018). We have plenary authority to determine whether sovereign immunity deprived the District Court of jurisdiction.[5] 28 **[—11—]** U.S.C. § 1291; *In re*

---

[3] The parties disagree as to whether this suit was properly filed in the Commission's name. We need not resolve that dispute.

[4] We do not reach issues implicated in challenges by the Governor and Legislature to "all other orders and rulings adverse to" them. J.A. 2, 4.

[5] Although the District Court did not revisit the sovereign immunity issue at summary judgment, the Legislature and amicus NYSA pursue that issue on appeal as a jurisdictional matter. We have jurisdiction over an appeal of an order granting summary judgment to address an underlying issue going to the District Court's jurisdiction. *See MCI Telecomm. Corp. v. Bell Atl.-Pa.*, 271 F.3d 491, 502–03 (3d Cir. 2001) (examining denial of sovereign immunity on appeal of summary judgment); *cf. Edelman v. Jordan*, 415 U.S. 651, 677–78 (1974) (observing "the **[—11—]** Eleventh Amendment defense sufficiently partakes of the

PennEast Pipeline Co., 938 F.3d 96, 103 (3d Cir. 2019), *petition for cert. filed*, No. 19-1039 (Feb. 18, 2020).

III

State sovereign immunity dates back to our Nation's Founding, and is deeply rooted in English law. *See Franchise Tax Bd. of Cal. v. Hyatt*, 139 S. Ct. 1485, 1493–94 (2019); 1 William Blackstone, Commentaries on the Laws of England 234–35 (1765). Assurances that States would remain immune from federal suit—absent their consent—were instrumental in securing sufficient support for the Constitution's adoption. *Edelman v. Jordan*, 415 U.S. 651, 660 & n.9 (1974). Although the Eleventh Amendment expressly protects a State from federal suits by citizens of another State or country,[6] case law recognizes that the actual scope of immunity extends beyond the Amendment's text. *Alden v. Maine*, 527 U.S. 706, 727–28 (1999). As a rule, "federal courts may not **[—12—]** entertain a private person's suit against a State" unless the State has waived its immunity or Congress has permissibly abrogated it. *Va. Office for Prot. & Advocacy v. Stewart*, 563 U.S. 247, 253–54 (2011) [hereinafter *VOPA*].

An "important limit" to that rule allows federal suits against state *officials* in certain circumstances. *Id.* at 254–55. Under the *Ex parte Young* doctrine, a state official is "stripped of his official or representative character" and thereby deprived of the State's immunity, *Ex parte Young*, 209 U.S. 123, 159–60 (1908), when he commits an "ongoing violation of federal law." *VOPA*, 563 U.S. at 254–55 (quoting *Verizon Md. Inc. v. Pub. Serv. Comm'n of Md.*, 535 U.S. 635, 645 (2002)). A person who is aggrieved may therefore seek prospective relief by suing him in his official capacity. *See id.* But *Ex parte Young*'s "authority-stripping theory . . . is a fiction that has been narrowly construed." *Pennhurst*, 465 U.S. at 114 n.25. *Ex parte Young* applies only to the "precise situation" of "a federal court command[ing] a state official to do nothing more than refrain from violating federal law." *VOPA*, 563 U.S. at 255.

Consistent with this narrow construction of *Ex parte Young*, the doctrine "does not apply 'when the state is the real, substantial party in interest.'" *Id.* (quoting *Pennhurst*, 465 U.S. at 101). Courts determine whether "relief sought nominally against an officer is in fact **{–239–}** against the sovereign" based on whether the relief would **[—13—]** "operate against" the sovereign. *Pennhurst*, 465 U.S. at 101 (quoting *Hawaii v. Gordon*, 373 U.S. 57, 58 (1963) (per curiam)). In other words, we examine "the *effect* of the relief sought." *Id.* at 107. If such relief would operate against the State, then we forego the fiction of *Ex parte Young* in favor of the bedrock principle of state sovereign immunity.

The Supreme Court has been "willing to police abuses of the [*Ex parte Young*] doctrine that threaten to evade sovereign immunity" because the relief would operate against the State. *VOPA*, 563 U.S. at 256. A State is generally the real, substantial party in interest if the "judgment sought would expend itself on the public treasury or domain, or interfere with public administration," *id.* at 255 (quoting *Pennhurst*, 465 U.S. at 101 n.11) (internal quotation marks omitted), or if relief consists of "an injunction requiring the payment of funds from the State's treasury, or an order for specific performance of a State's contract," *id.* at 256–57 (citation omitted) (citing *Edelman*, 415 U.S. at 666–67; *In re Ayers*, 123 U.S. 443 (1887)).[7] **[—14—]**

The Court has concluded that the sovereign was the real, substantial party in interest in suits nominally against officials where relief would effectively force the restructuring of

---

nature of a jurisdictional bar so that it need not be raised in the trial court").

[6] "The Judicial power of the United States shall not be construed to extend to any suit in law or equity, commenced or prosecuted against one of the United States by Citizens of another State, or by Citizens or Subjects of any Foreign State." U.S. Const. amend. XI.

[7] Even if the relief would affect the State's treasury, the State may not be the real, substantial party in interest if the effect on the public fisc is merely "ancillary" to permissible prospective relief, as was the case in *Ex parte Young*. *Edelman*, 415 U.S. at 667–68.

state mental health care at the State's expense, *see Pennhurst*, 465 U.S. at 93, 101 & n.11, 107; confer money damages for a State's disability benefit processing deficiencies, *see Edelman*, 415 U.S. at 655–56, 668–69; enjoin activity that would breach a State's contract, *see In re Ayers*, 123 U.S. at 502–03, 507; require substantial, unbudgeted expansion of a federal water project, *see Dugan v. Rank*, 372 U.S. 609, 610–11, 616, 620–21 (1963);[8] or quiet title to, and preclude state control of, territory within the State's regulatory jurisdiction, *see Idaho v. Coeur d'Alene Tribe of Idaho*, 521 U.S. 261, 281–82, 287–88 (1997) (permitting suit would be "as intrusive **[—15—]** as almost any conceivable retroactive levy upon funds in its Treasury").[9]

IV

Here, the Commission does not directly challenge the general rule of state sovereign immunity. It simply chose not to **{-240-}** name the State of New Jersey as a defendant in its Complaint. By naming the Governor instead, the Commission attempts to bring this case within the reach of *Ex parte Young*. That attempt is unavailing. Because the relief nominally sought from the Governor in this case would operate against the State itself, New Jersey is the real, substantial party in interest.[10] **[—16—]**

A

The Commission seeks a judgment that "would expend itself on the public treasury or domain." *VOPA*, 563 U.S. at 255 (quoting *Pennhurst*, 465 U.S. at 101 n.11). **[—17—]**

The Complaint is frank in its recitation of the expected financial effects of Chapter 324 on the Commission:

> [Chapter 324] would take away the Commission's primary revenue stream. . . . [T]he Commission is not funded with tax dollars, and its budget derives entirely from the assessments that it collects from Port employers. Inasmuch as the vast majority of commercial Port operations occurs on the New Jersey side, [Chapter 324]—which purports to remove the Commission's authority to assess fees on New Jersey employers—will virtually eliminate the Commission's budget.

J.A. 69–70.

The Commission's dim prognosis is consistent with the text of Chapter 324. Whereas the Commission has been collecting

---

[8] *Dugan* reached this conclusion as to claims against federal officials, but *Pennhurst* imported *Dugan*'s principles into an *Ex parte Young* suit against state officials. *See Pennhurst*, 465 U.S. at 101 n.11 (citing *Dugan*, 372 U.S. at 620); *see also Gordon*, 373 U.S. at 58 (suit against federal official was effectively against United States because prospective relief would, *inter alia*, "affect the public administration of government agencies" impacted by official's action).

[9] By contrast, the sovereign was *not* the real, substantial party in interest in suits against state officials to prevent enforcement of a State's railroad rate regulation, *see Ex parte Young*, 209 U.S. at 129–31, 159–60; secure access to a State's mental hospital records, *see VOPA*, 563 U.S. at 252, 256–57; or, as this Court decided, alter a state-approved agreement between competitors, *see MCI Telecomm.*, 271 F.3d at 514–15.

[10] Although we agree with the Legislature on this conclusion, we do not embrace the grounds upon which it argues for such an outcome. The Legislature contends that the Governor's enforcement duty was not sufficiently specific to permit an *Ex parte Young* action against him. **[—16—]** Indeed, *Ex parte Young* suggests that we consider the nature of the state officer's duty to enforce a challenged law. *See* 209 U.S. at 157, 161. But we think the Governor has sufficiently specific statutory obligations that an *Ex parte Young* claim cannot be precluded on that basis.

Chapter 324 expressly requires the Governor to notify Congress, the New York Governor, and the Commission of New Jersey's impending withdrawal—which triggers the ninety-day countdown to consummation—and then tell the Legislature's presiding officers that he did so. §§ 2, 31. The Complaint objects to the Governor's "taking any action to implement or enforce" Chapter 324 and identifies the portion of the Governor's obligations that triggers the withdrawal countdown. J.A. 55–56, 67–68. For this reason, we are not persuaded we should dismiss on grounds that the suit alleges insufficiently specific obligations to make out an *Ex parte Young* claim. *Cf. Constitution Party of Pa. v. Cortes*, 824 F.3d 386, 396 (3d Cir. 2016) (recognizing ministerial duties are amenable to *Ex parte Young* claims).

assessments on work within New Jersey, Chapter 324 tabs those assessments for the budget of the New Jersey Division of State Police. *See* § 25.b. The result will be that those assessments will now flow into New Jersey's coffers: "Each employer shall pay to the State Treasurer, for placement within the General Fund, an assessment . . . ." *Id.*; *see also* § 26.a(10) ("All funds of the division received as payment of any assessment or penalty under this section shall be deposited with the State **[—18—]** Treasurer."). The same goes for the Commission's current liquid assets. Chapter 324 requires the Commission to deposit "the funds of the commission applicable to this State . . . into the custody of the State Treasurer." § 4.b(2). At bottom, Chapter 324 redirects the Commission's present and anticipated future funding from New Jersey employers into New Jersey's treasury.

This suit is no mere attempt to compel or forestall a state official's actions consistent with *Ex parte Young*'s holding. Rather, when we compare the Commission's **{–241–}** allegations about Chapter 324 with the chapter's text, we observe that the Commission attempts to pry back its authority to assess employers, in direct conflict with Chapter 324's provisions. On these facts, where a judgment for the Commission would divert state treasury funding and thereby operate against the State,[11] we **[—19—]** conclude that New Jersey is the real, substantial party in interest.

B

We reach the same outcome when considering this suit from a different angle: the Commission effectively seeks "specific performance of a State's contract." *VOPA*, 563 U.S. at 257.

Like other interstate compacts, the Waterfront Commission Compact is a contract subject to our construction. *Tarrant Reg'l Water Dist. v. Herrmann*, 569 U.S. 614, 628 (2013). Our inquiry begins with the Compact's express terms, *id.*, and we need go no further. Each State "deemed" the Compact's regulation of the waterfront "an exercise of the police power of the two states for the protection of the public safety, welfare, prosperity, health, peace and living conditions of the people of the two states." N.Y. Unconsol. Law § 9805. And the Commission is empowered to "administer and enforce" the Compact's regulations. § 9810. New **[—20—]** Jersey's contractual performance therefore consists primarily of permitting the Commission to carry out regulation of hiring on the New Jersey side of the Harbor that otherwise falls within the State's police powers.

By enacting Chapter 324, the State of New Jersey has chosen to discontinue its performance of the Compact and to resume the full exercise of its police powers on its own side of the Harbor. Yet the Complaint seeks invalidation of Chapter 324. Granting this relief would compel New Jersey to continue to abide by the terms of an agreement it has decided to renounce. Such relief tantamount to specific performance would operate against the State itself, demonstrating that New Jersey is the real, substantial party in interest.

***

We are convinced that this suit seeks relief beyond the *Ex parte Young* doctrine's narrow

---

[11] Even if the effect on New Jersey's treasury can be deemed ancillary to permissible prospective relief, *see supra* note 7, this suit falls beyond *Ex parte Young*'s bounds for the independent reason that it effectively seeks specific performance of the Compact.

Separately, we do not view our fact-specific holding to create tension with cases allowing suits to enjoin future taxation to proceed under *Ex parte Young*. *E.g.*, *CSX Transp., Inc. v. Bd. of Pub. Works of W. Va.*, 138 F.3d 537, 541–43 (4th Cir. 1998) (determining whether relief sought was prospective or retrospective, without commenting on **[—19—]** whether State was real, substantial party in interest). We have no occasion to take a position on that issue. Here we are faced with a suit seeking prospective relief that unquestionably operates against the State itself: The Commission has no quibble with the assessments continuing but wants to keep the revenue coming to its own account instead of New Jersey's.

confines by asking that we invalidate Chapter 324. Invalidation would necessarily have an adverse impact on the State of New Jersey's treasury and compel the State to perform consistent with the Compact.[12] Because such relief would **[—21—]** operate against New Jersey as the real, substantial party in interest, the State is entitled to the protection of sovereign immunity. **{–242–}**[13] Accordingly, we lack jurisdiction to address the other threshold concerns raised by the Governor and Legislature, nor can we reach the merits of New Jersey's anticipated withdrawal from the Compact.

V

Because this suit impinges on the State of New Jersey's sovereignty, thereby depriving the District Court of jurisdiction, we will vacate the order granting summary judgment to the Commission, reverse the order denying the Governor's motion to dismiss, and vacate that order in all other respects. The case will be remanded for dismissal.

---

[12] *Cf. MSA Realty Corp. v. Illinois*, 990 F.2d 288, 289–90, 295 (7th Cir. 1993) (rejecting *Ex parte Young* claim that would effectively compel State to comply with its program **[—21—]** promising return of state sales taxes to participating municipalities).

[13] New Jersey has not waived its immunity from this suit, nor has Congress abrogated it. *See VOPA*, 563 U.S. at 253–54.

United States Court of Appeals
for the Third Circuit

No. 19-3542

WILSON
VS.
DIRECTOR, OFFICE OF WORKERS' COMPENSATION PROGRAMS

On Petition for Review of an Order of the Benefits Review Board

Decided: December 31, 2020

Citation: 984 F.3d 265, 8 Adm. R. 88 (3d Cir. 2020).

Before **KRAUSE**, **RESTREPO**, and **BIBAS**, Circuit Judges.

[—2—] {-268-} RESTREPO, Circuit Judge:

Petitioner Richard Wilson sustained hearing loss while working on a marine construction project and subsequently sought compensation benefits under the Longshore and Harbor Workers' Compensation Act ("LHWCA"), 33 U.S.C. §§ 901–50. An Administrative Law Judge ("ALJ") and the Benefits Review Board ("Board") dismissed Wilson's claim, finding that he was not covered under the LHWCA because he was not injured on navigable waters of the United States. Because we conclude that the ALJ and Board misconstrued the definition of navigable waters and that the waters where Wilson was injured were in fact navigable, we will reverse and remand for a determination of benefits.

I. BACKGROUND

Congress enacted the LHWCA to provide compensation for maritime workers who are injured on the job. *Pa. Tidewater Dock Co. v. Dir., Office of Workers' Comp. Programs*, **[—3—]** 202 F.3d 656, 658 (3d Cir. 2000). To be eligible for coverage, the LHWCA requires (1) that a worker be "engaged in maritime employment," 33 U.S.C. § 902(3); and (2) that his injury occur on "navigable waters of the Unites States" or an "adjoining [land] area," *id.* **{-269-}** § 903(a). These two requirements are respectively known as the "status" and "situs" requirements. *Ne. Marine Terminal Co. v. Caputo*, 432 U.S. 249, 265 (1977). If "a worker is injured on the actual navigable waters in the course of his employment on those waters," then he also "satisfies the status requirement," for he was "required to perform [his] employment duties" "in a historically maritime locale." *Dir., Office of Workers' Comp. Programs v. Perini N. River Assocs.*, 459 U.S. 297, 324 (1983). Because this case does not concern any injury on land, the success of Wilson's claim hinges on whether he satisfied the situs requirement, *i.e.*, whether the waters on which he was injured were in fact navigable.

The facts are not disputed. From approximately 2010 to 2014, Respondent Creamer-Sanzari Joint Venture ("Creamer") employed Wilson as a marine construction worker on the New Jersey Route 3 bridge replacement project. The Route 3 Bridge spans the Lower Passaic River from Clifton to Rutherford, New Jersey at River Mile 11.8. At that location, the navigation channel was authorized to be 150 feet wide and ten feet deep. Wilson's primary job on that project was to drive steel piles for a cofferdam, which is a watertight structure that allows for construction below the waterline. From a float stage on the river, Wilson positioned and secured piles while a crane operator hammered the piles into the riverbed. This process routinely exposed Wilson to extremely loud working conditions and, in 2014, he was diagnosed with a permanent hearing impairment resulting from such conditions. **[—4—]**

A few days after his diagnosis, Wilson filed a claim for benefits under the LHWCA. Creamer disputed Wilson's claim and the case was referred to an ALJ. Although the ALJ found that Creamer was a responsible employer and that Wilson's injuries were caused by his work on the Route 3 bridge, she dismissed Wilson's claim after finding that he was not covered under the LHWCA. Specifically, the ALJ concluded that Wilson failed to show that the Lower Passaic River was navigable at River Mile 11.8. Wilson appealed the ALJ's decision and the Board affirmed. Wilson now seeks judicial review of the Board's order.

II. DISCUSSION

Wilson raises two issues on appeal. First, he asserts that § 920(a) of the LHWCA creates a situs presumption and argues that the ALJ erred by failing to apply it in her situs analysis. Second, Wilson argues, even if situs is not presumed, he provided sufficient evidence to show that the Lower Passaic River was navigable at River Mile 11.8, and that the ALJ and Board incorrectly reached the opposite conclusion by applying too narrow a definition of navigable waters. Although we find Wilson's presumption argument unavailing, we agree with Wilson that the ALJ and Board erred in finding that the Lower Passaic River was not navigable at River Mile 11.8.

A. Standard of Review

We have appellate jurisdiction over this case under 33 U.S.C. § 921(c). We review the Board's decision only "to determine whether the Board acted in conformance with applicable law and within its proper scope of review." *Consolidation Coal Co. v. Benefits Review Bd.*, 629 F.3d 322, 326 (3d Cir. 2010) (internal quotations omitted). We exercise plenary review of the Board's legal conclusions, *Del. River Stevedores v. DiFidelto*, 440 **[—5—]** F.3d 615, 619 (3d Cir. 2006), and "must independently review the record and decide whether the ALJ's [factual] findings are rational, consistent **{-270-}** with applicable law and supported by substantial evidence" if those findings are challenged by a petitioner, *Helen Mining Co. v. Elliott*, 859 F.3d 226, 233 (3d Cir. 2017) (citations omitted).

B. Situs Requirement

We can preliminarily dispose of Wilson's presumption argument. Section 920(a) states: "it shall be presumed, in the absence of substantial evidence to the contrary[,] . . . [t]hat [a] claim [for compensation under this chapter] comes within the provisions of this chapter." 33 U.S.C. § 920(a). Wilson argues (1) that § 920(a) creates a situs presumption for claimants, and (2) that it shifts the burden of proving (or disproving) situs to respondents.

Both arguments are unavailing. First, situs is a threshold issue that must be resolved before § 920(a) can be applied. Congress enacted the LHWCA under its "admiralty and maritime jurisdiction," which gives it the authority to "alter or revise the maritime law which shall prevail throughout the country." *Crowell v. Benson*, 285 U.S. 22, 39 (1932) (citing U.S. Const. art. III, § 2). When Congress uses that authority, it is constrained by "the constitutional limits . . . [of] admiralty and maritime jurisdiction," *id.* at 55; *see also Ex parte Garnett*, 141 U.S. 1, 14 (1891), *Sea-Land Serv., Inc. v. Dir., Office of Workers' Comp. Programs*, 540 F.2d 629, 635 (3d Cir. 1976), which for maritime torts includes only injuries that occur on navigable waters of the United States and certain adjoining land areas, *see Victory Carriers, Inc. v. Law*, 404 U.S. 202, 205 (1971); *Herb's Welding, Inc. v. Gray*, 470 U.S. 414, 423 (1985) (explaining that the LHWCA definition of navigable waters was **[—6—]** expanded to include certain shoreside areas). Thus, the LHWCA's situs requirement is essentially a jurisdictional determination, which means its "existence is a condition precedent to the operation of the statutory scheme." *Crowell*, 285 U.S. at 54.

Second, the burden of proving situs lies with the claimant. Under the LHWCA, administrative adjudications "shall be conducted in accordance with the [Administrative Procedure Act ("APA")]," 33 U.S.C. § 919(d), and the APA states that, "[e]xcept as otherwise provided by statute, the proponent of a[n] . . . order has the burden of proof." 5 U.S.C. § 556(d). In *Greenwich Collieries*, the Supreme Court concluded that courts should "not lightly presume exemptions to the APA." *Dir., Office of Workers' Comp. Programs v. Greenwich Collieries*, 512 U.S. 267, 271 (1994). In that case, the Director argued that § 923(a) exempted the LHWCA from the APA's burden of proof rule. *Id.* That provision of the statute states that the Board is not bound by certain rules of evidence and procedure. *Id.* The Supreme Court disagreed with the Director, however, because it was reluctant to assume that Congress intended to group the burden of proof in the same category as evidentiary and procedural rules, noting that the burden of proof is a rule of substantive law. *Id.* Moreover, the Court explained, the LHWCA explicitly states that the APA is applicable "notwithstanding any other provisions of this chapter." *Id.* (quoting 33 U.S.C. § 919(d)).

We have subsequently held that a claimant who "seeks to have an order issued that she is entitled to benefits under the [LHWCA] . . . bears the burden of proving entitlement to benefits by a preponderance of the evidence." **{-271-}** *Maher Terminals, Inc. v. Dir., Office of Workers' Comp. Programs*, 992 F.2d 1277, 1282 (3d Cir. 1993). For the reasons explained above, we do not think § 920(a) applies to situs determinations. Even if it did, however, § **[—7—]** 920(a) does nothing more than create a rebuttable presumption that eases the claimant's burden of proof. *See Greenwich Collieries*, 512 U.S. at 280. It does not shift the burden of proof to the respondent. *See id.* at 279–80 (explaining that a rebuttable presumption only places a burden of production on the respondent).

C. Navigable Waters

We thus turn to the dispositive issue in this case: whether Wilson established that the Lower Passaic River was navigable at River Mile 11.8. Wilson argues that the ALJ and Board misconstrued the definition of navigable waters and, when the proper definition is applied, it is apparent that there is sufficient evidence showing the river was navigable at the Route 3 bridge location. We agree.

Navigability is a vast concept. Depending on the legal context, the definition greatly varies. *See Kaiser Aetna v. United States*, 444 U.S. 164, 170–72 (1979). In this instance, because the LHWCA is federal maritime law, we must apply a definition of navigable waters that is used for demarcating Article III admiralty jurisdiction. *See Perini N. River Assocs.*, 459 U.S. at 306, 323; *Lockheed Martin Corp. v. Morganti*, 412 F.3d 407, 412 n.2 (2d Cir. 2005). The ALJ, Board, and parties used the "navigable-in-fact" definition. Therefore, we will as well.[1] Under that standard, "[a] body of water is navigable for purposes of **[—8—]** federal admiralty jurisdiction if it is one that, by itself or by uniting with other waterways, forms a continuous highway capable of sustaining interstate or foreign commerce." *Reeves v. Mobile Dredging & Pumping Co.*, 26 F.3d 1247, 1253 (3d Cir. 1994) (citing *The Daniel Ball*, 77 U.S. (10 Wall.) 557, 563 (1870)).

The ALJ and Board seemed to misunderstand that a waterway can be found navigable in fact only if there is evidence that the waterway is capable of sustaining "commonly-used large commercial ships"[2] or if there is evidence of "*present* commercial use." App. 14, 15, 22. A waterway, however, is navigable in fact simply if it is capable of sustaining any type of interstate or foreign commerce. *See Morganti*, 412 F.3d at 413 (applying navigable-in-fact test with a focus on physical characteristics of the waterway to determine if it was capable of supporting interstate commerce). Demonstrating present commercial use is only one of the acceptable methods that a claimant may use to establish navigability. *See Price v. Price*, 929 F.2d 131, 135 (4th Cir. 1991). By construing the navigable-in-fact standard **{-272-}** too narrowly, the ALJ and Board overlooked evidence

---

[1] Due to the fact that the Lower Passaic River is tidally influenced at River Mile 11.8, the Director pointed out that Wilson also could have argued the river was navigable in that location because "waters that are affected by the ebb and flow of the tide are part of the 'navigable waters of the United States' for purposes of the federal government's admiralty jurisdiction." Dir. Supp. Ltr. Br. at 3 (Sept. 2, 2020). But, Wilson did not raise that argument before the agency, and we can resolve the situs issue based on the Lower Passaic River being navigable in fact. Therefore, we need not address any alternative bases for admiralty jurisdiction, including our "ebb-and-flow" test. *See United States v. Stoeco* **[—8—]** *Homes, Inc.*, 498 F.2d 597, 610 (3d Cir. 1974); *American Dredging Co. v. Selleck*, 556 F.2d 180, 181 (3d Cir. 1977). The Court also extends its gratitude to the Director for her supplemental letter brief and participation in argument in response to the Court's requests.

[2] The ALJ defined such vessels as "ocean-going cargo carrying vessels—container-ships, car carriers, and bulk carriers." App. 14.

which established that the Lower Passaic River was navigable in fact at River Mile 11.8.

The record shows that commercial vessels operating on the Lower Passaic River were able to transit portions of the river where the channel was as shallow as four feet and **[—9—]** as wide as seventy-two feet.[3] In 2008, the United States Army Corps of Engineers ("ACE") conducted a survey of the river and noted that the "authorized federal navigation channel . . . [extends from] the mouth of the river . . . [through River Mile] 15.4,"App. 32 and that the river "has been utilized primarily for commerce and industry for almost two centuries," App. 36. The report found that from 1997 to 2006 approximately twenty-eight million tons of liquid fuel were transported on the river. In one of the busiest stretches, from River Mile 1.2 to 2.5, the controlling depth of the channel was four feet and, at River Mile 4.6, the channel was seventy-two feet wide.

At River Mile 11.8, the channel depth exceeded four feet and was 150 feet wide. The ALJ and Board acknowledged that the channel was dredged to ten feet deep and 150 feet wide but reasoned that such evidence did not establish navigability because River Mile 11.8 had not been dredged since 1931 and it was unclear whether the "[c]hannel depth . . . [had] been constrained by . . . the natural siltation process." App. 14 (edit in original), 23 n.5. The ACE report notes, however, that River Mile 8.1 was last dredged to ten feet in 1932 yet, in 2008, the depth at River Mile 8.1 was nine feet. Moreover, in his briefing to the ALJ and Board, Wilson cited the National Oceanic and Atmospheric Administration ("NOAA") Navigation Chart for the Passaic River, which reported that the segment of the channel containing River Mile 11.8 was seven feet deep in 2017. *See* NOAA Chart 12337, https://www.charts.noaa.gov /OnLineViewer/12337.shtml (last visited Dec. 11, 2020) **[—10—]** (The Route 3 bridge is located between the Nutley and Rutherford Reach and the corresponding depths are located in the lower-right quadrant of the chart).

In light of such evidence, we are able to conclude that the Lower Passaic River at Mile 11.8 was navigable in fact in 2010. The record shows that there were no impediments blocking the navigation channel between its confluence with the Newark Bay and the Route 3 bridge. And, at all points in between, the channel exceeded four feet in depth and seventy-two feet in width. Because we look to whether a waterway "by itself or by uniting with other waterways, forms a continuous [commercial] highway," *Reeves*, 26 F.3d at 1253, and because commercial vessels could navigate within the noted physical constraints, we conclude that the river was navigable in fact at River Mile 11.8.

III. Conclusion

For the foregoing reasons, we reverse and remand to the Benefits Review Board for a determination of benefits.

[3] All depths are reported in terms of Mean Low Water, which is the average depth at low tide.

This page intentionally left blank

United States Court of Appeals for the Fourth Circuit

United States Court of Appeals
for the Fourth Circuit

No. 18-2366

GUNVOR SA
vs.
KAYABLIAN

Appeal from the United States District Court for the Eastern District of Virginia, at Alexandria

Decided: January 22, 2020

Citation: 948 F.3d 214, 8 Adm. R. 94 (4th Cir. 2020).

Before MOTZ and KEENAN, Circuit Judges, and TRAXLER, Senior Circuit Judge.

[—2—] **{–216–}** MOTZ, Circuit Judge:

Gunvor SA, a Swiss corporate business entity, sued United States citizens Arman and Lawrence Kayablian and the Amira Group Company, LLC, in the Eastern District of Virginia. Invoking the court's alienage diversity jurisdiction, Gunvor asserted various state-law claims. The defendants moved to dismiss pursuant to Federal Rule of Civil Procedure 12(b)(7) on the ground that Gunvor had failed to join Nemsss Petroleum Ltd., a British Virgin Islands corporation, which the defendants asserted was necessary and indispensable to the action. The district court agreed and, because joining Nemsss, another foreign entity, as a defendant would have destroyed complete diversity and so subject matter jurisdiction, dismissed the complaint without prejudice. Gunvor now appeals that **{–217–}** order. For the reasons that follow, we affirm.

I.

A.

We set forth the facts as alleged in Gunvor's verified complaint and in the contracts at issue here. Gunvor is a global commodities firm that trades crude oil and refined oil products. The Kayablians are officers of Amira and officers and directors of Nemsss, a subsidiary of Amira.

In spring 2016, the Kayablians approached Gunvor about a possible business relationship involving sales of Iraqi fuel oil. The Kayablians had access to Iraqi fuel oil through Gulf Energy for Petroleum Services, an Iraqi subsidiary of Nemsss. As an Iraqi company, Gulf Energy was able to purchase Iraqi fuel oil at the below-market domestic **[—3—]** price from the Iraqi Oil Tankers Corporation, a state-owned Iraqi company. But the Kayablians lacked the capacity and expertise to sell the fuel oil on the international market, where it would command a higher price. The Kayablians sought out Gunvor as a financing partner to provide upfront capital and logistical support to purchase the fuel oil in volume and resell it on the international market. The proposal envisioned both parties profiting from the transactions.

The parties discussed how best to structure the deal. Gunvor alleges in its complaint that the parties considered forming a joint venture, but ultimately decided to use "a series of one-off contracts that mimicked the structure of a [joint venture] without the formality." The contracts that enabled the deal included: (1) a contract for the Iraqi Oil Tankers Corp. to sell fuel to Gulf Energy; (2) a contract for Gulf Energy to sell the fuel to Nemsss; and (3) four contracts (the "Fuel Oil Contracts") for Nemsss to sell the fuel to Gunvor. In this way, the fuel would pass from the Iraqi Oil Tankers Corp., which would convey it at the lower Iraqi domestic price, through Gulf Energy and Nemsss to Gunvor, which would sell it to third parties at the higher international market price.

The Fuel Oil Contracts are especially relevant here. Each included an integration clause:

> This contract contains the entire agreement between the parties and supersedes all previous negotiations, representations, agreements or commitments with regard to its subject matter.
>
> Each party acknowledges that in entering into this contract it has not relied on any representations, warranties, statements or undertakings except

those which are expressly set out herein. **[—4—]**

Each Fuel Oil Contract also included a dispute resolution clause:

> This contract shall be governed by and construed in accordance with English law. Any controversy, dispute or claim whatsoever arising out of or in connection with this contract or the breach thereof shall be referred to arbitration in London . . . . For the avoidance of doubt this will not prevent either party from taking proceedings in any other jurisdiction to obtain security or ancillary relief or to enforce any order or award.

Gunvor drafted the Fuel Oil Contracts, including both the integration and dispute resolution clauses.

The Fuel Oil Contracts required Gunvor to provide the upfront capital for the arrangement in the form of "prepayments," in amounts ranging from $3 million to $12 million. Gunvor was to remit the prepayments to Nemsss, which would remit the funds to Gulf Energy, which would in turn remit them to the Iraqi Oil Tankers Corp. in order to procure the fuel. Gunvor alleges **{-218-}** in its complaint that these prepayments were to function as "credit [that] would be applied against the sale price of the fuel charged to Gunvor."

Gunvor made its contractually obligated payments to Nemsss, in total remitting nearly $125 million. Gunvor alleges, however, that it received only about $101 million worth of fuel oil. Increasingly concerned, Gunvor asked the Kayablians to account for the missing $24 million, to no avail. When Gunvor then asked the Kayablians to refund the disputed funds, they refused.

B.

Maintaining that the Kayablians and Amira had defrauded it, Gunvor brought this action in federal court in Virginia. Gunvor invoked the court's diversity jurisdiction for suits between citizens of a U.S. state and a citizen of a foreign state. Gunvor asserted state- **[—5—]** law claims for fraud, fraudulent inducement, conversion, unjust enrichment, negligent misrepresentation, and civil conspiracy. The complaint identified Nemsss and Gulf Energy as nonparties and sought to impose alter ego liability on the defendants for these nonparties' acts.

The Kayablians and Amira moved to dismiss the suit for nonjoinder of a necessary and indispensable party—Nemsss—that, as another foreign entity, would destroy complete diversity. In the alternative, they moved to compel arbitration.

The district court granted the motion to dismiss. In an oral ruling, the court held "that Nemsss . . . would be a necessary and indispensable party," notwithstanding Gunvor's "artful pleading . . . to try to avoid that reality." The court reasoned that the "core" of the parties' arrangement was the "agreement . . . for Gunvor to purchase quantities of oil from Iraq," which Gunvor was to do "through Nemsss." The district court found it "significant" that the Fuel Oil Contracts included "a complete integration clause, which contains very broad language indicating that any and all prior understandings or agreements, etc., are subsumed or integrated into these individual contracts." The court noted that these contracts "are between Gunvor and Nemsss, not the individuals who are named as defendants." Because joining Nemsss, a foreign corporation, would "destroy the diversity jurisdiction," the district court dismissed the complaint without prejudice.[1] **[—6—]**

In addition, the district court stated "for the record that if I had jurisdiction, I would have granted the motion to compel arbi-

[1] Because Gunvor could not cure the defect in its complaint without destroying jurisdiction, we may consider its appeal even though the dismissal was without prejudice. *See Domino Sugar Corp. v. Sugar Workers Local Union 392*, 10 F.3d 1064, 1066–67 (4th Cir. 1993); *see also Teamsters Local Union No. 171 v. Keal Driveaway Co.*, 173 F.3d 915, 916 (4th Cir. 1999).

tration." The court continued, "[I]t's crystal clear the parties' contemplation was that English law would apply, that arbitration of any disputes in any respect related to these oil contracts would be governed by English law and would be resolved in arbitration in London."

Gunvor timely appealed.

II.

When adjudicating a motion under Federal Rule of Civil Procedure 19, a district court asks first whether the nonjoined party is necessary under Rule 19(a) and then whether the party is indispensable under Rule 19(b). *See Nat'l Union Fire Ins. Co. v. Rite Aid of S.C., Inc.*, 210 F.3d 246, 249 (4th Cir. 2000). If the nonjoined **{–219–}** party is necessary and indispensable to the action, but joinder would destroy subject matter jurisdiction, the court must dismiss the action. *See Owens-Illinois, Inc. v. Meade*, 186 F.3d 435, 440 (4th Cir. 1999). Dismissal, though "a drastic remedy that should be employed only sparingly," is "required" if the nonjoined party "is both necessary and indispensable." *Home Buyers Warranty Corp. v. Hanna*, 750 F.3d 427, 433 (4th Cir. 2014) (alteration and internal quotation marks omitted). That determination "must be made pragmatically, in the context of the 'substance' of each case, rather than by procedural formula." *Provident Tradesmens Bank & Tr. Co. v. Patterson*, 390 U.S. 102, 119 n.16 (1968).

We review a district court's Rule 19 dismissal for abuse of discretion, reviewing the underlying findings of fact for clear error. *Nat'l Union*, 210 F.3d at 250. **[—7—]**

A.

This case hinges on a factual finding by the district court. The court found that the parties' "core agreement was for Gunvor to purchase quantities of oil from Iraq," which Gunvor was to do "through Nemsss."

In its appellate briefs, Gunvor disputes this characterization. Gunvor's briefing instead describes its agreement as a broad joint venture with the Kayablians and Amira, with Nemsss as one small cog in a much bigger machine. Gunvor claims that "the common purpose was for *the parties to the [joint venture]*—the Kayablians, Amira, and Gunvor—to share the profits from the sale of Iraqi fuel oil and the losses incurred to transport and ship the oil." Opening Br. at 16. Gunvor further contends in its briefs that the Fuel Oil Contracts between Gunvor and Nemsss "were only four of *many* contracts executed in furtherance of the [joint venture]," alongside other contracts between the Iraqi Oil Tankers Corp. and Gulf Energy, between Gulf Energy and Nemsss, and between Gunvor and its shipping charter parties. *Id.* at 17–18.

But Gunvor's briefs on appeal lie at odds with its complaint. Gunvor's opening brief, for example, describes its fuel oil arrangement as involving a fourteen-step plan, eleven steps of which involve Amira "direct[ing]" its subsidiaries to take various actions. *Id.* at 5–6. Gunvor's complaint, however, paints a different picture. The complaint alleges that by "the terms of the proposed joint venture[,] (1) Gunvor would remit the prepayment funds to Nemsss; (2) Nemsss would remit the prepayment funds to [Gulf Energy]; and (3) [Gulf Energy] would deposit the prepayment funds in full into [the Iraqi Oil Tanker Corp.]'s bank account in order to lift fuel from the Iraqi refinery." Pursuant to this **[—8—]** agreement, "Nemsss would make all arrangements and incur all expenses on the shore-side . . . and Gunvor would make all shipping arrangements and incur all the shipping-related expenses." "Nemsss and Gunvor," the complaint continues, "would then share their expenses and their income from their respective sales of the fuel oil on a 50:50 basis."

Thus, pursuant to the allegations in the complaint, the Fuel Oil Contracts were indeed the core of the parties' agreement, as the district court found. Nemsss, pursuant to the Fuel Oil Contracts, acted as the middleman, enabling the flow of money from Gunvor to the Iraqi-based companies and facilitating the flow of fuel oil from the refinery back to Gunvor in exchange. Even construing the agreement as a broader joint venture, Nemsss was its keystone.

The remainder of Gunvor's complaint also comports with this account. The complaint **{-220-}** articulates Gunvor's fundamental grievance: that it made the payments required by the Fuel Oil Contracts but did not receive the benefit of its bargain. The sole parties to those contracts were Gunvor and Nemsss. Despite Gunvor's current efforts to reframe the agreement as a joint venture, Gunvor stated in its complaint that it *declined* to form a joint venture and instead freely chose to enter "a series of one-off contracts." And the complaint lays bare that the Fuel Oil Contracts and Nemsss were the linchpin of that arrangement. For instance, the complaint describes in its first sentence Gunvor's intent "to recover damages suffered as a result of Defendants' fraudulent conduct in connection with purported fuel oil contracts"; notes that the Kayablians' initial proposal sought investments in Nemsss; and lists disputed payments Gunvor made, all pursuant to the Fuel Oil Contracts. Given that Gunvor peppered its complaint with claims against Nemsss, **[—9—]** Gunvor's attempt in its appellate briefs to downplay Nemsss's role in the scheme strains credulity.

In short, Gunvor's own complaint places Nemsss at the heart of this case, and the district court's factual findings follow inexorably from that account. Taking Gunvor at its word in its complaint, its present about-face notwithstanding, we find no error (let alone clear error) in the district court's factual findings and proceed to the Rule 19 inquiry.

B.

"The first question under Rule 19(a) is whether a party is necessary to a proceeding because of its relationship to the matter under consideration." *Home Buyers*, 750 F.3d at 433 (internal quotation marks omitted). "A party might be necessary under either Rule 19(a)(1)(A) or (B)." *Id.* at 434. In this case, we look to the latter. Nemsss is necessary if it "claims an interest relating to the subject of the action," Fed R. Civ. P. 19(a)(1)(B), and adjudicating the matter in Nemsss's absence could either "as a practical matter impair or impede [its] ability to protect the interest," *id.* 19(a)(1)(B)(i), or "leave an existing party subject to a substantial risk of incurring double, multiple, or otherwise inconsistent obligations because of the interest," *id.* 19(a)(1)(B)(ii).

Nemsss claims an interest in the Fuel Oil Contracts, which the district court correctly found to be the "core" of the parties' agreement and dispute, as explained above. Though a nonparty may formally claim an interest in an action, a "court with proper jurisdiction may also consider *sua sponte* the absence of a required person and dismiss for failure to join." *Republic of Philippines v. Pimentel*, 553 U.S. 851, 861 (2008). To the extent that Rule 19(a) requires *any* affirmative action from the nonjoined party at issue, the **[—10—]** declaration submitted by Lawrence Kayablian, Nemsss's chief executive officer, was sufficient for Nemss to claim an interest. That affidavit described Nemsss's agreements and relationship with Gunvor and emphasized that "[a]t no time did Nemsss Petroleum waive its right to arbitrate, which right arises from the [Fuel Oil C]ontracts." Nemsss asserted an interest in the enforcement of the Fuel Oil Contracts, thus satisfying Rule 19(a)(1)(B)'s first requirement.

Turning to the second requirement —found in Rule 19(a)(1)(B)(i)—litigating this action in Nemsss's absence could certainly impair its interest in the Fuel Oil Contracts. Gunvor now claims that "the damages and rights at issue here relate exclusively to the relationship between the Kayablians, Amira, and Gunvor" and that it does not seek to attack the Fuel Oil Contracts. Opening Br. at 24. Once **{-221-}** again, Gunvor sings a different tune now than it did in its complaint. Gunvor's complaint alleges that the Kayablians owe it "the missing prepayment funds"—that is, the difference between the payments Gunvor made and the value of the fuel oil it received. Gunvor made these payments *to Nemsss*, pursuant to *the Fuel Oil Contracts*, under which *Nemsss* was to supply Gunvor with the volume of fuel in question.

Behind the smoke and mirrors of Gunvor's "artful pleading," as the district court put it, Gunvor signed contracts with Nemsss and now seeks damages from the Kayablians and Amira for Nemsss's alleged failure to perform under those contracts. *See F&M Distribs., Inc. v. Am. Hardware Supply Co.*, 129 F.R.D. 494, 498 (W.D. Pa. 1990). Litigating this dispute would require the court to adjudicate Nemsss's rights and obligations under the Fuel Oil Contracts, and the outcome would turn on Nemsss's conduct **[—11—]** pursuant to them. Consequently, "fairness dictates" that Nemsss "be given the opportunity to protect its separate and distinct interest as a party." *Nat'l Union*, 210 F.3d at 251. Nemsss is therefore necessary under Rule 19(a)(1)(B)(i).

Aside from the substance of the inquiry, Gunvor protests that the district court failed to expressly evaluate the Rule 19(a) factors. We have seen no authority suggesting that such explicit and detailed consideration is required.[2] A Rule 19 dismissal requires explanation, but demanding a talismanic recitation from the district court would run afoul of the "pragmatic analysis" Rule 19 requires. *Provident Tradesmens*, 390 U.S. at 119 n.16.

The district court did not abuse its discretion in deeming Nemsss a necessary party under Rule 19(a).

C.

"[I]f the party is necessary but joining it to the action would destroy complete diversity, the court must decide under Rule 19(b) whether the proceeding can continue in that party's absence." *Home Buyers*, 750 F.3d at 433 (internal quotation marks omitted). Because Nemsss is a necessary party to the action and, as a foreign corporation, its joinder would destroy the complete diversity necessary for alienage jurisdiction, *see Slavchev v. Royal Caribbean Cruises, Ltd.*, 559 F.3d 251, 254 (4th Cir. 2009), we ask whether Nemsss **[—12—]** is an indispensable party under Rule 19(b). "At the outset, we note that precedent supports the proposition that a contracting party is the paradigm of an indispensable party." *Nat'l Union*, 210 F.3d at 252 (internal quotation marks omitted). Keeping that in mind, we consider, "in equity and good conscience," the four factors set forth in Rule 19(b). The "analysis is not mechanical; rather it is conducted in light of the equities at the particular case at bar." *Schlumberger Indus., Inc., v. Nat'l Sur. Corp.*, 36 F.3d 1274, 1287 (4th Cir. 1994).

The first factor, which concerns "the extent to which a judgment rendered in the person's absence might prejudice that person or the existing parties," Fed. R. Civ. P. 19(b)(1), "speaks to many of the same concerns addressed by the necessity analysis under Rule 19(a)(1)(B)," **{-222-}** *Home Buyers*, 750 F.3d at 435. For the reasons discussed above, an adverse judgment rendered in Nemsss's absence would surely prejudice Nemsss.

The second factor addresses "the extent to which any prejudice could be lessened or avoided by" "protective provisions in the judgment," "shaping the relief," or "other measures." Fed. R. Civ. P. 19(b)(2). Gunvor contends that the district court "certainly could structure any judgment" to avoid prejudice to Nemsss. Opening Br. at 28. But Gunvor offers no support for this proposition or explanation of just how the court could structure a judgment, and we do not see how the court could grant the judgment Gunvor requests without prejudicing Nemsss.

The third factor asks "whether a judgment rendered in the person's absence would be adequate." Fed R. Civ. P. 19(b)(3). This factor "focuses on the interest of the courts and the public in complete, consistent, and efficient settlement of controversies." *Home* **[—13—]** *Buyers*, 750 F.3d at 436 (internal quotation

[2] The only case Gunvor cites in support of its contrary view, *In re Lloyd's Register N. Am., Inc.*, 780 F.3d 283, 3 Adm. R. 273 (5th Cir. 2015), is clearly inapposite. There, the court denied a defendant's motion to dismiss for *forum non conveniens* without offering any rationale. *See id.* at 288, 3 Adm. R. at 273–74. Here, the district court addressed a very different question and offered concise but sound reasoning for rejecting Gunvor's argument: the Fuel Oil Contracts were the "core agreement" at issue in the dispute, and only Gunvor and Nemsss were parties to those contracts.

marks omitted). Given the allegations against Nemsss in Gunvor's complaint, not joining Nemsss here could lead to parallel or subsequent litigation or indemnification actions, all of which could produce incomplete, inconsistent, and inefficient settlement of this dispute.

The fourth and final factor looks to "whether the plaintiff would have an adequate remedy if the action were dismissed for nonjoinder." Fed. R. Civ. P. 19(b)(4). Gunvor has an adequate remedy in the absence of federal litigation: Gunvor is free to seek relief in state court, as Gunvor's counsel admitted at oral argument. *See Home Buyers*, 750 F.3d at 436; *Schlumberger*, 36 F.3d at 1288.

In sum, all four factors support the district court's determination. The court therefore did not abuse its discretion in concluding that Nemsss is an indispensable party and accordingly did not err in dismissing the complaint.

III.

For the foregoing reasons, the judgment of the district court is

AFFIRMED.

This page intentionally left blank

United States Court of Appeals for the Fifth Circuit

United States Court of Appeals
for the Fifth Circuit

No. 19-60337

BOURGEOIS
VS.
DIRECTOR, OFFICE OF WORKERS' COMPENSATION PROGRAMS

Petition for Review of an Order of the Benefits Review Board

Decided: January 2, 2020

Citation: 946 F.3d 263, 8 Adm. R. 102 (5th Cir. 2020).

Before **DAVIS, SMITH,** and **HIGGINSON,** Circuit Judges.

[—1—] {-264-} HIGGINSON, Circuit Judge:

Petitioner-appellant Tramond Bourgeois, a former employee of appellee Fab-Con, Inc., filed a claim for benefits under the Longshore and Harbor Workers' Compensation Act ("LHWCA") after he was injured while working on navigable waters on May 31, 2014. The Administrative Law Judge ("ALJ") found that Bourgeois suffered injuries to his right shoulder, right ankle, and lower back as a result of the accident and ordered his employer to pay disability benefits from June 1 through November 14, 2014. Bourgeois appealed the **[—2—]** ALJ's findings to the Benefits Review Board ("Board"), arguing that the ALJ erred in concluding that he did not suffer more severe shoulder and back injuries, including a labrum tear and lumbar facet arthrosis. The Board affirmed the ALJ's decision and denied Bourgeois's motion for reconsideration. For the following reasons, we deny the petition for review.

"We review a decision of the Board 'under the same standard as it reviews the decision of the ALJ: Whether the decision is supported by substantial evidence and is in accordance with the law.'" *Craven v. Director, OWCP*, 604 F.3d 902, 905 (5th Cir. 2010) (quoting *Empire United Stevedores v. Gatlin*, 936 F.2d 819, 822 (5th Cir. 1991)). "Substantial evidence is relevant evidence that is more than a scintilla but less than a preponderance." *Hill v. Director, OWCP*, 195 F.3d 790, 793 (5th Cir. 1999). In conducting this analysis, "we may not substitute our judgment of the facts for that of the ALJ or reweigh or reappraise the evidence." *Id.* We will affirm as long as the evidence provides "a substantial basis of fact from which the fact in issue can be reasonably inferred." **{-265-}** *Diamond M. Drilling Co. v. Marshall*, 577 F.2d 1003, 1006 (5th Cir. 1978) (internal quotation marks and citation omitted).

Bourgeois first argues that the Board erred when it affirmed the ALJ's finding that he did not suffer a labral tear to his right shoulder as a result of the accident. Under section 920 of the LHWCA, a claimant is entitled to a presumption that an injury is causally related to his employment as long as he proves "(1) that he . . . suffered harm, and (2) that conditions existed at work, or an accident occurred at work, that could have caused, aggravated, or accelerated the condition." *Port Cooper/T. Smith Stevedoring Co. v. Hunter*, 227 F.3d 285, 287 (5th Cir. 2000). The employer may rebut that presumption by pointing to "substantial evidence" establishing the lack of a causal nexus. *Id.* (quoting 33 U.S.C. § 920). Here, the ALJ did not err in concluding that Dr. Sweeney, appellee's medical expert, "presented a more thorough and credible **[—3—]** opinion . . . than [Bourgeois's treating physician,] Dr. Johnston," thus rebutting the presumption of a causal nexus. Though a June 24, 2014 MRI suggested that Bourgeois suffered a small ventral tear immediately after the accident, Dr. Johnston testified that he treated Bourgeois for a superior tear three years later, in 2017. Based on these disparities, Dr. Sweeney opined that "the obvious conclusion is [that Dr. Johnston] found tears in structures that were not present . . . in 2014,"[1]

[1] To the extent that Dr. Johnston testified later that the tear he observed in Bourgeois's shoulder was "a little bit anterior and a little bit posterior this testimony was inconsistent with his operative note, which did not describe a tear in the anterior region of Bourgeois's shoulder. Therefore, the ALJ did not err in concluding that Dr. Sweeney's opinion was more credible and "better supported by the objective medical evidence." *See, e.g., Turner v. Director, OWCP*, 334 F. App'x 693, 696 (5th Cir. 2009) ("As the fact finder, the ALJ is entitled to

and thus determined that the accident did not cause Bourgeois's labral tear.

Bourgeois argues that Dr. Sweeney was bound to accept Dr. Johnston's conclusion that Bourgeois suffered a single tear at the time of the accident, which progressed over time as a result of normal use. However, Dr. Johnston himself admitted that Bourgeois's labral tear could have been caused by an intervening injury, as opposed to the initial 2014 injury. Contrary to Bourgeois's position, the ALJ was not required to credit Dr. Johnston's testimony. *See Ceres Gulf, Inc. v. Director, OWCP*, 143 F. App'x 589, 593 (5th Cir. 2005) ("The ALJ [is] well within his province to reject [a treating physician's] testimony, especially [where] there [is] no other medical evidence presented to corroborate the doctor's position."). The ALJ properly considered the testimony and opinions of both experts and found Dr. Sweeney's explanation more credible. We may not disturb this determination, even if the ALJ could have plausibly drawn an alternate conclusion from the evidence. *New Thoughts Finishing Co. v. Chilton*, 118 F.3d 1028, 1030–31 (5th Cir. 1997) **[—4—]** ("[W]e may not substitute our judgment for that of the ALJ, nor reweigh or reappraise he evidence, but may only determine whether evidence exists to support the ALJ's findings.").

Second, the Board did not err when it refused to consider Bourgeois's new argument, presented for the first time in his motion for reconsideration, that the 2017 shoulder surgery was intended to address an AC joint sprain. Though Bourgeois argues that this theory was supported by "significant testimonial and documentary evidence," he fails to point to any portion **{-266-}** of the record that demonstrates that he asserted this claim before the ALJ. *See Johnston v. Hayward Baker*, 48 Ben. Rev. Bd. Serv. 59 (2014). By failing to brief the issue, Bourgeois also waived any objections to the ALJ's conclusions that his AC joint sprain was resolved by November 2014. Furthermore, to the extent that Bourgeois believed that the ALJ made a mistake in fact, he failed to file a motion for modification, as instructed by the Board in its order on the motion for reconsideration. *See* 33 U.S.C. § 922; 20 C.F.R. § 702.373.

Finally, the ALJ's finding that Bourgeois did not suffer from lumbar facet arthrosis was supported by substantial evidence. Though the low-resolution June 2, 2014 MRI suggests that Bourgeois might have sustained facet arthrosis, the higher resolution June 24, 2014 MRI presents no evidence of the condition. Moreover, as the factfinder, the ALJ was "exclusively entitled to assess both the weight of the evidence and the credibility of the witnesses." *Ceres Gulf, Inc.*, 683 F.3d at 228. There was substantial evidence to support the ALJ's determination that Bourgeois's statements about his pain were not credible, especially given Dr. Sweeney's physical examination of Bourgeois and his determination that Bourgeois exhibited no objective lumbar problems.

Thus, because substantial evidence supports the ALJ's determination, we deny the petition for review. *Bia Salamis, Inc. v. Director, OWCP*, 819 F.3d 116, 131, 4 Adm. R. 209, 220 (5th Cir. 2016) (internal quotation marks and citation omitted).

---

make credibility determinations and accept or reject any part of an expert's testimony." (citation omitted)).

United States Court of Appeals
for the Fifth Circuit

No. 18-31019

PHI, INC.
vs.
APICAL INDUS., INC.

Appeal from the United States District Court for the Western District of Louisiana

Decided: January 9, 2020

Citation: 946 F.3d 772, 8 Adm. R. 104 (5th Cir. 2020).

Before **OWEN,** Chief Judge, and **SMITH** and **DENNIS,** Circuit Judges.

[—1—] {-773-} DENNIS, Circuit Judge:

PHI, Inc. sued Rolls-Royce, Apical Industries, and Offshore Helicopter Support Services (OHS), after a helicopter PHI owned was required to make an emergency landing in the Gulf of Mexico when its Rolls-Royce-manufactured engine failed. After the landing, the emergency flotation system manufactured by Apical and serviced by OHS partially deflated, causing the helicopter to turn over in the water and resulting in a total loss due to salt water incursion. Relatively early in the case, PHI's action against Rolls-Royce was severed and transferred to federal court in Indiana. That action later settled. **[—2—]**

Ahead of a jury trial in the Western District of Louisiana on PHI's claims of redhibition (a Louisiana warranty claim sounding in contract law) against Apical and breach of contract against OHS, the magistrate judge presiding over the case by the parties' consent excluded all evidence regarding the cause of the engine failure and determined that he would not submit the issue of Rolls-Royce's liability to the jury as a basis for reduction in the damages award against Apical. The magistrate judge premised these rulings on the mistaken belief that Rolls-Royce could not, as a matter of law, be held solidarily liable along with Apical and OHS for the loss of the helicopter. The jury ultimately found Apical liable for the loss of the helicopter. Because, under Louisiana law, Rolls-Royce is a potential solidary obligor along with Apical, and because a finding of solidary liability would result in a reduction of damages award against Apical due to Rolls-Royce's earlier settlement with PHI, the magistrate judge's pretrial exclusion and verdict form rulings were in error. Accordingly, we VACATE and REMAND for trial on the issue of solidary liability. **{-774-}**

I

On December 1, 2011, a helicopter owned by PHI, Inc., formerly known as Petroleum Helicopters Inc., "sustained an engine failure and made an emergency water landing." In doing so, the helicopter pilot activated an emergency flotation system and executed a water landing. The pilot and the sole passenger escaped the helicopter unharmed on life rafts. A rescue boat picked up the pilot and passenger, dropped them off at a nearby oil platform, and returned to the helicopter. As the rescue boat then towed the helicopter to the platform, the right section of the flotation system deflated, causing the helicopter to flip over in the Gulf of Mexico. Although PHI recovered the helicopter from the Gulf, the incursion of salt water into the helicopter caused it to be a total loss. A post-accident inspection revealed that the right rear float was punctured, and, unlike the left rear float, it did not have a "doubler," a **[—3—]** patch used to protect from chafing damage where the float connected to the helicopter's railing.

PHI sued Apical Industries, Inc. (Apical), the manufacturer of the flotation system that failed while the helicopter was being towed, as well as Rolls-Royce and Offshore Helicopter Support Services, Inc. (OHS), in Louisiana state court. Rolls-Royce was the engine manufacturer, and OHS serviced the float system before the accident. After removal to federal court,[1] PHI's claims against Rolls-

[1] Also after removal, PHI filed an amended complaint alleging Louisiana redhibition claims against Rolls-Royce, as well as a breach of contract claim against OHS. PHI also brought a strict liability claim under the Louisiana Products Liability Act against Apical. However, the district

Royce were severed and transferred to Indiana based on a forum-selection clause.[2] The forum-selection clause was contained in a warranty agreement provided in connection with Rolls-Royce's 2011 sale of a replacement part to PHI called a No. 2 bearing.[3] PHI's case against Rolls-Royce in Indiana settled after that court denied summary judgment for Rolls-Royce on PHI's claim.

Ahead of trial against Apical and OHS, the magistrate judge excluded evidence regarding the cause of the Rolls-Royce engine failure, determining that this evidence was not relevant to PHI's claims against Apical or OHS, or to any of Apical or OHS's defenses.[4] The magistrate judge also refused to **[—4—]** submit to the jury a question about Rolls-Royce's liability. After a two-day trial, the jury found Apical's floats contained a redhibitory defect and OHS did not breach its contract with PHI. The jury awarded PHI $2,180,000 in damages, from which the magistrate judge later deducted $450,230 to account for the value of the engine, the loss of which Apical was not responsible for. Apical appealed. **{-775-}**

II

Apical asserts on appeal that the magistrate judge was incorrect to exclude evidence of the cause of the Rolls-Royce engine failure and to refuse to submit the issue of Rolls-Royce's liability to the jury. These contentions turn on two points: First, whether a limited warranty agreement between PHI and Rolls-Royce forecloses all potential liability on the part of Rolls-Royce for the salt-water damage caused to the helicopter; and second, if damages for salt-water incursion are in fact allowed, whether their availability makes Rolls-Royce a potential solidary obligor, entitling Apical to submit this question and evidence supporting it to a jury. We address each issue in turn.

A

The magistrate judge concluded that Rolls-Royce could not be solidarily liable with Apical and OHS, based on a limited warranty agreement executed between PHI and Rolls-Royce in connection with the sale of the No. 2 bearing in 2011 that waived consequential damages.[5] The magistrate judge reasoned **[—5—]** that under the limited warranty, "Rolls[-]Royce would not be liable for the same performance as Apical and OHS, and therefore, Rolls-Royce would not be solidarily liable with them." The warranty the magistrate judge relied on provided:

> THIS WARRANTY IS GIVEN EXPRESSLY AND IN PLACE OF ALL OTHER WARRANTIES, EXPRESS OR IMPLIED, INCLUDING ANY IMPLIED WARRANTIES OF MERCHANTABIL-ITY OR FITNESS FOR PARTICULAR

court dismissed this claim early in the litigation, and that dismissal is not appealed here.

[2] The district court initially denied the motion to sever and transfer. A panel of this court subsequently granted Rolls-Royce's petition for writ of mandamus, *In re Rolls Royce Corp.*, 775 F.3d 671, 2 Adm. R. 398 (5th Cir. 2014), directing the district court to sever PHI's claims against Rolls-Royce and transfer them to the United States District Court for the Southern District of Indiana. *See* 775 F.3d at 674, 683, 2 Adm. R. at 398, 406.

[3] The Rolls-Royce engine was installed by Bell Helicopters after its manufacture by Rolls-Royce in 1999. *Petroleum Helicopters, Inc. v. Rolls-Royce Corp.*, 1:15-CV-00840-TWP-DML, 2016 WL 7179362, at *1 (S.D. Ind. Dec. 9, 2016). The No. 2 bearing, the bearing alleged as one potential cause of the Helicopter's engine failure, was sold to PHI and installed in 2011.

[4] The magistrate judge specifically excluded evidence that someone improperly hammered on the No. 2 bearing, causing the engine to fail, as well as "the entirety of the **[—4—]** deposition testimony of Dr. Edney in his capacity as the corporate representative of Rolls Royce."

[5] The parties do not dispute that the total loss of the helicopter would constitute "consequential damages," as opposed to some other form of damages. This assumption appears correct. *See* UNIF. COMM.CODE § 2-715 ("Consequential damages resulting from the seller's breach include . . . injury to person or property proximately resulting from any breach of warranty."); *Damages*, BLACK'S LAW DICTIONARY (11th ed. 2019) (defining consequential damages as "[l]osses that do not flow directly and immediately from an injurious act but that result indirectly from the act. — Also termed indirect damages" (emphasis omitted)).

PURPOSE. THERE ARE NOT UNDERSTANDINGS, AGREEMENTS, REPRESENTATIONS, OR WARRANTIES NOT SPECIFIED HEREIN.

***

The obligations of Rolls-Royce under this Limited Warranty are limited to the repair of the spare module/part as provided herein. In no event, whether as a result of breach of contract or warranty, alleged negligence, or otherwise, shall Rolls-Royce be subject to liability for incidental, consequential, indirect, special or punitive damages of any kind, including without limitation to damage to the engine, airframe or other property, commercial losses, lost profits, loss of use, grounding of engines or aircrafts, inconvenience, loss of time, cost of capital, cost of substitute equipment, downtime, claims of customers, or changes in retirement lives and overhaul periods.

Apical argues that this warranty, which the magistrate judge found valid and enforceable under Indiana law, only applies to a bearing added to the engine ten years after installation of the engine itself, and therefore Rolls-Royce could still potentially be liable for damages to the extent the engine failed for reasons unrelated to the No. 2 bearing. We agree.[6] The Southern District of Indiana's order on Rolls-Royce's motion for summary judgment in **{-776-}** the severed action is informative on this point. There, the Indiana federal **[—6—]** court determined that PHI had not only brought an action regarding a defect in the No. 2 bearing, which would be covered by the warranty provision, but also a broader design defect claim asserting a defect in a "piccolo tube," which allegedly reduced the amount of oil that could reach the No. 2 bearing and potentially caused the engine failure. *See Petroleum Helicopters, Inc. v. Rolls-Royce Corp.*, 1:15-CV-00840-TWP-DML, 2016 WL 7179362, at *3–*4 (S.D. Ind. Dec. 9, 2016). Moreover, according to the Indiana federal court, "the [l]imited [w]arranty applies only to the No. 2 bearing," such that a claim asserting design defect beyond the No. 2 bearing could go forward. *Id.* at *4. This analysis is persuasive, and we adopt it. The warranty's plain terms apply only to the Rolls-Royce engine's "spare modules and parts." Moreover, PHI's response brief does not meaningfully challenge this point.[7]

Because the warranty's waiver of consequential damages does not apply to the claim that the engine failed due at least in part to a defect outside the No. 2 bearing, a dispute of fact exists as to whether damages for any non-waived defects are recoverable. *See Rolls-Royce Corp.*, 2016 WL 7179362, at *4 ("Accordingly, because the Limited Warranty applies only to the No. 2 bearing, a genuine issue of material fact remains regarding whether the engine contained a design defect, and summary judgment is denied on this issue." (emphasis omitted)). As discussed in the following section, this dispute of fact is material, and thus should have been put to the jury, because Rolls-Royce may be a solidary obligor under Louisiana law along with Apical. Should a **[—7—]** jury so find, Apical would be entitled to a reduction in the damages award against it.

B

Under Louisiana law, solidary liability arises when multiple obligors are liable for the same debt, and when performance by one would relieve the others' liability to the

---

[6] Although Apical did not specifically raise this distinction before the magistrate judge, the magistrate judge prohibited the parties from briefing the issue of solidary liability in their trial briefs. Under these circumstances, we decline to hold that Apical forfeited the argument.

[7] PHI also argued in Indiana federal court that the warranty failed in its essential purpose and was therefore unenforceable. The magistrate judge in the case at bar ruled that even if the warranty failed in its essential purpose, the warranty's waiver of consequential damages was still enforceable under governing Indiana law. Apical did not challenge this portion of the magistrate judge's ruling below, and does not do so on appeal. Accordingly, Apical forfeited any assertion of error on this point. *See Noatex Corp. v. King Const. of Houston, L.L.C.*, 732 F.3d 479, 485 n.4 (5th Cir. 2013) (issues not briefed are waived).

obligee.[8] LA. CIV. CODE art. 1794 (2019). Such a solidary obligation is not to be presumed but can arise from either "a clear expression of the parties' intent or from the law."[9] *Id.* art. 1796. "An **{–777–}** obligation may be solidary though it derives from a different source for each obligor." *Id.* art. 1797. Solidary liability is designed to protect the obligee by placing responsibility for the debt fully on the obligors, who can then seek contribution from one another. *Id.* art. 1790; *see also id.* art. 1805 ("A party sued on an obligation that would be solidary if it exists may seek to enforce contribution against any solidary co-obligor by making him a third[-]party defendant . . . ."). If a co-obligor has been released by his obligee, including through settlement, that potential co-obligor can no longer be made a party to the case; however, because solidary obligors are liable for the same debt, a settlement between the obligee and a solidary obligor reduces the obligation owed by the other obligors "in the amount of the remitted share," which means reduction by an **[—8—]** equal share of the liability. *Id.* art. 1803, rev. cmt. (a) (2019); *id.* art. 1804. "Among solidary obligors, each is liable for his virile portion. If the obligation arises from a contract or quasi-contract, virile portions are equal in the absence of agreement or judgment to the contrary." *Id.* art. 1804.

PHI argues that, even assuming some disputes of fact exist with respect to the scope of the limited warranty, Rolls-Royce cannot be a solidary obligor because it and Apical cannot as a factual matter be liable for the same dollar amounts in damages. As the argument goes, Apical is undisputedly not responsible for damage to the Rolls-Royce-manufactured engine, which the parties agree was destroyed prior to the helicopter landing in the water. Rolls-Royce, on the other hand, could potentially be responsible for the engine loss (assuming, for sake of this argument, that the claim against Rolls-Royce had not settled) in addition to the later losses caused by salt water incursion.

We disagree. Because Louisiana law does not require that damages amounts be identical for two parties to be held liable in solido, the magistrate judge erred in refusing to submit the issue of solidary liability to the jury.

The Louisiana Supreme Court has devised a three-part test based on the Louisiana Civil Code to determine when an obligation is solidary: (1) "when [the obligors] are obliged to the same thing," (2) "so that each may be compelled for the whole," and (3) "when payment by one exonerates the other toward the creditor." *Hoefly v. Gov't Employees Ins. Co.*, 418 So. 2d 575, 576 (La. 1982);[10] **[—9—]** *In re de la Vergne*, 205 F.3d 864, 866 (5th Cir. 2000) (recognizing Louisiana's three-part test). In establishing this test, the Louisiana

[8] The parties do not dispute that Louisiana law applies to the substantive claims for damages in this case. In determining what state's laws apply in this diversity action, we apply Louisiana conflicts of law principles. *See Klaxon Co. v. Stentor Elec. Mfg. Co.*, 313 U.S. 487, 496 (1941). Louisiana's conflicts of law regime requires, for a contract claim like redhibition, a determination as to "the state whose policies would be most seriously impaired if its law were not applied to that issue," including consideration of, inter alia, "the pertinent contacts of each state to the parties and the transaction . . . [and] the nature, type, and purpose of the contract." LA. CIV. CODE art. 3537. Because the magistrate judge has made no findings relevant to these considerations and the parties have not briefed nor submitted evidence pointing to the laws of any state other than Louisiana for PHI's substantive claims, we proceed on the assumption that Louisiana law applies to these claims.

[9] For example, in redhibition suits against the sellers and manufacturers of the thing sold, solidary liability arises by law. *See* LA. CIV. CODE art. 2545, rev. cmt. (c), (d) (2019).

[10] The Louisiana Supreme Court relied on former Louisiana Civil Code article 2091 in formulating this test: "There is an obligation *in solido* on the part of the debtors, when they are all obliged to the same thing, so that each may be compelled for the whole, and when the payment which is made by one of them, exonerates the others toward the creditor." LA. CIV. CODE art. 2091 (1976). The article has since been revised, and now appears as article 1794: "An obligation is solidary for the obligors when each obligor is liable for the whole performance. A performance rendered by one of the solidary obligors relieves the others of liability toward the obligee." LA. CIV. CODE art. 1794 (2019). The revision comments clarify that article 1794 "restates the principle contained in C.C. Art. 2091" and "does not change the law." *Id.* art. 1794, rev. cmt. (2019).

Supreme Court held that obligors can be solidarily liable even though "obligations . . . ar[o]se from separate acts or by different reasons."[11] **{-778-}** *Hoefly*, 418 So. 2d at 579; *see also* LA. CIV. CODE art. 1797 (2019) ("An obligation may be solidary though it derives from a different source for each obligor.").

Louisiana courts have held that "when two obligors are coextensively liable for at least *part* of the obligee's damages, the obligation is solidary as to their common liability." *Yarbrough v. Federal Land Bank Assn.*, 616 So. 2d 1327, 1335 (La. Ct. App. 2d Cir. 1993) (emphasis added). Co-obligors, then, may be solidarily liable for some but not all of an obligee's damages, depending on the resolution of various factual and causation issues. *See id.* For example, in *Steptoe v. Lallie Kemp Hosp.*,[12] Murphy Steptoe died from medical malpractice following an automobile accident. 634 So.2d at 334. Steptoe's death was caused by two "separate and distinct acts of negligence," where the **[—10—]** car accident tortfeasors caused Steptoe's initial injury and the medical malpractice tortfeasors caused Steptoe's death. *Id.* at 335. The Louisiana Supreme Court held that while only the car accident tortfeasors were liable for Steptoe's initial injury, both sets of parties were liable for Steptoe's death, and "[t]hus, the two groups now have solidary liability for the death." *Id.* at 336.

Similarly, here, only Rolls-Royce could have been liable for the helicopter's engine failure. Like the car accident tortfeasors in *Steptoe*, Rolls-Royce alone was liable for the initial injury—here, damage to the engine. According to the jury, Apical's faulty flotation system later caused the loss of the helicopter. This intervening cause should not exonerate the initial tortfeasor in our case (Rolls-Royce) any more than it did in *Steptoe*. *Cf. id.* As PHI argued in Indiana federal court: "[W]hen an engine fails in flight, it is reasonably foreseeable that the helicopter could be lost." Though Rolls-Royce and Apical may not be solidarily liable for the entire debt (as Apical shares no liability for the engine damage), they may be solidarily liable for the portion of PHI's damages that they may have co-extensively caused—the loss of the helicopter due to salt water incursion. *See Yarbrough*, 616 So. 2d at 1335; *see also Glasgow v. PAR Minerals Corp.*, 70 So.3d 765, 772 (La. 2011) ("[P]arties are solidarily liable to the extent that they share coextensive liability to repair certain elements of the same damage." (quotation marks omitted)).

Thus, the magistrate judge erred as a matter of law in refusing to submit to the jury the question of Rolls-Royce's liability as a basis for reduction in the damages award against Apical.

---

[11] This principle—that obligors are solidary when they are obligated to repair the same damage—holds true in a variety of factual scenarios in Louisiana jurisprudence. For example, "[w]here the combined fault of a contractor and a manufacturer of materials results in a loss [i.e., the defective condition of a fireplace and chimney] for which each defendant would be liable for the whole, the defendants' liability may be solidary." *Reeves v. Dixie Brick, Inc.*, 403 So. 2d 792, 795 (La. Ct. App. 2d Cir. 1981). Similarly, car accident tortfeasors and medical malpractice tortfeasors may be held solidarily liable for a victim's death. *See Steptoe v. Lallie Kemp Hosp.*, 634 So. 2d 331, 335–36 (La. 1994). A check depositor and a depository bank may also be held solidarily liable where their combined acts resulted in the improper deposit of a restrictively endorsed check, even though the depositor and bank engaged in "separate acts of conversion." *Schulingkamp v. Carter*, 984 So. 2d 795, 799 (La. Ct. App. 1st Cir. 2008) *rev'd*, 992 So. 2d 973 (La. 2008). These examples further illustrate that the underlying test is whether co-obligors are co-extensively liable for the same debt, regardless of how each party's debt arose. *See Joiner v. Diamond M Drilling Co.*, 688 F.2d 256, 263 (5th Cir. 1982) (finding a vessel owner, manufacturer, and physician solidary liable despite the fact that "their obligations ar[o]se from different acts and for different reasons" because "they are each obligated for the same thing," i.e., the victim's death).

[12] Although *Steptoe* is a personal injury case, the solidary liability regime applicable here applied in that case because it preceded Louisiana's 1996 revision to convert to a pure comparative fault regime in tort cases.

III

Having determined the magistrate judge erred in concluding solidary liability could **{-779-}** not exist between Apical and Rolls-Royce, we must determine the remedy for this error. Apical seeks a full retrial as to its own liability **[—11—]** because the magistrate judge failed to include a jury question as to Rolls-Royce's liability.

The magistrate judge reversibly erred in failing to submit the question of Rolls-Royce's liability to the jury for purposes of determining its status as a solidary obligor. His resulting exclusion of evidence relevant to that question was also, therefore, erroneous. As Apical points out and we have previously concluded, Rolls-Royce may be a solidary obligor with respect to the loss of the helicopter, for which Apical is currently obligated to pay $1,729,770. This obligation is cut in half if Rolls-Royce is a solidary obligor, because Rolls-Royce and PHI have settled all claims between themselves in the Indiana action, which, under Louisiana law, results in a reduction in any damages award by half. *See* LA. CIV. CODE art. 1803, rev. cmt. (a), (b) (2019); *Osborne v. Ladner*, 691 So. 2d 1245, 1257 (La. Ct. App. 1st Cir. 1997) (reducing award by half against one of two solidary obligors in contract case to account for settlement of the other solidary obligor). And the question of solidary liability "is a mixed question of law and fact," *Jackson v. Rubicon, Inc.*, 844 So. 2d 394, 397 (La. Ct. App. 3d Cir. 2003), such that a jury finding on this issue is required, *see United States v. Gaudin*, 515 U.S. 506, 512 (1995) ("[T]he application-of-legal-standard-to-fact sort of question . . . , commonly called a 'mixed question of law and fact,' has typically been resolved by juries.").

We need not vacate the jury's finding of liability as to Apical to cure this error, however.[13] We need only require a trial on whether Rolls-Royce is also **[—12—]** responsible for the loss of the helicopter such that it is a solidary obligor, along with Apical, entitling Apical to a reduction in the amount of damages it owes to PHI. *See Taylor v. U.S. Fid. & Guar. Ins. Co.*, 630 So. 2d 237, 239 (La. 1993) (pointing out, in a pre-comparative fault tort case applying solidary liability regime when one party settled, that "the reduction applies only when the remaining defendants prove at trial that the released party was a joint tortfeasor and therefore solidarily liable"); *see also Carter v. EPSCO, Inc.*, 681 F.2d 1062, 1067 (5th Cir. 1982) (remanding for factual finding as to solidary liability where district court erroneously concluded that one potential co-obligor could not be solidarily liable as a matter of law); *Bank of New Orleans & Tr. Co. v. Monco Agency, Inc.*, 823 F.2d 888, 889 (5th Cir. 1987) (remanding for trial as to the liability of one of several potential solidary obligors where district court erroneously held prescription had run as to that potential obligor). In requiring a trial on this issue, we intimate no view on the merit of the parties' respective arguments except to the **{-780-}** extent set out herein, the evidence supporting such arguments, or any additional evidentiary or legal rulings the magistrate judge may deem necessary to pass upon on remand.

***

[13] Apical also argues that the exclusion of evidence pertaining to Rolls-Royce's liability also justified full retrial on Apical's own liability, because the jury was allegedly tainted by the lack of context and background that evidence about the cause of the engine failure would have provided. We reject this argument. The parties stipulated that the engine failed, and the cause for the engine's failure is not relevant to the Float System's functionality and purpose, about which the magistrate judge specifically allowed evidence. Accordingly, Apical cannot show reversible error as to its own liability. *See E.E.O.C. v. Manville Sales Corp.*, 27 F.3d 1089, 1093 (5th Cir. 1994) ("In order to vacate a judgment based on an error in an **[—12—]** evidentiary ruling, this court must find that the substantial rights of the parties were affected." (internal quotation marks omitted)); *Kelly v. Boeing Petroleum Services, Inc.*, 61 F.3d 350, 361 (5th Cir. 1995) ("An error does not affect substantial rights if the court is sure, after reviewing the entire record, that the error did not influence the jury or had but a very slight effect on its verdict." (internal quotation marks omitted)).

For these reasons, we VACATE in part and REMAND for further proceedings consistent with this opinion.

United States Court of Appeals for the Fifth Circuit

No. 19-40071

PSARA ENERGY, LTD.
VS.
ADVANTAGE ARROW SHIPPING, L.L.C.

Appeal from the United States District Court for the Eastern District of Texas

Decided: January 9, 2020

Citation: 946 F.3d 803, 8 Adm. R. 111 (5th Cir. 2020).

Before **KING, JONES,** and **DENNIS,** Circuit Judges.

[—2—] {-805-} JONES, Circuit Judge:

Plaintiff Psara Energy Limited appeals the district court's January 2019 Order granting a motion to refer to arbitration this suit filed against Defendant-Appellees, Advantage Arrow Shipping, LLC; Advantage Holdings, LLC; Advantage Tankers, LLC; and Forward Holdings, LLC, (collectively, "the Advantage Defendants" or "Advantage"). We DISMISS this appeal for lack of appellate jurisdiction because the district court's Order, which administratively closed the case, is not a final, appealable order either as we have construed the Federal Arbitration Act ("FAA") or under any other theory.

BACKGROUND

In 2010, Psara entered into a bareboat charter agreement with Defendant Space Shipping, Ltd. ("Space Shipping") to charter the vessel CV STEALTH.[1] Through an amendment to the charter party later that year, Geden Holdings, Ltd. ("Geden") was made the "performance guarantor" of Space Shipping.

In 2014, the CV STEALTH was detained in Venezuela for more than three years by prosecutorial authorities, and Space Shipping failed to return the ship by the latest contractual redelivery date of June 22, 2015. When the CV STEALTH was finally released from Venezuela, it was out-of-class and so **[—3—]** extensively damaged due to neglect that it was incapable of sailing and in need of extensive repairs. Space Shipping towed the CV STEALTH to Trinidad where Psara took possession on March 24, 2018. She was sold as scrap. As a result of the damage, Psara initiated a London maritime arbitration claim against Space Shipping and Geden for damages equivalent to the repaired market value of the ship ($18,000,000.00) and amounts for unpaid charter hire, legal costs, interest, and other costs (an additional $1,860,063.80).

Shortly after the contractual redelivery date but before it commenced arbitration, Psara discovered that Geden Holdings had transferred its entire fleet of vessels to other corporate entities (including the Advantage Defendants). Based on the transfer of the fleet, Psara brought the instant suit in April 2018 against Space Shipping, Geden, and the Advantage Defendants alleging **{-806-}** breach of contract, fraudulent transfer and corporate succession theories. In conjunction with its lawsuit, Psara sought and obtained a maritime attachment against the ADVANTAGE ARROW, one of the defendants' vessels found within the Eastern District of Texas. Psara obtained similar relief against the MV ADVANTAGE START in the Eastern District of Louisiana. The Louisiana case was transferred to the Eastern District of Texas under 28 U.S.C. § 1404(a) and consolidated with Psara's case pending there.

The Advantage Defendants' motions under Supplemental Admiralty Rule E(4)(f) to vacate

---

[1] The Bareboat Charter agreement also included a provision that:

> (a) This Contract shall be governed by and construed in accordance with English law and any dispute arising out of or in connection with this Contract shall be referred to arbitration in London in accordance with the Arbitration Act 1996 or any statutory modification or re-enactment thereof save to the extent necessary to give effect to the provisions of the Clause.

The charter party refers "any dispute arising out of or in connection with the Contract" to arbitration in London, England.

the respective attachments were rejected, but the vessels were released upon the posting of substitute security.[2] In the case of the ADVANTAGE ARROW, the district court's order stated, "[t]he court will address the 'Motion to Vacate Attachment' at a later time." **[—4—]**

In June 2018, the Advantage Defendants moved for referral to arbitration in London on the basis that Psara's claims all arise from the charter party between Psara and Space Shipping, which contains a valid and enforceable arbitration clause. The Advantage Defendants contended that they should be included in Psara's ongoing arbitration proceedings against Space Shipping because Psara claims that the Advantage Defendants are a successor to Space Shipping and therefore liable for Psara's losses under the charter party. As Psara points out, however, the Advantage Defendants are non-signatories to the charter party and should not normally benefit from its arbitration provision. *Al Rushaid v. Nat'l Oilwell Varco, Inc.*, 814 F.3d 300, 305 (5th Cir. 2016) (describing limited theories of nonsignatory participation in arbitrations).

The district court granted the motion to refer to arbitration. The court found that the Advantage Defendants invoked the intertwined claims rule because without the underlying charter party and performance guarantee, Psara has no claims against the Advantage Defendants. Moreover, Psara cannot be permitted to sue the Advantage Defendants for contractual claims while insisting they are not entitled to the benefit of the arbitration clause in those underlying agreements. The district court further held that, while the dispute is being arbitrated, the Rule B attachments (for the vessels ARROW and START) remain in effect with posted security for Psara's potential arbitral award pursuant to the district court's jurisdiction under Sections 8 and 207 of the FAA. The district court then "administratively closed" the case, denied pending motions as moot, and retained jurisdiction to enforce any arbitration award. **[—5—]**

Months later, the district court denied Psara's motion to stay the referral to arbitration pending appeal, and this court denied an identical motion. Psara timely appealed.

DISCUSSION

A preliminary, and here dispositive, issue is whether the district court's order referring the suit to arbitration and administratively closing the case constitutes an appealable order. "If not, then this Court lacks jurisdiction and the appeal should be dismissed, which would pretermit any consideration of the merits of [the Appellant's] appeal." *Mire v. Full Spectrum Lending, Inc.*, 389 F.3d 163, 165 (5th Cir. 2004).

The Advantage Defendants question our appellate jurisdiction, and Psara responds that either the district court's order compelling **{-807-}** arbitration is final and appealable under 9 U.S.C. § 16(a)(3), or it is appeable pursuant to the collateral order doctrine. We discuss each theory in turn.

Psara's first theory turns on whether the district court's order is final. Section 16 of the FAA "governs appellate review of arbitration orders." *Apache Bohai Corp., LDC v. Texaco China, B.V.*, 330 F.3d 307, 309 (5th Cir. 2003). The statute accomplishes Congress's intent to favor arbitration "by authorizing immediate appeals from orders disfavoring arbitration and forbidding immediate appeals from orders favoring arbitration." *S. La. Cement, Inc. v. Van Aalst Bulk Handling, B.V.*, 383 F.3d 297, 300 (5th Cir. 2004). Thus, 9 U.S.C. § 16(a)(3) permits appeals taken from "a final decision with respect to an arbitration that is subject to this title," but § 16(b)(3) explicitly denies appellate jurisdiction over *nonfinal* orders "compelling arbitration under section 206." *See also S. La. Cement*, 383 F.3d at 300.

The Supreme Court has explained that a "final decision with respect to an arbitration" means "a decision that ends the litigation on

[2] The ADVANTAGE ARROW was secured for the amount of $4,000,000 and the ADVANTAGE START was secured for $800,000. After transfer, the total amount of substitute security for the vessels stands at $4,800,000.

the merits and **[—6—]** leaves nothing more for the court to do but execute the judgment." *Green Tree Fin. Corp.–Ala. v. Randolph*, 531 U.S. 79, 86 (2000) (quoting *Dig. Equip. Corp. v. Desktop Direct, Inc.*, 511 U.S. 863, 867 (1994). In *Green Tree*, because the district court "ordered the parties to proceed to arbitration, and dismissed all the claims before it," the order constituted a final, appealable decision. *Id.* at 89. Crucially, the Supreme Court went on to state that "[h]ad the District Court entered a stay instead of a dismissal in this case, that order would not be appealable." *Id.* at 87 n.2; *see also Mire*, 389 F.3d at 165.

Acknowledging the dichotomy expressed in *Green Tree*, this Circuit has repeatedly held that "[a]n arbitration order entering a stay, as opposed to a dismissal, is not an appealable final order." *S. La. Cement*, 383 F.3d at 300; *see also Apache*, 330 F.3d at 309 ("An arbitration order entering a stay, as opposed to a dismissal, is not an appealable final order."); *Cargill Ferrous Int'l v. SEA PHOENIX MV*, 325 F.3d 695, 697, 701–02 (5th Cir.2003) (dismissing for lack of appellate jurisdiction because the stay pending arbitration was not "a final judgment by the district court"). Nearly on point with this case, the court held in *Mire* that administratively closing a case "is the functional equivalent of a stay" and "thus not an appealable order under the FAA." *Mire*, 389 F.3d at 167. This is because the entry of a stay, as opposed to a dismissal, indicates that "the district court perceives that it might have more to do than execute the judgement once arbitration has been completed." *Apache*, 330 F.3d at 309 (quoting *ATAC Corp. v. Arthur Treacher's Inc.*, 280 F.3d 1091, 1099 (6th Cir. 2002)).

In contrast, "[a] district court order that compels arbitration and dismisses or closes a case outright possesses finality and confers jurisdiction on this court." *Sw. Elec. Power Co. v. Certain Underwriters at Lloyds of London*, 772 F.3d 384, 387 (5th Cir. 2014); *see also Am. Heritage Life Ins. Co.* **[—7—]** *v. Orr*, 294 F.3d 702, 707–08 (5th Cir. 2002) (holding an order final and appealable that "closed" the case; the only claim before the court was one seeking to compel arbitration, hence there was "no practical distinction between 'dismiss' and 'close' for the purposes of [that] appeal").

The district court here adopted the magistrate judge's report and recommendation ("R&R"), "granting the [referral to arbitration], directing the parties to arbitration, and staying the case pending **{–808–}** resolution of the arbitrable issues" in London. The district court then ordered the case "administratively closed" and retained jurisdiction to enforce any arbitration award. By adopting the R&R, the district court stayed the case, and by ordering administrative closure, it provided itself an additional safe harbor from the district courts' periodic reporting conditions. Moreover, this case commenced not as a suit simply to compel arbitration pursuant to the FAA, but to obtain relief against the defendants for, *inter alia*, breach of the charter party agreements and fraudulent transfer of assets. It is not inconceivable in such a situation that, although the defendants prevailed on a claim seeking arbitration, some aspects of the case might not be resolved in the arbitral forum, and the district court would have to reopen the case for purposes other than to enforce the arbitral award. The court's order aligns with "our case law [that] has developed clear distinction between final orders dismissing cases after compelling arbitration and interlocutory orders staying and administratively closing cases pending arbitration." *Sw. Electric*, 772 F.3d at 387. "The effect of an administrative closure is no different from a simple stay," which district courts often use "to remove from their pending cases suits which are temporarily active elsewhere (such as before an arbitration panel) or stayed (such as where a bankruptcy is pending)." *Mire*, 389 F.3d at 167. The court's order staying and **[—8—]** administratively closing the case pending arbitration was nonfinal for purposes of appellate review.

As an alternative ground for jurisdiction, Psara does not argue that its appeal satisfies the standards of 28 U.S.C. § 1292(b), which renders only some interlocutory orders appealable. Instead, Psara contends that the collateral order doctrine, an exception to the statute, authorizes appellate jurisdiction over interlocutory appeals from orders compelling arbitration. We rejected this argument in *Al Rushaid,* following the Supreme Court's admonition that, as a "narrow exception" to finality provisions, the collateral order doctrine should "never be allowed to swallow the general rule." *Dig. Equip. Corp.*, 511 U.S. at 868. Plainly, "[s]ection 16 provides a specific framework for determining whether and when an appeal is proper, and we will not interfere with the statutory design." *Al Rushaid,* 814 F.3d at 304. Every other circuit has reached the same outcome on this issue. *See Johnson v. Consumerinfo.com, Inc.*, 745 F.3d 1019, 1022 (9th Cir. 2014); *ConArt, Inc. v. Hellmuth, Obata + Kassabaum, Inc.*, 504 F.3d 1208, 1211 (11th Cir. 2007); *ATAC Corp.*, 280 F.3d at 1101–02.

Against this conclusion, Psara draws our attention to two cases, *Atl. Fertilizer & Chem. Corp. v. Italmare, S.p.A. of Ravenna*, 117 F.3d 266 (5th Cir. 1997) and *Heidmar, Inc. v. Anomina Ravennate di Armamento Sp.A*, 132 F.3d 264 (5th Cir. 1998). Neither case, however, applied the collateral order doctrine to authorize appellate review of interlocutory orders compelling arbitration, nor did either case consider the interaction between the clear statutory directive in FAA § 16(b) and the collateral order doctrine. *Atlantic Fertilizer* dealt with the district court's summary denial of a request for counter-security in light of a pending arbitration. 117 F.3d at 269. In *Heidmar,* the appellate court reviewed, pursuant to the collateral order **[—9—]** doctrine, an order vacating attachment pending arbitration because conducting appellate review of the order at a later date "would be an empty rite after the vessel had been released and the restoration of the attachment only theoretically possible." 132 F.3d at 267 (quoting *Swift & Co. Packers v. Compania Colombiana Del Caribe, S.A.*, 339 U.S. 684, 689 (1950)). But in this case, Psara has the security it sought because "the Rule B **{-809-}** attachment still remains in effect in this court and applies as valid security for the claim," and the district court held than any arbitral award "could come from the Rule B attachment."

Finally, we are obliged to consider whether appellate jurisdiction exists over the order compelling arbitration under 28 U.S.C. § 1292(a)(3), which confers jurisdiction over "[i]nterlocutory decrees of such district courts or the judges thereof determining the rights and liabilities of the parties to admiralty cases in which appeals from final decrees are allowed." We hold this avenue is also closed to Psara.

In reaching this conclusion, we adopt the reasoning provided in dicta from a previous unpublished decision, *Bordelon Marine, L.L.C. v. Bibby Subsea Rov, L.L.C.*, 685 F. App'x. 330 (5th Cir. 2017). In *Bordelon,* this court considered whether to exercise jurisdiction over the district court's denial of the appellant's motion to re-open to enforce the method of selecting arbitrators. The court held that Appellant waived his argument under § 1292(a)(3) because it was raised for the first time at oral argument. *Id.* at 335. Nevertheless, the court explained in a footnote that the appellant's argument was unavailing even if it had not been forfeited. *Id.* at 335 n.5. The court reasoned that compelling arbitration and determining the appointment of arbitrators "was not a determination of the rights and liabilities of the parties; rather, it merely settled 'how and where the rights and liabilities would be determined.'" *Id.* **[—10—]** (quoting *In re Ingram Towing Co.*, 59 F.3d 513, 517 (5th Cir. 1995)). We agree with that reasoning and find it equally applicable here.

This holding is consistent with our precedent limiting the applicability of § 1292(a)(3) to orders determining the parties' substantive rights and liabilities. These cases take a strict view of the statute's language about "determining the rights and liabilities." *See, e.g., Celtic Marine Corp. v. James C. Justice Cos., Inc.*, 760 F.3d 477, 480–81, 2 Adm. R. 288, 289–90 (5th Cir. 2014) (finding jurisdiction to review the district court's grant of summary judgment but not jurisdiction to review a Rule 60(b) order); *In re Ingram Towing Co.*, 59 F.3d 513, 517 (5th Cir. 1995) ("Orders which do not determine parties' substantive rights or liabilities . . . are not appealable under section 1292(a)(3) even if those orders have important procedural consequences." (quoting *Francis v. Forest Oil Corp.*, 798 F.2d 147, 150 (5th Cir. 1986))); *In re Patton–Tully Transp. Co.*, 715 F.2d 219, 222 (5th Cir. 1983) (holding that the appealed order must "finally determine the rights or liabilities of either party to this dispute"); *MS Tabea Schiffahrtsgesellschaft MBH & Co. KG v. Bd. of Comm'rs of Port of New Orleans*, 636 F.3d 161, 165 (5th Cir. 2011).

The district court's order to stay and administratively close Psara's case is not a final order for purposes of FAA § 16(a)(3); the collateral order doctrine does not apply to orders concerning arbitration governed by the FAA; and § 1292(a)(3) is inapplicable to referrals to arbitration in admiralty cases that do not determine a party's substantive rights or liabilities. Consequently, this court lacks jurisdiction to review this appeal and does not reach the merits of Psara's other issues.

CONCLUSION

For the foregoing reasons, the appeal is **DISMISSED**.

United States Court of Appeals
for the Fifth Circuit

No. 18-31115

BP EXPLORATION & PROD., INC.
VS.
CLAIMANT ID 100354107

Appeal from the United States District Court for the Eastern District of Louisiana

Decided: January 14, 2020

Citation: 947 F.3d 295, 8 Adm. R. 116 (5th Cir. 2020).

Before **SOUTHWICK, GRAVES,** and **ENGELHARDT,** Circuit Judges.

[—1—] {-296-} SOUTHWICK, Circuit Judge:

In these consolidated cases, BP appeals the district court's denial of discretionary review of five awards made to Walmart under the Settlement Agreement arising from the 2010 Deepwater Horizon disaster. The arguments before us arise from the change in accounting systems Walmart adopted in May 2010. We AFFIRM. **[—2—]**

FACTUAL AND PROCEDURAL BACKGROUND

On April 20, 2010, an explosion and fire caused the collapse of the Deepwater Horizon drilling rig in the Gulf of Mexico. Among other effects of that disaster was an enormous release of oil into the Gulf. In time, a Settlement Agreement was negotiated between BP, which was leasing the rig at the time of the disaster, and class-action representatives for those who claimed damage from the disaster. In that agreement were provisions for business economic loss ("BEL") claims. Such claims are initially decided by a Claims Administrator as part of a Court Supervised Settlement Program ("CSSP"). PricewaterhouseCoopers ("PWC") is one of the accounting firms that perform initial analysis of the claims for the Claims Administrator. **{-297-}**

The current appeal concerns BP's challenge to BEL awards made to Wal-Mart Stores East, L.P. The arguments center on the fact that Walmart changed its accounting system in May 2010, the month after the Deepwater Horizon explosion, which BP argues resulted in artificially inflated award amounts. The accounting change complicated the review of Walmart's BEL claims, which depend in part on showing expenses both before and after the disaster.

In June 2015, Walmart submitted a separate BEL claim to the Claims Administrator for each of Walmart's nine stores along the Gulf Coast. Only five of the claims are at issue here. Each of the five claims was the basis for a separate appeal from BP to this court. The five appeals were consolidated for decision by this panel. In April 2017, Walmart submitted supplemental documentation to the Claims Administrator for each claim. This documentation included a notification to the Claims Administrator that Walmart had changed its accounting system. In these submissions, Walmart sought to reconcile the differences between the two accounting systems. **[—3—]**

The Claims Administrator reviewed Walmart's claims with the assistance of PWC accountants. In July and December 2017, PWC and Walmart exchanged emails discussing the changes in Walmart's accounting system. The Claims Administrator's calculation notes give some indication that Walmart's explanations were considered. In February 2018, the Claims Administrator issued awards totaling just over $17.4 million.

BP appealed each of the CSSP's five awards, arguing that Walmart's accounting system change made its profit and loss data for the pre-May 2010 period inconsistent with the same data in the subsequent period. BP identified three accounts that had been treated differently in the pre-May 2010 accounting system than the post-May 2010 accounting system. Specifically, BP noted that "Tires" and "Trailer Parts" were categorized as fixed costs in the pre-May 2010 accounting system, but those two categories did not appear in the post-May 2010 accounting system. A new category, "Trailer Tires," had appeared, though, labeled as a variable cost.

According to BP's argument to the Appeal Panels, the result was that, at least for these accounts, Walmart's change in accounting systems caused the pre-disaster period to appear more profitable in comparison to the later period than it really was, thus artificially inflating Walmart's awards. Without stating a position as to whether the three specific accounts were handled appropriately, Walmart in its proposals to the five Appeal Panels agreed to treat all three accounts as variable.

Each of the five Appeal Panels selected Walmart's proposal for the final award amount. Regarding BP's claims that Walmart's change in accounting system skewed the calculations, the Appeal Panels addressed the matter to varying degrees. One Appeal Panel expressly concluded that the CSSP adequately addressed the changes, and all the Appeal Panels concluded that the amount in question BP had identified was minimal and that Walmart's **[—4—]** treatment of the three identified expense accounts as variable across time periods was adequate.

After the variable adjustment in addition to an agreed-upon downward adjustment not relevant here, the final total award amount was just over $15 million. The district court later denied BP's request for discretionary review. This appeal followed.

DISCUSSION

The issue before us is whether we should reverse the district court for **{-298-}** refusing to review the final awards for the five claims. This court applies an abuse-of-discretion standard to the district court's refusal to review a final award under the Settlement Program. *Claimant ID 100212278 v. BP Expl. & Prod., Inc.*, 848 F.3d 407, 410, 5 Adm. R. 202, 203 (5th Cir. 2017). That standard of review requires us to decide whether the final award "actually contradicted or misapplied the Settlement Agreement or had the clear potential to contradict or misapply the Settlement Agreement." *Id.*, 5 Adm. R. at 203 (punctuation edited) (quoting *Holmes Motors, Inc. v. BP Expl. & Prod., Inc.*, 829 F.3d 313, 315, 4 Adm. R. 263, 263 (5th Cir. 2016)). "It may [also] be an abuse of discretion to deny a request for review that raises a recurring issue on which the Appeal Panels are split if the resolution of the question will substantially impact the administration of the Agreement." *Id.*, 5 Adm. R. at 203 (quotation marks omitted).

On the other hand, the district court does not abuse its discretion if it denies a request for review that "involves no pressing question of how the Settlement Agreement should be interpreted and implemented, but simply raises the correctness of a discretionary administrative decision in the facts of a single claimant's case." *BP Expl. & Prod., Inc. v. Claimant ID 100094497 (Texas Gulf Seafood)*, 910 F.3d 797, 800, 6 Adm. R. 273, 274 (5th Cir. 2018). **[—5—]**

To decide whether the district court's refusal to review these final awards should be reversed, we must understand both how BEL claims under the Deepwater Horizon Settlement Agreement are to be processed, and whether the claims before us now resulted from a misapplication or contradiction of those requirements. Claimants must provide evidence to allow the CSSP to compare the actual profits of a business during a claimant-selected pre-disaster period ("Benchmark Period") to the profit that the claimant might have expected to earn in the comparable post-disaster period ("Compensation Period"). The Benchmark Period is the "time period which [a] claimant chooses as the baseline for measuring its historical financial performance." For the Benchmark Period, a claimant may choose "2009; the average of 2008–2009; or the average of 2007–2009." The Compensation Period is the time period after the calamity "selected by the Claimant to include three or more consecutive months between May and December 2010." Awards are calculated by adding together two compensation amounts, calculated in "Step 1" and "Step 2," and then multiplying the sum by an agreed upon "Risk Transfer Premium."

Step 1 Compensation is the difference between Benchmark Period Variable Profit and Compensation Period Variable Profit.

Variable Profit, in turn, is the sum of monthly revenue over the relevant period minus variable costs identified in Attachment A to the Settlement Agreement, the variable portion of salaries, and the variable portion of Costs of Goods Sold, for that respective period. Attachment A contains a list of "Variable Costs," which are used to calculate Variable Profit, as well as a list of "Fixed Costs," which are not used to calculate Variable Profit. Thus, whether a cost is defined as "Variable" or "Fixed" alters the size of the award. Step 1 Compensation reflects a claimant's reduction in Variable Profit (revenue minus variable costs) from the Benchmark Period to the Compensation Period. **[—6—]**

Step 2 of the calculation is "intended to compensate claimants for incremental profits the claimant might have been expected to generate in 2010 in the absence of the spill, based on the claimant's growth in revenue in January–April 2010 relative to the claimant-selected Benchmark Period." Step 2 Compensation is not at issue here. **{-299-}**

Once Step 1 and Step 2 Compensation are determined, they are added together, and then the agreed-upon "Risk Transfer Premium" is applied to determine the total award. The Claims Administrator makes these calculations to determine the final compensation award. Either party, the Claimant or BP, may appeal the Claims Administrator's final award determination to a CSSP Appeal Panel. Then, the Claimant or BP can request discretionary review from the district court.

Walmart supported its BEL claims with two sets of financial statements. First were financial statements from the pre-May 2010 accounting system, which covered Walmart's Benchmark Period of 2007 through 2009 as well as January through April 2010. Second, it included financial statements from the post-May 2010 accounting system, which covered May through December 2010, the remaining eight months of Walmart's Compensation Period. In a memorandum accompanying these submissions, Walmart explained the reconciliation of what it describes as "several dozen" accounts between the pre-May 2010 financial statements and the post-May 2010 financial statements. For variable costs, Walmart noted that "there is greater granularity in the ledger categories in the May–December 2010 financials." By that, Walmart meant "there are additional ledger categories included in the May–December 2010 Financials that are relevant to the compensation calculation."

BP argues that the district court's refusal to review these awards should be reversed because that court's denial of review failed both parts of our review **[—7—]** standard: the Appeal Panels contradicted or misapplied the Settlement Agreement, and there is a split in Appeal Panels on how to address a change in accounting systems when calculating compensation. We consider the arguments separately.

I. Contradiction or misapplication of Settlement Agreement

In its first argument, BP relies on a decision in which we held that the Settlement Agreement required "claims administrators to use their independent judgment and classify expenses as 'fixed' or 'variable' according to their substantive nature, rather than rational basis review of the claimants' own descriptions." *Texas Gulf Seafood*, 910 F.3d at 802, 6 Adm. R. at 276. In that precedent, we vacated the district court's denial of BP's request for discretionary review and remanded for further proceedings. *See id.* at 803, 6 Adm. R. at 276–77. That claimant conceded it had misclassified certain costs as fixed when those costs should have been classified as variable, but the claimant argued the Appeal Panel had correctly evaluated the claimant's categorizations under a rational-basis standard and thus had correctly accepted such categorizations. *Id.* at 801, 6 Adm. R. at 275. We characterized the claimant's argument as one "for a claims regime that essentially takes claimants at their word and classifies items as they request." *Id.*, 6 Adm. R. at 275. We concluded that "such an approach would lead to absurd results, in which the CSSP could find itself classifying identical costs enumerated in [Attachment A] as fixed in one claim and variable in another, depending on each claimant's choice." *Id.*, 6 Adm. R. at 275.

BP argues that our reasoning in *Texas Gulf Seafood* means a claimant who changed its accounting system during the relevant time period, like Walmart did, must provide a comprehensive map detailing how each expense was categorized before and after the change. BP argues that Walmart's change in classification of expenses regarding "Tires," "Trailer Parts," and "Trailer **[—8—]** Tires" is exemplary of the kind of changes that took place. Further, without exhaustive information regarding every expense account, BP argues that neither it nor those involved with evaluating **{-300-}** Walmart's claim can know whether there were other relevant changes in classification.

Walmart responds that by providing the supplemental information and reconciliation memorandum to the Claims Administrator, it provided the information necessary for the change in its accounting system to be factored into the calculations. Further, the Claims Administrator took the change into account in making the awards. Walmart also refers us to the Claims Administrator's calculation notes, which indicate awareness of the change in accounting system and that the accounts had been reconciled across systems and time periods as necessary. Further evidence is in Walmart's email exchanges with PWC in which those accountants asked for explanations of certain account changes between the old and new accounting systems. Admitting to the "Tires," "Trailer Parts," and "Trailer Tires" discrepancy, which Walmart asserts it properly resolved before the Appeal Panels by treating the expenses as variable throughout, Walmart argues BP has not identified any other discrepancies even after having access to Walmart's financial statements.

BP is correct that Walmart controlled the information it provided to the Claims Administrator and Appeal Panels. BP argues this information should have been more exhaustive. Nevertheless, BP has not shown that the Claims Administrator or any Appeal Panel contradicted or misapplied the Settlement Agreement, or that there was a clear potential for such contradiction or misapplication. As far as this record shows, the Claims Administrator conducted a searching review of the financial statements Walmart provided from both its old and new accounting system, and the PWC accountants **[—9—]** brought specific clarification questions to Walmart regarding the changes. Walmart responded to the satisfaction of the Claims Administrator. The Appeal Panels considered the parties' positions and concluded that BP had not shown sufficient evidence to warrant remand to the Claims Administrator and that the effect of any identified discrepancy was minimal.

There was not a showing of a misapplication or contradiction of the Settlement Agreement requiring the district court's review.

II. Split among Appeal Panels

BP also insists there is a split among Appeal Panels on how to address changes in accounting systems like the one at issue here. On one side of the supposed split, BP places two of the five Appeal Panels' decisions at issue here regarding Walmart's change in accounting system, and also one other Appeal Panel decision of which the district court denied BP's request for discretionary review. On the other side of the supposed split, BP places one Appeal Panel decision that remanded a claim to the CSSP after the claimant had shown that, due to a change in the claimant's accounting system, certain accounts were incorrectly classified as variable costs for the Benchmark Period but were correctly classified as fixed costs for the Compensation Period.

Walmart responds that the one Appeal Panel BP has identified, which remanded to the CSSP, was presented with a specific list of 27 accounts that had been classified differently, and from that the Appeal Panel determined that there was sufficient doubt regarding appropriate classification of accounts to justify remand. Walmart argues the Appeal Panel there was presented with specific instances of misclassifications, while the Appeal Panels here were only presented with potential inconsistences. **[—10—]**

BP replies that the only reason the Appeal Panel was presented with a specific **{-301-}** list of misclassified accounts was that it was the claimant there, not BP, who appealed the CSSP's award determination. The claimant had access to the information necessary to show specific inconsistencies. Here, BP argues, it could not possibly have identified specific misclassifications because it did not have the information necessary to do so. For BP to identify misclassifications, it argues, Walmart was required to provide a comprehensive map describing how each expense classified in Walmart's pre-May 2010 accounting system was classified in its post-May 2010 accounting system.

Although we are sympathetic, we are unconvinced by BP's pleas for more information. Before us is an exercise of judgment, not only by the district court but also by Appeal Panels and the Claims Administrator in deciding when there is enough evidence under the terms of the Settlement Agreement to make an award. In the single Appeal Panel decision that has created BP's purported split, there was extensive evidence that there had been misclassifications that significantly altered the award amount and ordered remand to address the changes. Here, BP is unsatisfied with the amount of information Walmart provided to the Claims Administrator and how extensively the Claims Administrator and its accountants investigated the accounting system change. We see this as a challenge to the Appeal Panels' decisions that "simply raises the correctness of a discretionary administrative decision in the facts of a single claimant's case." *Texas Gulf Seafood*, 910 F.3d at 800, 6 Adm. R. at 274.

The district court's denial of a request for discretionary review of such a decision is not an abuse of discretion. AFFIRMED.

United States Court of Appeals
for the Fifth Circuit

No. 19-30213

STATE OF LOUISIANA
VS.
UNITED STATES

Appeal from the United States District Court for the Western District of Louisiana

Decided: January 21, 2020

Citation: 948 F.3d 317, 8 Adm. R. 121 (5th Cir. 2020).

Before **DAVIS**, **SMITH**, and **COSTA**, Circuit Judges.

[—1—] {-318-} **DAVIS**, Circuit Judge: **{-319-}**

The State of Louisiana sued the United States for injunctive relief alleging that the United States Army Corps of Engineers ("Corps") has failed to maintain the Gulf Intracoastal Waterway in compliance with the River and Harbor Improvements Act. The State asserts that the United States has waived its sovereign immunity for such a claim under the Administrative Procedure Act ("APA"), specifically 5 U.S.C. § 702, because the State has been "adversely affected or aggrieved by agency action within the meaning of a relevant statute." We conclude that the State fails to satisfy the requirements for the waiver of sovereign immunity under § 702 in that it does not challenge "agency action" and the State's alleged injury does not fall within the "zone of **[—2—]** interests" of the River and Harbor Improvements Act. We additionally hold that the State's "failure to act" claim is not subject to judicial review under the APA because the Corps is not legally required to preserve and/or maintain the Gulf Intracoastal Waterway at a certain width. Therefore, we AFFIRM the district court's judgment dismissing the State's complaint under Rule 12(b)(1) for lack of subject matter jurisdiction.

I. Background

In 1925 the United States Congress enacted the River and Harbor Improvements Act ("Act"), which authorized the construction of the Gulf Intracoastal Waterway ("Waterway"), 100 feet in width, from New Orleans to Galveston.[1] In 1942 Congress expanded the authorized width of the Waterway to 125 feet.[2] The United States, in furtherance of the Act's mandate, entered into a servitude agreement with Louisiana landowners, obtaining a servitude limited to 300 feet in width affecting property in Vermilion Parish. The State later acquired property known as White Lake Wetlands Conservation Area ("White Lake Property") in Vermilion Parish. The United States' servitude runs across a portion of the White Lake Property.

In its complaint,[3] the State alleges that the Corps has failed to confine the Waterway to the parcel of ground upon which it holds its servitude and that the Waterway now extends onto land owned by the State. The State asserts that jurisdiction is proper under § 702 of the APA because the loss of **[—3—]** its property "aris[es] from inaction on the part of the [Corps]" and a "continuing failure to act to rectify the physical encroachment **{-320-}** in violation of Defendant's legal duties owed to Plaintiff." The State also asserts that jurisdiction is proper under § 702 because it "is not seeking monetary damages, rather injunctive relief." The State requests an injunction requiring abatement and removal of the encroachment, as well as restoration of the property to its prior condition.

In response to the State's complaint, the United States filed a motion to dismiss for

---

[1] River & Harbor Improvements Act of 1925, Pub. L. No. 68-585, ch. 467, 43 Stat. 1186, 1187; H.R. Rep. No. 1122 (1925).

[2] Pub. L. No. 77-675, ch. 520, 56 Stat. 703, 703 (1942).

[3] The State's initial complaint asserted a claim against the United States under the Federal Tort Claims Act ("FTCA"). In response to the United States' motion to dismiss asserting that it had not waived its sovereign immunity under the FTCA, the State requested leave to amend its complaint to set forth claims under the Little Tucker Act and the APA. The district court granted the State leave to amend and denied the United States' motion to dismiss without prejudice to re-urge the motion later. In its amended complaint, at issue in this appeal, the State asserts a claim against the United States under the APA only.

lack of subject matter jurisdiction under Rule 12(b)(1) based on its sovereign immunity. The United States asserted that in the absence of a waiver of its sovereign immunity, the district court lacked subject matter jurisdiction over a claim against it. The United States argued that although the APA provides a limited waiver of its sovereign immunity, express exceptions to the waiver found in § 704 of the APA deprived the district court of subject matter jurisdiction. Specifically, the United States contended that the State has an adequate remedy for an alleged breach of the servitude agreement under the Tucker Act in the Court of Federal Claims. The United States further argued that there has been no "final" agency action by the Corps.

The State responded by asserting that § 702 of the APA waives the United States' sovereign immunity where a person is "adversely affected or aggrieved by agency action within the meaning of a relevant statute" and seeks nonmonetary relief. The State argued that under that provision of the § 702 waiver, there is no requirement of "finality." It further contended that its claim arises from a "relevant statute," the River and Harbor Improvements Act ("Act") and its amendments, which allocated funds for and authorized the construction and maintenance of the Waterway. The State further contended that the Corps has failed to act on its responsibility to maintain the Waterway within the agreed-to and authorized parameters. **[—4—]**

In reply, the United States argued that neither the Act nor its amendments provide the State with any statutory cause of action. The United States additionally asserted that neither the Act nor its amendments impose any affirmative obligation on the Corps with regard to the width of the Waterway. Furthermore, the United States contended that the State's interest did not fall within the "zone of interests" of the Act or its amendments. The United States finally maintained that "failure to act" claims implicate § 706(1) of the APA which provides that the "reviewing court shall . . . compel agency action unlawfully withheld or unreasonably delayed." The United States asserted that because there is no statute or regulation requiring the Corps to maintain the Waterway as requested by the State, then it cannot be compelled to do so, and its sovereign immunity has not been waived under the APA.

The magistrate judge issued a report recommending that the United States' motion be granted. Over the State's objection, the district court adopted the report and recommendation and dismissed the State's complaint for lack of subject matter jurisdiction pursuant to Rule 12(b)(1). The State timely appealed.

II. DISCUSSION

This court reviews a district court's Rule 12(b)(1) dismissal for lack of subject matter jurisdiction de novo.[4] "Whether the United States is entitled to sovereign immunity is a question of law which this court reviews de novo."[5] The **{-321-}** State contends that the United States has waived its sovereign immunity in this matter under § 702 of the APA. Section 702 of the APA "waives sovereign immunity for actions against federal government agencies, seeking **[—5—]** nonmonetary relief, if the agency conduct is otherwise subject to judicial review."[6] Section 702, entitled "Right of review," provides:

> A person [1] suffering legal wrong because of agency action, or [2] adversely affected or aggrieved by agency action within the meaning of a relevant statute, is entitled to judicial review thereof. An action in a court of the United States seeking relief other than money damages and stating a claim that an agency or an officer or employee thereof acted or failed to act in an official capacity or under color of legal authority shall not be dismissed . . . on the ground that it is against the United States . . . .[7]

---

4 *Alabama-Coushatta Tribe of Tex. v. United States*, 757 F.3d 484, 487 (5th Cir. 2014).

5 *Id.* at 488.

6 *Id.*

7 5 U.S.C. § 702.

As explained by the Supreme Court in *Lujan v. National Wildlife Federation*,[8] § 702 of the APA contains two separate requirements. First, the person claiming a right to sue must identify some "agency action."[9] As defined by § 551(13) of the APA, "agency action" includes "an agency rule, order, license, sanction, relief, or the equivalent or denial thereof, or failure to act."[10] Second, the party seeking review under § 702 must show that he has suffered legal wrong because of the challenged agency action or that he has been "adversely affected or aggrieved" by the challenged agency action "within the meaning of a relevant statute."[11] The *Lujan* Court explained that "to be 'adversely affected or aggrieved . . . within the meaning' of a statute, the plaintiff must establish that the injury he complains of . . . falls within the 'zone of interests' sought to be protected by the statutory provision whose violation forms the legal basis for his complaint."[12] **[—6—]**

As to the first requirement, the State fails to point to any identifiable "agency action" within the meaning of § 702. The State contends that the Corps "has failed to maintain, preserve, and repair the Waterway so as to not infringe on Louisiana's property rights." As noted by one of our sister circuits, however, the term "action" as used in the APA "is a term of art that does not include all conduct such as, for example, constructing a building, operating a program, or performing a contract."[13] Moreover, the agency action being challenged must be "circumscribed [and] discrete."[14] As this court has noted, in interpreting the APA, *Lujan* "announced a prohibition on programmatic challenges—challenges that seek wholesale improvement of an agency's programs by court decree, rather than through Congress or the agency itself where such changes are normally made."[15] **{–322–}**

The State's allegations focus on decades of inaction by the Corps in failing to keep the Waterway from expanding beyond the width authorized by Congress in 1942. The State's "complaint fails to point to any identifiable action or event."[16] Consequently, the State has not satisfied the first requirement under § 702 of identifying specific agency action and, thus, fails to establish the United States has waived its sovereign immunity in this matter.[17]

We also conclude that the State has not established that it meets the second requirement under § 702 for a waiver of sovereign immunity, i.e., that **[—7—]** it has been adversely affected and aggrieved within the meaning of a relevant statute. As stated by the *Lujan* Court, to satisfy this requirement "the plaintiff must establish that the injury he complains of . . . falls within the 'zone of interests' sought to be protected by the statutory provision whose violation forms the legal basis for his complaint."[18] Louisiana asserts that it has been adversely affected and aggrieved within the meaning of a "relevant statute"—the River and Harbor Improvements Act—because the Act (and its amendment) provided for a width of 125 feet. Under the *Lujan* Court's explanation of § 702's "adversely affected" clause, however, Louisiana must establish that the encroachment of its land "falls within the 'zone of interests' sought to be protected by" the Act.[19]

---

8 497 U.S. 871 (1990).

9 *Id.* at 882.

10 5 U.S.C. § 551(13).

11 *Lujan*, 497 U.S. at 882.

12 *Id.* at 883 (citation omitted). Although *Lujan* involved Article III standing under the APA, and not sovereign immunity, the Court's decision required interpretation of the same APA provisions at issue here.

13 *Vill. of Bald Head Island v. U.S. Army Corps of Eng'rs*, 714 F.3d 186, 193, 1 Adm. R. 123, 127 (4th Cir. 2013).

14 *Id.* at 194, 1 Adm. R. at 127 (internal quotation marks and citation omitted).

15 *Alabama-Coushatta Tribe*, 757 F.3d at 490 (internal quotation marks and citation omitted).

16 *Id.* (internal quotation marks and citation omitted).

17 *Id.* at 490–91 (holding that plaintiff failed to point to "any identifiable 'agency action' within the meaning of § 702" because complaint brought "a challenge to the federal management of the natural resources on the land in question" and "not to a particular and identifiable action taken by the Government").

18 *Lujan*, 497 U.S. at 883 (citation omitted).

19 *Id.* (citation omitted).

Review of the legislative history of the River and Harbor Improvements Act and its amendment indicate that the purpose of the construction of the Waterway was to promote commerce, and the purpose of the amendment expanding the Waterway was to facilitate the transport of materials and supplies for the military during World War II. Specifically, the Act provided as an explanation for its enactment that "the railroads of the country are unable to carry all of its commerce and we can only provide for transportation of all the shipments offered by utilizing our waterways."[20] The amendment to the Act providing for the enlargement of the Waterway states that it was enacted "to promote the national defense and to promptly facilitate and protect the transport of materials and supplies needful to the Military Establishment."[21] This language indicates that the delineation of the Waterway to a width of 125 feet was motivated by the need for commerce on a **[—8—]** national scale. The interests of the landowners surrounding the Waterway do not appear to have been within the Act's "zone of interests."[22] Based on the foregoing, we conclude that the State has not met its burden of establishing that § 702 of the APA provides for **{-323-}** a waiver of the United States' sovereign immunity.[23]

In its reply brief and at oral argument, the State insists that it is not making a programmatic challenge to the Corps' maintenance of the Waterway. Instead, the State asserts that it is challenging the Corps' failure to act in a discrete way and seeks to compel the Corps to act in accordance with law. The State asserts that the Corps should be made to carry out "its basic duty to maintain the [Waterway] banks in the White Lake area, and prevent erosion—a legally required discrete action." Specifically, the State contends that under 33 U.S.C. § 426i of the Act, the Corps has a discrete duty to maintain and repair the Waterway within the specified dimensions and to repair shoreline erosion in the White Lake area. As described below, however, such an argument implicates a different section of the APA, § 706(1), which also has requirements for judicial review the State fails to satisfy.

As explained by the Supreme Court in *Norton v. Southern Utah Wilderness Alliance*, the APA places limits on "judicial review of agency **[—9—]** inaction."[24] "Failures to act are sometimes remediable under the APA, but not always."[25] The APA provides relief for a "failure to act" in § 706(1), which provides that a reviewing court shall "compel agency action unlawfully withheld or unreasonably delayed." After examining the definition of agency action under § 551(13) of the APA and noting that the definition includes a "failure to act," the *Norton* Court determined that "a claim under § 706(1) can proceed only where a plaintiff asserts that an agency failed to take a *discrete* agency action that it is *required to take*."[26] This "required-action" limitation "rules out judicial direction of even discrete agency action that is not demanded by law."[27]

Although the River and Harbor Improvements Act authorized a width of 125 feet for construction of the Waterway, no provision of the Act *requires* the Corps to maintain the Waterway at that width. The State contends that under 33 U.S.C. § 426i of the Act, the Corps has a discrete duty to

---

[20] H.R. Rep. No. 68-1122, at 1 (statement of Rep. Dempsey).

[21] 56 Stat. at 703.

[22] Moreover, the only case the State points to regarding the Act's "zone of interests" is a district court case which determined that a particular provision of the Act "was enacted for the benefit of *vessels*, and with respect to passengers and crews of vessels, as opposed to the general public." *See Cruise Lines Int'l Ass'n Alaska v. City and Borough of Juneau,* 356 F.Supp.3d 831, 847 (D. Alaska 2018) (emphasis added).

[23] Although the State relies heavily on *Weyerhaeuser Co. v. United States Fish and Wildlife Service,* 139 S. Ct. 361 (2018), it was not disputed in that case that there was agency action. The Supreme Court instead addressed a provision that excludes from APA review "agency action [that] is committed to agency discretion by law." 5 U.S.C. § 701(a)(2). That APA provision is not at issue here. As we have determined, the State has failed at the threshold requirement of showing agency action.

[24] 542 U.S. 55, 61 (2004).

[25] *Id.*

[26] *Id.* at 64.

[27] *Id.* at 65.

maintain and repair the Waterway within the specified dimensions and to repair shoreline erosion in the White Lake area. Contrary to the State's contentions, the statute imposes no such obligation on the Corps. Specifically, § 426i authorizes the Corps "to investigate, study, plan, and implement structural and nonstructural measures for the prevention or mitigation of shore damages attributable to . . . [the] Waterway, if a non-Federal public body agrees to operate and maintain such measures . . . ."[28]

The plain language of § 426i authorizes the Corps to take measures to prevent or mitigate shore damage caused by the Waterway; it does *not direct* the Corps to take such measures. Moreover, even if the Corps exercises its **[—10—]** discretionary authority **{–324–}** to act pursuant to § 426i, the statute facially places the duty of operating and maintaining any preventative or mitigative measures not on the Corps, but on the non-Federal public body that agrees to operate and maintain those measures. In sum, the State's argument that the Corps' inaction is subject to judicial review under the APA has no merit.

III. Conclusion

Based on the foregoing, we hold that the United States has not waived its sovereign immunity under the APA from the State's claims in this matter. Accordingly, the district court's judgment dismissing the State's complaint for lack of subject matter jurisdiction under Rule 12(b)(1) is AFFIRMED.

[28] 33 U.S.C. § 426i(a).

United States Court of Appeals
for the Fifth Circuit

No. 18-31275

BP EXPLORATION & PROD., INC.
vs.
CLAIMANT ID 100354107

Appeal from the United States District Court for the Eastern District of Louisiana

Decided: January 28, 2020

Citation: 948 F.3d 680, 8 Adm. R. 126 (5th Cir. 2020).

Before **OWEN,** Chief Judge, and **BARKSDALE** and **DUNCAN,** Circuit Judges.

[—1—] {-682-} DUNCAN, Circuit Judge: **{-683-}**

Following the disastrous Deepwater Horizon oil spill in 2010, Walmart submitted an economic loss claim under the Deepwater Horizon Settlement Agreement for one of its stores located on the Mississippi Gulf Coast. That store, it turns out, had reopened a mere six months before the oil spill, having been closed ever since it was destroyed by Hurricane Katrina several years earlier. The Settlement Program classified Walmart's submission as a "start-up business" claim and issued a compensation award of nearly $1 million. An appeal panel subsequently affirmed that award. BP sought review in the district court, arguing that Walmart should have been treated as a regular **[—2—]** business, not a start-up, and denied compensation altogether. The district court declined discretionary review. We affirm.[1]

I.

In 2003, Walmart opened "supercenter" #5079 in Pass Christian, Mississippi, just across U.S. Highway 90 from the Gulf of Mexico. The company operated the store for approximately two years, until Hurricane Katrina decimated Pass Christian in August 2005. The hurricane destroyed the store, and what was left of the building was demolished. This photo, looking out over the store's parking lot toward the beach, shows a portion of the destruction:

This is a photo of the structure itself, after cleanup: **[—3—] {-684-}**

In the wake of the hurricane, Walmart immediately announced plans to reopen the store. By early 2007, the company had purchased an additional 34 acres of land for the purpose of expanding its Pass Christian operation. Construction of the expanded store began in late 2008 and continued until Fall 2009. All the while, from September 2005 through early October 2009, the Pass Christian Walmart had no revenue. In late July 2009, the City of Pass Christian issued a new annual privilege tax license for the store, effective October 1, 2009 through September 30, 2010. Finally, on October 14, 2009, the rebuilt Walmart #5079 opened to the public.

[1] Chief Judge Owen dissents because, in her view, the district court abused its discretion by declining to review the appeal panel's decision.

On April 20, 2010, just six months after the Pass Christian Walmart reopened, the Deepwater Horizon drilling rig exploded in the Gulf of Mexico. Following the spill, BP entered into the Economic and Property Damages Class Action Settlement Agreement with entities that suffered spill-related economic losses. *See generally In re Deepwater Horizon*, 785 F.3d 986, 989, 3 Adm. R. 341, 341 (5th Cir. 2015) (describing history of the Settlement Agreement). **[—4—]**

The Settlement Agreement provides several compensation frameworks for business entities, including one for regular Business Economic Loss ("BEL") claims and another for Start-Up Business Economic Loss ("SBEL") claims.[2] Both frameworks allow businesses to submit claims for economic losses computed in part by comparing *actual* profits during a post-spill "Compensation Period" to *expected* profits for the same timeframe. The "Compensation Period" is a period of three or more consecutive months selected by the claimant from between May 2010 and December 2010 (for regular BEL claims) or between May 2010 and April 2011 (for **{-685-}** SBEL claims). A primary difference between the BEL and SBEL frameworks involves how expected profits are calculated. As described in Exhibit 4C to the Settlement Agreement, the regular BEL framework determines expected profits by looking to a *pre*-spill "Benchmark Period." Specifically, a regular BEL claimant can use financial figures from 2009, the average of 2008–2009, or the average of 2007–2009. To account for the fact that a start-up business would lack such pre-spill figures, the SBEL framework provides for a *post*-spill Benchmark Period.[3] The Benchmark Period for SBEL claimants consists of a period between May 2011 and April 2012 (*i.e.*, one year after the spill) corresponding to the months selected for the claimant's Compensation Period. In other words, regular BEL claimants recover under the Settlement Agreement by showing that profits during the spill year were less than profits during the *preceding* year(s), whereas SBEL claimants recover by showing that profits during the spill year were less than profits the *subsequent* year. **[—5—]**

The choice of filing a BEL or SBEL claim is not left entirely to the claimant. Rather, the Settlement Agreement expressly defines a "Start[-]Up Business" as one with "less than 18 months of operating history at the time of the Deepwater Horizon Incident." Some early claim-processing paperwork listed "11/1/08" as the cutoff date for SBEL treatment, but the Claims Administrator later issued Policy 381 v.3 explaining that "the correct application of [the Settlement Agreement] is to classify as a Start-Up Business one that commenced operations after 10/20/08 and classify as a general BEL business one that commenced operations on or before 10/20/08." In policy 362 v.2, which addressed how to tell if a start-up business sufficiently established its operations prior to the spill (so as to be eligible for compensation), the Claims Administrator prescribed a "totality of circumstances" analysis focused on, *inter alia*, when the business "began" to sell products or "incur substantial costs or expenses of a nature indicative of the actual start-up of business operations."

In June 2015, Walmart filed an SBEL claim for its Pass Christian store, selecting July 2010–January 2011 as its Compensation Period and July 2011–January 2012 as its Benchmark Period.[4] Based on financial documentation provided by Walmart, the Settlement Program computed a total net compensation of $817,392.13 and issued an award for that amount.

BP challenged this award before an appeal panel, urging that because the Pass Christian Walmart had a "longstanding" history dating back to its 2003 opening, it had more than 18 months of operating history and therefore

[2] The Settlement Agreement also provides compensation frameworks for "Failed Business" and "Failed Start-Up Business" claims, but those frameworks are not at issue here.

[3] Alternatively, SBEL claimants may choose to rely on qualifying financial projections prepared prior to the spill, but that option is not at issue here.

[4] The Settlement Program later dropped January 2011 from the Compensation Period and January 2012 from the Benchmark Period due to insufficient financial records.

should not have been treated under the SBEL framework. BP asserted that **[—6—]** Walmart's claim properly belonged within the BEL framework, which, according to BP, would yield an award of $0.

The appeal panel noted BP's arguments but affirmed the award. The panel acknowledged a prior decision finding that a business with no sales to customers from January 2008 until April 2009 did not qualify for SBEL treatment, but observed that Walmart distinguished that case while supplying several other decisions holding that periods of dormancy did not preclude start-up treatment. The appeal panel **{–686–}** "agree[d] with the majority" of the decisions and adopted Walmart's Final Proposal.

BP promptly sought discretionary review of the appeal panel decision in the district court. On November 14, 2018, the district court denied BP's request without comment. BP timely appealed.

II.

"We review the district court's denial of discretionary review for abuse of discretion." *Claimant ID 100235033 v. BP Expl. & Prod., Inc.*, 941 F.3d 801, 805, 7 Adm. R. 318, 321 (5th Cir. 2019) (citing *Holmes Motors, Inc. v. BP Expl. & Prod., Inc.*, 829 F.3d 313, 315, 4 Adm. R. 263, 263 (5th Cir. 2016)). Typically, we assess "whether the decision not reviewed by the district court actually contradicted or misapplied the Settlement Agreement, or had the clear potential to contradict or misapply the Settlement Agreement." *Id.*, 7 Adm. R. at 321 (quoting *Holmes Motors*, 829 F.3d at 315, 4 Adm. R. at 263); *see also Claimant ID 100250022 v. BP Expl. & Prod., Inc.*, 847 F.3d 167, 170, 5 Adm. R. 199, 200 (5th Cir. 2017) (per curiam) ("[W]e need not examine whether the [Settlement Program] was actually correct[.]"). However, "it is 'wrong to suggest that the district court must grant review of *all* claims that raise a question about the proper interpretation of the Settlement Agreement.'" *Claimant ID 100212278 v. BP Expl. & Prod., Inc.*, 848 F.3d 407, 410, 5 Adm. R. 202, 203 (5th Cir. 2017) (per curiam) (quoting *Holmes Motors*, 829 F.3d at 316, 4 Adm. R. at 264); *see also In re Deepwater Horizon*, 785 F.3d at 999, 3 Adm. R. at 350 (noting that "to turn the district court's discretionary review into a **[—7—]** mandatory review . . . would frustrate the clear purpose of the Settlement Agreement to curtail litigation"). "It is not an abuse of discretion to deny a request for review that involves no pressing question of how the Settlement Agreement should be interpreted or implemented, but simply raises the correctness of a discretionary administrative decision in the facts of a single claimant's case." *Claimant ID 100212278*, 848 F.3d at 410, 5 Adm. R. at 203 (quoting *In re Deepwater Horizon*, 641 F. App'x 405, 410 (5th Cir. 2016) (per curiam) (cleaned up)). "It may be an abuse, however, if the district court denies a request for review that raises a recurring issue on which the Appeal Panels are split if the resolution of the question will substantially impact the administration of the Agreement." *Claimant ID 100235033*, 941 F.3d at 806, 7 Adm. R. at 321 (quoting *Claimant ID 100212278*, 848 F.3d at 410, 5 Adm. R. at 203) (cleaned up).

III.

A.

BP argues that the appeal panel misapplied and contradicted the Settlement Agreement by ignoring its plain language. BP emphasizes that nothing in the Settlement Agreement indicates that the start-up classification requires a *continuous* 18-month period of revenue generation leading up to the spill. Pointing to Policy 381 v.3, BP asserts that a business does not count as a "start-up" if it "commenced operations" on or before October 20, 2008. Further, BP notes that Policy 362 v.2 specifies that the Settlement Program will determine a claimant's operating history based on when the claimant "began doing business or operating in the Gulf Coast Areas[.]" BP thus contends that, because Walmart began doing business in Pass Christian in 2003 and had well over 18 months of operating history by the time of the spill, its claim should have been treated under the regular BEL framework. BP bolsters this argument by stressing that Settlement Agreement terminology like "start-up business" should be interpreted according to ordinary usage, and Walmart's **[—8—]** Pass Christian store, insofar as it opened in 2003, would not be considered a "start-up business" in the ordinary sense. **{-687-}**

Walmart responds that the appeal panel properly applied the terms of the Settlement Agreement in light of Policy 362 v.2's "totality of circumstances" test. Walmart contrasts the "previous" Pass Christian store with the "new" store, contending that the former was totally destroyed by Hurricane Katrina and the latter was "not in operation or existence until October 2009." Walmart submits that, at most, BP's appeal raises a question about the correctness of a discretionary decision on the facts of a single case, not a pressing question about how the Settlement Agreement should be interpreted and implemented. Lastly, Walmart argues that BP's position "undermine[s] the entire structure and intent" of the Settlement Agreement because it denies businesses in Walmart's position any compensation. Walmart explains that under BP's view it (1) would not qualify for SBEL treatment because the prior Pass Christian store operated in 2003–2005, and (2) would not qualify for regular BEL treatment because—due to its nonoperation—it lacks financial records for the 2009 Benchmark Period. Walmart dubs this an "absolute Catch-22."

While BP's plain language argument does raise a question about the proper interpretation of the Settlement Agreement, we are not persuaded that the appeal panel decision "actually contradicted or misapplied" the Settlement Agreement or had the "clear potential" to do so. The reason is that the language of the Settlement Agreement does not unambiguously support BP's position, *i.e.*, that a business destroyed by Hurricane Katrina and relaunched too close in time to the Deepwater Horizon oil spill to have sufficient financial records to benchmark a regular BEL claim is nevertheless precluded from treatment under the start-up framework.

In reaching this conclusion, we are guided by the fact that the Settlement Agreement is a maritime contract interpreted in accordance with federal **[—9—]** admiralty law, which dictates that a contract "should be read as a whole and its words given their plain meaning unless the provision is ambiguous." *Holmes Motors*, 829 F.3d at 315, 4 Adm. R. at 264 (quoting *Breaux v. Halliburton Energy Servs.*, 562 F.3d 358, 364 (5th Cir. 2009)). "A provision is not ambiguous if 'its language as a whole is clear, explicit, and leads to no absurd consequences, and as such it can be given only one reasonable interpretation.'" *BP Expl. & Prod., Inc. v. Claimant ID 100262795*, 759 F. App'x 249, 252 (5th Cir. 2019) (per curiam) (quoting *Chembulk Trading LLC v. Chemex Ltd.*, 393 F.3d 550, 555 n.6 (5th Cir. 2004)). An appeal panel contradicts or misapplies the Settlement Agreement if its finding is "incongruent with the language of the Settlement Agreement[.]" *Claimant ID 100250022*, 847 F.3d at 170, 5 Adm. R. at 201; *cf. In re Deepwater Horizon*, 858 F.3d 298, 303–04, 5 Adm. R. 259, 261–62 (5th Cir. 2017) (reversing district court's approval of policies "inconsistent" with unambiguous text of Settlement Agreement).

As we read it, the definition of "Start-Up Business" in the Settlement Agreement is subject to at least two reasonable interpretations. "[L]ess than 18 months of operating history at the time of the Deepwater Horizon Incident" could mean less than 18 months of *total* operating history. On that interpretation, which BP favors, a business that reopened (after an extended period of dormancy) less than 18 months before the spill would be precluded from SBEL classification if the business previously operated for some substantial period adding up to a total of 18 months or more. But the language could also be read to mean less than 18 months of *continuous* operating history prior to the spill. On that reading, a business with a previous operating history followed by an extended period **{-688-}** of dormancy could still be eligible for SBEL classification if its reopening took place less than 18 months before the spill.

At first glance, Policy 381 v.3 appears to provide some clarity, classifying as a regular business one that "commenced operations on or before 10/20/08." **[—10—]** That language seems to suggest—as BP urges—a blanket rule that any business having ever "commenced operations" more than 18 months before the spill must be treated as a regular BEL claimant regardless of dormancies. But such a reading misconceives the applicability of Policy 381 v.3. The stated purpose of the policy was to resolve a discrepancy about the commencement date for SBEL claims because some forms listed "11/1/08" and others listed "10/20/08." The intended effect of the policy was to clarify that a business which "commenced operations" between 10/20/08 and 11/1/08 should be treated under the SBEL framework, not the BEL framework. The policy is silent regarding how to treat a business that, due to an extended period of dormancy, might be said to have *two* operating histories and *two* commencement dates.

Similarly, Policy 362 v.2's instruction to focus on when a business "began" doing business or operating does not resolve the ambiguity. Policy 362 v.2 is addressed to the question of whether a start-up business managed to attain sufficient operational status early enough to be eligible for compensation, *i.e.*, before the date of the spill. The policy does not bear on whether some *prior* operational history, followed by a period of dormancy, disqualifies a business from SBEL classification.[5]

Walmart's structural argument provides evidence that the circumstance here was never even contemplated by the parties to the Settlement Agreement. We find it difficult to believe that the parties intended to foreclose recovery by businesses that suffered spill-related losses mere months after finally resurfacing from the Gulf Coast's previous catastrophe, Hurricane Katrina. Quite to the contrary, the Settlement Agreement instructs the Claims **[—11—]** Administrator to select the framework and information that will "produce the greatest economic damage compensation amount[.]" The different frameworks for BEL and SBEL claims were not implemented to favor a particular type of business or restrict recovery for others, but rather "[t]o account for specific circumstances" in a claimant's business that might impede its ability to file a claim under one or the other framework.[6]

In sum, we hold that the appeal panel made a discretionary decision not incongruent with the language of the Settlement Agreement.

B.

Even though the appeal panel did not actually contradict or misapply the Settlement Agreement on a pressing question of implementation, we might still find abuse of discretion if the district court ignored a split among appeal panels on the issue **{–689–}** presented. Indeed, BP argues that appeal panels have "reached different conclusions about how a period of dormancy during which a business generates no revenue affects the classification of the business." BP submits that the panel here flagged this as a recurring issue, and simply adopted the majority approach without independent analysis. This, BP contends, "is precisely the type of issue the district court is required to review." Walmart responds that there is no split "involving claims truly analogous to this claim and the specific facts surrounding it." We agree with Walmart.

To determine whether the district court may have abused its discretion, "we examine a set of appeal panel decisions to see whether they have split on recurring issues with a substantial impact on the Settlement

[5] In any event, it is the Settlement Agreement that binds the parties, not policies later promulgated by the Claims Administrator. *See BP Expl. & Prod., Inc. v. Claimant ID 100195328*, 766 F. App'x 141, 145 (5th Cir. 2019) (per curiam) (citing *In re Deepwater Horizon*, 858 F.3d at 300–01, 5 Adm. R. at 259).

[6] To be sure, we have not been receptive to structural "catch-22" arguments that "ignore[] the settlement agreement itself." *Claimant ID 100068924 v. BP Expl. & Prod., Inc.*, 765 F. App'x 956, 960 (5th Cir. 2019) (per curiam). Nevertheless, Walmart's structural argument undermines the notion that the appeal panel *actually* contradicted or misapplied the Settlement Agreement, especially where, as here, the relevant provision is ambiguous.

Program." **[—12—]** *Claimant ID 100235033*, 941 F.3d at 808, 7 Adm. R. at 323. In addition to the underlying decision, the parties focus our attention on two other appeal panel decisions—one that classified a business with a period of dormancy as a regular BEL claimant and another that classified a business with a period of dormancy as an SBEL.

In APD 2017-3537, the claimant, a Louisville, Mississippi, metal products manufacturer, commenced operations in 2001. According to the Claims Administrator, the business "experienced a dormancy period" with no sales from January 2008 to April 2009. BP pointed out that the business went from paying $58,528 in utility bills in January 2008 to less than $100 in April 2008, and reported no salary or contract labor expenses for 2008 or 2009. Records from 2010 showed that the business began to recognize some sales again in April of that year. In front of the appeal panel, the claimant sought regular BEL treatment, explaining that—due to a "downtrend in the ability to sell its products"—it discontinued production in 2007 and focused on sales of existing inventory until finally ceasing operations in 2013. BP argued for SBEL treatment, pointing out that the claimant "went dormant in January 2008 . . . until April 2010." In what it described as a "close call," the appeal panel rejected BP's argument and applied the regular BEL framework.

In APD 2017-3813, the claimant, a Gulfport, Mississippi, sporting goods store that sold sailboats and watersports equipment, began operations in 2001 but was forced to close in 2005 after Hurricane Katrina. According to the claimant, the business was "completely lost," with no location, inventory, or sales after the hurricane. Eventually, in 2008, the decision was made to re-launch the business. Using the same Employer Identification Number as before, the business began incurring advertising and administrative expenses in July 2008 and recorded its first income in November and December of that year. After a "soft try opening" in 2009, the business fully reopened in 2010 **[—13—]** and continued operating until July 2012. The Settlement Program applied the regular BEL framework to the claim, producing an award of $0, but the claimant appealed, arguing for SBEL treatment. The appeal panel found that the criteria for SBEL treatment were satisfied, noting the claimant's "second operating history" commenced less than eighteen months before the spill.

BP argues that APD 2017-3537 is inconsistent with both APD 2017-3813 and the underlying decision in the present case. Walmart responds that APD 2017-3537 is distinguishable, whereas APD 2017-3813 is directly on point. The real debate seems to be about framing. BP frames the issue broadly, contending that appeal panels have split on how to treat claims where a "business experiences a period of dormancy during which no new revenue is generated." **{-690-}** Walmart frames the issue more narrowly, suggesting there is no split about how to treat "businesses that were completely destroyed by Hurricane Katrina and then opened new stores that commenced operations within 18 months of the spill." Walmart insists that the claim in APD 2017-3537 is "completely different" because it involved an ongoing business that merely suffered a "downtrend" and "never lost its physical facility, never lost all of its customers, and never left the Gulf Coast community."

In our view, Walmart's narrower framing of the issue (which accounts for the circumstances of the dormancy) is more appropriate and, on that framing, there is no split.[7] BP's attempt to frame the issue broadly is belied by BP's own inconsistent positions in the cited appeal panel decisions. One would expect BP—a party to the Settlement Agreement—to maintain a consistent position on discrete issues recurring before appeal panels. Yet on the issue as **[—14—]** BP frames it, BP has advocated for contradictory positions.

[7] Indeed, BP admitted at oral argument that besides this case and APD 2017-3813 it was not aware of any other appeal panel decisions involving business claimants whose operations were wiped out by Hurricane Katrina and then resumed in the immediate pre-spill period.

Although BP relies heavily on APD 2017-3537 for the sweeping proposition that a period of dormancy can never trigger SBEL treatment, it was BP that argued *for* SBEL treatment in that case *on the very basis of* the metal products manufacturer's period of dormancy.[8]

To be sure, appeal panel decisions need not be factually identical to create a split. In *Claimant ID 100235033*, we held that a split may exist where "each set of facts is unique to some degree, but comparison still is reasonable." 941 F.3d at 810, 7 Adm. R. at 324. In that case, we evaluated six other appeal panel decisions and determined that "those panels would likely have reached a different conclusion [than the underlying panel reached] had they handled the Claimant's case." *Id.* at 808, 7 Adm. R. at 323. In contrast, nothing in APD 2017-3537 indicates the panel would have reached a different conclusion had it handled Walmart's claim. The metal manufacturer in APD 2017-3537 suffered a business downturn and decided to cease new production and simply sell off its remaining unfinished inventory, which it did until closing for good in 2013. The appeal panel applied regular BEL treatment in what it described as a "close call." Nothing about this outcome indicates that the panel would "likely" have applied regular BEL treatment to Walmart's claim, where Hurricane Katrina destroyed the store and the surrounding community, and where over four years passed before the store managed to commence its second operating history.

Moreover, even if BP was correct that APD 2017-3537 contradicts both APD 2017-3813 and the decision at issue here, that would not be enough to mandate discretionary review. "[O]ne allegedly variant decision will not 'substantially impact the administration of the agreement' and therefore does **[—15—]** not require the district court's review." *Claimant ID 100262194 v. BP Expl. & Prod., Inc.*, 745 F. App'x 539, 541 (5th Cir. 2019) (per curiam) (quoting *Claimant ID 100212278*, 848 F.3d at 410, 5 Adm. R. at 203); *see also Claimant ID 100051301 v. BP Expl. & Prod., Inc.*, 694 F. App'x 236, 240 (5th Cir. 2017) (per curiam) ("[T]he fact that Appeal Panels have reached different **{–691–}** conclusions for this issue depending on the circumstances of each case does not represent the type of Appeal Panel split that would require the district court's review."). Here, where a singular decision only possibly diverges from the others in a fact-bound "close call," there is little likelihood of substantial impact on the administration of the Settlement Agreement.

In sum, we discern no split among appeal panels on the issue presented, let alone a split likely to have a substantial impact on the Settlement Program.

* * *

Because the underlying appeal panel decision did not actually contradict or misapply the Settlement Agreement on a pressing question of implementation, and because there was no split among appeal panels on the issue presented, the district court did not abuse its discretion by denying review.

AFFIRMED.

[8] We also note that BP argued for SBEL treatment in APD 2015-1586 and APD 2015-1762, other cases that involved extended dormancy periods.

United States Court of Appeals for the Fifth Circuit

No. 18-60698

SEA-LAND SERVS., INC.
vs.
DIRECTOR, OFFICE OF WORKERS' COMPENSATION PROGRAMS

Petition for Review of an Order of the Benefits Review Board

Decided: February 14, 2020

Citation: 949 F.3d 921, 8 Adm. R. 133 (5th Cir. 2020).

Before **JOLLY, SMITH,** and **STEWART,** Circuit Judges.

[—1—] {-923-} SMITH, Circuit Judge: **{-924-}**

Sea-Land Services, Inc. ("Sea-Land"), petitions for review of an order of the Benefits Review Board ("BRB"). The BRB upheld the determination of an administrative law judge ("ALJ") that Clarence Ceasar, Jr., did not aggravate his 1997 injury at Sea-Land while working for Universal Maritime Service **[—2—]** Company ("UMS") in 2011. Because the BRB did not err, we deny the petition.

I.

Ceasar injured his neck and back while working as a longshoreman for Sea-Land in 1997. Because of those injuries, Ceasar was unable to work and had to undergo several medical procedures. Thirteen years later, Ceasar and Sea-Land reached a settlement, under which Ceasar received a lump sum instead of continuing disability payments. Sea-Land remained on the hook for Ceasar's ongoing medical expenses.

In 2010, Ceasar's physician, Dr. Dan Eidman, approved his return to work with no restrictions, even though Ceasar continued to "describe[] his symptoms of neck and lower back pain as constant." Soon thereafter, Ceasar started working as a longshoreman for UMS but was injured again a year later when a coworker lowered a cargo container onto his hands.

Ceasar filed a claim for compensation under the Longshore and Harbor Workers' Compensation Act ("LHWCA"), 33 U.S.C. § 901 *et seq.* The LHWCA "provides compensation for the death or disability of any person engaged in 'maritime employment'" under certain circumstances. *Herb's Welding, Inc. v. Gray*, 470 U.S. 414, 415 (1985). Ceasar claimed that he injured his shoulder, neck, and back when he tried to free his hands from the container.

Sea-Land and UMS contested responsibility for treating Ceasar's neck and back injuries following the 2011 accident. Sea-Land (and Ceasar) contended that UMS was responsible because the 2011 accident either caused new injuries or aggravated old ones. UMS countered that Ceasar's neck and back injuries stemmed exclusively from the 1997 accident, so Sea-Land remains responsible for treatment. A Department of Labor ALJ sided with UMS and ordered Sea-Land to continue paying Ceasar's medical expenses. **[—3—]**

A claimant with a preexisting condition is entitled to LHWCA compensation if a workplace incident aggravates that condition. *Bis Salamis, Inc. v. Dir., OWCP*, 819 F.3d 116, 128, 4 Adm. R. 209, 217. Aggravation occurs where "an employment injury worsens or combines with a preexisting impairment to produce a disability greater than that which would have resulted from the employment injury alone." *Id.*, 4 Adm. R. at 217. An employer whose employee aggravates a preexisting condition must compensate the claimant for the entire resulting liability, *id.*, 4 Adm. R. at 217, regardless of whether the preexisting condition is the result of an accident at a prior employer's workplace. *Operators & Consulting Servs., Inc. v. Dir., OWCP*, 170 F. App'x 931, 934 (5th Cir. 2006); *see also Metro. Stevedore Co. v. Crescent Wharf & Warehouse Co.*, 339 F.3d 1102, 1104–05 (9th Cir. 2003). But if the disability results **{-925-}** only from the natural progression of injuries sustained while working for a former employer, then there is no aggravation, and the previous employer remains responsible. *Operators & Consulting Servs.*, 170 F. App'x at 934; *see also Metro. Stevedore*, 339 F.3d at 1105. At issue is whether Ceasar's injuries were aggravated in the 2011 incident or were the natural progression of his 1997 injuries.

LHWCA claims are evaluated using a three-step framework. First, the claimant must establish a *prima facie* case by showing "that (1) he suffered harm and (2) conditions of the workplace, or an accident at the workplace, could have caused, aggravated, or accelerated the harm." *Bis Salamis*, 819 F.3d at 127, 4 Adm. R. at 216. Establishing a *prima facie* case raises a presumption under Section 20(a) of the LHWCA that the claimant's injury is work-related and that the claimant is entitled to compensation. *Ortco Contractors, Inc. v. Charpentier*, 332 F.3d 283, 287 (5th Cir. 2003); *see also* 33 U.S.C. § 920(a). The employer can rebut that presumption by presenting substantial evidence that its workplace did not cause or aggravate the injury. *Bis Salamis*, 819 F.3d **[—4—]** at 127, 4 Adm. R. at 216. If the employer rebuts that presumption, the burden of proof falls to the claimant to demonstrate by a preponderance of the evidence that the employer's workplace caused or aggravated his injury. *Id.*, 4 Adm. R. at 216.

The ALJ applied that three-step framework. The ALJ first found that the testimony of Ceasar's treating physician, Dr. Eidman—who opined that the 2011 accident aggravated Ceasar's existing injuries—raised the Section 20(a) presumption. The ALJ then found that UMS successfully rebutted that presumption with reports by Doctors David Vanderweide, Robert Kagan, and Stephen Brown. Those doctors independently reviewed Ceasar's medical records and concluded that his neck and back pains reflected the natural progresssion of his 1997 injury. With the presumption out of the picture, the ALJ determined that Ceasar's injuries were "more likely than not a natural progression of his pre-existing condition." To reach that conclusion, the ALJ favored the reports of the independent physicians over Dr. Eidman's, reasoning that Ceasar's medical records better supported their conclusions. The ALJ assigned little weight to Ceasar's testimony, observing that he contradicted his own medical records and had a motive to ascribe his injury to UMS.[1]

II.

Our review of the BRB's decision is limited. We ensure only that it "adhered to its proper scope of review—i.e., whether the ALJ's findings of fact are supported by substantial evidence and are consistent with the law." *Gulf Best Elec., Inc. v. Methe*, 396 F.3d 601, 603 (5th Cir. 2004). "Substantial evidence is that relevant evidence—more than a scintilla but less than a **[—5—]** preponderance—that would cause a reasonable person to accept the fact finding." *Ceres Gulf, Inc. v. Dir., OWCP*, 683 F.3d 225, 228 (5th Cir. 2012) (quotation marks omitted). That deferential standard reflects the ALJ's role as "the factfinder who is exclusively entitled to assess both the weight of the evidence and the credibility of witnesses." *Id.*

Sea-Land attacks the ALJ's decision on two grounds. First, it asserts that the ALJ "erred in finding that the opinions of [Doctors] Vanderwiede [*sic*], Kagan, and Brown **{-926-}** constituted substantial evidence needed to rebut the opinion of Dr. Eidman, [Ceasar's] long-time treating physician." Sea-Land emphasizes that Dr. Eidman's testimony was entitled to greater weight than the opinion of non-treating physicians. Sea-Land critiques the weight given to the independent doctors in several ways, contending that: (1) the independent doctors based their evaluations on incomplete copies of Ceasar's medical records; (2) only one of the independent doctors, Dr. Brown, examined Ceasar in person; (3) the independent doctors' credentials are not in the record; and (4) the independent doctors' reports are flawed.

UMS responds that the independent doctors relied on complete copies of Ceasar's records and that Sea-Land mischaracterizes

[1] The terms of Ceasar's settlement with Sea-Land limit his compensation to medical expenses if his injuries stem from his 1997 accident. If, however, Ceasar aggravated his injuries in 2011, he would receive medical benefits *and* disability from UMS in addition to the lump-sum disability payment from his settlement with Sea-Land.

the doctors' reports. UMS also points to the opinions of the three independent physicians. Dr. Brown reported that Ceasar's "cervical and lumbar symptoms are a result of the original injury of August 17, 1997." "[A]lthough the more recent injury may have caused a temporary exacerbation of [Ceasar's] symptoms, the base-line amount of pain and the baseline issues the claimant was having [are] related to the 1997 injury." Dr. Kagan stated that "aggravations of a pre-existing condition occur at the time of the incident. There is no delayed reaction." He also stated that "[i]n this case, the hospital records follow the injury to his hands (07-27-11) as well as the first visit to Eidman (08-07-11) **[—6—]** approximately three weeks later mak[ing] no mention of any possible aggravation of the patient's pre-existing condition involving the cervical or lumbar spine." Dr. Vanderweide opined that "it is unreasonable to suggest a material aggravation or acceleration of [Ceasar's] cervical or lumbar complaints based upon the injury event of 2011. While the possibility of an exacerbation or flare-up of his symptoms may have occurred, there is insufficient evidence to suggest that the underlying pre-existing musculoskeletal condition was advanced in severity beyond its natural course by the injury event."

Although Sea-Land's criticisms have some force, they do not establish that the Section 20(a) presumption should have remained in effect. The "substantial evidence" showing needed to rebut the presumption is a "*minimal* requirement" less demanding than a preponderance of the evidence. *Ortco Contractors*, 332 F.3d at 289; *see also Ceres Gulf*, 683 F.3d at 231. As the ALJ and BRB concluded, the contrary opinions of three independent doctors that reviewed Ceasar's medical records met that low burden.[2]

Sea-Land's second contention goes to the ultimate issue: whether the ALJ erroneously attributed Ceasar's injuries to the 1997 accident. In making its case, Sea-Land avers that the ALJ discredited Ceasar's testimony irrationally in light of corroborating evidence and that Dr. Eidman's opinion is superior to that of the other three physicians. Some of Sea-Land's points may have convinced another factfinder. But to obtain the relief it seeks, Sea-Land must demonstrate that no reasonable mind could have arrived at the ALJ's conclusion. *Avondale Indus., Inc. v. Dir., OWCP*, 977 F.2d 186, 189 (5th Cir. 1992). Sea-Land fails to clear that high hurdle. **[—7—]**

It is true, for instance, that the opinion of a treating physician may be entitled to "considerable weight in determining disability." *Loza v. Apfel*, 219 F.3d 378, 395 (5th Cir. 2000). Nevertheless, an **{–927–}** "ALJ may give less weight to a treating physician's opinion when there is good cause shown to the contrary."[3] In this case, the ALJ was within his power to discount Dr. Eidman's testimony based on finding that (1) "much of his testimony and many of his reports are totally inconsistent with the testimony of his patient, who also accused him and his staff of falsifying records"; (2) his "testimony was at times internally inconsistent"; and (3) his conclusions were undermined by the "credible and well-reasoned opinions" of three independent physicians.

Moreover, it isn't this court's role to reevaluate each piece of evidence presented to the ALJ, as Sea-Land asks this court to do. The ALJ carefully considered Dr. Eidman's testimony, Ceasar's treatment records, and the reports of three independent physicians. In a thorough opinion, the ALJ determined that the independent physicians' reports and Ceasar's medical records indicated that Ceasar's injuries stemmed from the 1997 accident. "Although another factfinder might have reached a different conclusion, the ALJ thoroughly explained his reasons in this disputed case." *Ceres Gulf*, 683 F.3d at 232. Where confronted with factual disputes

[2] *See Ortco Contractors*, 332 F.3d at 286–87, 290 (holding that the BRB erroneously determined that three physicians' opinions insufficiently rebutted the Section 20(a) presumption).

[3] *Id.* (cleaned up); *see also Avondale Indus.*, 977 F.2d at 189 ("As fact finder, the ALJ determines questions of credibility of witnesses and of conflicting evidence. He is not required to accept the opinion or theory of a medical expert that contradicts the ALJ's findings based on common sense.").

surrounding a claim for LHWCA compensation, "[n]either we nor the [BRB] may substitute our judgment for that of the ALJ." *Bis Salamis*, 819 F.3d at 126, 4 Adm. R. at 215.

Because the ALJ's decision is supported by substantial evidence and is consistent with the law, the petition for review is DENIED.

United States Court of Appeals
for the Fifth Circuit

No. 18-20453

CERTAIN UNDERWRITERS AT LLOYD'S, LONDON
vs.
AXON PRESSURE PRODS., INC.

Appeal from the United States District Court for the Southern District of Texas

Decided: February 21, 2020

Citation: 951 F.3d 248, 8 Adm. R. 137 (5th Cir. 2020).

Before **CLEMENT**, **ELROD**, and **DUNCAN**, Circuit Judges.

[—2—] {-253-} DUNCAN, Circuit Judge:

This byzantine dispute arises out of a catastrophic oil well blowout that occurred in 2013 on the HERCULES 265 drilling rig in the Gulf of Mexico. The rig's charterer brought products-liability claims **{-254-}** against a refurbisher of the rig's blowout-prevention components, setting off a cascade of counterclaims and third-party claims based on various indemnity provisions in the web of contracts among the parties. Eventually, the district court granted a series of summary judgments, based both on contractual indemnity and also on the merits of the liability claims. For the reasons discussed below, we AFFIRM in part, REVERSE in part, and REMAND for further proceedings.

I.

We here provide a sketch of the background facts and proceedings. We dive later into deeper detail as needed when addressing specific issues.

Axon Pressure Products, Inc. and Axon EP, Inc. (together, "Axon") manufacture and service equipment used in offshore oil rigs. In 2010, Axon was hired by non-party Seahawk Drilling, Inc. to work on equipment on the rig that would eventually feature in this case—the HERCULES 265 drilling unit. Axon refurbished and remanufactured various parts on the rig designed to help prevent well blowouts.

In 2011, Hercules Drilling Company, at that point the owner of the HERCULES 265, entered an Offshore Daywork Drilling Contract (the "Drilling Contract") with Walter Oil & Gas Corporation. Under that agreement (as later amended), Walter chartered the HERCULES 265, located in the Gulf of Mexico. Hercules provided the rig and crew to Walter for re-working the A-3 well, located about 84 miles south of Houma, Louisiana. The Drilling Contract contained various provisions allocating liabilities between Walter and Hercules. **[—3—]**

In 2013, a blowout occurred at the A-3 well that the crew was unable to contain. Oil, gas, and other materials blasted up through the well at dangerously high pressure. The blowout caught fire and burned for several hours before sealing itself off, in the process causing extensive damage to the rig and other property. As required by federal law, Walter assembled a team of independent well-control experts to investigate the incident. The experts eventually produced multiple reports suggesting that human error led to the blowout.

Walter incurred over $70,000,000 in expenses resulting from the blowout. It tendered various claims to its insurers, Certain Underwriters at Lloyd's, London and Certain Insurance Companies Subscribing to Policy Nos. JHB CJP-1861, JHB CJP-1959, and 13PKGN9161 (together, "Underwriters"). Underwriters paid out over $48,000,000 in claims to Walter.

Walter and Underwriters (as a subrogee of some of Walter's claims) then sued Axon.[1] Walter asserted products-liability claims against Axon, alleging that the parts it had worked on malfunctioned, causing the blowout. Tana Exploration Company and Helis Oil & Gas Company—which both owned non-operating working interests in the A-3 well—also sued Axon. (Together, we refer to

[1] Other defendants were also named, but Plaintiffs have either dismissed or settled the claims against them.

Underwriters, Walter, Tana, and Helis as "Plaintiffs.")

In response, Axon filed counterclaims against Walter for indemnity as a third-party beneficiary under the Drilling Contract, as well as a breach of contract claim against Underwriters as a third-party beneficiary of Underwriters' promise to release claims against anyone Walter had released from liability. Axon also brought a third-party complaint against Hercules.[2] **[—4—]** **{-255-}** Axon asserted that it was the failure of Walter or Hercules personnel to operate the rig correctly that caused the blowout. Axon sought defense, indemnity, and attorney's fees from both Walter and Hercules.

In response to Axon's lawsuit, Hercules tendered its defense and indemnity to Walter, asserting that Walter had contractually assumed the liabilities Hercules then faced as a result of Axon's claims. Walter did not respond, and later moved for summary judgment on the issue. It sought a declaration that it did not owe defense and indemnity to Hercules for Axon's claims. In response, Hercules filed a third-party complaint against Axon and Walter. It sought indemnity and contribution from both.

The parties moved for summary judgment on various issues.[3] Axon sought a ruling that Hercules owed Axon indemnity for all claims by Walter and the other plaintiffs. The district court granted the motion and held that Hercules was obligated to defend and indemnify Axon for any losses from Plaintiffs' claims. Axon also moved for summary judgment against Plaintiffs on the substance of their products-liability claims. First, Axon contended that Plaintiffs failed both to prove causation and to show that Axon's products were defective. Separately, Axon asserted that Plaintiffs failed to produce evidence of damages. The district court eventually granted each of Axon's motions, though it did not provide a reasoned opinion for some of its decisions.

Hercules moved for summary judgment, seeking a ruling that Walter was required to defend and indemnify Hercules for any losses resulting from Axon's claims against Hercules. The court granted the motion.

To sum up: an oil well blowout caused millions in damage. Plaintiffs sued Axon for products liability. Axon then counterclaimed against Plaintiffs and **[—5—]** brought a third-party complaint against Hercules. Hercules then brought a third-party complaint against Axon and Plaintiffs. The district court granted summary judgment on various indemnity and merits issues and also struck several expert reports and evidence, with Axon winning on most issues.

Plaintiffs and Hercules now appeal different decisions by the district court. Plaintiffs appeal the grant of summary judgment in Axon's favor on the merits of the products-liability claims. They also appeal the district court's decisions striking various expert reports and evidence. Walter appeals the district court's decision that it owes a duty to release and indemnify both Hercules and Axon. Hercules appeals the court's determination that it owes duties to defend and indemnify Axon.

II.

We review a grant of summary judgment *de novo*, applying the same standard as the district court. *Rogers v. Bromac Title Servs., L.L.C.*, 755 F.3d 347, 350 (5th Cir. 2014). "Summary judgment is proper 'if the movant shows that there is no genuine dispute as to any material fact and the movant is entitled to judgment as a matter of law.'" *Id.* (quoting Fed. R. Civ. P. 56(a)). A genuine dispute of material fact exists "if the evidence is such that a reasonable jury could return a verdict for the nonmoving party." *Anderson v. Liberty Lobby, Inc.*, 477 U.S. 242, 248 (1986). "We construe all facts and inferences in the light most favorable to the nonmoving party," *Dillon v. Rogers*, 596 F.3d 260, 266 (5th Cir.

---

[2] Axon also sued Hercules Offshore, Inc. "Hercules" collectively refers to Hercules Offshore, Inc. and Hercules Drilling Company.

[3] Axon also filed multiple motions to strike various expert evidence, which the district court granted. We turn to these motions in Part IV(B) below.

2010) (quoting {-256-} *Murray v. Earle*, 405 F.3d 278, 284 (5th Cir. 2005)), but "[s]ummary judgment may not be thwarted by conclusional allegations, unsupported assertions, or presentation of only a scintilla of evidence," *McFaul v. Valenzuela*, 684 F.3d 564, 571 (5th Cir. 2012). Finally, "we are not limited to the district court's reasons for its grant of summary judgment and may affirm . . . on any ground raised below and supported by the **[—6—]** record." *Boyett v. Redland Ins. Co.*, 741 F.3d 604, 606–07 (5th Cir. 2014) (cleaned up).

We review the exclusion of expert testimony for abuse of discretion. *Sims v. Kia Motors of Am., Inc.*, 839 F.3d 393, 400 (5th Cir. 2016). "A district court abuses its discretion if it bases its decision on an erroneous view of the law or on a clearly erroneous assessment of the evidence." *CenterPoint Energy Hous. Elec. LLC v. Harris Cty. Toll Rd. Auth.*, 436 F.3d 541, 550 (5th Cir. 2006) (quoting *Ross v. Marshall*, 426 F.3d 745, 763 (5th Cir. 2005)).

III.

We turn first to the various indemnity issues. The parties' indemnity obligations are governed by a web of contracts. This simple diagram outlines the contours of those contractual relationships:

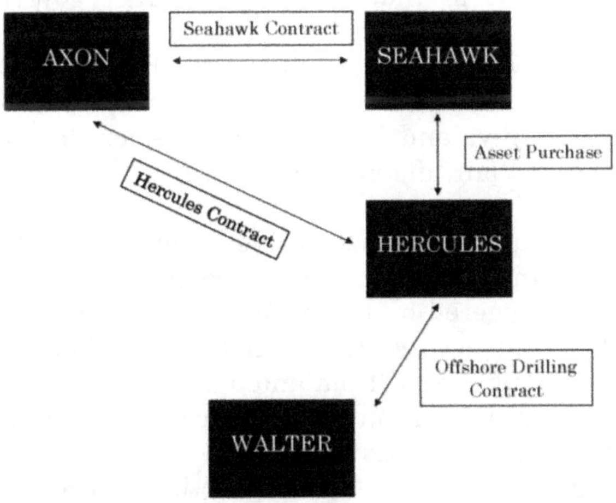

We will detail the relevant contractual provisions as needed. **[—7—]**

Defending the district court's decisions in its favor, Axon posits a scheme that extinguishes Plaintiffs' claims against it. It asserts that either (1) Walter must directly indemnify Axon for Walter's own claims against Axon, or (2) Walter must indemnify and defend Hercules against Axon's claims, which would result in circular indemnity, such that Walter would ultimately pay for its own successful claims against Axon. **{-257-}**

Resolution of these indemnity questions requires multiple steps. We first address whether Hercules must defend and indemnify Axon against Walter's claims. We then address whether Walter must directly indemnify Axon for Walter's own claims. Last, we address whether Walter must defend and indemnify Hercules against Axon's claims, which in turn arise from Walter's claims against Axon.

A. *Hercules' Duty to Indemnify Axon under the Seahawk Contract*

The district court concluded that Hercules was required to indemnify Axon under the Seahawk Contract. We agree.

1.

On June 16, 2010, Axon entered a Master Service Agreement (the "Seahawk Contract") with a company called Seahawk Drilling, Inc. At the time, Seahawk owned the HERCULES 265. Under the Seahawk Contract, Axon was placed on a list of providers who could perform work for Seahawk. When Seahawk had work for Axon, it would submit a work or purchase order for a specific job. Seahawk hired Axon to work on the HERCULES 265. Specifically, Axon was hired to refurbish—among other blowout preventer ("BOP") equipment—the blind shear rams ("BSRs"), which were part of the BOP stack.

The Seahawk Contract provided that it would "remain in force and effect until canceled by either party by giving the other party ten (10) days prior written notice." An indemnity clause required Seahawk to "release, [d]efend, **[—8—]** indemnify, and hold harmless [Axon] from and against any and all

[l]osses arising out of personal or bodily injury, sickness, disease or death or property damage, destruction or loss suffered by any member of Company Group in connection with this [a]greement." "Company Group" included Axon, its parent, subsidiaries, affiliates, and contractors, and various other parties.

Two days after Axon signed the Seahawk Contract, it entered into a similar service agreement with Hercules (the "Hercules Contract"). The Hercules Contract stated that it was to "supersede, amend, and restate any prior service or supply agreements or access agreements between [Hercules] and [Axon]." It was to "apply as a master service agreement to new [w]ork commenced during this Contract." An indemnity clause provided that "the parties . . . shall release, protect, defend, indemnify and hold harmless the other party and their insurers and subrogees . . . to the extent in each case . . . that such [liability] is caused by the negligence or other legal fault of the indemnifying party."

Seahawk ran into financial trouble and filed for bankruptcy. As part of that proceeding, Seahawk sold assets to Hercules, including the HERCULES 265 and the equipment Axon worked on. Hercules also bought "all of the interests, rights, [c]laims, and benefits arising or accruing to [Seahawk] under any [c]ontracts to which [Seahawk] is a party." Hercules assumed "the [l]iabilities of [Seahawk] under the terms of any [a]ssigned [c]ontract to the extent that such [l]iabilities are performance obligations, or otherwise attributable to the period from and after the [c]losing."

The Seahawk Contract was assigned to Hercules. The bankruptcy court specifically approved the purchase. The court also indicated that the transactions under the asset purchase agreement ("Purchase Agreement") would "be specifically performable and enforceable against and binding upon, and not subject to rejection or avoidance by, the [p]urchasers and [s]ellers." **[—9—]** The agreement closed on April 27, 2011. *See* **{-258-}** *In re Seahawk Drilling, Inc.*, No. 11-20089-RSS, 2011 WL 13323774 (Bankr. S.D. Tex. Apr. 27, 2011).

When Plaintiffs sued Axon, it sought defense and indemnity from Hercules under the Seahawk Contract. The district court granted summary judgment for Axon on the issue, holding that the Seahawk Contract controlled the parties' indemnity obligations for purposes of Plaintiffs' claims, and that under the contract, Hercules owed Axon defense and indemnity.

2.

The question of indemnity under the applicable contract is reviewed *de novo*. *Chevron USA, Inc. v. Aker Mar. Inc.*, 689 F.3d 497, 501 (5th Cir. 2012). We may affirm on any ground that was presented to the district court even if it did not ultimately form the basis of the district court's decision. *CQ, Inc. v. TXU Mining Co.*, 565 F.3d 268, 274 (5th Cir. 2009).

3.

Hercules asserts that the Hercules Contract, not the Seahawk Contract, governs indemnity between Hercules and Axon. Its core argument is that, since the Hercules Contract superseded all previous contracts between the parties, and because Hercules "stepped into the shoes" of Seahawk by assuming its contracts through the Purchase Agreement, the Hercules Contract supersedes the Seahawk Contract and the indemnity provision in the Hercules Contract governs here. We disagree and conclude that the Seahawk Contract governs. We therefore hold that Hercules must release, defend, indemnify, and hold harmless Axon for the claims Plaintiffs make against it.

As an initial matter, we conclude that the indemnity provision in the Seahawk Contract was triggered by Plaintiffs' suit against Axon. The contract requires Hercules to defend and indemnify Axon "from and against any and all [l]osses arising out of . . . property damage, destruction or loss suffered by any member of Company Group in connection with this [a]greement." "Company **[—10—]** Group" included "any entities for whom [Hercules] is performing services or providing goods." The group thus includes Walter because Hercules was "performing services" for Walter under the Drilling Contract. And Plaintiffs' claims against Axon arise in connection with the Seahawk Contract—that is, Plaintiffs claim Axon's work on the BOP was defective.

The next question is whether, as Hercules claims, the Hercules Contract superseded the Seahawk Contract. We hold that it did not, for several reasons. First, the Seahawk Contract was not a prior contract between Hercules and Axon. Axon and *Seahawk* entered the Seahawk Contract on June 16, 2010. Axon and Hercules entered the Hercules Contract on June 18, 2010. As of that date, Hercules was not a party to the Seahawk Contract, and therefore by its own terms the Hercules Contract could not have "supersede[d], amend[ed], and restate[d]" the Seahawk Contract. *See Breaux v. Halliburton Energy Servs.*, 562 F.3d 358, 366 (5th Cir. 2009) ("no sound basis" for concluding that later contract superseded earlier contract when contracts were not "*between the same parties*").

Second, the parties to the Seahawk Contract did not cancel it. By its own terms, the Seahawk Contract would "remain in force and effect until canceled by either party by giving the other party ten (10) days prior written notice." Hercules points to no evidence that any party to the contract gave the required notice to cancel the contract. **{-259-}**

Third, Hercules fails to point to evidence that Axon's work on the BOP was performed pursuant to the Hercules Contract. The Hercules Contract provided that it applied "as a master service agreement to new [w]ork commenced during this [c]ontract." But the record evidence shows that the work Axon did on the BOP was under the Seahawk Contract. The purchase order for the work on the BOP body lists Seahawk as the customer. So do the **[—11—]** purchase orders for the rams. Hercules does not point to contradictory evidence.

Contrary to Hercules' arguments, the revision of a repair data book does not create a fact question on this issue. An Axon executive testified that a revised repair data book was provided to Hercules after its purchase from Seahawk in order to reflect the change. He also testified that the revised version of the work orders "identify and describe the same work performed by Axon" pursuant to the purchase order that identifies Seahawk as the customer. In other words, the records establish that Axon performed work on the BOP and other equipment for *Seahawk*, and that after Hercules purchased Seahawk's assets the books were changed to reflect the new ownership, not to show that Axon performed work for *Hercules* on the BOP equipment.

Similarly, the district court's statement that the BOP was "refurbished by Axon after the [Hercules Contract] was executed" does not show the existence of a material fact dispute. Even assuming that the district court's statement, without any accompanying citation to evidence, could create a fact dispute, this statement does not establish that Axon performed work *for Hercules* on the BOP. Rather, it states that at some point after June 18, 2010—the date of the Hercules Contract—Axon performed work on the BOP. The evidence shows that the work on the BOP was performed for Seahawk. Further, Hercules did not finalize its purchase of Seahawk's assets—including the HERCULES 265—until April 27, 2011. *See Seahawk*, 2011 WL 13323774. Any work performed on the rig before then would necessarily have been performed on a rig owned by Seahawk, so whether work was performed on the BOP after June 18, 2010 is irrelevant—the relevant question is whether work was performed on the BOP after April 27, 2011. Hercules points to no such evidence. **[—12—]**

For these reasons, we hold that the Seahawk Contract governed the obligations of Axon and Hercules with regard to the underlying lawsuit. The district court correctly granted summary judgment for Axon on this issue.[4]

---

[4] Hercules makes a drive-by assertion that the district court erred by dismissing its counterclaims against Axon for indemnity at law, contribution, and breach of contract. Hercules' argument on the issue is brief and wholly conclusory, and it fails to respond to Axon's argument that Hercules has waived the issue. We agree with Axon and hold

B. *Walter's Duty to Indemnify Axon under the Drilling Contract*

The second indemnity question is whether Walter was required, by virtue of the Drilling Contract, to directly indemnify Axon for the very claims Plaintiffs brought against Axon. Contrary to the district court's ruling, we conclude that Walter was not required to do so.

1.

Hercules and Walter entered into the **{-260-}** Drilling Contract in 2011.[5] Section 501 of the contract outlines "[Walter]'s Standard of Performance." It provides that "[e]xcept for . . . obligations and liabilities specifically assumed by" Hercules, Walter is "solely responsible and assumes liability for all consequences of operations by both parties while on a daywork basis." Those consequences include "results and all other risks or liabilities incurred in or incident to or connected with, directly or indirectly, such operations."

Other provisions in the Drilling Contract allocate specific risks between the two parties. Article IX contains several provisions relevant to this appeal. **[—13—]** Section 902[6] obligates Walter to indemnify Hercules for damage to or loss of the hole or downhole property. Section 905(b)[7] requires Walter to indemnify Hercules for losses caused directly or indirectly by "pollution or contamination." Section 906[8] mandates indemnity for Hercules "for the cost of removal of all wreck and debris" and for the cost of "regaining control of any wild well." And section 907[9] obligates Walter to indemnify Hercules for loss to the mineral formation or strata, as well as the loss of oil, gas, or other minerals that had not yet "been reduced to physical possession above the seabed."

The relevant subsections further specify risks for which Walter is obligated to indemnify not only Hercules, but also its suppliers, contractors, **{-261-}** or subcontractors. For example, sections 902, 905(b),

---

that the issue is waived. *See United States v. Scroggins*, 599 F.3d 433, 446–47 (5th Cir. 2010) (argument not pressed on appeal is waived).

[5] Under the Drilling Contract, Walter was the "Operator" and Hercules was the "Contractor." "An operator is the company that serves as the overall manager and decisionmaker of a drilling project." *Zenergy, Inc. v. Performance Drilling Co.*, 603 F. App'x 289, 290 n.1 (5th Cir. 2015) (unpublished) (cleaned up). "A contractor is the company that owns and operates a drilling rig." *Id.* at 290 n.2 (cleaned up). For ease of reading, we substitute "Walter" for "Operator" and "Hercules" for "Contractor" when quoting the contract.

[6] "In the event the hole should be lost or damaged at any time, [Walter] shall, except as provided in Paragraph 705(f), be responsible for and hold harmless and indemnify [Hercules] and its suppliers, contractors and subcontractors of any tier from such damage to or loss of the hole, including all downhole property therein."

[7] "[Walter] shall be responsible for and hold harmless and indemnify [Hercules] and its suppliers, contractors and subcontractors of any tier against all claims, demands, causes of action, losses, and liabilities of every kind and character (including without limitation fines, penalties, assessments, third party claims, property damage, and control and removal of the pollutant involved) arising directly or indirectly from all pollution or contamination . . . which may occur including, but not limited to, that which may result from fire, blowout, cratering, seepage or any other uncontrolled flow of oil, gas, water or other substance . . . ."

[8] "[Walter] shall at all times be responsible for and hold harmless and indemnify [Hercules] for the cost of removal of all wreck and debris (including [Hercules'] Items as provided below). [Hercules] shall be responsible for and hold harmless and indemnify [Walter] for the cost of wreck and debris removal of [Hercules'] Items to the extent required by law or to prevent interference with [Walter's] operations. [Walter] shall at all times be responsible for and hold harmless and indemnify [Hercules] for the cost of regaining control of any wild well."

[9] "[Walter] shall at all times be responsible for and hold harmless and indemnify [Hercules] and its suppliers, contractors and subcontractors of any tier from and against any and all claims on account of injury to, destruction of or loss or impairment of any property right in or to oil, gas or other mineral substance or water, if at the time of the act or omission causing such injury, destruction, loss, or impairment, said substance had not been reduced to physical possession above the seabed, and for any loss or damage to any formation, strata, or reservoir beneath the seabed."

and 907 require Walter to **[—14—]** indemnify not only Hercules, but also its "suppliers, contractors, or subcontractors of any tier." In contrast, section 906 requires indemnification of only Hercules.

Two other sections in Article IX need our attention. First, section 911(c)[10] states that the words "be responsible for and hold harmless and indemnify" as used throughout Article IX "shall have no application to claims or causes of action asserted against [Walter] or [Hercules] which arise solely by reason of any agreement of indemnity with a person or entity" that is not a party to the Drilling Contract. Finally, section 912 explains that the provisions of Article IX, together with sections 605, 606, and 805, "shall exclusively govern the allocation of risks and liabilities of said parties without regard to cause."[11]

2.

We read contracts as a whole and give words "their plain meaning unless the provision is ambiguous." *Breaux*, 562 F.3d at 364 (quoting *Weathersby v.* **[—15—]** *Conoco Oil Co.*, 752 F.2d 953, 955 (5th Cir. 1984)).[12] "Disagreement as to the meaning of a contract does not make it ambiguous, nor does uncertainty or lack of clarity in the language chosen by the parties." *Id.* (quoting *Weir v. Fed. Asset Disposition Ass'n*, 123 F.3d 281, 286 (5th Cir. 1997)).

Axon makes two general arguments in support of affirmance. First, Axon asserts that, since Hercules did not specifically assume liability for a blowout, Walter assumed those risks under section 501 of the Drilling Contract. According to Axon, it **{-262-}** follows that Walter thus assumed the very liability that it now seeks to transfer to Axon by virtue of its products-liability suit. Second, Axon contends that the losses Walter seeks from Axon as damages fall into specific categories of loss for which Walter is required to directly indemnify Axon under the Drilling Contract.

Walter disagrees. In its view, the text of section 501 does not mention, and thus fails to create, any indemnity obligations at all.

10 "Except as otherwise provided herein, the parties intend and agree that the phrase 'be responsible for and hold harmless and indemnify' or other similar words of release or indemnity (including limitation or exclusion of damages and all other exculpatory provisions) in this Contract including without limitation Paragraphs 605, 606, 805, and 901 through 910 shall have no application to claims or causes of action asserted against [Walter] or [Hercules] which arise solely by reason of any agreement of indemnity with a person or entity not a party hereto. Except as otherwise provided herein, nothing contained herein shall confer any rights upon any third party beneficiary. Nothing contained herein shall confer any right of action in any person not a party hereto or identified as an indemnitee herein."

11 "The parties recognize that the performance of well drilling, workover and associated activities such as those to be performed under this Contract have resulted in bodily injury, death, damage or loss of property, well loss or damage, pollution, loss of well control, reservoir damage and other losses and liabilities. It is the intention of the parties hereto that the provisions of this Article IX and Paragraphs 605, 606 and 805 shall exclusively govern the allocation of risks and liabilities of said parties without regard to cause (as more particularly specified in Paragraph 911), it being acknowledged that the compensation payable to [Hercules] as specified herein has been based upon the express understanding that risks and liabilities shall be determined in accordance with the provisions of this Contract."

12 The parties do not appear to contest that maritime law applies to the contracts at issue. We do not address whether that is correct because it is irrelevant: wherever derived, the applicable principles of contract interpretation are general ones that are broadly applied. *See, e.g.*, Restatement (Second) of Contracts § 202(2) ("A writing is interpreted as a whole, and all writings that are part of the same transaction are interpreted together."); *see also Forbau v. Aetna Life Ins. Co.*, 876 S.W.2d 132, 133 (Tex. 1994) ("This court is bound to read all parts of a contract together to ascertain the agreement of the parties. The contract must be considered as a whole. Moreover, each part of the contract should be given effect." (citations omitted)); *Lewis v. Hamilton*, 652 So. 2d 1327, 1329–30 (La. 1995) ("The words of a contract must be given their generally prevailing meaning . . . . Each provision of a contract must be interpreted in light of the other provisions, and a provision susceptible of different meanings must be interpreted with a meaning that renders it effective rather than one which renders it ineffective.").

Walter also argues that Axon's broad reading of section 501 would render many other provisions meaningless. Regarding Axon's second argument, Walter argues that none of **[—16—]** the losses it seeks are covered by specific sections of the Drilling Contract that would require it to directly indemnify Axon.

The district court concluded section 501 established that "Walter, as operator, assumes all obligations and 'shall be solely responsible and assume[] all liability for all consequences of operations[,]' including Hercules' subcontractors[,] on any theory of law including strict liability." We disagree for the following reasons.

First, section 501 does not require Walter to directly indemnify Axon. Its plain text does not purport to create any indemnity obligations. Rather, it explains that Walter is solely responsible and assumes liabilities for any consequences of operations by both parties (*i.e.*, Walter and Hercules) that are not elsewhere specifically assumed by Hercules. "A contract of indemnity . . . should not be read to impose liability for those losses or liabilities which are neither expressly within its terms nor of such a character that it can be reasonably inferred that the parties intended to include them within the indemnity coverage." *Corbitt v. Diamond M. Drilling Co.*, 654 F.2d 329, 333 (5th Cir. Unit A Aug. 1981).[13]

Accepting the district court's interpretation would leave several sections in Article IX without purpose. Take an example. If, on these facts, Walter was required to directly indemnify Axon for the losses it seeks through its lawsuit, what would be left of section 906, which obligates Walter to indemnify **[—17—]** Hercules—but *not* its subcontractors or contractors, like Axon—"for the cost of removal of all wreck and debris" as well as costs for controlling wild wells? Another hypothetical. Imagine a scenario in which the blowout here caused a massive oil spill. Section 905(b) requires Walter to indemnify Hercules and its contractors for losses caused directly or indirectly by "pollution or contamination." If section 501 actually means that Hercules must indemnify Axon directly for those losses, what work is section 905(b) doing? There are other examples, but these two make the point: Axon's reading—and the district court's—would render much of Article IX redundant. To the extent possible, we interpret contracts to avoid that result. *Chembulk Trading LLC v. Chemex Ltd.*, 393 F.3d 550, 555 (5th Cir. 2004).[14] **{-263-}**

The district court's reading of section 501 also ignores the fact that Walter and Hercules agreed on a different scope of indemnification for different risks. For some risks, such as damage to the hole, Walter agreed to indemnify Hercules *and* its subcontractors, contractors, and suppliers. But for other risks, such as the cost of debris removal and costs to control a wild well, Walter agreed to indemnify only Hercules.

Further, Axon's reading conflicts with section 912. As noted above, that section makes the provisions of Article IX, along with sections 605, 606, and 805, the exclusive provisions "govern[ing] the allocation of risks and liabilities of said parties without regard to cause." Section 501 is not on that list. Whatever work section 501 is doing, then, the

---

[13] *See also Int'l Marine, L.L.C. v. Integrity Fisheries, Inc.*, 860 F.3d 754, 759, 5 Adm. R. 277, 279 (5th Cir. 2017) (reciting same principle "[u]nder federal maritime law"); *MEMC Elec. Materials, Inc. v. Albemarle Corp.*, 241 S.W.3d 67, 71 (Tex. App. 2007) ("Indemnity provisions are to be strictly construed, pursuant to the usual principles of contract interpretation, in order to give effect to the parties' intent as expressed in the agreement."); *Liem v. Austin Power, Inc.*, 569 So. 2d 601, 608 (La. Ct. App. 1990) (general contract interpretation principles apply to indemnity agreements; interpretation is determination of common intent of parties "and when the words of the contract are clear and explicit and lead to no absurd consequences, no further interpretation may be made").

[14] *See also In re Deepwater Horizon*, 785 F.3d 1003, 1011, 3 Adm. R. 325, 329 (5th Cir. 2015) (contracts to be interpreted to give effect to all terms without rendering any of them meaningless); *Ewing Constr. Co. v. Amerisure Ins. Co.*, 420 S.W.3d 30, 37 (Tex. 2014) ("[I]nterpretations of contracts as a whole are favored so that none of the language in them is rendered surplusage."); *Hamilton*, 652 So. 2d at 1330.

parties explicitly agreed that it is not doing the work Axon thinks it is. **[—18—]**

Second, we disagree with Axon that Hercules seeks damages for which Walter is required to directly indemnify Axon under Article IX of the Drilling Contract. Axon primarily asserts that three provisions of Article IX—sections 902, 905(b), and 907—give it a right to direct indemnity from Walter against Walter's own claims. Each of those sections requires Walter to indemnify and release not only Hercules, but also its suppliers, contractors, and subcontractors. Section 902 covers losses for damage to the hole; section 905(b) covers losses caused directly or indirectly by pollution or contamination; and section 907 covers losses for damage to the mineral formation or strata as well as losses from oil, gas, or other minerals that had not been reduced to physical possession above the seabed. *See supra* notes 6–7, 9.

Plaintiffs seek only the cost of regaining control of the well, plugging and abandoning the well, replacing the original platform, and removing the wreckage of the damaged platform. Axon contends these damages fall into categories covered by sections 902, 905(b), or 907, and since Axon asserts it qualifies as a supplier or subcontractor of Hercules, Walter owed Axon direct indemnity under the Drilling Contract between Walter and Hercules.[15]

We disagree. Plaintiffs did not seek damages for damage to the hole itself or any downhole equipment or property. So, section 902 does not cover the damages. Similarly, Plaintiffs did not seek damages for the loss of any subsurface oil or gas, so section 907 is not implicated. Thus, neither section requires Hercules to directly indemnify Axon.

Neither does section 905(b), on which Axon places particular emphasis. That section provides that Walter "shall be responsible for and hold harmless **[—19—]** and indemnify" Hercules (and its suppliers, contractors, or subcontractors) for liability caused directly or indirectly by "all pollution or contamination . . . which may occur including . . . that which may result from fire, blowout, cratering, seepage or any other uncontrolled flow of oil, gas, water or other substance." Axon asserts that the losses Plaintiffs seek are all included in this provision's broad language.

Axon's argument goes like this. The materials ejected during the blowout qualify as pollutants or contaminants. The losses **{-264-}** Plaintiffs claim—well control, plugging and abandoning the well, replacing the platform, and removing wreckage—were all caused, directly or indirectly, by the expulsion of those pollutants or contaminants during the blowout, or were caused by attempts to prevent further expulsion of those substances. Thus, Plaintiffs' claimed damages are all covered by the broad language of section 905(b).

We disagree with Axon's interpretation. First, Axon's argument is hard to square with the text of the provision itself. Take, for example, Plaintiffs' damages for the costs of replacing the original platform and removing the wreckage of the old one. Those damages were caused by the fire that resulted from the blowout, not by contamination or pollution. Thus the plain meaning of section 905(b) counsels against Axon's interpretation. *See Breaux*, 562 F.3d at 364 (words in contracts given plain meaning unless ambiguous); Restatement (Second) of Contracts § 202(3) ("Unless a different intention is manifested, . . . where language has a generally prevailing meaning, it is interpreted in accordance with that meaning."). Axon does not argue that 905(b) is ambiguous, and we find no ambiguity.

Second, Axon's reading of section 905(b) would render other provisions in Article IX meaningless, an outcome courts strive to avoid. *See Chembulk*, 393 F.3d at 555. Under Axon's reading, *any* possible expenses incurred by Walter as a result of the blowout would be covered by section 905(b) because

[15] We assume without deciding that Axon qualifies as either a supplier or subcontractor under the contract. Nothing in our decision precludes the district court reaching a determination on this issue should it be necessary to resolving the case on remand.

[—20—] they would have been caused, directly or indirectly, by the escape of materials qualifying as contaminants or pollutants. For example, Axon's reading would render part of section 906, which requires indemnity for the cost of controlling a wild well, superfluous—all costs of controlling a wild well would conceivably be costs incurred trying to prevent further escape of pollutants or contaminants. If section 905(b) was meant to be read that broadly, why include section 906 at all?

Third, Axon's reading again ignores the careful allocation of liability evidenced by Article IX. Hercules and Walter agreed that for some damages, Walter would indemnify only Hercules, while for others, Walter would also indemnify suppliers, contractors, and subcontractors. Reading section 905(b) as broadly as Axon does would make Hercules liable to contractors, subcontractors, and suppliers in essentially all instances, instead of only in those instances delineated in the particular sections of Article IX.

For these reasons, we hold that the district court erred by granting summary judgment to Axon on the ground that Walter was required to directly indemnify Axon for the claims Walter itself brought against Axon. We make no determination as to which provision or provisions of Article IX apply to Plaintiffs' claimed damages. We hold only that Axon's interpretation of sections 501 and 905(b)—with which the district court apparently agreed—do not justify summary judgment in its favor. We therefore reverse the summary judgment in Axon's favor on this ground.

C. *Walter's Duty to Release and Indemnify Hercules under the Drilling Contract*

The third indemnity question we address is whether Walter was required by the contract to release and indemnify Hercules for the claims Axon brought against Hercules—resulting in "circular indemnity," where liability is simply passed from Walter, to Axon, to Hercules, and then back to Walter. This [—21—] interpretation, which Axon urges, would essentially extinguish any liability from Axon to Walter. We conclude that the contract does not support **{–265–}** this interpretation, and so we reverse the judgment in Axon's favor on this issue.

1.

The provisions of the Drilling Contract discussed in Part III(B) are also relevant here. The key section is 911(c), which establishes that the indemnity provisions of the contract "shall have no application to claims or causes of action asserted against [Walter] or [Hercules] which arise solely by reason of any agreement of indemnity with a person or entity not a party hereto." The district court held that, notwithstanding this language, Walter was required to defend and indemnify Hercules against Axon's claims because "Axon's suit against Hercules is triggered by Underwriters' suit against Axon. In turn, Axon's suit against Hercules is based on contractual obligations between Hercules and Axon contained in an indemnity agreement."

2.

Walter argues on appeal that the district court's conclusion ignored section 911(c) and destroyed the careful distribution of liability in Article IX. We agree.

Section 911(c) exempts Walter from any obligation to indemnify Hercules for any claims brought by a third party against Hercules arising "solely by reason of any agreement of indemnity." As the district court itself acknowledged, Axon's claims against Hercules primarily arise out of the agreement between the two parties—the Seahawk Contract. *See supra* Part III(A).

Although Axon's complaint against Hercules also references claims for indemnity at law and common law contribution, creative pleading cannot disguise the fact that Axon's claim for indemnity against Hercules arises out of the Seahawk Contract. [—22—]

The Drilling Contract's provisions—specifically, section 501—do not expressly obligate Walter to indemnify Hercules for purely contractual claims brought by third parties against Hercules. "[E]xpress notice is required where a party seeks to shift his contractual liability to indemnify a third party." *Corbitt,* 654 F.2d at 333.[16] No provision in the Drilling Contract provides such notice. And section 911(c) expressly prohibits that scenario.

In *Corbitt,* we stated that indemnity agreements "should not be read to impose liability for those losses or liabilities which are neither expressly within its terms nor of such a character that it can be reasonably inferred that the parties intended to include them within the indemnity coverage." *Id.* Because the contract at issue there provided for indemnity "against all claims, suits, liabilities and expenses on account of personal injury . . . arising out of or in connection with performance of this Order," but did not "expressly provide" for indemnification against claims brought by third parties, we held that Sladco (analogous here to Walter) was not bound to indemnify Shell (analogous to Hercules) for claims arising out of "Shell's own separate contractual obligations." *Id.*

So too here. Section 501 says nothing about Walter being required to indemnify Hercules for claims brought by third parties against Hercules that arise out of a contract. In fact, section 501 says nothing about indemnity at all. Adopting Axon's reading of section 501 would impose liability on Walter for Hercules' liability to Axon, a third party, and it would do so without any express acceptance of that responsibility by Walter. That interpretation would contravene the rule set forth in *Corbitt.* **{-266-}**

To read section 501 as broadly as Axon and Hercules urge would also destroy the distinction carefully drawn between situations where Walter is **[—23—]** required to indemnify only Hercules and situations where Walter must also indemnify Hercules' suppliers, contractors, or subcontrators. As previously discussed, section 906 requires Walter to indemnify Hercules—and only Hercules—for costs associated with the removal of wreckage and debris and for the costs to control any wild wells. Those are precisely the sorts of damages claimed by Plaintiffs here. To read section 501 as requiring Walter to indemnify Hercules for Axon's claims would be to ignore the limitation imposed by section 906. We decline to do so. *See Chembulk,* 393 F.3d at 555. A limitation that can be avoided simply by having a third party sue Hercules is no limitation at all.

Axon's and Hercules' arguments to the contrary are unavailing. They assert that section 501 expressly provides that all liabilities not specifically assumed by Hercules are to be borne by Walter. Since Hercules did not specifically assume the risk of removing debris or controlling a wild well, the argument goes, Walter must ultimately bear the costs. But that argument ignores section 911(c), in which Hercules *did* specifically assume liabilities caused by third-party claims arising out of agreements of indemnity between Hercules and those third parties.

Hercules also argues that section 906 demonstrates that Walter expressly assumed any costs to remove wreck or debris or the costs of controlling any wild well. But, as with the previous argument, this argument also fails to account for section 911(c), under which, as just discussed, Hercules assumed liabilities caused by third-party claims arising out of contract. If Hercules brought its own claim for the costs of removing debris or controlling a wild well, those costs may well be covered by section 906. But to read section **[—24—]** 906 as requiring indemnification for third-party claims is to ignore section 911(c).[17]

Because section 911(c) specifically forecloses the possibility that Walter is required to indemnify Hercules for contractual obligations to third parties, and nothing else in the contract expressly provides otherwise,

[16] *See also MEMC Elec. Materials,* 241 S.W.3d at 71; *Liem,* 569 So. 2d at 608.

[17] Hercules also makes the same arguments regarding sections 902, 905(b), and 907 that we discussed in Part III(B)(3), *supra.* For the same reasons those sections do not require Walter to indemnify Axon directly, they also do not require Walter to indemnify Hercules.

we hold that Walter is not obligated to indemnify Hercules for the claims Axon brings against it. We therefore conclude that the district court's contrary conclusion was error and reverse the summary judgment in Hercules' favor on this issue.

IV.

We now turn to the district court's decisions regarding various expert evidence, as well as the merits of Plaintiffs' Louisiana Products Liability Act ("LPLA") claims. To establish their products-liability claim under the LPLA, Plaintiffs were required to show that (1) a characteristic of Axon's parts proximately caused the damage; (2) the damage arose from a reasonably anticipated use of the parts; and (3) the parts at issue were unreasonably dangerous. *See* La. Stat. Ann. § 9:2800.54(A). We first examine the district court's rulings regarding expert evidence because that analysis informs our review of the summary judgment decisions. We then turn to the individual summary judgment decisions.

A. *Factual Background*

Oil, natural gas, and other subsurface deposits are often contained within their **{-267-}** formations at high pressure. This poses a problem for those who want to drill into those formations. If a well is drilled into the formation and the pressures are not controlled, explosive blowouts can occur. To prevent **[—25—]** materials from the deposit from entering the wellbore, fluids from the drilling rig are pumped into the wellbore to create downward pressure on the formation. If this pressure is not carefully maintained, material from the formation can enter the wellbore. If that happens, the return rate of the pressure-maintenance fluid will increase suddenly. This is referred to in the industry as a "kick." Uncontrolled kicks can lead to blowouts.

Various pieces of equipment on the drilling rig help the crew control kicks and prevent blowouts. The key piece in this case is the blowout preventer stack ("BOP stack"). For ease of reference, we include the following illustration of a BOP stack provided in Axon's brief.

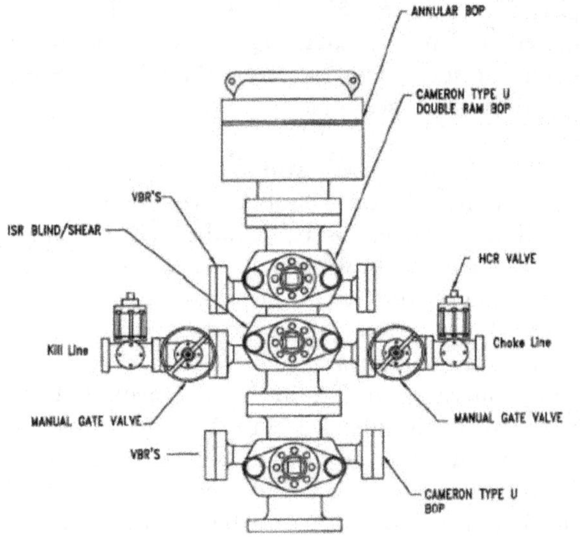

The BOP stack is placed near the top end of the drill pipe. As can be seen, the BOP at issue in this case contained an annular BOP, a double ram BOP, and a single ram BOP. The annular BOP is used to seal the space around the **[—26—]** drill pipe known as the annulus. The single ram BOP also seals the area around the drill pipe. The double ram BOP has two sets of rams. The top set of rams, like the single ram BOP, seals the area around the drill pipe. The bottom set of rams are BSRs. When activated, they cut and seal the drill pipe itself. **{-268-}**

Beneath the BSRs are outlets known as the kill and choke lines. The kill line pumps pressure-maintenance materials into the wellbore, and the choke line controls flow out of the wellbore. The choke line can be opened and closed manually at two different points, or it can be closed using the high closing ratio ("HCR") valve. The choke line plays a key role in this story.

The rams and HCR valve are all powered by the same source: the accumulator. The accumulator can be used to activate the rams or the HCR valve from one of three locations on the rig: the rig floor, the driller's shack, or the toolpusher's office.

In July 2013, the Hercules rig crew was removing drill pipe from the A-3 well. A kick occurred but went unnoticed. A short time later, fluid began erupting from the annulus and drill pipe onto the rig. The fluid erupted with enough force that it jammed the drill pipe into equipment overhead. This made it impossible for the crew to install a drill pipe safety valve, the usual first step in such a situation. The crew closed the annular BOP, but that did not stop the problem.

The blowout intensified. The crew decided to close the upper and lower rams from the toolpusher's office. They then activated the BSRs, which would shear and seal the pipe. They also tried to remotely close the HCR valve, which would have cut off the flow spewing out of the choke line. But the HCR valve never closed. For a moment, however, the flow from the well slowed. Three crew members decided to return to the rig floor to turn off engines there that could accidentally ignite the growing gas cloud. But as they were returning, the blowout picked up again, and they were unable to make it back to the rig **[—27—]** floor. Instead, they joined the rest of the crew and evacuated. After a few hours, the blowout ignited and burned for several days until the well eventually sealed itself. The rig suffered extensive damage.

As required by regulation, Walter assembled a team of independent well-control experts to investigate the blowout. *See* 30 C.F.R. § 250.1919. The experts produced a report (the "first SEMS report") and submitted it to the Bureau of Safety and Environmental Enforcement ("BSEE"). A second SEMS report was submitted later. The BSEE conducted its own investigation and issued another report, concluding that "the actions to close the rams came too late." The BSEE report states that "by the time the attempt to close [the rams] was made, the well was already flowing at a pressure exceeding the BOP's capabilities." The reports all concluded that the HCR valve had never closed, and so the choke line remained open as a path for flow from the well throughout the blowout. Ultimately, BSEE fined Walter for the crew's "inability to maintain proper completion fluid density throughout the well operations, and their failure to detect a well bore influx in a timely manner."

B. *Exclusion of Expert Evidence*

To begin, we consider the district court's evidentiary rulings that could have affected the summary judgments awarded. *See Curtis v. M&S Petroleum, Inc.*, 174 F.3d 661, 667–68 (5th Cir. 1999) ("We must first review the trial court's evidentiary rulings . . . . Then, with the record defined, we must review *de novo* the order granting judgment as a matter of law." (citation omitted)).

1.

We first examine the district court's decision to grant Axon's motion to exclude "any expert testimony offered by Simon Bellemare relating to Plaintiffs' products liability claims." We vacate the district **{-269-}** court's order excluding Bellemare's evidence because it failed to explain its decision. **[—28—]**

Plaintiffs proffered evidence from Bellemare regarding the allegedly dangerous condition of Axon's products, the third prong of Plaintiffs' LPLA claim. *See* La. Stat. Ann. § 9:2800.54(A). Axon moved to exclude his testimony, arguing that Bellemare was unqualified and that his analysis was unreliable. The district court, in a document styled "Plenary Order," stated: "Axon's motion to exclude testimony of Simon Bellemare – GRANTED." It offered no reasons for its decision.

Axon believes this was not reversible error because the district court's decision was clearly correct based on the record, and a remand would simply waste time and resources. It relies on our decision in *North Cypress Medical Center Operating Co. v. Aetna Life Insurance Co.*, 898 F.3d 461 (5th Cir. 2018), to argue that even if the district court abused its discretion by not providing reasons for a decision, we may examine the issue on our own to decide whether the district court's ultimate decision was correct.

In *North Cypress*, we concluded that even though the district court abused its discretion by failing to explain why it denied leave to amend, remand was not the appropriate remedy because it "would likely 'be an exercise in futility.'" *Id.* at 479 (quoting *Wiwa v. Royal Dutch Petroleum Co.*, 392 F.3d 812, 819 (5th Cir. 2004)). We reached that determination after observing that our precedent did not require reversal and remand, and that we have statutory authority to "affirm, modify, vacate, set aside or reverse any judgment, decree, or order of a court lawfully brought before it for review, and [we] may remand the cause and direct the entry of such appropriate judgment . . . or require such further proceedings to be had as may be just." *Id.* (quoting 28 U.S.C. § 2106). We then considered several factors and concluded after our own review of the record that the district court's decision was ultimately correct. *Id.* at 479–80.

We decline to extend *North Cypress* to this context. Here, the district court was tasked with determining the reliability of expert evidence. District **[—29—]** courts serve as gatekeepers and are responsible for ensuring the reliability and relevance of all expert evidence. *See Kumho Tire Co. v. Carmichael*, 526 U.S. 137, 152 (1999). The court must ensure that the expert "employs in the courtroom the same level of intellectual rigor that characterizes the practice of an expert in the relevant field." *Id.*

When a district court fails to give reasons for its decision to exclude expert testimony, a reviewing court has no way of knowing whether that gatekeeping responsibility has been adequately performed. "A statement of reasons is one of the handmaidens of judging." *Schwarz v. Folloder*, 767 F.2d 125, 133 (5th Cir. 1985). "Where a district court fails to explain its decision . . . we do not know whether the decision was within the bounds of its discretion or was based on an erroneous legal theory." *Id.* As *North Cypress* acknowledges, generally, "[r]emanding to provide the district court with an opportunity to explain its [decision] is preferred." 898 F.3d at 479.

Here, the need for the district court to explain its decision was particularly high given the stakes—the exclusion of Bellemare's testimony could devastate Plaintiffs' case. His testimony forms much of the evidentiary basis on which Plaintiffs opposed summary judgment on the "unreasonably dangerous condition" issue under the LPLA. *See* La. Stat. Ann. § 9:2800.54(A). While we do not hold that **{–270–}** all instances in which a district court fails to give reasons for excluding expert evidence constitute reversible error, we do hold that, in this circumstance, the district court abused its discretion in failing to do so. On remand, the district court should examine afresh the admissibility of Bellemare's expert testimony and give reasons for its decision.

2.

We next examine the court's two orders striking evidence from various other experts. Axon moved to exclude supplemental expert reports from Sones, Bourgoyne, Williams, Rusnak, Bellemare, and Adair, arguing that the reports **[—30—]** were untimely and therefore violated the court's scheduling order. It later moved to strike summary judgment affidavits from Sones and Bourgoyne on timeliness grounds, arguing that the affidavits disclosed new opinions beyond the district court's deadline for such disclosures. The district court appeared to grant both motions.

In an order dated January 8, 2018, the district court declined to strike the expert reports. The court then cryptically stated, "However, affidavits as opposed to reports that were filed are STRICKEN. The Court will not admit into evidence expert reports or affidavits, and reserves the right to strike, deny, or exclude part or all of any expert's testimony." No further explanation of the court's decision was given, and so the precise grounds for the decision are unclear. For purposes of our analysis, we assume the district court struck the affidavits on the grounds urged by Axon—timeliness.

District courts consider four factors when determining whether to exclude expert evidence as a sanction for the violation of a scheduling order. *In re Complaint of C.F. Bean*

L.L.C., 841 F.3d 365, 372, 4 Adm. R. 298, 301 (5th Cir. 2016). Those factors are: "(1) the explanation for the failure to identify the witness; (2) the importance of the testimony; (3) potential prejudice in allowing the testimony; and (4) the availability of a continuance to cure such prejudice." *Id.*, 4 Adm. R. at 301 (quoting *Geiserman v. MacDonald*, 893 F.2d 787, 791 (5th Cir. 1990)).

The district court failed to examine (or even acknowledge) these factors when it excluded the expert reports as untimely. In fact, it gave no reasons for its decision at all. We are tasked with determining whether the district court "base[d] its decision on an erroneous view of the law or on a clearly erroneous assessment of the evidence." *CenterPoint Energy*, 436 F.3d at 550 (quoting *Ross*, 426 F.3d at 763). But "[w]here a district court fails to explain its decision . . . we do not know whether the decision was within the bounds of its discretion or was based on an erroneous legal theory." *Schwarz*, 767 F.2d at 133. We **[—31—]** therefore hold that to the extent the district court's order excluded the expert reports of Sones, Bourgoyne, Williams, Rusnak, Bellemare, and Adair on timeliness grounds, the order must be vacated and remanded to allow the district court to explain its decision after considering the proper factors.

In an order dated February 14, 2018, the district court granted Axon's motion to exclude the Sones and Bourgoyne summary judgment affidavits and offered a brief explanation. It concluded that both experts' affidavits "merely distort issues already resolved by the same affiants' report (SEMS) to the federal government." It further explained that, in its view, the affidavits failed to scientifically establish that the BSRs were defective. Finally, the court noted that "[e]qually important to this decision, no dispute exists concerning the nature of the well blowout or the factors that caused[] or contributed to it." **{-271-}**

Like the first order, this second order also failed to examine the required factors. *See In re C.F. Bean*, 841 F.3d at 372, 4 Adm. R. at 301–02. And the brief reasoning the district court did give is questionable. The district court concluded that the affidavits contradicted issues in the SEMS Report. It then perplexingly concluded that—even though it had just recognized a conflict in the evidence—"no dispute exists concerning the nature of the well blowout or the factors that caused[] or contributed to it." But expert testimony is not subject to exclusion just because it contradicts other evidence in the record—to the contrary, at summary judgment that is the main point of expert evidence. *Cf.* Fed. R. Civ. P. 56(a) ("The court shall grant summary judgment if the movant shows that there is no genuine dispute as to any material fact . . . ."). The district court's explanation therefore did not justify the exclusion.

We do not decide here, however, what the result of the proper legal analysis should be. Rather, because the district court failed to examine the required factors, and the brief explanation it did offer is dubious, we vacate the **[—32—]** order denying the Sones and Bourgoyne affidavits and remand to allow the court to undertake the proper analysis in the first instance.[18]

C. *LPLA Products-Liability Claim*

We now proceed to the district court's grant of summary judgment on the merits of the products-liability claim. As previously discussed, Plaintiffs were required to show that (1) a characteristic of Axon's parts proximately caused the damage; (2) the damage arose from a reasonably anticipated use of the parts; and (3) the parts at issue were unreasonably dangerous. *See* La. Stat. Ann. § 9:2800.54(A). The district court granted Axon summary judgment because it concluded that Plaintiffs failed to show that a question of material fact existed regarding causation and the unreasonably dangerous

[18] The district court's summary judgment order on causation discusses the exclusion of expert evidence. This order suffers from the same lack-of-reasoned-explanation flaw as the two orders discussed. To the extent this order operates to exclude the expert evidence discussed, it must be vacated as well.

nature of the equipment. Axon urges affirmance on these grounds and asserts that the "reasonably anticipated use" prong provides an alternative ground for affirmance. We address each of these elements in turn.

1.

To establish causation, Plaintiffs were required to establish that the equipment Axon worked on proximately caused the blowout. In Louisiana, "[a] proximate cause is generally defined as any cause which, in natural and continuous sequence, unbroken by any efficient, intervening cause, produces the result complained of and without which the result would not have occurred." *Hutto v. McNeil-PPC, Inc.*, 79 So. 3d 1199, 1213 (La. Ct. App. 2011) (quoting *Sutton v. Duplessis*, 584 So. 2d 362, 365 (La. Ct. App. 1991)).

In granting Axon summary judgment, the district court concluded that Plaintiffs failed to meet this burden. It based its decision "for the most part[] **[—33—]** on the SEMS and BSEE Reports and the testimony of Walter's on[-]site personnel." The court specifically concluded that "the SEMS Report of findings is unimpeached." Though not entirely clear, it appears that the district court believed that the SEMS and BSEE reports were dispositive on the issue of causation, and that summary judgment for Axon was therefore appropriate.

We disagree. Our *de novo* review of the evidence finds disputes of material fact regarding causation. **{-272-}**

First, Plaintiffs produced evidence that the BSRs did not seal the drill pipe as they should have. Defense expert Bill Abel testified that flow from the well through the BOP would have stopped had the BSRs sealed properly. Another witness, Wilson, concurred. And a third witness, Bradley Pitts, testified that after the BSRs had been activated, gas continued to flow up through the rig floor and drill pipe. In fact, Pitts testified that the flow was not coming from the still-open choke line but was "all coming up the annulus . . . [a]nd the drill pipe." A jury could conclude, based on this evidence, that the BSRs did not seal the drill pipe as they should have.

Next, there is evidence that the continued flow from the annulus and drill pipe prevented the crew from successfully shutting in the well. Wilson testified that the crew had been unable to undertake "normal well control procedures" because the flow continued. Abel testified that, after activating the BSRs, the crew's next step would have been to close the choke line by whatever means necessary. Wilson testified that after the BSRs had been remotely activated, three workers attempted to return to the rig floor, but were unable to because the well started blowing out again. And one of the expert witnesses, Terry Brittenham, stated that it is likely that the crew may have been trying to access the rig floor to manually close the choke valve, and that if they had been able to do so, that would have been enough to stop the blowout had the BOP parts worked as intended. **[—34—]**

This evidence creates a material fact dispute that precludes summary judgment. A fact-finder could reasonably conclude, based on this evidence, that the alleged defect in the BSRs prevented the flow from stopping after the BSRs had been activated. The fact-finder could also conclude that the continued flow prevented the rig crew from being able to manually close the choke flow path. In other words, a fact-finder could conclude that the alleged BSR defect was a "cause which, in natural and continuous sequence, unbroken by any efficient, intervening cause," produced the blowout and that without the BSR defect the blowout would have been contained. *Hutto*, 79 So. 3d at 1213.

While other evidence also suggests that crew error may have been an additional cause of the blowout, a reasonable fact-finder still could conclude that a non-defective BOP would have, under the circumstances, allowed the crew to prevent the blowout. *See Stewart v. Capital Safety USA*, 867 F.3d 517, 521 (5th Cir. 2017) ("To find injury causation here, a jury would at least have to conclude that a different lifeline cable or a different warning would have, under the circumstances of this accident, prevented [the accident]."). A jury could have returned a verdict in Plaintiffs' favor on this issue, *see Liberty Lobby*, 477 U.S. at 248, and we therefore hold that the district court erred by granting summary judgment in Axon's favor on the issue of causation.

2.

The district court also granted Axon summary judgment on the grounds that Plaintiffs failed to create a question of material fact on the "unreasonably dangerous condition" prong of the LPLA test. Because the court gave no reasons for doing so, however, we cannot know the basis for its ruling.

When ruling on a summary judgment motion, "[t]he court should state on the record the reasons for granting or denying the motion." Fed. R. Civ. P. 56(a). This court has "many times emphasized the importance of a detailed discussion by the trial judge." *McIncrow v. Harris County*, 878 F.2d 835, 835– **[—35—]** 36 (5th Cir. 1989). When **{-273-}** district courts have failed to do so, we have on occasion vacated and remanded. *See D'Onofrio v. Vacation Publ'ns, Inc.*, 888 F.3d 197, 210 n.13 (5th Cir. 2018) (district court erred by "failing to state the reasons for granting summary judgment . . . as is required by Rule 56(a)"); *Baker v. TDCJ-CID*, 774 F. App'x 198, 199 (5th Cir. 2019) (unpublished) (same). However, because our review here is *de novo*, we need not vacate and remand if we can ourselves determine whether summary judgment is appropriate.

Vacatur and remand is appropriate here for two reasons. First, the district court's opinion is "pithy to the point of being incomplete." *Myers v. Gulf Oil Corp.*, 731 F.2d 281, 283 (5th Cir. 1984). The entire ruling consists of a single sentence. Second, vacatur here is appropriate because of our decision to vacate the exclusion of Bellemare's testimony. *Cf. 103 Inv'rs I, L.P. v. Square D Co.*, 372 F.3d 1213, 1218 (10th Cir. 2004) ("Because the decision to grant summary judgment was premised upon its exclusion of the expert reports, we REVERSE the district court's decision to grant summary judgment . . . ."). As we previously noted, Bellemare's testimony forms much of Plaintiffs' case on this issue. Thus the district court's decision regarding Bellemare's testimony will have a substantial impact on the appropriateness of summary judgment. We express no view on the outcome of the issue, but vacate so that the district court, having reviewed anew the admissibility of Bellemare's testimony, can then explain its decision on this issue. **[—36—]**

3.

Axon next offers the LPLA's "reasonably anticipated use" prong as an alternate ground for affirmance. We hold that questions of fact exist on this issue as well and that summary judgment is therefore inappropriate.[19]

Axon makes two primary contentions. First, it asserts that the BOP and BSRs are blowout *preventers*, but not blowout *stoppers*. Thus, the argument goes, using the BSRs to stop a blowout already in progress is not a reasonably anticipated use. Second, it asserts that it was not reasonably anticipated that the BSRs would be used in a situation where a rig crew attempted to close the BSRs but not the HCR valve.[20]

---

[19] Axon believes Underwriters has waived its arguments on this issue because Underwriters' opening brief did not spend much time on it. We disagree. The district court's summary judgment decision did not rest on the reasonably anticipated use prong, and so Underwriters had no occasion to address it in its opening brief. After Axon raised the issue as an alternative ground for affirmance, Underwriters sufficiently addressed the issue in its reply. That distinguishes this case from the case Axon cites, *MM Steel, L.P. v. JSW Steel (USA) Inc.*, 771 F.3d 301 (5th Cir. 2014). There, the petitioner "d[id] not brief [the waived] argument beyond [a] conclusory statement" and a citation to an unpublished district court order containing no reasoning on the point. *Id.* at 303 n.2. That is not the case here.

[20] Axon also asserts that it was not reasonably anticipated that the crew would use the BSRs in a situation in which the accumulator—the device that operated the BSRs—malfunctioned. But Axon never made that argument in the district court. Its summary judgment motion on the "reasonably anticipated use" prong did not make arguments regarding the accumulator. "Arguments not raised in the district court cannot be asserted for the first time on appeal." *Greenberg v. Crossroads Sys., Inc.*, 364 F.3d 657, 669 (5th Cir. 2004). We therefore do not consider this argument.

Fact questions exist on both issues. Louisiana defines "reasonably anticipated use" as "a use or handling of a product that the product's manufacturer **{-274-}** should reasonably expect of an ordinary person in the same or similar circumstances." La. Stat. Ann. § 9:2800.53(7). Obviously dangerous uses and uses contrary to industry practice are not reasonably anticipated. *Kampen v. Am. Isuzu Motors, Inc.*, 157 F.3d 306, 312 (5th Cir. 1998) (en banc). **[—37—]** Courts do not define a product's "use" at a high level of generality and may consider the user's negligent conduct. *Id.*

Plaintiffs produced evidence that would allow a fact-finder to conclude that the rig crew's attempt to use the BSRs to stop the in-progress blowout was reasonably anticipated. Axon contends that "the evidence shows that no one expects BOPs to be operated during a blowout." But the report of one of Plaintiffs' experts, Sones,[21] stated that BOPs are regularly used in the industry to prevent blowouts in progress. In fact, the report states that "situations involving the decision to activate blind shear rams are even more likely to occur when a well is already flowing, possibly even flowing onto the rig floor, as this closure is considered a last resort. . . . There is little if any reason to use the shear/blind rams if a well is not flowing." For that reason, the report opines that it is often *expected* that the well will be flowing when the BSRs are activated. The expert thus testified that the crew's actions were "reasonable and consistent with industry standards."

Regarding Axon's second contention—*i.e.*, that it was not anticipated that the crew would try to close the BSRs while leaving the HCR valve open—Plaintiffs' expert testified that the rig crew's actions were "normal in the industry." The testimony was that during a "soft shut in" procedure, the crew would have closed the annular first, followed by the other rams, and then the HCR valve would have been closed last. This procedure, the expert testified, is "normal" and "a reasonable method for controlling a kick."

A jury could conclude, based on this expert evidence, that the rig crew's use of the BOP and BSRs in an attempt to stop an in-progress blowout was **[—38—]** reasonably anticipated. Summary judgment is thus inappropriate on this element of Plaintiffs' LPLA claim. *See Liberty Lobby*, 477 U.S. at 248.

V.

Lastly, we address the district court's award of fees. Because our conclusions regarding multiple summary judgment decisions by the district court mean that the judgment no longer reflects an accurate disposition of the case, we VACATE the judgment, as well as the various orders entered awarding fees to the parties based on its summary judgment decisions.

* * *

We AFFIRM the summary judgment as to Hercules' duty to defend, hold harmless, and indemnify Axon. We REVERSE the summary judgment as to Walter's duty to directly indemnify Axon. We REVERSE the summary judgment as to Walter's duty to indemnify Hercules for Axon's claims. We VACATE the district court's order excluding Bellemare's testimony. We VACATE the district court's orders excluding the expert reports of Sones, Bourgoyne, Williams, Rusnak, Bellemare, and Adair, as well as the orders excluding the affidavits of Sones and Bourgoyne. We REVERSE the summary judgment as to the causation and "unreasonably dangerous condition" prongs of the LPLA. And we VACATE the district court's final judgment and fee orders. The case is REMANDED **{-275-}** for proceedings consistent with this opinion.

[21] Although Axon moved to strike deposition testimony from Sones that it argued constituted new opinions not found in his original report, it never moved to strike his original expert report, the source of this testimony.

United States Court of Appeals
for the Fifth Circuit

No. 18-30652

LATIOLAIS
VS.
HUNTINGTON INGALLS, INC.

Appeal from the United States District Court for the Eastern District of Louisiana

ON PETITION FOR REHEARING EN BANC

Decided: February 24, 2020

Citation: 951 F.3d 286, 8 Adm. R. 155 (5th Cir. 2020) (en banc).

Before **OWEN,** Chief Judge, and **JONES, SMITH, STEWART, DENNIS, ELROD, SOUTHWICK, HAYNES, GRAVES, HIGGINSON, WILLETT, HO, DUNCAN** and **OLDHAM,** Circuit Judges.[1]

[—1—] {-288-} JONES, Circuit Judge: **{-289-}**

This appeal was reconsidered en banc because Fifth Circuit precedents concerning the scope of the revised Federal Officer Removal Statute, 28 U.S.C. § 1442(a)(1), were extraordinarily confused. *See Latiolais v. Huntington Ingalls, Inc.*, 918 F.3d 406, 412–13, 7 Adm. R. 196, 200–01 (5th Cir. 2019). Having reconsidered, we **[—2—]** strip away the confusion, align with sister circuits, and rely on the plain language of the statute, as broadened in 2011. As a result, Avondale[2] was entitled to remove this negligence case filed by a former Navy machinist because of his exposure to asbestos while the Navy's ship was being repaired at the Avondale shipyard under a federal contract. We VACATE the contrary district court judgment and REMAND for further proceedings in federal court.

BACKGROUND AND PROCEDURE

During the 1960s and 1970s, the United States Navy contracted with the Defendant-Appellant, Avondale, to build and refurbish naval vessels. Most of the contracts in the 1960s required asbestos for thermal insulation. According to Avondale's expert, a marine engineer and naval historian, the contracts obliged Avondale "to comply with government plans and specifications, and the federal government had the right to and did exercise supervision over the process to ensure such compliance."

The Plaintiff-Appellee, James Latiolais, then a machinist aboard the USS *Tappahannock*, was exposed to asbestos while his ship underwent refurbishing at Avondale for several months. In 2017, Latiolais was diagnosed with mesothelioma. He died in October 2017.[3] **{-290-}**

Latiolais sued Avondale in Louisiana state court for causing him to contract mesothelioma. He asserted, *inter alia*, that Avondale negligently failed to warn him about asbestos hazards and failed to provide adequate safety equipment. He did not allege strict liability claims against Avondale. **[—3—]**

Avondale removed the case to federal court under 28 U.S.C. § 1442(a)(1). Latiolais sought remand, however, and the district court granted the motion. Observing this court's "causal nexus" requirement for federal officer removal, the district court asked whether the United States or any of its officials controlled Avondale's safety practices. The court found no such control and concluded that removal under § 1442(a)(1) was improper. Avondale timely appealed.

STANDARD OF REVIEW

Although an order remanding a case to state court is not generally reviewable, "an order remanding a case to the State court from which it was removed pursuant to

[1] Judges Dennis and Haynes concur in the judgment only. Judges Costa and Engelhardt are recused.

[2] The Defendant-Appellant has borne many names, including Huntington Ingalls, Northrop Grumman Shipbuilding, and Avondale Industries. Because the parties refer to the Defendant-Appellant as Avondale, the court does the same.

[3] Although Latiolais died shortly after filing his petition in Louisiana state court, no party argues that his death affects any issue in this appeal.

section 1442 or 1443 of this title shall be reviewable by appeal or otherwise." 28 U.S.C. § 1447(d). "We review the district court's remand order de novo, 'without a thumb on the remand side of the scale.'" *Legendre v. Huntington Ingalls, Inc.*, 885 F.3d 398, 400, 6 Adm. R. 193, 193 (5th Cir. 2018) (quoting *Savoie v. Huntington Ingalls, Inc.*, 817 F.3d 457, 462, 4 Adm. R. 225, 227 (5th Cir. 2016)).

DISCUSSION

As amended in 2011 and still effective, the Federal Officer Removal Statute states in pertinent part:

> (a) A civil action or criminal prosecution that is commenced in a State court and that is against or directed to any of the following may be removed by them to the district court of the United States . . . :
>
> (1) The United States or any agency thereof or any officer (or any person acting under that officer) of the United States or of any agency thereof, in an official or individual capacity, for or relating to any act under color of such office . . . .

28 U.S.C. § 1442(a)(1) (2018).

Some version of this statute has been in effect since 1815. *Watson v. Philip Morris Cos.*, 551 U.S. 142, 147–49, 127 S. Ct. 2301, 2305 (2007). At first, Congress authorized only some federal officials sued in connection with their **[—4—]** official duties to seek a federal forum rather than face possibly prejudicial resolution of disputes in state courts. *Willingham v. Morgan*, 395 U.S. 402, 405, 89 S. Ct. 1813, 1815 (1969). Over time, though, Congress has broadened the removal statute repeatedly until it reached the coverage quoted above. *See Watson*, 551 U.S. at 147–49, 127 S. Ct. at 2305; 28 U.S.C.A. § 1442 (West).

Federal officers may remove cases to federal court that ordinary federal question removal would not reach. In particular, section 1442(a) permits an officer to remove a case even if no federal question is raised in the well-pleaded complaint, so long as the officer asserts a federal defense in the response. As the Supreme Court has explained, "the raising of a federal question in the officer's removal petition . . . constitutes the federal law under which the action against the federal officer arises for Art. III purposes." *Mesa v. California*, 489 U.S. 121, 136, 109 S. Ct. 959, 968 (1989). The Court has consistently urged courts to avoid "a narrow, grudging interpretation of § 1442(a)(1)." *Willingham*, 395 U.S. at 407, 89 S. Ct. at 1816; *Arizona v. Manypenny*, 451 U.S. 232, 242, 101 S. Ct. 1657, 1664 (1981); **{–291–}** *Jefferson County v. Acker*, 527 U.S. 423, 431, 119 S. Ct. 2069, 2075 (1999).

Clearly, a defendant removing under section 1442(a)(1) must show (1) it is a "person" within the meaning of the statute, (2) it acted "pursuant to a federal officer's directions," and (3) it asserts a "colorable federal defense." *Winters v. Diamond Shamrock Chem. Co.*, 149 F.3d 387, 396–400 (5th Cir. 1998). This court's cases have also required pleading (4) "a causal nexus" between the defendant's acts under color of federal office and the plaintiff's claims. *E.g.*, *id.* at 398. Avondale's status as a "person" and its federal contract with the Navy for repairs to the *Tappahannock* satisfy the first and second conditions. Whether any "causal nexus" was required is the focal point of dispute, but the parties also debate the "colorable federal defense" criterion. **[—5—]**

I. The Connection Prong

The parties first join issue over the status of the "causal nexus" requirement. This requirement began as a restatement of part of the Supreme Court's test in *Willingham*, in which the Court interpreted "for any act under color of such office," 28 U.S.C. § 1442(a) (1948), to limit federal officer removal to suits that "grow[] out of conduct under color of office." 395 U.S. at 407, 89 S. Ct. at 1816. A civil suit "grows," the Court held, if the defendant's "acts or [his] presence at the place in performance of [his] official duty constitute the basis, though mistaken or false," of the plaintiff's action. *Id.* at 407, 409, 1816, 1817. To establish that much was to establish a "'causal connection' between the charged conduct and asserted official authority." *Id.* at 409, 1817 (quoting *Maryland v. Soper*, 270 U.S. 9, 33, 46 S. Ct. 185, 190–91 (1926)).

Three decades later, in *Winters*, this court restated *Willingham*'s "under color of office" or "causal connection" test as providing "that the defendants acted pursuant to a federal officer's directions and that a causal nexus exists between the defendants' actions under color of federal office and the plaintiff's claims." 149 F.3d at 398. In *Winters,* the defendant's formulation, packaging, and delivery of Agent Orange took place under direct governmental specification and supervision. *Id.* at 400. Consequently, the court determined that "a *direct* causal nexus exists between the defendants' actions taken under color of federal office and Winters's claims" for strict product liability and failure to provide adequate warnings. *Id.* at 399–400 (emphasis added). Notably, in applying *Willingham*'s color-of-office test, the *Winters* court asserted only that a "direct causal nexus" existed, not that it was necessary.

In this court's decisions following *Winters,* the "direct causal nexus" test became a talisman even after Congress, in 2011, amended section 1442(a), altering the requirement that a removable case be "for" any act under color of federal office and permitting removability of a case "for *or relating to*" such **[—6—]** acts, 28 U.S.C. § 1442(a) (2012) (emphasis added). Thus, in *Bartel v. Alcoa Steamship Co.*, the court accurately quoted the amended statute, but did not discuss the textual change and still applied a "direct causal nexus" test. 805 F.3d 169, 172–75, 3 Adm. R. 422, 422–25 (5th Cir. 2015). Subsequent panels of this court relied on *Bartel* and attempted to discern what kinds of plaintiffs' claims articulated causes of action sufficiently related to federal officers or directions to satisfy the "direct causal nexus" test. *See Savoie*, 817 F.3d at 462–66, 4 Adm. R. at 227–31; *Zeringue v. Crane Co.*, 846 F.3d 785, 793–94, 5 Adm. R. 193, 197–98 (5th Cir. 2017); *Legendre,* 885 F.3d at 400–403, 6 Adm. R. at 193–97; *see also* **{-292-}** *IntegraNet Physician Res., Inc. v. Tex. Indep. Providers, L.L.C.*, 945 F.3d 232, 240[4] (5th Cir. 2019); *Schexnayder v. Huntington Ingalls, Inc.*, No. CV 19-11773, 2020 WL 114136, at *2 (E.D. La. Jan. 10, 2020). The original *Latiolais* panel highlighted the tension between the amended statute and our precedents. 918 F.3d at 408–10, 7 Adm. R. at 196–98.

Unsurprisingly, Latiolais no longer relies on our case law alone and takes the position that, even as amended, section 1442(a) requires a direct causal nexus test. He contends that the added language applies to a narrow class of civil proceedings, not including this suit against Avondale; that the application of interpretive canons to the amended statute's language establishes the narrower interpretation; and that in any event the amendment cannot have been meant to dispense with all functional limitations on removal. Avondale asserts that the amendment broadened the availability of federal officer removal. Our analysis therefore turns to statutory interpretation. We conclude that Avondale has the better of the arguments. **[—7—]**

A.

The always primary, and here decisive, interpretive tool is the text itself. The amending legislation, the Removal Clarification Act of 2011, states, "Section 1442(a) of title 28, United States Code, is amended-- (1) in paragraph (1)-- (A) by striking 'capacity for' and inserting 'capacity, for or relating to'." Pub. L. No. 112-51, § 2(b)(1)(A), 125 Stat. 545. Following this amendment, section 1442(a) makes removable to federal court "[a] civil action . . . that is against or directed to . . . any person acting under [a federal] officer . . . for or relating to any act under color of such office."

This change plainly expresses that a civil action *relating to* an act under color of federal office may be removed (if the other statutory requirements are met). Further, the Supreme Court has recognized, "[t]he ordinary meaning of the[ ] words ['relating to'] is a broad one—'to

[4] *But cf.* 945 F.3d at 238 n. 18 (stating that the "causal nexus" test is "not outcome determinative in this case").

stand in some relation; to have bearing or concern; to pertain; refer; to bring into association with or connection with.'" *Morales v. Trans World Airlines, Inc.*, 504 U.S. 374, 383, 112 S. Ct. 2031, 2037 (1992). Congress added this "broad" term to "for," the preposition relied on in the Supreme Court's discussion of the "causal connection" test, *Jefferson County*, 527 U.S. at 431–32, 119 S. Ct. at 2075. By the Removal Clarification Act, Congress broadened federal officer removal to actions, not just *causally* connected, but alternatively *connected* or *associated*, with acts under color of federal office.

Two other circuit courts have acknowledged the impact of the amendment and formally adopted a "connection" test. *See Sawyer v. Foster Wheeler, L.L.C.*, 860 F.3d 249, 258, 5 Adm. R. 167, 172 (4th Cir. 2017); *In re Commonwealth's Mot. to Appoint Counsel Against or Directed to Defender Ass'n of Phila.*, 790 F.3d 457, 470–71 (3d Cir. 2015). The Eleventh Circuit, while persisting with the "causal connection" test, has cited the amended "relating to" language and **[—8—]** essentially implemented a connection rationale for removal. *Caver v. Cent. Ala. Elec. Coop.*, 845 F.3d 1135, 1144 & n.8 (11th Cir. 2017).

B.

Against this perfectly natural interpretation, Latiolais sets a creative alternative. He contends that "for" and "relating to" **{-293-}** modify different "civil action[s] or criminal prosecution[s]." To support this counter-intuitive proposal, Latiolais emphasizes a subsection title in the Removal Clarification Act. He deploys the canon against surplusage. He insists that the plain-meaning interpretation would be a radical, implicit change in law. And he deplores the consequences for courts and plaintiffs if the amendment permits wholesale removal of actions to the federal courts. We must address each of these arguments.[5]

Latiolais stresses a construction of the Removal Clarification Act, which amended section 1442 in 2011. The provision inserting "or relating to" into section 1442(a)(1) is part of a subsection entitled "Conforming Amendments." § 2(b), 125 Stat. at 545. According to Latiolais, "relating to" must "conform" to the Act's immediately preceding subsection, which "clarifies" that standalone subpoenas and other discovery matters are to be defined among the "civil action[s] or criminal prosecution[s]" that may be removed.[6] Because the insertion of "relating to" conforms to that "clarification," the amended section **[—9—]** 1442(a) means that only "pre-suit discovery matters" "relating to" an act under color of federal office are removable. Every other "civil action or criminal prosecution" that is not a pre-suit discovery matter, however, is removable only if it is "for" an act under color of federal office. The amendments, taken together, effectuate broader removability for pre-suit discovery matters, while the removal of liability suits or prosecutions remains in thrall to the direct causal nexus test.

For several reasons, this alternative interpretation based on "Conforming Amendments" is untenable. First, an act's subsection title cannot defeat the ordinary meaning of the statutory text it amends. Reading the language inserted into section 1442(a) via the Conforming Amendments yields that any "civil action or criminal prosecution [more broadly defined to include pre-suit discovery matters]" that otherwise meets the statutory requirements may be removed if it "relates to" an act under color of federal office. Any subsection title with contrary meaning would be unavailing

[5] Latiolais also presents a mélange of legislative history for consideration, but such history is to be avoided in statutory interpretation. Antonin Scalia & Bryan A. Garner, *Reading Law* 31–33, 56–58, 369–90 (2012).

[6] In the "Clarification," Congress broadened the definition of removable proceedings as follows: "As used in subsection (a), the terms 'civil action' and 'criminal prosecution' include any proceeding (whether or not ancillary to another proceeding) to the extent that in such proceeding a judicial order, including a subpoena for testimony or documents, is sought or issued. If removal is sought for a proceeding described in the previous sentence, and there is no other basis for removal, only that proceeding may be removed to the district court." § 2(a)(2), 125 Stat. at 545 (codified as amended at 28 U.S.C. § 1442(d)(1) (2018)).

because, in a war between text and title, text wins. Scalia & Garner, *supra*, at 222–23.

Moreover, the relevant title is not contrary to the statutory changes communicated in the text. One "clarifying" subsection of the Removal Clarification Act broadened the types of proceedings that are removable, no longer limiting removal to liability suits or criminal prosecutions against covered persons. § 2(a)(2), 125 Stat. at 545. The "conforming" subsection broadened the universe of acts that enable federal officers to remove. § 2(b)(1)(A), 125 Stat. at 545. Establishing a broader class of removable acts in section 2(b) conforms to establishing a broader class of removable proceedings in section 2(a). **{-294-}**

Ultimately, Latiolais's exegesis of the Removal Clarification Act and thus of section 1442(a) depends on the possibility of distinguishing pre-suit discovery matters from other proceedings. The text does not justify this **[—10—]** distinction. Instead, the amendment simply broadens the scope of removable proceedings. Had Congress sought to afford easier removability for pre-suit discovery matters than lawsuits, it could easily have drafted an entirely new provision in section 1442 to address the narrow category of state judicial orders of the type currently contemplated in section 1442(d). Instead, within section 1442, Congress both broadened the definition of "civil action" to include such orders and chose to add "relating to"—a term well known for its breadth. These changes neither signal ambiguity nor artificially limit the plain meaning of the provision. *See Advocate Health Care Network v. Stapleton*, 137 S. Ct. 1652, 1659 (2017) ("When legislators did not adopt 'obvious alternative' language, 'the natural implication is that they did not intend' the alternative." (quoting *Lozano v. Montoya Alvarez*, 572 U.S. 1, 16, 134 S. Ct. 1224, 1235 (2014)).

Latiolais's next thrust concerns the word "for," which remains in section 1442(a)(1). According to Latiolais, if "relating to" modifies "[a] civil action or criminal prosecution" without qualification, then "for" is superfluous, in violation of the interpretive canon against surplusage, *cf. Corley v. United States*, 556 U.S. 303, 314, 129 S. Ct. 1558, 1566 (2009) ("[O]ne of the most basic interpretive canons [is] that '[a] statute should be construed so that effect is given to all its provisions, so that no part will be inoperative or superfluous, void or insignificant.'" (quoting *Hibbs v. Winn*, 542 U.S. 88, 101, 124 S. Ct. 2276, 2286 (2004)). Accordingly, "relating to" must apply only to a subclass of "civil action or criminal prosecution."

This reading is also unpersuasive. To start, the canon against surplusage yields to context as it expresses courts' "*general* 'reluctan[ce] to treat statutory terms as surplusage.'" *Bd. of Trs. of Leland Stanford Junior Univ. v. Roche Molecular Sys., Inc.*, 563 U.S. 776, 788, 131 S. Ct. 2188, 2196 (2011) (alteration in original) (emphasis added) (quoting *Duncan v. Walker*, 533 U.S. 167, 174, 121 S. Ct. 2120, 2125 (2001)). Congress may in fact use "a **[—11—]** perhaps regrettable but not uncommon sort of lawyerly iteration" in which each word of a series means nearly the same thing. *Freeman v. Quicken Loans, Inc.*, 566 U.S. 624, 635, 132 S. Ct. 2034, 2043 (2012). If the meaning of a text is discernibly redundant, courts should not invent new meaning to avoid superfluity at all costs.

Anyway, such invention would be inappropriate in this case because "for" is not redundant. Instead, by keeping "for," Congress left no doubt that cases previously removable under the Federal Officer Removal Statute remained removable even as Congress broadened the universe of acts that could sustain removability. *Cf. Ali v. Fed. Bureau of Prisons*, 552 U.S. 214, 226, 128 S. Ct. 831, 840 (2008) ("The construction we adopt today does not render 'any officer of customs or excise' superfluous; Congress may have simply intended to remove any doubt that officers of customs or excise were included in 'law enforcement officer[s].'"). Lacking superfluity, section 1442(a)(1) leaves no work for the canon against surplusage to do.

Latiolais advances another interpretive doctrine, asserting that, should "or relating to" achieve broader removability of civil suits and criminal prosecutions, it **{-295-}** would "make radical—but entirely implicit—changes through technical and conforming amendments," which Congress does not do. *Cyan, Inc. v. Beaver Cty. Emps. Ret. Fund*, 138 S. Ct. 1061, 1071 (2018). In fact, the revision of section 1442(a)(1) was neither radical nor implicit.

Permitting removal of all acts "relating to" an act under color of federal office that meet the other requirements of removal did not radically change the Federal Officer Removal Statute. Congress had consistently broadened the statute before 2011.[7] *See Watson*, 551 U.S. at 147–49, 127 S. Ct. at 2305; **[—12—]** 28 U.S.C.A. § 1442 (West). In *Willingham* and *Acker*, the Supreme Court had read the amended statute to require only a minimal "causal connection." 395 U.S. at 409, 89 S. Ct. at 1817; 527 U.S. at 432–33, 119 S. Ct. at 2075–76. Given this series of events, moving from the causal connection test under "for" to a connection test under "for or relating to" was not a radical change.[8]

Nor was the change "entirely implicit." The *Cyan* case is inapposite. In *Cyan*, a defendant sought dismissal of a 1933 Securities Act class action from state court, contending that a definition in a subpart of a statutory section referenced by a newly added exception required removal. *See* 138 S. Ct. at 1068–70. The Supreme Court rejected the argument that the alleged change, discernible only implicitly, had, for the first time, required removal of 1933 Act claims. *Id.* at 1071–72. In this case, by contrast, Congress changed the operative statutory text, inserting into a phrase identified as the source of the causal connection test a term that is broad in ordinary and legal usage. If not preached on the housetops, this explicit change was far from just whispered in the ear.

Rather than *Cyan*, the better analogue to this case is *Burgess v. United States*. In 1994, Congress used a "conforming amendment" to define "felony drug offense" in the Controlled Substances Act ("CSA"). 553 U.S. 124, 134–35. 128 S. Ct. 1572, 1579 (2008). *Burgess* interpreted this conforming amendment **[—13—]** to have broadened the universe of acts that require a judge to impose a sentence enhancement under the CSA. *See id.* at 129, 1577. The Court noted that "Congress did not disavow any intent to make substantive changes; rather, the amendments were 'conforming' because they harmonized sentencing provisions in the CSA and the Controlled Substances Import and Export Act." *Id.* at 135, 1579. Likewise here, Congress did not disavow any intent to make substantive changes, and its "conforming amendment" harmonized the scope of removal-causing **{–296–}** acts with the scope of removable proceedings. Latiolais's text-focused arguments fail.

Latiolais caps his argument with the policy-related complaints that a plain reading of "relating to" enables removal of cases in a way that conflicts with past case law and suffuses indeterminacy in place of "workable standards" based on a "federal interest" in removal. Latiolais, however, articulates nothing about how to expound such a "federal interest." Moreover, if the causal connection test had provided such "workable standards," this court would have had clearer decisions. Finally, the statute's requirement that a removing party assert a colorable federal defense remains a constitutional, viable, and

---

[7] Indeed, after 2011, Congress continued to broaden section 1442 by amending 28 U.S.C. § 1442(c), National Defense Authorization Act for Fiscal Year 2013, Pub. L. No. 112-239, § 1087, 126 Stat. 1632, 1970–71.

[8] If any further confirmation of this point were necessary, it is available in various decisions by circuit courts that still seek a causal connection between action and act. In part because these courts interpret the "causal nexus" or "causal connection" requirement more expansively—and more in line with *Willingham*, 395 U.S. at 409, 89 S. Ct. at 1817, and *Soper*, 270 U.S. at 33, 46 S. Ct. at 190–91—than our court has done in recent cases, the outcomes in these cases have not been affected by failure to give effect to the new "relating to" language in section 1442(a). *See Betzner v. Boeing Co.*, 910 F.3d 1010, 1015 (7th Cir. 2018); *Ruppel v. CBS Corp.*, 701 F.3d 1176, 1179, 1181 (7th Cir. 2012); *Jacks v. Meridian Res. Co.*, 701 F.3d 1224, 1230 & n. 3 (8th Cir. 2012); *see also Bennett v. MIS Corp.*, 607 F.3d 1076, 1088 (6th Cir. 2010). *Compare Cabalce v. Thomas E. Blanchard & Assocs.*, 797 F.3d 720, 727–30 (9th Cir. 2015), *with Goncalves ex rel. Goncalves v. Rady Children's Hosp. San Diego*, 865 F.3d 1237, 1244–45 (9th Cir. 2017).

significant limitation on removability. *See Mesa*, 489 U.S. at 136–37, 109 S. Ct. at 968–69; *see generally* Anthony J. Bellia, Jr., *The Origins of Article III "Arising Under" Jurisdiction,* 57 Duke L.J. 263 (2007).

C.

For all these reasons, Latiolais's interpretation falls to the more natural reading that Congress applied "relating to" to all "civil action[s] or criminal prosecutions" without distinction. Subject to the other requirements of section 1442(a), any civil action that is connected or associated with an act under color of federal office may be removed. Accordingly, we overrule *Bartel* and its **[—14—]** progeny[9] to the extent that those cases erroneously relied on a "causal nexus" test after Congress amended section 1442(a) to add "relating to." Henceforth, to remove under section 1442(a), a defendant must show (1) it has asserted a colorable federal defense, (2) it is a "person" within the meaning of the statute, (3) that has acted pursuant to a federal officer's directions, and (4) the charged conduct is connected or associated with an act pursuant to a federal officer's directions.

In addition, the pleadings here satisfy the "connection" condition of removal. Latiolais alleges that Avondale failed to warn him of the dangers of asbestos and failed to take measures to prevent exposure. This negligence is connected with the installation of asbestos during the refurbishment of the USS *Tappahannock*. Avondale performed the refurbishment and, allegedly, the installation of asbestos pursuant to directions of the U.S. Navy. Thus, this civil action relates to an act under color of federal office.

II. Colorable Federal Defense

The remaining issue of law is whether Avondale asserted a colorable federal defense to Latiolais's claim. *See, e.g., Bell v. Thornburg*, 743 F.3d 84, 89–91 (5th Cir. 2014). It was briefed, but not decided, in the district court, and we may reach the issue as a matter of discretion. *See Singleton v. Wulff*, 428 U.S. 106, 121, 96 S. Ct. 2868, 2877 (1976); *see also Pinney Dock & Transp. Co. v. Penn Cent. Corp.*, 838 F.2d 1445, 1461 (6th Cir. 1988) ("[T]o the extent the issue is presented with sufficient clarity and completeness and its **[—15—]** resolution will materially advance the progress of this already protracted litigation, we should address it.").

To be "colorable," the asserted federal defense need not be "clearly sustainable," as section 1442 does not require a federal official or person acting under him "to 'win his case before he can have it removed.'" **{-297-}** *Jefferson County*, 527 U.S. at 431, 119 S. Ct. at 2075 (quoting *Willingham*, 395 U.S. at 407, 89 S. Ct. at 1816). Instead, an asserted federal defense is colorable unless it is "immaterial and made solely for the purpose of obtaining jurisdiction" or "wholly insubstantial and frivolous." *See Zeringue*, 846 F.3d at 790, 5 Adm. R. at 194; *see also Bell*, 743 F.3d at 89–91 (deeming an asserted federal defense colorable simply because it satisfied the "causal connection" requirement). Certainly, if a defense is plausible, it is colorable. *Compare Ashcroft v. Iqbal*, 556 U.S. 662, 678–79, 129 S. Ct. 1937, 1949–50 (2009) (plausible claim survives a motion to dismiss), *with Steel Co. v. Citizens for a Better Env't*, 523 U.S. 83, 89, 118 S. Ct. 1003, 1010 (1998) ("It is firmly established in our cases that the absence of a valid (as opposed to arguable) cause of action does not implicate subject-matter jurisdiction."), *and Montana-Dakota Utils Co. v. Nw. Pub. Serv. Co.*, 341 U.S. 246, 249, 71 S. Ct. 692, 694 (1951) ("If the complaint raises a federal question, the mere claim confers power to decide that it has no merit, as well as to decide that it has.").[10]

---

[9] *IntegraNet Physician Res., Inc. v. Tex. Indep. Providers, L.L.C.*, 945 F.3d 232 (5th Cir. 2019); *Legendre v. Huntington Ingalls, Inc.*, 885 F.3d 398, 6 Adm. R. 193 (5th Cir. 2018); *Zeringue v. Crane Co.*, 846 F.3d 785, 5 Adm. R. 193 (5th Cir. 2017); *Savoie v. Huntington Ingalls, Inc.*, 817 F.3d 457, 4 Adm. R. 225 (5th Cir. 2016).

[10] It may well be that courts, "in resolving a motion to remand, should first ask if the defendant offers a colorable federal defense." *See Legendre*, 885 F.3d at 405, 6 Adm. R. at 198 (Higginbotham, J., concurring). Still, in doing so, courts must avoid premature merits determination. *See id.*, 6 Adm. R. at 198. Thus, even if a federal defense makes "sharp demands," *id.*, 6 Adm. R. at 198, a court

In this case, Avondale asserts the federal defense outlined in *Boyle v. United Technologies Corp.*, 487 U.S. 500, 108 S. Ct. 2510 (1988). This defense **[—16—]** extends to federal contractors an immunity enjoyed by the federal government in the performance of discretionary actions. *Zeringue*, 846 F.3d at 790, 5 Adm. R. at 195.[11] Accordingly, federal contractors are not liable for design defects if "(1) the United States approved reasonably precise specifications; (2) the equipment conformed to those specifications; and (3) the supplier warned the United States about the dangers in the use of the equipment that were known to the supplier but not to the United States." *Boyle*, 487 U.S. at 512, 108 S. Ct. at 2510 (quoted in *Zeringue*, 846 F.3d at 790, 5 Adm. R. at 195). Furthermore, "the government contractor defense does not necessarily apply only to claims labeled 'design defect.'" *Bailey v. McDonnell Douglas Corp.*, 989 F.2d 794, 801 (5th Cir. 1993). Instead, "[w]hether it will apply to a particular claim depends *only* upon whether *Boyle*'s three conditions are met with respect to the *particular product feature* upon which the claim is based." *Id.* at 801–02.

In this case, Avondale offered evidence that the three *Boyle* conditions are met. First, Avondale submitted one affidavit and deposition testimony alleging that the Navy required installation of asbestos on the *Tappahannock*, as well as another affidavit alleging that the Navy generally required Avondale to install asbestos and to comply with certain related safety practices. These documents make colorable that the government approved reasonably precise specifications about the installation of asbestos. Second, Latiolais does not challenge that Avondale complied with those specifications, if they existed. Indeed, Latiolais himself testified that Avondale used asbestos in refurbishing the **{–298–}** *Tappahannock*. Third, Avondale's evidence tends to support that the federal government knew more than Avondale knew about asbestos-related **[—17—]** hazards and related safety measures. From such evidence, it is colorable that Avondale did not omit warning the government about any dangers about which the government did not know.

In light of the evidence submitted, Avondale's assertion of a federal defense is not wholly insubstantial and frivolous. We, of course, do not speculate on what further evidence may come to light as the case proceeds and conclude only that Avondale has a colorable federal defense.

CONCLUSION

As the foregoing discussion demonstrates, this action meets the conditions for removal under section 1442(a). The district court's remand order is VACATED, and we REMAND for further proceedings in federal court.

---

should not base removal on whether the defendant actually meets those demands. Only a colorable assertion of the federal defense is necessary.

[11] As the *Boyle* Court explained, "[i]t makes little sense to insulate the Government against financial liability for the judgment that a particular feature of military equipment is necessary when the Government produces the equipment itself, but not when it contracts for the production." 487 U.S. at 512, 108 S. Ct. at 2510 (quoted in *Zeringue*, 846 F.3d at 790, 5 Adm. R. at 195).

United States Court of Appeals
for the Fifth Circuit

No. 19-30313

GENESIS MARINE, L.L.C. OF DEL.
VS.
HORNBECK OFFSHORE SERVS., L.L.C.

Appeal from the United States District Court for the Eastern District of Louisiana

Decided: February 26, 2020

Citation: 951 F.3d 629, 8 Adm. R. 163 (5th Cir. 2020).

Before **KING, COSTA,** and **HO,** Circuit Judges.

[—1—] {-630-} **HO,** Circuit Judge:

Following a bench trial for breach of contract in admiralty, the district court denied both parties attorney's fees. Both parties now appeal seeking fees. We affirm.

I.

In 2013, Hornbeck Offshore Services sold nine sea vessels to Genesis Marine, a commercial operator of tugboats and barges. At the time, Hornbeck already had charter agreements for the vessels in place with third-party customers. In order to continue providing services to these existing customers without interruption, Genesis and Hornbeck entered into a series of contracts. **[—2—]**

First, the parties entered into a crew management ("crewman") agreement. Under the crewman agreement, Hornbeck would staff all vessels with appropriate crew, billing Genesis for the costs of personnel.

A second set of contracts concerned ship management ("shipman") fees. Each vessel had its own shipman agreement. Under the terms of the shipman contracts, Genesis agreed to pay Hornbeck $2,250 per vessel per day for management services, as well as expenses and fees for certain enumerated technical services. Each shipman agreement was to last twelve months and contained a termination clause in case Genesis sought to exit the contract early.

The third agreement was a set of "back-to-back" contracts, again particularized to each vessel. Hornbeck agreed to continue honoring existing charters for its current customers and to provide services until the charters could either be assigned to Genesis or Genesis entered into new agreements altogether. Hornbeck agreed to staff and operate the vessels it had just sold to Genesis, collect payment for charters, and then remit the funds back to Genesis within ten days. In this case, the relevant back-to-back agreement concerns Hornbeck and its preexisting charter customer Anadarko Petroleum Corporation ("Anadarko").

The back-to-back agreement in turn incorporated and was made subject to provisions of the "Master Time Charter" between Hornbeck and Anadarko. The Master Time Charter included, in relevant part, a paragraph stating:

> If the Master Agreement is placed in the hands of an attorney on account of any dispute under the Master Agreement, or if suit is brought on same, or if sums due under the Master Agreement are collected through bankruptcy or probate proceedings, then the prevailing party shall be entitled to recover reasonable attorneys' fees and costs from the other party. **[—3—] {-631-}**

The Master Time Charter also specified that Genesis would be responsible for paying Hornbeck costs for fuel, lube, and shorebase ("FLS") services.

Genesis sought to terminate all the shipman agreements. A dispute over the propriety of termination resulted in litigation. Under the back-to-back agreement, Genesis sued for breach of contract for the unpaid balance on the Anadarko charter hire, for a total of $722,346.36. Hornbeck replied with affirmative defenses of setoff and accord and satisfaction, and argued that Genesis had an outstanding balance of $117,284.54 for FLS services. Hornbeck further asserted counterclaims for unpaid management fees totaling nearly $3 million under the various shipman agreements.

Following a bench trial, the district court dismissed the shipman fees counterclaims and rendered judgment in favor of Genesis for $722,346.35 for the unpaid charter hire. The district court also awarded $117,284.54 to Hornbeck for FLS services.

Both parties asked for attorney's fees as the "prevailing party." The district court denied fees, reasoning that: (1) fees were not authorized by the shipman agreement, which controlled the litigation, and, in the alternative, (2) both Genesis and Hornbeck were prevailing parties, thus nullifying any award.

II.

"Factual determinations underlying the denial of fees are reviewed for clear error; legal conclusions, including whether a party is 'prevailing' . . . are reviewed de novo." *Grisham v. City of Fort Worth*, 837 F.3d 564, 568 (5th Cir. 2016). The actual award of attorney's fees is reviewed for abuse of discretion. *Mathis v. Exxon Corp.*, 302 F.3d 448, 461 (5th Cir. 2002). **[—4—]**

III.

"The general rule in admiralty is that attorneys' fees are not recoverable by the prevailing party." *Delta Steamship Lines, Inc. v. Avondale Shipyards, Inc.*, 747 F.2d 995, 1011 (5th Cir. 1984). But parties are entitled to contract for attorney's fees in the event of a dispute. *See Alyeska Pipeline Serv. Co. v. Wilderness Soc'y*, 421 U.S. 240, 257 (1975). This appeal asks us, for the first time, to determine what constitutes a "prevailing party" in the context of a maritime contract dispute.

Neither the Supreme Court nor our circuit has addressed this question within the specific context of a maritime dispute. But the Court has explained what constitutes a "prevailing party" in non-maritime contexts. Under 42 U.S.C. § 1988, a "plaintiff 'prevails' when actual relief on the merits of his claim materially alters the legal relationship between the parties by modifying the defendant's behavior in a way that directly benefits the plaintiff." *Farrar v. Hobby*, 506 U.S. 103, 111–12 (1992). *See also Grisham*, 837 F.3d at 568 ("The 'touchstone' of the prevailing party analysis is whether there has been 'a material alteration of the legal relationship' between the parties.") (citations omitted). And "[a] judgment for damages in any amount . . . modifies the defendant's behavior for the plaintiff's benefit by forcing the defendant to pay an amount of money he otherwise would not pay." *Farrar*, 506 U.S. at 113.

This understanding of "prevailing party" in the § 1988 context guides our decision here. We see no reason to apply a different definition in the maritime context. We therefore adopt the same definition of "prevailing party" here as in the § 1988 context. **{–632–}**

Under this definition, Genesis has prevailed. It has obtained a judgment for $722,346.35 that materially alters the relationship between the parties and **[—5—]** places Hornbeck in Genesis's debt. But Hornbeck has prevailed as well. It has obtained a $117,284.54 judgment that "forc[es] [Genesis] to pay an amount of money [it] otherwise would not pay."

Consequently, there are two prevailing parties. *See Fox v. Vice*, 563 U.S. 826, 835 (2011) (concluding, in the § 1988 context, that "a court could properly award fees to both parties" when a plaintiff prevailed on one claim and when a defendant defeated a separate, frivolous claim). And given that fact, the district court was entitled in its discretion to make an assessment as to the reasonableness of awarding fees to both parties or, conversely, neither. *See Cable Marine, Inc. v. M/V Trust Me II*, 632 F.2d 1344, 1345 (5th Cir. 1980) (per curiam) (concluding that "a court in its sound discretion may decline to award attorney's fees authorized by a contractual provision when it believes that such an award would be inequitable and unreasonable"); *Malin Int'l Ship Repair & Drydock, Inc. v. M/V SEIM SWORDFISH*, 611 F. Supp. 2d 627, 634 (E.D. La. 2009) (noting that the Fifth Circuit "has recognized the discretion of a maritime court to adjust a contract-based fee award for reasonability").

The district court here concluded that, because both parties prevailed, neither should be awarded attorney's fees. It did not abuse its considerable discretion in so deciding. Because we affirm on this basis, we do not consider the district court's alternative rationale that the shipman agreements did not authorize fees.[1] **[—6—]**

* * *

The denial of attorney's fees is affirmed.

[1] In addition, Hornbeck makes a last-ditch attempt to argue that Genesis is not entitled to attorney's fees because it failed to submit to arbitration per the Master Time Charter. Hornbeck alleges that, by failing to go to an arbitrator first as required under Paragraph 1312 of the contract, Genesis forfeited its right to fees. But as Hornbeck concedes, it never invoked arbitration at any point in prior proceedings. It cannot do so for the first time on appeal. *See Miller Brewing Co. v. Fort Worth Distrib. Co., Inc.*, 781 F.2d 494, 497 (5th Cir. 1986).

United States Court of Appeals
for the Fifth Circuit

No. 19-30264

BP EXPLORATION & PROD., INC.
vs.
CLAIMANT ID 100191715

Appeal from the United States District Court for the Eastern District of Louisiana

Decided: March 3, 2020

Citation: 951 F.3d 646, 8 Adm. R. 166 (5th Cir. 2020).

Before **CLEMENT, HIGGINSON,** and **ENGELHARDT,** Circuit Judges.

[—1—] {-647-} ENGELHARDT, Circuit Judge:

This appeal stems from the protracted *Deepwater Horizon* litigation. BP challenges the district court's order granting discretionary review and affirming a $77 million award against it. Because the district court did not consider investigating credible evidence of a sole, superseding cause for the Claimant's loss, we reverse and remand.

I.

After the April 20, 2010 Deepwater Horizon Oil Spill, BP negotiated and entered into the Economic and Property Damages Class Action Settlement **[—2—]** Agreement ("Settlement Agreement") to resolve the claims of those individuals and businesses who suffered damages as a result of the spill.

Relevant Provisions of the Settlement Agreement

To participate in the Settlement Agreement, a claimant must first submit a "claim form." The claim form is signed under penalty of perjury and requires claimants to attest that their damage was due to the Deepwater Horizon disaster. *See In re Deepwater Horizon* (*Deepwater Horizon III*), 744 F.3d 370, 377, 2 Adm. R. 183, 186 (5th Cir. 2014). Claimants who suffered a Business Economic Loss ("BEL") are classified into one of four geographic zones, which range from most impacted (Zone A) to least impacted (Zone D). Exhibit 4B to the Settlement Agreement addresses the causation requirements claimants must meet according to their assigned zone. It "provides for the use of proof of loss as a substitute for proof of causation." *Id.* at 375, 2 Adm. R. at 185.

Some claimants are entirely exempt from presenting any evidence that their loss was caused by the spill. Claimants located in Zone D, such as the claimant here, must pass one of seven qualitative tests to demonstrate that their loss was caused by the oil spill. One of those tests is the "V-Shaped Revenue Pattern," which is demonstrated by: (a) a 15% or more drop in revenue in three consecutive months between May-December 2010 compared to **{-648-}** the same months in other benchmark year(s), and (b) a 10% upturn in the same months in 2011 compared to 2010. Once causation is proved under Exhibit 4B, the Claims Administrator, as part of the Court Supervised Settlement Program ("CSSP"), calculates the amount of the award due under the formulae set forth in Exhibit 4C.

Claimant's award and BP's appeal

Appellee, Trammo, Inc. ("Claimant"), filed its BEL claim under the Settlement Agreement on March 8, 2013. Claimant is a global commodities merchandiser that purchases and supplies ammonia and fertilizers around the **[—3—]** world. It has a distribution port in Zone D in Tampa, Florida, and its claim was based on alleged damages it suffered at that location. After it satisfied the "V-Shaped Revenue Pattern" in Exhibit 4B, Claimant was allotted $77,688,762.55 under the Settlement Agreement's award calculations.

BP unsuccessfully appealed the award to an appeals panel. It then sought discretionary review from the district court, which granted review but affirmed Claimant's award. Striking out below, BP finally appealed to this court. BP argues that Claimant passed the V-Shaped Revenue Pattern due solely to a price spike and drop in the price of fertilizer that was unrelated to the oil spill. According to BP, the spike caused Claimant's revenues to soar and crash back down to normal rates thereafter. And, only because Claimant used months during the price spike as its benchmark period was it able to satisfy the "V-Shape Revenue Pattern" test in Exhibit 4B. In other words, Claimant's loss was not due to the spill; rather, the price spike in fertilizer was the sole, superseding cause for its loss.[1] Claimant disputes BP's interpretation of the Settlement Agreement and maintains that because its revenue curve passed one of the tests in Exhibit 4B, it was not required to proffer any additional evidence that its loss was caused by the oil spill.[2] **[—4—]**

II.

The interpretation of a settlement agreement is a question of contract law that is reviewed de novo. *Deepwater Horizon III*, 744 F.3d at 374, 2 Adm. R. at 184 (citing *Waterfowl L.L.C. v. United States*, 473 F.3d 135, 141 (5th Cir. 2006)). We recently confirmed that when the district court grants discretionary review and affirms the appeal panel, we review interpretive issues de novo. *Claimant ID 100081155 v. BP Expl. & Prod., Inc.*, 920 F.3d 925, 928, 7 Adm. R. 235, 236 (5th Cir. 2019). While the standard of review is less clear for factual findings, we need not address that issue because this appeal turns on matters of legal interpretation only. **{-649-}** *Claimant ID 100222322 v. BP Expl. & Prod., Inc.*, 773 F. App'x 775, 777 (5th Cir. 2019) (per curiam).

III.

The issue before us is a narrow one: is an investigation into a claimant's attestation required when BP presents credible evidence that the purported loss is not due to the spill but a sole, superseding cause?

The appeals panel answered in the negative. The district court did not specifically consider the issue but affirmed without qualification the appeals panel decision, which found that (1) Claimant "satisfied the requirements of Exhibit 4B of the Settlement agreement and that is all that [was] required of it"; and (2) BP's "alternative causation argument [has been] soundly rejected in recent federal court pronouncements interpreting the requirements of the Settlement Agreement."

To the contrary, we recognized that such an investigation may be warranted in one of our earliest decisions in the *Deepwater Horizon* progeny, *Deepwater Horizon III*. 744 F.3d at 377—78, 2 Adm. R. at 186–87. There, we held that causation was "certainly subordinated" in the Settlement Agreement and we therefore refused to impose a gatekeeping function on the CSSP. *Id.*, 2 Adm. R. at 186–87. However, we also caveated that not "all claims must be accepted no matter how clear the absence **[—5—]** of the required nexus may be." *Id.* at 378, 2 Adm. R. at 187. We left open the possibility that "real examples of implausible claims" could be resolved by "[t]he claims administrator, parties and district court... as they resolve other questions that arise in the handling of specific claims." *Id.*, 2 Adm. R. at 187.

But it was not until 2019, in *West*, that we found an example of such an "implausible claim." 919 F.3d at 288, 7 Adm. R. at 211. We vacated the award in *West* after finding that

[1] BP also argues that Claimant cannot recover because it cannot prove that it suffered a "loss," as defined in *BP Expl. & Prod., Inc. v. Claimant ID 100281817* (*West*), 919 F.3d 284, 7 Adm. R. 209 (5th Cir. 2019). *West*'s majority opinion found that because the Settlement Agreement did not define the word "loss," the word's plain meaning controlled. *Id.* at 287, 7 Adm. R. at 210. Thus, before the individual economic loss ("IEL") claimant in *West* was entitled to recompense, he was required to show that he suffered "unexpected diminutions in wages or other income that could otherwise support a claim for civil damages." *Id.* at 288, 7 Adm. R. at 210. We decline to extend this "plain meaning" requirement beyond the type of IEL claim that was before this court in *West*. Therefore, BP's argument in this regard has no merit.

[2] After oral argument, Claimant filed a letter with the court purporting to identify instances where it sought to prove causation during proceedings before the Claims Administrator. The record cites are less than clear examples, and Claimant has otherwise consistently maintained that it "need not show any causal nexus under the Settlement Agreement" because it "fully met the requirements of Exhibit 4B."

the "loss" the claimant suffered was not caused by the spill but was instead due solely to the front-loaded compensation scheme in his employment contract. *Id.* at 288–89, 7 Adm. R. at 211. *West* was followed shortly thereafter by *BP Expl. & Prod., Inc. v. Claimant ID 100141850 (Howard Industries),* 919 F.3d 887, 7 Adm. R. 214 (5th Cir. 2019) (per curiam). Though it did not exist in *Howard Industries*, we advised that "credible evidence of a sole, superseding cause for a claimant's loss" may warrant "an investigation into the plausibility of the attestation." *Id.* at 891, 7 Adm. R. at 217. Since *Howard Industries*, we have remanded two other claims for consideration of whether there was a sole, superseding cause of the claimant's purported loss. *BP Expl. & Prod., Inc. v. Claimant ID 100238083*, 778 F. App'x 296, 297 (5th Cir. 2019) (per curiam); *BP Expl. & Prod., Inc. v. Claimant ID 100296061*, 777 F. App'x 772 (5th Cir. 2019) (per curiam).

Thus, reversal is warranted because the appeal panel's categorical rejection of credible evidence of a sole, superseding cause stands in conflict with this court's precedent. In addition, the district court's decision was made without the benefit of our recent guidance on causation in *West* and *Howard Industries*. Because the district court has not considered whether there was credible evidence of a sole, superseding cause and because we are not the factfinder, the district court should review this argument in the first instance and determine whether to remand to the Claims Administrator for additional factfinding. **[—6—]**

IV.

Finally, we emphasize that the reach of today's holding is limited: an investigation into the plausibility of a claimant's attestation is required only when BP presents credible evidence of a sole, superseding cause. Accordingly, we REVERSE the district **{-650-}** court's order and REMAND for proceedings consistent with this opinion.

United States Court of Appeals
for the Fifth Circuit

No. 19-30418

ING BANK N.V.
vs.
BOMIN BUNKER OIL CORP.

Appeal from the United States District Court for the Eastern District of Louisiana

Decided: March 24, 2020

Citation: 953 F.3d 390, 8 Adm. R. 169 (5th Cir. 2020).

Before **SMITH**, **HO**, and **OLDHAM**, Circuit Judges.

[—2—] {-391-} SMITH, Circuit Judge:

Bomin Bunker Oil Corporation ("Bomin") asserted an *in rem* claim for a maritime lien against the *Bulk Finland M/V* ("the Vessel"), a ship to which it supplied fuel bunkers under a contract with one of the affiliates of O.W. Bunker & Trading A/S's ("OW Bunker"). The district court granted summary judgment, holding that Bomin wasn't entitled to a maritime lien because it hadn't supplied the bunkers on the order of someone with authority to procure necessaries on behalf of the Vessel. We affirm.

I.

"This lawsuit is the latest round in the maritime litigation spawned by the collapse of OW Bunker, formerly the world's largest supplier of fuel for ships." *NuStar Energy Servs., Inc. v. M/V COSCO Auckland*, 760 F. App'x 245, 246 (5th Cir.), *cert. dismissed*, 140 S. Ct. 339 (2019). In those other **{-392-}** cases, OW Bunker's fuel suppliers asserted *in rem* claims for maritime liens on the relevant ships, which, if successful, would allow them to recover the full costs of the fuel as opposed to "the pennies on the dollar they would likely receive in bankruptcy court." *Id.* We confront essentially that situation here.

A.

To ensure that the Vessel could refuel while at port in Balboa, Panama, three separate contracts were executed. First, Tatsuo Consulting Limited ("Tatsuo"), a charterer of the Vessel,[1] contracted with O.W. Bunker Malta Ltd. ("OW Malta") to arrange for a supply of fuel. As part of the contract, Tatsuo **[—3—]** agreed to incorporate "OW Bunker Group's Terms and Conditions of sale(s) for Marine Bunkers." Neither the contract nor its incorporated terms designated OW Malta as Tatsuo's agent. Nor did the contract direct OW Malta to use Bomin to supply the bunkers. The contract did, however, identify "BOMINFLOT" as the fuel supplier.

Next, OW Malta subcontracted with O.W. Bunker U.S.A. Inc. ("OW USA") to supply the bunkers that the Vessel required. Like the Tatsuo–OW Malta contract, the OW Malta–OW USA contract didn't direct OW USA to use Bomin to supply the fuel and didn't designate OW USA as an agent of either OW Malta or Tatsuo.

Finally, OW USA further subcontracted with Bomin to deliver the fuel. The OW USA–Bomin contract was addressed to OW USA, but it listed the account name as "Master a/o Owner a/o Charterer a/o Operator a/o Manager a/o M/V 'Bulk Finland' a/s 'O.W. Bunker USA Inc.'" That contract also specified that it would "be governed by [Bomin's] General Conditions of Sale and Delivery," which Bomin viewed as "an integral part" of the contract. Neither Tatsuo nor OW Malta was a party to that contract.

After Bomin physically delivered the fuel, it issued a Bunker Delivery Receipt. That receipt confirmed the types and quantities of fuel delivered, and it contained fine print stating that "[t]he vessel [was] ultimately responsible for the debt incurred through this transaction." The Vessel's chief engineer accepted delivery and signed the receipt.

Following delivery, OW Malta, OW USA, and Bomin each issued an invoice to its respective contractual counterparty. Before

---

[1] ING alleges that Tatsuo was acting as a charterer, which DryLog repeatedly disputes. Because whether Tatsuo was a charterer doesn't affect the outcome, we assume *arguendo* that it was.

those invoices came due, OW Bunker—OW Malta and OW USA's corporate parent—went belly up. As a result, OW Malta and OW USA filed for bankruptcy. To date, none of the parties has been paid for its performance under the contracts. **[—4—]**

B.

After OW Bunker collapsed, ING Bank N.V. ("ING")—one of OW Bunker's secured creditors—filed an *in rem* action against the Vessel under the Commercial Instruments and Maritime Liens Act ("CIMLA"), 46 U.S.C. §§ 31341 *et seq.* ING averred that it was entitled to a maritime lien because Tatsuo hadn't paid OW Malta for the full cost of the bunkers.[2] **{-393-}** The Vessel was served with an arrest warrant the same day.

Bomin filed a separate complaint against the Vessel, also *in rem*, asserting its right to a maritime lien related to the same fuel bunkers. Bomin didn't assert any other claims, whether *in personam* or *in rem*, against any other party. The district court consolidated ING's and Bomin's cases.

DryLog Bulkcarriers Limited ("DryLog"), the Vessel's long-term charterer, made a restrictive appearance to defend the *in rem* actions. To avoid arrest of the Vessel, DryLog agreed to post a $1.08 million bond to serve as a substitute res. DryLog then answered ING's and Bomin's complaints. After realizing that both liens related to the same fuel bunkers, DryLog moved to amend its pleadings to assert an interpleader.

Before the district court held a hearing on DryLog's motion to amend, ING and DryLog moved for summary judgment on Bomin's complaint. Bomin moved shortly thereafter to stay resolution of those motions, asserting that our resolution of *NuStar* would be "issue-determinative," because that case "present[ed] a fact pattern that [wa]s in all relevant aspects identical to the fact pattern in the instant action." The district court granted the stay and denied **[—5—]** ING's and DryLog's motions without prejudice.

Once the opinion in *NuStar* was issued, the district court ordered ING to file a joint supplemental brief in support of its summary judgment motion. ING did so, raising two principal positions: (1) Bomin didn't have a "maritime lien . . . because Bomin supplied the bunkers ordered by OW USA, a subcontractor of OW Malta"; and (2) Bomin didn't have a "breach of contract claim . . . because OW USA was not an agent of the BULK FINLAND."

Bomin opposed ING's motion on three grounds: (1) Bomin should be allowed to take discovery before the court ruled; (2) the court should hold a hearing on DryLog's motion to amend; and (3) three other decisions[3] supported that Bomin had a maritime lien on the Vessel. Bomin didn't address *NuStar*.

The district court granted summary judgment to ING and DryLog, deciding that Bomin didn't have a maritime lien because it didn't "furnish the fuel bunkers to BULK FINLAND on the order of the owner of the vessel or a person authorized by the owner . . . ." Bomin appeals.

II.

Bomin raises a single issue on appeal: whether the district court erred when it dismissed Bomin's *in rem* maritime lien claim against the Vessel.[4]

---

[2] ING asserted its lien "based on a $700 million revolving credit facility that a group of lenders provided OW Bunker and its affiliates almost a year before they went under." *NuStar*, 760 F. App'x at 246. To secure the credit, OW Bunker "assigned all of its rights, title and interests as of December 19, 2013, in certain assets, including customer accounts receivable for bunker deliveries, to ING."

[3] Bomin cited (1) *Martin Energy Services, LLC v. M/V Bourbon Petrel*, No. CV 14-2986, 2018 WL 6104718 (E.D. La. Nov. 21, 2018), (2) *NCL (Bahamas) Ltd. v. O.W. Bunker USA, Inc.*, 745 F. App'x 416 (2d Cir. 2018) (per curiam), and (3) *Canpotex Shipping Services Limited v. Marine Petrobulk Ltd.*, 2018 F.C. 957 (Fed. Ct. of Canada 2018).

[4] Bomin has abandoned its contentions related to discovery and to DryLog's motion to amend. *See Cinel v. Connick*, 15 F.3d 1338, 1345 (5th Cir. 1994) ("An appellant abandons all issues not raised and argued in its *initial* brief on appeal.").

A.

CIMLA "governs the circumstances under which a party is entitled to a **[—6—]** maritime lien." *Valero Mktg. & Supply Co. v. M/V Almi Sun*, 893 F.3d 290, 292, 6 Adm. R. 205, 205 (5th Cir. 2018). Under CIMLA, a party supplying goods or services can assert a maritime lien if (1) the goods or services provided were "necessaries," (2) the party "provid[ed] [the] necessaries to a vessel," **{-394-}** and (3) it did so "on the order of the owner or a person authorized by the owner."[5] "We apply the provisions of CIMLA *stricti juris* to ensure that maritime liens are not lightly extended by construction, analogy, or inference." *Id.*, 6 Adm. R. at 206 (quotation marks omitted). The parties don't dispute that the bunkers qualify as "necessaries" or that Bomin provided them to the Vessel. Instead, just as in *Valero* and *NuStar*, this case turns on the third element.

It's normal "for an entity supplying necessaries to a vessel to lack privity of contract with the owner of that vessel, and to instead contract with an intermediary." *Id.* at 293, 6 Adm. R. at 206. The caselaw has branched into two competing lines to address those realities: (1) "the general/subcontractor line of cases" and (2) "the principal/agent, or 'middle-man,' line of cases." *Id.*, 6 Adm. R. at 206. When confronted with contractual chains similar to the one in this case, we have treated physical fuel suppliers (*e.g.*, Bomin) as subcontractors and fuel traders (*e.g.*, OW Malta) as general contractors.[6] As best we can tell, every other circuit has too.[7] **[—7—]**

That distinction between subcontractor and general contractor is crucial. "[G]eneral contractor[s] supplying necessaries on the order of an entity with authority to bind the vessel ha[ve] a maritime lien." *Lake Charles Stevedores, Inc. v. Professor Vladimir Popov MV*, 199 F.3d 220, 229 (5th Cir. 1999). But "subcontractors hired by those general contractors" aren't entitled to one unless they can show "that an entity authorized to bind the ship controlled the selection of the subcontractor and/or its performance." *Id.*

B.

Bomin provided the bunkers to the Vessel under a contract with OW USA into which OW USA entered so as to satisfy its obligations under its contract with OW Malta. And OW Malta contracted with OW USA so that it could fulfill its contract with **{-395-}** Tatsuo. That places Bomin at the end of a three-linked chain: contractor-subcontractor-

[5] 46 U.S.C. § 31342(a); *see also Valero*, 893 F.3d at 292, 6 Adm. R. at 205; *ING Bank N.V. v. M/V Temara*, 892 F.3d 511, 519, 6 Adm. R. 44, 47–48 (2d Cir. 2018). CIMLA identifies the following parties who "are presumed to have authority to procure necessaries for a vessel: (1) the owner; (2) the master; (3) a person entrusted with the management of the vessel at the port of supply; or (4) an officer or agent appointed by–(A) the owner; (B) a charterer; (C) an owner pro hac vice; or (D) an agreed buyer in possession of the vessel." 46 U.S.C. § 31341(a).

[6] *See Valero*, 893 F.3d at 294, 6 Adm. R. at 207–08 ("These facts are more akin to those in which general contractors have been engaged to supply a service and have called upon other firms to assist them in meeting their contractual obligations." (quotation marks omitted)); *NuStar*, 760 F. App'x at 248 ("As NuStar's counsel acknowledged at oral argument, our recent decision in [*Valero*] controls the first half of this one."). In *Valero,* 893 F.3d at 295, 6 Adm. R. at 208, we considered applying the middleman line of cases—specifically, *Marine Fuel Supply & Towing, Inc. v. M/V Ken Lucky*, 869 F.2d 473 (9th Cir. 1988)—but declined to do so.

[7] *See, e.g., Bunker Holdings Ltd. v. Yang Ming Liber. Corp.*, 906 F.3d 843, 846, 6 Adm. R. 386, 387 (9th **[—7—]** Cir. 2018) ("The general rule stated in *Port of Portland* and *Farwest Steel* governs this case because OWB Far East occupied a position no different from that of a general contractor."); *Temara*, 892 F.3d at 515, 6 Adm. R. at 44 ("We agree with the District Court that the subcontractor physical supplier was not entitled to a maritime lien because it did not provide the bunkers on the order of an entity specified in CIMLA."); *Barcliff, LLC v. M/V Deep Blue*, 876 F.3d 1063, 1071, 5 Adm. R. 518, 523 (11th Cir. 2017) ("Where the owner directs a general contractor to provide necessaries to its vessel, a subcontractor retained by the general contractor to perform the work or provide the supplies is generally not entitled to a maritime lien."). The decision in *Bunker Holdings*, 906 F.3d at 846, 6 Adm. R. at 387, is particularly important because it distinguished *Ken Lucky*, which was binding precedent, in favor of applying the general/sub-contractor framework.

subcontractor. Accordingly, to be entitled to a maritime lien, Bomin must show "that an entity authorized to bind the ship controlled" its selection or its performance. *Id.* Bomin establishes neither.

1.

First, Bomin suggests that the OW USA–Bomin and Tatsuo–OW Malta contracts establish the requisite authority, quoting extensively from those **[—8—]** contracts and their corresponding terms. Bomin also repeatedly posits that it can enforce the terms governing the OW USA–Bomin contract up the contractual chain against OW Malta and Tatsuo.

Bomin's theory boils down to two steps. First, under Article 7.14 of the OW USA–Bomin contract's terms, Bomin reserved the right to assert a maritime lien.[8] And second, under Clause L.4 of the Tatsuo–OW Malta contract's conditions,[9] the terms of that contract were "varied" to comport with the terms that Bomin insisted upon in its contract with OW USA.

But that contention misses the point. It doesn't matter whether Article 7.14, or any contractual provision for that matter, states that Bomin has a right to a maritime lien. Maritime liens can't be created as a matter of contract; CIMLA provides the *only* means to obtain one.[10] The contractual terms **[—9—]** are relevant only to the extent that they show authorization by the Vessel's owners or their agents, *i.e.*, that Tatsuo controlled Bomin's selection as the fuel supplier or Bomin's performance under its contract with OW USA.

The provisions on which Bomin relies don't support any agency theory.[11] Nothing in the language that Bomin quotes establishes that Tatsuo required or instructed OW Malta or OW USA to contract with Bomin to supply the bunkers. Moreover, neither the Tatsuo–OW Malta contract nor the OW Malta–OW USA contract charged the OW Bunker entities with procuring necessaries for the Vessel on Tatsuo's behalf. **{-396-}** [12] Those contracts are merely "a series of counterparty transactions," *Temara*, 892 F.3d at 522, 6 Adm. R. at 51, and OW Malta and OW USA were free to complete performance by subcontracting *with anyone or no one at all*.[13]

---

[8] Article 7.14 provides that "Products and Services delivered under a Contract shall be made not only on the account of Buyer but also on the account of the receiving Vessel." Article 7.14 also indicates that OW USA, as "Buyer," warranted that (1) the Vessel's owner gave OW USA permission to purchase the bunkers, (2) Bomin had "the right to assert and enforce a lien" against the Vessel, and (3) the Vessel was "ultimately responsible for the debt incurred through the Contract."

For the first time on appeal, Bomin contends that Article 17 of those terms—in which Bomin purports to retain title to the bunkers until paid in full—also entitles it to a maritime lien. But because Bomin never raised that position before the district court, it can't assert it "for the first time on appeal." *Greenberg v. Crossroads Sys., Inc.*, 364 F.3d 657, 669 (5th Cir. 2004).

[9] Clause L.4 states,

> These Terms and Conditions are subject to variation in circumstances where the physical supply of the Bunkers is being undertaken by a third party which insists that the Buyer is also bound by its own terms and conditions. In such circumstances, these Terms and Conditions shall be varied accordingly, and the Buyer shall be deemed to have read and accepted the terms and conditions imposed by the said third party.

[10] *See, e.g.*, *Valero*, 893 F.3d at 292, 6 Adm. R. at 206 ("We apply the provisions of CIMLA *stricti juris* . . . ."); *Temara*, 892 F.3d at 519, 6 Adm. R. at 48 ("Maritime liens arise only by operation of law and not by contract."); *Bominflot, Inc. v. The M/V Henrich S*, 465 F.3d 144, 146 (4th Cir. 2006) ("[M]aritime liens are *stricti juris* and cannot be created by agreement between the parties.").

[11] Bomin bears the burden to show that OW Malta and OW USA were Tatsuo's agents. *See Karl Rove & Co. v. Thornburgh*, 39 F.3d 1273, 1296 (5th Cir. 1994).

[12] And because OW Malta and OW USA aren't the Vessel's owners, masters, managers, officers, or agents, neither is an entity "presumed to have authority to procure necessaries" on the Vessel's behalf. 46 U.S.C. § 31341(a).

[13] Moreover, "[i]t is a settled principle of contract law that a contract requiring A to supply X to C is satisfied if B, hired by A, provides X to C." *Lake Charles*, 199 F.3d at 232. As a result, Bomin physically delivering the fuel constituted both OW USA's performance under the OW Malta–OW USA contract and OW Malta's performance under the

Bomin can't reverse-engineer CIMLA's required authorization by contractually reserving a right to a maritime lien or by insisting that OW USA warrant that it had vessel-owner permission to purchase the bunkers.

2.

Bomin alternatively avers that Tatsuo "controlled Bomin's performance" through "its contract with Bomin facilitated through OW's Terms." Bomin contends that it "would have never been able to perform" if the Vessel hadn't accepted its services. It points out that Tatsuo, not OW Bunker, "selected the **[—10—]** bunkers Bomin provided," and the Vessel's crew made all the necessary connections to permit delivery of the fuel. Furthermore, the Tatsuo–OW Malta contract specified that "BOMINFLOT" would supply the fuel; Bomin's invoice was addressed to "MASTER AND/OR OWNER AND/OR CHARTERER AND/OR OPERATOR AND/OR MANAGER OF MV BULK FINLAND"; and the Vessel's chief engineer signed the Bunker Delivery Receipt.

But the most that those facts can show is that Tatsuo and the Vessel's chief engineer were aware that Bomin was the physical supplier and that neither objected to its performance. That isn't enough. A vessel owner or charterer's "[m]ere awareness" of a subcontractor's involvement "does not constitute authorization under CIMLA." *Valero*, 893 F.3d at 295, 6 Adm. R. at 208. Nor could it. "[H]olding that awareness that necessaries are being supplied [i]s sufficient, even though those necessaries were procured by an entity without authority to bind the vessel, would render [CIMLA's] authority requirement meaningless." *Lake Charles*, 199 F.3d at 232.

Valero is instructive. There, Almi Tankers (the vessel owner's authorized agent) contracted with OW Malta, who subcontracted with OW USA, who further subcontracted with Valero. *Valero*, 893 F.3d at 291, 6 Adm. R. at 205. The record showed that (1) Almi Tankers knew that Valero was "the bunker fuel supplier" and "did not object to Valero's selection," (2) "the sales order confirmation listed Valero as the supplier," (3) "Valero provided the entire bunkering service . . . with no assistance from O.W. or its affiliates," and (4) "the Vessel's agents monitored and tested Valero's performance." *Id.* at 294, 6 Adm. R. at 207. We held that those facts "prove[d] no more than the Vessel's awareness of Valero, not that the Vessel 'controlled' the selection or performance of Valero." *Id.* at 295, 6 Adm. R. at 208. The panel in *NuStar*, 760 F. App'x at 248, confronted almost identical facts and reached the same conclusion. There is no reason the result here should be **[—11—]** different. Bomin's reliance on *Martin, NCL*, and *Canpotex* is misplaced.[14] **{-397-}**

* * * * *

Because Bomin wasn't acting on the orders of either the Vessel's owners or their authorized agent when it supplied the fuel, Bomin doesn't have a maritime lien. The summary judgments are AFFIRMED.

Tatsuo–OW Malta contract. It didn't somehow create a *de facto* contract between Tatsuo and Bomin.

[14] *Martin*'s facts are distinct from the ones we confront. There, the relevant vessel's charterer (CGG) contracted with OW USA for fuel, and OW USA then solicited bids from fuel suppliers like Martin and Stone Oil. *See Martin*, 2018 WL 6104718, at *1. OW USA then presented those bids to CGG, which always told OW USA "to choose Martin Energy's lower bid." *Id.* at *6. In other words, "unlike *Valero* [or *NuStar* or this case], an entity authorized to bind the vessel controlled the selection of Martin Energy as physical supplier." *Id.* Bomin relies on an inapposite section of *Martin* discussing whether Martin had waived its right to a maritime lien by refusing to extend credit to the vessel's charterer. *See id.* at *4–5.

NCL and *Canpotex* similarly provide no safe harbor. In *NCL*, 745 F. App'x at 420, though the court remanded "for the district court to consider whether EKO [(the fuel supplier)] insisted that its terms and conditions appl[ied] to NCL [(the vessel's charterer)]," it did so only as it related to a *contract dispute* between NCL and OW Bunker. The court didn't evaluate whether EKO—the party occupying the same relative position as Bomin—was entitled to a maritime lien. And in *Canpotex*, 2018 F.C. 957, at 15 ¶ 37, the court didn't consider whether a maritime lien existed under either CIMLA or Canadian law.

United States Court of Appeals
for the Fifth Circuit

No. 19-60027

MMR CONSTRUCTORS, INC.
vs.
DIRECTOR, OFFICE OF WORKERS' COMPENSATION PROGRAMS

Petition for Review of an Order of the Benefits Review Board

Decided: March 26, 2020

Citation: 954 F.3d 259, 8 Adm. R. 174 (5th Cir. 2020).

Before **DAVIS, HAYNES,** and **OLDHAM,** Circuit Judges.

[—1—] {-261-} **DAVIS,** Circuit Judge:

Petitioner MMR Constructors appeals the Benefits Review Board's order awarding benefits to claimant Henry Flores under the Longshore and Harbor Workers' Compensation Act. Concluding that Flores was on navigable waters at the time of injury and that his case is controlled by *Perini*,[1] we AFFIRM. **[—2—]**

I. BACKGROUND

The facts are straightforward and uncontested. Henry Flores worked for MMR Constructors ("MMR") as a quality assurance and control technician for electrical systems. He assisted with electrical wiring for the construction of Chevron's tension-leg platform named Big Foot.[2] While working on the platform on January 20, 2014, Flores's left foot got caught on a cable, and he tore his Achilles tendon. The parties do not dispute that the injury occurred during the course and scope of his employment.

While Big Foot is currently located at its permanent home in the outer Continental Shelf of the Gulf of Mexico, at the time of Flores's accident, it was under construction at a shipyard in Corpus Christi Bay. During construction of what would ultimately become Big Foot, the platform floated in the bay on pontoons, connected to land by steel cables and utility lines.

An Administrative Law Judge (ALJ) held a formal hearing to assess Flores's claim for benefits, both under the Longshore and Harbor Workers' Compensation Act[3] (LHWCA or the Act) and as extended by the Outer Continental Shelf Lands **{-262-}** Act[4] (OCSLA). The ALJ initially found that, although there was "no question" Flores was injured on navigable waters, he was not a maritime employee and thus failed the LHWCA's status test under the 1972 amendments.[5] The Benefits Review Board (BRB) overturned the ALJ's order, relying on the Supreme Court's decision in *Perini* to conclude that Flores was **[—3—]** covered under the LHWCA because he was injured on navigable waters.[6] MMR timely filed a petition for review.

II. DISCUSSION

A. Standard of Review

This court reviews the BRB's legal conclusions de novo.[7] Because the facts here are not in dispute, "whether LHWCA coverage exists is a question of statutory interpretation and thus is reviewed as a pure question of law."[8]

---

[1] *Dir., OWCP, U.S. Dep't of Labor v. Perini N. River Assocs.*, 459 U.S. 297, 299 (1983) (hereinafter "*Perini*").

[2] Big Foot is an offshore oil platform used for deep water drilling that currently sits 225 miles south of New Orleans. It is anchored to the sea floor by over sixteen miles of tendons. Some estimates have Big Foot as high as 30 stories tall.

[3] 33 U.S.C. § 901, et seq.

[4] 43 U.S.C. § 1333(b).

[5] The ALJ also found that Flores was not entitled to compensation under the LHWCA as incorporated by the OCSLA. Because we hold that Flores is covered under the LHWCA directly, we need not reach this issue.

[6] *Flores v. MMR Constructors, Inc.*, 50 BRBS 47, 50–51 (2016).

[7] *B & D Contracting v. Pearley*, 548 F.3d 338, 340 (5th Cir. 2008).

[8] *Baker v. Dir., OWCP*, 834 F.3d 542, 545, 4 Adm. R. 276, 277 (5th Cir. 2016).

B. Injury on Navigable Waters

The LHWCA establishes a federal statutory workers' compensation scheme providing certain maritime workers with "medical, disability, and survivor benefits for work-related injuries and death."[9] Prior to 1972, the LHWCA's "situs" requirement only extended coverage to employees injured or killed on "navigable waters of the United States (including any dry dock)."[10] When Congress amended the LHWCA in 1972, it (1) expanded the situs requirement to include certain adjoining land areas and (2) added a "status" component in 33 U.S.C. § 902(3), requiring that employees be engaged in maritime employment within the meaning of the Act.[11]

We start with the Supreme Court's decision in *Perini*, decided after the LHWCA was amended in 1972. The facts in *Perini* bear some resemblance to the facts here: an employee was denied benefits after being injured on navigable waters because he was not engaged in maritime employment and, thus, could not satisfy the status test under the LHWCA as amended in 1972.[12] **[—4—]** The Supreme Court reversed.[13] It held that the 1972 amendments to the LHWCA sought to expand, not limit, coverage.[14] Before 1972, any claimant injured upon navigable waters in the course of his employment who satisfied the definition of "employee" would have been covered under the Act if employed by a statutory "employer."[15] The Court concluded that such claimants—"injured on the actual navigable waters in the course of [their] employment"—were still eligible under the amended LHWCA because the Court "consider[ed] these employees to be engaged **{-263-}** in maritime employment."[16] Thus, these claimants satisfied the amended Act's status requirement, the other statutory provisions notwithstanding.[17]

Our first challenge is to determine whether Flores, injured on a floating platform, would have satisfied the "situs" test under the LHWCA prior to 1972. In short, if Big Foot was on navigable waters, then Flores would have been covered under the pre-1972 LHWCA, and *Perini* teaches that he would also be eligible for coverage under the amended Act, despite his inability to otherwise meet the "status" test.[18] If, however, Big Foot did not rest on navigable waters, then Flores's claim fails because he cannot satisfy the situs or the status test required by the post-1972 amendments to the LHWCA. Two pre-1972 Fifth Circuit cases are helpful in determining whether Flores was injured on navigable waters. **[—5—]**

First, MMR contends that because this court previously held that Big Foot is not a vessel, it must be considered an extension of land.[19] But *Williams v. Avondale Shipyards, Inc.* reveals that this case does not hinge on whether Flores was injured on a vessel.[20] In *Williams*, a claimant was injured on a not-yet-commissioned Coast Guard cutter on its final sea trial.[21] The claimant filed multiple claims for relief under the Jones Act, general maritime law, and the LHWCA.[22] The court followed settled law and first held that the Coast Guard cutter was not a vessel since it was uncompleted, thereby barring coverage under the Jones Act.[23] Despite this fact, the court held that the claimant could still seek relief under the LHWCA if injured on navigable waters of the United States as

---

9 *Howlett v. Birkdale Shipping Co., S.A.*, 512 U.S. 92, 96 (1994).

10 33 U.S.C. § 903(a), 44 Stat. 1426; *see Perini*, 459 U.S. 297, 299 (1983).

11 *Perini*, 459 U.S. at 299; 33 U.S.C. §§ 903(a), 902(3).

12 *Perini*, 459 U.S. at 300–01.

13 *Id.* at 325.

14 *Id.* at 299.

15 *Id.* at 305.

16 *Id.* at 324; *see also Bienvenu v. Texaco, Inc.*, 164 F.3d 901, 904 (5th Cir. 1999) (en banc).

17 *Id.*

18 Flores's presence on navigable waters may not be "transient or fortuitous," *Bienvenu*, 164 F.3d at 908, but that issue does not present itself here.

19 *See Baker v. Director, OWCP*, 834 F.3d 542, 545, 4 Adm. R. 276, 277 (5th Cir. 2016).

20 452 F.2d 955 (5th Cir. 1971).

21 *Id.* at 957.

22 *Id.*

23 *Id.* at 958.

opposed to international waters.[24] *Williams*, then, stands for the solid proposition that an injury on a non-vessel located on navigable waters of the United States satisfies the situs requirement for purposes of coverage under the pre-1972 LHWCA. MMR's attempt to distinguish *Williams* fails. MMR relies upon cases that deal with whether crafts in various forms are vessels for purposes of the Jones Act or general maritime law.[25] Those **{-264-}** cases are irrelevant for our purposes in determining coverage under the LHWCA. **[—6—]**

Travelers Insurance Co. v. Shea is also helpful in our effort to determine whether Flores was injured on navigable waters. It teaches us that, pre-1972, if an employee was injured on a floating structure permanently attached to land, he was not covered under the LHWCA.[26] In *Shea*, the claimant was injured on a floating outfitting pier, which was an extension of a ramp that had been permanently anchored to both the shore and seabed with steel pillars.[27] We determined the pier was not on navigable waters and should instead be considered an extension of land.[28] Indeed, "[i]ts permanent home was in the water, and the waters below it had been completely removed from navigation."[29] Despite the fact that it was floating, the court treated it as a pier or extension of land because it was "permanently anchored . . . for eighteen years" with no plans to ever move it from its fixed position.[30]

We have since followed this analysis, emphasizing that the extent to which a craft or pier is permanently attached to land is critical. In *Peytavin v. Government Employees Insurance Co.*, for example, the court held that a floating pontoon fastened to the shore by means of cables could not be considered an extension of land.[31] Structures typically deemed extensions of land, the court noted, "were in some manner firmly and permanently fastened to the land."[32] "A vessel moored to a dock does not become an extension of the **[—7—]** land *nor do other structures secured to the shore by cables, or other temporary means*."[33]

From these cases, it is clear that if a craft resting on navigable waters is permanently attached to land, then the water underneath the craft is removed from navigation and is not navigable under the LHWCA.[34] While Big

[24] *Id.* at 959. It ultimately remanded the case to the district court to determine whether the accident occurred on navigable waters of the United States, as opposed to the high seas (since the LHWCA only extends to the former, whereas general maritime law extends to both). *Id.* at 960–61.

[25] *See, e.g., Lozman v. City of Riviera Beach, Fla.*, 568 U.S. 115, 122, 1 Adm. R. 2, 4 (2013) (a house boat could not be considered a vessel because it was not designed for transportation on water); *Cope v. Vallette Dry-Dock Co*, 119 U.S. 625, 630 (1887) (a floating drydock cannot be considered a vessel); *Manuel v. P.A.W. Drilling & Well Serv., Inc.*, 135 F.3d 344, 352 (5th Cir. 1998) (a rig bolted to a barge was a vessel under the Jones Act); *Leonard v. Exxon Corp.*, 581 F.2d 522, 524 (5th Cir. 1978) (a floating work platform was not a vessel for purposes of the Jones Act); *Cook v. Belden Concrete Prod., Inc.*, 472 F.2d 999, 1002 (5th Cir. 1973) (a floating dry dock is not a vessel within the scope of the Jones Act or general maritime jurisdiction).

[26] 382 F.2d 344, 349 (5th Cir. 1967).

[27] *Id.* at 345–46.

[28] *Id.* at 349.

[29] *Id. See also Nat'l Maint. & Repair v. Illinois Workers' Comp. Comm'n*, 395 Ill. App. 3d 1097 (2009). The Appellate Court of Illinois there held that the barge in question was an extension of land, because it had been affixed to the shore with mooring lines and a "spud" (essentially a temporary piling) for five or six years. *Id.* at 1102.

[30] *Shea*, 382 F.2d at 349.

[31] 453 F.2d 1121, 1126 (5th Cir. 1972).

[32] *Id.* at 1125.

[33] *Id.* at 1126 (quoting *Hastings v. Mann*, 340 F.2d 910, 911 (4th Cir. 1965)). *See also Nacirema Operating Co. v. Johnson*, 396 U.S. 212, 214–15 (1969) ("Since long before the Longshoremen's Act was passed, it has been settled law that structures such as wharves and piers, *permanently affixed to land*, are extensions of the land.") (emphasis added).

[34] The Second Circuit has adopted a different test. In *Lockheed Martin Corp. v. Morganti*, 412 F.3d 407, 414 (2d Cir. 2005), the court considered whether a research barge attached to a buoy rested on navigable waters. The court did not consider the permanence of the barge. *Id.* at 415. Instead, the court held that "a person on any object floating in actual navigable waters must be considered to be on actual navigable waters" for LHWCA coverage.

Foot was attached to land bordering Corpus Christi Bay, its attachment was not permanent. Big Foot was attached only temporarily while under construction—it was built to be moved offshore to drill for oil and gas in the Gulf of Mexico. Because it was not permanently attached to land, the water underneath it **{-265-}** was not removed from navigation. Thus, Flores was injured on navigable waters and is entitled to benefits under the Act if MMR was a statutory "employer." We now turn to that question.

C. "Employer" Requirement

Both the original and amended LHWCA define "employer" as "an employer any of whose employees are employed in maritime employment, in whole or in part, upon the navigable waters of the United States."[35] MMR argues that because neither Flores nor any other employee of MMR was engaged in "maritime employment" as defined by the post-1972 LHWCA's **[—8—]** "status" test, MMR does not qualify as a statutory "employer" under § 902(4). As set forth below, we conclude that MMR was a statutory employer.

Because *Perini* teaches us that the 1972 amendments to the LHWCA did not intend to limit coverage, the definition of both "employee" and "employer" under the Act become relevant. Before the amendments, "employee" was defined negatively to read: "[t]he term 'employee' does not include a master or member of a crew of any vessel, nor any person engaged by the master to load or unload or repair any small vessel under eighteen tons net."[36] The amended LHWCA substantially changed the definition of "employee" from a negative definition to: "any person engaged in maritime employment, including any longshoreman or other person engaged in longshoring operations, and any harbor-worker including a ship repairman, shipbuilder, and ship-breaker."[37] This new definition of "employee" became the "status" test.

It is noteworthy that the pre-1972 LHWCA definition of employee did not specify the type of maritime work that qualified as "maritime employment"; we read that definition to include anyone who met the situs test, subject to the two exceptions in the "employee" definition.[38] Our pre-1972 case law confirms that if the claimant qualified as an employee under the pre-1972 Act by being injured on navigable waters where he was regularly employed, the employer also qualified as a statutory "employer" under § 902(4): the employer had at least one employee engaged in maritime employment.[39] **[—9—]**

In 1965, this court addressed the definition of "employer" in *Nalco Chemical Corp. v. Shea*.[40] The claimant in that case was employed as a combination airplane pilot/salesman and was injured on navigable water.[41] The claimant's sales duties required him to call on customers on rigs located on navigable waters.[42] His injury on navigable waters satisfied the Act's situs requirement, and he was an "employee" **{-266-}** under the pre-1972 Act.[43] Important for this discussion, the statutory "employer" requirement was also satisfied—we held that to be an "employer," the LHWCA merely required that at least one of the employer's employees be engaged in maritime employment "in whole or in part."[44] The court concluded that the employee's sales

---

Id. at 416. The test we have established in *Shea* and *Peytavin* is not as broad as the Second Circuit's test.

35 Longshore Harbor Workers Compensation Act of 1927, Pub. L. No. 92-576, § 2(b), 86 Stat. 1251 (Oct. 27, 1972); § 903(2)(4). Congress amended the employer definition in 1972 to reflect the expanded situs requirements, but the definition otherwise remained unchanged. *Id.*

36 33 U.S.C. § 902(3) (1970).

37 § 903(2)(3) (1972). The definition excludes certain employees, none of which is at issue here.

38 § 902(3) (1970).

39 *See Hullinghorst Industries, Inc. v. Carroll*, 650 F.2d 750, 758 n.8 (5th Cir. 1981) ("We find no decision of this circuit which holds that 'employer' status may not be predicated upon the status of the injured claimant as a maritime employee under the Act.").

40 419 F.2d 572, 574 (5th Cir. 1969) (per curiam).

41 *Id.*

42 *Id.*

43 *Id.*

44 *Id.*

activities on navigable waters amounted to "maritime employment" under § 902(4).[45] Thus, the employer had at least one employee engaged in maritime employment and was an "employer" under the Act.

In the post-1972 cases, we have followed the same analysis in our interpretation of "employer" under the LHWCA. We have held that if the injured employee meets the Act's amended definition of "employee," the employer is ipso facto a covered employer—it has at least one employee engaged in maritime employment.[46]

MMR disagrees with this analysis and contends that it is important that the post-1972 "employer" requirement of § 902(4) be enforced and Flores be required to show that MMR has at least one employee who can satisfy the post- **[—10—]** 1972 definition of "employee." To make its argument, MMR points to language in *Perini*:

> In holding that we can find no congressional intent to affect adversely the pre-1972 coverage afforded to workers injured upon the actual navigable waters in the course of their employment, we emphasize that we in no way hold that Congress meant for such employees to receive LHWCA coverage merely by meeting the situs test, and without any regard to the "maritime employment" language. We hold only that when a worker is injured on the actual navigable waters in the course of his employment on those waters, he satisfies the status requirement in § 2(3), and is covered under the LHWCA, *providing, of course, that he is the employee of a statutory "employer,"* and is not excluded by any other provision of the Act.[47]

The Court clarified in a footnote that its holding "extends only to those persons 'traditionally covered' before the 1972 amendments."[48] It expressed "no opinion" on whether such coverage extended to workers injured while transiently or fortuitously on navigable water.[49] "Rather, our holding is simply a recognition that a worker's performance of his duties upon actual navigable waters is necessarily a very important factor in determining whether he is engaged in 'maritime employment.'"[50]

We read this language as leaving open the question of whether an employer of an employee injured after 1972 who is covered because of his injury on navigable waters (but who does not otherwise meet the status test) is an "employer" under the Act. In the footnote quoted above, the Court indicated concern about an employer unfairly being held responsible for LHWCA benefits when it had no notice its **{–267–}** employee was working on navigable waters. **[—11—]** Indeed, this court has recognized the legitimacy of such a concern.[51] To address this issue, we held that a worker injured in the course of his employment on navigable waters is not covered by the LHWCA if his presence on the water is "transient or fortuitous," so that the employer may not have notice of its potential exposure under the LHWCA.[52] It is clear, however, that the facts here do not raise this concern, because Flores had been working on Big Foot for MMR on navigable waters for several months before his injury.

We therefore hold that because Flores was regularly employed by MMR on navigable

---

[45] *Id.*

[46] *See Hullinghorst Industries, Inc. v. Carroll*, 650 F.2d 750, 758 (5th Cir. 1981) (holding the addition of an "employee" status requirement rendered the "employer" status requirement "largely tautological" since "the injured claimant himself must be engaged in maritime employment").

[47] *Perini*, 459 U.S. 297, 323–24 (1983) (emphasis added).

[48] *Id.* at 324 n.34.

[49] *Id.*

[50] *Id.*

[51] *See Carroll*, 650 F.2d at 757 ("Congress intended that liability should be imposed only where the employer had real or constructive notice of the likelihood of coverage.").

[52] *Bienvenu v. Texaco, Inc.*, 164 F.3d 901, 908 (5th Cir. 1999) (en banc).

waters and, under *Perini*, meets the "employee" definition, it follows that MMR had at least one employee engaged in maritime employment. Our conclusion that we should not read the "status" test as narrowing the definition of a statutory employer is consistent with both our holding in *Nalco Chemical Corp.* and the BRB's finding.[53] Our conclusion also follows the reasoning of the Supreme Court in *Perini*: Congress sought to expand, not limit, coverage under the LHWCA with the 1972 amendments.[54] MMR was thus an employer under the Act.

D. The Constitutionality of the LHWCA

MMR contends that applying the LHWCA to accidents with no connections to traditional maritime activity exceeds the constitutional limits of federal maritime jurisdiction.[55] To makes its argument that the Supreme **[—12—]** Court abrogated *Perini*, it relies on *Jerome B. Grubart, Inc. v. Great Lakes Dredge & Dock Co.*[56]

MMR has failed to show that the Court in *Grubart* sought to proscribe the reach of Congress's admiralty jurisdiction concerning the LHWCA. *Grubart* articulated a jurisdictional test for maritime torts for cases brought under 28 U.S.C. § 1333(1), which states that federal district courts have original and exclusive jurisdiction over civil cases of admiralty jurisdiction.[57] The Supreme Court has explained that the test for maritime tort jurisdiction is distinguishable. "Although the term 'maritime' occurs both in 28 U.S.C. § 1333(1) and in § 2(3) of the [LHWCA], these are two different statutes 'each with different legislative histories and jurisprudential interpretations over the course of decades.'"[58] *Grubart* also addressed the Extension of **{-268-}** Admiralty Jurisdiction Act, which expanded maritime jurisdiction to injuries occurring on land or sea caused by a vessel on navigable water.[59] The Supreme Court held in *Nacirema Operating Co. v. Johnson* that Congress did not "intend[] to amend or affect the coverage of the Longshoremen's Act" in passing the Extension Act, and that "the Act has no bearing whatsoever on [claimants'] right to a compensation remedy under the Longshoremen's Act."[60] Thus, nothing in *Grubart* suggests that the Court sought to abrogate *Perini* and limit admiralty jurisdiction under the LHWCA.

In addition, when numerous cases from the Supreme Court seemingly speak to an issue, "the Court of Appeals should follow the case which directly **[—13—]** controls, leaving to [the Supreme Court] the prerogative of overruling its own decisions."[61] Relying on *Parker v. Motor Boat Sales*, the Court in *Perini* made very clear: "when a worker is injured on the actual navigable waters in the course of his employment on those waters, he . . . is covered under the LHWCA."[62] In *Parker*, the injured worker, a janitor/porter, drowned while riding in a boat to look for hidden objects in muddy water.[63] One issue the Court had to consider was whether Congress had the authority to award compensation under the LHWCA for such a predominantly "non-maritime employee."[64]

[53] *Flores v. MMR Constructors, Inc.*, 50 BRBS 47, 51 (2016).

[54] *See Perini*, 459 U.S. at 315–16 (1983) (quoting *Voris v. Eikel*, 346 U.S. 328, 333 (1953)) ("We are unable to find any congressional intent to withdraw coverage of the LHWCA from those workers injured on navigable waters in the course of their employment, and who would have been covered by the Act before 1972. As we have long held, 'This Act must be liberally construed in conformance with its purpose, and in a way which avoids harsh and incongruous results.'").

[55] *See* U.S. CONST. art. III, § 2 ("The judicial Power shall extend to all Cases . . . of admiralty and maritime Jurisdiction . . .").

[56] 513 U.S. 527 (1995).

[57] *See id.* at 534 ("a party seeking to invoke federal admiralty jurisdiction pursuant to 28 U.S.C. § 1333(1) over a tort claim must satisfy conditions both of location and connection with maritime activity").

[58] *Perini*, 459 U.S. at 320 n.29 (quoting *Boudreaux v. American Workover, Inc.*, 680 F.2d 1034, 1035, 1050 (5th Cir. Unit A 1982)).

[59] *Grubart*, 513 U.S. at 532; *see* 46 U.S.C.A. § 30101.

[60] 396 U.S. 212, 223 (1969).

[61] *Rodriguez de Quijas v. Shearson/Am. Exp., Inc.*, 490 U.S. 477, 484 (1989).

[62] 459 U.S. 297, 310, 324 (1983).

[63] 314 U.S. 244, 246 (1941).

[64] *Id.* at 246, 248.

The Court held that "it is not doubted that Congress could constitutionally have provided for recovery under a federal statute in this kind of situation."[65] *Grubart*, which was decided twenty-five years ago and twelve years after *Perini*, made no mention of *Perini* or *Parker*, and the Supreme Court has not called either case into question since. Absent clear language abrogating *Perini*, we are bound by the Court's understanding of maritime jurisdiction in that case.

III. CONCLUSION

For the aforementioned reasons, we AFFIRM the BRB's award of compensation to Flores.

---

[65] *Id.* at 248. This court has similarly acknowledged the "long-standing judicial recognition of Congress' broad powers to expand the reach of admiralty jurisdiction" when discussing the constitutionality of the LHWCA. *Jacksonville Shipyards Inc. v. Perdue*, 539 F.2d 533, 545 (5th Cir. 1976), *aff'd, P.C. Pfeiffer Co. v. Ford*, 444 U.S. 69 (1979) (intervening subsequent history omitted).

United States Court of Appeals for the Fifth Circuit

No. 19-30499

LUWISCH
vs.
AMERICAN MARINE CORP.

Appeal from the United States District Court for the Eastern District of Louisiana

Decided: April 15, 2020

Citation: 956 F.3d 320, 8 Adm. R. 181 (5th Cir. 2020).

Before **KING, JONES,** and **COSTA,** Circuit Judges.

[—1—] {–324–} PER CURIAM:

This case pits an injured seaman against his former employer. After a bench trial, the district court found that the employer was liable for most of the seaman's injuries **{–325–}** and entered judgment accordingly. The employer now appeals, claiming a host of errors. Seeing none, we affirm.

I.

A.

On November 2, 2014, plaintiff–appellee Henry Luwisch was on board the M/V American Challenger, a vessel owned by his employer, defendant–appellant American Marine Corp. Luwisch was the chief engineer of the vessel, and one of his jobs that day was to store line on board. Luwisch climbed to the **[—2—]** upper deck of the vessel, where he had never previously been, to see whether there was room to store the line. He discovered that there was already line lying on the upper deck and that it was obstructing part of the walkway, creating a hazard. Luwisch then attempted to climb back down the ladder but in doing so tripped over the line and fell ten feet, to the lower deck. He was taken to the hospital, where a CT scan revealed damage to several of his cervical discs. Luwisch never returned to work for American Marine.

In December 2014 and again in February 2015, Luwisch saw Dr. William Alden, complaining of pain and numbness in his left arm and headaches, among other things. Dr. Alden found that Luwisch had damage to three of his cervical discs and referred him to Dr. Troy Beaucoudray for treatment. Between March 2015 and February 2016, Dr. Beaucoudray gave Luwisch a series of epidural steroid injections. These injections provided Luwisch only short-term relief, so Dr. Beaucoudray ultimately referred him to Dr. Bradley Bartholomew for surgery. But because of disagreements over who would pay, the surgery never took place.

Between March 2015 and June 2016, Luwisch worked intermittently as a mechanic for a series of different employers. In July 2016, Luwisch resumed working as a chief engineer. When applying for employment as a chief engineer, Luwisch denied having any previous neck injuries or neck pain. In May 2018, Luwisch quit his job and moved to Georgia to sell shrimp and run an RV park.

B.

In April 2017, when he was still living in Louisiana, Luwisch filed suit against American Marine, seeking maintenance and cure as well as compensatory damages. The case was tried without a jury, from July 23 to July 25, 2018. **[—3—]**

Based on the evidence presented at trial, the district court determined that, after an unrelated workplace accident in 2011, Luwisch had been diagnosed with degenerative disc disease and a herniated disc. Because Luwisch had not disclosed this condition to American Marine when he applied for employment, the district court ruled that Luwisch was not entitled to maintenance and cure.

But the district court found that the placement of the line on the upper deck of the American Challenger rendered the vessel unseaworthy, and it also found that American Marine had violated its duty to provide Luwisch with a reasonably safe place to work. The court determined that the placement of the line directly contributed to Luwisch's fall and that American Marine was eighty-percent responsible for the accident. The court determined that Luwisch himself was twenty-percent responsible.

The district court heard medical expert testimony from both sides and determined that although Luwisch had degenerative disc disease before the accident, his condition was asymptomatic until the fall exacerbated it. The district court agreed with **{-326-}** Luwisch that he could not continue to work as a chief engineer in the long term and thus had a diminished earning capacity. The district court awarded Luwisch damages—reduced by twenty percent due to his comparative negligence—based on his past medical expenses, past wage loss, loss of future earning capacity, and pain and suffering.

American Marine now appeals most aspects of the district court's decision. American Marine argues that (1) the American Challenger was not unseaworthy, (2) the district court incorrectly apportioned fault between the parties, (3) Luwisch's fall did not exacerbate his medical condition, (4) Luwisch does not have a diminished earning capacity, (5) Luwisch was not entitled to recover his medical expenses, and (6) the district court's pain-and-suffering award was excessive. We address each argument in turn. **[—4—]**

II.

"The standard of review for a bench trial is well established: findings of fact are reviewed for clear error and legal issues are reviewed de novo." *Barto v. Shore Constr., LLC*, 801 F.3d 465, 471, 3 Adm. R. 415, 416 (5th Cir. 2015) (quoting *Becker v. Tidewater, Inc.*, 586 F.3d 358, 365 (5th Cir. 2009)). As such, we will upset the district court's findings of fact only if we are "left with the definite and firm conviction that a mistake has been committed." *Id.*, 3 Adm. R. at 416 (quoting *Jauch v. Nautical Servs., Inc.*, 470 F.3d 207, 213 (5th Cir. 2006)). As relevant here, findings of fact include determinations of negligence, apportionment of fault, and calculation of damages. *See DePerrodil v. Bozovic Marine, Inc.*, 842 F.3d 352, 356, 358, 361, 4 Adm. R. 308, 309, 310, 313 (5th Cir. 2016). "Moreover, and of particular relevance here, the clearly erroneous standard of review following a bench trial requires even 'greater deference to the trial court's findings when they are based on determinations of credibility.'" *Guzman v. Hacienda Records & Recording Studio, Inc.*, 808 F.3d 1031, 1036 (5th Cir. 2015) (quoting *In re Luhr Bros.*, 157 F.3d 333, 338 (5th Cir. 1998)). Accordingly, "[w]e entertain a strong presumption that the court's findings must be sustained even though this court might have weighed the evidence differently." *Johnson v. Cenac Towing, Inc.*, 544 F.3d 296, 303 (5th Cir. 2008).

A.

"General maritime law imposes a duty upon shipowners to provide a seaworthy vessel." *Hlodan v. Ohio Barge Line, Inc.*, 611 F.2d 71, 74 (5th Cir. 1980) (citing *Carlisle Packing Co. v. Sandanger*, 259 U.S. 255 (1922)). "To be seaworthy, a vessel and its appurtenances must be reasonably fit for their intended uses." *Manderson v. Chet Morrison Contractors, Inc.*, 666 F.3d 373, 379 (5th Cir. 2012) (citing *Mitchell v. Trawler Racer, Inc.*, 362 U.S. 539, 550 (1960)). "Liability under the doctrine of unseaworthiness does not rest upon fault or negligence." *Johnson v. Offshore Express, Inc.*, 845 F.2d 1347, 1354 **[—5—]** (5th Cir. 1988). Instead, "a plaintiff must prove that the unseaworthy condition played a substantial part in bringing about or actually causing [an] injury and that the injury was either a direct result or a reasonably probable consequence of the unseaworthiness." *Id.*

The district court found that "[t]he placement of the rope at the top of the ladder to the upper deck . . . rendered the vessel unseaworthy." It also found that the line "was not the result of an isolated negligent act" and that it "played a substantial part in causing Plaintiff's injury, and the injury was a reasonably probable consequence of the unseaworthiness." Although American Marine argues that the **{-327-}** line's presence on the upper deck was "transitory in nature," it cites no caselaw for the proposition that the line must have lain on the deck for a particular amount of time to render the American Challenger unseaworthy, nor does it cite any evidence regarding how long the line had in fact lain there. Luwisch testified that he had never been to the upper deck before, and neither of the two deckhands—who were the only other people working on the boat—provided testimony. The district court thus concluded that the line had been there "for an extended period of time." American Marine has failed to demonstrate that the district court's finding of unseaworthiness was clear error.

B.

"A seaman is entitled to recovery under the Jones Act . . . if his employer's negligence is the cause, in whole or in part, of his injury." *Gautreaux v. Scurlock Marine, Inc.* (*Gautreaux II*), 107 F.3d 331, 335 (5th Cir. 1997) (en banc). Under the Jones Act, the employer's duty of care "retains the usual and familiar definition of ordinary prudence." *Id.*

Although "Jones Act negligence and unseaworthiness under general maritime law are two distinct causes of action," *Offshore Express*, 845 F.2d at 1354, they largely provide for the same remedies. Consequently, when we rule **[—6—]** "for [a] plaintiff on the issue of unseaworthiness, we [ordinarily] need not consider the question of Jones Act negligence." *Miles v. Melrose*, 882 F.2d 976, 983 (5th Cir. 1989), *aff'd sub nom. Miles v. Apex Marine Corp.*, 489 U.S. 19 (1990); *see, e.g., Colburn v. Bunge Towing, Inc.*, 883 F.2d 372, 375 n.3 (5th Cir. 1989).

"Comparative negligence applies in both Jones Act and unseaworthiness actions, barring an injured party from recovering for the damages sustained as a result of his own fault." *Miles*, 882 F.2d at 984. "Under the Jones Act and the law of unseaworthiness, contributory negligence, however gross, does not bar recovery, but only mitigates damages." *Offshore Express*, 845 F.2d at 1355.

American Marine has failed to establish that Luwisch's accident was mostly his own fault. The district court found that Luwisch was physically incapable of moving the line himself, in part because the rope had heavy wooden boards piled on top of it. And the court also found that Luwisch noticed a junction box with a loose electrical wire on the upper deck, near the line, that Luwisch determined needed to be repaired before the deckhands could safely climb up to help him move the line. These findings were supported by Luwisch's testimony at trial.

American Marine argues that Luwisch's testimony here is inconsistent, since Luwisch suggested that he noticed the loose wire only after he had decided to climb back down to the lower deck. But Luwisch also testified that he did not know where the two deckhands were at the time, because he could not see them from the upper deck. Luwisch testified that he intended to find the deckhands and, once he had noticed the loose wire, to find his tools for fixing the junction box as well. The district court evidently credited Luwisch's uncontroverted testimony and found that Luwisch was twenty percent at fault. American Marine has not shown this apportionment to be clearly erroneous. **[—7—]**

American Marine observes that, under the Jones Act, an "employer must have notice and the opportunity to correct an unsafe condition before liability attaches." *Colburn*, 883 F.2d at 374. Yet "[t]he standard of care is not 'what the employer subjectively knew, but rather what it objectively should have known.'" **{-328-}** *Id.* (citation omitted). "[A] corporate shipowner may be deemed to have constructive knowledge if the . . . negligent condition could have been discovered through the exercise of reasonable diligence." *Brister v. A.W.I., Inc.*, 946 F.2d 350, 356 (5th Cir. 1991). Here, the district court found that "[t]he rope was routinely stored in that location by the vessel's regular crew" and "had been in that position for an extended period of time." Because American Marine points to no evidence contradicting this finding, constructive knowledge could be imputed to it.[1]

[1] What is more, American Marine's liability for unseaworthiness, as opposed to negligence, does not require notice. *See Mitchell*, 362 U.S. at 549 ("[T]he shipowner's actual or constructive knowledge of the unseaworthy condition is not essential to his liability."); *Allen v. Seacoast Prods., Inc.*, 623 F.2d 355, 364 (5th Cir. 1980) ("Lack of

American Marine also seeks to rely on the primary-duty rule. In its original formulation, this rule barred an injured plaintiff from recovering from his employer if his injury resulted from his own failure to perform a duty of his employment. *See Walker v. Lykes Bros. S.S. Co.*, 193 F.2d 772, 774 (2d Cir. 1952). In this circuit, however, we have refused to adopt so strict a rule:

> [E]ven if an employee's injury resulted in part from his own negligence, whether in failing to carry out his duties or in some other respect, such negligence would only reduce, not bar, recovery unless the employer were not negligent at all and the employee's negligence was the sole cause of his injury.

Kendrick v. Ill. Cent. Gulf R.R. Co., 669 F.2d 341, 344 (5th Cir. 1982); *see also Gautreaux v. Scurlock Marine, Inc.*, 84 F.3d 776, 782 (5th Cir. 1996), *reinstated* **[—8—]** *in pertinent part by Gautreaux II*, 107 F.3d at 339. This rule does not bar Luwisch from recovery.

Nevertheless, American Marine insists that Luwisch was more than twenty percent at fault because he was responsible for correcting any safety hazards on the vessel. But the district court found that Luwisch had not seen the line prior to the incident, and American Marine does not contest this finding. Because Luwisch could not have corrected a dangerous condition that he knew nothing about, we see no basis to conclude that Luwisch violated any purported duty to American Marine.

Finally, American Marine argues that Luwisch contributed to his injury by concealing his prior injury when he applied for employment. American Marine cites to *Cenac Towing*, in which we concluded that, under the Jones Act, "contributory negligence may be found where a seaman has concealed material information about a pre-existing injury or physical condition from his employer; exposes his body to a risk of reinjury or aggravation of the condition; and then suffers reinjury or aggravation injury." 544 F.3d at 303-04.

In *Cenac Towing*, we vacated a district court's decision for "reevaluat[ion]" where the district court had held that the plaintiff was not negligent at all despite finding a "causal link" between the plaintiff's injury and the plaintiff's intentional concealment of his medical condition. *Id.* at 302-04. To be sure, this case presents similar facts, insofar as Luwisch concealed his preexisting neck injury in order to obtain employment with American Marine and then, in the course of that employment, aggravated his neck injury. Here, however, the district court clearly evaluated the evidence and **{-329-}** made no inconsistent findings about causation; indeed, it found that Luwisch was twenty percent at fault. *Cenac Towing* does not require vacatur, much less reversal. **[—9—]**

C.

American Marine asserts that Luwisch's present ailments do not stem from his fall aboard the American Challenger, but it does not carry its heavy burden of demonstrating clear error in the district court's choice between competing experts. At trial, American Marine's expert, Dr. Everett Robert, testified that images from MRIs that Luwisch underwent in 2011 and 2015 did not show "any clinically appreciable changes" but only "some mild degenerative changes that [became] more advanced." Dr. Bartholomew, however, testified that some of the changes on the MRIs "were out of proportion to the time period." Similarly, Dr. Beaucoudray testified that there "appeared to be more than the normal rate of degenerative changes." Combining that with Luwisch's failure to complain of radicular pain until after his 2014 fall, Dr. Beaucoudray concluded that, "more probably than not," the 2014 fall caused Luwisch's symptoms. Crediting Dr. Beaucoudray's medical opinion on this point was not clear error.

Additionally, although some medical records indicated that Luwisch suffered from radiculopathy in 2011, Dr. Beaucoudray

---

knowledge of or opportunity to correct [unseaworthy] conditions does not mitigate the vessel owner's duty."), *overruled on other grounds by Gautreaux II*, 107 F.3d at 339.

testified that this appeared to have been an intentional misdiagnosis designed to justify the cost of an MRI, and even Dr. Robert testified that Luwisch did not seem to have radiculopathy in 2011. The district court was not required to accept Dr. Robert's theory that Luwisch's symptoms were a delayed consequence of his 2011 accident.

D.

"A damages award for future lost wages should generally be based upon a seaman's work-life expectancy, meaning 'the average number of years that a person of a certain age will both live *and* work.'" *Barto*, 801 F.3d at 475, 3 Adm. R. at 420 (quoting *Madore v. Ingram Tank Ships, Inc.*, 732 F.2d 475, 478 (5th Cir. 1984)). A court may also consider "evidence that a particular person, by virtue of his health or **[—10—]** occupation or other factors, is likely to live and work a longer, or shorter, period than the average." *DePerrodil*, 842 F.3d at 361, 4 Adm. R. at 313 (quoting *Madore*, 732 F.2d at 478).

Dr. Bartholomew testified that someone with Luwisch's injuries should not work on boats because the labor could aggravate his condition. Similarly, Dr. Alden testified that, for someone with Luwisch's cervical-disc injuries, working as a chief engineer would exacerbate his condition and, on a long-term basis, cause intolerable pain. The district court credited this testimony and found that Luwisch "is not able to return to his job as a chief engineer on offshore vessels and has suffered a loss of earning capacity." American Marine objects that Dr. Alden did not reexamine Luwisch before trial but presents no reason to infer that Luwisch's condition would have improved since his 2015 examination.

American Marine's observation that Luwisch did, in fact, work as a chief engineer after his fall does not compel reversal. The district court found that Luwisch was in pain throughout his post-accident employment despite taking over-the-counter pain medication—a finding that American Marine does not dispute—and consequently the court found that Luwisch worked only "out of economic necessity" and "would not be able to do so long-term." **{-330-}** [2] Moreover, the evidence at trial was that Luwisch likely would not have been able to obtain these jobs had he been forthright with his employers about his injuries. American Marine does not dispute this either. Because Luwisch could not continue to work as a chief engineer without misrepresenting his condition to **[—11—]** his employers and experiencing pain, the district court's finding of diminished earning capacity was not clearly erroneous.

Neither does Luwisch's subsequent decision to quit working as a chief engineer compel reversal. Although American Marine makes much of Luwisch calling this his "retirement," the evidence at trial was that Luwisch was planning to "start selling seafood and running an RV park in Georgia." That is to say, Luwisch was seeking to move into a less physically demanding line of work. As one of the experts correctly noted at trial, the calculation of future income is based on what Luwisch's future earnings would have been "[i]f the accident hadn't occurred." American Marine's only evidence that Luwisch would have taken an early retirement even if he had not gotten injured is Luwisch's statement at trial that, when he was working as a mechanic *after* his fall, he hoped that he would be "ready to retire" in five years. This is weak evidence that Luwisch would have intended to "retire" on the same timeframe had he not been so physically impaired.

E.

Although the district court ruled that Luwisch was not entitled to maintenance and cure, the court nevertheless awarded Luwisch past medical expenses because of American Marine's negligence. American Marine suggests that the award of medical expenses

[2] American Marine's argument that nearly everyone works "out of economic necessity" misses the point. Luwisch testified at trial that he returned to work only after liquidating his retirement account and spending all of his savings. In other words, the district court's finding was that Luwisch forced himself to do work that he physically should not have been doing because he needed money to pay his bills.

vitiates the denial of maintenance and cure, but that argument is unavailing. *See Jauch*, 470 F.3d at 214 ("[T]he district court's denial of [the plaintiff]'s claim for maintenance and cure had no legal effect on his entitlement to recover Jones Act damages for his past medical expenses.").

American Marine also objects that Luwisch's medical expenses were paid for by his attorneys, but because the medical expenses were awarded on the Jones Act claim, the collateral-source rule applies. *See, e.g., Davis v. Odeco, Inc.*, 18 F.3d 1237, 1245 (5th Cir. 1994). "The collateral-source rule bars a **[—12—]** tortfeasor from reducing his liability by the amount the plaintiff recovers from independent sources." *DePerrodil*, 842 F.3d at 358, 4 Adm. R. at 311. "In its simplest form, the rule asks whether the tortfeasor contributed to, or was otherwise responsible for, a particular income source. If not, the income is considered 'independent of (or collateral to) the tortfeasor,' and the tortfeasor may not reduce its damages by that amount." *Id.* at 358-59, 4 Adm. R. at 311 (citation omitted) (quoting *Davis*, 18 F.3d at 1243). "Sources of compensation that have no connection to the tortfeasor are inevitably collateral." *Davis*, 18 F.3d at 1244.

As such, Luwisch's failure to prove that he was obliged to reimburse his attorneys for his medical expenses is irrelevant.[3] "In practice, the [collateral-source] **{-331-}** rule allows plaintiffs to recover expenses that they did not personally have to pay." *DePerrodil*, 842 F.3d at 359, 4 Adm. R. at 311. That is a permissible result: "better a potential windfall for the injured plaintiff than the liable tortfeasor." *Id.*, 4 Adm. R. at 311.

F.

"[A]ny amount awarded for pain and suffering depends to a great extent on the trial court's observation of the plaintiff and its subjective determination of the amount needed to achieve full compensation." *Offshore Express*, 845 F.2d at 1357 (quoting *Hernandez v. M/V Rajaan*, 841 F.2d 582, 590 (5th Cir. 1988)). Nevertheless, American Marine asserts that Luwisch is a serial liar whose testimony should not be credited and concludes that Luwisch "probably" "significantly exaggerated his complaints" such that his pain-and-suffering award "should be reduced by 80%."

Although the district court knew that Luwisch concealed his medical history from his employers, it nevertheless found Luwisch's trial testimony **[—13—]** about his current condition credible. American Marine also points to evidence that Luwisch concealed his employment from Drs. Bartholomew and Beaucoudray, and it notes that Luwisch made some inconsistent statements at trial, regarding the date when his property was foreclosed upon and the length of time that he was unemployed. But again, all this information was before the district court, which had the unique ability to observe Luwisch and to judge his credibility. Because Luwisch "has told a coherent and facially plausible story that is not contradicted by extrinsic evidence," *Guzman*, 808 F.3d at 1036 (quoting *Anderson v. City of Bessemer City*, 470 U.S. 564, 575 (1985)), we cannot say that the district court clearly erred in crediting his testimony.

III.

For the foregoing reasons, we AFFIRM the judgment of the district court.

---

[3] Because American Marine indisputably had "no connection with" the payment of Luwisch's medical expenses, it is "not a difficult task" to conclude that, under the rule, Luwisch's recovery should not be reduced. *Phillips v. W. Co. of N. Am.*, 953 F.2d 923, 930-31 (5th Cir. 1992). Indeed, American Marine does not argue to the contrary.

United States Court of Appeals
for the Fifth Circuit

No. 17-60817

GRAY
vs.
ALABAMA GREAT S. R.R. CO.

Appeal from the United States District Court for the Southern District of Mississippi

Decided: May 28, 2020

Citation: 960 F.3d 212, 8 Adm. R. 187 (5th Cir. 2020).

Before **OWEN,** Chief Judge, and **DENNIS** and **SOUTHWICK,** Circuit Judges.

[—1—] {-214-} **SOUTHWICK,** Circuit Judge:

Gregory Tramaine Miller was crushed to death between the couplers of two rail cars while working as a conductor trainee with Alabama Great Southern Railroad Company. Summary judgment dismissing all claims was granted on the basis that there was no evidence to support imposing any liability on the railroad. The administrators of Miller's estate argue on appeal that there was evidence to create a jury issue. We AFFIRM. **[—2—]**

FACTUAL AND PROCEDURAL BACKGROUND

On August 12, 2015, Gregory Miller was assigned to an Alabama Great Southern train crew consisting of a conductor, M.A. Sillimon; a brakeman, J.D. Henderson; and an engineer, A.C. Clearman. Miller rode the train to a facility in Petal, Mississippi, in order to couple empty rail cars that would then be taken to a different facility. Miller rode on one side of the train to the Petal facility. Upon arrival, he safely crossed over the tracks on foot to the other side of the train, using a safety procedure called "3-Step Protection" for crossing between standing rail cars.

The Alabama Great Southern is a wholly owned subsidiary of the Norfolk Southern Railway Company. Each company uses the same Operating Rules and Safety & General Conduct Rules. Operating Rule 22 prohibits an employee from going between standing equipment on the tracks for any reason unless 3-Step Protection is first established. Going between moving equipment on the tracks is never permitted. To establish 3-Step Protection, an employee must first orally request passage between cars from the engineer. If the request is made via radio, the employee must provide his or her occupation, job symbol, and engine number. Once such a request is made, the second step is for the engineer to take the following action: "apply the independent brake"; next, "[p]lace the reverser lever in neutral position"; and finally, "[o]pen the generator field switch." Third, before the employee is permitted to go between equipment on the tracks, the **{-215-}** engineer "must acknowledge to each requesting employee that '3-Step Protection' is established."

After Miller successfully established 3-Step Protection and crossed the tracks to the other side of the train, the train crew began to couple 11 rail cars. At the start, each rail car was approximately ten feet from the next one. The crew's train coupled the first uncoupled car waiting on the switch track, and the train was brought to a safety stop to ensure that coupling was successful. **[—3—]**

After the first coupling, Henderson was positioned at the north end of the line of cars and Sillimon was at the south end. Miller was about one-half of a car length south of Henderson, who was supervising Miller that night. Henderson, while facing north toward the train coupled to the engine and away from Miller, radioed the crew, "Everybody let me get big half to a bunch," meaning that the engineer should begin a "rolling coupling" of the remaining ten rail cars by slowly shoving the train south at a speed never exceeding two miles per hour, impacting and coupling each car, one right after the other, without stopping.

As the train approached, Henderson walked backward while facing north toward the train to give "full attention on the engine coming down," then started to turn south to observe the couplings. At this time, for reasons unknown and without 3-Step

Protection, Miller went between two rail cars during the rolling coupling. Henderson testified that as he was turning to the south, he noticed a "flash" and told Clearman to cease coupling by radioing, "That will do." Henderson could not see Miller, so he began walking south and found Miller fatally injured, caught in the coupling between two rail cars, the second of three couplings made during the shove.

As co-administrators of Miller's estate, Shaquere Myleshia Gray and Hannah Lasha Hoze filed suit against the Alabama Great Southern Railroad Company. They claimed the railroad was negligent in failing to train, instruct, and supervise Miller, that the railroad also was negligent in failing to provide a safe place to work for Miller, and that it was foreseeable that Miller would go between rail cars, which was the cause of his death.

In granting summary judgment for the railroad, the district court concluded that Miller's failure to establish 3-Step Protection before going between rail cars was the sole cause of his death, that his going between moving rail cars was unforeseeable, and that the plaintiffs failed to produce **[—4—]** evidence of any negligent acts by the railroad attributable to causing Miller's death. This timely appeal followed.

DISCUSSION

The suit was brought under the Federal Employers Liability Act ("FELA"), 45 U.S.C. § 51. The FELA provides the exclusive remedy for a railroad employee engaged in interstate commerce whose injury resulted from the negligence of the railroad. *Rivera v. Union Pac. R.R. Co.*, 378 F.3d 502, 507 (5th Cir. 2004). The FELA allows an injured railroad employee to recover damages for "injury or death resulting in whole or in part from the negligence" of the railroad. § 51. "Under FELA the test of a jury case is simply whether the proofs justify with reason the conclusion that employer negligence played any part, even the slightest, in producing the injury or death for which damages are sought." *CSX Transp., Inc., v. McBride*, 564 U.S. 685, 692 (2011). This standard leaves in place, though, the plaintiff's burden to provide evidence of "all the same elements as are found in a common law negligence action." **{-216-}** *Armstrong v. Kansas City S. Ry. Co.*, 752 F.2d 1110, 1113 (5th Cir. 1985). Indeed, "foreseeability is an essential ingredient of negligence under the Act." *Id.*

The FELA eliminated a variety of traditional defenses, such as the fellow-servant rule, the assumption-of-the-risk defense, and the doctrine of contributory negligence. *Consolidated Rail Corp. v. Gottshall*, 512 U.S. 532, 542–43 (1994); 45 U.S.C. §§ 51, 53–55. Even so, if a plaintiff's negligence is the sole cause of the injury, a defendant has no liability under the Act. *Southern Ry. Co. v. Youngblood*, 286 U.S. 313, 317 (1932).

We review a grant of summary judgment *de novo*, meaning this court considers the evidence and law in the same manner as the district court was required to do. *Ibarra v. UPS*, 695 F.3d 354, 355 (5th Cir. 2012). Summary **[—5—]** judgment is appropriate if the movant demonstrates "there is no genuine dispute as to any material fact and the movant is entitled to judgment as a matter of law." FED. R. CIV. P. 56(a). Under the FELA, awarding summary judgment to the defendant railroad is appropriate "[o]nly when there is a complete absence of probative facts" to support a jury verdict in the plaintiff's favor. *See Lavender v. Kurn*, 327 U.S. 645, 653 (1946). "This standard is highly favorable to the plaintiff and recognizes that the FELA is protective of the plaintiff's right to a jury trial." *Wooden v. Mo. Pac. R.R. Co.*, 862 F.2d 560, 561 (5th Cir. 1989) (punctuation edited).

The plaintiffs argue that Miller's failure to establish 3-Step Protection was not the sole cause of his death because the railroad's negligence must also have had a role in the accident. They contend that there was "overwhelming evidence" of at least some negligence by the railroad. Among their arguments is that Henderson negligently supervised Miller. There was evidence that the railroad used a supervisor/trainee system for on-the-job training. On the night of the accident, Henderson was Miller's supervisor. Although Henderson was working as a brakeman that night, he was a certified conductor, making it appropriate for him to supervise a conductor trainee. The plaintiffs say that Henderson was negligent because "a mentor should know where his mentee is at all times as he is in charge of ensuring the mentee's safety." At the time of the incident, though, "Henderson had his back to Mr. Miller, did not know where he was, and did not know what Mr. Miller was doing at any point while the shoving movement was occurring." The plaintiffs also argue that Henderson violated the railroad's procedure by failing "to observe the coupling that was occurring when Mr. Miller was injured."

There is no record evidence of any policy requiring that a supervisor never stop looking at a conductor-trainee. Plaintiffs say such evidence does exist, as Sillimon in his deposition testified that a trainee should always be **[—6—]** "within eyesight" of the supervisor. We do not interpret that testimony as supporting that the supervisor cannot as necessary look a different direction than the trainee during performance of the job. Instead, the supervisor must always be in a position to "keep an eye" on the trainee, meaning no obstruction to the view, even though at times the supervisor must concentrate on other tasks. The plaintiffs agree that Henderson was required to observe the couplings, which means he would have had to take his eyes off Miller during the first coupling, apparently just before Miller went between the second set of rail cars. **{-217-}**

The only evidence as to rules for coupling is testimony vaguely describing a conductor and brakeman's duty of "observing a coupling." We know from the record that Henderson was in the process of turning to observe a coupling when he saw a "flash," which was Miller's going between the rail cars. Henderson radioed Clearman to stop the train. Having considered plaintiffs' contentions to the contrary, we conclude there was no evidence that Henderson violated any procedure that played a part in Miller's death.

The plaintiffs also contend that the railroad negligently trained Miller because he "was never trained on the procedures of a rolling couple and the only evidence in the record suggests that he had never heard of such a move." The plaintiffs also argue the failure of Miller's crew members to "adequately job brief this procedure . . . played a central role in bringing about this injury." Thus, according to the plaintiffs, "[t]here is no evidence in the record to show that Mr. Miller had any reason to believe that the cars would continue to move or that he would be in danger if he needed to get between cars."

The plaintiffs' point is that if Miller had not been made aware of rolling couplings, then his undisputed knowledge of the procedures to be followed prior to going between cars would, at the time of his fatal violation of those procedures, have been joined by his ignorance that the cars would keep moving **[—7—]** after the initial coupling. Certainly, it was negligent for Miller to have gone between the cars, but a failure of others to explain what was occurring could have left him unaware of just how dangerous his actions would be. The only evidence of a source for Miller's knowledge was not identified by the railroad until oral argument in this court. We may, but are not required, to consider this evidence despite its late identification because we may affirm a judgment on any ground that appears in the record. *S&W Enters., L.L.C. v. SouthTrust Bank of Ala., NA*, 315 F.3d 533, 537 (5th Cir. 2003). We discuss the evidence.

The evidence comes from Sillimon's deposition. The dissent does not see that testimony in quite the same way we do, viewing it as a possibly generic description of how the work should be done as opposed to what was done that night. We will summarize the immediately preceding testimony, then quote at some length the relevant statements. Sillimon was asked about the coupling that had been completed by this same crew at other locations earlier on the night of Miller's death. He mentioned the first location but did not explicitly describe any rolling coupling there. The railroad's counsel then asked Sillimon to describe what happened at the second location, which still was not the job site where Miller was fatally injured that same day:

> Q: All right. And how many cars did y'all work that night [at the second location]? Do you know?
>
> A: It was 20 -- it was 20 in, 20 out.
>
> Q. Okay. And y'all have to spot all 20 of them?
>
> A. That's correct.
>
> Q. And how do y'all go about spotting these cars? How do y'all handle that?
>
> A. You spot each car up one at a time.
>
> Q. Okay. And take me through what you would do as the conductor, what the brakeman would do, and what the engineer would do in spotting these cars. **[—8—]**
>
> A. As far as the brakeman and the conductor, it can go either or.
>
> Q. Okay.
>
> A. I can walk down and do a C-100 [which he would later describe as checking each car prior to starting the coupling] and check everything, make sure **{-218-}** the hoses are -- make sure there's no one in the tracks, make sure the hoses are down, make sure any chocks or anything that we couple up to -- so it won't derail anything. Or the brakeman can walk down and do a C-100. And after we do a C-100, I'll be in position at the bottom. The brakeman be in position at the top. He will make the first coupling, and the rest of the couplings be run-in coupling.
>
> Q. And you refer to that as a running couple?
>
> A. That's correct.
>
> Q. And what -- what is a running couple?
>
> A. When you couple up to the -- you got to make sure you coupled up to the first car. Once you coupled up to the first car, you bunch to the next car. Then you bunch and then you bunch until you get to the last two cars. You stop the move. You couple up to that second to the last car, and then you couple up to the next car.

In summary, Sillimon started by saying it was necessary to "spot all 20" cars at the earlier location. He then was asked how the crew would accomplish that spotting. Certainly, some of his lengthy answer could be taken as a general description of how the tasks are done, particularly in stating that either the brakeman or the conductor could perform certain of the functions. The key to us, though, is that Sillimon testified that a series of rolling couplings had to be made at the job site preceding the one where Miller was fatally injured. Perhaps there were shortcomings in initial training or otherwise in making Miller aware of the dangers of a rolling coupling, specifically that the train keeps moving as the closely spaced but not yet coupled cars are sequentially linked. Regardless of that possibility, Sillimon testified that Miller had just experienced that sort of coupling. **[—9—]**

The plaintiffs also argue that it is a fact dispute whether Miller requested 3-Step Protection. They discuss evidence that requesting over the radio is not always heard. There is a protection for that built into the three steps, though, *i.e.,* the requesting employee must wait for the engineer to "acknowledge to each requesting employee that '3-Step Protection' is established." It is undisputed that Sillimon did not acknowledge 3-Step Protection to any employee during the time Miller went between the rail cars and suffered his fatal injuries.

Last, the plaintiffs contend that "[i]t is wholly foreseeable that an employee will get between cars during the course of his work, especially when as here he is expecting the movement to stop for some period of time." They rely on a Supreme Court decision in which the decedent stepped between standing rail cars to detach a damaged car. *Chicago Great W. R.R. v. Schendel*, 267 U.S. 287, 289 (1925). There, the rail cars sat on a downward grade and gravity caused the rail car to slide into the decedent, fatally injuring him. *Id.* The Court held that although the decedent was partially negligent, the railroad was liable because there was evidence that the damaged rail car did not meet the statutory requirements to protect him, and that damage was the reason he had stepped between the cars. *Id.* at 292. Unlike in *Schendel*, though,

Miller was killed during continuous coupling of cars, a process he had just witnessed elsewhere, and during a time in which he knew not to cross between cars without following the described protocols. In some circumstances it of course is foreseeable that railroad employees will get between cars. In the circumstances here, stepping between **{-219-}** cars was prohibited and the reasons for the prohibition would have been clear.

Finally, we consider whether plaintiffs are correct that the district court improperly relied at least in part on a finding that Miller assumed the risk of injury by stepping between the cars. As we stated, the FELA abolished **[—10—]** assumption of the risk and similar defenses. *See Gottshall*, 512 U.S. at 542–43. According to the plaintiffs, the district court's reliance on the fact that Miller knew how to utilize 3-Step Protection based on training and experience means that it concluded that Miller assumed the risk of ignoring that protocol.

We see no application of this discarded defense by the district court. Though the district court mentioned that Miller was trained and tested on the safety procedure before he went to field training, the court was merely explaining Miller's negligence. The district court stated that the plaintiffs "ha[d] not produced evidence of any negligent acts attributable to [the railroad] that caused the accident." *Gray*, 2017 WL 6805046, at *3. That is a reference to a lack of evidence, not to an assumption of risk.

"If the employee's negligence was the sole proximate cause of his injury, he cannot recover." *Atlantic Coast Line R. Co. v. Dixon*, 189 F.2d 525, 527 (5th Cir. 1951). Though there is a lack of clarity as to exactly what happened, Miller, unfortunately, negligently went between the two cars. In the absence of any evidence to support a jury finding that some negligence on the part of the railroad contributed to the accident, summary judgment was proper.

AFFIRMED.

(Reporter's Note: Dissenting Opinion follows on p. 192).

[—11—] {-219-} **DENNIS**, Circuit Judge, dissenting:

I respectfully dissent. In my view, the record contains evidence from which a reasonable jury could find that Miller's death resulted at least in part from AGS's negligence: Miller was a new hire of about forty-five days with no prior railroad experience, and he had not been schooled, trained, or instructed in the multi-car rolling coupling procedure that resulted in his death. Miller, therefore, may not have understood that more than a single car would be coupled, and Henderson, the brakeman responsible for Miller's supervision, failed to keep Miller close to him and within his eyesight during the rolling coupling. A reasonable jury could thus infer that the railroad's negligence played a part, *even the slightest*, in producing the injury or death for which damages are sought, such that this case should proceed to a jury trial.

I.

FELA prescribes that:

> Every common carrier by railroad . . . shall be liable in damages to any person suffering injury while he is employed by such carrier . . . for such injury or death *resulting in whole or in part* from the negligence of any of the officers, agents, or employees of such carrier . . . .

45 U.S.C. § 51 (emphasis added). Congress enacted FELA in response to the dangers inherent in working on the railroad, and its language on causation "is as broad as could be framed." *Urie v. Thompson*, 337 U.S. 163, 181 (1949); *see Consolidated Rail Corp. v. Gottshall*, 512 U.S. 532, 542-43 (1994). The Supreme Court has recognized that "in comparison to tort litigation at common law, 'a relaxed standard of causation applies under FELA.'" *CSX Transportation, Inc., v. McBride*, 564 U.S. 685, 692 (2011) (quoting *Gottshall*, 512 U.S. at 542-43). "Under {-220-} FELA the test of a jury case is simply whether the proofs justify with reason the conclusion that employer negligence played any part, *even the slightest*, in producing the injury or death for which damages are [—12—] sought." *Id.* (emphasis added) (quoting *Rogers v. Missouri Pac. R. Co.*, 352 U.S. 500, 506 (1957)).

We review a district court's grant of summary judgment for the railroad de novo, and "we must resolve all ambiguities, permissible inferences, and material issues of fact in favor of the non-moving parties." *Total E & P USA Inc. v. Kerr-McGee Oil & Gas Corp.*, 719 F.3d 424, 429 (5th Cir. 2013). In a FELA case, it is the province of the jury to weigh many factors, including the nature of the task and the hazards it entails, in determining whether employer fault "played any part, even the slightest," in the employee's injury. *McBride*, 564 U.S. at 692; *see Bailey v. Central Vt. Ry.*, 319 U.S. 350, 353-54 (1943).

The majority concludes that Plaintiffs have not produced evidence of any negligent acts attributable to AGS that caused the accident and that Miller's negligence in going between the moving rail cars was not foreseeable. I disagree. Plaintiffs point to several acts or omissions by AGS and its employees that a reasonable jury could find were negligent and "played [a] part, even the slightest, in producing" Miller's death. *McBride*, 564 U.S. at 692.

First, the record reveals that Miller had been employed in railroad work only forty-five days at the time of his death, and though he attended a classroom training center in Georgia for nineteen days, the center did not instruct conductor trainees like Miller on rolling couplings, the procedure the crew employed at the time Miller was killed. The written rules and guidance provided to Miller as a conductor trainee also did not describe the rolling coupling procedure. In the classroom, trainees were taught a different procedure for coupling a single railcar—the engineer slowly drives the train until it makes the connection with the car being coupled, the engineer stops the train, and the crew members go between the cars to finalize the coupling. Crew members then walk to the next rail car on the track to prepare for the next coupling. In practice, however, AGS employees also used a "rolling [—13—] coupling" procedure to couple more than a single rail car at a time, the procedure that the crew utilized at the time Miller was killed. When executing a rolling coupling, the engineer stops once after the first standing car is coupled to the train, then, when signaled, he shoves the train at walking speed, impacting and coupling each remaining uncoupled car, one right after the other, without stopping until the next to last standing uncoupled car is coupled. Once the second to last rail car is coupled, the train stops briefly, then the engineer drives the train into the last car until it is coupled. Then the crew makes sure that all couplings are secure, connects the air hoses between the cars, and cuts the air in to the now-coupled cars.

Though the trainees were taught the rules prohibiting employees from going between moving railcars and that they must request 3-Step Protection before moving between standing cars on a track,[1] they **{-221-}** were not specifically trained or given any written or oral instruction on how the rules applied to rolling couplings of a "bunch" of cars or the additional dangers inherent in the rolling coupling of as many as nine to ten cars without stopping between individual couplings. A reasonable jury could conclude that the railroad was negligent in failing to provide Miller with basic training in rolling couplings before he was required to participate in such a dangerous procedure in his work.

Second, a reasonable jury could find that, as in his classroom training, Miller was not instructed during his on-the-job training as to how to participate in a rolling coupling, nor was he provided notice that the crew was going to perform a rolling coupling prior to the crew activating that dangerous **[—14—]** procedure in which he was killed. For the on-the-job stage of their training, conductor trainees like Miller were assigned to a variety of jobs for a little over three months, with different crews and conductors in charge of each job. During the job briefing on the night of the accident, Sillimon, the senior conductor and leader of the crew, did not provide Miller with any information or instruction about rolling couplings or tell him that the crew would use a rolling coupling at any location, and no one mentioned Miller's lack of experience or instructed him as to what he was expected to do or was responsible for during a rolling coupling. As noted in AGS's expert's report, at the worksite where Miller was killed, the crew first used a single car coupling to connect the first uncoupled standing car on the track to the rest of the train—once the first car was connected, the train stopped. A jury could infer that Miller, because of his inexperience and lack of schooling, instruction and training, would have expected the next coupling to be a single-car coupling as well, after which the train would stop moving. However, Henderson called for a rolling coupling, saying, "Everybody let me get a big half to a bunch," a phrase that would inform only knowledgeable workers—those familiar with a rolling coupling and the terminology used to call for one—that Henderson was calling for a rolling coupling of as many as ten cars. It is undisputed that this jargon was not taught in the rulebook or classroom training and is instead something that employees must pick up on from their work in the field. From the facts in the record, a jury could find that Miller, who had been out of the classroom for less than a month, did not know what Henderson's instruction meant, and therefore had no reason to understand that the train would not stop after another coupling, but would continue rolling, impacting and coupling cars up to the point where he was killed. A jury could conclude these failures by the railroad and by Miller's supervisors were also negligent. **[—15—]**

Moreover, Plaintiffs have consistently contended that Miller did not know what a rolling coupling was, had not been informed that the maneuver would be used at the work site, and was only familiar with the standard single-car coupling procedure. AGS did not dispute any of these facts in the district court or in its brief to this court. At oral argument before this court, however, counsel for AGS cited to Sillimon's deposition and contended

---

[1] Another rule explains that employees must not cross tracks "between standing separated cars or locomotives unless the equipment is separated by at least 50 feet and the employee maintains at least 10 feet of separation between themselves and the nearest equipment." Three-step protection is required where, as here, "a locomotive is coupled to standing equipment or is on the same track in a position to couple to the equipment."

that it showed Miller had been exposed to a rolling coupling earlier on the night that he was killed.

I disagree with the defense counsel's oral argument and the majority's contention that Sillimon's deposition testimony provides conclusive evidence that Miller had previously witnesses a rolling coupling earlier on the night he was killed. Maj. Op. at 7-9. At the start of the relevant portion of the deposition, Sillimon was answering questions about a job the crew worked the night of the accident. He was **{-222-}** then asked: "And how do y'all go about spotting these cars? How do y'all handle that?" After an explanation of what the brakeman and conductors typically do, Sillimon concluded: "He will make the first coupling, and the rest of the couplings be run-in coupling." Sillimon then explained in general the process of a running or rolling coupling.

The pretrial deposition does not specify that Sillimon, in speaking of rolling couplings, was describing the process employed by the crew at a different facility earlier on the night of the accident instead of simply describing the process of a rolling coupling generally. Given the ambiguity of the testimony and our obligation to resolve such ambiguity in Miller's favor, I would conclude that there is at least a genuine issue of material fact as to whether Miller had seen a rolling coupling earlier in the evening on the night of the accident. *See Total E & P USA Inc.*, 719 F.3d at 429 ("[I]n reviewing the summary judgment de novo, we must resolve all ambiguities, permissible **[—16—]** inferences, and material issues of fact in favor of the non-moving parties . . . .").

Finally, Plaintiffs have presented evidence in opposition to AGS's motion for summary judgment that AGS employees failed to reasonably mentor or supervise Miller. Though Sillimon was the senior conductor and Henderson had only eight months of experience as a conductor, Sillimon put Henderson in charge of mentoring and supervising Miller at the time of the accident. Henderson had been cited five times for rules violations in 2015 and 2016. On the night of the accident, when Henderson instructed the engineer to start the rolling coupling, Henderson had his back turned toward Miller who was half a car length away from Henderson. Henderson then walked backward, still facing away from Miller, as the engineer proceeded to couple up three railroad cars, all with Miller being out of Henderson's eyesight. As Henderson turned to face the south, he noticed a "flash" in his *peripheral* vision, providing further evidence that Miller was out of Henderson's sight and close supervision. Together, these facts would support a reasonable jury in finding that Henderson, for whose acts and omissions AGS is vicariously responsible, was an inattentive and careless supervisor whose failure to mentor and supervise Miller contributed to the accident that caused his death.

The majority claims that "[t]here is no record evidence of any policy for which a conductor-trainee must always be within view of their supervisor." However, Darren Gooch, a trainmaster who worked for AGS, testified that the "rule" when supervising conductor trainees was to keep them "within sight distance and close," and Sillimon acknowledged in his deposition that when he was a conductor-trainee, the brakeman or conductor kept him "within eyesight." This is an issue for the jury, who could reasonably conclude that AGS was responsible for Henderson's failure to mentor, closely supervise, and watch Miller during the dangerous rolling coupling procedure. **[—17—]**

II.

Though Miller may have been negligent in assuming only a single car was to be coupled and in moving between the railcars without requesting 3-Step Protection, it is well-established in FELA law that the railroad can still be liable if its negligence contributed in part to the danger even when the employee's negligence was the more direct cause of the injury. *McBride*, 564 U.S. at 695 (rejecting the argument that "the railroad's part . . . was too indirect" a cause when compared to the employee's negligence). When executing **{-223-}** a single car coupling that Miller was taught in the classroom, the engineer would stop after each coupling, and employees would go between each of the newly coupled cars to turn on the air and check the connection for the cars. A reasonable jury could conclude, then, that due to his lack of supervision, training, and experience, Miller went between the cars because he did not understand that the crew was executing a rolling coupling and that the impacts and movements of the rail cars would not stop after a single car had been coupled.

Though no case presents identical facts, the Supreme Court has required the submission of FELA cases to juries based on even slighter proof of negligence and causation. *See Lavender v. Kurn*, 327 U.S. 645, 648-49, 652 (1946) (circumstantial evidence that worker killed by skull fracture was struck on head by mail hook swinging from side of railway company's mail car was sufficient for jury); *Gallick v. Baltimore & Ohio R.R. Co.*, 372 U.S. 108, 109-10, 122 (1963) (upholding a jury verdict for a plaintiff who lost both his legs as a result of an infected insect bite because railroad was negligent in maintaining a stagnant pool of water attractive to vermin and insects).

* * *

The Supreme Court has instructed that "the test of a jury case [under FELA] is simply whether the proofs justify with reason the conclusion that **[—18—]** employer negligence played any part, even the slightest, in producing the injury or death for which damages are sought." *Rogers*, 352 U.S. at 506. "The burden of the employee is met . . . when there is proof, even though entirely circumstantial, from which the jury may with reason make that inference." *Id.* at 508. It is irrelevant that "the jury may also with reason, on grounds of probability, attribute the result to other causes, including the employee's contributory negligence." *Id.* at 506.

Submission of a FELA case to the jury is required "in all but the infrequent cases where fair-minded jurors cannot honestly differ whether fault of the employer played any part in the employee's injury." *Id.* at 510. This case is clearly not one of those rare cases in which every reasonable juror must conclude that the employer's negligence played no part—not even the slightest—in the employee's injury and death. *See id.*; *McBride*, 564 U.S. at 692. The majority opinion, in failing to account for the special features of FELA's negligence action that make it significantly different from the ordinary common-law negligence action, contributes to the steady erosion and undermining of the right to a jury trial under FELA in this Circuit. *See also Huffman v. Union Pac. R.R.*, 675 F.3d 412, 426, 433 (5th Cir. 2012) (Dennis, J., dissenting) ("The evidence in this case is manifestly sufficient to meet the test of a jury case under the FELA, which is simply whether employer negligence played any part, even the slightest, in producing the injury."). For the foregoing reasons, I dissent.

United States Court of Appeals
for the Fifth Circuit

No. 19-30612

MARTIN ENERGY SERVS., L.L.C.
VS.
BOURBON PETREL M/V

Appeal from the United States District Court for the Eastern District of Louisiana

Decided: June 17, 2020

Citation: 962 F.3d 827, 8 Adm. R. 196 (5th Cir. 2020).

Before **BARKSDALE**, **HIGGINSON**, and **DUNCAN**, Circuit Judges.

[—2—] {-829-} DUNCAN, Circuit Judge:

Under the Commercial Instruments and Maritime Liens Act ("CIMLA"), 46 U.S.C. §§ 31301–31343, a person may obtain a maritime lien against a vessel by providing it with "necessaries." Here, plaintiff Martin Energy Services ("Martin") delivered fuel to three support vessels owned by C.G.G. Services, U.S., Inc. ("CGG"). The support vessels carried the fuel in their cargo tanks to refuel three other vessels performing seismic surveys off Louisiana's coast. When CGG failed to pay for the fuel, Martin sued, and the district court **[—3—]** concluded Martin had a maritime lien on the support vessels. That result unduly expands our maritime lien precedents. Fuel may be "necessary" to a vessel if it fuels the vessel. But the fuel transported by the support vessels was for refueling *other* vessels. That fuel was not "necessary" to the support vessels. We therefore reverse and render judgment for CGG.

I.

In 2014, CGG was conducting seismic surveying operations off the coast of Louisiana with three vessels, the *Geo Celtic*, *Oceanic Sirius*, and *Oceanic Vega* (the "Seismic Vessels"). CGG was responsible for ensuring the Seismic Vessels were supplied with fuel, supplies, and equipment. To do so, CGG used three other vessels, the *Bourbon Petrel*, *OMS Resolution*, and *Miss Lilly* (the "Support Vessels"), which made deliveries to the Seismic Vessels from Port Fourchon, Louisiana. At first, CGG purchased fuel directly from Martin, **{-830-}** but credit problems eventually led it to buy through a trader, O.W. Bunker USA, Inc. ("O.W. Bunker"). For the purchases at issue in this case, O.W. Bunker arranged for fuel deliveries through Martin.

Those fuel deliveries occurred in October and November 2014. Pursuant to purchase orders from O.W. Bunker, Martin delivered fuel to each of the three Support Vessels. Each vessel had a cargo tank for carrying fuel to the Seismic Vessels, as distinct from a "day tank" holding fuel for the Support Vessels themselves. On three separate occasions during this time, the Support Vessels transported thousands of gallons of fuel in their cargo tanks to refuel the Seismic Vessels.

Shortly after, O.W. Bunker filed for bankruptcy.[1] CGG had not yet paid O.W. Bunker's invoices for the Martin fuel. CGG eventually settled with O.W. **[—4—]** Bunker, but O.W. Bunker never forwarded payment to Martin. Martin then sued CGG in federal district court, asserting *in rem* claims against the Support Vessels and *in personam* claims against the vessels' owners. The *in personam* claims were disposed of on summary judgment, and the *in rem* claims were tried to the court.

The district court ruled for Martin. The court concluded that Martin's delivery of fuel gave rise to a maritime lien against the Support Vessels. It reasoned that the Martin fuel qualified as "necessaries" to those vessels under CIMLA. *See* 46 U.S.C. § 31342(a). The court also concluded the fuel was provided "on the order" of CGG or its authorized agent, as

[1] This case is yet another "round in the maritime litigation spawned by the collapse of OW Bunker, formerly the world's largest supplier of fuel for ships." *ING Bank N.V. v. Bomin* **[—4—]** *Bunker Oil Corp.*, 953 F.3d 390, 391, 8 Adm. R. 169, 169 (5th Cir. 2020) (quoting *NuStar Energy Servs., Inc. v. M/V COSCO Auckland*, 760 F. App'x 245, 246 (5th Cir.), *cert. dismissed*, --- U.S. ---,140 S. Ct. 339 (2019)).

CIMLA requires. *See id.* Finally, the court awarded Martin pre-judgment interest dating from each fuel purchase. CGG timely appealed.

II.

On appeal from a bench trial, we review fact findings for clear error and legal conclusions *de novo*. *Maritrend, Inc. v. Serac & Co. (Shipping) Ltd.*, 348 F.3d 469, 470 (5th Cir. 2003) (citation omitted). "Whether a maritime lien exists is a question of law, reviewed *de novo*." *Comar Marine, Corp. v. Raider Marine Logistics, LLC*, 792 F.3d 564, 575, 3 Adm. R. 371, 377 (5th Cir. 2015).

III.

CIMLA[2] governs entitlement to maritime liens. *ING Bank N.V. v. Bomin Bunker Oil Corp.*, 953 F.3d 390, 393, 8 Adm. R. 169, 171 (5th Cir. 2020) (quoting *Valero Mktg. & Supply Co. v. M/V Almi Sun, IMO No. 9579535*, 893 F.3d 290, 292, 6 Adm. R. 205, 205 (5th Cir. 2018)). It states, in relevant part, that "a person providing *necessaries to a* **[—5—]** *vessel* on the order of the owner or a person authorized by the owner . . . has a maritime lien on the vessel [and] may bring a civil action in rem to enforce the lien." 46 U.S.C. § 31342(a)(1), (2) (emphasis added). The lien "is a special property right in the vessel," which "grants the creditor the right to appropriate the vessel, have it sold, and be repaid the debt from the proceeds." *Equilease Corp. v. M/V Sampson*, 793 F.2d 598, 602 (5th Cir. 1986) (en banc) (citation omitted).[3] "We apply the **{-831-}** provisions of CIMLA *stricti juris* to ensure that maritime liens are not 'lightly extended by construction, analogy, or inference.'" *Valero*, 893 F.3d at 292, 6 Adm. R. at 206 (quoting *Atl. & Gulf Stevedores, Inc. v. M.V. Grand Loyalty*, 608 F.2d 197, 200–01 (5th Cir. 1979)).

While not defining "necessaries," CIMLA furnishes an illustrative list: "repairs, supplies, towage, and the use of a dry dock or marine railway." 46 U.S.C. § 31301(4). In that regard, "[n]ecessaries are the things that a prudent owner would provide to enable a ship to perform well the functions for which she has been engaged." *Equilease*, 793 F.2d at 603 (citing 2 Benedict on Admiralty § 34 (7th ed. 1984)). The term, which has a "broad meaning,"[4] includes "most goods or services that are useful to the vessel, keep her out of danger, and enable her to perform her particular function." *Id.* These are items useful "to vessel operations"[5] and "necessary to keep the ship going."[6] **[—6—]**

A.

It is undisputed that the Martin fuel was put into the cargo tanks of the Support Vessels, each of which transported it to refuel the Seismic Vessels. The issue is whether, as the district court concluded, that fuel constituted "necessaries" to the Support Vessels, giving rise to a maritime lien under CIMLA. The court reasoned that two of the Support Vessels, the *Bourbon Petrel* and the *OMS Resolution*, served as "floating gas stations" for the Seismic Vessels and that the fuel was "necessary" for the Support Vessels to perform this function. Similarly, the court reasoned the fuel was "necessary" for the third Support Vessel, the *Miss Lilly*, to function as an "offshore supply vessel," transporting fuel, equipment, and personnel to the Seismic Vessels. On appeal, CGG argues this was error. It contends the Martin fuel supported operation of the Seismic Vessels, not the Support Vessels. The fuel was merely cargo carried by the Support Vessels, and no

---

[2] In 1988, CIMLA recodified the 1910 Federal Maritime Lien Act ("FMLA"), 46 U.S.C. §§ 971–975, without changing its substance. *See Maritrend*, 348 F.3d at 470–71.

[3] *See also Racal Survey, U.S.A., Inc. v. M/V Count Fleet*, 231 F.3d 183, 191 (5th Cir. 2000) (necessaries are "designated for specific vessels").

[4] *J. Ray McDermott & Co. v. Off-Shore Menhaden Co.*, 262 F.2d 523, 525 (5th Cir. 1959).

[5] *Gulf Marine & Indus. Supplies, Inc. v. Golden Prince M/V*, 230 F.3d 178, 180 (5th Cir. 2000) (discussing *Equilease*); *see also Silver Star Enterprises, Inc. v. Saramacca M/V*, 82 F.3d 666, 668 (5th Cir. 1996) (maritime liens "developed as a necessary incident of the operation of vessels") (quoting *Piedmont & George's Creek Coal Co. v. Seaboard Fisheries Co.*, 245 U.S. 1, 9 (1920)).

[6] *Silver Star*, 82 F.3d at 668 (quoting *Dampskibsselskabet Dannebrog v. Signal Oil & Gas Co.*, 310 U.S. 268, 280 (1940)).

authority supports deeming cargo "necessaries" for purposes of a maritime lien. We agree.

Fuel may qualify as a "necessary" to a vessel under CIMLA when it is supplied to refuel that vessel. *See, e.g., Valero*, 893 F.3d at 291, 294, 6 Adm. R. at 205, 207 (there was "no dispute that [fuel] bunkers qualify as necessaries . . . to the Vessel" when plaintiff supplied fuel to a vessel that "needed refueling"). In such a case, fuel could be akin to "repairs, supplies, [or] towage," 46 U.S.C. § 31301(4): like those things, the fuel would be "necessary to keep the ship going." *Silver Star Enterprises, Inc. v. Saramacca M/V*, 82 F.3d 666, 668 (5th Cir. 1996) (quoting *Dampskibsselskabet Dannebrog v. Signal Oil & Gas Co.*, 310 U.S. 268, 280 (1940)). Therefore, the Martin fuel may have qualified as a "necessary" vis-à- **[—7—]** vis the Seismic Vessels.[7] We need not decide that question, **{-832-}** however, because the Seismic Vessels are not parties here.

The Support Vessels present a different scenario. As the district court found, CGG utilized the Support Vessels "for ensuring that the Seismic Vessels were supplied with fuel and water." To that end, the fuel deliveries at issue "were put in the cargo tanks of the [Support Vessels]," and the entire amount was transported to the Seismic Vessels for their refueling. The district court did not find that any part of the Martin fuel was used to fuel the Support Vessels.[8]

Given those undisputed facts, there is no basis for concluding that the Martin fuel was a "necessary" as to the Support Vessels. To do so would, as CGG persuasively argues, "represent an unprecedented expansion of the CIMLA" by extending the concept of "necessaries" to *cargo* transported by a vessel. The parties cite no precedent—nor can we find any—supporting that expansion.[9] Based on that absence alone, we would reject the proposition. "The **[—8—]** absence of precedent signifies the weakness of [Martin's] position, since admiralty enjoys an unusually rich legal tradition and, more than nearly any other contemporary area of federal law, relies on venerable precedents where they exist." *Gulf Marine & Indus. Supplies, Inc. v. Golden Prince M/V*, 230 F.3d 178, 180 (5th Cir. 2000).

B.

We are unpersuaded by the district court's reasoning and by Martin's arguments on appeal. The court reasoned the Martin fuel was necessary for the Support Vessels to perform their "particular function"—that is, as "floating gas stations" (the *Bourbon Petrel* and *OMS Resolution*), or an "offshore supply vessel" (the *Miss Lilly*). The court relied on decisions concluding maritime liens existed where goods and services (*e.g.*, liquor, linens, cigarettes, or advertising) were provided to assist vessels in their "particular functions" (*e.g.*, as a pleasure yacht, floating hotel, shrimper, or cruise ship).[10] On appeal, Martin

[7] *See, e.g., Belcher Co. of Ala. v. M/V Maratha Mariner*, 724 F.2d 1161, 1163 (5th Cir. 1984) (stating in *dicta* that, "when Belcher supplied fuel to the M/V Marantha Mariner, a maritime lien [under the FMLA] may have arisen by operation of law").

[8] As to the *Bourbon Petrel* and *OMS Resolution*, the district court found the Martin fuel *could not* have been used to refuel those vessels because their cargo tanks were "physically separated" from the "day tanks" used for their own fuel. The situation was more complex as to the *Miss Lilly*, because her cargo and day tanks were connected by piping and, during the period at issue, some fuel was transferred from her cargo to day tanks. The district court found this immaterial, however, because the amount of fuel transferred was *less* than the amount already aboard before the Martin deliveries. Consequently, the district court found the *Miss Lilly* "had sufficient fuel onboard to reach the Seismic Vessels prior to being loaded with the Martin Energy fuel." Martin does not argue that this finding is clearly erroneous. In any event, the district court did not base its conclusion on the *Miss Lilly*'s putative consumption of any of the Martin fuel.

[9] As CGG points out, some precedent supports the idea that the physical "containers" that enable cargo ships to transport cargo may qualify as "necessaries" for the cargo ship. *See Foss Launch & Tug Co. v. Char Ching Shipping U.S.A., Ltd.*, 808 F.2d 697, 700 (9th Cir. 1996). But, as CGG correctly argues, that precedent does not support the quite different idea that the *cargo itself* is a "necessary" as to the cargo ship.

[10] *See, e.g., Portland Pilots, Inc. v. Nova Star M/V*, 875 F.3d 38, 41, 45, 5 Adm. R. 85, 85, 89 (1st

continues **{–833–}** to rely on these decisions. They are off point. In each, the good or service was provided for use by the vessel itself, and the resulting lien ran against that vessel. Here, by contrast, the Martin fuel was provided for use by the Seismic Vessels, not the Support Vessels. Any lien based on the fuel as a "necessary" would presumably run against the Seismic Vessels (something, again, we do not decide). *See Trico Marine Operators, Inc. v. Falcon Drilling Co.*, 116 F.3d 159, 161–62 (5th Cir. 1997) (supply boat services ferrying provisions to drilling rig were "necessaries" as to rig). The cases cited by the **[—9—]** district court (and Martin) fail to support the different proposition that the lien would run against the *Support* Vessels, which were merely carrying the fuel for other vessels' consumption.

Finally, claiming we must view the situation "from the vendor's perspective," Martin argues it had no way of knowing the fuel it delivered was destined for refueling the Seismic Vessels, not the Support Vessels. The district court did not rely on this proposition. To support it, Martin cites only our statement in *Equilease* that a "necessary" turns on the "present, apparent want of the vessel, not the character of the thing supplied." 793 F.2d at 603 (quoting 2 Benedict on Admiralty § 34). Martin misreads the quote. It means only that a "necessary" is determined by the need of the vessel; it says nothing about the "perspective of the vendor." Martin cites no other authority for introducing this element of subjectivity into the maritime lien analysis, because there is none.

In sum, we conclude that, contrary to the district court's conclusion, the fuel supplied for refueling the Seismic Vessels did not qualify as a "necessary" with respect to the Support Vessels and so did not create a maritime lien under CIMLA as to the Support Vessels.[11]

CONCLUSION

The district court's judgment is REVERSED and judgment is RENDERED in favor of CGG.

Cir. 2017) (recognizing maritime lien for providing linens to a "floating hotel"); *Stern, Hays, & Lang, Inc. v. M/V Nili*, 407 F.2d 549, 551 (5th Cir. 1969) (recognizing maritime lien for providing advertising services to a cruise ship) (citing *Colonial Press of Miami, Inc. v. The Allen's Cay*, 277 F.2d 540 (5th Cir. 1960)); *Allen v. The M/V Contessa*, 196 F. Supp. 649, 651 (S.D. Tex. 1961) (recognizing maritime lien for cigarettes provided as part of crew provisions on shrimper); *Walker-Skageth Food Stores v. The Bavois*, 43 F. Supp. 109, 111 (S.D.N.Y. 1942) (recognizing maritime lien for providing liquor to a pleasure yacht).

[11] Given our resolution of the appeal, we do not reach CGG's argument that the fuel was not provided "on its order," nor its argument concerning pre-judgment interest.

United States Court of Appeals
for the Fifth Circuit

No. 20-20035

NATIONAL SHIPPING CO. OF SAUDI ARABIA
vs.
VALERO MKTG. & SUPPLY CO.

Appeal from the United States District Court for the Southern District of Texas

Decided: June 30, 2020

Citation: 963 F.3d 479, 8 Adm. R. 200 (5th Cir. 2020).

Before **STEWART**, **HIGGINSON**, and **COSTA**, Circuit Judges.

[—1—] {–480–} STEWART, Circuit Judge:

Valero Marketing and Supply Company ("Valero") files this appeal pursuant to 28 U.S.C. § 1292(a)(3) after the district court denied its motion for certification for interlocutory appeal under 28 U.S.C. § 1292(b). Because we lack jurisdiction, we dismiss Valero's appeal.

I. Facts & Procedural History

In March 2019, two shipping companies—the National Shipping Company of Saudi Arabia ("National Shipping") and Indelpro S.A. DE C.V. **[—2—]** ("Indelpro")—sued Valero, in two separate actions,[1] alleging that it had supplied them with contaminated fuel. Valero answered both complaints and filed a third-party complaint against Trafigura Trading L.L.C. ("Trafigura"). In its third-party complaint against Trafigura, Valero alleged claims for breach of contract, negligence, express and implied warranty breach, products liability, and violations of the Texas Civil Practice and Remedies Code. Valero also invoked Rule 14(c)[2] to "tender" Trafigura as a direct defendant in the National Shipping case on grounds that it was wholly liable for the damages alleged therein.

Trafigura, the third-party defendant, asserted that Valero's claims fell under three contracts (Nos. 1654384, 1659403, & 1669270) between Trafigura and Valero—one with a mandatory arbitration clause and two with exclusive forum selection clauses. On these grounds, Trafigura moved to sever and transfer the claims subject to the forum selection clauses to the Southern District of New York (the designated forum) and to dismiss the **{–481–}** claims subject to the arbitration clause in favor of arbitration.

On December 26, 2019, the district court addressed Trafigura's motions in both shipping cases in a single opinion. It granted Trafigura's motion to sever and transfer the claims under the two contracts with the forum selection clauses and to sever and dismiss the claims under the contract with the arbitration clause. In its memorandum and opinion, the district court **[—3—]** explained that Contract No. 1654384 contained a valid agreement to arbitrate and that several of Valero's claims fell within the scope of that agreement so severance and dismissal in favor of arbitration was warranted. As to Contract Nos. 1659403 and 1669270, the district court noted that they contained exclusive forum selection clauses identifying the Southern District of New York as having exclusive jurisdiction. Upon analyzing the applicable private and public-interest factors, the court determined that severance and transfer was appropriate. *See* 28 U.S.C. § 1404(a). Finally, citing this court's opinion in *Texaco Exploration & Production Company v. AmClyde Engineered Products Company*, 243 F.3d 906, 908, 910 (5th Cir. 2001), the district court held that the Rule 14(c) tender did not overcome the contractually agreed upon arbitration and forum selection clauses.

---

[1] *The Nat'l Shipping Co. of Saudi Arabia v. Valero Mktg. & Supply Co.*, Civil Action No. 19-1096; *Indelpro S.A. DE C.V. v. Valero Mktg. & Supply Co.*, Civil Action No. 19-4115.

[2] *See* Fed. R. Civ. P. 14(c)(1)-(2) ("If a plaintiff asserts an admiralty or maritime claim under Rule 9(h), the defendant . . . may, as a third-party plaintiff, bring in a third-party defendant who may be wholly or partly liable—either to the plaintiff or to the third-party plaintiff—for remedy over, contribution, or otherwise on account of the same transaction, occurrence, or series of transactions or occurrences . . . . The third-party plaintiff may demand judgment in the plaintiff's favor against the third-party defendant.").

After the district court's December 2019 opinion issued, Valero filed a notice of appeal pursuant to 28 U.S.C. § 1292(a)(3). Valero then filed a motion for clarification as to what effect the transfer and dismissal of its third-party claims against Trafigura had on its Rule 14(c) tender of Trafigura in the National Shipping case. In its motion, Valero stated that if the district court intended to "fully dismiss Trafigura," it would seek certification of the issue for interlocutory appeal to the Fifth Circuit under 28 U.S.C. § 1292(b).

The district court granted Valero's motion for clarification and explained that there was "no Rule 14(c) tender that overcomes the arbitration and forum-selection clauses at issue in this case [so] Trafigura is no longer a party to this litigation." The district court then denied Valero's motion to conditionally certify the issue for interlocutory appeal under 28 U.S.C. § 1292(b) observing that:

> The December 2019, opinion did not determine the rights and obligations of Valero and Trafigura, but merely ruled on the forum for determining those rights and obligations. The issue does not involve a **[—4—]** "controlling issue of law" nor will it "materially advance the ultimate termination of the litigation."

Valero then appealed the district court's March 3, 2020 order pursuant to 28 U.S.C. § 1292(a)(3) noting that the order "merely makes clear that the prior [December 2019] opinion did, in fact, have the effect of dismissing Valero's Rule 14(c) tender of Trafigura as a direct-defendant to Plaintiff National Shipping Company of Saudi Arabia."

II. Standard of Review

"[T]his court has a duty to analyze its own jurisdiction de novo." *See Providence Behavioral Health v. Grant Rd. Pub. Util. Dist.*, 902 F.3d 448, 455 (5th Cir. 2018) (citing *Smith v. Booth*, 823 F.2d 94, 96 (5th Cir. 1987)).

III. Discussion

On appeal, Valero argues that the district court erred in concluding that the dismissal and transfer of its third-party claims against Trafigura necessitated dismissal of its Rule 14(c) tender of Trafigura in the National Shipping case. Trafigura counters that this court lacks jurisdiction to entertain Valero's appeal under 28 U.S.C. § 1292(a)(3) because the district **{–482–}** court's ruling did not constitute a final determination of the rights and liabilities of the parties. We agree.

"This court's appellate jurisdiction is ordinarily limited to 'final decisions of the district courts of the United States.'" *SCF Waxler Marine, LLC v. Aris T M/V*, 902 F.3d 461, 464, 6 Adm. R. 246, 247 (5th Cir. 2018) (citing 28 U.S.C. § 1291). However, where permitted by statute, we may hear certain interlocutory appeals. *Id.*, 6 Adm. R. at 247. Section 1292(a)(3) provides that appellate courts shall have jurisdiction over appeals from interlocutory decrees of district courts "determining the rights and liabilities of the parties to admiralty cases." We have "construed [this] grant narrowly, hewing closely to the statute's 'original purpose of permitting appeals from orders finally determining one party's liability to another and **[—5—]** referring the action for a computation of damages.'" *Waxler Marine*, 902 F.3d at 464, 6 Adm. R. at 247 (citation omitted). We do not look at the "characterization of the ruling at issue [but rather] to the substance of what the lower court decided." *Id.*, 6 Adm. R. at 248. We have acknowledged "that appellate jurisdiction is generally appropriate 'whenever an order in an admiralty case dismisses a claim for relief on the merits.'" *Id.* at 464–65, 6 Adm. R. at 248.

Valero contends that under *Waxler Marine*, the "district court's dismissal of the Rule 14(c) tender of Trafigura to [National Shipping] as a direct-defendant has the effect of finally determining the liability of Trafigura as non-existent with respect to those claims." We disagree. As the district court stated in its March 2020 order, "[t]he December 2019[] opinion did not determine the rights and obligations of Valero and Trafigura, but merely ruled on the forum for determining those rights and obligations."[3] Moreover, Valero's own liability in the shipping cases has yet to be established in the underlying litigation and consequently, as Trafigura concedes in its appellate brief, "Trafigura's potential liability to Valero remains a live issue" although it must be resolved in a different forum. Because we conclude that the district court's December 2019 order granting Trafigura's motions to sever and transfer and to sever and dismiss did not determine the rights and liabilities of the parties, we hold that we do not have jurisdiction over Valero's appeal taken pursuant to 28 U.S.C. § 1292(a)(3).

IV. Conclusion

Valero's appeal is dismissed for lack of jurisdiction.

---

[3] *See In re Ingram Towing Co.*, 59 F.3d 513, 517 (5th Cir. 1995) (rejecting jurisdiction under section 1292(a)(3) for decision staying state court action because "[t]he district court did not determine the rights and liabilities of the parties, it 'merely settled how and where the rights and liabilities would be determined.'" (quoting *State Establishment v. M/V Wesermunde*, 770 F.2d 987, 990 (11th Cir. 1985))); *see also Psara Energy, Ltd. v. Advantage Arrow Shipping, L.L.C.*, 946 F.3d 803, 809, 8 Adm. R. 111, 114–15 (5th Cir. 2020).

United States Court of Appeals
for the Fifth Circuit

No. 19-20435

VANTAGE DEEPWATER CO.
vs.
PETROBAS AM., INC.

Appeal from the United States District Court for the Southern District of Texas

Decided: July 16, 2020

Citation: 966 F.3d 361, 8 Adm. R. 203 (5th Cir. 2020).

Before **SOUTHWICK, COSTA,** and **DUNCAN,** Circuit Judges.

[—1—] {-365-} **SOUTHWICK,** Circuit Judge:

This is an appeal of a district court's order confirming a $622 million arbitration award. The defendants argue that, because public policy precludes enforcing the award, it should have been vacated. The defendants also argue that the district court erred in denying the defendants' discovery motions.

We AFFIRM.

FACTUAL AND PROCEDURAL BACKGROUND

The parties in this case are oil and gas companies, incorporated and based in different countries. Vantage Deepwater Company is a Cayman Islands company; Vantage Deepwater Drilling, Inc., is a Delaware corporation **[—2—]** with its principal place of business in Texas (collectively, "Vantage"). Vantage operates a fleet of oil rigs. Petrobras Venezuela Investments & Services B.V. is a Dutch company; Petrobras America Inc. is a Delaware corporation; and Petróleo Brasileiro S.A. – Petrobras is a Brazilian company (the three collectively, "Petrobras").

In 2007, Petrobras had not listed Vantage as an approved drilling service contractor. In exchange for help procuring drilling-services contracts, Vantage's largest shareholder and board member Nobu Su, also known as Hsin-Chi-Su, agreed to pay approximately $30 million in bribes, distributed as kickbacks to three individuals: Jorge Zelada, Eduardo Musa, and Hamylton Pinheiro Padilha, Jr. By 2016, a Brazilian criminal investigation revealed the bribery was part of a larger scheme dubbed *Lava Jato* (Operation Carwash). Zelada, Musa, and Padilha were convicted of crimes arising from the scheme in Brazil. Su and Vantage's former CEO, Paul Bragg, also were indicted in Brazil, but briefing states they have not returned to that country. Vantage told United States regulators in 2017 that it had discovered some evidence that its then-CEO Bragg and then–board member John O'Leary were at least willfully blind to Padilha and Su's bribery. In 2018, the United States **{-366-}** Department of Justice entered a non-prosecution agreement with Petrobras relating to the fraud. The Justice Department stated that multiple Petrobras individuals had received bribes to assist Vantage in winning the drilling contract with Petrobras.

In 2009, Vantage Deepwater Company and Petrobras Venezuela executed the Agreement for the Provision of Drilling Services ("DSA"). Under the DSA, Vantage would perform offshore drilling services for Petrobras for an eight-year term. Also in 2009, Petróleo Brasileiro executed a Form of Payment and Performance Guaranty, in which it "unconditionally, absolutely and irrevocably guarantee[d]" Petrobras Venezuela's obligations under the DSA. **[—3—]** To fulfill Vantage's obligations, Vantage's parent company purchased an ultra–deepwater oil rig called the *Titanium Explorer* for over $948 million. The DSA's eight-year term began in December 2012.

In August 2013, a Brazilian magazine published an article claiming that a Vantage shareholder had paid $14.5 million to João Augusto Henriques, a lobbyist for the Brazilian Democratic Movement Party, to secure a drilling contract with Petrobras. Petrobras then conducted an internal investigation into the allegations. The investigatory report recorded attempts to interview Henriques, but in the end, the report could not "prove the veracity" of the bribery allegations. The report acknowledged, however, that "Petrobras's good practices ceased to be observed" and that there were "deficiencies in the process of contracting." The report suggested submitting the report to Brazilian prosecutors. The report also found that the DSA was "at market value." A few months later, the parties executed the Second Novation and Third Amendment, in which they reaffirmed that the DSA was binding.

About two years into the DSA's term, in October 2014, Vantage and Petrobras executed the Third Novation and Amendment Agreement. It was this agreement that included an arbitration clause, which provided that any disputes arising out of the DSA as amended by the Third Novation would be "exclusively and finally resolve[d]" through arbitration conducted by the International Center for Dispute Resolution of the American Arbitration Association ("AAA") in Houston, Texas. Vantage and Petrobras agreed that the arbitrators would have the "power to rule on objections concerning jurisdiction, including the existence or validity of [the] arbitration clause and existence or the validity of" the DSA. The Third Novation also stated that "[t]he parties waive irrevocably their right to any form of appeal, review or recourse to any court or other judicial authority, to the extent that such waiver may be validly made." **[—4—]**

The DSA prohibited terminating the contract for convenience but allowed termination if Vantage materially breached or failed to provide its services. In August 2015, several years before the end of the DSA's term, Petrobras terminated the DSA. Immediately thereafter, Vantage demanded arbitration pursuant to the Third Novation, claiming over $450 million in expectancy damages and over $800 million in reliance damages. The asserted expectancy damages were based on lost profit calculations, and the asserted reliance damages were primarily based on Vantage's incurring debt to acquire the *Titanium Explorer*.

Petrobras responded by arguing it had terminated the DSA for operational reasons because Vantage materially breached the contract. Petrobras also argued that the DSA was procured through bribery and corruption, making the agreement invalid. Petrobras claims it first had actual knowledge of the bribery only in 2015, after Padilha pled guilty to his role in the **{–367–}** scheme in a Brazilian court. Vantage claims that Petrobras actually had knowledge after the magazine article was published in 2013, and that Petrobras ratified the DSA when it agreed to the Third Novation.

Throughout 2016, the parties and the arbitration tribunal, once it was selected, addressed a variety of procedural issues. The tribunal consisted of three arbitrators. After Vantage's first pick, David Keltner, was removed due to a conflict of interest, Vantage appointed Charles N. Brower, who is a judge on the Iran–United States Claims Tribunal, an international arbitral tribunal. Petrobras appointed Mr. James Gaitis. Keltner and Gaitis selected as chairman Professor William Park of Boston University.

The tribunal held evidentiary hearings between May 16 and June 1, 2017. On June 7, Petrobras moved the AAA to disqualify and remove Judge Brower. Petrobras gave four reasons to support its motion. First, Petrobras asserted that Brower appeared partial because he "continuously made **[—5—]** inappropriate, off-the-record comments under his breath while [Petrobras's] witnesses were being cross-examined, and while [Petrobras's] counsel cross-examined [Vantage's] witnesses." Second, Petrobras asserted that Brower continually and "improperly advocated" for Vantage including by cross-examining one of Petrobras's fact witnesses for nearly two hours. Third, Petrobras asserted that during the hearing Brower incorrectly summarized the direct evidence of bribery, which must have been because he was either "intentionally ignoring other evidence" or "intentionally misstating the evidence related to bribery and corruption." Last, Petrobras asserted that Brower frequently dozed off during the hearing, indicating that he could not diligently perform his duties.

The AAA spent some time investigating the assertions of bias. Chairman Park's billing statement, for example, showed he communicated with the AAA for about five and a half hours. The AAA denied the motion in a sentence.

The final award was issued on June 29, 2018. A majority of the arbitrators — Chairman Park and Judge Brower — awarded Vantage over $620 million. Gaitis wrote a one-paragraph dissent that claimed unfairness in the proceedings:

> I object to, and I dissent from, the tribunal majority's Final Award. This Objection and Dissent is based not only on my differing conclusions regarding the merits of the parties' dispute, but also on my belief and conclusion that the prehearing, hearing, and posthearing processes that led to the issuance of the Final Award have denied [Petrobras] in this proceeding the fundamental fairness and due process protections meant to be provided to arbitrating parties by Sections 10(a)(1), 10(a)(2), 10(a)(3), 10(a)(4), and Chapters 2 and 3 of the Federal Arbitration Act, 9 U.S.C. § 1, *et seq.*

In July 2018, Vantage filed a petition to confirm the arbitration award in the United States District Court for the Southern District of Texas. Petrobras opposed confirmation and moved the district court to vacate the **[—6—]** award. To support its motion for vacatur, Petrobras sought leave to depose Gaitis. Petrobras claimed that the additional testimony would provide a more complete record on which the district court could evaluate the arbitral award. After a hearing in December 2018, the district court denied the motion to subpoena Gaitis. Two months later, Petrobras moved for leave to serve a subpoena on the AAA. Petrobras sought the AAA's documents in connection with the challenges to Brower in the arbitration. The district court also denied that motion. **{-368-}**

In May 2019, the district court denied the motion to vacate and granted Vantage's petition to confirm the award. The court entered final judgment and ordered Petrobras to pay $733,968,000 (the arbitration award plus interest), and post-judgment interest. Petrobras appealed.

DISCUSSION

This case implicates Chapter 3 of the Federal Arbitration Act ("FAA"), 9 U.S.C. §§ 301–307, which governs nondomestic arbitration awards subject to the Inter-American Convention on International Commercial Arbitration of January 30, 1975, T.I.A.S. No. 90-1027, *reprinted following* Pub. L. 101-369, 104 Stat. 448 (1990) (the "Panama Convention"). The FAA requires that a court confirm an arbitration award unless there is a ground for refusing to enforce the award as specified in the Panama Convention. 9 U.S.C. § 207; *see id.* § 302 (applying Section 207 to cases governed by Panama Convention). The Supreme Court has recognized an "emphatic federal policy in favor of arbitral dispute resolution." *Mitsubishi Motors Corp. v. Soler Chrysler-Plymouth, Inc.*, 473 U.S. 614, 631 (1985). "A court may not review the merits of an [arbitration] award — it must accept the facts found by the arbitrator and the arbitrator's interpretation of the contract and applicable law." *Manville Forest Prods. Corp. v. United Paperworkers Int'l Union*, 831 F.2d 72, 74 (5th Cir. 1987). **[—7—]**

We review the district court's legal determinations *de novo* and findings of fact for clear error. *Hughes Training Inc. v. Cook*, 254 F.3d 588, 592 (5th Cir. 2001). Review of the underlying arbitral award is "exceedingly deferential," though. *Petrofac, Inc. v. DynMcDermott Petroleum Operations Co.*, 687 F.3d 671, 674 (5th Cir. 2012). Although we "grant arbitrators considerable leeway when reviewing most arbitration decisions," we do not "give *extra* leeway to district courts that uphold arbitrators." *First Options of Chicago, Inc. v. Kaplan*, 514 U.S. 938, 948 (1995).

Petrobras argues that public policy precluded confirming the arbitration award. Petrobras also argues that the district court's denial of its discovery motions led the court to base its confirmation order and denial of vacatur on an incomplete record. Vacatur is warranted, Petrobras contends, because the arbitrators failed to issue a "reasoned award" as to Petróleo Brasileiro. In addition to responding to Petrobras's arguments, Vantage argues that Petrobras waived its right to appeal. We will start by addressing the appeal waiver. Because in the end we do not need to decide that question, we then turn to Petrobras's claims of error.

I. Appeal waiver

A valid appeal waiver does not deprive the court of jurisdiction; accordingly, if affirming the judgment is a clearer resolution than deciding the validity of the appeal waiver, we can affirm. *See In re Deepwater Horizon*, 934 F.3d 434, 441, 7 Adm. R. 297, 299 (5th Cir. 2019). The waiver appears in the Third Novation: "The Parties waive irrevocably their right to any form of appeal, review or recourse to any court or other judicial authority, to the extent that such waiver may be validly made." Courts "rigorously enforce arbitration agreements according to their terms." *American Exp. Co. v. Italian Colors Rest.*, 570 U.S. 228, 233 (2013). Contractual clauses must be "clear and unequivocal," though, in order **[—8—]** to waive a right. *Ensco Int'l, Inc. v. Certain Underwriters at Lloyd's*, 579 F.3d 442, 443 (5th Cir. 2009) (waiving the right to removal). **{–369–}**

Vantage reasons that because federal and Texas law enforce appeal waivers, we should enforce the appeal waiver here. *See id.*; *Bennett v. Comm'n for Lawyer Discipline*, 489 S.W.3d 58, 69 n.1 (Tex. App.— Houston [14th Dist.] 2016, no pet.). To be clear, Vantage does not argue on appeal that the Third Novation barred the district court's review of the award, only that *appellate* review of the district court's judgment is barred. Petrobras replies that it could not waive its right to appeal under the Panama Convention or the FAA and that there was no clear and unequivocal indication of waiver.

The parties cite competing persuasive authorities from other circuits. The Ninth Circuit held that "the statutory grounds for vacatur in the FAA may not be waived or eliminated by contract." *In re Wal-Mart Wage & Hour Emp. Practices Litig.*, 737 F.3d 1262, 1268 (9th Cir. 2013). The court was rejecting a waiver clause that would have precluded *all* federal-court review. *Id.* at 1266 n.3. Because parties may not contract for expanded judicial review, *see Hall St.*, 552 U.S. at 578, the Ninth Circuit reasoned that private agreements eliminating judicial review of arbitration awards also are not enforceable. *Wal-Mart*, 737 F.3d at 1267.

The Second Circuit stated that those "seeking to enforce arbitration awards through federal-court confirmation judgments may not divest the courts of their statutory and common-law authority to review both the substance of the awards and the arbitral process for compliance with § 10(a)." *Hoeft v. MVL Grp., Inc.*, 343 F.3d 57, 66 (2d Cir. 2003), *overruled on other grounds by Hall St. Assocs. L.L.C. v. Mattel, Inc.*, 552 U.S. 576 (2008).

The Tenth Circuit enforced the following contractual provision that it considered to waive appellate review only: "Judgment upon the award rendered by the arbitrator shall be final and nonappealable and may be **[—9—]** entered in any court having jurisdiction thereof." *MACTEC, Inc. v. Gorelick*, 427 F.3d 821, 827 (10th Cir. 2005). The court concluded "that contractual provisions limiting the right to appeal from a district court's judgment confirming or vacating an arbitration award are permissible, so long as the intent to do so is clear and unequivocal." *Id.* at 830.

Vantage argues that *MACTEC* supplies the applicable rule while Petrobras calls that rule "legally doubtful." Petrobras instead would have us extend *Wal-Mart* to waivers of appellate review as well. Petrobras further contends that parties cannot contractually deprive this court of its authority to review arbitration awards.

The parties agree that if the waiver clause barred all federal court review—namely, the ability to oppose confirmation and move for vacatur in district court—then the waiver would not be enforceable. The waiver provision in the DSA, unlike the one in *MACTEC*, states that the waiver applies only to the extent legally permissible. *MACTEC*, 427 F.3d at 829. This does not make the waiver equivocal. The "to the extent" clause preserves valid applications of the appeal waiver, even if other applications of the clause are invalid.

Wal-Mart neither contradicted nor endorsed *MACTEC*; the two cases dealt with different issues. *Wal-Mart*, 737 F.3d at 1266 n.3. We are inclined to think the Tenth Circuit's approach is persuasive. Still, if the district court's judgment is affirmable on the merits, we do not need to discern the law for this circuit on such appeal waivers. We therefore will now examine the merits.

II. Motion to confirm

Article V(2)(b) of the Panama Convention allows a country to refuse to **{–370–}** recognize or execute an arbitration decision under the Convention if "the recognition or execution of the decision would be contrary to the public policy" of that country. The party asserting the public policy defense bears the burden **[—10—]** of proving United States public policy would be violated by enforcing the award. *Asignacion* v. *Rickmers Genoa Schiffahrts-gesellschaft mbH & Cie KG*, 783 F.3d 1010, 1016–17, 3 Adm. R. 304, 306–07 (5th Cir. 2015). "The public policy defense is to be 'construed narrowly to be applied only where enforcement would violate the forum state's most basic notions of morality and justice.'" *Karaha Bodas Co. v. Perusahaan Pertambangan Minyak Dan Gas Bumi Negara (Karaha Bodas II)*, 364 F.3d 274, 306 (5th Cir. 2004). Further, a public policy rendering a contract unenforceable "must be 'explicit,' 'well defined,' and 'dominant.' It must be 'ascertained by reference to the laws and legal precedents and not from general considerations of supposed public interests.'" *East Associated Coal Corp. v. United Mine Workers of Am., Dist. 17*, 531 U.S. 57, 62 (2000) (quoting *W.R. Grace & Co. v. Rubber Workers*, 461 U.S. 757, 766 (1983)). The public policy defense under the Panama Convention is "substantively identical" to the one set forth in the Convention on the Recognition and Enforcement of Foreign Arbitral Awards, commonly called the "New York Convention." *See, e.g., TermoRio S.A. E.S.P. v. Electranta S.P.*, 487 F.3d 928, 933 (D.C. Cir. 2007).

Petrobras argues that enforcing the arbitration award violates United States public policy because the award requires Petrobras to pay damages based on a contract illegally procured through bribery. Even if this country's public policy would bar enforcement of such contracts, the district court relied on the arbitrators' findings, first, that Petrobras had not proved Vantage was guilty of bribery and, second, that Petrobras "knowingly ratified the DSA." Accepting those fact findings, the district court then considered whether public policy would bar enforcing a bribery-procured but ratified contract. The court accepted another district court's rejection of a public policy defense if both parties engaged in the same fraudulent misconduct. *See Tamimi Glob. Co. v. Kellogg Brown & Root L.L.C.*, No. CIV.A. H-11-0585, 2011 WL 1157634, at *3 (S.D. Tex. Mar. 24, 2011). Because both Vantage and Petrobras allegedly **[—11—]** engaged in misconduct, and the contract was later ratified, the district court concluded there was no public policy impediment to enforcement.

A. How much deference

The first question on this issue is whether the district court erroneously deferred to the arbitrators' ratification finding. Petrobras asserts that the district court mistakenly deferred to the arbitrators' public policy conclusions rather than reviewing those conclusions *de novo*. Petrobras does not dispute that if ratification occurred, then enforcing the arbitration award does not violate public policy; rather, Petrobras argues that the arbitrators' findings do not amount to legal ratification.

"Under the New York Convention, the rulings of the Tribunal interpreting the parties' contract are entitled to deference." *Karaha Bodas II*, 364 F.3d at 290. "The court may not refuse to enforce an arbitral award solely on the ground that the arbitrator may have made a mistake of law or fact." *Id.* at 288. This is because "[t]he parties did not bargain for the facts to be found by a court, but by an arbitrator . . . . Nor does the fact that it is inquiring into a possible violation of public policy excuse a court for doing the arbitrator's task." **{-371-}** *United Paperworkers Int'l Union v. Misco, Inc.*, 484 U.S. 29, 45 (1987).

Petrobas relies on one of this court's opinions to support that the district court should have considered the public policy issue *de novo*. *See Gulf Coast Industries Workers Union v. Exxon Co.*, 991 F.2d 244, 248 n.5 (5th Cir. 1993). The case involved a dispute about whether an employee was discharged for just cause. *Id.* at 247. We stated that a court "enjoy[s] more latitude in reviewing the arbitrator's decision" when public policy violations are alleged. *Id.* at 249. A court defers to an arbitrator's findings of fact "but review[s] his conclusions *de novo*," because "[c]ourts are the ultimate arbiters of public policy, not arbitrators." *Id.* at 248 n.5, 249. The Supreme Court has similarly stated that "the question of public policy is ultimately one for resolution by the **[—12—]** courts." *W.R. Grace & Co.*, 461 U.S. at 766. Still, courts must "tak[e] the facts as found by the arbitrator." *Gulf Coast*, 991 F.2d at 249. The *Gulf Coast* arbitration award would have reinstated an employee to a position working with dangerous equipment. *Id.* at 250, 255. Though it was clear that an employee's use of a controlled substance violated public policy, the problem with the arbitration award was elsewhere. Public policy prohibited reinstating a worker who posed a safety hazard. *Id.* at 250, 255. We set aside the reinstatement of the worker under *de novo* review of public policy. *Id.* at 257.

Petrobras is not seeking our review of whether the final award violated public policy. Instead, Petrobras wants us to decide whether the underlying contract violated public policy. Petrobras questions whether any ratification occurred that would obviate any public policy problem in the DSA. We agree with the district court that "[t]he public policy exception cannot be used to simply question the merits of the underlying award." *Hardy Expl. & Prod., (India), Inc. v. Gov't of India, Ministry of Petroleum & Nat. Gas*, 314 F. Supp. 3d 95, 109 (D.D.C. 2018).

The Second Circuit applied this principle in *Europcar Italia, S.p.A. v. Maiellano Tours, Inc.*, 156 F.3d 310 (2d Cir. 1998). We have cited *Europcar* favorably for the proposition that a reviewing court should not reconsider an arbitrator's findings. *Karaha Bodas II*, 364 F.3d at 288 n.2. In *Europcar*, the appellant argued enforcing an arbitration award would violate public policy where the award was based on an allegedly forged agreement. 156 F.3d at 315. The Second Circuit distinguished between fraud that may lead to application of the public policy exception under the Convention and fraud that would not:

> [The defendant-appellant] has apparently confused the issue of a fraudulently obtained arbitration agreement or award, which might violate public policy and therefore preclude enforcement, with the issue of whether the underlying contract that is subject of **[—13—]** the arbitrated dispute was forged or fraudulently induced—a matter to be determined exclusively by the arbitrators.

Id. (citations omitted). The *Europcar* court observed that the appellant did not dispute the validity of the supplemental arbitration agreement. *Id.* Further, the appellant could not "seek to relitigate" the arbitrators' determination of whether the parties' underlying agreement was forged — even if the arbitrators had made an error of law or fact. *Id.* at 315–16. "[W]hether the underlying contract that is the subject of the arbitrated dispute was forged or fraudulently induced" was a question for the arbitrators and was not the basis of a public policy defense. *Id.* Therefore, enforcing the arbitration award did not violate public policy. *Id.* at 316. **{-372-}**

Like the underlying conduct in *Gulf Coast*, the underlying conduct here, bribery, does violate public policy. *See* 991 F.2d at 250. Unlike in *Gulf Coast*, though, enforcing the arbitration award does not create a situation contrary to public policy, such as putting anyone's safety at risk. The arbitrators found Petrobras ratified the DSA. When we defer to that finding, the legal conclusion follows that the DSA, and the arbitration award, did not violate public policy.

Further, as in *Europcar*, the arbitration agreement here is external to the underlying contract and the arbitration agreement's validity is not disputed. 156 F.3d at 315. Also, both in *Europcar* and here, the arbitrators had the power to rule on the underlying contract's validity. *Id.* The arbitration clause in the Third Novation provided that the arbitrators would have power to rule on the existence and validity of the DSA. Whether a contract should be voided because of bribery is a question about the validity of the DSA. The tribunal answered that question when it found that Petrobras ratified the DSA and thus waived bribery objections. The arbitrators also found that Petrobras had not established that "Vantage knew of or participated in any bribery." These findings were within the tribunal's authority to rule on the DSA's **[—14—]** validity. As such, the validity of the DSA was rightly a question for the arbitrators rather than the district court.

Petrobras also argues that the district court and the arbitrators relied on a flawed definition of ratification. Even if that is so, mistakes of law or fact are not grounds for denying confirmation. *Karaha Bodas II*, 364 F.3d at 288.

We conclude that the district court did not engage in inappropriate deference to the arbitrator's decision.

B. "Mutual misconduct"

Petrobras also takes issue with what it perceives as the district court's ultimate conclusion that "[i]t does not violate public policy to enforce an arbitration award against parties who were alleged to have mutually engaged in mutual misconduct during the formation of a contract, particularly when that contract was later ratified." Petrobras disputes that Petrobras engaged in misconduct in the contracting process and that mutual misconduct does not override public policy defenses. Mutual misconduct was not the basis of the district court's confirmation order, though. The district court accurately defined ratification, recognized the arbitrators' ratification finding, and thus concluded that "Petrobras has not met its burden of showing that the Tribunal's contract interpretation violates some explicit public policy." The court continued:

> Petrobras's attempt to relitigate the merits of its contract dispute and the general appeal to public policy against paying and accepting bribes to form contracts does not meet the high burden of showing that enforcement of the actual arbitration decision in this case would violate the most basic notions of morality and justice.

The district court did not base its decision just on "mutual misconduct." We also need not concern ourselves with the precise reasoning by the district court, because we review *de novo* whether the award should have been confirmed. **[—15—]** *Asignacion*, 783 F.3d at 1014–15, 3 Adm. R. at 305. There was no public policy bar to confirmation.

III. Discovery motions

District courts occasionally allow discovery in vacatur and confirmation proceedings. *See* FED. R. CIV. P. 81(a)(6)(B). Previously we have endorsed a flexible inquiry for district courts to use when **{-373-}** assessing discovery requests in the context of such proceedings: "the court must weigh the asserted need for hitherto undisclosed information and assess the impact of granting such discovery on the arbitral process." *Karaha Bodas II*, 364 F.3d at 305 (quoting *Lummus Glob. Amazonas S.A. v. Aguaytia Energy del Peru S.R. Ltda.*, 256 F. Supp. 2d 594, 626 (S.D. Tex. 2002)). The court should focus on "specific issues raised by the party challenging the award and the degree to which those issues implicated factual questions that cannot be reliably resolved without some further disclosure." *Id.* "The party seeking discovery bears the burden of showing its necessity." *Freeman v. United States*, 556 F.3d 326, 341 (5th Cir. 2009). Moreover, "[t]he loser in arbitration cannot freeze the confirmation proceedings in their tracks and indefinitely postpone judgment by merely requesting discovery." *Imperial Ethiopian Gov't v. Baruch-Foster Corp.*, 535 F.2d 334, 337 (5th Cir. 1976). We review a district court's order denying discovery for an abuse of discretion. *JP Morgan Chase Bank, N.A. v. Datatreasury Corp.*, 936 F.3d 251, 255–56 (2019).

Two refusals to subpoena witnesses are at issue. First, the district court disallowed a deposition of Gaitis, the dissenting arbitrator. Second, the court refused to authorize a *subpoena* on the AAA itself, regarding its investigation into the request to disqualify Judge Brower. We discuss both.

A. Motion for leave to depose Gaitis

Petrobras asserts that discovery was necessary to resolve the question of the arbitrators' bias and that "glaring red flags" in the record indicate evident **[—16—]** partiality and misconduct, 9 U.S.C. § 10(a)(2), (3). Before identifying these red flags, we will address the parties' agreement not to depose the arbitrators.

When an organization's arbitration rules are incorporated into the underlying agreement, those rules are treated the same as any other contractual provision. *See C & L Enters., Inc. v. Citizens Band Potawatomi Indian Tribe of Okla.*, 532 U.S. 411, 419 n.1 (2001). We seek to "give effect to the intent of the parties," including to any contractual limitations. *Stolt-Nielsen S.A. v. AnimalFeeds Int'l Corp.*, 559 U.S. 662, 684 (2010).

Here, the arbitration clause in the Third Novation incorporates the AAA's Commercial Arbitration Rules. Rule 52(e) of the AAA's rules provides that "[p]arties to an arbitration under these rules may not call the arbitrator . . . as a witness in litigation or any other proceeding relating to the arbitration" and an arbitrator is "not competent to testify as [a] witness[] in such proceeding." Vantage says this provision was enforceable, so the district court did not abuse its discretion in denying Petrobras's motion. Petrobras does not raise any general contract defenses against enforcing Rule 52(e), but it asserts that enforcing the rule here would "eviscerate the integrity of the arbitral process." This general policy concern does not persuade us that the district court erred in enforcing the incorporated terms of the contract.

Further, even without Rule 52(e), Petrobras was not entitled to depose Gaitis. Petrobras points to the unusual and strong statement in the dissent: that the entire arbitration, "the prehearing, hearing, and posthearing processes," denied Petrobras "fundamental fairness and due process protections." Petrobras also claims that several moments during the arbitration hearings substantiate the dissent's assertion, such as when Judge Brower made comments that Petrobras perceived as hostile to Petrobras. For example, Judge **{-374-}** Brower allegedly made off-the-record comments such as "already talked about" and "asked and answered." We agree with the district **[—17—]** court's view of these matters: "Although Petrobras may feel that the comments allegedly made by Judge Brower were abrasive, critical, or rude, these same comments can be viewed as Judge Brower's efforts to move the proceeding along . . . ."

The examples of Judge Brower's allegedly biased conduct at the hearings do not establish that the district court abused its discretion when it refused to allow Petrobras to depose Gaitis. We have not discovered any court of appeals decision holding that a district court abused its discretion in denying discovery from an arbitrator about the substance of the award. We see nothing in this record to cause us to be the first.

B. Motion to subpoena the AAA

After the district court denied the motion for leave to subpoena Gaitis, Petrobras moved for leave to serve a subpoena on the AAA. Petrobras sought to discover documents from the AAA's investigation into Judge Brower's alleged bias. That investigation occurred because Petrobras moved to disqualify Judge Brower after the merits hearing.

First, we conclude that the AAA's ultimate finding that Judge Brower was *not* biased is hardly a "red flag" indicating that discovery was needed. Likewise, the arbitral record did not show signs of partiality or misconduct that compelled the district court to delay the case in order for Petrobras to serve a subpoena on the AAA.

It is relevant that there was no motion for this discovery against the AAA until all the parties had finished briefing the respective motions to confirm and vacate. It is true the deadlines for discovery and for new motions were still ahead. The discovery motion came, though, only a few weeks before the merits hearing on the motions to confirm and to vacate. Although Petrobras's motion was not technically overdue, the district court reasonably considered that **[—18—]** additional discovery would cause further delay to the final resolution of the case. *See Karaha Bodas II*, 364 F.3d at 304.[1]

Moreover, several circuits have held that arbitral immunity extends to organizations like the AAA. *Olson v. Nat'l Ass'n of Sec. Dealers*, 85 F.3d 381, 382 (8th Cir. 1996); *New England Cleaning Servs. v. AAA*, 199 F.3d 542, 545 (1st Cir. 1999). In an unpublished decisions, a panel of this court found arbitral immunity for the AAA. *Jason v. AAA, Inc.*, 62 F. App'x 557 (5th Cir. 2003).

Regardless of the exact dimensions of arbitral immunity, Petrobras has not shown that the district court abused its discretion in denying the discovery motions.

IV. Motion to vacate

The extent of judicial review of arbitral awards under the Panama Convention depends in part on where the award was made. Relevant in this case is that when the United States is the country of primary jurisdiction, meaning the country where the arbitration took place, our courts "have much broader discretion to set aside an award." **{-375-}** *Karaha Bodas Co. v. Perusahaan Pertambangan Minyak Dan Gas Bumi Negara (Karaha Bodas I)*, 335 F.3d 357, 368 (5th Cir. 2003). The arbitration at issue here was held in Texas, so the district court could entertain Petrobras's motion to vacate the award "in accordance with the country's domestic arbitral law and its full panoply of express and implied grounds for relief." *Gulf Petro Trading Co. v. Nigerian Nat'l Petroleum Corp.*, 512 F.3d 742, 746 (5th Cir. 2008). **[—19—]**

Petrobras moved to vacate the arbitration award based on Section 10(a)(2), (3), and (4) of the FAA.[2] Under Section 10(a)(2), Petrobras argued Judge Brower's alleged bias indicated partiality. Under Section 10(a)(3), Petrobras argued the tribunal had failed to consider certain evidence. Last, under Section 10(a)(4), Petrobras argued that the award was not reasoned with respect to Petróleo Brasileiro. The district court disagreed on each point. On appeal, Petrobras argues that the district court should not have denied the vacatur motion with respect to subsections (a)(2) and (a)(3) without first allowing discovery. We already held that the district court did not

[1] In an unpublished decision, this court considered the denial of discovery that was first requested after all the merits briefs were filed and after the agreed-to discovery deadline. *Woods v. P.A.M. Transp. Inc.-L.U.*, 440 F. App'x 265, 268 (5th Cir. 2011). We emphasized that discovery cannot be used just to delay confirmation proceedings, "particularly considering the strong policy favoring expeditious enforcement of arbitration awards." *Id.* That reasoning appears sound to us.

[2] Although the FAA provides default rules, parties can contract to apply other rules. *Volt Info. Scis., Inc. v. Bd. of Trustees*, 489 U.S. 468, 474–75 (1989). Here, the dispute-resolution section of the Third Novation contains a choice-of-law provision selecting Texas law. Thus, one might ask whether Texas or federal vacatur standards apply. *See BNSF Ry. Co. v. Alstom Transp., Inc.*, 777 F.3d 785, 790–91 (5th Cir. 2015). In one case, we found federal vacatur standards applied because the choice-of-law clause did not expressly reference California's arbitration law. *Cooper v. WestEnd Capital Mgmt., L.L.C.*, 832 F.3d 534, 544 (5th Cir. 2016). Here, though, the choice-of-law clause is specific to the "arbitration provisions" of the Third Novation. Although the clause does not name the Texas General Arbitration Act, the clause is expressly about arbitration, and the clause is in the section establishing how the parties may enforce an arbitration award. We are therefore not persuaded that the FAA's vacatur standards are the right ones to apply in this case. Texas and federal vacatur standards do not significantly differ, though, *compare* 9 U.S.C. § 10, *with* TEX. CIV. PRAC. & REM. § 171.088, and the parties discuss only the federal vacatur standards. Because the relevant bases for vacatur exist in both federal and state law, we will consider the arguments under the FAA as presented by the parties.

abuse its discretion in denying the discovery motions, and Petrobras raises no other arguments in support of vacatur under Section 10(a)(2) and (3).

What remains is Petrobras's argument under Section 10(a)(4). That section provides for vacatur "where the arbitrators exceeded their powers, or so imperfectly executed them that a mutual, final, and definite award upon the subject matter submitted was not made." 9 U.S.C. § 10(a)(4). An argument for vacatur under Section 10(a)(4) must be balanced against the parties' agreement to have arbitrators interpret their agreement, which means that **[—20—]** "an arbitral decision even arguably construing or applying the contract must stand, regardless of a court's views of its (de)merits." *Oxford Health Plans LLC v. Sutter*, 569 U.S. 564, 569 (2013) (quotation marks omitted). "[T]he substantive question of whether an arbitrator has exceeded his arbitration powers is a function of [our] highly deferential standard of review in such cases: an arbitrator has not exceeded his powers unless he has utterly contorted . . . the essence of the contract." *Timegate Studios, Inc. v. Southpeak Interactive, L.L.C.*, 713 F.3d 797, 802–03 (5th Cir. 2013). In other words, the arbitrator exceeds his authority where he acts "contrary to an express contractual provision." *PoolRe Ins. Corp. v. Organizational Strategies, Inc.*, 783 F.3d 256, 265 (5th Cir. 2015). We resolve any doubts in favor of arbitration. *Rain CII Carbon, LLC v. ConocoPhillips Co.*, 674 F.3d 469, 472 (5th Cir. 2012). **{-376-}**

The Third Novation specified that the arbitrators were required to "render a reasoned award in writing." In one recent opinion, we outlined a "reasoned award" continuum. *YPF S.A. v. Apache Overseas, Inc.*, 924 F.3d 815, 820 (5th Cir. 2019). There is no specific definition of the term, but it requires "something short of findings and conclusions but more than a simple result." *Id.* (quoting *Sarofim v. Trust Co. of the W.*, 440 F.3d 213, 215 n.1 (5th Cir. 2006)). In other words, we ask whether the arbitrators "issued more than a mere announcement." *Id.*

Petrobras argues that the arbitration award was not reasoned at least as it relates to Petróleo Brasileiro. That company is not a party to the DSA or its amendments but rather is party to the Form of Payment and Performance Guaranty. Thus, Petróleo Brasileiro contested the arbitrators' jurisdiction. The guaranty says that the laws of England and Wales apply to disputes arising out of the document. Under English law, Petrobas argued that Vantage's claim against Petróleo Brasileiro was "premature because the Guaranty is a secondary suretyship obligation, not an independent first **[—21—]** demand instrument." Vantage, though, argued that Petróleo Brasileiro was bound to all the provisions of the parties' agreements, including the arbitration clause in the Third Novation. Vantage also argued that the guaranty's choice-of-law clause was superseded by the Third Novation's.

On appeal, Petrobras argues that the arbitration award was not reasoned because it did not address the arguments that the guaranty did not create immediate liability for Petróleo Brasileiro. The arbitrators determined that because Petróleo Brasileiro was a "primary obligor under the DSA and the Guaranty," Petróleo Brasileiro "remain[ed] responsible for breaches of [the DSA]." The arbitration award discusses whether Petróleo Brasileiro was a proper defendant, explaining the claimants' position, the respondents' position, and the tribunal's own analysis. This is "more than a simple result." *Sarofim*, 440 F.3d at 215 n.1. Or "[i]t is, at the very least, doubtful that the award is not more than a simple result." *Rain CII Carbon*, 674 F.3d at 474. Accordingly, vacatur as to Petróleo Brasileiro was not warranted.

AFFIRMED.

United States Court of Appeals for the Fifth Circuit

No. 19-30535

MAYS
VS.
CHEVRON PIPE LINE CO.

Appeal from the United States District Court for the Western District of Louisiana

Decided: August 3, 2020
Revised: August 4, 2020

Citation: 968 F.3d 442, 8 Adm. R. 213 (5th Cir. 2020).

Before **BARKSDALE, HIGGINSON,** and **DUNCAN,** Circuit Judges.

[—1—] {-444-} DUNCAN, Circuit Judge:

James Mays was killed in an explosion on an offshore platform owned by appellant Chevron Pipe Line Company ("Chevron"). Mays was directly employed by a Chevron subcontractor, Furmanite American ("Furmanite"), which serviced valves on Chevron's platforms. Mays' widow and children sued Chevron for state-law wrongful death, and Chevron **[—2—]** claimed immunity under the state workers' compensation scheme. The parties agree that state immunity does not protect Chevron if Mays' accident was covered by the federal Longshore and Harbor Workers' Compensation Act ("LHWCA"), 33 U.S.C. §§ 901–50, which extends to injuries "occurring as the result of" natural-resource extraction on the Outer Continental Shelf ("OCS"). 43 U.S.C. § 1333(b). This question of LHWCA coverage was submitted to the jury, based on evidence that even though the platform Mays was working on was in Louisiana waters, it was connected to Chevron's OCS platforms; that the fatal explosion was caused by gas flowing from those platforms; and that those platforms had to be shut down due to the accident. The jury found Mays' death was caused by Chevron's OCS activities, which meant that the LHWCA applied and that Chevron did not enjoy state immunity. The jury found Chevron 70% at fault for Mays' death and awarded his widow $2 million for her loss of Mays' affection.

Chevron's central argument on appeal concerns the jury instructions. Chevron insists they violated the Supreme Court's decision in *Pacific Operators Offshore, LLP v. Valladolid*, which interpreted the federal law extending LHWCA coverage to OCS activities. 565 U.S. 207 (2012). Chevron argues that under *Valladolid*, the jury should have been asked only whether the OCS activities of Mays' *direct* employer, Furmanite, caused his death. According to Chevron, Furmanite had no OCS activities, and so the LHWCA could not have applied to supplant Chevron's state immunity. Asking instead about the link between Mays' death and *Chevron's* OCS operations, Chevron urges, was legal error that **{-445-}** requires reversing the jury verdict and rendering judgment in Chevron's favor.

Chevron misreads *Valladolid*. That decision, consistent with the language of the statute it interpreted, requires only a link "between the injury and extractive operations on the shelf." *Id.* at 211. It does not specify which **[—3—]** employer's OCS operations are relevant in a case, like this one, where a subcontractor's employee does work for a contractor with OCS operations. Chevron would extract from *Valladolid* a limitation it does not contain. We therefore reject Chevron's argument that the jury instructions violated *Valladolid*. We also reject Chevron's alternative arguments that the evidence failed to link Mays' death with Chevron's OCS operations and that the district court abused its discretion in not reducing Mrs. Mays' damages.

The judgment of the district court is affirmed.

I.

James Mays worked as a valve technician for Furmanite. On September 13, 2014, Mays was killed while servicing a valve at the Lighthouse Point natural gas platform, which is part of Chevron's Henry Gas Gathering System ("Henry System"). The platform lies in Louisiana's territorial waters, but the Henry System includes other platforms outside

Louisiana waters on the OCS.[1] Two such platforms are connected by pipeline to the platform on which Mays was killed. To stop the gas flowing through the breached valve that caused Mays' death, Chevron had to shut off gas flow from the two connected OCS platforms. At the time of the accident, Mays was working pursuant to a contract between Chevron and Furmanite, under which Furmanite provided maintenance and repair services to several Henry System platforms.

Mays' estate, wife, and children (collectively, "plaintiffs") sued Chevron in federal district court, invoking the court's diversity jurisdiction **[—4—]** and raising tort claims under Louisiana law. Specifically, they alleged Chevron failed to maintain the valve Mays was working on and also misinformed him about the valve's manufacturer. They asserted these mistakes led Mays to inadvertently breach the pipeline's pressure barrier, triggering an explosion that killed him.

Chevron moved for summary judgment, claiming immunity as Mays' "statutory employer" under the Louisiana Workers' Compensation Act ("LWCA"), LA. REV. STAT. ANN. §§ 23:1020–1470. A statutory employer is one that receives work from someone by contracting with his direct employer. *See id.* § 23:1061(A)(1). The statutory employer may owe the employee workers' compensation under certain circumstances. In exchange, the statutory employer, like the direct employer, is immune from tort liability. *Id.*; *see also id.* § 23:1032(A)(1).

In response, the plaintiffs argued this state-law immunity did not apply because Mays was covered by the federal LHWCA. By its terms, the state LWCA does not apply where the LHWCA does.[2] **{-446-}** The plaintiffs argued the LHWCA applied to Mays' death because of the accident's ties to the OCS. Another federal law, the Outer Continental Shelf Lands Act ("OCSLA"), 43 U.S.C. §§ 1331–56, extends the LHWCA to injuries "occurring as the result of" OCS operations. 43 U.S.C. § 1333(b). This extension applies where (1) an employee's injury "result[s] from" OCS extractive operations, and (2) his employer is an "employer" under **[—5—]** OCSLA.[3] *See Barger v. Petroleum Helicopters, Inc.*, 692 F.2d 337, 340 (5th Cir. 1982); *Stansbury v. Sikorski Aircraft*, 681 F.2d 948, 950 (5th Cir. 1982).[4] An injury "result[s] from" OCS extractive operations if it has a "substantial nexus" to those operations. *Valladolid*, 565 U.S. at 222. Chevron responded that it was not Mays' "employer" under OCSLA and that Mays' death could have had no nexus to OCS operations because his direct employer, Furmanite, had no such operations.

The district court initially agreed with Chevron and granted summary judgment. It ruled that whoever the relevant employer might be under OCSLA (Chevron or Furmanite), the plaintiffs failed to identify any evidence showing a "substantial nexus"

[1] The OCS comprises "all submerged lands lying seaward" of state-controlled navigable waters but within the United States' exclusive economic zone. 43 U.S.C. § 1331(a); *see also id.* § 1301(a).

[2] *See* LA. REV. STAT. ANN. § 23:1035.2 (providing that "[n]o [LWCA] compensation shall be payable" to employees "covered by . . . the [LHWCA], or any of its extensions"); *see also, e.g.*, *Johnson v. ACE Am. Ins. Co.*, 2015-0277 (La. App. 4 Cir. 9/23/15), 176 So. 3d 609, 610–11 (explaining LWCA is inapplicable "if [employee] is eligible to receive benefits under the LHWCA or other federal compensation scheme").

[3] An "employer" under OCSLA is

> an employer any of whose employees are employed in . . . operations conducted on the [OCS] for the purpose of exploring for, developing, removing, or transporting by pipeline the natural resources, or involving rights to the natural resources, of the subsoil and seabed of the [OCS].

43 U.S.C. § 1333(b)(2).

[4] Ordinarily, to qualify for LHWCA coverage, an employee must meet maritime "situs" and "status" tests. *See* 33 U.S.C. §§ 903(a), 902(3); *see also generally Wood Grp. Prod. Servs. v. Malta*, 930 F.3d 733, 737, 743, 7 Adm. R. 287, 289, 294 (5th Cir. 2019) (discussing situs and status). Because OCSLA has its own status test, however, "there is no need for an employee to whom OCSLA applies to satisfy independently the two-fold situs and status test for LHWCA coverage." *Stansbury*, 681 F.2d at 950–51.

between Chevron's OCS operations and Mays' death. On the plaintiffs' motion to alter or amend the judgment, however, the court changed its mind. It found a genuine dispute of material fact as to the substantial-nexus requirement because, contrary to its prior understanding, the incident involved "gas being transported by pipeline from the [OCS]" and caused Chevron to shut down two OCS platforms. The court denied Chevron's motion to certify that ruling for interlocutory appeal. **[—6—]**

The case proceeded to trial before a different district judge.[5] At the close of the plaintiffs' case and again at the close of evidence, Chevron moved for judgment as a matter of law ("JMOL"), relying on its contention that there was no connection between Mays' death and any OCS operations of Furmanite. The motions were denied, and the jury was instructed to determine whether there was a substantial nexus between Mays' death and Chevron's OCS operations. The jury found there was. It assigned 70% of the fault for Mays' death to Chevron and 30% to Mays, and awarded damages of over $2.9 million, including $2 million to Mrs. Mays for loss of affection. The district court denied Chevron's renewed motion for JMOL. Chevron also moved for remittitur of the $2 million awarded to Mrs. Mays. The district court sustained all but $527.54 of the award and entered an amended judgment. Chevron timely appealed.

II.

We review a district court's ruling on a renewed JMOL motion *de novo*, applying the same standards as the district **{–447–}** court. *MultiPlan, Inc. v. Holland*, 937 F.3d 487, 494 (5th Cir. 2019) (quoting *N. Cypress Med. Ctr. Operating Co. v. Aetna Life Ins. Co.*, 898 F.3d 461, 473 (5th Cir. 2018)). A party is entitled to JMOL when "[the] party has been fully heard on an issue . . . and the court finds that a reasonable jury would not have a legally sufficient evidentiary basis to find for the party on that issue." FED. R. CIV. P. 50(a)(1). We examine the evidence as a whole and "in the light most favorable to the non-moving party." *Herster v. Bd. of Supervisors of La. State Univ.*, 887 F.3d 177, 184 (5th Cir. 2018) (quoting *Carmona v. Sw. Airlines Co.*, 604 F.3d 848, 854 (5th Cir. 2010)). A jury verdict lacks a legally sufficient **[—7—]** evidentiary basis "where the facts and inferences point so strongly and overwhelmingly in favor of the moving party that reasonable jurors could not arrive at a contrary verdict." *Id.* "[T]he court may not make credibility determinations or weigh the evidence, as those are jury functions." *N. Cypress Med. Ctr.*, 898 F.3d at 473 (quoting *Fairchild v. All Am. Check Cashing, Inc.*, 815 F.3d 959, 966 (5th Cir. 2016)). "Where a jury verdict has been rendered, . . . we are 'especially deferential' to the verdict." *MultiPlan*, 937 F.3d at 494 (quoting *Johnson v. Thibodaux City*, 887 F.3d 726, 731 (5th Cir. 2018)).

We review the district court's ruling on a remittitur motion for abuse of discretion. *Longoria v. Hunter*, 932 F.3d 360, 364 (5th Cir. 2019); *Esposito v. Davis*, 47 F.3d 164, 167 (5th Cir. 1995).

III.

Chevron raises three issues on appeal. First, it claims the district court misapplied the Supreme Court's *Valladolid* decision by instructing the jury to determine whether there was a substantial nexus between Mays' death and *Chevron's*—as opposed to *Furmanite's*—OCS operations. Second, even assuming the focus was correctly on Chevron's OCS operations, Chevron argues the link between those operations and Mays' death was so "indirect" and "tenuous" that it failed the substantial nexus test as a matter of law. Third, Chevron argues the district court abused its discretion by refusing to reduce Mrs. Mays' $2 million because the facts were not "especially tragic" compared to other cases and supported at most a $700,000 award. We address each issue in turn. **[—8—]**

A.

Chevron first argues the district court erred in instructing the jury to focus on the connection between its own OCS operations

[5] The original judge retired.

and the accident.[6] Instead, it claims, the jury should have been instructed to consider the nexus between Mays' death and Furmanite's operations. Because Furmanite had no OCS operations, Chevron argues, it was entitled to JMOL. Chevron's argument turns on what it calls the "plain language" of the Supreme Court's "holding" in *Valladolid*, and so we examine that decision in some detail.

Valladolid resolved a circuit split over the causation standard in 43 U.S.C. § 1333(b), the OCSLA provision that extends LHWCA coverage to OCS extraction–related injuries. The provision applies the LHWCA to injuries "occurring as the result of operations conducted on the [OCS]." *Id.* Our circuit had held this language established a narrow "situs-of-injury" test, covering injuries on an OCS platform **{-448-}** or on waters above the OCS. *Mills v. McDermott, Inc.*, 877 F.2d 356, 362 (5th Cir. 1989) (en banc). By contrast, the Third Circuit had read the same language to establish a broader test covering any injuries that would not have occurred "but for" OCS operations. *See Curtis v. Schlumberger Offshore Serv., Inc.*, 849 F.2d 805, 811 (3d Cir. 1988). In *Valladolid*, the Supreme Court rejected both formulas in favor of the Ninth Circuit's middle-ground test, which required a "substantial nexus between the injury and extractive operations on the shelf." 565 U.S. at 211 (quoting *Valladolid v. Pac. Operations Offshore, LLP*, 604 F.3d 1126, 1139 (9th Cir. **[—9—]** 2010)); *see id.* at 222 (concluding "the Ninth Circuit's 'substantial-nexus' test is more faithful to the text of § 1333(b)").

As it did in the district court, Chevron insists that *Valladolid*'s "plain language" resolves the question here—namely which employer's OCS activities inform the substantial nexus test when a case involves a subcontractor (*i.e.*, a "direct" employer) and a contractor (an "indirect" employer). Chevron focuses on *Valladolid*'s statement that the test requires "a significant causal link between the injury that [the employee] suffered and *his employer's* on-OCS operations." 565 U.S. at 222 (emphasis added). In Chevron's view, this language means that the only relevant employer is the "direct, payroll employer."

But *Valladolid* does not stand for that proposition. As the district court explained in rejecting this argument, *Valladolid* involved only a benefits claim against a direct employer. *See id.* at 210. The decision did not involve the situation where a subcontractor's employee claims benefits vis-à-vis a contractor, and so had no occasion to explore how the nexus test would apply there. Moreover, as discussed, *Valladolid* asked only what causation standard to extract from § 1333(b); it did not address who may qualify as an "employer" under OCSLA. Chevron's fixation on the phrase "his employer" in *Valladolid* thus commits two errors. First, it extends a judicial decision beyond its holding, parsing the opinion as if it were a statute. *See, e.g., Reiter v. Sonotone Corp.*, 442 U.S. 330, 341 (1979) ("[T]he language of an opinion is not always to be parsed as though we were dealing with the language of a statute."). Second, Chevron overlooks that *Valladolid* phrased the test elsewhere in the opinion without mentioning a "employer" at all. *See* 565 U.S. at 211 (asking whether "'the claimant must establish a substantial nexus between the injury and extractive operations on the shelf' to qualify for workers' compensation benefits under the OCSLA" (quoting *Valladolid*, 604 **[—10—]** F.3d at 1139)); *id.* at 216–17 (stating "§ 1333(b) extends LHWCA workers' compensation coverage to any employee injury, regardless of where it happens, as long as it occurs 'as the result of operations conducted on the [OCS]").[7]

[6] As noted, the reason for asking this jury question was to determine whether Mays was covered by OCSLA's extension of the LHWCA to OCS-related injuries. 43 U.S.C. § 1333(b). The parties agree that if the LHWCA applies to Mays via OCSLA, Chevron cannot benefit from the Louisiana statutory-employer defense.

[7] Justice Scalia's concurrence—which advanced a "proximate cause" formulation—did the same. *See id.* at 223 (Scalia, J., concurring in part and concurring in the judgment) ("I would hold that an employee may recover under § 1333(b) if his injury was proximately caused by operations on the [OCS]."). These alternative formulations underscore that Chevron's argument is, at bottom, an attempt to construct a holding out of one out-of-context phrase from *Valladolid*.

Chevron also relies on our post-*Valladolid* decision in *Baker v. Gulf Island Marine Fabricators, L.L.C.*, 834 F.3d 542, 4 Adm. R. 276 (5th Cir. 2016), but only because it quotes Chevron's preferred "his employer" phrase from *Valladolid*. *See id.* at 548, 4 Adm. R. at 279 (quoting *Valladolid*, 565 U.S. at 222). **{-449-}** Like *Valladolid*, *Baker* involved only claims against a direct employer. *See id.* at 544 & n.1, 4 Adm. R. at 276 & n.1. And, like *Valladolid*, *Baker* at times phrased the nexus test without referring to the claimant's "employer." *See id.* at 548, 4 Adm. R. at 279 (asking whether Baker's activities had "a sufficiently substantial nexus to OCS operations"). Even worse for Chevron, in applying the nexus test, *Baker* did not limit itself to asking about the direct employer's OCS operations but also considered the operations of the platform the employee was working on. *See id.* at 549, 4 Adm. R. at 279–80 (asking whether employee's work was "too attenuated from [the platform's] future purpose of extracting natural resources from the OCS for the OCSLA to cover his injury").[8] **[—11—]**

We find more guidance on this issue from the language of § 1333(b). That provision requires a link only between the employee's "injury" and extractive "operations conducted on the [OCS]." *See* 43 U.S.C. § 1333(b) (applying LHWCA "[w]ith respect to disability or death of an employee resulting from any injury occurring as the result of operations conducted on the [OCS]"). It does not restrict the relevant operations to those conducted by the employee's "direct, payroll employer," as Chevron claims. Given that OCSLA and the LHWCA contain numerous, express references to an "employer,"[9] § 1333(b)'s omission of the term is presumed purposeful. *See Russello v. United States*, 464 U.S. 16, 23 (1983). Similarly, we see no language that would indicate Congress intended OCSLA to alter the relationship between a statutory employer and employee. Neither we nor the Supreme Court has authority to edit the text, as Chevron evidently imagines. *See, e.g., In re Gardenhire*, 209 F.3d 1145, 1152 (9th Cir. 2000) ("As judges, of course, we must apply statutes as written, not as they should have been written with the benefit of hindsight.").

Beyond its misplaced reliance on *Valladolid* and *Baker*, Chevron's other arguments also fail to support its view that the nexus test must consider only a direct employer's OCS operations. For instance, Chevron argues that **[—12—]** failing to restrict the test to direct employers "eliminates the need for a direct employer-employee relationship" under the LHWCA and would give an employee benefits "because of a completely unrelated company's on-OCS operations." We disagree. First of all, Chevron is mistaken that LHWCA benefits necessarily demand a "direct employer-employee relationship." To the contrary, the LHWCA expressly provides that an **{-450-}** "employer" includes a "contractor" (*i.e.*, an indirect employer) who may sometimes be liable for benefits to a "subcontractor['s]" (direct employer's) employee. 33 U.S.C. § 904(a). Nor is it true that failing to limit the nexus test as

[8] The employee in *Baker*, whose direct employer was Gulf Island, was working on a "tension leg offshore oil platform (TLP) named Big Foot," *id.* at 544, 4 Adm. R. at 276, co-owned by Chevron and other companies, *see Lloyd's Syndicate 457 v. FloaTEC, L.L.C.*, 921 F.3d 508, 511, 7 Adm. R. 240, 240 (5th Cir. 2019). In concluding there was no substantial nexus, *Baker* looked to the OCS contacts of both Gulf Island and the platform owners. *See* 834 F.3d at 549, 4 Adm. R. at 279–80 (discussing Big Foot's OCS operations as well as Gulf Island's lack of OCS operations). *Baker* did not **[—11—]** squarely address the question before us, however, and we decline to overread the opinion. We note Chevron does not argue that the jury should have been asked about the OCS activities of *both* Furmanite *and* Chevron. Whether that would be the proper inquiry in a case involving a contractor and subcontractor is therefore not before us.

[9] *See, e.g.*, 43 U.S.C. § 1333(b)(2) (defining "employer" for OCSLA purposes); 33 U.S.C. § 902(4) (defining "employer" for LHWCA purposes); *id.* § 904(a) (discussing liability of an "employer" for compensation and specifying when an "employer" is liable as "contractor" for compensation to employees of a "subcontractor"); *id.* § 905(a) (setting out conditions under which an "employer" enjoys exclusive liability under LHWCA); *id.* § 930 (detailing "employers'" reporting requirements); *id.* § 938 (penalizing an "employer" for certain malfeasance).

Chevron urges would allow an employee to obtain benefits because of an "unrelated company's on-OCS operations." OCSLA's nexus requirement is separate from its "employer" requirement. An employee may satisfy the first but not the second. *See, e.g.*, *Barger*, 692 F.2d at 340 (treating these as separate requirements). Nor does the nexus requirement override other LHWCA provisions that limit who is liable to pay benefits to non-immediate employees. *See, e.g.*, 33 U.S.C. § 904(a) (contractor liable for benefits "only if . . . subcontractor fails to secure the payment of compensation"). Chevron's arguments pertain only to *Valladolid*'s substantial-nexus test, and it raises no separate argument about its status as an "employer" under the LHWCA.[10] We thus express no view on whether Chevron is Mays' "employer" under the LHWCA, as extended by OCSLA.[11] **[—13—]**

Finally, Chevron contends that including its OCS operations in the nexus inquiry violates our decisions in *Frederick v. Mobil Oil Corp.*, 765 F.2d 442 (5th Cir. 1985), and *Gates v. Shell Oil*, 812 F.2d 1509 (5th Cir. 1987). We again disagree. Chevron emphasizes that both decisions held a contractor was not an LHWCA "employer" of a subcontractor's employee—and was thus suable in tort—because the subcontractor paid the employee LHWCA benefits. *See Frederick*, 765 F.2d at 446; *Gates*, 812 F.2d at 1513; *see also* 33 U.S.C. § 905(a). These decisions, however, have nothing to say about the connection between an injury and the OCS. Neither applied (indeed, both long predated) the substantial-nexus test. Instead, the decisions concern when a contractor is an "employer" under the LHWCA, an issue Chevron does not raise. And even had Chevron raised the argument, it is unclear whether these decisions would help it: Chevron disputes[12] that Mays' survivors actually received LHWCA benefits from his direct employer, which was the determinative factor in *Frederick* and *Gates*.[13] **[—14—] {-451-}**

In sum, we reject Chevron's argument that the district court erred by instructing the jury to consider Chevron's OCS operations in answering the substantial nexus question.

B.

Chevron argues in the alternative that the evidence linking its OCS operations to Mays' death is so "indirect" and "tenuous" that it fails the substantial nexus test as a matter of law. Although Chevron's brief frames this as a legal challenge, it is actually an attack on the jury's factual finding that there was "a significant causal link" between Mays' death and Chevron's OCS operations. That argument faces steep odds: Chevron must show the evidence "point[s] so strongly and

---

10 Chevron argues in passing that its OCS operations should not factor into the nexus test because it could lead to the "absurd" result of Chevron being considered Mays' "employer" for other purposes, such as liability for LHWCA benefits. But there would be nothing "absurd" about that outcome. As already noted, the LHWCA expressly foresees circumstances under which a contractor is liable for LHWCA benefits to a subcontractor's employee. *See* 33 U.S.C. § 904(a).

11 For instance, Chevron does not argue it is not Mays' employer because Mays' survivors may have received LHWCA benefits from Furmanite's insurer. *See* 33 U.S.C. [—13—] § 905(a) (for exclusive liability purposes, "a contractor shall be deemed the employer of a subcontractor's employees only if the subcontractor fails to secure the payment of compensation as required by section 904 of this title"); *see also Stansbury*, 681 F.2d at 951 (explaining "OCSLA incorporated only the remedies, not the criteria, of the LHWCA," which "includes 33 U.S.C. § 933(i), which provides that the workers' compensation is the exclusive remedy of an injured employee"). That issue is not before us.

12 In a post-argument supplemental brief, Chevron argues that the plaintiffs "did not introduce any evidence of LHWCA benefits at trial" and that a letter from Furmanite's insurance carrier stating that Mays' survivors "would receive LHWCA benefits" was inconclusive.

13 *Gates* is unhelpful to Chevron for another reason. It involved a suit under OCSLA § 1333(a)(2)(A), which incorporates state law only to the extent it is "not inconsistent with" federal law. We concluded Louisiana's statutory-employer defense was inconsistent with the LHWCA immunity scheme (under which the contractor was suable). *See* 812 F.2d at 1513–14. In this case, however, we are sitting in diversity, and so it does not matter whether the statutory-employer defense is "inconsistent" with federal law.

overwhelmingly in [Chevron's] favor" that no reasonable jury could have ruled as this one did. *Herster*, 887 F.3d at 184. We must view the evidence in the light most favorable to the plaintiffs, *id.*, and we cannot "make credibility determinations or weigh the evidence, as those are jury functions." *N. Cypress Med. Ctr.*, 898 F.3d at 473 (cleaned up). On top of all that, we are "especially deferential" to jury verdicts. *MultiPlan*, 937 F.3d at 494 (citation omitted). Measured against those daunting standards, Chevron's argument falls short.

The substantial nexus question submitted to the jury is "fact-specific" and "depend[s] on the individual circumstances of each case." *Baker*, 834 F.3d at 548–49, 4 Adm. R. at 279 (quoting *Valladolid*, 565 U.S. at 222). Chevron essentially quarrels with the weight the jury gave certain facts. For instance, it argues that only "some" of the gas released from the valve Mays breached "originated from on-OCS facilities." Similarly, it points out that only "some" of the Henry System platforms shut down in the wake of Mays' accident were on the OCS. Chevron claims these facts show "neither a significant nor direct link" between Mays' death and Chevron's OCS operations. But the jury could have drawn different inferences from the **[—15—]** evidence as a whole. For example, the jury heard expert testimony from an engineer that the gas that escaped from the breached valve was extracted from the OCS and was a "direct factor in Mr. Mays' fatal injury." The jury also heard uncontested evidence that the platform Mays was working on when he was killed was connected to two OCS platforms and that gas flow from those specific platforms had to be shut down because of the accident.[14] There was also testimony that Furmanite maintained and repaired Chevron's valves "extensively" and that Chevron had contracted with Furmanite for valve services on the Henry System, including for its on-OCS platforms. As the district court correctly concluded, this evidence presented a jury question as to whether there was a significant causal link between Mays' death and OCS activities. Chevron fails to explain why the jury's affirmative finding was so contrary to the overwhelming weight of the evidence as to be irrational. *See Herster*, 887 F.3d at 184. Instead, **{-452-}** Chevron effectively asks us to reweigh the evidence, something we cannot do. *See MultiPlan*, 937 F.3d at 494; *N. Cypress Med. Ctr.*, 898 F.3d at 473.

Chevron relies heavily on our decisions in *Herb's Welding v. Gray*, 766 F.2d 898 (5th Cir. 1985), and *Baker*, 834 F.3d 542, 4 Adm. R. 276, but neither is on point. *Herb's Welding* is superficially similar to Mays' case: it involved an OCSLA benefits claim by a welder injured while working on a fixed rig in Louisiana waters connected indirectly to an OCS platform. *See* 766 F.2d at 899–900. **[—16—]** The likeness ends there, however. Unlike our case, the injury in *Herb's Welding* was not linked in any way to gas produced on the OCS, nor did the incident cause the shut-down of OCS platforms.[15] Furthermore, the decision (from 1985) applied an embryonic version of our court's "situs-of-injury" test, which was eventually rejected in *Valladolid*.[16] *Baker* is

[14] This is precisely the kind of evidence that led the district court to reverse its initial summary judgment in Chevron's favor. As the court explained, the plaintiffs' evidence showed that "pressurized natural gas *originating from the OCS* was being transported by pipeline *through the valve on the Lighthouse platform which Mr. Mays was attempting to repair at the time of his death*." The court also relied on evidence that "at least one OCS platform transported natural gas by pipeline to and through the valve at issue (Tiger Shoals A – 217A), and two OCS platforms had to be shut in to stop the release of pressurized gas through the pipeline and valve involved in Mr. Mays' death."

[15] Gray injured his knee running away from an explosion caused when he burned through a gas flow line. *See Herb's Welding v. Gray*, 470 U.S. 414, 416–17 (1985). Nothing in the various opinions suggests any concrete link between Gray's injury and gas from the OCS. Nor, unlike our case, was Gray's rig directly connected to an OCS platform. Rather, "the platform on which [Gray] was injured was connected by a gas flow line to a second platform within state waters which in turn was connected by a flow line to a third platform located on the shelf." *Herb's Welding*, 766 F.2d at 899–900. Because this case lends no help to Chevron in any event, we need not consider how the substantial-nexus test might apply to it.

[16] *See id.* at 900 ("Under our decision, an employee's [OCSLA] coverage will change depending on the rig to which he is assigned on a particular day."); *see also Valladolid*, 565 U.S. at

even further afield: it involved a marine carpenter injured on land while building a housing module "which would ultimately be integrated into an [offshore platform], which would ultimately be placed on the OCS." 834 F.3d at 544, 548, 4 Adm. R. at 279. We affirmed the Benefit Review Board's ("BRB") decision that Baker's work was "too attenuated" from OCS activities to satisfy the substantial nexus test. *Id.* at 549, 4 Adm. R. at 279–80. We reject Chevron's argument that *Baker* is "analogous" to this case because Mays also spent much of his employment on land[17] and **[—17—]** because Furmanite was not "direct[ly]" involved in Chevron's OCS activities. Baker's injury had a wafer-thin connection to OCS extraction, whereas the evidence here supports finding a more substantial connection between Mays' death and OCS extractive operations. Finally, both *Herb's Welding* and *Baker* involved our *de novo* review of BRB decisions, whereas this case involves our review of a jury verdict to which we are "especially deferential." *MultiPlan*, 937 F.3d at 494 (citation omitted); *cf. Baker*, 834 F.3d at 545, 4 Adm. R. at 277 (reviewing existence of LHWCA coverage as "a pure question of law," where facts undisputed).

In sum, we reject Chevron's argument that the evidence linking its OCS operations to Mays' death failed to meet the **{-453-}** substantial nexus test as a matter of law. We therefore cannot disturb the jury's finding on that issue.

C.

Finally, Chevron claims the district court abused its discretion by refusing to reduce the jury's $2 million loss-of-affection award to Mrs. Mays. We disagree.

A federal court sitting in diversity applies state remittitur standards. *Foradori v. Harris*, 523 F.3d 477, 497 (5th Cir. 2008) (citation omitted). Under Louisiana law, "[a]n appellate court may disturb a damages award only after an articulated analysis of the facts discloses an abuse of discretion." *Miller v. LAMMICO*, 2007-1352 (La. 1/16/08), 973 So.2d 693, 711 (citations omitted). The reviewing court first examines the specific case's "facts and circumstances," and only if that reveals an abuse of discretion does the court "resort to a review of prior similar awards." *Id.* (citations omitted). "It is **[—18—]** well-settled that vast discretion is accorded to the trier of fact in fixing general damages awards . . . such that an appellate court should rarely disturb an award of general damages." *Purvis v. Grant Par. Sch. Bd.*, 2013-1424 (La. 2/14/14), 144 So. 3d 922, 927–28 (citations omitted); *see also* LA. CIV. CODE art. 2324.1.

Chevron highlights three facts which, it claims, show abuse of discretion in the damages award. First, Mays died "instantly," with no "pre-death pain and suffering." Second, Mrs. Mays did not witness her husband's death nor "suffer any distress associated with watching her husband's condition become progressively worse." Third, Chevron claims the record does not show Mrs. Mays suffered "extraordinary" mental distress, requiring "medical or psychiatric treatment due to the accident." Claiming the district court abused its discretion by overlooking these facts, Chevron cites eight "comparable" wrongful-death cases with awards ranging from $300,000 to $1.5 million, urging that Mrs. Mays' award should have been reduced to $700,000 at most.

---

215 (rejecting our situs-of-injury test because "nothing in [the] language [of § 1333(b)] suggests that the injury to the employee must occur on the OCS").

[17] Chevron argues in passing that the district court wrongly excluded evidence that Mays spent 90% of his time working on land. We need not consider whether this was an abuse of discretion because Chevron—in barely one page devoted to this issue—makes no attempt to explain why the exclusion affected Chevron's "substantial rights." *EEOC v. Manville Sales Corp.*, 27 F.3d 1089, 1093 (5th Cir. 1994); *see, e.g., JTB Tools & Oilfield Servs., L.L.C. v. United States*, 831 F.3d 597, 601 (5th Cir. 2016) (explaining an issue is waived if brief "only repeat[s] conclusory assertions" and "fail[s] to offer any supporting argument or citation to authority" (citing Fed. R. App. P. 28(a)(8)); *Willis v. Cleco Corp.*, 749 F.3d 314, 319 (5th Cir. 2014); *see also United States v. Scroggins*, 599 F.3d 433, 446–47 **[—17—]** (5th Cir. 2010) ("It is not enough to merely mention or allude to a legal theory." (citation omitted)).

We are not persuaded. In rejecting Chevron's remittitur motion, the district court found that Mrs. Mays "provided compelling testimony" about the loss of her husband's affection. They were married nearly 40 years. Asked to name her favorite memory of her husband, she testified, "[H]e is my memory. I was with him from the time I was 17." Mrs. Mays also testified that she and Mays had nearly finished building their retirement home, where they planned to "sit on the back porch and drink coffee all day." On the day Mays was killed, Mrs. Mays received news of his death while waiting for him at a casino in Marksville, where they had planned to spend the weekend to celebrate their 39th wedding anniversary. She collapsed and had to be carried out. The district court also observed that Mrs. Mays "could not see [Mays'] body post-accident because it was so badly mangled." And because of the **[—19—]** time spent floating in the gas-tainted water, Mays' body had such a strong odor that he could not be buried in the wooden casket he had chosen before he died.

In sum, we are not persuaded that the district court abused its discretion in refusing to reduce Mrs. Mays' award.

***

The judgment of the district court is AFFIRMED.

United States Court of Appeals
for the Fifth Circuit

No. 19-20506

SANCHEZ
vs.
SMART FABRICATORS OF TEX., L.L.C.***

Appeal from the United States District Court for the Southern District of Texas

Decided: August 14, 2020

***Petition for rehearing en banc granted on Oct. 30, 2020.

Citation: 970 F.3d 550, 8 Adm. R. 222 (5th Cir. 2020).

Before **DAVIS, JONES,** and **WILLETT,** Circuit Judges.

[—1—] {-551-} DAVIS, Circuit Judge:

Plaintiff Gilbert Sanchez appeals the district court's denial of his motion to remand **{-552-}** and grant of summary judgment in favor of Defendant Smart Fabricators of Texas ("SmartFab"). Both rulings rested on the district court's holding that Sanchez did not qualify as a seaman under the Jones Act. Concluding that Sanchez is a seaman, we REVERSE and REMAND WITH INSTRUCTIONS to remand the matter to state court. **[—2—]**

I. BACKGROUND

Sanchez, a welder hired by SmartFab, was injured when he tripped on a pipe welded to the deck of a jack-up drilling rig. The rig was owned and operated by Enterprise Offshore Drilling LLC ("Enterprise").

Sanchez worked for SmartFab as a welder for 67 days. Of those 67 days, Sanchez worked two jobs that do not count in the seaman calculus: two days (3% of his total employment) in SmartFab's onshore shop, and four days (6% of his total employment) on the ENSCO 75, a vessel not owned by Enterprise or part of its fleet. He spent the remaining days—those pertinent to our calculus—on Enterprise's jack-up drilling rigs. Sanchez worked 48 of those days (72% of his total employment) on the ENTERPRISE WFD 350, a rig adjacent to an inland pier, and 13 of those days (19% of his total employment) on the ENTERPRISE 263, a rig on the Outer Continental Shelf.

Although Sanchez's injury occurred on the ENTERPRISE 263, the vast majority of his time with SmartFab was spent on the ENTERPRISE WFD 350. Thus, it becomes critical whether his work aboard that rig was substantial in terms of both its duration and nature. For all 48 days he spent on the ENTERPRISE WFD 350, the rig was jacked up above water, a step away from and adjacent to the shoreside pier. Sanchez only worked day shifts, returning home every evening.

After his accident, Sanchez sued SmartFab in state court under the Jones Act. SmartFab removed the case, but Sanchez argued that the Jones Act precluded removal. The district court denied Sanchez's motion to remand and granted SmartFab's motion for summary judgment, each for the **[—3—]** same reason: Sanchez could not qualify as a Jones Act seaman.[1] Sanchez timely appealed both orders.

II. DISCUSSION

We review both the denial of a motion to remand and the grant of summary judgment de novo.[2]

The Jones Act grants "any seaman" a cause of action in negligence against the vessel owner, master, or fellow crewmembers.[3] Only seamen may sue under the Jones Act. Generally, Jones Act claims are "not subject to removal to federal court."[4] Sanchez argues that because he was a seaman who brought

---

1 *See Sanchez v. Enter. Offshore Drilling LLC*, No. CV H-19-110, 2019 WL 2515307, at *4 (S.D. Tex. June 18, 2019); *Sanchez v. Enter. Offshore Drilling LLC*, 376 F. Supp. 3d 726, 733 (S.D. Tex. 2019).

2 *Holmes v. Atl. Sounding Co.*, 437 F.3d 441, 445 (5th Cir. 2006), *abrogated on other grounds by Lozman v. City of Riviera Beach, Fla.*, 568 U.S. 115, 1 Adm. R. 2 (2013).

3 *Chandris, Inc. v. Latsis*, 515 U.S. 347, 354 (1995); 46 U.S.C. § 30104.

4 *Lewis v. Lewis & Clark Marine, Inc.*, 531 U.S. 438, 455 (2001).

his negligence claim under the Jones Act in state court, the district court erred in granting **{-553-}** summary judgment for SmartFab and denying his motion to remand. So, the only issue for us to decide on appeal is whether Sanchez is a Jones Act seaman. If he is, the district court must be reversed and the case remanded.

Congress has not defined the term "seaman," and the "difficult . . . task of giving a cogent meaning to [the] term has been left to the courts."[5] We are guided by the Supreme Court's two-prong test, set forth in *Chandris, Inc. v. Latsis*:[6] (1) the employee's duties "must contribute to the function of **[—4—]** the vessel or to the accomplishment of its mission,"[7] and (2) the employee "must have a connection to a vessel in navigation (or an identifiable group of such vessels) that is substantial in terms of both its duration and its nature."[8] The parties agree that Sanchez meets the first prong—he was "doing the ship's work" as a welder and fitter. But SmartFab argues, and the district court found, that Sanchez fails the second.

The Court's substantial-connection prong was designed "to separate the sea-based maritime employees who are entitled to Jones Act protection from those land-based workers who have only a transitory or sporadic connection to a vessel in navigation."[9] The Court has explained that "the total circumstances of an individual's employment must be weighed to determine whether he had a sufficient relation to the navigation of the vessels and the perils attendant thereon."[10]

To make this determination, *Chandris* instructs us to address both the quantity (duration) and quality (nature) of the worker's duties aboard a vessel during his employment with his current employer. As to duration, the Court held in *Chandris* that, as a rule of thumb, a "worker who spends less than about 30 percent of his time in the service of a vessel in navigation should not qualify as a seaman under the Jones Act."[11] And as to nature, the Court emphasized that we focus on the nature of the claimant's connection with the vessel.[12] The Court then reiterated in *Harbor Tug & Barge Co. v. Papai* that **[—5—]** the Jones Act should only extend to "those workers who face regular exposure to the perils of the sea."[13] It explained, "For the substantial connection requirement to serve its purpose, the inquiry into the nature of the employee's connection to the vessel must concentrate on whether the employee's duties take him to sea."[14]

The district court held, and we agree, that Sanchez satisfies the duration **{-554-}** requirement of the *Chandris* test.[15] Indeed, he spent over 70% of his employment with SmartFab aboard the ENTERPRISE WFD 350, and around 19% of his employment aboard the ENTERPRISE 263, two jack-up drilling rigs owned by Enterprise Offshore Drilling.[16] The question of whether he

[5] *In re Endeavor Marine Inc.*, 234 F.3d 287, 290 (5th Cir. 2000) (per curiam).

[6] 515 U.S. 347, 368 (1995).

[7] *Id.* This threshold requirement is "very broad." *Id.*

[8] *Id.*

[9] *Id.* at 368.

[10] *Id.* at 370.

[11] *Id.* at 371.

[12] *Id.* at 370.

[13] 520 U.S. 548, 560 (1997).

[14] *Id.* at 555. Papai engaged in maintenance—chipping rust and painting—aboard the docked vessels. *Id.* at 551. The court observed that his actual duty "did not include any seagoing activity; he was hired for one day to paint the vessel at dockside and he was not going to sail with the vessel after he finished painting it." *Id.* at 559. The court ultimately held that Papai did not establish seaman status under the group of vessels concept (i.e., the fleet doctrine). *Id.* at 560.

[15] *Sanchez v. Enter. Offshore Drilling LLC*, 376 F. Supp. 3d 726, 732 (S.D. Tex. 2019).

[16] On appeal, SmartFab argues that we may only look at Sanchez's time spent on vessels on the Outer Continental Shelf. This is wrong. "[J]ack-up drilling platforms . . . are considered vessels under maritime law." *Barker v. Hercules Offshore, Inc.*, 713 F.3d 208, 215, 1 Adm. R. 206, 209 (5th Cir. 2013), SmartFab has made no showing that the docked jack-up drilling rigs had lost their vessel status, either because they were "withdrawn from the water for extended periods," *Cain v. Transocean Offshore USA, Inc.*, 518 F.3d 295, 300 (5th Cir. 2008), or "being transformed through 'major overhauls or renovations,'" *Chandris, Inc. v. Latsis*, 515 U.S. 347, 374 (1995) (citation omitted). Thus, the district court did not err in considering

qualifies as a seaman thus narrows to whether the circumstances of his employment meet the nature test. **[—6—]**

The district court answered that question in the negative and concluded that Sanchez was a shoreside worker.[17] The court observed that his work on vessels—primarily the work he completed on ENTERPRISE WFD 350—did not expose him to the perils of the sea, and the court therefore concluded that Sanchez was not a seaman.[18]

Our case law rejects such a narrow reading of the substantial-in-nature requirement. In *In re Endeavor Marine*, the plaintiff, a crane operator, worked on a moored derrick barge on the Mississippi River, where he loaded and unloaded cargo and helped to maintain the crane.[19] He was rarely required to board a moving vessel, and he never traveled beyond the immediate dock area.[20] The district court held that because his duties did not "take him to sea," as *Papai* required, he did not qualify as a seaman.[21] We disagreed.[22] We held the plaintiff's connection to the vessel was substantial in nature, because his connection to the barge regularly exposed him to the perils of the sea—namely, being "on the brown waters of the Mississippi River"—regardless of whether he actually went to sea.[23] **[—7—]**

We followed *Endeavor Marine* fourteen years later in *Naquin v. Elevating Boats, L.L.C.*[24] There, the plaintiff, a vessel repair supervisor, was injured in a shipyard while working on a fleet of liftboats.[25] The liftboats he worked on were either moored, jacked up, or docked in the shipyard canal.[26] We rejected the argument that the work upon those vessels did not expose the plaintiff to the perils of the sea, even if the vessels were docked in a canal and rarely ventured beyond.[27] Finding "no basis to distinguish *Endeavor Marine*," we held **{-555-}** that working on a vessel docked or at anchor in navigable water satisfied the substantial in nature requirement.[28]

The nature of Sanchez's employment cannot be distinguished from that of plaintiffs' in *Endeavor Marine* and *Naquin*. First, *Endeavor Marine* makes clear that Sanchez can qualify as a Jones Act seaman so long as he is exposed to the perils of the sea, even if his duties are on a vessel jacked up next to a dockside pier.[29] Second, *Naquin* establishes that Sanchez can qualify as a seaman if he was "doing [a] ship's work on vessels docked or at anchor in navigable water."[30] This is true regardless of whether Sanchez was welding or operating marine cranes like the plaintiff in *Naquin*. "While . . . near-shore workers may face fewer risks, they still remain exposed to the **[—8—]** perils of a maritime work environment."[31] The district court underscored that the drilling rigs on which Sanchez worked were jacked up above the water, but the same was true for some of the liftboats in *Naquin*.[32] And, while the court emphasized that Sanchez was a land-based welder who went home every evening, we held in *Naquin* that such work aboard vessels was not disqualifying.[33] The cases are indistinguishable.

Sanchez's time aboard the ENTERPRISE WFD 350.

17 *Sanchez*, 376 F. Supp. 3d 726, 732–733.

18 *Id.*

19 234 F.3d 287, 298 (5th Cir. 2000) (per curiam); *see also In re Complaint of Endeavor Marine, Inc.*, No. CIV.A. 98-0779, 1999 WL 76586, at *1 (E.D. La. Feb. 11, 1999).

20 *Endeavor Marine*, 234 F.3d at 289.

21 *Id.* at 291.

22 *Id.*

23 *Id.* at 291–92, 292 n.3.

24 744 F.3d 927, 2 Adm. R. 200 (5th Cir. 2014).

25 *Id.* at 930, 2 Adm. R. at 200.

26 *Id.*, 2 Adm. R. at 200.

27 *Id.* at 934–35, 2 Adm. R. at 203–04.

28 *Id.* at 935, 2 Adm. R. at 204. *See also Grab v. Boh Bros. Const. Co.*, 506 F. App'x 271, 276 (5th Cir. 2013) (unpublished) (ironworker foreman on stationary crane barge on Lake Ponchartrain was exposed to perils of the sea).

29 *In re Endeavor Marine Inc.*, 234 F.3d 287, 292 (5th Cir. 2000) (per curiam).

30 *Naquin*, 744 F.3d 927, 935, 2 Adm. R. 200, 204 (5th Cir. 2014).

31 *Id.* at 934, 2 Adm. R. at 203.

32 *Id.*, 2 Adm. R. at 203. The other liftboats were moored or docked. *Id.*, 2 Adm. R. at 203.

33 *Id.* at 934, 2 Adm. R. at 203. *See also Grab v. Boh Bros. Constr. Co., L.L.C.*, 506 Fed. App'x. 271, 276 (5th Cir. 2013) (unpublished) ("[T]he fact that [the injured employee] returned home daily did not

Sanchez has therefore shown that he had a substantial connection both in nature and duration to the vessels on which he worked. The district court erred in holding that Sanchez was not a Jones Act seaman.

III. CONCLUSION

We REVERSE the district court's judgment and REMAND WITH INSTRUCTIONS to remand the matter to the 165th Judicial District Court of Harris County, Texas.

(Reporter's Note: Concurring Opinion follows on p. 226).

******(Reporter's Note: On October 30, 2020, the U.S. Fifth Circuit ordered that this case be reheard en banc, with oral argument, on a date thereafter to be fixed.)******

---

remove him from his exposure to cognizable dangers of the sea.").

[—9—] {-555-} **DAVIS,** Circuit Judge, specially concurring in the judgment, joined by **JONES** and **WILLETT,** Circuit Judges:

Although this panel is bound by our precedent, for reasons discussed below, I am persuaded that our case law is inconsistent with the teaching of the Supreme Court. It is clear to me that Sanchez was a land-based fitter and welder whose duties did not take him to sea; consequently, he does not qualify as a seaman.

I.

The undisputed facts of this case are outlined in the majority opinion. Basically, Sanchez was a welder and fitter, who worked on jobs where his employer sent him to satisfy customer orders. He was land-based, lived at home, and traveled to and from work every day. During the 48 days he worked on the ENTERPRISE WFD 350, the barge was jacked up adjacent to and one step away from the dock. While he performed welding repair services on the barge, it was never jacked down into the water or moved away from the dock. {-556-}

Three Supreme Court cases are important to our analysis of whether Sanchez was a seaman. The first is *McDermott International, Inc. v. Wilander*.[1] Most relevant to today's case, the Court emphasized that maritime workers are covered under two acts—the Longshore and Harbor Workers' Compensation Act and the Jones Act—and that coverage under the two acts is mutually exclusive.[2] As such, the Court underscored the important distinction between land-based and sea-based maritime workers.[3] Only [—10—] "[t]he latter, who owe their allegiance to a vessel and not solely to a land-based employer, are seamen."[4] The Court went on to define seamen as workers who "contribute to the function of the vessel" or are "employed on board a vessel in furtherance of its purpose."[5]

The Court further developed the relationship a worker must have to a vessel in order to be a seaman four years later in *Chandris, Inc. v. Latsis*.[6] The Court held that "the ultimate inquiry is whether the worker in question is a member of the vessel's crew or simply a land-based employee who happens to be working on the vessel at a given time."[7] The Court required that a seaman have a substantial connection to a vessel that is substantial in terms of both its duration and nature.[8]

While the Court did not expand on the "nature" element in *Chandris*, it did provide some important details to the requirement in *Harbor Tug & Barge Co. v. Papai*.[9] The plaintiff in *Papai* was land-based and worked on a group of tugs owned by three tugboat operators in the San Francisco Bay, where he did maintenance, longshoring, and deckhand work.[10] He was injured while doing painting work on one of the defendant's tugs, the *Pt. Barrow*.[11] The Court first held that the plaintiff failed to establish seaman [—11—] status under the "fleet doctrine."[12] The Court also held that the plaintiff's work was not substantial in nature.[13] It stressed: "For the substantial connection requirement to serve its purpose, the inquiry into the nature of the employee's connection to the vessel must concentrate on whether the employee's duties *take him to sea*."[14] Such an inquiry, the Court explained, is "helpful in distinguishing land-based from sea-based employees."[15] The Court then noted that the plaintiff's "actual duty on the *Pt. Barrow* throughout the employment in

1 498 U.S. 337 (1991).
2 *Id.* at 347.
3 *Id.*
4 *Id.*
5 *Id.* at 346, 355 (cleaned up).

6 515 U.S. 347 (1995).
7 *Id.* at 370.
8 *Id.* at 376.
9 520 U.S. 548 (1997).
10 *Id.* at 551.
11 *Id.*
12 *Id.* at 559–60. The Court rejected Papai's argument that the group of tugs operating in the San Francisco Bay Area served by Papai's union was an identifiable group of vessels to which he had a substantial connection. *Id.* The Court explained that a worker could have a connection to a fleet of vessels only if those vessels are under common ownership and control. *Id.*
13 *Id.* at 559.
14 *Id.* at 555 (emphasis added).
15 *Id.*

question {-557-} did not include any seagoing activity; he was hired for one day to paint the vessel at dockside and he was not going to sail with the vessel after he finished painting it."[16] The Court concluded no percentage of his work "subject[ed] him to the perils of the sea."[17]

II.

Moving to the instant case, I am persuaded that our precedent has failed to apply the above Supreme Court authority correctly. **[—12—]**

As the panel discusses, in *In re Endeavor Marine Inc.*, the plaintiff worked as a crane operator unloading barges at a dock on the Mississippi River.[18] He also performed routine maintenance work on the same barge.[19] The plaintiff was land-based, and his duties did not take him to sea or even out on the waters of the Mississippi River.[20]

In *Naquin v. Elevating Boats, L.L.C.*, we relied on *Endeavor Marine* and held that plaintiff satisfied the nature element of the substantial connection requirement.[21] Our reliance was misplaced. The land-based plaintiff worked on dockside vessels and in a canal adjacent to the shipyard—his duties did not take him to sea or expose him to its perils.[22]

Applying the aforementioned Supreme Court caselaw, I agree that because Sanchez spent more than 70% of his employment time with SmartFab aboard the ENTERPRISE WFD 350, he satisfied the duration prong of the substantial connection requirement. Yet, as discussed above, I am persuaded that we did not correctly follow the Court's dictates in holding that Sanchez satisfied the nature element of the substantial connection requirement. All of his welding work on the ENTERPRISE WFD 350 was done while the rig was jacked up adjacent to the dock. He was never assigned to sail on the vessel, and instead only had to take two steps off the rig and onto land every evening at the end of his shift. His work was essentially land- **[—13—]** based, never exposing him to the perils of the sea. I believe that we should take this case en banc and bring our jurisprudence in line with Supreme Court caselaw.[23]

******(Reporter's Note: On October 30, 2020, the U.S. Fifth Circuit ordered that this case be reheard en banc, with oral argument, on a date thereafter to be fixed.)******

---

[16] *Id.* at 559.

[17] *Id.* at 560. For an excellent discussion on the difficulties distinguishing between land-based and sea-based employment, see Kenneth Engerrand's article, *Escape from the Labyrinth: Call for the Admiralty Judges of the Supreme Court to Reconsider Seaman Status*, 40 HOUS. J. INT'L L. 741, 779 (2018). *See also* Robert Force and Martin J. Norris, 1 THE LAW OF SEAMEN § 2:5–8 (5th ed. 2019) (for a comprehensive discussion of the cases on the subject).

[18] 234 F.3d 287, 289 (5th Cir. 2000) (per curiam).

[19] *Id.* at 289, 293.

[20] *Id.* at 292 n.3.

[21] *Naquin v. Elevating Boats, L.L.C.*, 744 F.3d 927, 935, 2 Adm. R. 200, 203–04 (5th Cir. 2014).

[22] *Id.* at 930–31, 2 Adm. R. at 200. *See also id.* at 943, 2 Adm. R. at 211–12 (Jones, J., dissenting) (arguing that the plaintiff was not exposed to the perils of the sea because he "spent nearly all of his time dockside, repairing boats that were secured in the shipyard canal, or operating a land-based crane, or working in the shipyard fabrication shop").

[23] This would also be consistent with the Second Circuit's approach in *Matter of Buchanan Marine, L.P.*, 874 F.3d 356, 5 Adm. R. 100 (2d Cir. 2017). The plaintiff in that case worked on the Hudson River as a barge maintainer. *Id.* at 361, 5 Adm. R. at 100. The court determined that the plaintiff's work on the barges did not regularly expose him to the perils of the sea, because the barges were always moored in the Hudson. *Id.* at 367, 5 Adm. R. at 105–06. Although the Second Circuit distinguished *Naquin*, its distinction is suspect—under our case law, the plaintiff there would most certainly satisfy the nature element of the substantial connection requirement.

United States Court of Appeals
for the Fifth Circuit

No. 19-30311

DELOACH MARINE SERVS., L.L.C.
VS.
MARQUETTE TRANSP. CO., L.L.C.

Appeal from the United States District Court for the Eastern District of Louisiana

Decided: September 11, 2020

Citation: 974 F.3d 601, 8 Adm. R. 228 (5th Cir. 2020).

Before **SMITH, WILLETT,** and **DUNCAN,** Circuit Judges.

[—1—] {–603–} DUNCAN, Circuit Judge:

Two barge towboats collided on the Mississippi River. After a bench trial, the district court found the captains of both vessels negligent to varying degrees. Both parties appeal. Finding no clear error, we affirm the district court's apportionment of fault. We remand to consider prejudgment interest.

I.

A.

On January 26, 2016, the M/V JUSTIN PAUL ECKSTEIN ("JUSTIN") and M/V VANPORT ("VANPORT") collided near mile **[—2—]** marker 131 on the Mississippi River. Both vessels are barge towboats, and each had several barges attached to it. Before the collision, the JUSTIN sat idle on the west bank of the river, south of a barge-storage area called a fleeting facility. The JUSTIN was facing north ("upriver") and needed to enter the channel to move south ("downriver"). In order to turn around, the JUSTIN's captain, Billy Jackson, hoped to "top around" the JUSTIN, a maneuver through which her bow (or, more precisely, the bows of her barges) would be extended out of the river's "slack" water and into its navigational channel, where the current would turn her bow to face south. At 12:49 pm, Jackson made a radio call to announce to vessels in the area that he intended to top around into the channel.

Ten minutes before Jackson's call, the VANPORT was a few miles upstream of the JUSTIN, traveling downriver. The VANPORT had made a "passing agreement" with a larger ship, the BEATRICE, whereby the BEATRICE would pass the VANPORT to the VANPORT's port (left). In reaching this agreement, the BEATRICE asked the VANPORT to stay as far to the right (*i.e.*, as close to the west bank) as she could, because the BEATRICE—an oceangoing vessel with a deep hull—needed to stay in the deepest part of the river channel. The VANPORT's captain, Matthew Vidrine, put the vessel in idle and moved out of the navigational channel. The BEATRICE began to overtake the VANPORT as agreed.

At 12:54 pm, as the BEATRICE was overtaking the VANPORT, Jackson called **{–604–}** the VANPORT. The following exchange took place:

> JUSTIN: I straightened her up there with all the traffic coming. I think you're down far enough now that I can go ahead and start letting her spin.
>
> VANPORT: Yeah, you sure can. I'm just slowed down to get this ship by me . . . .
>
> JUSTIN: Yeah, seeing as how I'm going to be about abreast here **[—3—]** and I got her crossways, I didn't want to have my head stuck out there in nobody's way.
>
> VANPORT: I appreciate it. I saw that, but I had confidence.

The two captains interpreted this exchange differently. Vidrine thought the JUSTIN planned to execute the top-around maneuver *after* the VANPORT passed by. Vidrine therefore believed the JUSTIN would remain outside the navigational channel until the VANPORT passed. When Vidrine agreed to allow the JUSTIN to "start letting her spin," he thought Jackson planned to "spin in behind the VANPORT and fall in behind it." For his part, however, Jackson believed Vidrine had agreed to keep the VANPORT clear of the JUSTIN while she topped around *ahead* of the

VANPORT. Jackson also believed he had enough time to execute the maneuver before the VANPORT passed, in part because Vidrine told him he had "slowed down." Jackson therefore began to top around immediately after the radio exchange, pushing the JUSTIN's bow into the navigational channel.

Computerized navigational data (called "Rose Point data"[1]) shows that immediately after the captains' radio exchange, the VANPORT continued on a straight course, on the edge of the navigational channel, "hugging" the fleeting facility along the west bank. Just as the JUSTIN began pulling out from the bank to top around, the BEATRICE reached the VANPORT's port and began its passing maneuver. At 12:58 pm, the BEATRICE cleared the VANPORT, and Vidrine realized the JUSTIN was turning directly into the VANPORT's path. As the VANPORT immediately **[—4—]** turned to port to avoid the JUSTIN, Vidrine radioed the JUSTIN, "I hope you're backing down," to which Jackson responded, "Roger, roger, I'm backing away from you."

Too late. Not a minute after, the barges the JUSTIN was towing struck the VANPORT's lead barge. After the collision, Jackson told Vidrine: "[T]hat's why I asked you whether you thought it would be all right for me to go ahead and start turning . . . . I ain't but six foot off the bank." The collision caused about $1.2 million in damage to the VANPORT's cargo. Insurers of the VANPORT reimbursed the cargo owner for the full amount, and Deloach, the VANPORT's owner, took an assignment of any claim against the JUSTIN's owner, Marquette.

Litigation ensued.

B.

Deloach first sued Marquette, alleging Jackson's negligence caused the collision. Marquette counterclaimed, alleging Vidrine was contributorily negligent. The district court held a two-day bench trial, hearing testimony from both captains as well as two expert witnesses. The court found both captains at fault, apportioning 70% to Jackson and 30% to Vidrine. Its **{-605-}** findings were based on ordinary negligence, the *Pennsylvania* Rule,[2] and negligence by violating an industry custom.

As to ordinary negligence, the court "determine[d] that both captains failed to adhere to a standard of reasonable care under the circumstances, but that defendant [the JUSTIN] was more at fault than plaintiff [the **[—5—]** VANPORT]." This was primarily because "the JUSTIN's decision to perform the top around maneuver in front of oncoming traffic created the unsafe circumstances that led to the collision." As the downriver vessel, the VANPORT had the right of way, and Jackson knew the BEATRICE was passing the VANPORT. Therefore, "the JUSTIN should have waited until the channel was clear before topping around." The JUSTIN was also negligent "in failing to clearly communicate its intent to turn in front of, rather than behind or to the side of, the VANPORT." Jackson's ambiguous communications "did not adequately convey [his] intent to reverse the typical right-of-way pattern."

On the other hand, the district court found the VANPORT negligent in agreeing "that the JUSTIN could begin the top around maneuver before the VANPORT had safely passed the JUSTIN." Vidrine should have realized from Rose Point data that "it was too early for the JUSTIN to begin its turn." Accordingly, the

---

[1] According to the district court, "Rose Point is a marine navigation software program that allows vessel captains to see their vessel's trajectory as well as the position of other vessels near them." Courts have recognized Rose Point as "the industry standard," which "automatically and objectively record[s] vessel location and movement on a proven industry standard electronic chart." *Marquette Transp. Co., LLC v. M/V Century Dream*, No. CV 16-522, 2017 WL 677814, at *2 (E.D. La. Feb. 21, 2017).

[2] Under the so-called *Pennsylvania* Rule, a ship that violates a statute designed to prevent collisions is liable unless it can prove its violation "could not have been a cause of the collision." *Pennzoil Producing Co. v. Offshore Exp., Inc.*, 943 F.2d 1465, 1472 (5th Cir. 1991) (citing inter alia *The Pennsylvania*, 86 U.S. 125, 136 (1873)).

VANPORT should have instructed the JUSTIN to wait to begin its turn until the VANPORT was clear.

The court also concluded both captains violated several of the Inland Navigational Rules and that their violations caused the collision. *See generally Marine Transp. Lines, Inc. v. M/V Tako Invader*, 37 F.3d 1138, 1144 (5th Cir. 1994) (discussing enactment of Inland Navigational Rules in 1980 "to unify the rules governing navigation in the inland waters of the United States"). According to the court, both captains violated Rule 2, which obliges captains to keep "the ordinary practice of seamen," 33 C.F.R. § 83.02, for the same reasons that both were negligent.[3] The court next found the JUSTIN violated **[—6—]** Rule 14(d), which gives downbound vessels the right-of-way over upbound vessels when two vessels are proceeding head-on. *Id.* § 83.14.[4] The VANPORT had right-of-way as the downriver vessel, and the JUSTIN violated Rule 14(d) "when it performed the top around maneuver in front of the VANPORT." The district court rejected Marquette's argument that the VANPORT violated Rule 14(d) by failing to "propose the manner of passage" as the rule requires. *Id.* The VANPORT had no notice "that the JUSTIN was planning to **{-606-}** move in front of it," and "it was reasonable for the VANPORT to understand that the JUSTIN would turn behind it."

Finally, the district court also found that "neither captain violated Rule 5," which requires captains to maintain a "proper look-out," *id.* § 83.05;[5] that the VANPORT did not violate Rule 6, which requires vessels to "proceed at a safe speed," *id.* § 83.06;[6] and that "both captains violated **[—7—]** Rules 7 and 8," which require captains to use "all available means" to assess risk of collision, *id.* § 83.07(a),[7] and to take appropriate action to avoid collision, *id.* § 83.08.[8] But the court's findings regarding these rules "[did] not

---

[3] Rule 2 (*see* 33 C.F.R. § 83.02(a)) relevantly provides:

> (a) Nothing in these Rules shall exonerate any vessel, or the owner, master, or crew thereof, from the consequences of any neglect to comply with these Rules or of the **[—6—]** neglect of any precaution which may be required by the ordinary practice of seamen, or by the special circumstances of the case.

[4] Rule 14(d) (*see* 33 C.F.R. § 83.14(d)) provides:

> (d) Notwithstanding paragraph (a) of this Rule, a power-driven vessel operating on the Great Lakes, Western Rivers, or waters specified by the Secretary, and proceeding downbound with a following current shall have the right-of-way over an upbound vessel, shall propose the manner of passage, and shall initiate the maneuvering signals prescribed by Rule 34(a)(i) (§ 83.34(a)(i)), as appropriate.

[5] Rule 5 (*see* 33 C.F.R. § 83.05) provides:

> Every vessel shall at all times maintain a proper look-out by sight and hearing as well as by all available means appropriate in the prevailing circumstances and conditions so as to make a full appraisal of the situation and of the risk of collision.

[6] Rule 6 (*see* 33 C.F.R. § 83.06) relevantly provides:

> Every vessel shall at all times proceed at a safe speed so that she can take proper and effective action to avoid collision and be stopped within a distance appropriate to the prevailing circumstances and conditions.

See also id. § 83.06(a), (b) (enumerating various factors for "determining a safe speed").

[7] Rule 7 (*see* 33 C.F.R. § 83.07(a)) relevantly provides:

> (a) Every vessel shall use all available means appropriate to the prevailing circumstances and conditions to determine if risk of collision exists. If there is any doubt such risk shall be deemed to exist.

[8] Rule 8 (*see* 33 C.F.R. § 83.08(a)) relevantly provides:

> (a) Any action taken to avoid collision shall be taken in accordance with the Rules of this subpart (Rules 4–19) (§§ 83.04 through 83.19) and shall, if the circumstances of the case admit, be positive, made in ample time and with due regard to the observance of good seamanship.

See also id. § 83.08(b)–(f) (specifying avoidance measures in specific circumstances).

change the Court's conclusions about the nature of the parties' negligence."[9]

The district court allocated 70% of the liability for the collision to Marquette as owner of the JUSTIN and the remaining 30% to Deloach as owner of the VANPORT, finding that the JUSTIN played a larger role in the collision by "mov[ing] into the channel in front of downstream traffic without taking due care." The VANPORT shared fault because it gave "the JUSTIN permission to begin topping around."

Both parties timely appeal, contesting the district court's allocation of fault. Marquette's argument hinges principally on its contention that, contrary to the district court's ruling, Rule 14(d) required the VANPORT to propose the manner of passage and that the VANPORT's failure to do so led to the collision. Marquette further argues that the district court's **[—8—]** misinterpretation of Rule 14(d) led to errors in its holdings regarding Rules 5, 6, 7, and 8. Deloach claims the district court erred in apportioning 30% liability to the VANPORT and in omitting prejudgment interest from Deloach's damage award.

II.

"The standard of review for a bench trial is well established: findings of fact are reviewed for clear error and legal issues are reviewed *de novo*." *Luwisch v. Am. Marine Corp.*, 956 F.3d 320, 326, 8 Adm. R. 181, 182 (5th Cir. 2020) (quoting *Barto v. Shore Constr., LLC*, 801 F.3d 465, 471, 3 Adm. R. 415, 416 (5th Cir. 2015)). "[W]e will upset the district court's findings **{-607-}** of fact only if we are 'left with the definite and firm conviction that a mistake has been committed.'" *Id.*, 8 Adm. R. at 182 (citation omitted). "[F]indings of fact include determinations of negligence, apportionment of fault, and calculation of damages." *Id.*, 8 Adm. R. at 182 (citing *DePerrodil v. Bozovic Marine, Inc.*, 842 F.3d 352, 356, 358, 361, 4 Adm. R. 308, 309, 310, 313 (5th Cir. 2016)). We grant "even 'greater deference to the trial court's findings when they are based on determinations of credibility.'" *Id.*, 8 Adm. R. at 182 (quoting *Guzman v. Hacienda Records & Recording Studio, Inc.*, 808 F.3d 1031, 1036 (5th Cir. 2015)). And we employ "a strong presumption that the court's findings must be sustained even though this court might have weighed the evidence differently." *Id.*, 8 Adm. R. at 182 (quoting *Johnson v. Cenac Towing, Inc.*, 544 F.3d 296, 303 (5th Cir. 2008)).

III.

A.

We first address Marquette's argument that the district court misinterpreted Rule 14(d) when it held that the VANPORT was under no duty to "propose the manner of passage." We disagree.

The Inland Navigational Rules contain eight rules governing vessels' rights-of-way. *See* 33 C.F.R. §§ 83.11–83.18. Rule 14, which the parties agree **[—9—]** applies to the collision, covers "[h]ead-on situation[s]." *Id.* § 83.14. It provides in relevant part:

> [A] power-driven vessel operating on the Great Lakes, Western Rivers, or waters specified by the Secretary, and proceeding downbound with a following current shall have the right-of-way over an upbound vessel, shall propose the manner of passage, and shall initiate . . . maneuvering signals . . . as appropriate.

Id. § 83.14(d).

Marquette argues that the district court ignored Rule 14(d)'s requirement that the downriver vessel "propose the manner of passage" and initiate appropriate maneuvering signals. According to Marquette, "the VANPORT . . . instructed the JUSTIN she could begin her downriver turn." Marquette argues the district court "defiantly . . . ignored the overarching purpose of Rule 14"—namely, that the downbound vessel "with the right of way, must use its right of way appropriately and communicate with the JUSTIN." It claims

[9] The district court also rejected Marquette's argument that pursuant to industry custom, the vessels had "established a top around agreement" and that the VANPORT violated that agreement. Marquette does not contest this conclusion.

"[t]hat 'right of way' does not mean that the JUSTIN must 'yield,' only that the right of way vessel like VANPORT gets to dictate how the two vessels meet." According to Marquette, the district court erred in finding the VANPORT lacked notice of the situation to trigger its obligation to propose passage, as the VANPORT "knew that she was heading downriver in the direction of the JUSTIN."

We disagree for two reasons. First, while Marquette paints its appeal as a *de novo* attack on the district court's legal reasoning, its Rule 14(d) argument turns on whether the court was correct that the VANPORT lacked notice that the two vessels were on a collision course. That is a fact finding we review only for clear error. *See Luwisch*, 956 F.3d at 326, 8 Adm. R. at 182. Marquette insists that Vidrine knew the VANPORT was heading towards the JUSTIN and that the district court's ruling therefore "sidestep[ped] the VANPORT's **[—10—]** obligation to propose a safe manner of passage." But this argument contradicts the district court's findings that the VANPORT lacked notice "that the JUSTIN was planning to move in front of it" and that "it was reasonable for the VANPORT to understand that the JUSTIN would turn behind it." If Marquette wishes to challenge those findings, it must show they were not only incorrect but clearly erroneous. Marquette does not try to meet this standard, and our review of the record detects no clear error.

Second, even applying *de novo* review, we reject Marquette's interpretation of Rule 14(d). At the outset, we disagree **{-608-}** with Marquette's unfounded claim that the VANPORT's right-of-way "does not mean that the JUSTIN must 'yield.'" The term "right-of-way" means precisely that: it is "[t]he right to take precedence in traffic." *Right-of-way*, BLACK'S LAW DICTIONARY (11th ed. 2019). As the district court noted, we have previously recognized the "failure to yield the right-of-way" as an act of negligence. *Union Oil Co. of Cal. v. Tug Mary Malloy*, 414 F.2d 669, 673 (5th Cir. 1969). Marquette tries to distinguish *Mary Malloy* merely because it was not a head-on case involving Rule 14(d), but instead involved a collision between two ships traveling in the same direction. *See id.* at 671. That is immaterial. The decision is still premised on the commonsense notion that the corollary of one vessel's right-of-way is the other's duty to yield.[10] Here, the district court found that the upbound JUSTIN's failure to yield to the downbound VANPORT violated the VANPORT's right-of-way. And, as **[—11—]** explained, Marquette has failed to show any clear error in the district court's findings concerning the circumstances of the collision.

We similarly reject Marquette's reading of Rule 14(d) to impose a "mandatory duty to propose safe passage," notwithstanding the VANPORT's lack of notice of the JUSTIN's planned maneuver. To begin with, Marquette misreads Rule 14(d)'s text, which states that the downbound vessel "shall propose the manner of passage," but only "as appropriate." 33 C.F.R. § 83.14(d).[11] Marquette also cites *Marine Transport Lines, Inc., v. M/V Tako Invader*, 37 F.3d at 1145, but that decision does not help its argument. There, we held that a downbound vessel "may force a departure from" the usual rule that head-on vessels pass on their port sides, *see* 33 C.F.R. § 83.14(a), "provided" the downbound vessel "propose[s] the manner of passage" in compliance with Rule 14(d). *Marine Transport Lines* does not hold or even suggest that a downbound vessel has an affirmative duty, notwithstanding its right-of-way, to propose the manner of passage. Rather, it treats the "manner of passage" language in Rule 14(d) as a means for the downbound vessel to bypass

[10] *See, e.g., id.* at 672 (stating the "primary issue" was whether the record "sustain[ed] the trial court's finding that the MARY MAL[L]OY's *failure to yield the right-of-way* to the PURE OIL was the proximate cause of the collision" (emphasis added)); *id.* at 672 n.3 (rejecting appellant's "halfhearted[]" attack on district court's negligence finding based on the argument that "the MARY MALLOY was under no duty to *yield the right-of-way* to the PURE OIL" (emphasis added)).

[11] Under the series-qualifier canon, "as appropriate" modifies the "shall propose" obligation, because the phrase is separated by a comma from a list of three parallel "shall" verbs. *See* ANTONIN SCALIA & BRYAN A. GARNER, READING LAW: THE INTERPRETATION OF LEGAL TEXTS 147–51 (2012).

the ordinary port-to-port passage standard in Rule 14(a). *See id.*[12] Neither party argues that such a situation was presented here. *Marine Transport Lines* is therefore irrelevant. **[—12—]**

B.

Marquette next argues that the district court misinterpreted Rules 5, 6, 7, and 8. It contends the district court's misreading of Rule 14(d) and its holding that the VANPORT had the right-of-way infected its analyses under these other rules.

We reject this argument for three reasons. First, as discussed above, Marquette has not shown the district court misinterpreted **{–609–}** Rule 14(d) or that the VANPORT's right-of-way was ineffective. Because its arguments regarding Rules 5 through 8 flow from the district court's putative misreading of Rule 14(d), we reject these arguments too. Second, the district court's holdings regarding Rules 5 through 8 were made alternatively to its determinations on ordinary negligence. The court found "that these rules [did] not change [its] conclusions about the nature of the parties' negligence." Marquette acknowledges this but fails to develop any argument that the district court erred in its findings regarding ordinary negligence. Accordingly, even if we agreed with Marquette's positions regarding these rules (something we do not decide), the district court's other findings would remain unaffected. Finally, as with Rule 14(d), Marquette's challenges under Rules 5 through 8 repeatedly contest the district court's fact findings without showing clear error. For example, Marquette argues the court erred in finding the VANPORT "maintained a safe speed," claiming that the VANPORT's pre-collision speed increase "could not have been due to 'a fast river current.'" But Marquette fails to develop an argument that this conclusion was clearly erroneous.

[12] Moreover, *Marine Transport Lines* also involved the "Narrow Channel Rule" in Rule 9. *Id.* at 1142–44; *see* 33 C.F.R. § 83.09. That rule for "[a] vessel proceeding along the course of a narrow channel or fairway," *id.* § 83.09(a)(i), has no application to this case.

C.

We turn to Deloach's cross-appeal. Deloach contends the district court erred in assigning the VANPORT 30% of the liability for the collision. We disagree. **[—13—]**

We review "a trial court's finding on apportionment of relative fault in a maritime collision" only for clear error. *In re Settoon Towing, L.L.C.*, 859 F.3d 340, 344, 5 Adm. R. 266, 267 (5th Cir. 2017) (citing *Tokio Marine & Fire Ins. Co. v. FLORA MV*, 235 F.3d 963, 970 (5th Cir. 2001)). Our review is "deferential," and we will not second-guess the district court's weighing of the facts. *Id.* at 353, 5 Adm. R. at 275. "Even if we might have given different weight to different pieces of evidence than did the district court, this is not a reason to disturb that court's findings of relative responsibility, absent a showing of clear error." *Id.*, 5 Adm. R. at 275 (alteration omitted) (quoting *Tokio Marine*, 235 F.3d at 971). Our deference "is particularly important in a bench trial where the district court's opportunity to judge the witnesses' credibility weighs strongly." *Id.*, 5 Adm. R. at 275 (citing *Canal Barge Co. v. Torco Oil Co.*, 220 F.3d 370, 375 (5th Cir. 2000)). Even if the district court fails to "provide a detailed explanation for its apportionment of fault," we presume that "it made the requisite allocation of fault based on the facts before it." *Id.* at 353, 5 Adm. R. at 275.

Deloach fails to identify clear error. Deloach first argues Vidrine was "the essentially innocent party," claiming the court's allocation of fault to Deloach "was based solely on Vidrine's verbal assent . . . to Jackson's dual message that he would begin topping-around but knew he had to stay out [sic] VANPORT's way." This ignores the court's findings that Vidrine could have seen the JUSTIN on the VANPORT's Rose Point display and that he "should have known that it was too early for the JUSTIN to begin its turn." Moreover, Deloach's argument does not touch the court's finding that Vidrine should have clarified his understanding of the JUSTIN's position and intentions and that this failure was partially responsible for the collision.

For the same reason, we reject Deloach's argument that Vidrine "was not negligent in giving his assent" to the JUSTIN to top around. According to Deloach, Vidrine's understanding that the JUSTIN intended to stay in the slack water under the fleet instead of swinging out into the channel was **[—14—]** objectively reasonable, such that Vidrine cannot be faulted for approving that plan. But this argument founders on the district court's fact finding that **{–610–}** Vidrine should have clarified his understanding and that his failure to do so led to the collision.[13] Here, again, we see no clear error.

Relatedly, Deloach argues Vidrine did not give the JUSTIN permission to top around in the navigational channel. It claims that had the JUSTIN stayed in the slack water as Vidrine had understood, the accident would not have taken place, and that "Vidrine had no choice but to rely on Jackson to perform his maneuver competently." This argument again fails to grapple with the district court's finding that Vidrine could have prevented the incident by making clearer his understanding of the JUSTIN's location and intentions.

In sum, Deloach fails to pinpoint any clear error in the district court's allocation of 30% liability to the VANPORT.

D.

Finally, we address Deloach's argument that it was owed prejudgment interest as a prevailing maritime party. We remand the matter to consider whether prejudgment interest is appropriate.

"Under maritime law, the awarding of prejudgment interest is the rule rather than the exception, and, in practice, is well-nigh automatic." *Reeled Tubing, Inc. v. M/V Chad G*, 794 F.2d 1026, 1028 (5th Cir. 1986) (citing *Inland Oil & Transp. Co. v. Ark-White Towing Co.*, 696 F.2d 321, 327 (5th Cir. 1983)). The district court's decision to award or withhold prejudgment **[—15—]** interest is reviewed for abuse of discretion, but "[a] trial court has the discretion to deny prejudgment interest only where peculiar circumstances would make such an award inequitable." *Id.* (citing *Inland Oil*, 696 F.2d at 327).

Here, neither the district court's order nor its judgment awards or denies prejudgment interest. Unable to locate any findings about the propriety of prejudgment interest, we are unable to review Deloach's argument. We therefore remand for the limited purpose of considering prejudgment interest. *Cf. Whitfield v. Lindemann*, 853 F.2d 1298, 1306 (5th Cir. 1988) (remanding to determine propriety of prejudgment interest and noting lack of analysis "makes it difficult to weigh the propriety of the district court's exercise of discretion").

* * *

We AFFIRM the district court's judgment apportioning fault between the parties. We REMAND solely to determine whether prejudgment interest is proper and, if so, in what amount.

---

[13] For similar reasons, we also reject Deloach's argument that Vidrine's failure to "remind Jackson" to stay clear of the VANPORT was not negligent. Vidrine's understanding about how the JUSTIN intended to maneuver, even if reasonable, did not alleviate the need for Vidrine to communicate clearly with Jackson to avoid a collision.

United States Court of Appeals
for the Fifth Circuit

No. 19-20506

SANCHEZ
vs.
SMART FABRICATORS OF TEX., L.L.C.

Appeal from the United States District Court for the Southern District of Texas

ON PETITION FOR REHEARING EN BANC

(Opinion March 11, 2020, 5 Cir., 2020, 952 F.3d 620, withdrawn)
(Opinion August 14, 2020, 5 Cir., 2020, 970 F.3d 550, 8 Adm. R. 222)

Decided: October 30, 2020

Citation: 978 F.3d 976, 8 Adm. R. 235 (5th Cir. 2020) (en banc).

Before **OWEN,** Chief Judge, and **JONES, SMITH, STEWART, DENNIS, ELROD, SOUTHWICK, HAYNES, GRAVES, HIGGINSON, COSTA, WILLETT, HO, DUNCAN, ENGELHARDT, OLDHAM,** and **WILSON,** Circuit Judges.

[—1—] {-976-} PER CURIAM: [—2—]

A member of the court having requested a poll on the petition for rehearing en banc, and a majority of the circuit judges in regular active service and not disqualified having voted in favor,

IT IS ORDERED that this cause shall be reheard by the court en banc with oral argument on a date hereafter to be fixed. The Clerk will specify a briefing schedule for the filing of supplemental briefs. Pursuant to 5th Cir. R. 41.3, the panel opinion in this case dated August 14, 2020, is vacated.

United States Court of Appeals
for the Fifth Circuit

No. 19-40580

RAICEVIC
vs.
FIELDWOOD ENERGY, L.L.C.

Appeal from the United States District Court for the Southern District of Texas

Decided: October 28, 2020
Published: November 10, 2020

Citation: 979 F.3d 1027, 8 Adm. R. 236 (5th Cir. 2020).

Before **SMITH, WILLETT,** and **DUNCAN,** Circuit Judges.

[—1—] {-1029-} PER CURIAM: **{-1030-}**

After injuring his back while working on Fieldwood Energy's offshore platform, Milorad Raicevic sued Fieldwood (and the platform operators) for negligence. The jury found that Fieldwood was the only defendant that was negligent, attributing 50% of the responsibility to the company. The jury attributed the other 50% to Raicevic. After trial, and before entering judgment, the district court requested further briefing on Fieldwood's defense under the exclusive-remedy provision of the Longshore and Harbor Workers' Compensation Act. The district court entered judgment for **[—2—]** Defendants (including Fieldwood) because it found that Raicevic was Fieldwood's borrowed employee, and thus the LHWCA's exclusive-remedy provision gave Fieldwood tort immunity. Because we agree that the LHWCA was Raicevic's exclusive remedy, we affirm.

I

Waukesha Pearce Industries, Inc. (not a defendant in this case) employed Raicevic as an offshore platform mechanic beginning in 2008. While still employed by Waukesha Pearce, Raicevic worked on Fieldwood's offshore platform located on the outer continental shelf in the Gulf of Mexico. Almost a year into working (and sleeping) on Fieldwood's platform, Raicevic awoke after midnight to an alarm blaring in the mechanic's room. Raicevic slipped and fell twice, due to oil that had leaked on the floor, while trying to address the mechanical issue that triggered the alarm.

Raicevic suffered back injuries that necessitated various treatments, including surgery, physical therapy, and steroid injections. Raicevic received coverage for these treatments through Waukesha Pearce's workers' compensation benefits, but it is unclear whether the benefits came from state plans or the LHWCA.

Raicevic sued Fieldwood and the platform operators for negligence. Fieldwood countered that Raicevic was its borrowed employee, so various workers' compensation schemes, including the LHWCA, precluded Raicevic's tort claim. Raicivec filed a motion in limine to bar any discussion of workers' compensation insurance at trial, and the district court granted the motion.

At trial, the jury found that Fieldwood and Raicevic were each 50% responsible for Raicevic's injuries. The jury also made special findings about the factors that a court weighs to decide borrowed employee status. But **[—3—]** because of the motion in limine, the jury made no findings about any other issues related to Fieldwood's LHWCA defense.

After trial, but before entering judgment, the district court requested further briefing on Fieldwood's LHWCA defense. The post-trial briefing focused on two necessary conditions for the LHWCA to apply and thus bar Raicevic's negligence claim: (1) Was Raicevic Fieldwood's borrowed employee? and (2) Did Fieldwood secure workers' compensation benefits under the LHWCA? Considering the jury's findings on the factors of borrowed-employee status and the post-trial briefing, the district court concluded that both conditions were met. Accordingly, the court rendered judgment for all defendants because the LHWCA gave Fieldwood tort immunity, and the jury found that the other defendants were not negligent. Raicevic now appeals, challenging the district court's two findings on the LHWCA defense.

II

After a trial, we review questions of law de novo, "while questions of fact are reviewed for clear error." **{-1031-}** *Anne Harding v. Cty. of Dallas*, 948 F.3d 302, 306–07 (5th Cir. 2020). So here, we review anew the core legal question: whether Raicevic was Fieldwood's borrowed employee. *See Billizon v. Conoco, Inc.*, 993 F.2d 104, 105 (5th Cir. 1993). And we review for clear error the key factual finding: that Fieldwood secured benefits under the LHWCA.

III

Under the Outer Continental Shelf Lands Act, an employee's exclusive remedy for a work-related injury is the LHWCA. 43 U.S.C. § 1333(a)(1) and (b); 33 U.S.C. § 905(a). This means that, if applicable, the LHWCA would preclude a tort action like Raicevic's. But this exclusivity provision only applies to (1) employers who (2) "secure payment of **[—4—]** compensation" under the LHWCA. 33 U.S.C. § 905(a). Raicevic argues that Fieldwood cannot satisfy either requirement.

A

Turning first to the question of Raicevic's employer, Fieldwood must show that Raicevic was its borrowed employee in order to have tort immunity under the LHWCA. *Melancon v. Amoco Prod. Co.*, 834 F.2d 1238, 1243 (5th Cir.), *amended on reh'g in part sub nom. Melancon v. Amoco Prods. Co.*, 841 F.2d 572 (5th Cir. 1988). To determine whether an employee is a "borrowed employee," we consider the nine factors articulated in *Ruiz v. Shell Oil Company*:

1. Who had control over the employee and the work he was performing, beyond mere suggestion of details or cooperation?
2. Whose work was being performed?
3. Was there an agreement, understanding, or meeting of the minds between the original and the borrowing employer?
4. Did the employee acquiesce in the new work situation?
5. Did the original employer terminate his relationship with the employee?
6. Who furnished tools and place for performance?
7. Was the new employment over a considerable length of time?
8. Who had the right to discharge the employee?
9. Who had the obligation to pay the employee?

413 F.2d 310 (5th Cir. 1969); *see also Melancon*, 834 F.2d at 1244.

These nine factual inquiries underlie borrowed-employee status, but the ultimate determination of whether an employee is a borrowed employee is a question of law for the court to decide. *Melancon*, 834 F.2d at 1244.

The district court submitted these nine questions to the jury. And the parties acknowledge that the jury's findings do not point uniformly in one **[—5—]** direction. After considering the jury's findings and the parties' post-trial briefing on the issue, the district court determined that Raicevic was Fieldwood's borrowed employee. Raicevic now challenges that determination; he does not challenge the jury's factual findings.

Determining borrowed-employee status, particularly in the LHWCA context, is a complex question of law. *Gaudet v. Exxon Corp.*, 562 F.2d 351, 358 (5th Cir. 1977). A court must consider not only the nine factors, "but the implications to be drawn from" them. *Id.* And "in different cases, [] certain of these factors may be more important than others, at least in the light of the facts [] before the court." *Alday v. Patterson Truck Line, Inc.*, 750 F.2d 375, 376 (5th Cir. 1985).

Further, we originally created the nine-factor test in the respondeat-superior **{-1032-}** context. *See Gaudet*, 562 F.2d at 356. But in the LHWCA context, the test is not used to impute liability but "to escape it through the exclusive remedy provisions." *Id.* As we have explained:

> Although the coverage of the LHWCA is not contractual and does not depend

> upon the consent of the parties, nonetheless when an employee begins work for an employer under the coverage of the LHWCA, he is presumed to have consented to the Act's trade-off of possibly large common law damages for smaller but certain LHWCA benefits. And by the very act of continuing in employment, he may be assumed to agree that, considering the likelihood of injury and the likely severity of injury within the working conditions he experiences, the benefits offered by the LHWCA in the event of injury are acceptable.

Id. So in assessing the nine factors, we focus on whether the employee has consented (implicitly or explicitly) to this statutory trade-off. **[—6—]**

With that focus in mind, we now briefly review the nine factors. And we conclude that Raicevic was Fieldwood's borrowed employee, although we do so for reasons somewhat different from those given by the district court.[1]

We start with the easier factors in this case. The jury's findings as to factors 2, 4, and 6—that Raicevic was performing Fieldwood's work, Raicevic acquiesced in the work situation, and Fieldwood provided the tools and place of work—clearly favor Fieldwood (borrowed-employee status). But the jury's finding as to factor 5—that Waukesha Pearce did not terminate its relationship with Raicevic prior to his injury—favors Raicevic (no borrowed-employee status).

For the remaining factors, there is considerable dispute about the implications we should draw from the jury's findings.

Factor One. The jury found that Fieldwood did not have control over Raicevic's work beyond merely suggesting details. Raicevic argues that the **[—7—]** jury's finding should weigh in his favor because Waukesha Pearce, not Fieldwood, told him to work on Fieldwood's platform; no one from Fieldwood told him exactly how to do the repairs; and his direct supervisor was a Waukesha Pearce field service manager. Fieldwood, on the other hand, argues that it told Raicevic what to inspect on the platform, and when and where to conduct **{–1033–}** those inspections; two Fieldwood employees supervised Raicevic—Raicevic even claimed that one was the "best boss" he ever had; and the Waukesha Pearce supervisor was never on Fieldwood's platform and didn't provide any guidance as to Raicevic's actual work for Fieldwood.

In the LHWCA context, we have previously rejected the arguments Raicevic makes and held that the arguments Fieldwood makes indicate borrowed-employee status. *See, e.g.*, *Melancon*, 834 F.2d at 1245 (holding that control factor favored borrowed-employee status where employee took orders from borrowed employer about what work to do and when and where to do it). We thus conclude that the jury's finding—that Fieldwood didn't control Raicevic—does not preclude, or even

[1] While the district court came to the correct conclusion, it did so via an improper interpretation of our cases. The court gave a thorough overview of our caselaw discussing how to weigh the nine factors and noted that our decision in *Gaudet v. Exxon Corporation* stated that factors 4–7 were "most pertinent when the borrowed employee doctrine is used as a defense to common law liability in the LHWCA context." 562 F.2d at 357. So far so good. But then, the district court analyzed only those four factors, claiming that the other five factors were not "essential" and treating them as if they were completely disposable. *Gaudet* does not support this nor, as Raicevic points out, do the cases that followed. In *Gaudet*, we said that looking at factors 4–7 was a "suggested focus within" the nine-factor test. *Gaudet*, 562 F.2d at 359. And since *Gaudet*, we have repeatedly stated that out of the nine factors, no single factor or combination of them is determinative. *Brown v. Union Oil Co.*, 984 F.2d 674, 676 (5th Cir. 1993); *Fontenot v. Mobil Oil Expl. & Producing Se., Inc.*, 997 F.2d 881 (5th Cir. 1993) (per curiam) (stating that *Gaudet*'s holding was that the nine "factors are to be weighed as appropriate in each particular case"); *Mosley v. Wood Grp. PSN, Inc.*, 760 F. App'x 352, 359 n.8 (5th Cir. 2019) (per curiam). We have also said that "in many of our prior cases," the first of the nine factors—who controlled the employee's work—was "central" to the analysis even though *Gaudet* "deemphasized" this factor. *Brown*, 984 F.2d at 676. While determining how to weigh the nine factors will depend on the facts of the case, no factor can be categorically excluded from the analysis.

necessarily weigh against, borrowed-employee status.

Factor Three. The jury found, and no one disputes, that Waukesha Pearce and Fieldwood had a written agreement that said Raicevic was an independent contractor, not Fieldwood's employee. But even Raicevic acknowledges that this type of contract "does not automatically prevent borrowed employee status." *Brown v. Union Oil Co.*, 984 F.2d 674, 677–78 (5th Cir. 1993). The parties' actions can waive or modify an independent-contractor provision. *Id.* And we have previously found an independent-contractor agreement modified by the parties' behavior when there is evidence showing that all parties understood that the employee "would be taking his instructions from" the borrowed employer. *Melancon*, 834 F.2d at 1245. The jury's finding that there was a contract says nothing about whether the parties modified or waived that contract. **[—8—]**

Here, there is evidence that Raicevic took instructions from and was supervised by Fieldwood employees. Raicevic admitted that he had to follow Fieldwood's instructions and get Fieldwood's permission for major repairs. Raicevic counters only that the contract itself is clear, and that the jury's finding that Fieldwood didn't control Raicevic suggests that there was no waiver or modification. Without deciding whether the parties modified the contract, we hold that the evidence demonstrating Fieldwood's supervision of and instruction to Raicevic is enough to make this factor neutral. In other words, the existence of the contract does not counsel against finding borrowed-employee status.

Factor Seven. We have often found that the length of the new employment is a neutral factor unless the new employment lasted for years. If it did, that favors borrowed-employee status. *Mays v. Dir., Office of Workers' Comp. Programs*, 938 F.3d 637, 646, 7 Adm. R. 309, 314 (5th Cir. 2019) (collecting cases). The jury found that Raicevic's one year on the Fieldwood platform was not a "considerable" length of time. But in the LHWCA context, one year seems long enough to accept the risks of the job and consent to the statutory trade-off of receiving benefits in lieu of the possibility of winning a tort suit. Thus, this factor tilts in Fieldwood's favor (borrowed-employee status).

Factors Eight and Nine. The jury found that Fieldwood did not have the right to discharge or the obligation to pay Raicevic, suggesting that these last two factors weigh in favor of no borrowed-employee status. But as Fieldwood points out, we weigh these factors differently in the LHWCA and respondeat-superior contexts.

As to the right to discharge—factor eight—the focus is on whether Fieldwood had the right to "terminate [Raicevic's] services" for Fieldwood, not whether it had the right to terminate his employment in general. **{-1034-}** *Capps v.* **[—9—]** *N.L. Baroid-NL Indus., Inc.*, 784 F.2d 615, 618 (5th Cir. 1986). Because Fieldwood had the right to remove Raicevic from working on its platform at any time, factor eight favors borrowed-employee status.

The obligation to pay—factor nine—does not focus on who paid Raicevic. The more helpful question is: Where did the funds originally come from? *Id.* Here, Fieldwood paid Waukesha Pearce for Raicevic's work, then Waukesha Pearce paid Raicevic. That is enough to skew the factor in Fieldwood's favor. *See Melancon*, 834 F.2d at 1246.

All in all, only one factor (five) plainly favors Raicevic. We therefore agree with the district court that Raicevic was Fieldwood's borrowed employee, meaning Fieldwood can invoke the LHWCA as a bar to Raicevic's tort claim unless any exceptions apply.

B

One exception to LHWCA tort immunity is relevant here. Raicevic's tort claim is not barred if Fieldwood "fail[ed] to secure payment of compensation as required by" the LHWCA. 33 U.S.C. § 905(a); *Total Marine Servs., Inc. v. Dir., Office of Worker's Comp. Programs*, 87 F.3d 774, 778 (5th Cir. 1996). The parties did not submit this issue to the jury, so the district court made a fact finding under Federal Rule of Civil Procedure 49(a)(3). *See also Taherzadeh v. Clements*, 781 F.2d 1093, 1100 (5th Cir. 1986) ("In the absence of a demand by the parties that an issue be submitted, and if such issue is omitted, [Rule 49(a)] allows the Court to make its own findings on the omitted issue.").

The district court found that Fieldwood had LHWCA workers' compensation insurance at the time of Raicevic's injury, and therefore Fieldwood could invoke the LHWCA as a bar to Raicevic's tort claim. As noted above, we review the district court's factual finding for clear error. *Heck v. Triche*, 775 F.3d 265, 282 (5th Cir. 2014). **[—10—]**

Raicevic argues that the question is not just whether Fieldwood had LHWCA insurance, but whether any employer (Waukesha Pearce or Fieldwood) paid Raicevic benefits specifically under the LHWCA. Raicevic also says that the district court erred because the post-trial evidence Fieldwood submitted on the issue was untimely. Both arguments fail.

We have never directly addressed Raicevic's first argument—that to invoke the LHWCA as a defense, an employer must prove not just that it had LHWCA insurance, but that it paid benefits under that insurance to the employee. As the language of the LHWCA and our cases show, that standard is too demanding. In *Thibodeaux v. J. Ray McDermott & Company*, the employee argued that the employer failed to "secure payment of compensation" because it did not properly post the required notice about the LHWCA. 276 F.2d 42, 46 (5th Cir. 1960). We held that even assuming the notice was inadequate, the employer had purchased LHWCA insurance, and that's all it needed to do to "secure payment." *Id.* The statute contains specific provisions about "how and in what manner an employer shall comply with the obligation to secure payment of compensation." *Id.* In other words, the statute makes clear what it means to "secure payment"—buy insurance or receive approval to pay compensation benefits directly. 33 U.S.C. § 932(a). *See also Melancon*, 834 F.2d at 1247 n.17 ("There is no requirement that tort immunity under § 905(a) attaches only to an employer who actually pays for his employees' worker's compensation (i.e. the premiums for the worker's compensation insurance coverage)."). **{-1035-}**

Here, the evidence showed that both Fieldwood and Waukesha Pearce had LHWCA insurance at the time of Raicevic's injury. That is **[—11—]** enough for Fieldwood to invoke the LHWCA's exclusive-recovery provision.[2]

Finally, the district court's consideration of Fieldwood's post-trial evidence was proper. The parties did not submit the issue of workers' compensation insurance to the jury. In fact, Raicevic filed a motion in limine, which the district court granted, to bar any discussion of workers' compensation insurance at trial. So after trial, the district court asked for further briefing on these issues, and Fieldwood submitted an affidavit with its briefing to prove it had LHWCA insurance at the time of Raicevic's injury. Raicevic points to no cases that would prohibit the court, as the factfinder on this issue, from considering the post-trial evidence and briefing. The district court committed no error.

IV

Because we find that Fieldwood has tort immunity, the district court correctly entered judgment for the Defendants. We AFFIRM.

---

[2] It appears that just two district courts have addressed this issue, and both have found that securing payment means only obtaining LHWCA insurance. *Birkenbach v. Nat'l Gypsum Co.*, No. 13-14607, 2014 WL 2931795, at *5 (E.D. Mich. June 30, 2014); *In re Natures Way Marine, LLC*, 984 F. Supp. 2d 1231, 1243 (S.D. Ala. 2013). "The LHWCA provides that the employer must secure payment of compensation, and binding case law explains this as the long-range method whereby the employer satisfies the Department of Labor that it can, that is, *it has the potential,* to pay compensation payments when/if required to do so under the Act. The LHWCA does not place any additional burden on the employer to immediately and actually make compensation payments to individual injured employees." *See In re Natures Way Marine*, 984 F. Supp. 2d at 1243 (emphasis in original).

United States Court of Appeals for the Fifth Circuit

No. 20-40274

IN RE SOUTHERN RECYCLING, L.L.C.

Appeal from the United States District Court for the Southern District of Texas

Decided: December 7, 2020

Citation: 982 F.3d 374, 8 Adm. R. 241 (5th Cir. 2020).

Before **CLEMENT, HO,** and **DUNCAN,** Circuit Judges.

[—2—] {-377-} CLEMENT, Circuit Judge:

After an accident during shipbreaking operations killed one worker and injured another, Southern Recycling, L.L.C., brought a petition for exoneration or limitation of liability under the Limitation of Liability Act. 46 U.S.C. § 30501, *et seq.* **{-378-}** Claimants Nestor Aguilar (the injured worker), Lorena Aguilar, Dora Mendieta (individually, as next friend of Jorge Loredo's son, J.L. III, and on behalf of the estate of Jorge Loredo), and Jane Mary Loredo (collectively, "Claimants") moved to dismiss under Rule 12(b)(1) for lack of admiralty jurisdiction. Claimants argued that the barge Aguilar and Loredo had been working on was no longer a "vessel," and was instead a "dead ship." The district court agreed and dismissed for lack of subject matter jurisdiction. We AFFIRM.

I. Facts and Proceedings

Southern Recycling contracted with Kirby Offshore Marine Operating, LLC ("Kirby") to purchase an articulated tug/barge unit ("ATB") for shipbreaking and recycling. The ATB comprised a tugboat, the M/V Viking, and an oceangoing tanker barge, DBL 134. The parties to the contract agreed that the vessels should be "cleaned of all chemicals, petroleum products, and sludge," so Kirby hired a contractor to clean the vessels. Kirby then transported the ATB from New York to the International Shipbreaking Limited, L.L.C. ("ISL") shipyard in Brownsville, Texas.

ISL, which is an affiliate of Southern Recycling and had custody of the ATB for shipbreaking, began to conduct preliminary shipbreaking activities, including removing deck plates, cutting "small doors" in the cargo tanks, and making cuts to the bow of the barge. ISL workers also began to remove pipes that were part of a heating coil system in the cargo tanks. Unfortunately, because the barge had been used to transport gasoline, other petroleum **[—3—]** products, and ethanol, the pipes contained an unknown amount of gasoline. While Aguilar and Loredo were cutting through one such pipe, a spark ignited a pocket of gasoline vapors, causing an explosion and fire that killed Loredo and severely injured Aguilar. Claimants sued for damages in Texas state court. Shortly thereafter, Southern Recycling brought this suit for limitation or exoneration under the Limitation of Liability Act.

"The Limitation of Liability Act does not confer jurisdiction upon federal courts." *Guillory v. Outboard Motor Corp.*, 956 F.2d 114, 115 (5th Cir. 1992) (per curiam). Instead, courts turn to 28 U.S.C. § 1333(1), which confers admiralty jurisdiction "exclusive of the courts of the States." Admiralty jurisdiction can only attach for Limitation Act purposes when the structure at issue is a "vessel." 46 U.S.C. § 30502. Claimants argued that, because DBL 134 was being broken for scrap when the accident happened, it was a "dead ship"—not a vessel—and the court was without subject matter jurisdiction to hear the limitation claim. In the alternative, Claimants argued that the district court should dismiss under Rule 12(b)(6) or grant summary judgment under Rule 56 for failure to state a claim upon which relief could be granted for the same reason (that the Limitation Act applies only to vessels).

Southern Recycling noted that DBL 134 is still floating in the Brownsville Shipyard and had even been moved since the accident (albeit within the ISL facility). Southern Recycling contended that the cuts were minor and preparatory only, and that DBL 134 retained the essential characteristics of a vessel—including that it still floats. The district court, however, considered photographs of the barge submitted by the parties, including one that depicted "a **gaping hole open to the sea** down to or below its waterline." The district court concluded in a brief opinion that DBL 134 was a dead ship, not a vessel, that it lacked subject matter jurisdiction, and that the **{-379-}** motion to dismiss should be granted. Southern Recycling timely appealed. **[—4—]**

II. STANDARD OF REVIEW

"We review a dismissal for lack of subject matter jurisdiction under Rule 12(b)(1) de novo," applying the same standard as the district court. *Flores v. Pompeo*, 936 F.3d 273, 276 (5th Cir. 2019) (citation omitted). A district court may dismiss a case under Rule 12(b)(1) based on "(1) the complaint alone; (2) the complaint supplemented by undisputed facts evidenced in the record; or (3) the complaint supplemented by undisputed facts plus the court's resolution of disputed facts." *Barrera-Montenegro v. United States*, 74 F.3d 657, 659 (5th Cir. 1996) (quotations omitted). Where, as here, the district court has expressly relied on its resolution of disputed jurisdictional facts, "those findings are reviewed for clear error." *Robinson v. TCI/US W. Commc'ns, Inc.*, 117 F.3d 900, 904 (5th Cir. 1997).

The burden of proving subject matter jurisdiction lies with the party asserting jurisdiction, and it must be proved by a preponderance of the evidence. *Ballew v. Cont'l Airlines, Inc.*, 668 F.3d 777, 781 (5th Cir. 2012) ("The plaintiff must prove by a preponderance of the evidence that the court has jurisdiction based on the complaint and evidence.") (citation omitted).

"We review evidentiary rulings," including both denial of an evidentiary hearing and denial of a request for discovery, "for abuse of discretion." *Freeman v. United States*, 556 F.3d 326, 341 (5th Cir. 2009) (citations omitted).

III. DISCUSSION

Southern Recycling argues first on appeal that the district court applied an inadequately deferential standard of review and should have applied a standard more akin to Rule 12(b)(6) or Rule 56; that is, that the district court should have looked either to the pleadings alone or to the pleadings supported only by undisputed facts. Southern Recycling also contends that the district court substantively erred in its analysis of DBL 134. **[—5—]** Because DBL 134 still floats and has been moved on navigable waters since the accident, Southern Recycling argues that it remains a vessel. Finally, Southern Recycling asks us, in the alternative, to find the district court erred in denying Southern Recycling's request for further discovery and to remand.

A.

We address first Southern Recycling's argument regarding the standard of review. The rule is that courts may resolve disputed jurisdictional facts to decide a 12(b)(1) motion, and a district court that does so is entitled to deference unless the decision is "clearly erroneous." *Williamson v. Tucker*, 645 F.2d 404, 413–14 (5th Cir. 1981). There is, however, an exception to this rule. Citing *M.D.C.G. v. United States*, Southern Recycling argues that "when the issue of jurisdiction is intertwined with the merits, district courts should 'deal with the objection as a direct attack on the merits of the plaintiff's case under either Rule 12(b)(6) or Rule 56.'" 956 F.3d 762, 768–69 (5th Cir. 2020) (quoting *Montez v. Dep't of Navy*, 392 F.3d 147, 150 (5th Cir. 2004)). Because the existence of a vessel is a precondition for the Limitation Act to apply, 46 U.S.C. § 30502, Southern Recycling argues that the issue is intertwined with the merits of its limitation claim and that it is entitled to the heightened Rule 12(b)(6) or Rule 56 standards.

Southern Recycling had submitted an affidavit by ISL's president, Chris Green, claiming that "ISL made no cuts to the **{-380-}** DBL134's hull below the fully loaded waterline and did not otherwise alter the integrity of the DBL134's hull. In other words, DBL134 still floats." Southern Recycling argues now that this proves DBL 134 remains a vessel, or at least that there are genuine disputes of material fact that preclude summary judgment under the Rule 56 standard. FED. R. CIV. P. 56(a). Because the district court expressly decided the motion to dismiss based on resolution of disputed facts under Rule 12(b)(1), we must first decide whether it was correct to do so. **[—6—]**

There is no clear test for when the "intertwined with the merits" exception applies. Southern Recycling argues that it should apply any time the jurisdictional ruling could be dispositive of the claim as a whole. Southern Recycling cites dicta in *Ramming v. United States* that a dismissal for lack of subject matter jurisdiction "does not prevent the plaintiff from pursuing a claim in a court that does have proper jurisdiction" as implying that the usual 12(b)(1) rule only applies where a party can take their claim elsewhere. 281 F.3d 158, 161 (5th Cir. 2001) (per curiam) (citation omitted). This is not the correct implication to take from *Ramming*, and we decline to adopt "dispositive" as the test for when the exception applies.

Following the above comment, the *Ramming* court affirmed dismissal of a suit as time-barred where timeliness was a jurisdictional requirement. *Id.* at 165. In other words, *Ramming* did *not* leave the plaintiff with an alternative forum to pursue his case; the jurisdictional ruling ended it. Although questions about when a claim has accrued typically present a pure (or nearly pure) question of law, both the district court and this court weighed competing fact narratives to make findings about when Ramming should have been on notice that his claim had accrued. *See id.* at 163; *Cloud v. United States*, 126 F. Supp. 2d 1012, 1019–20 (S.D. Tex. 2000); *see also Gonzalez v. United States*, 284 F.3d 281, 287–91 (1st Cir. 2002) (resolving a "*nearly* pure" question of law about when a claim accrued by reference to affidavits, depositions, and other evidence outside the pleadings, before dismissing case for lack of jurisdiction as time-barred under the FTCA) (emphasis added).

To determine whether the exception applies, we look instead to the *extent* to which the jurisdictional question is intertwined with the merits, considering such factors as whether the statutory source of jurisdiction differs from the source of the federal claim and whether judicial economy favors early resolution of the jurisdictional issue. We have also noted that "where the jurisdictional issue can be extricated from the merits and tried as **[—7—]** a separate issue the findings of the district court must be accepted unless they are clearly erroneous." *Williamson*, 645 F.2d at 416 n.10 (citing *McLain v. Real Est. Bd. of New Orleans, Inc.*, 583 F.2d 1315, 1322–23 (5th Cir. 1978)).

We begin with a factor emphasized by our colleagues on the First and Tenth Circuits: whether the court's subject matter jurisdiction is derived from the same statute as the cause of action. *See, e.g., Gonzalez*, 284 F.3d at 287 ("A jurisdictional issue is intertwined with the merits where the court's subject matter jurisdiction depends upon the statute that governs the substantive claims in the case."); *Sizova v. Nat'l Inst. of Standards & Tech.*, 282 F.3d 1320, 1324 (10th Cir. 2002) ("We have stated that subject matter jurisdiction and the merits are considered intertwined when subject matter jurisdiction is dependent upon the same statute which provides the substantive claim in the case." (cleaned up)). **{-381-}**

Here, jurisdiction depends on federal courts' general admiralty jurisdiction, as granted in 28 U.S.C. § 1333(1) and authorized in Article 3, section 2, of the U.S. Constitution, whereas Southern Recycling's claim depends on the Limitation of Liability Act, 46 U.S.C. § 30501, *et seq.* This implies that "vessel" is best understood as an antecedent jurisdictional question. That is, a court must establish that it has admiralty jurisdiction—in this context, because a vessel is involved—to "satisfy itself as to the existence of its power to hear the case." *Williamson*, 645 F.2d at 413. The existence of a vessel in the Limitation Act is better understood to be assumed—since it was required by the antecedent jurisdictional question—than to be a separate element of a limitation claim.

We consider next whether "the jurisdictional issue can be extricated from the merits and tried as a separate issue." *Id.* at

416 n.10. Where vessel status has been addressed in prior cases, it is almost always treated as an independent inquiry. *See, e.g.*, *Lozman v. City of Riviera Beach*, 568 U.S. 115, **[—8—]** 130, 1 Adm. R. 2, 8 (2013) (floating home is not a vessel); *Stewart v. Dutra Constr. Co.*, 543 U.S. 481, 492 (2005) (dredge is a vessel); *Baker v. Dir., Office of Worker's Comp. Programs*, 834 F.3d 542, 547, 4 Adm. R. 276, 278 (5th Cir. 2016) (stationary oil platform is not a vessel). This case is complicated by factual disputes about the physical characteristics of DBL 134 (e.g., whether the hole in the bow is above or below the waterline), but Southern Recycling puts forward no reason why determining basic physical characteristics of the barge should be too complex to extricate from the remainder of a complex limitation action.

By contrast, in the cases Southern Recycling cites,[1] the alleged jurisdictional issues are consistently so intertwined with the underlying causes of action as to be inextricable, such as FTCA cases in which the issue is whether a government employee was "acting within the scope of his employment when he committed [a] tort[ ]." *M.D.C.G.*, 956 F.3d at 768; *see e.g.*, *Montez*, 392 F.3d at 149 (same). The Supreme Court dealt with a similarly inextricable merits issue in *Bell v. Hood*, 327 U.S. 678 (1946). The question was whether the Constitution implied a cause of action for damages when federal officials violated a plaintiff's Fourth and Fifth Amendment rights. *Id.* at 683. *Bell* predated *Bivens v. Six Unknown Named Agents of Fed. Bureau of Narcotics*, 403 U.S. 388 (1971), so it was undecided whether the Constitution implied such a remedy. *Bell*, 327 U.S. at 684. The legal issue was *identical* to the key issue of law (that is, the merits issue): is there a cause **[—9—]** of action for money damages when federal officials violate the Fourth and Fifth Amendments? *Id.* Here, the jurisdictional issue (is DBL 134 a vessel?) is readily extricable from the primary merits issues. **{-382-}**

The ability to extricate the jurisdictional issue is closely related to considerations of judicial economy, which also support treating vessel status as an antecedent jurisdictional inquiry. This court has explained the exception to the normal 12(b)(1) rule by noting that "no purpose is served by indirectly arguing the merits" and that "[j]udicial economy is best promoted when the existence of a federal right is directly reached." *Williamson*, 645 F.2d at 415. The question of whether DBL 134 is a vessel, if treated as an antecedent inquiry, promotes judicial economy.

A limitation action, at its core, is not about whether a structure is or is not a vessel. Rather, it's about consolidating what could otherwise be a multiplicity of separate actions following a maritime incident into a single forum "for determining (1) whether the vessel and its owner are liable at all; (2) whether the owner may in fact limit liability to the value of the vessel and pending freight; (3) the amount of just claims; and (4) how the funds should be distributed to the claimants." THOMAS J. SCHOENBAUM, 2 ADMIRALTY & MAR. L. § 15:6 (6th ed. 2018). We could add to that questions about whether the incident occurred without the "privity and knowledge of the owner," 46 U.S.C. § 30505, and whether there is a dispute as to the value of the vessel. This case involves disputes between Southern Recycling and Claimants, claims and counterclaims among Southern Recycling, Kirby, and Clean Water of New York (the company hired to clean DBL 134), a motion for preliminary injunction and rescission of the contract between Southern Recycling and Kirby, and numerous other claims and counterclaims among various parties to this action—none of

[1] We note that several of the cases Southern Recycling relies on are simply inapposite. For example, Southern Recycling cites to *Williams v. Reeves* for the proposition that a "dismissal for lack of jurisdiction will not be affirmed unless it appears certain that the plaintiff cannot prove any set of facts in support of his claim that would entitle plaintiff to relief." 954 F.3d 729, 734 (5th Cir. 2020) (cleaned up). However, the *Williams* court was looking at a Rule 12(b)(1) motion that was decided on the pleadings, not on the resolution of disputed fact issues. *Williams v. Bryant*, No. 3:17-cv-404-WHB-LRA, 2018 WL 8996382, at *1 (S.D. Miss. Mar. 28, 2018). When a motion to dismiss is decided solely on the pleadings, the plaintiff is entitled to a generous construction similar to a 12(b)(6) dismissal.

which, at their core, center on whether DBL 134 was or was not a vessel. In other words, a limitation action is extremely complex; the vessel inquiry is not. Judicial **[—10—]** economy is served by addressing the antecedent question of jurisdiction at the outset, prior to the remaining merits inquiry.

Because the jurisdictional question of whether DBL 134 is a vessel is antecedent to the merits in a limitation action, rather than intertwined with the merits, the district court did not err in applying the usual Rule 12(b)(1) standard and resolving factual disputes about the physical characteristics of the structure. We review findings of fact for clear error and will only reverse if, "on the entire evidence," we are "left with the definite and firm conviction that a mistake has been committed." *Flores*, 936 F.3d at 276.

B.

We turn now to whether the district court erred in determining that DBL 134 was no longer a vessel. Southern Recycling submits that, when we conduct this analysis, it would be inappropriate for us to consider any evidence in the record that was submitted after the briefs and replies related to Claimant's 12(b)(1) motion. This would include filings in the record associated with Southern Recycling's motion for preliminary injunction against Kirby, since these were submitted over a month after the 12(b)(1) filings. Because (1) the district court had the opportunity to review these materials, (2) Southern Recycling offers no authority to support its argument, (3) Southern Recycling had an opportunity to reply (and did reply) to Kirby's evidence, (4) Southern Recycling does not allege that any of the photos or technical materials are inaccurate or misleading, and (5) this court may "affirm on any ground supported by the record, including one not reached by the district court," *Ballew*, 668 F.3d at 781, we decline Southern Recycling's invitation to ignore evidence.

To understand whether a structure is a vessel, the Supreme Court directs **{-383-}** us to the definition of a vessel Congress provided in 1 U.S.C. § 3: "The word 'vessel' includes every description of watercraft or other artificial **[—11—]** contrivance used, or capable of being used, as a means of transportation on water." *See Stewart*, 543 U.S. at 489. The Supreme Court has emphasized that "the term 'contrivance' refers to something contrived for, or employed in contriving to effect a purpose." *Lozman*, 568 U.S. at 123, 1 Adm. R. at 4 (cleaned up). Thus, the test for whether a structure is a vessel is whether "a reasonable observer, looking to the [structure's] physical characteristics and activities, would consider it designed to a practical degree for carrying people or things over water." *Id.* at 121, 1 Adm. R. at 3. Courts should "avoid subjective elements, such as owner's intent," and should consider only "objective evidence of a waterborne transportation purpose." *Id.* at 128, 1 Adm. R. at 7.

There is no question that an oceangoing cargo barge is a vessel. Nor can there be any doubt that Southern Recycling's subjective intent to dismantle DBL 134 for scrap is insufficient to render it a dead ship.[2] *See Blake Marine Grp., LLC v. Epic Ala. Recyclers, LLC*, No. 19-0468-CG-B at *4 (S.D. Ala. Dec. 30, 2019) ("The fact that it was towed as a 'dead ship' and that EPIC had contractually agreed not to use the AMOS RUNNER to engage in any maritime commerce does not change the physical attributes and behavior of the structure.") DBL 134, at a minimum, *was* a vessel when it arrived at ISL's shipyard in Brownsville. The question is whether it had become a dead ship yet when the accident happened.

To determine whether DBL 134 was a dead ship, we ask whether it "had or had not been withdrawn from navigation and maritime

[2] We note here Southern Recycling's argument that the district court took insufficient notice of an affidavit by Southern Recycling's Vice President, Douglas Higginbotham. The affidavit discusses the contract between Southern Recycling and Kirby, the accident, and Southern Recycling's subjective intent t return DBL 134 to Kirby. Because subjective intent is irrelevant to whether DBL 134 was a vessel or a dead ship, the district court did not err in disregarding Mr. Higginbotham's affidavit.

commerce." *Amoco Oil v. M/V Montclair*, 766 F.2d 473, 477 (11th Cir. 1986). Whether a **[—12—]** vessel has been withdrawn from navigation is a question of the physical characteristics of and modifications to the structure. *See* THOMAS J. SCHOENBAUM, 1 ADMIRALTY & MAR. L. § 3:6 (6th ed. 2018) ("Only if a ship is so changed in function that is has no further navigation function will it be considered to have lost vessel status.").

The plaintiff bears the burden to "prove by a preponderance of the evidence that the court has jurisdiction based on the complaint and evidence," *Ballew*, 668 F.3d at 781 (citation omitted), but DBL 134 was unquestionably a vessel when it arrived at ISL's facility. Thus, where the line between "vessel" and "dead ship" is in dispute, the party challenging vessel status must show evidence of structural changes sufficient to give rise to a question of whether a vessel's function has been so altered as to withdraw it from navigation. Then, the party asserting jurisdiction bears the burden to demonstrate that a structure retains sufficient navigation function to remain a vessel.

The district court cited "photographs provided by Claimants" showing "a **gaping hole open to the sea** down to or below [DBL 134's] waterline" and information indicating that "another large opening had been cut into the bottom side of the liquid cargo tank and large holes had been cut through the deck." Claimants add that, in **{–384–}** response to Southern Recycling's motion for a preliminary injunction requiring Kirby to take possession of DBL 134 and remove it from ISL's facility, Kirby submitted additional photos of DBL 134, technical manuals and diagrams, and several affidavits, including that of Christopher Nash, the former Captain of the M/V Viking.

The technical manuals indicate that the waterline, when the barge is fully loaded, is as little as four feet, nine inches (4'9") below the deck in the winter, four feet, two and a half inches (4'2.5") in summer, and three feet, eight inches (3'8") in tropical waters. Contrary to Southern Recycling's **[—13—]** claim, the photographs do not depict a minor preparatory cut to the bow above "the fully loaded waterline [that] did not otherwise alter the integrity of the hull." To the contrary, both the image supplied by Claimants in their motion and the images supplied by Kirby clearly depict, as the district court found, "a gaping hole open to the sea."

The photographs make clear that, at the time of the accident, a large portion of the bow had been severed cleanly off the front, leaving a hole that spans the barge from starboard to port, and is approximately one quarter as deep as it is wide. Although the record does not disclose a precise measurement, the cut is clearly about ten to twenty feet deep. The technical specifications (the accuracy and authenticity of which Southern Recycling does not dispute) indicate a fully loaded waterline 3'8" to 4'9" below the deck, depending on season. The cut, therefore, *visibly* extends to well below the fully loaded waterline.

The district court also had the benefit of a photo submitted by Southern Recycling in its opposition to Claimant's motion to dismiss, depicting DBL 134 as it was prior to any shipbreaking work. The portion of the bow that is missing from Claimants' picture is visible in Southern Recycling's picture, providing the district court (and this court) an adequate comparison to conclude that the portion of bow that had been severed was significant and sizeable. Further, the photo shows how the front of the barge had been fully enclosed, rather than wide open, allowing a reasonable observer to conclude that, should this formerly ocean-going barge be taken back out into open waters, it would be at a substantially increased risk of taking on water through the gaping hole in its bow. In weighing these photographs against Southern Recycling's visibly false assertion that "DBL 134's hull is intact" and its misleading implication that the only preparatory work done was "the minor removal of piping and deck plates to access same," or against Mr. Green's visibly implausible contention that no cuts **[—14—]** were made below the fully loaded waterline, the district court did not clearly err in concluding that "DBL 134 could not navigate over water."

Southern Recycling contends that, notwithstanding the district court's conclusion about the gaping hole in the front of the barge, DBL 134 could not be a dead ship because it still floats, and has even been moved on the Brownsville Ship Channel (from one part of ISL's facility to another).[3] The conclusion that the hole is "down to or below the waterline," Southern Recycling argues, must be false because, if true, the barge would sink.

But a structure is not a vessel merely because it is "capable of floating, **{-385-}** moving under tow, and incidentally carrying even a fair-sized item or two when [it] do[es] so." *Lozman*, 568 U.S. at 121, 1 Adm. R. at 3. The physical structure of a vessel must give a reasonable observer evidence that the structure is "designed to a practical degree for transportation on water"—that is, transportation of persons or things over water. *Id.* at 122, 1 Adm. R. at 4 (cleaned up). Even if Claimants' evidence had been insufficient to prove that DBL 134 could no longer safely navigate over water, it was at least enough to show that major structural changes had been made and to implicate Southern Recycling's burden to show that DBL 134 was a vessel—that is, to show that DBL 134 could still serve a useful purpose. Southern Recycling failed to do so.

In its motion for a preliminary injunction against Kirby, Southern Recycling alleged that "DBL 134 [is] a ticking bomb awaiting one spark to ignite it." The barge is so unsafe that Southern Recycling is, "quite frankly, lucky that another accident has not occurred," and when an expert discovered the condition the barge was in he had to "immediately order[ ] all **[—15—]** personnel to evacuate the DBL 134." Southern Recycling does not allege that the barge could carry people over water; to the contrary, it is unsafe for personnel to board.

Southern Recycling also alleges that its preparatory work has included "cutting small 'doors' in the cargo tanks." This implies that it can no longer carry the liquid cargo for which it was designed. To be sure, a limitation on what a vessel can do does not necessarily render it a dead ship. For example, the heating pipe system involved in the accident had been deactivated since 2012, limiting the types of cargo DBL 134 could transport; it was, nonetheless, still a vessel because it could carry different cargo. Now, however, the tanks have been cut open, the barge is unsafe for humans to board, and there is a large hole in the bow that visibly prevents the barge from being loaded to capacity (if *any* loading capacity remains, Southern Recycling does not say so). The standard is permissive, and transporting people or things over water need not be a vessel's *primary* purpose—in *Stewart v. Dutra Constr. Co.*, it was enough that a dredge carried "machinery, equipment, and crew over water." 543 U.S. at 492. But Southern Recycling has failed to identify *any* transportation purpose that DBL 134 could serve or *anything* that it could carry over water.

Southern Recycling points to objective characteristics like "a raked hull, bow, deck, ten cargo tanks, etc." It contrasts these characteristics against the floating home that was held not to be a vessel in *Lozman* because it had an unraked hull, nonmaritime livings quarters, etc. 568 U.S. at 121–22, 1 Adm. R. at 3–4. However, a reasonable observer would not see a raked hull and bow, but a severed bow and part of a raked hull—with a gaping hole in it. A reasonable observer would note that much of the deck has been removed, and the cargo tanks can no longer hold a cargo. A reasonable observer would not see a vessel ready to transport persons or cargo, but a dead ship in the process of being scrapped. **[—16—]**

Southern Recycling failed to demonstrate that, based on its physical characteristics, DBL 134 had not been removed from navigation. The district court did not err in concluding that DBL 134 was a dead ship. It lacked subject matter jurisdiction and properly dismissed under Rule 12(b)(1).

[3] Southern Recycling makes much of the fact that the barge was moved four times within the ISL facility since its arrival. This is immaterial—Southern Recycling only alleges clearly that it moved the barge once since the accident and identifies no other moves made *before* Southern Recycling cut a large hole in DBL 134's bow.

C.

Because Southern Recycling had requested and been denied further discovery, it now requests, in the alternative to a reversal on the merits, that we **{-386-}** remand for further factual development. We decline to do so. A plaintiff should be ready to present some amount of basic jurisdictional evidence, or at least raise an inference that further discovery will uncover such evidence, from the outset of litigation. "[A] 'factual attack' under Rule 12(b)(1) may occur at any stage of the proceedings, and plaintiff bears the burden of proof that jurisdiction does in fact exist." *Menchaca v. Chrysler Credit Corp.*, 613 F.2d 507, 511 (5th Cir. 1980) (citations omitted).

Although a ruling that decides disputed facts should ordinarily be subject to an evidentiary hearing, "an evidentiary hearing is not required." *Moran v. Kingdom of Saudi Arabia*, 27 F.3d 169, 173 (5th Cir. 1994) (citation omitted). "The party seeking discovery bears the burden of showing its necessity," *Freeman*, 556 F.3d at 341, but Southern Recycling did not make any compelling showing that it would need time to conduct discovery to explain away the hole in the bow of DBL 134. The bid package for DBL 134 included engineering drawings. Southern Recycling's affiliate, ISL, had custody of the barge. Yet Southern Recycling made no effort to show why it could not take pictures of its own to explain away the hole in the bow or provide its own measurements of the depth of the hole compared to the waterline based on the engineering drawings in response to Claimants' evidence. **[—17—]**

"It hardly bears repeating that control of discovery is committed to the sound discretion of the trial court and its discovery rulings will be reversed only where they are arbitrary or clearly unreasonable." *Williamson v. U. S. Dep't of Agric.*, 815 F.2d 369, 382 (5th Cir. 1987) (citation omitted). Southern Recycling has not shown why it needed further discovery or what material evidence further discovery could have produced that was not already available to it, so Southern Recycling has not shown that the district court's ruling was arbitrary or clearly unreasonable.

IV. CONCLUSION

The precise moment a ship is withdrawn from navigation can be a difficult, fact-intensive inquiry. We are fortunate that we need not decide precisely how many rotted planks must be removed before Theseus's ship ceases to be Theseus's ship. When her bow has been severed, leaving a gaping hole open to the sea, her cargo tanks have been rendered inoperable, and the party asserting jurisdiction is unable even to allege any types of people or things that she is capable of carrying over navigable water, we can readily conclude that DBL 134 is no longer a vessel.

AFFIRMED.

United States Court of Appeals
for the Fifth Circuit

No. 19-20160

STELLY
vs.
DURISO

Appeal from the United States District Court for the Southern District of Texas

Decided: December 11, 2020

Citation: 982 F.3d 403, 8 Adm. R. 249 (5th Cir. 2020).

Before **JONES, HAYNES,** and **HO,**[1] Circuit Judges.

[—1—] {-405-} HAYNES, Circuit Judge:

Plaintiff Rhonda Stelly worked with Defendant Paul Duriso at two union hiring halls in south Texas for over a year. In that time, Stelly alleged that Duriso repeatedly asked her offensive, threatening, and humiliating questions relating to her gender. Stelly eventually sued the unions she was affiliated with, as well as a maritime association that used the hiring halls, for **[—2—]** sexual harassment under federal employment law, arguing that Duriso's conduct created a hostile work environment. Stelly also sued Duriso himself for intentional infliction of emotional distress ("IIED") under Texas state law. The district court entered a default judgment in Stelly's favor on the IIED claim against Duriso, and Stelly ultimately prevailed at trial against one of the other defendants. We conclude that Stelly could not pursue IIED claim against Duriso in light of the other statutory remedies available to Stelly. We therefore VACATE the default judgment on the IIED claim and REMAND for further proceedings.

I. Background

Because this is an appeal of a default judgment, we take all well-pleaded factual allegations in Stelly's complaint as true; this section, therefore, reflects the facts as alleged therein. *U.S. ex rel. M-CO Constr., Inc. v. Shipco Gen., Inc.*, 814 F.2d 1011, 1014 (5th Cir. 1987). In January 2014, Stelly began working as a longshoreman for West Gulf Maritime Association ("WGMA"), an organization that employs skilled longshoremen. Stelly affiliated with two local unions of the International Longshoremen's Association ("ILA"): ILA local union 1316 ("ILA Local 1316") and ILA local union 21 ("ILA Local 21"). Stelly worked alongside Duriso, a board member of both local unions.

Duriso started sexually harassing Stelly shortly after she started coming to the unions' hiring halls. On a number of occasions, Duriso asked Stelly if she needed a "sugar daddy"—that is, someone who could help her in exchange for romantic or sexual favors. Duriso clearly had himself in mind for that role: he regularly described to Stelly the sexual acts he wanted to perform on her. The consequences of rejecting Duriso's advances were similarly made apparent to Stelly: Duriso threatened Stelly that, if Stelly did **[—3—]** not "learn how to 'play ball' like the other women there," Stelly would stop getting work.

Several months into her time at the hiring halls, Stelly filed an internal complaint with ILA Local 21 about Duriso's conduct. Duriso responded by screaming at Stelly, threatening Stelly, and ordering the foremen to pass Stelly over for jobs. ILA Local 21 did nothing to stop the **{-406-}** harassment, so Stelly filed another complaint, this time with WGMA, which ultimately resulted in Duriso being suspended pending investigation. But, even then, Duriso continued to come to the hiring halls and harass Stelly.

Stelly eventually sued Duriso, ILA Local 1316, ILA Local 21, and WGMA in federal district court. Stelly asserted employment discrimination and retaliation claims against ILA Local 1316, ILA Local 21, and WGMA under Title VII of the Civil Rights Act of 1964, 42 U.S.C. §§ 2000e–2000e-17, and an IIED claim against Duriso under Texas state law. Duriso evaded service and did not defend the suit. The district court entered a default

[1] Judge Ho concurs in Sections I, II, and III.A. He would certify the question addressed in Section III.B to the Texas Supreme Court for consideration. *See, e.g., JCB, Inc. v. The Horsburgh & Scott Co.*, 941 F.3d 144, 145 (5th Cir. 2019).

judgment against Duriso on Stelly's IIED claim and awarded Stelly $75,000 in damages. The other three defendants, meanwhile, went to trial on the Title VII claims, where Stelly ultimately prevailed against ILA Local 21. *Stelly v. W. Gulf Mar. Ass'n*, 407 F. Supp. 3d 673, 689 (S.D. Tex. 2019), *appeal dismissed sub nom. Stelly v. Int'l Longshoremen's Ass'n Local 21*, No. 19-20730, 2019 WL 8504706 (5th Cir. Oct. 30, 2019).[2] Before that trial was held, the district court certified the judgment against Duriso as a final **[—4—]** judgment under Federal Rule of Civil Procedure 54(b). Duriso timely appealed.

II. Jurisdiction & Standard of Review

The district court had federal question jurisdiction over the Title VII claims under 28 U.S.C. § 1331. The district court also had supplemental jurisdiction over the IIED claim against Duriso under 28 U.S.C. § 1367(a) because it arose out of the same case or controversy as the Title VII claims. We have jurisdiction to review the district court's judgment under 28 U.S.C. § 1291. *See Recreational Props., Inc. v. Sw. Mortg. Serv. Corp.*, 804 F.2d 311, 313 (5th Cir. 1986) ("The appeal of a default judgment . . . [is] a final judgment under 28 U.S.C. § 1291 . . . .").

We review the entry of a default judgment for abuse of discretion and any underlying factual determinations for clear error. *Wooten v. McDonald Transit Assocs., Inc.*, 788 F.3d 490, 495 (5th Cir. 2015). Because we generally prefer that cases be resolved on the merits, however, we perform that review "with a grain of salt": even a "slight abuse of discretion may justify reversal." *Id.* at 496 (internal quotation marks and citation omitted).

III. Discussion

A. Rule 60

We first consider whether Duriso can appeal from the default judgment without having first moved to set aside that default judgment in the district court. Our court has previously identified a circuit split on whether a party must file a Rule 60(b) motion challenging a default judgment in the district court prior to appealing, but we have thus far declined to opine on the subject in a published opinion. *See BHTT Ent., Inc. v. Brickhouse Café & Lounge, L.L.C.*, 858 F.3d 310, 314 (5th Cir. 2017); *cf. SUA Ins. Co. v. Buras*, **[—5—]** 421 F. App'x 384, 385 n.2 (5th Cir. 2011) (per curiam[3]) **{-407-}** (identifying that a party "[o]rdinarily" files a Rule 60(b) motion but concluding that doing so is not necessary for an appeal).

We now hold that a party's failure to file a motion to set aside a default judgment in the district court does not prevent the party from appealing that judgment to our court.[4] A final default judgment is, at bottom, a final judgment capable of immediate appellate review. *See Recreational Props.*, 804 F.2d at 313; *see also* 10A CHARLES ALAN WRIGHT & ARTHUR R. MILLER, FEDERAL PRACTICE AND PROCEDURE § 2684 (4th ed. 2020) ("As a final judgment, a judgment entered pursuant to Rule 55(b)(2) may be reviewed immediately by the court of appeals."). No statute or rule of civil procedure requires a defaulting party to first contest the default judgment in district

---

[2] At trial, the district court granted WGMA's motion for judgment as a matter of law at the close of Stelly's affirmative case. *Stelly*, 407 F. Supp. 3d at 677 n.2. After the jury initially awarded Stelly $5,400 in lost wages and $200,000 in punitive damages against ILA Local 21 and $600 in lost wages and $100,000 in punitive damages against ILA Local 1316, *id.* at 677, the district court granted ILA Local 1316 judgment as a matter of law and directed remittitur with respect to ILA Local 21, proposing an amended judgment in the amount of $60,400, *id.* at 689. Stelly accepted the amended judgment.

[3] Because this opinion is unpublished, it is non-precedential, but we cite it due to the similarity to the issue presented here.

[4] We accordingly agree with the Second and Sixth Circuits (which generally allow a party to appeal a default judgment without first filing a Rule 60(b) motion) and disagree with the Ninth and Eleventh Circuits (which generally do not). *Compare Pecarsky v. Galaxiworld.com Ltd.*, 249 F.3d 167, 170–71 (2d Cir. 2001), *and Prime Rate Premium Fin. Corp. v. Larson*, 930 F.3d 759, 768 (6th Cir. 2019), *with Consorzio Del Prosciutto Di Parma v. Domain Name Clearing Co., LLC*, 346 F.3d 1193, 1195 (9th Cir. 2003), *and Commodity Futures Trading Comm'n v. Am. Commodity Grp. Corp.*, 753 F.2d 862, 866 (11th Cir. 1984) (per curiam).

court. In particular, Rule 55(c) itself makes clear that a party *may* move under Rule 60(b) to set aside a default judgment, but it does nothing to suggest that the party *must* do so. *See* FED. R. CIV. P. 55(c).[5] **[—6—]**

To be sure, in most circumstances, a party will benefit from using such a motion to develop the record. *See Wooten*, 788 F.3d at 495–96. The defaulting party will be unable to raise any fact questions that were not brought before the district court. *See U.S. ex rel. M-CO Constr.*, 814 F.2d at 1014 ("The default judgment establishes the truth of these factual allegations."). Unpled affirmative defenses are also off the table. *See Henry v. First Nat'l Bank of Clarksdale*, 595 F.2d 291, 298 n.1 (5th Cir. 1979) (noting that affirmative defenses "are considered waived if not pleaded in the trial court"). But the lack of a Rule 60(b) motion is not an absolute barrier: if the existing record and pleadings do not support the judgment, the defaulting party can prevail on appeal without having raised the issues first in the district court with a Rule 60(b) motion. *See, e.g., Pecarsky v. Galaxiworld.com, Ltd.*, 249 F.3d 167, 173–74 (2d Cir. 2001) (vacating a default judgment in large part because the defendant's existing filings before the district court suggested a complete defense).

[5] The Supreme Court has made clear that only statutory provisions can be jurisdictional, not "court-made" procedural rules. *Hamer v. Neighborhood Hous. Servs. of Chi.*, 138 S. Ct. 13, 16 (2017). Therefore, even if we were to conclude that a Rule 60 motion is a prerequisite to appealing a default judgment, that requirement could only be a mandatory claim-processing rule, not a jurisdictional one. *Cf. Recreational Props.*, 804 F.2d at 313; *accord Prime Rate*, 930 F.3d at 768 ("Any Rule 60(b) exhaustion mandate—which would not flow out of any federal statute—instead would count as a non-jurisdictional **[—6—]** claims-processing rule." (quotation omitted)). Arguments concerning mandatory claim-processing rules are generally forfeited if the relevant party does not brief them. *See Hamer*, 138 S. Ct. at 16. Stelly did not raise any argument with respect to Rule 60(b) in her briefs, conceding same on oral argument; therefore, any such argument would be forfeited.

B. IIED Claim

That brings us to the merits: whether the district court appropriately entered a default judgment against Duriso on Stelly's IIED claim. Under Texas law, a plaintiff bringing an IIED claim must **{–408–}** demonstrate that the defendant intentionally or recklessly engaged in extreme or outrageous conduct that resulted in severe emotional distress. *Standard Fruit & Vegetable Co. v. Johnson*, 985 S.W.2d 62, 66 (Tex. 1998). But not all such conduct is actionable under IIED—the plaintiff must also demonstrate that there is no alternative cause of action available to address the alleged **[—7—]** misconduct. *Hoffmann-La Roche Inc. v. Zeltwanger*, 144 S.W.3d 438, 447 (Tex. 2004). That is because IIED is a "gap-filler" tort reserved for "those rare instances in which a defendant intentionally inflicts severe emotional distress in a manner so unusual that the victim has no other recognized theory of redress." *Id.*

Accordingly, a plaintiff generally cannot sustain an IIED claim if the plaintiff could have brought a sexual harassment claim premised on the same facts: "when the gravamen of the plaintiff's complaint is for sexual harassment, the plaintiff must proceed solely under a statutory claim unless there are additional facts, unrelated to sexual harassment, to support an independent tort claim for intentional infliction of emotional distress." *Id.* at 441. In particular, the Texas Supreme Court has noted that IIED claims against both employers and individual employees premised on sexually harassing conduct can be foreclosed by alternative causes of action under Title VII or the Texas Commission on Human Rights Act ("TCHRA"). *See id.* at 447; *Creditwatch, Inc. v. Jackson*, 157 S.W.3d 814, 815–16 (Tex. 2005) (rejecting IIED claims against both an employer and an individual employee because the claims were premised on sexual harassment actionable under other statutes).[6] **[—8—]**

[6] The Texas Courts of Appeals and federal district courts are split on whether the lack of individual liability under Title VII and the TCHRA constitutes a "gap" with respect to coworkers and supervisors that IIED can fill. *See generally Grant*

The gravamen of Stelly's IIED claim here is for sexual harassment. All of Stelly's IIED allegations against Duriso stem from Duriso's sexually harassing conduct in the hiring halls and Duriso's related attempts to retaliate against Stelly for reporting that conduct. Stelly alleged that Duriso repeatedly asked her offensive, threatening, and humiliating questions because **{–409–}** of her sex, including direct invitations to help Stelly advance professionally if she gave him sexual favors. Stelly further alleged that Duriso talked "constantly" about sexual things he wanted to do to her. These are all sexual harassment allegations. Indeed, in both the internal complaints Stelly filed and the IIED section of the complaint Stelly filed in federal district court, Stelly characterized Duriso's conduct as such: Duriso, Stelly alleged, had engaged in "sexual harassment" and thereby created a "hostile work environment."

From the beginning of recognizing this tort, the Texas Supreme Court has made clear that IIED is a high threshold to establish. *See Twyman v. Twyman*, 855 S.W.2d 619, 621–22 (Tex. 1993) (adopting cause of action and emphasizing IIED is subject to "rigorous legal standards"). Because of our determination above, we need not consider whether Stelly's allegations identify a disturbing pattern of behavior that would give rise to an IIED claim **[—9—]** in other settings. Stelly had alternative remedies here. Specifically, because Duriso's conduct happened entirely in connection with the workplace, Stelly could seek redress against WGMA, ILA Local 1316, and ILA Local 21 under Title VII.[7] Indeed, Stelly did just that, using Duriso's conduct as a basis for her Title VII claims against those defendants. Further, Stelly ultimately prevailed on such claims against ILA Local 21. *See Stelly*, 407 F. Supp. 3d at 678–81. The availability of those statutory remedies on the same facts forecloses Stelly's IIED claim against Duriso. *See Hoffmann-La Roche*, 144 S.W.3d at 447; *CreditWatch*, 157 S.W.3d at 816. There is, in short, no "gap" that IIED needs to fill in this case. *Hoffmann-La Roche*, 144 S.W.3d at 447. The district court therefore abused its discretion in entering a default judgment on that claim.

Accordingly, we VACATE the district court's default judgment on the IIED claim

v. Lone Star Co., 21 F.3d 649, 653–54 (5th Cir. 1994) ("Only 'employers,' not individuals acting in their individual capacity who do not otherwise meet the definition of 'employers,' can be liable under [T]itle VII."); *Jenkins v. Guardian Indus. Corp.*, 16 S.W.3d 431, 742 (Tex. App.—Waco 2000, pet. denied) ("[S]upervisors and managers are not liable in their individual capacities for alleged acts of discrimination under the TCHRA."). Some courts have found a "gap." *See Garcia v. Shell Oil Co.*, 355 S.W.3d 768, 778 (Tex. App.—Houston [1st Dist.] 2011, no pet.); *Dixon v. State Farm Mut. Auto. Ins. Cos.*, 433 F. Supp. 2d 785, 790 (N.D. Tex. 2006); *Sauceda v. Bank of Tex., N.A.*, No. CIV.A.3:04-CV-2201-P, 2005 WL 578474, at *5 (N.D. Tex. Mar. 9, 2005). Others have not. *See Roane v. Dean*, Nos. 03-19-00307-CV, 3- **[—8—]** 19-00352-CV, 2020 WL 2078252, at *4–5 (Tex. App.—Austin Apr. 30, 2020, pet. filed); *Swafford v. Bank of Am. Corp.*, 401 F. Supp. 2d 761, 764 (S.D. Tex. 2005).

Although we recognize that the Texas Supreme Court has not definitively resolved whether the lack of individual liability under Title VII or the TCHRA leaves a "gap" fillable by IIED, the court's decision in *CreditWatch* strongly suggests that its answer is "no." In that case, the court rejected IIED claims against both an employer *and* an individual because those claims "stemmed from [the employee]'s lewd advances" and were therefore "covered by other statutory remedies." 157 S.W.3d at 816. We predict the Texas Supreme Court would follow a similar approach here, where the allegations underlying Stelly's IIED claim all stem from Duriso's sexual harassment. *See Ironshore Eur. DAC v. Schiff Hardin, L.L.P.*, 912 F.3d 759, 764 (5th Cir. 2019) ("If the Texas Supreme Court has not ruled on an issue, we make an *Erie* guess, predicting what the Texas Supreme Court would do if faced with the same facts." (cleaned up)).

[7] In its ruling on the other defendants' post-trial motions for judgment as a matter of law, the district court identified that we have not expressly determined whether Title VII applies to labor organizations. *Stelly*, 407 F. Supp. 3d at 678 (concluding that the weight of authority from other circuits indicates that labor organizations can be sued under Title VII). Neither party to this appeal suggests that Stelly was unable to pursue Title VII claims against ILA Local 1316 and ILA Local 21, and so we need not (and do not) resolve the question of labor organization liability under Title VII generally.

and REMAND to the district court for further proceedings consistent with this opinion.[8]

[8] Because we conclude that the district court erred in determining that Stelly could sustain an IIED claim against Duriso, we do not address Duriso's arguments that the district court's default judgment did not comply with Rule 54.

United States Court of Appeals
for the Fifth Circuit

No. 19-30756

KNIGHT
vs.
KIRBY OFFSHORE MARINE PAC., L.L.C.

Appeal from the United States District Court for the Eastern District of Louisiana

Decided: December 17, 2020

Citation: 983 F.3d 172, 8 Adm. R. 254 (5th Cir. 2020).

Before **BARKSDALE, ELROD,** and **HO,** Circuit Judges.

[—1—] {-175-} BARKSDALE, Circuit Judge:

Primarily at issue is whether, as a matter of law, Andrew Lee Knight can be held contributorily negligent for his ankle injury underlying his Jones Act negligence claim against Kirby Offshore Marine Pacific, L.L.C. (Kirby). The district court concluded, *inter alia*: Kirby was negligent, based on an order by its vessel's captain to replace the stern line in unfavorable weather; and Knight was contributorily negligent for placing the removed stern line near him and subsequently stepping on it while carrying out that order, reducing his damages award in proportion to his **{-176-}** fault. AFFIRMED IN PART; VACATED IN PART; REMANDED. **[—2—]**

I.

Knight was a seaman aboard the M/V SEA HAWK, a tugboat owned by Kirby that was then towing a barge from the State of Washington to Alaska. As an offshore tankerman, Knight was responsible for, *inter alia*, all the deck labor: loading and discharging cargo, assisting with repairs, and general heavy lifting for both vessels.

The SEA HAWK housed a stern line used when entering and exiting ports to secure the barge to the tug. The line was more than 100-feet long and several inches thick. At one point the line chafed. Once the vessels were in the open sea and the stern line was no longer in use, the captain ordered Knight and another crewmember, Ladd, to change out the line. When the order was given, four-foot seas and winds of at least 20 miles an hour caused the SEA HAWK to roll.

After Knight and Ladd removed the chafed line, they placed it on the deck next to them. As they were installing the new line, Knight stepped on the chafed line and injured his ankle. He testified that the rocking of the SEA HAWK caused him to lose his balance. As discussed *infra*, Knight's injury prevents his returning to work in the same capacity.

Following the accident, Knight filed, *inter alia*, this Jones Act negligence claim under 46 U.S.C. § 30104 *et seq.* Following a two-day bench trial, the court concluded: Kirby was negligent because "there were safer times to issue the order to change the line"; and Knight was contributorily negligent because he failed to "watch his footing while replacing the chafed stern line" and failed to "move the chafed stern line to a location on the boat where he would not have stepped on it". The court assigned equal fault to each party.

For Knight's injury, the court awarded, *inter alia*, $60,000 for past-and-future general damages for pain and suffering, based on Knight's **[—3—]** continued complaints of pain and his doctor's finding he had suffered, *inter alia*, a 10% lower-extremity impairment. His total damages of approximately $344,000 were reduced proportionate to his assignment of 50% fault.

In denying Knight's Federal Rule of Civil Procedure 59(e) post-trial motion to alter or amend judgment, the court rejected: Knight's contention that, as a matter of law, a seaman may not be held contributorily negligent for carrying out an order; his challenge that Ladd must be equally at fault for the placement of the stern line; and his claim that the award of $60,000 in general damages was manifestly unjust.

II.

Knight maintains: the court erred, as a matter of law, by concluding he was contributorily negligent, even though he was following an order at the time of his injury;

and, in the alternative, it clearly erred in finding him contributorily negligent. Knight also contends the court clearly erred in awarding him only $60,000 in general damages.

A.

We first consider whether, as a matter of law, a seaman may be held contributorily negligent when he is complying with an order from his superior. If he can, we turn to the district court's finding Knight 50% at fault.

1.

The district court's legal conclusions are reviewed *de novo*. *E.g.*, **{-177-}** *Becker v. Tidewater, Inc.*, 586 F.3d 358, 365 (5th Cir. 2009). In challenging the application of contributory negligence, Knight primarily relies on *Williams v. Brasea, Inc.*, 497 F.2d 67 (5th Cir. 1974), in which this court stated in *dictum*, "a seaman may not be contributorily negligent for carrying out orders that result in his own injury, even if he recognizes possible danger", *id.* at 73. Knight asserts this principle was reiterated and affirmed in an **[—4—]** unpublished opinion in *Ledet v. Smith Marine Towing Corp.*, 455 F. App'x 417 (5th Cir. 2011). Accordingly, Knight maintains that, as a matter of law, he cannot be held negligent because he was following his captain's order.

In its denial of Knight's Rule 59(e) post-trial motion, the district court correctly noted that Knight failed, before entry of judgment, to raise his challenge to the application of contributory negligence. *See Simon v. United States*, 891 F.2d 1154, 1159 (5th Cir. 1990) ("[Rule 59(e) motions] cannot be used to raise arguments which could, and should, have been made before the judgment issued. . . . [T]hey cannot be used to argue a case under a new legal theory") (citation omitted). Further, as previously stated, the proposition urged by Knight is *dictum* in *Williams*; we lack any binding precedent applying *Williams* to deny application of contributory negligence. In any event, Knight's contention fails.

The above-described *dictum* in *Williams* undeniably modifies the rule in Jones Act negligence claims that "contributory negligence is an affirmative defense that diminishes recovery in proportion to the seaman's fault". *Johnson v. Cenac Towing, Inc.*, 544 F.3d 296, 302 (5th Cir. 2008); 45 U.S.C. § 53 (mandating contributory negligence under the Federal Employees Liability Act (FELA)), 46 U.S.C. § 30104 (incorporating FELA into the Jones Act). In *Williams*, a supervisor was untangling a line caught on a winch when he allegedly ordered his crewman to turn on the power, trapping the supervisor's hands and causing significant injury. *Williams*, 497 F.2d at 71. Our court held: if the order was in fact given, the crewman could not be found contributorily negligent for failing to ensure the supervisor was free from danger before following the command. *Id.* at 73. More pertinent to this appeal, *Williams* stated in *dictum*: a seaman cannot be held contributorily negligent for following an order that results in *his own* injury. *Id.* (citation omitted). **[—5—]**

Judges Ho and Elrod in their concurring and dissenting opinions, respectively, do not agree that the above statement in *Williams* about a seaman's own injury is *dictum*. As discussed, the issue in *Williams* was a supervisor's, not a seaman's, injury. Accordingly, the statement in *Williams* concerning an injury to a seaman was unnecessary for deciding the issue before the court: the supervisor's injury. Therefore, the statement about the seaman is *dictum* and, concomitantly, not binding precedent. *E.g.*, *United States v. Segura*, 747 F.3d 323, 328–29 (5th Cir. 2014) ("A statement is dictum if it could have been deleted without seriously impairing the analytical foundations of the holding and[,] being peripheral, may not have received the full and careful consideration of the court that uttered it. A statement is not dictum if it is necessary to the result or constitutes an explication of the governing rules of law. If a statement is dictum, we are free to disregard it from prior panel opinions when we find it unpersuasive.") (cleaned up); *United States v. Rubin*, 609 F.2d 51, 69 n.2 (2d Cir. 1979), *aff'd*, 449 U.S. 424 (1981) (Friendly, J., concurring) ("A judge's power to bind is limited to the issue that is before him; he cannot transmute dictum into decision by waving a wand and uttering the word 'hold[ing]'."). **{–178–}**

The *dictum* in *Williams*, or a similar limit on contributory negligence, has been applied in other jurisdictions. The ninth circuit adopted a categorical interpretation of *Williams*, applying the bar on contributory negligence to all orders from a captain. *See Simeonoff v. Hiner*, 249 F.3d 883, 890 (9th Cir. 2001) (declaring *Williams* "persuasive, fair to crew and vessel owners alike" because "[c]ompliance with orders from supervisors will promote vessel safety and will aid efficacy of command at sea"). Other courts, by comparison, apply *Williams* only to a supervisor's *specific orders*, allowing contributory negligence when there was a *general order*. *See Weeks Marine, Inc. v. Garza*, 371 S.W.3d 157, 167 (Tex. 2012) (holding the rule in *Williams* applies solely "when the seaman is ordered to do a specific task in **[—6—]** a specific manner or is ordered to do a task that can be accomplished in only one way"). Notably, but with no mention of *Williams*, both the third and eighth circuits rely on the same distinction between general and specific orders when considering contributory negligence under FELA, which, as noted *supra*, is incorporated by the Jones Act. *See Fashauer v. New Jersey Transit Rail Operations, Inc.*, 57 F.3d 1269, 1279 (3d Cir. 1995) ("when the employee is given a specific order—that is, where he or she is told to perform a specific task in a particular way—he is not contributorily negligent") (internal quotation marks and citation omitted); *Alholm v. Am. Steamship Co.*, 144 F.3d 1172, 1179 (8th Cir. 1998) ("A seaman cannot be found comparatively negligent [] when following an order to complete a task in a specific manner.").

Our court's analysis of Jones Act negligence claims tracks the distinction between general and specific orders. In *Boudreaux v. United States*, 280 F.3d 461 (5th Cir. 2002), a supervisor ordered a seaman to perform two jobs but "did not specifically instruct [plaintiff] on the order of these tasks", *id.* at 464. While the seaman and a fellow crewmember were performing one of the tasks (involving transporting a 300-pound valve), one of the seamen slipped on piping they had previously exposed, injuring plaintiff. *Id.* at 464–65. Our court upheld the attribution of 50% fault to both seamen. *Id.* at 467.

Similarly, in *Pallis v. United States*, 369 F. App'x 538 (5th Cir. 2010), our court upheld the assignment of 75% fault to a seaman when he was ordered to move trash and elected to carry the heavier objects without any help, *id.* at 540, 546. In reducing the seaman's award proportional to his fault, we explained that a rule barring contributory negligence for all orders would make "automatons of seamen" and abrogate the principle that a seaman must perform his tasks with ordinary prudence. *Id.* at 542. **[—7—]**

This principle—seamen must act with ordinary prudence under the circumstances—was affirmed by our court in *Gautreaux v. Scurlock Marine, Inc.*, 107 F.3d 331 (5th Cir. 1997) (en banc). There, we observed that prior fifth circuit cases had "vacillated" in their pronunciations of the proper standard of care for seamen in Jones Act negligence claims, describing the duty as either "slight care", "ordinary prudence", or both. *Id.* at 337–38. After extensive review, we held a seaman owes more than a "slight duty" to look after his own safety. *Id.* at 339. Rather, a seaman is obligated to act "with ordinary prudence under the circumstances" because "nothing in the text or structure of the FELA–Jones Act legislation suggests that the standard of care to be attributed to either an employer or an employee is anything different than ordinary prudence". *Id.* at 338–39.

On the other hand, in the earlier-referenced opinion for *Ledet*, after the captain **{–179–}** ordered a seaman to perform a highly specific task (tying a pendant wire to a norman pin at a designated time), the seaman was injured. *Ledet*, 455 F. App'x at 420. Although plaintiff was not found negligent, our court observed that, even if he were, *Williams* would foreclose any reduction of the award. *Id.* at 422. Unlike in the cases discussed *supra* (*Boudreaux*, *Pallis*, and

Gautreaux), we referenced *Williams* and expressly stated that it remains applicable.

Of course, because *Pallis* and *Ledet* are unpublished, they are not precedential; but, their reasoning can be persuasive. *See* 5th Cir. R. 47.5.4; *Ballard v. Burton*, 444 F.3d 391, 401 n.7 (5th Cir. 2006) (recognizing unpublished opinions issued after 1 January 1996 are not controlling precedent but may be considered persuasive authority).

This survey of our case law shows the *dictum* in *Williams*, at most, stands for the proposition that a seaman may not be found contributorily negligent for carrying out a specific order from his superior that results in the **[—8—]** seaman's injury. A specific order is one that must be accomplished using a specific manner and method and leaving the seaman with no reasonable alternative to complete the assigned task. *See Alholm*, 144 F.3d at 1179; *Fashauer*, 57 F.3d at 1278; *see also Simeonoff*, 249 F.3d at 891 n.4 (applying *Williams* categorically while noting, "[w]hen a seaman completes an ordinary task at sea, even if requested by a superior, contributory negligence may mitigate damages if an injured seaman had alternatives available, and chose the unreasonable course in completing that task"). Such a rule accepts the earlier-referenced importance of a superior's efficacious command at sea while avoiding awarding unreasonable conduct. *See Gautreaux*, 107 F.3d at 339.

The order given Knight and Ladd was a general order and, therefore, does not trigger the *Williams' dictum*. As in *Boudreaux*, the order was simply to change out equipment on the vessel—no additional instructions or specifications were provided. *See Boudreaux*, 280 F.3d at 464 (reducing seaman's award of damages in proportion to his fault when he was ordered to, *inter alia*, replace a valve). Changing out the chafed line fell within the class of ordinary "heavy lifting" Knight performed routinely. Therefore, the district court was not precluded, as a matter of law, from reducing his award proportional to his fault.

2.

Accordingly, we address the contributory-negligence finding; findings of fact are reviewed for clear error. *E.g.*, *Becker*, 586 F.3d at 365. A finding is clearly erroneous when the reviewing court is left with the definite and firm conviction that a mistake has been made. *E.g.*, *Jackson v. OMI Corp.*, 245 F.3d 525, 528 (5th Cir. 2001).

Knight contends the district court clearly erred in finding him 50% at fault. It did not clearly err in finding Knight was negligent in stepping on the **[—9—]** chafed line, but it did in finding him negligent for failing to move it. (Knight's claim that Ladd must be equally at fault for Knight's injuries was not raised until Knight's above-discussed post-trial motion and was properly denied. Obviously, this should have been raised before trial. Fed. R. Civ. P. 59(e); *Boudreaux*, 280 F.3d at 467 n.3.)

Again, the standard of care for a seaman under the Jones Act is that of an ordinarily prudent seaman under like circumstances. *Gautreaux*, 107 F.3d at 339. Regarding the court's first finding of negligence, Knight had the duty to watch where **{-180-}** he stepped. The record shows he was an experienced tankerman, was trained to change the line safely, had experience with rolling vessels, and knew the chafed line was on the deck while he was preparing to load the new one. As stated *supra*, the court did not clearly err in imputing negligence to Knight for stepping on the line.

The court's second negligence finding, pertaining to the placement of the chafed line on the deck, lacks any record evidence. Knight testified he stepped on the line after it was taken off the winch but before the new one was installed. Ladd, who was working with Knight, testified that placing the chafed line to the side was the standard operating procedure. Commonsensically, a seaman should not place obstacles near his working area. But Kirby does not present any evidence showing Knight placed the chafed line on the deck in an imprudent manner. Moreover, the SEA HAWK's captain, who gave the order to Knight and Ladd, watched the entire procedure and testified there were no irregularities in how they performed their task. He further explained they did not haphazardly throw the chafed line on the deck.

In the absence of any evidence, the court's finding of 50% negligence on the basis, in part, of Knight's placement of the chafed stern line is clearly erroneous. *See Boudreaux*, 280 F.3d at 467 (finding seaman 50% negligent for **[—10—]** stepping on piping he had previously exposed because he, *inter alia*, conceded there was a safer procedure).

B.

A court's damages award is a finding of fact reviewed for clear error. *Barto v. Shore Constr., L.L.C.*, 801 F.3d 465, 473, 3 Adm. R. 415, 418–19 (5th Cir. 2015). As such, the award is not clearly erroneous if it is plausible in the light of the record. *Comar Marine, Corp. v. Raider Marine Logistics, L.L.C.*, 792 F.3d 564, 574, 3 Adm. R. 371, 376 (5th Cir. 2015). General damages are available for pain and suffering and their negative impact on one's normal life routines. *Barto*, 801 F.3d at 473, 3 Adm. R. at 419. "Any amount to be awarded for pain and suffering must necessarily depend to a great extent on the trial court's observation of . . . plaintiff and its subjective determination of the amount needed to achieve full compensation." *Hyde v. Chevron U.S.A., Inc.*, 697 F.2d 614, 632 (5th Cir. 1983).

As mentioned above, the court denied Knight's contention in his post-trial motion that the general damages award of $60,000 was manifestly unjust. The court observed that there are factually analogous cases where courts awarded lower or similar damages for plaintiffs with comparable disabilities. Accordingly, the court reasoned, Knight's insistence that his award was unjust failed. We agree.

Neither party disputes the court's factual findings regarding Knight's injuries or recovery. Knight underwent three reconstructive surgeries on his ankle and attended approximately 100 physical-therapy sessions. His orthopedic surgeon assigned him a 14% foot-and-ankle impairment, 10% lower-extremity impairment, and 4% whole-person impairment. Knight cannot return as an offshore tankerman, but he can work as a shore tankerman (a position requiring less strenuous activity).

Knight maintains the court's findings support an award greater than $60,000 in general damages. In addition to a Louisiana federal-court case, **[—11—]** he relies heavily on analogous Louisiana state-court cases. In that regard, our court looks to relevant federal and state cases within the district court's jurisdiction in determining whether damages were excessive. *See* **{-181-}** *Moore v. M/V ANGELA*, 353 F.3d 376, 385 (5th Cir. 2003) (holding award was excessive because of, *inter alia*, factually similar Louisiana appellate-court decisions); *Lebron v. United States*, 279 F.3d 321, 326 (5th Cir. 2002) ("we will decline to reduce damages where the amount awarded is not disproportionate to at least one factually similar case from the relevant jurisdiction") (internal quotations and citation omitted). We see no reason for not applying a similar standard in assessing whether damages were inadequate. *See, e.g., Dominique v. Georgia Gulf Corp.*, No. 96-30418, 1996 WL 670315, at *3 (5th Cir. Nov. 7, 1996) (acknowledging "factually similar cases in Louisiana" and holding damages award was not inadequate).

Knight compares his injury to that in *Wynne v. Trotter*, 46 So. 3d 678 (La. Ct. App. 2010). There, plaintiff suffered a fracture in his right heel, causing a 12% foot-and-leg impairment. *Id.* at 685. Plaintiff developed a permanent limp, lost his ability to run and stand for extended periods of time, and did not undergo surgery to repair the injury. *Id.* The court upheld an award of $185,000. *Id.* at 685–86. The present-day value of the award, according to Knight, is roughly $217,000. *See Ledet*, 455 F. App'x at 423 (calculating present-day value of prior award using Bureau of Labor Statistics' CPI Inflation Calculator, *available* at *http://data.bls.gov/cgi-bin/cpicalc.pl*).

Knight also cites *Baham v. Nabors Drilling USA, LP*, 721 F. Supp. 2d 499 (W.D. La.

2010): plaintiff fractured his ankle, precipitating surgery and the insertion of two screws, *id.* at 516. Plaintiff suffered a 35% foot-and-ankle impairment, 25% lower-extremity impairment, and 10% whole-person impairment. *Id.* at 517. The court awarded $250,000 in general damages. *Id.* at 520. **[—12—]**

Although Knight insists *Wynne* and *Baham* necessitate a greater award, other Louisiana state-court cases with comparable injuries affirm amounts similar to Knight's. In *Seymour v. Cigna Ins. Co.*, 622 So. 2d 839 (La. Ct. App. 1993), plaintiff fractured his ankle, underwent two surgeries, received monthly treatment from his orthopedic surgeon for four years, and required injections of anesthesia into his sympathetic nervous system. *Id.* at 844. The court upheld $35,000 in general damages, *id.*, the equivalent of $63,000 today (conversion done using earlier-referenced CPI Inflation Calculator).

Relatedly, in *Broussard v. Oak Trace Apartments*, 69 So. 3d 1257 (La. Ct. App. 2011), plaintiff sustained a broken ankle, underwent surgery, and testified "she [was] no longer able to do things she used to do", including basic activities like walking on a treadmill. *Id.* at 1262–63. The court upheld a $50,000 award. *Id.* at 1263. And in *Laborde v. St. James Place Apartments*, 928 So. 2d 643 (La. Ct. App. 2006), plaintiff suffered a sprained ankle and underwent surgery, *id.* at 646. She was diagnosed with a 5% total-body disability and attended two months of physical therapy. *Id.* The court upheld an award of $20,000. *Id.* at 648.

Granted that prior general-damage awards are not always controlling, our clearly-erroneous standard of review and the range of awards in factually analogous cases preclude reversing the award of $60,000. *See Lebron*, 279 F.3d at 326. While it may be lower on the scale of adequate amounts, it is not outside the bounds of plausibility to constitute clear error.

III.

For the foregoing reasons, the judgment is AFFIRMED IN PART and VACATED IN PART; this matter is REMANDED for the district court, consistent with this opinion, **{-182-}** to find the percentage of contributory **[—13—]** negligence based solely on Knight's stepping on the line and, concomitantly, to decide his total damages award. **[—14—]**

(Reporter's Note: Concurring Opinion follows on p. 260).

[—14—] {-182-} HO, Circuit Judge, concurring:

I join parts I, II.A.2, II.B, and III of the majority opinion. As for part II.A.1, I agree that our decision in *Williams v. Brasea*, 497 F.2d 67 (5th Cir. 1974), does not control the outcome of this case. *Williams* states that "a seaman may not be contributorily negligent for carrying out orders that result in his own injury, even if he recognizes possible danger." *Id.* at 73. Judge Barksdale dismisses this statement as mere *dicta* (because *Williams* involved a supervisor rather than a seaman), while Judge Elrod regards this statement as essential to the *ratio decidendi* of our decision. But we surely all agree that "[a] court [may] distinguish[] a precedent by discerning material differences between it and the present dispute." BRYAN A. GARNER ET AL., THE LAW OF JUDICIAL PRECEDENT 97 (2016). After all, "'[i]t is common to see a later narrowing of a [holding] that, in the heat of the moment and of the argument, was too broadly phrased. The original judge, later courts will say, did not have the other possible sorts of cases in mind.'" *Id.* at 98 (quoting KARL LLEWELLYN, THE CASE LAW SYSTEM IN AMERICA 15 (Paul Gewirtz ed., 1989)). That is precisely the approach we are taking here. "*Williams*, at most, stands for the proposition that a seaman may not be found contributorily negligent for carrying out a *specific order* from his superior that results in the seaman's injury." *Ante*, at 8 (emphasis added). *See generally ante*, at 5–7 (collecting cases distinguishing between general and specific orders). And the order given to Knight and Ladd was a general order, not a specific one. So *Williams* is distinguishable from this case. Accordingly, I agree that the district court was not precluded from finding Knight contributorily negligent. [—15—]

(Reporter's Note: Dissenting Opinion follows on p. 261).

[—15—] {-182-} **ELROD,** Circuit Judge, dissenting:

Andrew Knight suffered a severe injury aboard the *M/V Sea Hawk*. He argues that the district court erred, as a matter of law, by holding him contributorily negligent even though he was following orders at the time of his injury. Because our binding and longstanding precedent under the rule of orderliness precludes a finding of contributory negligence, I dissent.

I.

Under our precedent in *Williams v. Brasea, Inc.*, 497 F.2d 67 (5th Cir. 1974), we should hold that the district court erred by holding Knight contributorily negligent. In *Williams*, we stated that "a seaman may not be contributorily negligent for carrying out orders that result in his own injury, even if he recognizes possible danger." *Id.* at 73. In this case, it is undisputed that Knight was following orders at the time of his injury. Therefore, the district court erred by holding him contributorily negligent—plain and simple.

The majority does not alter *Williams*'s binding effect. Although one member of the panel would declare our longstanding rule in *Williams* dictum, the majority of this panel holds that it is not. *Williams* remains the law of this circuit.

Indeed, we reaffirmed the *Williams* rule in *Ledet v. Smith Marine Towing Corp.*, 455 F. App'x 417 (5th Cir. 2011). In *Ledet*, the vessel owner argued that the seaman was contributorily negligent while attempting to comply with the captain's orders. *Id.* at 422. We concluded, however, that "[b]ecause the district court found that Ledet was following orders, Smith **[—16—]** Marine's argument **{-183-}** about Ledet's own negligence is foreclosed by *Williams*." *Id.*[1]

The majority concludes that Knight's circumstances do not fall under *Williams*—reasoning that *Williams* can be distinguished because it dealt with a "specific" rather than "general" order and that Knight was given a general order. However, this reasoning fails in two ways.

First, we have never before read *Williams* as a case that only deals with "specific orders." Nor did the Ninth Circuit when they adopted the *Williams* rule. *See Simeonoff v. Hiner*, 249 F.3d 883, 890 (9th Cir. 2001) (adopting *Williams*'s rule and rejecting the specific-order distinction on the ground that it "fails to consider the effect of even a general order on a seaman" and that compliance with all orders from supervisors "will promote vessel safety and will aid efficacy of command at sea.").[2]

Second, while I reject the contention that *Williams* contained a general-and-specific-order distinction, even if we applied such a distinction in this case, *Williams* would still require holding that Knight was not contributorily negligent. Knight was given a specific order—he was ordered to perform a specific task at a specific time. That order was to change out the **[—17—]** stern line at a time when four-foot seas and winds of at least twenty miles an hour were causing the vessel to rock. He was then injured after stepping on the chafed line, which he testified was due to the rocking of the vessel. Knight followed his captain's order—exhibiting a compliance which "promote[s] vessel safety and . . . aid[s] efficacy of command at sea." *Simeonoff*, 249 F.3d at 890.

---

[1] The post-*Williams* cases Judge Barksdale relies on in Part II.A.1 of the opinion do not mention or modify *Williams*. *See Gautreaux v. Scurlock Marine, Inc.*, 107 F.3d 331, 333–39 (5th Cir. 1997) (*en banc*) (discussing negligence standard generally in a situation that did not involve following orders); *Boudreaux v. United States*, 280 F.3d 461, 466–74 (5th Cir. 2002) (assuming that the seaman following orders could be held contributorily negligent and analyzing whether the district court's distribution of fault was correct, not whether any fault should have been assigned to the seaman in the first place); *Pallis v. United States*, 369 F. App'x 538, 541–42 (5th Cir. 2010) (same).

[2] Some other circuits have crafted a narrower rule. *See Alholm v. Am. S.S. Co.*, 144 F.3d 1172, 1179 (8th Cir. 1998); *Burden v. Evansville Materials, Inc.*, 840 F.2d 343, 346 (6th Cir. 1988). We are bound by ours, which does not make a distinction between "general" and "specific" orders.

Simply put, following our longstanding precedent in *Williams*, I would hold that the district court erred by finding Knight contributorily negligent even though he sustained his injury while following orders.[3]

II.

Knight also contends that the district court clearly erred by awarding him only $60,000 in general damages, despite the multiple surgeries, lengthy physical therapy, and permanent impairment, which caused him to no longer be able to work on a vessel. I would reverse the district court judgment on this ground as well.

General damages are available "for pain and suffering and impact on one's normal life routines." *Barto v. Shore Constr., L.L.C.*, 801 F.3d 465, 473, 3 Adm. R. 415, 419 (5th Cir. 2015) (quoting *Crador v. La. Dep't of Highways*, 625 F.2d 1227, 1230 (5th Cir. 1980)). As a result of his injury, Knight needed to undergo **{-184-}** three reconstructive surgeries (which included the insertion of screws) and to attend approximately 100 physical therapy sessions. His doctor assigned him 14% foot-and-ankle impairment, 10% lower-extremity impairment, and 4% whole-person impairment. Examining the undisputed extent of Knight's injuries and impairment, the district court found $60,000 a sufficient **[—18—]** amount. However, factually analogous cases in both the Louisiana federal and state courts support a greater award.

In *Wynne v. Trotter*, 10-90 (La. App. 4 Cir. 6/30/10), 46 So.3d 678, 681, 685, for example, the plaintiff suffered a fracture in his right heel, causing a 12% leg-and-foot impairment. The plaintiff developed a permanent limp and lost his ability to run and stand for extended periods of time. *Id.* at 685. There was no indication that the plaintiff underwent surgery to repair the injury. *Id.* The court upheld an award of $185,000.[4] *Id.*

In another case, *Baham v. Nabors Drilling USA, LP*, 721 F. Supp. 2d 499, 516 (W.D. La. 2010), *aff'd*, 449 F. App'x 334 (5th Cir. 2011), the plaintiff fractured his ankle, precipitating surgery and the insertion of two screws. The court awarded $250,000 in general damages.[5] *Id.* at 520.

In its order denying Knight's motion to alter or amend the judgment, the district court distinguished *Wynne* on the ground that the plaintiff there suffered a fracture, whereas Knight merely "rolled his ankle." The court's description does not seem to capture an injury that entailed multiple surgeries and the insertion of screws. Whatever label is used, Knight's injury was severe enough to require him to undergo three surgeries and attend over a hundred physical therapy classes.

Furthermore, the cases relied upon by the district court in denying Knight's motion are not analogous. In the first, *Broussard v. Oak Trace Apartments*, 11-125 (La. App. 3 Cir. 7/13/11), 69 So.3d 1257, 1262–63, the plaintiff sustained a broken ankle, had to have surgery, and testified that "she **[—19—]** is no longer able to do things she used to do." However, she was also in a car accident unrelated to the lawsuit that aggravated her ankle injury. *Id.* at 1259. The court upheld a $50,000 award.[6] *Id.* at 1263. In the other case, *LaBorde v. St. James Place Apartments*, 2005-0007 (La. App. 1 Cir. 2/15/06), 928 So.2d 643, 646, the plaintiff suffered a sprained ankle and underwent surgery. She was diagnosed with a 5% post-surgery disability and attended weeks of physical therapy. *Id.* The court upheld a general damages award of

3 Because of this conclusion, I would not reach the issue of whether the district court erred in finding he acted negligently based on the facts in this case.

4 The present-day value of the award, according to Knight, is roughly $217,000. *See Ledet*, 455 F. App'x at 423 (calculating the present-day value of a prior award using the Bureau of Labor Statistics's CPI Inflation Calculator).

5 This is the equivalent of $298,000 today, using the CPI Inflation Calculator.

6 This is the equivalent of $57,000 today, using the CPI Inflation Calculator.

$20,000.[7] *Id.* at 648. Knight's injuries are much more severe.

The majority opinion also relies on *Seymour v. Cigna Ins. Co.*, 93-229 (La. App. 5 Cir. 1993), 622 So.2d 839, *writ denied*, 629 So.2d 1136 (La. 1993), which the district court did not cite. In that case, the plaintiff fractured his ankle, underwent two surgeries, required monthly treatment from his orthopedic surgeon for four years, and required injections of anesthesia into his sympathetic nervous system. *Id.* at 844. However, an orthopedic surgeon who examined the plaintiff determined that he did not walk with a limp, and the plaintiff testified that although he had to give up **{–185–}** some sports activities like roller skating, he still walked, drove, and took care of his young children. *Id.* There, the court upheld an award of $35,000.[8] *Id.*

On the spectrum between *LaBorde/Broussard* and *Wynne/Baham*, *Seymour* is closer to *Broussard/LaBorde*. These cases involved fewer surgeries and less impairment on the plaintiff's ability to perform his or her line of work.

While the "clear error" standard is high, it is not insurmountable. *See Graham v. Milky Way Barge, Inc.*, 824 F.2d 376, 389–90 (5th Cir. 1987) **[—20—]** (holding that district court erred in awarding inadequate damages). I would hold that the district court clearly erred in assessing a general damages award of only $60,000.

* * *

In this case, I would conclude that the district court erred twice: once by ignoring our binding and longstanding precedent in *Williams* that seamen who are injured while following orders cannot be held contributorily negligent and again by awarding insufficient damages. I respectfully dissent.

---

[7] This is the equivalent of $26,000 today, using the CPI Inflation Calculator.

[8] This is the equivalent of $63,000 today, using the CPI Inflation Calculator.

United States Court of Appeals
for the Fifth Circuit

No. 19-40799

RIVERA
VS.
KIRBY OFFSHORE MARINE, L.L.C.

Appeal from the United States District Court for the Southern District of Texas

Decided: December 22, 2020

Citation: 983 F.3d 811, 8 Adm. R. 264 (5th Cir. 2020).

Before **KING, STEWART,** and **SOUTHWICK,** Circuit Judges.

[—1—] {-814-} STEWART, Circuit Judge:

Captain Jay Rivera was hired by Kirby Offshore Marine, L.L.C. ("Kirby") to pilot the M/V TARPON ("Tarpon"), a 120-foot seagoing vessel. While aboard the Tarpon, Captain Rivera injured his foot when he tripped over a stair inside a hatch door. Captain Rivera's injuries prevented him from continuing to work as a harbor pilot, and he sued Kirby for his lost wages. The district court held a seven-day bench trial on Captain Rivera's claims. At the end of trial, the court determined that Kirby was liable to Captain Rivera on his claim of *Sieracki* seaworthiness and that Kirby was alternatively liable under the Longshore and Harbor Workers' **[—2—]** Compensation Act ("LHWCA"). The court awarded Captain Rivera $11,695,136.00 in damages. Kirby appealed. We AFFIRM. **{-815-}**

I. Facts and Procedural History

From June 2007 to July 2018, Captain Rivera was a state-commissioned Branch Pilot for the Port Aransas Bar and Corpus Christi Bay. As a Branch Pilot, he assisted vessels in navigating the Port Corpus Christi Ship Channel and the LaQuinta Channel.

Through July 2018, Captain Rivera was a member of the Aransas-Corpus Christi Pilots Association ("Association"), an unincorporated pilots association. The Association regulates the rules and procedures of licensed pilots practicing on the Port Aransas Bar, the Corpus Christi Bay, and the surrounding tributaries. The Association collects pilotage fees earned by the members, uses the fees in a common fund, and makes pro rata distributions to its members.

Captain Rivera was also the sole owner and officer of Riben Marine, Inc., an S-Corporation. Captain Rivera incorporated Riben Marine to receive his various forms of revenue. In addition to his pilot earnings, Captain Rivera also earned money as an expert witness and as a charter service provider.

On August 19, 2016, Captain Rivera was dispatched to pilot the Tarpon from the Port Aransas sea buoy to Oil Dock # 11 in the Corpus Christi Harbor. The Tarpon was indirectly owned and operated by Kirby. The Tarpon was attached to a tug and barge unit,[1] and Captain Rivera could not board the Tarpon without first boarding the barge. Captain Rivera traveled to the Tarpon by pilot boat and boarded the Tarpon using a ladder affixed to **[—3—]** the barge. Having just come from outside, Captain Rivera continued to wear his sunglasses while on the Tarpon.

After boarding, Captain Rivera was greeted by David Hudgins, a Kirby employee who was assigned to escort him to the Tarpon's wheelhouse.[2] Hudgins had only been working aboard the Tarpon for two days, and he had not been formally trained on how to escort pilots. Hudgins and Captain Rivera "transited to the stern of the barge where they both climbed down onto the deck" of the Tarpon. As they headed toward the Tarpon's wheelhouse, Captain Rivera slowed down and lost sight of Hudgins. Captain Rivera continued his journey to the Tarpon's wheelhouse without Hudgins escorting him.

[1] In a tug and barge unit, the tug fits into a notch on the barge's stern and is connected to the barge by a set of pins.

[2] The wheelhouse or house is the vessel's enclosed area that normally contains the vessel's navigation quarters or engine room. *See St. Phillip Offshore Towing Co. v. Wis. Barge Lines*, 466 F. Supp. 403, 406 (E.D. La. 1979).

To enter the wheelhouse, Captain Rivera had to climb over a two-foot-high bulkhead and through a watertight door. From the door, he had to use another step inside the engine-room hatch access door to step down to the interior deck area. The area was not well illuminated. When Captain Rivera reached the inside step, he stepped down toward the deck with his left foot. He landed on the hatch cover, rolled his ankle, and fell. Captain Rivera lay on the deck after his injury, and Hudgins eventually found him. Hudgins helped Captain Rivera the rest of the way to the wheelhouse. Once inside the wheelhouse, Captain Rivera requested ice and ibuprofen and reported his injury to Captain Crossman, the Tarpon's captain. Captain Rivera then piloted the Tarpon to its intended destination.

After exiting the Tarpon, Captain Rivera sought medical attention for his injury. Doctors confirmed that Captain Rivera fractured his fifth **[—4—]** metatarsal of his left **{-816-}** foot and placed his foot in an air cast. Captain Rivera experienced lingering injuries during his recovery, and doctors eventually diagnosed him with Complex Regional Pain Syndrome ("CRPS"). Captain Rivera was declared medically unfit for his mariner certification due to his condition and lingering injuries. On recommendation from the Board of Pilot Commissioners, the Governor of Texas revoked Captain Rivera's state harbor commission. After his commission was revoked, Captain Rivera lost his Association membership as well.

Captain Rivera sued Kirby under various maritime laws for negligence and vessel seaworthiness. Captain Rivera sought relief on alternative grounds for: Kirby's negligence under the common law, Kirby's breach of the duty of a seaworthy ship under *Seas Shipping Co., Inc. v. Sieracki*, 328 U.S. 85 (1946), and Kirby's negligently maintained vessel under § 905(b) of the LHWCA.

After a seven-day bench trial, the district court issued a Findings of Fact and Conclusions of Law order that concluded that the Tarpon was unseaworthy under *Sieracki* and that, in the alternative, Kirby was negligent under § 905(b) of the LHWCA. The district court also concluded that Captain Rivera was not contributorily negligent for wearing sunglasses aboard the Tarpon.

Because Captain Rivera's injuries prevented him from working as a harbor pilot, the district court awarded him damages for his past and future harbor pilot wages. Captain Rivera did not seek damages for his chartering or expert work because his injuries did not prevent him from working in these roles. The district court relied on Captain Rivera's economic expert's calculations and entered a judgment for Captain Rivera in the amount of $11,695,136.00. Kirby now appeals. **[—5—]**

II. Standard of Review

"We review legal conclusions and mixed questions of law and fact following a bench trial de novo." *In re Luhr Bros. Inc.*, 325 F.3d 681, 684 (5th Cir. 2003). The district court's factual findings are binding unless clearly erroneous. *Id.* "Questions concerning the existence of negligence and causation are treated as factual issues subject to the clearly erroneous standard." *Id.* (quoting *Avondale Indus. v. Int'l Marine Carriers, Inc.*, 15 F.3d 489, 492 (5th Cir. 1994)). We review the district court's finding of contributory negligence for clear error. *See Fisher v. Agios Nicolaos V*, 628 F.2d 308, 311–312 (5th Cir. 1980).

We review the district court's evidentiary rulings for abuse of discretion. *Am. Int'l Specialty Lines Ins. Co. v. Res-Care, Inc.*, 529 F.3d 649, 656 (5th Cir. 2008). We review damages calculations for clear error. *Deperrodil v. Bozovic Marine, Inc.*, 842 F.3d 352, 361, 4 Adm. R. 308, 313 (5th Cir. 2016).

III. Discussion

On appeal, Kirby argues that the district court committed five errors. First, it argues that Captain Rivera is a proper plaintiff under § 905(b) of the LHWCA and is therefore ineligible to bring a claim under *Sieracki*. Second, it argues that it was error to hold it liable under § 905(b). Third, it asserts that the district court erred in holding that Captain

Rivera was not contributorily negligent. Fourth, it asserts that the district court erred by permitting Captain Rivera to introduce evidence of Kirby's subsequent remedial measures. Lastly, it argues that even if it is liable for Captain Rivera's injuries, the district court improperly calculated damages because it overestimated his future earnings. **[—6—] {-817-}**

1. Captain Rivera's Status Under the LHWCA

Kirby argues that Captain Rivera is an employee of Riben Marine and is therefore an eligible plaintiff under 33 U.S.C. § 905(b). Kirby further argues that if Captain Rivera is eligible to bring a claim under the LHWCA, he is ineligible to bring a claim under *Sieracki*. Captain Rivera argues that he is not an employee of Riben Marine and therefore is not eligible to sue under § 905(b). We agree with Captain Rivera.

The district court concluded that Captain Rivera was not covered by the LHWCA because it was not clear "that [he] was the employee of anyone." *Bach v. Trident Steamship Co., Inc.* 920 F.2d 322, 327 n.5 (5th Cir. 1991), *vacated* 500 U.S. 949 (1991), *reinstated* 947 F.2d 1290 (5th Cir. 1991). Having determined that the record was unclear as to Captain Rivera's status as an LHWCA-covered employer, the district court analyzed his *Sieracki* unseaworthiness claim. *See id.* We review the district court's conclusion about Captain Rivera's status under the LHWCA de novo. *See New Orleans Depot Servs. Inc., v. Dir., Off. of Worker's Comp. Programs*, 718 F.3d 384, 387, 1 Adm. R. 228, 229 (5th Cir. 2013) (en banc).

Captain Rivera's potential LHWCA claim falls under 33 U.S.C. § 905(b). Section 905(b) states that "[i]n the event of injury to a person covered under this chapter caused by the negligence of a vessel, then such person, or anyone otherwise entitled to recover damages by reason thereof, may bring an action against such vessel . . . ." 33 U.S.C. § 905(b). To be "a person covered under this chapter," Captain Rivera must be the employee of someone. *See Bach*, 920 F.2d at 327 n.5. Since there is no evidence that Captain Rivera was an employee while aboard the Tarpon, he cannot be covered by the LHWCA.

Kirby argues that Captain Rivera was employed by Riben Marine when he was injured upon the Tarpon. But the facts do not support such a **[—7—]** conclusion. Captain Rivera was requested, hired, and paid through his affiliation with the Association. Kirby does not argue that Captain Rivera is an employee of the Association,[3] and we consider harbor pilots akin to independent contractors. *See, e.g., Steinhort v. Comm'r of Internal Revenue*, 335 F.2d 496, 499 (5th Cir. 1964).

Our holding is consistent with *Manuel v. Cameron Offshore Boats, Inc.* In *Manuel*, we analyzed a § 905(b) claim brought by an employee of an independent contractor. 103 F.3d 31, 32–33 (5th Cir. 1997). Because Manuel was an employee of a contractor, he was a proper plaintiff under the LHWCA. *See id.* at 33.

Captain Rivera is an independent contractor rather than someone's employee, and he is thus not covered by the LHWCA. Since he is also not a Jones Act seaman[4], he may proceed on a seaworthiness claim under *Sieracki*. *See* **{-818-}** *Aparicio v. Swan Lake*, 643 F.2d 1109, 1110 (5th Cir. Unit A Apr. 1981) ("If the harbor worker is not covered by the LHWCA, the Sieracki cause of action and the concomitant indemnification action afforded the vessel owner are both still seaworthy."). We therefore affirm the district court's conclusion that Captain Rivera is a *Sieracki* seaman. **[—8—]**

---

[3] Even if Kirby raised the argument that Captain Rivera is an employee of the Association, we would reject that argument. Associations are generally not liable for the actions of pilots. *See Steinhort v. Comm'r of Internal Revenue*, 335 F.2d 496, 499 (5th Cir. 1964). Beyond that, an association "does no business except as an agent of its individual members." *Mobile Bar Pilots Ass'n v. Comm'r of Internal Revenue* 97 F.2d 695, 697 (5th Cir. 1938).

[4] A Jones Act seaman is a "master or member of a crew of any vessel." *Chandris, Inc. v. Latsis*, 515 U.S. 347, 355–56 (1995). Neither party argues that Captain Rivera is a Jones Act seaman.

2. Captain Rivera's Sieracki seaworthiness claim

Having determined that Captain Rivera is a *Sieracki* seaman, we next turn to analyze his seaworthiness claim under *Sieracki.* Kirby reiterates its argument that Captain Rivera is covered by the LHWCA and thus ineligible to bring a claim under *Sieracki.* As we have already shown, that argument fails.

The district court determined that Captain Rivera's seaworthiness claim was meritorious. We review the district court's finding of unseaworthiness for clear error. *Jackson v. OMI Corp.*, 245 F.3d 525, 528 (5th Cir. 2001).

To prevail on his *Sieracki* unseaworthiness cause of action, Captain Rivera must prove that Kirby "failed to provide a vessel, including her equipment and crew, which is reasonably fit and safe for the purposes for which it is to be used." *Id.* at 527. He must also "establish a causal connection between his injury and the breach of duty that rendered the vessel unseaworthy." *Id.* at 527–28. "To establish the requisite proximate cause in an unseaworthiness claim, a plaintiff must prove that the unseaworthy condition played a substantial part in bringing about or actually causing the injury and that the injury was either a direct result or a reasonably probable consequence of the unseaworthiness." *Johnson v. Offshore Exp., Inc.*, 845 F.2d 1347, 1354 (5th Cir. 1988).

We cannot conclude that the district court committed clear error in concluding that the Tarpon was unseaworthy. Captain Rivera sufficiently demonstrated that his injuries were caused by his fall over the unmarked hatch door and that the door was a tripping hazard. Tripping hazards may render a vessel unseaworthy. *See Jussila v. M/T La. Brimstone*, 691 F.2d 217, 219–20 (5th Cir. 1982). We therefore affirm the district court's finding that the Tarpon was unseaworthy. **[—9—]**

3. Captain Rivera's Contributory Negligence

Kirby next argues that Captain Rivera was contributorily negligent by wearing sunglasses aboard the Tarpon. In the alternative, Kirby argues that the district court made insufficient findings on the contributory negligence issue. We disagree in both regards.

The district court concluded that Captain Rivera was not contributorily negligent. We review the district court's finding on the issue of contributory negligence for clear error. *See In re Luhr Bros. Inc.*, 325 F.3d at 684. "[A] finding is 'clearly erroneous' when although there is evidence to support it, the reviewing court on the entire evidence is left with the definite and firm conviction that a mistake has been committed." *Hobbs v. Petroplex Pipe and Constr., Inc.*, 946 F.3d 824, 829 (5th Cir. 2020) (alteration in original) (quoting *Anderson v. City of Bessemer City*, 470 U.S. 564, 573 (1985)).

Here, the district court did not err in determining that Captain Rivera was not contributorily negligent. The district court determined that Captain Rivera did not act unreasonably when he wore sunglasses aboard the Tarpon on a sunny August day. The district court also determined that the hazardous condition that caused Captain Rivera's injuries was not **{-819-}** open and obvious. Even if he had not been wearing the sunglasses, it is not clear that he could have seen the hatch doorstep and avoided his injury. Kirby has failed to demonstrate that the district court's contributory negligence determination was clearly erroneous.

Kirby also argues that the district court made insufficient factual findings on the contributory negligence question. We again disagree.

Federal Rule of Civil Procedure 52 requires that the district court "find the facts specially and state its conclusions of law separately." FED. R. CIV. P. 52(a). The district court's findings of fact and conclusions of law **[—10—]** must be "sufficient in detail and exactness to indicate the factual basis for the ultimate conclusion reached by the court." *Lettsome v. United States*, 434 F.2d 907, 909 (5th Cir. 1970).

The record indicates that the district court gave Kirby's contributory negligence argument full consideration. The district court's findings of fact and conclusions of law on the contributory negligence question are well within the specificity required by Rule 52. Beyond its legal conclusions, the district court also made several factual findings that indicate the basis for its determination. The district court determined that the edges of the hatch cover were not marked, that the hatch was unusually placed, and that the hatch cover was oddly positioned and difficult to see. We conclude that the district court's findings of fact were sufficient to indicate the basis for its ultimate conclusion that Captain Rivera was not contributorily negligent.

4. Subsequent Remedial Measures

Kirby next argues that the district court erred by allowing Captain Rivera to introduce evidence of a subsequent remedial measure. We disagree.

We review evidentiary rulings during a bench trial for abuse of discretion. *Am. Int'l Specialty Lines Ins. Co.*, 529 F.3d at 656. Even where the district court committed an error, we reverse only where the error affects a party's substantial rights. *See* FED. R. EVID. 103(a).

The district court allowed Captain Rivera to admit evidence of a photo showing that Kirby later placed reflective tape near the area where Captain Rivera was injured. Though the district court initially precluded Captain Rivera from introducing the evidence, it eventually let him after determining that Kirby opened the door. **[—11—]**

Assuming *arguendo* that the district court erroneously admitted evidence of a subsequent remedial measure, Kirby has not demonstrated that the error affected its substantial rights.

Kirby points to the district court's mention of the photo as evidence that its substantial rights were violated. Even without the photograph, there was evidence from which the court could conclude that Kirby was negligent. The district court's findings that the hazard was not visible and that the hatch was in an unusual place support a ruling for Captain Rivera, and this evidence exists independent of the photograph that Kirby takes issue with. We therefore hold that the district court did not abuse its discretion by admitting evidence of Kirby's subsequent remedial measures.

5. Damages

Kirby's final argument is that the district court erred in assessing Captain Rivera's lost future earnings. We disagree here as well. **{-820-}**

The district court determined that Captain Rivera was entitled to damages for his lost future earnings. Using Captain Rivera's expert's calculations, the district court awarded him damages of $11,695,136.00. We review the district court's calculation of damages for clear error. *Deperrodil*, 842 F.3d at 361, 4 Adm. R. at 313.

To determine lost future earnings in a maritime case, we (1) estimate the plaintiff's loss of work-life or expected remaining work-life; (2) calculate the lost income stream; (3) compute the total damage; and (4) discount that total to present value. *Culver v. Slater Boat Co.*, 722 F.2d 114, 117 (5th Cir. 1983). Kirby disputes the second step of the *Culver* analysis, the district court's calculation of Captain Rivera's lost income stream.

The district court adopted the recommendation of Captain Rivera's economic expert. Captain Rivera's expert used Riben Marine's Schedule K- **[—12—]** 1 tax forms to gauge his income rather than his personal tax returns. Riben Marine received Captain Rivera's pilot income as well as the income from his work as an expert and a charterer. Riben Marine's K-1 documents reflected the income that he earned from his pilot earnings. Captain Rivera's personal tax returns reflected the total income from his various income streams.

Had the district court relied on Captain Rivera's personal tax returns as Kirby suggests, the damages calculation would have been in error. Captain Rivera sought damages for his lost future wages as a harbor pilot. He did not seek damages for his work as an expert or a charterer because he was able to continue working in those roles after he was injured. His personal tax returns reflected his income from all three roles whereas Riben Marine's K-1 forms reflected his pilot earnings separately. Had the district court actually relied on his personal tax returns, the returns would have inflated his pilot income. The district court did not err when it used Riben Marine's K-1 forms.

Lastly, Kirby cites *Tran v. Abdon Callais Offshore, LLC*, No. 12-0999, 2014 WL 12538905, at *2 (E.D. La. Sept. 22, 2014) for the proposition that tax returns should be used as evidence of earnings. *Tran* says that tax returns can be used to estimate earnings, but it does not say that using tax returns to estimate earnings is required. Kirby has thus not demonstrated that the use of tax returns was clearly erroneous.

IV. Conclusion

For the foregoing reasons, we AFFIRM the district court's conclusion that Captain Rivera was a *Sieracki* seaman and prevails on his unseaworthiness claim. We also AFFIRM the court's conclusions as to Captain Rivera's lack of contributory negligence, the admission of the photo evidence, and Captain Rivera's damages.

This page intentionally left blank

United States Court of Appeals for the Sixth Circuit

United States Court of Appeals
for the Sixth Circuit

No. 20-5378

PROGRESSIVE RAIL INC.
vs.
CSX TRANSP., INC.

Appeal from the United States District Court for the Eastern District of Kentucky at Frankfort

Decided: December 2, 2020

Citation: 981 F.3d 529, 8 Adm. R. 272 (6th Cir. 2020).

Before **NORRIS**, **SUTTON**, and **KETHLEDGE**, Circuit Judges.

[—2—] {-530-} SUTTON, Circuit Judge: **{-531-}**

It took a ship and a train to transport two electrical transformers from Germany to Kentucky. The ocean leg was uneventful, and the transformers reached Maryland unscathed. But one of the transformers suffered damage during the inland rail leg to the Bluegrass State. The rail carrier, CSX, sought shelter under a provision of the original transportation contract that insulated subcontractors from liability. Because the terms of the contract apply to this dispute, we affirm the district court's decision to grant summary judgment to CSX.

I.

The controversy arises out of an international shipment of two electrical transformers from Bremerhaven, Germany, to Ghent, Kentucky. Siemens AG, a German company, sells electrical transformers and other industrial manufacturing equipment. It does business in the United States through a wholly owned subsidiary, Siemens Energy. K+N International arranges shipping contracts by putting sellers, like Siemens AG, in touch with carriers. It does business in Germany through a subsidiary, K+N AG, and does business in the United States through another subsidiary, K+N Inc.

In 2011, Siemens Energy, on behalf of Siemens AG, sold two transformers to Gallatin Steel, located in Ghent. Siemens AG retained freight forwarder K+N AG to make the necessary transportation arrangements. K+N AG retained Blue Anchor Line, which issued a bill of lading for the trip that provided "the terms of the carriage." *Norfolk S. Ry. Co. v. Kirby*, 543 U.S. 14, 19 (2004). Through the bill of lading, Siemens Energy agreed not to sue downstream subcontractors of Blue Anchor Line for any problems arising out of the transport from Germany to Kentucky.

K+N AG subcontracted with K-Line to complete the ocean leg of the transportation. And Siemens Energy contracted with another K+N entity, K+N Inc., to complete the land leg of the trip from Baltimore to Ghent. K+N Inc. contacted Progressive Rail, a rail logistics coordinator, **[—3—]** to identify a rail carrier. They settled on CSX, which agreed to complete the trip from Maryland to Kentucky.

During the rail leg from Maryland to Kentucky, one of the transformers was damaged. The problem allegedly cost Siemens Energy more than $1,500,000 to fix.

Progressive Rail filed a lawsuit in 2015 in federal district court in Kentucky against CSX, seeking to limit its liability for these costs. That same year, Siemens Energy filed a lawsuit in federal district court in Maryland against CSX, seeking recovery for the damage to the transformer. The actions were consolidated in the Kentucky federal district court.

The district court granted summary judgment for CSX because the rail carrier qualified as a subcontractor under the Blue Anchor bill and could invoke its liability-shielding provisions. Siemens Energy appeals.

II.

At stake is whether CSX is liable to Siemens Energy for the damaged transformer. There is a simple way to think about the dispute and a more complicated way. Either way, CSX is not liable.

The simple way turns on the terms of the initial transportation contract. Under the contract, the manufacturer agreed to ship the transformers from Germany to Kentucky. The contract accounts for the reality that water and land separate Germany **{-532-}** from Kentucky, arranging a trip with segments by ship and by train. And it accounts for the reality that subcontracts would be arranged for each stretch of the trip. Through it all, the contract says that "[t]he merchant undertakes . . . that no claim or allegation shall be made against any Sub-Contractor whatsoever, whether directly or indirectly, which imposes or attempts to impose upon any Sub-Contractor any liability whatsoever in connection with the Goods or the Carriage of the Goods." R.94-3 at 3. Because the contract defines Siemens Energy as a "merchant," it cannot sue a "Sub-Contractor," defined to include "rail . . . transport operators" like CSX. R.94-3 at 3. Thus: CSX is exempt from this lawsuit by Siemens Energy. **[—4—]**

That conclusion does not change if we account for some complications—the maritime nature of this contract and the terms of art and statutes that go with it: bills of lading, through bills, multimodal transportation, a Himalaya Clause, a Clause Paramount, the Carriage of Goods by Sea Act, *see* 46 U.S.C. § 30701, the Carmack Amendment, *see* 49 U.S.C. § 11706(a), and so forth.

The parties agree that the Blue Anchor bill of lading is a maritime contract. One objective of the bill after all is to transport goods by sea. *See Kirby*, 543 U.S. at 27. Under the federal common law for interpreting such contracts, as with most contracts, we respect the terms used by the parties in the agreement and give that language a fair reading. *Id.* at 22–23, 31; *Royal Ins. Co. of Am. v. Orient Overseas Container Line Ltd.*, 525 F.3d 409, 421 (6th Cir. 2008).

A maritime contract may set the liability rules for an entire trip, including any land-leg part of the trip, and it may exempt downstream subcontractors. Two things are required to accomplish both ends. One is that the contract must amount to a "through bill of lading," which covers "both the ocean and inland portions of the transport in a single document." *Kawasaki Kisen Kaisha Ltd. v. Regal-Beloit Corp.*, 561 U.S. 89, 94 (2010). The other is that the contract must include a "Himalaya Clause," one that extends liability protection to all subcontractors along the way. 46 U.S.C. § 30701 (Notes § 7); *Kirby*, 543 U.S. at 29. A Himalaya Clause, on the off chance you are wondering, takes its name from an English case about the steamship *Himalaya*, not from the far-above-sea-level mountain range. *See Dimond Rigging Co. v. BDP Int'l, Inc.*, 914 F.3d 435, 439 n.5, 7 Adm. R. 362, 363 n.5 (6th Cir. 2019).

With both provisions in place, the downstream subcontractor becomes insulated from liability. *See CNA Ins. Co. v. Hyundai Merch. Marine Co.*, 747 F.3d 339, 361, 2 Adm. R. 410, 426–27 (6th Cir. 2014); *Fortis Corp. Ins., SA v. Viken Ship Mgmt. AS*, 597 F.3d 784, 792 (6th Cir. 2010). Those are the rules. How do they apply here?

Is the Blue Anchor bill of lading a through bill? Yes. In the contract's top-right corner, it refers to the "Multimodal Transport" covered by the bill, hence contemplating sea and land legs. R.94-3. The contract defines multimodal transport to happen when "the Carrier has indicated a place of receipt and/or a place of delivery on the front hereof in the relevant spaces." R.94-3 at **[—5—]** 3. The carrier did just that. It indicated that Bremerhaven, Germany would be the port of loading, Baltimore, Maryland the port of discharge, and Ghent, Kentucky the "Place of Delivery." R.94-3 at 1; R.96-9 at 1. By its terms, the contract gave the parties every reason to "anticipate[] that a land carrier's services would be necessary for the contract's performance"—that **{-533-}** it contemplated a multimodal trip, that it indeed was a through bill of lading. *Kirby*, 543 U.S. at 32.

Does this through bill of lading exempt CSX from liability? Yes. The bill of lading contains a Himalaya Clause. It first allows the carrier to "sub-contract" any part of the carriage, including by "rail . . . transport operators" as well as by "any independent contractors, servants or agents employed by the Carrier in performance of the Carriage and any direct or indirect sub-contractors, servants or agents thereof, whether in direct contractual privity with the Carrier or not." R.94-3 at 3. It then provides every subcontractor with the "benefit of all provisions . . . benefiting the Carrier," including the covenant not to sue. R.94-3 at 3. It then provides that the merchants—defined to include the shipper (Siemens AG) and the consignee (Siemens Energy)—agree that "no claim or allegation shall be made against any Sub-Contractor whatsoever, whether directly or indirectly, in connection with the Goods or the Carriage of the Goods." R.94-3 at 3. Siemens Energy, a merchant, thus cannot sue CSX, a subcontractor, under the covenant not to sue.

As is their right, the upstream parties extended liability-limiting provisions to downstream rail carriers like CSX, opting to take on the risks of transport (and perhaps insurance) for themselves. *See Fortis Corp. Ins.*, 597 F.3d at 792; *CNA Ins. Co.*, 747 F.3d at 372, 2 Adm. R. at 436–37. In the context of a Himalaya Clause like this one, it makes no difference that the downstream carrier was not in privity of contract with either of the Siemens entities. *Kirby*, 543 U.S. at 34.

Trying to head off this conclusion, Siemens Energy maintains that the Blue Anchor bill of lading is not a through bill. But if that is the case, why does the bill refer to "multimodal" transportation and to "Ghent, Kentucky"? In reality, nothing in the text of the Blue Anchor bill helps Siemens Energy's case. It instead pivots to the claim that extrinsic evidence shows this language was a "glaring administrative error." Appellant Br. 26. But we do not use words **[—6—]** discovered through extrinsic evidence to contradict the direct and most reliable evidence of the meaning of a contract: the words within its four corners. *CITGO Asphalt Refin. Co. v. Frescati Shipping Co.*, 140 S. Ct. 1081, 1088, 8 Adm. R. 2, 4 (2020); *Royal SMIT Transformers BV v. Onego Shipping & Chartering, BV*, 898 F.3d 543, 551, 6 Adm. R. 238, 243 (5th Cir. 2018). Otherwise, downstream carriers in through bills of lading could not rely on the language of the upstream contracts. *See Kirby*, 543 U.S. at 25–27.

For what it is worth, Siemens Energy never offers cognizable evidence of an error anyway. The sole citation to the record used to support this argument involves the deposition of a K+N Inc. employee. But the individual was not involved in negotiating or drafting the contract, making his statement after-the-fact speculation that a mistake occurred. That does not suffice. "Oops" is not a reason for overriding the terms of a contract. That's especially so when employees of Siemens AG and Siemens Energy reviewed the bill of lading and did not notice any error until this accident occurred.

That CSX issued its own contract for the Maryland-to-Kentucky part of the trip does not alter this conclusion. The original contract referred to the need for downstream subcontracts. What was anticipated thus was needed. And giving the contract its special transportation label—a second bill of lading—hardly makes a difference. It just situates the new bill of lading in the context of the contract, an arrangement **{–534–}** for transportation. More than one bill of lading is not unusual. Sometimes they are even duplicative. *See Regal-Beloit*, 561 U.S. at 103–04.

That Siemens AG paid for the ocean leg and Siemens Energy paid for the land leg does not change things either. Why? The method of payment does not alter the method of liability. It was still a multimodal bill of lading and still a through bill of lading.

Siemens Energy says that these transportation arrangements usually work differently. That's a strange argument, for starters, given that *it* was a signatory to the original contract. But even if that is correct, it makes no difference. Sure, *Norfolk South Railway Co. v. Kirby*, 543 U.S. 14 (2004) and *Kawasaki Kisen Kaisha Ltd. v. Regal-Beloit Corp.*, 561 U.S. 89 (2010), involved contracts in which the shipping intermediary retained the rail carrier. But that does not mean all transportation agreements use this model. Otherwise, there would be few through bills **[—7—]** of lading from the manufacturer to the buyer. Nor at any rate is it unusual for subsidiaries of a parent corporation, in this case K+N AG and K+N Inc., to aid one another in carrying out a contract for multimodal transport. Cooperation between separate and distinct, yet related, subsidiaries is a mainstay of modern contractual arrangements. *Tenn. Valley Auth. v. Exxon Nuclear Co.*, 753 F.2d 493, 497 (6th Cir. 1985); *see United States v. Bestfoods*, 524 U.S. 51, 61 (1998); *Schenley Distillers Corp. v. United States*, 326 U.S. 432, 436–37 (1946).

Siemens Energy claims last of all that the covenant not to sue is unenforceable because a federal statute, the Carriage of Goods by Sea Act, guarantees a certain level of recovery. But it failed to raise the argument below and thus forfeited it here. *See Scottsdale Ins. Co. v. Flowers*, 513 F.3d 546, 552 (6th Cir. 2008). Several courts have rejected the argument anyway. *See, e.g., Sompo Japan Ins. Co. of Am. v. Norfolk S. Ry. Co.*, 762 F.3d 165, 183, 2 Adm. R. 78, 91 (2d Cir. 2014); *Royal SMIT Transformers*, 898 F.3d at 549–50, 6 Adm. R. at 241–42; *Fed. Ins. Co. v. Union Pac. R. Co.*, 651 F.3d 1175, 1180 (9th Cir. 2011).

We affirm.

This page intentionally left blank

United States Court of Appeals for the Seventh Circuit

United States Court of Appeals
for the Seventh Circuit

No. 19-2164

LEDURE
VS.
UNION PAC. R.R. CO.

Appeal from the United States District Court for the Southern District of Illinois

Decided: June 17, 2020

Citation: 962 F.3d 907, 8 Adm. R. 278 (7th Cir. 2020).

Before **BAUER, KANNE,** and **BARRETT,** Circuit Judges.

[—1—] {-909-} BAUER, Circuit Judge:

Bradley LeDure, a conductor for Union Pacific Railroad Company, slipped and fell while preparing a locomotive for departure. LeDure brought suit for negligence against Union Pacific under the Locomotive Inspection Act and the Federal Employers' Liability Act. The district court granted summary judgment for Union Pacific. It **[—2—]** found the Locomotive Inspection Act inapplicable and then determined that LeDure's injuries were otherwise unforeseeable because he slipped on a small "slick spot" unknown to Union Pacific. For the following reasons, we affirm.

I. BACKGROUND

On August 12, 2016, at about 2:10 a.m., LeDure reported to work at a rail yard in Salem, Illinois. His job was to assemble a train for a trip to Dexter, Missouri. The first step was to determine how many locomotives were necessary and tag each one to indicate whether or not they would operate.

Three locomotives were coupled together on a sidetrack. The locomotives arrived at 2:00 a.m. from Chicago, Illinois. LeDure decided that only one locomotive would be powered on. LeDure tagged the first locomotive for operation and the second for non-operation. He moved to the final locomotive, UP5683, to shut it down and tag it accordingly.

While on the exterior walkway of UP5683, LeDure slipped and fell down its steps. LeDure got up and proceeded to power down and tag the locomotive. He returned to where he fell and, using a flashlight, bent down to identify a "slick" substance. LeDure reported the incident to his supervisor. He gave a written statement before going home. Union Pacific conducted an inspection and reported cleaning a "small amount of oil" on the walkway.

LeDure sued Union Pacific for negligence. He alleged violations of the Locomotive Inspection Act and the Federal Employers' Liability Act, arguing that Union Pacific failed to maintain the walkway free of hazards. Both parties moved for **[—3—]** summary judgment. The district court agreed with Union Pacific and dismissed LeDure's claims with prejudice. The court found the Locomotive Inspection Act inapplicable since UP5683 was not "in use" **{-910-}** during the incident. It also held LeDure's injuries were not reasonably foreseeable because they resulted from a small "slick spot" unknown to Union Pacific. LeDure moved to alter or amend the judgment, and the court denied the motion. LeDure timely appealed.

II. DISCUSSION

We review *de novo* the grant of summary judgment. *Kopplin v. Wis. Cent. Ltd.*, 914 F.3d 1099, 1102, 7 Adm. R. 382, 383 (7th Cir. 2019). Summary judgment is required if "there is no genuine dispute as to any material fact and the movant is entitled to judgment as a matter of law." Fed.R.Civ.P. 56(a). A court will grant summary judgment against a party "who fails to make a showing sufficient to establish the existence of an element essential to that party's case, and on which that party will bear the burden of proof at trial." *Bio v. Fed. Express Corp.*, 424 F.3d 593, 596 (7th Cir. 2005).

The Locomotive Inspection Act and the Federal Employers' Liability Act together provide redress for injured railroad workers. Specifically, the Locomotive Inspection Act supplements a Federal Employers' Liability Act negligence claim. The Locomotive

Inspection Act delegates authority to the Secretary of Transportation to create regulations delineating the safe "use" of locomotives. 49 U.S.C. § 20701. If the plaintiff shows a regulatory violation, this establishes negligence per se. The plaintiff must still show, per the Federal Employers' Liability Act, the injury resulted "in whole or in part" from this negli- **[—4—]** gence. *Crane v. Cedar Rapids Iowa City Ry.*, 395 U.S. 166 (1969) (citing 45 U.S.C. § 51).

The first question for the Locomotive Inspection Act is whether the locomotive was "in use" at the time of the accident. *Brady v. Terminal Rail Ass'n of St. Louis*, 303 U.S. 10, 13 (1938); *Lyle v. Atchison T. & S.F. Ry. Co.*, 177 F.2d 221, 222 (7th Cir. 1949). The district court noted the circuit courts' various tests. For instance, while the Fourth Circuit created a totality of the circumstances analysis, the Fifth Circuit has said a locomotive is "in use" if it is assembled and the crew has completed pre-departure procedures. *Deans v. CSX Transportation, Inc.*, 152 F.3d 326, 329 (4th Cir. 1998); *Trinidad v. Southern Pacific Transportation Co.*, 949 F.2d 187, 189 (5th Cir. 1991).

In determining that UP5683 was not in use, the district court properly applied *Lyle* and its holding that "to service an engine while it is out of use, to put it in readiness for use, is the antithesis of using it." *Lyle*, 177 F.2d at 223. LeDure essentially seeks to limit this holding to say a locomotive is not "in use" only when it is being repaired, but this is an unduly narrow reading of *Lyle* and its progeny. *See Tisneros v. Chicago & N.W. Ry. Co.*, 197 F.2d 466 (7th Cir. 1952). The district court reasoned that UP5683 was stationary, on a sidetrack, and part of a train needing to be assembled before its use in interstate commerce. For those reasons, we agree it was not "in use" and that the Locomotive Inspection Act and its regulations are inapplicable.

LeDure argues that Union Pacific is nevertheless liable because it did not clean up the slick spot or alternatively because UP5683's walkway traction was not adequately maintained. For claims about unsafe work conditions, an **[—5—]** essential element of a Federal Employers' Liability Act claim is foreseeability, or whether there were "circumstances which a reasonable person would foresee as creating a potential for harm." *Holbrook v. Norfolk Southern Ry. Co.*, 414 F.3d 739, 742 (7th Cir. 2005) (quoting *McGinn v. Burlington N. R.R.*, 102 F.3d 295, 300 (7th Cir. 1996)). **{-911-}** The plaintiff "must show that the employer had actual or constructive notice of those harmful circumstances." *Id.* (citing *Williams v. Nat'l R.R. Passenger Corp.*, 161 F.3d 1059, 1063 (7th Cir.1998)).

The district court correctly held that LeDure failed to provide evidence sufficient to prove his injuries were reasonably foreseeable. Whereas the *Holbrook* plaintiff identified the potential source of oil he slipped on, LeDure does not claim Union Pacific had notice of the slick spot or any hazardous condition that could have leaked the oil. Instead, he argues that Union Pacific should have inspected UP5683 and cleaned the spot beforehand. But, as in *Holbrook*, there is no evidence that an earlier inspection would have cured the hazard. This is problematic when LeDure testified the spot was small, isolated, and without explanation. Under these facts, a jury could not find Union Pacific knew or should have known about the oil or its hazard to LeDure.

Finally, LeDure argues the district court failed to address his argument that UP5683's walkway was not adequately maintained. This is inaccurate. LeDure introduced pictures of UP5683's walkway two years after the incident and pictures of another locomotive walkway that did not use metal studs for traction. As the district court noted, LeDure presented evidence to support a design-defect theory but nothing to show negligence. Just as importantly, the cause of his injury was **[—6—]** undisputedly the slick spot and there is no evidence—aside from LeDure's lay testimony—to suggest the alternate design pattern could have prevented his injury.

III. CONCLUSION

We conclude that the Locomotive Inspection Act and its regulations are inapplicable since UP5683 was not "in use" at the time of LeDure's injury. We further hold that LeDure's injuries were not reasonably foreseeable under the Federal Employers' Liability Act and thus Union Pacific breached no duty of care. For those reasons, we AFFIRM the grant of summary judgment for Union Pacific.

United States Court of Appeals for the Eighth Circuit

United States Court of Appeals
for the Eighth Circuit

No. 18-3126

HALL
VS.
BNSF RY. CO.

Appeal from the United States District Court for the Western District of Missouri- Kansas City

Decided: May 1, 2020

Citation: 958 F.3d 672, 8 Adm. R. 282 (8th Cir. 2020).

Before **SHEPHERD, GRASZ,** and **KOBES,** Circuit Judges.

[—1—] {-673-} KOBES, Circuit Judge:

Joseph Hall appeals the district court's[1] denial of his motion for a new trial. He argues the court abused its discretion by refusing to provide the jury with a specific damages instruction. We find no abuse of discretion and affirm. **[—2—]**

Hall suffered a shoulder injury when he fell on a defective train crossover platform. He sued BNSF Railway Company for violating the Safety Appliance Act and sought damages under the Federal Employers' Liability Act (FELA). Before trial, Hall and BNSF proposed an identical, generic damages instruction based on Eighth Circuit Manual of Model Jury Instructions 15.70. Later, Hall submitted a new, more specific proposal instructing the jury that it could consider damages arising from Hall's pain and mental suffering, future pain and suffering, and lost earnings. This more specific instruction was based on Model Instruction 15.70's optional list of damages.

The district court rejected Hall's more specific instruction because it did "not believe that the evidence [was] sufficient to support a claim of future damages." July 11 Tr., D. Ct. Dkt. 117 at 304:6–9. Hall countered that the evidence at least showed both wage losses and pain and **{-674-}** suffering, *id.* at 304:14–17, and he requested that the court "use the bullet points in the [proposed] instruction so the jury understands that they're appropriately presented to them for consideration, even though its not future [damages]," *id.* at 304:14–22. The court also rejected this suggestion and submitted the initial generic instruction to the jury. Final Instruction No. 13 permitted the jury to award Hall an amount that "will fairly and justly compensate the Plaintiff for any damages you find the Plaintiff sustained as a direct result of the occurrence mentioned in evidence." D. Ct. Dkt. 105 at 19. The jury awarded Hall $35,000—an amount similar to his claim for lost wages. On appeal, Hall argues he was entitled to the more specific jury instruction.

Typically, we review jury instructions for an abuse of discretion. *Retz v. Seaton*, 741 F.3d 913, 919 (8th Cir. 2014). BNSF contends plain error review applies because Hall failed to provide *another* proposed instruction after the court rejected his more specific instruction. We disagree. Hall preserved his objection when he asked the court to use some of the bullet points for categories of available damages **[—3—]** after it rejected his specific damages instruction. *See Kehoe v. Anheuser-Busch, Inc.*, 96 F.3d 1095, 1104 (8th Cir. 1996). As a result, we will review for an abuse of discretion.

"A district court possesses broad discretion in instructing the jury, and jury instructions do not need to be technically perfect or even a model of clarity." *McCoy v. Augusta Fiberglass Coatings, Inc.*, 593 F.3d 737, 744 (8th Cir. 2010) (citation omitted). Our review is "limited to determining whether the instructions, taken as a whole and viewed in the light of the evidence and applicable law, fairly and accurately submitted the issues to the jury." *Lincoln Composites, Inc. v. Firetrace USA, LLC*, 825 F.3d 453, 461 (8th Cir. 2016) (citation omitted). "There is no abuse of discretion in denying a party's requested instruction if the instructions actually given by the trial court adequately and correctly cover the substance of the requested instruction." *Retz*, 741 F.3d at 919 (cleaned up). Finally, we will reverse only if "we find that the [instructional] error affected the

[1] The Honorable Gary A. Fenner, United States District Judge for the Western District of Missouri.

substantial rights of the parties." *Phillips v. Collings*, 256 F.3d 843, 851 (8th Cir. 2001).

Hall argues that he was entitled to the more specific damages instruction because in *Chicago & N.W. Railway Company v. Green*, 164 F.2d 55, 61 (8th Cir. 1947), we held that if the evidence is sufficient to support a party's theory of the case, he is entitled a "specific instruction" on that theory. Hall misreads *Green*, which involved the defendant's "theory of the accident." *Id.* Here, the instructions permitted Hall to present his theory of the case—that BNSF breached a duty it owed to him causing his shoulder injury.

Instruction No. 13 only dealt with damages and directed the jury to award Hall "any damages [they] find [Hall] sustained." D. Ct. Dkt. 105 at 19. We restate the obvious: the jury could award *any damages* to compensate Hall's injuries under FELA. As our model jury instructions state, the "list of [specific] damages is *optional* and is intended to include those items of damage for which recovery is commonly **[—4—]** sought in the ordinary F.E.L.A. case." *Eighth Circuit Manual of Model Jury Instructions* 15.70 (2017) (emphasis added). A district court does not abuse its broad discretion when it refuses to instruct on specific subsets of damages—especially when the jury is instructed to award recovery for any damages. *See Bd. of Water Works Tr. of Des Moines v. Alvord, Burdick & Howson*, 706 F.2d 820, 823 (8th Cir. 1983) **{–675–}** ("[T]he trial court is not bound to give the party's requested instruction.").

In any case, the generic instruction did not impact Hall's substantial rights. The district court invited Hall to argue each category of damages in closing. Hall told the jury that it should "keep in mind that there are other elements of damages that [it] should consider, including any pain and suffering, [and] disability [he] has from the time of the incident until his testimony." July 11 Tr., D. Ct. Dkt. 117 at 331:3–7. He then recounted all the evidence he believed supported those damages. After hearing that evidence, Instruction No. 13 permitted the jury to consider the full range of his alleged damages, including future damages.

We affirm the district court's denial of Hall's motion for a new trial.

United States Court of Appeals
for the Eighth Circuit

No. 19-2536

MILLER
VS.
UNION PAC. R.R. CO.

Appeal from the United States District Court for the District of Nebraska- Omaha

Decided: August 26, 2020

Citation: 972 F.3d 979, 8 Adm. R. 284 (8th Cir. 2020).

Before **COLLOTON** and **BENTON**, Circuit Judges, and **WILLIAMS**,[1] District Judge.

[—1—] {–981–} WILLIAMS, District Judge:

Gary W. Miller sustained injuries while serving as an engineer for Union Pacific Railroad Company (UP) when the train he was operating partially derailed **[—2—]** because a misaligned switch sent the train onto an unused siding track. Miller brought suit seeking compensation under the Federal Employers' Liability Act (FELA), 45 U.S.C. § 51 et seq., asserting FELA negligence per se and negligence claims. Specifically, in his negligence per se claim, Miller alleged UP failed to comply with federal regulations requiring it to align the switch for mainline movement. In his negligence claim, Miller alleged UP was negligent by failing to align the switch for mainline movement, properly secure switch keys to prevent a third party from changing the switch, install additional or different devices to lock the switch in place, or remove the switch when UP stopped using the siding track. Miller appeals the district court's[2] order denying his motion for partial **{–982–}** summary judgment and granting UP's motion for summary judgment. We affirm.

[1] The Honorable C.J. Williams, United States District Judge for the Northern District of Iowa, sitting by designation.

[2] The Honorable Laurie Smith Camp, United States District Judge for the District of Nebraska.

I.

At about 8:00 p.m., on September 20, 2015, Miller and a conductor were operating a train from Oklahoma City to Enid, Oklahoma along a mainline track. Near Enid was a switch that could divert a train from the mainline track to a siding track. UP had not used the siding track for about ten years and generally had not maintained the siding track. The siding track was short and there was a ravine past the end of the track. The siding track was not intended for high speeds.

Federal Railroad Administration (FRA) regulation 49 C.F.R. § 218.105 requires railroads to adopt policies designating the default position for switches. In compliance with this regulation, UP adopted an operating rule requiring switches to be lined for mainline travel when not in use. FRA regulations also require railroad switches to have reflectorized "switch targets" that tell the train crew whether a switch is lined for mainline travel or onto a siding track. A green square indicates the **[—3—]** switch is lined for mainline travel, and a red circle with a silver stripe indicates that the switch is lined for the siding track.

As the train neared Enid and was about 1,500 feet from the switch, Miller noticed the small silver stripe on the switch indicator. When Miller realized the switch was lined toward the siding track, he activated various braking mechanisms. The event data recorder for the train shows that Miller began braking just more than 800 feet from the switch. The train continued down the track and when the train was about 500 feet from the switch Miller could first see part of the red target. The lead locomotive went through the switch onto the siding track. The second locomotive derailed and pulled the lead locomotive to a stop. The remaining cars piled up near the switch. Miller was injured in the incident.

UP had inspected the switch just days before the accident, on both September 15 and 18, 2015, finding it aligned for mainline movement. The switch was secured by a standard switch lock that could be unlocked with a universal "102 key." These 102 keys worked on numerous UP switches and were distributed to various UP employees. Amtrak employees also had access to 102 keys. Those two inspections also showed the switch was spiked and anchored to prevent the switch from being misaligned to the unused siding track. The day before the accident, another train passed over the switch on the mainline without incident. Between that train's passage and the accident, there was no evidence that any UP employees were at the switch location within the scope of their duties.

After the accident, UP inspected the switch again. This time the switch was partially lined to the siding track but was not latched in that position. Someone had used a 102 key to unlock the switch. At some point before September 20, 2015, there was a burglary of an Amtrak building in nearby Oklahoma City, and a number of 102 keys were stolen. The side of the lock looked like it had recently been "beat on." **[—4—]** Locks that have not been opened for a while can be difficult to open, and sometimes it is necessary to strike the side of locks to get keys to work.

UP contacted the authorities, and Special Agent Scott Bybee ("Bybee") of the Railroad Police Department investigated the incident. In addition to the marks on the lock, Bybee also noted that the spikes and rail anchors holding the switch in place had been removed and were left near the switch. Bybee believed that the derailment was the result of a criminal act. **{-983-}**

In granting summary judgment in UP's favor, the district court concluded that a third party, not UP, had misaligned the switch causing the accident. The district court found that UP was not negligent per se because Miller could not prove UP violated the switch position regulation when it did not know or should have known that the switch had become misaligned. The district court also found that even if UP violated the regulation, its violation was excused because it exercised reasonable care to comply with the regulation. As to Miller's negligence claim, the district court found that Miller failed to produce facts raising a genuine issue for trial about whether UP breached a general duty of care.

II.

This Court reviews a grant of summary judgment de novo. *See Torgerson v. City of Rochester*, 643 F.3d 1031, 1042 (8th Cir. 2011) (en banc). "Summary judgment should be granted when—viewing the facts most favorably to the nonmoving party and giving that party the benefit of all reasonable inferences—the record shows that there is no genuine issue of material fact." *Schilf v. Eli Lilly & Co.*, 687 F.3d 947, 948 (8th Cir. 2012) (citing FED. R. CIV. P. 56(c)). "At summary judgment, the court's function is not to weigh the evidence and determine the truth of the matter itself, but to determine whether there is a genuine issue for trial." *Id.* at 949 (citing *Anderson v. Liberty Lobby, Inc.*, 477 U.S. 242, 249 (1986)). "There is a **[—5—]** genuine dispute when the evidence is such that a reasonable jury could return a verdict for the non-moving party." *Dick v. Dickinson State Univ.*, 826 F.3d 1054, 1061 (8th Cir. 2016) (citation and internal quotation marks omitted); *see also Odom v. Kaizer*, 864 F.3d 920, 921 (8th Cir. 2017) (reviewing grant of summary judgment de novo; summary judgment is proper when there is no genuine issue of material fact and party is entitled to judgment as a matter of law; evidence is viewed and all reasonable inferences are drawn in nonmoving party's favor). In summary judgment, however, "[t]he nonmovant 'must do more than simply show that there is some metaphysical doubt as to the material facts,' and must come forward with 'specific facts showing that there is a genuine issue for trial.'" *Torgerson*, 643 F.3d at 1042 (citing *Matsushita Elec. Indus. Co. v. Zenith Radio Corp.*, 475 U.S. 574, 586–87 (1986)).

III.

Enacted in 1908, FELA provides railroad employees with a federal cause of action for injuries. FELA states, in relevant part:

> Every common carrier by railroad . . . shall be liable in damages to any person suffering injury while he is employed by such carrier . . . for such injury or death resulting in whole or in part from the

negligence of any of the officers, agents, or employees of such carrier[.]

45 U.S.C. § 51. FELA imposes upon employers a continuous duty to provide a reasonably safe place to work. *Cowden v. BNSF Ry. Co.*, 690 F.3d 884, 889 (8th Cir. 2012). "Cognizant of the physical dangers of railroading that resulted in the death or maiming of thousands of workers every year, Congress crafted a federal remedy that shifted part of the 'human overhead' of doing business from employees to their employers." *Consol. Rail Corp. v. Gottshall*, 512 U.S. 532, 542 (1994) (quoting *Tiller v. Atl. Coast Line R.R. Co.*, 318 U.S. 54, 58 (1943)). "In order to further FELA's humanitarian purposes," Congress removed various common-law obstacles **[—6—]** to an employee's recovery, *id.*, and courts have "liberally **{-984-}** construed FELA to further Congress'[s] remedial goal," *id.* at 543. Nevertheless, "although common-law principles are not necessarily dispositive of questions arising under FELA, unless they are expressly rejected in the text of the statute, they are entitled to great weight in our analysis." *Id.* at 544.

"Under the FELA,'[a] railroad will be liable if its or its agent's negligence played any part, *even the slightest*, in producing the employee's injury.'" *Ybarra v. Burlington Northern, Inc.*, 689 F.2d 147, 149 (8th Cir. 1982) (quoting *Richardson v. Mo. Pac. R.R. Co.*, 677 F.2d 663, 665 (8th Cir. 1982) (emphasis in original)). "FELA's language on causation . . . 'is as broad as could be framed.'" *CSX Transp., Inc. v. McBride*, 564 U.S. 685, 691 (2011) (quoting *Urie v. Thompson*, 337 U.S. 163, 181 (1949)); *see also Fletcher v. Union Pac. R.R. Co.*, 621 F.2d 902, 909 (8th Cir.1980) ("The test of causation under the FELA is whether the railroad's negligence played any part, however small, in the injury which is the subject of the suit."). "That FELA is to be liberally construed, however, does not mean that it is a workers' compensation statute." *Gottshall*, 512 U.S. at 543. The basis of liability remains "negligence, not the fact that injuries occur." *Id.* (quoting *Ellis v. Union Pac. R.R. Co.*, 329 U.S. 649, 653 (1947)).

Under FELA, an employer's "fault may consist of a breach of the duty of care . . . or of a breach of some statutory duty." *Kernan v. Am. Dredging Co.*, 355 U.S. 426, 432 (1958). If a plaintiff proves a railroad violated a statutory duty, then the plaintiff need not prove the common law elements of foreseeability, duty, or breach. *Edwards v. CSX Transp. Inc.*, 821 F.3d 758, 760, 4 Adm. R. 316, 317 (6th Cir. 2016). Moreover, a violation of a safety statute "creates liability under FELA . . .without regard to whether the injury flowing from the breach was the injury the statute sought to prevent." *Kernan*, 355 U.S. at 433. Thus, "a railroad's violation of a safety statute . . . is negligence per se." *McBride*, 564 U.S. at 703 n.12. **[—7—]**

Under the Federal Railroad Safety Act (FRSA), 49 U.S.C. §§ 20101, et seq., the Secretary of Transportation delegated to the FRA the responsibility of prescribing regulations for the operation of railroads. One such regulation at issue here addressed the designation of switch positions. It provides, in relevant part:

> (a) Each railroad shall adopt and comply with an operating rule which complies with the requirements of this section. When any person including, but not limited to, each railroad, railroad officer, supervisor, and employee violates any requirement of an operating rule which complies with the requirements of this section, that person shall be considered to have violated the requirements of this section.
>
> (b) Designating switch position. The normal position of a hand-operated main track switch shall be designated by the railroad in writing and the switch shall be lined and locked in that position when not in use except when:
>
>> (1) The train dispatcher directs otherwise with respect to the position of a hand-operated main track switch and the necessary protection is provided; or

(2) The hand-operated switch is left in the charge of a crewmember of another train, a switchtender, or a roadway worker in charge.

49 C.F.R. § 218.105. A separate regulation requires railroads to inspect "each switch . . . at least monthly." 49 C.F.R. § 213.235. **{-985-}**

IV.

Miller alleges UP was negligent per se for violating the regulation requiring that the main track switch be lined and locked for main line movement per UP's policy. The relevant portions of Section 218.105 require two things of railroads: 1) adopt a written operating rule designating the normal position of a hand-operating **[—8—]** main track switch; and 2) line and lock the switch in that position when it is not in use. Here, there is no question that UP adopted a written operating rule that switches be lined and locked for mainline movement when not in use. The question is whether UP complied with the rule by lining and locking the switch for mainline movement. There is no doubt that UP did line and lock the switch for mainline movement, and beyond that inspected the switch twice within days of the accident to ensure its proper alignment. There is also no doubt that, at the time of the accident, the switch was no longer lined and locked for mainline movement.

Miller posits that the fact the switch was not aligned for mainline movement at the time of the accident means UP failed to comply with Section 218.105. In short, Miller would have UP be strictly liable for any injuries resulting from the state of the switch, no matter who was responsible for the state of the switch. Throughout his briefing, Miller conflates "strict liability" with "negligence per se." That argument is not consistent with FELA, which is not a strict liability statute. *See Gottshall*, 512 U.S. at 543. Nor is it consistent with the plain language of Section 218.105, which imposes liability when any person, including any railroad, violates the rule. *See* 49 C.F.R. § 218.105(a) (assigning fault to "that person" who "violates any requirement of an operating rule which complies with the requirements of this section"). Liability lies, then, with the actor responsible for the violation—the person who caused the switch not to be aligned as designated. Thus, for UP to be liable, Miller would need to show that UP caused the switch to be moved out of its designated position.

Edwards, a Sixth Circuit case, is instructive. *See* Edwards, 821 F.3d at 762, 4 Adm. R. at 318–19. There, plaintiff suffered injury because of an unsanitary bathroom in a lead locomotive. *Id.*, 4 Adm. R. at 318–19. He sued under FELA, alleging negligence per se and arguing that the railroad violated a regulation that stated that the "sanitation compartment of each lead locomotive in use *shall* be sanitary." *Id.*, 4 Adm. R. at 318 (citing 49 C.F.R. § 229.139(a) (emphasis added)). A different regulation required the railroad to inspect each sanitation compartment daily. *Id.*, 4 Adm. R. at 318 (citing 49 C.F.R. § 229.21). The facts were **[—9—]** uncontested that the bathroom was unsanitary at the time of plaintiff's accident, and that the railroad had cleaned the bathroom less than 24 hours prior. *Id.* at 759–60, 4 Adm. R. at 316–17. The court rejected plaintiff's argument, ruling that it "reads too much into [the regulation] and too little into the context in which it appears." *Id.*, 4 Adm. R. at 318. The court read the two regulations together to require sanitary conditions at the time of daily inspection, instead of creating a regulatory scheme "creat[ing] a 24/7 strict liability duty—one that, as the district court pointed out, would require a full-time bathroom supervisor." *Id.*, 4 Adm. R. at 318; *see also Maracich v. Spears*, 570 U.S. 48, 68 (2013) (citing A. Scalia & B. Garner, *Reading Law: The Interpretation of Legal Texts* 180 (2012) ("The provisions of a text should be interpreted in a way that renders them compatible, not contradictory.")). This case is analogous. A different regulation requires railroads to inspect each switch monthly. *See* 49 C.F.R. § 213.235(a). Section 213.235 and Section 218.105 should be read as compatible, so that a railroad must inspect each switch monthly and it must not cause a switch to **{-986-}** be not aligned as designated. To do otherwise, as Miller contends, would nullify the monthly inspection requirement and require a "full-time" supervisor for every switch. *See Edwards*, 821 F.3d at 762, 4 Adm. R. at 318.

Here, Miller did not present any evidence that would raise a genuine issue of material fact that UP "played any part, even the slightest" to cause the switch to be moved from its designated position. *See Ybarra*, 689 F.2d at 149. Rather, the evidence showed the switch was misaligned by a criminal act of a third party. The evidence showed that someone had tampered with the lock and other safety devices to change the switch. A UP employee inspected the switch only two days before the accident and found it locked in proper alignment. Plaintiff offered evidence that at some unspecified time UP used the siding for storing equipment during maintenance. There was, however, no evidence that any UP employee was in the area between the time a train passed safely over the switch the day before and the accident. The lack of evidence of such activity is both a deficiency in plaintiff's burden to generate an issue of material fact and affirmative evidence that no UP employee used the siding in an official capacity at the relevant time. *See Torgerson*, 643 F.3d at 1042; *see also* **[—10—]** FED. R. EVID. 803(7). Any conclusion that UP changed the switch alignment because at some point in the past UP used the siding would rely on pure speculation or conjecture. Thus, the evidence failed to show that UP caused the switch to be moved out of its designated position.

Miller's focus on the other elements of a FELA claim are misplaced. It is true that under a FELA negligence per se theory, Miller need not show that UP acted negligently in violating a safety regulation. Thus, for example, UP would still be liable if a UP employee aligned the switch for mainline movement, but failed to adequately lock it in place. Even if the employee was not negligent and took reasonable efforts to lock the switch in place, UP would still be liable for any injuries resulting from the misaligned switch. But Miller must still show that UP committed the act that constitutes the violation. Here, there was no evidence a UP employee had anything to do with the improper alignment of the switch.[3] **[—11—]**

Similarly, under FELA a railroad would be liable if the railroad's conduct contributed to the injury, no matter how slight or small that railroad's conduct was in contributing **{-987-}** to the injury. For example, if a UP employee properly aligned the switch, but failed to properly lock it (even if that failure was not negligent), and a third party criminally moved the unlocked switch to the siding track, UP would still be liable even though the criminal was primarily responsible for the resulting injuries. Here, again, there is no evidence a UP employee played any role in the changing of the switch. The switch had been properly aligned and locked, a train had safely passed over the switch a day before, and the evidence showed that someone had tampered with the switch, lock, and other preventive measures. There is no evidence in the record that any act

[3] The dissent argues that the court's holding is foreclosed by the Supreme Court's holding in *Kernan v. American Dredging Co.*, and that the Supreme Court's ruling in *O'Donnell v. Elgin, Joliet & Eastern Railway Co.* illustrates that a railroad is liable when it violates a safety statute or regulation. These cases are factually distinguishable. In *Kernan* and *O'Donnell*, the facts show that the employer engaged in conduct that violated the statute or regulation. In *Kernan*, the employer set an open-flame kerosene lamp closer to the water than the statute allowed, which led to the ignition of inflammable vapors on the water and the seaman's death. 355 U.S. at 427-28. There was no evidence or suggestion that anyone but the employer was responsible for the location of the lamp. In *O'Donnell*, the railroad used a railcar that did not have a statutorily-prescribed coupler, leading to a worker's death. 338 U.S. 384, 385-86 (1949). In *O'Donnell*, there was no evidence or suggestion that a third party installed the improper coupler on the railcar. Here, the employer complied with the regulation. The evidence was uncontested that UP had properly aligned and locked the switch. The question before the district court, then, was whether plaintiff had presented evidence that generated a genuine issue of material fact whether UP, or a third party, then violated the regulation by changing the alignment. The district court found, and we agree, that plaintiff presented only speculation that a UP employee changed the alignment and, even if a UP employee did so, the employee acted outside the scope of employment.

of a UP employee contributed to the misalignment.

Miller repeatedly asserts that FELA imposes an "absolute duty" on railroads to comply with safety regulations. Neither the Supreme Court nor this Court has held that to be the case. When we have used the phrase "absolute duty," it was with respect to that portion of FELA that allows for causes of action based on other statutes. This Court has said, for example, that "[t]he [Federal Safety Appliance Acts, 49 U.S.C. § 20301 et seq.,] impose[s] [an] absolute dut[y] on railroads to provide required safety equipment on their trains, including safe power braking systems." *Grogg v. Mo. Pac. R.R. Co.*, 841 F.2d 210, 212 (8th Cir. 1988) (citations omitted). *Cf. O'Donnell*, 338 U.S.at 389, 390 n.7 (ruling that even the Federal Safety Appliance Act that requires railroads to ensure secure coupling–"in no way dependent on negligence"–has a limited defense for intervening acts, such as saboteur). Similarly, the Locomotive Inspection Act, 49 U.S.C. § 20701 et seq. imposes "an absolute and continuing duty to maintain [a] locomotive." *Lilly v. Grand Trunk W. R.R. Co.*, 317 U.S. 481, 485 (1943). The same is true of the Locomotive Inspection Act's predecessor, the Boiler Inspection Act. *Urie*, 337 U.S. at 188 (1949). In contrast, neither the Supreme Court nor this Court has found that the FRSA regulation at issue here imposes an absolute duty on railroads to ensure employee safety. The provisions of 45 U.S.C. § 51 which establish a negligence cause of action under **[—12—]** FELA do not establish absolute liability. "[FELA] does not make the railroad an absolute insurer against personal injury damages suffered by its employees." *Wilkerson v. McCarthy*, 336 U.S. 53, 61 (1949).

Because UP committed no act violating the regulation requiring switches to be aligned per the railroad's written policy, the district court did not err in granting summary judgment on Count II of Miller's complaint.[4]

V.

Miller also alleged that UP breached its duty of care under FELA because it failed to: (1) properly align the switch for main track movement; (2) protect its keys; (3) remove the unused sidetrack and switch; (4) use other methods to secure the switch; and (5) keep the switch position indicator clearly visible and clear of vegetation. To prove a FELA negligence claim, a plaintiff must prove the common law elements of negligence. This includes an element of foreseeability. *See McBride*, 564 U.S. at 703 **{-988-}** (emphasizing that "reasonable foreseeability of harm . . . is indeed 'an essential ingredient of FELA *negligence*.'" (alteration omitted, emphasis original) (quoting *Gallick v. Balt. & Ohio R.R.*, 372 U.S. 108, 117 (1963)). Thus, UP's knowledge is an affirmative element of Miller's negligence claim. In other words, summary judgment was appropriate unless Miller proffered evidence showing a genuine issue of material fact that UP had a "reasonable ground to anticipate that a **[—13—]** particular condition . . . would or might result in a mishap and injury[.]" *Burckhard v. BNSF Ry. Co.*, 837 F.3d 848, 853–54, 4 Adm. R. 360, 362 (8th Cir. 2016) (first alteration in original).

Here, UP cannot be liable under a negligence theory for failing to properly align the switch unless it knew or had reason to know it was misaligned. There was no evidence that UP was aware the switch was not properly aligned. As noted, UP twice inspected the switch within days of the accident and another train safely passed over the switch the day before the accident. Miller produced no evidence that UP was aware or had reason to believe that the switch had been or would be misaligned by a third party.[5]

[4] The district court ruled that Section 218.105 has a knowledge requirement Miller did not satisfy, and in the alternative, ruled that if UP failed to comply with the regulation, its conduct was excused because it took reasonable care to comply with the regulation. We need not address these issues. *See Reasonover v. St. Louis Cty.*, 447 F.3d 569, 578–79 (8th Cir. 2006) ("We may affirm summary judgment for any reason supported by the record, even if it differs from the rationale of the district court.").

[5] As the district court noted, even if the person who misaligned the switch was a UP employee, Miller did not point to any evidence that the employee was acting within the scope of

Likewise, Miller presented no evidence that UP failed to reasonably protect its keys or had reason to know that the security of its keys or locks were compromised. There was no evidence proffered that keys were stolen from UP or any of its facilities. The only evidence was that someone stole 102 keys from an Amtrak facility in Oklahoma City. Miller presented no evidence that UP was aware of that burglary before the accident or had reason to believe additional steps were needed to protect its switches from the criminal who had stolen the 102 keys.

And although removal of the switch or unused siding track would have prevented this accident, that does not mean that UP was negligent if it failed to do so. Miller proffered no evidence of an industry standard or other evidence that could lead a jury to find UP negligent for failing to remove the switch or track. The mere **[—14—]** existence of alternate safer methods alone does not establish negligence under FELA. *See Abernathy v. E. Ill. R.R. Co.*, 940 F.3d 982, 988, 7 Adm. R. 403, 405 (7th Cir. 2019); *Wright v. BNSF Ry. Co.*, 177 F. Supp. 3d 1310, 1316 (N.D. Okla. 2016).

Miller relies on *Stone v. New York, C., & St. L. R. Co.*, 344 U.S. 407 (1953), to support his argument that the existence of alternate safer methods to perform the job is evidence that the defendant did not act reasonably. In *Stone*, the plaintiff injured his back while he and one other employee were removing track ties using tongs. In determining if the employer was negligent, the Court considered the existence of three alternate methods to remove the ties other than the method used at the time of the injury. The Court also considered other evidence in the record of the employer's negligence, including the fact that there were other difficult ties on the stretch of track, that normally difficult ties were removed using four men instead of two, and the fact that plaintiff told his boss he was pulling as hard as he could but the boss ordered him to pull harder before the injury. The Supreme Court held "all these facts comprise the situation to be appraised in determining **{-989-}** whether respondent was negligent. Those circumstances were for the trier of facts to appraise." *Id.* at 409.

Courts have harmonized *Stone* with the principle that the employers need only take reasonable precautions, not every possible precaution, by holding that evidence of alternate safer methods is only relevant when the plaintiff can present some evidence that the method chosen by the employer was negligent. *See Molczyk v. Chic., Cent. & Pac. R.R. Co.*, No. 1:15-cv-00049-CFB, 2018 WL 6356068, at *2 (S.D. Iowa May 4, 2018) ("A plaintiff cannot attempt to prove that the defendant was negligent simply by pointing to alternative methods; he must first present evidence that the method actually employed was not reasonably safe, and may then seek to introduce evidence that safer alternative methods existed, that those methods were available at the time, and that they had been used under similar circumstances." (citing *Myrick v. Union Pac. R.R. Co.*, 84 N.E.3d 504, 531 (Ill. Ct. App. 2017) (internal quotation marks omitted)); *Miller v. BNSF Ry. Co.*, Civil Action No. **[—15—]** 15-cv-2268-WJM-NYW, 2017 WL 2001678, at *5 (D. Colo. May 11, 2017) ("The evidence in *Stone* reflected a dispute as to whether the method actually used had been reasonably safe. The fact that alternative methods had been available was therefore relevant [to] the jury's determination[.]"); *Uhl v. CSX Transp.*, Civil Action No. 3:08-0064, 2009 WL 1749372, at *7 (S.D. W. Va. June 18, 2009) (holding that evidence of alternative boarding locations was admissible because plaintiff represented he would present evidence that the chosen boarding location was dangerous).

Here, UP took significant steps to ensure that the switch was not lined toward the unused industry track. The switch was spiked, locked, and anchored to prevent mis-alignment. UP also periodically inspected the switch to make sure it was still properly lined and locked for mainline travel. The only

---

employment. Thus, UP would not be liable for the purported rogue employee's act under a respondeat superior theory. Miller did not challenge that finding on appeal. *Beasley v. Warren Unilube, Inc.*, 933 F.3d 932, 936 n.3 (8th Cir. 2019) ("Because Beasley failed to raise this claim in his opening brief on appeal, the argument is waived.").

evidence that arguably shows that the chosen method was unreasonable is that numerous people, including employees from other railroads, had access to 102 keys. This is not enough to show that UP's failure to adopt yet more measures to ensure safe travel on the mainline track constituted negligence.

Similarly, Miller failed to point to any evidence that would establish that UP was negligent if it failed to install additional or different devices to prevent someone from tampering with the switch. Miller suggests that UP could have used a "clamping" method to further protect the switch. Railroads use a clamp to temporarily protect tracks while performing maintenance and a UP employee testified that the method could have been used on the switch here. Miller also suggests that UP could have used a combination lock on which a universal 102 key would not work. Although it is again possible that these other measures could have prevented the accident in this case, there is no evidence that these measures constituted the standard of care in the industry or that the measures UP did take were unreasonable such that failure to implement the additional measures Miller advocates in hindsight constituted negligence. **[—16—]**

Finally, Miller alleged that UP was negligent for failing to maintain the switch position indicator such that it was visible at a reasonable distance of 1,000 feet. Here, at 1,500 feet Miller saw a silver stripe on the position indicator. He began breaking at least 800 feet before the switch. There was no evidence before the district court to generate an issue of fact about whether the accident could have been prevented had Miller seen the reflector sooner than he did. Miller adduced no evidence that a switch must always be **{-990-}** visible from a thousand feet because other factors, including geometry and geography, can affect its visibility. Miller presented no evidence that vegetation interfered with the visibility of the switch. The district court also noted that Miller presented no evidence about the physical condition of the switch reflector itself, the curvature of the track, or other factors important in assessing the distance from which the switch indicator should have been visible.[6] Moreover, the evidence here showed that the switch had not been fully locked into its misaligned position, which may also have affected its visibility. UP is responsible for ensuring the position indicator is sufficiently visible when the switch is fully locked in one position or another. Here, plaintiff offered nothing but "mere speculation, conjecture, or fantasy" to support his claim that the switch should have been visible from a greater distance and whether the accident could have been avoided if it had been. *Putman*, 348 F.3d at733-34.

In sum, the district court did not err in concluding that there was no genuine issue of material fact whether UP was negligent. **[—17—]**

VI.

Accordingly, we affirm the judgment of the district court.

(Reporter's Note: Dissenting opinion on p. 292).

[6] On appeal, Miller points to evidence in the record that the track was straight at this location, but failed to point to such evidence before the district court. The district court was not "obligated to wade through and search the entire record for some specific facts that might support the nonmoving party's claim." *White v. McDonnell Douglas Corp.*, 904 F.2d 456, 458 (8th Cir. 1990).

[—17—] **{-990-}** **COLLOTON,** Circuit Judge, dissenting:

Appellant Miller sued Union Pacific for negligence under the Federal Employers' Liability Act (FELA). As the court acknowledges, "a railroad's violation of a safety statute . . . is negligence per se" under the FELA. *CSX Transp., Inc. v. McBride*, 564 U.S. 685, 703 n.12 (2011). Negligence per se is a "label for what is simply a violation of an absolute duty." *Carter v. Atlanta St. & A.B. R. Co.*, 338 U.S. 430, 434 (1949). As the court also recognizes, if a plaintiff shows that a railroad violated a statutory duty, then he has established negligence for purposes of the FELA and need not prove the common-law elements of foreseeability, duty, or breach. "Once the violation is established, only causal relation is at issue." *Id.*

Miller contends that Union Pacific violated a federal regulation promulgated under the Federal Railroad Safety Act (FRSA), 49 U.S.C. § 20103. The regulation governs main track switches, and provides as follows: "The normal position of a hand-operated main track switch shall be designated by the railroad in writing and *the switch shall be lined and locked in that position when not in use*," except in circumstances not applicable here. 49 C.F.R. § 218.105(b) (emphasis added). Each railroad must have an operating rule that complies with that requirement. *Id.* § 218.105(a). Union Pacific has such a rule, to wit: "The normal position of a main track switch is for main track movement, and *it must be lined and locked in that position*." R. Doc. 41-2, at 2 (emphasis added). When a railroad violates a requirement of the operating rule, the railroad "shall be considered to have violated the requirements of" the federal regulation. 49 C.F.R. § 218.105(a). **[—18—]**

Whether Union Pacific violated the safety regulation depends on the meaning of the operating rule and the regulation. The rule requires that a main track switch "must be lined and locked" for main track **{-991-}** movement. Miller was injured when a misaligned switch caused the train that he was operating partially to derail. Union Pacific operated the railroad track and the main track switch, so it was the "person" responsible for complying with the regulation and ensuring that the switch was lined and locked. *See* 49 C.F.R. § 218.105(a). At the time of Miller's injury, the switch was not "lined and locked" for main track movement. It follows that Union Pacific violated the safety regulation requiring that the switch must be lined and locked in the normal position. The railroad was therefore negligent per se under the FELA, subject to a possible defense based on an intervening and independent cause. *See O'Donnell v. Elgin, J. & E. R. Co.*, 338 U.S. 384, 394 n.7 (1949).

Union Pacific and the court advance several arguments to avoid this straightforward conclusion. First, the court accepts the railroad's contention that while the Safety Appliance Act and Locomotive Inspection Act impose absolute duties on railroads that are enforced through the FELA, Union Pacific has no "absolute duty" to comply with safety regulations promulgated under the FRSA. Ante, at 11. Given that violation of an "absolute duty" is synonymous with "negligence per se," *Carter*, 338 U.S. at 434, the court's reasoning effectively eliminates a claim of negligence per se under the FELA when it is based on a violation of railroad safety regulations.

The court's conclusion was effectively rejected more than sixty years ago in *Kernan v. American Dredging Company*, 355 U.S. 426 (1958). There, the Supreme Court held that the FELA and the Jones Act both "impose upon the employer the duty of paying damages when injury to the worker is caused, in whole or in part, by the employer's fault." "This fault may consist of a breach of the duty of care . . . or of *a breach of some statutory duty*." *Id.* at 432-33 (emphasis added). The Court rejected the contention that "fault" was limited to violations of the Safety Appliance Act and **[—19—]** the Boiler Inspection Act, or that an employee's injury flowing from a statutory violation must be the injury the statute sought to prevent. *Id.* at 433.

The employer in *Kernan* violated a rule promulgated by the Coast Guard, *id.* at 427 & n.1, and the Court deemed the infraction to be a violation of the statute under which the regulation was promulgated. *Id.* at 428, 438 n.8. The dissenting opinion in *Kernan* argued for a narrower view of the FELA, but acknowledged the Court's contrary conclusion based on earlier precedent: "The Court thus reads these decisions to establish a doctrine under the FELA that *injuries following any violation of any statute, not simply the Safety Appliance and Boiler Inspection Acts, are actionable without any showing of negligence* . . . ." *Id.* at 445 (Harlan, J., dissenting) (emphasis added).

Kernan guides the analysis here. Under the FELA, there is "a bright-line rule" that an "employer's violation of a statutory or regulatory duty gives rise to FELA liability for a resulting employee injury." *Schmitz v. Canadian Pac. R. Co.*, 454 F.3d 678, 683 (7th Cir. 2006). As with the breach of the Jones Act regulation in *Kernan*, a violation of a regulation promulgated under the Federal Railroad Safety Act is the equivalent of a statutory violation that establishes negligence per se under the FELA. *See id.* at 682-83; *Eckert v. Aliquippa & S. R. Co.*, 828 F.2d 183, 187 (3d Cir. 1987); *Mosco v. Baltimore & Ohio R.R.*, 817 F.2d 1088, 1091 (4th Cir. 1987).

Second, Union Pacific and the court maintain that the railroad does not violate the safety regulation at **{-992-}** 49 C.F.R. § 218.105(b) unless it undertakes an "act" that causes a switch to be out of alignment. Whether the railroad violated a regulation, however, depends simply on the meaning of the regulation. The regulation at issue says flatly that a track switch operated by the railroad "shall be lined and locked" in the normal position. The rule does not merely provide that railroad employees must refrain from acts that cause a switch to be misaligned. Where the text of the regulation does not define a violation in terms of a causative act of the railroad, the **[—20—]** employee need not prove such an act to establish a violation. The court's inquiry into whether the railroad "played any part, even the slightest," in causing the switch to be moved, *ante*, at 9, confuses the question whether the railroad violated the regulation (and was therefore negligent per se) with the separate element of whether the employer's negligence (*i.e.*, the violation of the regulation) caused the employee's injury. *See Rogers v. Mo. Pac. R. Co.*, 352 U.S. 500, 506 (1957) ("Under [the FELA] the test of a jury case is simply whether the proofs justify with reason the conclusion that *employer negligence* played any part, even the slightest, in producing the injury or death for which damages are sought.") (emphasis added).

O'Donnell is illustrative. The Safety Appliance Act made it unlawful for a railroad to use any car that was "not equipped with couplers" that would remain coupled until set free by some purposeful act of control. 338 U.S. at 387 & n.2, 389. When an employee presented evidence "showing the breaking of the coupler," he established a violation of the Act, *id.* at 393, because the statutory requirement was simply to refrain from using any car that was "not equipped" with couplers that would remain coupled. The employee was not required to show that an act by the railroad caused the coupler to break. A railroad, the Court explained, could not "escape liability for a coupler's inadequacy by showing that too much was demanded of it, nor by showing that while the coupler broke it had been properly manufactured, diligently inspected and showed no visible defects." *Id.* at 393.

To justify reading a causal act requirement into the regulation on track switches, the railroad and the court invoke *Edwards v. CSX Transp. Inc.*, 821 F.3d 758, 4 Adm. R. 316 (6th Cir. 2016), but the analogy is wanting. *Edwards* held that because a regulatory requirement that restrooms "shall be sanitary" was tied to a daily inspection routine, and the next required inspection had not "become due" when a particular restroom was found unsanitary, the complaining employee did not establish a violation of the rule. *Id.* at 761, 4 Adm. R. at 317–18. The court attempts to draw a parallel by citing a regulation from Track Safety Standards that requires a monthly inspection of each **[—21—]** track switch. 49 C.F.R. § 213.235. The required inspections, however, are designed only to "detect deviations from the standards prescribed *in this part*," that is, Part 213 of the regulations. 49 C.F.R. § 213.231 (emphasis added). The rule that a main track switch must be "lined and locked" appears in Part 218 on Railroad Operating Practices. The inspections under Part 213 are not aimed at detecting deviations from a standard prescribed in Part 218. The Part 213 inspection regime thus does not qualify the requirement of § 218.105(b) that a main track switch "shall be lined and locked" or absolve the railroad of responsibility for alignment of switches during the period between monthly inspections.[7] **{-993-}**

Third, Union Pacific defends the district court's conclusion that the safety rule on track switches includes a knowledge element, such that the railroad violates the regulation only if it knows or has notice that a switch is misaligned. The court does not adopt this argument, *ante*, at 12 n.4, and the railroad's interpretation is incorrect. The rule on alignment of main track switches appears in Part 218 of the regulations on Railroad Operating Practices. The railroad derives the knowledge requirement from a provision that appears in Part 213 on Track Safety Standards, which states: "any owner of track to which *this part* applies who knows or has notice that the track **[—22—]** does not comply with the requirements of *this part*," must take certain actions. 49 C.F.R. § 213.5(a) (emphases added). The directive does not apply to Part 218 and the regulation on main track switches.

When the Federal Railroad Administration adopted the Track Safety Standards in 1998, the agency recognized that the "knowledge standard is unique to the track regulations; other FRA regulations are based on strict liability." *Track Safety Standards*, 63 Fed. Reg. 33,992-01, 33,995 (June 22, 1998). Ten years later, when the agency promulgated Part 218 and the rule on main track switches, it did not incorporate the "unique" knowledge requirement from Part 213. Therefore, a railroad violates the terms of § 218.105(b) if a switch is not "lined and locked" in the normal position, regardless of the railroad's knowledge.

Fourth, the railroad defends the district court's conclusion that the railroad's violation of the regulation was excused. The district court cited the common-law principle that "[a]n actor's violation of a statute is excused and not negligent if . . . the actor exercises reasonable care in attempting to comply with the statute." Restatement (Third) of Torts: Phys. & Emot. Harm § 15 (Am. Law Inst. 2010). The court does not endorse this conclusion either, *ante*, at 12 n.4, and the argument fails because the FELA does not incorporate such a common-law rule. The duty under the FELA to comply with a statute "is an absolute one, and the carrier is not excused by any showing of care, however assiduous." *Brady v. Terminal R. Ass'n of St. Louis*, 303 U.S. 10, 15 (1938). Liability "cannot be escaped by proof of care or diligence." *O'Donnell*, 338 U.S. at 390.

Based on the undisputed fact that the main track switch was not locked and lined in the normal position at the time of the accident, Miller has established that the railroad violated the safety regulation at 49 C.F.R. § 218.105(b). With one possible caveat, that is sufficient to establish negligence per se. In *O'Donnell*, the Supreme Court declined to say that a railroad may never effectively defend under the FELA by **[—23—]** showing that noncompliance with a statutory command was the result of an "intervening and independent

---

[7] Even if a violation of the regulation were premised on a casual act by the railroad, there likely would be a genuine dispute of fact about who caused the switch to be misaligned. Opening the switch required a key that Union Pacific provided to numerous employees, and Miller marshals circumstantial evidence in support of an inference that a railroad employee unlocked the switch and misaligned it while performing maintenance or otherwise. Reply Br. 17. While there is no *direct* evidence that a railroad employee was at the switch location within the scope of his duties, there also is no direct evidence that a third-party criminal or rogue employee misaligned the switch. The court refers to evidence that switch keys were stolen in a burglary, *ante*, at 3, but even if that would be circumstantial evidence of a crime at the switch, the only evidence of stolen keys is inadmissible hearsay, *see* R. Doc. 69-1, at 2, which "may not be used to support or defeat a motion for summary judgment." *Brooks v. Tri-Systems, Inc.*, 425 F.3d 1109, 1111 (8th Cir. 2005).

cause" such as "the work of a saboteur." 338 U.S. at 394 n.7. The parties and the district court have not addressed that issue **{–994–}** in this case. On remand, the district court could determine in the first instance whether an "intervening and independent cause" defense is available under the FELA and, if so, could allow the railroad to present evidence of its saboteur theory as a defense at trial.

For these reasons, I would reverse the grant of summary judgment and remand the case for further proceedings.

This page intentionally left blank

United States Court of Appeals for the Ninth Circuit

United States Court of Appeals for the Ninth Circuit

No. 19-50134

UNITED STATES
vs.
MORAN-GARCIA

Appeal from the United States District Court for the Southern District of California

Decided: July 23, 2020

Citation: 966 F.3d 966, 8 Adm. R. 298 (9th Cir. 2020).

Before **KLEINFELD** and **NGUYEN,** Circuit Judges, and **PAULEY III,*** District Judge.

* The Honorable William H. Pauley III, United States District Judge for the Southern District of New York, sitting by designation.

[—4—] {–968–} KLEINFELD, Senior Circuit Judge:

We vacate the conviction and remand for dismissal of the indictment without prejudice because venue was not established.

Ezequiel Francisco Moran-Garcia was among the passengers caught late at night six miles off the California coast in a small, disguised boat. He was indicted for attempting to enter the United States after having been deported, in violation of 8 U.S.C. § 1326(a) and (b), and for attempting to enter the United States other than at a place designated, in violation of 8 U.S.C. § 1325. The indictment alleged that these offenses had occurred "within the Southern District of California."

Before trial, the government argued that the district court should take judicial notice that the Southern District of California extended twelve miles out to sea and so instruct the jury. The evidence at trial established that Moran was apprehended six miles off the coast, within sight of the lights of San Diego. San Diego is within the Southern District of California. At the conclusion of the government's evidence, defense counsel moved under Federal Rule of Criminal Procedure 29 for a judgment of acquittal based on insufficient evidence of venue. Defense counsel argued that the Southern District extended only three miles out to sea, not twelve, so the government had failed to prove that the offense was committed within the Southern District. The district court denied the motion, accepting the government's argument that the location where the boat was captured was within the Southern District. The court then ruled that no jury **[—5—]** instruction on venue was appropriate because, in its view, venue was not a question of fact for the jury but instead a legal question that it had already decided by denying defense counsel's Rule 29 motion.

The government attorney gave bad counsel to the district court. Defense counsel was correct, and the court erred by taking the question from the jury. The Southern District of California as defined by Congress "comprises the counties of Imperial and San Diego."[1] Imperial County is landlocked, so only San Diego County matters to this case. "The territorial sea of the United States . . . extends to 12 nautical **{–969–}** miles,"[2] but that is not true of the Southern District of California. California law defines the western border of San Diego County as extending "to a point three English miles [into the] Pacific Ocean."[3] Thus it is beyond debate that the location of the putative offense was within the territorial waters of the United States but was not within the Southern District of California.

Controlling circuit law establishes that, although venue is not an element of the offense, nevertheless "it must still be proved by the government at trial."[4] "Venue is a question of fact that the government must prove by a preponderance of **[—6—]** the evidence."[5] It is a jury question. "[N]ormally it is not for the court to determine venue" and "it is error to not give a requested instruction on

---

1 28 U.S.C. § 84(d).

2 Proclamation No. 5928, 54 Fed. Reg. 777 (Dec. 27, 1988).

3 Cal. Gov't Code § 23137.

4 *United States v. Jensen*, 93 F.3d 667, 669 n.2 (9th Cir. 1996) (citing *United States v. Kaytso*, 868 F.2d 1020, 1021 (9th Cir. 1988)).

5 *United States v. Lukashov*, 694 F.3d 1107, 1120 (9th Cir. 2012) (citing *United States v. Casch*, 448 F.3d 1115, 1117 (9th Cir. 2006)).

venue."[6] Venue is "part of the bedrock of our federal system,"[7] and proper venue is a "constitutional right," "not a mere technicality."[8] The district court therefore could not properly decide venue itself and should have submitted the issue to the jury. The district court could not properly take judicial notice that the location where the boat was captured fell within the Southern District of California, since it did not.

The government argues a new theory of venue on appeal, one it did not urge at trial. Its new argument is that venue was proper in the Southern District of California under 18 U.S.C. § 3238, which provides that the trial of an offense begun or committed outside any judicial district "shall be in the district in which the offender . . . is arrested or is *first brought*."[9] The government argues that a rational juror could **[—7—]** have found it more likely than not that Moran was first brought to the Southern District of California. Therefore, the government claims, the errors of taking venue away from the jury and deciding the issue on an erroneous theory were harmless. This argument is colorable because, as we have held, error in taking venue away from the jury, though of "constitutional magnitude, . . . is not structural," and is "consequently susceptible of harmless error analysis."[10]

The government would thus have us apply the usual test for insufficiency of evidence: whether "*any* rational juror" could have concluded that Moran was "first brought" to the Southern District of California.[11] This would be the correct test if the jury had concluded that venue was **{–970–}** proper, but it is the wrong test for harmless error in this case where the question was not put to the jury and the jury made no determination.

"[W]hen a court has failed to give a venue instruction to the jury, that error will be viewed as harmless if the evidence viewed rationally by a jury could only support a conclusion that venue existed."[12] Thus, the test for harmless error is not **[—8—]** whether "*any* rational juror" could have concluded that Moran was first brought to the Southern District of California, but rather whether the evidence, had it been viewed by a rational jury, could *only* have led to that conclusion. This is a kind of converse of the sufficiency of the evidence test applicable where a jury has made a determination: Instead of asking whether a rational juror could have reached the conclusion, we ask whether a rational juror could have rejected the urged conclusion. Applying the correct test, the government has not established harmlessness of the error.

Sometimes "proof of venue may be so clear that failure to instruct on the issue is not reversible error."[13] In this case, though, the proof was not so clear. No witness testified to where Moran was first brought. The question was not asked. Government testimony established only that the boat was apprehended six miles offshore within sight of the lights of San Diego, and that the government's marine interdiction unit agent, who testified to the capture, was based in San Diego.

Venue, like most facts, can be proved as effectively by circumstantial evidence as by

---

[6] *Lukashov*, 694 F.3d at 1112 (citing *Casch*, 448 F.3d at 1117).

[7] *Casch*, 448 F.3d at 1117.

[8] *Lukashov*, 694 F.3d at 1119; *see also* U.S.CONST. art. III, § 2, cl. 3.

[9] 18 U.S.C. § 3238 (emphasis added). 18 U.S.C. § 3238 reads in full:

> The trial of all offenses begun or committed upon the high seas, or elsewhere out of the jurisdiction of any particular State or district, shall be in the district in which the offender, or any one of two or more joint offenders, is arrested or is first brought; but if such offender or offenders are not so arrested or brought into **[—7—]** any district, an indictment or information may be filed in the district of the last known residence of the offender or of any one of two or more joint offenders, or if no such residence is known the indictment or information may be filed in the District of Columbia.

[10] *Casch*, 448 F.3d at 1117.

[11] *United States v. Nevils*, 598 F.3d 1158, 1166 (9th Cir. 2010) (en banc).

[12] *Lukashov*, 694 F.3d at 1120.

[13] *Casch*, 448 F.3d at 1118 (quoting *United States v. Martinez*, 901 F.2d 374, 376 (4th Cir. 1990)).

direct evidence.[14] The government argues that this case is like *United States v. Trenary*, where we held the jury could infer that the defendants passed through the Southern District of California based on their drive from Newport Beach, California, to **[—9—]** Punta Bandera, Mexico.[15] But this analogy is poor. In *Trenary*, the smugglers driving from Newport Beach—on the coast in the Central District of California—to Punta Bandera—on the Baja California coast southwest of Tijuana—would almost certainly have passed through the Southern District of California.[16] But in the case before us, it is nowhere near so certain and obvious that the agents would have brought their arrestees to the Southern District of California. Though a rational juror could have so inferred, we cannot say that no rational juror could have concluded otherwise, considering that the government had the burden of proof.

Had they been instructed on venue, the jurors could have rationally concluded that, since no agent was asked where Moran was first brought, and it was within the power of the prosecutor to ask, that the agents did not know. Jurors might have rationally inferred from the absence of easily available evidence, as jurors often do, that if the government did not present evidence that Moran was first brought to San Diego, and had the burden of proving it, he probably was not brought there. The evidence demonstrated that the agents patrolled from San Diego all the way north to San Francisco. The agents did not testify that they stopped patrolling as soon as **{-971-}** they caught an offender to bring him or her in, so a juror might have inferred that the agents likely continued their patrol north, at least until their boat was too full to continue.

The government urges that we reach a contrary conclusion based on two documents that were not introduced **[—10—]** at trial. This argument is hard to understand, since rational jurors could not have drawn an inference from evidence never presented to them. Nor are the documents much help. The government says that Moran neither does nor could raise any actual doubt as to venue, perhaps suggesting that Moran could not have proved that he was not first brought into the Southern District. But this is irrelevant, since the burden of proof was and is on the prosecution. The documents are of limited force regardless.

One is the presentence report, which did not exist until after the trial and was under seal. Jurors never see these. The presentence report says that Moran and the other illegal aliens caught "were turned over" to border-protection agents at Point Loma Naval Base in San Diego. But the probation officer who wrote the report had no personal knowledge of this fact, and therefore must have been relying on what the prosecutors or agents told him, or assumed it, since this fact was of no importance to the sentencing recommendation.

The other document is an internal memorandum from one interdiction agent in the agency to another saying that the aliens on the boat "were transported to U.S. Naval Base Point Loma [in San Diego] for further inspection" and then "transported by U.S. Border Patrol Agents to the San Clemente Border Patrol Station for processing" and "arrested" at the dock in San Clemente. This document was submitted during motion practice but not at trial. No juror could have inferred anything from it, never having seen it. San Clemente, where Moran was arrested, is in the Central District of California, not the Southern District of California. Since the statute says venue "shall be in the district in which **[—11—]** the offender . . . is *arrested* or is first brought,"[17] had jurors seen this document, it might have added to their uncertainty. Neither they nor we, from what evidence was presented at trial—and even what was not presented at trial but has been put before us—would know from the record why Moran was arrested in the Central District of California rather than in the Southern District.

---

14 *United States v. Powell*, 498 F.2d 890, 891 (9th Cir. 1974).

15 473 F.2d 680, 681–82 (9th Cir. 1973) (per curiam).

16 *Id.* at 682.

17 18 U.S.C. § 3238 (emphasis added).

Venue is not an element of the crime.[18] Unlike an element, it need not be proved beyond a reasonable doubt.[19] But venue does need to be put to the jury, and proved by the government, albeit only by a preponderance of the evidence.[20] Neither was done here, and the evidence viewed rationally by a jury would not necessarily support the conclusion that venue lay in the Southern District of California. The errors, not being harmless under the applicable standard, require that Moran's conviction be vacated.

The parties agree that the case should be dismissed upon remand if we do not deem the error to have been harmless. They differ on whether dismissal should be with or without prejudice. Citing *Kaytso*, we noted in *United States v. Ruelas-Arreguin* that in the absence of a request by the **[—12—]** defendant for transfer to a proper venue, the indictment should be dismissed without prejudice.[21] **{-972-}**

Generally, under the Double Jeopardy Clause, the government does not get a second trial to prove what it failed to prove by sufficient evidence in the first trial.[22] But double jeopardy does not apply in the same way to a failure to prove venue as it does to a failure to prove an element of an offense. Unlike the typical reversal for sufficiency of the evidence, the missing evidence here did not go to guilt or innocence; that is, it had nothing to do with whether the defendant did or did not do the criminal acts alleged in the indictment. We held in *United States v. Kaytso* that double jeopardy does not bar a conviction where the defendant was re-indicted after dismissal of the first indictment based on the government's failure to prove venue in the first trial.[23] The reason was that "[w]hile venue presents a question of fact and must be proved by the government, it is not an essential element of the offense," and "failure to establish venue does not go to guilt or innocence."[24] Dismissal of the first indictment "cannot be **[—13—]** considered an acquittal and so is not shielded by the double jeopardy clause."[25]

The decision whether to apply the doctrine of collateral estoppel, urged by the defense, is within the discretion of the trial court, but retrial is not necessarily barred and requirements of fundamental fairness ultimately control.[26] Retrial was allowed in *Kaytso* even though venue was put to the jury, and the government's witness could not remember the exact location where the crime occurred.[27] Moran's case for collateral estoppel here is weaker than in *Kaytso* because the factual question was never put to the jury, so retrial would not upset a jury determination of a fact.

Accordingly, we vacate Moran's conviction, and remand with instructions for the district court to dismiss the indictment without prejudice. The district court has discretion with regard to collateral estoppel, in accord with the guidance in *Kaytso*, if that is raised in a motion before it.

VACATED and REMANDED.

---

18 *Jensen*, 93 F.3d at 669 n.2.

19 *Lukashov*, 694 F.3d at 1120.

20 *Id.*

21 *United States v. Ruelas-Arreguin*, 219 F.3d 1056, 1060 n.1 (9th Cir. 2000). Our attention has also been drawn to *United States v. Lozoya*, 920 F.3d 1231 (9th Cir. 2019), but that case has been taken en banc and has no effect on this decision. Nor could it have an effect, since the case does not modify the rule of *Kaytso* and *Ruelas-Arreguin*.

22 *See United States v. Scott*, 437 U.S. 82, 87 (1978).

23 *Kaytso*, 868 F.2d at 1021.

24 *Id.*

25 *Id.*

26 *Id.* at 1022.

27 *Id.* at 1021–22.

United States Court of Appeals
for the Ninth Circuit

No. 18-16026

GLOBAL COMMODITIES TRADING GROUP, INC.
vs.
BENEFICIO DE ARROZ CHOLOMA, S.A.

Appeal from the United States District Court for the Eastern District of California

Decided: August 26, 2020

Citation: 972 F.3d 1101, 8 Adm. R. 302 (9th Cir. 2020).

Before **THOMAS,** Chief Judge, and **FLETCHER** and **MILLER,** Circuit Judges.

[—4—] {–1104–} **FLETCHER,** Circuit Judge:

From 2008 through 2012, Global Commodities Trading Group, Inc. ("Global"), sold over fifty million dollars of agricultural commodities to Beneficio de Arroz Choloma, S.A. ("Bachosa"). After Bachosa fell behind on its payments on two contracts, Global brought suit against the corporation and two of its officers in the United States District Court for the Eastern District of California. The district court dismissed Global's claims for lack of personal jurisdiction and denied as moot the defendants' motion to dismiss for *forum non conveniens*. We hold that the district court had personal jurisdiction over both the corporate and individual defendants and that litigation in the Eastern District of California would not result in disproportionate inconvenience. We therefore reverse in part, vacate in part, and remand with instructions to deny the *forum non conveniens* motion on the merits.

I. Facts and Procedural History

Global is a California corporation with its headquarters in Placer County, California. At the time of the events giving rise to this action, it was engaged in the business of international sales of agricultural commodities. Bachosa is a corporation organized under the laws of Honduras with its principal place of business in Choloma, Cortés, Honduras. It is engaged in the business of importing and processing rice and corn from countries including the **{–1105–}** United States. Bachosa has no offices, real property, or employees in California. **[—5—]**

From 2008 through 2012, Bachosa purchased approximately 137,450 metric tons of agricultural commodities from Global for more than $50 million pursuant to hundreds of separately negotiated contracts. The contracts generally were cost, insurance, freight ("CIF") contracts, meaning Global's contractual performance was considered complete when the goods were loaded at the point of shipment. Global and Bachosa primarily negotiated their contracts by phone and email. Global's President, Ramiro Velasquez, stated in his declaration that several Bachosa employees also made business trips to Global's office in California. Those employees included the individual defendants in this case—Bachosa's President, Sady Farid Andonie Reyes ("Andonie"), and Secretary, Joyce Mary Jarufe Dox ("Jarufe").

On December 17, 2011, Bachosa entered into a contract with Global to purchase 14,500 metric tons of U.S. No. 2 or better long grain rough rice and a separate contract to purchase 5,000 metric tons of U.S. No. 2 or better white corn. According to Velasquez's declaration, Andonie and Jarufe met with Global employees at Global's California office in January 2012 in connection with the contracts. Andonie and Jarufe represented to Global that they had successfully extended their Honduran import permits to allow receipt of the rice and corn under the contracts. Andonie and Jarufe dispute that such a meeting ever occurred. They claim to have traveled to California only on two occasions, each for purposes of tourism.

Following the alleged January meeting in California, Global arranged for shipment under the contracts. The United States Department of Agriculture issued an inspection **[—6—]** certificate for the rice and corn in Woodland, California. The goods were shipped from the United States from Port of Darrow, Louisiana to Puerto Cortes, Honduras on the *MV UBC Sacramento* on January 19, 2012.

Upon arrival of the *Sacramento* in Honduras, Honduran authorities did not allow the goods to be offloaded. Global alleges that, contrary to the representations Bachosa's employees had made in California earlier that month, the company's import permits were invalid. While held in port in Honduras, the *Sacramento* incurred demurrage charges of approximately $644,000. Bachosa failed to make timely payment under its two contracts with Global, which it attributed to being assessed a 45% import duty on the goods. After further negotiations, Global and Bachosa entered into a memorandum of understanding, under which Bachosa acknowledged that it owed Global $7,073,648 for the goods and $644,697.92 for the shipping delays, and agreed to pay those sums. Andonie signed the memorandum as "Owner and Legal Representative" of the corporation.

Contemporaneously with the execution of the memorandum, Bachosa executed a promissory note in favor of Global for $11,000,000, and Andonie and Jarufe executed a personal guaranty that designated Jarufe a surety of the note. Although the document purports to bear her signature, Jarufe stated in her declaration that she "did not sign the guaranty," had "never spoken with Global or any of its agents regarding the guaranty," and "[n]ever saw the guaranty" before seeing the complaint in this action. In his declaration, Andonie claimed that Velasquez told him that he needed the memorandum, promissory note, and guaranty only so that he "could have something to show the banks," and that the **[—7—]** agreements would not be legally binding. Global provided the memorandum, note, and guaranty to its bank in order to maintain its line of credit. **{-1106-}**

In the spring of 2014, Bachosa defaulted on its obligations under the memorandum and note, and neither Andonie nor Jarufe made payment pursuant to the guaranty. Global lost its line of credit and shuttered its office.

Global and its insurer brought suit in California state court later that year against Bachosa, Andonie, and Jarufe. The defendants removed the action to the United States District Court for the Eastern District of California. Once in federal court, they moved to dismiss for lack of personal jurisdiction and for *forum non conveniens*. The district court allowed limited jurisdictional discovery. Without holding an evidentiary hearing, the district court granted the motion to dismiss for lack of personal jurisdiction. It denied Global's motion for leave to amend its complaint to add claims for fraud related to Jarufe's purported signature on the guaranty and denied as moot defendants' motion to dismiss for *forum non conveniens*. The district court reasoned that negotiations conducted through international communications were insufficient to support personal jurisdiction when the defendants were not physically present in the forum state. It discounted the visits Andonie and Jarufe made to Global's California office on behalf of Bachosa because those visits, if made, dealt with the underlying commodities contracts, not the subsequently executed memorandum, note, and guaranty.

Global timely appealed. **[—8—]**

II. Standard of Review

"We review *de novo* a district court's dismissal for lack of personal jurisdiction." *Picot v. Weston*, 780 F.3d 1206, 1211 (9th Cir. 2015). The plaintiff bears the burden of demonstrating that personal jurisdiction is proper. *Schwarzenegger v. Fred Martin Motor Co.*, 374 F.3d 797, 800 (9th Cir. 2004). However, "[w]here, as here, the motion is based on written materials rather than an evidentiary hearing, 'the plaintiff need only make a prima facie showing of jurisdictional facts.'" *Id.* (quoting *Sher v. Johnson*, 911 F.2d 1357, 1361 (9th Cir. 1990)). In this posture, we take as true all uncontroverted allegations in the complaint and resolve all genuine factual disputes in the plaintiff's favor. *See id.*

III. Discussion

A. Personal Jurisdiction

"'Federal courts ordinarily follow state law in determining the bounds of their jurisdiction over persons.' Because 'California's long-arm statute allows the exercise of personal jurisdiction to the full extent permissible under the U.S. Constitution,' our inquiry centers on whether exercising jurisdiction comports with due process." *Picot*, 780 F.3d at 1211 (internal citations omitted) (quoting *Daimler AG v. Bauman*, 571 U.S. 117, 125 (2014)); *see* Cal. Code Civ. Proc. § 410.10.

Federal due process permits a court to exercise personal jurisdiction over a nonresident defendant if that defendant has "at least 'minimum contacts' with the relevant forum **[—9—]** such that the exercise of jurisdiction 'does not offend traditional notions of fair play and substantial justice.'" *Schwarzenegger*, 374 F.3d at 801 (quoting *Int'l Shoe Co. v. Washington*, 326 U.S. 310, 316 (1945)). Those contacts may be so continuous and systematic as to render a defendant essentially at home in the forum state and amenable to any suit there. Alternatively, a court may exercise jurisdiction over "issues deriving from, or connected with, the very controversy that establishes jurisdiction." *Goodyear Dunlop Tires Operations, S.A. v. Brown*, 564 U.S. 915, 919 (2011). The Supreme Court has referred to these different **{-1107-}** bases for personal jurisdiction as "general" and "specific" jurisdiction. *See, e.g.*, *id.*; *Bristol-Myers Squibb Co. v. Superior Court of Cal.*, 137 S. Ct. 1773, 1779–80 (2017).

Global does not contend that either Bachosa or the individual defendants have contacts so continuous and systematic as to render them essentially at home in California and thus amenable to general jurisdiction. We consider whether their contacts with the State of California in connection with this controversy are enough to allow the exercise of specific jurisdiction.

1. Specific Jurisdiction over Bachosa

We use a three-prong test for analyzing claims of specific jurisdiction. First, "[t]he non-resident defendant must purposefully direct his activities or consummate some transaction with the forum or resident thereof; or perform some act by which he purposefully avails himself of the privilege of conducting activities in the forum, thereby invoking the benefits and protections of its laws." *Schwarzenegger*, 374 F.3d at 802 (quoting *Lake v. Lake*, **[—10—]** 817 F.2d 1416, 1421 (9th Cir. 1987)). Second, the claim must arise out of or relate to the defendant's forum-related activities. *Id.* Finally, the exercise of jurisdiction must be reasonable. *Id.* The plaintiff must satisfy the first two prongs of this test. "If the plaintiff succeeds in satisfying both of the first two prongs, the burden then shifts to the defendant to 'present a compelling case' that the exercise of jurisdiction would not be reasonable." *Id.* (quoting *Burger King Corp. v. Rudzewicz*, 471 U.S. 462, 476–78 (1985)).

Under the first prong of the specific-jurisdiction inquiry, "purposeful availment" and "purposeful direction" are distinct concepts. *Id.* at 802. Purposeful availment generally provides a more useful frame of analysis for claims sounding in contract, while purposeful direction is often the better approach for analyzing claims in tort. *See id.*; *Picot*, 780 F.3d at 1212. However, our cases do not impose a rigid dividing line between these two types of claims. When both contract and tort claims are at issue, both tests are relevant. *See Picot*, 780 F.3d at 1212. At bottom, both purposeful availment and purposeful direction ask whether defendants have voluntarily derived some benefit from their interstate activities such that they "will not be haled into a jurisdiction solely as a result of 'random,' 'fortuitous,' or 'attenuated' contacts." *Burger King*, 471 U.S. at 474–75 (quoting *Keeton v. Hustler Magazine, Inc.*, 465 U.S. 770, 773–74 (1984)).

The Supreme Court's decision in *Burger King* guides our analysis in this case. Burger King Corporation sued a Michigan franchisee in federal court in Florida—where Burger King had its principal place of business—for breach of the franchise agreement. *Id.* at 466–68. The defendant franchisee was a Michigan resident with no physical **[—11—]** connection to Florida. *Id.* at 479. Indeed, he had never been to Florida. Nonetheless, the Court held that because Burger King and the franchisee had agreed to an ongoing business relationship with foreseeable consequences in Florida, the franchisee was amenable to suit there. The franchise agreement was not an isolated or fleeting business contact. Instead, it was a contract that contemplated a long-term relationship between the parties and "continuing and widereaching contacts with Burger King in Florida." *Id.* at 480.

The Court rejected any sort of "mechanical test[]" based on "conceptualistic theories of the place or contracting or of performance." *Id.* at 478–79 (internal citations and quotation marks **{–1108–}** omitted). Whether performance was to be rendered in Michigan or in Florida was disputed in the case. *See id.* at 476; *id.* at 488 (Stevens, J., dissenting). Rather than looking to the place of performance, the Court looked to the business reality behind the particular contract at issue. The Court wrote, "[W]e have emphasized the need for a highly realistic approach that recognizes that a contract is ordinarily but an intermediate step serving to tie up prior business negotiations with future consequences which themselves are the real object of the business transaction. It is these factors—prior negotiations and contemplated future consequences, along with the terms of the contract and the parties' actual course of dealing—that must be evaluated in determining whether the defendant purposefully established minimum contacts within the forum." *Id.* at 479 (internal citations and quotation marks omitted).

Following the lead of the Court in *Burger King*, we have emphasized that courts must evaluate the parties' entire course of dealing, not solely the particular contract or tortious **[—12—]** conduct giving rise to the claim, when assessing whether a defendant has minimum contacts with a forum. *See, e.g., Picot*, 780 F.3d at 1212; *Sher*, 911 F.2d at 1363–64; *see also Yahoo! Inc. v. La Ligue Contre Le Racisme Et L'Antisemitisme*, 433 F.3d 1199, 1207–08 (9th Cir. 2006) (en banc) (per curiam) (collecting cases). In cases where we have held that a contract between a forum resident and a nonresident did not give rise to specific jurisdiction in the forum, we have done so because the business relationship between the parties was fleeting or its center of gravity lay elsewhere. *See, e.g., Boschetto v. Hansing*, 539 F.3d 1011 (9th Cir. 2008) (holding that a single eBay sale to a California resident did not give rise to personal jurisdiction there); *Thomas P. Gonzales Corp. v. Consejo Nacional De Produccion De Costa Rica*, 614 F.2d 1247 (9th Cir. 1980) (holding that a contract resulting from public bidding in Costa Rica did not give rise to personal jurisdiction in California).

Interpreting genuine factual disputes in Global's favor—as we must in this posture—we conclude that Global has made a prima facie showing that Bachosa "reach[ed] out beyond [Honduras]" to "create continuing relationships and obligations with citizens of [California]." *Burger King*, 471 U.S. at 473. Bachosa sustained a relationship with Global over several years and hundreds of contracts, purchasing millions of dollars of goods to be shipped from the United States. The goods Bachosa purchased were graded according to American standards, and inspection certificates were issued in California. Bachosa consistently made payments on the contracts to Global in California. When difficulties arose concerning the two contracts at issue here, Bachosa induced Global to continue doing business with it by acknowledging its ongoing obligations to make payments in **[—13—]** California. The promise was made for the purpose of obtaining benefits from a California corporation. Although *Burger King* does not require physical presence, Global further alleges that Bachosa's officers came to Global's office in California and while there made the promises central to this dispute.

The district court erred by considering the memorandum, note, and guaranty in isolation, ignoring the business reality in which they were embedded. As just described, those agreements followed a lengthy and ongoing course of dealing. They recognized a continuing obligation in connection with past sales on which Bachosa had allegedly failed to make payments. Moreover, Global's claims here are not limited to breach of the memorandum, note, and guaranty. Global's complaint also included two claims in indebitatus assumpsit—"common counts," in the parlance of **{–1109–}** California pleading—alleging, independently of the agreements, that Bachosa had failed to pay for goods it had received. Those claims related to the underlying commodities transactions, not to the subsequently executed memorandum, note, and guaranty.

In sum, Bachosa maintained numerous contacts with California during the course of its years-long business relationship with Global. Those contacts gave rise to this dispute, and it was reasonable for Bachosa to expect that it would be haled into court in California to fulfill its obligations and to account for harm it foreseeably caused there. We therefore hold that the district court had personal jurisdiction over Bachosa in this action. **[—14—]**

2. Specific Jurisdiction over Andonie and Jarufe

Specific jurisdiction over Andonie and Jarufe presents a different question: when may a court exercise jurisdiction over individuals based on their contacts with a forum on behalf of a corporation? Andonie and Jarufe contend that a court may not consider such contacts at all. Instead, they argue, a court may consider only the actions they took in an individual capacity on their own behalf.

Our precedent rejects this limitation on personal jurisdiction over corporate officers. In *Davis v. Metro Prods., Inc.*, 885 F.2d 515 (9th Cir. 1989), employees of a corporation contended that their actions on behalf of the corporation could only subject them to jurisdiction in circumstances that would allow the court to pierce the corporate veil for purposes of liability. We held that constitutional due process imposed no such limitation. We noted that the Supreme Court had allowed the exercise of specific jurisdiction over employees based on actions they took on behalf of a corporation. *See id.* at 521; *see, e.g., Calder v. Jones*, 465 U.S. 783, 790 (1984) ("their status as employees does not somehow insulate them from jurisdiction"); *Keeton*, 465 U.S. at 781 n.13. As a matter of Arizona law, we held that the state's long-arm statute allowed the exercise of personal jurisdiction to the limits of the federal Constitution, and therefore did not shield corporate officers from jurisdiction over their persons based on actions within the scope of their employment. *Davis*, 885 F.2d at 522.

California's long-arm statute, like Arizona's, imposes no limitations on personal jurisdiction beyond those required by **[—15—]** due process. *See Picot*, 780 F.3d at 1211. Andonie and Jarufe's actions on behalf on Bachosa, like the actions of the employees in *Davis*, *Calder*, and *Keeton*, may therefore give rise to personal jurisdiction over them as individuals.

Although their status as officers of Bachosa does not foreclose personal jurisdiction over Andonie and Jarufe, their status also does not guarantee it. Personal jurisdiction over an individual who acts as an agent of a third party must be assessed on the individual's actions alone. *See Sher*, 911 F.2d at 1366; *see also Keeton*, 465 U.S. at 781 n.13 ("[J]urisdiction over an employee does not automatically follow from jurisdiction over the corporation which employs him. . . ."). We do not impute a corporation's forum contacts to each of the corporation's employees. Instead, we assess whether each individual had minimum contacts with the forum such that the exercise of jurisdiction over that individual would comport with traditional notions of fair play and substantial justice. *Calder*, 465 U.S. at 790.

Two of our cases are illustrative. In *Davis*, we held that two corporate officers had sufficient contacts with Arizona when they conducted meetings with clients in **{-1110-}** Arizona and ultimately entered into six agreements with Arizona residents on behalf of the corporation. *See Davis*, 885 F.2d at 522–23. In *In re Boon Global Ltd.*, 923 F.3d 643 (9th Cir. 2019), on the other hand, we suggested that signing a single contract with a forum resident on behalf of a corporation would not subject a corporate officer to personal jurisdiction in a claim for breach of that contract. However, with the limited factual record before us on a petition for writ of mandamus, we stopped short of holding in that case that the district court clearly erred in exercising jurisdiction. *See id.* at 652. **[—16—]**

Interpreting genuine factual disputes in Global's favor, Andonie and Jarufe had extensive contacts with California. Like the corporate officers in *Davis*, Andonie and Jarufe met with Global's employees in the forum state to negotiate the commodities transactions at issue in the suit. While in Global's office in California, Andonie and Jarufe falsely assured Global that Bachosa had extended its importation permits. Further, they had previously traveled to California on multiple occasions as part of the ongoing business relationship between Global and Bachosa. We hold that these contacts are sufficient to support the exercise of specific jurisdiction over Andonie and Jarufe.

The guaranty signed by Andonie and Jarufe may provide an independent basis for personal jurisdiction over the individual defendants. Global contends that in the guaranty Andonie and Jarufe assumed personal liability for the note. We have held that a corporate officer who personally guarantees a corporation's obligation "interject[s] himself into the transaction," subjecting the officer to personal jurisdiction on like terms as the corporation. *Forsythe v. Overmyer*, 576 F.2d 779, 783 (9th Cir. 1978).

Not all of our holding in *Forsythe* survived the Supreme Court's subsequent decisions in *Calder* and *Keeton*. Our statement in *Forsythe* that "a corporate officer who has contact with a forum only with regard to the performance of his official duties is not subject to personal jurisdiction in that forum," *Forsythe*, 576 F.2d at 783–84, is clearly irreconcilable with the Supreme Court's decisions subjecting corporate employees to suit in exactly those circumstances. *See Miller v. Gammie*, 335 F.3d 889, 900 (9th Cir. 2003) (en banc); *see also Davis*, 885 F.2d at 521 (rejecting the fiduciary **[—17—]** shield doctrine based on *Calder* and *Keeton*). However, our holding in *Forsythe* that a personal guaranty of a corporation's debt may give rise to personal jurisdiction over a corporate officer remains good law.

Global presented evidence that Andonie and Jarufe were key players in Bachosa's years-long business relationship with Global and that they personally assumed liability for Bachosa's obligations under the note. In these circumstances, they "could have reasonably foreseen that they would be haled into [California's] courts" if their actions caused harm there. *Davis*, 885 F.2d at 523. We therefore conclude that the district court had personal jurisdiction over them in this action.

Because we hold that the district court had personal jurisdiction over Andonie and Jarufe based on Global's claims in its initial complaint, we do not reach the question whether its proposed amendments to the complaint would cure any jurisdictional defect.

B. *Forum Non Conveniens*

"We have discretion to reach *forum non conveniens* even if the district court declined to consider it." *Ranza v. Nike, Inc.*, 793 F.3d 1059, 1076 (9th Cir. 2015). It is proper to do so where "the record is sufficiently developed and the issue has been presented and argued to **{–1111–}** us." *Id.* (quoting *Dole Food Co. v. Watts*, 303 F.3d 1104, 1117 (9th Cir. 2002)). The parties briefed the issue at length and agreed during oral argument that we should reach it. In the interest of judicial economy, we exercise our discretion to do so. **[—18—]**

We decide questions of *forum non conveniens* as a matter of federal law even in cases where state or foreign substantive law governs. *Ravelo Monegro v. Rosa*, 211 F.3d 509 (9th Cir. 2000). "To prevail on a motion to dismiss based upon *forum non conveniens*, a defendant bears the burden of demonstrating an adequate alternative forum, and that the balance of private and public interest factors favors dismissal." *Ranza*, 793 F.3d at 1076 (quoting *Carijano v. Occidental Petroleum Corp.*, 643 F.3d 1216, 1224 (9th Cir. 2011)). "[F]orum non conveniens [i]s an exceptional tool to be employed sparingly . . . ." *Ravelo Monegro*, 211 F.3d at 514. To succeed, a defendant must make "a clear showing of facts which . . . establish such oppression and vexation of a defendant as to be out of proportion to plaintiff's convenience." *Id.* (alteration in original) (quoting *Cheng v.*

Boeing Co., 708 F.2d 1406, 1410 (9th Cir. 1983)).

We hold that the balance of private and public interest factors does not favor dismissal. Both sides identify witnesses for whom appearance in their home country would be more convenient. Most of the key documentary evidence, although originally in Spanish, has already been translated into English. The defendants contend that evidence related to Honduran importation permits and the demurrage charges incurred by the *Sacramento* would be more easily accessible in Honduras. However, evidence related to the negotiations in California would be more easily accessible in California. That some witnesses would prefer to appear in Honduras falls well short of a clear showing of facts which establish such oppression and vexation of a defendant as to be out of proportion to plaintiff's convenience. *Ravelo Monegro*, 211 F.3d at 514. Moreover, Global submitted evidence of significant safety concerns with travel to Honduras, **[—19—]** particularly for those who travel to the country for the purpose of collecting debt owed by Honduran companies.

The defendants contend that the public interest factors favor dismissal because Honduran law would govern this dispute. They point to California Civil Code § 1646, which requires the terms of a contract "to be interpreted according to the law and usage of the place where it is to be performed; or, if it does not indicate a place of performance, according to the law and usage of the place where it is made." In their view, the contracts for rice and corn did not indicate the place of performance. Therefore, in their view, the law of Honduras would apply, because that is where they contend they accepted the contracts.

We do not agree with the defendants' choice-of-law analysis. Section 1646 governs only the interpretation of contractual terms. Under California's choice-of-law rules, all other issues in a contract dispute, including the validity of a contract, are governed by governmental interest analysis. *See Frontier Oil Corp. v. RLI Ins. Co.*, 153 Cal. App. 4th 1436 (Cal. Ct. App. 2007); *see, e.g., Bernkrant v. Fowler*, 360 P.2d 906 (Cal. 1961) (en banc) (applying governmental interest analysis to determine which state's statute of frauds governed the validity of a contract). California law presumptively applies under the governmental interest approach unless there is a true conflict of governmental interests and the foreign jurisdiction's interests would be more severely impaired by the application of California law. *See* **{-1112-}** *S. A. Empresa De Viacao Aerea Rio Grandense v. Boeing Co.*, 641 F.2d 746 (9th Cir. 1981); *Kearney v. Salomon Smith Barney, Inc.*, 137 P.3d 914 (Cal. 2006). Thus, California law will likely **[—20—]** govern key issues in this dispute, including the validity and enforceability of the memorandum, note, and guaranty.

A plaintiff's choice of forum—particularly a plaintiff's "home forum"—is entitled to considerable deference. *Ranza*, 793 F.3d at 1076 (quoting *Piper Aircraft Co. v. Reyno*, 454 U.S. 235, 255 (1981)); *see also Ravelo Monegro*, 211 F.3d at 512 (noting that dismissal for *forum non conveniens* is typically only appropriate where a plaintiff chooses a forum wholly unrelated to the dispute). This case presents no more than the ordinary burdens any foreign defendant will bear when called to defend an action in the United States against a domestic plaintiff. Those burdens are insufficient to overcome the presumption in favor of Global's choice of its home forum.

Conclusion

We reverse the district court's order dismissing the action for lack of personal jurisdiction, vacate its orders on the parties' remaining motions, and remand with instructions to deny the *forum non conveniens* motion on the merits.

REVERSED in part, VACATED in part, and REMANDED.

United States Court of Appeals for the Ninth Circuit

No. 19-70521

JORDAN
vs.
SSA TERMINALS, LLC

On Petition for Review of an Order of the Benefits Review Board

Decided: August 28, 2020

Citation: 973 F.3d 930, 8 Adm. R. 309 (9th Cir. 2020).

Before **NELSON** and **BRESS,** Circuit Judges, and **BLOCK,*** District Judge.

* The Honorable Frederic Block, Senior United States District Judge for the Eastern District of New York, sitting by designation.

[—3—] {-933-} BLOCK, District Judge:

Anthony Jordan petitions for review of the denial of his claim for disability benefits under the Longshore and Harbor Workers' Compensation Act ("LHWCA" or "the Act"), 33 U.S.C. §§ 901–50. Because the Administrative Law Judge ("ALJ") applied an improper legal standard in assessing Jordan's disability, we grant the petition and remand. We write principally to set forth the standards for evaluating pain under the Act.

I

Jordan worked for SSA Terminals, LLC ("SSA"), as a longshoreman. Approximately 85% of the time, he was assigned to drive a heavy truck (called a "tractor") to move cargo containers around the terminal. Jordan also owned and operated a small landscaping business. **[—4—]**

On September 17, 2014, the tractor Jordan was driving was lifted and dropped by a crane. He suffered extensive damage to his lower back, including herniated discs, stenosis and nerve impingement. He was initially treated with medication and physical therapy, but continued to complain of back pain and spasms, as well as pain and numbness in his legs. These symptoms reduced his mobility and made him prone to falling.

Jordan saw Dr. James Reynolds, a spine surgeon, on three occasions beginning in November 2015. Dr. Reynolds recommended spinal fusion surgery, which was successfully performed on March 28, 2018.

Several years before the surgery, Jordan filed a claim for benefits under the LHWCA with SSA and its insurer, Homeport Insurance Company ("Homeport"). SSA and Homeport agreed that Jordan was totally disabled immediately following the accident and again as he recovered from surgery.

At some point during the claim process, Homeport ordered surveillance of Jordan. The surveillance videos, recorded in January 2015 and between February and June 2016, showed Jordan lifting and carrying various objects; engaging in physical activities such as bending, tossing a baseball, and doing push-ups; and attending sporting events where he appeared to sit and stand for long periods without difficulty.

Presumably based on the videos, SSA and Homeport took the position that Jordan was able to perform his usual work for a period of time between his accident and his surgery. Accordingly, the claim was assigned to an administrative law judge to determine whether Jordan was disabled between April 14, 2016, and March 27, 2018. **[—5—] {-934-}**

A. Testimony of Claimant and Treating Physician

The ALJ held an evidentiary hearing at which Jordan and Dr. Reynolds testified. Jordan testified, "There's nothing I can't do, but it all either is painful, elevates the pain, or I can't do it for the amount of time that would be considered a job." He further testified that his landscaping business required "[p]ushing a lawnmower, walking around with a blower, watering plants, some grooming, a lot of pointing, telling people what to do," as well as lifting "[m]aybe 35 pounds." Jordan continued to do landscaping work after his injury, but testified that it was "not at the capacity that [he] was." Instead of doing "every aspect of the job" as he did before, he was "more in the supervisor-type role" after his injury. He still did some physical tasks, but only "because [he had] no choice."

Dr. Reynolds corroborated Jordan's complaints of pain, testifying that MRIs revealed "modic changes," a condition "generally associated with a lot of back pain." Dr. Reynolds testified in particular that "bouncing around in a truck" would be "very painful" and "assume[d] it would accelerate the already significant degeneration that's present in the [lower back]." In sum, Dr. Reynolds opined that Jordan was totally disabled from work as a longshoreman, principally because he could not work "an eight-hour day in a regular fashion" and would have to "take breaks and do things to decrease the pressure on his back." He acknowledged that Jordan continued to work "about five hours a day" at his landscaping business, but "didn't discourage him from doing that" because he could "take breaks or lie down or lean against a wall."

Dr. Reynolds did not view the surveillance videos, but saw references to them in the reports of one of the non-treating physicians discussed below. **[—6—]**

B. Evidence from Non-Treating Physicians

The ALJ also received evidence in the form of the reports and depositions of three non-treating physicians retained to perform independent medical examinations: Dr. Yi Chiang, an osteopath; Dr. Charles Skomer, a neurologist; and Dr. Brian Su, an orthopedist.

Dr. Chiang saw Jordan on four occasions. At one point, Jordan asked Dr. Chiang to become his treating physician, but she declined. After the first three examinations, Dr. Chiang opined that Jordan was unable to work as a longshoreman; after the fourth, on February 26, 2016, she opined that he could return to work provided he did not need to bend at the waist more than 50% of the time, lift or carry greater than 20 pounds, or walk more than one hour at a time; she specifically opined that Jordan was "[a]ble to drive autos, cars, tractors." After viewing the surveillance videos, Dr. Chiang testified at a deposition that she would have said that Jordan could work without restrictions on February 26, 2016, because the videos showed him "surpassing those [restrictions] effortlessly."

Dr. Skomer examined Jordan on two occasions. After an examination on June 10, 2015, he opined that Jordan was totally temporarily disabled. After an examination on August 12, 2015, he opined that Jordan could perform "semi-sedentary" work for up to four hours a day, with "breaks for stretching" every 30 minutes. As with Dr. Chiang, Dr. Skomer changed his opinion after viewing the surveillance videos. In an October 2016 report, he stated that Jordan could perform his "normal employment full time, without restrictions," and that his prior opinions were "not valid or accurate" because it was not "reasonable" to conclude that Jordan "was experiencing lumbar and lower **[—7—]** extremity pain while able to **{-935-}** perform the activities observed on the video tapes."

Dr. Su examined Jordan on October 6, 2017, and reviewed the reports of Drs. Chiang and Skomer, as well as the surveillance videos. He opined that the surveillance videos were inconsistent with Jordan's complaints of pain, and that he could "return to his job as a longshoreman." Since Dr. Su viewed the surveillance videos prior to preparing his report, there was no need for him to revise his opinions.

C. Agency Decisions

The ALJ rendered his decision on May 29, 2018. He began by describing "the most difficult issue in this case" as "the difference between 'can' and 'cannot'":

> Mr. Jackson [sic] argues it may be literally true he "can" endure some level of physical exertion, but only at such a cost in extraordinary effort and suffering the court cannot fairly require it of him under the circumstances of this case. [SSA], by contrast, argues the

> court cannot rationally conclude Mr. Jordan "cannot" exert himself physically when he in fact does. Thus the court finds itself in the Twilight Zone separating difficulty from impossibility—the difference between "can" and "cannot."

The ALJ then summarized the evidence set forth above. He described Jordan's testimony that he could do anything he wanted, "but only with pain, and only for shorter periods than before the injury," as "unhelpful." He apparently did not accept SSA and Homeport's assertion that Jordan was **[—8—]** not credible, instead describing him as "focusing on the wrong question." In the ALJ's mind, the relevant question was "whether [Jordan's] remaining abilities would allow him to return to work." "On this point," the ALJ thought, "Mr. Jordan's testimony is, at best, ambiguous."

Turning to Dr. Reynolds, the ALJ described him as "well-qualified" and "credible." He nevertheless rejected his opinion that Jordan could not work as a longshoreman "for one reason only: he has never seen [the] surveillance footage." The ALJ stated that the difference between Jordan's self-described limitations and the activities shown in the videos was "striking, even to the untrained eye." Stressing the changed opinions of Drs. Chiang and Skomer, he further noted that the videos' "effect on the medical opinions in this case is remarkable."

The ALJ described Jordan's complaints of pain as "not wildly improbable" and acknowledged that "[a] lazier person in Mr. Jordan's position might well have simply stayed at home and made no effort to work after the accident." But the ALJ reasoned that "[i]f Mr. Jordan 'can' work, the Act presumes that he will, and denies him benefits," and that "if Mr. Jordan's financial needs compel him to work unwillingly, he has plenty of company in the workforce." Accordingly, the ALJ found that Jordan had not carried his burden of proving that he was totally disabled between April 14, 2016, and March 27, 2018.

Jordan appealed to the Benefits Review Board ("BRB"), which affirmed. It held that the ALJ (1) "rationally determined that [Jordan's] statements regarding his inability to return to work are not creditable" in light of the surveillance videos, and (2) "permissibly gave greater weight to the opinions of the physicians who viewed the **[—9—]** surveillance videos." Jordan timely petitioned for judicial review.

II

The BRB must accept the ALJ's findings of fact unless they are "contrary to the law, irrational, or unsupported by substantial evidence." *Chugach Mgmt. Servs. v. Jetnil*, 863 F.3d 1168, 1173 (9th Cir. 2017). We then "conduct an independent review of the administrative record to **{-936-}** determine if the Board adhered to this standard." *Stevedoring Servs. of Am. v. Price*, 382 F.3d 878, 883 (9th Cir. 2004). The interpretation of the LHWCA, by contrast, "is a question of law reviewed de novo and is not entitled to any special deference." *Id.*

Under the LHWCA, the employee has the initial burden of proving that "his work related injury prevented him from performing his former job." *Hairston v. Todd Shipyards Corp.*, 849 F.2d 1194, 1196 (9th Cir. 1988). The burden then shifts to the employer to prove "that suitable alternate work was available in the community." *Id.*

A. Pain and Disability

The central issue in this case is whether Jordan's complaints of pain described a covered disability. The LHWCA defines "disability" as the "incapacity because of injury to earn the wages which the employee was receiving at the time of injury in the same or other employment." 33 U.S.C. § 902(10).

We have occasionally alluded to the effect of pain on a claimant's ability to do work and earn wages. The claimant in *Carrion v. SSA Marine Terminals, LLC*, 821 F.3d 1168, 4 Adm. R. 386 (9th Cir. 2016), for example, "had endured decades of **[—10—]** persistent [knee] pain without any actual or expected improvement." *Id.* at 1170, 4 Adm. R. at 386. We said that "[w]ithout doubt, he is disabled." *Id.*, 4 Adm. R. at 386. In *Container Stevedoring Co. v. Director, Office of Workers Compensation Programs*, 935 F.2d 1544 (9th Cir. 1991), we upheld the ALJ's finding that the claimant's post-injury wages did not reflect his earning capacity because he was able to work after his injury only with "pain and limitations." *Id.* at 1550.

Other circuit courts have been more explicit that pain can be disabling. *See, e.g.*, *Bath Iron Works Corp. v. White*, 584 F.2d 569, 575 (1st Cir. 1978) ("[A]n employee need not be in pain, nor is he required, after injury, to continue in employment which is medically contraindicated until his condition and pain render it impossible for him to work at all."). Perhaps the clearest statement comes from the Fifth Circuit: "Even if able to work, [a claimant] may be found to be totally disabled if he is working with extraordinary effort and in excruciating pain." *La. Ins. Guar. Ass'n v. Bunol*, 211 F.3d 294, 297 (5th Cir. 2000). The BRB has itself endorsed a virtually identical formulation: "An employee may be found to be totally disabled despite continued employment if he works only through extraordinary effort and in spite of excruciating pain, or is provided a position only through employer's beneficence." *Ramirez v. Sea-Land Servs., Inc.*, 33 BRBS 41, 1999 WL 284793, at *5 (BRB Apr. 20, 1999); *see also Haughton Elevator Co. v. Lewis*, 572 F.2d 447, 451 (4th Cir. 1978) (Winter, J., concurring) ("I agree with the Board that 'it would be unfair to penalize [the claimant] by denying him compensation for permanent total disability because he made an extraordinary effort to keep working" and that a man "having a severe physical disability as a result of an employment-related injury should not be required to continue enduring **[—11—]** excruciating pain and subjecting himself to the possibility of further injury . . . .").

SSA and Homeport do not dispute the idea that pain can be disabling, but point out that the complaints of pain must be credible. We agree.

We hold, as a matter of first impression, that credible complaints of severe, persistent, and prolonged pain can establish a prima facie case of disability, even if the claimant can literally perform his or her past work. *See, e.g., Bunol*, 211 F.3d at 297. **{-937-}**

Our holding should not be taken to mean that any amount of pain is per se disabling. As the Sixth Circuit observed in *Paducah Marine Ways v. Thompson*, 82 F.3d 130 (6th Cir. 1996), there are some "aches and pains that are not disabling and thus not compensable" under the LHWCA. *Id.* at 134. Even judges must endure some degree of physical discomfort inherent in their work.

On the other hand, a claimant need not experience excruciating pain to be considered disabled. According to one reputable dictionary, "excruciating" is defined as "so intense as to cause great pain or anguish," Webster's Third New International Dictionary 794 (2002), and is synonymous with "agonizing, harrowing, racking, raging, tormenting, torturing, torturous [and] wrenching," Merriam-Webster Online, https://merriam-webster.com/dictionary/excruciating (last visited Aug. 21, 2020). Torture should not be the benchmark for disability under the LHWCA, a statute which "is to be liberally construed in favor of injured employees." *Saipan Stevedore Co. v. Dir., Office of Workers' Comp. Programs*, 133 F.3d 717, 722 (9th Cir. 1998) (citing *Voris v. Eikel*, 346 U.S. 328, 333 (1953)). **[—12—]**

Moreover, although the Fifth Circuit and the BRB have made reference to the term, neither has suggested that "excruciating" is the threshold for disabling pain. Both the circuit court and the agency simply rejected the proposition that continued employment precluded a finding of disability in the face of evidence that the work subjected the claimant to such extreme pain. *See Bunol*, 211 F.3d at 297; *Ramirez*, 1999 WL 284793, at *5 n.5. Indeed, the Fifth Circuit has elsewhere acknowledged that the LHWCA does not "require[] that a longshoreman be bed-ridden before he is considered totally disabled." *Watson v. Gulf Stevedore Corp.*, 400 F.2d 649,

654 (5th Cir. 1968); *see also John W. McGrath Corp. v. Hughes*, 289 F.2d 403, 405 (2d Cir. 1961) (noting that, under the LHWCA, "[a] person may be permanently totally disabled in an economic sense and still be ambulatory").

Between the poles of "any" pain (which is not sufficient), *see Paducah Marine Ways*, 82 F.3d at 134, and "excruciating" pain (which is not necessary to show), *see Bunol*, 211 F.3d at 297, lies a considerable range. There is, in other words, a vast middle ground between occasional discomfort and torture. Although the cases have not clearly identified the quantum of pain that is sufficient to create a disability under the LHWCA, the statute's definition of "disability" and the case law in this area support our holding that the level of pain must be sufficiently severe, persistent, and prolonged to significantly interfere with the claimant's ability to do his or her past work. *See id.* (upholding disability benefits based on testimony that the claimant worked only with "substantial" and "constant pain"); *see also Mijangos v. Avondale Shipyards, Inc.*, 948 F.2d 941, 944–45 (5th Cir. 1991) (reinstating disability award when "there was much expert testimony indicating that [the claimant] could physically perform certain jobs" but "[t]here **[—13—]** was also testimony indicating that [the claimant] would have constant pain in any of these jobs"); *see also Nardella v. Campbell Mach., Inc.*, 525 F.2d 46, 49 (9th Cir. 1975) ("Even a relatively minor injury must lead to a finding of total disability if it prevents the employee from engaging in the only type of gainful employment for which he is qualified.").

We leave it to ALJs to determine, based on consideration of all the facts and circumstances of a particular case, whether a claimant's complaints of pain are (1) credible and (2) if so, whether the level of pain described is so severe, persistent, and **{-938-}** prolonged that it significantly interferes with the claimant's ability to do his or her past work. Although we do not attempt an across-the-board definition of disabling pain, we offer the following guideposts.

First, the pain must relate to an injury "arising out of and in the course of employment." 33 U.S.C. § 902(2); *see also Kalama Servs., Inc. v. Office of Workers' Comp. Programs*, 354 F.3d 1085, 1091 (9th Cir. 2004). Pain unrelated to such an injury will not suffice.

In addition, the pain must be sufficiently severe, persistent, and prolonged to adversely impact the claimant's ability to do his or her job in some significant way. This certainly includes impossibility; an injury might make an activity so painful that the employee literally cannot do it, "render[ing] it impossible for him to work at all." *See White*, 584 F.2d at 575. It would also cover a situation in which the employee can perform a task only by enduring extreme or "excruciating" pain. *Bunol*, 211 F.3d at 297. But it might also impact the employee's ability to perform the activity over a full workday. *See Eller & Co. v. Golden*, 620 F.2d 71, 72 (5th Cir. 1980) (upholding a disability benefits award when, among other things, the claimant credibly testified **[—14—]** that he could "not continue to work beyond four hours due to pain in his lower back and the 'giving way' of his left knee which caused him to fall when he attempted to lift cargo"). Or it might simply cause the severe, persistent, and prolonged pain that would make a reasonable employee stop doing the activity. *See Bunol*, 211 F.3d at 297 (upholding disability benefits based on "substantial" and "constant pain"); *Mijangos*, 948 F.2d at 944–45 (5th Cir. 1991) (reinstating disability award based on "constant pain"). In other words, whatever the level of pain, the employee need not make an "extraordinary effort" to overcome it and should not be penalized if he or she does so. *Bunol*, 211 F.3d at 297.

Relatedly, and although somewhat distinct from the issue of the required quantum of pain, an employee need not perform work that, according to the medical evidence, will exacerbate his or her injury to a degree that significantly impedes the claimant's ability to perform his or her past work. As the First Circuit explained in *Bath Iron Works*, a claimant is not "required, after injury, to continue in employment which is medically contraindicated until his condition and pain render it impossible for him to work at all."

584 F.2d at 575; *see also Container Stevedoring*, 935 F.2d at 1550 (upholding an award of disability benefits based in part on a treating physician's view that continuing to work would "lead to worsening symptoms and worsening disability" for the claimant) (quotations omitted); *Haughton Elevator Co.*, 572 F.2d at 451 (Winter, J., concurring) (agreeing that, under the LHWCA, a claimant "should not be required to continue enduring excruciating pain and subjecting himself to the possibility of further injury"); *Care v. Wa. Metro. Area Transit Auth.*, 21 BRBS 248, 251 (1988) ("A doctor's opinion that [a claimant's] return to his usual work would aggravate his condition may support a finding of total disability."); *Lobue v. Army & Air Force Exch. Serv.*, **[—15—]** 15 BRBS 407, 408–09 (1983) (affirming an ALJ's finding that the claimant was disabled based on a physician's statement that continued work would "aggravate" the claimant's spondylolisthesis); *cf. Haw. Stevedores, Inc. v. Ogawa*, 608 F.3d 642, 653 (9th Cir. 2010) (affirming ALJ's consideration of work restrictions that would allow claimant to "avert more pronounced cognitive difficulties").

B. Application

The ALJ in this case framed his analysis as an inquiry into the difference **{-939-}** between "difficulty" and "impossibility," or between "can" and "cannot." As we explained above, our answer to that inquiry is that disability does not mean that it is completely impossible for the claimant to do his or her past work. Our review of the ALJ's decision indicates that he applied an improperly high standard to Jordan's claim.

First, in the ALJ's view, SSA and Homeport argued that "the court cannot rationally conclude Mr. Jordan 'cannot' exert himself physically when in fact he does." That he found in favor of SSA and Homeport implies, absent any indication to the contrary, that he adopted the impossibility standard he said they advocated.

Second, the ALJ described Jordan's testimony about his pain as "unhelpful," "focused on the wrong question," and "at best, ambiguous." To the contrary, Jordan relevantly and unambiguously testified that he could do anything he wanted to, but "it all either is painful, elevates the pain, or I can't do it for the amount of time that would be considered a job." If the ALJ did not believe that testimony, he could have said so. Instead, he described Jordan as "human" and "hardly unusual." Such descriptions shed no light on the ALJ's view of Jordan's credibility. Instead, and notwithstanding the ALJ's apparent reliance on the opinions of the different **[—16—]** physicians and the surveillance video footage of Jordan, the ALJ's opinion as a whole suggests that the ALJ believed Jordan had to establish that it was literally impossible for him to do his past work. That was error.[1]

Therefore, we remand to the BRB with instructions to remand to the ALJ. On remand, the ALJ must first determine whether Jordan's complaints of pain were credible. If so, then the ALJ must decide whether the pain described significantly affected Jordan's ability to do his past work in the manner we have described in this opinion. If the ALJ finds Jordan's complaints of pain *not* credible, then they need not be taken into account.

C. Other Issues

Jordan makes two additional claims of error. First, he argues that the ALJ's decision to credit the opinions of the non-treating physicians over those of Dr. Reynolds was irrational.[2] Second, he argues that the

---

[1] The BRB described the ALJ's decision as a "rational[] determin[ation]" that Jordan's testimony about his limitations were "not creditable." Unlike many final administrative decisionmakers, the BRB is not free to reach an independent conclusion; its review of the ALJ's decision is limited by the "substantial evidence" standard. *See Chiguch*, 863 F.3d at 1173. We therefore do not defer to the BRB's description of the ALJ's decision.

[2] As in Social Security cases, the opinions of treating physicians in LHWCA cases are "entitled to special weight." *Amos v. Dir., Office of Workers Comp. Programs*, 153 F.3d 1051, 1054 (9th Cir. 1998). However, that deference is given because a treating physician "has a greater opportunity to know and observe the patient as an individual." *Id.*

surveillance videos alone are not substantial evidence of his ability to work. **[—17—]**

Both those issues are potentially relevant to Jordan's credibility regarding his pain. Jordan's self-described pain was corroborated by Dr. Reynolds but called into question by the non-treating physicians. The surveillance videos show Jordan engaged in activities arguably inconsistent with his description of his limitations. **{-940-}**

In addition to whatever independent evidentiary weight they might have, the surveillance videos provided a basis from which the medical experts could draw inferences regarding Jordan's ability to work full-time as a longshoreman. The ALJ can give those inferences the weight he thinks they deserve. Indeed, we expect that the ALJ will consider all the evidence—Jordan's testimony, the opinions of treating and non-treating physicians, and the surveillance videos—in deciding whether Jordan's complaints of pain are credible, and if so, whether that pain significantly impacted his ability to do his past work.

III

Jordan's petition for review is **GRANTED**. The matter is **REMANDED** to the BRB with instructions to remand to the ALJ for further proceedings consistent with this opinion.

(quoting *Magallanes v. Bowen*, 881 F.2d 747, 751 (9th Cir. 1989)). **[—17—]** Here, Dr. Reynolds saw Jordan on only three occasions, while Dr. Chiang saw him four times. Jordan does not argue that Dr. Reynolds's status as a treating physician entitled his opinion to any particular deference.

United States Court of Appeals
for the Ninth Circuit

No. 19-55136

LOPEZ
vs.
CATALINA CHANNEL EXPRESS, INC.

Appeal from the United States District Court for the Central District of California

Decided: September 9, 2020

Citation: 974 F.3d 1030, 8 Adm. R. 316 (9th Cir. 2020).

Before **MURGUIA** and **CHRISTEN,** Circuit Judges, and **HELLERSTEIN,*** District Judge.

* The Honorable Alvin K. Hellerstein, United States District Judge for the Southern District of New York, sitting by designation.

[—3—] {-1031-} **MURGUIA,** Circuit Judge: **{-1032-}**

Daniel Lopez is confined to a wheelchair due to a disability and he alleges that he was unable to use the restroom aboard the Jet Cat Express, a passenger vessel sailing between Long Beach and Santa Catalina Island, California, because the restroom's door was too narrow to allow his wheelchair to enter. Lopez sued Catalina Channel Express, Inc. ("Catalina"), which owns and operates the vessel, under the Americans with Disabilities Act of 1990 ("ADA") and California's Unruh Civil Rights Act ("Unruh **[—4—]** Act") for failing to widen the vessel's restroom door. The district court denied Lopez's motion for summary judgment and instead granted summary judgment to Catalina on Lopez's ADA claim. The district court also refused to exercise supplemental jurisdiction over Lopez's Unruh Act claim.

We have jurisdiction pursuant to 28 U.S.C. § 1291, and we reverse and remand.

I. Factual and Procedural Background

Daniel Lopez is a T-10 paraplegic, which means he is unable to walk and is dependent on a wheelchair for mobility. In April 2017, Lopez returned from Catalina Island to Long Beach on the Jet Cat Express, a passenger vessel owned and operated by Catalina. While aboard, Lopez soiled himself because the restroom's door was too narrow for his wheelchair to enter.

Catalina has not altered the restroom in the Jet Cat Express since it was built in 2001. According to Tony Ross, Catalina's Vice President of Vessel Engineering, no passenger—other than Lopez—has ever reported any difficulty accessing the restroom. Ross also testified that the sliding "pocket door" creates a 26-inch-wide entryway when fully opened and the door cannot be widened because its handle is placed three inches from the outer edge of the door.

According to Ross, there are two reasons why widening the restroom door is not readily achievable. First, "installing a different type of handle at the outer edge of the 'pocket door' . . . may make it more likely that passengers' hands would be injured in the doorway when closing the door, due to the constant movement of the vessel." Second, Catalina "cannot structurally alter the restroom without negatively **[—5—]** impacting the stability of the vessel . . . [which] is a threat to the safety of navigation." Specifically, Ross explained:

> [M]odifications and alterations to a vessel can negatively impact the stability of the vessel in many ways. For example, here, in order to expand the doorway of the disabled-accessible restroom on the Jet Cat Express, the structure of the restroom itself would need to be expanded which, in turn, would impact the structure of the adjoining restroom. As walls shift, the vessel's overall weight changes. These changes may cause the overall center of gravity ("COG") of the vessel to move, and the freeboard to be reduced. *These two factors affect the stability of a vessel.*
>
> . . . Simply put, as the COG moves and the amount of freeboard becomes lower, the vessel becomes more susceptible to unstable situations.

In other words, Ross declared that widening the vessel's restroom door is not readily achievable. **{–1033–}**

Lopez sued Catalina alleging violations of the ADA, 42 U.S.C. §§ 12101–12213, and the Unruh Act, Cal. Civ. Code § 51. The district court bifurcated Lopez's ADA claims from his state law claim, and after some discovery, granted summary judgment to Catalina on Lopez's ADA claims and declined to exercise supplemental jurisdiction over his Unruh Act claim. Lopez timely appealed. **[—6—]**

II. Standard of Review

We review a district court's grant of summary judgment de novo. *Tauscher v. Phx. Bd. of Realtors, Inc.*, 931 F.3d 959, 962 (9th Cir. 2019) (citing *Furnace v. Sullivan*, 705 F.3d 1021, 1026 (9th Cir. 2013)). Summary judgment is appropriate only if, taking the evidence and all reasonable inferences in the light most favorable to the non-moving party, there are no genuine issues of material fact, and the movant is entitled to judgment as a matter of law. Fed. R. Civ. P. 56(a). "An issue of material fact is genuine if there is sufficient evidence for a reasonable jury to return a verdict for the non-moving party." *Tauscher*, 931 F.3d at 962 (quoting *Thomas v. Ponder*, 611 F.3d 1144, 1150 (9th Cir. 2010)).

"The interpretation of [the ADA] is a question of law subject to de novo review." *Molski v. Foley Estates Vineyard & Winery, LLC*, 531 F.3d 1043, 1046 (9th Cir. 2008) (alteration in original) (quoting *Barden v. City of Sacramento*, 292 F.3d 1073, 1075 (9th Cir. 2002)). We also review the district court's allocation of the burden of proof de novo. *Id.* (citing *Ferrari, Alvarez, Olsen & Ottoboni v. Home Ins. Co.*, 940 F.2d 550, 555 (9th Cir. 1991)).

III. Analysis

Congress enacted the ADA to address discrimination against individuals with disabilities. 42 U.S.C. §§ 12101(b)(1)–(4). Title III, at issue in this case, provides that "[n]o individual shall be discriminated against on the basis of disability in the full and equal enjoyment of the goods, services, facilities, privileges, advantages, or accommodations of any place of public accommodation by any person who owns, leases (or leases to), or operates a place of public accommodation." *Id.* § 12182(a). In simpler **[—7—]** terms, owners of "places of public accommodation"—which include a passenger vessel like the Jet Cat Express—have a duty to make sure that individuals with disabilities can fully enjoy the facilities.[1]

To prevail on a Title III discrimination claim, Lopez must establish that: (1) he is disabled within the meaning of the ADA; (2) Catalina is a private entity that owns, leases, or operates a place of public accommodation; and (3) Catalina discriminated against him by denying him public accommodations because of his disability. *Molski v. M.J. Cable, Inc.*, 481 F.3d 724, 730 (9th Cir. 2007) (citing 42 U.S.C. §§ 12182(a)–(b)). Here, the first two elements of Lopez's discrimination claim are met because neither party disputes that Lopez is disabled, *see* 42 U.S.C. § 12102, or that the Jet Cat Express is a place of public accommodation within the meaning of the ADA, *see id.* § 12181(7); 28 C.F.R. § 36.104. Only the third element is at issue: whether the inaccessibility of the restroom on the Jet Cat Express constitutes discrimination under the ADA. *See* **{–1034–}** *Strong v. Valdez Fine Foods*, 724 F.3d 1042, 1044 (9th Cir. 2013) ("There is no dispute that [the plaintiff] is disabled, [or] that the restaurant is covered by the ADA . . . . The only question is whether any barriers interfered with [the plaintiff's] ability 'to participate in or benefit from the goods, services, facilities, privileges, advantages, or **[—8—]** accommodations' of the restaurant." (quoting *Chapman v. Pier 1 Imps.*

---

[1] Catalina argues that the ADA does not apply to Lopez's claims because its operations do not affect commerce for the purposes of 42 U.S.C. § 12184. Section 12184 prohibits discrimination "in specified public transportation services provided by private entities." *Id.* But Lopez's claims arise under 42 U.S.C. § 12182, not § 12184, and § 12182 prohibits discrimination "by public accommodations." Catalina admitted in its answer that it was a place of public accommodation, and this admission is binding. *Am. Title Ins. Co. v. Lacelaw Corp.*, 961 F.2d 224, 226 (9th Cir. 1988).

(*U.S.), Inc.* ("*Chapman I*"), 631 F.3d 939, 945 (9th Cir. 2011) (en banc))). Lopez alleges that Catalina's failure to widen the restroom door—an "architectural barrier" under the statute—prevented him from fully enjoying the facilities aboard the Jet Cat Express.[2]

A. Removal of Architectural Barriers Under the ADA

Discrimination under Title III of the ADA specifically includes "a failure to *remove* architectural barriers . . . in existing facilities . . . where such removal is *readily achievable*." 42 U.S.C. § 12182(b)(2)(A)(iv) (emphases added). In addition, even if "an entity can demonstrate that the removal of a barrier . . . is *not* readily achievable," the entity is still liable under the ADA if it fails to "make [its] goods, services, facilities, privileges, advantages, or accommodations available through alternative methods" so long as "such methods are *readily achievable*." *Id.* § 12182(b)(2)(A)(v) (emphases added). The ADA defines the phrase "readily achievable" as "easily accomplishable and able to be carried out without much difficulty or expense." *Id.* § 12181(9).

Examples of architectural barriers that are subject to the ADA include slopes and cross-slopes in a parking lot that are too steep (more than two percent incline), *Kohler v. Bed Bath & Beyond of Cal., LLC,* 780 F.3d 1260, 1262 (9th Cir. 2015); **[—9—]** aisles in a store that are not wide enough for wheelchairs, *Chapman v. Pier 1 Imps. (U.S.), Inc.* ("*Chapman II*"), 779 F.3d 1001, 1005 (9th Cir. 2015); seating in a restaurant that does not accommodate wheelchairs; *Strong*, 724 F.3d at 1044; soap dispensers and hand dryers that are mounted too high (more than forty inches from the floor), *Oliver v. Ralphs Grocery Co.*, 654 F.3d 903, 905 n.5 (9th Cir. 2011); and a bar that is too high to drink from, *Jankey v. Poop Deck*, 537 F.3d 1122, 1123 (9th Cir. 2008).

Accordingly, to prevail on his discrimination claim, Lopez must establish either: (1) that Catalina failed to alter the restroom door when doing so was readily achievable; or (2) even if the alteration was not readily achievable, that Catalina could have made the restroom available to Lopez through alternative methods without much difficulty or expense. 42 U.S.C. §§ 12182(b)(2)(A)(iv)–(v). We address each of these alleged bases of liability in turn.

B. Readily Achievable

The district court granted summary judgment to Catalina largely because it concluded that Lopez bore—and failed to carry—the burden of establishing that altering the Jet Cat Express's restroom door was "readily achievable." Our court has not decided which party bears the burden to establish that removal of an architectural barrier is or is not readily achievable. The district court recognized this was an undecided question and decided to "follow[] the lead of 'the overwhelming majority of federal courts that apply **{–1035–}** the burden-shifting framework of" the Tenth Circuit's decision in *Colorado Cross Disability Coalition v. Hermanson Family Limited Partnership,* 264 F.3d 999 (10th Cir. 2001). In affirming the district court's conclusion that Lopez failed to meet his initial burden, we join the Second Circuit and adopt a burden-shifting framework that slightly differs from **[—10—]** the Tenth Circuit's framework in *Colorado Cross*. Under the Second Circuit's approach, plaintiffs have the initial burden at summary judgment of *plausibly showing* that the cost of removing an architectural barrier does not exceed the benefits under the particular circumstances. *See Roberts v. Royal Atl. Corp.*, 542 F.3d 363, 373 (2d Cir. 2008).

Title III of the ADA is silent as to who bears the burden of proving at summary judgment that removal of an architectural barrier is, or is not, readily achievable. The Tenth Circuit was the first court of appeals to articulate a two-part burden-shifting

[2] Lopez's complaint also raises claims that Catalina failed to make "reasonable modifications in policies, practices, or procedures" and "alterations." 42 U.S.C. §§ 12182(b)(2)(A)(ii), 12183(a)(2). However, he moved for summary judgment only on his claim that Catalina did not remove an architectural barrier, in violation of §§ 12182(b)(2)(A)(iv)–(v).

framework for evaluating whether removing an architectural barrier is "readily achievable" under the ADA. *Colo. Cross*, 264 F.3d at 1002–07. Under *Colorado Cross*, the plaintiff "must initially present evidence tending to show that the suggested method of barrier removal is readily achievable under the particular circumstances." *Id.* at 1002. If the plaintiff meets that initial burden, the defendant "then bears the ultimate burden of persuasion that barrier removal is *not* readily achievable." *Id.* at 1002–03 (emphasis added). In other words, the defendant "bears the *ultimate* burden of persuasion regarding its *affirmative defense* that a suggested method of barrier removal is not readily achievable." *Id.* at 1006 (emphasis added).

The Eighth and Eleventh Circuits have adopted *Colorado Cross*'s burden-shifting framework for evaluating barrier removal claims. *See Wright v. RL Liquor*, 887 F.3d 361, 364 (8th Cir. 2018) ("[T]his court holds that the district court properly required [the plaintiff] to initially present evidence tending to show that the suggested method of barrier removal was readily achievable under the circumstances."); *Gathright-Dietrich v. Atlanta Landmarks, Inc.*, 452 F.3d 1269, 1274 (11th Cir. 2006) ("The district **[—11—]** court did not err in following the burden of proof enunciated in *Colorado Cross*, and we adopt that burden shifting framework for the reasons articulated by the *Colorado Cross* court.").[3] The Second Circuit tweaked the test slightly, requiring plaintiffs to first "articulate a *plausible proposal* for barrier removal" and recognizing that "the defendant may counter the plaintiff's showing by meeting its own burden of persuasion and establishing that the costs of a plaintiff's proposal would in fact exceed the benefits." *Roberts*, 542 F.3d at 373 (emphasis added). Importantly, while it is clear that the defendant bears the ultimate burden of proving the affirmative defense, all of our sister circuits have placed the initial burden of proof on the plaintiff. This makes sense because at a minimum, at the outset, a plaintiff must make clear what accommodation is needed, and disability accommodations can be idiosyncratic.

Indeed, placing the initial burden on the plaintiff of plausibly showing how removal of an architectural barrier is readily **{–1036–}** achievable under the circumstances is sensible for several reasons. First, subsections 12182(b)(2)(A)(iv) and (v)—which, read together, require the removal of an architectural barrier unless such removal is not readily achievable—place the ultimate burden on the *defendant* to **[—12—]** prove the *affirmative defense* that removal of an architectural barrier is not readily achievable. *Colo. Cross*, 264 F.3d at 1002. Subsection (iv) starts by requiring defendants to remove architectural barriers if that removal is readily achievable. 42 U.S.C. § 12182(b)(2)(A)(iv). Subsection (v), in turn, offers the defendant an opportunity to avoid liability by "demonstrat[ing] that the removal of a barrier under clause (iv) is *not* readily achievable[.]" *Id.* § 12182(b)(2)(A)(v) (emphasis added). In other words, *only if* the plaintiff first makes a plausible showing that the barrier removal *is* readily achievable, does the defendant then have to negate that showing and prove that the removal is *not* readily achievable. This is consistent with the ADA's mandate that an entity must remove an architectural barrier *unless* it can show that removal is *not* readily achievable. *Colo. Cross*, 264 F.3d at 1002.

Second, applying a burden-shifting framework in this context is consistent with our application of burden-shifting frameworks to other similarly worded subsections of Title III. For example, the first clause of subsection 12182(b)(2)(A)(ii) requires defendants to make reasonable modifications to their policies, practices, or procedures to allow individuals

[3] In the absence of direction from us, most district courts in our circuit have also followed *Colorado Cross*, assigning plaintiffs the initial burden of establishing that removing an architectural barrier is readily achievable. *See, e.g.*, *Vogel v. Rite Aid Corp.*, 992 F. Supp. 2d 998, 1010–11 (C.D. Cal. 2014); *Paulsen v. PS Bus. Parks, LP*, No. C10-1031, 2011 WL 3419894, at *2 (W.D. Wash. Aug. 4, 2011); *Moeller v. Taco Bell Corp.*, 816 F. Supp. 2d 831, 854 (N.D. Cal. 2011); *Vesecky v. Garick, Inc.*, No. 07-1173, 2008 WL 4446714, at *3 (D. Ariz. Sept. 30, 2008); *Wilson v. Pier 1 Imps. (US), Inc.*, 439 F. Supp. 2d 1054, 1067 (E.D. Cal. 2006); *Hubbard v. Rite Aid Corp.*, 433 F. Supp. 2d 1150, 1159 (S.D. Cal. 2006).

with disabilities to enjoy their goods and services. 42 U.S.C. § 12182(b)(2)(A)(ii). The second clause of subsection (ii), in turn, offers defendants an opportunity to avoid liability by "demonstrat[ing] that making such modifications *would fundamentally alter the nature* of such goods [or] services." 42 U.S.C. § 12182(b)(2)(A)(ii) (emphases added). In *Lentini v. California Center for the Arts*, we endorsed the Fifth Circuit's holding that, under subsection (ii), the plaintiff must initially prove that a modification was requested and that the requested modification was reasonable. 370 F.3d 837, 845 (9th Cir. 2004) (citing *Johnson v. Gambrinus Co./Spoetzl Brewery*, **[—13—]** 116 F.3d 1052, 1059 (5th Cir. 1997)). If the plaintiff meets that initial burden, then the defendant bears the ultimate burden of persuasion that the requested modification would fundamentally alter the nature of the public accommodation. *See id.* More recently, in *Karczewski v. DCH Mission Valley LLC*, we confirmed that to prevail on a claim under subsection (ii) the plaintiff must first establish a prima facie case that the defendant "fail[ed] to make a requested reasonable modification that was . . . necessary to accommodate the plaintiff's disability." 862 F.3d 1006, 1010 (9th Cir. 2017) (quoting *Fortyune v. Am. Multi-Cinema, Inc.*, 364 F.3d 1075, 1082 (9th Cir. 2004)). Only then must the defendant "make the requested modification unless it proves that doing so would alter the fundamental nature of its business." *Id.*

Finally, a burden-shifting approach is congruent with how we adjudicate employment claims under Title I of the ADA. For example, under Title I, a disabled employee seeking an employment accommodation under 42 U.S.C. § 12112(b)(5)(A)–(B)[4] must **{-1037-}** initially prove that the **[—14—]** accommodation "seems reasonable on its face[.]" *U.S. Airways, Inc. v. Barnett*, 535 U.S. 391, 401 (2002). If the employee meets that initial burden, then the defendant "must show special (typically case-specific) circumstances that demonstrate undue hardship in the particular circumstances." *Id.* at 402. Similarly, when it comes to disparate-treatment employment claims under the ADA, the Supreme Court has clarified that once an employee makes "a prima facie showing of discrimination, the next question . . . [is] whether [the employer] offered a legitimate, nondiscriminatory reason for its actions so as to demonstrate that its actions were not motivated by [the employee's] disability." *Raytheon Co. v. Hernandez*, 540 U.S. 44, 55 (2003).

Lopez argues that, under our decision in *Molski*, Catalina bears the initial burden of establishing that removal of the restroom door is not readily achievable. 531 F.3d at 1043. In *Molski*, a paraplegic man sued a winery because it refused to remove external architectural barriers that prevented wheelchair access to its historic wine-tasting room. *Id.* at 1045–46. We held that, under those circumstances, the defendant had the initial burden of proving that removal of the barriers was not readily achievable because federal regulations "do[] not place that burden on the party advocating for remedial measures," but "on the party with the best access to information *regarding the historical significance of the building*." *Id.* at 1048 (emphasis added). Indeed, 28 C.F.R. § 36.405 requires qualified historic buildings to "comply to the maximum extent feasible with" **[—15—]** the Americans with Disabilities Act Accessibility Guidelines for Buildings and Facilities, § 4.1.7 ("§ 4.1.7"). In turn, § 4.1.7 requires entities who own historic places of

---

[4] Discrimination under these subsections includes, among other things,

> (A) not making *reasonable accommodations* to the known physical or mental limitations of an otherwise qualified individual with a disability who is an applicant or employee, *unless such covered entity can demonstrate that the accommodation would impose an undue hardship* on the operation of the business of such covered entity; or (B) denying employment opportunities to a job applicant or employee who is an otherwise qualified individual with a disability, if such denial is based on the need of such covered entity to **[—14—]** make *reasonable accommodation* to the physical or mental impairments of the employee or applicant."

42 U.S.C. § 12112(b)(5) (emphases added).

public accommodation to "consult with the State Historic Preservation Officer" if they "believe[] that compliance with the requirements would threaten or destroy the historic significance of the building." Therefore, the *Molski* court concluded "§ 4.1.7 counsels in favor of placing the burden of production on the defendant." *Molski*, 531 F.3d at 1048.

Molski applies only to the removal of architectural barriers "in historic facilities." *Id.* Notably, the plaintiff had identified the nature of the accommodation requested. We reasoned in *Molski* that:

> The defendant sought the *historical designation* in this case. Thus, the defendant possesses the best understanding of the circumstances under which that designation might be threatened. The defendant is also in the best position to discuss the matter with the Santa Barbara County Historic Landmarks Advisory Commission and to request an opinion on proposed methods of barrier removal. As a result, the defendant is in a better position to introduce, as part of its affirmative defense, detailed evidence and expert testimony concerning whether the *historic significance* of a structure would be threatened or destroyed by the proposed barrier removal plan.

Id. (emphases added). Here, by contrast, the Jet Cat Express is not a historic facility. Catalina need not consult with a historic preservation entity on proposed methods of barrier **[—16—]** removal to evaluate how the alteration of the vessel's restroom door might threaten the vessel's historic significance. *Molski* only applies in cases that involve removal of architectural barriers to historic facilities—it is the exception, not the rule.[5] **{-1038-}**

Although every circuit applies a burden-shifting framework when addressing claims for removal of architectural barriers at summary judgment, the initial burden placed on plaintiffs varies. For example, the Tenth Circuit requires plaintiffs to provide "precise cost estimates" and "a specific design" regarding their proposed accommodation, *Colo. Cross*, 264 F.3d at 1009, whereas the Second Circuit requires plaintiffs only to "articulate a plausible proposal for barrier removal, 'the costs of which, facially, do not clearly exceed its benefits,'" *Roberts*, 542 F.3d at 373 (quoting *Borkowski v. Valley Cent. Sch. Dist.*, 63 F.3d 131, 138 (2d Cir. 1995)). We believe that the **[—17—]** Second Circuit's approach is most sensible because otherwise we would be asking too much of plaintiffs, especially considering that defendants have more knowledge and information regarding their own facilities, which allows them to quickly and easily counter implausible barrier-removal proposals. *See Roberts*, 542 F.3d at 373 ("Neither the estimates nor the proposal are required to be exact or detailed, for the defendant may counter the plaintiff's showing by meeting its own burden of persuasion and establishing that the costs of a plaintiff's proposal would in fact exceed the benefits."). Accordingly, we hold that to satisfy their initial burden, ADA plaintiffs must plausibly show how the cost of removing the architectural barrier at issue does not exceed the benefits under the circumstances.

---

[5] Unsurprisingly, most district courts in our circuit have declined to apply *Molski* when a case does not involve a historic facility. *See, e.g., Vogel*, 992 F. Supp. 2d at 1011 n. 35 ("*Molski* appears to be limited to the historic building context . . . . The decision does not address non-historic building compliance and is not controlling in this case."); *Vesecky*, 2018 WL 4446714, at *3 ("[U]ntil the Ninth Circuit provides additional and specific instruction to the lower courts this Court will follow the overwhelming majority of federal courts that apply the burden-shifting framework of [*Colorado*] *Cross*, specifically in cases where a historic building is not at issue."); *Ridola v. Chao*, No. 16-CV-02246-BLF, 2018 WL 2287668, at *10 (N.D. Cal. May 18, 2018) (same); *Gonzalez v. Riverrock Properties, LLC*, No. 2:14-CV-2362-TLN-EFB, 2016 WL 3267116, at *3 (E.D. Cal. June 14, 2016) (same); *Paulsen*, 2011 WL 3419894, at *2 (same); *but see Rodriguez*, 2012 WL 3538014, at *11 ("While it is true that [*Molski*] is, by its terms, limited to cases where the historical exception is asserted, its concerns regarding the availability of evidence have equal weight when defendant claims that remediation would be too costly or impractical.").

Additionally, the ADA requires courts to consider four enumerated factors when "determining whether an action is readily achievable," including:

> (A) the nature and cost of the action needed [];
>
> (B) the overall financial resources of the facility or facilities involved in the action; the number of persons employed at such facility; the effect on expenses and resources, or the impact otherwise of such action upon the operation of the facility;
>
> (C) the overall financial resources of the covered entity; the overall size of the business of a covered entity with respect to the number of its employees; the number, type, and location of its facilities; and **[—18—]**
>
> (D) the type of operation or operations of the covered entity, including the composition, structure, and functions of the workforce of such entity; the geographic separateness, administrative or fiscal relationship of the facility or facilities in question to the covered entity.

42 U.S.C. § 12181(9)(A)–(D). Lopez argues that ADA plaintiffs will not have the information required by § 12181(9), but under the test we adopt, plaintiffs are not required to address in detail each of the four factors to meet their initial burden of plausibly explaining why it is readily achievable to remove an architectural barrier. If the plaintiff makes a plausible showing **{-1039-}** that the requested accommodation is readily achievable, the burden shifts to the defendant to counter the plaintiff's initial showing, and at that point the district court is required under the statute to weigh each of the § 12181(9) factors to determine whether removal of the architectural barrier is readily achievable or not. Therefore, it is in plaintiffs' best interest to submit as much evidence as possible pertaining to each of the § 12181(9) factors in their initial barrier-removal proposal, even if it is not required to satisfy their initial burden of plausibly showing how the costs of removal outweigh the benefits. Otherwise, plaintiffs risk meeting their initial burden but failing to ultimately prevail on summary judgment.[6] **[—19—]**

In this case, the district court correctly found that Lopez not only failed to address the § 12181(9) factors, but that he also did not meet his initial burden of plausibly showing how the cost of widening the Jet Cat Express's restroom door does not exceed the benefits. The only evidence that Lopez submitted to that effect was a two-page declaration from Corey Taylor, a private investigator who conducted "an investigation" consisting of "taking photographs and measurements of the restroom at the Catalina Express Jet Cat Express." The extent of Taylor's testimony is that the restroom pocket door at issue in this case "opens only 25 inches in width" but "could have opened 34 inches, if not blocked by the metal pin, located on the top of the sliding door." Taylor does not estimate why he is qualified to opine on this issue, or even how he reached his conclusion. Taylor also attaches three photographs of the door, none of which display any measurements, and one of which, construed generously, seems to depict what looks like a "pin" on the pocket door's top rail. The district court correctly concluded that, even if Taylor's statement that the pin is blocking the door from opening more widely is true, it "only identifies the problem; it does not bear on the question of whether remediating the problem is readily achievable." Nowhere does Lopez explain how much he thinks widening the door would cost, let alone why that cost does not exceed the potential benefits of a wider door. Therefore, Taylor's declaration is patently insufficient for Lopez to meet his initial burden.

Accordingly, we affirm the district court's conclusion that Lopez failed to meet his initial burden of plausibly showing that the costs of widening the Jet Cat Express's restroom door

[6] *See e.g., Garibay v. Rodriguez*, No. CV 18-09187, 2019 WL 8060795, at *4 (C.D. Cal. Dec. 19, 2019); *Lopez v. Lopez*, No. CV 18-6473, 2019 WL 7905742, at *6 (C.D. Cal. Oct. 17, 2019); *Mannick v. Kaiser Found. Health Plan, Inc.*, No. C 03-5905, 2006 WL 1626909, at *12 (N.D. Cal. June 9, 2006).

do not exceed the benefits such that widening the door was shown to be "readily achievable." **[—20—]**

C. Alternative Methods

Even if widening the Jet Cat Express's restroom door was not readily achievable, Lopez could still prevail on his Title III discrimination claim if he establishes that Catalina chose not to make the restroom available to him even though it could have done so through alternative methods without much difficulty or expense. 42 U.S.C. §§ 12182(b)(2)(A)(v).

On appeal, Catalina argues that it offers narrow wheelchairs to individuals with disabilities who need to use the restroom on the Jet Cat Express. Lopez does not dispute that evidence; rather, he argues that he was never offered a different wheelchair that would fit through the restroom's door. Lopez did testify, however, that he rejected Catalina's offer to transfer him from his wheelchair to the toilet directly: **{-1040-}** "I'm a hefty guy, and I've had bad experiences with people trying to help me. They assume they can. I've been dropped, so I wouldn't." It is therefore unclear whether Lopez would have accepted an offer to use a narrower wheelchair or whether an offer to transfer him directly to the toilet would satisfy Catalina's duty to offer "alternative methods" to use the restroom. In any case, the district court did not evaluate whether Catalina made the restroom available to Lopez through alternative methods.[7] **[—21—]**

Accordingly, we reverse the district court's grant of summary judgment to Catalina and remand for the district court to determine in the first instance whether there is sufficient evidence that Catalina made the restroom "available through alternative methods" pursuant to § 12182(b)(2)(A)(v).

IV. Conclusion

We affirm the district court's conclusion that Lopez failed to meet his initial burden of plausibly showing that widening the Jet Cat Express's restroom door was "readily achievable" under 42 U.S.C. §§ 12182(b)(2)(A)(iv). In doing so, we adopt a burden-shifting framework whereby plaintiffs have the initial burden at summary judgment of plausibly showing that the cost of removing an architectural barrier does not exceed the benefits under the particular circumstances. The defendant then bears the ultimate burden of persuasion that barrier removal is not readily achievable.

We reverse the district court's grant of summary judgment, however, because the district court did not evaluate whether Catalina made the restroom available to Lopez through "alternative methods." On remand, the district court should determine in the first instance whether there is sufficient evidence that Catalina made the restroom "available through alternative methods" pursuant to § 12182(b)(2)(A)(v).

REVERSED and REMANDED with instructions. Each party shall bear its own costs.

---

[7] The district court did address Lopez's alternative argument that "even if 'full barrier removal' is not readily achievable, readily achievable partial accommodations must still be made." This appears to be a different argument having to do with Catalina's duty to remove architectural barriers that is unrelated to Catalina's duty to make the restroom available to Lopez through "alternative methods." 42 U.S.C. §§ 12182(b)(2)(A)(v).

United States Court of Appeals
for the Ninth Circuit

No. 18-15455

PACIFIC CHOICE SEAFOOD CO.
vs.
ROSS

Appeal from the United States District Court for the Northern District of California

Decided: September 25, 2020

Citation: 976 F.3d 932, 8 Adm. R. 324 (9th Cir. 2020).

Before **THOMAS**, Chief Judge, and **FLETCHER** and **MILLER**, Circuit Judges.

[—4—] {-934-} MILLER, Circuit Judge: **{-935-}**

In 2010, the National Marine Fisheries Service implemented a quota system for the Pacific non-whiting groundfish fishery, one of several stocks of fish that the Service administers in the Pacific Ocean. Acting under the Magnuson-Stevens Fishery Conservation and Management Act of 1976, 16 U.S.C. §§ 1801–1891d (the Magnuson-Stevens Act or the Act), the Service imposed a quota limiting the total allowable catch, divided it among the participants in the fishery, and prohibited any one entity from "own[ing] or control[ling]" more than 2.7 percent of the outstanding quota share. 50 C.F.R. § 660.140(d)(4)(i). The Service **[—5—]** defined "control" to include "the ability through any means whatsoever to control or have a controlling influence over" an entity with quota share. *Id.* § 660.140(d)(4)(iii)(H).

In 2015, the Service determined that Pacific Choice Seafood Company and related entities (collectively, Pacific Choice) together owned or controlled at least 3.8 percent of the quota share. After the Service ordered Pacific Choice to divest its excess share, Pacific Choice brought this action, alleging that the Service's 2.7 percent maximum share and its "control" rule exceeded its authority under the Magnuson-Stevens Act and violated the Administrative Procedure Act. The district court granted summary judgment to the Service. We affirm.

I

Congress enacted the Magnuson-Stevens Act to prevent overfishing and to ensure that "fisheries [are] conserved and maintained so as to provide optimum yields on a continuing basis." 16 U.S.C. § 1801(a)(5). The Act establishes eight regional fishery management councils, each of which is charged with developing a "fishery management plan" for the fisheries in its region. *Id.* § 1852(a)(1), (h)(1). A management plan must prescribe measures "necessary and appropriate for the conservation and management of the fishery." *Id.* § 1853(a)(1), (b)(3). Once a council develops a plan, the Secretary of Commerce must evaluate it and either approve or reject it. *Id.* § 1854(b)(1). The Secretary has delegated that responsibility to the Service. *See Pacific Dawn LLC v. Pritzker*, 831 F.3d 1166, 1170 (9th Cir. 2016).

In 1990, the regional fishery councils began to regulate some fisheries by adopting quota programs under which the councils divided up the total allowable catch and gave participants in the fishery the right to harvest a specified **[—6—]** quantity of fish. *See Pacific Coast Fed'n of Fishermen's Ass'ns v. Blank*, 693 F.3d 1084, 1087 (9th Cir. 2012). Such programs proved controversial, and in 1996, Congress imposed a temporary moratorium on new quota programs. Sustainable Fisheries Act, Pub. L. No. 104-297, § 108(e), 110 Stat. 3559, 3576–77 (1996). In 2007, after the National Academy of Sciences concluded that quota programs "can be effective solutions to a host of fishery-related problems, including **{-936-}** economic inefficiency, over-capitalization . . . and overfishing," Congress reauthorized new quota programs, which it called "limited access privilege programs." *Pacific Coast*, 693 F.3d at 1087–88; *see* Magnuson-Stevens Fishery Conservation and Management Reauthorization Act of 2006, Pub. L. No. 109-479, § 106, 120 Stat. 3575, 3586 (2007).

Congress set out several requirements for limited access privilege programs. Most relevant here, a council must ensure that no one entity acquires "an excessive share" of the total privileges. 16 U.S.C. § 1853a(c)(5)(D). To that end, a council must establish "a maximum share, expressed as a percentage of the total limited access privileges, that a limited access privilege holder is permitted to hold, acquire, or use," along with "any other limitations or measures necessary to prevent an inequitable concentration of limited access privileges." *Id.*

This case involves the limited access privilege program for the Pacific non-whiting groundfish fishery. As their name suggests, groundfish live near the bottom of the ocean. *See West Coast Groundfish*, National Oceanic and Atmospheric Administration, https://www.fisheries.noaa.gov/species/west-coast-groundfish. The fishery consists of more than 90 species of groundfish in the Pacific Ocean off the coast of California, Oregon, and Washington, including **[—7—]** lingcod, sablefish, sole, and rockfish, but not including the Pacific whiting, or hake, which is regulated separately. *See* 50 C.F.R. § 660.140, table 1 to paragraph (d)(1)(ii)(D). The relevant regional council for the fishery is the Pacific Fishery Management Council, which has representatives from California, Oregon, Washington, and Idaho, as well as from Indian tribes with federally recognized fishing rights in those States. 16 U.S.C. § 1852(a)(1)(F).

Even before Congress reauthorized limited access privilege programs in 2007, the Council had started to implement a rationalization program for the Pacific fisheries it manages. In this context, "rationalization" means avoiding overcapacity—the presence of more fishing vessels than necessary to catch a sustainable number of fish—by, among other things, reducing the number of vessels operating in the Council's fisheries. In addition to reducing overfishing, the Council aimed to "increase net economic benefits" from its fisheries and to create "individual economic stability" for vessels that operated within them. *Pacific Coast*, 693 F.3d at 1089.

The Council's years-long deliberative process began with the Trawl Individual Quota Committee, a committee of industry representatives formed to analyze possible quota limits on both an aggregate and per-species level. In 2003, relying on data from aggregate average catches from 1994 to 2003, the Quota Committee proposed several possible limits on the aggregate quota share that could be held by any one entity, ranging from 1.5 to 5 percent of the total allowable catch.

After the Quota Committee completed its analysis, the Groundfish Allocation Committee reviewed the recommendations and "added three options for the Council's consideration," ranging from the average maximum share **[—8—]** for the 1994–2003 period to 1.5 times those limits. The Allocation Committee's report paid particular attention to the "maximum fleet consolidation level" that each option would create—in other words, how much market concentration would result. Part of the Allocation Committee's analysis involved calculating a Herfindahl-Hirschman index, or "HHI," a measure of market concentration commonly employed in the antitrust context. *See* **{-937-}** *Saint Alphonsus Med. Ctr.-Nampa Inc. v. St. Luke's Health Sys., Ltd.*, 778 F.3d 775, 786 (9th Cir. 2015). That analysis suggested that the Council could set aggregate catch limits up to about 18 percent without creating anticompetitive effects in the fishery.

But after significant deliberation among the Quota Committee, the Allocation Committee, and the Council, the Allocation Committee failed to agree on a single recommendation. After proposing two new options, the Allocation Committee asked yet another committee—the Groundfish Management Team—to evaluate all of the options that had been proposed.

The Management Team began by noting that while "[a]ntitrust concerns define the upper extreme of where limits can be set," fishing quotas are also "a tool for balancing the Council's social objectives against the undesired effects of the . . . drive toward increased economic efficiency." In contrast to the Quota Committee and the Allocation Committee, which had focused on aggregate revenues, the Management Team focused on per-vessel profitability. It analyzed historical data on a per-vessel basis to determine the current profitability of the fishery. It then projected profitability based on varying fleet sizes, and it cautioned that "concerns about control" resulting from higher quota share maximums "go beyond revenues" and **[—9—]** involve "other issues such as bargaining, market power, and types of relationships that may influence the operation of the fishery." In light of its conclusion that a fleet size of 40 to 50 vessels would provide optimal profitability while minimizing "control and consolidation of quota ownership," the Management Team presented possible maximum quota shares ranging from approximately 1.3 to 3.8 percent but ultimately recommended a limit of 2.3 to 2.7 percent depending on the desired amount of consolidation.

The Management Team's per-vessel approach mostly won out. In March 2009, the Groundfish Advisory Subpanel evaluated proposals from the Management Team and the Allocation Committee and issued a brief report. The Advisory Subpanel acknowledged the "trade-off" recognized by the Management Team "between preventing excessive market control . . . and the lower revenues and efficiency associated with control limits that are set too low." It recommended a 2.7 percent maximum aggregate quota share, which it noted was the "mid range of the data" in the Management Team's report. The Advisory Subpanel did not completely adopt the Management Team's recommendations; some of its proposed limits for individual species instead matched the Allocation Committee's recommendations, or proposed a limit not recommended by either committee.

After further deliberation on several matters not at issue here, the Council proposed Amendment 20 to the overall fishery plan implementing the limited access privilege program, including the 2.7 percent aggregate catch limit. 75 Fed. Reg. 53,380 (Aug. 31, 2010); 75 Fed. Reg. 32,994 (June 10, 2010). The Service approved the plan in August 2010 with some technical changes, and it finalized the relevant rules in October and December of that year. *See* **[—10—]** 75 Fed. Reg. 78,344 (Dec. 15, 2010); 75 Fed. Reg. 60,868 (Oct. 1, 2013). The Service and the Council also jointly published a final environmental impact statement containing an extensive discussion of the agency's development of the limited access privilege program.

At the same time, the Service adopted a "control" rule to enforce the provision of section 1853a that prohibits anyone with limited access privileges from "hold[ing], acquir[ing], or us[ing]" any quota share exceeding the regulatory maximum. 16 U.S.C. § 1853a(c)(5)(D)(i); *see* 75 Fed. Reg. at 60,954–55. In the final rule, the Service interpreted section 1853a as authorizing it **{-938-}** to prohibit permit holders from "own[ing] or control[ling]" quota share above the maximum. 50 C.F.R. § 660.140(d)(4)(i)(A). It then defined "control" as, among other things, the "ability through any means whatsoever to control or have a controlling influence" over an entity holding quota share. 50 C.F.R. § 660.140(d)(4)(iii)(H).

Not everyone welcomed the new rule. Pacific Choice operates a seafood-processing facility in Eureka, California, and indirectly controls several vessels that participate in the fishery. After significant delay while the Service worked out divestiture procedures for entities holding excess share, the Service eventually implemented the 2010 rule and notified Pacific Choice that it held at least 3.8 percent of the fishery's quota share. That share exceeded the 2.7 percent maximum and triggered the divestiture provisions. *See* 50 C.F.R. § 660.140(d)(4)(v). The Service issued various moratoria on the requirement to transfer excess quota share after an initial allocation, but in November 2015, it issued a final rule requiring divestiture. *See* 80 Fed. Reg. 69,138 (Nov. 9, 2015). **[—11—]**

Pacific Choice complied with the divestiture requirement and brought this action against the Service soon thereafter. On cross-motions for summary judgment, the district court granted summary judgment for the Service, concluding that Pacific Choice had not established that either the 2.7 percent maximum share or the Service's control rule violated the Act or the APA.

II

We begin by considering whether we have jurisdiction to hear this case. Neither party has raised the issue, but we have a duty to determine whether we have jurisdiction, "even though the parties are prepared to concede it." *Spencer Enters., Inc. v. United States*, 345 F.3d 683, 687 (9th Cir. 2003) (quoting *Bender v. Williamsport Area Sch. Dist.*, 475 U.S. 534, 541 (1986)).

The question is whether Pacific Choice's suit was timely. The Act requires any challenge to agency actions or "[r]egulations promulgated by the Secretary" to be filed within 30 days of "the date on which the regulations are promulgated or the action is published in the Federal Register." 16 U.S.C. § 1855(f)(1). We have held that the Act's time limits are jurisdictional. *See Sea Hawk Seafoods, Inc. v. Locke*, 568 F.3d 757, 765 (9th Cir. 2009). There is reason to doubt whether that characterization is consistent with more recent Supreme Court decisions, which have clarified that filing deadlines are generally non-jurisdictional claim-processing rules. *See, e.g., Henderson ex rel. Henderson v. Shinseki*, 562 U.S. 428, 434–36 (2011). But even under the Court's newer, more restrictive approach, at least some time limits for claims against the government remain jurisdictional. *See John R. Sand & Gravel Co. v. United States*, 552 U.S. 130, 139 (2008). Our prior cases are not "clearly irreconcilable" with any intervening Supreme **[—12—]** Court decision, and we remain bound by them. *Miller v. Gammie*, 335 F.3d 889, 893 (9th Cir. 2003) (en banc).

Pacific Choice filed suit on December 4, 2015, which obviously was more than 30 days after the Service's 2010 rule. The lawsuit also came more than 30 days after the Service enforced the 2010 rule against Pacific Choice through its July 28, 2015 letter.

We nevertheless conclude that Pacific Choice's suit was timely because it was brought within 30 days of the Service's publication of the 2015 rule requiring divestiture. A timely challenge to an agency's action "may challenge both the action **{–939–}** and the regulation under which the action is taken." *Oregon Troller's Ass'n v. Gutierrez*, 452 F.3d 1104, 1113 (9th Cir. 2006). The 2015 rule constituted an "action," which the Act defines to include any "actions . . . taken by the Secretary under regulations which implement a fishery management plan." 16 U.S.C. § 1855(f)(2); *see also Oregon Troller's Ass'n*, 452 F.3d at 1115–16. And although Pacific Choice does not reassert on appeal the challenges it raised below to the 2015 rule, if it prevailed in this case, it could regain the share it was required to divest. We therefore conclude that Pacific Choice's suit was timely under section 1855(f)(1). *See Oregon Troller's Ass'n*, 452 F.3d at 1113–14; *see also California Sea Urchin Comm'n v. Bean*, 828 F.3d 1046, 1049 (9th Cir. 2016).

III

Pacific Choice raises two challenges to the 2.7 percent quota share limit. First, it argues that the Service misinterpreted the term "excessive share" in section 1853a(c)(5)(D) by sidelining considerations of market power in favor of per-vessel profitability. Second, it argues that the Service acted arbitrarily and capriciously by failing **[—13—]** to consider all relevant factors and relying on insufficient analysis in choosing the 2.7 percent limit. We review the district court's decision de novo, *see Pacific Dawn*, 831 F.3d at 1173, and we reject both challenges.

A

We begin with Pacific Choice's argument that the 2.7 percent maximum share contravenes the Magnuson-Stevens Act. At the outset, we acknowledge some uncertainty as to exactly what Pacific Choice believes the Service's interpretive error to be. In its opening brief, Pacific Choice asserted that "'[e]xcessive share,' as used in 16 U.S.C. § 1853a(c)(5)(D) . . . means 'conditions of monopoly or oligopoly,'" and that the Service violated the Act because it "relied on . . . factors outside the scope of [section 1853a(c)(5)(D)] by setting a maximum share that reflected 'a chance of generating a reasonable profit.'" That language suggests that it is improper for the Service to consider any factors other than market power, or at least that it is improper for the Service to consider whether a maximum share will allow reasonable profits. But in its reply brief, Pacific Choice rejected that suggestion as "a straw man," disclaiming the argument that the Service "may *only* consider market power" and arguing instead that "market power is *an essential and indispensable factor*" for determining a maximum share, which the Service ignored by "bas[ing] the limit *solely on other factors*."

To the extent Pacific Choice means that market power is one of many factors that the Service must consider, we do not think the Service disagrees. To the contrary, when asked at oral argument if the Service is required to consider market power, counsel for the Service said yes. And in promulgating the 2010 rule, the Service explained that the Council had "considered a wide range of factors such as social benefits, **[—14—]** impact on labor, impacts on processors, impacts on harvesters, impacts on the public, the number and sizes of firms, within-sector competition, *market power*, efficiency, geographic distribution, communities, and fairness and equity." 75 Fed. Reg. at 33,004 (emphasis added). The Service advanced a similar interpretation in a 2007 guidance document instructing fishery councils to consider "market power including monopoly . . . or monopsony" in designing limited access privilege programs.

Pacific Choice appears to believe, however, that considering market power as one of several factors is not enough. Instead, we understand Pacific Choice's statutory argument to be that whatever limit **{-940-}** the Service sets, it must in some sense be "based on" market-power considerations. In other words, Pacific Choice's argument implies that it would be improper for the Service to determine that a particular limit would prevent any market participant from exercising market power but then to set a lower limit that reflects other considerations. We note that where, as here, market power could be avoided with a higher limit than is needed to achieve other objectives, Pacific Choice's position is not so different, in practice, from a rule that the Service may consider only market power.

In assessing Pacific Choice's statutory argument, we apply the framework of *Chevron U.S.A. Inc. v. NRDC, Inc.*, 467 U.S. 837 (1984). "[W]hen an agency is authorized by Congress to issue regulations and promulgates a regulation interpreting a statute it enforces, the interpretation receives deference if the statute is ambiguous and if the agency's interpretation is reasonable." *Encino Motorcars, LLC v. Navarro*, 136 S. Ct. 2117, 2124 (2016).

Our first step is to determine whether Congress has "directly addressed the precise question at issue." *Chevron*, **[—15—]** 467 U.S. at 843. We conclude that it has not. The relevant statutory text directs the Service to

> (D) ensure that limited access privilege holders do not acquire an excessive share of the total limited access privileges in the program by—
>
> > (i) establishing a maximum share, expressed as a percentage of the total limited access privileges, that a limited access privilege holder is permitted to hold, acquire, or use; and
> >
> > (ii) establishing any other limitations or measures necessary to prevent an inequitable concentration of limited access privileges.

16 U.S.C. § 1853a(c)(5)(D). That provision defines neither "excessive share" nor "maximum share," and it contains no reference to market power. Other provisions of the same section make clear that limited access privilege programs are to serve a variety of objectives. Specifically, such programs "shall . . . promote—(i) fishing safety; (ii) fishery conservation and management; and (iii) social and economic benefits." *Id.* § 1853a(c)(1)(C).

Pacific Choice points to a separate section of the Act that outlines standards for fishery management and instructs the Service to ensure that allocations of quota share are "(A) fair and equitable to all such fishermen; (B) reasonably calculated to promote conservation; and (C) carried out in such manner that no particular individual, corporation, or other entity acquires an excessive share of such privileges." 16 U.S.C. § 1851(a)(4). Like section 1853a(c)(5)(D), **[—16—]** however, that provision does not say what Congress meant by "excessive share." And the next paragraph makes clear that although the Service must "consider efficiency" in developing fishery management measures, economic efficiency is *not* the only goal: "no such measure shall have economic allocation as its sole purpose." *Id.* § 1851(a)(5).

Pacific Choice emphasizes that the Service previously interpreted section 1851(a)(4)'s "excessive share" clause to "imply conditions of monopoly or oligopoly." 60 Fed. Reg. 61,200, 61,202 (Nov. 29, 1995). The Service's prior interpretations cannot transform otherwise ambiguous statutory text into an unambiguous command because "the whole point of *Chevron* is to leave the discretion provided by the ambiguities of a statute with the implementing agency." **{-941-}** *Smiley v. Citibank (S.D.), N.A.*, 517 U.S. 735, 742 (1996). In any event, the Service's belief that the term "excessive share" "impl[ies]" market power is itself far from an unambiguous statement that market power must have singular importance—almost by definition, one cannot "directly address[]" an issue by implication. *Chevron*, 467 U.S. at 843.

Pacific Choice also relies on the Act's legislative history, but legislative history cannot "supply mandatory requirements not found within the [Magnuson-Stevenson Act] itself." *Pacific Coast*, 693 F.3d at 1093. Even if it could, the legislative history here does not do so. Pacific Choice points to two floor statements from individual Representatives indicating that Congress was concerned about preventing "excessive and inequitable consolidation at the expense of small-scale fishermen," 152 Cong. Rec. 23,359 (Dec. 8, 2006) (statement of Rep. Allen), and wanted to "protect[] small fishermen from those who would like to consolidate fisheries," *id.* at 23,360 (statement of Rep. **[—17—]** Rahall). Those statements reflect a desire to protect small fishing operations, but, like the statutory text, they do not suggest that the maximum share must be no more restrictive than necessary to avoid excessive concentration.

Because the Act is ambiguous as to what factors the Service must consider in setting a maximum share, we turn to step two of the *Chevron* framework: whether the Service has adopted a "reasonable interpretation" of the statute. 467 U.S. at 844. We have previously held that the Act gives the Service "broad discretion" to carry out its provisions. *Northwest Envtl. Def. Ctr. v. Brennan*, 958 F.2d 930, 935 n.3 (9th Cir. 1992). Congress directed the Service to consider a wide range of factors in establishing limited access privilege programs, including "the basic cultural and social framework of the fishery" and "the sustained participation of small owner-operated fishing vessels and fishing communities that depend on the fisheries." 16 U.S.C. § 1853a(c)(5)(B). In light of those objectives, it was reasonable for the Service to conclude that other factors can dictate a lower maximum share than might be required by a singular focus on preventing excessive market power—or, in other words, that the Service may attempt to do something more than act simply as a fishery-specific version of the Federal Trade Commission or the Justice Department's Antitrust Division.

Pacific Choice suggests that the Service erred in interpreting the Act to permit consideration of whether vessels would have a "chance at generating a reasonable profit." We disagree. The Act requires the Service to "include measures to assist, when necessary and appropriate, entry-level and small vessel owner-operators, captains, crew, and fishing communities." 16 U.S.C. § 1853a(c)(5)(C). While Congress noted that those measures **[—18—]** might "includ[e] . . . set-asides of harvesting allocations" or "economic assistance," it did not say that those actions were the only such measures the Service could adopt. *Id.* Instead, Congress left it to the

Service to determine when and how assisting small vessel owner-operators might be "necessary and appropriate." *Id.* Giving weight to the chance of generating a profit was a reasonable way to implement Congress's directive.

B

Although the Service permissibly interpreted the Act, we still must ensure that the 2.7 percent maximum share is not "arbitrary, capricious, [or] an abuse of discretion." 5 U.S.C. § 706(2)(A). That standard is deferential: as long as an agency has "examine[d] the relevant data and articulate[d] a satisfactory explanation for its action including a 'rational connection between **{-942-}** the facts found and the choice made,'" the Supreme Court has made clear that "a court is not to substitute its judgment for that of the agency." *Motor Vehicle Mfrs. Ass'n of U.S., Inc. v. State Farm Mut. Auto. Ins. Co.*, 463 U.S. 29, 43 (1983) (quoting *Burlington Truck Lines v. United States*, 371 U.S. 156, 168 (1962)); *accord FCC v. Fox Television Stations, Inc.*, 556 U.S. 502, 513–14 (2009).

As an initial matter, the Service asks us to disregard Pacific Choice's objections because Pacific Choice did not raise them before the agency. Generally, a "party forfeits arguments that are not raised during the administrative process." *Lands Council v. McNair*, 629 F.3d 1070, 1076 (9th Cir. 2010). But we will consider any issue that was "raised with sufficient clarity to allow the decision maker to understand and rule on the issue raised, whether the issue was considered sua sponte by the agency or was raised by someone other than the petitioning party." *Glacier Fish Co., LLC v. Pritzer*, 832 F.3d 1113, 1120 n.6 (9th Cir. 2016) **[—19—]** (internal quotation marks and citation omitted). Because the Service in fact examined the issues that Pacific Choice now raises, including in response to other commenters during the notice-and-comment period, we consider them on the merits.

In assessing the Service's decision, we "review the whole record," 5 U.S.C. § 706, which includes "everything that was before the agency pertaining to the merits of its decision." *Portland Audubon Soc. v. Endangered Species Comm.*, 984 F.2d 1534, 1548 (9th Cir. 1993). Pacific Choice urges us to examine only the Service's decision memoranda while ignoring the Council's materials, including analyses by the Quota Committee, the Allocation Committee, the Management Team, and the Advisory Subpanel. Although the Act requires the Service to "evaluat[e]" the Council's proposed regulations to "determine whether they are consistent with the fishery management plan" and with the Act, it does not require the Service to engage in a lengthy discussion of every aspect of the plan or to repeat points already made by the Council and its committees. 16 U.S.C. § 1854(b)(1). Instead, when the Service finds that an amendment is consistent with a fishery plan, the Act requires it to do no more than "publish such regulations in the Federal Register," along with any "technical changes as may be necessary for clarity and an explanation of those changes." *Id.* § 1854(b)(1)(A). Pacific Choice offers no authority supporting its assertion that we should focus exclusively on the Service's memoranda from the very end of the administrative process. To the contrary, we have previously upheld the Service's regulations on the basis of findings by the Council and its committees. *See Fisherman's Finest, Inc. v. Locke*, 593 F.3d 886, 896 (9th Cir. 2010).

Pacific Choice contends that the Service's decision-making process was flawed in two ways: the Service "failed **[—20—]** to consider an important aspect of the problem" by ignoring market power altogether, *State Farm*, 463 U.S. at 43, and it also failed to articulate "the methods by which, and the purposes for which" it set the maximum share at 2.7 percent rather than at some other percentage, *San Antonio, Tex. ex rel. City Pub. Serv. Bd. v. United States*, 631 F.2d 831, 852 (D.C. Cir. 1980). We reject both of those arguments.

First, the record shows that the Service did consider market power. After the Quota Committee completed its initial analysis based on historical aggregate revenue, the

Allocation Committee examined the degree of concentration within the fishery, calculating an HHI. Relying on Department of {-943-} Justice antitrust guidelines defining a concentrated market based on HHI, the Allocation Committee concluded that all of the options then under consideration—ranging from 1.5 to 5 percent—were "unlikely" to "affect market power." With the conclusion in hand that market-power considerations were unlikely to be significant factors in establishing a maximum share, the Service might have understandably decided to ignore market power.

But contrary to Pacific Choice's representations, market-power considerations and economic analyses continued to play a prominent role in the agency's consideration of the maximum share. Building on the Allocation Committee's analysis, the Management Team acknowledged the dual purposes of setting maximum shares: the limits not only serve as "preventative measures against anticompetitive market conditions" but also "ensure that the benefits . . . arising from the public fishery resource accrue to a minimum number of [quota-share] owners." The Management Team then conducted an in-depth analysis of the degree of concentration in the fishery, projecting vessel profitability [—21—] based on varying levels of market concentration. After cautioning against the effect that higher quota-share maximums might have on "bargaining, market power, and . . . . undue influence over other aspects of the fishery," the Management Team presented a range of options from 1.3 to 3.8 percent depending on the Service's desired degree of "consolidation" within the fishery. While Pacific Choice might prefer the higher limits suggested by the Allocation Committee's HHI analysis rather than the lower ones suggested by the Management Team's economist, we see no reason to second-guess the Management Team's economic analysis.

Nor did the Management Team offer the final word on market power—the Council itself detailed its reasoning in an exhaustive overview in the 2010 environmental impact statement, which it issued jointly with the Service. While it is true that the Council stated that its quota-share limits were "aimed at more than just preventing market power or other anticompetitive situations," that is not the same as ignoring market power.

Second, we conclude that the agency engaged in a reasoned process from which its path to the 2.7 percent limit "may reasonably be discerned." *Alaska Dep't of Envtl. Conservation v. EPA*, 540 U.S. 461, 497 (2004) (quoting *Bowman Transp., Inc. v. Arkansas-Best Freight Sys., Inc.*, 419 U.S. 281, 286 (1974)). Pacific Choice argues that the Advisory Subpanel picked 2.7 percent only because it was the "mid range of the data presented" in the Management Team's economic analysis. Even if that were an accurate characterization of the Advisory Subpanel's recommendation, it would not necessarily establish that the Service's decision was unreasoned given the extensive discussion of Act's factors presented at each step of the [—22—] rulemaking process. We have upheld similar determinations in the past where the agency "had to choose some number from a broad range" and selected "a reasonable figure." *San Luis & Delta-Mendota Water Auth. v. Jewell*, 747 F.3d 581, 616 (9th Cir. 2014); *see Missouri Pub. Serv. Comm'n v. FERC*, 215 F.3d 1, 5–6 (D.C. Cir. 2000).

In any event, Pacific Choice's interpretation of the administrative record is not persuasive. Pacific Choice misconstrues the Advisory Subpanel's recommendation, which did not state that the panel recommended 2.7 percent *because* that figure was in the middle of the Management Team's recommendations. Instead, the Advisory Subpanel adopted the Management Team's recommendation because it concluded {-944-} that the "revenue-based approach . . . [was] a useful conceptual approach" for setting a maximum share. The Advisory Subpanel's recommendation is brief, but it reveals independent judgment on each aspect of the recommendations from the Allocation Committee and the Management Team, most notably on individual species limits.

More generally, we see no reason to focus only on the Advisory Subpanel's memo when it constituted just one step in the lengthy administrative process. Viewed as a whole, the record contains extensive justification for the 2.7 percent limit. As the Management Team concluded, that limit accommodates a variety of the Council's objectives for setting a maximum share, including "cap[ping] the initial allocation of quota share at a level that is consistent with" historical quota distributions on the 2003 control date, and allowing more consolidation in the fishery than a lower limit—such as 2.3 percent—would accomplish. The Service's environmental impact statement fully explains how the agency arrived at the 2.7 percent limit from the **[—23—]** Quota Committee's initial recommendation of 1.5 to 5 percent.

Under the APA, "we will uphold a decision of less than ideal clarity if the agency's path may reasonably be discerned." *Bowman*, 419 U.S. at 286. We have no difficulty in following the Service's path to the 2.7 percent maximum share, and we hold that the Service did not act arbitrarily or capriciously in setting it.

IV

Pacific Choice also advances statutory and APA challenges to the Service's control rule. We reject both.

The Magnuson-Stevens Act requires that the Service "establish[] a maximum share . . . that a [share] holder is permitted to hold, acquire, or use." 16 U.S.C. § 1853a(c)(5)(D)(i). According to Pacific Choice, the Service exceeded the authority granted by that statute when it interpreted "hold, acquire, or use" to include "control" and proceeded to define "control" to include, among other things, "the ability through any means whatsoever to control or have a controlling influence over the entity to which [quota share] is registered." 50 C.F.R. §660.140(d)(4)(iii)(H). Pacific Choice argues that the rule "effectively re-writes Congress's definition" by using the word "control," which does not appear in the statute. But the word "acquire," which does appear in the statute, means "to come into possession, *control*, or power of disposal of." *Webster's Third New International Dictionary* 18 (2002) (emphasis added). If that were not enough, the word "use" easily encompasses the concept of control. *See Friends of Animals v. United States Fish & Wildlife Serv.*, 879 F.3d 1000, 1006–09 (9th Cir. 2018). Beyond that, section 1853a(c)(5)(D)(ii) gives the Service even broader authority **[—24—]** to establish "any other limitations or measures necessary to prevent an inequitable concentration of limited access privileges." 16 U.S.C. § 1853a(c)(5)(D)(ii).

Pacific Choice responds that we must read the statute against a background of ordinary corporate-law principles, under which a corporation is a distinct entity from its owners. We agree that Congress drafts laws while "aware of settled principles of corporate law." *Dole Food Co. v. Patrickson*, 538 U.S. 468, 474 (2003). It is also true that Congress defined the term "person" in the Act to mean "any individual . . . corporation, partnership, association, or other entity." 16 U.S.C. § 1802(36). But the Service's control rule does not purport to redefine personhood. Instead, it defines when a person "own[s] or control[s]" quota share nominally held by *other* people. 50 C.F.R. § 660.140(d)(4)(i)(A). That is in no **{-945-}** way inconsistent with the common-law understanding of corporate ownership.

Because the Service's interpretation of "hold, acquire, or use" represents an exercise of delegated authority, our review of it is governed by *Chevron*, and we see nothing in the statute that unambiguously forecloses the Service's approach. Instead, the Service's rule represents a reasonable implementation of Congress's directive that quota allocations be "fair and equitable" and be "carried out in such manner that no particular individual, corporation, or other entity acquires an excessive share of such privileges." 16 U.S.C. § 1851(a)(4).

Nor are we persuaded that the rule is arbitrary and capricious. Pacific Choice does not identify a deficiency in the Service's rulemaking process but instead argues that the Service's definition of "control" is so broad—and thus so vague—that it constitutes an abuse of discretion. In limited situations, we have recognized that an agency might act

[—25—] arbitrarily and capriciously by "fail[ing] to properly specify" its rules such that it leaves "no method by which" a regulated party "can gauge [its] performance." *Arizona Cattle Grower's Ass'n v. United States Fish & Wildlife Serv.*, 273 F.3d 1229, 1250–51 (9th Cir. 2001). This is not such a situation.

The rule is indeed broad. Its broadest provision covers any person who "has the ability through any means whatsoever to control or have a controlling influence over" an entity holding quota share. 50 C.F.R. § 660.140(d)(4)(iii)(H). But breadth is not the same thing as vagueness. *See Pennsylvania Dep't of Corrections v. Yeskey*, 524 U.S. 206, 212 (1998). The rule's terms have clear meanings sufficient to inform regulated entities about what types of conduct the Service will prohibit: ownership or control that evades the Service's maximum share limits. For example, clause (d)(4)(iii)(A) deems control satisfied when a person "has the right to direct . . . the business of [an] entity," clause (d)(4)(iii)(B) when a person "has the right to limit the actions of or replace" corporate officers, and clause (d)(4)(iii)(C) when a person "has the right to direct . . . the transfer of" quota share. It requires no great leap to read the more general language of clause (d)(4)(iii)(H) as prohibiting the same sort of thing. *See Yates v. United States*, 574 U.S. 528, 545, 3 Adm. R. 2, 9 (2015).

Crucially, we see no ambiguity about whether Pacific Choice "own[ed] or control[led]" the related entities at issue here. Pacific Choice's brief discloses that each of the six entities that held quota share are wholly owned either by Frank Dulcich or by a corporation that Dulcich owns. Under any plausible definition of "control," Dulcich controls the Pacific Choice entities. Because Pacific Choice is subject to the control rule even under its narrowest construction, we **[—26—]** need not consider the rule's outermost limits or whether, in some other case, the Service might abuse its discretion by applying the rule in a surprising or unforeseeable way. *See Village of Hoffman Estates v. Flipside, Hoffman Estates, Inc.*, 455 U.S. 489, 495 (1982) ("A plaintiff who engages in some conduct that is clearly proscribed cannot complain of the vagueness of the law as applied to the conduct of others.").

AFFIRMED.

United States Court of Appeals
for the Ninth Circuit

No. 19-70297

INTERNATIONAL LONGSHORE & WAREHOUSE UNION
VS.
NATIONAL LABOR RELATIONS BD.

On Petition for Review of an Order of the National Labor Relations Board

Decided: October 14, 2020

Citation: 978 F.3d 625, 8 Adm. R. 334 (9th Cir. 2020).

Before **HAWKINS** and **MCKEOWN**, Circuit Judges, and **KENDALL,*** District Judge.

* The Honorable Virginia M. Kendall, United States District Judge for the Northern District of Illinois, sitting by designation.

[—6—] {-628-} **HAWKINS**, Circuit Judge:

We address a years-long intra-union dispute over the right to perform certain maintenance and repair (M&R) work for Kinder Morgan Terminals (Kinder Morgan) **{-629-}** at its Bulk Terminal facility in Vancouver, Washington. In 2008, Local 4 of the International Longshore and Warehouse Union (the Longshoremen)[1] and the Pacific Maritime Association (PMA), an association of West Coast port operators, negotiated a collective bargaining agreement (CBA) with the Longshoremen in which they agreed to offset anticipated future losses of longshore jobs to automation by expanding the Longshoremen's jurisdiction to include additional work at facilities run by PMA members. One such member, Kinder Morgan, had previously subcontracted the electrical **[—7—]** M&R work at its Vancouver facility to a company that employed electricians represented by Local 48 of the International Brotherhood of Electrical Workers (the Electrical Workers).[2] Relying on CBA language that covered the work in question, the Longshoremen filed several grievances to enforce the new CBA when Kinder Morgan continued using Electrical Workers even after the agreement took effect. When the Electrical Workers responded by threatening to picket the Vancouver facility, Kinder Morgan asked the National Labor Relations Board (the Board) to intervene.

A cacophony of agency and arbitral decisions ensued. Following a 2011 hearing under section 10(k) of the National Labor Relations Act (NLRA), 29 U.S.C. § 160(k), the Board awarded the disputed work to the Electrical Workers over the Longshoremen's defense that they were preserving work secured under the new CBA. Meanwhile, the arbitrator assigned to the Longshoremen's grievances found as a matter of contract interpretation that the CBA covered the disputed work. As the Longshoremen took steps to enforce their arbitral victory, the Electrical Workers filed unfair labor practices (ULP) charges, and the Board filed a complaint alleging that the Longshoremen's continued pursuit of the disputed work violated section 8(b)(4) of the NLRA, 29 U.S.C. § 158(b)(4). In 2014, an administrative law judge (ALJ), after a seven-day hearing, found the Longshoremen's actions were aimed at preserving bargained-for work and dismissed the complaint.

Five years later, the Board disagreed. Reversing the ALJ, the Board again rejected the Longshoremen's work **[—8—]** preservation defense, found them in violation of the NLRA, and ordered them to cease all attempts to obtain the disputed work, to withdraw its grievances, and to request vacatur of their favorable arbitral award. The Longshoremen and PMA[3] now seek review of this order, and,

[1] The union's international organization is also a Petitioner. Since their differences are immaterial here, and for ease of reference, we refer to them collectively as "the Longshoremen" and to their members as "Longshoremen."

[2] In addition to referring to the union organization as "the Electrical Workers," we similarly refer to its members as "Electrical Workers."

[3] We previously denied without prejudice the Board's motion to dismiss PMA's petition because it was not a party to the underlying proceedings. The Board has since conceded the petition's timeliness and declined to renew its motion "because PMA

in a counterpetition, the Board seeks its enforcement.[4] **{–630–}**

We resolve three issues here. *First*, we reaffirm the well-settled rule that 10(k) decisions are not res judicata in subsequent ULP proceedings. Indeed, our and the Board's own case law expressly allow parties in ULP proceedings to relitigate arguments previously rejected in 10(k) decisions. We therefore hold that the Board erred in deeming its 10(k) decision "dispositive" of the Longshoremen's work preservation defense. *Second*, we reject the Board's construction of the work preservation defense. The Supreme Court has twice disallowed such a narrow focus on past performance of the precise work in dispute as ill-suited to the holistic, circumstantial inquiry that is indispensable where, as here, parties strike agreements aimed at preserving union jobs in the face of technological threats to traditional **[—9—]** union work. We hold that the Board erred by disregarding this binding precedent and instead making past performance of the specific work at issue the beginning and end of its analysis. *Third*, we hold that the 2008 CBA encompasses the disputed work which both unions claim. Subject only to exceptions not at issue here, the plain language of the agreement unambiguously assigns to the Longshoremen all M&R work, on all present and future stevedore cargo handling equipment—including its technological equipment and electronics—for all PMA members, at all West Coast ports. The Board erred by using extrinsic evidence to inject ambiguity into the CBA's unambiguous terms and, by extension, assessing the Longshoremen's work preservation defense based on that erroneous construction.

Accordingly, we grant the petitions for review, deny the cross-petition for enforcement, vacate the Board's order, and remand for further proceedings.

BACKGROUND

The Longshoremen and PMA have a decades-long collective bargaining relationship. *Int'l Longshoremen's & Warehousemen's Union (Cal. Cartage)*, 208 NLRB 986, 987 (1974). The Longshoremen have represented a coastwide collective bargaining unit of longshore workers at West Coast ports since 1938. *Shipowners' Ass'n of the Pac. Coast*, 7 NLRB 1002, 1025 (1938). As a multiemployer association whose members, including Kinder Morgan, employ Longshoremen at ports along the West Coast, PMA is responsible for negotiating and administering CBAs on its members' behalf. Kinder Morgan operates marine terminals at several West Coast ports, including its Vancouver facility, which it has operated since the 1990s. *Int'l Brotherhood of Elec. Workers, Local 48 (IBEW)*, 357 NLRB 2217, 2217 (2011). **[—10—]**

Virtually all longshore work at West Coast ports is covered by a single CBA called the Pacific Coast Longshore Contract Document (PCLCD). Most relevant for our purposes is the version negotiated in 2008—specifically, its terms addressing the anticipated introduction of labor-saving automation technologies at West Coast ports. The language in section 1.71 of the agreement remained the same as in previous iterations, providing that the PCLCD "shall apply to the maintenance and repair of all stevedore cargo handling equipment." The parties then added two new provisions. In section 1.72, the Longshoremen and PMA stipulated:

> It is recognized that the introduction of new technologies, including fully mechanized and robotic-operated marine terminals, necessarily displaces traditional longshore work and workers, including the operating, maintenance and repair, and associated cleaning of

makes essentially the same arguments as ILWU, which undisputably has standing." We do not address it further.

[4] On July 2, 2019, we consolidated the Longshoremen's and PMA's petitions for review and the Board's cross-petition for enforcement—all of which arise from the same Board order. We also granted Kinder Morgan and the Electrical Workers leave to intervene, and each has filed a brief in support of the Board's cross-petition. Finally, we granted leave to the Maritime Union of Australia and the International Longshoremen's Association, AFL-CIO, to participate as amici, and each has filed an amicus brief in support of the petitions for review.

> stevedore cargo **{–631–}** handling equipment. The parties recognize robotics and other technologies will replace a certain number of equipment operators and other traditional longshore classifications. It is agreed that the jurisdiction of the ILWU shall apply to the maintenance and repair of all present and forthcoming stevedore cargo handling equipment in accordance with Sections 1.7 and 1.71 and shall constitute the functional equivalent of such traditional ILWU work.

And in section 1.73, they further agreed that

> [t]he scope of work shall include . . . maintenance and repair . . . of all present and **[—11—]** forthcoming technological equipment related to the operation of stevedore cargo handling equipment (which term includes containers and chassis) and its electronics, that are controlled or interchanged by PMA companies, in all West Coast ports.

Simply put, the parties decided that PMA members could increase their use of automated equipment, and in exchange, the Longshoremen's jurisdiction would expand to offset the corresponding loss of traditional longshore work.[5]

This case emanates from conflicting constructions of these new terms—specifically, whether they encompass the disputed work at Kinder Morgan's Vancouver facility. Before 2008, Kinder Morgan had subcontracted such work to a subcontractor which employed workers under its own CBA with the Electrical Workers. *See ILWU*, 367 NLRB **[—12—]** No. 64, slip op. at 2. When this arrangement continued beyond the 2008 PCLCD's operational date, the Longshoremen filed several grievances arguing that Kinder Morgan's use of Electrical Workers violated sections 1.71 through 1.73 of the agreement. The Longshoremen's local president also penned a letter demanding that Kinder Morgan hire Longshoremen to perform the disputed work. The Electrical Workers responded by threatening to picket the Vancouver facility if Kinder Morgan capitulated to the Longshoremen's demands.[6] Caught in the middle, Kinder Morgan then filed charges against the Electrical Workers with the Board and requested a 10(k) hearing, *see* 29 U.S.C. § 160(k).

On December 31, 2011, the Board issued its 10(k) determination. After a three-day hearing and briefing from Kinder Morgan, the Electrical Workers, and the Longshoremen, the Board awarded the disputed **{–632–}** work to the Electrical Workers. *IBEW*, 357 NLRB at 2221. Citing the unions' competing claims to the same work, the Electrical Workers' use of picketing threats against Kinder Morgan, and the absence of an agreed-upon method to resolve the dispute, the Board made its threshold finding of a bona fide jurisdictional dispute. *Id.* at 2218. It then rejected the

---

[5] For PMA members that already had contracts with other unions, Section 1.81 of the PCLCD states that

> ILWU jurisdiction of maintenance and repair work shall not apply at those specific marine terminals that are listed as being "red-circled" in the July 1, 2008 Letter of Understanding on this subject. Red-circled facilities, as they are modified/upgraded (e.g., introduction of new technologies), or expanded, while maintaining the fundamental identity of the pre-existing facility, shall not result in the displacement of the recognized workforce and shall not be disturbed, unless as determined by the terminal owner or tenant.

Since the Board found that the 2008 PCLCD does not encompass the disputed work, it did not decide whether Section 1.81 excludes electrical M&R work performed at Kinder Morgan's Vancouver facility from the Longshoremen's jurisdiction. *See Int'l Longshore & Warehouse Union (ILWU)*, 367 NLRB No. 64 (Jan. 31, 2019).

[6] The Longshoremen and PMA question the sincerity of the Electrical Workers' picketing threats by claiming that Kinder Morgan and the Electrical Workers concocted a superficially jurisdictional dispute to invite Board intervention. The Board twice rejected, and the ALJ did not consider, this argument. *See IBEW*, 357 NLRB at 2218; *ILWU*, 367 NLRB No. 64, slip op. at 5 n.6. Because we vacate the Board's order based on antecedent legal errors, we, too, decline to address it.

Longshoremen's defense that they had acted lawfully to preserve work bargained for under the 2008 PCLCD. The Board instead noted the disputed work's past performance **[—13—]** by Electrical Workers, a concomitant lack thereof by the Longshoremen, and an absence of contractual language explicitly assigning *electrical* maintenance work to the Longshoremen. *Id.* at 2218–19. It then discounted the language in sections 1.71 through 1.73 as too "general" to support the work's reassignment to the Longshoremen, credited Kinder Morgan's preference for Electrical Workers, dismissed the Longshoremen's evidence of past performance of electrical M&R work as too sparse, noted Electrical Workers' superior skills and training, and thus deemed their continued use more economical. *Id.* at 2219–20.

The Area Arbitrator assigned to the Longshoremen's earlier-filed grievances reached the opposite conclusion.[7] On February 21, 2012, the arbitrator issued an award finding that the Longshoremen's jurisdiction under the 2008 PCLCD encompasses the disputed work and referred the matter to the Coast Labor Relations Committee (CLRC), which ordered Kinder Morgan to "take the necessary steps to assign the work in dispute" to Longshoremen. Over the next several months, Kinder Morgan and the Longshoremen worked with the CLRC to implement the order, including preparing job postings for the work in question and interviewing Longshoremen candidates. While that was being accomplished, Kinder Morgan continued sending the work to its subcontractor and its Electrical Workers, to which the Longshoremen responded by physically **[—14—]** obstructing Electrical Workers' access to the Vancouver facility.

On November 8, 2012, the Electrical Workers went back to the Board and filed ULP charges against the Longshoremen. On June 28, 2013,[8] the Board filed a complaint alleging that the Longshoremen's actions violated section 8(b)(4) of the NLRA, 29 U.S.C. § 158(b)(4). The Board based its allegations on the Longshoremen's failure to withdraw its grievances, its efforts to enforce its favorable arbitral award, and its attempts to prevent Electrical Workers from performing electrical M&R work at Kinder Morgan's Vancouver facility.

An ALJ dismissed the complaint on August 13, 2013. Following a seven-day hearing, the ALJ found that (1) Longshoremen had previously performed electrical M&R work at "numerous" PMA-affiliated facilities; (2) contrary to the Board's 10(k) decision, the 2008 PCLCD encompasses both present and future electrical M&R work, including the disputed work here; (3) the work preservation doctrine recognizes the validity of such agreements; and (4) Kinder Morgan, as a PMA member, is bound by its terms.

The Board disagreed. On January 31, 2019, it reversed the ALJ's dismissal and **{-633-}** found that the Longshoremen's use of the grievance process and physical obstruction of jobsites constituted ULP under the NLRA. The Board began by stating that its initial 10(k) decision precluded the Longshoremen from reasserting its work preservation defense against the ULP charges. It also rejected the ALJ's **[—15—]** finding of past performance of the disputed work by Longshoremen, as well as the ALJ's constructions of the PCLCD and the work preservation doctrine. The Board then ordered the Longshoremen to cease and desist from said activities, to withdraw its grievances against Kinder Morgan, and to request vacatur of the arbitrator's decision concluding that the terms of the 2008 PCLCD encompass electrical M&R work.

These petitions for review and cross-petition for enforcement followed.[9]

---

[7] The designated Area Arbitrator had originally found that a July 28, 2008 Letter of Understanding (LOU) exempted Kinder Morgan's Vancouver facility from the relevant provisions of the PCLCD. On appeal, however, the Coast Arbitrator concluded that the LOU included no such exemption and remanded to the Area Arbitrator.

[8] After amending its complaint several times, the Board filed the operative consolidated complaint on October 22, 2013.

[9] The Longshoremen and PMA filed their petitions on February 1 and June 13, 2019, respectively, and the Board filed its cross-petition on March 28, 2019.

JURISDICTION AND STANDARD OF REVIEW

We have jurisdiction to review the petitions and cross-petition under 29 U.S.C. § 160(e) and (f). We will enforce the Board's order if it "correctly applied the law and if its factual findings are supported by substantial evidence in the record as a whole." *Plaza Auto Ctr., Inc. v. NLRB*, 664 F.3d 286, 291 (9th Cir. 2011) (quotation marks omitted). While we accord the Board's interpretations of the NLRA "considerable deference," *Recon Refractory & Constr., Inc. v. NLRB*, 424 F.3d 980, 987 (9th Cir. 2005) (quotation marks omitted), its legal interpretations generally must follow Supreme Court and circuit case law, *NLRB v. Ashkenazy Prop. Mgmt. Corp.*, 817 F.2d 74, 75 (9th Cir. 1987), and absent explanation, adhere to its own precedent, *NLRB v. Great W. Produce, Inc.*, 839 F.2d 555, 557 (9th Cir. 1988). Substantial evidence supports a factual finding if a **[—16—]** reasonable juror could have reached the Board's conclusion. *Plaza Auto*, 664 F.3d at 291.

ANALYSIS

Congress enacted the ULP provisions in section 8(b)(4) of the NLRA, 29 U.S.C. § 158(b)(4), to protect "neutral employer[s]" caught between competing unions. *Nat'l Woodwork Mfrs. Ass'n v. NLRB*, 386 U.S. 612, 625–26 (1967). We limit our discussion to one of these provisions.[10] Subsection (D) makes it a ULP for a union to threaten or coerce any person with the object of "forcing or requiring any employer to assign particular work to employees in a particular labor organization . . . rather than to employees in another labor organization." 29 U.S.C. § 158(b)(4)(D).

"Section 8(b)(4)(D), however, must be read in light of [section] 10(k) with which it is interlocked." *NLRB v. Plasterers' Local Union No. 79*, 404 U.S. 116, 123 (1971). If the Board has reasonable cause to believe section 8(b)(4)(D) was violated, *Int'l Tel. & Tel. Corp. v. Local 134, Int'l Brotherhood of Elec. Workers (ITT)*, 419 U.S. 428, 445 n.16 (1975), section 10(k) "empower[s] and direct[s]" **{-634-}** the Board "to hear and determine" the dispute unless the parties can timely demonstrate that "they have adjusted, or agreed upon methods for the voluntary adjustment of, the dispute." 29 U.S.C. § 160(k). This scheme encourages the swift, often **[—17—]** informal resolution of disputes by giving the parties a sort of "advisory opinion" that previews the Board's probable assessment of the merits before the long slog of formal ULP proceedings begins in earnest. *ITT*, 419 U.S. at 446; *see also id.* at 441–47 (describing purpose, function, and limitations of 10(k) proceedings). It is not, however, a binding, final disposition. *Id.* at 444.

I. The Board's 10(k) Decision Does Not Bar Re-Litigation of the Longshoremen's Work Preservation Defense

We begin with the Board's determination that its 10(k) decision precluded the Longshoremen from reasserting their work preservation defense in the subsequent ULP proceeding. The Board found its prior decision "dispositive of the question whether the Longshoremen had a valid work preservation objective" and deemed the Longshoremen's continued invocation of the defense an invalid attempt "to relitigate the Board's assignment of the disputed electrical M&R work to IBEW-represented employees." Though it now calls this finding "largely immaterial" given its purported reconsideration of the 10(k) decision later in the order, the Board still maintains that it "reasonably relied on precedent precluding such re-litigation." Not as we see it.

The Supreme Court has long held that "[t]he findings and conclusions in a [section] 10(k) proceeding are not res judicata on the unfair labor practice issue in the later [section] 8(b)(4)(D) determination." *ITT*, 419

[10] Although the underlying complaint alleges that the Longshoremen's actions violated Section 8(b)(4)(ii)(B) and (D), the Board's analysis focuses almost entirely on subsection (D), save for a two-sentence paragraph at the end stating that the same actions by the Longshoremen also violated subsection (B)'s secondary boycott prohibition. *See ILWU*, 367 NLRB No. 64, slip op. at 8. Because the latter finding depends entirely on the Board's erroneous application of subsection (D), we do not address subsection (B) separately here.

U.S. at 446. If a union does not follow the Board's 10(k) decision, "the Board must prove [by a preponderance of the evidence] the union guilty of a [section] 8(b)(4)(D) violation before a cease-and-desist order can issue." *Plasterers' Local*, 404 U.S. at 122 n.10. This typically entails revisiting some of the arguments rejected during a 10(k) proceeding, at which **[—18—]** time the Board need only have found reasonable cause to believe section 8(b)(4)(D) was violated before issuing an award. *See id.*; *ITT*, 419 U.S. at 445 n.16. "Indeed, reconsideration of [section] 10(k) rulings appears implicitly contemplated by the statutory scheme, given that a [section] 8(b)(4)(D) proceeding involves a full adversarial adjudication, in contrast with the informal proceedings required under [section] 10(k)." *Pac. Maritime Ass'n v. NLRB (PMA)*, 827 F.3d 1203, 1211 (9th Cir. 2016).

Board case law has long observed this anti-preclusion rule. *See Longshoremen ILWU Local 6 (Golden Grain)*, 289 NLRB 1, 2 (1988) ("[W]e overrule prior Board cases to the extent they suggest that a respondent in an 8(b)(4)(D) proceeding is not entitled to relitigate factual issues concerning the elements of the 8(b)(4)(D) violation that were raised in an underlying 10(k) proceeding unless it presents new or previously unavailable evidence."); *accord Plumbers Local 290 (Streimer Sheet Metal Works)*, 323 NLRB 1101, 1101 n.3 (1997) ("In light of the Respondent's election . . . to relitigate the unfair labor practice issue, we find no need to review the Board's decision reached under a different evidentiary standard in the Sec. 10(k) proceeding."); *Tile, Marble, Terrazzo Finishers & Shopworkers, Local 47-T (Grazzini Bros.)*, 315 NLRB 520, 521 (1994) ("[A] respondent is entitled to a hearing . . . if the respondent denies the existence of an element of the 8(b)(4)(D) violation, either directly **{-635-}** or by raising an affirmative defense."); *Teamsters Local 216 (Granite Rock Co.)*, 296 NLRB 250, 250 (1989) ("[A] respondent may relitigate factual issues concerning the elements of the 8(b)(4)(D) violation that were raised in the underlying 10(k) proceeding."). Yet the Board offered no explanation before it departed from that rule here. *See Great W. Produce*, 839 F.2d at 557. Nevertheless, that does not end our analysis. **[—19—]**

Even as it has eschewed giving certain findings in 10(k) decisions res judicata effect, the Board has concurrently maintained that parties cannot "relitigate threshold matters that are not necessary to prove an 8(b)(4)(D) violation." *Golden Grain*, 289 NLRB at 2 n.4. Albeit passingly, the Board seizes upon such language here by suggesting that it reasonably relied on this rule in barring re-litigation of the Longshoremen's work preservation defense in the subsequent ULP proceedings. We disagree.

The "threshold matters" mentioned in *Golden Grain* refer to the initial jurisdictional assessment. Indeed, the decision's immediately subsequent reference to "the threshold issue of whether there had been an agreed method of settlement," *see id.*, points directly to the initial "three-step inquiry" used to determine whether there is a valid jurisdictional dispute warranting Board intervention under section 10(k), *see Recon Refractory*, 424 F.3d at 988. This threshold inquiry asks whether "(1) a union has used a proscribed means—such as picketing or threatening to picket—to enforce its claim to the work in dispute; (2) there are competing claims to the disputed work between rival groups of employees; and (3) there is no agreed-upon method for resolving the dispute voluntarily." *Id.* If the Board answers each of these in the affirmative, it then proceeds to the heart of the 10(k) inquiry by awarding the disputed work "based on considerations such as the employer's past practice, industry custom, and contract rights." *Id.*

This is not merely the most reasonable reading of a "threshold matters" exception, but the only one that rests within the bounds set by our previous decisions and those of the Supreme Court. *See ITT*, 419 U.S. at 446; *PMA*, 827 F.3d at 1211. Not so of the Board's preferred approach, **[—20—]** which would effectively nullify *Golden Grain*'s distinction of some issues as "threshold" by converting the entire 10(k) process into a threshold inquiry, and by extension, creating an exception that swallows the anti-preclusion rule. *See Ashkenazy Prop.*, 817 F.2d at 75.

The Board fell into this very trap in *Grazzini Brothers*, upon which the Board now relies in defending its use of a more expansive exception. There, after acknowledging the anti-preclusion rule, the Board nevertheless granted dispositive weight to the findings supporting its earlier 10(k) award—in that instance, concerning the existence of a CBA between the respondent and the employer. 315 NLRB at 521–22. Citing its "well settled" rule that a party cannot relitigate a 10(k) work assignment in a later ULP proceeding,[11] the Board announced that "[i]t logically follows that a party cannot relitigate the various factors, including the existence or nonexistence, of a collective-bargaining agreement, that the Board considers in making its 10(k) determination." *Id.* at 522. Addressing *Golden Grain*'s "threshold matters" exception in a footnote, the Board simply stated that barring re-litigation of the factors going to the merits of a 10(k) **{-636-}** award "is consistent with the Board's holding that it will not permit renewed litigation of threshold or preliminary matters not necessary to prove an 8(b)(4)(D) violation." *Id.* at 522 n.7. Not really.

We begin by noting the rather breathtaking scope of such an exception. The entire 10(k) proceeding consists of two components: an initial jurisdictional finding and an award **[—21—]** based on considerations like past practice, industry custom, and CBAs. *See Recon Refractory*, 424 F.3d at 988. If, as *Grazzini Brothers* suggests, *Golden Grain*'s bar on relitigating "threshold matters" encompasses both parts, then the anti-preclusion rule loses all practical meaning. But that is not the case.

Nothing in *Golden Grain* supports the more expansive "threshold matters" exception that the Board recognized in *Grazzini Brothers* and now relies upon here. To the contrary, *Golden Grain* and its progeny reinforce our stated view that the exception refers exclusively to the Board's initial jurisdictional inquiry. *See* 289 NLRB at 2 n.4 (using "agreed upon method of settlement" inquiry as example of a "threshold matter"); *Granite Rock Co.*, 296 NLRB at 250 n.2 (same); *Streimer Sheet Metal Works*, 323 NLRB at 1103–04 ("[W]hile I am bound by the Board's 10(k) findings as to certain 'threshold matters,' I am nevertheless required to judge the lawfulness of the picketing in the light of the parties' 'relitigation' during this trial of certain 'factual issues concerning the elements of the [alleged] 8(b)(4)(D) violation,' *including their relitigation of certain matters as to which the Board made findings in the 10(k) decision*, and on which the General Counsel now relies as evidence that the picketing had a 'proscribed,' work-reassignment 'object.'" (emphasis added, footnote omitted)); *Architectural Metal Workers Local 513 (Custom Contracting)*, 292 NLRB 792, 793 (1989) ("The Respondent's affirmative defense does not raise such purely preliminary or threshold matters. This would be the case had the Respondent asserted that the Employer did not meet the Board's jurisdictional standards."). Thus, even if we were to accept the Board's claim that its 10(k) work assignments are unreviewable, *see Grazzini Bros.*, 315 NLRB at 522, that presumption necessarily excludes those parts of the 10(k) **[—22—]** determination that go to the merits of subsequent ULP charges, including affirmative defenses like work preservation. *See id.* at 521 ("[A] respondent is entitled to a hearing . . . if the respondent denies the existence of an element of the 8(b)(4)(D) violation, either directly or by raising an affirmative defense.").

In sum, the Board's expansion of the "threshold matters" exception in *Grazzini Brothers* and its later reliance on the same here find no support in the precedents of the Supreme Court, of this Court, or of the Board itself. And in neither instance did the Board either distinguish its finding from the anti-preclusion rule, *see Ashkenazy Prop.*, 817 F.2d at 75, or explain its departure from the narrower construction advanced by the *Golden Grain* line of cases, *see Great W. Produce*, 839 F.2d at 557. We therefore hold

---

[11] Because Board case law explicitly excludes affirmative defenses from those "threshold matters" excepted under *Golden Grain*, we need not address the Board's potentially narrower rule against relitigating 10(k) work assignments.

that the Board erred in finding its 10(k) determination dispositive of the Longshoremen's work preservation defense, and we overrule *Grazzini Brothers* to the extent it holds to the contrary.[12] **{–637–}**

II. The Board's Application of the Work Preservation Doctrine

We turn next to the Board's analysis of the Longshoremen's work preservation defense. Unmoved by the Board's preclusion argument, the ALJ proceeded to the merits and found that the Longshoremen's negotiation of and **[—23—]** attempts to enforce the 2008 PCLCD had aimed "to limit the more recent outsourcing of unit jobs to nonunit employees in order to diminish these looming adverse consequences on unit employees who face the loss of the jobs they have been performing for years." When the Board reversed, it followed its initial preclusion finding with an alternative analysis concluding that the ALJ had misconstrued the work preservation doctrine; that the relevant terms of the 2008 PCLCD do not encompass the disputed work; and that only the electrical M&R work performed at Kinder Morgan's Vancouver facility was relevant to the Longshoremen's defense. This was also error.

A valid work preservation objective provides a complete defense against alleged violations of section 8(b)(4)(D), as well as against jurisdictional disputes under section 10(k). *See Nat'l Woodwork*, 386 U.S. at 644–46; *Recon Refractory*, 424 F.3d at 988–89. "The touchstone is whether the agreement or its maintenance is addressed to the labor relations of the contracting employer vis-à-vis his own employees." *Nat'l Woodwork*, 386 U.S. at 645. "The effect of work preservation agreements on the employment opportunities of employees not represented by the union, no matter how severe, is of course irrelevant to the validity of the agreement so long as the union had no forbidden secondary purpose to affect the employment relations of the neutral employer." *NLRB v. Int'l Longshoremen's Ass'n (ILA I)*, 447 U.S. 490, 507 n.22 (1980); *accord The N.Y. Presbyterian Hosp.*, 354 NLRB 71, 77 (2009) ("[U]nions and employers are entitled to negotiate contracts that 'preserve' unit work by way of no-subcontracting or similar clauses, *even if the enforcement of such agreements may cause the contracting employer to cease doing business with someone else.*"). In a word, the dispositive measure is purpose, not effect. **[—24—]**

A. The Board's Doctrinal Framework

The first friction point concerns the contours of the work preservation doctrine itself. Central to this dispute are the parties' assessments of the Supreme Court's elaboration of the doctrine in *ILA I* and *NLRB v. International Longshoremen's Association (ILA II)*, 473 U.S. 61 (1985). The Longshoremen and PMA predictably prefer the ALJ's view, which characterized these cases as a rejection of "the Board's highly restrictive view that the work preservation doctrine is confined only to work traditionally performed by unit employees." The Board meanwhile falls back on its own view that these cases examine only "one aspect of the work preservation doctrine—identifying the 'work in controversy' in a 'complex case of technological displacement'"—and thus offer little assistance here. In fact, the *ILA* cases are not unlike this one.

In *ILA I*, the Court began by reiterating a two-part test for determining whether a CBA provision constitutes a lawful work preservation agreement. The first part requires that the agreement "have as its objective the preservation of work traditionally performed by employees represented by the union." **{–638–}** *ILA I*, 447 U.S. at 504. The second provides that "the contracting employer must have the power to give the employees the work in question," or rather, the "right of control." *Id.* "The rationale of the second test is that if the

[12] The Board also refused to consider the Longshoremen's collusion argument, *see supra* note 5, based on the Board's erroneous conclusion that its 10(k) determination precluded the issue's reconsideration during the ULP proceedings. It did not, however, offer an alternative analysis of the argument as it did with the Longshoremen's work preservation defense. We therefore decline to address the issue before remanding to the Board for consideration under the appropriate legal standard.

contracting employer has no power to assign the work, it is reasonable to infer that the agreement has a secondary objective, that is, to influence whoever does have such power over the work." *Id.* at 504–05.

The sticking point in *ILA I* was the doctrine's application in cases where, as here, "employees' traditional work is displaced, or threatened with displacement, by technological innovation." *Id.* at 505. Because the union workers there **[—25—]** had never performed the precise work at issue at the precise location in question, the Board found that the union's objective had been work acquisition rather than work preservation, and thus, secondary in nature. *Id.* at 506. The Court disagreed. Since technology often alters altogether the way that work gets done, the Court explained that the doctrine "must also apply to situations where unions attempt to accommodate change while preserving as much of their traditional work patterns as possible." *Id.* at 506. Otherwise, only those agreements that "respond to change with intransigence" would be valid—something Congress had never intended. *Id.*

The Court instead advanced a more holistic approach to defining disputed work. That assessment requires "a careful analysis of the traditional work patterns that the parties are allegedly seeking to preserve, and of how the agreement seeks to accomplish that result under the changed circumstances created by the technological advance." *Id.* at 507. The greater the complexity, the broader the industrial and vocational scope of the analysis. *Id.* But in all cases, the focus must be "on the work of the bargaining unit employees, not on the work of other employees who may be doing the same or similar work," and on how the agreement attempts to preserve jobs impacted by the introduction of new technologies. *Id.*

Five years later, the Court in *ILA II* repudiated once more the Board's preoccupation with "employees outside the bargaining unit." 473 U.S. at 82. First, the Court familiarly renounced concerns with the "extra-unit effects" of an otherwise legitimately motivated agreement. *Id.* at 79. There was no question that the union's motive for executing the agreement was preserving its members' jobs, and thus, no reasonable inference of aggrandizement was to be **[—26—]** gleaned from evidence of the agreement's effects on others. *Id.* Second, the Court rejected the Board's understanding that work eliminated by innovation cannot possibly be preserved. *Id.* at 80–81. But as the Court observed, job elimination itself often forms the impetus for such agreements. *Id.* Thus, the relevant inquiry must remain whether

> a union's activity is primary or secondary—that is, whether the union's efforts are directed at its own employer on a topic affecting employees' wages, hours, or working conditions that the employer can control, or, instead, are directed at affecting the business relations of neutral employers and are "tactically calculated" to achieve union objectives outside the primary employer-employee relationship.

Id. at 81. Of course, the "preservation/acquisition dichotomy" might still, in certain cases, help to detect tactical agreements aimed at acquiring work even absent any threat of job losses. *Id.* at 79 n.19. The Board's error there was making acquisition a talisman. As happened here. **{-639-}**

Two compounding errors beset the Board's work preservation analysis. It erred first by deeming the *ILA* cases inapplicable here. Neither case suggests its work preservation framework should be reserved only for particularly complex cases of technological displacement. To the contrary, *ILA I* specifically contemplates its application to both the "simple case" and "more complex cases." 447 U.S. at 507. "Whatever its scope," the inquiry remains the same: focused on bargaining unit workers rather than non-unit workers currently doing the same or similar **[—27—]** work; unconcerned with the work's precise location; and accommodative toward change (or even the threat of change), including the elimination of traditional work. *See id.* at 505, 507–08 & n.22; *ILA II*, 473 U.S. at 79–82.

The Board subsequently erred by limiting its work preservation inquiry to whether Longshoremen had historically performed electrical M&R work at Kinder Morgan's Vancouver facility. The *ILA* cases underscore the primacy of the work preservation agreement's purpose, even if its enforcement comes at a cost to extra-unit workers. For the ALJ, the terms of the PCLCD left little doubt about the Longshoremen's intent—perhaps most notably, the parties' mutual anticipation of robotics- and other technology-inflicted displacements of existing longshore work under section 1.72. If the PCLCD indeed covers the disputed work, then it at least stands to reason that the Longshoremen sought the disputed work, not to achieve some unrelated union objective or to inflict harm on Electrical Workers or the subcontractor that employed them, but "to limit the more recent outsourcing of unit jobs to nonunit employees in order to diminish these looming adverse consequences on unit employees who face the loss of the jobs they have been performing for years." *See ILA II*, 473 U.S. at 79 n.19 ("An agreement bargained for with the objective of work preservation in the face of a genuine job threat . . . is not 'acquisitive' . . . even though it may have the incidental effect of displacing work that otherwise might be done elsewhere or not be done at all."). The Board's order does not mention this possibility, much less address it.

Instead, the Board appears to have fallen "into the same analytical trap" about which the *ILA* cases warn. *See ILA II*, 473 U.S. at 82. Its ULP order is preoccupied with the precise location of the disputed work and with those non-unit **[—28—]** employees who stood to lose work were it to enforce the Longshoremen's (and PMA's) interpretation of the PCLCD. *See ILA I*, 447 U.S. at 506–08; *ILA II*, 473 U.S. at 79. So, too, of its initial 10(k) decision. *See IBEW*, 357 NLRB at 2218–19. As a result, neither engages the fundamental inquiry of work preservation—namely, whether the Longshoremen negotiated and attempted to enforce the 2008 PCLCD in pursuit of a primary or secondary purpose. *See ILA II*, 473 U.S. at 81. The Board instead employs the same "wooden application" of the preservation/acquisition dichotomy, wherein the Longshoremen's purpose is presumed secondary once it is determined that Longshoremen have not performed the precise work in question, irrespective of the parties' contractually enshrined aim of preempting automation-induced job losses. *See ILA II*, 473 U.S. at 80 n.19; *cf. id.* at 75–76 (secondary purpose possible where "union engaged in activity to reach out to monopolize jobs or acquire new job tasks when their own jobs are not threatened" (quotation marks omitted)). But that is not the rule. **{-640-}**

The *ILA* cases make clear that not all bargained-for work in a legitimate work preservation agreement must be work that was traditionally performed by that union's workers. *See id.* at 80–81 ("'Elimination' of work in the sense that it is made unnecessary by innovation is not of itself a reason to condemn work preservation agreements . . . to the contrary, such elimination provides the very premise for such agreements."); *ILA I*, 447 U.S. at 506 (doctrine applies "where unions attempt to accommodate change while preserving as much of their traditional work patterns as possible" (emphasis added)). To be sure, the acquisition of previously unperformed work may, in certain circumstances—for example, where union jobs have not been threatened, *see ILA II*, 473 U.S. at 75–76, or where that **[—29—]** work is markedly different from the union's traditional work, *see id.* at 81—suggest a secondary purpose. The Board made no such finding here. Rather, it made prior performance of electrical M&R work at Kinder Morgan's Vancouver facility a talisman, and in so doing, it eluded the "inferential and fact-based" inquiry that the doctrine requires. *See id.* at 81.

Simply put, the Board's narrow work preservation analysis is incompatible with the Supreme Court's holistic, circumstantial inquiry. We therefore hold that the Board erred in finding the *ILA* cases inapplicable here and instead making past performance and extra-unit effects the beginning and end of its analysis. The success of any work preservation defense here, however, depends upon one final, antecedent issue to which we now turn.

B. The 2008 PCLCD Encompasses Electrical M&R Work

The Longshoremen's work preservation defense necessarily assumes that the disputed electrical M&R work is covered by the agreement it claims to defend. Otherwise, its grievance actions and attempts to physically prevent Electrical Workers from performing electrical M&R work for Kinder Morgan lose their inference of a primary objective. In its 10(k) decision, the Board concluded that the 2008 PCLCD does not encompass electrical M&R work because its terms are "very general" and contain "no explicit mention of electrical work." *IBEW*, 357 NLRB at 2219. It also found that the 2008 changes to the PCLCD anticipating automation-related displacement "were directed at new work to be based on the introduction of new technologies." *Id.* The Board then deferred to these findings without offering any additional analysis in its ULP order. This, too, was error. **[—30—]**

The Board and the intervenors overstate the deference owed to the Board's contract interpretations. "Although the Board has occasion to interpret collective-bargaining agreements in the context of unfair labor practice adjudication, the Board is neither the sole nor the primary source of authority in such matters." *Litton Fin. Printing Div. v. NLRB*, 501 U.S. 190, 202 (1991) (citation omitted); *accord NLRB v. Dist. Council of Iron Workers*, 124 F.3d 1094, 1098 (9th Cir. 1997) (de novo review of collective bargaining agreements). Courts and arbitrators fill that role. *Litton*, 501 U.S. at 202. We therefore owe no deference to the Board's construction of CBAs. *See Local Joint Exec. Bd. of Las Vegas v. NLRB*, 540 F.3d 1072, 1078 (9th Cir. 2008); *accord Wilkes-Barre Hosp. Co. v. NLRB*, 857 F.3d 364, 373 (D.C. Cir. 2017) ("[W]e owe no deference to the Board's interpretation of a disputed collective bargaining agreement." (citation omitted)). We instead construe such agreements "according **{-641-}** to ordinary principles of contract law" unless federal labor policy dictates otherwise. *M & G Polymers USA, LLC v. Tackett*, 574 U.S. 427, 435 (2015).

As with all contracts, the intent of the parties is paramount. *Id.* And in this case, that inquiry begins and ends with the plain language of the 2008 PCLCD. *See id.* ("Where the words of a contract in writing are clear and unambiguous, its meaning is to be ascertained in accordance with its plainly expressed intent." (quotation marks omitted)).

Section 1.71 of the PCLCD provides, as it long has, that the agreement "shall apply to the maintenance and repair of all stevedore cargo handling equipment." Citing the parties' expectation of automation-induced displacement of traditional longshore work, however, the parties in 2008 added two new terms. The first (section 1.72) provides "that **[—31—]** the jurisdiction of the ILWU shall apply to the maintenance and repair of all present and forthcoming stevedore cargo handling equipment in accordance with Sections 1.7 and 1.71 and shall constitute the functional equivalent of such traditional ILWU work." And the second (section 1.73) relevantly states that

> [t]he scope of work shall include . . . maintenance and repair . . . of all present and forthcoming technological equipment related to the operation of stevedore cargo handling equipment (which term includes containers and chassis) and its electronics, that are controlled or interchanged by PMA companies, in all West Coast ports.

Neither supports the Board's proscribed limitations.

First, neither term reinforces the Board's conclusion that the "contract language demonstrate[s] that the collective-bargaining agreement changes were directed at new work to be based on the introduction of new technologies." *See IBEW*, 357 NLRB at 2219. The Board's analysis does not specify what language led to its "new work only" construction. Meanwhile, the terms' application to "all present and forthcoming stevedore cargo handling equipment" and to "all present and forthcoming technological equipment related to the operation of stevedore cargo handling equipment" express a contrary intention. Such language unambiguously encompasses both new and preexisting M&R work, and therefore, the parties' negotiations, post-agreement conduct, and industry customs bear no relevance to its meaning. *See Pierce Cnty. Hotel Emps. & Rest. Emps. Health Tr. v. Elks Lodge*, 827 F.2d 1324, 1327 (9th Cir. 1987) ("Extrinsic evidence is **[—32—]** inadmissible to contradict a clear contract term." (citation omitted)).

Second, the Board was not free to ignore the plain meaning of the phrase "maintenance and repair of all stevedore cargo handling equipment" simply because such language is "very general." *See IBEW*, 357 NLRB at 2219. A contractual term bearing a broad general meaning is no more inherently ambiguous than a similarly sweeping statutory provision. *See Arizona v. Tohono O'odham Nation*, 818 F.3d 549, 557 (9th Cir. 2016). In either case, mere generality tends to denote breadth, not ambiguity. *See id.* Neither the Board nor the intervenors point to a contractual provision suggesting an intent to limit the scope to mechanical M&R work. Nor do they explain how this more general language is inherently susceptible to conflicting meanings.

Regardless, the parties' inclusion of the phrase "and its electronics" in section 1.73 resolves whatever ambiguity the phrase "maintenance and repair of all stevedore cargo handling equipment" alone might **{-642-}** have embodied—at least insofar as it concerns the inclusion of electrical M&R work. And it directly contradicts the Board's conclusion that the PCLCD omits an "explicit mention of electrical work." *See IBEW*, 357 NLRB at 2219. Neither the Board nor the intervenors suggest how work on the "electronics" of "all stevedore cargo handling equipment" might reasonably entail something other than electrical maintenance and repair work. As we see it, it is unlikely that it does. Thus, the Board again erred in looking outside the four corners of the 2008 PCLCD to inject ambiguity into this otherwise clear contract term. *See Pierce*, 827 F.2d at 1327.

Third, we conclude that the Board's view that section 1.72's functional equivalence clause pertains only to the **[—33—]** work previously encompassed by section 1.71 is untenable. This construction not only misreads section 1.72 and ignores section 1.73, but also renders the functional equivalence clause itself superfluous.

Read in relevant part, the functional equivalence clause of section 1.72 states "that the jurisdiction of the ILWU . . . shall constitute the functional equivalent of such traditional ILWU work." The Board's attempt to anchor this language to section 1.72's intervening reference to section 1.71 ignores section 1.72's compound predicate structure. The correct reading of the functional equivalence clause does not define the scope of work. Section 1.73 does that. The clause instead enshrines the parties' agreement that the scope of work included within the Longshoremen's jurisdiction will be considered the functional equivalent of its traditional work.

> More fundamentally, the Board's reading of the functional equivalence clause impermissibly renders sections 1.72 and 1.73 redundant. *See Alday v. Raytheon Co.*, 693 F.3d 772, 784 (9th Cir. 2012) ("As in all contracts, the collective bargaining agreement's terms must be construed so as to render none nugatory and avoid illusory promises." (quotation marks omitted)). All parties agree that section 1.71 did not change in 2008. However, if, as the Board suggests, section 1.72's functional equivalence clause only reiterates the scope of work covered by previous versions of the PCLCD, then the parties' addition of sections 1.72 and 1.73 in 2008 accomplished nothing. The parties would have no need for a functional **[—34—]** equivalence clause if the 2008 PCLCD merely continued to encompass the same scope of work covered by previous versions. And likewise, the parties would have had no reason to add a term defining the scope of work if section 1.71 had already done so.

All told, the Board misconstrued the 2008 PCLCD in its 10(k) decision and, by extension, in its ULP order. The Board erred by consulting extrinsic evidence without first providing a legitimate basis for finding any of the relevant terms ambiguous. It then compounded that error by relying on such evidence to construe sections 1.72 and 1.73 in a manner that not only ignored their plain language, but also rendered much of their newly bargained-for provisions illusory. We hold that, subject only to exceptions not at issue here, the plain language of the 2008 PCLCD unambiguously assigns to the Longshoremen all M&R work, on all present and future stevedore cargo handling equipment—including its technological equipment and electronics—for all PMA members, at all West Coast ports.

CONCLUSION

For these reasons, we conclude that the Board erred by according the findings in its 10(k) determination preclusive weight, by ignoring Supreme Court precedent in **{–643–}** favor of an impermissibly narrow construction of the work preservation doctrine, and in construing the 2008 PCLCD as excluding the disputed work. We accordingly **GRANT** both petitions for review, **DENY** the cross-petition for enforcement, **VACATE** the Board's order, and **REMAND** for further proceedings consistent with this opinion.

United States Court of Appeals for the Ninth Circuit

No. 20-35127

IN RE GARRETT

Appeal from the United States District Court for the District of Montana

Decided: December 2, 2020

Citation: 981 F.3d 739, 8 Adm. R. 347 (9th Cir. 2020).

Before **TASHIMA**, **GRABER**, and **IKUTA**, Circuit Judges.

[—3—] {-741-} TASHIMA, Circuit Judge:

Caleb Garrett filed a complaint for exoneration from or limitation of liability under 46 U.S.C. §§ 30501–30512, invoking the district court's admiralty jurisdiction, 28 U.S.C. § 1333(1). The district court dismissed his complaint for want of jurisdiction. We have jurisdiction under 28 U.S.C. § 1291, we review de novo, *Rattlesnake Coal. v. U.S. EPA*, 509 F.3d 1095, 1100 (9th Cir. 2007), and we affirm.

"A party seeking to invoke federal admiralty jurisdiction over a tort claim must satisfy both a location test and a connection test." *In re Mission Bay Jet Sports, LLC*, 570 F.3d 1124, 1126, (9th Cir. 2009) (internal quotation marks omitted). Here, the complaint fails the location test. Under the location test, "[t]he tort must occur on navigable waters." Waters are navigable "when they form in their ordinary condition by themselves, or by uniting with other waters, a continued highway over which commerce is or may be carried on with other States or foreign countries in the customary modes in which such commerce is conducted by water." *The Daniel Ball*, 77 U.S. (10 Wall.) 557 (1870).

It is undisputed that this boating accident occurred on Holter Lake, that Holter Lake is located on a stretch of the Missouri River located wholly within Montana, and that this stretch of river is "completely obstructed by Hauser dam at one end and by Holter dam at the other," precluding it from serving as an artery of interstate commerce. *Adams v. Mont. Power Co.*, 528 F2d 437, 439 (9th Cir. 1975). Consequently, Holter Lake is not navigable for purposes of admiralty jurisdiction, and "[a] cause of action sounding in tort is not **[—4—]** cognizable under admiralty jurisdiction unless the alleged wrong occurs on navigable waters." *Id.* Thus, because the alleged tort here did not occur on navigable waters, the complaint here is not cognizable under the district court's admiralty jurisdiction.[1]

Garrett urges us to reject *Adams*' "outdated view of the locality test," but because *Adams* has not been overruled by a higher authority, it remains binding precedent. *Miller v. Gammie*, 335 F.3d 889, 893 (9th Cir. 2003) (en banc). Further, the cases on which Garrett relies are readily distinguishable. In *Sanders v. Placid Oil Co.*, 861 F.2d 1374, 1377–78 (5th Cir. 1988), the river was navigable because it served as an artery of interstate commerce during significant portions of the year. In *Sawczyk v. U.S. Coast Guard*, 499 F. Supp. 1034, 1039 (W.D.N.Y. 1980), the **{-742-}** river was navigable because it formed an international boundary between the United States and Canada. In *Mission Bay Jet Sports*, 570 F.3d at 1127, the body of water was navigable because it was "open to the Pacific Ocean," "subject to the ebb and flow of tides," and "neither enclosed nor obstructed." And in *Taghadomi v. United States*, 401 F.3d 1080, 1086 (9th Cir. 2005), the accident occurred at sea, in waters off Hawaii.

Garrett points out that maritime jurisdiction can extend to recreational boating.[2] *See Foremost Ins. Co. v. Richardson*, **[—5—]** 457 U.S. 668, 674 (1982). Regardless of the type of vessel or activity involved, however, the tort "must occur on or over navigable waters." *Taghadomi*, 401 F.3d at 1084. As we explained in *Mission Bay Jet Sports*, "[t]he tort must occur on navigable waters and bear a 'significant relationship to

---

[1] Garrett's argument that "the Coast Guard has designated Holder Lake a navigable waterway for purposes of its regulatory jurisdiction," citing 33 C.F.R. § 66.05-100, is inapposite. The regulation has no effect on federal courts' admiralty or maritime jurisdiction under 28 US.C. § 1333.

[2] The accident here involved a recreational fishing boat.

traditional maritime activity.'" 570 F.3d at 1126 (emphasis added) (quoting *Foremost*, 457 U.S. at 674).

Because Garrett has not met the location test for navigable waters, we need not reach the connection test. The district court properly dismissed this action for lack of jurisdiction under 28 U.S.C. § 1333(1).

AFFIRMED.

United States Court of Appeals for the Tenth Circuit

United States Court of Appeals
for the Tenth Circuit

No. 19-1025

HILL
vs.
WARSEWA

Appeal from the United States District Court for the District of Colorado

Decided: January 23, 2020

Citation: 947 F.3d 1305, 8 Adm. R. 350 (10th Cir. 2020).

Before **HOLMES, KELLY,** and **BACHARACH,** Circuit Judges.

[—2—] {-1306-} **KELLY,** Circuit Judge:

Plaintiff-Appellant Roger Hill appeals from the district court's dismissal of his complaint pursuant to Fed. R. Civ. P. 12(b)(6) for lack of prudential standing. Mr. Hill is a fly fisherman who prefers to fish at a favorite spot in the Arkansas River. Defendants-Appellees Mark Everett Warsewa and Linda Joseph (Landowners) contend that they own the Arkansas riverbed up to its centerline at the spot at which Mr. Hill prefers to fish. Mr. Hill contends that this segment of the river was navigable for title at the time Colorado was admitted to the United States and that title to the riverbed consequently vested in the state at admission under Article IV of the Constitution and the Equal Footing Doctrine. According to Mr. Hill, the state holds this title in trust for the public, **[—3—]** subject to an easement for public **{-1307-}** uses such as fishing. Defendant-Appellee State of Colorado (Colorado or the State) agrees with the Landowner Appellees that this segment of the river was non-navigable for title at statehood and is privately owned. The district court[1] found that Mr. Hill lacked prudential standing because he asserted a generalized grievance and rested his claims on the rights of the state. We have jurisdiction pursuant to 28 U.S.C. § 1291 and we reverse.

Background

Mr. Hill believes that he, as a member of the public, has a right to fish at the disputed segment of the Arkansas River. The dispute over title has led to conflict between Mr. Hill and the Landowners. Mr. Hill alleges that the Landowners have sought to exclude him from the property by chasing him off by force and threats of force, throwing rocks at him, threatening legal action, and shooting a gun at one of his friends. Aplt. Br. at 9.

The Landowners contend that they own the riverbed and are within their rights to exclude Mr. Hill. They claim that the chain of record title for the land[2] originates with a federal patent and that only private owners are within that chain. The Landowners purchased the Warsewa Parcel by warranty deed in 2006. The subdivision plat for the Warsewa Parcel, which is designated Lot 5 of Block 2 in that document, indicates that its boundaries extend up to the center line of the river. Aplt. App. 41–42. **[—4—]**

Below, Mr. Hill alleged facts in support of his navigability claim. Colorado was admitted as a state on August 1, 1876. Mr. Hill alleged that fur trappers used the Arkansas River to transport goods prior to that date. *Id.* at 31. He also asserted that contemporaneous newspaper reports describe commercial use of the river to float logs and railroad ties downstream. *Id.* at 32.

Mr. Hill first filed an action in the district court. *See Hill v. Warsewa*, 18-cv- 00277-PAB-KLM (D. Colo.). The Landowners defaulted in that action, while Colorado moved to intervene and asked the district court to dismiss on Eleventh Amendment grounds. *See* Motion to Intervene, *id.* (May 7, 2018) (ECF No. 17). Before that motion was resolved, Mr. Hill moved for, and was granted, voluntary dismissal of the action. *See* Notice of

---

[1] Magistrate Judge Kathleen M. Tafoya, sitting by consent of all parties. *See* Consent to Jurisdiction of Magistrate Judge, *Hill v. Warsewa et al.*, No. 18-cv-01710- KMT (Aug. 3, 2018) (ECF No. 25).

[2] We follow the parties by referring to this land as the "Warsewa Parcel."

Voluntary Dismissal, *id.* (May 29, 2018) (ECF No. 23).

Mr. Hill then filed substantially the same action in Colorado state court. Aplt. App. 6. Colorado was named as an "interested party" and later appeared in the action. The landowners appeared and removed the action to the district court on the basis of federal question jurisdiction. *See id.* at 18. Mr. Hill added Colorado as a named Defendant in the federal action. *See id.* at 26.

Both the Landowner Appellees and Colorado moved the district court to dismiss, alleging defects in constitutional and prudential standing and failure to state a claim. *See id.* at 45, 62. Mr. Hill responded with various motions of his own, moving to remand for lack of subject matter jurisdiction, asking the court to stay consideration of opposing motions until resolution of his motion to remand, and moving to certify the question of the nature of Colorado's title to the Colorado Supreme Court. *See id.* 77, 83. **[—5—] {-1308-}**

The district court declined to stay consideration and resolved the remaining motions. *See id.* at 177. First, the court held that Mr. Hill lacked prudential standing to bring his claims because he asserted the rights of a third party—Colorado—and alleged only a generalized grievance. *Id.* at 184–86. The court rejected Mr. Hill's motion to remand because it was dismissing on the "threshold issue" of prudential standing, rather than the jurisdictional issues of constitutional standing or sovereign immunity. *Id.* at 186–87. It then denied Mr. Hill's motion to certify a question to the Colorado Supreme Court as moot. *Id.* at 187. On appeal, Mr. Hill argues that the district court erred by finding that he lacked prudential standing to bring his claims. Because we agree and conclude that this error requires a remand, we do not reach Mr. Hill's other contentions.

Discussion

We review a district court's dismissal under Fed. R. Civ. Pro. 12(b)(6) de novo. *Safe Streets All. v. Hickenlooper*, 859 F.3d 865, 878 (10th Cir. 2017). We review dismissals for lack of prudential standing de novo. *Wilderness Soc'y v. Kane County*, 632 F.3d 1162, 1168 (10th Cir. 2011) (en banc). We accept as true all well-pleaded factual allegations in the complaint. *Safe Streets All.*, 859 F.3d at 878. For standing purposes, "we must assume the Plaintiffs' claim has legal validity." *Wilderness Soc'y*, 632 F.3d at 1168 (quoting *Initiative & Referendum Inst. v. Walker*, 450 F.3d 1082, 1093 (10th Cir. 2006) (en banc)).

This case presents questions about (1) the order in which constitutional standing and other threshold jurisdictional issues should be approached by federal courts, and (2) **[—6—]** the content and application of the constitutional and prudential standing doctrines. We address each in turn.

A. Threshold Issues

Mr. Hill initially argues that the district court erred by analyzing prudential standing before sovereign immunity and constitutional standing. According to Mr. Hill, the Supreme Court has "limited courts' ability to skip jurisdictional issues when, as here, the case has been removed." Aplt. Br. at 41. Mr. Hill concedes that courts "can dismiss on other preliminary issues before considering subject matter jurisdiction" in some circumstances. *Id.* at 40. He contends, however, that the district court was required to find that constitutional standing and other subject matter jurisdiction issues were "more difficult" to resolve before it used this order. *Id.* at 41–42.

We do not believe that the cases establish such a rigid sequence. The very cases Mr. Hill cites hold that "there is no unyielding jurisdictional hierarchy." *Gadlin v. Sybron Int'l Corp.*, 222 F.3d 797, 799 (2000) (quoting *Ruhrgas AG v. Marathon Oil Co.*, 526 U.S. 574, 578 (1999)). The Supreme Court has observed that "[i]t is hardly novel for a federal court to choose among threshold grounds for denying audience to a case on the merits." *Ruhrgas AG*, 526 U.S. at 585. As the district court noted, both this court and the Supreme Court have relied on *Ruhrgas* to proceed directly to prudential standing without addressing other jurisdictional issues. *See Wilderness Soc'y*, 632 F.3d at 1168 ("Because [The Wilderness Society] lacks prudential standing, we proceed directly to that issue without deciding whether [The Wilderness Society] has constitutional standing or whether the case is moot."); *see also Tenet v. Doe*, 544 U.S. 1, 6 n.4 (2005) ("[t]he **[—7—]** prudential standing doctrine[] represents the sort of 'threshold question' we have recognized may be resolved before addressing jurisdiction"). Mr. Hill's argument to the contrary relies on the idea **{–1309–}** that *Lexmark International Inc. v. Static Control Components, Inc.* limited prudential standing to such a degree that it is no longer appropriate to treat it as a threshold inquiry. 572 U.S. 118, 125–26 (2014); *see also infra* Part B. A member of this court has already suggested that prior decisions related to the third party standing strand of prudential standing "remain[] sound" after *Lexmark* because the Supreme Court did not "revisit the doctrine of third party standing" in that case. *Kane County v. United States*, 928 F.3d 877, 900–01 (10th Cir. 2019) (Tymkovich, C.J., dissenting). We agree and hold that third party standing should continue to be analyzed under the framework of prudential standing. If Mr. Hill is correct that what remains of prudential standing is a loose end, then we will have to wait for the Supreme Court to tie it up. The district court did not err by sequencing the issues in the way it did.

B. Prudential Standing Analysis

Prudential standing represents "judicially self-imposed limits on the exercise of federal jurisdiction" that are "founded in concern about the proper—and properly limited—role of the courts in a democratic society." *Bennett v. Spear*, 520 U.S. 154, 162 (1997) (quoting *Allen v. Wright*, 468 U.S. 737, 751 (1984), *Warth v. Seldin*, 422 U.S. 490, 498 (1975)). Prudential standing must exist in all cases except where the requirement is "expressly negated," for example by statutory directive from Congress. *Id.* at 163. Traditionally, the doctrine encompassed three broad principles: "[1] the general prohibition on a litigant's raising another person's legal rights, [2] the rule **[—8—]** barring adjudication of generalized grievances more appropriately addressed in the representative branches, and [3] the requirement that a plaintiff's complaint fall within the zone of interests protected by the law invoked." *Lexmark*, 572 U.S. at 126 (quoting *Elk Grove Unified Sch. Dist. v. Newdow*, 542 U.S. 1, 12 (2004)).

In *Lexmark*, the Supreme Court sought to untangle the traditional strands of prudential standing analysis and dispel "misleading" labels. *Id.* at 125. The Court concluded that the zone of interests test is not prudential in origin and is indeed not a standing inquiry at all, while the generalized grievance test is properly part of the Article III constitutional standing inquiry. *Id.* at 127 n.3. The third party rights inquiry's "proper place in the standing firmament" was left to "await another day." *Id.*[3] For the reasons stated above, we continue to analyze third party standing as an element of prudential standing and apply our pre-*Lexmark* decisions bearing on that analysis. *See supra* Part A.

1. Third Party Standing

Under the prudential standing doctrine, a party may not "rest its claims" **{–1310–}** on the rights of third parties where it cannot "assert a valid right to relief of its own." *Wilderness Soc'y*, 632 F.3d at 1170. Prudential standing "imposes different demands **[—9—]** than injury in fact." *Id.* at 1171. Accordingly, "[a] party may suffer a cognizable injury but still not possess a right to relief." *Id.* Injury to "a party's interest for the purposes of

[3] Mr. Hill argues that *Lexmark* held "that the generalized grievance and zone of interest doctrines in fact fall within the jurisdictional Article III standing inquiry." Aplt. Br. at 22. That is not correct. We have said that "the zone-of-interests doctrine *isn't actually a matter of standing at all*; instead, it merely asks whether a particular federal cause of action 'encompasses a particular plaintiff's claim.'" *In re Peeples*, 880 F.3d 1207, 1213 (10th Cir. 2018) (emphasis added) (quoting *Lexmark*, 572 U.S. at 127). Mr. Hill is correct that the generalized grievance inquiry is now part of constitutional standing. *See Kerr v. Polis*, 930 F.3d 1190, 1194 n.3 (10th Cir. 2019) (stating that "generalized grievances are 'barred for constitutional reasons, not prudential ones'" quoting *Lexmark*, 572 U.S. at 127 n.3)).

constitutional standing does not automatically confer prudential standing."

The fact that Mr. Hill alleges violation of a right he contends is his own distinguishes this case from *Wilderness Society*. In that case, an environmental group could point to no specific right "of its own" that the county violated by seeking to enforce its alleged rights of way over federal lands. *Wilderness Soc'y*, 632 F.3d at 1170. Instead, it characterized itself as "working to protect its conservation interests" after suffering "aesthetic or recreational injury." *Id.* at 1171, 1174. We observed that Wilderness Society's asserted injuries might be enough to establish constitutional standing, but that "prudential standing moves beyond injury in fact and addresses whether a plaintiff is asserting its own legal rights rather than resting on the rights or interests of third parties." *Id.* at 1174.

The Wilderness Society asserted a general interest in conservation and freedom from recreational or aesthetic injury. By contrast, Mr. Hill is asserting that *he* has a right to fish. *See* Aplt. App. 33–34 (Mr. Hill alleging, in his complaint, that "he has a right of public access to the subject real property by virtue of the State's title."). The fact that resolving the dispute requires determining whether this segment of the Arkansas River was navigable in 1876 and therefore titled to the state by operation of law does not erase the fact that Mr. Hill is claiming a right in himself.

An example we examined in *Wilderness Society* is instructive here. In the panel decision, Judge McConnell's dissent posed the following hypothetical: **[—10—]**

> Imagine that my next-door neighbor, who keeps his property neat and tidy, is faced with a competing claimant to the land, who is likely to allow the property to fill with weeds. I might very much hope my neighbor wins. My property values and aesthetic interests could seriously be affected. I may be impatient with my neighbor's inclination toward compromise and apparent disinclination to go to court. But no one would say I have standing to sue in defense of my neighbor's property rights. The Wilderness Society is in precisely that situation.

Wilderness Soc'y v. Kane County, 581 F.3d 1198, 1232 (10th Cir. 2009) (McConnell, J., dissenting).

Mr. Hill finds himself in a very different situation. He is more like the purported holder of an easement he alleges was granted by the competing claimant than a neighbor who fears aesthetic harm from lack of upkeep. In this hypothetical, determining whether Mr. Hill has any right to use the easement will require an examination of the underlying title. It would make little sense to deny Mr. Hill prudential standing to determine his rights in the easement because of the existence of a dispute between the underlying property owners. The right he asserts is his own, even if it exists by virtue of the actions of another.

Mr. Hill concedes that this purported right comes to him "by virtue of the State's title." Aplt. Br. at 27. However, Mr. Hill's claims do not "turn on the superiority" of a sovereign's property right. *Wilderness Soc'y*, 632. F.3d at 1171. In Mr. Hill's telling, title vested in the state over a century ago because the river was navigable for title under Article IV and the Equal Footing Doctrine. Mr. Hill alleges that he has a specific, legally protected **{-1311-}** right to fish resulting from these alleged facts and law. The other parties and amici may ultimately be correct that Colorado law does not actually afford Mr. Hill the **[—11—]** right to fish that he asserts, even if he can prove navigability as a factual matter. But in this regard "far-fetchedness is a question to be determined on the merits." *Walker*, 450 F.3d at 1092. We assume that Mr. Hill's claim has "legal validity" and conclude that he asserts his own rights, not those of Colorado, for prudential standing purposes. *Wilderness Soc'y*, 632 F.3d at 1168.

2. Generalized Grievance

The district court concluded that Mr. Hill "[did] not show that his claim is more than a generalized grievance based on a desire for the general public, including himself, to be able to fish in certain spots." Order at 8, 18-cv-01710-KMT (D. Colo. Jan. 8, 2019) (ECF No. 47). The parties disagree about whether the district court rested its prudential standing finding on this conclusion. It is unnecessary to resolve this dispute because, in any event, the district court misconstrued the generalized grievance analysis as applying to prudential rather than constitutional standing. *See* Order at 8, *id.* (D. Colo. Jan. 8, 2019) (ECF No. 47) ("To satisfy the prudential standing requirement . . . the plaintiff's claim must not be a 'generalized grievance.'"). *Lexmark* made clear that the generalized grievance analysis is part of constitutional standing, not prudential standing. 572 U.S. at 127 n.3; *see also Kerr*, 930 F.3d at 1194 n.3. At this stage, we do not examine whether the district court's conclusion that Mr. Hill asserted a generalized grievance was correct.[4] **[—12—]** The district court's discussion of this issue may be relevant to questions of constitutional standing on remand, but it erred by construing this inquiry as bearing on prudential standing.

The district court erred by concluding that Mr. Hill lacked prudential standing to bring his claims. We take no position on whether Mr. Hill has demonstrated constitutional standing and we do not reach any of the merits issues presented by this case.

We **REVERSE** the judgment of the district court and **REMAND** the case for further proceedings consistent with this opinion.

(Reporter's Note: Dissenting Opinion follows on p. 355).

---

[4] The dissent urges that "we should decide this issue and conclude that Mr. Hill's claim constitutes a generalized grievance." The dissent may be proven right that "the district court will presumably rule again [on remand] that the claim constitutes a generalized grievance," but that is mere speculation at this stage. We respectfully disagree with the dissent's assertion that "we should tell the district court whether **[—12—]** such a ruling would be correct." We do not issue advisory opinions. *Flast v. Cohen*, 392 U.S. 83, 96 (1968).

[—1—] {-1311-} **BACHARACH,** Circuit Judge, dissenting:

I agree with the majority that as a member of the public, Mr. Hill has an interest in the homeowners' parcel that does not rest on "the legal rights or interests" of the state of Colorado. *Warth v. Seldin*, 422 U.S. 490, 499 (1975). And I agree that "the district court misconstrued the generalized grievance analysis as applying to prudential rather than constitutional standing." Majority Op. at 11. Given this error, the majority remands to the district court without deciding whether Mr. Hill's claim involves a generalized grievance. I believe that we should decide this issue and conclude that Mr. Hill's claim constitutes a generalized grievance.

I. Mr. Hill has asserted a generalized grievance.

An injury is considered "generalized" when it is "shared in substantially equal {-1312-} measure by all or a large class of citizens." *Warth*, 422 U.S. at 499. For example, when a plaintiff asserts only a harm to rights shared with every other citizen, the claim falls outside the constitutional constraints on federal jurisdiction. *Lujan v. Defs. of Wildlife*, 504 U.S. 555, 573–74 (1992).

Mr. Hill denies that his harms are generalized, pointing to his allegations of individualized harassment, violence, and threats. According to Mr. Hill, these individualized harms convert "an otherwise public-rights [—2—] claim" into a private action. Appellant's Opening Br. at 33. But Mr. Hill is not suing for assault and battery; he is suing to obtain a declaration that he has a protected right to fish in this river on the ground that this is a right enjoyed by every Colorado citizen. In my view, this is a classic example of a generalized grievance.

Mr. Hill also argues that "particularly in the context of a declaratory judgement action, it is enough for standing purposes to say that real harm may occur absent the declaration" because "the Declaratory Judgment Act is supposed to prevent a plaintiff from having to actually incur a harm before bringing suit." Appellant's Opening Br. at 34 (citing *MedImmune, Inc. v. Genentech, Inc.*, 549 U.S. 118, 129 (2007)). Thus, Mr. Hill argues, we should address his claim now without requiring him to prove individualized injury by returning to the fishing hole. But claims for declaratory judgments are subject to constitutional restraints on jurisdiction. *MedImmune*, 549 U.S. at 126. So even if the Declaratory Judgment Act provided a remedy, the district court could not skirt the jurisdictional constraint on generalized grievances.

II. Because Mr. Hill has asserted a generalized grievance, the district court lacks constitutional jurisdiction.

Mr. Hill's generalized grievance strips the district court of constitutional jurisdiction. [—3—]

Prior cases have described the restriction on generalized grievances as prudential rather than constitutional. *E.g., Valley Forge Christian Coll. v. Ams. United for Separation of Church & State, Inc.*, 454 U.S. 464, 474–75 (1982). But as the majority observes, the Supreme Court clarified in *Lexmark International, Inc. v. Static Control Components, Inc.* that its "reluctance to entertain generalized grievances" is a constitutional mandate grounded in Article III—not a matter of prudence. 572 U.S. 118, 127 n.3 (2014); *see also Lujan v. Defenders of Wildlife*, 504 U.S. 555, 573–74 (1992) ("We have consistently held that a plaintiff raising only a generally available grievance about government . . . does not state an Article III case or controversy.").

Our circuit recently took heed of this clarification, observing that "*Lexmark* made clear that the first two principles previously labelled as prudential standing [the zone of interests test and the bar on generalized grievances] are not independent jurisdictional hurdles." *Kerr v. Polis*, 930 F.3d 1190, 1194 n.3 (10th Cir. 2019). We cited *Lexmark*'s declaration that generalized grievances are "barred for constitutional reasons, not 'prudential' ones." *Id.* (quoting 572 U.S. at 127 n.3). Thus, the majority correctly characterizes the existence of a generalized grievance as a constitutional limitation on the federal courts' jurisdiction, not a prudential limitation. **[—4—] {-1313-}**

III. We should decide whether the claim involves a generalized grievance.

The majority correctly concludes that (1) the restriction on generalized grievances is jurisdictional and (2) the district court should not have treated the issue as a prudential concern. But the majority stops there, declining to address whether the district court was right to characterize Mr. Hill's claim as a generalized grievance. I think that we should decide this issue.

We know that the district court will decide whether Mr. Hill's claim constitutes a generalized grievance because that court must ensure its own jurisdiction. *Arbaugh v. Y&H Corp.*, 546 U.S. 500, 514 (2006). Indeed, the district court has already ruled that Mr. Hill asserted a generalized grievance.

As the majority points out, the district court incorrectly treated the issue as prudential. Though the issue is constitutional, rather than prudential, the content of the test for generalized grievances does not turn on whether the test itself is constitutional or prudential. So the district court will presumably rule again that the claim constitutes a generalized grievance. If the court does so, it will need to remand the case to state court. 28 U.S.C. § 1447(c).

I think that we should tell the district court whether such a ruling would be correct. After all, the district court has already decided whether **[—5—]** the claim constitutes a generalized grievance, and the parties have briefed the issue on appeal.[1] I would tell the district court that it was right to regard the claim as a generalized grievance and that the only error was in dismissing the case rather than remanding it to state court. I would thus reverse and remand to the district court with instructions to remand this case to Colorado state court.

[1] The majority acknowledges that the federal courts lack subject-matter jurisdiction to decide generalized grievances, but concludes that "[i]t is unnecessary to resolve" whether Mr. Hill has asserted one. Majority Op. at 11. In my view, however, resolving the issue is both advisable and arguably necessary because we must ensure the existence of subject-matter jurisdiction in district court. *Steel Co. v. Citizens for a Better Env't*, 523 U.S. 83, 95 (1998). Given the absence of a prudential basis for dismissal, we may incur an obligation to decide whether Mr. Hill's claim involves a generalized grievance. Even in the absence of an obligation, however, we should decide the issue now because the district court's characterization as a generalized grievance is unlikely to change.

United States Court of Appeals
for the Tenth Circuit

No. 19-6018

EZELL
VS.
BNSF RY. CO.

Appeal from the United States District Court for the Western District of Oklahoma

Decided: February 5, 2020

Citation: 949 F.3d 1274, 8 Adm. R. 357 (10th Cir. 2020).

Before **MATHESON**, **PHILLIPS**, and **MORITZ**, Circuit Judges.

[—1—] **{-1275-}** **PHILLIPS**, Circuit Judge: **{-1276-}**

Throughout American history, railroad workers have risked their lives and limbs to satisfy our Nation's need to have freight shipped across the United States. To recompense those workers for the injuries they suffer from their occupation, **[—2—]** Congress enacted the Federal Employers Liability Act (FELA), 45 U.S.C. §§ 51–60. FELA permits injured railroad workers to sue their railroad employers for negligence. To succeed, employees must present some evidence showing that their workplaces were not reasonably safe. For purposes of summary judgment, we credit George Ezell's account that to complete his assigned task, he had to climb railcar ladders to see which railcars were more than half full of ballast. Even with that, the evidence establishes that to do their jobs railroad conductors need to climb the ladders and that this is a reasonably safe activity. For that reason, we agree with the district court's dismissal of this case. Ezell's proffering what he believes are safer alternatives does not show negligence. We affirm.

BACKGROUND

I. Factual Background

Ezell was a conductor for BNSF Railway Company. On May 2, 2014, the trainmaster, Michael Castleberry, directed Ezell to detach twenty ballast-loaded railcars from a train about to enter the Enid, Oklahoma train yard. Earlier that day, a maintenance-of-way crew had used ballast from at least some of the railcars while working to maintain the track. Ezell testified that Castleberry did not tell him what counted as a loaded railcar. But Ezell testified that Shawn Jernigan, the yardmaster, had previously told him to treat ballast railcars as loaded if they were more than half full.[1] Jernigan contested ever doing so. **[—3—]**

As Ezell took charge of the entering train, two crews previously with the train left it. The first was the maintenance-of-way crew, and the second was a crew that Ezell's crew was relieving. Despite internal rules that Ezell asserts required them to "keep a good list"—a list that he says would have documented "empties and loads"—neither crew provided him with such a list. Appellant's Opening Br. 8.[2]

---

[1] Ezell also testified that he had been previously told that a railcar is fully loaded if an employee, standing on the ground, can see the ballast's peak above the **[—3—]** railcar. This prompted BNSF's attorney to ask Ezell who had told him "that for a rock car to be considered *a load*, you had to be able to see the peak of the mound from the ground?" Appellant's App. vol. 2 at 185 (emphasis added). But this mischaracterized Ezell's testimony that the mound had to be visible for a car to be considered *fully loaded*, not for it to be considered *loaded*. Even though Ezell responded that Jernigan had told him about such a rule, we understand Ezell's testimony as being that he was told a car was *fully loaded* if a mound was visible and *loaded* if it was more than half full. *Genberg v. Porter*, 882 F.3d 1249, 1253 (10th Cir. 2018) ("On an appeal from a grant of summary judgment, we draw all reasonable factual inferences in favor of the non-moving party." (citation omitted)).

[2] We do not read these rules to provide the clear direction that Ezell claims they do: "Follow these requirements when unloading ballast cars: 14. Make sure ballast cars are empty with the doors properly closed and locked before releasing the cars. 15. Keep a good list of car numbers and release them promptly." Appellant's App. vol. 2 at 146; *see also* Appellant's App. vol. 1 at 64 ("Comply with all company safety rules, engineering instructions, training practices and policies.").

Before Ezell's crew moved the train into the Enid railyard, Devon Miller, its brakeman, went ahead to configure the yard {-1277-} switches. Earlier, Miller had obtained a list of the train's railcars from Jernigan. As the train slowly entered the railyard, Miller noted for each railcar whether its wheel-assembly springs were compressed. He marked the railcars with compressed springs as loaded. Miller testified that he gave the list to Ezell. But Ezell could not remember getting the list. Whether he did or not, Ezell testified that even with Miller's list he would still have needed to climb [—4—] the railcar ladders to see which were more than half full of ballast—a more precise determination than compressed springs would give.[3]

During his three years with BNSF, Ezell had been involved with several ballast trains. He testified that he had often checked the content of the railcars by climbing the railcar ladders and looking inside. On this day, he used that same method for each inspection—he would climb the railcar ladder, reach with his left hand to grab "the top lip" (or flange), and then pull himself up to look inside the railcar.

Ezell safely performed this method for five or six railcars, but while inspecting the next railcar, his left hand slipped from the flange after he had let go of the ladder rung with his right hand. He was unable to resecure a grip with either hand and fell several feet to the ground, fracturing his right leg, right ankle, and left foot.

[3] BNSF makes much of Ezell's choosing to climb the railcar ladders despite having safer alternatives to determine whether a railcar was loaded. It argues that he could have (1) used a list, (2) checked the compression of the springs, (3) banged on the side of the railcar, or (4) thrown a rock into the railcar and listened for a hollow sound. But on summary judgment, we credit Ezell's testimony that these four alternative methods would not have enabled him to complete his assigned task of accurately identifying twenty loaded railcars to detach—that is, twenty railcars more than half full of ballast. Accordingly, the other four methods play no role in our analysis.

II. Procedural Background

Under FELA and the Federal Safety Appliance Act (FSAA), 49 U.S.C. §§ 20301–20306, Ezell sued BNSF for failing to provide him with a reasonably safe place to work. BNSF moved for summary judgment, arguing that its railcar complied [—5—] with the governing safety regulations and that Ezell had offered no evidence of BNSF's negligence. Ezell partially opposed that motion, claiming that BNSF had breached its duty to him in three ways: (1) by not having the maintenance-of-way crew or the train crew provide him with a list of the empty railcars, (2) by failing to provide him a tool to eliminate any need to climb the railcar ladders (a stick of some sort with a mirror), and (3) by failing to implement a policy defining what constituted a loaded railcar. Ezell conceded that his FSAA claim should be dismissed.

The district court granted summary judgment for BNSF on Ezell's FELA claim. On two bases, it ruled that "the undisputed evidence show[ed] that BNSF fulfilled its duty to provide Ezell with a safe place to work and with adequate and reasonably safe tools and equipment." Appellant's App. vol. 2 at 286. First, as Ezell admits, the railcar complied with federal regulations and was in good condition. Second, after considering testimony from Ezell's expert, Colon R. Fulk, the district court concluded that climbing a railcar is a safe activity and that it "is a regularly performed function of a conductor." *Id.* at 287. Because the evidence showed that BNSF provided a safe workplace even with conductors climbing railcar ladders, the district court concluded that Ezell's argument that BNSF could have provided even safer alternatives to climbing would not suffice to show any BNSF negligence. {-1278-} This appeal followed. We have appellate jurisdiction under 28 U.S.C. § 1291. [—6—]

DISCUSSION

I. Standard of Review

We review de novo the district court's grant of summary judgment against Ezell's FELA claim. *May v. Segovia*, 929 F.3d 1223, 1234

(10th Cir. 2019) (quoting *Tuckel v. Grover*, 660 F.3d 1249, 1251 (10th Cir. 2011)). We affirm "if the movant show[ed] that there [was] no genuine dispute as to any material fact and the movant [was] entitled to judgment as a matter of law." Fed. R. Civ. P. 56(a). In making that decision, we view the evidence "in the light most favorable to the non-moving party." *Schulenberg v. BNSF Ry. Co.*, 911 F.3d 1276, 1285, 6 Adm. R. 405, 410 (10th Cir. 2018) (internal quotation marks omitted) (quoting *Libertarian Party of N.M. v. Herrera*, 506 F.3d 1303, 1309 (10th Cir. 2007)). After "the moving party has identified a lack of a genuine issue of material fact, the nonmoving party has the burden to cite to 'specific facts showing that there is a genuine issue for trial.'" *May*, 929 F.3d at 1234 (quoting *Schneider v. City of Grand Junction Police Dep't*, 717 F.3d 760, 767 (10th Cir. 2013)). The nonmoving party must be specific to satisfy its burden, either by "citing to particular parts of materials in the record" or by showing that the moving party has relied on insufficient or inadmissible evidence. Fed. R. Civ. P. 56(c)(1)(A)–(B).

II. Deficient Appendix and New Theories

BNSF argues that we should not reach the substantive issues because Ezell has made procedural errors.

First, BNSF points out that Ezell failed to include in his appendix the summary-judgment briefing in the district court. BNSF argues that comparing his **[—7—]** district court briefing with his appellate briefing shows that Ezell is making new arguments on appeal. The issue is easily resolved. BNSF may cure the problem and "file a supplemental appendix of [its] own." *Milligan-Hitt v. Bd. of Trs.*, 523 F.3d 1219, 1231 (10th Cir. 2008) (citing 10th Cir. R. 30.2(A)(1)). BNSF has done so, and we now have what we need to consider BNSF's argument.

Next, BNSF claims that in the district court Ezell "failed to raise the bulk of theories that he [now] offers." Appellee's Resp. Br. 17. BNSF lists the following as new "theories":

1. FELA plaintiffs only have the burden of showing slight negligence by the defendant.
2. BNSF's failure to follow its own rules creates a jury question.
3. By enacting its rules, BNSF recognized a need for them.
4. BNSF's work methods were inadequate since they were subjective.
5. BNSF had an obligation to provide better tools—that is, tools that would allow employees to determine if a railcar was loaded without requiring them to climb railcars.
6. Ezell's testimony creates a genuine issue of material fact.

But Ezell raised all six of these theories before the district court:

1. Ezell argued that BNSF could be liable if he showed that, "no matter how small" it was, BNSF's negligence played a role in causing his injury. Appellee's Suppl. App. vol. 2 at 165 (citation omitted).
2. Ezell claimed that the jury could find that BNSF breached its duty because it failed to provide him "with a list showing cars which were loaded versus empty." *Id.* at 166.
3. Ezell stated that providing a list was the "best practice[]" and that BNSF **{–1279–}** was negligent for not following its "best practice." *Id.* at 164, 166.
4. Ezell claimed that BNSF breached its duty because it did not adopt specific guidelines or procedures to determine whether railcars were empty, instead simply requiring employees to bang on the sides to decide if they thought the railcars sounded hollow.
5. Ezell argued that BNSF was negligent for not using a modified brake stick, a tool that would "allow[] workers to inspect the inside of cars for loads without having to climb on the car." *Id.* at 166–67. **[—8—]**
6. Ezell stated that there were "[a]dditional facts precluding judgment as a matter of law." *Id.* at 160. To support that contention, he cited his deposition to dispute numerous facts asserted by BNSF—such as whether he

was instructed that a railcar was loaded if it was more than half full and that "BNSF had no written guidelines with respect to whether a ballast car was loaded or empty." *Id.* at 161.

Though Ezell might be expanding on these theories now, he did present them in some form to the district court—he is not relying on different theories of liability. For instance, this situation is unlike one in which a plaintiff raises a negligent-failure-to-warn claim in the district court but then argues a negligent-design claim on appeal. *See, e.g., Lyons v. Jefferson Bank & Tr.*, 994 F.2d 716, 722 (10th Cir. 1993) (citing *Grasmick v. Otis Elevator Co.*, 817 F.2d 88, 89–90 (10th Cir. 1987)). Instead, all of Ezell's claims are FELA claims rooted in one theory: BNSF was negligent because it did not take precautions that would enable Ezell to avoid climbing the railcar ladders to complete his assigned job task.

Furthermore, BNSF argues that all of these theories can and should be "distilled" into one inquiry: "whether the method prescribed by BNSF . . . was reasonably safe, not whether BNSF could have used a safer[,] alternative method for performing the task." Appellee's Resp. Br. 25–26. The district court agreed and found that BNSF's method was reasonably safe, and BNSF argues that we should now affirm on the same basis. But because BNSF casts Ezell's various arguments—old or new—as all part of one inquiry, the same inquiry as that made by the district court, we fail to see how BNSF can, at the same time, argue that Ezell's "new theories" present new issues. **[—9—]**

III. Elements of a FELA Claim

FELA is a remedial law designed to "shift[] part of the 'human overhead' of doing business from employees to their employers." *Consol. Rail Corp. v. Gottshall*, 512 U.S. 532, 542 (1994) (quoting *Tiller v. Atl. Coast Line R.R.*, 318 U.S. 54, 58 (1943)). In part, FELA states:

> Every common carrier by railroad while engaging in [interstate] commerce . . . shall be liable in damages to any person suffering injury while he is employed by such carrier in such commerce . . . for such injury or death resulting in whole or in part from the negligence of any of the officers, agents, or employees of such carrier, or by reason of any defect or insufficiency, due to its negligence, in its cars, engines, appliances, machinery, track, roadbed, works, boats, wharves, or other equipment.

45 U.S.C. § 51. We have derived from this four elements to a FELA claim: (1) the employee was injured within the scope of his employment, (2) the employment was in furtherance of the employer's interstate transportation business, (3) the employer was negligent, and (4) the employer's negligence played some part in causing the injury for which the employee seeks compensation **{–1280–}** under FELA. *Van Gorder v. Grand Trunk W. R.R.*, 509 F.3d 265, 269 (6th Cir. 2007); *see also Volner v. Union Pac. R.R.*, 509 F. App'x 706, 708 (10th Cir. 2013) (unpublished) (adopting *Van Gorder*'s elements).

Here, Ezell indisputably satisfies the first two elements, but BNSF argues that he fails on elements three and four.

All negligence questions start the same: did the defendant owe and breach a duty to the plaintiff? Without a duty to the plaintiff, courts and juries cannot say that **[—10—]** a defendant did anything wrongful vis-à-vis the plaintiff by acting or failing to act. *See CSX Transp., Inc. v. McBride*, 564 U.S. 685, 703 (2011) (citing *Gallick v. Balt. & Ohio R.R.*, 372 U.S. 108, 119 n.7 (1963)). So, before we can consider causation, we must first determine whether Ezell has raised a genuine dispute about BNSF's owing and breaching a duty to him.

"A railroad has a duty to use reasonable care in furnishing its employees with a safe place to work." *Atchison, Topeka & Santa Fe Ry. Co. v. Buell*, 480 U.S. 557, 558 (1987). The degree of that duty depends on the magnitude of risk—the greater the risk the greater the duty. *Bailey v. Cent. Vt. Ry.*, 319 U.S. 350, 353 (1943) ("[The employer's duty] is a duty which becomes more imperative as the risk increases." (internal quotation marks and citation omitted)). In considering whether a railroad has breached its duty, the Supreme Court has instructed us to ask whether the railroad "observe[d] that degree of care which people of ordinary prudence and sagacity would use under the same or similar circumstances[.]" *CSX Transp.*, 564 U.S. at 703 (internal quotation marks omitted) (quoting *Gallick*, 372 U.S. at 118).

Appraising negligence under FELA "turns on principles of common law . . . , subject to such qualifications [that] Congress" introduces. *Gottshall*, 512 U.S. at 543 (internal quotation marks omitted) (quoting *Urie v. Thompson*, 337 U.S. 163, 182 (1949)). And "[a]t common law the duty of the employer to use reasonable care in furnishing his employees with a safe place to work was plain." *Bailey*, 319 U.S. at 352 (citations omitted); *see also* Dan B. Dobbs et al., The Law of Torts § 420 (2d ed.) (June 2019 update) ("[T]he employer owes a duty of reasonable care to furnish a **[—11—]** safe place in which to work." (citations omitted)). The duty is "measured by what is reasonably foreseeable under like circumstances." *CSX Transp.*, 564 U.S. at 703 (internal quotation marks omitted) (quoting *Gallick*, 372 U.S. at 118).

Thus, the Supreme Court has ruled that the railroad's duty to provide a safe workplace is a duty of reasonable care.[4] *E.g.*, *id.*; **{-1281-}** *Buell*, 480 U.S. at 558; *Gallick*, 372 U.S. at 118. Having outlined BNSF's duty, we will now address whether a genuine dispute exists about BNSF breaching that duty.[5] **[—12—]**

IV. Ezell Has Failed to Show That Climbing a Railcar Ladder Is Not Reasonably Safe.

Ezell claims that he needed to climb the railcar ladders to complete his assigned task—to determine whether each railcar was loaded, that is, more than half full of ballast. At the summary-judgment stage, we credit Ezell's testimony that Jernigan had defined a loaded railcar this way.

---

[4] In a few older cases, some circuits have concluded that a railroad's duty is a heightened one and can be breached just by "slight negligence." *See, e.g.*, *Ulfik v. Metro-N. Commuter R.R.*, 77 F.3d 54, 58 n.1 (2d Cir. 1996) (citing *Mullahon v. Union Pac. R.R.*, 64 F.3d 1358, 1364 (9th Cir. 1995); *Syverson v. Consol. Rail Corp.*, 19 F.3d 824, 825 (2d Cir. 1994); *Hines v. Consol. Rail Corp.*, 926 F.2d 262, 267 (3d Cir. 1991)); *see also Ackley v. Chi. & N. W. Transp. Co.*, 820 F.2d 263, 267 n.6 (8th Cir. 1987) (analogizing a railroad's "special dut[y]" under FELA to the relationship between a school and its pupils). We too have used the slight-negligence term, albeit without specifying whether we were referring to fault or causation. *See Mo.-Kan.-Tex. Ry. Co. v. Hearson*, 422 F.2d 1037, 1040 (10th Cir. 1970). At other times, we have spoken of the need for railroads to "use ordinary care" and "do what a reasonably prudent person would do to make the work environment safe." *Volner*, 509 F. App'x at 709 (citing *Van Gorder*, 509 F.3d at 269). Whatever our earlier approach, in view of *CSX Transportation*, we conclude that the Supreme Court has discredited the notion that a railroad's duty to its employees is a heightened one that can be breached by slight negligence. 564 U.S. at 703; *see also Gautreaux v. Scurlock Marine, Inc.*, 107 F.3d 331, 335–36 (5th Cir. 1997) (en banc) (noting that the slight-negligence rule was derived from misreading Supreme Court precedent). But once an employee shows that the railroad has breached its duty, then the employee's burden of establishing causation is relaxed. *Rogers v. Mo. Pac. R.R.*, 352 U.S. 500, 506 (1957); *see also CSX Transp.*, 564 U.S. at 693–95, 697 (noting that *Rogers*'s relaxed-standard test refers to causation); *Gottshall*, 512 U.S. at 542–43 (same).

[5] Ezell asserts that even if BNSF had a duty of ordinary prudence BNSF's internal rules "ratcheted up" its duty. Oral Argument at 12:13–12:24. Assuming that BNSF's internal rules apply here and that Ezell did need to receive a "good list" indicating which cars were more than half full, we disagree that those rules **[—12—]** augmented BNSF's duty. While a company's internal rules "are admissible to show negligence," those rules "do not alter the applicable standard of care." *Robinson v. Mo. Pac. R.R.*, 16 F.3d 1083, 1091 (10th Cir. 1994); *Fulton v. St. Louis–S.F. Ry.*, 675 F.2d 1130, 1133 (10th Cir. 1982); *see also Therrien v. Target Corp.*, 617 F.3d 1242, 1256 (10th Cir. 2010) (approving a jury instruction that allowed admission of Target's internal policies with the limitation that "the finding of a violation of policy or procedure should not be equated with a finding of negligence"). Here, Ezell offers BNSF's internal rules to heighten—or ratchet up—BNSF's duty, but these cases preclude such an enhancement of the standard of care.

That takes us to the next step—did BNSF provide Ezell an unsafe workplace by requiring him to climb the railcar ladder to make a more precise determination? No, according to Ezell's expert witness, Colon Fulk. Fulk testified that it would not be "unreasonable for a railroad to expect a conductor to climb on a railcar" and conceded that conductors "do it all the time." Appellant's App. vol. 2 at 266. He also agreed that "it is not an unreasonable risk for BNSF or any railroad to expect its railroad . . . employees to climb a railcar" as "part of the[ir] job requirements[.]" *Id.* at 268–69. He opined that there would be "[n]othing unreasonable about a yardmaster" ordering a conductor "to visually inspect every car." *Id.* at 267. And **[—13—]** when asked if he "st[oo]d by [his] testimony that asking a conductor to climb a railcar is not an unsafe task," he said, "[t]hat's true." *Id.* at 270.[6]

To operate its railroad, BNSF must sometimes have its employees climb railcar ladders. In addition to checking how full railcars are, expert Fulk identified another **{-1282-}** reason that BNSF employees might need to climb the ladders—BNSF policy requires maintenance-of-way crew members to "climb ballast cars to ensure that the loads are balanced[.]" *Id.* at 272–73. He also testified that conductors "often have to [climb] to set hand brakes[.]" *Id.* at 266.

BNSF met its initial burden of showing a safe workplace, even when requiring employees to climb railcar ladders. In response, Ezell impermissibly expands the safe-workplace standard as requiring the safest alternative available. For instance, Ezell argues that he never would have had to climb the ladder if BNSF had supplied him some sort of mirror on a stick. And he argues that he would not have had to climb the railcar ladder had BNSF enforced its internal rules requiring the maintenance-of-way and train crews supply him with a list of loads and empties. But to show railroad negligence, FELA requires plaintiffs to show an unsafe workplace—not a failure to provide the safest possible workplace. *E.g., Darrough v. CSX Transp.,* **[—14—]** *Inc.*, 321 F.3d 674, 676 (7th Cir. 2003) ("CSXT did not have to create the safest possible work environment . . . only a reasonably safe one."); *Walker v. Ne. Reg'l Commuter R.R.*, 225 F.3d 895, 899 (7th Cir. 2000) ("Safer methods of lifting may be available, but Metra need only use a reasonably safe method for lifting the blade." (citation omitted)); *Stillman v. Norfolk & W. Ry. Co.*, 811 F.2d 834, 838 (4th Cir. 1987) (explaining that the district court did not even need to admit evidence that the railroad had access to a safer, alternative method when the primary method was itself safe); *Soto v. S. Pac. Transp. Co.*, 644 F.2d 1147, 1148 (5th Cir. 1981) (per curiam) ("That there were other, arguably more advanced, methods in use by the defendant for cleaning these pits is of no significance where the method in use by Mr. Soto was not an inherently unsafe one.").

Because BNSF did provide Ezell a safe workplace, even according to his own expert witness, we agree with the district court that it is entitled to summary judgment. Accordingly, we affirm.

---

[6] Importantly, BNSF has a safety rule imposing requirements on its employees climbing railcar ladders. Employees must "[m]aintain three-point contact"—that is, maintain contact with "both feet and one hand or both hands and one foot"—while "ascending or descending ladders or platforms." Appellee's Suppl. App. vol. 1 at 83. Although the rule itself does not state what employees must maintain three-point contact with, Ezell's expert testified that one purpose of the rule is to require "contact with safety appliance[s]" that will hold an employee's weight. Appellant's App. vol. 2 at 254. The flange above the ladder does not qualify as a safety appliance.

United States Court of Appeals for the Eleventh Circuit

United States Court of Appeals
for the Eleventh Circuit

No. 17-14294

UNITED STATES
vs.
CABEZAS-MONTANO

Appeal from the United States District Court for the Southern District of Florida

Decided: January 30, 2020

Citation: 949 F.3d 567, 8 Adm. R. 364 (11th Cir. 2020).

Before **ROSENBAUM, TJOFLAT,** and **HULL,** Circuit Judges.

[—1—] {-576-} HULL, Circuit Judge: **{-577-}**

After a jury trial, defendants Trinity Rolando Cabezas-Montano, Hector Leonardo Guagua-Alarcon, and Adalberto Frickson Palacios-Solis appeal their **[—2—]** convictions and sentences under the Maritime Drug Law Enforcement Act ("MDLEA"). *See* 46 U.S.C. §§ 70501-70508. They were convicted of conspiracy to possess with intent to distribute over five kilograms of cocaine while on board a vessel subject to the jurisdiction of the United States, in violation of 46 U.S.C. § 70506(b), and possession with intent to distribute over five kilograms of cocaine while on board a vessel subject to the jurisdiction of the United States, in violation of 46 U.S.C. § 70503(a)(1).

As to their convictions, the defendants, either together or separately, challenge: (1) the constitutionality of the MDLEA; (2) the district court's determination of MDLEA subject matter jurisdiction; (3) the delay in presentment for a probable cause hearing; (4) the denial of their motion in limine to exclude evidence of post-arrest, pre-*Miranda*[1] silence; (5) the sufficiency of the evidence; and (6) the denial of their motions for a mistrial based on the government's alleged *Brady*[2] violation. As to their sentences, the defendants, either together or separately, challenge: (1) the constitutionality of the denial of safety-valve relief in their MDLEA case; (2) the denial of a minor-role reduction; and (3) the denial of their motions for a downward variance. They also claim the sentencing court committed procedural error and imposed substantively unreasonable sentences. **[—3—]**

After careful review of the record and the parties' briefs, and with the benefit of oral argument, we affirm the defendants' convictions and sentences. We start by recounting the trial evidence about the defendants' crimes.[3]

I. FACTUAL BACKGROUND

A. Coast Guard's Detection of the Go-Fast Vessel

On the night of October 24, 2016, the U.S. Coast Guard cutter *Hamilton* was patrolling in the eastern Pacific Ocean at 10 degrees latitude and 91 degrees longitude, which was approximately 200 miles off the coast of Central America, namely Guatemala and El Salvador. During the patrol, around 9:05 p.m., a Coast Guard marine patrol aircraft notified the *Hamilton* cutter that it had detected a go-fast vessel ("GFV") that was traveling northbound at a high rate of speed and was approximately six nautical miles away from the cutter.[4]

The target GFV was 30-to-35 feet long, had two outboard engines, and was carrying three passengers on board. GFVs, also known as a "Panga" or "Panga-style" vessels, are small vessels designed to cut through the water with less friction so that they can travel at higher speeds. GFVs are low-profile and have a very **[—4—]** different shape, style, and speed than a fishing boat. **{-578-}** Drug smugglers

---

1 *Miranda v. Arizona*, 384 U.S. 436, 86 S. Ct. 1602 (1966).

2 *Brady v. Maryland*, 373 U.S. 83, 83 S. Ct. 1194 (1963).

3 While there were two jury trials, the first resulted in a mistrial. The facts we recount are based on the evidence from the second jury trial.

4 Coast Guard personnel testified that, while at sea, they use an international military unit of time called "Zulu." While it was 9:05 p.m. on October 24, local time when the Coast Guard aircraft contacted the *Hamilton* cutter, under Zulu time it was 2:05 a.m. on October 25. To avoid confusion, we will refer to local time.

commonly use GFVs to transport drugs and travel at night without navigation lights to avoid detection.

After being notified of the GFV, the *Hamilton* crew met for a briefing in the cutter's Combat Information Center ("CIC"). The CIC was equipped with a Forward-Looking Infrared Radar ("FLIR") system and various other radars that enabled the Coast Guard to monitor nighttime vessel activity on the high seas. The FLIR system uses heat-based infrared detection to create a video in black (the objects emitting more heat) and white (the objects emitting less heat) depicting the activities or objects being monitored. The FLIR system allowed the Coast Guard to see vessels, passengers, and any jettisoned objects at night.

Generally speaking, Coast Guard members in the CIC stay in contact with all other *Hamilton* units throughout interdictions and keep them updated on the course and distance of target vessels. The three *Hamilton* units included (1) a helicopter, (2) an over-the-horizon ("OTH") vessel, and (3) a long-range interceptor ("LRI") vessel. The helicopter also was equipped with a FLIR monitoring system that recorded its observations on video too. The OTH vessel was equipped with search lights, radar, and weapons. The crew on these *Hamilton* units were equipped with and used night-vision goggles.

After the CIC briefing, the *Hamilton* crew decided to dispatch all three **[—5—]** units—the helicopter, OTH vessel, and LRI vessel—to intercept the target GFV. At launch time, it was very dark due to lack of moonlight, but the weather and sea conditions were calm and without wind.

B. Helicopter Chase

At 9:34 p.m., the *Hamilton* helicopter launched. At 9:45 p.m., the helicopter located the 30-to-35-foot GFV with two outboard engines that was carrying three individuals. The GFV appeared to be "dead-in-water" but started moving again.[5] The helicopter moved alongside the GFV. At this point, the GFV and the helicopter still were approximately 200 to 250 nautical miles from the coast of Central America. The CIC on the *Hamilton* cutter eventually picked up the GFV on its FLIR and other radar systems and continuously monitored it.

While pursuing the GFV, the *Hamilton* helicopter crew obtained a statement of no objection from Coast Guard headquarters, entitling it to request that the vessel stop and to fire warning and disabling shots if necessary. The helicopter crew broadcasted orders in English and Spanish for the GFV to stop, ordered the passengers to put their hands up and move to the front of the vessel, and flashed its blue law enforcement lights and Coast Guard emblem. The GFV disregarded the instructions and continued moving in an evasive, zig-zag path. This prompted the helicopter crew to continue its chase and to fire three rounds of warning shots. **[—6—]** Every fifth round that the helicopter crew fired contained a "tracer round," a large and easily-visible red glow that detached from the projectile before entering the water. The GFV continued to disobey the orders.

As the helicopter continued to chase the GFV, its crew saw the GFV's passengers jettisoning packages overboard. One package remained attached to the vessel and dragged behind in the water. The helicopter crew marked the location where the packages were jettisoned with chemical lights and relayed the coordinate positions to the *Hamilton* cutter. The helicopter FLIR video showed that the GFV's left **{-579-}** side engine was cooler than the right side engine.

The GFV slowed down and came to a stop, at which point the passengers appeared to crank the engines to restart them. The GFV began moving again. Because the GFV passengers were next to the vessel's engines, the helicopter crew fired two rounds of warning shots near the aft of the GFV to get

---

[5] "Dead-in-water" means that the vessel has stopped and is motionless in the water.

them to move toward the front of the vessel. The passengers complied, but the helicopter crew was unable to fire disabling shots at the GFV's engines without endangering the passengers. At this point, the helicopter was running low on fuel, so it communicated to the *Hamilton* cutter the GFV's last-known coordinate position and headed back to the cutter to refuel. Around 11:00 p.m., the helicopter crew lost its visual of the GFV and landed back at the *Hamilton* cutter at 11:05 p.m.

C. OTH and LRI Vessel Searches and Recovery of a Cocaine Bale [—7—]

Around 10:00 p.m., the OTH vessel launched. After the helicopter headed back to the *Hamilton* cutter, the OTH vessel spent 20 to 30 minutes searching the area that the helicopter crew indicated was the last known coordinate location of the GFV but was unsuccessful. The *Hamilton* cutter instructed the OTH crew to suspend its search for the GFV and instead head to the scene of the jettisoned packages. The OTH crew found the chemical lights left by the helicopter crew and searched the area but found no packages.

Approximately 31 minutes after the helicopter crew lost its visual of the GFV, the *Hamilton* cutter reacquired the GFV's location using its CIC's FLIR and other radar systems. The *Hamilton* cutter crew observed on the CIC's FLIR system that the GFV was dead-in-water and that one of the passengers was flailing and frantically trying to fix the engine. The cutter crew informed the OTH crew that it had reacquired sight of the GFV and redirected the OTH vessel to that coordinate position. While en route to the specified location, the OTH crew recovered a 20-kilogram cocaine bale floating in the water along with a buoy tied to a black line. The OTH crew relayed to the *Hamilton* cutter the coordinate location of the recovered cocaine bale and continued its search for the GFV.

While the OTH crew was recovering the bale, the LRI vessel launched around 11:33 to 11:43 p.m. Soon thereafter, the *Hamilton* cutter instructed the OTH crew to resume its search for the jettisoned packages because the LRI vessel **[—8—]** had reached the GFV and was preparing to approach. The *Hamilton* cutter crew observed the LRI's approach of the GFV on the CIC's FLIR system. Meanwhile, the OTH crew searched for about two hours but recovered no additional bales. Samples of the recovered bale's contents, which consisted of 20 individually wrapped 1-kilogram packages, field-tested positive for cocaine.

D. LRI Crew's Boarding and Search of the GFV

The LRI vessel approached a dead-in-water GFV that had two outboard engines and three passengers. The GFV, which had no navigation lights, was in international waters, 200-plus miles away from the closest land mass. The LRI vessel illuminated its blue law enforcement light and announced over a loud hailer in English and Spanish, "United States Coast Guard, put your hands in the air and move towards the front of the vessel." The GFV's passengers complied with these orders.

After receiving permission for right-of-visit boarding, a boarding team from the LRI vessel then boarded the GFV. While **{-580-}** conducting an initial safety sweep, the LRI boarding team members observed that much of the GFV had been wiped down with fuel.

The LRI boarding team, which included a Spanish translator, began asking right-of-visit questions to determine the nationality of the vessel. The team noticed the vessel was not flying any flag and had no other indicia of nationality. The team **[—9—]** twice asked the GFV's passengers if anyone wished to make a claim of nationality for the vessel. The passengers—Cabezas-Montano, Guagua-Alarcon, and Palacios-Solis—did not respond either time. When asked to identify the master of the vessel, the defendants did not respond. When asked a second time, Guagua-Alarcon and Palacios-Solis pointed to Cabezas-Montano, who in turn pointed to Palacios-Solis. The boarding team asked Cabezas-Montano and Palacios-Solis if either of them was the master, but they did not answer and continued to point at each other. The LRI boarding team concluded that there was no claim of nationality for the vessel and that no one claimed to be the master.

When asked about the GFV's last port of call, Palacios-Solis stated that it was Manta, Ecuador. According to one LRI boarding team member, without a claim of nationality for the vessel or a master to take the claim from, the Coast Guard "take[s] the last port of call as the nationality of the vessel." The boarding team also observed an Ecuadorian maker's mark on the back of the GFV indicating that the vessel was manufactured in Ecuador. When asked about the date of last port of call, Palacios-Solis stated that he and the other two defendants had gone fishing but ended up lost at sea for 32 days. The team observed, however, that the defendants did not seem happy to see Coast Guard personnel and declined the Coast Guard's offer of food and water.

The LRI boarding team conveyed to the *Hamilton* cutter that the GFV bore **[—10—]** an Ecuadorian maker's mark and that its last port of call was in Ecuador. The *Hamilton* cutter contacted Ecuador to obtain a statement of no objection to permit the U.S. Coast Guard to conduct a full law enforcement boarding. According to the Coast Guard personnel's testimony, a foreign government, in response to the Coast Guard's request for a statement-of-no-objection, could claim the vessel and deny boarding, make no claim, or claim the vessel and permit boarding. Here, Ecuador provided its statement of no objection to a Coast Guard Flag Officer early on the morning of October 25. The LRI boarding team detained the defendants, placed them on the LRI vessel, and began its full boarding onto the GFV.

The LRI boarding team swabbed the GFV's surfaces that were not saturated with fuel and the defendants' hands for trace quantities of drugs. The defendants appeared visibly concerned when the swabbing began. Ultimately, the Coast Guard found trace amounts of drugs: (1) one defendant tested positive for trace amounts of cocaine and PCP; and (2) trace amounts of cocaine were detected on the GFV's bow and tiller.

The LRI boarding team also conducted a full search of the GFV. The team found: (1) a buoy and black line similar in appearance to the buoy and black line that were recovered where the jettisoned cocaine bale was found; (2) the same brown packing tape that was wrapped around the recovered bale; (3) eleven 25-gallon fuel drums, most of which were full; (4) a phone charger; (5) a satellite **[—11—]** phone battery; (6) a document containing satellite phone numbers; and (7) a document containing coordinates. Although no phones were on board, a team member testified that drug smugglers in GFVs sometimes **{–581–}** throw their electronic equipment overboard to prevent the Coast Guard from recovering stored data. The team observed a wet shirt covering the left engine, which lessened the engine's heat signature and made detection more difficult.

As to the defendants' fishing trip story, the LRI boarding team found fishing hooks and knives but did not find any bait, fish, or remnants of fish. The team found lines, but they appeared to be unserviceable and not usable for fishing. The team also found large quantities of water and sports drinks, as well as fresh fruit and food items that did not appear to be 32 days old. The bottom of the GFV appeared extremely clean and free from growth, which was an unusual state for a vessel that was allegedly adrift at sea for 32 days.

After being onboard for 12 hours, the LRI crew left the GFV and sank the vessel because it was a navigation hazard. The LRI vessel headed back to the *Hamilton* cutter, where the defendants were taken for processing.

E. Coast Guard's Recovery of 24 More Cocaine Bales

After conducting a drift analysis based on factors such as current and wind movement to determine where to search for the jettisoned packages, the OTH vessel dispatched in the daytime, responded to the designated area, and recovered **[—12—]** 24 additional bales along with buoys equipped with GPS trackers. The 25 total recovered bales collectively weighed 614 kilograms. Lab testing, based on a representative 10-kilogram sample, confirmed that the substance in the recovered bales was cocaine. The tested sample had an estimated purity level of 86 and 89 percent, which was very high and indicated that the drugs were close to their original source. The cocaine bales' total wholesale value was over $10 million.

The Coast Guard also found GPS trackers attached to some of the cocaine bales themselves, which charted their movement as follows. Three trackers launched between October 15 and 16, 2016, some from the coast of Esmeraldas, Ecuador and others from the coast of the Ecuadorian and Colombian border. All three trackers converged when they traveled within the coastal region of Ecuador. Next, the trackers moved away from the coast of Ecuador, northwest towards the Galapagos Islands. The trackers then changed course and moved northeast towards the coast of the Guatemalan and El Salvadorian border. However, the GPS trackers suddenly stopped moving and then started drifting slowly in a south or southeast direction—indicating that the trackers were no longer on a vessel—in the area where the Coast Guard found them on October 24 and 25. The GPS trackers' trajectories were consistent with the *Hamilton* cutter's and helicopter's coordinate range data for the target GFV and the document containing coordinates found on the defendants' vessel. Four Coast Guard personnel testified that they **[—13—]** neither saw nor heard any other vessels in the vicinity during the entirety of the interdiction.

F. Defendants' Version of Events

The defendants told a different story. According to Palacios-Solis's testimony at trial, he and his codefendants departed from the Esmeraldas, Ecuador, port for a short, four-day fishing trip on the boat. Palacios-Solis testified that the boat, of which he was the captain, was a typical Ecuadorian fishing boat. Palacios-Solis claimed that, while he initially lied to the Coast Guard about not being the captain, he admitted to his role once he arrived in Florida. The defendants quickly returned to the Esmeraldas port because the boat's engines were not working well. They had a **{-582-}** mechanic fix the engine, but Palacios-Solis forgot to change the oil after the engine was fixed.

They again set out for their fishing trip. On the second day of their fishing trip, once they were approximately 150 to 200 miles from the Esmeraldas, the engines failed and Palacios-Solis was not able to repair them. They assumed that another fishing boat would come along and help them, but none did and they were left adrift for 27 to 30 days.

According to Palacios-Solis's testimony, he intentionally covered the engines to protect them from pirates. The documents discovered during the search of the GFV were left by previous users and Palacios-Solis denied any knowledge **[—14—]** of their contents. He testified that the lines on the vessel were for fishing and that they were rendered unusable by the Coast Guard personnel during their search. He conceded that the buoy and black line found in the water looked just like the buoy and black line found on the vessel, which were his. The brown packing tape on the vessel, however, was not his and Palacios-Solis denied knowing where it came from. Palacios-Solis testified that the food was 30 days old and was not fresh and that there was not much food left over by the time the Coast Guard arrived. The defendants were asleep when the Coast Guard approached their boat, they were confused by the lights and yelling, and they were scared that the Coast Guard personnel were going to kill them.

Throughout trial, the government's witnesses testified as to the coordinate locations of the critical points during the interdiction of the GFV and of the recovered cocaine bales. In their case, however, the defendants called a maritime expert who created a model pointing out discrepancies in the government's plotted coordinates. Nonetheless, on cross-examination, the maritime expert conceded that at least some portions of his method and model were erroneous, incomplete, and/or misleading.

Notably too, a Coast Guard maritime expert, who conducted a drift analysis, testified that the defendants' story about being adrift for about 30 days was physically impossible given the claimed starting point of the fishing trip, the **[—15—]** weather and currents, and the coordinate location of the interdiction. The Coast Guard expert disagreed with the accuracy of the defense expert's model. The Coast Guard expert testified that the southward location, where the *Hamilton* crew searched for and recovered the bales, was consistent with information regarding the direction of the GFV.

A Coast Guard health services technician also testified that she observed and examined the defendants once they were detained and brought aboard the *Hamilton* cutter on October 25. The health services technician testified the defendants did not require any medical intervention and exhibited no signs of malnourishment, dehydration, malnutrition, lethargy, or extended exposure to the elements.

II. FIRST JURY TRIAL

On December 12, 2016, Palacios-Solis, Cabezas-Montano, and Guagua-Alarcon made their first entry into the United States, when they were brought to Key West, Florida, in the Southern District of Florida.

On December 13, a criminal complaint issued against the defendants and their initial appearances were held before a magistrate judge. The complaint charged all defendants with conspiracy to possess with intent to distribute five kilograms or more of cocaine on board a vessel subject to the jurisdiction of the United States. In **{-583-}** an attached probable-cause affidavit, a Drug Enforcement Agency ("DEA") Special Agent stated how: (1) on October 25, the Coast Guard **[—16—]** detained the defendants and the GFV and then transferred the defendants to the *Hamilton* cutter, approximately 215 nautical miles off the coast of Guatemala/El Salvador; and (2) on December 12, the Coast Guard brought the defendants to Key West.

On December 16, the defendants were indicted on charges of: (1) conspiracy to possess with intent to distribute five or more kilograms of cocaine on board a vessel subject to the jurisdiction of the United States, in violation of 46 U.S.C. §§ 70503(a)(1), 70506(a) and (b), and 21 U.S.C. § 960(b)(1)(B) (Count 1); and (2) possession with intent to distribute five or more kilograms of cocaine on board a vessel subject to the jurisdiction of the United States, in violation of 46 U.S.C. §§ 70503(a)(1) and 70506(a), 21 U.S.C. § 960(b)(1)(B), and 18 U.S.C. § 2 (Count 2).

On February 4, 2017, the government filed a motion for the district court to make a pretrial determination of jurisdiction regarding whether the defendants' vessel was subject to the jurisdiction of the United States. The government submitted that: (1) the stateless GFV was interdicted in international waters and upon high seas by the Coast Guard on October 24, 2016; (2) at the time of the interdiction, there were three passengers on board, who were the defendants; (3) when asked by the Coast Guard, none of the defendants claimed to be the master of the vessel and none made a claim of nationality for it; and (4) thus, the **[—17—]** United States determined the vessel to be "without nationality" subjecting the vessel to the jurisdiction of the United States under 46 U.S.C. § 70502(c)(1)(A) and (d)(1)(B).

The first trial resulted in a mistrial after the jury was unable to reach a unanimous verdict. As outlined below, the district court explicitly addressed its jurisdiction before the second trial.

III. SECOND JURY TRIAL

A. Defendants' Motion to Dismiss the Indictment

Prior to the second jury trial, all defendants moved to dismiss the indictment for lack of subject-matter jurisdiction on three enumerated grounds containing multiple sub-issues.[6] The defendants argued that: (1) there was no evidence that their vessel was outside the territorial waters of a foreign nation, precluding jurisdiction based on the vessel's

[6] While Palacios-Solis filed the motion to dismiss the indictment, the district court granted Cabezas-Montano's and Guagua-Alarcon's motion to adopt it.

status as one without nationality; (2) there was no evidence that the cocaine allegedly being transported by the vessel was destined for the United States, such that there was no U.S. "nexus" permitting the exercise of extraterritorial jurisdiction; (3) without a requirement that the trafficking crime have a "nexus" to the United States, the MDLEA's jurisdictional element violates due process; (4) the MDLEA's requirement that the district court determine the **[—18—]** jurisdictional element, rather than the jury, violates the Fifth and Sixth Amendment, especially in cases where a vessel is declared "stateless" and the parties dispute material facts regarding the alleged statelessness; and (5) the admission of a certification of the Secretary of State to establish extraterritorial jurisdiction in such a case would violate the Confrontation Clause and constitute inadmissible hearsay.

In response, the government argued, *inter alia*, that: (1) the defendants were interdicted in international waters and upon **{–584–}** the high seas when their GFV was stopped approximately 215 nautical miles southwest of the coast of Guatemala in the Pacific Ocean; (2) their GFV was without nationality and was subject to the jurisdiction of the United States; and (3) the defendants' remaining arguments were foreclosed by this Court's precedent.

At a pretrial hearing before a magistrate judge, defendants' counsel made their jurisdictional arguments. The magistrate judge's report ("R&R") recommended the denial of the defendants' motion to dismiss the indictment. The magistrate judge found that: (1) the vessel was in international waters at the time it was intercepted by the Coast Guard; (2) jurisdiction existed under § 70502(c)(1)(A) of the MDLEA because the defendants' vessel was "without nationality"; and (3) this Court's precedent foreclosed the defendants' constitutional arguments. Over the defendants' objections, the district court **[—19—]** adopted the R&R and denied their motion to dismiss the indictment.

B. Defendants' Post-Arrest, Pre-*Miranda* Silence

Next, Palacios-Solis filed a motion in limine to exclude evidence of the defendants' post-arrest, pre-*Miranda* silence in response to the Coast Guard's interrogation. Palacios-Solis conceded that this Court's precedent foreclosed his argument but sought to preserve the issue. Guagua-Alarcon adopted the motion.

In response, the government submitted that it did not intend to elicit, in its case-in-chief, the defendants' silence or statements other than their silence or answers to the Coast Guard's questions regarding: (1) the master or captain of the GFV; (2) the nationality of the GFV; (3) the last port of call; and (4) the next port of call. The government reserved the right to elicit any silence or statements during the defense's case and in rebuttal.[7]

The district court denied Palacios-Solis's and Guagua-Alarcon's motion in limine as moot. The district court highlighted: (1) the defendants' concession that this Court's precedent foreclosed their challenge; (2) the admissibility of their silence or answers to the questions identified by the government; (3) the government's indication that it otherwise would not elicit any other silence or statements by the defendants; and (4) the government's rights pertaining to cross-**[—20—]** examination during the defense's case and in rebuttal.

C. Pretrial Hearing

Before trial, the district court held a pretrial hearing during which it granted the defendants' motion to deem any objection made by one defendant as adopted by all defendants, unless a defendant opted out. The government clarified that it intended to elicit during their case-in-chief: (1) the defendants' silence when asked about the GFV's nationality; (2) their actions of pointing to Cabezas-Montano and Palacios-Solis when

[7] As explained later, the defendants on appeal challenge only the admission of their post-arrest, pre-*Miranda* silence.

asked about the vessel's master; (3) any statements or silence about the last and next ports of call; and (4) the defendants' statement that they were adrift at sea for about 30 days. Palacios-Solis reiterated that this Court's precedent permitted the admission of such evidence, but that he preserved his challenge to it.

D. Government's Case-In-Chief

The second jury trial began on July 17, 2017. The government called seven witnesses: **{-585-}** (1) six Coast Guard members who carried out the October 24-through-25 interdiction operation and testified about the above events; and (2) the DEA forensic chemist who tested the seized evidence for cocaine.

When Petty Officer Robert Tetzlaff testified as to his observations from the CIC's FLIR system—namely, that he observed one of the GFV passengers flailing and frantically trying to fix the engine—Palacios-Solis moved for a mistrial on **[—21—]** *Brady* grounds. Palacios-Solis asserted that Officer Tetzlaff's testimony indicated that there was a CIC FLIR video—showing the GFV passengers flailing and trying to restart the vessel—which the government had not turned over to the defense. The government responded that it learned of this aspect of Officer Tetzlaff's testimony only the day before trial, that it did not possess the CIC's FLIR video because it was already recorded over, and that it did not notify the defense because it did not view the evidence as exculpatory.

The district court agreed that the evidence was inculpatory, not exculpatory, but directed the government to investigate whether the FLIR video actually was recorded and/or recorded over. The next day, the government notified the district court that, while the Coast Guard records its FLIR videos, it records over them if no preservation request is made, and that it no longer had the October 24/25, 2016 FLIR video. Palacios-Solis renewed his mistrial motion, which Cabezas-Montano and Guagua-Alarcon joined. The district court denied the motion and the trial continued.[8]

E. Defendants' Evidence, Government's Rebuttal, and Rule 29 Motions

The government rested on the third day of trial. The defendants moved for a **[—22—]** judgment of acquittal under Rule 29 of the Federal Rules of Criminal Procedure. They argued that there was insufficient evidence of their guilt and the court lacked subject-matter jurisdiction.[9] The district court denied the defendants' Rule 29 motions.

The defense then called a maritime expert who prepared a coordinate model for this case. Palacios-Solis also testified. The defense rested. In rebuttal, the government called the Coast Guard health services technician and its own maritime expert who conducted a drift analysis of the defendants' vessel. The defendants renewed their Rule 29 motions, which the district court denied.

F. Jury Verdict and Post-Trial Motions

After deliberations, the jury found all three defendants guilty on both counts. Palacios-Solis filed a post-trial Rule 29 motion claiming again that: (1) there was insufficient evidence to support his convictions; (2) the court lacked subject-matter jurisdiction; and (3) the government's introduction of the defendants' post-arrest, **{-586-}** pre-*Miranda* silence violated his Fifth Amendment rights against self-incrimination. Ultimately, at sentencing,

---

[8] On direct examination, Officer Tetzlaff testified that the October 24/25 FLIR video likely was recorded over. During the defense's cross-examination, Officer Tetzlaff agreed that it would have been helpful to compare the CIC's and the helicopter's FLIR videos and testified further about his observations from the CIC's FLIR video on the night of the interdiction. Then, on redirect examination, Officer Tetzlaff confirmed that he did not tell prosecutors about his CIC FLIR observations until just before the second trial.

[9] Palacios-Solis renewed his motion to dismiss the indictment. Guagua-Alarcon adopted both codefendants' Rule 29 arguments. The district court stated that after trial it would revisit the renewed motion to dismiss but that it did not hear anything that would change its prior determination.

the district court denied Palacios-Solis's post-trial Rule 29 motion. Among other things, the district court determined that no defendant had claimed to be the master of the vessel or claimed any nationality, **[—23—]** that the Coast Guard could not confirm or deny the vessel's nationality, and thus the vessel was without nationality and subject to the jurisdiction of the United States. This is the defendants' appeal.

IV. MDLEA

Before addressing the defendants' appellate claims, we give some background about the MDLEA.

The Constitution empowers Congress "[t]o define and punish Piracies and Felonies committed on the high Seas, and Offences against the Law of Nations." U.S. Const. Art. I, § 8, cl. 10. "The Supreme Court has interpreted that Clause to contain three distinct grants of power: to define and punish piracies, to define and punish felonies committed on the high seas, and to define and punish offenses against the law of nations." *United States v. Campbell*, 743 F.3d 802, 805, 2 Adm. R. 543, 544 (11th Cir. 2014). This MDLEA appeal involves a conviction for a felony offense defined by an act of Congress under the second grant of power. *See id.*, 2 Adm. R. at 544.

Congress enacted the MDLEA to prohibit any person from "knowingly or intentionally . . . possess[ing] with intent to manufacture or distribute, a controlled substance" on board "a vessel subject to the jurisdiction of the United States," 46 U.S.C. § 70503(a)(1) and (e)(1), and from conspiring to do the same, *id.* § 70506(b). Specifically, § 70503(a)(1) provides that, "[w]hile on board *a covered vessel*, an individual may not knowingly or intentionally . . . possess with intent to **[—24—]** manufacture or distribute, a controlled substance. *Id.* § 70503(a)(1) (emphasis added). The MDLEA defines a "covered vessel" to include, among other things, "a vessel subject to the jurisdiction of the United States." *Id.* § 70503(e). In turn, the MDLEA defines a "vessel subject to the jurisdiction of the United States" to include, among other things, "a vessel without nationality." *Id.* § 70502(c)(1)(A).

In 1996, Congress amended the MDLEA to provide that "[j]urisdiction of the United States with respect to a vessel subject to this chapter is not an element of an offense." *Id.* § 70504(a); *see Campbell*, 743 F.3d at 805, 2 Adm. R. at 545. That section continues that "[j]urisdictional issues arising under this chapter are preliminary questions of law to be determined solely by the trial judge." 46 U.S.C. § 70504(a). Congress made clear that the MDLEA "applies even though the act is committed outside the territorial jurisdiction of the United States." *Id.* § 70503(b).

V. DEFENDANTS' CONSTITUTIONAL CLAIMS

As a threshold matter, all defendants argue that the MDLEA is unconstitutional because: (1) Congress's power to define and punish felonies on the high seas is limited to felonies bearing a "nexus" to the United States; (2) due process prohibits the prosecution of foreign nationals for offenses bearing no "nexus" to the United States; and (3) the MDLEA violates the Fifth and Sixth **[—25—]** Amendments by removing the determination of jurisdictional facts from the jury.[10] **{-587-}**

As the defendants concede, each of these constitutional arguments is foreclosed by our binding precedent. First, this Court has held that the MDLEA is a valid exercise of Congress's power under the Felonies Clause as applied to drug trafficking crimes without a "nexus" to the United States. *See Campbell*, 743 F.3d at 809-10, 2 Adm. R. at 548; *see also United States v. Valois*, 915 F.3d 717, 722, 7 Adm. R. 452, 452 (11th Cir.) (following *Campbell* and reaching the same holding), *cert. denied*, 140 S. Ct. 263 (2019); *United States v. Cruickshank*, 837 F.3d 1182, 1187-88, 4 Adm. R. 472, 472–73 (11th Cir. 2016) (following *Campbell* and reaching the same

[10] We review *de novo* a district court's interpretation of a statute and whether a statute is constitutional. *United States v. Valois*, 915 F.3d 717, 722 n.1, 7 Adm. R. 452, 452 n.1 (11th Cir.), *cert. denied*, 140 S. Ct. 263 (2019).

holding); *United States v. Estupinan*, 453 F.3d 1336, 1338-39 (11th Cir. 2006).

Second, this Court has held that the Fifth Amendment's Due Process Clause does not prohibit the trial and conviction of aliens captured on the high seas while drug trafficking because the MDLEA provides clear notice that all nations prohibit and condemn drug trafficking aboard stateless vessels on the high seas. *See United States v. Rendon*, 354 F.3d 1320, 1326 (11th Cir. 2003); *see also Valois*, 915 F.3d at 722, 7 Adm. R. at 452 (following *Rendon* and reaching the same holding). The defendants' MDLEA convictions thus do not violate their due process rights even if their offenses lack a "nexus" to the United States. *See, e.g., United States v.* **[—26—]** *Wilchcombe*, 838 F.3d 1179, 1186 (11th Cir. 2016); *Campbell*, 743 F.3d at 812, 2 Adm. R. at 550.

Third, this Court has held that, because the MDLEA's jurisdictional requirement goes to the subject-matter jurisdiction of the courts and is not an essential element of the MDLEA substantive offense, it does not have to be submitted to the jury for proof beyond a reasonable doubt. *See United States v. Tinoco*, 304 F.3d 1088, 1109-12 (11th Cir. 2002); *see also Valois*, 915 F.3d at 722, 7 Adm. R. at 452 (following *Tinoco* and reaching the same holding); *Cruickshank*, 837 F.3d at 1192, 4 Adm. R. at 476 (following *Tinoco* and reaching the same holding); *Campbell*, 743 F.3d at 809, 2 Adm. R. at 547–48 (following *Tinoco* and *Rendon* and reaching the same holding); *Rendon*, 354 F.3d at 1326-28 (following *Tinoco* and reaching the same holding).

The defendants also claim that: (1) the admission of a certification of the U.S. Secretary of State to establish extraterritorial jurisdiction, especially where a vessel is declared "stateless," violates the Confrontation Clause and constitutes inadmissible hearsay; and (2) the certification procedure as to the jurisdictional element violates the Due Process Clause of the Fifth Amendment by allowing an act of foreign omission to substitute for the government's burden of proof on a "material element." *See* 46 U.S.C. § 70502(d)(2) (providing that, when a master or individual in charge makes a claim of registry, the foreign nation may respond "by radio, telephone, or similar oral or electronic means," and the foreign nation's response "is proved conclusively by certification of the Secretary of State or the **[—27—]** Secretary's designee"). Ultimately, the government never introduced a certification from the Secretary of State, and thus we need not address these issues.

In any event, as the government points out, this Court has already held that the introduction of a Secretary of State certification to establish extraterritorial jurisdiction under the MDLEA does not violate the Confrontation Clause and does not constitute inadmissible hearsay. *See Campbell*, 743 F.3d at 806-08, 2 Adm. R. at 545–47 ("The Confrontation Clause does not bar the admission of hearsay to make a pretrial determination of jurisdiction when that hearsay does not pertain to an element of the offense."); *Cruickshank*, 837 F.3d at 1192, 4 Adm. R. at 476 ("A United States Department of State certification of jurisdiction under the MDLEA does not implicate the Confrontation **{-588-}** Clause because it does not affect the guilt or innocence of a defendant."); *see also Valois*, 915 F.3d at 722-23, 7 Adm. R. at 453 (following *Campbell* and *Cruickshank* and reaching the same holding). In *Campbell*, we determined that because the stateless nature of the defendant's vessel was not an element of his MDLEA offense to be proved at trial, the admission of the Secretary of State certification did not violate a defendant's right to confront the witnesses against him. 743 F.3d at 806, 2 Adm. R. at 545.[11] **[—28—]**

[11] In his brief, Guagua-Alarcon argues that the MDLEA's certification procedure also violates separation of powers by unconstitutionally delegating the jurisdiction determination to the executive branch, as opposed to the judiciary or the jury. Prior to the 1996 amendment to the MDLEA, this Court held that the MDLEA's certification procedure did not implicate separation of powers. *United States v. Rojas*, 53 F.3d 1212, 1214-15 (11th Cir. 1995), *superseded by statute as recognized in Campbell*, 743 F.3d at 803-04, 2 Adm. R. at 543. We explained that the certification **[—28—]** procedure "merely provide[d] a method by which the Executive Branch [could] evidence that it ha[d]

Based on our binding precedent, we conclude that the defendants have not shown that the MDLEA is unconstitutional.[12]

VI. MDLEA SUBJECT-MATTER JURISDICTION

Guagua-Alarcon and Palacios-Solis contend that, even if the MDLEA is constitutional, the district court erred in concluding that its statutory requirements for subject-matter jurisdiction were met.[13] The government bears the burden of establishing that the statutory requirements of MDLEA subject-matter jurisdiction are met. *Tinoco*, 304 F.3d at 1114. **[—29—]**

As noted above, a vessel is covered by the MDLEA if it is "subject to the jurisdiction of the United States." 46 U.S.C. § 70503(e)(1). Here, the government asserted subject-matter jurisdiction under 46 U.S.C. § 70502(c)(1)(A): that the vessel was "subject to the jurisdiction of the United States" because it was "a vessel without nationality." In § 70502(d)(1), the MDLEA defines "a vessel without nationality" as including each of the following three statutory options: **{–589–}**

> (A) a vessel aboard which the master or individual in charge makes a claim of registry that is denied by the nation whose registry is claimed;
>
> (B) a vessel aboard which the master or individual in charge fails, on request of an officer of the United States authorized to enforce applicable provisions of United States law, to make a claim of nationality or registry for that vessel; and
>
> (C) a vessel aboard which the master or individual in charge makes a claim of registry and for which the claimed nation of registry does not affirmatively and unequivocally assert that the vessel is of its nationality.

Id. § 70502(d)(1)(A)-(C). From the outset, the government invoked jurisdiction over the defendants' vessel under § 70502(d)(1)(B), based on the defendants' failure to make a claim of nationality for the vessel.

Based on the record evidence, we conclude that the government established that the defendants' vessel was a "vessel without nationality" under the § 70502(d)(1)(B) definition and was thus subject to the jurisdiction of the United States under § 70502(c)(1)(A). At trial, the Coast Guard boarding team members **[—30—]** testified that they asked the defendants to identify the

---

obtained a foreign nation's consent to jurisdiction," and that nothing in the procedure "deprive[d] the court of its ability and obligation to determine whether the requirements of the MDLEA ha[d] been met." *Id.* at 1214-15 (explaining that the MDLEA left courts "free to determine, and [t]o decide, whether a proffered certificate [was] sufficient evidence of jurisdiction").

While we have not directly addressed in a published case whether the revised MDLEA statute's certification procedure implicates separation of powers, we have stated that "courts must still determine whether the MDLEA's jurisdictional requirements have been met," regardless of the MDLEA assigning conclusive proof to a certification provided by the Secretary of State or designee. *Wilchcombe*, 838 F.3d at 1186-88; *accord United States v. Mejia*, 734 F. App'x 731, 734-35 (11th Cir.) (unpublished), *cert. denied*, 139 S. Ct. 593 (2018) (rejecting, in dicta, the defendant's separation of powers challenge under *Rojas* and *Wilchcombe* and concluding that "nothing in [§ 70502(d)(2)] deprives the district court of its power to determine whether the MDLEA's jurisdictional requirements have been met"). Ultimately, because the district court did not rely on a Secretary of State certification in finding that the defendants' vessel was subject to the jurisdiction of the United States, we need not rule on Guagua-Alarcon's separation of powers claim.

[12] In a letter notice of supplemental authority, Palacios-Solis argues that the MDLEA is void for vagueness. Because Palacios-Solis failed to raise this issue at all in his brief, he has abandoned it. *See United States v. Jernigan*, 341 F.3d 1273, 1283 n.8 (11th Cir. 2003).

[13] We review *de novo* a district court's interpretation and application of statutory provisions regarding whether the district court has subject-matter jurisdiction. *Tinoco*, 304 F.3d at 1114. However, we review for clear error the district court's factual findings with respect to jurisdiction. *Id.*

master of the vessel and in response the defendants pointed at each other but no one identified himself as the master.

The LRI boarding team then also asked the defendants individually if anyone wished to make a claim of nationality for the vessel, but no one responded.[14] Despite being given two opportunities, the defendants did not produce any nationality documents, did not fly any nation's flags, and did not make any verbal claim of nationality or registry. *Id.* § 70502(e)(1)-(3).

We recognize that, on appeal, Guagua-Alarcon alleges that the defendants verbally claimed Ecuadorian nationality for the vessel, that the Ecuadorian government was unable to confirm the claim, and that, without a Secretary of State certification, the Coast Guard improperly assumed that the vessel was stateless, seized the defendants, and destroyed the vessel. The record evidence, however, does not show that any defendant claimed a nationality in response to the LRI boarding team's questions. Rather, the record shows that the LRI boarding team asked the defendants individually if anyone wished to make a claim of nationality for the vessel and the defendants did not respond. Because the defendants made no **[—31—]** claim of nationality, the statelessness of their vessel is clear under subsection (d)(1)(B), and a Secretary of State certification was unnecessary. *Id.* § 70502(d)(1)(B), (d)(2).[15]

We do acknowledge that the Coast Guard learned that the vessel's last port of **{-590-}** call was Ecuador, found the vessel's Ecuadorian maker's mark, and took an additional step beyond its statutory obligation when it contacted Ecuador to receive its statement of no objection. This courtesy call, however, did not create a nationality claim on behalf of the defendants and their vessel where no master presented himself or actively made a claim of nationality. *See United States v. Obando*, 891 F.3d 929, 933, 938, 6 Adm. R. 442, 444, 448 (11th Cir. 2018) (explaining that, because no crew member made a claim of nationality for their vessel, their vessel was "without nationality" under § 70502(d)(1)(B) even though the Coast Guard "out of an abundance of caution" did more than what was required by the MDLEA by contacting the Ecuadorian government when the vessel's master indicated that a painted flag on the vessel's hull was Ecuadorian); *United States v. Hernandez*, 864 F.3d 1292, 1304, 5 Adm. R. 477, 483 (11th Cir. 2017) (recognizing that, once "the statutory requirements for MDLEA prosecution in U.S. courts have been met . . . any further **[—32—]** jurisdictional complaint over that U.S. prosecution is to be handled by the executive branch, nation-to-nation, in the international arena"). Rather, the vessel remained stateless under § 70502(d)(1)(B).

It also is of no matter that the Coast Guard takes the last port of call as the nationality of the vessel and contacts that corresponding government when no claim is made. Whatever the foreign government's response (or non-response), the Coast Guard's taking of that additional step does not void a statelessness finding under §§ 70502(c)(1)(A) and 70502(d)(1)(B).

Consequently, the defendants' vessel was a "vessel without nationality," 46 U.S.C. § 70502(d)(1), and thus a "vessel subject to the jurisdiction of the United States," *id.* § 70502(c)(1)(A), and therefore a "covered vessel," *id.* § 70503(e)(1), to which the MDLEA's criminal prohibition against possessing a controlled substance with distributary intent extends, *id.* § 70503(a)(1). The district court properly exercised

---

[14] We recognize that the LRI boarding team did not also ask who was "the individual in charge," but the team's questions were nevertheless sufficient because they did ask all defendants if anyone wished to make a claim of nationality for the vessel. As such, any individual who possessed the authority to make a claim of registry or nationality for the vessel was given the opportunity to do so at the request of a duly authorized officer. *See* 46 U.S.C. § 70502(d)(1)(B).

[15] Even so, the defendants' claim that the government must produce a certification when subject-matter jurisdiction is based on subsections (d)(1)(A) or (C) is unsupported by the language of subsection (d)(2). While a certification provides *conclusive* proof of the foreign nation's response, the subsection does not state that the response cannot be proven by other means. *See* 46 U.S.C. § 70502(d)(2).

jurisdiction over the defendants and their offenses under the MDLEA.

VII. DELAY IN GUAGUA-ALARCON'S PRESENTMENT

For the first time on appeal, Guagua-Alarcon argues that his convictions should be vacated because the government deliberately and tactically took seven weeks in order to transport him to Florida—rather than bringing him promptly before a magistrate judge in California, the closest U.S. state—for a probable cause **[—33—]** determination.[16] He asserts that the government purposely delayed his presentment to a magistrate judge in order to forum shop because federal courts in California require the government to prove a U.S. "nexus" to establish subject-matter jurisdiction, whereas federal courts in Florida do not.

Nonetheless, Guagua-Alarcon concedes that we should review his delay challenge for plain error since he raises it for the first time on appeal. Under the plain-error standard, we will vacate a judgment only if there is (1) an error, (2) that is plain, and the error both (3) affected the defendant's substantial rights, and (4) seriously affected the fairness of the judicial proceedings. *United States v. Hernandez*, 906 F.3d 1367, 1370 (11th Cir. 2018); *United States v. Ramirez-Flores*, 743 F.3d 816, 822 (11th Cir. 2014). A defendant cannot prevail on plain-error review "where there is no precedent from the Supreme Court or this Court directly resolving" the issue in favor of the defendant. **{-591-}** *United States v. Lange*, 862 F.3d 1290, 1296 (11th Cir. 2017) (quotation marks omitted).

As a preliminary matter, we note that the MDLEA does not prohibit the government from taking offenders to Florida rather than California. A person violating the MDLEA "may be tried in any district," "if the offense was begun or committed upon the high seas," as was the case here. 46 U.S.C. § 70504(b)(2); *see also* 18 U.S.C. § 3238 (assigning jurisdiction over all offenses committed upon the **[—34—]** high seas to the district in which the offender is arrested or is first brought). Accordingly, the issue here is not *where* the defendant was taken, but *why* it took the government 49 days to present the defendant arrested outside the United States before a magistrate judge in the United States for a probable cause hearing.

In this regard, Rule 5(a)(1)(B) of the Federal Rules of Criminal Procedure expressly provides that "[a] person making an arrest outside the United States must take the defendant *without unnecessary delay* before a magistrate judge, unless a statute provides otherwise." Fed. R. Crim. P. 5(a)(1)(B) (emphasis added). In *Mallory v. United States*, the Supreme Court indicated that the purpose of Rule 5(a) is to prevent oppressive police interrogations and other "third-degree" tactics before bringing the accused in front of an officer of the court; the remedy was the exclusion of evidence which was gained during the delay by the use of such tactics. 354 U.S. 449, 451-54, 77 S. Ct. 1356, 1357-59 (1957); *see McNabb v. United States*, 318 U.S. 332, 345, 63 S. Ct. 608, 615 (1943) ("[T]o permit such evidence to be made the basis of a conviction in the federal courts would stultify the policy which Congress has enacted into law.");[17] *United States v. Mendoza*, 473 F.2d 697, **[—35—]** 702 (5th Cir. 1973) ("A violation of [Rule 5(a)] renders the evidence obtained *per se* inadmissible.").[18]

In *United States v. Purvis*, this Court expressly addressed "unnecessary delay"

[16] Only Guagua-Alarcon makes this delay claim on appeal.

[17] The *McNabb-Mallory* exclusionary rule—under which an arrestee's confession, whether voluntary or involuntary, is inadmissible if given after an unreasonable delay in bringing him before a judge—was superseded in part by 18 U.S.C. § 3501, which immunizes voluntary confessions given within six hours of a suspect's arrest. *See Corley v. United States*, 556 U.S. 303, 306-11, 322, 129 S. Ct. 1558, 1562-64, 1571 (2009). The Supreme Court in *Corley* held that Congress intended merely to modify *McNabb-Mallory*'s exclusionary rule, rather than supplant it, when it enacted § 3501. *Id.* at 306, 322, 129 S. Ct. at 1562, 1571.

[18] This Court adopted as binding precedent all Fifth Circuit decisions prior to October 1, 1981. *Bonner v. City of Prichard*, 661 F.2d 1206, 1209 (11th Cir. 1981) (en banc).

under Rule 5(a)(1)(B). 768 F.2d 1237, 1238-39 (11th Cir. 1985). This Court held that various factors are considered in determining whether a delay was unnecessary, including: (1) the distance between the location of the defendant's arrest in international waters and the U.S. port he was brought to; (2) the time between the defendant's arrival at the U.S. port and his presentment to the magistrate judge; (3) any evidence of mistreatment or improper interrogation during the delay; and (4) any reason for the delay, like exigent circumstances or emergencies. *Id.*

Here, the timeline and location of defendant Guagua-Alarcon's arrest are not disputed. Guagua-Alarcon was brought onboard the *Hamilton* cutter on October 25, and the cutter was located 200-plus miles off the coast of Guatemala/El Salvador. On December 12, Guagua-Alarcon made his first entry into the Key West port. On December 13, he was presented for his initial appearance before a magistrate **{-592-}** judge. There was a 49-day delay between Guagua-Alarcon's arrest and his presentment. **[—36—]**

As to the first *Purvis* factor, the distance between the arrest location outside the United States and Key West was quite lengthy. As to the second *Purvis* factor, Guagua-Alarcon arrived at Key West on December 12 and was presented immediately to the magistrate judge on December 13. As to the third *Purvis* factor, there is no claim that Guagua-Alarcon was mistreated or improperly interrogated during transit. Thus, the first, second, and third *Purvis* factors arguably help the government.

As to the fourth *Purvis* factor, the problem for Guagua-Alarcon is that he did not raise this delay issue below, much less claim the delay was "unnecessary," and thus he has presented no evidence (at trial or a pretrial hearing) indicating the reasons or circumstances behind the delay. Guagua-Alarcon's allegation that the government deliberately and tactically delayed in order to forum shop is pure speculation and unsupported by any record evidence.[19] By failing to develop the factual predicates for his claim in the district court, Guagua-Alarcon has failed to carry his burden to show the particular delay here was "unnecessary" and thus a Rule 5(a) violation.[20] **[—37—]**

Given this problem, Guagua-Alarcon argues that we should remand for an evidentiary hearing, but such further hearing and fact finding at this point in the proceedings would undermine the plain-error doctrine. *See United States v. Bonavia*, 927 F.2d 565, 570 (11th Cir. 1991) ("We note that the plain error doctrine should be applied sparingly lest the contemporaneous objection rule, requiring timely objections to preserve issues for appeal, be swallowed by the plain error exception.").

In any event, Guagua-Alarcon points to no controlling precedent from the Supreme Court or the Eleventh Circuit establishing that a 49-day delay, no matter the circumstances of this interdiction on the high seas 200 miles off the coast of Guatemala/El Salvador, presumptively constitutes "unnecessary delay" under Rule 5(a). In other MDLEA cases, this Court has concluded that delays, albeit shorter ones,

---

[19] Guagua-Alarcon argues that California was closer to the location of his arrest than Florida. There is no record evidence regarding the distances between Guagua-Alarcon's arrest and those U.S. states. Because of the Panama Canal route, geographical calculations are needed to reveal the distances.

[20] The government (without evidence too) asserts that the delay could have been caused by any number of valid reasons, such as the Coast Guard opting to continue their normal law enforcement patrolling activities through the conclusion of their mission, "diplomatic wrangling" **[—37—]** between the U.S. and Ecuadorian governments, a mechanical mishap, or some other emergency. In short, both Guagua-Alarcon and the government speculate as to the cause of the delay.

However, on appeal, Guagua-Alarcon has moved to vacate his convictions based on "unnecessary delay" under Rule 5(a), and thus he as movant has the burden to establish the delay was "unnecessary." Yet, he has not developed the required factual predicate to do so. To be clear, our ruling is based on the lack of evidence or factual predicate for the "unnecessary delay" claim, not on the merits of the claim.

were reasonable. *See Purvis*, 768 F.2d at 1239 (holding that a five-day delay was reasonable for defendants arrested on the high seas approximately 350 miles from Key West); *United States v. Odom*, 526 F.2d 339, 342-43 (5th Cir. 1976) (holding that a five-day delay was reasonable for a defendant arrested on the high **[—38—]** seas approximately 200 miles from the United States); *see also* **{-593-}** *United States v. Castillo*, 899 F.3d 1208, 1217-18, 6 Adm. R. 463, 469–70 (11th Cir. 2018) (Martin, J., concurring) (discussing Rule 5(a)(1)(B) and determining that a 19-day delay was reasonable for a defendant arrested off of "[t]he Pacific coast of Guatemala," "approx.-imately 1,000 miles from the port of Miami"), *cert. denied*, 139 S. Ct. 796 (2019).[21] No case, however, has addressed a 49-day delay or held what circumstances or reasons would make such a delay unnecessary. Because no Supreme Court or Eleventh Circuit precedent has ruled whether a delay in presentment similar to Guagua-Alarcon's was "unnecessary delay" under Rule 5(a), Guagua-Alarcon has failed to show plain error.

Despite Rule 5(a), Guagua-Alarcon asserts that his case is controlled by the constitutional, 48-hour rule established by the Supreme Court in *County of Riverside v. McLaughlin*, 500 U.S. 44, 111 S. Ct. 1661 (1991). Prior to *McLaughlin*, the Supreme Court held that "the Fourth Amendment requires a timely judicial determination of probable cause as a prerequisite to detention." *Gerstein v. Pugh*, 420 U.S. 103, 126, 95 S. Ct. 854, 869 (1975). Then, in *McLaughlin*, the Supreme Court ruled that "a jurisdiction that provides judicial determinations of probable cause within 48 hours of arrest will, as a general matter, **[—39—]** comply with the promptness requirements of *Gerstein*." *McLaughlin*, 500 U.S. at 56, 111 S. Ct. at 1670.

Guagua-Alarcon contends *McLaughlin* established a per se 48-hour outer-limit rule and thus his detention violated the Fourth Amendment. However, *McLaughlin* did not establish 48 hours as a per se outer limit. *See id.* at 56, 111 S. Ct. at 1670 ("[W]e hesitate to announce that the Constitution compels a specific time limit."). Rather, in *McLaughlin*, the Supreme Court held that, generally, when a probable cause determination does not happen within 48 hours, "the burden shifts to the government to demonstrate the existence of a bona fide emergency or other extraordinary circumstance." *Id.* at 47, 56, 111 S. Ct. at 1665, 1670; *Powell v. Nevada*, 511 U.S. 79, 83-84, 114 S. Ct. 1280, 1283 (1994). Again, because Guagua-Alarcon did not raise his *McLaughlin* claim in the district court, we must review his *McLaughlin* claim too for plain error.

Here, Guagua-Alarcon has not shown error, much less plain error, because the Fourth Amendment does not apply to searches and seizures (arrests) by the United States of a non-citizen/non-resident alien *arrested in international waters or a foreign country*. *See United States v. Verdugo-Urquidez*, 494 U.S. 259, 274-75, 110 S. Ct. 1056, 1066 (1990) (holding that the Fourth Amendment protects only "the people" of the United States and has no application to search-and-seizure challenges where the challenger is a non-citizen/non-resident alien with no **[—40—]** voluntary attachment to the United States and the area searched is located outside of the United States);[22] *United States v. Vilches-Navarrete*, 523 F.3d 1, 13 (1st Cir. 2008) (applying *Verdugo-Urquidez* and holding the district court **{-594-}** properly dismissed the MDLEA defendant's Fourth Amendment claim regarding the U.S. Coast Guard's actions because the defendant was Chilean, he was not residing in the United States, and the Coast Guard's actions occurred in

---

[21] The majority in *Castillo* held that the defendant's guilty plea waived his right to challenge his detention and did not address the Rule 5(a) issue. 899 F.3d at 1214-15, 6 Adm. R. at 466.

[22] The Supreme Court explained in *Verdugo-Urquidez* that, "[t]here is likewise no indication that the Fourth Amendment was understood by contemporaries of the Framers to apply to activities of the United States directed against aliens in foreign territory or in international waters." 494 U.S. at 267, 110 S. Ct. at 1061. Rather, "aliens receive constitutional protections when they have come within the territory of the United States and developed substantial connections with this country." *Id.* at 271, 110 S. Ct. at 1064.

international waters); *United States v. Bravo*, 489 F.3d 1, 8-9 (1st Cir. 2007) (holding the district court properly denied the MDLEA defendants' motion to suppress evidence seized from their vessel because, under *Verdugo-Urquidez*, "the Fourth Amendment does not apply to activities of the United States against aliens in international waters"); *United States v. Zakharov*, 468 F.3d 1171, 1179-80 (9th Cir. 2006) (holding that, because the alleged unconstitutional delay took place outside of the United States in international waters and there was no suggestion that Zakharov, as neither a U.S. citizen nor U.S. resident, had any substantial connection to this country, the Fourth Amendment did not apply to him and his claim); *see also United States v. Rojas*, 812 F.3d 382, 388, 397-98 (5th Cir. 2016) (holding that, under *Verdugo-Urquidez*, the defendants—Colombian citizens and residents—had no Fourth Amendment **[—41—]** protections to challenge the admission of wiretap conversations, which were recorded in Colombia, in their drug trafficking prosecutions under 21 U.S.C. §§ 959, 960, and 963).

While not in a drug trafficking case under the MDLEA, this Court similarly has applied the *Verdugo-Urquidez* rule in drug trafficking cases brought against non-resident aliens. *See, e.g., United States v. Valencia-Trujillo*, 573 F.3d 1171, 1173, 1182-83 (11th Cir. 2009) (holding that, under *Verdugo-Urquidez*, "[t]he Fourth Amendment . . . does not apply to actions against foreign citizens on foreign soil" and thus a non-resident alien charged with drug smuggling crimes could not challenge on Fourth Amendment grounds the district court's denial of an evidentiary hearing in which he sought to invalidate his arrest and involuntary extradition in Colombia);[23] *United States v. Emmanuel*, 565 F.3d 1324, 1332 (11th Cir. 2009) (holding, in a drug trafficking case, that "[t]he Fourth Amendment exclusionary rule does not apply to the interception of wire communications in the Bahamas of a Bahamian resident").

In this drug trafficking case under the MDLEA, we too must follow *Verdugo-Urquidez* and conclude that defendant Guagua-Alarcon, who is a non-U.S. citizen and non-U.S. resident, and who has no significant connection to the **[—42—]** United States, cannot challenge under the Fourth Amendment and *McLaughlin* the Coast Guard's conduct in taking 49 days on the high seas outside of the United States to transport him to Florida for presentment to the magistrate judge.[24] Rather, the correct analytical framework for Guagua-Alarcon's delay-in-presentment challenge is under Rule 5(a) and the *Purvis* factors as outlined above. Thus, Guagua-Alarcon has shown no plain error to establish his Fourth Amendment and *McLaughlin* claims.[25] **{-595-}**

VIII. DEFENDANTS' POST-ARREST, PRE-*MIRANDA* SILENCE

Palacios-Solis argues that the district court erred in denying his motion in limine to preclude the government from presenting

[23] In *Valencia-Trujillo*, this Court added that "[t]he allegedly improper seizure of Valencia-Trujillo occurred in Colombia," and "[b]ecause there can be no violation of our Fourth Amendment in that country, there can be no entitlement to a *Franks* hearing to establish that one occurred there." *Id.* at 1183.

[24] Once Guagua-Alarcon was brought to Florida on December 12, he appeared before a magistrate judge on December 13. The issue here is only about the Coast Guard's conduct in taking 49 days to transport Guagua-Alarcon to Florida (or, as Guagua-Alarcon alleges, deliberately delaying his transit).

[25] In his initial brief, Guagua-Alarcon stated that his remedy for the unreasonable delay in presentment was to vacate his convictions. While we need not, and do not, reach this issue, we note that federal courts have concluded that the remedy for a *McLaughlin* or Rule 5(a) delay-in-presentment violation is suppression of the evidence obtained during the delay, not the vacatur of a conviction. *See Corley*, 556 U.S. at 309, 129 S. Ct. at 1563 (explaining that, generally, confessions made during periods of detention that violate the prompt presentment requirement of Rule 5(a) are rendered inadmissible); *Gerstein*, 420 U.S. at 119, 95 S. Ct. at 865 (explaining the "established rule that illegal arrest or detention does not void a subsequent conviction" and that "a conviction will not be vacated on the ground that the defendant was detained pending trial without a determination of probable cause"); *Mendoza*, 473 F.2d at 702.

evidence of the defendants' post-arrest, pre-*Miranda* silence as "consciousness of guilt."[26]

As Palacios-Solis concedes, this Court's binding precedent forecloses his **[—43—]** argument. Once a defendant is in custody and receives *Miranda* warnings, he indisputably has a Fifth Amendment right to remain silent. *See Oregon v. Elstad*, 470 U.S. 298, 304-05, 311, 105 S. Ct. 1285, 1290-91, 1294 (1985). Yet, the Supreme Court has expressly held that the Fifth Amendment allows the use of a defendant's post-arrest, pre-*Miranda* silence to impeach the defendant. *Brecht v. Abrahamson*, 507 U.S. 619, 628, 113 S. Ct. 1710, 1716 (1993). This Court, in *United States v. Rivera,* went one step further. 944 F.2d 1563, 1568 (11th Cir. 1991). In *Rivera,* this Court held that, in its case-in-chief, the government may use a defendant's post-arrest, pre-*Miranda* silence as direct evidence tending to prove the defendant's guilt. *Id.*

Palacios-Solis points out a circuit split on this issue. This Court has already noted this circuit split in *Wilchcombe* and again upheld our precedent in *Rivera*. *Wilchcombe*, 838 F.3d at 1190-91 ("Whatever the state of the law in other circuits, in our circuit it was permissible for the government to comment on [the defendant's] silence."). Given our precedent, the district court did not abuse its discretion in denying Palacios-Solis's motion in limine on this basis.

IX. SUFFICIENCY OF THE EVIDENCE

As to both counts, Cabezas-Montano and Palacio-Solis argue that there was insufficient evidence to convict them of violating the MDLEA because the government offered no evidence that they were the ones responsible for the drugs **[—44—]** the Coast Guard found floating in the Pacific Ocean two-and-a-half hours after the helicopter initially spotted the target GFV's passengers jettisoning packages.[27] **{-596-}**

To prove the existence of a conspiracy, "the government must establish that an agreement existed between two or more persons and that the defendant knowingly and voluntarily participated in it." *Tinoco*, 304 F.3d at 1122 (quotation marks omitted) (reviewing the sufficiency of the evidence supporting conspiracy and substantive MDLEA convictions). The government may meet its burden using circumstantial evidence. *Id.* While a defendant's presence is not determinative, it is a material factor when weighing evidence of a conspiracy. *Id.* at 1122-23.

The government also may use circumstantial evidence to meet its burden of proving possession of a controlled substance with intent to distribute. *Id.* A defendant's possession may be either actual or constructive. *Id.* A defendant constructively possesses contraband when he exercises some measure of dominion or control over it, either exclusively or in association with others. *Id.* Moreover, we may infer a defendant's intent to distribute from the large quantity of narcotics seized. *Id.* **[—45—]**

As this Court has pointed out, "conspiracy and possession cases involving narcotics-laden vessels present repetitive fact patterns." *Id.* In *Tinoco*, we identified these factors to consider when determining whether a jury reasonably could conclude that a defendant found on the target vessel was guilty of the drug conspiracy and possession charges:

> (1) probable length of the voyage, (2) the size of the contraband shipment, (3) the necessarily close relationship between captain and crew, (4) the obviousness of

---

[26] We review evidentiary rulings for an abuse of discretion. *United States v. Turner*, 474 F.3d 1265, 1275 (11th Cir. 2007).

[27] We review *de novo* whether the record contains sufficient evidence to support the jury's guilty verdict, viewing the evidence in the light most favorable to the government and resolving all reasonable inferences and credibility evaluations in favor of the verdict. *Tinoco*, 304 F.3d at 1122. We will not overturn the jury's verdict "unless no trier of fact could have found guilt beyond a reasonable doubt." *Id.* (quotation marks omitted). The evidence need not "exclude every reasonable hypothesis of innocence or be wholly inconsistent with every conclusion except that of guilt, provided that a reasonable trier of fact could find that the evidence established guilt beyond a reasonable doubt." *Id.* (quotation marks omitted).

> the contraband, and (5) other factors, such as suspicious behavior or diversionary maneuvers before apprehension, attempts to flee, inculpatory statements made after apprehension, witnessed participation of the crew, and the absence of supplies or equipment necessary to the vessel's intended use.

Id. Once the government shows that a large quantity of contraband was present on a vessel, its "remaining burden of showing that the crew knowingly participated in the drug trafficking operation is 'relatively light,'" and can be met by proving any one of the other *Tinoco* factors. *Id.*

In this case, the jury had ample evidence demonstrating that the defendants were guilty of the MDLEA conspiracy and possession crimes. First, the evidence showed that the defendants' vessel was the same GFV the Coast Guard was targeting on the night of October 24. Multiple units of the *Hamilton* cutter monitored and chased the target GFV for almost three hours, stayed in contact with each other and shared coordinate locations throughout this time period, and only lost its visual of the GFV for 31 minutes. The target GFV was a 30-to-35-foot **[—46—]** high-speed vessel with two outboard engines carrying three passengers, and the three defendants and their vessel matched that description. The *Hamilton* crew found the defendants' vessel in the vicinity it had been searching for and chasing the GFV. And, importantly, the *Hamilton* crew neither saw nor heard of any other vessels in the vicinity during the entirety of the interdiction.

Additionally, the results of the Coast Guard's searches of the defendants' vessel and the GPS trackers matched their observations during the chase of the GFV. The FLIR video showed that the GFV's left side engine was emitting less heat than the right side engine, which was consistent with the LRI boarding team's discovery of a wet shirt covering the left engine. The buoys and black line recovered from the water matched those discovered on the defendants' vessel and claimed **{-597-}** by Palacios-Solis. And the trajectories of the GPS trackers on the recovered bales were consistent with the *Hamilton* cutter's and helicopter's coordinate range data for the target GFV as well as the coordinate document found on the defendants' vessel.

Moreover, the defendants' story that they had gone on a four-day fishing trip but had been lost or adrift at sea for about 30 days was contradicted by substantial evidence: (1) the defendants' vessel was a GFV and not a fishing boat; (2) the GFV's bottom side was clean and had no growth; (3) the defendants had no bait, fish, or useable fishing lines onboard; (4) they had a substantial amount of fuel for **[—47—]** a short fishing trip; (5) they had large quantities of food and liquids, which appeared to be fresh; (6) they did not seem happy to see the Coast Guard after being adrift for about 30 days; (7) they needed no medical care and showed no signs of lethargy, extended exposure to the elements, or malnutrition; and (8) a drift analysis showed that their story was impossible based on their claimed starting point, the weather and currents, and the coordinate location of the interdiction.

In short, while the *Hamilton* crew lost a visual of the GFV for 31 minutes, there was a wealth of other evidence establishing that the defendants' later-captured vessel was the observed target GFV which was jettisoning the bales of cocaine.

Second, the evidence also showed that the recovered bales of cocaine were the same ones that were jettisoned by the target GFV, which was the defendants' vessel. While aboard the target GFV, the defendants jettisoned numerous packages overboard during the chase and then the helicopter crew communicated the location of the jettisoned packages by using chemical lights and relaying the coordinate position. Although the OTH crew did not find the jettisoned packages at the specified location, the OTH crew recovered one package of cocaine and a buoy with a black line floating in the water while en route to the location where the defendants' vessel had been visually reacquired. Then, the OTH crew recovered **[—48—]** 24 more bales of cocaine and buoys equipped with GPS trackers after conducting a drift analysis to calculate the likely location of the jettisoned packages given the current and wind movement. And, according to the Coast Guard maritime expert's testimony, the southward location where the *Hamilton* crew searched for and recovered the bales was consistent with information regarding the direction of the GFV.

Once again, the results of the vessel and GPS-tracker searches matched the *Hamilton* crew's observations during the chase of the GFV. The buoys, black line, and brown packing tape wrapped around the cocaine bales matched those discovered on the defendants' vessel. The GPS trackers' trajectories on the recovered bales were consistent with the coordinate range data for the GFV, the coordinate document found on the defendants' vessel, and Palacios-Solis's statement to the LRI boarding team that the defendants' last port of call was in Ecuador. The GPS trackers also showed the sudden stopping and slow drifting of the bales, which is consistent with the defendants jettisoning the bales off the GFV and the bales drifting in the water into the area where the Coast Guard eventually found them.

Still yet, other evidence established the link between the defendants and the recovered bales of drugs. By the time the LRI boarding team boarded the defendants' vessel, it had been wiped down almost entirely with fuel, so as to hide **[—49—]** any remaining evidence of drugs. The defendants appeared visibly concerned when the LRI boarding team began the swabbing process, which revealed that one of the defendants **{-598-}** and the GFV's bow and tiller recently were in contact with trace amounts of cocaine. And, as discussed earlier, the defendants' fishing story was contradicted by substantial evidence.

Although the *Hamilton* crew discovered the bales of cocaine in areas outside of the immediate location where they reacquired sight of the GFV and where they dropped chemical lights, there was plenty of other evidence establishing that these were the packages that the defendants jettisoned off their vessel. In sum, sufficient evidence established that the defendants' vessel was the target GFV and that the recovered cocaine bales were the ones that had been jettisoned from the GFV.

With that established, we now turn to the *Tinoco* factors and why a jury could reasonably find the defendants were involved in a conspiracy to traffic and possess the drugs on their vessel. The size of the contraband shipment is relevant to show: (1) the passengers' knowledge of the contraband's presence on the vessel; (2) the passengers' intent to use the contraband for large-scale distribution, rather than for personal use; and (3) participation in the drug trafficking conspiracy by all the vessel's passengers. *See Tinoco*, 304 F.3d at 1121, 1123 ("The value of the cocaine also was relevant to showing that the cocaine most likely was not for personal consumption, but for large-scale distribution, which went to whether the **[—50—]** appellants acted with an intent to distribute the cocaine."); *United States v. Cruz-Valdez*, 773 F.2d 1541, 1546 (11th Cir. 1985) (explaining that large drug quantities on a small vessel "make it most unlikely that the persons on board will be ignorant of its presence" and that "it is highly improbable that drug smugglers would allow an outsider on board a vessel filled with millions of dollars worth of contraband").

Indeed, the packages jettisoned from the defendants' vessel contained a large amount of cocaine—25 total bales of cocaine collectively weighing 614 kilograms and worth $10 million wholesale. *See United States v. Hernandez*, 864 F.3d 1292, 1304-05, 5 Adm. R. 477, 484 (11th Cir. 2017) (stating that 290 kilograms of cocaine within ten previously jettisoned bales indicated cocaine smuggling). Although the defendants' vessel was carrying a large cocaine shipment, only three crew members were aboard. *See Tinoco*, 304 F.3d at 1123 ("The presence of a large amount of contraband on a small vessel with a small crew evidenced the defendants' knowing participation in the drug smuggling operation."). And, at trial, Palacios-Solis testified and eventually admitted that he was the captain aboard a small 30-to-35-foot vessel for possibly up to ten days, given the GPS tracker evidence. Given the small size of the boat, the few number of crew members, and the large amount of cocaine, that evidence made it reasonable for the jury to find beyond a reasonable doubt that the defendants knew of and agreed to participate in the charged drug conspiracy and possession crimes. **[—51—]**

Yet, the government also proved three other *Tinoco* factors indicative of guilt of the charged crimes: (1) suspicious behavior or diversionary maneuvers before apprehension; (2) attempts to flee; and (3) absence of equipment necessary to the vessel's purported use as a fishing boat. The evidence established that the defendants led the *Hamilton* crew on a two-hour chase, despite the crew's repeated orders and warning shots to signal the vessel to heave to. The defendants covered at least one of their engines to reduce its visibility, restarted their engines and began moving each time the Coast Guard reacquired them, and engaged in evasive, zig-zag movements. The defendants also wiped down their vessel with fuel before the **{-599-}** boarding crew came aboard. And, other than some fishing hooks and knives, there were no usable fishing supplies or equipment aboard.

Ultimately, a jury reasonably could conclude that the defendants were guilty of the drug conspiracy and possession charges given their presence and close proximity on the small GFV for several days, the large amount and high monetary value of the cocaine, their diversionary maneuvers and attempts to flee, and the absence of necessary fishing supplies on their vessel. *Id.* at 1122-23. We thus conclude sufficient evidence supported the defendants' convictions.[28]

X. PALACIOS-SOLIS'S MOTION FOR A MISTRIAL [—52—]

Palacios-Solis argues that the district court abused its discretion in denying his motion for a mistrial based on the government's alleged *Brady* violation for not disclosing the CIC's FLIR video on the *Hamilton* cutter and the fact that Petty Officer Tetzlaff observed critical events as recorded by that video.[29] Palacios-Solis takes issue with Officer Tetzlaff's testimony that he observed on the video that one of the defendants "looked . . . very frantic trying to get the engine fixed."

Palacios-Solis has not shown that the prosecution's failure to disclose this evidence violated his rights under *Brady*. The Supreme Court in *Brady* held that "the suppression by the prosecution of evidence *favorable* to an accused upon request violates due process where the evidence is material either to guilt or to punishment, irrespective of the good faith or bad faith of the prosecution." 373 U.S. at 87, 83 S. Ct. at 1196-97 (emphasis added). Here, Palacios-Solis has not shown that the subject evidence was "favorable" or exculpatory, but concedes that Officer Tetzlaff's testimony about the contents of the CIC's FLIR video was "highly-incriminating" and "contradicted" the defendants' innocent version of events. Palacios-Solis made the same concession when arguing his motion for a mistrial before the district court. Because the purportedly suppressed evidence is neither favorable nor material, Palacios-Solis failed to show a *Brady* violation and **[—53—]** the district court did not abuse its discretion in denying his motion for a mistrial.

XI. SENTENCING

A. Defendants' Presentence Investigation Reports ("PSR")

Cabezas-Montano's and Guagua-Alarcon's PSRs assigned them a base offense level of 38 for Counts 1 and 2, under U.S.S.G. § 2D1.1(a)(5) and (c)(1), because they were responsible for transporting 614 kilograms of cocaine.[30] The PSRs did not apply either an

[28] We recognize that the government stresses that the defendants did not verbally respond when asked the right-of-visit questions and pointed at each other when asked to identify the master of the vessel. However, we need not rely on that evidence to uphold the jury's verdict here.

[29] We review for abuse of discretion the denial of a motion for a mistrial." *Valois,* 915 F.3d at 723 n.2, 7 Adm. R. at 453 n.2.

[30] The base-offense-level paragraph in Guagua-Alarcon's PSR actually states that he was held accountable for "612 kilograms" of cocaine, but this appears to be a typo, as the quantity of cocaine is

aggravating or mitigating role adjustment. Their total offense level of 38 and criminal history category of I yielded an advisory guidelines range of 235 **{-600-}** to 293 months' imprisonment for both counts.

Palacios-Solis's PSR assigned him a base offense level of 38 for Counts 1 and 2, under § 2D1.1(a)(5) and (c)(1), because he too was responsible for transporting 614 kilograms of cocaine.[31] The PSR added a two-level increase for his role as the captain of the vessel and a two-level increase for obstruction of justice by giving false trial testimony about being adrift for about 30 days. The PSR pointed out that Palacios-Solis admitted at trial to being the captain of the vessel. Palacios-Solis's total offense level of 42 and criminal history category of I yielded an advisory guidelines range of 360 months' to life imprisonment for both **[—54—]** counts.

B. Defendants' Objections and Motions for Downward Variance

All defendants filed written objections to their PSRs and then made or expanded upon their objections at the sentencing hearing. All defendants objected to not receiving a two-level minor-role reduction under U.S.S.G. § 3B1.2(b). Palacios-Solis also objected: (1) to the PSR's factual basis, maintaining his innocence; (2) to his two-level aggravating role increase under U.S.S.G. § 2D1.1(b)(3)(C); (3) to his not receiving a two-level reduction under the "safety valve" provision of U.S.S.G. § 5C1.2; and (4) to his receiving the two-level increase for obstruction of justice.

All defendants also moved for downward variances pursuant to 18 U.S.C. § 3553(a), requesting the 120-month statutory mandatory minimum sentence. Guagua-Alarcon highlighted his poverty, poor education, physical disabilities, familial relationships in Ecuador, efforts to support his family, and minor role in the offense. Cabezas-Montano emphasized his age, lack of prior crimes, minor role in the offense, familial relationships in Colombia, and efforts to support his family. Palacios-Solis stressed his "background and characteristics" and the severity of a 360-month sentence. Each defendant made only $80 to $100 a week, lived in poverty, was poorly educated, and had family members in their home countries who depended upon them financially. **[—55—]**

C. Government's Response

In response, the government argued that none of the defendants should receive a minor-role reduction because: (1) they were held accountable only for the quantity of cocaine they jettisoned from their vessel; (2) they jettisoned a huge quantity of cocaine; (3) they each played a vital role in the drug trafficking conspiracy and in attempting to destroy the evidence of their crimes; and (4) their transportation of such a large cocaine shipment was an essential component of their drug trafficking. The government emphasized that Palacios-Solis's role increase applied given his admission that he was the captain. The government stressed that Palacios-Solis was not eligible for the safety-valve relief because he had not provided the government with any information about his offenses and there was no precedent supporting his Fifth Amendment challenge to that requirement for safety-valve relief. And his false trial testimony warranted his obstruction-of-justice increase.

D. Sentencing Hearing

The defendants were sentenced together at a combined hearing. The district court addressed the defendants' arguments as to their alleged minor roles, which largely **{-601-}** overlapped with their arguments for downward variances. Cabezas-Montano and his counsel led these arguments, which were adopted and briefly **[—56—]** expanded upon by Palacios-Solis's and Guagua-Alarcon's attorneys.

The defendants argued that they were the "little guys" in the drug trafficking operation, as they did not own the drugs, package the drugs, make arrangements for the drugs'

---

otherwise documented as "614 kilograms" elsewhere in his PSR.

31 The base-offense-level paragraph of Palacios-Solis's PSR includes the same "612 kilogram" typo as in Guagua-Alarcon's PSR.

transportation or receipt, or make "millions and millions" of dollars off of the drugs' distribution. For example, Cabezas-Montano, as a "little guy," lived in poverty in his home country, only made up to a hundred dollars a week as a career fisherman, and stood to make more money in one week than he'd make in 20 years if he succeeded in this drug trafficking trip. While the defendants were not minor participants with respect to the transported drugs in this case, they were "very small fish in a very large [drug trafficking] pond" with respect to "the real world." While the "little fish" risked long sentences if they got caught, the "big guys" would continue to run the operation and make millions. The defendants also had no decision-making authority within the conspiracy. The defendants did not plan or organize the drug operation but only transported the drugs. They pointed out that the Guidelines reference transporting drugs as an example of conduct that could be eligible for a minor-role reduction.[32]

The government reiterated that the defendants were not entitled to a minor-role reduction because they were entrusted with a large quantity of cocaine, they **[—57—]** evaded the Coast Guard and created a substantial risk to those involved in the interdiction efforts, and they acted together in navigating the vessel and throwing the cocaine overboard.

The district court then engaged in a lengthy colloquy with Cabezas-Montano's counsel regarding his argument that the defendants were just the "little guys" in a larger operation. The district court asked how it would know whether a defendant aboard a vessel was a "little guy" or was a "big guy" representing the owners of the cocaine. Cabezas-Montano stated that those facts would be based on the government's intelligence on particular trafficking organizations or networks, investigation into the particular case, or cooperation of the defendants. Cabezas-Montano argued that the government presented no evidence indicating he was anything other than what he said: a low-income fisherman.

The district court also inquired about deterrence and asked about how much couriers typically make for successfully transporting cocaine. Cabezas-Montano stated that a typical courier could make $20,000 for transporting a load of cocaine, which was a lot more than he made per week back at home. The district court was concerned that an individual like Cabezas-Montano would not be deterred from attempting a successful run given the possible reward. Cabezas-Montano responded that he already was deterred by the remorse of being separated from his family and the guilt of no longer being able to provide for them. He argued that **[—58—]** many people in his home country do not realize the risk they face by transporting drugs and that general deterrence would be better served if he were able to return home and relay what happened to him. Cabezas-Montano reiterated that 120 months was very severe and would be sufficient to deter him. **{-602-}**

Ultimately, the district court was unpersuaded by the defendants' deterrence argument given the number of individuals who make similar trips, some of which are successful and report their successes to their villages. The district court indicated that MDLEA penalties were significant partly because of the harm these drug offenses wreak on our society. The district court concluded: (1) that transportation was a critical role in the drug trafficking industry; (2) that defendants are accountable for their role in the conspiracy that was charged, not in a larger conspiracy that involved drug manufacturers or distributors somewhere else; and (3) that each of the defendants was an essential member of this conspiracy. The district court overruled the defendants' minor-role objections. After hearing from Cabezas-Montano's counsel, the district court denied Cabezas-Montano's downward-variance request.

Palacios-Solis and his counsel went next. The district court overruled Palacios-Solis's objections to the PSR's factual basis, noting that it had heard the trial evidence and found

[32] This is a compilation of the defendants' arguments in their written objections and at sentencing.

that the evidence supported that factual basis. Palacios-Solis again raised his mitigating-role objection, which the district court overruled **[—59—]** as well. Palacios-Solis then raised his objection to the denial of safety-valve relief. Although claiming he met the first four requirements of the safety valve, Palacios-Solis conceded that he did not meet the fifth requirement (to provide the government with information about his offenses), but argued that the fifth requirement violated his right against self-incrimination under the Fifth Amendment. The district court observed that Palacios-Solis did not provide all he knew about the case and lied about his role at trial and in any event controlling precedent foreclosed his Fifth Amendment challenge. The district court overruled the safety-valve objection.

Palacios-Solis also challenged his obstruction-of-justice increase and argued he did not lie at trial. Overruling the objection, the district court found that Palacios-Solis testified about being adrift for about 30 days, that the Coast Guard expert testified that this story was physically impossible, and that there was plenty of evidence that the defendants attempted to conceal and destroy evidence during the chase.

Palacios-Solis also raised his request for a downward variance to the 120-month statutory mandatory minimum sentence. The district court denied his request. After ruling on each of Palacios-Solis's PSR objections, the district court found that his total offense level was 42, his criminal history category was I, and his advisory guidelines range was 360 months to life. **[—60—]**

Guagua-Alarcon and his counsel went last, but noted that his only remaining objection was to not receiving the minor-role reduction, which the district court overruled.[33] The district court found that Guagua-Alarcon's total offense level was 38, his criminal history category was I, and his advisory guidelines range was 235 to 293 months.

E. Counsel's Final Sentencing Arguments

After the defendants' personal allocutions,[34] their counsel presented arguments **{-603-}** for sentences well below the guidelines range. For example, the defendants argued that a shorter term of U.S. imprisonment would better promote general deterrence because they could go home and relay what happened. They also argued that: (1) they came from poverty and had a poor education; (2) the large drug quantity was irrelevant because they had no control over the amount transported; (3) they would not do well in a U.S. prison as non-English speakers with no family or support system here; and (4) a within-guidelines-range sentence would be extreme and unwarranted. Cabeza-Montano's counsel also stressed that, **[—61—]** in two of his other MDLEA cases, his clients had been found guilty after a trial but nevertheless were granted large downward variances and received sentences between 120 and 188 months' imprisonment.

In opposing 120-month sentences, the government argued that sentences must have meaning and that if a defendant goes to trial, loses, and then receives a downward variance to the bare statutory mandatory minimum sentence of 120 months, there would be no incentive for defendants to take responsibility for their criminal actions. The government noted that only one district court judge had granted the downward variances Cabezas-Montano's counsel referred to and that none of the judges in the district who presided over MDLEA cases had ever given a minor-role

---

[33] At this juncture, Guagua-Alarcon did not mention his motion for a downward variance but appeared to assume the district court had already denied his motion too when the district court denied those of Cabezas-Montano and Palacios-Solis.

[34] In allocution, Cabezas-Montano stated that he was concerned about his family's welfare and asked to be deported back to his home country. Palacios-Solis stressed that there was no cocaine found on the defendants' vessel, that they were asleep when the Coast Guard apprehended them, and that he was concerned about his inability to provide for his family, and he asked for mercy. Guagua-Alarcon maintained his innocence, denied being involved with coçaine, and asked to be deported back to his home country to be with his family.

reduction, whether the defendants pled guilty or went to trial. The government emphasized that the defendants' advisory guidelines ranges were reasonable and requested 240-month sentences for Cabezas-Montano and Guagua-Alarcon and at least a 360-month sentence for Palacios-Solis.

F. District Court's Sentences

The district court then addressed the § 3553(a) factors. The district court explained that it had presided over several MDLEA cases in the past and would seek to be consistent with himself, rather than with other judges, especially given the defendants' advisory guidelines ranges in this case. The district court noted: (1) the large quantity of drugs involved in this case; (2) the drugs were valued at **[—62—]** many millions of dollars; (3) there had been an uptick in MDLEA cases recently; and (4) these drug trafficking operations have a profound impact on U.S. communities and law enforcement. The district court observed that, in order to promote respect for the law and to provide deterrence, "the message needs to be sent home to these individuals who are contemplating engaging in this kind of criminal behavior, that the United States intends on doing something about" drug trafficking. The district court explicitly stated that it considered the parties' statements, the PSRs containing the advisory guidelines ranges, and the § 3553(a) factors. The district court determined that, for each defendant, sentences at the lower end of the advisory guidelines range would provide sufficient punishment and deterrence.

The district court sentenced: (1) Cabezas-Montano and Guagua-Alarcon to 240 months' imprisonment, concurrently on both counts; and (2) Palacios-Solis to 360 months' imprisonment, concurrently on both counts. The defendants renewed all prior objections, but made no new objections.

XII. SAFETY-VALVE RELIEF

Turning back to the arguments on appeal, Palacios-Solis and Cabezas-Montano **{–604–}** challenge the constitutionality of the "safety-valve" provisions of 18 **[—63—]** U.S.C. § 3553(f) and U.S.S.G. § 5C1.2.[35] They concede, however, that they are not eligible for safety-valve relief because, at the time of their MDLEA convictions under Title 46, no Title 46 offense was covered by the safety valve in § 3553(f) or § 5C1.2. *See United States v. Pertuz-Pertuz*, 679 F.3d 1327, 1328 (11th Cir. 2012) (holding that, because no Title 46 offense appeared in the plain terms of the safety valve, defendants convicted under Title 46—which includes MDLEA offenses— were not eligible for safety-valve relief).[36]

---

[35] We review *de novo* a district court's interpretation of a statute and whether a statute is constitutional. *Valois*, 915 F.3d at 722 n.1, 7 Adm. R. at 452 n.1.

[36] Congress recently amended § 3553(f) to add MDLEA offenses to the list of crimes eligible for safety-valve relief. *See* First Step Act of 2018, Pub. L. No. 115-391, § 402(a)(1)(A)(ii), 132 Stat. 5194, 5221 (2018). However, Congress made the amendment applicable to convictions entered on or after the date of enactment, December 21, 2018. First Step Act § 402(b), 132 Stat. at 5221. That amendment thus does not apply to the defendants in this case because they were convicted in 2017.

The prior version of § 3553(f) in effect in 2017 provided that, "in the case of an offense under section 401, 404, or 406 of the Controlled Substances Act (21 U.S.C. [§§] 841, 844, 846) or section 1010 or 1013 of the Controlled Substances Import and Export Act (21 U.S.C. [§§] 960, 963), the court shall impose a sentence pursuant to guidelines . . . without regard to any statutory minimum sentence, if the court finds at sentencing, after the Government has been afforded the opportunity to make a recommendation, that" the defendant has met five requirements. 18 U.S.C. § 3553(f) (effective May 27, 2010, to Dec. 20, 2018). Importantly, the fifth requirement was that, "not later than the time of the sentencing hearing, the defendant has truthfully provided to the Government all information and evidence the defendant has concerning the offense or offenses that were part of the same course of conduct or of a common scheme or plan." *Id.* § 3553(f)(5).

Similarly, § 5C1.2 provides that, "in the case of an offense under 21 U.S.C. § 841, § 844, § 846, § 960, or § 963, the court shall impose a sentence in accordance with the applicable guidelines without regard to any statutory minimum sentence, if the court finds that the defendant meets the criteria in 18 U.S.C. § 3553(f)(1)-(5)." U.S.S.G. § 5C1.2(a). Both provisions are known as the "safety valve." *United States v. Johnson*, 375 F.3d 1300, 1302 (11th Cir. 2004).

Further, this Court has held that the safety valve's prior exclusion of Title 46 defendants does not violate the Fifth Amendment's Equal Protection Clause. **[—64—]** *Castillo*, 899 F.3d at 1212-13, 6 Adm. R. at 464–65; *see also Valois*, 915 F.3d at 729, 7 Adm. R. at 458 (following *Castillo* and reaching the same holding). In doing so, we applied rational-basis review and concluded that Congress had "legitimate reasons to craft strict sentences for violations of the [MDLEA]." *Castillo*, 899 F.3d at 1213, 6 Adm. R. at 465. We highlighted the "pressing concerns about foreign relations and global organizations" and the difficulties inherent in policing "drug trafficking on the vast expanses of international waters." *Id.*, 6 Adm. R. at 465. Palacio-Solis's and Cabezas-Montano's equal-protection challenges to the safety-valve thus are foreclosed by *Castillo*.

Palacio-Solis and Cabezas-Montano also contend that the safety-valve's fifth requirement—that defendants provide information to the government about their offenses—violates their Fifth Amendment right against self-incrimination. "[T]his Court has not addressed in a published opinion this Fifth Amendment issue as to the safety valve." *See Valois*, 915 F.3d at 730, 7 Adm. R. at 459. In *Valois*, we briefly discussed the issue but ultimately did not decide it. *Id.*, 7 Adm. R. at 459. Namely, we pointed out that, in *United States v. Henry*, 883 F.2d 1010, 1011 (11th Cir. 1989), this Court concluded that "U.S.S.G. § 3E1.1, the acceptance-of-responsibility provision of the Guidelines, does not violate the Fifth Amendment **{-605-}** right against self-incrimination." *Valois*, 915 F.3d at 730, 7 Adm. R. at 459 (explaining that "[s]ection 3E1.1(a) is not a punishment; rather, the reduction for acceptance of responsibility is a reward for those defendants who express genuine remorse for their criminal conduct" (quotation marks omitted)). **[—65—]** We also pointed out that "[s]everal of our sister circuits have concluded that the same is true for the safety valve in 18 U.S.C. § 3553(f) and U.S.S.G. § 5C1.2(a)." *Id.*, 7 Adm. R. at 459 (citing *United States v. Warren*, 338 F.3d 258, 266-67 (3d Cir. 2003); *United States v. Cruz*, 156 F.3d 366, 374 (2d Cir. 1998); *United States v. Washman*, 128 F.3d 1305, 1307 (9th Cir. 1997); *United States v. Arrington*, 73 F.3d 144, 149-50 (7th Cir. 1996)).

Nevertheless, in *Valois*, we declined to decide the issue given our conclusions that safety-valve relief was unavailable to the Title 46 MDLEA defendants in that case and that such unavailability did not violate the Equal Protection Clause and is constitutional. *Id.*, 7 Adm. R. at 459. Similarly, here, because Palacio-Solis and Cabezas-Montano are not eligible for safety-valve relief in the first place, we need not consider these defendants' claim that the substantive requirements for safety-valve relief violate their Fifth Amendment right against self-incrimination. *See id.*, 7 Adm. R. at 459.

XIII. PROCEDURAL AND SUBSTANTIVE REASONABLENESS

All defendants raise various procedural and substantive reasonableness arguments related to their sentences. Generally, we review the reasonableness of a sentence under a deferential abuse-of-discretion standard using a two-step process. *United States v. Pugh*, 515 F.3d 1179, 1190 (11th Cir. 2008). First, we look at whether the district court committed any significant procedural error, such as **[—66—]** miscalculating the advisory guidelines range, treating the guidelines as mandatory, failing to consider the § 3553(a) factors, selecting a sentence based on clearly erroneous facts, or failing to explain adequately the chosen sentence.[37] *Id.* Then, we examine whether the sentence is substantively unreasonable in light of the § 3553(a) factors and the totality of the circumstances. *Id.* The defendants, as the parties challenging their sentences, bear the

[37] The § 3553(a) factors include, of relevance: (1) the nature and circumstances of the offense and the history and characteristics of the defendant; (2) the need to reflect the seriousness of the offense, to promote respect for the law, and to provide just punishment for the offense; (3) the need for deterrence; (4) the need to protect the public from the defendant's future crimes; (5) the sentencing guidelines range; and (6) the need to avoid unwarranted sentence disparities. 18 U.S.C. § 3553(a)(1)-(2), (4), (6).

burden to show that their sentences are unreasonable. *Id.* at 1189.

A. Minor-Role Reduction

All three defendants argue that the district court erred in denying them a two-level minor-role reduction under U.S.S.G. § 3B1.2(b).[38]

Section 3B1.2(b) provides that a defendant is entitled to a two-level decrease in **{–606–}** his offense level if he was a "minor participant in any criminal activity." U.S.S.G. § 3B1.2(b). A defendant is a "minor participant" if he was "less culpable **[—67—]** than most other participants in the criminal activity," but his role "could not be described as minimal." *Id.* § 3B1.2, cmt. n.5. In determining whether a defendant is entitled to a minor-role reduction, the district court must consider the totality of the circumstances and the facts of the particular case. *Id.* § 3B1.2, cmt. n.3(C).

In *United States v. De Varon*, this Court established two principles to "guide the determination of whether a defendant played a minor role in the criminal scheme: (1) 'the defendant's role in the relevant conduct for which [he] has been held accountable at sentencing,' and (2) '[his] role as compared to that of other participants in [his] relevant conduct.'" *United States v. Presendieu*, 880 F.3d 1228, 1249 (11th Cir. 2018) (quoting *United States v. De Varon*, 175 F.3d 930, 940 (11th Cir. 1999) (en banc)). "In making the ultimate finding as to role in the offense, the district court should look to each of these principles and measure the discernable facts against them." *De Varon*, 175 F.3d at 945.

In *De Varon*, this Court pointed to these examples of relevant factors for the district court to consider in the drug courier context: "amount of drugs, fair market value of drugs, amount of money to be paid to the courier, equity interest in the drugs, role in planning the criminal scheme, and role in the distribution." *Id.* (stressing that this is a non-exhaustive list, wherein no one factor is more important than another). This determination is highly fact-intensive and "falls within the sound discretion of the trial court." *Id.* **[—68—]**

The amended commentary to § 3B1.2 presents a non-exhaustive list of factors "[s]imilar to the fact-intensive, multi-faceted approach this Court established in *De Varon*." *Presendieu*, 880 F.3d at 1249; *see also Cruickshank*, 837 F.3d at 1193, 4 Adm. R. at 478 (explaining that the purpose of Amendment 794 to the commentary to § 3B1.2 was to "further clarify the factors for a court to consider for a minor-role adjustment" in a way that "still continue[s] to embrace the approach we took in *De Varon*"). These factors include: (1) "the degree to which the defendant understood the scope and structure of the criminal activity"; (2) "the degree to which the defendant participated in planning or organizing the criminal activity"; (3) "the degree to which the defendant exercised decision-making authority or influenced the exercise of decision-making authority"; (4) "the nature and extent of the defendant's participation in the commission of the criminal activity"; and (5) "the degree to which the defendant stood to benefit from the criminal activity." U.S.S.G. Supp. to App. C, Amend. 794; U.S.S.G. § 3B1.2, cmt. n.3(C) (2015).

"The court must consider all of [the § 3B1.2] factors to the extent applicable, and it commits legal error in making a minor role decision based solely on one factor." *Valois*, 915 F.3d at 732, 7 Adm. R. at 460–61 (quotation marks omitted); *see, e.g.*, *Cruickshank*, 837 F.3d at 1194-95, 4 Adm. R. at 479 (concluding that, "although nothing in

[38] We review a district court's denial of a role reduction for clear error." *Valois*, 915 F.3d at 730 n.8, 7 Adm. R. at 459 n.8. This Court will not disturb a district court's findings regarding the denial of a role reduction "unless we are left with a definite and firm conviction that a mistake has been made." *Id.* at 731, 7 Adm. R. at 460. "The court's choice between two permissible views of the evidence will rarely constitute clear error, so long as the basis of the trial court's decision is supported by the record and the court did not misapply a rule of law." *Id.*, 7 Adm. R. at 460. The defendant bears the burden of establishing, by a preponderance of the evidence, his minor role in the offense. *Id.*, 7 Adm. R. at 460.

De Varon or Amendment 794 [to § 3B1.2's commentary] precludes a district court from **[—69—]** considering the drug quantity with which the defendant was involved as an indicator of his role, we think it was legal error for the district court to say that this is the *only* factor to be considered in a case like this one").

Here, based on the totality of the circumstances, the district court did not clearly err in denying the defendants' request for a minor-role reduction. Under *De Varon*'s first principle, the inquiry is whether the defendant "played a relatively **{-607-}** minor role in the conduct for which [he] has already been held accountable—not a minor role in any larger criminal conspiracy." *De Varon*, 175 F.3d at 944; *United States v. Martin*, 803 F.3d 581, 591 (11th Cir. 2015). The record shows that all three defendants knowingly participated in the illegal transportation of a large quantity of high-purity and high-value cocaine, that they and their transportation roles were important to that scheme, and that they were held accountable for that conduct only. *See* U.S.S.G. § 3B1.2, cmt. n.3(C); *De Varon*, 175 F.3d at 941-43; *see also United States v. Monzo*, 852 F.3d 1343, 1347 (11th Cir. 2017) (considering, as part of the totality of the circumstances, that the defendant "participated in the distribution of high-purity [drugs], . . . that he was responsible only for his direct role in the conspiracy, and that he was important to the scheme").

While these facts do not render the defendants ineligible for the minor-role reduction, they support the district court's denial of the reduction. Further, the fact **[—70—]** that the defendants' transportation roles—moving a large quantity of high-purity cocaine through international waters—were important, and indeed critical, to the drug trafficking scheme was relevant to the fourth factor in § 3B1.2's commentary about the nature of the defendants' participation in the criminal activity. *See* U.S.S.G. § 3B1.2, cmt. n.3(C). That the defendants each were to receive $20,000 for their significant transportation roles showed the defendants stood to benefit from the criminal act, which is the fifth factor in § 3B1.2's commentary. *See id.*

In addition, under *De Varon*'s second principle, the record indicates that none of the defendants were "less culpable than most other participants in the criminal activity." U.S.S.G. § 3B1.2, cmt. n.5. If anything, Palacios-Solis was the most culpable of the three defendants because, as he testified, he was the captain of the vessel. While Cabezas-Montano and Guagua-Alarcon appear to have had less of a role than Palacios-Solis, that fact alone does not make them minor participants. "The fact that a defendant's role may be less than that of other participants engaged in the relevant conduct may not be dispositive of role in the offense, since it is possible that none are minor or minimal participants." *De Varon*, 175 F.3d at 944. Simply put, the three defendants here did not carry their burden to show how they were less culpable than "most other participants" in the criminal activity, as they presented no supporting evidence at trial or at sentencing. *See* U.S.S.G. § 3B1.2, cmt. n.5; *Valois*, 915 F.3d at 731, 7 Adm. R. at 460. **[—71—]**

The defendants do principally argue that they were less culpable than other participants in the larger conspiracy, such as those who recruited and trained the defendants, those who planned the scheme, and those with a financial interest in the drugs. In this vein, the defendants argue that the district court denied them minor-role adjustments solely because the other participants were not charged and the defendants were held accountable only for the drug amounts charged against them.

Subsequent amendments to the Sentencing Guidelines clarify that, "[i]n considering a § 3B1.2 adjustment, a court must measure the defendant's role against the relevant conduct for which the defendant is held accountable at sentencing, whether or not other defendants are charged." *See* U.S.S.G. App. C, Amend. 635, Reason for Amendment. We also recognize the Sentencing Commission's statement, in agreement with our decision in *De Varon*, that "§ 3B1.2 does not automatically preclude a defendant from being considered for a mitigating role adjustment in a case in which the defendant is held accountable under **{–608–}** § 1B1.3 solely for the amount of drugs the defendant personally handled." *See id.*

Nevertheless, the district court is not required to consider the culpability of any *unknown* conspirators or a hypothetical conspiracy. *See De Varon*, 175 F.3d at 944. This Court has explained that the district court should consider "other **[—72—]** participants only to the extent that they are identifiable or discernable from the evidence" and "may consider only those participants who were involved in the relevant conduct attributed to the defendant." *Id.* The trial evidence pointed to only the three defendants as participants involved in the relevant conduct that was attributed to each of them. The defendants submitted no evidence at trial or at sentencing regarding any other co-conspirators, let alone anyone who recruited or trained the defendants, plotted the offense, or owned the drugs. "Despite having the burden of proof, [the defendants] did not put forth evidence showing who else was involved or what their roles were. Without such evidence, the district court could not compare the roles of the other conspirators or 'determine that the defendant[s] w[ere] less culpable than *most other participants* in [their] relevant conduct.'" *See United States v. Wright*, 862 F.3d 1265, 1278 (11th Cir. 2017) (quoting *De Varon*, 175 F.3d at 944).

To the extent that the defendants argue that the district court denied them minor-role reductions on the sole ground that they were being held accountable for only their conduct and the drug amount on their vessel, the record shows that the district court considered not one but several grounds in denying the reduction. *See* U.S.S.G. App. C, Amend. 635, Reason for Amendment; *Valois*, 915 F.3d at 732, 7 Adm. R. at 460–61. During the sentencing colloquy, Cabezas-Montano's counsel argued and the district court considered: (1) the defendants' argument that they were just the "little **[—73—]** guys" in a larger operation, rather than, as the district court put it, "big guy[s]" representing the owners of the cocaine; (2) how much money couriers stood to make in these operations; (3) the critical role of transportation within the drug trafficking industry; and (4) that the defendants were being held accountable under § 1B1.3 solely for the amount of drugs they personally handled. This discussion related to numerous factors outlined by *De Varon* and the commentary to § 3B1.2, and the defendants have failed to show that any of these factors was improper. *See* U.S.S.G. § 3B1.2, cmt. n.3(C); *De Varon*, 175 F.3d at 945.

Based on the totality of the circumstances and the record in this case, the district court did not clearly err in denying the defendants minor-role reductions under § 3B1.2.

B. 18 U.S.C. § 3553(c)(1)

Cabezas-Montano and Palacios-Solis argue that the district court procedurally erred under 18 U.S.C. § 3553(c)(1) because it "gave no indication or explanation" as to why it chose a sentence at the particular point in the advisory guidelines range or as to why a sentence at the low-end of that range was sufficient.[39] Under § 3553(c)(1), a district court "at the time of sentencing, shall state in open court the reasons for its imposition of the particular sentence." 18 **[—74—]** U.S.C. § 3553(c)(1). In doing so, the district court should "tailor its comments to show that the sentence imposed **{–609–}** is appropriate" in light of the § 3553(a) factors. *United States v. Bonilla*, 463 F.3d 1176, 1181 (11th Cir. 2006) (quotation marks omitted).

That said, the district court is not required to incant specific language or articulate its consideration of each individual § 3553(a) factor, so long as the whole record reflects the district court's consideration of the § 3553(a) factors. *Id.* at 1181-82. When the district court fails to mention the § 3553(a) factors, we look to the record to see if the district court did, in

---

[39] We review *de novo* whether the district court's explanation of its sentence complied with § 3553(c)(1), regardless of whether the defendant objected on such grounds at sentencing. *United States v. Bonilla*, 463 F.3d 1176, 1181 (11th Cir. 2006); *United States v. Williams*, 438 F.3d 1272, 1274 (11th Cir. 2006).

fact, consider the relevant factors. *See United States v. Dorman*, 488 F.3d 936, 944 (11th Cir. 2007). When pronouncing its chosen sentence, the district court need only set forth enough to satisfy us that it considered the parties' arguments and had a reasoned basis for exercising its own legal decisionmaking authority. *United States v. Carpenter*, 803 F.3d 1224, 1232 (11th Cir. 2015).

Here, the record shows that the district court provided a sufficient explanation of its imposed sentences under § 3553(c)(1). Before pronouncing its sentences, the district court judge expressly articulated that it had considered the parties' arguments, the PSRs containing the advisory guidelines ranges, and the § 3553(a) factors. In the downward-variance arguments before the district court, the parties had also discussed the majority of the § 3553(a) factors—namely, the **[—75—]** nature and circumstances of the offenses, the defendants' histories and characteristics, the advisory guidelines ranges, and the needs for deterrence, to reflect the seriousness of the offenses, to protect the public, and to promote respect for the law. Though the district court did not discuss the defendants' individual circumstances, the district court stated it had considered the parties' arguments and the PSRs, both of which contained discussions of the defendants' individual circumstances. That is sufficient. *See Bonilla*, 463 F.3d at 1181; *United States v. Irey*, 612 F.3d 1160, 1194-95 (11th Cir. 2010) (en banc) (explaining that the district court need not discuss each individual factor on the record).

In fact, the district court provided a sufficiently in-depth explanation of its sentences, explicitly highlighting several § 3553(a) factors, including: (1) the sentences given in other recent MDLEA cases in comparison to the applicable advisory guidelines ranges; (2) the seriousness of the defendants' drug trafficking crime, which involved a large quantity of drugs with high monetary value; and (3) the needs to promote respect for the law, to protect the public, and for deterrence, given the recent uptick in MDLEA cases and their profound impact on communities and law enforcement. The district court stated that low-end guidelines range sentences would provide sufficient punishment and deterrence and sentenced Cabezas-Montano to 240 months' imprisonment (towards the bottom of the applicable 235-to-293-months advisory guide-lines range) and **[—76—]** Palacios-Solis to 360 months' imprisonment (at the very bottom of the applicable 360-months-to-life advisory guide-lines range).

Therefore, the district court complied with § 3553(c)(1)'s mandate to "state in open court the reasons for its imposition of the particular sentence." 18 U.S.C. § 3553(c)(1). Cabezas-Montano and Palacios-Solis have not shown that the district court erred in explaining their sentences. *See Pugh*, 515 F.3d at 1190; *Bonilla*, 463 F.3d at 1181.

C. Denial of Downward Variances

All defendants argue that, in denying their motions for a downward variance, the district court erroneously considered that they exercised their right to trial, thereby unconstitutionally penalizing them for exercising **{–610–}** this right and violating § 3553(a). The defendants allege that their decision to go to trial was the determining factor in the district court's decision to impose high sentences.

Generally, when a district court recognizes its authority to grant a variance, we review for abuse of discretion its decision not to grant a downward variance. *United States v. Cubero*, 754 F.3d 888, 897-98 & 897 n.8 (11th Cir. 2014). However, while the defendants moved for downward variances below, none raised any argument regarding the district court's alleged reliance on their exercise of their right to trial in denying the motions. Thus, their new challenge on appeal is reviewed for plain error. *See Ramirez-Flores*, 743 F.3d at 822. **[—77—]**

"[T]he district court has considerable discretion in deciding whether the § 3553(a) factors justify a variance and the extent of such a variance." *United States v. Croteau*, 819 F.3d 1293, 1309 (11th Cir. 2016). "We give that decision due deference because the district court has an institutional advantage in making sentencing determinations." *Cubero*, 754 F.3d at 892 (quotation marks omitted).

Here, the record shows no error regarding the district court's denial of the defendants' downward-variance motions, let alone any plain error affecting their substantial rights. Cabezas-Montano and Guagua-Alarcon have not shown any error because, in denying their specific downward-variance motions, the district court never mentioned that they exercised their right to trial. Rather, in denying their motions, the district court: (1) rejected the defendants' argument that they were just the "little guys" in a larger operation; (2) rejected their argument that they and/or other couriers would be deterred from making future trafficking trips when the possible reward for a successful trip was so high; (3) noted that MDLEA penalties were significant because of the harm drug offenses wreak on society; and (4) found that each defendant was an essential member of the conspiracy.

It was not until Palacios-Solis raised his downward-variance argument—several pages of transcript after Cabeza-Montano's and Guagua-Alarcon's motions already were denied—that the district court made the complained-of comments. In denying Palacios-Solis's downward-variance motion, the district court commented: **[—78—]**

> Also, the motion for a downward variance, I think we're treading on some difficult waters if we come in and say—I mean, I think every defendant has an absolute right to go to trial and exercise it and understand what the consequences are.
>
> But what I'm hearing from you and others in these types of cases is that the guideline amount of time is just a lot of time; so why not just give us the mandatory-minimum every time. So let us have two bites at the apple: Let us go to trial and maybe we'll be acquitted, we can all go home. And sometimes we have acquittals in these cases and sometimes we have mistrials.
>
> But if we don't get acquitted, then at least give us the minimum-mandatory with a downward departure so that we can kind of hedge our bets. We want our cake and eat it. We don't want to have to face the guideline sentence. We want to go to trial and hopefully get acquitted. But if we do go to trial and we get convicted, then we want the mandatory-minimum. You know, if we start setting up that precedent, then everybody is going to want to roll the dice with one hand tied behind their back.
>
> Anyway, I don't think a downward departure or variance is justified. **{-611-}**

In making the comments, the district court made no reference to Cabeza-Montano or Guagua-Alarcon, or their motions.

Even if the district court's comments were made in reference to each of the defendants' downward-variance motions, the defendants still have not shown error. The defendants describe the district court's comments as denying their downward-variance motions solely in an effort to punish them for going to trial. The record does not support such a portrayal. Rather, the district court actually acknowledged the defendants' "absolute right to go to trial," and then the remainder of the district **[—79—]** court's comments were its efforts at characterizing the nature of Palacios-Solis's argument for the statutory mandatory minimum sentence. Notably, the district court characterized Palacios-Solis's argument as being that, no matter what, a defendant every time should still receive only the mandatory statutory minimum sentence after trial because the length of the guidelines sentences in these types of drug cases is "just a lot of time." The district court rejected this argument and stated, "Anyway, I don't think a downward departure or variance is justified," indicating that it was denying Palacios-Solis's motion on the merits, just as it had earlier denied Cabeza-Montano's and Guagua-Alarcon's motions on the merits. Thus, given the record as a whole, the defendants have not shown that the district court's denial of their downward-variance motions was an effort to penalize them for going to trial.

D. Substantive Reasonableness

Cabezas-Montano, and Palacios-Solis by adoption, argue that their sentences are substantively unreasonable.[40] Yet, when a district court imposes a sentence within the advisory guidelines range, we ordinarily will expect the sentence to be a reasonable one. *Carpenter*, 803 F.3d at 1234; *United States v. Docampo*, 573 F.3d 1091, 1101 (11th Cir. 2009). Further, a district court may attach great weight to one factor over others, and the weight it attaches to any one factor is committed to **[—80—]** its sound discretion. *United States v. Rosales-Bruno*, 789 F.3d 1249, 1254 (11th Cir. 2015).

Under the abuse-of-discretion standard, we will vacate a sentence on substantive reasonableness grounds only if "we are left with the definite and firm conviction that the district court committed a clear error of judgment in weighing the § 3553(a) factors by arriving at a sentence that lies outside the range of reasonable sentences dictated by the facts of the case." *Irey*, 612 F.3d at 1190 (quotation marks omitted). We will not "set aside a sentence merely because we would have decided that another one is more appropriate" and we ensure only that the district court's sentence is a reasonable one. *Id.* at 1191.

Here, Cabezas-Montano's 240-month sentence falls near the bottom of the 235-to-293-months advisory guidelines range, a strong indication of reasonableness. *See Carpenter*, 803 F.3d at 1234; *Docampo*, 573 F.3d at 1101. Similarly, Palacios-Solis's 360-month sentence falls at the very bottom of the 360-months-to-life advisory guidelines range, also suggesting reasonableness. *See id.* Nevertheless, they argue that their within-guidelines-range sentences are still substantively unreasonable because the district court considered only the seriousness of the defendants' offenses and the need to promote general deterrence and failed to consider (1) their individual histories and circumstances, and (2) the sentences imposed by different judges **{-612-}** on similarly situated defendants in Cabezas- **[—81—]** Montano's counsel's other MDLEA cases.

While the district court did not expressly discuss these defendants' individual histories and circumstances, the record belies their assertion that it did not *consider* them. As outlined above, the district court explicitly considered the defendants' PSRs and downward-variance arguments, and it also heard their allocutions, all of which reflected their individual histories and characteristics. Namely, Cabezas-Montano and Palacios-Solis highlighted their familial relationships in Colombia and Ecuador, guilt and remorse from being separated from their family members, poverty, efforts to support their families as low-income fishermen, lack of prior crimes, and alleged minor roles in the offense. Similarly, the district court heard Cabezas-Montano's counsel's arguments regarding the large downward variances received by purported similarly situated MDLEA defendants in his other cases, heard the government's opposing argument that only one district court judge had granted those large downward variances, and even asked the parties clarifying questions about those other cases. The district court was not required to discuss these factors in more detail. *See Irey*, 612 F.3d at 1194-95.

Cabezas-Montano and Palacios-Solis also contend that the district court imposed a within-guidelines-range sentence based on the highest drug quantity and did not meaningfully distinguish their individual conduct from that of a "drug **[—82—]** kingpin." This contention is unsupported, speculative, and ignores that the district court sentenced Cabezas-Montano at the low-end of his applicable advisory guidelines range and his total sentence was 120 months less than his more culpable codefendant, Palacios-Solis, who admitted to being the vessel's captain. And given Palacios-Solis's role as the captain, we cannot say the district court erred in imposing his low-end 360-month guidelines sentence.

[40] The record does not indicate that Guagua-Alarcon has adopted this argument.

While Cabezas-Montano and Palacios-Solis focus on their individual histories and circumstances and the sentences received by purported similarly situated defendants in other MDLEA cases, these are only two factors in the § 3553(a) analysis. *See* 18 U.S.C. § 3553(a)(1), (6). The district court was well within its substantial discretion to weigh more heavily other considerations, like: (1) the applicable advisory guidelines range; (2) the seriousness of the defendants' high-quantity and high-value drug trafficking crime; and (3) the needs to promote respect for the law, to protect the public, and for deterrence, given the prevalence and profound impact of MDLEA cases. *See id.* § 3553(a)(1)-(2), (4); *Rosales-Bruno*, 789 F.3d at 1254.

All in all, Cabezas-Montano and Palacios-Solis have failed to show that "the district court committed a clear error of judgment in weighing the § 3553(a) factors by arriving at a sentence that lies outside the range of reasonable sentences dictated by the facts of [this] case." *See Irey*, 612 F.3d at 1190 (quotation marks omitted). **[—83—]**

XIV. CONCLUSION

For the reasons discussed above, we affirm the defendants' convictions and sentences.

AFFIRMED.

(Reporter's Note: Concurring Opinion follows on p. 396).

[—84—] **{-612-}** **ROSENBAUM,** Circuit Judge, concurring:

I concur in the panel's opinion but write separately to address two points. First, I am deeply troubled that the government took seven weeks between arresting the defendants and bringing them before a magistrate judge for a probable-cause determination. And second, I am concerned **{-613-}** that one of our holdings in *United States v. Rivera*, 944 F.2d 1563, 1568 (11th Cir. 1991), on which the panel opinion relies, is incorrect. While I urge the Court to reconsider that holding *en banc* in an appropriate case, I do not think our error in *Riviera* affects the ultimate outcome here.

I.

The government is fortunate that the defendants did not raise the Coast Guard's apparent seven-week odyssey in the district court.[1] Had the defendants done so, the government would have had to establish under Rule 5(a)(1)(B), Fed. R. **[—85—]** Crim. P., that its seven-week delay was not "unnecessary." Since the defendants did not press this claim in the district court, though, we have no information about the reason for the delay, so we cannot say the district court plainly erred in not, on its own, realizing that a seven-week delay occurred and finding that the delay was unnecessary.

But seven weeks! That's a long time. Christopher Columbus's first voyage across the entire Atlantic Ocean, from the Canary Islands to the Bahamas, took only roughly five weeks. *How Long Did It Take Columbus and His Crew to Cross the Atlantic*, Reference, https://www.reference.com/history/long-did-columbus-his-crew-cross-atlantic-ocean-81eb6768c230a21c (last visited Jan. 27, 2020). And in 1873, Jules Verne contemplated a voyage around the whole world (by sea and rail) would take only 80 days. In fact, Nellie Bly[2] beat his **{-614-}** estimate in 1890 by completing the journey in 72 days, six hours, eleven minutes, and fourteen seconds.[3] It's hard **[—86—]** to believe that the Coast Guard, nearly 126 years later, needed 70% of Bly's travel period to go only between Central and North America.

Surely at some point a delay becomes presumptively "unnecessary," even by plain-error standards. Perhaps we cannot say definitively that seven weeks for this trip is

---

[1] The map below shows the point where the Coast Guard encountered the defendants, southwest of El Salvador, and the place to which the Coast Guard took the defendants, Key West, Florida.

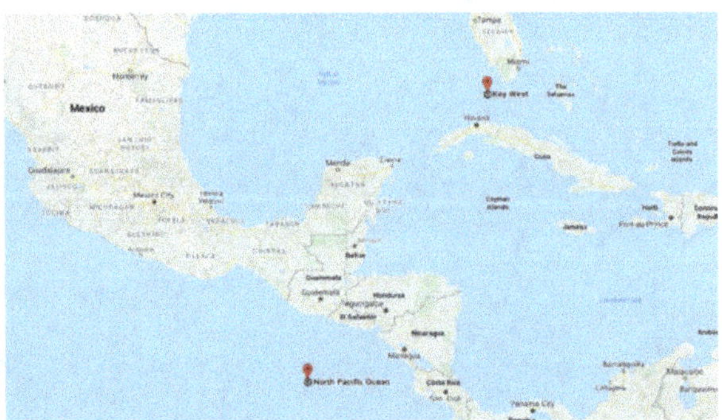

[2] Nellie Bly was born Elizabeth Jane Cochran. She began using the pseudonym Nellie Bly when she started writing for the *Pittsburgh Dispatch*. Arlisha R. Norwood, *Nellie Bly*, National Woman's History Museum, https://www.womenshistory.org/education-resources/biographies/nellie-bly (last visited Jan. 27, 2020). At a time when women were not welcomed as reporters, Bly's work established her as one of the most well-known journalists in the country. *Id.* Among her groundbreaking work, Bly helped pioneer the field of investigative journalism, going undercover as a mentally ill person to investigate the notorious insane asylum on Blackwell's Island (now Roosevelt Island). *Id.* As a result of Bly's exposé for the *New York World* on her time at the asylum, the New York District Attorney's Office undertook a major investigation of the facility, culminating in significant changes in New York City's Department of Public Charities and Corrections. *Nellie Bly*, Biography (Nov. 6, 2019), https://www.biography.com/activist/nellie-bly (last visited Jan. 27, 2020).

[3] *Jan 25, 1890 CE: Around the World in 72 Days*, National Geographic, https://www.nationalgeographic.org/thisday/jan25/around-world-72-days/ (last visited Jan. 27, 2020); *129 years ago, Nellie Bly passed through Lancaster on her '72 days around the world'*, **[—86—]** LancasterOnline, https://lancasteronline.com/features/years-ago-nellie-bly-passed-through-lancaster-on-her-days/article_01fe8868-1e8d-11e9-9be8-13475110aeb6.html (last visited Jan. 27, 2020).

presumptively "unnecessary," but what if the Coast Guard had taken an extra month? What about an entire year? The government might be able to explain such delays—and again, we have no record in this case—but a lengthy trip like this raises more than a few questions.

Plus, if the government could have delivered the defendants to a closer jurisdiction in less time, it seems to me that Rule 5(a)(1)(B) required it to do so—regardless of the fact that 46 U.S.C. § 70504(b)(2) allows an alleged MDLEA offender to "be tried in any district," "if the offense was begun or committed upon the high seas." Any delay occasioned by shipping the defendants to a further jurisdiction, for forum-shopping purposes (as the defendants assert), certainly would have been "unnecessary."[4]

In addition to violating Rule 5, "unnecessary" delay in presentment may also be unconstitutional. True, the Supreme Court has suggested that the Fourth **[—87—]** Amendment "has no application" outside the United States to "a citizen and resident of [a foreign country] with no voluntary attachment to the United States." *United States v. Verdugo-Urquidez,* 494 U.S. 259, 274-75 (1989). But that does not mean that the Constitution does not constrain the government's powers at all. "Even when the United States acts outside its borders, its power are not absolute and unlimited but are subject to such restrictions as are expressed in the Constitution." *Boumediene v. Bush,* 553 U.S. 723, 765 (2008) (cleaned up).

Depending on the necessity for the length of the detention during the delay in **{-615-}** presentment, one of those limitations may include the Suspension Clause. The Supreme Court has explained that the writ of habeas corpus is "an essential mechanism in the separation-of-powers scheme." *Id.* at 743. That is so since habeas "preserves limited government" by allowing a detainee to challenge his detention when a branch of the government has exceeded its constitutional powers in imprisoning him. *See id.* at 744. And since "the Constitution's separation-of-powers structure, like the substantive guarantees of the Fifth and Fourteenth Amendments, protects persons as well as citizens, foreign nationals who have the privilege of litigating in our courts can seek to enforce separation-of-power principles" such as the Suspension Clause. *Id.* at 743 (citations omitted); *cf. Nishimura Ekiu v. United States,* 142 U.S. 651, 660 (1892) ("An alien immigrant, prevented from landing by any such officer claiming authority to do so under an act of congress, and thereby **[—88—]** restrained of his liberty, is doubtless entitled to a writ of *habeas corpus* to ascertain whether the restraint is lawful.").

The Supreme Court has concluded that we must consider at least three factors in evaluating the reach of the Suspension Clause: "(1) the citizenship and status of the detainee and the adequacy of the process through which that status determination was made; (2) the nature of the sites where apprehension and then detention took place; and (3) the practical obstacles inherent in resolving the prisoner's entitlement to the writ." *Boumediene,* 553 U.S. at 766. When we do so, it seems likely that the Suspension Clause applies to foreign-national criminal detainees in sole United States custody before they have been charged—even if the United States is holding them outside this country.

To understand why, we must review *Boumediene.* In *Boumediene,* the petitioners were aliens designated as enemy combatants and detained at the United States Naval Station at Guantanamo Bay, Cuba. *Id.* at 732. They denied they were enemy combatants and sought the issuance of writs of habeas corpus for their release. *Id.* at 734. Applying the three factors listed above, the Supreme Court concluded that the *Boumediene* petitioners could seek habeas in United States courts, since Congress had not acted in conformance with the requirements of the Suspension Clause when it enacted a statute stripping the courts of jurisdiction to issue the writ. *Id.* at 766-771, 792. **[—89—]**

[4] Once again, though, the problem here is that the record is devoid of evidence that, under the marine conditions at the time of the journey, any other jurisdiction would have been materially closer than Key West, so we cannot find plain error on that basis on this record.

With respect to the first factor—the citizenship and status of the detainee and the adequacy of the process through which that status determination was made—the Court noted that the detainees were not American citizens but emphasized that they objected to their characterization as enemy combatants. *Id.* at 766. For that reason, the Court examined the procedural protections the detainees received in the hearings where the government determined them to be enemy combatants. **{–616–}** *Id.* at 766-67. In so doing, the Court concluded that these protections—where the detainee received a "personal representative" (though not a lawyer or advocate) and was able to present "reasonably available evidence"—fell "well short of the procedures and adversarial mechanisms that would eliminate the need for habeas corpus review." *Id.* at 767

Turning to the second consideration—the nature of the sites where apprehension and then detention occurred—the Court observed that the detainees had been taken into custody outside the United States and detained in a place that is "technically outside the sovereign territory of the United States." *Id.* at 768. Though these facts weighed against a finding that the detainees had rights under the Suspension Clause, the Court chose to instead stress that the United States enjoyed absolute and indefinite control over the facility at Guantanamo Bay. *Id.* at 768-69. As a result, the Court reasoned that "[i]n every practical sense Guantanamo is not abroad; it is within the constant jurisdiction of the United States." *Id.* at 769. **[—90—]**

As to the third factor—the practical obstacles inherent in resolving the prisoner's entitlement to the writ—the Court first conceded "that there are costs to holding the Suspension Clause applicable in a case of military detention abroad." *Id.* at 769. Nevertheless, it did not find the costs dispositive. *Id.* Rather, the Court focused on the government's lack of credible arguments that the military mission at Guantanamo would be "compromised" if United States courts heard the detainees' habeas claims. *Id.* It further noted that it had no reason to believe that adjudicating a habeas corpus petition would somehow upset Cuba. *Id.* at 770. And finally, it observed that "the United States is, for all practical purposes, answerable to no other sovereign for its acts" on Guantanamo. *Id.* Indeed, the Court recognized, the detainees were "held in a territory that, while technically not part of the United States, [was] under the complete and total control of our Government." *Id.* at 771.

The case of MDLEA detainees in the Coast Guard's sole custody on the high seas is even more compelling. First, at the time they are detained on the Coast Guard's vessel, MDLEA arrestees, unlike Guantanamo detainees, receive no process at all. They do not enjoy a proceeding of any type to determine whether the Coast Guard has correctly concluded that probable cause supporting their arrest and detention exists until after their detention on the high seas ends; they cannot present evidence contesting their detention; and they do not receive "personal representatives." If the process available to the Guantanamo detainees did not **[—91—]** satisfy the Suspension Clause, then certainly the absence of process altogether cannot.

Second, while Coast Guard vessels on the high seas are not within the jurisdiction of the United States, as with Guantanamo, the United States enjoys absolute and indefinite control over its own ships while they are in international waters.

And finally, like the detainees at Guantanamo, MDLEA detainees onboard a Coast Guard ship operating in international waters also are "under the complete and total control of our Government." For **{–617–}** these reasons, it seems likely that, at least theoretically,[5] an MDLEA detainee onboard a

[5] As a practical matter, such a right may not amount to much. While an MDLEA detainee is in custody on a government vessel—even assuming he has the knowledge to prepare a petition seeking habeas—he may not have a way to actually file such a petition. As a result, an MDLEA detainee's habeas rights might rely on whether others have knowledge of the detention and are in a position to be able to file a habeas petition on behalf of the detainee. Of course, even if, as a practical matter, a remedy is unattainable, that does not relieve the

government vessel for an unnecessary period enjoys the right to seek habeas corpus in a court of the United States.

In any case, at a minimum, the United States should give some serious consideration to its procedures for presenting an MDLEA detainee arrested in international waters. In the absence of a very good reason, detaining a person on the high seas for seven weeks before formally charging him with a crime is just wrong.

II. [—92—]

Next, though I recognize that we are bound by *Rivera*, I respectfully disagree with its holding that, in the government's case in chief, the government may present testimony or otherwise comment on a defendant's silence when the defendant was in custody but before he received his *Miranda*[6] warnings. *Rivera*, 944 F.2d at 1568.

As I read *Miranda*, its purpose was to avoid precisely this result. In fact, *Miranda* described its own holding as follows: "the prosecution may not use statements, whether exculpatory or inculpatory, stemming from ***custodial interrogation*** of the defendant unless it demonstrates the use of [*Miranda* rights] effective to secure the privilege against self-incrimination." 384 U.S. at 444 (emphasis added). The Supreme Court noted, "[T]here can be no doubt that the Fifth Amendment privilege is available outside of criminal court proceedings and serves to protect persons in all settings in which their freedom of action is curtailed in any significant way . . . ." *Id.* at 467. *Miranda* further explained that the reading of *Miranda* rights must occur "[p]rior to any questioning" because the rights are designed "to inform accused persons of their ***right of silence*** and to ***assure a continuous opportunity to exercise it***[.]" *Id.* at 444 (emphasis added).

If an in-custody person's silence before the administration of *Miranda* rights may be used against that person, then, in violation of *Miranda*, that person is not "assured a continuous opportunity to exercise" his right of silence while subject to **[—93—]** the "inherently compelling pressures" of unwarned custodial interrogation. *See Salinas v. Texas*, 570 U.S. 178, 184 (2013) (plurality opinion) (quoting *Miranda*, 384 U.S. at 467-68 & n.37). As a result, allowing a detainee's silence while in custody, but before administration of this procedure, to be used against that person in the government's case in chief eviscerates the purpose of *Miranda*. Admissibility of in-custody, pre-*Miranda* silence in response to an officer's questions or comments also rewards the delayed administration of *Miranda* rights, so it can encourage law enforcement to engage in such a practice.

Not only is our *Rivera* holding contrary to *Miranda*, but **{-618-}** *Fletcher v. Weir*, 455 U.S. 603 (1982), the sole authority on which we relied in reaching our *Rivera* holding, cannot bear the weight we have thrust upon its shoulders. In *Fletcher*, the Supreme Court held only that using in-custody, pre-*Miranda* silence *to impeach* a defendant who has taken the stand does not violate due process. *Id.* at 607. The Court never endorsed or even suggested that due process condones relying on a defendant's in-custody, pre-*Miranda* silence in the government's case in chief.

In particular, to justify the rule in *Fletcher*, the Court invoked common law, noting that it "traditionally has allowed witnesses to be *impeached* by their previous failure to state a fact in circumstances in which that fact naturally would have been asserted." *Fletcher*, 455 U.S. at 606 (citation and internal quotation marks omitted) (emphasis added). Our *Rivera* analysis cites no common-law authority for the **[—94—]** proposition that in-custody, pre-*Miranda* silence may be used against a defendant in the government's case in chief. Nor does it explain why the fact that the common law authorized admissibility of such reticence for impeachment purposes somehow means that in-custody, pre-*Miranda*-rights silence may also be used against a defendant in the government's case in chief.

---

government of its obligation to comply with the Constitution.

[6] 384 U.S. 436 (1966).

And the Supreme Court's more recent caselaw—*Salinas*, 570 U.S. 178 (plurality opinion)—undermines our holding in *Rivera*. In *Salinas*, the Supreme Court held that in *non-custodial* settings (before *Miranda* warnings are issued), a person who wishes to rely on his right to remain silent must expressly invoke that right. *Id.* at 190 (plurality opinion). But significantly, the Court noted that "a witness' failure to invoke the privilege must be excused where governmental coercion makes his forfeiture of the privilege involuntary." *Id.* at 184 (plurality opinion). Citing to *Miranda*, 384 U.S. at 467-68 & n.37, the Court then went on to explain that "a suspect who is subjected to the inherently compelling pressures of an unwarned custodial interrogation need not invoke the privilege." *Id.* (internal quotation marks omitted). In other words, as recently as 2013, the Court reaffirmed *Miranda*'s principle that an in-custody person's silence, pre-*Miranda* rights, may not be used against him, even if he does not expressly invoke his right to remain silent. **[—95—]**

For these reasons, I respectfully disagree with our holding in *Rivera* authorizing the use of an arrestee's silence against him, pre-*Miranda* rights. And I urge my colleagues to reconsider this rule *en banc*.

Nevertheless, I think that use of the defendant's in-custody, pre-*Miranda*-rights silence does not affect the outcome here.

First, to the extent that the government relied on the defendants' silence here to establish subject-matter jurisdiction under the MDLEA, that was not error, even if *Rivera* is wrong. "To qualify for the Fifth Amendment privilege, a communication must be testimonial, incriminating, and compelled." *Hiibel v. Sixth Judicial Dist. Court of Nevada, Humboldt Cty.*, 542 U.S. 177, 189 (2004). The privilege covers testimony that would either directly "support a conviction under a federal criminal statute" or merely "furnish a link in the chain of evidence needed to prosecute the claimant for a federal crime[.]" *Hoffman v. United States*, 341 U.S. 479, 486 (1951). But as the panel opinion points out, the "jurisdictional requirement is not an . . . essential element of the MDLEA substantive offense," *Tinoco*, 304 F.3d at 1109, so it need not be submitted **{-619-}** to the jury for proof beyond a reasonable doubt. Panel Op. at 26 (collecting cases). As a result, an MDLEA detainee's testimonial communication (including silence) is not "incriminating" for the purposes of the Fifth Amendment's privilege against self-incrimination. More simply put, the government's use of an MDLEA detainee's silence to prove statutory subject-matter **[—96—]** jurisdiction has nothing to do with proving that the detainee substantively violated the MDLEA, so it does not implicate the Fifth Amendment.

And second, as it relates to the government's use of the defendants' silence as evidence of their guilt on the substantive charges of drug-trafficking, on this record, application of *Rivera*—even if, as I believe, it was wrongly decided—was harmless beyond a reasonable doubt. *See Chapman v. California*, 386 U.S. 18, 24 (1967). We have explained that "[o]verwhelming evidence of guilt" is relevant to assessing whether an error of constitutional dimension is harmless beyond a reasonable doubt. *United States v. Guzman*, 167 F.3d 1350, 1353 (11th Cir. 1999).

Here, the record is rife with such evidence. For starters, Palacios-Solis testified that the defendants were adrift at sea for 27 to 30 days. Yet when the Coast Guard encountered them, it found large amounts of water and sports drinks, as well as fresh fruit and food items that did not appear to be that old. Nor did the defendants show any signs of having been adrift at sea for four weeks. Plus, the bottom of the vessel was clean and free from growth, also belying the defendants' story. Besides that, while Palacios-Solis said the defendants had been on a fishing trip, the Coast Guard discovered no bait, fish, or fish remnants onboard. And the lines the Coast Guard did recover appeared to be unserviceable and not usable for fishing. Then there were the 25 bales of cocaine, located in a place consistent with the currents from where the defendants allegedly ditched them. Not only that, but the Coast **[—97—]** Guard found onboard the defendants' boat the same kind of buoy and black line recovered with the bales.

The defendants also put gasoline on their boat's surface—a dangerous practice that did not appear to serve any legitimate purpose. Even so, though, the Coast Guard still found traces of cocaine onboard the defendants' boat.

In short, the defendants' silence in response to the Coast Guards' questions about the boat's captain and nationality pales in comparison to the torrent of other evidence the government presented of the defendants' guilt. As a result, even if *Rivera* wrongly authorizes admission of defendants' in-custody, pre-*Miranda*-rights statements—which, for the reasons I have explained, I think it does—allowing the government to rely in its case in chief on the defendants' silence here would not require reversal.

United States Court of Appeals
for the Eleventh Circuit

No. 18-13282

UNITED STATES
vs.
GOLDMAN

Appeal from the United States District Court for the Southern District of Florida

Decided: March 25, 2020

Citation: 953 F.3d 1213, 8 Adm. R. 402 (11th Cir. 2020).

Before **ROSENBAUM**, **TJOFLAT**, and **HULL**, Circuit Judges.

[—1—] {-1215-} ROSENBAUM, Circuit Judge:

In Robert Louis Stevenson's *Treasure Island*, Jim Hawkins memorably hunted for Captain Flint's hidden treasure. *The Goonies* put its own spin on treasure **[—2—]** hunting when the title band of friends defied One-Eyed Willy's maze of booby traps to find his hidden treasure and save their beloved neighborhood. But for real-life treasure-hunting stories, perhaps nothing beats the quests of the aptly named Mel Fisher and his company Treasure Salvors, Inc.

Fisher and his team specialized in finding and salvaging shipwrecks of Spanish galleons and other vessels from the Spanish Colonial era, off the coasts of Florida and its Keys. As of the mid-1980s, Fisher's operation had recovered treasure worth approximately $400 million at that time.

Among that treasure was Gold Bar 27, which Fisher donated to the Mel Fisher Maritime Heritage Museum (the "Museum") in Key West, Florida. There, Gold **{-1216-}** Bar 27 became iconic, and three to four million Museum visitors handled it over the years.

Enter Defendant-Appellant Jarred Alexander Goldman (sometimes truth can be stranger than fiction) and Codefendant Richard Steven Johnson. In 2010, Goldman and Johnson stole Gold Bar 27 from the Museum. This appeal requires us to consider the proper standard—we might call it the gold standard—for determining, for purposes of ordering restitution under the Mandatory Victims Restitution Act, 18 U.S.C. § 3663A ("MVRA"), the value of Gold Bar 27.

Today we take this golden opportunity to reaffirm that in a case like this one, where the loss is of a unique artifact for which market value cannot fully compensate, **[—3—]** courts must use replacement cost in determining restitution. While absolute precision is not required under the MVRA, the district court must base its restitution order on evidence. And that evidence must show that the restitution will make the victim whole—nothing more and nothing less. Because the district court, without the benefit of our decision today, did not ascertain replacement value when it determined market value was insufficient and then imposed restitution, we vacate the restitution order and remand for valuation that applies the proper legal *bar*ometer to the gold bar here.

Goldman also challenges the loss amount used to determine his offense level. But here, we part ways with Goldman's analysis. The district court explained that it would impose the same sentence, even if it had the loss figure wrong. For that reason and because the sentence the district court imposed is not substantively unreasonable, we affirm Goldman's sentence.

I.

We pick up Gold Bar 27's story in 1622. A Spanish fleet of ships set sail from Spain to various parts of the Americas to pick up cargos of gold, silver, tobacco, copper, and other goods to take back to Spain.[1] After they obtained their cargos, the **[—4—]** ships convened in Havana, Cuba. Among these ships was the *Santa Margarita*, which carried Gold Bar 27. In all, 28 vessels—including the

[1] Regrettably, slave labor and other deplorable practices were used to procure some of these goods. *See Gold, silver and sugar*, Discovering Bristol – an online history of the port and its people, http://www.discoveringbristol.org.uk/slavery/routes/places-involved/south-america/gold-silver-sugar/ (last visited Mar. 25, 2020).

Tierra Firme Fleet and its guard ships—then launched from Cuba to begin their return to Spain with their bounty. The idea was that there was safety in numbers.[2]

Unfortunately, though, traveling in a group could not protect the ships from severe weather. Without the benefit of modern weather technology, the ships left Havana on September 4, 1622, smack in the thick of hurricane season. And sure enough, within 24 hours of the fleet's departure, a hurricane descended upon the **{–1217–}** vessels. Seven of the 28 ships sank in the waters between Cuba and the Florida Keys or smashed on the reefs of the Florida Keys. Among these were the *Nuestra Señora de Atocha*[3] ("*Atocha*") and the *Santa Margarita*. So Gold Bar 27, onboard the sunken *Santa Margarita*, sat on the bottom of the ocean for hundreds of years.

Then, in 1969, Fisher and his team began searching the waters of the Florida **[—5—]** Keys for the *Atocha*. While they were looking for the cargo of that vessel,[4] in 1980, they came across the *Santa Margarita* wreckage site. Fisher and his team recovered from that wreck, among other items, gold ingots, including Gold Bar 27.

Later, to promote interest in the maritime history of Florida and the Caribbean, Fisher founded the Museum in nearby Key West. *See MISSION*, Mel Fisher Maritime Museum, https://www.melfisher.org/mission-values-goals (last visited Mar. 25, 2020). As we have noted, among other things, Fisher donated to the Museum the item Treasure Salvors inventoried as "Gold Bar 27" from the *Santa Margarita*.

At the Museum, Gold Bar 27 lived its best life. It became the focus of the Museum's "lift a gold bar" exhibit.[5] This exhibit allowed visitors to enjoy a close encounter with Gold Bar 27: visitors could place their hands in a display case and touch, handle, and raise the gold bar without removing it. As we have noted, during the bar's display in the Museum, probably three to four million visitors picked up the gold bar. The bar became so famous that the Museum centered its marketing on it. **[—6—]**

The marketing must have worked better than the Museum had hoped because in 2010, Goldman and Johnson drove all the way from West Palm Beach to the Museum in Key West, Florida.[6] There, Goldman served as a lookout while Johnson wandered around trying to find something to steal. Surveillance video showed Johnson unsuccessfully attempting to pry open several display cases, while Goldman stood watch. Eventually, Johnson broke off a piece of the case displaying Gold Bar 27, and unfortunately, he did indeed lift the gold bar

---

[2] The Spanish ships sought to protect themselves from several threats. At this time, pirate attacks occurred. *See Atocha & Margarita Story*, Mel Fisher's Treasures, https://www.melfisher.com/Library/AtochaMargStory.asp (last visited Mar. 25, 2020). In addition, the Tierra Firme Fleet sailed during the course of the Thirty Years War (1618-1648) and the Eighty Years War (1568-1648). *Id.*; *Thirty Years' War*, HISTORY, https://www.history.com/topics/reformation/thirty-years-war (last visited Mar. 25, 2020); *Eighty Years' War*, Encyclopædia Britannica, https://www.britannica.com/event/Eighty-Years-War (last visited Mar. 25, 2020). And just a year before the Tierra Firme Fleet left Havana, in 1621, Spain ended a twelve-year truce with its Dutch provinces, which had been in a state of rebellion. *Atocha & Margarita Story, supra*. The Dutch then began attacking Spanish naval and merchant vessels. *Id.*

[3] The *Atocha*, which was built in Havana, was named for "the most revered religious shrine in Spain." *Atocha & Margarita Story, supra* note 2.

[4] Five years earlier, in 1975, Fisher's team had found part of the *Atocha*, including some of its bronze cannons. Jay Amberg, *They Were a Ragtag Band of Treasure Hunters Who Spent 16 Years*, Chicago Tribune (July 20, 1990), https://www.chicagotribune.com/news/ct-xpm-1990-07-20-9003010506-story.html. But it would take another 10 years, until July 20, 1985, for the team to locate a site containing much of the *Atocha*'s cargo. *Id.*

[5] At the time of the theft in 2010, the Museum had in its collection a total of eight gold bars recovered from shipwrecks.

[6] For readers unfamiliar with Florida's geography, this is roughly a five-hour drive in no traffic. Federal Bureau of Investigation Special Agent Rhonda Squizzero testified at trial that it took her six hours to make the drive in traffic.

(in a way the display certainly did not contemplate). Then he and Goldman, the iconic Gold Bar 27 in hand, left the Museum and drove back to West Palm Beach.

That's where Gold Bar 27's luck finally ran out. After stealing the bar, Johnson used the bar as his personal treasure stash, sawing off pieces as he needed money, until just a small piece remained.[7] **{–1218–}**

B.

Eventually the law caught up with Goldman and Johnson. A grand jury indicted them for conspiracy to commit an offense against the United States, in violation of 18 U.S.C. § 371, and theft of major artwork, in violation of 18 U.S.C. § 668. Goldman pled not guilty, and the court set the case for trial. **[—7—]**

Johnson, however, pled guilty to both counts of the indictment. In his factual proffer, Johnson agreed that Gold Bar 27 was worth approximately $556,000.

At Goldman's trial, the government presented evidence detailing the history of Gold Bar 27 and Goldman's role in stealing it, which we have already noted. It also put on evidence explaining how the government eventually discovered that Goldman and Johnson had been responsible for the theft. Specifically, while Johnson was attempting to steal Gold Bar 27, he left an identifiable fingerprint on the display case.

The crime remained unsolved until 2015, when the Monroe County Sheriff's Office received an anonymous tip through "Crime Stoppers." The caller led investigators to Goldman.

In 2016 law enforcement interviewed Goldman, who admitted to serving as a lookout for Johnson while he stole the antique gold bar. During trial, Goldman also stipulated that the gold bar was more than 100 years old and was worth in excess of $100,000. The jury found Goldman guilty as charged.

C.

Goldman's pre-sentence investigation report ("PSI") valued the stolen gold bar at approximately $556,000, the value the Museum placed on it. It noted that the victims included the Museum and an insurance company (AXA Art Insurance), which had paid a $100,000 insurance claim to the Museum for the theft. **[—8—]**

As relevant to this appeal, the PSI recommended finding Goldman responsible for a loss amount greater than $550,000, which would result in a 14-level enhancement under U.S.S.G. § 2B1.1(b)(1)(H) and § 2B1.5(b)(1)(B) to Goldman's offense level. The PSI also noted that restitution was mandatory, and it concluded that the total loss in the case was $556,000, with $456,000 owed to the Museum and $100,000 owed to AXA Art Insurance Corporation.

Johnson, who faced the same recommendations, challenged the PSI's valuation of the gold bar, despite his earlier stipulation to that valuation in his factual proffer at the change-of-plea hearing. In particular, he objected to how the value would impact his guidelines offense level and his restitution obligation.

In support of his objections to the valuation, Johnson submitted insurance documents by the Museum's insurance provider, AXA Art Insurance, describing how AXA calculated the value of the gold bar and what the insurance settlement amount would be. According to those documents, AXA did not agree with the Museum's $555,696 valuation of Gold Bar 27. It noted that it had asked the Museum for information as to how a "point system" the Museum used to value artifacts worked, but the Museum had failed to respond.

---

[7] Johnson's counsel asserted that Johnson gave a sawed-off piece of the bar to Goldman as payment, but Goldman told law enforcement that Johnson left town without paying him the $2,000 Johnson had promised for Goldman's role in the crime. In any case, Gold Bar 27 was destroyed.

AXA stated that it valued the gold bar using the methodology set forth in the policy language, which provided coverage for liability for the "current market value" of the property at the time of loss. The policy further explained that "[m]arket value **[—9—]** for fine art and collectible property is generally interpreted to be 'the price at which an asset would trade in a competitive auction setting.'"

To calculate what that price would be, AXA identified five auctioned shipwreck gold bars from the *Atocha*, which it **{-1219-}** deemed comparable to Gold Bar 27. Of those five, AXA relied on the three that had sold at auction in 2009 (the other two bars sold in 2007 and 2008) to determine "current market conditions." Based on its review of the auction prices for the three bars, AXA determined that similar gold bars "sell on average 45 percent above their melt value." Then, AXA calculated Gold Bar 27's melt value to be $63,228.13, based on its weight and purity. Next, AXA added 45 percent to that value for Gold Bar 27's status as a *Santa Margarita* shipwreck bar, along with another 15 percent for Gold Bar 27's "notoriety" and iconic value. Altogether, the sum amounted to $101,165.01.

The district court scheduled Goldman and Johnson to be sentenced on the same day.

D.

The district court convened Johnson's sentencing hearing first. During the hearing, the government presented evidence on the value of Gold Bar 27.[8] Goldman **[—10—]** and his attorney participated in that portion of Johnson's sentencing hearing, since the court was determining the value of the gold bar.

Melissa Kendrick, the President and CEO of the Museum, testified that at the time that Gold Bar 27 was stolen, the Museum estimated its value at roughly $550,000. She explained that the Museum arrived at this valuation based on a point system used by the Mel Fisher Investor Division:

> Every artifact . . . when it is found, is appraised and given a value. That value is expressed in points. So for example, this pen in 1985 might have been given 100 points. Today, it is still 100 points. But what changes is the valuation of a point. So that would move with the market, because that is the number of points times the point value would give you the fair market value. The price that a willing buyer and a willing seller would reach in a transaction.

According to Kendrick, when Gold Bar 27 was recovered, it was assigned a value of 8,178 points. Multiplying those 8,178 points by the value of a point at the time of the theft, the Museum determined Gold Bar 27's value to be $556,000.

Kendrick admitted to "hav[ing] no idea what the ongoing value and the fluctuation in points" was. Nor did she explain how the value of a point was determined or why Gold Bar 27 was assigned 8,178 points at the time it was recovered from the wreck of the *Santa Margarita*.

After opining that Gold Bar 27 was worth $556,000, Kendrick recounted that when Gold Bar 27 was stolen, AXA paid out only approximately $100,000. Although Kendrick acknowledged that several other comparably sized gold bars **[—11—]** recovered from the wrecks of the *Atocha* and the *Santa Margarita* had sold for much less than $556,000, she offered a couple of reasons for that.

First, Kendrick said, the other bars were sold at auctions. Therefore, Kendrick reasoned, "the only thing that you can derive from those sales is what a willing buyer and willing seller was prepared to pay. So very, very close to melt value."

Second, Kendrick continued, other gold bars did not have the pedigree that Gold Bar 27 did, as the stolen gold bar was "iconic," unlike the others, which were "ordinary

[8] Counsel for Johnson argued that he was not bound by his previous agreement as to value in the factual proffer because the government had subsequently received information of comparable gold bars that had sold for less. The government acquiesced in its need to prove the value, since it had to do so with respect to Goldman, regardless.

shipwreck bars." She emphasized {-1220-} that during the nearly thirty years Gold Bar 27 was on display at the Museum, about three to four million people had touched it, which, in Kendrick's opinion, had greatly increased the value of the bar:

> Yes, but if a bar is brought up from either of those two shipwrecks and they're put in somebody's sock drawer they don't continue to gather the value for the story that that artifact could tell. If a gold bar belonged to Elvis and Elvis had that bar and did certain things with it, then that would become part of the story and it would enrich the value of that object. We, at the museum, enrich the value of that object by putting it on display and having every one of our visitors have the opportunity to interact firsthand with history.

In short, Kendrick considered Gold Bar 27 to be "priceless" because "there is not another bar to buy to replace it, in all likelihood."

Nevertheless, Kendrick conceded that "[t]he museum is not in the business of buying and selling gold bars or any particular artifacts, so I have no personal knowledge as to what—as to the prices that artifacts have sold for." Kendrick also admitted that she was not aware of a single gold bar from the *Atocha* or *Santa* **[—12—]** *Margarita* wrecks that had sold for even half the price of $550,000.

Kendrick stated that the Museum had not replaced Gold Bar 27 because that would require both the money to pay for a replacement bar and the availability of a replacement bar from a private collector willing to sell it.

The district court accepted the Museum's valuation as proper:

> You know, the thing that troubles me about this particular item is that you can find a value by melting it down and selling it for its weight in gold. And that may be what the people that were selling it and buying it were doing. But if these were rare books, what are they worth, 12 cents? Yet they're worth $100,000. And I think somebody that has something like this in a museum is entitled to place a value, and I think that particularly when one of the parties has agreed that the value is 500-some thousand dollars, I'm not going to go below that.

The district court then sentenced Johnson to a total of 63 months of imprisonment and ordered him to pay restitution in the amount of $580,195.43, jointly and severally with Goldman.[9]

Next, the court convened Goldman's sentencing hearing. After calculating Goldman's offense level at 24 and his criminal-history category at I, with a corresponding guidelines range of 51 to 63 months' imprisonment, the court sentenced Goldman to 40 months of imprisonment for each count, to be served concurrently, followed by three years of supervised release. The court also ordered **[—13—]** Goldman to pay $570,195.43 in restitution, jointly and severally with Johnson.[10]

For the record, Goldman objected to the court's determination of Gold Bar 27's value. Then the government asked the district court whether it would have imposed the same sentence had it not made the determination as to value. The district court responded, "Yes. I would have made the {-1221-} same determination because my position is that it was a priceless work of art."

Goldman now appeals. In Section II, we address his sentencing claim, and in Section III, we consider his objection to the restitution order.

---

9 The difference between $580,195.43 and $556,000, or $24,195.43, reflected an additional insurance company loss. The amount included in the written judgment was for $10,000 less, however, apparently due to a mathematical error in Johnson's favor.

10 The court's restitution amount for Goldman apparently contained the same $10,000 mathematical error that was in Johnson's judgment. *See supra* n.9.

II.

We begin with Goldman's sentencing challenge. As we have noted, Goldman objects to the district court's valuation of Gold Bar 27 that figured into the court's total offense calculation under the Sentencing Guidelines.

In particular, United States Sentencing Guidelines Manual ("U.S.S.G.") § 2B1.5 sets forth the offense guideline applicable to the crime of theft of cultural-heritage resources. It imposes an enhancement to the basic offense level, depending on the value of the item involved in the crime.[11] *See* U.S.S.G. §§ 2B1.5(b)(1), **[—14—]** 2B1.1(b) (2016).[12] For example, a value greater than $550,000 but less than $1,500,000.01 results in an enhancement of 14 points to the basic offense level. *Id.*

But in this case, we do not dwell on whether the district court correctly ascertained the "value" of Gold Bar 27 for purposes of the Sentencing Guidelines because the court stated that it would have imposed the same sentence regardless of the "value" of Gold Bar 27 as properly calculated under § 2B1.5(b)(1). And under our precedent in the form of *United States v. Keene*, 470 F.3d 1347, 1349 (11th Cir. 2006), we need not review an issue when (1) the district court states it would have imposed the same sentence, even absent an alleged error, and (2) the sentence is substantively reasonable. That is so because under those circumstances, we have explained, any error in the guidelines calculation is harmless. *See id.*

Therefore, we turn to the question of substantive reasonableness. When we consider the substantive reasonableness of the sentence under a *Keene* analysis, we assume the guidelines error the defendant alleges and reduce the guidelines calculation and its corresponding sentencing range accordingly. *Id.*; *United States v. Lozano*, 490 F.3d 1317, 1324 (11th Cir. 2007). Then we assess the substantive reasonableness of the sentence actually imposed, in light of the reduced sentencing range. *Keene*, 470 F.3d at 1349. **[—15—]**

Here, Goldman contends that the court should have calculated the value of Gold Bar 27 at more than $95,000 but less than $150,000.01. Had the court done so, Goldman's resulting offense level would have been 18, with a corresponding guidelines range of 27-33 months. As we have noted, Goldman was, in fact, sentenced to 40 months' imprisonment.

So we must consider whether the 40-month sentence that the district court imposed was substantively reasonable, in light of the 27-33-month guidelines range and the rest of the sentencing record. To conduct this evaluation, we consider the totality of the circumstances and whether the sentence achieves the sentencing purposes stated in § 3553(a). **{-1222-}** *Gall v. United States*, 552 U.S. 38, 51 (2007). The district court must impose a sentence that is sufficient, but not greater than necessary, to comply with the factors and purposes listed in § 3553(a)(2), including the need to reflect the seriousness of the offense, promote respect for the law, provide just punishment for the offense, deter criminal conduct, and protect the public from the defendant's future criminal conduct. 18 U.S.C. § 3553(a)(2); *United States v. Croteau*, 819 F.3d 1293, 1309 (11th Cir. 2016). The district court also must consider the nature and circumstances of the offense and the history and characteristics of the defendant. 18 U.S.C. § 3553(a)(1). Although the district court must take into account each of the § 3553(a) factors, it need not discuss them specifically; rather, the court's acknowledgement that it has considered the § 3553(a) factors will suffice.

---

[11] The Application Notes to § 2B1.5(b)(1) instruct, as potentially relevant here, that "the value . . . shall include" both the "archaeological value" and the "commercial value" of the item. U.S.S.G. § 2B1.5(b)(1), cmt. n.2(A). Nevertheless, in determining the "value" for purposes of this guideline, the court may "make a reasonable estimate . . . based on available information." *Id.* at cmt. n.2(B).

[12] As Goldman's sentencing occurred on July 30, 2018, this is the applicable edition of the Sentencing Guidelines. *See* U.S.S.G. § 1B1.11(a) ("The court shall use the Guidelines Manual in effect on the date that the defendant is sentenced.").

[—16—] *United States v. Turner*, 474 F.3d 1265, 1281 (11th Cir. 2007).

When it comes to weighing the § 3553(a) factors, the district court enjoys great discretion. *United States v. Clay*, 483 F.3d 739, 743 (11th Cir. 2007). Nevertheless, a district court abuses its discretion if it (1) fails to consider relevant factors that were due significant weight, (2) gives an improper or irrelevant factor significant weight, or (3) commits a clear error of judgment by unreasonably balancing the proper factors. *United States v. Irey*, 612 F.3d 1160, 1189 (11th Cir. 2010) (en banc). The defendant bears the burden of proving his sentence is substantively unreasonable, in view of the § 3553(a) factors and the record. *Keene*, 470 F.3d at 1350.

We will vacate a sentence only if we are left with the "definite and firm" conviction that the district court committed a clear error of judgment in weighing the § 3553(a) factors by arriving at a sentence that is outside the range of reasonable sentences dictated by the facts of the case. *Irey*, 612 F.3d at 1190. We do not presume that a sentence outside the guideline range is unreasonable and must give due deference to the district court's decision that the § 3553(a) factors, as a whole, justify the extent of the variance. *United States v. Rosales-Bruno*, 789 F.3d 1249, 1254–55. A sentence imposed well below the statutory maximum penalty is an indicator of reasonableness. *See United States v. Gonzalez*, 550 F.3d 1319, 1324 (11th Cir. 2008). **[—17—]**

Accounting for these considerations, we review the substantive reasonableness of Goldman's 40-month sentence. In imposing Goldman's sentence, the district court stated that it had given thought to all the § 3553(a) factors. In particular, with respect to the "nature and circumstances of the offense," 18 U.S.C. § 3553(a)(1), the court emphasized that Gold Bar 27 was a "priceless work of art" and that the "destruction of an artifact that is priceless" is a "bad crime." Indeed, the record reflects that Goldman's actions deprived the Museum and its millions of visitors of the Museum's centerpiece exhibit—an artifact and an experience that, in the Museum's view, can never be replaced. Even though the guidelines had already accounted for the value of the gold bar, we cannot say that, on this record, the district abused its discretion in further accounting for that factor. *See United States v. Amedeo*, 487 F.3d 823, 833–34 (11th Cir. 2007).

Goldman's sentence was approximately two-thirds that of his more responsible codefendant Johnson. And the 40-month sentence fell significantly below the statutory maximum sentence the court could have imposed (60 months for Count 1 and 120 months for Count 2), further indicating the sentence's reasonableness. *See Gonzalez*, 550 F.3d at 1324. **{-1223-}**

Ultimately, we conclude that Goldman's sentence did not fall outside the range of reasonable sentences dictated by the facts of the case. *Irey*, 612 F.3d at 1190. So we find no abuse of discretion in the district court's sentencing decision, **[—18—]** and we affirm Goldman's sentence.

III.

Next, we address Goldman's restitution challenge.

A.

We review *de novo* questions of law concerning a restitution order, and we review for clear error the factual findings supporting a restitution order. *United States v. Edwards*, 728 F.3d 1286, 1291 (11th Cir. 2013).

B.

A district court may order restitution only as a statute authorizes. *Id.* The MVRA requires the district court to grant restitution to all victims once a defendant is convicted of "any offense . . . in which an identifiable victim or victims has suffered a . . . pecuniary loss." 18 U.S.C. § 3663A(c)(1)(B). Section 3664 sets forth the procedures a court must follow under the MVRA. *Id.* § 3663A(d). It requires the court to "order restitution to each victim in the full amount of each victim's losses as determined by the court and without consideration of the economic circumstances of the defendant." *Id.* § 3664(f)(1)(A).

We have said that "[t]he primary and overarching purpose of the MVRA . . . is to make victims of crime whole, to fully compensate these victims for their losses and to restore these victims to their original state of well-being." *United States v. Collins*, 854 F.3d 1324, 1329 (11th Cir. 2017) (citation and internal quotation marks **[—19—]** omitted). Restitution should not "provide a windfall for crime victims." *United States v. Martin*, 803 F.3d 581, 594 (11th Cir. 2015) (citations and internal quotation marks omitted). Nor is restitution intended to punish the defendant. *Id.* at 595. For these reasons, "[a] restitution award must be based on the amount of loss *actually* caused by the defendant's conduct." *United States v. Huff*, 609 F.3d 1240, 1247 (11th Cir 2010) (citation and internal quotation marks omitted) (emphasis in original). Where, as here, "return of the property . . . is impossible," the MVRA demands that the defendant shall "pay an amount equal to [ ] the greater of [ ] the value of the property on the date of the damage, loss, or destruction; or the value of the property on the date of sentencing," minus the value of any property returned. 18 U.S.C. § 3663A(b)(1)(B). The government bears the burden of proving the loss amount—the "value"—by a preponderance of the evidence. *Id.* § 3664(e).

We first considered the meaning of "value" in § 3663A(b)(1) in *United States v. Shugart*, 176 F.3d 1373 (11th Cir. 1999). We noted that for fungible commodities, "value" means "the actual cash value, or fair market value, of the item—that is, '[t]he fair or reasonable cash price for which the property could be sold in the market in the ordinary course of business.'" *Id.* at 1375 (quoting Black's Law Dictionary (6th ed. 1990)); *see also* Value, Black's Law Dictionary (11th ed. 2019) (defining "fair market value" as "[t]he price that a seller is willing to accept and a buyer is willing to pay on the open market and in an arm's-length transaction; the point at which **[—20—]** supply and demand intersect"); *cf.* 26 C.F.R. § 20.2031-1(b) ("The fair market value is the price at which the property would change hands between a willing buyer and a willing seller, neither being under any compulsion to buy or to sell and both having reasonable knowledge of relevant facts."). **{-1224-}**

But when the loss involves a unique item or when no ready market for it exists, fair market value may not be an option. *See Shugart*, 176 F.3d at 1375. So we have explained that when "actual cash value is unavailable or unreliable," we determine value under § 3663A by looking to "replacement cost." *Id.* Replacement cost is "[t]he cost of a substitute asset that is equivalent to an asset currently held." *United States v. Steele*, 897 F.3d 606, 610–11 (4th Cir. 2018) (quoting Replacement Cost, Black's Law Dictionary (10th ed. 2014)).

We have no precedent that directly articulates how a court should determine the value of a unique item stolen from a museum, such as Gold Bar 27. But *Shugart* and its progeny are instructive.

In *Shugart*, we held that the district court did not abuse its discretion in ordering restitution in an amount necessary to rebuild a century-old church that the defendants had burned down. 176 F.3d at 1375. We explained that a church is not a fungible commodity, but rather is unique and "valued by its members, precisely because of its location, its design, and the memories it evokes." *Id.* For these reasons, we observed that simply purchasing a different existing structure **[—21—]** elsewhere—that is, determining loss based on actual cash value—could not fill those voids in the same way that "rebuild[ing] a church comparable in size and design on the same lot where the original church stood" could. *Id.* On that basis, we affirmed the district court's use of replacement cost to determine the value of the church.

The Sixth Circuit adopted our *Shugart* analysis in *United States v. Genschow*, 645 F.3d 803, 814 (6th Cir. 2011). There, the defendant had, without authorization, cleared five acres of unpopulated, tribal trust land on the Ontonagon Reservation, owned by the

Keweenaw Bay Indian Community ("Community"). *Id.* at 805, 808. The president of the Community submitted a victim-impact statement that described the sacred traditions of the Chippewa and Ojibwe carried out on the land. *Id.* at 810. As the president explained, the unauthorized clearing of the land destroyed the Community's resources and offended its traditions. *Id.* The Sixth Circuit upheld restitution for "the value of the removed timber and the cost of restoring the Property," despite the defendant's objection that the restitution amount should have been based on the fair market value of the land, which would have been lower. *Id.* at 814. The court reasoned that "when destroyed property is unique or lacks an active market such that the actual cash value is unreliable or unavailable, using replacement value as a measure for restitution is proper under the MVRA." *Id.* at 815.

For purposes of ascertaining the best way to establish value under the MVRA, **[—22—]** artifacts like Gold Bar 27 are roughly analogous to the unique items lost in *Shugart* and *Genschow*. Like the special aspects of the church in *Shugart* and the sacred ground in *Genschow*, Gold Bar 27's unique properties render actual cash value unreliable and unavailable. So it makes sense to treat Gold Bar 27, the *Shugart* church, and the *Genschow* sacred lands the same way for purposes of valuing them under the MVRA. For that reason, today we reaffirm our holding in *Shugart*: where, because of the unique nature of an item, cash value does not sufficiently compensate under the MVRA for actual loss, a district court should use replacement value to determine restitution.

Of course, using replacement value in a case like this one may be easier said than done. Depending on the nature of the item lost or destroyed, the district court may have to account for various components in determining a replacement **{-1225-}** cost—some easier to quantify than others. Yet we have recognized that determining the restitution amount "is by nature an inexact science." *Martin*, 803 F.3d at 595 (citation and internal quotation marks omitted). And so where, as here, a precise valuation of a stolen item might not be possible, a court does not abuse its discretion in making a "reasonable estimate of the loss, given the available information." *United States v. Futrell*, 209 F.3d 1286, 1291 (11th Cir. 2000) (citation and internal quotation marks omitted); *see also id.* at 1292. Nevertheless, the district court must explain how it arrived at its loss figure, so we can conduct a review of that **[—23—]** determination and ensure it is based on sufficient evidence. *Huff*, 609 F.3d at 1248.

Here, we are not able to do that. We know that the district court rejected the idea of valuing Gold Bar 27 based on the auction prices of other gold bars discovered in the wrecks of the *Atocha* and the *Santa Margarita*. We also know that the court identified the value of Gold Bar 27 to be $556,000, based on Kendrick's testimony that the bar was worth that amount. Indeed, the court explained that "somebody that has something like this in a museum is entitled to place a value." But allowing Kendrick to establish the gold bar's value, absent any evidence of her own training in valuating artifacts or of any explanation of the Museum's point system, is not appropriate. *See United States v. Renick*, 273 F.3d 1009, 1027 (11th Cir. 2001) ("Alleged victims cannot determine their own 'losses.'").[13]

And here, the record contains no explanation of how the Mel Fisher Investor Division's point system, on which the Museum blindly based its $556,000 valuation, works. Silence in this situation is not golden. We have no idea, for instance, what the purpose of the Mel Fisher Investor Division point system is.[14] We also do not **[—24—]** know how the

---

[13] Nor can Johnson's factual stipulation of the value in connection with his own plea somehow satisfy the government's burden as to value for Goldman. Goldman, in contrast, stipulated at his trial to only a value in excess of $100,000. And nothing indicates that Johnson is trained in the appraisal of shipwreck treasure. Nor is the Museum, it appears, for that matter.

[14] Perhaps the Mel Fisher Investor Division point system may be a system Fisher's business devised for distributing recovered treasure items to investors in his operation, based on their investments. *See Mel Fisher*, The Treasure Wrecks Chronicles: Treasure Wrecks & Their Discoverers,

Mel Fisher Investor Division determined that Gold Bar 27 was assigned 8,178 points when it was recovered. Nor do we know how many points were assigned to other comparable gold bars recovered at the same time from the same wrecks. We likewise lack information concerning whether any of these comparable gold bars assigned point values were sold at auction or otherwise, and if so, for how much. Also missing is any information about how the valuation of a single point is determined.

In the absence of any evidence establishing the basis for the Mel Fisher Investment Division's point system, we cannot evaluate whether the district court's valuation based on that system was a reasonable estimate of the replacement cost of Gold Bar 27. For that reason, we must vacate the order of restitution and remand to the district court to conduct an evidentiary hearing to determine a reasonable **{–1226–}** estimate of the replacement cost of Gold Bar 27.

Perhaps the government will be able to put on evidence to establish the reliability of the Mel Fisher Investment Division's point system in determining replacement cost. Perhaps it won't. Or perhaps AXA's valuation better establishes replacement value. Its components appear to attempt to account for what would seem to be all the necessary considerations: (1) melt value; (2) based on sales of **[—25—]** comparable gold bars, a premium for the fact that Gold Bar 27 was recovered from the *Santa Margarita*; and (3) a premium for the iconic lift-a-bar-exhibit aspect of Gold Bar 27. But the record contains no indication of how AXA arrived at the 15% premium for Gold Bar 27's unique lift-a-bar-exhibit status. So we do not know whether that 15% premium is reasonable. The district court must consider these questions in the first instance.

---

http://thethunderchild.com/GhostGunsVirginia/TreasureWrecks/MelFisher.html (last visited Mar. 25, 2020); John Rothchild, *Mel Fisher $44 Million Later or Maybe It's $200 million. But after that Incredible Memorial Day Discovery, Who's Counting?*, Sun Sentinel (Feb. **[—24—]** 9, 1986), http://www.sun-sentinel.com/news/fl-xpm-1986-02-09-8601090476-story.html. If so, it may not tell us much, if anything, about the replacement cost of Gold Bar 27.

IV.

For the reasons we have explained, we affirm Goldman's sentence, but we vacate the order of restitution and remand for the district court to ascertain the amount of restitution in a manner consistent with this opinion.

AFFIRMED IN PART, VACATED IN PART, and REMANDED.

United States Court of Appeals
for the Eleventh Circuit

No. 17-13602

CARROLL
VS.
CARNIVAL CORP.

Appeal from the United States District Court for the Southern District of Florida

Decided: April 15, 2020

Citation: 955 F.3d 1260, 8 Adm. R. 412 (11th Cir. 2020).

Before **JORDAN, PRYOR,** and **WALKER,*** Circuit Judges.

*The Honorable John M. Walker, Jr., United States Circuit Judge for the Second Circuit, sitting by designation.

[—1—] {-1262-} JORDAN, Circuit Judge: **[—2—]**

Elaine Carroll tripped over the leg of a lounge chair while she was walking through a narrow pathway on a Carnival cruise ship. She sued Carnival, alleging that it negligently failed to maintain a safe walkway and failed to warn her of that dangerous condition. The district court granted summary judgment in favor of Carnival on both claims, concluding that the condition was open and obvious and that Carnival lacked actual or constructive notice of the hazard.

After review of the record and the parties' briefs, and with the benefit of oral argument, we reverse. In concluding that the condition was open and obvious and that Carnival lacked notice, the district court failed to draw all factual inferences in favor of Mrs. Carroll. In addition, even if the allegedly dangerous condition were open and obvious, that would only defeat the failure to warn claim, and would not bar the claim for negligently failing to maintain a safe walkway.

I

In March of 2015, Mrs. Carroll and her husband Michael were passengers on board the *Carnival Pride*. On the first full day of the cruise, Mrs. and Mr. Carroll **{-1263-}** were walking to one of the restaurants, David's Steakhouse, on Deck 11 of the ship. The outer glass wall of David's Steakhouse is curved in the shape of a semi-circle. Lounge chairs are set up in a semi-circular shape along the curved glass wall of the restaurant. **[—3—]**

To get to the restaurant, the Carrolls had to walk on a curved walkway between the foot-end of the row of lounge chairs (on their right side) and the ship's railing (on their left side). When they initially approached the walkway, there were approximately two to three feet between the chairs and the railing, so they were able to walk side-by-side. At some point after passing the first chair, however, the distance between the chairs and the railway narrowed, so Mrs. Carroll's husband walked in front of her and she followed behind him. While Mrs. Carroll was walking behind her husband, her right foot clipped the leg of one of the lounge chairs, causing her to fall and suffer injuries.

Mrs. Carroll sued Carnival for negligence. She asserted, among other things, that Carnival negligently maintained a dangerous condition—"lounge chairs that narrowed and protruded onto a pedestrian walkway"—and negligently failed to warn passengers of the danger associated with that condition.

Carnival moved for summary judgment, arguing that the lounge chairs did not constitute a dangerous condition, and even if they did, it had no duty to warn of the condition for two reasons. First, the condition was open and obvious. Second, Carnival lacked notice of the hazard. Mrs. Carroll opposed the motion, responding that although the lounge chair that she tripped on was not hazardous in and of itself, the location of the lounge chairs and the manner in which they were arranged constituted a dangerous condition. She also argued that the condition was not open **[—4—]** and obvious because, due to the layout of the lounge chairs and the narrowness of the path, she was forced walk behind her husband, obstructing her view. And she asserted that she did not need to prove that Carnival had notice of the hazard because it created the unsafe condition.

Both parties presented evidence in support of their positions, including the deposition testimony of Mrs. and Mr. Carroll and several Carnival employees. Mrs. Carroll also presented the affidavit of an expert, Randall Jaques, who opined that the walkway was unsafe and fell below industry standards.

The district court granted summary judgment in favor of Carnival. In doing so, the district court concluded that Carnival had no duty to warn Mrs. Carroll of the allegedly dangerous condition because it was open and obvious. The district court stated that, because the condition was open and obvious, it did not need to reach whether Carnival had actual or constructive notice of the risk-creating condition. It nevertheless also concluded that Carnival lacked notice of the danger.

II

We review a district court's grant of summary judgment *de novo. See Guevara v. NCL (Bahamas) Ltd.*, 920 F.3d 710, 720, 7 Adm. R. 476, 480 (11th Cir. 2019). "Generally speaking, we will affirm if, after construing the evidence in the light most favorable to the non-moving party, we find that no genuine issue of material fact exists and the moving party is entitled to judgment as a matter of law." *Sorrels v. NCL (Bahamas)* **[—5—]** *Ltd.*, 796 F.3d 1275, 1286, 3 Adm. R. 659, 665 (11th Cir. 2015) (citation and internal quotation marks omitted).

III

This action is governed by federal maritime law because Mrs. Carroll's injury **{-1264-}** occurred on a ship sailing in navigable waters. *See Guevara*, 920 F.3d at 720, 7 Adm. R. at 481. "In analyzing a maritime tort case, we rely on general principles of negligence law." *Chaparro v. Carnival Corp.*, 693 F.3d 1333, 1336 (11th Cir. 2012) (quoting *Daigle v. Point Landing, Inc.*, 616 F.2d 825, 827 (5th Cir. 1980)). To prevail on her maritime negligence claims, therefore, Mrs. Carroll had to prove that (1) Carnival had a duty to protect her from a particular injury; (2) Carnival breached that duty; (3) the breach actually and proximately caused her injury; and (4) she suffered actual harm. *See Sorrels*, 796 F.3d at 1280, 3 Adm. R. at 660.

With respect to the duty element, a cruise line like Carnival owes its passengers "a 'duty of reasonable care' under the circumstances." *Id.* at 1279, 3 Adm. R. at 659. This requires, as "a prerequisite to imposing liability," that Carnival "have had actual or constructive notice of the risk-creating condition[.]" *Keefe v. Bahama Cruise Line, Inc.*, 867 F.2d 1318, 1322 (11th Cir. 1989). Thus, Carnival's liability "hinges on whether it knew or should have known" of the dangerous condition. *Id.* **[—6—]**

We begin by analyzing Mrs. Carroll's claim that Carnival negligently failed to warn her of a dangerous condition, and then evaluate her claim that Carnival negligently failed to maintain a safe walkway.

A

1

"An operator of a cruise ship has a duty to warn only of known dangers that are not open and obvious." *Guevara*, 920 F.3d at 720 n.5, 7 Adm. R. at 481 n.5. In evaluating whether a danger is "open and obvious" we are guided—as in general tort law—by the "reasonable person" standard. *Cf. Lamb by Shepard v. Sears, Roebuck & Co.*, 1 F.3d 1184, 1189–90 (11th Cir. 1993) (explaining in the products liability context that whether a danger is open and obvious is determined "on the basis of an objective view of the product, and the subjective perceptions of the . . . injured party are irrelevant") (citations omitted); *McCarty v. Menard, Inc.*, 927 F.3d 468, 471 (7th Cir. 2019) (explaining in the premises liability context that "[w]hether a hazardous condition is open and obvious is an objective inquiry"). The question, therefore, is whether a reasonable person would have observed the chair leg and appreciated the risk of walking through the narrow passageway under the circumstances.[1] **[—7—]**

[1] We have repeatedly acknowledged and applied this reasonable person standard in unpublished maritime decisions. *See, e.g., Frasca v.*

The district court concluded that Carnival had no duty to warn Mrs. Carroll of the dangers associated with the walkway because the "placement of deck chairs on an open deck, on a clear and sunny day, was an open and obvious condition." D.E. 84 at 10. In reaching this decision, the **{-1265-}** district court relied on Mrs. Carroll's deposition testimony that she could have seen the chair leg had she looked down. *See id.* at 9. The district court also relied on Mrs. Carroll's testimony "that she did not walk behind her husband because the area narrowed, as her husband explained, but rather, because 'you do that.'" *See id.* at 2.

But there was also evidence in the record—which the district court did not acknowledge—that Mrs. Carroll was *forced* to walk behind her husband after passing the first lounge chair because the walkway narrowed. Mrs. Carroll testified that, as a result, her view was blocked by her husband, who has a large profile, so she could not see the foot of the lounge chair that she tripped on nor around the curve of the walkway.

In our view, the district court erred by crediting some statements by Mrs. Carroll—which favored Carnival's open and obvious argument—over her other **[—8—]** statements that she was forced to follow behind her husband due the layout of the chairs and the narrowness of the walkway. Viewing the facts in the light most favorable to Mrs. Carroll, as we must, the record supports an inference that a reasonable person in Mrs. Carroll's circumstances would not have observed the chair leg obstructing her path. There is a genuine dispute of material fact as to whether the danger associated with the walkway was open and obvious.

2

After concluding that Carnival had no duty to warn Mrs. Carroll because the allegedly dangerous condition was open and obvious, the district court stated that it need not decide whether Carnival had actual or constructive notice of the condition. It nevertheless determined that Carnival lacked such notice. In reaching this conclusion, the district court again failed to view the evidence in the light most favorable to Mrs. Carroll and overlooked evidence in the record from which a reasonable jury could find that Carnival had notice.[2] **[—9—]**

Evidence that a ship owner has taken corrective action can establish notice of a dangerous or defective condition. *See Guevara*, 920 F.3d at 720–22, 7 Adm. R. at 481–83 (holding that a warning sign alerting passengers to "watch [their] step" was

---

NCL (Bahamas), Ltd., 654 F. App'x 949, 952 (11th Cir. 2016) (explaining that an operator of a cruise ship has no duty to warn of dangers that are open and obvious and that whether a danger is open and obvious is based on a "reasonable person" standard); *Horne v. Carnival Corp.*, 741 F. App'x 607, 609 (11th Cir. 2018) ("A cruise line does **[—7—]** not need to warn passengers or make special arrangements for open-and-obvious risks. . . . In determining whether a risk is open and obvious, we focus on 'what an objectively reasonable person would observe and do[ ] not take into account the plaintiff's subjective perceptions.") (internal quotation marks and citations omitted); *Krug v. Celebrity Cruises, Inc.*, 745 F. App'x 863, 866 (11th Cir. 2018) ("Under federal admiralty law, a cruise ship has no duty to warn of known dangers that are open and obvious. . . . We evaluate whether a danger would be open and obvious from an objectively reasonable person's point of view and do not focus on the plaintiff's subjective perspective.").

[2] Mrs. Carroll contends that evidence of notice should not be required if the owner of the cruise ship created the dangerous condition. She urges us to modify or reject our decision in *Everett v. Carnival Cruise Lines*, 912 F.2d 1355, 1358–59 (11th Cir. 1990), which held that the district court's jury instructions were erroneous because they did not require the plaintiff to prove notice if she established that the cruise line created the dangerous condition. As a panel, we are bound by *Everett* even if we had misgivings about it. *See Smith v. GTE Corp.*, 236 F.3d 1292, 1300 n.8 (11th Cir. 2001) ("Under the well-established prior panel precedent rule of this Circuit, the holding of the first panel to address an issue is the law of this Circuit, thereby binding all subsequent panels unless and until the first panel's holding is overruled by the Court sitting en banc or by the Supreme Court."). In any event, we need not address *Everett* because, as explained in the text, Mrs. Carroll presented sufficient evidence to create a genuine dispute of material fact on notice.

sufficient to create an issue of material fact on whether the cruise ship had notice of the dangerous nature of the step down); *Sorrels*, 796 F.3d at 1288, 3 Adm. R. at 666–67 (holding that a ship employee's testimony that the ship would sometimes post a warning sign on the pool deck after it rained was enough to create an issue of material fact on whether there was notice that the deck could be slippery when wet). Here, there is evidence reflecting that Carnival took corrective measures to prevent people from tripping over the lounge chairs in the walkway on Deck 11. **{–1266–}**

For example, Mrs. Carroll presented evidence, including the testimony of one of Carnival's employees, that if the lounge chairs were arranged in the "lay-flat position," rather than upright, they would protrude further into the walkway—making the walkway even narrower. As a result, Carnival required them to be set up in the upright position, and employees regularly patrolled the area to fix the chairs. *See* D.E. 49 at ¶¶ 12–13, 32–36.

Specifically, one of Carnival's pool deck supervisors, Viktor Symotiuk, testified that the lounge chairs on Deck 11 were supposed to be arranged in the upright position, and he was instructed (and trained other employees that he supervised) to make sure that the chairs were not protruding into or blocking the **[—10—]** walkway. *See* D.E. 49 at ¶ 12; D.E. 48-5 at 30, 36–38. Although he testified that a lounge chair may be used in the lay-flat position if it is occupied, he also stated that "[y]ou never leave the chair unattended and flat in that area." D.E. 48-5 at 33. He further acknowledged that "[i]f the lounge chair is set on the passenger walkway, it would be an obstruction[ ], it's a reason why a person can get injured." *Id.* at 64.

The district court relied on the deposition of another pool deck supervisor, Denys Stavyts'ky, who testified that that the chairs could be set up in either the upright or lay-flat position. *See* D.E. 84 at 12. But the conflict in the testimony of Mr. Symotiuk and Mr. Stavyts'ky demonstrates that there is a dispute of material fact, making summary judgment inappropriate.[3]

In addition to the testimony of Mr. Symotiuk, there was also the testimony of a Carnival security officer, Manolyn Saldo. She testified that part of her duties included patrolling Deck 11 and moving any lounge chairs that were blocking the walkway. *See* D.E. 44 at ¶¶ 39–41. The assistant chief security officer, Siddhartha Kokate, likewise testified that because passengers sometimes pull out chairs and do not put them back in place, they can create an "unsafe condition," so it is part of the staff's duties to take corrective action and remove that hazard. *See* D.E. 44-6 at 14; D.E. 44 ¶¶ 45–47. **[—11—]**

As in *Guevara* and *Sorrels*, a reasonable jury could view this testimony as evidence that Carnival has taken corrective measures—i.e., adopting a policy of keeping the chairs in-line and/or in the upright position and instructing employees to ensure that they are not blocking the walkway—due to a known danger. This is enough to withstand summary judgment on the issue of Carnival's notice.

In sum, there were disputes of fact on both the obviousness of the condition and Carnival's notice of the danger. The district court therefore erred in granting summary judgment on Mrs. Carroll's failure to warn claim.[4]

---

[3] We note that Mr. Stavyts'ky also testified that hotel stewards were required to inspect that the chairs were arranged properly every 15-20 minutes. *See* D.E. 44-3 at 45–46.

[4] Mrs. Carroll also asserts that Carnival had notice of the dangerous condition because there were 12 separate instances where passengers tripped and fell over lounge chairs aboard ships in the same class as the *Carnival Pride*. The parties dispute whether these prior incidents were sufficiently similar to Mrs. Carroll's accident to put Carnival on notice of the risks associated with the walkway on Deck 11 of the *Carnival Pride*. We do not reach this issue because, as discussed above, there is other evidence in the record establishing that there is a genuine dispute of material fact as to whether Carnival had notice of the dangerous condition.

B

The district court appears to have concluded that Carnival was entitled to summary judgment on both Mrs. Carroll's failure to warn and negligent maintenance **{-1267-}** theories because of the open and obvious nature of the condition. The district court reasoned that it need not reach notice after determining that the condition was open and obvious, suggesting that its decision on the latter was dispositive of the entire case. That initial conclusion, however, should not have ended the analysis for Mrs. Carroll's negligent maintenance claim. As Mrs. Carroll correctly argues, Carnival **[—12—]** may still be liable for maintaining a dangerous condition even if the danger was obvious.

1

As noted earlier, this action is governed by federal maritime law. *See Guevara*, 920 F.3d at 720, 7 Adm. R. at 481. "Subject to direction from Congress, the federal courts fashion federal maritime law." *Air & Liquid Sys. Corp. v. DeVries*, 139 S. Ct. 986, 992, 7 Adm. R. 2, 3 (2019). In doing so, we "may examine, among other sources, judicial opinions, legislation, treatises, and scholarly writing." *Id.*, 7 Adm. R. at 3. *See also E. River S.S. Corp. v. Transamerica*, 476 U.S. 858, 864–65 (1986) ("Drawn from state and federal sources, the general maritime law is an amalgam of traditional common-law rules, modifications of those rules, and newly created rules.") (footnote omitted); *Franza v. Royal Caribbean Cruises, Ltd.*, 772 F.3d 1225, 1231–32, 2 Adm. R. 582, 585–86 (11th Cir. 2014) (discussing our "broad discretion in admiralty and maritime" cases to "develop th[e] law").

The open and obvious nature of a dangerous condition negates liability for failure to warn. *See, e.g., Guevara*, 920 F.3d at 720 n.5, 7 Adm. R. at 481 n.5 (noting that the duty to warn only applies to "dangers that are not open and obvious"); Benedict on Admiralty § 5.04 (7th ed. 2019) (stating that the duty of cruise lines to give notice of defective conditions "extends only to those dangers which are not apparent or obvious"); Thomas J. Schoenbaum, Admiralty & Maritime Law § 5:11 (6th ed. 2018) ("[T]here **[—13—]** is a duty to warn passengers only of dangers that are not apparent and obvious."). We have not squarely addressed, however, whether the open and obvious nature of a dangerous condition also bars liability for a maritime negligent maintenance claim. Because Congress has not spoken on this issue, "[w]e start with basic tort-law principles" to determine whether such a distinction exists (or should exist) in maritime law. *Air & Liquid Sys. Corp.*, 139 S. Ct. at 993, 7 Adm. R. at 4.

The Third Restatement of Torts imposes a duty of reasonable care on possessors of land—even if a danger is open and obvious—if the possessor should anticipate harm. *See* Restatement (Third) of Torts § 51 cmt. k (2012). It notes that that such a duty is consistent with § 343A(1) of the Second Restatement of Torts, which requires land possessors to take reasonable precautions for known or obvious dangers when the possessor "should anticipate the harm despite such knowledge or obviousness." Restatement (Second) of Torts § 343A(1) (1965). As relevant here, the Second Restatement of Torts illustrates this principle with the following example:

> Through the negligence of A Grocery Store a fallen rainspout is permitted to lie across a footpath alongside the store, which is used by customers as an exit. B, a customer, leaves the store with her arms full of bundles which obstruct her vision, and does not see the spout. She trips over it, and is injured. If it is found that A should reasonably have anticipated this, A is subject to liability to B.

Restatement (Second) of Torts § 343A cmt. f, illus. 4. **[—14—]**

The Third Restatement of Torts distinguishes between failure to warn claims and negligent maintenance claims, explaining that the open and obvious nature of a risk negates the duty to warn because "[t]he **{-1268-}** primary purpose of a warning is to give notice of the existence of the risk. . . . Risks that are known, open, or obvious already provide notice to those who might be exposed to the risk, making a warning superfluous." Restatement (Third) of Torts § 51 cmt. k. By contrast, the open and obvious nature of a risk does not render the duty to exercise reasonable care superfluous:

> Known or obvious dangers pose less of a risk than comparable latent dangers because those exposed can take precautions to protect themselves. Nevertheless, despite the opportunity of entrants to avoid an open and obvious risk, in some circumstances, a residual risk will remain. Land possessors have a duty of reasonable care with regard to those residual risks. Thus, the fact that a dangerous condition is open and obvious bears on the assessment of whether reasonable care was employed, *but it does not pretermit the land possessor's liability.*

Id. (emphasis added).

Thus, the Third Restatement of Torts treats the open and obvious nature of a dangerous condition as a factor to be considered in a comparative fault analysis—not as a bar to liability for negligently maintaining premises. *See id.* ("An entrant who encounters an obviously dangerous condition and who fails to exercise reasonable self-protective care is contributorily negligent. Because of comparative fault, however, the issue of the defendant's duty and breach must be kept distinct **[—15—]** from the question of the plaintiff's negligence."). As the Third Restatement of Torts notes, a contrary rule that would preclude liability because a risk is open and obvious would "sit[ ] more comfortably—if not entirely congruently—with the older rule of contributory negligence as a bar to recovery." *Id.*

We think the approach of the Third Restatement of Torts is consistent with maritime tort principles, and we adopt it. For starters, it aligns with the Supreme Court's adoption of comparative negligence in maritime cases. *See Kermarec v. Compagnie Generale Transatlantique*, 358 U.S. 625, 628–29 (1959) (holding that because maritime law governed the plaintiff's negligence claim, the district court erred "in instructing the jury that contributory negligence . . . would operate as a complete bar to recovery," and that "[t]he jury should have been told instead that [the plaintiff's] contributory negligence was to be considered only in mitigation of damages"); *Smith & Kelly Co. v. S/S Concordia TADJ*, 718 F.2d 1022, 1029–30 (11th Cir. 1983) (applying comparative fault principles in a maritime case).

The approach of the Third Restatement of Torts is also dictated by the former Fifth Circuit's opinion in *Arthur v. Flota Mercante Gran Centro Americana S.A.*, 487 F.2d 561 (5th Cir. 1973). In *Arthur*, the plaintiff set out to board the defendant's vessel to inspect the loading of grain. *See id.* at 562. To board the ship, he had to cross a brow gangway and step down a bulwark ladder. *See id.* As he stepped down on the ladder, he slipped and fell, causing injury. *See id.* The case proceeded to trial **[—16—]** solely on the plaintiff's negligence claim against the shipowner. *See id.* After a jury verdict in the plaintiff's favor, the defendant appealed, arguing in pertinent part that "it owed no duty to protect the plaintiff from the risk of harm created by the dangerous condition of the vessel because [the] plaintiff, as an experienced seaman [an inspector], knew or should have known of the dangerous condition." *Id.* at 563. The *Arthur* panel rejected this argument, explaining that "[t]he trial court properly considered this contention as relating to plaintiff's negligence in boarding the vessel in the **{-1269-}** condition in which it existed. Comparative negligence is the rule to be followed; the negligence of the plaintiff, regardless of how gross, does not preclude recovery, but only mitigates damages." *Id.* Though *Arthur* is not often cited for this principle, it constitutes binding precedent and demonstrates that the open and obvious nature of a dangerous condition does not bar a claim against a shipowner for negligent failure to maintain safe premises.[5] **[—17—]**

---

[5] It is unclear from *Arthur* whether the plaintiff was covered by the Longshore and Harbor Workers' Compensation Act, 33 U.S.C. § 901 *et seq.* But even if the plaintiff would have been covered by the

Accordingly, even if the risk was open and obvious, that does not preclude Mrs. Carroll's negligent maintenance claim. *See Lewis v. Langenfelder & Son*, No. 2:01cv804 & 2:02cv622, 2004 WL 2996780, at *6 (E.D. Va. Aug. 17, 2004) ("If the nature of the gap between the vessel and the shore was a dangerous condition, it was created by the defendant through its employees, and the defendant had a duty to correct this condition, regardless of whether it was open and obvious. The decedent's decision to proceed despite this condition may have been contributorily negligent, but this conclusion is not a per se bar to recovery under the law of admiralty.").

2

Mrs. Carroll presented evidence creating a genuine dispute of material fact as to whether Carnival negligently maintained an unsafe walkway. This included an affidavit from her expert, Mr. Jaques, who opined that the width of the walkway would have been below industry standards if the chairs were in the lay flat position. This testimony is relevant in determining whether Carnival's conduct fell below the standard of care. *See, e.g., Sorrels*, 796 F.3d at 1282, 3 Adm. R. at 661–62 ("[E]vidence of custom within a particular industry, group, or organization is admissible as bearing on the standard of care in determining negligence . . . Compliance or noncompliance with such custom, though not conclusive on the issue of negligence, is one of the factors the trier of fact may consider in applying the standard of care.") (citation and internal quotation marks omitted). **[—18—]**

According to Mr. Jaques, the maximum amount of room possible in the walkway was 35–36 inches if the lounge chairs were in the upright position and pushed up against the glass wall of David's Steakhouse. If the lounge chairs were in the lay-flat position, however, the width of the walkway would be 28 ½ inches if the chairs were only two inches from the glass, and between 23 and 25 inches if the chairs were approximately six inches from the glass. If some of the chairs were in the lay flat position or pulled out a few inches, Mr. Jaques opined that the walkway would violate industry standards, including but not limited to the ADA standards, which require "a clear width of not less than 36 inches[.]" D.E. 49 at 37.

The record further reflects that there are disputes of material fact regarding whether the chairs were in the upright or lay-flat position at the time of the accident, and whether the chairs were in line or out **{–1270–}** of position. For example, both Mrs. and Mr. Carroll testified in their depositions that at least some of the deck chairs were in the lay flat position. Mrs. Carroll also testified, however, that at the time of the accident the chairs "weren't messed up." D.E. 48-1 at 41. In contrast, Mr. Carroll testified that the chairs were not "orderly," explaining that three or four of the chairs were "out of position" and "were pulled back from the glass several feet[.]" D.E. 48-3 at 25. He explained that the chairs "were in the walkway," which he described as being "more like an obstacle course," and estimated that the width of the walkway was about 20 inches. *See id.* at 25, 29. **[—19—]**

A reasonable jury could find that at least some chairs were in the lay-flat position and out of order, and thus conclude—in conjunction with Mr. Jaques' testimony—that Carnival negligently maintained an unsafe walkway that fell below industry standards. The district court therefore erred in granting summary judgment on Mrs. Carroll's negligent maintenance claim.

LHWCA, *Arthur* is still controlling because the plaintiff's claims arose prior to the enactment of the 1972 Amendments to the LHWCA, which added § 905(b), a statutory negligence action against the ship. *See Scindia Steam Nav. Co., Ltd. v. De Los Santos*, 451 U.S. 156, 165 (1981). Prior to 1972, a longshoreman injured in the course of his employment could receive compensation from the shipowner if he could prove that his injury was caused by the shipowner's negligence or the ship's unseaworthiness. *See id.* at 164; *Clark v. Bothelho Shipping Corp.*, 784 F.2d 1563, 1564–65 (11th Cir. 1986). *Arthur* was decided on negligence grounds and involved—as here—the duty a shipowner owes to an invitee.

IV

We reverse the district court's grant of summary judgment in favor of Carnival and remand for further proceedings consistent with this opinion.

REVERSED AND REMANDED.

United States Court of Appeals
for the Eleventh Circuit

No. 19-10533

TROUTMAN
vs.
SEABOARD ATL. LTD.

Appeal from the United States District Court for the Southern District of Florida

Decided: May 13, 2020

Citation: 958 F.3d 1143, 8 Adm. R. 420 (11th Cir. 2020).

Before **MARTIN, NEWSOM,** and **CARNES,** Circuit Judges.

[—2—] {–1144–} MARTIN, Circuit Judge:

Anthony Troutman was injured when he fell from a walkway on the upper deck of the ship where he was working as a longshoreman. He sued the ship and its owners (collectively, "Seaboard"), seeking to hold them liable under the Longshore and Harbor Workers' Compensation Act (the "LHWCA"), 33 U.S.C. § 901 *et seq.* Seaboard moved for summary judgment, arguing that the LHWCA does not permit Mr. Troutman's negligence claim. The District Court granted Seaboard's motion. It held that Mr. Troutman's suit was barred because, among other reasons, the hazardous condition that led to his injury was open and obvious.

With the benefit of oral argument, we affirm.

I.

A. FACTUAL BACKGROUND

On April 22, 2016, Mr. Troutman was working for a stevedoring company named Eller ITO to secure containers being loaded onto the *M/V Seaboard Atlantic* (the "Vessel"). The Vessel is owned and chartered by Defendants Seaboard Atlantic Ltd. and Seaboard Marine Ltd. Prior to the incident, Mr. Troutman had been employed as a longshoreman for over 19 years.

This case centers around the cargo-loading process for two of the Vessel's bays, Bay 28 and Bay 32. Bay 28 is raised above Bay 32. An elevated walkway **[—3—]** runs along the bottom of Bay 28, above Bay 32. Usually, cargo is loaded into the lower Bay 32 before Bay 28. When this happens, the cargo fills Bay 32 and the tops of the containers are higher than the walkway **{–1145–}** above. This alleviates the risk of falling off the walkway, since the person on the walkway is even with the tops of the cargo in Bay 32. However, when Bay 32 is empty, there is a six-to-eight-foot drop from the walkway to the deck.

Before April 22, 2016, Mr. Troutman had worked on the Vessel over 20 times. Sometimes when Mr. Troutman worked on the Vessel, the elevated walkway was protected by a rope fence. Other times, Mr. Troutman and other longshoremen had to ask Seaboard to put up the rope fence. When he worked on the Vessel, including on the day in question, Mr. Troutman worked as a lasher. A lasher works to secure, and to release securing mechanisms for, cargo being loaded onto the ship.

On the day of the incident, the superintendent of Eller ITO, Gilberto Perez, decided to load Bay 28 first because of a delay in readying the containers that were to be loaded into Bay 32. There was no rope fence protecting the walkway that day. Mr. Troutman and Mr. Perez both knew that the walkway was unsafe without the rope fence. Mr. Troutman also knew that he was not obligated to put himself in danger to perform his job, and that if a dangerous condition was present he was not required to work through it. Mr. Troutman did not ask Seaboard to put up the **[—4—]** rope fence that day. No party disputes that the walkway, in its exposed state, was an open and obvious hazard.

While Mr. Perez did direct that Bay 28 be loaded first, he did not instruct Mr. Troutman to start lashing the cargo on Bay 28. Had Mr. Troutman asked, Mr. Perez would have told him not to start lashing the cargo on Bay 28 until Bay 32 was loaded. Mr. Perez also testified that Eller ITO would have provided Mr. Troutman with safety equipment to prevent him from falling if he asked for it.

Nevertheless, Mr. Troutman began to lash the cargo loaded into Bay 28 before cargo had been loaded into Bay 32. While walking on the elevated walkway, he tripped on loose lashing materials left there by another longshoreman. He lost his balance and fell to the deck below. He was seriously injured and had to undergo surgery.

B. PROCEDURAL HISTORY

Mr. Troutman sued Seaboard, alleging it was negligent in breach of (1) the duty to turn over a safe vessel to the stevedore company; (2) the duty to intervene; and (3) the duty to exercise ordinary care to keep the vessel in reasonably safe condition. Seaboard answered the complaint and the parties proceeded to discovery. Following discovery, Seaboard moved for summary judgment.

The District Court granted summary judgment for Seaboard on all of Mr. Troutman's claims. Relevant to this appeal, the court held that Mr. Troutman **[—5—]** could not succeed on his first claim—breach of what is known as the LHWCA's "turnover duty"—because the walkway was an open and obvious hazard which he could have avoided. Mr. Troutman timely appealed. His appeal challenges the grant of summary judgment on this basis alone.

II.

"We review *de novo* the district court's grant of summary judgment, considering all of the evidence in the light most favorable to the nonmoving party." *Nesbitt v. Candler County*, 945 F.3d 1355, 1357 (11th Cir. 2020). "Summary judgment is proper 'if the movant shows that there is no genuine dispute as to any material fact and the movant is entitled to judgment as a matter of law.'" *Id.* (quoting Fed. R. Civ. P. 56(a)). **{-1146-}**

III.

This appeal requires us to address a question of first impression in this circuit: when, if ever, a negligence claim for breach of the shipowner's duty to turn over a vessel in safe condition properly lies where the plaintiff was injured by an open and obvious hazard. We conclude that, generally, a shipowner does not breach this duty when the injurious hazard was open and obvious and could have been avoided by a reasonably competent stevedore. Although this rule is not absolute, Mr. Troutman cannot show any exception to the rule that would deprive **[—6—]** Seaboard of an open-and-obvious defense here. We therefore affirm the District Court's order granting summary judgment in favor of Seaboard.

A.

The LHWCA "establishes a comprehensive federal workers' compensation program that provides longshoremen and their families with medical, disability, and survivor benefits for work-related injuries and death." *Howlett v. Birkdale Shipping Co., S.A.*, 512 U.S. 92, 96, 114 S. Ct. 2057, 2062 (1994). The statute was amended in 1972 to permit a longshoreman to "seek damages in a third-party negligence action against the owner of the vessel on which he was injured." *Id.*; *see* Longshoremen's and Harbor Workers' Compensation Act Amendments of 1972, Pub. L. No. 92-576, § 18(a), 86 Stat. 1251, 1263 (codified as amended at 33 U.S.C. § 905(b)). It is this section of the LHWCA that governs Mr. Troutman's claim for relief.

Under § 905(b), a shipowner owes the longshoreman three general duties: "(1) a turnover duty, (2) a duty to exercise reasonable care in the areas of the ship under the active control of the vessel, and (3) a duty to intervene." *Kirksey v. Tonghai Mar.*, 535 F.3d 388, 391 (5th Cir. 2008) (citing, *inter alia*, *Howlett*, 512 U.S. at 98, 114 S. Ct. at 2063); *see Scindia Steam Nav. Co. v. De Los Santos*, 451 U.S. 156, 167–68, 101 S. Ct. 1614, 1622–23 (1981). The 1972 amendments to the LHWCA also abrogated the shipowner's common-law defenses of assumption of **[—7—]** the risk and contributory negligence. *Kirsch v. Plovidba*, 971 F.2d 1026, 1031 n.6 (3d Cir. 1992) (citing *Scindia*, 451 U.S. at 165 n.13, 101 S. Ct. at 1621 n.13).

A shipowner's turnover duty consists of two corresponding duties. First, under the "duty of safe condition," the shipowner must exercise "ordinary care under the circumstances to have the ship and its equipment in such condition that an expert and experienced stevedore will be able by the exercise of reasonable care to carry on its cargo operations with reasonable safety to persons and property."[1] *Bjaranson v. Botelho Shipping Corp., Manila*, 873 F.2d 1204, 1207 (9th Cir. 1989) (quoting *Scindia*, 451 U.S. at 167, 101 S. Ct. at 1622); *see Roach v. M/V Aqua Grace*, 857 F.2d 1575, 1581 (11th Cir. 1988) ("[A] shipowner must turn over the ship and its equipment in a condition that permits a stevedore to do its work with reasonable safety . . . ."). Second, the shipowner has a "duty to warn" the longshoreman "of any hidden dangers of which [the shipowner] knows or should know." *Roach*, 857 F.2d at 1581; *see* **{-1147-}** *Howlett*, 512 U.S. at 98–99, 114 S. Ct. at 2063. The duty to warn is a "corollary" to the duty of safe condition. *Howlett*, 512 U.S. at 98, 114 S. Ct. at 2063. **[—8—]**

B.

The District Court granted summary judgment for Seaboard on both aspects of the turnover duty. The court held that Seaboard did not breach the duty of safe condition because "an expert and experienced stevedore could have loaded the Vessel with 'reasonable safety' by loading the lower deck first or . . . by staying off the walkway until *after* the lower deck was loaded." *Troutman v. Seaboard Atl. Ltd.*, No. 1:18-cv-21586-UU, 2019 WL 656259, at *4 (S.D. Fla. Jan. 8, 2019). The court also held that Seaboard did not breach the duty to warn because "[t]he undisputed facts show that the hazard posed by the exposed walkway was open and obvious to the stevedore." *Id.* On appeal, Mr. Troutman argues the District Court erred by granting Seaboard an open-and-obvious defense to its turnover duty of safe condition.

Under the LHWCA, the stevedoring company and the longshoreman have primary responsibility for avoiding hazards they should have anticipated. The LHWCA assumes the ability of "an expert and experienced stevedoring contractor, mindful of the dangers he should reasonably expect to encounter, . . . to carry on cargo operations with reasonable safety to persons and property." *Howlett*, 512 U.S. at 98, 114 S. Ct. at 2063 (quotation marks omitted). The shipowner does not have a duty "to turn over an absolutely safe vessel; the shipowner need only exercise reasonable care." 1 Thomas J. Schoenbaum, *Admiralty & Maritime Law* **[—9—]** § 7:14, at 708 (6th ed. 2018). Where a hazard exists, the question of negligence boils down to whether "an expert and experienced stevedore"—rather than an "unskilled person[]"—could safely avoid the hazard. *Bjaranson*, 873 F.2d at 1208. Generally, shipowners have "a rightful expectation" that a stevedoring company will "perform [its] task properly without supervision by the ship" and that the stevedore will "avoid exposing the longshoremen to unreasonable hazards." *Scindia*, 451 U.S. at 170, 101 S. Ct. at 1623–24; *see id.* at 180 (Powell, J., concurring) (stating that, under the majority opinion in *Scindia*, the "primary burden . . . for avoiding injuries caused by obvious hazards" is placed "on the stevedore").

We read this precedent to establish a general rule that the open-and-obvious defense applies to breach of the turnover duty of safe condition. This squares with the Supreme Court's pronouncements in *Scindia* and *Howlett*. A longshoreman can only be said to have carried out his work with "reasonable competence" if he "identif[ied] and cope[d] with defects" of which he was aware.[2]

[1] Although the turnover duty of safe condition is framed in terms of danger to the stevedore—the longshoreman's employer—"the focus of the factual inquiry is frequently directed at [whether] experienced longshore workers" could complete their work with reasonable safety. *See Thomas v. Newton Int'l Enters.*, 42 F.3d 1266, 1270 n.4 (9th Cir. 1994).

[2] To the extent that our pre-*Howlett* case law—in particular, *Lemon v. Bank Lines, Ltd.*, 656 F.2d 110 (5th Cir. Sept. 1981)—suggests that a shipowner breaches the duty of safe condition by turning over a ship with an open and obvious hazard, we agree with the current-day Fifth Circuit that these cases have been "undermine[d]" by *Howlett*. *See Kirksey*, 535 F.3d at 395–96; *see also*

Howlett, 512 U.S. at 104, 114 S. Ct. at 2066; *Scindia*, 451 U.S. at 172, 101 S. Ct. at 1624. Although **[—10—]** the Supreme Court's articulation of what it means to act as a reasonable longshoreman came in the context of the duty to warn, *see Howlett*, 512 U.S. at 99–100, 101 S. Ct. at 2064, this reasoning applies with equal force to the shipowner's defense "against a claim based on the general failure to provide a safe **{-1148-}** ship based on defects in the stow." *See Kirksey*, 535 F.3d at 393–94; *see also Howlett*, 512 U.S. at 102, 114 S. Ct. at 2065 (applying principles "taken from [*Scindia*'s] examination of the . . . duty to intervene" to analysis of the turnover duty). In contrast, Mr. Troutman's preferred rule—that a shipowner violates the duty of safe condition by turning over a ship with any hazard, no matter how obvious or avoidable—would violate several principles established in this area of law. For example, shipowners could no longer rely on the expertise and experience of the stevedoring company or longshoremen to deal with hazards that may arise. In addition, Mr. Troutman's rule would effectively require shipowners to turn over an absolutely safe vessel, a duty which the LHWCA does not impose. We thus conclude that the open and obvious nature of the exposed walkway is relevant to whether Seaboard violated its turnover duty of safe condition.

Mr. Troutman says the defense does not apply in this case because the walkway was inherently unsafe, comparing it to a hypothetical situation in which Seaboard allowed tigers to prowl the Vessel's deck. *See* Oral Argument Recording at 5:45–6:03. Mr. Troutman's analogy misses the mark because it would hardly be **[—11—]** reasonable for Seaboard to expect him to carry out his duties with safety if dangerous animals were roaming the ship. Here, by contrast, it is undisputed that Mr. Troutman could have waited to use the walkway until after Bay 32 was loaded with cargo, thereby avoiding the hazard. As a result, the general rule applies in this case.

Bonner v. City of Prichard, 661 F.2d 1206, 1207 (11th Cir. 1981) (en banc) (adopting as binding precedent all decisions of the former Fifth Circuit handed down prior to the close of business on September 30, 1981).

Finally, Mr. Troutman says that affirming the District Court in his case cannot be squared with Congress's abrogation of the shipowner's defenses of assumption of the risk and contributory negligence. This argument misunderstands whose negligence is at issue in this appeal. We do not hold that Mr. Troutman is barred from recovery because he acted negligently by crossing the walkway. Rather, we hold that, based on the undisputed facts of this case, Seaboard did not act negligently. As we have explained, Seaboard was entitled to rely on the "expertise in cargo operations" of Mr. Troutman and his employer. *See Kirsch*, 971 F.2d at 1031 n.6. Because "an 'expert and experienced stevedore' acting with 'reasonable care'" would have been able to avoid the walkway, Seaboard was not negligent in allowing the walkway to exist in its exposed state. *See Morris v. Compagnie Mar. Des Chargeurs Reunis, S.A.*, 832 F.2d 67, 71 (5th Cir. 1987) (quoting *Scindia*, 451 U.S. at 168, 101 S. Ct. at 1622). **[—12—]**

IV.

The exposed walkway was an open and obvious hazard that Mr. Troutman could have avoided with the exercise of reasonable care. For this reason, the District Court properly dismissed Mr. Troutman's claim for negligence under the LHWCA.

AFFIRMED.

United States Court of Appeals
for the Eleventh Circuit

No. 18-14917

AMY
vs.
CARNIVAL CORP.

Appeal from the United States District Court for the Southern District of Florida

Decided: June 16, 2020

Citation: 961 F.3d 1303, 8 Adm. R. 424 (11th Cir. 2020).

Before **WILSON**, **MARCUS**, and **THAPAR**,* Circuit Judges.

*The Honorable Amul R. Thapar, United States Circuit Judge for the Sixth Circuit, sitting by designation.

[—2—] {-1304-} **WILSON**, Circuit Judge: **{-1305-}**

This maritime-negligence case arises out of an accident that occurred at sea on Carnival's cruise ship *Liberty*. While on Deck 14 with her family, W.A., a three-year-old female child, climbed and—accounts differ—either fell over or through a guard rail onto Deck 12 and suffered head injuries. W.A.'s mother, Elizabeth Amy, sued Carnival on W.A.'s behalf for negligent creation and maintenance of the guard rail and failure to warn of the danger posed by the guard rail.[1] The district court granted summary judgment on both counts to Carnival. Amy appeals, arguing that the district court erred as to both counts. We agree with Amy. The district court erred, first, when it concluded that there was no genuine issue of material fact as to Carnival's notice of the alleged risk-creating condition because it failed to view the evidence in a light most favorable to Amy and to draw reasonable inferences in her favor. It also erred when it resolved the failure-to-warn claim on a basis that Carnival did not raise, without providing Amy notice or **[—3—]** an opportunity to respond. Therefore, we reverse the district court's grant of summary judgment and remand for further proceedings.[2]

I.

To set the scene, the *Liberty* has a Deck 12 and a Deck 14, but no Deck 13. Deck 14 overhangs Deck 12. Deck 14 has a guard rail, which is composed of a series of horizontal metal and wooden bars called courses. The courses are 7.87 inches apart. W.A. fell from Deck 14 onto Deck 12.

Witnesses told different stories about how W.A. fell. W.A.'s brother, who was standing on Deck 14 with her, testified that W.A. put her hands on the second course, tried to pull herself up and sit on the lower course, lost her grip, and slipped through the courses. But two brothers (minors unrelated to the Amy family), who were waiting to go down a waterslide at the time W.A. fell, said in separate depositions that W.A. had climbed the courses; was standing on the second course from the bottom; had her hands on the wooden, top course; leaned over it; and fell over the top of the guard rail.

Amy sued Carnival and alleged the following in her complaint. The guard rail posed a risk of falling and resulting injury to children because children could climb or pass through it and fall to a lower deck. **{-1306-}** W.A. fell and injured herself **[—4—]** doing just that. For multiple reasons, Carnival knew that the guard rail posed such a risk. And Carnival negligently created, maintained, and failed to warn about the danger the guard rail posed to small children.

Carnival answered. It denied negligence, asserted it had no actual or constructive notice of the dangerous condition, but did not raise a defense that the condition was open and obvious.

---

[1] Amy made a third, catch-all negligence allegation. But the district court declined to analyze that third count due to lack of record evidence about any other allegedly unsafe conditions, and Amy does not argue about it on appeal. So we do not address it further.

[2] The district court also entered an order awarding Carnival its costs. Amy separately appealed from that order, *see* D.E. 89, and we consolidated the two appeals. Because we reverse the district court's summary judgment order, we also vacate the award of costs.

During discovery, the parties deposed the following witnesses, among others. At least three *Liberty* passengers testified that Carnival warned passengers about the guard rails at safety meetings. Nancy Mitchell testified that, at the beginning of the cruise, she attended a mandatory safety drill at which crew members warned passengers in person not to "climb up rails," "try to sit on them," "try to get selfies [or] lean[] over" them. She also testified that crew members said that "accidents can happen, that there have been passengers [who] have fallen off." The two brothers, who witnessed W.A. fall while waiting in line for the water slide, testified similarly, albeit with less detail.

Frank Fore, Amy's engineering expert, executed an affidavit and a Rule 26 report. Per his affidavit, he inspected the *Liberty* and another cruise ship, the *M/S Disney Wonder*. It appears that Carnival never challenged or rebutted Fore's Rule 26 report and affidavit at any point in the district-court proceedings. **[—5—]**

In the executive summary of his report, Fore states the following. "Falls from heights, *e.g.,* buildings, have caused significant injuries and deaths among young children; and have been one of the most common reasons for emergency room visits." "Guards with horizontal metal courses present a 'ladder effect' which can attract small children and encourage them to attempt to climb through or over such guards." Some jurisdictions have proactively required safety "measures to protect small children from falls from heights (*e.g.,* window guards and making balcony railings difficult for small children to pass through or climb over)." Respected safety organizations "have long recommended that any open spaces between barriers and guardrails be narrowed so that a four (4) inch sphere (or a small child's head/torso) not be capable of passing through any such space." "Proactive structural measures, to make barriers and guardrails more difficult for small children to climb over or through, have found their way on to some cruise ships," such as the *Disney Wonder*. Carnival itself "utilizes flat clear panel barriers in lieu of open, ladder-effect (*i.e.,* climbable) horizontal metal guardrails; and . . . angles barriers and guardrails back toward potential child climbers (an effective form of anti-climb protection)." However, it does so "in some, but not all, locations aboard the *Carnival Liberty* and other vessels in its fleet."

More specifically, Fore analyzed the accident location. "Deck 14 forward of the *Carnival Liberty* is a location where a fall from height to the hard deck below **[—6—]** (Deck 12) is capable of producing sufficient forces to seriously injure or kill a toddler or small child." Therefore, this location "requires an effective barrier or guardrail that minimizes the risk of small children climbing through or over such a barrier." The Deck 14 guard rails "consist of horizontal metal railings with open, wide spaces that are sufficient for small children to pass through; and lack anti-climb measures such as" solid paneling or curved guard rails. The configuration of the Deck 14 guard rails contravenes the previously mentioned recommended safety standards.

Carnival's corporate representative, Suzanne Vasquez, testified to the following on Carnival's behalf. She confirmed that a **{-1307-}** "general purpose[] of the guard rails like the one involved in this case . . . includ[es] being efficient to contain humans [including small children] on one side from getting to the other side." And Carnival conceded that "a guard rail that for whatever reason would not be efficient to contain foreseeable human beings on one side, and not allow them to get to the other side . . . would be dangerous." Carnival knows that "if a guard rail has sufficient space between the lower [courses,] . . . in theory a small human being could get through there." Carnival was aware "[t]hat if you go over or somehow through [a guard rail], you could fall 10 feet and die or get very injured." The danger of falling over a railing is "apparent." For that reason, it is "common knowledge" that climbing a guard rail is "inherently dangerous" for a **[—7—]** child. She also explicitly acknowledged that the Deck 14 railing is climbable and has no climb protection and that Carnival knew the same. Carnival "do[es] everything we can to protect our guests and our crew" and "safety and security of guests and crew is of preeminent importance all the time."

Ben Clement, Carnival's Director of Shipbuilding since 2006 or 2007 and the senior vice president in charge of new build and dry-dock refurbishments, agreed that the primary purpose of having barriers or guard rails on balconies and other locations on Carnival's ships, including the accident location, is safety, "to keep people from falling." And he agreed that Carnival "understands that . . . people [who] need to be kept from falling include[] small children." He testified that Carnival "design[s] to the extreme safety." Carnival previously modified other railings to prevent climbing because it was aware of "the temptation of climbing" and that climbable railings "could be potentially unsafe." Finally, Clement testified that, in the context of his job with Carnival, he had heard of a safety recommendation that "[o]pen guards shall have balusters or ornamental patterns such that a four-inch diameter sphere cannot pass through any opening, up to a height of 34 inches." There was an internal discussion about that standard, and Carnival implemented that standard for ships at least as early as 2005 or so, when the planning for another ship, the *Dream*, began. **[—8—]**

Carnival moved for summary judgment based on lack of notice evidence. Amy opposed Carnival's motion and filed a statement of disputed material facts.

The district court granted summary judgment for Carnival, holding that Carnival owed W.A. no duty. As to the negligent-creation-and-maintenance claim, the court found no evidence that Carnival had actual or constructive notice of the risk-creating condition. Its analysis turned on specificity. The court concluded that "[n]othing in the record permits the conclusion that Carnival had actual notice that the <u>specific</u> alleged risk-creating conditions—that is, [the railing's exact measurements]—were dangerous."[3] It reasoned that "evidence of general railing dangers is not sufficient." The court said that Carnival's warning against climbing on railings at the mandatory muster drill was too general to serve as evidence of notice of the specific alleged risk-creating conditions. As for constructive notice, the court considered the safety recommendations and the *Disney Wonder*'s safety measures but concluded that neither indicated notice. **{–1308–}** The district court cited Clement's testimony once and Fore's never. As for the failure-to-warn count, the district court concluded that the danger posed by the rail was open and obvious; thus, Carnival had no duty to warn. Amy appealed.

II. **[—9—]**

"We review a district court's grant of summary judgment de novo, viewing all the evidence, and drawing all reasonable factual inferences, in favor of the nonmoving party." *Guevara v. NCL (Bahamas) Ltd.*, 920 F.3d 710, 720, 7 Adm. R. 476, 480 (11th Cir. 2019). A grant of summary judgment is proper "if the movant shows that there is no genuine dispute as to any material fact and the movant is entitled to judgment as a matter of law." Fed. R. Civ. P. 56(a). But it is improper if a reasonable jury could find for the non-moving party. *Guevara*, 920 F.3d at 720, 7 Adm. R. at 481.

III.

Because W.A.'s injury "occurred on a ship sailing in navigable waters," federal maritime law governs this action. *See Carroll v. Carnival Corp.*, 955 F.3d 1260, 1263–64, 8 Adm. R. 412, 413 (11th Cir. 2020). "In analyzing a maritime tort case, we rely on general principles of negligence law." *Id.* at 1264, 8 Adm. R. at 413.

To win on her maritime negligence claims, Amy must prove that, among other things not at issue here (i.e., breach, causation, and harm), Carnival had a duty to protect her from a particular injury.[4] *See id.*, 8 Adm. R.

[3] The district court also described the "specific risk-creating conditions" as "the alleged unreasonably wide distance between the courses, the alleged unreasonably short height of the railing, and the alleged unreasonably dangerous lack of plexiglass or other solid barriers."

[4] That duty is one of reasonable care under the circumstances. *Carroll*, 955 F.3d at 1264, 8 Adm. R.

at 413; *Sorrels v. NCL (Bahamas) Ltd.*, 796 F.3d 1275, 1280, 3 Adm. R. 659, 660 (11th Cir. 2015) (characterizing the "particular injury" there as a "slip and fall"). For a duty to arise, Carnival must "have had actual or **[—10—]** constructive notice of the risk-creating condition, at least where, as here, the menace is one commonly encountered on land and not clearly linked to nautical adventure. [Carnival's] liability thus hinges on whether it knew or should have known about the [risk-creating condition]." *Keefe*, 867 F.2d at 1322.

Unlike notice, which is material to both of Amy's claims, whether the condition is "open and obvious" impacts a negligent-maintenance claim differently than a failure-to-warn claim. For a negligent-maintenance claim, a shipowner "may still be liable for maintaining a dangerous condition even if the danger was obvious." *Carroll*, 955 F.3d at 1267, 8 Adm. R. at 416. Yet, with respect to a failure-to-warn claim, "[a]n operator of a cruise ship has a duty to warn only of known dangers that are not open and obvious." *Id.* at 1264, 8 Adm. R. at 413.

We begin by analyzing the notice issue. Then we turn to the district court's grant of summary judgment on the failure-to-warn claim because the dangerous condition was open and obvious.

A.

In concluding that Carnival lacked notice of the guard rail's alleged risk-creating conditions, the district court failed to view the evidence in a light most favorable to Amy, the non-moving party, and to draw reasonable factual inferences in her favor. Take, first, the evidence of Carnival's warnings to its passengers. **[—11—]**

"Evidence that a ship owner has taken corrective action can establish notice of a dangerous . . . condition." **{–1309–}** *Id.* at 1265, 8 Adm. R. at 414. Corrective action includes warning passengers about a danger posed by a condition. *See id.*, 8 Adm. R. at 414–15 (citing *Guevara*, 920 F.3d at 720–22, 7 Adm. R. at 481–83, and *Sorrels*, 796 F.3d at 1288, 3 Adm. R. at 666–67, for their holdings involving warning signs as evidence creating issues of material fact as to notice). But "[n]ot all warning[s] . . . will be evidence of notice; there must also be a connection between the warning and the danger." *Guevara*, 920 F.3d at 721, 7 Adm. R. at 482.

Guevara involved such a connection. There, a "watch your step" warning was sufficiently connected to a danger posed by a small step down to withstand summary judgment. *Id.* at 721–22, 7 Adm. R. at 481–83. The district court found no notice because the sign only "generically advise[s] passengers to 'hold the handrail' and 'watch your step' as they climb the three steps to the landing. It does not warn of a potential danger associated with the small step from the landing to the deck." *Id.* at 722, 7 Adm. R. at 482. We disagreed with the district court's reasoning about the warning's generic nature compared to a more specific danger because, we reiterated, we view the evidence and draw factual inferences in favor of the non-moving party at the summary judgment stage. *Id.*, 7 Adm. R. at 482–83. We held that there was a genuine issue of material fact as to notice. *Id.*, 7 Adm. R. at 482–83.

Here, starting with the danger of falling over the rail, Nancy Mitchell testified that Carnival warned passengers not to "climb up rails," "try to sit on **[—12—]** them," "try to get selfies [or] lean[] over" them because "accidents can happen" and "there have been passengers [who] have fallen off." Carnival's warning and the falling-over danger posed by the Deck 14 guard rail line up—certainly a "sufficient connection" exists between the warning and the danger, as in *Guevara*.[5] *See*

at 413; *Guevara*, 920 F.3d at 720, 7 Adm. R. at 481; *Keefe v. Bahama Cruise Line, Inc.*, 867 F.2d 1318, 1322 (11th Cir. 1989) (per curiam). Our prior precedent forecloses Amy's argument for a heightened duty of care. *See Smith v. GTE Corp.*, 236 F.3d 1292, 1300 n.8 (11th Cir. 2001) (stating our prior-precedent rule).

[5] We reject Carnival's argument that the warnings were directed at adult, not children, passengers. Not only do we fail to see such a distinction in the testimony, but also the required "connection" is not so narrowly defined.

id. at 721, 7 Adm. R. at 482. Viewed in a light most favorable to Amy, this warning evidence is enough to withstand summary judgment as to notice. *See id.* at 721–22, 7 Adm. R. at 481–83 (reversing summary judgment as to notice given evidence of a warning sufficiently related to the danger at issue); *Sorrels*, 796 F.3d at 1289, 3 Adm. R. at 667 (concluding, in a case where the plaintiff slipped on a deck that was wet from rain, that evidence that "slippery when wet" signs were sometimes posted on the ship's deck after rain was sufficient to withstand summary judgment as to notice).

In rejecting Carnival's warning as too generic, the district court failed to view Nancy Mitchell's testimony in a light most favorable to Amy. *See Guevara*, 920 F.3d at 722, 7 Adm. R. at 482–83. The district court here relied on the *Guevara* district court's grant of summary judgment and its reasoning that the warning was too generic compared to the specific danger at issue. But we explicitly addressed and rejected that reasoning on appeal in *Guevara*. *See id.*, 7 Adm. R. at 482–83. To be sure, the district court here did not **[—13—]** have the benefit of our decision in *Guevara* at the time it granted summary judgment in this case. But under *Guevara*, suffice it to say that the district court's focus on specificity here was too exacting for this notice issue at summary judgment. *See id.* at 721–22, 7 Adm. R. at 481–83.[6]

As for the danger of falling through the rail, a reasonable jury could find that Carnival **{-1310-}** had notice of this danger based on Vasquez's and Clement's testimony. Perhaps most accessible and intuitive to a reasonable jury was Vasquez's testimony (on Carnival's behalf) that (1) guard rails' general purpose is to prevent people from getting from one side to the other, which Clement corroborated; (2) a guard rail ineffective at serving that purpose is dangerous; (3) a child can get through a sufficiently wide space; (4) an obvious danger of falling results from climbing a guard rail; and (5) Carnival knew that the Deck 14 guard rail is climbable and has no climb protection. And a reasonable jury could understand Clement's testimony to show that Carnival knew of the dangers of climbable railings, as well as the 4-inch safety standard, and implemented that standard to prevent children from falling through the guard rails.

In light of the other evidence in the case, additional aspects of Vasquez's, Clement's, and Fore's testimony together fuel a dispute of fact as to whether **[—14—]** Carnival should have known of the guard rail's alleged risk-creating conditions. Both Vasquez and Clement testified that Carnival prioritized safety and went above and beyond to ensure passenger safety. Given their testimony, a reasonable jury could conclude that Carnival should have known about the subjects of Fore's testimony. Moreover, as Fore noted, Carnival in fact already utilized railing configurations on the *Liberty* and other ships in Carnival's fleet that complied with safety recommendations. And, as far as we can tell, Carnival never challenged or rebutted Fore's testimony. The district court made no mention of his testimony, which, as we see it, could have carried considerable weight for a jury.

It bears repeating that our task here is merely to decide whether the record contains evidence from which a reasonable jury could conclude that Carnival knew or should have known that children could climb or pass through the Deck 14 guard rail and fall. It does.[7] To be clear, a reasonable jury also could see other evidence to indicate that Carnival lacked notice. But it is not for us to weigh the evidence and decide; that task is for the jury. Because a genuine dispute of fact exists as to notice, the district court erred in granting summary judgment on that basis.

Also, we need not decide whether this warning was also evidence of notice of the falling-through condition because, for reasons discussed later, at least Vasquez's and Clement's testimony create a dispute of fact as to notice of that specific danger.

6 This case does not call for further discussion about how specific warnings must be relative to the alleged danger at issue to qualify as evidence of notice, so we will leave it at that.

7 Because there was evidence that Carnival had actual notice that the railing posed both dangers, we need not decide whether notice of one of the dangers would necessarily establish notice of the other.

B. **[—15—]**

As to the failure-to-warn claim, we must consider another basis that the district court offered for granting summary judgment: The dangerous condition was open and obvious. Sure enough, "[a]n operator of a cruise ship has a duty to warn only of known dangers that are not open and obvious." *Carroll*, 955 F.3d at 1264, 8 Adm. R. at 413. But a district court may "grant [a summary judgment] motion on grounds not raised by a party" *only* "[a]fter giving notice and a reasonable time to respond." Fed. R. Civ. P. 56(f).

The district court did not do so here. Neither in its answer nor in its summary judgment motion did Carnival raise an "open and obvious" defense, and it does not argue to the contrary on appeal. We see no sign that the district court gave Amy notice that it planned to decide the failure-to-warn claim on the condition's open and obvious nature, much less an opportunity to respond. Yet the district court indeed granted the motion on that basis for the failure-to-warn claim and even impliedly acknowledged what it was **{-1311-}** doing: "Carnival's motion is premised only on the notice issue." Therefore, the district court erred in granting summary judgment on this basis.

IV.

In conclusion, the district court erred in granting summary judgment for Carnival as to both claims. Therefore, we reverse and remand for further proceedings. We also vacate the award of costs to Carnival. *See Sorrels*, 796 F.3d **[—16—]** at 1279 n.1, 3 Adm. R. at 659 n.1 ("Because we vacate the district court's summary judgment order, we vacate the award of costs.").

REVERSED AND REMANDED.

United States Court of Appeals
for the Eleventh Circuit

No. 19-10177

UNITED STATES
vs.
TIGUA

Appeal from the United States District Court for the Middle District of Florida

Decided: June 26, 2020

Citation: 963 F.3d 1138, 8 Adm. R. 430 (11th Cir. 2020).

Before **PRYOR,** Chief Judge, **JORDAN** and **NEWSOM,** Circuit Judges.

[—2—] {-1140-} **PRYOR,** Chief Judge:

The key issue in these separate appeals is whether defendants adjudicated guilty before but sentenced after the effective date of the First Step Act of 2018 may qualify for relief under the amended statutory safety-valve provision. Pub. L. No. 115-391, § 402(a), 132 Stat. 5194, 5221. Eulogio Ramiro Yoza Tigua and Freddy Oswaldo Torres Castro appeal their mandatory minimum sentences of 120 **[—3—]** months of imprisonment imposed following their pleas of guilty to violating the Maritime Drug Law Enforcement Act. 46 U.S.C. §§ 70503(a), 70506(a), 70506(b); 21 U.S.C. § 960(b)(1)(B)(ii); 18 U.S.C. § 2. The First Step Act states that its amendment of the statutory safety-valve provision "shall apply only to a conviction entered on or after the date of [its] enactment" on December 21, 2018. First Step Act § 402(b). Because Tigua and Castro had their "conviction[s] entered" when the district court accepted their pleas of guilty before December 21, 2018, they are ineligible for relief from the statutory mandatory-minimum sentence under the amended statutory safety-valve provision. Castro also argues for a reduction of his sentence for his minor role, but any error the district court might have committed in denying the reduction is harmless. We affirm Tigua's and Castro's sentences.

I. BACKGROUND

Tigua and Castro served in a three-man crew on a go-fast boat transporting multiple bales of cocaine. On July 13, 2018, the United States Coast Guard intercepted the boat in international waters, about 267 miles west of the Galapagos Islands. The crew members jettisoned their cargo, but after a helicopter dispatched by the Coast Guard disabled the boat, officers recovered 846 kilograms of cocaine from the water. Although an Ecuadorian flag was painted on the hull of the boat, Ecuadorian officials refused to confirm or deny its registry. **[—4—]**

After indictment, both men pleaded guilty in separate proceedings. In September 2018, Castro pleaded guilty to conspiring to distribute and to possessing with intent to distribute 5 kilograms or more of cocaine while aboard a vessel subject to the jurisdiction of the United States. 46 U.S.C. §§ 70503(a), 70506(a), 70506(b); 18 U.S.C. § 2. The district court accepted Castro's plea in October 2018. That same month, Tigua agreed to plead guilty only to the conspiracy offense. 46 U.S.C. §§ 70503(a), 70506(b).

The presentence investigation reports stated that Tigua and Castro qualified for **{-1141-}** a two-level reduction of their offense levels, *see* United States Sentencing Guidelines Manual § 2D1.1(b)(18) (Nov. 2018) (cross-referencing U.S.S.G. § 5C1.2(a)), but that they were not entitled to be sentenced below the statutory mandatory-minimum sentence for first-time offenders whose crimes involved five kilograms or more of a mixture or substance containing a detectable amount of cocaine, 21 U.S.C. § 960(b)(l)(B)(ii); 18 U.S.C. § 3553(f) (amended December 21, 2018). Neither Tigua nor Castro objected to the factual statements in the presentence reports, but Tigua objected to the calculation of his offense level. He argued that he was eligible for relief from the mandatory-minimum sentence under the statutory safety valve notwithstanding precedent holding that the provision did not apply to maritime drug traffickers. **[—5—]**

In January 2019, Tigua and Casto each argued in separate sentencing hearings that he qualified for relief from the mandatory-minimum sentence, under section 402 of the First Step Act, which extended the statutory safety valve to maritime drug traffickers. First Step Act § 402(a). The government conceded that Tigua was eligible for safety-valve relief and did not object to Castro's request to reduce his sentence.

The district court ruled that Tigua and Castro were ineligible for safety-valve relief. The district court concluded that section 402 applies to a defendant who has his "conviction entered" on or after the effective date of the First Step Act, which refers to the date a defendant is adjudged guilty by a court or a jury, not to the date judgment is entered after sentencing. The district court ruled that section 402 did not apply to Tigua and Castro because the district court accepted their pleas of guilty before the effective date of the Act.

The district court also denied Castro's motion for a two-level reduction in his offense level for serving a minor role. *See* U.S.S.G. § 3B1.2(b). Castro admitted in his presentence report and the district court found that "three people were put at sea with tens of millions of dollars of cocaine"; they shared responsibility to navigate the vessel and made a collective decision to flee and jettison the cargo; Castro "participated in the execution of . . . the ocean-going voyage . . . [by] getting together his personal effects and planning and organizing **[—6—]** that part of it"; and he had "seen to it the vessel was [fueled], etc." Based on those facts and Castro's admission that he was promised $40,000 on delivery of the cocaine, the district court ruled that Castro failed to establish he was less culpable than an average participant.

The district court determined that Tigua had an adjusted total offense level of 26 and a criminal history category of I, which yielded an advisory guideline range of 63 to 78 months of imprisonment. The district court determined that Castro had an adjusted total offense level of 31 and a criminal history category of I, which yielded an advisory guideline range of 108 to 135 months of imprisonment. The district court sentenced Tigua and Castro each to the statutory mandatory-minimum sentence of 120 months of imprisonment.

II. STANDARDS OF REVIEW

We review *de novo* an issue of statutory interpretation. *United States v. Johnson*, 375 F.3d 1300, 1301 (11th Cir. 2004). "When reviewing the denial of safety-valve relief, we review for clear error a district court's factual determinations." *Id.* We also review for clear error the factual findings about a defendant's role in an offense. *United States v. Rodriguez De Varon*, 175 F.3d 930, 937 (11th Cir. 1999) (en banc). **[—7—]**

III. DISCUSSION

We divide our discussion in two parts. First, we address whether Tigua and Castro **{-1142-}** are eligible for safety-valve relief under section 402(b) of the First Step Act. Second, we address Castro's request for a reduction for minor role.

A. Tigua and Castro Are Ineligible for Safety-Valve Relief Under the First Step Act.

Section 402 of the First Step Act broadened the circumstances in which defendants may receive a sentence below the otherwise statutory mandatory-minimum sentence for their crimes. Before the Act, the safety-valve provision allowed district courts to sentence a defendant in accordance with the range recommended under the Sentencing Guidelines "without regard to" a statutory mandatory-minimum penalty for specified offenses, 21 U.S.C. §§ 841, 844, 846, 960, 963. 18 U.S.C. § 3553(f) (2012). Because section 3553(f) did not apply to violations of the Maritime Drug Act, a first-time offender whose crime involved five kilograms or more of a mixture or substance containing a detectable amount of cocaine was subject to a mandatory-minimum sentence of 120 months of imprisonment. *United States v. Castillo*, 899 F.3d 1208, 1212, 6 Adm. R. 463, 464 (11th Cir. 2018) (citing 21 U.S.C. § 960(b)(1)(B) and 46 U.S.C. § 70506(a)), *cert. denied*, 139 S. Ct. 796 (2019). The First Step Act amended section 3553(f) to apply to more criminal offenses, including "section[s] 70503 or 70506 of title 46," which punish defendants who conspire to distribute and who possess with intent to distribute **[—8—]** controlled substances while on board a vessel subject to the jurisdiction of the United States. First Step Act § 402(a).

By its terms, the amendment to section 3553(f) "appl[ies] only to a conviction entered on or after the date of enactment of [the First Step] Act." *Id.* § 402(b). We have yet to interpret the meaning of "conviction entered" in section 402 in a published opinion. In *United States v. Cabezas-Montano*, the defendants conceded that they were ineligible for safety-valve relief when "convicted in 2017" of maritime drug trafficking. 949 F.3d 567, 604 & n.36, 8 Adm. R. 364, 387 & n.36 (11th Cir. 2020).

Because the Act does not define the phrase "conviction entered," we begin with its ordinary meaning. *See Taniguchi v. Kan Pac. Saipan, Ltd.*, 566 U.S. 560, 566 (2012). "As in all cases involving statutory construction, our starting point must be the language employed by Congress, and we assume that the legislative purpose is expressed by the ordinary meaning of the words used." *United States v. Fisher*, 289 F.3d 1329, 1338 (11th Cir. 2002) (quoting *Am. Tobacco Co. v. Patterson*, 456 U.S. 63, 68 (1982)); *see also* Antonin Scalia & Bryan A. Garner, *Reading Law: The Interpretation of Legal Texts* § 2, at 56 (2012) ("[T]he purpose must be derived from the text . . . .").

Tigua and Castro argue that the term "conviction" in section 402(b) means "judgment of conviction," which is a legal term of art that includes "the plea, the verdict or findings, the adjudication, *and* the sentence." *Judgment of Conviction*, **[—9—]** *Black's Law Dictionary* (11th ed. 2019) (emphasis added); *see also* Fed. R. Crim. P. 32(k)(1) (stating that "the court must set forth the plea, the jury verdict or the court's findings, the adjudication, and the sentence" in the "judgment of conviction"). Because the district court had not sentenced them before December 21, 2018, Tigua and Castro contend that they are entitled to safety-valve relief. We disagree.

We understand the term "conviction" in section 402 to convey its ordinary meaning. *See* Scalia & Garner, *Reading Law* § 6, at 69 ("Words are to be understood in their ordinary, everyday meanings . . . ."). Conviction means "the judgment of a jury or **{–1143–}** judge that a person is guilty of a crime as charged." *Conviction*, *American Heritage Dictionary* (5th ed. 2015); *accord Conviction*, *Webster's Third New International Dictionary* (1993) ("[T]he act of proving, finding, or adjudging a person guilty of an offense or crime."). The legal meaning of conviction is the same. *See Conviction*, *Black's Law Dictionary*, *supra* ("The act or process of judicially finding someone guilty of a crime . . . ."). In this context, the term "conviction" conveys its ordinary meaning as distinct from the term "sentence." And to date, all other courts that have interpreted section 402 have reached the same conclusion. *See, e.g.*, *United States v. White*, 413 F.Supp.3d 15, 40 (D.D.C. 2019); *United States v. Havens*, 374 F.Supp.3d 628, 634 (E.D. Ky. 2019). **[—10—]**

The provisions surrounding section 402 support our reading. *See* Scalia & Garner, *Reading Law* § 24, at 167 ("The text must be construed as a whole."); *id.* § 39, at 252 ("Statutes *in pari materia* are to be interpreted together, as though they were one law."). Section 401 of the First Step Act, which amends the requirements to enhance sentences for repeat offenders with prior convictions for felony drug offenses, applies "to any offense that was committed before the date of enactment of this Act, if a sentence for the offense ha[d] not been imposed as of such date of enactment." § 401(c). Likewise, section 403, which amends the sentencing provisions for armed career criminals, applies if the defendant's "sentence for the offense has not been imposed" by the effective date of the Act. *Id.* § 403(b). "[W]e must presume that Congress said what it meant and meant what it said" in the Act, *United States v. Steele*, 147 F.3d 1316, 1318 (11th Cir.1998) (en banc), and "use[d] different language in similar sections . . . [to convey] different meanings," *Iraola & CIA, SA v. Kimberly–Clark Corp.*, 232 F.3d

854, 859 (11th Cir. 2000); *see also* Scalia & Garner, *Reading Law* § 25, at 170 ("[W]here [a] document has used one term in one place, and a materially different term in another, the presumption is that the different term denotes a different idea."). So the use of "conviction" in section 402 and "sentence" in surrounding provisions—sections 401 and 403—necessarily means that "conviction entered" does not refer to the date of sentencing. **[—11—]**

Tigua, Castro, and the government argue that *Deal v. United States*, 508 U.S. 129 (1993), supports their argument that "conviction entered" is synonymous with "judgment of conviction," but we disagree. In *Deal*, the Supreme Court interpreted the phrase "second or subsequent conviction" in the Armed Career Criminal Act, 18 U.S.C. § 924(c)(1). 508 U.S. at 131. It stated that "conviction" could refer to either the "adjudication of guilt" or the "judgment of conviction," *id.* at 131–32, but when read in context, the word had to bear the first meaning or else "the provision would be incoherent, prescribing that a sentence which has already been imposed (the defendant's second or subsequent 'conviction') shall be 5 or 20 years longer than it was." *Id.* at 132–33. As in *Deal*, were we to interpret "conviction" in section 402 to mean "judgment of conviction," then a defendant would not qualify for safety valve relief until *after* the district court imposed the mandatory-minimum sentence. To give the defendant the relief provided in section 402, the district court would have to vacate or otherwise modify the sentence, which is the same kind of counterintuitive result that the Supreme Court rejected in *Deal*. For maritime drug traffickers to obtain safety-valve relief under section 402, "conviction entered" must mean "adjudication of guilt."

Tigua, Castro, and the government also urge us to interpret "conviction entered" consistent with the purpose of eliminating **{-1144-}** sentencing disparities as the Supreme Court did in *Dorsey v. United States*, 567 U.S. 260 (2012), but the text of **[—12—]** the Act forecloses that reading. In *Dorsey*, the Supreme Court considered whether the reduced statutory penalties provided in the Fair Sentencing Act applied to defendants who had committed their crimes before and were sentenced after its effective date. 567 U.S. at 264. Because the text of the Act did not address the issue, the Court concluded that Congress must have intended the Act to apply to defendants who had not yet been sentenced based on several policy considerations, including the goals of reducing statutory penalties and eliminating sentencing disparities. *Id.* at 273–81. In contrast with the Fair Sentencing Act, the First Step Act makes clear which offenders qualify. And although we acknowledge that it will result in sentencing disparities, the text states that only an offender who has his "conviction entered on or after the date of enactment of this Act" is eligible to receive a sentence below the statutory mandatory minimum penalty. First Step Act § 402(b).

The district court did not err in determining that Tigua and Castro were ineligible for safety-valve relief under the First Step Act. The district court accepted Tigua's and Castro's pleas of guilty and adjudicated them guilty of maritime drug trafficking offenses in October 2018. Because Tigua and Castro had their "conviction[s] entered" before section 402 was enacted in December 2018, the statutory safety valve did not apply to their offenses and they were subject to mandatory-minimum sentences of 120 months of imprisonment. *See Castillo*, **[—13—]** 899 F.3d at 1212, 6 Adm. R. at 464. That the government would prefer that Tigua and Castro benefit from the Act does not affect our decision. *See United States v. Linville*, 228 F.3d 1330, 1331 n.2 (11th Cir. 2000). We must apply the Act as written.

B. Any Error in Denying Castro a Reduction for Minor Role Is Harmless.

Even if we were to assume that the district court erred by denying Castro a reduction for a minor role, the error would be harmless. Had Castro been entitled to a two-level reduction for being a minor participant in the criminal activity, U.S.S.G. § 3B1.2(b), it would have resulted in a total offense level of 29 and an advisory guideline range of 87 to 107 months of imprisonment. But the district court could not impose a sentence "below the statutory mandatory minimum unless the government filed a substantial assistance motion pursuant to 18 U.S.C. § 3553(e) and U.S.S.G. § 5K1.1 or [Castro] f[ell] within the safety-valve of 18 U.S.C. § 3553(f)," *United States v. Castaing–Sosa*, 530 F.3d 1358, 1360 (11th Cir. 2008), and neither of those exceptions applied to Castro. The denial of a reduction for a minor role had no effect on Castro's sentence.

IV. CONCLUSION

We **AFFIRM** Tigua's and Castro's sentences.

United States Court of Appeals for the Eleventh Circuit

No. 18-12619

DeROY vs. CARNIVAL CORP.

Appeal from the United States District Court for the Southern District of Florida

Decided: June 30, 2020

Citation: 963 F.3d 1302, 8 Adm. R. 435 (11th Cir. 2020).

Before **ROSENBAUM, GRANT,** and **HULL,** Circuit Judges.

[—1—] {-1306-} ROSENBAUM, Circuit Judge:

Fans of movies set in medieval times know that the narrow slits in otherwise seemingly impenetrable castle walls allowed castle defenders to launch arrows at **[—2—]** approaching castle attackers.[1] This architectural **{-1307-}** feature was designed to protect the archer while still allowing the archer to defend the castle.[2] It is known as a "loophole."[3]

But arrows were not the only thing that could fit through castle-wall loopholes. Sometimes children and small adults could as well.[4] And they could use them to escape the thick castle walls.[5]

It's not clear that the figurative usage of the term "loophole" derives from a reference to the architectural feature. But the parallels between the two usages are nonetheless obvious. Figuratively, "loophole" has come to mean "[a]n outlet or means of escape[;] [o]ften applied to an ambiguity or omission in a statute, etc., which affords opportunity for evading its intention." *Loop-hole*, Oxford English Dictionary, https://www.oed.com/view/Entry/110180 (last visited June 29, 2020).

Here, Plaintiff-Appellee Carmela DeRoy attempts to take advantage of a supposed loophole in the forum-selection clause of a contract she entered into with **[—3—]** Defendant-Appellant Carnival Corporation when she bought a ticket for a Carnival cruise. The forum-selection clause requires all litigation to proceed in federal court if federal jurisdiction lies for the claim. DeRoy, who injured her foot on a rug while onboard the Carnival *Valor*, simultaneously sued Carnival in both state and federal court. In her federal suit—this case—she attempted to plead her case to avoid invoking federal jurisdiction, even though federal jurisdiction could exist over a claim seeking damages for the injuries DeRoy allegedly suffered onboard the *Valor*. Then DeRoy sought for the district court to dismiss this federal case for lack of jurisdiction, so she could permissibly proceed with the state suit under the forum-selection clause.

It was a creative effort. But DeRoy's proposed loophole does not exist, so she cannot escape the forum-selection clause's ironclad consequences. Under the forum-selection clause's plain language, when jurisdiction for a claim could lie in federal district court, federal court is the *only* option for a plaintiff. Here, DeRoy's claim for negligence at sea falls well within the walls of the federal court's admiralty jurisdiction. Even without explicitly invoking admiralty jurisdiction—and in fact

---

1 *Loophole*, Grammarist, https://grammarist.com/interesting-words/loophole/ (last visited June 29, 2020); *Loophole*, Online Etymology Dictionary, https://www.etymonline.com/word/loophole (last visited June 29, 2020).

2 *Loophole*, Grammarist, *supra* note 1.

3 *What's the origin of "loophole"?*, The Straight Dope (Feb. 6, 2003), https://www.straightdope.com/columns/read/2071/whats-the-origin-of-loophole/; *see also Loophole*, Dictionary by Merriam-Webster, https://www.merriam-webster.com/dictionary/loophole (last visited June 29, 2020) (defining "loophole" secondarily as, among other things, "a small opening through which small arms may be fired" and noting this definition as the "first known use" of the term, in 1591); *Loop-hole*, Oxford English Dictionary, https://www.oed.com/view/Entry/110180 (last visited June 29, 2020).

4 The Straight Dope, *supra* note 3.

5 *See id.*

intentionally attempting to plead around it—DeRoy's complaint is subject to Federal Rule of Civil Procedure 9(h)'s provision rendering her claim an admiralty or maritime claim. Her claim is therefore subject to the forum-selection clause's federal-court-forum fortress. **[—4—]**

For these reasons, the district court erred in dismissing the action for lack of subject-matter jurisdiction. We therefore reverse and remand for further proceedings.

I. FACTUAL BACKGROUND

For purposes of reviewing a district court's dismissal for lack of subject-matter **{–1308–}** jurisdiction, we take the facts as the plaintiff has alleged them, unless the district court has made a contrary finding. *Giardiello v. Balboa Ins. Co.*, 837 F.2d 1566, 1568 n.1 (11th Cir. 1988).

Here, DeRoy asserted that in October 2016, she was a cruise passenger on the Carnival *Valor* ship. During her cruise, DeRoy tripped on a dip in the carpeting in one of the *Valor*'s inside hallways. As a result of her fall, DeRoy broke her right foot and suffered other damages.

On February 20, 2018, DeRoy simultaneously filed two complaints against Carnival Corporation: one in the United States District Court for the Southern District of Florida and one in the Eleventh Judicial Circuit Court in and for Miami-Dade County, Florida.[6] Each complaint contains a single negligence claim against Carnival.

DeRoy's ticket contract with Carnival contained a forum-selection clause that **[—5—]** required her to bring any claim in the United States District Court for the Southern District of Florida if it was jurisdictionally possible to do so:

> [I]t is agreed by and between the Guest and Carnival that all disputes and matters whatsoever arising under, in connection with or incident to this Contract or the Guest's cruise, including travel to and from the vessel, shall be litigated, if at all, before the United States District Court for the Southern District of Florida in Miami, or as to those lawsuits to which the Federal Courts of the United States lack subject matter jurisdiction, before a court located in Miami-Dade County, Florida, U.S.A. to the exclusion of the Courts of any other county, state or country.

In accordance with this provision, as we have noted, DeRoy filed the suit pending here.

Yet DeRoy devoted the majority of her complaint to attempting to establish that the district court lacked subject-matter jurisdiction—whether diversity, federal-question, or admiralty jurisdiction—to adjudicate her claims. In furtherance of this tactic, DeRoy noted that both she and Carnival were citizens of Florida, so no diversity jurisdiction existed. She next pointed out that since she brought a negligence claim only, federal-question jurisdiction was lacking. And then she asserted that she had elected to bring her *in personam* negligence action *at law*—not in admiralty. So, DeRoy concluded, admiralty jurisdiction did not exist, since admiralty jurisdiction does not extend to *in personam* claims brought *at law*.

For these reasons, DeRoy contended, the federal district court lacked subject-matter jurisdiction and was required to dismiss her suit. Indeed, DeRoy invited the **[—6—]** district court to "dismiss this case sua sponte because it lacks subject matter jurisdiction over the claims in this lawsuit." And the primary relief she sought in her negligence claim consisted of "[d]ismissal of this case for lack of subject matter jurisdiction," with damages as only an alternative request.[7] **{–1309–}**

[6] The record reflects that the state-court case is essentially on hold pending the outcome of this appeal.

[7] Certainly, pleading in the alternative is permissible in federal court. *United Techs. Corp. v. Mazer*, 556 F.3d 1260, 1273 (11th Cir. 2009) ("Rule 8(d) of the Federal Rules of Civil Procedure expressly permits the pleading of both alternative and inconsistent claims."). And "[t]he pleading of alternative jurisdictional bases is a common

Carnival responded with a motion to dismiss, or, in the alternative, for a more definite statement. In its motion, Carnival asserted that DeRoy undoubtedly could have invoked admiralty jurisdiction, since 28 U.S.C. § 1333 provides that "[t]he district courts have original jurisdiction, exclusive of the courts of the States," over "[a]ny civil case of admiralty or maritime jurisdiction, saving to suitors in all cases all other remedies to which they are entitled."[8] And it noted that, to the extent the saving-to-suitors clause of § 1333 guaranteed DeRoy the right to a jury trial under the Florida constitution, Carnival would not object to a jury trial as DeRoy requested **[—7—]** in her complaint.[9]

In her response to Carnival's motion, DeRoy clarified that she was not challenging the enforceability of the forum-selection clause, nor was she claiming that the saving-to-suitors clause in § 1333 gave her an inalienable right to litigate in state court, nor was she arguing that she would be deprived of her right to a jury trial under the Florida constitution. Rather, DeRoy claimed, she was simply exploiting a hole in Carnival's contract that no one had previously thought of: since, in DeRoy's view, the forum-selection clause allowed lawsuits where the federal courts had no jurisdiction to proceed in state court, DeRoy pleaded her case in a way intended to evade the federal district court's jurisdiction—specifically, by refusing to *invoke* admiralty jurisdiction.

The district court found DeRoy's position convincing and entered an order dismissing the complaint on May 22, 2018. In reaching this conclusion, the district court determined that the saving-to-suitors clause in § 1333 allowed DeRoy to evade the court's admiralty jurisdiction. In the district court's view, DeRoy, as the master of her own complaint, had deliberately avoided invoking admiralty jurisdiction. It did not matter, the district court said, that DeRoy *could* have brought her claim in admiralty because she affirmatively brought her claim at law. As a result, the district **[—8—]** court determined, it lacked subject-matter jurisdiction over DeRoy's claim as she pleaded it. And the forum-selection clause did not remedy the jurisdictional problem, the district court reasoned, because subject-matter jurisdiction cannot be created through consent. Nevertheless, the district court recognized that *had* DeRoy brought her claim in admiralty, the court would have enjoyed subject-matter jurisdiction.

Carnival now appeals.

II. STANDARD OF REVIEW

We review *de novo* the grant of a motion to dismiss for lack of subject-matter jurisdiction. *Tundidor v. Miami-Dade Cty.*, 831 F.3d 1328, 1331, 4 Adm. R. 460, 461 (11th Cir. 2016). In reviewing a facial challenge to a complaint, we consider only the allegations in the complaint, accepting them as true for this purpose. **{-1310-}** *McElmurray v. Consol. Gov't of Augusta-Richmond Cty.*, 501 F.3d 1244, 1251 (11th Cir. 2007). Finally, we review *de novo* the interpretation of a contract. *Grange Mut. Cas. Co. v. Woodard*, 861 F.3d 1224, 1230 (11th Cir. 2017).

III. DISCUSSION

This case comes before us in a peculiar procedural posture, with DeRoy's tacit invocation of federal jurisdiction—by filing her complaint in the district court—coupled with DeRoy's explicit disavowal of federal

practice." *State Establishment for Agr. Prod. Trading v. M/V Wesermunde*, 770 F.2d 987, 991 n.3 (11th Cir. 1985). Pleading a lack of jurisdiction as an alternative to her affirmative claim for negligence, while contradictory, is not fatal to DeRoy's complaint.

[8] We have referred to this latter provision of 28 U.S.C. § 1333 interchangeably as the "saving to suitors" clause and the "savings to suitors" clause. *See, e.g., Beiswenger Enters. Corp. v. Carletta*, 86 F.3d 1032, 1037 (11th Cir. 1996) ("saving to suitors" clause); *Murphy v. Fla. Keys Elec. Co-op. Ass'n, Inc.*, 329 F.3d 1311, 1319 (11th Cir. 2003) ("savings to suitors" clause). The Supreme Court has shown a preference for utilizing the singular moniker. *See Lewis v. Lewis & Clark Marine, Inc.*, 531 U.S. 438, 443 (2001) ("saving to suitors" clause). For consistency, in this opinion, we refer to the provision as the "saving-to-suitors clause."

[9] While admiralty cases do not guarantee the right to a jury trial, Federal Rule of Civil Procedure 39 permits trying such an action by jury with the parties' consent. Fed. R. Civ. P. 38, 39.

jurisdiction in her allegations **[—9—]** and claim for relief.[10] But regardless of what a complaint may say about a court's jurisdiction to entertain it, as we explain below, we look beyond the labels to the underlying facts of the complaint to evaluate jurisdiction.[11]

Here, the complaint alleges a simple personal-injury claim by a cruise-ship passenger who broke her foot while onboard Carnival's *Valor*. In dealing with claims like this, our precedent establishes four key principles that we must apply: (1) this type of claim falls comfortably within the admiralty jurisdiction of the district court; (2) a plaintiff need not expressly invoke admiralty jurisdiction for a **[—10—]** district court to be able to exercise it where it exists; (3) in cases such as the one here, the saving-to-suitors clause does not operate as a get-out-of-federal-court escape; and (4) federal forum-selection clauses are enforceable. When we apply these principles here, what DeRoy presents as a Gordian jurisdictional knot[12] turns out to require just a straightforward **{-1311-}** application of our existing precedent to gently untangle its strings.

A. Subject-Matter Jurisdiction

Federal courts have an obligation to examine *sua sponte* their own jurisdiction over a case, notwithstanding the contentions of the parties. *Univ. of S. Ala. v. Am. Tobacco Co.*, 168 F.3d 405, 410 (11th Cir. 1999). That is so because subject-matter jurisdiction underlies a court's power to hear a case. *United States v. Cotton*, 535 U.S. 625, 630 (2002). And for that same reason, subject-matter jurisdiction can never be forfeited or waived. *Id.*

---

[10] After the district court entered its order dismissing DeRoy's complaint, at least two other plaintiffs followed in her footsteps by filing their own complaints seeking immediate dismissal for want of jurisdiction. *See Diaz v. BPCL Mgmt.*, No. 18-cv-61379-BB (S.D. Fla. Jun. 19, 2018); *Siliakus v. Carnival Corp.*, No. 18-cv-25137-UU (Dec. 6, 2018).

[11] Carnival invites us to analyze the jurisdiction issue by analogizing to the artful-pleading doctrine. We decline to do so. That doctrine pertains to the right of a defendant to remove a cause of action over which federal subject-matter jurisdiction exists, despite the "artful pleading" or labels utilized by a plaintiff in the state court pleadings. *See Roe v. Michelin N. Am., Inc.*, 613 F.3d 1058, 1064 (11th Cir. 2010); *Pretka v. Kolter City Plaza II, Inc.*, 608 F.3d 744, 766 (11th Cir. 2010). According to the artful-pleading doctrine, a plaintiff who files suit in state court may not defeat removal simply by "omitting to plead necessary federal questions." *Rivet v. Regions Bank of La.*, 522 U.S. 470, 475 (1998) (quoting *Franchise Tax Bd. of Cal. v. Construction Laborers Vacation Trust for S. Cal.*, 463 U.S. 1, 22 (1983)). "If a court concludes that a plaintiff has 'artfully pleaded' claims in this fashion, it may uphold removal even though no federal question appears on the face of the plaintiff's complaint." *Id.* While the artful-pleading doctrine shows that sometimes courts exercise jurisdiction over the protest of the plaintiff, the doctrine is not a perfect analogy. Indeed, some have argued that the doctrine is limited to cases where "federal law completely preempts a plaintiff's state-law claim." *Id.*; *Caterpillar Inc. v. Williams*, 482 U.S. 386, 397 n.11 (1987) (explaining that while removal courts have occasionally sought to determine whether the real nature of a claim is federal, regardless of a plaintiff's characterization, most courts "correctly confine this practice to areas of the law pre-empted by federal substantive law" (citation and quotation marks omitted)). Here, we need not (and do not) consider the artful-pleading doctrine since it is clear federal jurisdiction exists, regardless. *See* 14C Fed. Prac. & Proc. Juris. § 3722.1 (Rev. 4th ed.) ("Unfortunately, the artful-pleading doctrine lacks precise definition and has bred considerable confusion.").

[12] The term "Gordian knot," which refers to a very difficult or unsolvable problem, finds its origins in a legend about Alexander the Great. Evan Andrews, *What Was the Gordian Knot?*, HISTORY (last updated Aug. 29, 2018), https://www.history.com/news/what-was-the-gordian-knot. According to the story, in 333 B.C.E., Alexander the Great entered the Phrygian capital of Gordium in what is now Turkey. *Id.* When he arrived, he found an ancient wagon with its yoke tied with "several knots all so tightly entangled that it was impossible to see how they were fastened." *Id.* (internal quotation marks omitted). An oracle had announced that whoever could untangle the knots was destined to become the ruler of all of Asia. *Id.* After Alexander the Great tried to manually untie it for some time, according to one version of the legend, he cut the knot in half with a single stroke of his sword, announcing that it made no difference how the knot was untied. *Id.*

The plaintiff bears the burden of affirmatively asserting facts that show the **[—11—]** existence of jurisdiction and including "a short and plain statement of the grounds upon which the court's jurisdiction depends." *Taylor v. Appleton*, 30 F.3d 1365, 1367 (11th Cir. 1994); Fed. R. Civ. P. 8(a). But even when the parties disclaim or fail to present requirements that go to the existence of subject-matter jurisdiction, courts must *sua sponte* consider such issues. *Gonzalez v. Thaler*, 565 U.S. 134, 141 (2012). And it is the facts and substance of the claims alleged, not the jurisdictional labels attached, that ultimately determine whether a court can hear a claim. *See Taylor*, 30 F.3d at 1367 (plaintiff must allege *facts* demonstrating jurisdiction); *see also In re Carter*, 618 F.2d 1093, 1101 (5th Cir. 1980)[13] (explaining that, in the context of examining a removed case, "[t]he reviewing court looks to the substance of the complaint, not the labels used in it").

Once the court establishes that jurisdiction exists, it has a duty to exercise that jurisdiction. *See Quackenbush v. Allstate Ins. Co.*, 517 U.S. 706, 716 (1996) ("[F]ederal courts have a strict duty to exercise the jurisdiction that is conferred upon them by Congress."); *Jackson-Platts v. Gen. Elec. Capital Corp.*, 727 F.3d 1127, 1143 (11th Cir. 2013). **[—12—]**

1. Admiralty jurisdiction covers personal-injury claims like DeRoy's that occur onboard cruise ships at sea

The Constitution provides that the federal judicial power "shall extend . . . to all Cases of admiralty and maritime Jurisdiction." U. S. Const., Art. III, § 2, cl. 1. Under 28 U.S.C. § 1333, district courts enjoy "original jurisdiction, exclusive of the courts of the States, of: (1) Any civil case of admiralty or maritime jurisdiction, saving to suitors in all cases all other remedies to which they are otherwise entitled." Citing this provision, we have held that when cruise-ship passengers bring personal-injury claims for injuries that occurred at sea, those claims fall squarely within the admiralty jurisdiction of the district courts. *Caron v. NCL (Bahamas), Ltd.*, 910 F.3d 1359, 1365, 6 Adm. R. 471, 473 (11th Cir. 2018).

As we have explained, to fall within admiralty jurisdiction, a tort claim must satisfy two criteria: (1) the incident **{–1312–}** must have taken place on navigable water or the injury must have been caused by a vessel on navigable water; and (2) the incident must have been "connected with maritime activity." *Id.*, 6 Adm. R. at 473. An incident qualifies as "connected with maritime activity" if, when we evaluate "the general features of the type of incident involved," we determine that that variety of occurrence has "a potentially disruptive impact on maritime commerce" and that "the general character of the activity giving rise to the incident shows a substantial relationship to traditional maritime activity." *Id.*, 6 Adm. R. at 473 (quoting *Jerome B. Grubart, Inc. v. Great Lakes Dredge & Dock Co.*, 513 U.S. 527, 534 (1995) (internal quotation marks omitted)). **[—13—]**

DeRoy's negligence claim here meets both of these criteria. First, the incident precipitating DeRoy's claim occurred while the *Valor* was traveling at sea. Second, unchecked personal injuries allegedly resulting from a cruise-ship operator's negligence have the potential to disrupt maritime commerce, and DeRoy suffered her injury while participating as a passenger on a cruise, which is a traditional maritime activity. *See id.*, 6 Adm. R. at 473 ("Personal-injury claims by cruise ship passengers, complaining of injuries suffered at sea, are within the admiralty jurisdiction of the district courts.").

2. DeRoy's failure to expressly allege admiralty jurisdiction here does not mean that admiralty jurisdiction ceases to exist

Sometimes, in addition to admiralty, a court enjoys another basis for subject-matter jurisdiction—say, diversity jurisdiction. In those cases, Rule 9(h) of the Federal Rules of

[13] *See Bonner v. City of Prichard*, 661 F.2d 1206, 1207 (11th Cir. 1981) (en banc) (holding that all decisions of the "old Fifth" Circuit handed down prior to the close of business on September 30, 1981, are binding precedent in the Eleventh Circuit).

Civil Procedure allows a party to elect to proceed at law via the other jurisdictional basis or to proceed through admiralty. Fed. R. Civ. P. 9(h)(1) ("If a claim for relief is within the admiralty or maritime jurisdiction and also within the court's subject-matter jurisdiction on some other ground, the pleading may designate the claim as an admiralty or maritime claim[.]"). And if a party has two or more viable bases for jurisdiction, one of which is admiralty, then the party's failure to designate her claim as arising in admiralty means that the case will instead proceed at law. *Murphy v. Fla. Keys Elec. Co-op. Ass'n, Inc.*, 329 F.3d 1311, 1319 (11th Cir. 2003) ("If a claim has multiple jurisdictional bases, one of which is **[—14—]** admiralty, . . . [f]ailure to identify a claim as an admiralty or maritime claim in these circumstances means that it is not one.").

Crucially, though, Rule 9(h) also provides that "[a] claim cognizable *only* in the admiralty or maritime jurisdiction is an admiralty or maritime claim for those purposes, *whether or not so designated*." Fed. R. Civ. P. 9(h)(1) (emphasis added). Although Rule 9(h) allows a plaintiff in a maritime case to choose whether to proceed at law or in admiralty, that choice is available only if there is a choice to be made—that is, if the plaintiff has a separate basis for subject-matter jurisdiction other than admiralty. But when admiralty is the only basis for jurisdiction, then admiralty jurisdiction applies, regardless of how the plaintiff designates her case.

Caron presents an example of a case where a claim proceeded in admiralty despite the plaintiff's failure to elect admiralty jurisdiction under Federal Rule of Civil Procedure 9(h) as his primary basis for jurisdiction. There, Caron, the plaintiff, impaired after drinking alcohol, fell down an escape hatch on a cruise ship. 910 F.3d at 1362, 6 Adm. R. at 471. He sued the cruise line for serving him too much alcohol. *Id.*, 6 Adm. R. at 471. In his complaint, Caron asserted both diversity of citizenship and admiralty jurisdiction. *Id.* at 1363, 6 Adm. R. at 471. On appeal, we addressed whether the district court had subject-matter jurisdiction of Caron's claim. Caron argued that alienage-diversity **{-1313-}** jurisdiction existed; as a backup, though, he also asserted that he had sufficiently invoked admiralty jurisdiction, notwithstanding his failure to officially designate admiralty **[—15—]** under Rule 9(h). *See id.* at 1364–65 & n.4, 6 Adm. R. at 472–73 & n.4.

We ruled that though alienage-diversity jurisdiction was lacking over Caron's case, we did have admiralty jurisdiction, as "[p]ersonal-injury claims by cruise ship passengers, complaining of injuries suffered at sea, are within the admiralty jurisdiction of the district courts." *Id.* at 1365, 6 Adm. R. at 473. We clarified that "[s]ince admiralty was the only proper source of jurisdiction, Caron was not required to elect it under Federal Rule of Civil Procedure 9(h)" to proceed on that basis. *Id.* at 1365 n.4, 6 Adm. R. at 473 n.4. Rather, we explained, we enjoyed jurisdiction because "Caron alleged sufficient *facts* to support the District Court's exercise of admiralty jurisdiction." *Id.* at 1366, 6 Adm. R. at 474 (emphasis added).

Like the claim at issue in *Caron*, DeRoy's negligence claim lies squarely within federal-court admiralty jurisdiction, since, as we have explained, the facts and tort claim she alleged satisfy admiralty jurisdiction. So despite DeRoy's attempt to avoid invoking admiralty jurisdiction, the district court enjoyed it nonetheless.

It makes no difference that in *Caron*, Caron affirmatively invoked admiralty jurisdiction in the alternative, and in DeRoy's case, DeRoy actively attempted to disclaim admiralty jurisdiction throughout her complaint. Admiralty jurisdiction turns on the *facts* and substance of the claims alleged in the complaint. And here, the complaint alleges sufficient facts demonstrating that the district court had admiralty subject-matter jurisdiction. *Cotton*, 535 U.S. at 630; *Taylor*, 30 F.3d at **[—16—]** 1367; *Gonzalez*, 565 U.S. at 141. Since admiralty jurisdiction is the only basis for federal jurisdiction under the facts and substance of DeRoy's complaint, the district court enjoyed admiralty jurisdiction in this case, whether DeRoy invoked it or not. Fed. R. Civ. P. 9(h).

3. The saving-to-suitors clause does not nullify admiralty jurisdiction over this action

Although the district court was aware that admiralty jurisdiction could lie for a claim like DeRoy's, it nonetheless concluded that under § 1333's saving-to-suitors clause, DeRoy could and did choose to avoid admiralty jurisdiction. That was error.

As we have noted, § 1333 vests district courts with original jurisdiction over civil admiralty or maritime disputes, but the statute "saves to suitors"—meaning plaintiffs—"all other remedies to which they are otherwise entitled." 28 U.S.C. § 1333(1). While the Supreme Court has noted that the drafters' intention behind what is now § 1333 "is not entirely clear and has been the subject of some debate," it has nonetheless concluded that "the saving to suitors clause preserves remedies and the concurrent jurisdiction of state courts over some admiralty and maritime claims."[14] *Lewis v. Lewis & Clark Marine, Inc.*, 531 U.S. 438, 444, 445 (2001). **[—17—]**

One remedy the saving-to-suitors clause safeguards is the right to a jury trial.[15] *Id.* at 454–55 ("Trial **{-1314-}** by jury is an obvious, but not exclusive, example of the remedies available to suitors."). Unlike with federal cases brought at law, no Seventh Amendment right to a jury trial applies in admiralty cases. *Fitzgerald v. U.S. Lines Co.*, 374 U.S. 16, 20 (1963). So we have said that the saving-to-suitors clause "embodies a presumption in favor of jury trial and common law remedies in the forum of the claimant's choice." *Beiswenger Enters. Corp. v. Carletta*, 86 F.3d 1032, 1037 (11th Cir. 1996).

For that reason, we have concluded that the saving-to-suitors clause generally provides a plaintiff in a maritime case alleging an *in personam* claim three options: "(1) the plaintiff may file suit in federal court under admiralty jurisdiction . . . ; (2) the plaintiff may file suit in federal court under diversity jurisdiction; or (3) the plaintiff may file suit in state court." *St. Paul Fire & Marine Ins. Co. v. Lago Canyon, Inc.*, 561 F.3d 1181, 1187 n.13 (11th Cir. 2009); *Diesel "Repower", Inc. v. Islander Invs. Ltd.*, 271 F.3d 1318, 1322 (11th Cir. 2001) ("The saving to suitors clause allows an *in personam* action, whether the action is instituted in a state court or in a federal court under diversity jurisdiction or in a federal court under maritime jurisdiction."). **[—18—]**

Nothing about the saving-to-suitors clause does anything to alter the fact that the district court enjoyed admiralty jurisdiction over DeRoy's claim, based on the facts she alleged in her complaint and given that DeRoy herself filed this action in federal court. Nor does the saving-to-suitors clause authorize a plaintiff who files in federal court to escape or sabotage existing admiralty jurisdiction by simply labeling her claims "at law," rather than "in admiralty." The saving-to-suitors clause of 28 U.S.C. § 1333 likewise does not relieve courts of their burden to examine their own jurisdiction. And when a plaintiff herself files a suit in federal court, the saving-to-suitors clause does not modify Rule 9(h) to permit a party to "elect" to proceed at law in federal court instead of in admiralty when admiralty provides the only basis for subject-matter jurisdiction—at least not when the defendant agrees to a jury trial.

Rather, the saving-to-suitors clause allowed DeRoy to choose to file her claim exclusively in state court. Because DeRoy did not, though, and because she voluntarily filed in federal court and alleged sufficient facts to satisfy admiralty jurisdiction, DeRoy's case could not be dismissed from federal district court for lack of subject-matter jurisdiction. And the saving-to-suitors clause is not even

[14] The saving-to-suitors clause does not provide concurrent state and federal jurisdiction over all admiralty claims. *In rem* proceedings, "where a vessel or thing is itself treated as the offender and made the defendant by name or description in order to enforce a lien," fall exclusively within the federal domain. *Madruga v. Superior Court of State of Cal. in & for San Diego Cty.*, 346 U.S. 556, 560 (1954).

[15] In the district court, DeRoy disclaimed any reliance on an argument that the saving-to-suitors clause gave her an inalienable right to litigate in state court or that she otherwise would be deprived of her right to a jury trial under the Florida constitution by proceeding in federal court.

arguably relevant to the analysis, since DeRoy filed in federal court and Carnival has agreed to a jury trial.

We also reject the notion that the saving-to-suitors clause's impact on removal jurisdiction has any relevance here. True, if the plaintiff elects to file a maritime **[—19—]** case in state court, that case may not be removed to federal court solely on the basis of admiralty jurisdiction. *Armstrong v. Ala. Power Co.*, 667 F.2d 1385, 1388 (11th Cir. 1982) ("[A] federal district court should not accept the removal of a saving clause case solely because of its general maritime nature: the maritime nature simply does not provide a ground for federal jurisdiction.").[16] But this is not a removal **{–1315–}** action. And neither the fact that the saving-to-suitors clause gives state and federal courts concurrent jurisdiction over admiralty *in personam* cases nor the fact that a defendant may not remove a saving-to-suitors claim solely on the basis of admiralty jurisdiction affects DeRoy's affirmative act of filing her own suit in federal court. Because DeRoy did so and the facts she alleged nonetheless established admiralty jurisdiction, the district court had admiralty jurisdiction over DeRoy's maritime negligence claim, regardless of the saving-to-suitors clause.

B. The forum-selection clause here required DeRoy to file in the U.S. District Court in Miami any claims over which federal jurisdiction could exist if properly pleaded

As we have discussed, the district court dismissed DeRoy's maritime negligence claim for lack of subject-matter jurisdiction, even though it recognized that admiralty jurisdiction could exist over DeRoy's claim. We have already **[—20—]** explained why that was error from a jurisdictional point of view. But it was also error for another reason: the forum-selection clause did not allow DeRoy to avoid federal jurisdiction for any claims she had against Carnival that could be brought in federal court.

While the saving-to-suitors clause gives state and federal courts concurrent jurisdiction over admiralty *in personam* cases such as this one, parties are free to contract for a federal forum for potential claims, provided, of course, that the federal forum has independent subject-matter jurisdiction. *M/S Bremen v. Zapata Off-Shore Co.*, 407 U.S. 1, 11(1972); *Ins. Corp. of Ireland v. Compagnie des Bauxites de Guinee*, 456 U.S. 694, 702 (1982). DeRoy has expressly disclaimed challenging the enforceability of the clause, so we must apply the clause here.

In interpreting a forum-selection clause's language, we turn to general contract principles to apply the plain meaning of the contract's language. *Slater v. Energy Servs. Grp. Int'l, Inc.*, 634 F.3d 1326, 1330 (11th Cir. 2011). We consider the contract as a whole, the parties, and the agreement's purpose to best determine the intent of the parties. *Id.* Where contract principles do not reveal a particular meaning of a clause in question and more than one reasonable construction is plausible, we choose the construction that favors the non-drafting party. *Id.*

We begin our analysis of the forum-selection clause here by considering whether it is permissive or mandatory. As its name suggests, a permissive clause **[—21—]** permits litigation in a jurisdiction other than the one designated. *Id.* But a mandatory clause requires the party to litigate exclusively within the designated forum. *Id.*

Here, as we have noted, the forum-selection clause provides, in relevant part, that "all disputes . . . shall be litigated, if at all, before the United States District Court for the Southern District of Florida in Miami, or as to those lawsuits to which the Federal Courts . . . lack subject matter jurisdiction, before a court located in Miami-Dade County, Florida." The plain meaning of the forum-selection clause at

[16] We decided *Armstrong* under a version of the removal statute, 28 U.S.C. § 1441, that has since been amended. Section 1441(b) was amended as part of the Federal Courts Jurisdiction and Venue Clarification Act of 2011, § 102, Pub. L. No. 112–63, 125 Stat. 758. We have yet to consider whether *Amstrong*'s holding withstands these amendments, nor need we do so now, as DeRoy's action is not before us as a result of removal.

issue here reflects that the clause is a mandatory one that requires a litigant to sue in Miami federal district court when her claims are amenable to federal jurisdiction. **{-1316-}**

Three aspects of the first half of the clause—"all disputes . . . shall be litigated, if at all, before the United States District Court for the Southern District of Florida in Miami"—stand out. First, the clause specifies that it pertains to "all" disputes arising from the cruise. We have recognized that "all" means "every" or "any." *See United States v. Castro*, 837 F.2d 441, 445 (11th Cir. 1988) (concluding "any" means "every" or "all"). So the forum-selection clause applies to every dispute that arises from the cruise. Second, the clause employs the term "shall." We have recognized that "the use of the term 'shall' is one of requirement." *See Slater*, 634 F.3d at 1330. So this word requires any litigation to occur in the United States District Court for the Southern District of Florida. And third, the clause uses the phrase "if at all" in describing litigation. In the context of the forum-selection clause at issue, this **[—22—]** language means that if a dispute can be litigated in the Southern District of Florida, that is the only place it can be litigated. If such a dispute is not litigated in the Southern District of Florida, it is not to be litigated "at all."

The second half of the forum-selection clause—"or as to those lawsuits to which the Federal Courts . . . lack subject matter jurisdiction, before a court located in Miami-Dade County, Florida"—does nothing to change the fact that all disputes arising from the cruise, that can be litigated in the Southern District of Florida, must be litigated there or not litigated at all. Rather, the second half of the clause permits a plaintiff to file in state court only when the federal court does not have subject-matter jurisdiction over the claim. It is a failsafe that guards against the possibility that a plaintiff with a potentially viable claim will not be able to have her claim heard because federal jurisdiction is lacking over the facts of the claim.

Contrary to DeRoy's argument, the "or" language is not an invitation for litigants to forum shop. Litigants who wish to be in state court cannot simply refuse to set forth the correct federal jurisdictional ground. DeRoy's construction would render the "shall" language meaningless and effectively nullify the forum-selection clause: a plaintiff could just "decline" to invoke diversity or admiralty jurisdiction to get into state court. We do not construe contracts that way. Rather, when, as here, we may reasonably construe a contract to give every provision meaning, we do so. *Fla. Polk Cty. v. Prison Health Servs., Inc.*, 170 F.3d 1081, 1084 (11th Cir. 1999). **[—23—]**

We further note that the Supreme Court has concluded that cruise lines have a special interest in clarifying where they can be sued, since their business involves transporting passengers through many jurisdictions. *Carnival Cruise Lines, Inc. v. Shute*, 499 U.S. 585, 593 (1991). Clarity in the forum for litigation spares parties time and expense, and it allows the cruise line to pass the savings to passengers. *Id.* at 594. We will not effectively repudiate a valid forum-selection clause by allowing a plaintiff to circumvent it by refusing to acknowledge the correct basis for federal jurisdiction over her case.

Indeed, DeRoy has conceded that she concurrently filed her complaint in federal court because, in the absence of a binding federal holding that the district court did not enjoy jurisdiction over her claim, binding case law in state court would have required the state court to dismiss her claim in accordance with the forum-selection clause. Courts in the jurisdiction where DeRoy filed her state-court complaint, Florida's Third District Court of Appeal, have found enforceable the very forum-selection clause at issue here, requiring other lawsuits to proceed in federal **{-1317-}** court where jurisdiction exists. *M.Z. v. Carnival Corp.*, 239 So. 3d 756, 758 (Fla. 3d DCA 2018), *reh'g denied* (Mar. 27, 2018) (enforcing the same forum-selection clause at issue here, because there was no evidence of overreaching or bad faith, or that "plaintiffs w[ould] be mistreated or short-changed by the judges of the United States District Court for the Southern District of Florida, or that federal judges **[—24—]** w[ould] routinely deny cruise ship passengers, such as these plaintiffs, jury trials if requested"); *Leslie v. Carnival Corp.*, 22 So. 3d 561, 562–63 (Fla. 3d DCA 2008), *upheld on reh'g en banc,* 22 So. 3d 567 (Fla. 3d DCA 2009) (enforcing the same forum-selection clause at issue here against the allegation that the clause deprives Florida citizens of their right to a jury trial under the saving-to-suitors clause); *Carnival Corp. v. Garcia,* 237 So. 3d 1110, 1114 (Fla. 3d DCA 2018) ("[O]nly in the absence of admiralty jurisdiction, will proper venue lie in a state court in Miami–Dade County.").

Put simply, DeRoy did not discover a "loophole" in the forum-selection clause, so she cannot escape its consequences. Rather, because her claim is capable of being pleaded to satisfy federal jurisdiction (and was, in fact, pleaded that way), the claim must proceed, if at all, in federal court.

IV. CONCLUSION

In short, the forum-selection clause does not contain the loophole DeRoy urges. To the contrary, it serves as a moat around the federal-court forum, ensuring that claims where federal jurisdiction could lie, if litigated at all, stay in federal court.

For the reasons we have explained, the district court enjoyed admiralty subject-matter jurisdiction over DeRoy's complaint. Therefore, we must reverse and vacate the order of dismissal for lack of subject-matter jurisdiction and remand for further proceedings consistent with this opinion. **[—25—]**

REVERSED, VACATED, and REMANDED.

United States Court of Appeals
for the Eleventh Circuit

No. 18-12663

OTTO CANDIES, LLC
vs.
CITIGROUP, INC.

Appeal from the United States District Court for the Southern District of Florida

Decided: July 1, 2020

Citation: 963 F.3d 1331, 8 Adm. R. 445 (11th Cir. 2020).

Before **JORDAN** and **NEWSOM,** Circuit Judges, and **HALL,*** District Judge.

*Honorable James Randal Hall, Chief United States District Judge for the Southern District of Georgia, sitting by designation.

[—1—] {-1334-} **JORDAN,** Circuit Judge: **[—2—] {-1335-}**

Two American plaintiffs. Thirty-seven foreign plaintiffs. One American defendant. A fraudulent scheme allegedly taking place here and in Mexico, with the American defendant allegedly engaging in fraudulent activity in the United States. Assumptions, but no evidence, about where the key documents and witnesses are located.

The district court, faced with this paradigm, granted the American defendant's motion to dismiss for *forum non conveniens*. After reviewing the record, and with the benefit of oral argument, we reverse and remand for further proceedings. First, the district court mistakenly gave only "reduced" deference to the American plaintiffs' choice of forum. Second, the American defendant—which had the burden of persuasion—did not support its claims that most of the relevant documents and witnesses are located in Mexico. **{-1336-}**

I

In reviewing a motion to dismiss for *forum non conveniens*, we accept as true the factual allegations in the complaint to the extent they are uncontroverted by affidavits or other evidence, or have not been challenged in the context of an evidentiary hearing. We also draw all reasonable inferences in favor of the plaintiffs. *See Delong Equip. Co. v. Washington Mills Abrasive Co.*, 840 F.2d 843, 845 (11th Cir. 1988) (reviewing Rule 12(b) motions to dismiss for ineffective service of process, lack of personal jurisdiction, and improper venue). *See also Shi v. New* **[—3—]** *Mighty U.S. Tr.*, 918 F.3d 944, 948 (D.C. Cir. 2019) (accepting the plaintiffs' allegations of facts as true on a motion to dismiss for *forum non conveniens*); *Aguas Lenders Recovery Grp. v. Suez, S.A.*, 585 F.3d 696, 697 (2d Cir. 2009) (explaining that, on appeal from a *forum non conveniens* dismissal without a factual hearing, the court accepts the plaintiff's facts as true). The following facts are taken from the plaintiffs' amended complaint and have not been contested by affidavits or other evidence. We set them out in detail because of their importance.

A

Oceanografía S.A. de C.V., a now-bankrupt Mexican company, provided oil drilling services to Petròleos Mexicanos S.A. ("Pemex" for short), Mexico's state-owned oil and gas company. Grupo Financiero Banamex S.A. de C.V. (the "Banamex Group") is a wholly owned subsidiary of Citigroup and has its principal place of business in Mexico. Banco Nacional de México, S.A. ("Banamex" for short), also based in Mexico, is a wholly owned subsidiary of the Banamex Group. Banamex is therefore an indirect subsidiary of Citigroup.

In 2008, Citigroup established credit facilities within Banamex to provide cash advances to Oceanografía and fund its operations with Pemex. A division of Citigroup based in New York, called the Institutional Clients Group, was responsible for developing and overseeing the credit facilities, and Citigroup supervised the entire arrangement. In exchange for the cash advances, Citigroup charged **[—4—]** Oceanografía a high interest rate and obtained the right to collect repayment directly from Pemex. Because Pemex is state-owned (and perhaps unlikely to default), Citigroup's credit facility was profitable and low risk. Citigroup increased its cash advances on several occasions, bloating Oceanografía with debt up to half of its annual net revenues and far exceeding the value of the underlying Pemex contracts.

Citigroup was aware that Oceanografía was overleveraged because Oceanografía sent audited financial statements and documents detailing its operational and financial condition. For each increase of the credit facility, Citigroup prepared a memorandum based on credit application forms that Oceanografía provided. The forms included work estimates for the Pemex contracts, as well as Pemex's signed authorizations, and were supposed to be subject to Citigroup's internal review procedures. Citigroup did not perform the review procedures, however, and granted advances knowing they were based on authorization documents with forged Pemex signatures.

Citigroup saved Oceanografía's credit forms to its internal network. Because Citigroup and Oceanografía communicated directly through Citigroup's servers in the United States, the falsified Pemex documents and related communications are also located in the United States and are in Citigroup's possession. Several Citigroup employees who oversaw the program and approved the cash advances are (or were) located in Miami and New York. **[—5—] {-1337-}**

Citigroup knew about Oceanografía's unstable financial condition not only through the cash advance program, but also because it became intimately involved in other aspects of Oceanografía's business. Citigroup acted as the trustee and paying agent on Oceanografía's 2008 bond issuance, advised Oceanografía on plans to acquire assets, represented the company in pursuing investors, and supervised the creation of payment trusts for the benefit of its trade creditors.

In 2014, the Mexican government discovered that Oceanografía had failed to provide insurance policies for its Pemex contracts and banned it from executing new contracts with Pemex. The government then learned of the cash advance scheme and investigated further. Mexican banking regulators found that ten Citigroup employees had violated Mexican criminal laws, and Mexican authorities pursued charges against Citigroup employees for causing Banamex to violate banking laws.

The scandal began to unfold in Mexico but reverberated in the United States. It prompted Citigroup to conduct an internal review of its cash advance program, and Samuel Libnic, based in Miami as Citigroup's head of legal matters for Latin America, led the project with support from at least one other Miami-based employee. Citigroup publicly admitted that some its employees had been criminally involved in the fraudulent scheme and announced that it had terminated employees both "inside and outside" of Mexico. **[—6—]**

The scandal also led the SEC and the Justice Department to open domestic investigations into Citigroup. Citigroup disclosed these investigations in its SEC annual report, stating that they had "included requests for documents and witness testimony." Several plaintiffs have now filed civil actions in the United States related to the fraudulent scheme.

B

In this case, thirty-nine plaintiffs—two American and thirty-seven foreign—sued Citigroup (and only Citigroup) in federal court. They claim that the fraudulent cash advances lured them into investing in or contracting with Oceanografía and that "Citigroup and/or Oceanografía" knowingly misrepresented Oceanografía's financial stability. They assert substantive and conspiracy claims under the RICO Act, 18 U.S.C. §§ 1962(c)–(d), as well as state-law claims for fraud, aiding and abetting fraud, conspiring to commit fraud, and breach of fiduciary duty. The plaintiffs allege that some of the misrepresentations were made during meetings in the United States, on telephone calls to and from the United States, in emails located on servers in the United States, and in written materials reviewed, revised, or approved by Citigroup personnel in the United States.

Some of the plaintiffs are shipping companies which leased vessels to Oceanografía. They allege that Citigroup's fraudulent misrepresentations and omissions induced them to transact with Oceanografía while it was financially **[—7—]** unstable, causing them to lose substantial amounts of money on their leases. One of those shipping lessors, Otto Candies, LLC, is a citizen of the United States and alleges that it received fraudulent communications in Louisiana.

Another group of plaintiffs comprises Oceanografía bondholders. They claim that Citigroup's fraudulent misrepresentations and omissions induced them to purchase Oceanografía bonds issued in the United States on which Oceanografía eventually defaulted. One of those bondholders, Waypoint Asset Management LLC, is an investment company based in the United States. It acquired bonds in part based on allegedly fraudulent communications made in New York. **{-1338-}**

Citigroup moved to dismiss the original complaint for *forum non conveniens* or, in the alternative, under Rules 9(b) and 12(b)(6) of the Federal Rules of Civil Procedure. In response, the plaintiffs moved for limited discovery concerning factual allegations that Citigroup had made in its motion—namely, that all of the witnesses and evidence germane to the claims are located in Mexico, that the cash advance contracts were negotiated and executed in Mexico, and that none of the alleged misconduct took place in the United States. The plaintiffs argued that Citigroup's assertions contradicted or misrepresented the allegations in the complaint or were not supported by evidence. Citigroup opposed discovery, arguing that its grounds for *forum non conveniens* dismissal were based entirely on information in the complaint. The district court denied the plaintiffs' motion, **[—8—]** concluding that the plaintiffs failed to establish good cause for discovery and that their requests were overbroad.

The plaintiffs then filed an amended complaint, and Citigroup again moved to dismiss on the same grounds. The district court heard argument and granted Citigroup's motion to dismiss for *forum non conveniens.*

II

Forum non conveniens, a common law doctrine, provides that a district court has inherent power to decline to hear a case in which there is proper jurisdiction and venue. *See Gulf Oil Corp. v. Gilbert*, 330 U.S. 501, 507 (1947). It is a flexible tool, used to prevent litigation that would "establish oppressiveness and vexation to a defendant out of all proportion to [the] plaintiff's convenience" or that is unsuitable for the domestic forum because of "the court's own administrative and legal problems." *Piper Aircraft Co. v. Reyno*, 454 U.S. 235, 241 (1981) (quoting *Koster v. Lumbermens Mut. Cas. Co.*, 330 U.S. 518, 524 (1947)) (alterations omitted).

Because the plaintiff's forum choice "should rarely be disturbed," *Gulf Oil*, 330 U.S. at 508, a *forum non conveniens* dismissal is subject to three conditions. First, as a threshold matter, a court should not dismiss an action for *forum non conveniens* unless there is an adequate and available alternative forum. *See Leon v. Millon Air, Inc.*, 251 F.3d 1305, 1310–11 (11th Cir. 2001). Second, the balance of the relative private and public interests must weigh in favor of dismissal to justify **[—9—]** invocation of the doctrine. *See id.* Private interests include the parties' relative ease of access to sources of proof, access to witnesses, ability to compel testimony, the possibility of viewing the premises, and the enforceability of a judgment. *See Gulf Oil*, 330 U.S. at 508. Public interests include a sovereign's interests in deciding the dispute, the administrative burdens posed by trial, and the need to apply foreign law. *See id.* at 508–09. Third, the plaintiffs must be able to reinstate their suit in the alternative forum without undue inconvenience or delay. *See Leon*, 251 F.3d at 1310–11. "A defendant has the burden of persuasion as to all elements of a *forum non conveniens* motion[.]" *Id.* at 1311.[1]

With respect to the private interests, courts begin with the presumption that a domestic plaintiff has chosen a sufficiently convenient forum, and it is therefore incumbent upon the defendant "to prove vexation and oppressiveness that are **{-1339-}** out of all proportion to the plaintiff's convenience." *Id.* at 1314 (internal quotation marks and citation omitted). A defendant invoking *forum non conveniens* with respect to a domestic plaintiff therefore "bears a heavy burden in opposing the plaintiff's chosen forum." *Sinochem Int'l Co. Ltd. v. Malaysia Int'l Shipping Corp.*, 549 U.S. 422, 430 (2007). The defendant must offer "positive evidence of unusually extreme **[—10—]** circumstances," and the district court must be "thoroughly convinced that material injustice is manifest before exercising any such discretion as may exist to deny a United States citizen access to the courts of this country." *SME Racks, Inc. v. Sistemas Mecánicos Para Electrónica*, 382 F.3d 1097, 1101 (11th Cir. 2004) (quoting *Burt v. Isthmus Dev. Co.*, 218 F.2d 353, 357 (5th Cir. 1955)).

Foreign plaintiffs are also entitled to a presumption in favor of their forum choice, albeit a presumption that "applies with less force." *Sinochem Int'l*, 549 U.S. at 430 (quoting *Piper Aircraft*, 454 U.S. at 255–56). Reduced deference is "not an invitation to accord a foreign plaintiff's selection of an American forum *no* deference since dismissal for *forum non conveniens* is the exception rather than the rule." *Lacey v. Cessna Aircraft Co.*, 862 F.2d 38, 45–46 (3d Cir. 1988) (citation omitted). *Accord R. Maganlal & Co. v. M.G. Chem. Co.*, 942 F.2d 164, 168 (2d Cir. 1991).[2]

We review a *forum non conveniens* dismissal for abuse of discretion, recognizing that a district court has wide latitude to assess the relevant private and public interest factors. *See Piper Aircraft*, 454 U.S. at 257. We may reverse when the district court makes a clear error of judgment or applies the wrong legal standard, **[—11—]** such as an incorrect presumption regarding the plaintiff's forum choice. *See SME Racks*, 382 F.3d at 1102 (reversing *forum non conveniens* dismissal because the district court "failed to articulate the relevant standards and failed to apply any presumption in its analysis").

III

Before assessing the private and public interest factors in this case, the district court acknowledged that the two American plaintiffs ordinarily would be entitled to a strong presumption in favor of their forum choice, whereas the remaining thirty-seven foreign plaintiffs would not be entitled to the same level of deference. But because all the plaintiffs had decided to invest in Oceanografía, a Mexican company doing business in Mexico, the district court determined that the plaintiffs could not "feign surprise at potentially having to litigate a resulting dispute in Mexico." It therefore applied only a "reduced" deference to the two domestic plaintiffs' forum choice, just as it did for the foreign plaintiffs. This, we conclude, was incorrect.

A

The deference owed to the forum choice of domestic plaintiffs cannot be reduced solely because they chose to invest in a foreign entity and may have expected **{-1340-}** to litigate abroad on certain matters. Neither the Supreme Court nor the Eleventh Circuit has adopted a "foreign investment" standard, and such a rule would be in tension with existing

---

[1] The district court concluded that Mexico was an adequate and available alternative forum, and that the plaintiffs would not be subject to undue inconvenience or delay if they had to refile there. The plaintiffs do not challenge these conclusions on appeal, so we do not address them further.

[2] The initial presumption is an important mooring for an otherwise flexible doctrine. *See Simon v. Republic of Hungary*, 911 F.3d 1172, 1182 (D.C. Cir. 2018) ("The *forum non conveniens* doctrine comes with ground rules. The starting point is a strong presumption in favor of the plaintiff's choice of the forum in which to press her suit."); 14D Charles Alan Wright, Arthur R. Miller, Edward H. Cooper, & Richard D. Freer, Federal Practice and Procedure § 3828 (4th ed. 2013) ("Without knowing the level of deference to accord the plaintiff's choice of forum, it is not clear how one would assess whether the *Gulf Oil* factors outweigh the plaintiff's choice.") (italics added).

precedent. After all, "the central purpose of any *forum* **[—12—]** *non conveniens* inquiry is to ensure that the trial is convenient[.]" *Piper Aircraft*, 454 U.S. at 256. *See also King v. Cessna Aircraft Co.*, 562 F.3d 1374, 1383 (11th Cir. 2009) ("[T]he appropriate inquiry is indeed convenience.").

A court begins with the reasonable assumption that "[w]hen the plaintiff has chosen the home forum . . . this choice is convenient." *Piper Aircraft*, 454 U.S. at 255–56. That a plaintiff invested in a foreign entity or country does not mean that the chosen domestic forum will be inconvenient, or even that it should be presumed to be inconvenient. It is possible that the most significant events giving rise to the plaintiff's claims took place in the United States or that most of the relevant documents or witnesses would be located here, even though foreign investment is involved. *See* 14D Charles Alan Wright, Arthur R. Miller, Edward H. Cooper, & Richard D. Freer, Federal Practice and Procedure § 3828 (4th ed. 2013) ("In some instances, controversies that at first blush appear to be foreign actually have a meaningful connection with the United States or its domestic policies because there have been relevant transnational contacts."). In short, investment in a foreign entity or country alone is not enough to dilute the threshold presumption that an American citizen has chosen the most convenient forum. And—except where there is a valid forum-selection clause, *see Atl. Marine Constr. Co. v. U.S. Dist. Court*, 571 U.S. 49, 63 (2013)—the plaintiff's reasonable expectations are beside the point. **[—13—]**

We acknowledge that at least one case supports the proposition which the district court applied and which Citigroup now urges us to adopt. In *EIG Energy Fund XIV, L.P. v. Petróleo Brasileiro S.A.*, 246 F. Supp. 3d 52, 78 (D.D.C. 2017), the district court discounted the presumption in favor of the forum choice of domestic plaintiffs because their decision to invest abroad "put them on notice that they might be required to litigate disputes in a foreign forum," such that litigation abroad was "reasonably foreseeable." Nevertheless, the court ultimately denied the defendants' motion to dismiss for *forum non conveniens*. *See id.* at 83.

In our view, the district court in *EIG* misread prior cases in deducing a broad rule that "plaintiffs involved in disputes arising from international commerce receive less choice-of-forum deference than plaintiffs engaging in domestic transactions." *Id.* at 78 (citing *DTEX, LLC v. BBVA Bancomer, S.A.*, 508 F.3d 785, 795 (5th Cir. 2007), *Intec USA, LLC v Engle*, 467 F.3d 1038, 1040 (7th Cir. 2006), and *Guidi v. Inter-Continental Hotels Corp.*, 224 F.3d 142, 147 (2d Cir. 2000)). Of the cases relied on by the district court in *EIG*, the Fifth Circuit's decision in *DTEX* is the only one arguably on point, and even that case did not reduce the deference given to the domestic plaintiff's forum choice solely because of foreign investment.[3] **[—14—] {-1341-}**

In *DTEX*, the operative fact was not that the plaintiff did business with a foreign entity, but that it sued for an "injury occurring in a foreign country" and that the "alleged torts all occurred in Mexico." 508 F.3d at 795, 802. This is an important distinction, and one that appears in other international commerce cases.

For example, in *Sussman v. Bank of Israel*, 801 F. Supp. 1068 (S.D.N.Y. 1992), *aff'd*, 990 F.2d 71 (2d Cir. 1993), the district court explained that "[w]here an American plaintiff chooses to invest in a foreign country *and then complains of fraudulent acts occurring primarily in that country*, the plaintiff's ability to rely upon citizenship as a talisman against *forum non conveniens* dismissal is

---

[3] The two other cases cited in *EIG* are not on point. The Second Circuit in *Guidi* reversed a *forum non conveniens* dismissal in part because the "failure to grant [the plaintiff's] choice of an American forum significant deference was unsound." 224 F.3d at 146. The Seventh Circuit in *Intec USA* offered some thoughts about *forum non conveniens* and expressed "doubt" that the threshold deference "has controlling force in litigation among firms all of which trade worldwide," **[—14—]** but it ultimately vacated the *forum non conveniens* dismissal because the district court lacked subject-matter jurisdiction. *See* 467 F.3d at 1040, 1044.

diminished." *Id.* at 1073 (emphasis added). In that case, the plaintiffs invested in an Israeli financial institution, alleged that they were defrauded "in Jerusalem" by the Israeli defendants, and "[a]ccording to [the] plaintiffs' theory, it was in Israel that the defendants hatched their illegal scheme," notwithstanding some "peripheral" activities in the United States. *See id.* at 1071, 1074. Given these allegations, the plaintiffs' citizenship and residence "d[id] not constitute the powerful, near-decisive factors for which they contend[ed]," although the ultimate burden of persuasion still rested with the defendant. *See id.* at 1074. *See also Howe v. Goldcorp Investments, Ltd.*, 946 F.2d 944, 951 (1st Cir. 1991) (because the "relevant events" surrounding **[—15—]** the plaintiff's claims took place in Canada, it was "not surprising" that most of the documents and witnesses were in Canada as well); *Reid-Walen v. Hansen*, 933 F.2d 1390, 1395 (8th Cir. 1991) ("When an American corporation doing extensive foreign business brings an action for injury occurring in a foreign country, many courts have partially discounted the plaintiff's United States citizenship."). The rule described in cases like *Sussman* is therefore narrower and more nuanced than the one which Citigroup asks us to adopt.

As Citigroup acknowledges, moreover, neither the Supreme Court nor the Eleventh Circuit has squarely addressed whether it would be appropriate to reduce deference to a domestic plaintiff's forum choice in cases like *Sussman*. Nor have we considered whether some form of intermediate deference is ever permissible for American plaintiffs. *Compare Carijano v. Occidental Petroleum Corp.*, 643 F.3d 1216, 1228 (9th Cir. 2011) (rejecting intermediate deference), *with Iragorri v. United Techs. Corp.*, 274 F.3d 65, 71 (2d Cir. 2001) (establishing "sliding scale" deference).

We need not answer those questions here. Although Citigroup vigorously argues that the claims here "arise from" foreign business dealings, the plaintiffs do not complain of conduct or injuries occurring primarily in Mexico. Taking the plaintiffs' allegations as true, Citigroup directed a scheme and engaged in acts in furtherance of that scheme from the United States, where it is based. The **[—16—]** Institutional Clients Group was responsible for administering the allegedly fraudulent cash advance program from New York. Several employees involved in the alleged fraud were based in New York or Miami. And several of the allegedly fraudulent communications occurred in meetings on United States soil or in emails or calls directed to or maintained in the United States. As we read the complaint, this is a dispute focused on Citigroup's conduct in the United States, and so one would presume—at least initially—that a trial here would be more convenient (or would at least not be inconvenient). **{-1342-}**

Citigroup argues that the fraud against the plaintiffs was really perpetrated by Mexican entities in Mexico. But Citigroup did not present any evidence to support this contention, and its argument mischaracterizes the complaint, the thrust of which is, again, that Citigroup directed the scheme and caused the plaintiffs' injuries from its offices in the United States. Accepting that Banamex and Oceanografía were key players in the scheme, the plaintiffs still allege that the Institutional Clients Group "developed and oversaw" the credit facility program, approved fraudulent credit applications with knowledge of the risks, and circumvented internal review procedures—all in the United States.

Citigroup points to obscurities in the complaint regarding who committed certain acts, noting that the plaintiffs frequently allege that Citigroup "and/or" Oceanografía made fraudulent misrepresentations. Citigroup argues that the more **[—17—]** specific allegations in the complaint confirm that Oceanografía and its controlling shareholder, Amado Yáñez, made "nearly all of the alleged misrepresentations." With respect to the domestic plaintiffs, Citigroup points out that they allege that "Mr. Yáñez and/or other Oceanografía principals traveled on dozens of occasions to Louisiana" to make the fraudulent misrepresentations to Otto Candies. Citigroup also submits that Waypoint's claims are "overwhelmingly directed towards" Oceanografía and Mr. Yáñez.

These points have some force, but the complaint's primary allegations are about Citigroup's involvement in the scheme *qua* administrator and supervisor. And, as Citigroup concedes, there are allegations in the complaint that Citigroup communicated directly with some of the plaintiffs in the United States. For example, the plaintiffs allege that Citigroup and Otto Candies discussed over email the mechanics of the cash advance facility and that Citigroup misrepresented Oceanografía's financial situation in those communications. The plaintiffs also allege that Citigroup misrepresented Oceanografía's financial situation to other plaintiffs and, for example, induced them to renegotiate their loans with Oceanografía. Citigroup's response is that the specific allegations about its conduct are not relevant to the causes of action and therefore immaterial to the *forum non conveniens* analysis. For reasons we explain later, however, we have no basis at this stage to assess which allegations are material and which are superfluous. **[—18—]**

Significantly, the plaintiffs chose to sue Citigroup—and no one else—for its alleged role in the fraud. They did not sue Mexican nationals—Banamex or Oceanografía, or their respective employees or agents—who *according to Citigroup* caused their injuries. We take no position on Citigroup's alternative grounds for dismissal under Rules 9(b) and 12(b)(6), but we note that when Citigroup argues for *forum non conveniens* dismissal because the complaint "directly implicate[s] an alleged fraud carried out by Mexican nationals in Mexico," it improperly assumes that it did not carry out the fraud. This is an argument on the merits, and not necessarily on whether the facts *as alleged* should be litigated in the United States.

Admittedly, it can sometimes be difficult to disentangle the merits of a complaint from a *forum non conveniens* inquiry. Whoever is ultimately responsible for the plaintiffs' alleged injuries may be a strong indicator of where the most convenient forum is. If Citigroup is correct that in the end only the Mexican entities can be liable, then the plaintiffs should have sued those entities instead, in which case Mexico would have been the presumptively most convenient forum. But, again, the plaintiffs **{-1343-}** sued Citigroup, and not the Mexican entities. *Cf.* 7 Charles Alan Wright, Arthur R. Miller, & Mary Kay Kane, Federal Practice and Procedure § 1623 (3d ed. 2019) (explaining that plaintiffs may sue one or more joint tortfeasors without joining others, and need not join every coconspirator if joinder is not feasible). If, on the other hand, the plaintiffs are correct that Citigroup is **[—19—]** independently liable for its alleged role in overseeing, directing, or participating in the scheme, then presumably the United States would be the most convenient forum. Because at this stage we accept the complaint's allegations as true, we determine the applicable presumption from the plaintiffs' perspective, and not Citigroup's. *See Delong Equip.*, 840 F.2d at 845; *Shi*, 918 F.3d at 948.

Even as the parties quarrel over the nature of the complaint and the locus of events, there remains an elephant in the room—Citigroup. It is the only defendant in this case, and it is based in the United States. Not only that, it has offices in Miami and conducts substantial activities throughout the United States, including New York—where the Institutional Clients Group is based. One would therefore think that it would be more convenient for Citigroup to litigate in the Southern District of Florida than in Mexico.

This is yet another reason to leave the presumption for the plaintiffs' chosen forum in place and require that Citigroup demonstrate—with positive evidence—why litigating on its home turf would be so oppressive and vexatious that a federal court should decline jurisdiction. When an American plaintiff sues an American defendant for conduct allegedly occurring in the United States, it should not be easy for the defendant to obtain a *forum non conveniens* dismissal. *See, e.g., Galustian v. Peter*, 591 F.3d 724, 732 (4th Cir. 2010) (providing greater deference in favor of a domestic forum where "the defendant is a resident and citizen of the forum he **[—20—]** seeks to have declared inconvenient for litigation"); *Peregrine Myanmar Ltd. v. Segal*, 89 F.3d 41,

46 (2d Cir. 1996) (in weighing the *Gulf Oil* factors, "the court starts with a presumption in favor of the plaintiff's choice of forum, especially if the defendant resides in the chosen forum, as here"); *Lony v. E.I. Du Pont de Nemours & Co.*, 935 F.2d 604, 608 (3d Cir. 1991) ("This case is puzzling in that frequently the *forum non conveniens* issue is raised by a defendant sued away from home who seeks to convince the court that the balance of relevant factors should be tipped against requiring it to defend in a forum far from its home jurisdiction."). *Cf. Piper Aircraft*, 454 at 256 n.24 (citing *Pain v. United Techs. Corp.*, 637 F.2d 775, 797 (D.C. Cir. 1980), for the proposition that "citizenship and residence are proxies for convenience").

B

We now turn to Citigroup's argument that "where foreign plaintiffs significantly outnumber domestic plaintiffs, diminished deference should be applied to all of the plaintiffs' forum choice." Appellee's Br. at 17. Though addressed preemptively by the plaintiffs in their initial brief, the district court did not reduce deference to the American plaintiffs based on the presence of foreign plaintiffs. It was only because the American plaintiffs invested in a foreign entity that the district court discounted the initial deference and placed them on par with their foreign counterparts. Because that was error, the district court on remand will need to afford **[—21—]** the requisite deference to the American plaintiffs. It will then have to deal with a mixed group of foreign and domestic plaintiffs, potentially turning Citigroup's argument into a live issue. We therefore provide a few observations. **{-1344-}**

We have not found any cases holding that reduced deference to American plaintiffs is warranted when they sue alongside foreigners, but we have located a couple that state the opposite. In *Carijano*, 643 F.3d at 1228, the Ninth Circuit rejected the argument that *Piper Aircraft* stands for the proposition that "when both domestic and foreign plaintiffs are present, the strong presumption in favor of the domestic plaintiff's choice of forum is somehow lessened." And in *Simon*, 911 F.3d at 1183, the D.C. Circuit explained that "the addition of foreign plaintiffs does not render for naught the weighty interest of Americans seeking justice in their own courts." Citigroup cites two unpublished district court cases in support of its argument, but neither is convincing.[4] **[—22—]**

There also does not appear to be any practical or doctrinal basis to reduce deference to domestic plaintiffs who sue alongside foreign plaintiffs, particularly when they all sue a single American defendant for conduct that they allege occurred in the United States. For one, the presence of foreign plaintiffs does not change the otherwise domestic nature of a complaint—here, that Citigroup committed wrongs in or from the United States, where it is based. *Cf. In re Air Crash Off Long Island, N.Y., on July 17, 1996*, 65 F. Supp. 2d 207, 217 (S.D.N.Y. 1999) (acknowledging that "the presence of foreign plaintiffs (who chose to sue in the United States) [did] not change the essentially American character of [the] case, which involve[d] a flight originating in the United States, a United States carrier, United States manufacturing defendants, and predominantly United States domiciliaries as passengers").

---

[4] In *Takiguchi v. MRI Int'l, Inc.*, No. 2:13-cv-01183, 2015 WL 6661479, at *3 (D. Nev. Oct. 29, 2015), the plaintiffs were entitled to limited deference not because the foreign plaintiffs outnumbered the American plaintiffs, but because the latter conceded that they were actually residents of Japan and Canada, and that one was a resident of Texas (not of Nevada, where the district court was located). The district court, in any event, denied the motion to dismiss for *forum non conveniens*.

In *Fasano v. Juoqing Li*, No. 16-cv-8759, 2017 WL 6764692, at *6 (S.D.N.Y. Dec. 29, 2017), *vacated and remanded sub nom., Fasano v. Yu Yu*, 921 F.3d 333 (2d Cir. 2019), the district court stated that "[b]ecause the foreign plaintiffs outnumber the domestic plaintiff, and because their financial interest in the action is much greater than the domestic plaintiff's interest, the Court accords diminished deference to Plaintiffs' choice of forum." But the *Fasano* district court did not cite any cases in support of that proposition, and its decision was vacated and remanded for failure to consider a forum selection clause in the contract at issue.

In addition, the purpose of *forum non conveniens* is to prevent the defendant from facing harassing and vexatious litigation out of all proportion to the plaintiffs' convenience. From Citigroup's perspective, then, the presence of numerous foreign plaintiffs may not make the case more difficult to litigate in the United States. Citigroup may wish to take numerous depositions because of the sheer number of plaintiffs, but that would be true if there were thirty-nine American plaintiffs. What is significant for our purposes is that the presence of foreign plaintiffs would not necessarily lead to unwarranted burdens or additional travel for Citigroup to depose those plaintiffs. The district court has broad discretion over the location of **[—23—]** depositions, *see DeepGulf, Inc. v. Moszkowski*, 330 F.R.D. 600, 609 (N.D. Fla. 2019) (collecting cases), and the general rule is that plaintiffs are required to make themselves available for examination in the district in which they bring suit. *See* 8A Charles Alan Wright, Arthur R. Miller, & Richard L. Marcus, Federal Practice and Procedure § 2112 (3d ed. 2010) (collecting cases). At the same time, the foreign plaintiffs will not be able to drag Citigroup to all corners **{-1345-}** of the globe to take corporate depositions, as there is a presumption that a defendant will be deposed in the district of its residence or principal place of business. *See DeepGulf*, 330 F.R.D. at 607 (collecting cases). All else being equal, the ratio of domestic to foreign plaintiffs does not necessarily have a bearing on Citigroup's convenience.[5]

There may be instances of blatant gamesmanship—for example, where a domestic plaintiff is added at the eleventh hour to strengthen the other plaintiffs' connections to the United States—such that reduced deference may be appropriate for all the plaintiffs. *See Vivendi SA v. T-Mobile USA Inc.*, 586 F.3d 689, 694–96 (9th Cir. 2009). But at this juncture, we see no evidence of improper forum shopping. Indeed, it would be ironic to fault the foreign plaintiffs for their willingness to travel to the United States to sue Citigroup in its country of citizenship. **[—24—]**

Rather than reduce or enhance the deference owed to domestic or foreign plaintiffs, some courts have conducted a separate *forum non conveniens* analysis for each group. A bifurcated analysis may be appropriate, for example, where foreign and domestic plaintiffs filed separate lawsuits that were consolidated for administrative purposes, or where parties can be dropped or claims can be severed under Rule 21. *See Kolawole v. Sellers*, 863 F.3d 1361, 1372 (11th Cir. 2017); *Tazoe v. Airbus S.A.S.*, 631 F.3d 1321, 1335 (11th Cir. 2011); *King*, 562 F.3d at 1383–84; *Banco Latino v. Gomez Lopez*, 17 F. Supp. 2d 1327, 1333 (S.D. Fla. 1998).

We leave it to the district court to determine whether a bifurcated analysis is permissible or warranted in this case once the domestic and foreign plaintiffs are afforded their appropriate deference on remand. But we note that—procedural issues aside—a split analysis might be problematic in some respects. If the domestic plaintiffs are permitted to move forward in the district court, then dismissing the foreign plaintiffs would force Citigroup to defend against two actions (assuming the foreign plaintiffs refile in Mexico). That could defeat the purpose of *forum non conveniens*, particularly if the parties intend to rely on the same documents and witnesses in both countries. *See In re Assicurazioni Generali S.p.A. Holocaust Ins. Litig.*, 228 F. Supp. 2d 348, 370 (S.D.N.Y. 2002) (declining to dismiss a foreign plaintiff with no *bona fide* connection to the chosen forum because the domestic plaintiffs in the consolidated action were permitted to move forward, and therefore **[—25—]** the bulk of evidence would already be in the United States). Then again, this potential problem would be moot if the claims of the domestic plaintiffs are dismissed for *forum non conveniens*. These matters are for the district court to consider on remand.

Finally, we address and reject Citigroup's argument that the two American plaintiffs are only "nominal" litigants entitled to reduced deference. The district court found that these

[5] We say "necessarily" because at this point Citigroup has not put forward any evidence to the contrary.

two plaintiffs were American citizens for purposes of its *forum non conveniens* analysis and said no more about whether their role in the lawsuit was legitimate. There has not been discovery on this issue and there is no evidence that these entities are not real parties-in-interest or that they otherwise lack standing to assert their claims.

C

In sum, it was inappropriate for the district court to discount or reduce the deference owed to the chosen forum of the **{-1346-}** American plaintiffs based on their decision to invest or transact business abroad. Nor was there any other reason to deviate from the normal rule that an American plaintiff suing in the United States is presumed to have chosen the most convenient forum. A remand is therefore warranted. *See SME Racks*, 382 F.3d at 1102 (reversing a *forum non conveniens* dismissal due to the district court's failure to afford the proper deference owed to domestic plaintiffs). **[—26—]**

Our decision today does not guarantee that plaintiffs can avoid *forum non conveniens* dismissal by making vague allegations, or by strategically joining foreign plaintiffs together with domestic ones and suing a single domestic defendant. The plaintiff-friendly, facial reading of the complaint leads only to an *initial* presumption. That presumption is not dispositive, and a defendant can always marshal positive evidence to overcome it. *See, e.g., Contact Lumber Co. v. P.T. Moges Shipping Co.*, 918 F.2d 1446, 1449 (9th Cir. 1990) ("Although a defendant must meet an almost impossible burden in order to deny a citizen access to the courts of this country, the cases demonstrate that defendants frequently rise to the challenge.") (internal quotation marks and citation omitted). Citigroup had the opportunity to engage in limited discovery related to *forum non conveniens* and to present evidence in support of its motion. But, as explained below, Citigroup opposed discovery and failed to carry its burden.

IV

We now consider the *Gulf Oil* private and public interest factors. Although the district court had wide latitude to weigh the evidence and determine whether those factors pointed clearly toward dismissal, the threshold error on the deference owed to the domestic plaintiffs tainted its analysis. The error in effect switched the burden of persuasion and allowed Citigroup to obtain a *forum non conveniens* dismissal without presenting any evidence on these factors. **[—27—]**

As noted earlier, Citigroup bore the burden of persuasion on all elements of its *forum non conveniens* motion. *See Leon*, 251 F.3d at 1311. A strong presumption in favor of the American plaintiffs should have forced Citigroup to offer "positive evidence of unusually extreme circumstances" and "material injustice" to oust those plaintiffs from their chosen domestic forum. *See SME Racks*, 382 F.3d at 1101 (quoting *Burt*, 218 F.2d at 357). Yet Citigroup opposed discovery and offered no evidence on the private interest factors.

The district court also erred with respect to the foreign plaintiffs. Even though they were entitled to "somewhat" less deference than their domestic counterparts, that lesser degree of deference should not have removed Citigroup's burden entirely. By failing to proffer *any* positive evidence of private inconvenience, Citigroup failed to carry its burden as to both the domestic and foreign plaintiffs.

A

We begin with *Piper Aircraft*, which involved only foreign plaintiffs and therefore established the floor of a defendant's *forum non conveniens* burden. That case arose from a plane crash in Scotland. *See* 454 U.S. at 238–39. The plane was subject to Scottish air traffic control and operated through a Scottish air taxi service, and the pilot and passengers were all Scottish subjects and residents. *See id.* at 239. The Supreme Court held that, under these circumstances, the defendant's burden to demonstrate private inconvenience was not particularly heavy; the defendant was **[—28—]** not required to "submit affidavits identifying the witnesses they would call and the testimony these witnesses would provide if the trial were held in the alternative forum." *Id.* at 258. At the same time, **{-1347-}** the defendant was required to "provide enough information to enable the [d]istrict [c]ourt to balance the parties' interests." *Id.* The Supreme Court did not explain what would constitute "enough" information, so it is useful to examine the facts and history of the case to better delineate its holding.

Before the case reached the Supreme Court, the Third Circuit had reversed the district court's dismissal for *forum non conveniens*, concluding that the defendant did not "set[ ] forth the requisite specific information" of private inconvenience. *See Reyno v. Piper Aircraft Co.*, 630 F.2d 149, 161 (3d Cir. 1980), *rev'd*, 454 U.S. 235 (1981). But the district court had in fact relied on affidavits, including one that attested to the defendant's witnesses and their testimony on certain topics, albeit in broad strokes. *See Piper Aircraft*, 454 U.S. at 259 & n.27. The relevant affidavit did not identify witnesses by name, but offered general categories of witnesses—for example, by occupation or by role in the incident in question—as well as some expected topics of testimony. *See id. See also* Petition for Writ of Certiorari, *Piper Aircraft Co. v. Reyno,* Nos. 80-848 & 80-883 (filed Nov. 25, 1980), at Ex. F (Affidavit of Charles J. McKelvey). On that record, the Supreme Court held that "sufficient information was provided" to allow the district court to assess the relevant interests. *See Piper Aircraft*, 454 U.S. at 258–59. We therefore do not read **[—29—]** *Piper Aircraft* as holding that any less information would have sufficed under the circumstances.[6]

When American plaintiffs sue in federal court, the defendant's burden is heavier. As we have long held, a defendant must come forward with "positive evidence of unusually extreme circumstances" such that the district court is "thoroughly convinced that material injustice is manifest before exercising any such discretion as may exist to deny a United States citizen access to the courts of this country." *SME Racks*, 382 F.3d at 1101 (quoting *Burt*, 218 F.2d at 357).[7] **[—30—]** **{-1348-}**

[6] The affidavit provided, for example, that the defendant "would call as witnesses the owners and employees of the Scottish air-taxi company which owned and operated the aircraft and hired the pilot," that their testimony "would concern the cause of and liability for this accident," and that all "such persons are residents and citizens of Scotland." The affidavit also provided that the defendant "would call as witnesses the persons who were responsible for the training and licensing of the pilot of this aircraft," that their testimony "would concern the cause of the accident and the liability thereof," and that those witnesses also were residents and citizens of Scotland. The affidavit continued like this for five categories of witnesses. *See* Petition for Certiorari, *Piper Aircraft Co. v. Reyno*, Nos. 80-848 & 80-883 (filed Nov. 25, 1980), at Ex. F.

[7] For cases reversing *forum non conveniens* dismissals because the defendant failed to proffer sufficient evidence in light of the circumstances of the case, see *Lacey*, 862 F.2d at 44 (holding that the evidence was insufficient because the defendants "submitted no evidence to support their contentions," whereas the plaintiff produced a report that the cause of a crash was a defective product manufactured in the United States, and submitted affidavits "that various witnesses on the product liability issue are located in Pennsylvania and throughout the United States and are available to testify here"), and *Baris v. Sulpicio Lines, Inc.*, 932 F.2d 1540, 1550 (5th Cir. 1991) (rejecting bare allegations of private inconvenience and holding that "in order to fulfill the requirements of *Gulf Oil*, a more detailed presentation must be made by the defendants concerning the private interest factors").

For cases holding that there was sufficient evidence of inconvenience, see *Interface Partners Int'l Ltd. v. Hananel*, 575 F.3d 97, 105 (1st Cir. 2009) (affirming *forum non conveniens* dismissal where the defendant "adequately identified the twenty-nine witnesses he intend[ed] to call in the proceedings[,] . . . indicated the relevance of at least ten" of those witnesses, and offered "affidavits from those ten" witnesses that they would testify to "various facts disputing the allegations of misconduct asserted"), *Delta Air Lines, Inc. v. Chimet, S.p.A.*, 619 F.3d 288, 300 (3d **[—30—]** Cir. 2010) (affirming a *forum non conveniens* dismissal because the defendant "identified the witnesses it intended to depose and proffered in oral argument the information that it expected to obtain"), and *Gschwind v. Cessna Aircraft Co.*, 161 F.3d 602, 610 (10th Cir. 1998) (holding that the defendants, who

We have not set out strict rules on what constitutes "unusually extreme circumstances," and it probably does not make sense to do so. That is because the quantum and quality of evidence needed will depend on the unique facts and circumstances of the given case. *See, e.g., Lacey*, 862 F.2d at 44 (holding that "on the particular facts of this case, the defendants did not submit sufficient information to allow the district court properly to undertake the *forum non conveniens* analysis"). In complex commercial cases—with elaborate legal claims and allegations involving transnational communications, or with multiple international and domestic parties—the locus of events may be difficult to pinpoint.

B

Because this is a complex commercial dispute with domestic and foreign plaintiffs, Citigroup should have offered some evidence of inconvenience and certainly no less than what the defendant provided in *Piper Aircraft*. After a thorough review of the record, we find very little if any positive evidence of Citigroup's inconvenience, especially regarding the location of documents and witnesses. **[—31—]**

In its *forum non conveniens* motion, Citigroup argued that "key individuals identified in the [amended complaint] that would be critical to Citigroup's defense include former Banamex employees located in Mexico." But it did not identify any of the former Banamex employees by name or position, attest to their residence in Mexico with affidavits, anticipate the basic topics of their testimony, or explain how these unidentified witnesses would be critical to its case. Citigroup also asserted that its defense would be based on corporate and banking records and communications in Mexico, including documents belonging to Citigroup's alleged Mexican co-conspirators. Again, however, it did not identify these documents, generally or specifically. Citigroup also speculated—again without details or evidence—that "[t]here is no reason to doubt that equally critical witnesses from [Oceanografía] and Pemex . . . are also located in Mexico."

The plaintiffs, on the other hand, allege that Citigroup employees involved in the cash advance program are in the United States and identify some of these employees by name. The plaintiffs also refer to Citigroup's public statement that it fired individuals involved in the fraud both "inside and outside" of the United States. We not only accept these allegations as true at this stage, we also draw from them appropriate reasonable inferences. *See Delong Equip.*, 840 F.2d at 845; *Shi*, 918 F.3d at 948. One reasonable inference is that these domestic witnesses have material information and are available or subject to compulsory process in the United States. **[—32—]**

Citigroup made some factual assertions in its motion, but it did so by either misconstruing the complaint or by contradicting the plaintiffs' allegations without discrete evidentiary support. For example, Citigroup argued that "Mexico is where the cash advance contracts were negotiated and executed," which implies that material evidence will be located there. The **{-1349-}** paragraph of the complaint to which Citigroup cited, however, alleges that "Citigroup, through Banamex, and Oceanografía entered into a Cash Advance Contract in September 2012." Nowhere do the plaintiffs allege that the cash advance program was negotiated and executed exclusively in Mexico. Indeed, they sought discovery on that very point (and others). Citigroup may be correct, but it had the burden to rebut the plaintiffs' allegations on these matters with positive evidence. No evidence, by definition, is an absence of positive evidence.

Even if we were to accept its unsupported factual claim that the cash advance program was negotiated and executed in Mexico, Citigroup did not rebut the plaintiffs' plausible allegations that it would have collected and stored the relevant documents

---

"c[a]me forward with documentary evidence," offered the "bare minimum of evidence necessary," although the court "certainly would have benefitted from additional evidence in the record").

during the SEC and Justice Department investigations. The plaintiffs, we note, allege that a Citigroup employee in Miami led an internal audit into the cash advance program. Citigroup did not contest this factual allegation with an affidavit from a corporate representative or otherwise explain why documents from that audit would not be available in the United States. **[—33—]**

Citigroup argued below that "Mexico is where [Oceanografía's] alleged falsification of Pemex work estimates and authorizations took place." This may be true, but the plaintiffs allege that the ordinary business practice was for Oceanografía to send those work estimate documents to Citigroup in the United States. Based on this unrebutted allegation, it is not clear why Citigroup does not already have—or could not easily access—the allegedly falsified work estimates and authorization documents, even if they were originally created in Mexico. The plaintiffs also plausibly allege that Citigroup controls all the email servers of its subsidiaries, including Banamex, from the United States. Given the absence of evidence to the contrary, it should be relatively easy for Citigroup to access the relevant documents from those servers. If that is not so, Citigroup should explain why not. *See Simon*, 911 F.3d at 1186 (explaining that "[d]igitization . . . has eased the burden of transcontinental document production and has increasingly become the norm in global litigation"); Maggie Gardner, *Retiring Forum Non Conveniens*, 92 N.Y.U. L. Rev. 390, 414 (2017) (arguing that, because of modern technology and digitization, "transnational evidence collection is far less burdensome today than it was even at the time of *Piper*," such that the defendant's burden of proving hardship should be harder to meet).

Citigroup's contentions about the location of key evidence and witnesses may well be plausible. They may even be correct. But Citigroup failed to support those **[—34—]** contentions with positive evidence on the *Gulf Oil* private interest factors, and therefore failed to carry its burden.[8] **{–1350–}**

C

Citigroup makes a more sweeping argument on appeal. It contends that the district court viewed the complaint as a whole and reasonably concluded that the relevant

---

[8] Citigroup did provide some positive evidence at the *forum non conveniens* stage, but its evidence did not speak to the location of documents and witnesses.

First, Citigroup cited to an expert affidavit and a copy of a complaint that a Mexican affiliate of Otto Candies had filed in Mexico against Banamex and Citibank, N.A. (a subsidiary of Citigroup not named in this case). Those documents tended to show that Mexico was an adequate and available forum. As noted above, the plaintiffs do not challenge this conclusion on appeal, and so this evidence is not relevant for our purposes.

Second, Citigroup referred to the same expert affidavit to show that it would be difficult to compel Mexican witnesses to testify in the United States and that Mexican banking laws would prevent Banamex from sharing information absent permission from the Mexican banking regulator. These contentions, however, presuppose (1) that material witnesses are in Mexico, and not in the United States, and (2) that Citigroup does not already have domestic access to the Banamex documents apparently protected by Mexican banking secrecy laws. Citigroup did not offer any evidence to establish these two implicit and necessary premises.

Third, Citigroup submitted various SEC filings to demonstrate that the Institutional Clients Group was a "business segment," not a legal entity, and that the Group had employees all over the world, including at subsidiaries such as Banamex. The district court did not rely on these documents, and it is not clear how the Group's status as a business segment rather than a distinct legal entity changes the *forum non conveniens* analysis. The complaint does not depend on that distinction, and instead focuses on the role that the Group played in developing and overseeing the credit facilities. The fact that the Group is a business segment with employees at Banamex, moreover, could be a double-edged sword. It might make it more plausible that New York-based executives of the Group directed the alleged scheme from the United States through their subordinates in Mexico. That would be consistent with the plaintiffs' claims, and it would also mean that evidence of the fraudulent conduct would be accessible in the United States.

evidence would be in Mexico. Citigroup relies on *Ford v. Brown*, 319 F.3d 1302, 1308 (11th Cir. 2003), for the proposition that district courts must analyze the elements of the plaintiffs' causes of action, consider what evidence is required to **[—35—]** prove and disprove each element, and make a reasoned assessment about the location of relevant evidence.

There are two problems with Citigroup's argument. The first is that the district court did not delineate the elements of each claim in order to sort through the relevant and irrelevant evidence. The second is that the court did not have positive evidence to sort through in the first place. This case is therefore similar to *La Seguridad v. Transytur Line*, 707 F.2d 1304, 1306–07, 1310 (11th Cir. 1983), where we reversed a *forum non conveniens* dismissal because the district court "did not attempt to go beyond [the] representations of counsel to ascertain the underlying facts of the case" and "did not attempt to pin counsel down to their theories of the case, and the facts that would support their theories." Likewise, the district court here stated—without further explanation—that it would be necessary for the plaintiffs to establish the "underlying fraud" in Mexico. It also accepted the contention of Citigroup that its defense would require documents in Mexico, even though Citigroup did not describe with any particularity the defense or the evidence necessary to establish it.

Citigroup assumes that the district court must have "appreciated" which facts would be relevant to the litigation, and therefore tries to reconstruct what it sees as the court's implicit reasoning. But that is not enough for us evaluate the factual and legal issues of the case. *See id.* at 1308 ("Without delineating the elements of the **[—36—]** claims and the defenses thereto, we simply cannot know the factual issues raised by these claims, and are left only to speculate as to what witnesses and documents might be relevant and where they might be located.").

Even if we were to accept Citigroup's reconstructed argument—that the RICO claims would require the plaintiffs to establish an "enterprise" with foreign entities and that the aiding and abetting fraud claims would require the plaintiffs to establish an underlying fraud in Mexico—it is still not clear why it wouldn't be just as easy to develop these theories in the United States. First, based on their allegations, it is plausible that the plaintiffs could establish the RICO enterprise and underlying fraud with documents already in Citigroup's possession. Indeed, the plaintiffs **{-1351-}** contend that there is no real dispute concerning the events in Mexico, so it seems they believe they can prove their case without resorting to additional documents or witnesses there. Second, the plaintiffs intend to prove that Citigroup controlled and directed the enterprise from the United States, so it is not clear why the bulk of evidence wouldn't be in the United States, even if some documents tending to establish the global enterprise could also be found in Mexico. Third, Citigroup's argument ignores the plaintiffs' direct fraud and fiduciary duty claims, which appear at first glance to require investigation into Citigroup's conduct in the United States. In any event, no matter how we try to dissect the various claims, this is a "fragmentary **[—37—]** record" on which it is "impossible to make a sound determination of relative convenience." That requires us to remand for further development. *See id.*

The district court erred in concluding that the "ease of access to evidence" factor supported dismissal. That conclusion was based on unsupported findings that the material documents and evidence "are all located in Mexico," and that "all of the key players in this dispute . . . will be available in Mexico." The court also erred in concluding that the "availability of witnesses and compulsory process" factor favors dismissal. That conclusion was based on the unsupported contention of Citigroup that it needed to rely on witnesses in Mexico for its defense. On this record, these errors were fatal to the *Gulf Oil* private interest analysis. *See Ford*, 319 F.3d at 1308 ("Perhaps the most important 'private interest' of the litigants is access to evidence."); 17 James Wm. Moore et al., Moore's Federal Practice § 111.74[3][c][iii] (3d ed. 2020) ("Of all the private interest factors . . . the relative ability of the forums to compel the attendance of significant unwilling witnesses at trial often is considered the most important factor, because the presentation of live testimony often is 'essential to a fair trial.'").

D

The district court also concluded that the public interest factors weighed in favor of litigation in Mexico. Although Citigroup is the only named defendant, the case involved "four primary players, three of which are unquestionably Mexican **[—38—]** entities"—Banamex, Oceanografía, and Pemex. The court reasoned that Mexico "clearly has a substantial interest in this case being litigated in Mexico as evidenced by numerous parallel proceedings underway and the fact that one of the key players in this dispute is owned by the Mexican government."

The district court did not ultimately find "such meaningful connections between any of the parties and [the Southern District of Florida] that would outweigh the clear interest Mexico has over this litigation." But that conclusion is questionable because the plaintiffs allege that Citigroup conducts substantial business in the Southern District of Florida and that two of its Miami-based employees audited the cash advance program after the scandal unfolded in Mexico. There is therefore some local interest in the case. On the other hand, there does not appear to be any local need to have the case dismissed. The district court did not cite, for example, any administrative difficulties or docket congestion in the Southern District that warranted a *forum non conveniens* dismissal.

But even if the district court adequately considered the administrative interests of the Southern District, it failed to consider the sovereign interests of the United States. *See SME Racks*, 382 F.3d at 1104 (explaining that although the district court "recognized that Florida had in interest in [that case], it failed to recognize any federal interest"). The United States has a **{-1352-}** stake in this litigation, and that should factor into the public interest analysis. *See Republic of Panama, v. BCCI Holdings* **[—39—]** *(Luxembourg) S.A.*, 119 F.3d 935, 953 (11th Cir.1997) ("Relevant public interest factors include the sovereigns' interests in deciding the dispute[.]").

As explained above, the plaintiffs opted to sue Citigroup for its alleged role in the fraud. If they succeed in proving the facts and legal claims, as alleged, then Citigroup—a United States corporation—would be liable to two American plaintiffs for causing them injuries from its United States offices. We have observed that "a sovereign has a very strong interest when its citizens are allegedly victims and the injury occurs on home soil." *SME Racks*, 382 F.3d at 1104. *See also Esfeld v. Costa Crociere, S.P.A.*, 289 F.3d 1300, 1311 (11th Cir. 2002) ("There is a strong federal interest in making sure that plaintiffs who are United States citizens generally get to choose an American forum for bringing suit, rather than having their case relegated to a foreign jurisdiction."). As further evidence that the United States has a substantial interest in this case, the Justice Department and SEC conducted domestic investigations into Citigroup for the cash advance program at issue. *See Carijano*, 643 F.3d at 1232 (explaining that the United States has a "significant interest in providing a forum for those harmed by the actions of its corporate citizens"). On remand, the district court must consider the interests of the United States in analyzing the *Gulf Oil* public interest factors. **[—40—]**

V

We now turn to the discovery conditions that the district court imposed in its order, as the parties dispute their propriety and efficacy. Because we are reversing on other grounds, we do not directly address whether the conditions, as phrased, were appropriate. But we provide some thoughts for the district court and the parties to consider on remand.

In *Piper Aircraft*, the Supreme Court suggested that, in order to mitigate the practical difficulties of *forum non conveniens* dismissals, "district courts might dismiss subject to the condition that defendant corporations agree to provide the records relevant to the plaintiff's claims." 454 U.S. at 257 n.25. The Supreme Court did not explain, however, how district courts should enforce discovery conditions as litigation proceeded abroad. Nonetheless, following the *Piper Aircraft* decision, it became common practice for courts to include stipulations, not only regarding discovery, but also involving the defendant's consent to foreign jurisdiction and final judgment, and the defendant's waiver of foreign statutes of limitation.

With respect to discovery, district courts have imposed conditions that range from the parties having to make "relevant" documents and witnesses available to the parties consenting to abide by the Federal Rules of Civil Procedure. We have approved of these types of discovery conditions and have even held that the imposition of such conditions supported the finding of an adequate, alternative **[—41—]** forum. *See Satz v. McDonnell Douglas Corp.*, 244 F.3d 1279, 1283 (11th Cir. 2001) (affirming the district court's finding that the foreign court was adequate in part because the defendant "agree[d] to conduct all discovery in accordance with the Federal Rules of Civil Procedure"); *Magnin v. Teledyne Cont'l Motors*, 91 F.3d 1424, 1430–31 (11th Cir. 1996) (affirming a *forum non conveniens* dismissal in part based on the condition that any domestic discovery "be done in accordance with the Federal Rules of Civil Procedure").[9] **{-1353-}**

In this case, the district court required Citigroup to "reasonably make available all relevant documents and witnesses within its control," and the plaintiffs would have been able "to move to reinstate the action within ninety (90) days of [Citigroup] failing to comply" with that or any other condition. Given our precedent, we do not fault the district court for imposing such a typical condition in its order. But we urge the parties and the court to re-evaluate the limits and contours of that condition in case the district court again dismisses for *forum non conveniens*.

For starters, what rules would govern the scope of "reasonableness," "relevance," and "control"? Would those concepts be defined by Mexican law or by the Federal Rules of Civil Procedure? The plaintiffs urge the latter, arguing that **[—42—]** we have "emphasized" dismissals conditioned on compliance with U.S. discovery rules. Although we have sanctioned that type of condition, we have also approved of a condition that only required disclosure of "relevant" documents without reference to the Federal Rules. *See Tazoe*, 631 F.3d at 1330.

Either type of condition could present problems. As the plaintiffs note, the required disclosure of "relevant" evidence is open-ended. If foreign law governs relevance, the condition subjects the parties to some uncertainty and to the idiosyncrasies of the foreign court, which to some extent undermines the purpose of *forum non conveniens*. *See* Maggie Gardner, *Parochial Procedure*, 69 Stan. L. Rev. 941, 987 (2017) (arguing that "it is hard for judges to forecast whether the alternative foreign forum will resolve the defendants evidentiary concerns" or "whether the foreign court's jurisdiction over evidence will actually translate into party access"). Requiring the parties to follow the Federal Rules, on the other hand, may provide them with more clarity about their ongoing obligations. But we have not given much more thought to what mechanisms, or legal authority, the district court has at its disposal to ensure compliance with the Federal Rules while a dismissed case is being litigated in a foreign court. What permits the district court to adjudicate discovery disputes in a case that it has already dismissed? Does the court need to retain some **[—43—]** sort of jurisdiction? And what happens if those disputes are also pending before a Mexican court?[10]

[9] Cases involving similar discovery conditions are voluminous. *See, e.g., Mercier v. Sheraton Int'l, Inc.*, 981 F.2d 1345, 1358 (1st Cir. 1992); *Stewart v. Dow Chem. Co.*, 865 F.2d 103, 104–05 (6th Cir. 1989); *Oto v. Airline Training Ctr. Arizona, Inc.*, 247 F. Supp. 3d 1098, 1109 (D. Ariz. 2017).

[10] Other courts have noted some of these issues in passing. *See In re Union Carbide Corp. Gas Plant Disaster at Bhopal, India in Dec., 1984*, 809 F.2d 195, 205 (2d Cir. 1987) (explaining that a discovery stipulation would be "subject to such

As noted, the district court included a "return jurisdiction" clause, which permits the plaintiffs to refile in the Southern District of Florida in the event of a breach of a condition and perhaps would encourage Citigroup's compliance with the discovery conditions. We have modified dismissal orders to *add* return jurisdiction clauses—at least where there was some indication that the foreign court would not assume jurisdiction. *See Leon*, 251 F.3d at 1316; *King*, 562 F.3d at 1384. But with the understanding that a return jurisdiction clause is permissible, we still foresee possible practical difficulties. **{-1354-}**

As one commentator has explained, the efficacy of a return jurisdiction clause depends on a "herculean conception of [the] plaintiffs' patience, litigiousness, and financial resources." Gardner, *Parochial Procedure*, 69 Stan. L. Rev. at 990. Some plaintiffs may not have the resources or appetite to refile and start anew in federal court, especially after protracted litigation abroad. That presupposes that the **[—44—]** plaintiffs even had the resources to travel to and refile in the foreign court in the first place. *See* Martin Davies, *Time to Change the Federal Forum Non Conveniens Analysis*, 77 Tul. L. Rev. 309, 319 (2002) (explaining that "few plaintiffs even bother to pursue their claim in the alternative foreign forum following *forum non conveniens* dismissal from a U.S. court.") (italics added).

For plaintiffs who do have resources for further litigation, they may actually seek out or manufacture disputes in the hopes that even a minor discovery disagreement could trigger a return jurisdiction clause and reopen the doors to federal court. The plaintiffs here, for example, might want to seek extremely broad discovery and then refile in the district court the moment that Citigroup withholds a document on relevance grounds.

Accordingly, on remand, the district court should consider whether a single breach would permit the plaintiffs to reinstitute their case in federal court, and whether a breach must be material. If so, what would constitute a "material" breach, and under whose law? Moreover, could Citigroup "cure" a breach if the plaintiffs file a discovery motion and the district court concludes that the withheld documents were relevant? That is, if the district court resumes jurisdiction and resolves a discovery dispute in the plaintiffs' favor, could Citigroup agree to produce the withheld documents and then simply return to the Mexican court? Or does Citigroup, like Julius Caesar, cross the Rubicon once it improperly withholds a **[—45—]** relevant document? Without considering these questions (and perhaps others), the district court may face practical problems down the road which could make litigation *less* convenient for everyone involved.

VI

The district court did not apply the deference owed to the domestic plaintiffs, and it erred in weighing the *Gulf Oil* private interest factors as to all the plaintiffs because Citigroup did not satisfy its burden. We therefore reverse and remand for further proceedings, including consideration of the United States' interests under the public interest factors.

The district court may in its discretion permit limited discovery, hold an evidentiary hearing, or accept additional evidence and supplemental briefing from the parties on the private and public interest factors. Because the plaintiffs have not challenged the district court's findings that Mexico is an adequate and available forum, or that they would not be subject to undue inconvenience or delay if they had to reinstate their case in Mexico, those findings stand. We also leave in place the district court's unchallenged findings with respect to the enforceability of the foreign judgment, though we take no view on the

approval as may be required of the [foreign] court," and otherwise "the parties will be limited by the applicable discovery rules of the [foreign] court in which the claims will be pending"); *Pinder v. Moscetti*, 666 F. Supp. 2d 1313, 1321 (S.D. Fla. 2008) (requiring the defendants to provide all relevant evidence within their custody and control, but recognizing that such a condition "d[id] not extend the discovery allowed under the Federal Rules of Civil Procedure to litigation in the Bahamas," as discovery "shall be governed by the applicable discovery rules of the Bahamas court").

weight of this fact in the district court's *Gulf Oil* analysis on remand.

We do not address at this time whether the district court erred in its understandable attempt to ensure that Citigroup would provide adequate discovery **[—46—]** in Mexico. We also do not take any view on Citigroup's alternative arguments for dismissal, which the district court did not reach.

REVERSED AND REMANDED.

United States Court of Appeals
for the Eleventh Circuit

No. 18-11638

TESORIERO
vs.
CARNIVAL CORP.

Appeal from the United States District Court for the Southern District of Florida

Decided: July 14, 2020

Citation: 965 F.3d 1170, 8 Adm. R. 463 (11th Cir. 2020).

Before **ROSENBAUM, GRANT,** and **HULL,** Circuit Judges.

[—1—] {-1174-} GRANT, Circuit Judge:

When Irina Tesoriero sat on the vanity chair in her Carnival Cruise ship cabin, she was in for a terrible surprise—it collapsed. While she and her husband **[—2—]** waited for help to arrive, they saw that a leg had fallen off the chair. Observing no other outward defects, they took some photos of the pegs that normally held the chair together, which became visible only after the chair broke. Still waiting for help, they let **{-1175-}** in a steward who came to replace the broken chair with a fresh one. Finally, the Tesorieros took matters into their own hands and went directly to the onboard medical center; there, they were told that Tesoriero's arm was not broken, and an x-ray was taken to be sure. The onboard doctor treated her with Tylenol, ice, and a sling and sent the couple on their way.

Understandably frustrated that her injury continued to bother her, Tesorerio sought treatment at home after the cruise. Still no broken arm, but she was suffering from a terrible case of medial epicondylitis and ulnar neurapraxia—a diagnosis Tesoriero describes as tennis elbow. Tesoriero was also understandably frustrated with Carnival, and filed suit against the cruise line, alleging that it had failed to inspect and maintain the cabin furniture (or else warn her of the danger the chair posed). Perhaps aware of the difficulty she may have in showing that Carnival had notice about the chair's dangers (especially given the photos suggesting no outward defects), she fought the usual notice requirement on two fronts: first, she alleged that res ipsa loquitur applied and meant that she did not need to show notice, and second, she claimed that Carnival should be sanctioned with an adverse inference on notice because it failed to preserve the broken chair.

The district court granted summary judgment in favor of Carnival. The court found that the cruise line did not have notice that the chair was dangerous, that res ipsa loquitur did not apply, and that the failure to save the chair was not **[—3—]** sanctionable. Tesoriero now appeals those three conclusions. After careful review, we agree with the district court that Tesoriero failed to show that Carnival had actual or constructive notice that the chair was broken. Unlike the district court, we decline to consider whether res ipsa loquitur applies; even if it does, that doctrine cannot cure a defect in notice. Nor can the requested spoliation sanctions; even setting aside whether we think the chair itself could have provided any evidence of notice, Carnival's failure to preserve the chair was not shown to be in bad faith and is therefore not sanctionable. For all those reasons, we affirm.

I.

On June 26, 2015, Irina Tesoriero was getting ready for dinner in her cabin aboard the Carnival *Splendor*. She pulled a wooden chair "about a foot" away from the vanity and attempted to sit down, but it collapsed beneath her. Her right collarbone struck the vanity and her right arm was injured; initially, she believed that her arm was broken. Her husband, Joseph Tesoriero, witnessed the incident and called the front desk for help.

While waiting for help to arrive, Joseph inspected and photographed the chair. He saw that it "did not have any obvious or observable outward defects" before it broke. He also saw that the right front leg, which had been attached to the seat by pegs, had fallen off, and that the glue on the pegs was dried and chipped. In his opinion, it "was obvious from the appearance of the pegs—visible only after it fell apart—that the pegs had been unglued and loose for a long time." A steward came to the cabin, took away the broken chair, and replaced it with a new one. **[—4—]** The chair was later disposed of by an unknown crew member because it could not be fixed.

Tesoriero and her husband waited around for medical staff, and went to the onboard medical center when in-cabin aid was not forthcoming. Tesoriero was then examined by a physician, who told her (correctly, as it turns out) that she did not have a fracture and gave her Tylenol, ice, and an arm sling. Although an x-ray was taken, it was sent to Miami for review **{-1176-}** because it could not be read on the ship. While at the medical center, Joseph Tesoriero completed a "passenger injury statement" on his wife's behalf. The statement collected basic information, including the time, date, and location of the incident.

In accordance with Carnival's policy, because Tesoriero's injury only required first aid—and because she did not request an accident report—the medical staff classified the accident as "non-reportable." That meant that the security department, which is responsible for investigating accidents and, when necessary, preserving evidence, was asked to do neither. The room stewards, on the other hand, dispose of broken furniture that cannot be repaired and only preserve it if asked to do so. That general policy was followed here, so the chair was not preserved.

After Tesoriero disembarked, she received confirmation that her x-ray results did not show a broken arm. But the arm was not ready to make peace, and Tesoriero continued to experience pain and swelling. She was ultimately diagnosed with medial epicondylitis and ulnar neurapraxia, which she described as "tennis elbow." Tesoriero struggled to get her arm back to full strength, **[—5—]** undergoing injections, therapy, and surgery, apparently with little success; she says that she continued to require medical treatment into this litigation, and that she struggles with basic tasks like cooking, taking out the garbage, and carrying groceries.

A little less than a year after the cruise, Tesoriero filed a complaint against Carnival in the Southern District of Florida, asserting a single claim of negligence based on Carnival's alleged failure to inspect and maintain the cabin furniture and failure to warn passengers of the unsafe condition. Both parties moved for summary judgment. For its part, Carnival invoked a familiar defense, arguing that it was not responsible for Tesoriero's injury because it had neither actual nor constructive knowledge that the chair was unsafe prior to the incident.

During discovery, Tesoriero deposed the housekeeping manager who was aboard the ship at the time of the accident. The manager testified that stewards cleaned the cabins daily and were responsible for inspecting the cabin furniture. He explained that that process involved physical movement of the chairs in the course of vacuuming, as well as visual inspection of the entire cabin, including the furniture, for signs of damage. Damaged furniture was reported to a floor supervisor, who was tasked with making a record of the problem and addressing it. When repairs were possible, they were made, and when repairs were not possible, the items were disposed of.

Tesoriero's arguments—considering both her response to Carnival's motion and her own motion for summary judgment—were threefold. *First*, she said that the condition of the chair, coupled with Carnival's regular inspections of the cabin **[—6—]** furniture, was enough to constitute constructive notice of the dangerous condition.[1] *Second*, she contended that the doctrine of res ipsa loquitur applied and eliminated the need for her to show that Carnival had notice in any event. *Finally*, she argued that Carnival's disposal of the broken chair amounted to spoliation of evidence and

[1] At the trial level, Tesoriero pressed additional arguments. She said that Carnival had constructive notice because of (1) a prior accident involving a collapsing metal balcony chair; and (2) internal documents from Carnival regarding the repair and replacement of cabin chairs. She also contended that her negligent maintenance claim did not require a showing of notice. The district court rejected all these arguments, and Tesoriero does not challenge those rulings on appeal.

entitled {-1177-} her to an inference that Carnival had notice of the risk-creating condition.

A magistrate judge issued a report and recommendation on the competing motions. He said that the evidence demonstrated that "no reasonable inspection could have discovered the dangerous condition without first deconstructing the cabin chair." As to the res ipsa loquitur issue, the magistrate first concluded that the doctrine, if applicable, would indeed absolve Tesoriero of any need to show that Carnival had actual or constructive notice of the dangerous condition. Ultimately though, he decided that the doctrine did not apply because a collapsing chair can easily happen even without negligence. Finally, the magistrate declined to sanction Carnival for spoliation of evidence, seeing no evidence that Carnival reasonably anticipated litigation following the accident.

Over Tesoriero's objections, the district court affirmed and adopted the magistrate judge's report and recommendation and granted Carnival summary judgment. In adopting the recommendation, the court specifically ruled that res ipsa loquitur did not apply and that the facts surrounding the disposal of the broken **[—7—]** chair did "not amount to spoliation such that an adverse inference is warranted." Tesoriero appealed.

II.

"We review a district court's grant of summary judgment *de novo*. Summary judgment is appropriate only when no genuine issue of material fact exists and the moving party is entitled to judgment as a matter of law." *Lewis v. City of Union City*, 918 F.3d 1213, 1220 n.4 (11th Cir. 2019) (en banc) (internal citation omitted). We view "the evidence and all reasonable inferences drawn from it in the light most favorable to the nonmoving party." *Hornsby-Culpepper v. Ware*, 906 F.3d 1302, 1311 (11th Cir. 2018). "Where the record taken as a whole could not lead a rational trier of fact to find for the non-moving party, there is no genuine issue for trial." *Id.* (quotation marks and citation omitted). "We review the district court's decision regarding spoliation sanctions for abuse of discretion." *Flury v. Daimler Chrysler Corp.*, 427 F.3d 939, 943 (11th Cir. 2005). We "may affirm for any reason supported by the record, even if not relied upon by the district court." *Lage v. Ocwen Loan Servicing LLC*, 839 F.3d 1003, 1009 (11th Cir. 2016) (citation omitted).

III.

On appeal, Tesoriero raises three arguments. *First*, she argues that her husband's observations about the broken cabin chair, coupled with Carnival's admitted regular inspections, show that Carnival had constructive notice that the chair was dangerous. *Second*, she argues that even if she cannot establish notice, the doctrine of res ipsa loquitur saves her claim because it eliminates the ordinary **[—8—]** notice requirement. *Finally*, she argues that she is entitled to an adverse inference against Carnival on the notice requirement in any event because Carnival spoliated evidence when it discarded the chair.

A.

Before turning to Tesoriero's constructive notice argument, we should say a few words about the background legal principles in play. "Maritime law governs actions arising from alleged torts committed aboard a ship sailing in navigable waters." *Guevara v. NCL (Bahamas) Ltd.*, 920 F.3d 710, 720, 7 Adm. R. 476, 481 (11th Cir. 2019). "Drawn from state and federal sources, the general maritime law is an amalgam of traditional common-law rules, modifications of those rules, and newly created rules." {-1178-} *Misener Marine Const., Inc. v. Norfolk Dredging Co.*, 594 F.3d 832, 838 (11th Cir. 2010) (quoting *E. River S.S. Corp. v. Transamerica Delaval, Inc.*, 476 U.S. 858, 864–65 (1986)). And in the absence of an established federal maritime rule, we "may borrow from a variety of sources in establishing common law admiralty rules to govern maritime liability where deemed appropriate." *Marastro Compania Naviera, S.A. v. Canadian Mar. Carriers, Ltd.*, 959 F.2d 49, 53 (5th Cir. 1992) (applying the "general common law and in particular the

Restatement (Second) of Torts" to "determine the law of maritime trespass"); *see also Wells v. Liddy*, 186 F.3d 505, 525 (4th Cir. 1999) (The "general maritime law may be supplemented by either state law or more general common law principles." (internal citation omitted)). For maritime tort cases in particular, "we rely on general principles of negligence law." *Chaparro v. Carnival Corp.*, 693 F.3d 1333, 1336 (11th Cir. 2012) (citation omitted). **[—9—]**

A few key principles have developed to guide our analysis of these torts. A cruise line "is not liable to passengers as an insurer," but instead is liable to passengers "only for its negligence." *Keefe v. Bahama Cruise Line, Inc.*, 867 F.2d 1318, 1322 (11th Cir. 1989) (citation omitted). The elements of a maritime negligence claim, in turn, are well-established, and stem from general principles of tort law. A cruise passenger must show that "(1) the defendant had a duty to protect the plaintiff from a particular injury, (2) the defendant breached that duty, (3) the breach actually and proximately caused the plaintiff's injury, and (4) the plaintiff suffered actual harm." *Guevara*, 920 F.3d at 720, 7 Adm. R. at 481 (quoting *Chaparro*, 693 F.3d at 1336).

Here, the first question for us is the scope of Carnival's duty to Tesoriero. Shipowners owe their passengers a duty of "ordinary reasonable care under the circumstances." *Keefe*, 867 F.2d at 1322. This standard requires, "as a prerequisite to imposing liability, that the carrier have had actual or constructive notice of the risk-creating condition," at least so long as "the menace is one commonly encountered on land and not clearly linked to nautical adventure." *Id.*; *Everett v. Carnival Cruise Lines*, 912 F.2d 1355, 1358 (11th Cir. 1990). In other words, a cruise ship operator's duty is to shield passengers from known dangers (and from dangers that should be known), whether by eliminating the risk or warning of it. Liability for a cruise ship operator thus "'hinges on whether it knew or should have **[—10—]** known' about the dangerous condition." *Guevara*, 920 F.3d at 720, 7 Adm. R. at 481 (quoting *Keefe*, 867 F.2d at 1322).[2]

We have identified at least two ways that constructive notice can be shown. *First*, a plaintiff can establish constructive notice by showing that a "defective condition existed for a sufficient period of time to invite corrective measures." *Id.*, 7 Adm. R. at 481 (alterations adopted) (quoting *Monteleone v. Bahama Cruise Line, Inc.*, 838 F.2d 63, 65 (2d Cir. 1988)). *Second*, a plaintiff can show evidence of "substantially similar incidents in which conditions substantially similar to the occurrence in **{-1179-}** question must have caused the prior accident." *Id.*, 7 Adm. R. at 481 (quotation marks and citation omitted). On the other hand, the fact that the cruise line runs the ship is not enough—constructive notice of a risk cannot be imputed merely because a shipowner "created or maintained" the premises. *Everett*, 912 F.2d at 1358–59.

Here, the evidence does not show—and Tesoriero does not contend—that Carnival had actual notice that the chair was dangerous. Nor do we have any evidence of substantially similar incidents involving wooden cabin chairs. Tesoriero's sole argument that Carnival had constructive notice relies on her husband's observations about the chair, along with Carnival's furniture-inspection policy. In her view, these facts demonstrate that Carnival should have known about **[—11—]** the chair's "hair-trigger condition." For Tesoriero to prevail on this theory, we would need to conclude that the

[2] This notice requirement is not unique to maritime law. For example, in a traditional negligence action against a landowner by an invitee, a "defect or danger is generally insufficient to establish liability, unless it is shown to be of such a character or of such duration that the jury may reasonably conclude that due care would have discovered it." W. Page Keeton et al., *Prosser and Keeton on the Law of Torts* § 61, at 426–27 (5th ed. 1984). So, for example, the "mere fact of the presence of a banana peel on a floor may not be sufficient to show that it has been there long enough for reasonable care to require the defendant to discover and remove it," while a "black, flattened out and gritty" peel might lead to a different conclusion. *Id.* § 39, at 243 (citation omitted). The key is notice.

chair existed in a defective condition "for a sufficient period of time to invite corrective measures." *Guevara*, 920 F.3d at 720, 7 Adm. R. at 481. A defect, however, must be reasonably detectable for it to "invite" corrective measures, and we cannot see how the chair's condition here issued any such invitation.

To begin, Carnival's "regular inspections weigh against a finding of constructive notice" that the chair was dangerous—not in favor of that finding. *Id.* at 723 n.8, 7 Adm. R. at 483 n.8; *see also Monteleone*, 838 F.2d at 66. The daily inspection policy required stewards to report damaged furniture to a floor supervisor, and the supervisor was then responsible for documenting and addressing the issue. The lack of a report noting structural damage to Tesoriero's cabin chair—or any wooden cabin chair for that matter—indicates that the chair was not in a condition that invited corrective measures.

And at a more basic level, Tesoriero's constructive notice argument is undermined by her own evidence. In Joseph Tesoriero's affidavit describing the incident, he observed that the glue on the pegs holding the chair together "appeared to be dried out or chipped away" and that it was "obvious" that "the pegs had been unglued and loose for a long time." But those observations, however obvious they may have been after the fall, could not have been made by the crew before the chair came apart. Joseph Tesoriero himself admitted that—before its collapse—the "chair did not have any obvious or observable outward defects." In fact, he added that the condition of the pegs was "visible only after it fell apart." **[—12—]**

The photographic evidence submitted by Tesoriero only reinforces her husband's observations. Though the pictures cannot reveal the state of the glue, it appears that the leg and seat of the chair were held together by four pegs that fit into opposing holes. With the chair intact, its cloth-covered frame would have enveloped and obscured the peg-and-hole assembly. So, consistent with Joseph Tesoriero's testimony, any defect relating to dried or chipped glue could not have been visible until the chair came apart.

Even beyond the lack of any outwardly visible defect, Tesoriero's characterization of the chair's "hair-trigger condition" is weakened by her own testimony. In her deposition, Tesoriero testified that she moved the chair back from the vanity, evidently without noticing any problem; the issue only became apparent after the chair broke under her full weight.

The combined effect of this evidence does not support a reasonable inference that Carnival should have known about the danger. Quite the opposite: it supports an inference that the defect in the chair was hidden, was not readily observable by sight or touch, and could only be discovered by either disassembling the chair to view the pegs or stress testing it. An implicit **{-1180-}** legal requirement that all furniture on a cruise ship be either disassembled or subjected to daily stress testing would be remarkable. Rather than establishing that Carnival should have known of the chair's defective condition, the evidence supports the cruise line's assertion that moving the chair during cleaning and conducting routine visual inspections did not reveal a risk-creating condition. **[—13—]**

B.

That brings us to res ipsa loquitur. Tesoriero argues that even if she cannot show that Carnival had notice of the chair's dangerous condition, the cruise line can still be held liable under that doctrine because it eliminates the usual notice requirement. Her theory, though, fails on several fronts: it not only misunderstands the relationship between duty and notice in a tort claim but would also dramatically expand the doctrine of res ipsa loquitur, which "in the admiralty context is not totally unique but neither is it routine." *United States v. Baycon Indus., Inc.*, 804 F.2d 630, 633 (11th Cir. 1986).

Res ipsa loquitur—Latin for "the thing speaks for itself"—is an evidentiary doctrine that permits a trier of fact to infer a defendant's negligence from unexplained circumstances.[3] *Sweeney v. Erving*, 228 U.S. 233, 238–39 (1913); *see also Johnson v. United States*, 333 U.S. 46, 49 (1948). In other words, it is a form of circumstantial evidence. *See Sweeney*, 228 U.S. at 240; *see also* W. Page Keeton et al., *Prosser and Keeton on the Law of Torts* § 39, at 243 (5th ed. 1984); *Restatement (Second) of Torts* § 328D cmt. b (Am. Law Inst. 1965). For the doctrine to apply, the plaintiff needs to show that "(1) the injured party was without fault, (2) the instrumentality causing the injury was under the exclusive control of the defendant, and (3) the mishap is of a type that ordinarily does not occur in the absence of negligence." *Baycon*, 804 F.2d at 633. **[—14—]**

But before we address the application of the doctrine to the facts of this case, we need to decide a threshold question that has divided the district courts in our Circuit—whether a maritime passenger who fails to establish the shipowner's notice of a dangerous condition can still survive summary judgment by invoking res ipsa loquitur. If not, the lack of notice is dispositive: no notice, no negligence. This is an open question in our Circuit.

Indeed, district courts have reached conflicting conclusions on the issue. In *Adams v. Carnival Corp.*—a maritime negligence action arising from a deck chair collapsing under a passenger—the district court considered the effect of res ipsa loquitur on the notice requirement. No. 08-22465-CIV, 2009 WL 4907547, at *1, *5 (S.D. Fla. Sept. 29, 2009). The evidence showed that Carnival conducted routine inspections of the chairs, and the court concluded that the plaintiff presented no evidence that the defect was "even capable of detection." *Id.* at *4. There, as here, the plaintiff attempted to get around the usual notice requirement with res ipsa loquitur. Ultimately, the district court held that the plaintiff's invocation of res ipsa loquitur did "not obviate the need to show that Carnival had notice." *Id.* at *5. "Without specific facts demonstrating, at least, that the purported defect was detectable with sufficient time to allow for corrective action," the case could not proceed to a jury. *Id.*

Since *Adams*, though, the tide has turned and a majority of the district courts **{-1181-}** in this Circuit have reached the opposite conclusion (including in this case).[4] A **[—15—]** leading example is *Millan v. Celebration Cruise Operator, Inc.*, where a piece of the ceiling fell and hit a passenger. 212 F. Supp. 3d 1301 (S.D. Fla. 2015). After initially distinguishing *Adams* on its facts, the court went on to conclude that "a plaintiff is not required to show the defendant's actual or constructive notice of the defective condition in order to raise a *res ipsa loquitur* inference

---

[3] As it turns out, the phrase itself does not "speak for itself"—the Latin terminology has long been criticized for adding unnecessary mystery "to a relatively simple problem" of circumstantial evidence. *Restatement (Second) of Torts* § 328D cmt. a (Am. Law Inst. 1965).

[4] Cases from other jurisdictions take a variety of approaches on res ipsa loquitur and notice. Following in *Adams*' footsteps, "several cases in the maritime context" support an argument **[—15—]** "that a predicate for a *res ipsa loquitur* finding is that the Defendant had notice of the defective condition." *Tillson v. Odyssey Cruises*, No. 08-10997-DPW, 2011 WL 309660, at *7 (D. Mass. Jan. 27, 2011). Others have concluded that res ipsa loquitur is incompatible with a notice requirement. *See, e.g., Krivokuca v. City of Chicago*, 73 N.E.3d 525, 532 (Ill. App. Ct. 2017) (holding that res ipsa loquitur was unavailable when statute required showing actual or constructive notice); *Mixon v. Wash. Metro. Area Transit Auth.*, 959 A.2d 55, 60 (D.C. 2008) (This "court and others have held that in cases in which notice is an essential element of a plaintiff's claim, *res ipsa loquitur* is inapplicable because it is inconsistent with the requirement of notice."). There is also considerable support for the opposite proposition. *See, e.g., Smith v. United States*, 860 F.3d 995, 998 n.2 (7th Cir. 2017) (noting that "the inference triggered by the res ipsa loquitur doctrine would include the proposition that the defendant had notice of the defective nature of the instrumentality that caused the plaintiff's injury"); *Miller v. Cincinnati, New Orleans & Tex. Pac. Ry. Co.*, 317 F.2d 693, 696 (6th Cir. 1963) ("If application of the doctrine permits an inference of *negligence*, such inference must necessarily include all the essential elements of negligence, including here an inference that defendant had actual or constructive knowledge of the defective condition."); *Burns v. Otis Elevator, Co.*, 550 So. 2d 21, 22 (Fla. Dist. Ct. App. 1989) (actual or constructive notice of the defect is "immaterial" if the conditions for the res ipsa doctrine are established).

of negligence under maritime law." *Id.* at 1306. In support of that conclusion, the district court cited our opinion in *United States v. Baycon Industries* as finding "no requirement of actual or constructive notice for *res ipsa* in maritime negligence action." *Id.* at 1305–06 (citing *Baycon*, 804 F.2d at 632–35). The problem is that *Baycon* does not say that (or even hint at it). Nevertheless, many district court opinions have embraced this view in the years that followed, often with little more than a citation to *Millan* itself. *See, e.g., Morhardt v. Carnival Corp.*, 304 F. Supp. 3d 1290, 1296 (S.D. Fla. 2017) (citing *Millan* and noting that "courts in this district have held that **[—16—]** a plaintiff in a maritime action based on negligence is not required to prove that the shipowner had notice of the defective condition when the doctrine of *res ipsa loquitur* applies"); *O'Brien v. NCL (Bahamas) Ltd.*, 288 F. Supp. 3d 1302, 1314 (S.D. Fla. 2017).

In resolving the apparent uncertainty within our Circuit about notice and res ipsa loquitur, we return to first principles.[5] "Res ipsa loquitur leads only to the conclusion that the defendant has not exercised reasonable care, and is not itself any proof that he was under a duty to do so." Keeton et al., *supra*, § 39, at 255. "It does not permit the imposition of liability without fault, and therefore does not help to establish the duty of care, which is essential to every negligence case." 1 Stuart M. Speiser, *The Negligence Case: Res Ipsa Loquitur* § 3:1, at 90 (1972). That means the doctrine does not apply unless the alleged negligence is "within the scope of the defendant's duty to the plaintiff." **{–1182–}** *Restatement (Second) of Torts* § 328D (Am. Law Inst. 1965). That same duty requirement is found in the res ipsa loquitur doctrines of many states, and at least one federal circuit court has already stated that it applies in the admiralty context as well. *See, e.g., Trigg v. City & County of Denver*, 784 F.2d 1058, 1060 (10th Cir. 1986) (applying Colorado law); *Biggs v. Logicon, Inc.*, 663 F.2d 52, 54 (8th Cir. 1981) (noting in an admiralty case that res ipsa loquitur only applies if the "negligence is within the scope of the defendant's duty to the plaintiff"); *Moon v. Dauphin County*, 129 A.3d 16, 26 (Pa. **[—17—]** Commw. Ct. 2015); *Crum v. Equity Inns, Inc.*, 685 S.E.2d 219, 229 (W. Va. 2009); *Linnear v. CenterPoint Energy Entex/Reliant Energy*, 966 So. 2d 36, 44 (La. 2007).

So res ipsa loquitur can allow a jury to infer from circumstantial evidence that the defendant must have breached its duty—but it cannot show that a defendant must have had that duty in the first place. The Supreme Court's description of the doctrine as "an aid to the plaintiff in sustaining the burden of proving *breach* of the duty of due care" is consistent with that understanding—a duty can only be breached if it exists. *Commercial Molasses Corp. v. N.Y. Tank Barge Corp.*, 314 U.S. 104, 113 (1941) (emphasis added). It would be quite odd to say that a party must have had a duty, but for reasons that cannot be discovered. As another court put it, "*res ipsa loquitur* provides no assistance to a plaintiff's obligation to demonstrate a defendant's duty, that a breach of that duty was a substantial factor in causing plaintiff harm, or that such harm resulted in actual damages. However, *res ipsa loquitur* does aid a plaintiff in proving a breach of duty." *Quinby v. Plumsteadville Family Practice, Inc.*, 907 A.2d 1061, 1071 n.15 (Pa. 2006). Well put.

For instance, a trespasser, to whom no duty of care was owed by a landowner, may not establish a landowner's liability for a defective condition by relying on res ipsa loquitur. *Restatement (Second) of Torts* § 328D cmt. j (Am. Law Inst. 1965). Similarly, if a statute provides that automobile drivers are only liable to their passengers for "wilful, wanton, or reckless conduct," a passenger relying on res ipsa loquitur to show a breach of ordinary care cannot establish liability under the higher statutory duty. *Id.* In other words, res ipsa loquitur "does not eliminate a **[—18—]** plaintiff's obligation to prove that the defendant owed a duty to the plaintiff in the

[5] Our Circuit is not alone in its uncertainty—at least as a general matter. Prosser and Keeton, for instance, describe "an uncertain 'doctrine' of res ipsa loquitur, which has been the source of some considerable trouble to the courts." Keeton et al., *supra*, § 39, at 243–44.

first place." *Ausherman v. Bank of Am. Corp.*, 352 F.3d 896, 901 (4th Cir. 2003).

With this foundation laid, our resolution of the notice issue is straightforward. If res ipsa loquitur cannot eliminate the duty requirement, it cannot eliminate the notice requirement; the two are intertwined in a maritime negligence tort. *Guevara*, 920 F.3d at 720, 7 Adm. R. at 481. Maritime passengers are owed a duty of "ordinary reasonable care under the circumstances, a standard which requires, as a prerequisite to imposing liability, that the carrier have had actual or constructive notice of the risk-creating condition." *Keefe*, 867 F.2d at 1322; *Everett*, 912 F.2d at 1358. And we have been clear that the scope of a cruise line's "duty to protect its passengers is informed, if not defined, by its knowledge of the dangers they face onboard." *K.T. v. Royal Caribbean Cruises, Ltd.*, 931 F.3d 1041, 1044, 7 Adm. R. 507, 508 (11th Cir. 2019).

The *Baycon* case, no matter how frequently it is cited, does not change that equation. In fact, it does not even use the term notice or explicitly consider the issue before us today. Instead, *Baycon* deals with shipowner liability for sunken vessels. *Baycon*, 804 F.2d at 631–32. The suit was brought under the Rivers and Harbors Act of 1899, which imposed a duty on shipowners to not "voluntarily or carelessly" sink a **{-1183-}** vessel. *Id.* at 631, 633 n.5 (citation omitted). Because the forty-year-old, long-idle ship in that case sunk on a clear and calm night, we allowed the doctrine of res ipsa loquitur to supply the inference that its sudden sinking was caused by negligence. *Id.* at 634. That is all. **[—19—]**

Even so, district courts in this Circuit have sometimes concluded—perhaps from the lack of any discussion about notice—that *Baycon* demonstrates that res ipsa loquitur eliminates any notice requirement. But that is just not right. To begin, though *Baycon* does not specifically address notice, the Court's discussion of the dredge's age, the length of time since it had been in service, and the preparation for travel without assessing "the condition of the external hull below the water line" rings in the tones of constructive notice. *Id.* And more to the point, absent so much as a word about notice in that earlier precedent on statutory negligence for sunken vessels, we cannot jump to the conclusion that res ipsa loquitur obviates the well-known notice requirement for cruise ship negligence cases brought by passengers.

* * *

In sum, a plaintiff who relies on res ipsa loquitur to show a breach of duty still bears the burden of proving that a duty existed in the first place. And because notice is an integral part of duty, a passenger who relies on res ipsa loquitur bears the burden of showing that the cruise line had notice. As it applies to this case, then, the doctrine does not help Tesoriero. Carnival's duty was to protect Tesoriero from dangerous conditions that it was aware of or should have been aware of. But as we have already explained, Tesoriero's own evidence shows that the chair's defect was hidden. Because res ipsa loquitur has no effect on our duty analysis, Tesoriero's failure to establish Carnival's actual or constructive notice is fatal to her case. And that is true whether or not res ipsa loquitur would otherwise apply to a broken chair fact pattern—a question we need not consider given our resolution of the notice issue. **[—20—]**

So, although we conclude that the district court erred by holding that res ipsa loquitur obviates the notice requirement, we ultimately reach the same result: Tesoriero's failure to prove that Carnival had notice cannot be cured by her reliance on res ipsa loquitur.

C.

Finally, we consider Tesoriero's argument that Carnival spoliated evidence by disposing of her broken cabin chair. She maintains here, as she did below, that Carnival should be sanctioned with an adverse inference that the cruise line had notice of the defect—an inference that would defeat its motion for summary judgment.

The district court declined to impose Tesoriero's requested sanction because, in its view, Carnival did not reasonably anticipate litigation, and therefore did not have a duty to preserve the chair. This was incorrect, and the district court's reasoning is undermined by Carnival's own admission. During discovery, in its response to a request for admissions under Federal Rule of Civil Procedure 36, Carnival admitted that it anticipated litigation "immediately after the incident was reported." "A matter admitted under this rule is conclusively established unless the court, on motion, permits the admission to be withdrawn or amended." Fed. R. Civ. P. 36(b). Because the record does not indicate that Carnival's admission was withdrawn or amended, we must conclude that the district court erred in holding that Carnival did not anticipate litigation.

But anticipation of litigation is not the standard for spoliation sanctions—bad faith is. So even though the district court **{-1184-}** incorrectly concluded that Carnival **[—21—]** did not anticipate litigation, the court's decision not to impose sanctions for spoliation would still be appropriate absent evidence that Carnival acted in bad faith. And even if bad faith were shown, the court's decision not to impose sanctions would be appropriate if "the practical importance of the evidence" was minimal. *Flury*, 427 F.3d at 945; *cf. Green Leaf Nursery v. E.I. DuPont De Nemours & Co.*, 341 F.3d 1292, 1308 (11th Cir. 2003) (no spoliation claim under Florida law without a "significant impairment in the ability to prove the lawsuit"); *Walter v. Carnival Corp.*, No. 09-20962-CIV, 2010 WL 2927962, at *2 (S.D. Fla. July 23, 2010) (evidence must be "crucial to the movant being able to prove its prima facie case or defense" to establish spoliation). We "may affirm for any reason supported by the record, even if not relied upon by the district court." *Lage*, 839 F.3d at 1009.

Spoliation is "defined as the destruction of evidence or the significant and meaningful alteration of a document or instrument." *Green Leaf Nursery*, 341 F.3d at 1308 (11th Cir. 2003) (quotation marks and citation omitted). In some circumstances, a party's "spoliation of critical evidence may warrant the imposition of sanctions." *Flury*, 427 F.3d at 945. Because spoliation is an evidentiary matter, "federal law governs the imposition of spoliation sanctions." *Id.* at 944. Sanctions for spoliation may include "(1) dismissal of the case; (2) exclusion of expert testimony; or (3) a jury instruction on spoliation of evidence which raises a presumption against the spoliator." *Id.* at 945.

When deciding whether to impose sanctions, a number of factors are relevant: "(1) whether the party seeking sanctions was prejudiced as a result of the **[—22—]** destruction of evidence and whether any prejudice could be cured, (2) the practical importance of the evidence, (3) whether the spoliating party acted in bad faith, and (4) the potential for abuse if sanctions are not imposed." *ML Healthcare Servs., LLC v. Publix Super Mkts., Inc.*, 881 F.3d 1293, 1307 (11th Cir. 2018) (citing *Flury*, 427 F.3d at 945).

Spoliation sanctions—and in particular adverse inferences—cannot be imposed for negligently losing or destroying evidence. Indeed, "an adverse inference is drawn from a party's failure to preserve evidence only when the absence of that evidence is predicated on bad faith." *Bashir v. Amtrak*, 119 F.3d 929, 931 (11th Cir. 1997). And bad faith "in the context of spoliation, generally means destruction for the purpose of hiding adverse evidence." *Guzman v. Jones*, 804 F.3d 707, 713 (5th Cir. 2015). This consideration is key in evaluating bad faith because the party's reason for destroying evidence is what justifies sanctions (or a lack thereof). "Mere negligence is not enough, for it does not sustain an inference of consciousness of a weak case." *Vick v. Tex. Emp't Comm'n*, 514 F.2d 734, 737 (5th Cir. 1975) (citation omitted).[6]

Some of our earlier cases illustrate the difference between bad faith and mere negligence. In *Bashir v. Amtrak*, we held on summary judgment that the unexplained absence of a train's speed record tape did not

[6] In *Bonner v. City of Prichard*, 661 F.2d 1206 (11th Cir. 1981) (en banc), this Court adopted as binding precedent all of the decisions of the former Fifth Circuit handed down prior to the close of business on September 30, 1981.

warrant an adverse inference that the train was traveling at an excessive speed when it struck and killed a pedestrian. 119 F.3d at 931. We would "not infer that the missing speed tape **[—23—]** contained evidence unfavorable to appellees unless the circumstances surrounding the tape's absence indicate bad faith, e.g., that appellees tampered with the evidence." *Id.* Because **{-1185-}** plaintiffs produced no evidence that the train company purposefully lost or destroyed the tape, we concluded that there was no showing of bad faith. And finding no bad faith, we declined to impose spoliation sanctions against the train company, which had already produced significant evidence that the train was not exceeding the statutory speed limit. *Id.* at 931–32.

In contrast, bad faith was evident, and spoliation sanctions were appropriate, in *Flury v. Daimler Chrysler Corp.* 427 F.3d at 944–47. There, the plaintiff sued a vehicle manufacturer alleging that he was injured when his car's airbags did not inflate during a crash. *Id.* at 940. Shortly after the lawsuit was filed, the defendant sent a letter requesting the location of the vehicle so that it could conduct an inspection. *Id.* at 941–42. The plaintiff did not respond to the letter. Although he was "fully aware that defendant wished to examine the vehicle," he "ignored defendant's request and allowed the vehicle to be sold for salvage without notification to defendant of its planned removal." *Id.* at 945. It is no surprise that we found bad faith on those facts.

But the facts here are different, and Tesoriero has not established that Carnival's failure to preserve the chair rose to the level of bad faith. Nothing in this record indicates that Carnival disposed of the broken chair in a manner inconsistent with its policies or that the policies themselves somehow establish bad faith.[7] And **[—24—]** unlike the plaintiff in *Flury*, Carnival cannot be said to have been "fully aware" of Tesoriero's desire to further inspect the chair. *See Flury*, 427 F.3d at 945; *see also Calixto v. Watson Bowman Acme Corp.*, No. 07-60077-CIV, 2009 WL 3823390, at *16 (S.D. Fla. Nov. 16, 2009) (concluding that bad faith can be established by circumstantial evidence only when the "act causing the loss cannot be credibly explained as not involving bad faith by the reason proffered by the spoliator").

The record shows that the cabin steward came to Tesoriero's cabin soon after the accident to remove and replace the broken chair. The steward was not there to investigate the accident, but simply to replace the chair. Of course, as the housekeeping manager aboard the Carnival *Splendor* explained, if Tesoriero had requested that the chair be saved, the steward would have done so. He also would have done so if the security department had requested retention. But without a request from Tesoriero or the security department, the chair was taken to maintenance for repair. When the maintenance department could not repair it, the chair was disposed of.

Even if the disposal of the chair were somehow improper, we do not see how it would give rise to anything more than an act of mere negligence. The security department at Carnival is responsible for investigating accidents and preserving evidence. Again, Tesoriero offers no evidence that she ever requested that the chair be preserved. Nor was the security department informed by the medical staff that a **[—25—]** passenger was injured seriously enough to require an investigation. Under Carnival's policy, injuries that only require first aid are classified as "nonreportable" and do not require an accident report and an investigation by the security department. By **{-1186-}** all accounts, on the ship, the injury

[7] It is unclear to us how—as the dissent suggests—three district court cases that declined to offer any relief based on spoliation or discarding evidence in accordance with Carnival's policies **[—24—]** should persuade us that sanctions are appropriate here. Dissenting Op. at 11–12. The point only sharpens when we consider that two out of the three cases involved collapsing chairs. *See Walter v. Carnival Corp.*, No. 09-20962-CIV, 2010 WL 2927962 (S.D. Fla. July 23, 2010); *Hickman v. Carnival Corp.*, No. 04-20044-CIV, 2005 WL 3675961 (S.D. Fla. July 11, 2005).

to Tesoriero's arm appeared minor.[8] Her arm was not broken and was only treated with basic first aid—ice, a sling, and Tylenol.[9]

In short, nothing in the record smacks of bad faith. Under these facts, Carnival's explanation reasonably suggests that the chair was not destroyed to hide adverse evidence. At most, Tesoriero has provided evidence that Carnival's shipboard medical staff were negligent in not anticipating that her injury could be more serious than it appeared. Mere negligence in losing or destroying evidence is not enough to warrant sanctions. *Bashir*, 119 F.3d at 931. And the right hand not talking to the left is not the same thing as the right hand telling the left to destroy evidence. Accordingly, we conclude that the district court properly declined to draw an adverse inference from Carnival's failure to retain the chair. **[—26—]**

To be sure, we would have little trouble affirming sanctions against Carnival if the factual circumstances were slightly different. For example, if Tesoriero's arm had been visibly fractured, it would be hard for Carnival to convince us that the decision not to report the injury to security was reasonable, or in keeping with its ordinary policy. Similarly, if there were any evidence that Tesoriero requested that the chair be preserved, we would be highly skeptical of a subsequent claim that the chair was disposed of pursuant to a routine policy. In both of those circumstances, the inference that the chair was destroyed to hide adverse evidence would be much stronger than it is here.

We will briefly add that even if there were evidence to somehow support a finding of bad faith, that would not justify the leap that the dissenting opinion takes. To begin, no party has cited a persuasive case to support a presumption of notice as a spoliation sanction, and the one identified by the dissent falls short.[10] But even **{-1187-}** more critically, we disagree with the dissent's view that "the practical importance of the evidence" supports sanctions in this case. *Flury*, 427 F.3d at 945; *ML Healthcare Servs., LLC*, 881 F.3d at 1307. Here, even if the chair had been **[—27—]** preserved, it is not clear what evidence of Carnival's notice could be deduced from the already-broken piece of furniture. Joseph Tesoriero testified that there was no outwardly visible defect, Tesoriero herself noticed no problem when she moved the chair back from the vanity, and the photographic evidence confirms that the peg-and-hole

[8] The dissent's quote from Tesoriero's independent medical examination that her initial x-ray "was read as a hairline fracture" (by whom, he does not say, and we do not know) does not change this fact. Dissenting Op. at 10. Tesoriero does not argue, even once, that her arm was broken. According to her own testimony, she was told it was not broken on the ship, she was told it was not broken on land, and her arm was, in fact, not broken. She was diagnosed with medial epicondylitis and ulnar neurapraxia—a condition that she describes as "tennis elbow"—and Tesoriero does not dispute this conclusion. At this point, of course, we have no doubt that her injury turned out to be serious.

[9] The dissent suggests that this treatment, because it was provided by a physician instead of a layperson, is not really first aid. Dissenting Op. at 8–9. In the context of Carnival's policy, however, first aid refers to the type of care provided, not on who is providing the treatment. We have no hesitation concluding that ice, a sling, and Tylenol together are nothing more than simple first aid in the context of this policy. The fact that an x-ray was taken, as a diagnostic step, to confirm the absence of a fracture does not move the needle.

[10] We note a few things about the exemplar magistrate judge order cited by the dissent as an example of spoliation leading to an inference-of-notice sanction. First, the sanction imposed was the "least-severe sanction available," and was a "rebuttable, permissible adverse inference that the destroyed evidence would have demonstrated the existence of a dangerous condition" that the defendant knew or should have known about. *In re the Complaint of Boston Boat III, LLC*, 310 F.R.D. 510, 523 (S.D. Fla. 2015) (parenthetical mark omitted). And that light-touch sanction was imposed in a case that involved dramatic evidence of bad faith: for starters, the defendant destroyed critical evidence well after litigation began. Not only that, but the defendant's attorney personally observed and failed to stop ongoing destruction, the plaintiff's attorney was not timely notified of the destruction, and the defendant presented inconsistent explanations for why the evidence was destroyed. *Id.* at 517–23. The differences between those facts and the ones in this case speak for themselves. Indeed, nothing in this case would preclude the sanction applied in that one.

assembly—as well as the state of the glue holding it together—would have been obscured before the accident. In light of the evidence, and given Tesoriero's failure to avail herself of Carnival's offer to inspect an identical unbroken cabin chair from the *Splendor*, we are unpersuaded that her ability to inspect the broken chair would have been so important to the notice issue as to warrant sanctions. We also note our disagreement with our dissenting colleague's apparent view that because evidence of notice would be necessary for Tesoriero to show a prima facie case of negligence, it must mean that the chair would have provided the evidence. Dissenting Op. at 18–19. Respectfully, we fail to see why one leads to the other; while notice has not been shown here, it is not because the chair is missing.

IV.

In conclusion, Tesoriero did not establish that Carnival had actual or constructive notice that the chair was dangerous. This is fatal to her case. Her failure to establish the duty element of her negligence claim cannot be cured by her invocation of the res ipsa loquitur doctrine. And because she has not shown that Carnival committed sanctionable spoliation of evidence, her case is not saved through an adverse inference sanction. Accordingly, although we disagree with the reasoning of the district court in some respects, we reach the same result.

AFFIRMED.

(Reporter's Note: Dissenting Opinion follows on p. 475).

[—28—] {-1187-} **ROSENBAUM,** Circuit Judge, dissenting:

When Irina Tesoriero boarded the Carnival *Splendor* to enjoy some special family time, she never expected the costs of her trip to include two surgeries and numerous doctor and physical-therapy appointments totaling more than $120,000 in medical bills. Nor did Tesoriero realize that her cruise would cost her much of the use of her dominant right arm and hand. But that's the price that Tesoriero has paid because a chair on the *Splendor* collapsed as she tried to sit on it.

This case is about who should pay for Tesoriero's damages. Under the law, of course, if Carnival was not negligent, it is entitled to a judgment in its favor, and Tesoriero must shoulder the burden. On the other hand, if Carnival was negligent, then it has a legal obligation to pay for Tesoriero's reasonable damages.

But we will never know whether Carnival was negligent because Carnival destroyed the chair that caused Tesoriero's injuries. So conveniently for Carnival, there is no evidence that Carnival had notice of the chair's dangerous condition. The panel opinion excuses Carnival's destruction of evidence by just accepting Carnival's word that it did not destroy the chair in bad faith. And the panel opinion does so even though Carnival has previously destroyed evidence in other cases and has been warned by a federal court that its destruction of evidence could result in sanctions, Carnival's so-called evidence-preservation procedures are designed to **{-1188-}** ensure that evidence will be destroyed in at least some cases and in fact have repeatedly resulted in the destruction of relevant evidence, and Carnival has failed **[—29—]** to follow its own evidence-preservation procedures in several cases, including this one.

To make matters worse—and in stark contrast to how Carnival allowed the chair here to be destroyed—Carnival calculatedly preserved evidence favorable to it from the moment Tesoriero reported her fall onboard the *Splendor*.

For these reasons and others I explain below, I respectfully disagree with the panel opinion. The record here raises a genuine issue of material fact concerning whether Carnival destroyed the chair in bad faith.

And if a jury were to conclude that Carnival had, in fact, disposed of the chair in bad faith, Tesoriero would be entitled to an inference that the chair was evidence favorable to her and detrimental to Carnival. In particular, that inference could establish that Carnival had notice of—that is, it knew or should have known about—the unsafe condition of the chair.

After all, Carnival testified that it repairs broken chairs when possible. ECF No. 39-1 at 19-20.[1] So an examination of the chair at issue here might have revealed a faulty repair, or it could have shown that the type of defect that occurred here has happened before on the very same chair. It also might have suggested that if, in fact, as Carnival testified, its employees conducted proper daily inspection of the furniture, Carnival should have known about the chair's defect through that program. **[—30—]** ECF No. 39-1 at 47-48. Any of these outcomes would have provided evidence that Carnival had notice of the chair's dangerous condition. And if Tesoriero could have shown an issue of fact concerning notice, her claim would have survived summary judgment. In short, this record raises a genuine issue of material fact concerning whether Carnival destroyed the chair in bad faith, and that, in turn, necessarily means that it raises a genuine issue of material fact as to whether Carnival had notice of the defect in the chair that injured Tesoriero.

---

[1] For reasons of transparency, I include pincite references to the evidence of record. That way, anyone who wishes to follow along from their armchair may evaluate firsthand the evidence I summarize. References are to the district-court ECF number and the CM/ECF-imprinted page number, except where evidence consists of deposition transcripts. In those cases, references are to the page numbers of the deposition transcript, since four deposition transcript pages appear on each CM/ECF-numbered page.

For that reason, Tesoriero is entitled to have a jury decide whether it believes Carnival's version of the story. So I would vacate the grant of summary judgment and remand for a trial. Because the panel opinion erroneously allows a judge (without so much as an evidentiary hearing), instead of a jury, to weigh credibility on the paper record and resolve this genuine issue of material fact—whether Carnival destroyed the defective chair in bad faith—I respectfully dissent.

I.

The panel opinion correctly sets forth the legal principles concerning spoliation. But it's worth emphasizing that the summary-judgment standard applies equally to spoliation-related facts and other facts material to the resolution of the legal issues before the district court. After all, "'bad faith' is a question of fact like any other." *Bracey v. Grondin*, 712 F.3d 1012, 1019 (7th Cir. 2013) (citation and internal quotation marks omitted).

So we must view the spoliation-related evidence and any reasonable inferences from it in the light most favorable to Tesoriero, **{–1189–}** since she is the non-moving party. *See Al-Rayes v. Willingham*, 914 F.3d 1302, 1306 (11th Cir. 2019). **[—31—]** That means that if a genuine dispute of material fact exists over bad faith, and a finding of bad faith would support an adverse inference against Carnival about a fact material to the resolution of the merits here, summary judgment must be denied. As I explain below, that's exactly the situation here.

My disagreement, then, lies with the panel opinion's statement of the facts and its application of spoliation law to those facts. Once we consider all the evidence—something the panel opinion did not do—we must conclude that the evidence raises a material issue of fact about whether Carnival destroyed the chair in bad faith. Specifically, a reasonable jury could find that Carnival devised and retained policies and procedures designed to result in the destruction of material evidence in at least some cases, or it created conditions that made compliance with its evidence-preservation policies and procedures unlikely, or both.

If a jury reached any of these conclusions, it reasonably could find that Carnival destroyed the chair here in bad faith. And if a jury made that finding, Tesoriero would be entitled to an adverse inference that Carnival destroyed the chair because an examination of it could have provided evidence that Carnival knew or should have known of the chair's defective condition—a crucial part of Tesoriero's *prima facie* case of negligence against Carnival.

A.

I begin with a little background against which we must view Carnival's policies and procedures covering the preservation of material evidence involved in an onboard injury. As the panel opinion notes, Carnival conceded in its responses to Tesoriero's requests for admissions that "immediately after the incident was **[—32—]** reported [by Tesoriero while onboard the *Splendor*, Carnival] anticipated litigation arising from the accident." ECF No. 65 at 25, 29. Indeed, as Monica Petisco, Carnival's corporate litigation representative, admitted, "anytime anything happens onboard, [Carnival] anticipate[s] litigation." ECF No. 39-2 at 24.

That is certainly clear from the Passenger Injury Statement form that Carnival requires its guests to fill out in their own handwriting as soon as they seek medical attention onboard. *See* ECF No. 44-8. That Carnival demands the injured passenger prepare the form in her own handwriting conveniently renders the form an admission by the passenger for future-litigation evidentiary purposes. *See United States v. Williams*, 837 F.2d 1009, 1014 (11th Cir. 1988). The form also seeks to seal the passenger into the details surrounding the injury, likely before all details are known.

For example, in addition to questions about where and when an injury occurred and how "in detail" it happened, the form asks the passenger to state what she "believe[s] caused this accident" and "what [she] could have done to avoid the accident." *Id.* Then the form requires the guest to identify all witnesses to the accident, whether the guest uses glasses or contact lenses and whether the guest was wearing them at the time of the accident, and "[w]hat kind of shoes" the guest was wearing when the accident happened. *Id.*

Put simply, the Passenger Injury Form appears designed to preserve for Carnival's benefit, from the instant an injury occurs, all evidence from the passenger that might assist Carnival in future litigation. Indeed, the specific information the questions seek suggests that Carnival has learned much from its past litigation about the evidence most helpful to it in litigation. **[—33—]**

Of course, there is nothing inherently wrong with that. But those steps differ strikingly from Carnival's policies and actual **{-1190-}** practices concerning preservation of material tangible evidence that might hurt Carnival and help a passenger in future litigation. And a reasonable jury might find that fact bears on whether Carnival, in good faith, has developed and executes its policies and procedures to preserve material tangible evidence.

B.

With this in mind, I review Carnival's applicable policies and procedures. According to Carnival's corporate representatives, Carnival's security department is ultimately responsible for maintaining material tangible evidence. ECF No. 39-2 at 48; ECF No. 39-1 at 42. Yet Carnival's security department does not even become involved in deciding whether to preserve such evidence unless an accident report is filed. ECF No. 39-2 at 48. According to Petisco, Carnival's litigation representative, an accident report can be filed in two circumstances. First, a guest can "request that [Carnival] create an accident report." *Id.* And, second, Carnival "entrusts . . . the [ship's] doctor to make the determination between reportable or non-reportable [accidents]," based on whether an injury requires "[a]nything beyond first aid." *Id.* at 48-49.

The panel opinion simply assumes without any analysis that these policies are reasonable. But on their face, these policies increase in three ways the likelihood that material evidence will be discarded. Indeed, as Carnival well knows, history has proven that true. Carnival's policies have previously resulted in the destruction **[—34—]** of material evidence. And, in fact, at least one district court has warned Carnival that a pattern of discarding material evidence could support spoliation sanctions.

1.

I begin by identifying the three ways Carnival's policies meaningfully increase the odds that Carnival will destroy material evidence. First, Carnival's housekeeping process has no mechanism requiring housekeeping employees to check with the security department before discarding broken furniture from a guest's room. Rather, when furniture in a guest's room breaks, Carnival's policy requires housekeeping staff to immediately remove and replace the object in question—even if, as happened here, housekeeping removes the item while the injured passenger remains in the room and waits for help. ECF No. 39-1 at 41-42.

Once the broken piece is removed, it is taken to be repaired. *Id.* at 42. If the furniture cannot be fixed, it is "usually disposed" of. *Id.* That does not happen if—and only if—Carnival's security department affirmatively intervenes and preserves the piece. *See id.* So unless the security department jumps in to save evidence before the housekeeping department throws it out, evidence is discarded. But of course, the security department does not intercede if an accident report is not filed.

Second, and compounding this problem, Carnival's shipboard processes falsely cause guests to believe that they have made an accident report when they seek medical attention from the ship's doctor. As I have noted, when a guest visits the ship's doctor to address an injury, she must fill out a Carnival document called "Passenger Injury Statement." Besides the other questions the thorough form lists, it asks, "Date [accident] reported," "Name of staff member accident reported to," **[—35—]** "Time reported," and "If not reported immediately, please explain why?" ECF No. 44-8. These questions suggest that a passenger can officially report an accident to any "staff member" and that the passenger has officially reported her injury to Carnival when she fills out the Passenger Injury Statement. So a passenger has no reason to ask whether she must do anything **{–1191–}** further to make an official report to Carnival to trigger the security department's preservation of material evidence. Some might say this form lulls passengers into a false sense of security that they have fully reported the incident.

Third, Carnival's policy leaving it to the discretion of the ship's doctor to decide whether an accident report should be filed (and the evidence thus preserved), ensures that accident reports will not be filed in at least some cases where evidence should be maintained. Carnival's policy calls for the ship's doctor to prepare an accident report only when the doctor must provide more than first aid. But Carnival does not define what it means by "first aid." Rather, that is up for interpretation by each individual doctor.[2] **[—36—]**

And even if we disregard this shortcoming and assume all doctors abide in precisely the same way by some (unidentified) universally applicable definition of "first aid," the policy wrongly equates a doctor's assessment that an injury requires no more than first aid with the determination that an injury is not serious and the piece of furniture causing it should not be preserved. In fact, as is common knowledge, some injuries, at first glance, may appear minor but later manifest themselves as severe.

Carnival has also not explained why a policy that depends on the provision of "first aid" satisfies its duty to preserve evidence in anticipation of litigation. And the relationship between the two is not obvious to me.

Nor is it obvious to Carnival, since Carnival anticipates litigation "anytime anything happens onboard" and preserves evidence favorable to it in *every* instance, regardless of whether the doctor provides only "first aid." To rubberstamp a policy that allows Carnival to treat plaintiff-favorable evidence in its control differently invites gamesmanship. Indeed, the policy knowingly results in destruction of evidence even though, by requiring the injured guest to fill out the Injury Statement Form to receive medical attention, Carnival simultaneously preserves evidence favorable to itself, in anticipation of litigation, when a doctor does not file an accident report.

2.

This case demonstrates some of these pitfalls.

First, this case appears to have involved more than first aid, but according to Carnival, the doctor did not file an accident report. Here, the doctor took X-rays of **[—37—]** Tesoriero's arm. X-ray equipment is not in any standard first-aid kit I've ever seen. Plus here, the doctor sent the X-rays off the ship to Miami to be read—a process that would not be completed until after Tesoriero left the ship. Seeking consultation **{–1192–}** from a specialist physician, like taking X-rays in the first place, seems like more than "first aid."

[2] Standard references do not uniformly define the term "first aid." For example, a medical dictionary defines "first aid" as "[i]mmediate assistance administered in the case of injury or sudden illness by a bystander or other layperson, before the arrival of trained medical personnel." *First Aid*, Stedman's Medical Dictionary (28th ed. 2006). A non-medical dictionary defines "first aid" as "emergency and sometimes makeshift treatment given to someone (as a victim of an accident) requiring immediate attention where regular medical or surgical care is not available." *First Aid*, Webster's Third New International Dictionary, Unabridged (2020), https://unabridged.merriam-webster.com/ (last visited Mar. 25, 2020). Setting aside the fact that a doctor technically does not render "first aid" under either definition, these definitions do not set forth medical standards that identify what treatments, procedures, or remedies are necessarily "first aid" and what are not. As a result, Carnival's policy does not clearly delineate when a doctor should prepare an accident form.

(But then again, we can't look to Carnival's policy for guidance on that). If the Miami doctor had found a break in Tesoriero's arm, neither Tesoriero nor the ship's doctor would have known until after the cruise ended. In fact, it is not clear the ship's doctor ever would have learned of the break. But because Carnival left filing an accident report to the doctor's discretion and, according to Carnival, the doctor did not do that (more on this later, *see infra* at 14-15), the chair was discarded—before the ship's doctor even had confirmation about whether Tesoriero's arm was broken.

As it turned out, according to Tesoriero's medical records, Tesoriero's X-ray "was read as a hairline fracture."[3] ECF No. 44-11 at 10. And her follow-up medical **[—38—]** care showed that she had "a focus of T2 hyperintensity at the insertion of the common extensor tendon on the lateral humeral epicondyle consistent with a partial tear." *Id.* As a result, Tesoriero was "unable to drive without pain and unable to carry anything."[4] *Id.* By any definition, that is certainly an injury requiring more than first aid.

Second, even if we assume Tesoriero's injury required only mere "first aid" while she was onboard the *Splendor*, there can be no question that Tesoriero, in fact, suffered a serious injury. I have already recounted the lasting pain the injury has caused Tesoriero. And because of her injury onboard the *Splendor*, Tesoriero had to undergo two surgeries, physical therapy, and other medical treatment after her cruise ended—resulting in medical expenses of more than $120,000. ECF No. 44-11 at 14. If the doctor's failure to file an accident report here was consistent with Carnival policy, a reasonable jury could conclude that Carnival's policy is unreasonable, **{-1193-}** or even that it was created in bad faith. After all, under the panel opinion's analysis, Carnival's policy that ensures destruction of evidence in these **[—39—]** circumstances is precisely what shields it from potential liability and any consequences of destroying the evidence.

Tellingly, this is not the first case where Carnival has destroyed material evidence, supposedly in accordance with its policies. For example, in *Morhardt v. Carnival Corp.*, Morhardt used a ship hair dryer, which electrocuted him and burned and blackened his hand. 304 F. Supp. 3d 1290, 1292-93 (S.D. Fla. 2017). He immediately went to the ship's infirmary for treatment. *Id.* at 1293. Yet

[3] The panel opinion takes issue with this statement because it says that "Tesoriero does not argue . . . that her arm was broken." *See* Maj. Op. at 25 n.8. True, she doesn't. But that misses the point. The point is that the X-ray taken by the ship's doctor was read by a medical professional as showing a serious enough injury to require more than simple first aid. As for the derivation of that statement, it comes from Tesoriero's independent medical examination report, which a Board-certified orthopedic surgeon conducted. More specifically, it appears in his review of Tesoriero's medical records from July 1, 2015, four days after the incident. The surgeon reported that a medical professional who examined Tesoriero on July 1 stated in Tesoriero's visit notes that Tesoriero "had an [X]-ray on the cruise that was read as a hairline fracture." ECF No. 44-11 at 10. Presumably, that refers to the Miami specialist's reading of the X-ray the ship's doctor took, because the ship's medical center advised Tesoriero that the ship's doctor (who told Tesoriero he didn't think her arm was broken but he couldn't confirm) "didn't have full expertise to read an X-ray, and it would be shipped to Miami, and they would give [Tesoriero] an answer," which would happen after she left the cruise ship. ECF No. 39-3 at 74. The medical facility Tesoriero visited on July 1 then took a new X-ray that "revealed no acute fracture." ECF No. 44-11 at 10. That a new X-ray taken four days after the incident did not show an "acute fracture" does not mean that **[—38—]** an X-ray taken four days earlier did not show a "hairline fracture." By their nature, "hairline" fractures can be difficult to see, and the intervening time between the initial X-ray and the later one could have made any "hairline" fracture that may have existed at one time even harder to see, to the extent that it continued to exist.

[4] Tesoriero also testified,

> I can't carry the garbage. I can't carry the laundry. I can't empty or pick up heavy pots. Cooking is very restrictive in terms of getting things in and out of an oven. Carrying groceries, doing grocery shopping, opening a bottle of water, twisting actions. I can't peel potatoes. I can't peel carrots. I can't flip pancakes. I can't put any pressure on—like when you peel an apple.

ECF No. 39-3 at 52.

Carnival threw out the hair dryer involved in the incident. *Id.* at 1297.

The district court in *Morhardt* described Carnival's actions as being "a matter of keen concern." *Id.* And the court noted that it was "aware of other cases in which a plaintiff passenger was injured aboard a Carnival cruise ship and the object that purportedly caused the injury was immediately discarded." *Id.* at 1297 n.6 (citing *Walter v. Carnival Corp.*, No. 09-20962-CIV, 2010 WL 2927962 (S.D. Fla. July 23, 2010)).[5] Significantly, the court "caution[ed] Carnival against establishing a pattern or practice of discarding such objects because such actions could potentially provide a basis for spoliation sanctions or liability in the future." *Id.*

The panel opinion finds it "unclear how . . . three district court cases that decline to offer any relief based on spoliation or discarding evidence should persuade [the panel opinion] that sanctions are appropriate here." Maj. Op. at 23-24 n.7. And somehow, it thinks the fact that "2 of the 3 cases involved collapsing chairs" **[—40—]** strengthens its view that sanctions are not appropriate here. *Id.* In my view, the opposite is true.

At some point, adherence to policies Carnival knows from past litigation result in the destruction of material evidence—especially when Carnival anticipates litigation and simultaneously employs policies designed to preserve evidence favorable to it—constitutes bad faith. This is particularly the case here because a federal court has already expressly warned Carnival that its continuing failure to maintain material evidence may result in spoliation sanctions. Surely, the mere fact of the existence of Carnival's policies (that it knows result in destruction of material evidence)—even if Carnival complied with them—cannot indefinitely shield Carnival from liability and consequences of any type.

Indeed, we suggested as much when we held that one of the factors relevant to whether spoliation sanctions should be imposed is "the potential for abuse if sanctions are not imposed." *ML Healthcare Servs., LLC v. Publix Super Mkts., Inc.*, 881 F.3d 1293, 1307 (11th Cir. 2018) (citing *Flury v. Daimler Chrysler Corp.*, 427 F.3d 939, 945 (11th Cir. 2005)). Yet to excuse Carnival's destruction of evidence, the panel opinion allows Carnival to continue to hide behind the very policies Carnival knows result in destruction of evidence. A jury should be allowed to determine whether Carnival has reached the point where its policies that have previously proven to result in destruction of evidence can no longer shield it from liability.

C. [—41—]

Even if a jury rejected the notion that Carnival's failure to modify its policies to prevent material evidence from being destroyed **{–1194–}** demonstrates bad faith, a reasonable jury could still conclude that Carnival failed to ensure compliance with its preservation policies here. And a jury that made that finding could conclude that Carnival's failure to abide by its own policies shows bad faith in and of itself.

To begin with, Tesoriero reported her incident with the chair literally at least five different ways to Carnival while she was still onboard her cruise.[6] And after she told Dr.

[5] *See also Hickman v. Carnival Corp.*, No. 04-20044-CIV, 2005 WL 3675961 (S.D. Fla. July 11, 2005) (Carnival "almost immediately" repaired bar stool involved in incident, instead of preserving it).

[6] First, Tesoriero's husband Joseph called Guest Services, reported the incident, and asked for immediate medical attention. ECF No. 39-3 at 65-66; ECF No. 44-3 at ¶ 5; ECF No. 39-6 at 3. Second, when the cabin steward went to the Tesorieros' room and removed the broken chair, the Tesorieros told him that Tesoriero believed she had broken her arm and that they had called for help, and they asked him whether a doctor would be coming to the room. ECF No. 39-3 at 67. Third, when no doctor arrived at the Tesorieros' room after half an hour, the Tesorieros went to the infirmary to seek medical attention. *Id.* at 72-73. It was closed, but they found a nurse and told her about Tesoriero's injury. *Id.* at 73. She got Dr. Potkonjak, and the Tesorieros told him about the injury. *Id.*; ECF No. 44-3 at ¶ 6. Fourth, Dr. Potkonjak gave the Tesorieros a Passenger Injury Statement to fill out, which reported the incident yet again. ECF No. 39-3 at 68; *see also* ECF No. 44-8. And finally, while still onboard the cruise, Tesoriero also reported her

Milos Potkonjak, the ship's doctor, he advised her that a health-and-safety official on the ship would speak with her about her injury. ECF No. 39-3 at 100-01. Even Carnival conceded in its answers to Tesoriero's requests for admissions that "the accident in this case was reported to the Defendant cruise line on the cruise on which the incident occurred." ECF No. 65 at 25, 29. Yet the chair was not preserved. **[—42—]**

Despite all these reports to Carnival employees in various cruise line positions, Carnival made no effort to preserve the chair involved in the injury. And though the ship's doctor advised Tesoriero that a health-and-safety official would speak with her concerning her injury, no one ever did.

This reference to a health-and-safety official appears to be a reference to Carnival's security department. If so, that means the doctor apparently thought he was making a report to the security department, even though Carnival has no record of any such report. But once again conveniently for Carnival but inconveniently for Tesoriero, sixteen days after Tesoriero's injury occurred, Carnival did not renew Dr. Potkonjak's contract and provided "his last known address" as, in its entirety, "Biograd, Croatia."[7] ECF No. 39-6 at 3. As a result, checking with Dr. Potkonjak would appear to be difficult, if not impossible.

If a reasonable jury concluded that the destruction of the chair was a consequence of Carnival's failure to follow its own policies, it could also reasonably find that Carnival's shortcomings resulted from its bad faith. First, the mere fact that Tesoriero made five different reports of the incident and the chair was still destroyed—even though Carnival anticipated litigation—could reasonably be construed as evidence that Carnival acted in bad faith when it failed to follow its policies here. **[—43—] {-1195-}**

Second, that Dr. Potkonjak apparently believed he reported the incident to the security department but no record of that was ever made and that he is now unavailable for questioning similarly could be viewed as suggesting that Carnival acted in bad faith when it threw away the chair.

And finally, this is not the first case where Carnival's failure to follow its own preservation policies has resulted in the destruction of evidence. In *Walter*, Carnival discarded a deck chair that collapsed under the passenger there. 2010 WL 2927962, at *1. The chair in that case was lost, even though Carnival employees prepared an accident report. *Id.* at *2. And just over a year ago, Carnival lost CCTV footage of a guest's fall, even though Carnival conceded it had a duty to preserve that evidence. *Sosa v. Carnival Corp.*, No. 18-20957-CIV, 2018 WL 6335178, *1 (S.D. Fla. Dec. 4, 2018). The magistrate judge considering a motion for sanctions against Carnival in that case described Carnival's position as (1) "'[c]'est la vie' ('that's life,' or 'that's how things happen') and (2) 'stuff happens.'"[8] *Id.*

No wonder Carnival has that attitude. Carnival keeps discarding material evidence, and that keeps working to its advantage. So why would it ever do anything to remedy its compliance with its own policies?

A reasonable jury viewing these facts could conclude that Carnival's failure to strictly

---

injury to the front-desk supervisor on the ship, seeking a document stating that she would get her X-rays back. ECF No. 39-3 at 100. Carnival's responses to Tesoriero's interrogatories also indicate that Tesoriero "interacted with . . . I Care personnel" about her injury, ECF No. 39-6 at 3, but it is not clear whether the "I Care personnel" she spoke with included any of the Carnival employees previously identified.

[7] Tesoriero testified that Dr. Potkonjak informed her when she went to the medical center that "it was his first day on the ship." ECF No. 39-3 at 73-74. If that also meant that the date of Tesoriero's injury was Dr. Potkonjak's first date of employment with Carnival, then Carnival employed Dr. Potkonjak for a total of seventeen days.

[8] *See also Wilford v. Carnival Corp.*, No. 17-21992-CIV, 2019 WL 2269155 (S.D. Fla. May 28, 2019) (Carnival could not locate and produce X-rays its medical personnel took in an onboard medical clinic after the plaintiff slipped and fell onboard).

adhere to its stated policies betrayed bad faith on Carnival's part.

And if a jury reached that conclusion, Tesoriero would be entitled to an inference that Carnival destroyed the chair because it would have provided evidence **[—44—]** that Carnival knew or should have known of the chair's unsafe condition. Though many courts have observed that "courts must not hold the prejudiced party to too strict a standard of proof regarding the likely contents of the destroyed evidence because doing so allows the spoliators to profit from the destruction of the evidence," *In the Matter of: the Complaint of Boston Boat III, LLC*, 310 F.R.D. 510, 521 (S.D. Fla. 2015) (citations and internal quotation marks omitted) (collecting cases); *see also Kronisch v. United States*, 150 F.3d 112, 128 (2d Cir. 1998), here, it is clear that the missing chair could have provided Tesoriero with critical evidence that Carnival knew or should have known that its chair was defective.

As I have explained, an examination of the chair that actually collapsed could have revealed that Carnival had previously fixed that same chair in the same place. Or it could have shown that Carnival had previously repaired another part of the chair, which caused stress on the joint that separated. Or it could have betrayed that its housekeeping staff did not in fact move and check the furniture daily, as Carnival testified it did, because if it did, it should have been aware of the chair's defective condition. Any of these revelations would have shown that Carnival either knew or should have known that the chair was not fit for continued use.

And contrary to the panel opinion's suggestion, *see* Maj. Op. at 26-27, it is obvious that examination of a similar chair would not reveal any of these things that, if they existed, would have occurred in only the chair involved in the incident.

Joseph's amateur photographs do not save the day for Carnival, either. *See id.* at 27. They are a poor substitute for the actual chair, which could have permitted sampling of the glue that allowed the joint **{-1196-}** to separate (as well as examination for **[—45—]** more than one application of glue, as in a repair of the chair joint) and inspection of the rest of the anatomy of the chair to determine whether a repair to a part of the chair that was not photographed could have placed extra stress on the part of the chair that separated.

Similarly, I respectfully disagree with the panel opinion that Joseph's brief looking over of the chair while his wife was writhing in pain and the two were waiting for medical attention qualifies as a thorough examination that would have revealed any of these problems with the defective chair if they existed. *See id.*

As for the panel opinion's contention that an examination would not have revealed that housekeeping staff knew or should have known of the defect because "Tesoriero herself noticed no problem when she moved the chair back from the vanity," *id.*, there is a significant difference between pulling a chair out about a foot from a vanity as a prerequisite to grooming, and cleaning and checking furniture as part of job duties, as the Carnival staff was charged with doing. Plus, even if we assume no difference, Tesoriero's failure to notice a problem with the chair when she pulled it out would not establish that Carnival had not previously repaired that same chair or that the chair had not broken before in the same place.

Notice is the one thing that Tesoriero could not establish on summary judgment without the benefit of an examination of the chair. Because showing notice is an element of her claim for negligence, and because inspecting the chair may well have provided the necessary evidence that Carnival knew or should have known of the chair's defective condition, the chair qualifies as crucial evidence. **[—46—]**

The panel opinion suggests that proof of notice is somehow exempt from the regular rules that govern the imposition of spoliation sanctions. *See id.* at 26. But the only support it offers for this novel notion is its assertion that "no party has cited a persuasive case to support a presumption of notice as a spoliation sanction, and the one identified by the dissent falls short." *Id.*

Most respectfully, the panel opinion is doubly wrong. First, as the panel opinion indicates, sanctions for bad faith are appropriate when "the practical importance of the evidence" is significant. Maj. Op. at 21 (quoting *Flury*, 427 F.3d at 942). It does not make a difference why the evidence is important; all that matters is that the evidence has "practical importance." Obviously, evidence that proves a necessary element of a plaintiff's *prima facie* case is "practical[ly] important" when the plaintiff cannot establish that element without it. *See Palmas & Bambu, S.A. v. E.I. Dupont De Nemours & Co., Inc.*, 881 So. 2d 565, 582 (Fla. Dist. Ct. App. 2004) (noting that "where evidence necessary to prove a *prima facie* case is missing due to actions of a party, an essential element of a claim may be presumed" (citing *Pub. Health Tr. of Dade Cty. v. Valcin*, 507 So. 2d 596, 599 (Fla 1987))).[9] Notice is a necessary element of Tesoriero's *prima facie* case of negligence. And as I have explained, an examination of the defective chair may well have proven that Carnival knew or should have known of the chair's condition. So upon a finding of bad faith, **[—47—]** it would have been appropriate for a court to give a spoliation sanction concerning that necessary evidence.[10] **{-1197-}**

Second, courts have in fact awarded spoliation sanctions when destroyed evidence might have proven notice. In *Boston Boat*, for example, the court imposed a spoliation presumption "that the destroyed evidence would have demonstrated the existence of a dangerous condition ***which Boston Boat knew about, should have known about or created***." 310 F.R.D. at 523 (emphasis added). The panel opinion's attempt to distinguish *Boston Boat* on the dual bases that it imposed only a "rebuttable, permissible adverse inference" and that it "involved dramatic evidence of bad faith" once again misses the point. The point here is that when a court finds that evidence was destroyed in bad faith, spoliation sanctions can appropriately be imposed to establish a presumption of notice where the destroyed evidence itself, had it not been discarded, could have proven notice.

Here, for the reasons I have explained, the defective chair that Carnival destroyed may well have proven that Carnival had notice of the chair's dangerous condition, had Carnival not discarded the piece of furniture. So given an opportunity **[—48—]** to evaluate the witnesses and other evidence at trial, a jury reasonably could have concluded, upon a sanctions-based presumption instruction, that an inspection of the chair would have revealed that Carnival knew or should have known of its dangerous condition. Since that is the case, particularly on a motion for summary judgment, where we must construe the facts in favor of the non-moving party, Tesoriero has established a material issue of fact concerning whether Carnival discarded the chair in bad faith.

Because a material question of fact exists as to the bad-faith issue, the district court should not have granted summary judgment. Rather, the court should have allowed a jury

---

9 We have explained that while federal law governs the imposition of spoliation sanctions, our opinion concerning sanctions can be "informed by [state] law" when, as here, it is consistent with federal spoliation principles. *Flury*, 427 F.3d at 943, 944.

10 The panel opinion asserts that I espouse the position "that because evidence of notice would be necessary for Tesoriero to show a prima facie case of negligence, it must mean that the chair would have provided the evidence." Maj. Op. at 27. Nonsense. No fair reading of my dissent could support the panel opinion's claim. Indeed, as I have explained two other times in this dissent, *see supra* at 29, 44, an examination of the defective chair in this case could have yielded evidence that Carnival knew or should have known of the chair's dangerous condition—that is, evidence of notice. Those explanations amply demonstrate the practical importance of the destroyed chair. *See Kronisch*, 150 F.3d at 128 ("[C]are should be taken not to require too specific a level of proof [because] . . . holding the prejudiced party to too strict a standard of proof regarding the likely contents of the destroyed evidence would subvert the prophylactic and punitive purposes of the adverse inference, and would allow parties who have intentionally destroyed evidence to profit from that destruction." (citation and internal quotation marks omitted)).

to resolve the bad-faith question of fact, along with all the other disputes of relevant fact in the case.[11] *Vodusek v. Bayliner Marine Corp.*, 71 F.3d 148, 157 (4th Cir. 1995) ("We conclude that the district court acted within its discretion in permitting the jury to draw an adverse inference if it found that Vodusek or her agents caused destruction or loss of relevant evidence. Rather than deciding the spoliation issue itself, the district court provided the jury with appropriate guidelines for evaluating the evidence."); *Kronisch*, 150 F.3d at 128 ("We believe that plaintiff has produced enough circumstantial evidence to support the inference that **{–1198–}** the destroyed MKULTRA files may have contained documents supporting (or potentially proving) his claim, and that the possibility that a jury would choose to **[—49—]** draw such an inference, combined with plaintiff's circumstantial evidence, is enough to entitle plaintiff to a jury trial."); *United States v. Laurent*, 607 F.3d 895, 902 (1st Cir. 2010) ("A 'spoliation' instruction, allowing an adverse inference, is commonly appropriate in both civil and criminal cases where there is evidence from which a reasonable jury might conclude that evidence favorable to one side was destroyed by the other." (citing 4 L. Sand et al., *Modern Federal Jury Instructions* § 75.01 (instruction 75-7), at 75-16 to -18 (2010))).

The panel opinion simply concludes that Carnival acted consistently with its policies and that its policies do not "somehow establish bad faith." Maj. Op. at 23. But for the reasons I have explained, the record viewed in the light most favorable to Tesoriero cannot support that conclusion. So vacatur of the district court's entry of summary judgment and remand for trial is warranted here.

II.

Because Tesoriero has shown a material issue of fact with respect to bad faith concerning Carnival's disposal of the chair, summary judgment should not have been granted in this case. I therefore respectfully dissent.

---

[11] At the very least, the district court should have held an evidentiary hearing on the issue instead of resolving the material issue of fact against Tesoriero on the papers. *Cf. McDonald's Corp. v. Robertson*, 147 F.3d 1301, 1311 (11th Cir. 1998) (noting in the context of a motion for preliminary injunction that it is an abuse of discretion to fail to hold an evidentiary hearing where facts central to a party's claims are disputed); *Oldfield v. Pueblo De Bahia Lora, S.A.*, 558 F.3d 1210, 1216 (11th Cir. 2009) ("Because the material facts relating to the personal jurisdiction issues were not in dispute, there was no need for an evidentiary hearing.").

United States Court of Appeals for the Eleventh Circuit

No. 18-10474

CORLEY
vs.
LONG-LEWIS, INC.

Appeal from the United States District Court for the Northern District of Alabama

Decided: July 16, 2020

Citation: 965 F.3d 1222, 8 Adm. R. 485 (11th Cir. 2020).

Before **PRYOR,** Chief Judge, **PRYOR** and **LUCK,** Circuit Judges.

[—1—] {-1224-} PRYOR, Chief Judge: **{-1225-}**

This appeal requires us to resolve three difficult questions of appellate jurisdiction before deciding a single issue on the merits. The jurisdictional issues are (1) whether an order granting a voluntary dismissal without prejudice, Fed. R. **[—2—]** Civ. P. 41(a)(2), is a "final decision[]," 28 U.S.C. § 1291; (2) whether we have territorial jurisdiction, *id.* § 1294, to review an interlocutory decision by an out-of-circuit district court that merged into the final judgment of a district court in this Circuit; and (3) whether an appellant has standing to appeal from a final judgment accompanying an order granting his motion for a voluntary dismissal. Charles Corley and his wife, Myra Corley, filed this lawsuit against dozens of companies that allegedly supplied products containing asbestos that caused Charles's malignant mesothelioma. Although the Corleys commenced their suit in an Alabama court, the companies removed it to the Northern District of Alabama. The Judicial Panel on Multidistrict Litigation then transferred the suit to the Eastern District of Pennsylvania, which eventually returned it to the Northern District of Alabama. After the Northern District of Alabama granted the Corleys' motion to voluntarily dismiss the last two companies in the suit, the Corleys sought our review of an order entered by the Eastern District of Pennsylvania that denied their motion to reconsider a partial summary judgment in favor of several companies. In that motion, the Corleys had argued for the first time that the district court should apply maritime law, not state law, to determine **{-1226-}** the merits of their claims. We conclude that the order granting a voluntary dismissal without prejudice is a final order, that we have territorial jurisdiction to hear this appeal, and that the Corleys have standing to appeal. We also affirm the judgment against the Corleys. **[—3 —]**

I. BACKGROUND

Charles and Myra Corley sued dozens of companies that allegedly supplied asbestos-laden products that Charles used when he served in the United States Navy and later when he was a self-employed mechanic and repairman. The Corleys alleged that these products caused Charles's malignant mesothelioma and sought damages under state law. After Charles's death, his son, Oscar Corley, joined the suit as the executor of Charles's estate. Oscar and Myra amended their complaint to add a claim under the Alabama Wrongful Death Act. The Corleys originally filed their complaint in an Alabama court, and the companies removed the suit to the Northern District of Alabama.

The Judicial Panel on Multidistrict Litigation transferred this action to the Eastern District of Pennsylvania, where several of the companies filed motions for summary judgment. As relevant to this appeal, the Pennsylvania district court granted summary judgment in favor of 17 companies that supplied products that Charles used when he was in the Navy—a group we will call the "Navy suppliers." The district court determined that the statute of limitations had expired on the claims against these companies. The Corleys filed a motion to reconsider, which asked for "leave to elect the application of maritime law and, in so doing, the [extended] statute of limitations recognized under maritime law." After explaining that the Corleys had not previously argued that maritime law applied, the district **[—4 —]** court denied the motion on the ground that a motion for reconsideration was far too late in the litigation for the Corleys to change their theory of liability.

Over the next year, the Pennsylvania district court whittled the suit down to what it thought were the final two companies in the suit—Honeywell International, Inc., and Ford Motor Company. The Judicial Panel on Multidistrict Litigation then remanded the suit to the Northern District of Alabama. The Alabama district court later dismissed Honeywell and Ford from the suit with prejudice.

The Corleys filed an appeal to this Court that challenged the Pennsylvania order denying their motion to reconsider the summary judgment in favor of the Navy suppliers. Two defendants, Fairbanks Morse Pump Corporation and Garlock Sealing Technologies, LLC, filed suggestions of bankruptcy in this Court. After investigation, we discovered that the Corley's claims against Fairbanks and Garlock were still pending in the district court and dismissed the Corleys' appeal.

On remand to the district court, the Corleys reported that Fairbanks and Garlock had filed petitions for relief in a bankruptcy court in 2010, which had stayed proceedings against them in this suit. Three months later, the bankruptcy court confirmed a reorganization plan that prevented the Corleys from litigating their claims against Fairbanks and Garlock in this suit. Because their claims against the two companies had "already been eliminated as a matter of law" in the bankruptcy court, the Corleys asked the district court to voluntarily dismiss those **[—5 —]** claims without prejudice. *See* Fed. R. Civ. P. 41(a)(2) (permitting the dismissal of "an action . . . at the plaintiff's request . . . by court order, on terms that the court considers proper"); *see also Plains Growers, Inc. ex rel. Florists' Mut. Ins. Co. v. Ickes-Braun Glasshouses, Inc.*, 474 F.2d 250, 253 (5th Cir. 1973) (holding that plaintiffs can voluntarily **{-1227-}** dismiss individual parties from a suit). The district court granted their motion and entered what it called a "final judgment with respect to all claims asserted in this action." The Corleys then filed this appeal, which again challenges the denial of their motion to reconsider the summary judgment in favor of the Navy suppliers.

II. JURISDICTION

We have a threshold obligation to ensure that we have jurisdiction to hear an appeal, for "[w]ithout jurisdiction [we] cannot proceed at all in any cause." *Ex parte McCardle*, 74 U.S. (7 Wall.) 506, 514 (1869); *accord Univ. of S. Ala. v. Am. Tobacco Co.*, 168 F.3d 405, 410 (11th Cir. 1999). Because we are a court of limited jurisdiction, adjudicating an appeal without jurisdiction would "offend[] fundamental principles of separation of powers." *Steel Co. v. Citizens for a Better Env't*, 523 U.S. 83, 94 (1998). In practical terms, our jurisdiction "must be both (1) authorized by statute and (2) within constitutional limits." *OFS Fitel, LLC v. Epstein, Becker & Green, P.C.*, 549 F.3d 1344, 1355 (11th Cir. 2008). **[—6 —]**

To say that the odd procedural history of this appeal tests the boundaries of our jurisdiction would be an understatement. The Corleys challenge an interlocutory order from a district court in another circuit, and they do so by appealing from an order granting their motion for a voluntary dismissal without prejudice. But even so, we conclude that we have jurisdiction to address the merits.

We divide our discussion of the jurisdictional issues into three parts. First, we address whether an order granting a motion to voluntarily dismiss an action without prejudice is a "final decision[]." 28 U.S.C. § 1291. Second, we consider whether we have territorial jurisdiction to hear an appeal challenging an interlocutory order issued by a district court outside this Circuit that merged into the final judgment of a district court in this Circuit. *See id.* § 1294. Finally, we examine whether the Corleys have standing to appeal from an order that granted their motion for a voluntary dismissal. *See* U.S. Const. art. III, § 2.

A. The Corleys Appealed a Final Decision.

The Corleys invoke our subject-matter jurisdiction over "appeals from all final decisions of the district courts of the United States." 28 U.S.C. § 1291. Because the district court entered an order granting the Corleys' motion to voluntarily dismiss their only remaining claims, *see* Fed. R. Civ. P. 41(a)(2), the Corleys contend that we can hear their appeal. The Navy suppliers respond that we still lack jurisdiction. They argue that an order granting a plaintiff's motion to **[—7—]** voluntarily dismiss an action without prejudice under Rule 41(a)(2) is not a final decision under section 1291.

Under section 1291, "[a] 'final decision' is one by which a district court disassociates itself from a case." *Gelboim v. Bank of Am. Corp.*, 574 U.S. 405, 408 (2015) (internal quotation marks omitted); *see also id.* at 409 ("[T]he statute's core application is to rulings that terminate an action."). The voluntary dismissal underlying this appeal arguably fits that definition. It ended the involvement of the district court, and the Corleys have conceded that the bankruptcy court "eliminated" their claims against Fairbanks and Garlock "as a matter of law." "That the dismissal was without prejudice to filing another suit does not make the cause unappealable, for denial of relief and dismissal of the case ended this suit so far as the District Court was concerned." **{–1228–}** *United States v. Wallace & Tiernan Co.*, 336 U.S. 793, 794 n.1 (1949).

But we do not write on a blank slate. Indeed, "the canvas looks like one that Jackson Pollock got to first." *Gunn v. Minton*, 568 U.S. 251, 258 (2013). Our precedent splinters in multiple directions on whether voluntary dismissals without prejudice are final. *Compare, e.g.*, *McGregor v. Bd. of Comm'rs*, 956 F.2d 1017, 1020 (11th Cir. 1992) ("An order granting a plaintiff's motion for voluntary dismissal pursuant to Rule 41(a)(2) qualifies as a final judgment for purposes of appeal." (internal quotation marks omitted)), *with, e.g.*, *State Treasurer v. Barry*, **[—8—]** 168 F.3d 8, 13 (11th Cir. 1999) ("[V]oluntary dismissals, granted without prejudice, are not final decisions themselves . . . ."), *with, e.g.*, *CSX Transp., Inc. v. City of Garden City*, 235 F.3d 1325, 1328–29 (11th Cir. 2000) (holding that a voluntary dismissal without prejudice was final when "there was no attempt to manufacture jurisdiction").

Our divergent decisions can be traced to two opinions of the former Fifth Circuit: *LeCompte v. Mr. Chip, Inc.*, 528 F.2d 601 (5th Cir. 1976), and *Ryan v. Occidental Petroleum Corp.*, 577 F.2d 298 (5th Cir. 1978). To "determine which of our precedents binds us," *CSX Transp., Inc. v. Gen. Mills, Inc.*, 846 F.3d 1333, 1337 (11th Cir. 2017), we must begin with them.

LeCompte involved a plaintiff's appeal from an order granting his motion under Rule 41(a)(2) to dismiss his complaint without prejudice subject to certain conditions. 528 F.2d at 602. Before reaching the merits, our predecessor court considered whether the order was appealable. *Id.* It devoted most of its attention to whether the plaintiff had standing to challenge the stringent conditions on refiling that the district court attached to its dismissal order. *See id.* at 603–04. But before it reached that issue, *LeCompte* addressed whether the order was final, *see id.* at 603, which was also necessary to its holding that the order was appealable, *see* 28 U.S.C. § 1291. It concluded that "[w]here the trial court allows the plaintiff to dismiss his action without prejudice, the judgment, of course, qualifies as a final **[—9—]** judgment for purposes of appeal." *LeCompte*, 528 F.2d at 603 (internal quotation marks omitted). After concluding that the voluntary dismissal order was final and that the plaintiff was adverse to that order, *LeCompte* vacated and remanded the order on the merits. *Id.* at 603–05.

Ryan v. Occidental Petroleum Corp., 577 F.2d 298, came two years later. After the district court in *Ryan* had dismissed all but one of the plaintiff's claims, the plaintiff moved to voluntarily dismiss the paragraph of his complaint that contained his remaining substantive allegation. *Id.* at 300. Although the district court granted the plaintiff's narrow motion, it "did not purport to dismiss the jurisdictional allegations of [the] complaint . . . and it specifically noted that the dismissal was without prejudice to [the plaintiff's] right to file again." *Id.* When the plaintiff tried to appeal, the former Fifth Circuit held that it lacked jurisdiction. *Id.* It concluded that no final judgment existed because "the torso of the plaintiff's complaint—including the identification of the parties and the jurisdictional allegations—remain[ed] before the district court." *Id.* at 301. *Ryan* later explained that the "chief problem" with finality in the appeal was that the plaintiff's dismissal motion was "more appropriately considered to be an amendment to the complaint under Rule 15" and that an order granting leave to amend "lacks finality" when it "permits judicial proceedings to continue." *Id.* at 302 n.2. *Ryan* separately concluded that the plaintiff could not take advantage of the *Jetco* exception to **[—10—]** finality, which allows parties to appeal interlocutory decisions that were part of a **{-1229-}** series of orders that "effectively terminated the entire litigation." *Id.* at 301–02; *see also Jetco Elec. Indus., Inc. v. Gardiner*, 473 F.2d 1228, 1231 (5th Cir. 1973). Because the "language of the district court's order, along with its retention of the jurisdictional allegations of the complaint, appeared to contemplate that [the plaintiff] would pursue this same action in the same court," the voluntary dismissal did "not amount to a termination of the litigation between the parties." *Ryan*, 577 F.2d at 302. And because the order "neither amount[ed] to an appealable final decision nor [met] the requirements of any exception to the finality rule," *Ryan* dismissed the appeal. *Id.* at 303.

LeCompte and *Ryan* are not in conflict. We can read *LeCompte* to establish that a voluntary dismissal under Rule 41(a)(2) is a final decision for the purposes of appeal at least when the court places stringent conditions on refiling. *See* 528 F.2d at 603. *Ryan* qualifies that voluntary dismissals are deprived of finality when part of the complaint remains before the district court, which occurs when a plaintiff moves to voluntarily dismiss only part of his remaining complaint without prejudice, the district court grants the motion without purporting to dismiss the remainder of the complaint, and the dismissal order contemplates future filings in the court. *See* 577 F.2d at 300–02 & n.2. Under these circumstances, the dismissal **[—11—]** is akin to an order granting leave to amend, which is not final when it "permits judicial proceedings to continue." *See id.* at 302 n.2.

Perhaps because no conflict existed, both the former Fifth Circuit and, at least initially, this Court held that voluntary dismissals without prejudice were final in a variety of circumstances. Shortly after *Ryan*, our predecessor court explained that *LeCompte* "stated the usual rule governing the appealability of orders granting motions for voluntary dismissal" and reiterated that voluntary dismissals under Rule 41(a)(2) are final decisions. *Yoffe v. Keller Indus., Inc.*, 580 F.2d 126, 129 (5th Cir. 1978). This Circuit initially allowed appeals from voluntary dismissals without prejudice without addressing whether a voluntary dismissal was final. *See, e.g., Black v. Broward Emp't & Training Admin.*, 846 F.2d 1311, 1312 & n.3 (11th Cir. 1988); *Studstill v. Borg Warner Leasing*, 806 F.2d 1005, 1007 (11th Cir. 1986); *McCants v. Ford Motor Co., Inc.*, 781 F.2d 855, 856 (11th Cir. 1986). But we later cited *LeCompte* and held that an "order granting voluntary dismissal without prejudice under Rule 41(a)(2) is final and appealable" by a defendant who had opposed the plaintiff's motion for voluntary dismissal. *Kirkland v. Nat'l Mortg. Network, Inc.*, 884 F.2d 1367, 1369–70 (11th Cir. 1989). Because the voluntary dismissal was a final judgment, we explained, "it incorporate[d] and [brought] up for review the preceding nonfinal order" that the defendant challenged. *Id.* at 1370. Finally, in *McGregor v. Board of Commissioners*, which **[—12—]** involved a plaintiff's challenge to several claims that the district court had dismissed on the merits before granting the plaintiff's motion to dismiss his remaining claims, we quoted *LeCompte* and *Yoffe* and held that "[a]n order granting a plaintiff's motion for voluntary dismissal pursuant to Rule 41(a)(2) qualifies as a final judgment for purposes of appeal." 956 F.2d at 1020 (internal quotation marks omitted).

The conflict came in *Mesa v. United States*, which also involved an order granting a motion to voluntarily dismiss a suit without prejudice. *See* 61 F.3d 20, 21 (11th Cir. 1995). *Mesa* held that the order of dismissal before it was not final. *See id.* It interpreted *Ryan* to hold that "the voluntary dismissal of [a] plaintiff's remaining claim could not be considered final because a voluntary dismissal is without prejudice **{–1230–}** to the moving party to file those claims again." *Id.* at 22. This understanding of finality became the standard in this Circuit for addressing voluntary dismissals without prejudice. *See State Treasurer*, 168 F.3d at 13; *Constr. Aggregates, Ltd. v. Forest Commodities Corp.*, 147 F.3d 1334, 1335–37 (11th Cir. 1998) (extending *Mesa* to stipulated dismissals under Rule 41(a)(1)).

We first spotted the tension in our precedent in *State Treasurer v. Barry*, 168 F.3d 8. After the district court in *State Treasurer* granted a partial summary judgment in favor of the defendants, the parties filed a joint stipulation to dismiss the remaining claim in the suit. *Id.* at 9–10; *see also* Fed. R. Civ. P. 41(a)(1)(A)(ii) **[—13—]** (allowing the plaintiff to dismiss an action without a court order if all parties sign a stipulation of dismissal). We dismissed the plaintiff's appeal because we concluded that *Mesa* and its reading of *Ryan* controlled. *See State Treasurer*, 168 F.3d at 16. Although we failed to mention *McGregor*, we acknowledged that *LeCompte* and *Kirkland* had allowed appeals from voluntary dismissals without prejudice. *Id.* at 14. But we concluded that the reasoning of these two decisions did not extend to stipulated dismissals. *Id.* at 15. *LeCompte* and *Kirkland*, we explained, involved court orders of dismissal under Rule 41(a)(2), not stipulated dismissals under Rule 41(a)(1). *Id.*; *see also Kirkland*, 884 F.2d at 1369–70 (concluding that a voluntary dismissal without prejudice "under Rule 41(a)(2) is final"); *LeCompte*, 528 F.2d at 603 (concluding that a voluntary dismissal without prejudice is final "[w]here *the trial court allows* the plaintiff to dismiss his action without prejudice" (emphasis added) (internal quotation marks omitted)). We added, in dicta, that *LeCompte* "is limited to a subset of Rule 41(a)(2) dismissals": dismissals in which the court "placed stringent conditions on the plaintiff's ability to re-file its dismissed claims." *State Treasurer*, 168 F.3d at 15.

This appeal picks up where *State Treasurer* left off. To be sure, we have revisited whether stipulated or noticed dismissals under Rule 41(a)(1) are final. *See, e.g.*, *Equity Inv. Partners, LP v. Lenz*, 594 F.3d 1338, 1341–42 n.2 (11th Cir. 2010); *Schoenfeld v. Babbitt*, 168 F.3d 1257, 1265–66 (11th Cir. 1999); *Univ. of S.* **[—14—]** *Ala.*, 168 F.3d at 408 n.1. But we have not addressed the tension between our earliest precedents and *Mesa* as applied to voluntary dismissals under Rule 41(a)(2). *Cf. Hood v. Plantation Gen. Med. Ctr., Ltd.*, 251 F.3d 932, 933–34 (11th Cir. 2001) (holding that an order granting a motion for voluntary dismissal was not final when a claim remained pending in the district court and that voluntarily dismissing the remaining claim did not trigger the *Jetco* exception). That tension is squarely presented in this appeal.

Two principles govern our approach to resolving conflicts in our precedent. First, we are "obligated, if at all possible, to distill from apparently conflicting prior panel decisions a basis of reconciliation and to apply that reconciled rule." *United States v. Hogan*, 986 F.2d 1364, 1369 (11th Cir. 1993). And second, if we cannot reconcile our precedent, we must follow the oldest decision that governs the issue. *See Gen. Mills*, 846 F.3d at 1338; *accord* Bryan A. Garner et al., *The Law of Judicial Precedent* § 36, at 303–04 (2016).

We see no way to give force to *Mesa* in the light of our earlier precedents. Even if *State Treasurer* is correct that we can limit *LeCompte* to situations in which the district court attached "stringent conditions" to the voluntary-dismissal order, 168 F.3d at 15, we must still reconcile *Mesa* with our other earlier decisions, at least one of which is materially identical to it. In both *McGregor* and *Mesa*, the plaintiff suffered **{–1231–}** an adverse decision on some of his claims and voluntarily **[—15—]** dismissed his remaining claims without prejudice to challenge the earlier decision on appeal. *See Mesa*, 61 F.3d at 21; *McGregor*, 956 F.2d at 1018–20. *McGregor* concluded that "an order granting a plaintiff's motion for voluntary dismissal pursuant to Rule 41(a)(2) 'qualifies as a final judgment for purposes of appeal.'" 956 F.2d at 1020 (quoting *Yoffe*, 580 F.2d at 129, and *LeCompte*, 528 F.2d at 603). Conversely, *Mesa* later concluded that these orders were not final. 61 F.3d at 21–22. Because *Mesa* did not even mention *McGregor*, it provided no reason to distinguish that decision. And we cannot find one.

Because we cannot harmonize our decisions, the earliest-precedent rule applies. *See Gen. Mills*, 846 F.3d at 1340. And under that rule, we must follow *McGregor*, which both predates *Mesa* and is consistent with our earlier decisions. So we hold that an order granting a motion to voluntarily dismiss the remainder of a complaint under Rule 41(a)(2) "qualifies as a final judgment for purposes of appeal." *McGregor*, 956 F.2d at 1020 (quoting *Yoffe*, 580 F.2d at 129, and *LeCompte*, 528 F.2d at 603). And because the Corleys appealed from such an order, we have jurisdiction under section 1291.

B. We Have Territorial Jurisdiction to Hear This Appeal.

The next issue concerns our territorial jurisdiction under section 1294, which mandates that "appeals from reviewable decisions of the district . . . courts shall be taken . . . to the court of appeals for the circuit embracing the district." 28 U.S.C. **[—16—]** § 1294. The Corleys urge us to hold that "reviewable decisions" in section 1294 refers to appealable decisions—that is, decisions that federal laws grant circuit courts jurisdiction to review. Here, that decision is the voluntary-dismissal order. *See id.* § 1291. Because the Northern District of Alabama issued that order, we would have jurisdiction to review the order as "the court of appeals for the circuit embracing [that] district." *Id.* § 1294; *see also id.* § 41. The Navy suppliers counter that the reviewable decision is the order that the Corleys challenge—that is, the denial of their motion for reconsideration by the Eastern District of Pennsylvania—which would deprive us of jurisdiction. *See id.* § 41.

The parties' disagreement tracks a circuit split over the application of section 1294 to interlocutory orders that precede an inter-circuit transfer. Most circuits to reach the question have concluded that they can review an out-of-circuit interlocutory decision so long as they have jurisdiction over the district court that issued the appealable decision. *See Kalama v. Matson Navigation Co.*, 875 F.3d 297, 305, 5 Adm. R. 346, 351 (6th Cir. 2017); *In re Briscoe*, 448 F.3d 201, 213–14 (3d Cir. 2006); *Jones v. InfoCure Corp.*, 310 F.3d 529, 532–34 (7th Cir. 2002); *Hill v. Henderson*, 195 F.3d 671, 674–75 (D.C. Cir. 1999); *Chaiken v. VV Publ'g Corp.*, 119 F.3d 1018, 1025 n.2 (2d Cir. 1997); *Tel-Phonic Servs., Inc. v. TBS Int'l, Inc.*, 975 F.2d 1134, 1138 (5th Cir. 1992). Conversely, the Tenth Circuit has held that it lacks jurisdiction to review interlocutory orders issued by an out-of-circuit district court, **[—17—]** even when the appealable decision comes from within its boundaries. *See McGeorge v. Cont'l Airlines, Inc.*, 871 F.2d 952, 954 (10th Cir. 1989). In its view, jurisdiction under section 1294 depends on whether the district court that issued the interlocutory order under review lies within its territorial boundaries. *See id.*

We agree with the majority interpretation and hold that the phrase "reviewable decisions" in section 1294 refers to appealable decisions. Congress has not given us the power to review interlocutory orders at will. Outside of narrow circumstances not **{-1232-}** relevant here, we can review those orders only when they "merge into a final judgment of the district court." *Akin v. PAFEC Ltd.*, 991 F.2d 1550, 1563 (11th Cir. 1993). So even when we consider the merits of an interlocutory order, we still "review" the final decision into which the earlier order merged. *See Kalama*, 875 F.3d at 305, 5 Adm. R. at 350–51 ("A partial dismissal is not 'reviewable' until it can be appealed—generally, when it 'merges' into a final, appealable judgment."). That final decision is necessarily the reviewable decision.

The rest of section 1294 dispels any lingering ambiguity about the meaning of "reviewable decision." *See Reno v. Koray*, 515 U.S. 50, 56 (1995) ("[I]t is a fundamental principle of statutory construction . . . that the meaning of a word cannot be determined in isolation, but must be drawn from the context in which it is used." (internal quotation marks omitted)). Section 1294 concerns "*appeals from* reviewable decisions." 28 U.S.C. § 1294 (emphasis added). This language, of **[—18—]** course, presumes that the "reviewable decision[]" is an appealable decision. After all, there can be no "appeal[] from" a non-appealable decision. *Cf. Cox v. Adm'r U.S. Steel & Carnegie*, 17 F.3d 1386, 1413 n.4 (11th Cir. 1994) ("When reviewing an appeal from a final judgment, this court can review rulings on previous interlocutory orders." (alteration adopted) (internal quotation marks omitted)). *See generally* 28 U.S.C. § 1291 (giving courts of appeals jurisdiction over "appeals from all final decisions" of district courts). Adopting the minority interpretation would require us to ignore this context, which we cannot do.

The Navy suppliers argue that our decision in *Roofing and Sheet Metal Services, Inc. v. La Quinta Motor Inns, Inc.*, 689 F.2d 982, 986 (11th Cir. 1982), requires a different interpretation of section 1294. In *Roofing*, the Western District of Arkansas transferred the underlying suit to the Southern District of Alabama, and the appellant sought to challenge that transfer order on appeal to this Court. *See id.* at 984–85. We held that section 1294 prevented us from reviewing the transfer order. *Id.* at 986–87; *see also Murray v. Scott*, 253 F.3d 1308, 1314 (11th Cir. 2001) (holding the same); *cf. In re Corrugated Container Anti-Trust Litig.*, 620 F.2d 1086, 1090–91 (5th Cir. 1980) (holding that section 1294 required dismissing an appeal from a final order of contempt issued by the Southern District of New York against a third-party witness). The Navy suppliers argue that *Roofing* demands that we dismiss the Corleys' appeal. **[—19—]**

We disagree. The holding of *Roofing* does not extend beyond transfer orders. *Roofing* reached its decision in the shadow of what it called the "well established" rule that "a transferee court cannot directly review the transfer order itself." 689 F.2d at 986 (quoting *Starnes v. McGuire*, 512 F.2d 918, 924 (D.C. Cir. 1974) (en banc)); *see also id.* at 987 ("[W]e know of no case in which [any] circuit . . . has in fact reviewed a transfer order issued by a district court in another circuit."). When *Roofing* held that it could not review the transfer order before it, it joined the uniform consensus of our sister circuits that an out-of-circuit transfer order is not reviewable on appeal in the transferee circuit. *See Posnanski v. Gibney*, 421 F.3d 977, 980 (9th Cir. 2005); *United States v. Copley*, 25 F.3d 660, 662 (8th Cir. 1994); *Lewelling v. Farmers Ins. of Columbus, Inc.*, 879 F.2d 212, 218 (6th Cir. 1989); *McGeorge*, 871 F.2d at 953–54; *Reyes v. Supervisor of the Drug Enf't Admin.*, 834 F.2d 1093, 1095 (1st Cir. 1987); *Linnell v. Sloan*, 636 F.2d 65, 67 (4th Cir. 1980); *Starnes*, 512 F.2d at 924; *Purex Corp. v. St. Louis Nat'l Stockyards Co.*, 374 F.2d 998, 1000 (7th Cir. 1967); *see also Songbyrd, Inc. v. Estate of Grossman*, 206 F.3d 172, 178 (2d Cir. 2000) **{-1233-}** (requiring a party to file a retransfer motion in the transferee court to appeal a transfer order). *But see Nascone v. Spudnuts, Inc.*, 735 F.2d 763, 772 n.9 (3d Cir. 1984) (suggesting in dicta that a transferee circuit could review a transfer order). This bar does not encompass other out-of-circuit interlocutory decisions. *See Hill*, 195 F.3d at 677 (concluding that **[—20—]** the "complex and somewhat conflicting pattern of reviewability" of transfer orders does not affect the reviewability of other pretransfer orders).

In sum, we have territorial jurisdiction. The term "reviewable decisions" in section 1294 refers to appealable decisions. The Northern District of Alabama issued the final, appealable decision in this suit. And, of course, we can hear appeals from that court.

C. The Corleys Have Standing to Appeal.

The final jurisdictional issue concerns our jurisdiction under Article III of the Constitution, which limits our authority to "Cases" and "Controversies." U.S. Const. art. III, § 2. Although the parties do not dispute this issue, "[l]ongstanding principles of federal law oblige us to inquire *sua sponte* whenever a doubt arises as to the existence of federal jurisdiction." *Green v. Graham*, 906 F.3d 955, 961 (11th Cir. 2018) (internal quotation marks omitted). Because our precedent leaves doubt about whether we have Article III jurisdiction to hear the Corleys' appeal from their own voluntary dismissal, we address the issue.

"To have a case or controversy, a litigant must establish that he has standing, which must exist 'throughout all stages of litigation,'" including on appeal. *United States v. Amodeo*, 916 F.3d 967, 971 (11th Cir. 2019) (quoting *Hollingsworth v. Perry*, 570 U.S. 693, 705 (2013)). Standing is an "irreducible constitutional minimum," and a "court is powerless to continue" in its absence. *CAMP Legal Def.* **[—21—]** *Fund, Inc. v. City of Atlanta*, 451 F.3d 1257, 1269 (11th Cir. 2006) (internal quotation marks omitted). To establish standing, a litigant must prove that "he has suffered a concrete and particularized injury." *Amodeo*, 916 F.3d at 971 (quoting *Hollingsworth*, 570 U.S. at 704). In the appellate context, "the primary meaning of the injury requirement is adverseness." *Id.* Specifically, the litigant "must be adverse as to the final judgment" to appeal from that judgment. *OFS Fitel*, 549 F.3d at 1356 (internal quotation marks omitted).

As a general rule, a plaintiff is not adverse to a voluntary dismissal that he requested. *See, e.g.*, *Druhan v. Am. Mut. Life*, 166 F.3d 1324, 1326 (11th Cir. 1999). This rule "can easily be understood," the former Fifth Circuit explained, because "the plaintiff has acquired that which he sought," so the order cannot be adverse. *LeCompte*, 528 F.2d at 603.

Appellate standing is murkier when a plaintiff appeals from a voluntary dismissal to challenge an adverse interlocutory order. On the one hand, we have held that plaintiffs have standing to appeal from a voluntary dismissal if the adverse interlocutory order is effectively "case-dispositive" and "the district court bases its dismissal with prejudice on the fact that its interlocutory decision disposed of the entire case." *OFS Fitel*, 549 F.3d at 1359 (order excluding expert testimony that was legally necessary to prevail). On the other hand, interlocutory orders that do not address the merits of a plaintiff's claim cannot establish **[—22—]** appellate standing. *See Druhan*, 166 F.3d at 1326 (order denying the plaintiff's motion to remand her suit to state court); *accord Woodard v. STP Corp.*, 170 F.3d 1043, 1044 (11th Cir. 1999). The second class of appeals lacks adverseness because there is "no contested court ruling, either interlocutory or final, as to **{-1234-}** the merits of the plaintiff's claims" and so "the dismissal on the merits derives only from the plaintiff's own written request." *OFS Fitel*, 549 F.3d at 1356.

This appeal does not fit neatly within our precedents on voluntary dismissals. Unlike the plaintiff in *OFS Fitel*, the Corleys did not voluntarily dismiss their claims to contest a "case-dispositive" order. They instead challenge a years-old order denying their motion to reconsider a summary judgment in favor of some defendants. But unlike the plaintiffs in *Druhan* and *Woodard*, the Corleys contest an order that completely resolved their claims against certain defendants on the merits and merged into the final judgment. *See Akin*, 991 F.2d at 1563 ("When a district court enters a final judgment, all prior non-final orders and rulings which produced the judgment are merged into the judgment and subject to review on appeal." (internal quotation marks omitted)). Because the Corleys never consented to that order, the final judgment contains an adverse decision on the merits that does not "derive[] only from the plaintiff's own written request." *OFS Fitel*, 549 F.3d at 1356. **[—23—]**

Although our precedent on voluntary dismissals does not resolve this appeal, a broader principle of appellate standing establishes that the Corleys are adverse to the final judgment: "a party is 'aggrieved' and ordinarily can appeal a decision 'granting in part and denying in part the remedy requested.'" *Forney v. Apfel*, 524 U.S. 266, 271 (1998) (quoting *United States v. Jose*, 519 U.S. 54, 56 (1996)). Even though the Corleys are not adverse to the order of voluntary dismissal, which granted their requested remedy for Fairbanks and Garlock, they are adverse to the order that denied their motion to reconsider the summary judgment in favor of the Navy suppliers. And the latter order is just as much a part of the final judgment as the voluntary-dismissal order. So, notwithstanding their voluntary dismissal, the Corleys are adverse to part of the final judgment, which is enough to establish appellate standing. *See Aaro, Inc. v. Daewoo Int'l (Am.) Corp.*, 755 F.2d 1398, 1400–01 (11th Cir. 1985) (holding that plaintiffs who prevailed at trial on some of their claims and consented to a remittitur order could still appeal because they challenged an adverse partial summary judgment that had merged into the final judgment); *see also Forney*, 524

U.S. at 271; *OFS Fitel*, 549 F.3d at 1359 ("[W]hen the appeal is from a final judgment, the fact that the appeal substantively concerns an interlocutory ruling is no bar to jurisdiction."). **[—24—]**

III. STANDARD OF REVIEW

We review the denial of a motion for reconsideration for an abuse of discretion. *See Richardson v. Johnson*, 598 F.3d 734, 740 (11th Cir. 2010).

IV. DISCUSSION

The merits of this appeal are straight-forward. The Corleys contend that the district court abused its discretion when it denied their motion for reconsideration, which argued that they had a valid claim against the Navy suppliers under maritime law. The Corleys argue that they had a right to "make an election between civil and admiralty law," even after the district court entered a summary judgment. We disagree.

When the district court denied the Corleys' motion, it explained that the Corleys had "never argued previously that maritime law should apply." In their complaint, the Corleys instead alleged that "no claim of admiralty or maritime law is raised." They maintained this position in their response **{-1235-}** to the Navy suppliers' motion for summary judgment, which discussed only Alabama law. The Corleys waited until after the district court granted summary judgment in favor of the Navy suppliers to argue, in a motion for reconsideration, that they had a valid claim under maritime law against the Navy suppliers. The district court ruled that the Corleys could not argue that a different substantive law governed their complaint at that late stage in the litigation. **[—25—]**

We have long held that district courts act well within their discretion when they refuse to consider arguments that a party made for the first time in a motion for reconsideration. *See, e.g., Bost v. Fed. Express Corp.*, 372 F.3d 1233, 1242–43 (11th Cir. 2004); *Hashwani v. Barbar*, 822 F.2d 1038, 1041 (11th Cir. 1987). As we have explained, "[t]here is a significant difference between pointing out errors in a court's decision on grounds that have already been urged before the court and raising altogether new arguments on a motion to amend; if accepted, the latter essentially affords a litigant two bites at the apple." *Am. Home Assur. Co. v. Glenn Estess & Assocs., Inc.*, 763 F.2d 1237, 1239 (11th Cir. 1985) (internal quotation marks omitted). This principle extends to plaintiffs' motions for reconsideration that urge district courts to apply a different law to govern their claims for relief. *See id.* (holding that the district court did not abuse its discretion when it rejected a choice-of-law argument that a party raised for the first time in a motion for reconsideration).

The Corleys contend that Federal Rule of Civil Procedure 9(h) gave them the right to invoke maritime law at any time, but they misread that rule. *See* Fed. R. Civ. P. 9(h)(1) ("If a claim for relief is within the admiralty or maritime jurisdiction and also within the court's subject-matter jurisdiction on some other ground, the pleading may designate the claim as an admiralty or maritime claim . . . ."). Rule 9(h)(1) "serves only as a device by which the pleader may claim the **[—26—]** special benefits of admiralty procedures and remedies, including a nonjury trial, when the pleadings show that both admiralty and some other basis of federal jurisdiction exist." *Romero v. Bethlehem Steel Corp.*, 515 F.2d 1249, 1252 (5th Cir. 1975). It does not determine whether maritime law governs a claim. *See Powell v. Offshore Nav., Inc.*, 644 F.2d 1063, 1065 & n.5 (5th Cir. Unit A May 1981).

The Corleys are not entitled to a second bite at the apple. They argued that Alabama law applied until the district court granted summary judgment in favor of the Navy suppliers. Their motion for reconsideration was the first time they even suggested that maritime law applied. And they do not offer a compelling explanation to justify their delay. For example, the Corleys' main argument is that the intervening decision of a district court in an unrelated suit, *Conner v. Alfa Laval, Inc.*, 799 F. Supp. 2d 455 (E.D. Pa. 2011), changed the law and allowed them to bring a maritime claim. But, of course, decisions of district courts "have no binding precedential authority beyond the case in which they are entered," *Dow Jones & Co. v. Kaye*, 256 F.3d 1251, 1258 n.10 (11th Cir. 2001); *accord* Garner et al., *The Law of Judicial Precedent* § 29, at 255, so *Conner* could not have affected their ability to bring a claim under maritime law. At bottom, the district court did not abuse its discretion when it concluded that this motion was an incorrect vehicle to change the substantive law governing the suit. **[—27—]**

V. CONCLUSION

We **AFFIRM** the judgment of the district court.

(Reporter's Note: Concurring Opinion follows on p. 495).

[—28—] {-1235-} **PRYOR,** Chief Judge, joined by **LUCK,** Circuit Judge, concurring:

Although this Court has jurisdiction to hear the Corleys' appeal from their voluntary **{-1236-}** dismissal, I write separately both to underscore the widespread problems that Federal Rule of Civil Procedure 41(a) creates in finality doctrine and to highlight better ways for many litigants to secure appellate review of decisions that resolve only some of their claims.

Rule 41(a) is a poor mechanism to accelerate appellate review. The rule contemplates the voluntary dismissal of "an action," Fed. R. Civ. P. 41(a), which, we have explained, refers to "the whole case" instead of particular claims, *Perry v. Schumacher Grp. of La.*, 891 F.3d 954, 958 (11th Cir. 2018) (internal quotation marks omitted). *But see Plains Growers, Inc. ex rel. Florists' Mut. Ins. Co. v. Ickes-Braun Glasshouses, Inc.*, 474 F.2d 250, 253 (5th Cir. 1973) ("[W]e hold that plaintiff is entitled to a dismissal against one defendant under Rule 41(a), even though the action against another defendant would remain pending."). The rule also presumes that a plaintiff will want to refile the "action" later. *See* Fed. R. Civ. P. 41(a) (mandating that unless the notice, stipulation, or order of dismissal "states otherwise, the dismissal is without prejudice"). Perhaps unsurprisingly, litigants' attempts to hijack this rule as a means to "home-brew their own approach to obtaining appellate review" of particular claims, *First Health Grp. Corp. v. BCE Emergis Corp.*, 269 F.3d 800, 801 (7th Cir. 2001), have not always been smooth. **[—29—]**

Nearly every circuit has encountered similar issues to those we considered in this appeal. We are not the first court to face an intracircuit split in our precedent. *See Robinson-Reeder v. Am. Council on Educ.*, 571 F.3d 1333, 1338–39 & n.6 (D.C. Cir. 2009) (explaining that several inter- and intra-circuit splits exist on the question); *Chappelle v. Beacon Commc'ns Corp.*, 84 F.3d 652, 654 (2d Cir. 1996) (listing intracircuit splits); *see also* Terry W. Schackmann & Barry L. Pickens, *The Finality Trap: Accidentally Losing Your Right to Appeal (Part I)*, 58 J. Mo. Bar 78, 84 (2002) (cautioning litigants that judicial decisions in this area are not "assured of adherence in the future" and are sometimes "ignore[d]"). And although the panel opinion compares this Circuit's finality doctrine on Rule 41(a) to a Jackson Pollock painting, we might have also called it an "egregious mess," *Williams v. Seidenbach*, 958 F.3d 341, 355 (5th Cir. 2020) (en banc) (Willett, J., concurring in the judgment) (internal quotation marks omitted), or lamented that "[i]t would be an understatement to say that our precedents . . . are difficult to harmonize," *West v. Macht*, 197 F.3d 1185, 1188 (7th Cir. 1999).

Nor are we the only circuit to riddle our doctrine with exceptions to the purported nonfinality of voluntary dismissals without prejudice. Many circuits, for example, assess the likelihood that the plaintiff will relitigate dismissed claims. *See, e.g., Spring Creek Expl. & Prod. Co., LLC v. Hess Bakken Inv., II, LLC*, 887 F.3d 1003, 1015–16 (10th Cir. 2018). In other circuits, this plaintiff can secure **[—30—]** appellate jurisdiction by recanting before the appellate panel any intention of pursuing the voluntarily dismissed claims. *See, e.g., Jewish People for the Betterment of Westhampton Beach v. Vill. of Westhampton Beach*, 778 F.3d 390, 394 (2d Cir. 2015). The plaintiff will receive a particularly good deal in the Third Circuit, which requires him to renounce pursuing the dismissed claims only in the same district court. *See Doe v. Hesketh*, 828 F.3d 159, 165 (3d Cir. 2016). The First Circuit will hear an appeal if he "unequivocally" reserved the right to appeal in the district court, *see Scanlon v. M.V. SUPER SERVANT 3*, 429 F.3d 6, 8 (1st Cir. 2005) (internal quotation marks omitted), while the Federal and Ninth Circuits will reach the merits if he persuades them that he acted in good faith and did not intend to manufacture appellate jurisdiction **{-1237-}** with the voluntary dismissal, *see Doe v. United States*, 513 F.3d 1348, 1353–54 (Fed. Cir. 2008); *James v. Price Stern Sloan, Inc.*, 283 F.3d 1064, 1070 (9th Cir. 2002). But the plaintiff should take the opposite approach if he finds himself in the Eighth Circuit, which has held that finality exists when the plaintiff tries to manufacture jurisdiction—that is, if the plaintiff voluntarily dismissed his claims without prejudice to "expedite appellate review" of other issues. *Helm Fin. Corp. v. MNVA R.R., Inc.*, 212 F.3d 1076, 1080 (8th Cir. 2000).

In the light of the volatility Rule 41(a) brings to appellate jurisdiction, district courts faced with voluntary-dismissal motions would act well within their **[—31—]** discretion to redirect litigants to other avenues to appeal. *See McCants v. Ford Motor Co., Inc.*, 781 F.2d 855, 857 (11th Cir. 1986) ("Dismissal on motion of the plaintiff pursuant to Rule 41(a)(2) is within the sound discretion of the district court, and its order may be reviewed only for an abuse of discretion."). The Federal Rules of Civil Procedure provide litigants with better options to secure an appeal.

For example, district courts can designate decisions on the merits as final under Rule 54(b). *See* Fed. R. Civ. P. 54(b) (allowing district courts to "direct entry of a final judgment as to one or more, but fewer than all, claims or parties" if they find that "there is no just reason for delay"). In this appeal, such a designation would have obviated any question about whether we could reach the merits. *See, e.g.*, *Perry*, 891 F.3d at 958 ("[I]t is likely that a plaintiff would have little trouble [satisfying Rule 54(b)] where . . . the nucleus of her multi-claim and multi-party suit has been destroyed and she is now faced with committing the time and expense of trying only one claim against only one defendant.").

Alternatively, district courts may sever a party's remaining claims. *See* Fed. R. Civ. P. 21 ("The court may . . . sever any claim against a party."). The severed claims would "proceed[] as a discrete suit and result[] in [their] own final judgment from which an appeal may be taken." *Hofmann v. De Marchena Kaluche & Asociados*, 642 F.3d 995, 998 (11th Cir. 2011). As with Rule 54(b), Rule 21 can form the basis of an appeal. *See, e.g.*, *Estate of Amergi ex rel. Amergi v.* **[—32—]** *Palestinian Auth.*, 611 F.3d 1350, 1367 (11th Cir. 2010) ("[I]t was no abuse of discretion to sever the claims so that Saperstein could proceed to trial on his FTA claim and that the Amergis could take an immediate appeal for the dismissal of their claims."). Here, the Corleys moved to sever their claims before they sought a voluntary dismissal without prejudice, but the district court denied their motion without explanation.

Still other possibilities remain open to explore. For example, a district court could grant leave to amend a complaint to drop lingering claims. *See* Fed. R. Civ. P. 15(a)(2) (empowering district courts to "freely give leave [to amend] when justice so requires"); *see also Nat'l Broiler Mktg. Ass'n v. United States*, 436 U.S. 816, 819 n.5 (1978); *Klay v. United Healthgroup, Inc.*, 376 F.3d 1092, 1106 (11th Cir. 2004). Or, if needed, a district court could drop parties. *See* Fed. R. Civ. P. 21 ("On motion . . . the court may at any time, on just terms, add or drop a party."); *see also Lampliter Dinner Theater, Inc. v. Liberty Mut. Ins. Co.*, 792 F.2d 1036, 1045–46 (11th Cir. 1986) (stressing the "great discretion" district courts have when using Rule 21 to drop a party).

District courts should consider the availability of these options when deciding whether to grant a voluntary dismissal without prejudice under Rule 41(a)(2). To **{-1238-}** be sure, the panel opinion paves the way for litigants to continue using Rule 41(a) to secure appellate review, but this result may not be permanent. Our **[—33—]** decision is largely grounded on the force of precedent, and an en banc court would have colorable arguments to reconsider our approach. *See, e.g.*, *Williams*, 958 F.3d at 362 (Oldham, J., dissenting) (arguing that litigants lack standing to appeal from a voluntary dismissal without prejudice because "a Rule 41(a) dismissal represents a voluntary abandonment of the entire action"). And in the light of the chaos both within and among the circuits, the Supreme Court might also intervene.

I express no opinion on the need for such a shift, much less on the merits of any future dispute over our appellate jurisdiction. Regardless of these issues, litigants have a number of more reliable tools to use when seeking appeals. They should look first to them before resorting to Rule 41(a).

United States Court of Appeals for the Eleventh Circuit

No. 19-10371

HIGGS
vs.
COSTA CROCIERE S.P.A. CO.

Appeal from the United States District Court for the Southern District of Florida

Decided: August 14, 2020

Citation: 969 F.3d 1295, 8 Adm. R. 497 (11th Cir. 2020).

Before **WILSON**, **MARCUS**, and **BUSH**,* Circuit Judges.

*Honorable John Kenneth Bush, United States Circuit Judge for the Sixth Circuit, sitting by designation.

[—2—] **{-1299-}** **MARCUS**, Circuit Judge:

On Christmas Eve, 2014, Joyce Higgs tripped over a bucket in a dining area of the cruise ship *Costa Luminosa* and sustained serious injuries to her left shoulder. She sued the cruise company, defendant Costa Crociere ("Costa"), for negligently placing the bucket behind a corner in a highly-trafficked area, and on September 27, 2018, a jury returned a verdict in her favor for over $1 million.

Costa challenges that verdict, arguing that the district court should have granted it judgment as a matter of law because Higgs failed to show that the cruise ship had notice of the hazard posed by the bucket. In the alternative, Costa claims that it is entitled to a new trial because the district court improperly addressed discovery disputes between the parties, unfairly prejudicing it at trial. After careful review, and with the benefit of oral argument, we find these arguments unpersuasive and affirm the verdict in Higgs's favor.

The more difficult question comes to us as a cross-appeal. Specifically, Higgs argues that the district court erred in reducing the jury's award of compensatory damages for past medical expenses from the amount the jury found to be reasonable—and which closely approximated the amount billed by Higgs's healthcare providers (roughly $61,000)—to the much lower amount actually paid in satisfaction of those charges by her and her insurer (some $16,000). This claim raises a question of first impression under maritime law. We hold that the **[—3—]** appropriate measure of medical damages in a maritime tort case is that reasonable value determined by the jury upon consideration of any relevant evidence, including the amount billed, the amount paid, and any expert testimony and other relevant evidence the parties may offer. Because the district court improperly reduced Higgs's damages by applying a bright-line rule that would categorically limit medical damages to the **{-1300-}** amount actually paid by an insurer, we vacate the district court's reduction of the medical damages award and remand for entry of judgment in the amount the jury found to be reasonable.

I.

On the morning of December 24, 2014, Joyce Higgs was on the fourth day of a Caribbean cruise with her family, including her daughter, son-in-law, and grandson. Higgs and her daughter, Christina Bartolo, were the first out of their rooms that morning. They went to the ship's breakfast buffet, where Higgs went to pick up food while Christina saved a table. As Higgs was returning from the buffet line and turning left around a busboy station, she was forced to take a step towards the station as diners at a nearby table moved their chairs back to stand. One or two steps around the corner of the station, while walking on a carpeted pathway, Higgs tripped over a cleaning bucket that she had not seen and sustained injuries to her shoulder, fracturing her humerus. She spent the remainder of the cruise bed- **[—4—]** bound, and she has been in and out of the offices of doctors and physical therapists ever since.

Higgs's grandson, Domingo Bartolo Jr., arrived on the scene shortly after the incident. He testified in his deposition, which was played for the jury, that his efforts to photograph the bucket over which his grandmother had tripped were frustrated by a female security officer who was taking photos of her own. Costa disputes this account. It says that the female security officer—Kavita Kamble—investigated the incident but took no contemporaneous photos of the scene. Instead, Costa claims that the only photos of the area were taken the following evening and reflect Kamble's own halfhearted attempt to reconstruct the scene—the photos show the water bucket not behind the corner but in front of it, clearly visible on approach from the buffet. Both parties agree this does not depict the bucket's location when Higgs tripped over it on December 24. Domingo Jr. also testified that he saw Kamble take down the names of eyewitnesses. In the end, Kamble composed an investigation report that blamed Higgs's poor judgment and inattentiveness for the accident.

Higgs filed her complaint against Costa in the United States District Court for the Southern District of Florida, alleging negligence under federal maritime law, on February 11, 2015. Discovery disputes began between the parties the following year. Costa did not disclose Kamble's identity in its initial disclosures, **[—5—]** nor did it turn over the photos it concedes she took. Citing Domingo Jr.'s deposition testimony, Higgs moved to compel production of "contemporaneous photographs of the scene" on January 29, 2016. Costa responded by asserting work product privilege and denying that the photos it had were "contemporaneous"; rather, it stated, they "were taken 1 to 2 days later." A magistrate judge found that Higgs's need for the photos, coupled with the fact that Costa had prevented her from taking her own, were sufficient to overcome any work product privilege. The court ordered Costa to "produce, within three days of this Order, copies of those photographs which were taken on December 24, 2014 and December 25, 2014, and which depict the scene of the incident as it existed on December 24, 2014."

But Costa didn't produce anything in response. Instead, it had Kamble execute an affidavit stating that the only photographs she took did not depict "the scene **{–1301–}** of Mrs. Higgs' incident as it existed on December 24, 2014 at the moment the guest fell," nor were they "designed to depict the scene of Mrs. Higgs' incident." Costa did not reveal this affidavit to anyone else and responded to the judge's order by denying, without elaboration, that it possessed any responsive photographs.

Higgs did not press the matter further, and the case proceeded to trial in March 2016. Costa did not call Kamble as a witness or introduce her photographs **[—6—]** into evidence. At trial, Costa's corporate representative testified that "there should never be a bucket on the carpet" and that the buckets must be "tucked to the [busboy] stations" to minimize the risk of tripping. The jury returned an approximately $1.1 million verdict for Higgs, finding her to be 15% at fault for the accident. Costa appealed, and a panel of this Court reversed and remanded for a new trial, finding that the district court had erred by excluding evidence of Higgs's propensity to fall. *See Higgs v. Costa Crociere S.p.A.*, 720 F. App'x 518, 520 (11th Cir. 2017) (per curiam).

On remand, the discovery disputes came to a head. Costa announced—a little more than one month before the second trial—that it intended to call a new corporate representative and expand the scope of his testimony to cover, among other things, "Costa's investigation following the subject incident" and "any other matter relating to Costa's knowledge or involvement with the facts alleged in the Complaint." Higgs responded with a subpoena for "[a]ny and all internal correspondence concerning the incident in question or any efforts to investigate the incident" and "[a]ll documents regarding Costa's knowledge and/or investigation of the subject incident." Costa refused to comply; thereafter, the district court granted Higgs's emergency motion to compel on August 30, 2018. The court ordered Costa to produce responsive documents or a privilege log by September 7 in anticipation of the deposition of its new corporate representative on September **[—7—]** 10. Costa produced the accident investigation report—revealing Kamble's identity—but did not produce Kamble's photos until September 11, 2018, one day after its corporate representative's deposition.

Incensed, Higgs filed a motion for discovery sanctions, seeking an adverse jury instruction regarding Kamble's identity and her photos. Costa moved *in limine* to preclude Higgs from raising discovery issues before the jury. The district court granted Higgs's sanctions motion and denied Costa's motion *in limine.* It found that Costa had committed "an egregious discovery violation" and adopted an adverse instruction that would permit but not require the jury to infer that earlier production of the photos and Kamble's identity would have been unfavorable to Costa. The adverse instruction read this way:

> You are instructed that the Court has found that the Defendant deliberately concealed from the Plaintiff the name of a witness with direct knowledge and participation in the investigation of this matter, Kavita Kamble. You are also instructed that the Defendant deliberately concealed from the Plaintiff photographs of the scene which were taken within 30 days of the incident, in violation of this Court's order.
>
> You may infer that Kavita Kamble would have offered testimony favorable to the Plaintiff had she been produced. You may also infer that the timely production of the photographs . . . would have been unfavorable to Defendant. **{-1302-}**

Before the trial started, the district court allowed Costa's counsel to voir dire the jury to ensure that the court's adverse instruction would not unduly prejudice Costa. **[—8—]**

At trial, Higgs's counsel argued at length that Costa's concealment of evidence suggested its consciousness of guilt. Costa did not object. Before the case was submitted to the jury, Costa moved for judgment as a matter of law on the ground that Higgs hadn't shown that it had notice of the hazard posed by the bucket. The motion was denied.

The jury returned a verdict for Higgs, awarding $650,000 in past general damages, $500,000 in future general damages, and $61,000 in past medical expenses, all to be discounted by 10% due to Higgs's comparative negligence. The award for past medical expenses roughly matched the amount billed by Higgs's healthcare providers. After briefing, however, the district court reduced the jury's award of medical expenses to $16,326.01, the amount it had determined was actually paid by Higgs and her insurer, United Healthcare, pursuant to United Healthcare's contractual discounts with the providers. The total award amounted to $1,143,061.34, including pre-judgment interest.

Thereafter, Costa renewed its motion for judgment as a matter of law. The district court denied the motion, finding ample evidence from which the jury could have concluded that Costa had notice of the hazard and that its adverse instruction was supported by both Federal Rule of Civil Procedure 37 and its own inherent power because of Costa's bad-faith pattern of discovery violations. This timely appeal followed. **[—9—]**

II.

Costa raises two challenges to the verdict. First, it argues that the district court erred in denying its motion for judgment as a matter of law because Higgs failed to produce evidence establishing that Costa was on notice of the hazard posed by the bucket, as required by maritime tort law. Second, Costa says it is entitled to a new trial because the district court's rulings on the discovery issues made the trial unfair. Specifically, it claims that the court abused its discretion by reading the adverse instruction to the jury. It also asserts that the district court should not have permitted Higgs's counsel to argue that Costa's alleged concealment of evidence suggested that it was liable for the fall.

A.

We review *de novo* a district court's denial of a motion for judgment as a matter of law. *See Doe v. Celebrity Cruises, Inc.*, 394 F.3d 891, 902 (11th Cir. 2004). Judgment as a matter of law is appropriate when "the plaintiff presents no legally sufficient evidentiary basis for a reasonable jury to find for him on a material element of his cause of action." *Pickett v. Tyson Fresh Meats, Inc.*, 420 F.3d 1272, 1278 (11th Cir. 2005). In entertaining a motion for judgment as a matter of law, "the court must draw all reasonable inferences in favor of the non-moving party, and it may not make credibility determinations or weigh the evidence." *Reeves v. Sanderson Plumbing Prods., Inc.*, 530 U.S. 133, 150 (2000). **[—10—]**

Higgs fell on a ship in navigable waters, so maritime law governs her lawsuit. *Kornberg v. Carnival Cruise Lines, Inc.*, 741 F.2d 1332, 1334 (11th Cir. 1984). Maritime law is "a species of judge-made federal common law," **{-1303-}** *Yamaha Motor Corp., U.S.A. v. Calhoun*, 516 U.S. 199, 206 (1996), under which the owner and operator of a ship owes certain duties to the ship's passengers, the breach of which is a "maritime tort," *Kornberg*, 741 F.2d at 1334 (quotation omitted). "A carrier by sea, however, is not liable to passengers as an insurer, but only for its negligence." *Id.* A shipowner's duty in this regard is limited to "exercising reasonable care towards those lawfully aboard the vessel who are not members of the crew." *Chaparro v. Carnival Corp.*, 693 F.3d 1333, 1336 (11th Cir. 2012) (per curiam) (emphasis and quotation omitted).

As we have explained, reasonable care "requires, as a prerequisite to imposing liability, that the carrier have had actual or constructive notice of the risk-creating condition." *Keefe v. Bahama Cruise Line, Inc.*, 867 F.2d 1318, 1322 (11th Cir. 1989) (per curiam). To show notice, it is not enough to demonstrate merely that the defendant negligently created or maintained its premises. *See Everett v. Carnival Cruise Lines*, 912 F.2d 1355, 1358–59 (11th Cir. 1990). Rather, the plaintiff must establish that a cruise line in fact knew or should have known that a particular hazard existed. *Id.* Costa argues that Higgs has not done so. **[—11—]**

We disagree. Higgs introduced sufficient evidence from which the jury could reasonably infer that Costa, through its employees, had actual knowledge of the danger. The evidence showed that a Costa employee placed a bucket—more than one foot tall and filled with dirty water—behind a blind corner in a highly-trafficked breakfast buffet pathway. That this placement would pose a danger of tripping would have been obvious to anyone, including to any employee who knowingly placed the bucket there. Moreover, the evidence was sufficient to allow the jury to infer that Costa was generally aware of the tripping hazard buckets can pose. At least one Costa employee must have actually known both where the bucket had been placed and that it posed a substantial danger in that location. This evidence is more than enough to establish Costa's actual notice of the hazard.

Higgs's daughter, Christina—the only eyewitness to testify at trial—stated that she saw her mother trip over a bucket placed "about 6 inches" around a corner and "about two" of her mother's small steps onto a carpeted area. She further testified that, when she had been in the dining room previously, she noticed Costa employees using buckets to clean the tables and never saw anyone other than Costa employees handling them. Domingo Jr. testified to the same effect. He said that he saw Costa keep buckets "in the areas where people walk through." He also testified that Costa was generally aware of the tripping danger buckets could pose, as there were "yellow caution signs" near some of the buckets in the dining room. **[—12—]** Finally, Higgs herself reported to the jury that after taking two steps around the corner she "knew [her] leg and foot had hit something because [she] started falling forward." She agreed with Christina that the bucket was "within 6 inches" of the corner and that she hadn't seen the bucket because she "was looking straight ahead." From these facts, the jury could reasonably infer that Costa had actual knowledge of the tripping hazard posed by the placement of the bucket on the carpeted pathway.

Moreover, even if this testimony was not sufficient to demonstrate actual knowledge, there was ample evidence from **{-1304-}** which the jury could have concluded that Costa had constructive knowledge (that is, it reasonably should have known) of the danger. Higgs's expert testified that the industry standard is to keep buckets "behind the scenes" because the "biggest concern" is "slip and falls." He further testified that none of the other major cruise companies permitted buckets to be placed in the dining area. Indeed, the testimony of Costa's corporate representative at the first trial, which was read to the jury the second time, conceded this point. The testimony made clear that Costa trained its employees to tuck buckets to busboy stations and that company policy prohibits placing the buckets in carpeted areas. Costa's corporate representative in the second trial disagreed, claiming "there are no rules that say[] where to place the buckets," but **[—13—]** even he admitted that buckets have to be placed "in a visible place and away from escape routes or emergency exits."

On this record, we are satisfied that a reasonable jury could find that Costa had actual or constructive notice that the bucket had been placed in the carpeted pathway, and actual or constructive notice of the danger presented. The district court did not err in denying Costa's motion for judgment as a matter of law.

B.

We review a district court's imposition of a discovery sanction, such as the district court's adverse jury instruction, for abuse of discretion, whether the sanction was imposed pursuant to Federal Rule of Civil Procedure 37 or the court's inherent power. *See Amlong & Amlong, P.A. v. Denny's, Inc.*, 500 F.3d 1230, 1237 (11th Cir. 2007) (inherent power); *Serra Chevrolet, Inc. v. Gen. Motors Corp.*, 446 F.3d 1137, 1146–47 (11th Cir. 2006) (Rule 37). Thus, we can only reverse discovery sanctions and grant a new trial if the court "made a clear error of judgment" or "applied the wrong legal standard." *Amlong & Amlong*, 500 F.3d at 1238 (quotation omitted). Costa argues that the district court committed a clear error of judgment by misinterpreting its good-faith efforts to comply with its discovery obligations. Again, we are unpersuaded.

Federal Rule of Civil Procedure 37(b) empowers a district court to issue sanctions, including providing a jury with adverse instructions, if a party "fails to **[—14—]** obey an order or to provide or permit discovery." *See* Fed. R. Civ. P. 37(b)(2)(A). Moreover, the trial courts of the United States have the inherent authority to issue sanctions as a punishment for bad-faith behavior in the proceedings before them. *See Chambers v. NASCO, Inc.*, 501 U.S. 32, 50 (1991). Unlike sanctions short of dismissal under Rule 37, which do not require a finding of bad faith, *see BankAtlantic v. Blythe Eastman Paine Webber, Inc.*, 12 F.3d 1045, 1049 (11th Cir. 1994), the "key to unlocking a court's inherent power is a finding of bad faith," *Purchasing Power, LLC v. Bluestem Brands, Inc.*, 851 F.3d 1218, 1223 (11th Cir. 2017). "The standard is a subjective standard with a narrow exception for conduct tantamount to bad faith." *Id.*

The district court found that Costa had engaged in a bad-faith pattern of discovery violations designed to conceal important evidence from Higgs. It based this finding on three incidents: (1) Costa's omission of Kavita Kamble's identity in its initial disclosures; (2) its non-compliance with the magistrate judge's order mandating **{–1305–}** the production of "copies of those photographs which were taken on December 24, 2014 and December 25, 2014, and which depict the scene of the incident as it existed on December 24, 2014"; and (3) its non-compliance with the district court's August 30, 2018 order requiring production of all documents related to Costa's investigation of the incident. The district court reasonably **[—15—]** concluded that Costa had acted in bad faith, and it granted Higgs a reasonable remedy.

The most serious violation was Costa's concealment of the identity of Kavita Kamble. Indeed, because Costa concealed her identity throughout the first trial and disclosed it only two weeks before the second, Higgs has never had the opportunity to depose her, and we still do not know what she might have said. As the Costa employee who conducted the company's initial investigation of the incident, Kamble's identity should have been revealed in the company's initial disclosures. Federal Rule of

Civil Procedure 26 requires a party, "without awaiting a discovery request," to disclose the identity "of each individual likely to have discoverable information" that "the disclosing party may use to support its claims or defenses." Fed. R. Civ. P. 26(a)(1)(A)(i).[1] Moreover, a party must supplement **[—16—]** that disclosure "in a timely manner if the party learns that in some material respect the disclosure" is "incomplete or incorrect." Fed. R. Civ. P. 26(e)(1)(A).

Kamble was obviously "likely to have discoverable information," but Costa claims it never intended to "use" it because it was not planning to call Kamble to testify at trial. This exceedingly narrow understanding of its disclosure obligations is at war with the spirit of openness and fair play the discovery rules embrace. *See, e.g., United States v. Procter & Gamble Co.*, 356 U.S. 677, 682 (1958) (the purpose of the broad discovery rules is to "make a trial less a game of blind man's bluff and more a fair contest with the basic issues and facts disclosed to the fullest practicable extent"). Rule 26 of the Federal Rules of Civil Procedure makes it abundantly clear that a party's discovery obligations extend far beyond disclosure of the identities of witnesses it intends to call at trial. *See* Fed. R. Civ. P. 26(a)(1) advisory committee's note to 2000 amendment ("'Use' includes any use at a pretrial conference, to support a motion, or at trial. The disclosure obligation is also triggered by intended use in discovery, apart from use to respond to a discovery request . . . ."). **[—17—]**

Moreover, at a minimum, Kamble's identity should have been disclosed pursuant to **{-1306-}** Rule 26(a) and (e) as soon as Costa announced that its corporate representative's testimony would cover "Costa's investigation following the subject incident" in August 2018. At that point, Costa announced its intent to use information it could only have received from Kamble. Yet it still only disclosed her identity in response to a court order, weeks later.

The two other discovery violations concerned Costa's refusal to turn over the photographs taken by Kamble. In February 2016, the magistrate judge ordered Costa to turn over "copies of those photographs which were taken on December 24, 2014 and December 25, 2014, and which depict the scene of the incident as it existed on December 24, 2014." Costa turned nothing over, claiming that it had no responsive photos after Kamble executed an affidavit, which it also did not reveal, to the effect that the only photos she took did not depict the scene at the moment Higgs fell. Years later and only a few weeks before the second trial, the district court ordered Costa to produce "[a]ll documents regarding Costa's knowledge and/or investigation of the subject incident," or a privilege log. Costa still did not specifically acknowledge the existence of the photographs until after the deadline set by the court, and after the deposition of its corporate representative.

Costa argues that it did not deliberately avoid disclosing the photographs. It says the

---

[1] That provision provides:

> Except as exempted by Rule 26(a)(1)(B) or as otherwise stipulated or ordered by the court, a party must, without awaiting a discovery request, provide to the other parties . . . the name and, if known, the address and telephone number of each individual likely to have discoverable information—along with the subjects of that information—that the disclosing party may use to support its claims or defenses, unless the use would be solely for impeachment.

Fed. R. Civ. P. 26(a)(1)(A)(i). Further, the Rules provide:

> A party who has made a disclosure under Rule 26(a)—or who has responded to an interrogatory, request for production, or request for admission—must supplement or correct its disclosure or response . . . in a timely manner if the party learns that in some material respect the disclosure or response is incomplete or incorrect, and if the additional or **[—16—]** corrective information has not otherwise been made known to the other parties during the discovery process or in writing; or . . . as ordered by the court.

Fed. R. Civ. P. 26(e)(1).

magistrate judge's order did not cover the photographs, since they did not **[—18—]** depict the scene of the incident "as it existed on December 24, 2014." This argument is too clever by half. For starters, Costa's much-too-literal interpretation of the magistrate judge's order is incorrect. That order contemplated production of photographs taken on "December 24, 2014 *and* December 25, 2014." A photograph taken on December 25 cannot literally depict the scene as it existed on December 24. The court's order is better understood as capturing photographs which roughly depict, or were intended to depict, the scene as it existed when Higgs tripped. Kamble's photographs fit that bill perfectly. That Kamble swears in her affidavit that the photographs do not depict the scene "at the moment the guest fell"—language which appears nowhere in the magistrate judge's order—is of little moment. Under Costa's interpretation, it would have been required to disclose only those photographs coincidentally taken just at the moment Higgs fell to the ground. That could not possibly be what the judge's order meant.

Moreover, if Costa genuinely believed in good faith that the photographs it had did not fall within the order it could and should have said so before now. It could have explained to the magistrate court or, for that matter, to the district court why it believed its photos were not responsive. It could have produced Kamble's affidavit, or it could have offered to produce the photos *in camera*. It did none of these things. It simply denied that it had any responsive photos. This is not the behavior of a party acting in good faith. **[—19—]**

Finally, the sanction the district court chose to apply—a permissive adverse-inference instruction—was among the most restrained in its arsenal. The district court also permitted Costa's counsel to voir dire the jurors to ensure they understood the instruction. The court instructed the jury that it had found that Costa violated court orders related to discovery and that the jury *could*, but was not required to infer that earlier disclosure of the information would have been unfavorable to Costa. But the district court could have **{-1307-}** gone further still: it could have "direct[ed] that the matters . . . be taken as established for purposes of the action" or it could even have "prohibit[ed] the disobedient party from supporting or opposing designated claims or defenses." Fed. R. Civ. P. 37(b)(2)(A)(i), (ii). In short, the district court did not abuse its considerable discretion in sanctioning Costa's conduct with a permissive adverse-inference instruction. Because the instruction was not an abuse of discretion, a new trial is not warranted on this basis.

C.

Next, Costa urges us to grant a new trial because the statements made by Higgs's counsel accusing Costa of concealing evidence unduly prejudiced it and encouraged the jury to resolve the case on an impermissible basis. Higgs's counsel, indeed, made much of Costa's pre-trial litigation conduct and the district court's adverse-inference instruction during his opening statement and closing **[—20—]** argument. Counsel argued that "concealment" was a theme in the case; that Costa "concealed for years photographs of the scene of the accident which would have showed us [the bucket was] exactly where Mrs. Higgs said it was"; and that Costa "intended to hide evidence" and "violate Court orders" as "part of a scheme and a plan to prejudice this case," as found by "the man in the black robe, nominated by the President of the United States and appointed by the United States Senate to sit as a federal district court judge."

But Costa did not object to any of those statements when they were made, and so our review is only for plain error.[2] *See United States v. Pielago*, 135 F.3d 703, 707 (11th Cir. 1998). "Under the plain error standard, before

[2] Costa argues our review should be for abuse of discretion, since the district court's order denying Costa's motion *in limine* implicitly authorized counsel's statements. *See Kropilak v. 21st Century Ins. Co.*, 806 F.3d 1062, 1067 (11th Cir. 2015). We disagree. It is well established that "'the overruling of a motion in limine does not suffice' for preservation of an objection on appeal." *United States v. Brown*, 665 F.3d 1239, 1247 (11th Cir. 2011) (per curiam) (quoting *United States v. Khoury*, 901 F.2d 948, 966 (11th Cir. 1990)). And where a party fails to renew its objection at trial, our review is only for plain error. *Id.*

an appellate court can correct an error not raised at trial, there must be (1) error, (2) that is plain, and (3) that affects substantial rights. If all three conditions are met, an appellate court may then exercise its discretion to notice a forfeited error, but only if (4) the error seriously affects the fairness, integrity, or public reputation of judicial proceedings." *United States v. Smith*, 459 F.3d 1276, 1283 (11th Cir. 2006) (quotation omitted). Because the interests at stake are less acute than in the **[—21—]** criminal context, "a finding of plain error is seldom justified in reviewing argument of counsel in a civil case." *Oxford Furniture Cos. v. Drexel Heritage Furnishings, Inc.*, 984 F.2d 1118, 1128 (11th Cir. 1993) (quotation omitted). To warrant reversal, an impermissible argument must "gravely" impair the "calm and dispassionate consideration of the case by the jury." *BankAtlantic*, 955 F.2d at 1474 (quotation omitted).

Those conditions are not met here. The statements to which Costa now objects—suggesting that it still had not turned over all of its photographs, that it failed to disclose the identity of Kamble because it knew her testimony would be unfavorable, and that Kamble knew the identities of eyewitnesses—all had a basis in evidence. That means they cannot clear the high bar required to demonstrate plain error in a **{-1308-}** civil case. *See Oxford Furniture*, 984 F.2d at 1129 (finding no plain error even where counsel in closing arguments made statements "for which there was no supporting evidence, outright misstatements of the evidence, [and] expressions of counsel's personal opinions"). Moreover, the district court repeatedly instructed the jury that statements by counsel are not evidence. *Cf. United States v. Lopez*, 590 F.3d 1238, 1256 (11th Cir. 2009) (explaining that, where the district court instructs the jury that counsel's statements are not evidence, "we will reverse only if the [statement] is so prejudicial as to be incurable"). Finally, Costa contemporaneously objected on other grounds to some **[—22—]** of the statements it now claims were prejudicial, and the district court sustained those objections. Thus, even if permitting these statements was error at all, it was not plain, nor did it affect the fairness, integrity, or public reputation of the court.

III.

Finally, we come to the matter of damages. In her cross-appeal, Higgs raises an important issue of first impression for this Court—how to calculate past medical expense damages in a maritime tort action where, as has become common, there is a dramatic disparity between the amount a healthcare provider bills a plaintiff for treatment and the amount her insurer actually pays the provider in satisfaction. This question has divided district courts in the Southern District of Florida. *Compare Bonnell v. Carnival Corp.*, No. 13-CV-22265, 2015 WL 12712609, at *3 (S.D. Fla. Jan. 20, 2015) (granting motion *in limine* to exclude evidence of the amount actually paid), *with Gharfeh v. Carnival Corp.*, No. 17-20499-CIV, 2019 WL 186864, at *6 (S.D. Fla. Jan. 14, 2019) (fixing the plaintiff's recovery at the amount actually paid as a matter of law).

Today, we adopt the rule that best reflects the idiosyncratic realities of the healthcare market, avoids reliance on arbitrary factors unrelated to the harm suffered by the plaintiff, and affirms our confidence in juries to resolve challenging questions of fact. We hold that the appropriate measure of medical damages is a reasonable value determined by the jury upon consideration of all relevant **[—23—]** evidence. Both the amount *billed* by healthcare providers and the amount *paid* by insurers are admissible as relevant to the question of fixing reasonable value. Because the district court erroneously reduced the jury's award of medical damages to Higgs under a *per se* rule that would cap the amount of damages at the amount paid, we reverse.

A.

After her injury at sea, Joyce Higgs was in and out of the offices of doctors and physical therapists for years. Based on the bills introduced into evidence, these healthcare providers billed her, in total, $60,944.11. But Higgs was responsible for making only her copayment—a small fraction of this amount. She has a Medicare Advantage plan with

United Healthcare, paid for by her pension from the public schools of Georgia, for which premiums are deducted from her retirement pay. United Healthcare overwhelmingly bore the costs of Higgs's treatment. But it didn't pay the $60,944.11 total either—no one did. According to the billing statements offered to the jury, Higgs paid $350 in copays. The bills reflect an outstanding balance of $2,794.70. United Healthcare was responsible for the remaining $57,799.41. But it didn't even pay that **{-1309-}** amount. Instead, pursuant to the generally applicable contract United Healthcare has with Higgs's medical **[—24—]** providers, the bills reflect that it paid only $12,313.67 in total in satisfaction of the charges, and the healthcare providers "wrote off" the remaining $45,485.74.[3]

This fact pattern—in which a medical provider ostensibly bills a certain amount to an insurer, but a preexisting contract between the two requires only a fraction of that amount to be paid—has become very common in the healthcare market. Many insurers have longstanding contracts with healthcare providers to settle bills at steep discounts from the amounts nominally charged for the treatment of insureds. This can result in, as here, a dramatic disparity between the amount billed and the amount paid for a plaintiff's medical treatment. Because this market structure may obscure the real value of medical services, courts have struggled to square tort law with the realities of modern healthcare finance.

In this case, the district court permitted Higgs to introduce into evidence unredacted billing records from her healthcare providers. Those records depict the total amount billed, the smaller amount paid by United Healthcare, and the amount written off. Accompanying these records were attestations that the amounts billed **[—25—]** "represent the necessary and reasonable expenses for the services provided to Joyce Higgs." After the close of evidence, the district court charged the jury to find the "reasonable value or expense of medical care and treatment necessarily or reasonably obtained by Mrs. Higgs in the past."[4] Based on its review of all of the evidence extant, the jury determined that the reasonable value of past medical expenses was $61,000.

After the verdict, however, Costa persuaded the district court to reduce the jury's award to the amount actually paid by Higgs and United Healthcare—approximately $16,000—on the theory that a plaintiff's recovery, as a matter of law, is limited to the amount paid for her medical treatment. Many district courts in the Southern District of Florida have adopted this rule in maritime tort cases. *See, e.g., Gharfeh*, 2019 WL 186864, at *6 (joining "*myriad* Southern District of Florida cases (most of them within the past three years)" and holding that "a plaintiff would obtain an improper windfall if he or she were permitted to recover damages for the billed-but-not-paid amount or to recover **{-1310-}** for bills that were written **[—26—]** off" (emphasis in original)); *Diczok v. Celebrity Cruises, Inc.*, No. 16-21011-CIV, 2017 WL 3206327, at *3 (S.D. Fla. July 26, 2017); *Smith v. Royal Caribbean Cruises, Ltd.*, No.

---

[3] These figures are based on the medical records that were admitted into evidence and considered by the jury in the second trial. The record indicates, however, that these were not the only medical bills Higgs in fact received and which were produced in discovery. In calculating the total amount paid by Higgs and her insurer, for the purpose of reducing her recovery to that amount, the district court relied on all the bills produced in discovery, not only those that were offered to the jury. Had the district court considered only the bills presented to the jury during the second trial, the corresponding figure would have been $15,458.37, not $16,326.01. Because we hold that it was error for the district court to reduce Higgs's recovery at all, we need not consider whether it reduced the recovery in an appropriate way.

[4] The district court's instruction read this way:

> You shall consider the . . . . reasonable value or expense of medical care and treatment necessarily or reasonably obtained by Mrs. Higgs in the past.
>
> You should not reduce the amount of compensation for past medical care to which Mrs. Higgs is otherwise entitled, on account of any payments made by health insurance, or by Medicare, or by any other source.

13-20697-Civ., 2014 WL 5312534, at *3 (S.D. Fla. Oct. 10, 2014).

Other district courts, however, have adopted the opposite rule—either fixing a plaintiff's recovery at the amount billed or excluding evidence of the amount paid. *See Milbrath v. NCL Bah., Ltd.*, No. 1:17-cv-22071, 2018 WL 2036081, at *5 (S.D. Fla. Feb. 28, 2018) ("A tortfeasor should not be able to escape its compensation duty through a reduction in its liability payment by a plaintiff who happens to have his or her medical expenses written off; this would reduce the deterrent effect of damages on the tortfeasor."); *Bonnell*, 2015 WL 12712609, at *3; *Jones v. Carnival Corp.*, No. 04-20407-CIV, 2006 WL 8209625, at *2 (S.D. Fla. Jan. 24, 2006).

The controversy surrounding this damages question is limited neither to the Southern District of Florida nor to maritime law—courts around the country have struggled to calculate medical damages in tort cases when medical bills overstate expenses. *See, e.g., Deperrodil v. Bozovic Marine, Inc.*, 842 F.3d 352, 360, 4 Adm. R. 308, 312 (5th Cir. 2016) ("State laws differ as to their approach to written-off expenses in tort cases; within our circuit alone, three different rules prevail."); *see also* Jacob A. Stein, 2 Stein on Personal Injury Damages Treatise § 7:36 (3d ed.) (noting that **[—27—]** "there is no consensus on the appropriate rule among the few courts that have reached the question").

B.

The resolution of this question turns on the construction of a principle of tort law known as the collateral source rule. The collateral source rule is both a substantive principle of damages and an evidentiary rule. In its substantive role, the collateral source rule provides that a plaintiff is entitled to recover the full value of the damages caused by a tortfeasor, without offset for any amounts received in compensation for the injury from a third party (like an insurance company or a family member). *See Bourque v. Diamond M. Drilling Co.*, 623 F.2d 351, 354 (5th Cir. 1980);[5] Restatement (Second) of Torts § 920A(2) ("Payments made to or benefits conferred on the injured party from other sources are not credited against the tortfeasor's liability, although they cover all or a part of the harm for which the tortfeasor is liable."). In its evidentiary role, the collateral source rule bars the admission of evidence of payments made by third parties. *Bourque*, 623 F.2d at 354 ("[T]he rule prohibits the introduction of evidence offered to show that [a plaintiff] already has been compensated for his injuries."). **[—28—]**

The collateral source rule is thus an exception to the basic tort principle that damages are designed to make the plaintiff whole—the rule allows a plaintiff to recover damages for a harm for which she has already been compensated. In fact, it makes her more than whole. 25 C.J.S. *Damages* § 189 ("The collateral-source rule is an exception to the general rule of damages preventing a double recovery by an injured party, or in other words, it is an exception to the general rule that in a tort action, the measure of damages is that that will compensate and make the plaintiff whole."). But the law conceptualizes the collateral source payment as necessarily a **{-1311-}** windfall—after all, a party other than the victim or the alleged tortfeasor has voluntarily chosen to bear the costs of the victim's injury—that is better awarded to the plaintiff than the tortfeasor. *See Sweep v. Lear Jet Corp.*, 412 F.2d 457, 459 (5th Cir. 1969) (summarizing justifications for the collateral source rule). Moreover, the rule is understood to avoid discouraging plaintiffs from prudently paying for insurance by limiting their recoveries, and it deters negligence by punishing tortfeasors for the full amount of their wrongdoing. *Id.*

It is also well established that the collateral source rule—both in its substantive and evidentiary roles—applies to maritime tort cases. *See Bourque*, 623 F.2d at 352, 354. Its proper application to contemporary

[5] In *Bonner v. City of Prichard*, we adopted as binding precedent all decisions of the former Fifth Circuit handed down prior to the close of business on September 30, 1981. 661 F.2d 1206, 1209 (11th Cir. 1981) (en banc).

medical expenses is a vexing question, however. *See McConnell v. Wal-Mart Stores, Inc.*, 995 F. Supp. 2d 1164, 1169 (D. Nev. 2014) ("As controversial as the collateral source rule is, **[—29—]** whether the rule should apply to 'write-downs' is even more so."). It is uncontested that as a substantive, general matter, the collateral source rule applies to the calculation of Higgs's medical damages. That is, Higgs is entitled to recover medical damages over and above the amount she paid out of pocket, even though those costs were settled by her insurer. Both parties agree—as they must—that Higgs is entitled to recover some amount for which United Healthcare was solely responsible. Thus, in some real way, she is *going* to receive a windfall. The question before us is how much, and how that figure should be calculated.

1.

Our guiding principle is that plaintiffs are entitled to recover the reasonable value of treatment for injuries they have sustained, regardless of whether their medical expenses have been paid and by whom. *See* Restatement (Second) of Torts § 924 ("One whose interests of personality have been tortiously invaded is entitled to recover damages for past . . . reasonable medical . . . expenses."); *see also Harrison v. Flota Mercante Grancolombiana, S.A.*, 577 F.2d 968, 977 (5th Cir. 1978) (recognizing that "[g]eneral maritime law incorporates the general law of torts when not inconsistent with the law of admiralty"); *Gorman v. Miller*, 415 F.2d 1137, 1138 (5th Cir. 1969) (per curiam) (affirming award of "usual, reasonable and customary" medical expenses to plaintiff); Restatement (Second) of Torts § 911 cmt. h ("When the plaintiff seeks to recover for expenditures made or **[—30—]** liability incurred to third persons for services rendered, normally the amount recovered is the reasonable value of the services rather than the amount paid or charged."); *id.* § 924 cmt. f ("The value of medical services made necessary by the tort can ordinarily be recovered although they have created no liability or expense to the injured person . . . .").

Because of the way in which healthcare is paid for in the United States, we simply cannot say that the amount healthcare providers charge categorically reflects that reasonable value. As the Supreme Judicial Court of Massachusetts has explained:

> With the increasing role played by public and private health insurers in the American health care delivery system, doctors, hospitals, and other medical care providers have developed charge structures that may have little or no relationship to the reasonable value of the medical services at issue, because the providers ultimately negotiate discounts from the listed charges and are **{–1312–}** reimbursed on the basis of the discounted rates. The only patients actually paying the stated charges are the uninsured, a small fraction of the medical bill payors.

Law v. Griffith, 930 N.E.2d 126, 133 (Mass. 2010); *see also* Mark A. Hall & Carl E. Schneider, *Patients as Consumers: Courts, Contracts, and the New Medical Marketplace*, 106 Mich. L. Rev. 643, 663 (2008) (noting that, over the past decade "markups over costs have more than doubled, from 74% to 164%"); James McGrath, *Overcharging the Uninsured in Hospitals: Shifting a Greater Share of Uncompensated Medical Care Costs to the Federal Government*, 26 Quinnipiac L. **[—31—]** Rev. 173, 185 (2007) (observing that the "nation's health care payment systems" have "evolved into a system where a hospital's list price is relatively meaningless"); George A. Nation III, *Hospitals Use the Pernicious Chargemaster Pricing System to Take Advantage of Accident Victims: Stopping Abusive Hospital Billing*, 66 Drake L. Rev. 645, 652–53 (2018) (noting that healthcare prices "are not set by the hospital to be paid; rather, they are set to be discounted in negotiations with insurance companies and to game the . . . system"). Indeed, many courts around the country in recent years have taken notice of the extent to which medical bills can overestimate the reasonable value of medical services.[6] Thus, categorically adopting the amount billed as the measure of recovery would routinely give plaintiffs unreasonably large damages awards, unjustifiable in law or fact. **[—32—]**

On the other hand, neither could we say that the amount paid—an amount established by broad contracts between insurers and providers, divorced from the treatment of a particular plaintiff—is categorically a better approximation of the reasonable value of a provider's medical services. *See, e.g.*, *Stayton v. Del. Health Corp.*, 117 A.3d 521, 532 (Del. 2015) ("Just as the amounts healthcare providers charge today are not, in any realistic sense, standard or going rates, neither are the amounts paid by particular payers."). Indeed, the amount paid for a plaintiff's treatment varies widely based often on factors entirely unrelated to the services provided, including the relationship between a particular insurer and a particular provider or whether the plaintiff is insured at all. *See, e.g.*, *Law*, 930 N.E.2d at 134 (explaining that "the discount from charges that the provider accepts is likely a function of a variety of factors, including **{–1313–}** the bargaining power of the insurer or, as here, limited by Federal or State law—factors that relate to the injured plaintiff's relationship with a collateral third-party payor and have nothing to do with the tortfeasor").

Many courts have likewise observed the extent to which the amount paid in a particular case is a function of unrelated and largely arbitrary factors.[7] Indeed, **[—33—]** fixing a plaintiff's recovery at the amount paid injects arbitrary variation into the recoveries of similarly situated plaintiffs based on the happenstance of their insurance—precisely the result the collateral source rule, which is based on the premise that plaintiffs who suffer the same injuries should receive the same recovery, is designed to prevent. *Cf.* *Sweep*, 412 F.2d at 459 ("The fact that an injured person receives from a collateral source payments which may have some tendency to mitigate the consequences of the injury which he otherwise would have suffered may not be taken into consideration in assessing the damages or other recovery to which the claimant may be entitled.").

---

[6] *See, e.g.*, *Weston v. AKHappytime, LLC*, 445 P.3d 1015, 1030–31 (Alaska 2019) (Stowers, C.J., dissenting) ("[T]here is nothing reasonable about the intentionally inflated and knowingly fictitious prices charged by the healthcare providers . . . . The amount originally billed by the healthcare providers has no rational relationship to the economic realities of modern healthcare payment practices."); *Kenney v. Liston*, 760 S.E.2d 434, 451 (W. Va. 2014) (Loughry, J., dissenting) ("Given the current complexities of health care pricing structures, it is simply absurd to conclude that the amount billed for a certain procedure reflects the 'reasonable value' of that medical service."); *Howell v. Hamilton Meats & Provisions, Inc.*, 257 P.3d 1130, 1142 (Cal. 2011) ("[M]aking any broad generalization about the relationship between the value or cost of medical services and the amounts providers bill for them—other than that the relationship is not always a close one—would be perilous."); *Martinez v. Milburn Enters., Inc.*, 233 P.3d 205, 223 (Kan. 2010) (identifying the "present tenuous relationship between medical charges and medical costs"); *Leitinger v. DBart, Inc.*, 736 N.W.2d 1, 24 (Wis. 2007) (Roggensack, J., dissenting) ("It has been said that the amount billed for medical expenses has become a fictitious amount.").

[7] *See, e.g.*, *Weston*, 445 P.3d at 1025 (describing "the inherent weakness in relying on the amounts paid as presumptive proof of reasonableness"); *Tri-County Equip. & Leasing, LLC v. Klinke*, 286 P.3d 593, 597 n.6 (Nev. 2012) ("[I]t is apparent that there are numerous reasons for medical provider discounts, including discounts that result when an injured party's insurance company has secured medical provider discounts as part of the health insurance plan."); *Howell*, 257 P.3d at 1144 ("For a given medical service to a given plaintiff . . . the amount of the **[—33—]** negotiated rate differential may be higher or lower than the average discount over the range of services offered."); *Stanley v. Walker*, 906 N.E.2d 852, 857 (Ind. 2009) ("Thus, based on the realities of health care finance, we are unconvinced that the reasonable value of medical services is necessarily represented by either the amount actually paid or the amount stated in the original medical bill."); *Leitinger*, 736 N.W.2d at 18 ("The reimbursement rate of a particular health insurance company generally arises out of a contractual relationship and reflects a multitude of factors related to the relationship of the insurance company and the provider . . . ."); *Radvany v. Davis*, 551 S.E.2d 347, 348 (Va. 2001) ("[N]egotiated amounts . . . do not reflect the 'prevailing cost' of [medical] services to other patients.").

Moreover, fixing recovery rigorously on the amount actually paid would harm insureds of larger insurance plans as opposed to the uninsured and would particularly limit the recoveries of poor and elderly people covered by Medicaid and Medicare. *See Stayton*, 117 A.3d at 532 ("Given the particularly hard bargain that government drives with providers, poor and disabled persons covered by government programs will receive the lowest recovery in litigation."). Thus, we cannot say as a matter of **[—34—]** law that the amount paid is any more likely to reflect reasonable value than the amount billed.

The long and the short of it is that, as the Indiana Supreme Court has observed, the "complexities of health care pricing structures make it difficult to determine whether the amount paid, the amount billed, or an amount in between represents the reasonable value of medical services." *Stanley v. Walker*, 906 N.E.2d 852, 857 (Ind. 2009). In this environment, as we see it, it would be inappropriate to impose a bright-line rule for the calculation of damages. Rather, in the absence of any legislation clarifying this measure of damage, it is wiser to leave the ultimate determination—the reasonable value of medical services received by a particular plaintiff in a particular case—to the jury, upon its consideration of all relevant evidence, notably including the amount billed, the amount paid, and any expert testimony and other relevant evidence the parties **{-1314-}** may offer.[8]

The supreme courts of several states have generally adopted this approach to the calculation of medical expenses in tort cases. *See id.*; *see also Martinez v. Milburn Enters., Inc.*, 233 P.3d 205, 222–23 (Kan. 2010); *Robinson v. Bates*, 857 **[—35—]** N.E.2d 1195, 1200 (Ohio 2006); *Haselden v. Davis*, 579 S.E.2d 293, 294–95 (S.C. 2003). Other jurisdictions have adopted a similar rule in which the jury is charged to determine the reasonable value of medical services and the defendant may "call a representative of the particular medical provider whose bill the defendant wishes to challenge, and to elicit evidence concerning the provider's stated charges and the range of payments that the provider accepts for the particular type or types of services the plaintiff received." *See Law*, 930 N.E.2d at 135–36; *see also Howell v. Hamilton Meats & Provisions, Inc.*, 257 P.3d 1130, 1152 (Cal. 2011) (Klein, J., dissenting) ("[T]he reasonable value of the patient's care is a question for the trier of fact. It may be that the sum the providers accepted in full payment is equivalent to the reasonable value of the care, or it may be that the reasonable value of the care is a higher figure.").

2.

We begin again observing that the collateral source rule plays two roles: a substantive one, which prohibits the reduction of a plaintiff's damages by amounts paid by a third party; and an evidentiary one, which prohibits admission of evidence that a third-party payment was made in compensation of a plaintiff's injuries. *See Bourque*, 623 F.2d at 354. The evidentiary role of the collateral source doctrine acts as a prophylactic, shielding the jury from evidence that is likely to encourage it to violate the substantive role of the rule. *See, e.g., Leitinger* **[—36—]** *v. DBart, Inc.*, 736 N.W.2d 1, 14 (Wis. 2007) (explaining that the evidentiary role of "the collateral source rule protects against the ever-present danger that the jury will misuse evidence of collateral payments to diminish the damage award" (alteration adopted and quotation omitted)). The two principal arguments against the approach we adopt in this case arise from disagreements about the scope of the evidentiary role of the collateral source rule.

First, some jurisdictions conceptualize a healthcare write-off *itself* as a "collateral payment," evidence of which cannot be admitted under the collateral source rule. *Id.* Because introducing a lower amount for which the bills were settled necessarily indicates

8 We note that some state legislatures have modified the scope of the collateral source rule by statute. *See, e.g., Jones v. Carnival Corp.*, No. 04-20407-CIV, 2006 WL 8209625, at *2 (S.D. Fla. Jan. 24, 2006) (noting that "Fla. Stat. § 768.76 . . . abrogates the common law collateral source rule"). No such legislation bears upon the determination of this question in maritime tort law.

that some sort of discount was made, these courts hold that any evidence of the amount paid is categorically inadmissible, even if they also ostensibly charge the jury to find the reasonable value of the medical expenses. *See, e.g., Olariu v. Marrero*, 549 S.E.2d 121, 123 (Ga. Ct. App. 2001) (noting that a prior Georgia case "establishes that a write-off of medical expenses is a collateral source of payment" that was properly excluded).

We do not find persuasive the argument that a contractual discount of medical expenses is properly considered as a payment **{-1315-}** for purposes of the collateral source rule. To do so ignores the reality of the contemporary healthcare market. It is, of course, true that in general a "discharge of a debt is a type of payment." *Jones*, 2006 WL 8209625, at *2. But application of that economic truism in this **[—37—]** context makes little sense where the "debt" only ever exists on paper and no one—not the insurer, not the provider, not the taxpayer, and not the plaintiff—was ever responsible for paying it. In the healthcare market, because the written-off amount was established by preexisting contracts, the healthcare providers could not have collected the amount nominally billed from *anyone, ever*. *See Suhor v. Lagasse*, 770 So. 2d 422, 427 (La. Ct. App. 2000) (characterizing the amount billed as "a non-existent debt"); *see also* John Dewar Gleissner, *Proving Medical Expenses: Time for a Change*, 28 Am. J. Trial Advoc. 649, 656 (2005) (describing medical bills as presenting "an amount that never was and never will be paid"). Indeed, because such a large percentage of medical expenses are paid under contracts that provide for discounts, the contracts themselves play a role in *setting* billed medical expenses by encouraging providers to bill arbitrarily large amounts with the knowledge and expectation that no one will ever be required to pay so high a figure. *See Kenney v. Liston*, 760 S.E.2d 434, 451 (W. Va. 2014) (Loughry, J., dissenting) ("Like retailers who raise the price of their goods by twenty-five percent before having a ten percent off sale, medical providers utilize the same sort of tactic to ensure a profit."). In other words, because the amount billed does not create a debt in any meaningful sense, the write-off is not a reduction of debt in any meaningful sense, and it is not subject to the evidentiary bar of the collateral source rule. **[—38—]**

Moreover, evidence of the amount paid is probative of the reasonable value of medical services in a way that evidence of other kinds of collateral payments is not. If a tortfeasor negligently destroys a car, the fact that the plaintiff's wealthy uncle bought her a replacement does not elucidate the reasonable value of the destroyed car in any way. Not so in the wild world of medical billing, where the jury needs all the help it can get—if, for example, it is standard that bills for a particular medical procedure are settled at a steep discount, the amount billed is unlikely to approximate the reasonable value of the provider's medical services. *Cf. id.* at 451–52 ("What more probative evidence of the reasonable value of the services could there be than the negotiated and paid rate for the services?"); *Scott v. Garfield*, 912 N.E.2d 1000, 1014 (Mass. 2009) (Cordy, J., concurring) ("[T]he plaintiff is only entitled to the reasonable value of his medical expenses, and the price that a medical provider is prepared to accept for the medical services rendered is highly relevant to that determination."). The evidentiary role of the collateral source rule was never intended to shield the jury from highly probative evidence of this kind. *See* Joel K. Jacobsen, *The Collateral Source Rule and the Role of the Jury*, 70 Or. L. Rev. 523, 541 (1991) ("[C]oncealing relevant **[—39—]** information from the jury does not further the legitimate purpose of the collateral source rule.").[9]

---

[9] For similar reasons, we are not persuaded by the argument—made by some courts that conceive of a write-off as a collateral source payment—that the collateral source rule always contemplates windfall and therefore that recovery of the entire amount billed is unobjectionable. *See Acuar v. Letourneau*, 531 S.E.2d 316, 323 (Va. 2000) ("To the extent that [our] result provides a windfall to the injured party, we have previously recognized that consequence and concluded that the victim of the wrong rather than the wrongdoer should receive the windfall."). This argument makes little sense. The collateral source rule necessarily contemplates *some* windfall, but it is agnostic as to *how much*. *See Diczok v. Celebrity Cruises, Inc.*, No. 16-21011-

Indeed, this conclusion—that a write-off of medical expenses is not a collateral **{–1316–}** source payment—appears to be the majority position among the district courts in the Southern District of Florida applying maritime law. *See Gharfeh*, 2019 WL 186864, at *6 ("Those cases, which now appear to generate the majority view in our district, hold that the collateral source rule in admiralty cases is not implicated by discounts or write-offs . . . ."). Though we disagree with the courts that cap a plaintiff's damages, as a matter of law, at the amount paid, we find their reasoning on the evidentiary question persuasive. *See id.* at *7 ("Moreover, prohibiting evidence of the discount or write-off gives the jury a skewed view of the financial reality surrounding the medical bills.").

The second criticism levied at the approach we adopt today is that introducing evidence of the amount paid necessarily injects the fact that the **[—40—]** plaintiff is insured into the trial, which encourages the jury to abandon the substantive aspect of the collateral source rule and award minimal medical expenses. *See, e.g., Leitinger*, 736 N.W.2d at 13 ("If evidence of the collateral source payments were admissible, even for consideration of the reasonable value of the medical treatment rendered, a plaintiff's recovery of medical expenses would be affected by the amount actually paid by a collateral source for medical services."). But to the extent a plaintiff worries she may be prejudiced by the jury's knowledge of the fact that she is insured, the district court may choose to admit into evidence only the total *amount* for which the medical bills were settled, without reference to *who* settled them.[10] *See Stanley*, 906 N.E.2d at 853 ("To the extent the discounted amounts may be introduced without referencing insurance, they may be used to determine the reasonable value of medical services."). In this way, admitting evidence of the paid amount—which could have been paid by the plaintiff (indeed, part of it was), the insurer, or anyone else—does not violate the letter or the spirit of the collateral source rule. It is simply a figure, described as the total actual amount of payment, that provides a benchmark for the jury's **[—41—]** consideration of the reasonable value of a provider's medical services. *See Martinez*, 233 P.3d at 226 ("[I]f the jury hears that '$5,000 has paid this $70,000 bill in full,' then the jury can still reasonably perceive that the plaintiff has paid it herself, *e.g.*, by receiving a cash discount.").

And, in the event that the plaintiff does not object to the admission into evidence of **{–1317–}** the settling party's identity, we trust the jury to follow a court's specific instruction that it may not offset the calculation of medical damages by any amounts paid by third parties. *See, e.g., ML Healthcare Servs., LLC v. Publix Super Markets, Inc.*, 881 F.3d 1293, 1303 (11th Cir. 2018) (finding sufficient a court's jury instruction "not to reduce any damages it might award on account of" a third party's payments, since few "tenets are more fundamental to our jury system than the presumption that juries obey the court's instructions" (quotation omitted)); *see also Marshall v. Lonberger*, 459 U.S. 422, 438 n.6 (1983); *Raulerson v. Wainwright*, 753 F.2d 869, 876 (11th Cir. 1985) (per curiam).[11] **[—42—]**

CIV, 2017 WL 3206327, at *3 (S.D. Fla. July 26, 2017) ("[T]he collateral source doctrine does not govern the *amount* of medical expenses a plaintiff may claim in damages." (emphasis added)). That is, the rule ensures that a plaintiff may recover the full value of the damage caused by the tortfeasor, but it says nothing about the value of that damage.

[10] This did not happen here because Higgs had no objection to the introduction of her medical bills in unredacted form—indeed, she offered the bills into evidence herself. Higgs's counsel conceded that he "couldn't really redact them without just complet[ely] butchering up the bills because the way it was, Medicare was referenced in there and her United Healthcare." The evidentiary role of the collateral source rule is designed to protect plaintiffs from prejudice, and we will not interfere with counsel's judgment that Higgs was unlikely to be prejudiced by acknowledgement of the fact that she was insured.

[11] In addition, we will not indulge the fiction that, in general, it would only be the introduction of evidence of the amount paid that could raise the specter of a plaintiff's health insurance in the jury's mind. That specter is always there. It is a matter of common knowledge that the overwhelming majority of Americans have some form of health insurance. *See Law*, 930 N.E.2d at 133 (observing

Our confidence in juries was vindicated by the events in this case. Because the evidence Higgs offered to prove her medical expenses also showed that most of those expenses were settled by United Healthcare, the district court instructed the jury that it "should not reduce the amount of compensation for past medical care to which Mrs. Higgs is otherwise entitled, on account of any payments made by health insurance, or by Medicare, or by any other source." We know that the jury followed this instruction because it awarded to Higgs the entire amount billed, without any offset for the portions settled by her insurer.

For these reasons, we hold that the appropriate measure of past medical expense damages in a maritime tort case is the amount determined to be reasonable by the jury upon its consideration of all relevant evidence, including the amount billed, the amount paid, and any expert testimony and other relevant evidence the parties may offer. We need not remand for further proceedings because the jury calculated its original damages award in a manner wholly consistent with this rule. In the trial court, Higgs introduced into evidence her unredacted medical bills, which itemized both the amount billed and the amount paid. The district court properly charged the jury to determine the reasonable value of the medical treatment Higgs received. The only evidence the jury heard as to the reasonableness of the charges were attestations accompanying the bills that the amounts billed "represent the necessary and reasonable expenses for the services **[—43—]** provided to Joyce Higgs." But Costa knew that it could introduce evidence of the unreasonableness of the billed amounts. Indeed, at the charge conference after the presentation of the evidence, Costa's counsel told the court it had chosen not to do so because Higgs had the burden of proving "the reasonableness of the bills," and Costa thought she had not met her burden. The jury disagreed, as it was plainly permitted to do.

Simply put, the jury arrived at its initial calculation of medical expenses consistent with the rule we adopt in this case. Only **{–1318–}** the district court's post-trial reduction of damages was error. Thus, we reverse the district court's reduction of the jury's damages award and remand with instructions for it to enter final judgment reinstating the amount of medical expenses found to be reasonable by the jury, discounted by 10% for Higgs's comparative negligence.

Accordingly, we **AFFIRM IN PART, VACATE IN PART** and **REMAND IN PART.**

---

that the uninsured are a "small fraction" of patients); U.S. Census Bureau, Health Insurance Coverage in the United States: 2018 2 (2019) (stating that 91.5% of Americans had health insurance coverage for some or all of 2018); *see also Martinez*, 233 P.3d at 228 (noting that juries "likely infer insurance coverage for defendants and plaintiffs in cases involving motor vehicle accidents" but in such cases "we routinely entrust our juries with . . . determining . . . damage amounts" (quotation marks omitted)).

United States Court of Appeals for the Eleventh Circuit

No. 17-12038

UNITED STATES
vs.
DAVILA-MENDOZA

Appeal from the United States District Court for the Southern District of Florida

Decided: August 26, 2020

Citation: 972 F.3d 1264, 8 Adm. R. 513 (11th Cir. 2020).

Before **PRYOR**, **BRANCH**, and **BOGGS**,* Circuit Judges.

*Honorable Danny J. Boggs, United States Circuit Judge for the Sixth Circuit, sitting by designation.

[—2—] **{-1266-}** **BRANCH**, Circuit Judge: **{-1267-}**

In this case, three foreign nationals in a foreign vessel in the territorial waters of a foreign nation were arrested by the United States Coast Guard with the consent of the foreign country and prosecuted in the United States for drug- **[—3—]** trafficking crimes under the Maritime Drug Law Enforcement Act (MDLEA), 46 U.S.C. §§ 70501–70508. The defendants unsuccessfully moved to dismiss the indictment, in relevant part, on the ground that the MDLEA was unconstitutional as applied to them because Congress lacks the authority to criminalize acts committed in the territorial waters of foreign nations. The defendants ultimately pleaded guilty to the drug-trafficking crimes, but preserved their right to appeal the denial of their motion to dismiss. This appeal followed and presents us with a question of first impression—whether the MDLEA exceeds Congress's authority pursuant to the Constitution's Foreign Commerce Clause or, alternatively, the Necessary and Proper Clause, as applied to the drug-trafficking activities of these defendants in the territorial waters of a consenting foreign country. After careful consideration, and with the benefit of oral argument, we conclude that the MDLEA, as applied to these defendants, exceeds Congress's constitutional authority, and we vacate their convictions.

I. BACKGROUND

The undisputed facts are as follows. On June 4, 2016, Andres Davila-Mendoza, Otmar Gonzalez, Julio Pineda, and a minor were on board a stalled go-fast vessel in the territorial waters of Jamaica. With the permission of the Jamaican government, U.S. Coast Guard officials who had been patrolling the area by air and sea boarded and searched the distressed vessel. They discovered that the **[—4—]** vessel was loaded with 3,500 kilograms of baled marijuana. Pineda told the Coast Guard officials that he was the captain, that he was Nicaraguan, that the vessel was Costa Rican, and that they were traveling from Jamaica to Costa Rica. Another crew member stated that the vessel was overloaded with marijuana and its engines had stopped working. With the further permission of the Jamaican government, the Coast Guard seized the boat occupants and the drugs, and the United States prosecuted the three men.

The three defendants were charged in an indictment with possessing and conspiring to possess with intent to distribute more than 1,000 kilograms of marijuana while on board a vessel, in violation of the MDLEA, 46 U.S.C. §§ 70503(a)(1), 70503(b); 70506(b). That statute provides in relevant part that: "While on board a covered vessel, an individual may not knowingly or intentionally . . . manufacture or distribute, or possess with intent to manufacture or distribute, a controlled substance." 46 U.S.C. § 70503(a)(1). This prohibition "applies even though the act is committed outside the territorial jurisdiction of the United States." *Id.* § 70503(b). For purposes of the MDLEA, a "covered vessel" includes "a vessel subject to the jurisdiction of the United States." *Id.* § 70503(e). And the MDLEA specifically provides that a vessel in the territorial waters of a foreign nation is subject to the jurisdiction of the United States "if the nation consents to the enforcement of United States law by the United States." *Id.* **[—5—]** § 70502(c)(1)(E).[1]

[1] The defendants' boat was a "vessel subject to the jurisdiction of the United States," by statutory definition, because Jamaica consented to the United States Coast Guard's enforcement of

Notably, in enacting the MDLEA, Congress found "that . . . trafficking in controlled substances aboard vessels is a serious international problem, is universally condemned, and presents a **{-1268-}** specific threat to the security and societal well-being of the United States." *Id.* at § 70501.

The defendants moved to dismiss the indictment on the grounds that the application of the MDLEA to them exceeded Congress's power under the Define and Punish Clause, U.S. Const. art. I, § 8, cl. 10. They also objected to the district court's exercise of *in personam* jurisdiction over them as a violation of their due-process rights. The government responded that the extraterritorial application of the MDLEA to the defendants was authorized by the Foreign Commerce Clause, *id.* art. I, § 8, cl. 3, and/or the Necessary and Proper Clause, *id.* art. I, § 8, cl. 18.

The magistrate judge heard oral argument on the issue and recommended that the defendants' motion be denied, finding that Congress had lawfully exercised its power under the Foreign Commerce Clause. The magistrate judge also found that international law provided adequate notice to the defendants, satisfying due process. The defendants filed objections, and the district court affirmed and adopted the report and recommendation of the magistrate judge. **[—6—]**

The defendants pleaded guilty under a conditional plea agreement that preserved their right to appeal the denial of their motion to dismiss the indictment. The district court sentenced each defendant to 59 months of imprisonment to be followed by removal proceedings and 5 years of non-reporting supervised release. The defendants now appeal on that preserved basis, and we consider their appeals together.

American laws in its territorial waters. 46 U.S.C. § 70502(c)(1)(E).

II. STANDARD OF REVIEW

"We review *de novo* the legal question of whether a statute is constitutional." *United States v. Campbell,* 743 F.3d 802, 805, 2 Adm. R. 543, 544 (11th Cir. 2014) (quoting *United States v. Tinoco,* 304 F.3d 1088, 1099 (11th Cir. 2002)).

III. DISCUSSION

The defendant-appellants in this consolidated appeal argue that the MDLEA, as applied to them, exceeds Congress's authority under Article I of the Constitution. The government contends that the MDLEA, as applied to the defendants, was a valid exercise of Congress's power under the Foreign Commerce Clause, or alternatively, under the Necessary and Proper Clause. We address whether Congress has such authority under each Clause in turn.

A. The Foreign Commerce Clause

As an initial matter, the district court correctly recognized that, under our Circuit precedent, the Constitution's Define and Punish Clause does not authorize **[—7—]** the MDLEA's operation in foreign territorial waters. *See United States v. Bellaizac-Hurtado,* 700 F.3d 1245, 1258 (11th Cir. 2012). That tripartite clause grants Congress power to "define and punish Piracies and Felonies committed on the high Seas, and Offenses against the Law of Nations." U.S. Const. art. I, § 8, cl. 10. Because the crimes here were not committed on the high seas,[2] the Piracies and Felonies Clauses do not

[2] The high seas lie beyond any nation's territorial sea and are "international waters not subject to the dominion of any single nation." *United States v. Louisiana,* 394 U.S. 11, 23 (1969). And we have frequently examined and upheld the constitutionality of the application of the MDLEA to conduct that occurred on the high seas. *See, e.g., United States v. Estupinan,* 453 F.3d 1336, 1338–39 (11th Cir. 2006); *United States v. Rendon,* 354 F.3d 1320, 1322–23 (11th Cir. 2003); *Tinoco,* 304 F.3d at 1092–95. But this case presents an altogether different question because the conduct at issue here involves foreign nationals aboard a foreign vessel in the territorial waters of a foreign nation, not the high seas.

apply. And we explained in *Bellaizac-Hurtado* that the use of the term **{-1269-}** "the law of nations" in the Offenses Clause limits its application to those offenses recognized by customary international law. 700 F.3d at 1249–53. Because drug trafficking is not such an offense, *id.* at 1253–57, we held that the MDLEA was unconstitutional under the Offenses Clause as applied to the *Bellaizac-Hurtado* defendants, who had been charged with drug trafficking on board a vessel in the territorial waters of Panama.

But we generally presume statutes to be constitutional. *United States v. Morrison*, 529 U.S. 598, 607 (2000). And our Court has suggested in passing, albeit dicta, that there may exist a different Article I authorization for the MDLEA's operation as applied to conduct that occurs in the territorial waters of a **[—8—]** foreign nation—the Foreign Commerce Clause. *United States v. Baston*, 818 F.3d 651, 667 (11th Cir. 2016) ("If the government had invoked the Foreign Commerce Clause in *Bellaizac-Hurtado*, we might have reached a different result."). The government here has taken us up on that suggestion and argues that the MDLEA as applied to the conduct of these defendants was a valid exercise of Congress's authority pursuant to the Foreign Commerce Clause. Accordingly, the question we must answer is whether the Foreign Commerce Clause authorizes the MDLEA's operation as applied to these defendants.

1. Legal Framework

The Constitution provides that "Congress shall have Power . . . [t]o regulate Commerce with foreign Nations, and among the several States, and with the Indian Tribes." U.S. Const. art. I, § 8, cl. 3. This tripartite clause is commonly known as the Foreign Commerce Clause, the Interstate Commerce Clause, and the Indian Commerce Clause, respectively. "The Commerce Clause emerged as the Framers' response to the central problem giving rise to the Constitution itself: the absence of any federal commerce power under the Articles of Confederation." *Gonzales v. Raich*, 545 U.S. 1, 16 (2005). The Supreme Court first defined the nature of Congress's commerce power in its 1824 decision in *Gibbons v. Ogden*, explaining that:

> [c]ommerce, undoubtedly, is traffic, but it is something more: it is intercourse. It describes the commercial intercourse between nations, **[—9—]** and parts of nations, in all its branches, and is regulated by prescribing rules for carrying on that intercourse. . . . It is the power to regulate; that is, to prescribe the rule by which commerce is to be governed. This power, like all others vested in Congress, is complete in itself, may be exercised to its utmost extent, and acknowledges no limitations, other than are prescribed in the constitution.

22 U.S. 1, 189–90, 196 (1824). Over time, the understanding and meaning of "regulate Commerce," at least in the context of the Interstate Commerce Clause, has expanded and three general categories of regulation have emerged as permissible exercises of Congress's commerce power. *See Raich*, 545 U.S. at 15–17 (discussing historical evolution of commerce power). "First, Congress can regulate the channels of interstate commerce. Second, Congress has authority to regulate and protect the instrumentalities of interstate commerce, and persons or things in interstate commerce. Third, Congress has the power to regulate activities that substantially affect interstate commerce." *Id.* at 16–17 (internal citations omitted).

With regard to the Foreign Commerce Clause, the Supreme Court has described the Foreign Commerce Clause as granting Congress a broad, "exclusive[,] **{-1270-}** and plenary" power to regulate commerce with foreign nations. *See Bd. of Trs. of Univ. of Ill. v. United States*, 289 U.S. 48, 56 (1933). Yet, jurisprudence addressing Congress's positive Foreign Commerce Clause power is sparse. Most of the Supreme Court's Foreign Commerce Clause precedents concern the foreign commerce power only in its negative, or dormant, sense. **[—10—]** Specifically, the dormant foreign commerce power operates to void acts of the states upon foreign commerce because of the Constitution's overriding concern for national uniformity in foreign commerce—even in instances when Congress has not affirmatively acted. *See, e.g.*, *Japan Line, Ltd. v. Cty. of L.A.*, 441 U.S. 434, 448 (1979) (striking down a state tax on imports); *see also Bd. of Trs. of Univ. of Ill.*, 289 U.S. at 57–58 (affirming a U.S. tariff over a state's protest). But the Supreme Court has never clearly articulated the bounds of the positive foreign commerce power.

And we have only one case in which we have addressed Congress's positive foreign commerce power, *Baston*. Specifically, the defendant in *Baston* was "an international sex trafficker" who trafficked women "around the world, from Florida to Australia to the United Arab Emirates." 818 F.3d at 656. Although Baston was a non-citizen, he was arrested at his mother's home in the United States and charged and convicted of violating 18 U.S.C. §§ 1596(a)(2) and 1591, which prohibits sex trafficking by force, fraud, or coercion.[3] *Id.* at 657–59. **[—11—]** Notably, § 1596(a)(2) grants the United States "extra-territorial jurisdiction over" sex trafficking by force, fraud, or coercion that occurs overseas by a person who is "present in the United States."[4]

As relevant background, Congress enacted §§ 1591 and 1596, respectively, as part of the Trafficking Victims Protection Act of 2000 and the Trafficking Victims Protection Reauthorization Act of 2008 (together, the "TVPA"). *Id.* at 666, 668. "The TVPA is part of a comprehensive regulatory scheme," *id.* at 668 (quotation omitted), designed to "combat trafficking in persons . . . to ensure just and effective punishment of traffickers, and to protect their victims," 22 U.S.C. **[—12—]** § 7101. In enacting the TVPA, Congress expressly found that "[t]rafficking in persons is a modern form of slavery," and "is the fastest growing **{–1271–}** source of profits for organized criminal enterprises worldwide. Profits from the trafficking industry contribute to the expansion of organized crime in the United States and worldwide." *Id.* § 7101(b)(1), (8). Further, Congress found that "[t]rafficking in persons substantially affects interstate and foreign commerce" as such trafficking "has an impact on the nationwide employment network and labor market." *Id.* § 7101(b)(12).

On appeal, Baston argued that he could not be ordered to pay restitution for his extraterritorial conduct, and that any holding to the contrary would exceed Congress's authority under Article I of the Constitution. 818 F.3d at 666. Thus, this Court examined

---

[3] 18 U.S.C. § 1591 provides:

(a) Whoever knowingly—

> (1) in or affecting interstate or foreign commerce, or within the special maritime and territorial jurisdiction of the United States, recruits, entices, harbors, transports, provides, obtains, advertises, maintains, patronizes, or solicits by any means a person; or **[—11—]**
>
> (2) benefits, financially or by receiving anything of value, from participation in a venture which has engaged in an act described in violation of paragraph (1),

knowing, or, except where the act constituting the violation of paragraph (1) is advertising, in reckless disregard of the fact, that means of force, threats of force, fraud, coercion described in subsection (e)(2), or any combination of such means will be used to cause the person to engage in a commercial sex act, or that the person has not attained the age of 18 years and will be caused to engage in a commercial sex act, shall be punished as provided in subsection (b).

[4] 18 U.S.C. § 1596(a) provides:

In addition to any domestic or extra-territorial jurisdiction otherwise provided by law, the courts of the United States have extra-territorial jurisdiction over any offense (or any attempt or conspiracy to commit an offense) under section . . . 1591 if—

> (1) an alleged offender is a national of the United States or an alien lawfully admitted for permanent residence (as those terms are defined in section 101 of the Immigration and Nationality Act (8 U.S.C. 1101)); or
>
> (2) an alleged offender is present in the United States, irrespective of the nationality of the alleged offender.

whether § 1596(a)(2), which confers extraterritorial jurisdiction over sex trafficking, was a constitutional exercise of Congress's authority under the Foreign Commerce Clause. *Id.* at 666–69. In addressing this question, we first noted that "nothing in the Foreign Commerce Clause" or in Article I itself "limits Congress's power to enact extraterritorial laws." *Id.* at 667. We then noted that the dormant Foreign Commerce Clause cases provided little insight into the bounds of Congress's positive foreign commerce power other than the suggestion in dicta that the foreign commerce power "may be broader" than the interstate commerce power (the bounds of which have been more thoroughly **[—13—]** explored). *Id.* at 668 (quoting *Atl. Cleaners & Dyers, Inc. v. United States*, 286 U.S. 427, 434 (1932)). Nevertheless, we declined to "demarcate the outer bounds of the Foreign Commerce Clause" and instead "assum[ed], for the sake of argument, that the Foreign Commerce Clause has the same scope as the Interstate Commerce Clause." *Id.*

> In other words, Congress's power under the Foreign Commerce Clause includes at least the power to regulate the "channels" of commerce between the United States and other countries, the "instrumentalities" of commerce between the United States and other countries, and activities that have a "substantial effect" on commerce between the United States and other countries.

Id.

We then concluded that § 1596(a)(2) was a valid exercise of Congress's foreign commerce power "at least as a regulation of activities that have a 'substantial effect' on foreign commerce." 818 F.3d at 668. Citing the congressional findings, we explained that "Congress had a 'rational basis' to conclude that [sex trafficking by force, fraud, or coercion]—even when it occurs exclusively overseas—is 'part of an economic "class of activities" that have a substantial effect on . . . commerce' between the United States and other countries." *Id.* at 668–69.

With *Baston* as our guide in the case at hand, we too, assume, without deciding, that the Foreign Commerce Clause has the same scope as the Interstate Commerce Clause. Under this assumption, the parties agree that, given the unique **[—14—]** facts of this case, if the application of the MDLEA to the defendants' conduct is to pass muster, it will be under the third category of regulated commerce: those activities that have a "substantial effect" on commerce between the United States and foreign nations.

The substantial-effects inquiry is most commonly conducted in the Interstate Commerce Clause context. For instance, in *United States v. Lopez*, 514 U.S. 549 (1995), the Supreme Court was tasked with determining whether the Gun-Free School Zones Act of 1990, which made it a federal offense "for any individual knowingly to possess a firearm at a place that the individual knows, or has reasonable cause to believe, is a school zone[,]" was a valid exercise **{-1272-}** of Congress's authority under the Interstate Commerce Clause. *Id.* at 551 (citing the Gun-Free School Zones Act of 1990, Pub. L. 101-647, § 1702 (1990), *codified at* 18 U.S.C. § 922(q) (1990)). Emphasizing that Congress's constitutionally enumerated powers have "judicially enforceable outer limits," the Court set out to define more clearly the limit on Congress's authority to regulate interstate commerce. *Id.* at 566. The Court acknowledged that, if the statute "[was] to be sustained, it must be under the third category as a regulation of an activity that substantially affects interstate commerce." *Id.* at 559. The Court then explained "[w]here economic activity substantially affects interstate commerce, legislation regulating that activity will be sustained." *Id.* at 560. But the Gun Free School Zones Act was "a **[—15—]** criminal statute that by its terms ha[d] nothing to do with 'commerce' or any sort of economic enterprise[.]" *Id.* at 561. The Court also noted that the statute "contain[ed] no jurisdictional element which would ensure, through case-by-case inquiry, that the firearm possession in question affect[ed] interstate commerce." *Id.* The Court further explained that although Congress is not required to make findings as to the burdens an activity has on interstate commerce and "[w]hether particular operations affect interstate commerce sufficiently to come under the constitutional power of Congress to regulate them is ultimately a judicial rather than a legislative question," it nevertheless would consider any legislative and congressional findings regarding the effect of the activity on interstate commerce as part of its independent inquiry into the constitutionality of the statute under the Commerce Clause. *Id.* at 557 n.2, 562–63 (quoting *Heart of Atlanta Motel, Inc. v. United States*, 379 U.S. 241, 273 (1964) (Black, J., concurring)). However, there were no such findings present in *Lopez* as "[n]either the statute nor its legislative history contain[ed] express congressional findings regarding the effects upon interstate commerce of gun possession in a school zone." *Id.* at 562 (first alteration in original) (quotations omitted). Finally, although the government made attenuated arguments about the substantial effects of gun possession in a local school zone on interstate commerce (*i.e.*, that possession of a firearm in a school zone might lead to violent crime and violent crime affects the economy by driving **[—16—]** up insurance costs and by deterring individuals from traveling to "unsafe areas") the Court rejected those arguments, concluding that such arguments would, logically extended, allow Congress to regulate almost every private activity. *Id.* at 563–64. Consequently, because the text and structure of the Constitution do not allow Congress a "general police power of the sort retained by the States," *id.* at 567, the Court struck down the Act as unconstitutional.

Five years later, in *United States v. Morrison*, 529 U.S. 598 (2000), the Supreme Court was again confronted with the question of whether a particular statute regulating a non-economic activity was a valid exercise of Congress's power under the Interstate Commerce Clause. The statute in question in *Morrison* created a civil right of action against perpetrators of gender-motivated crimes of violence. *Id.* at 601 (citing the Violence Against Women Act of 1994, Pub. L. 103-322, § 40302 (1994), *originally codified at* 42 U.S.C. § 13981 (1994), *now codified at* 34 U.S.C. § 12361). The government sought to sustain the statute "as a regulation of activity that substantially affects interstate commerce." *Id.* at 609. The Court noted that, similar to the **{–1273–}** statute at issue in *Lopez*, the statute in question did not seek to regulate an economic activity and "contain[ed] no jurisdictional element establishing that the federal cause of action is in pursuance of Congress'[s] power to regulate interstate commerce." *Id.* at 613. But, unlike in *Lopez*, in **[—17—]** *Morrison* Congress made express findings that gender-motivated violence affects interstate commerce

> "by deterring potential victims from traveling interstate, from engaging in employment in interstate business, and from transacting with business, and in places involved in interstate commerce; . . . by diminishing national productivity, increasing medical and other costs, and decreasing the supply of and the demand for interstate products."

Id. at 614–15 (quoting H.R. Conf. Rep. No. 103–711, at 385, U.S. Code Cong. & Admin. News 1994, pp. 1803, 1853). However, the Court reiterated that "the existence of congressional findings is not sufficient, by itself, to sustain the constitutionality of Commerce Clause legislation," and Congress's findings as to the *Morrison* statute suffered from the same flaw as the arguments proffered by the government in *Lopez*. *Id.* at 614–15. Specifically, the reasoning of Congress followed "the but-for causal chain from the initial occurrence of violent crime . . . to every attenuated effect upon interstate commerce[,]" which "[i]f accepted . . . would allow Congress to regulate any crime as long as the nationwide, aggregated impact of that crime has substantial effects on employment, production, transit, or consumption." *Id.* at 615. And, again the Court cautioned that such reasoning would allow the vast regulation of crime, family law, and other areas traditionally reserved to the states. *Id.* at 615–16. Accordingly, the Court concluded that Congress may not "regulate noneconomic, violent criminal conduct based solely on that conduct's aggregate effect on interstate commerce." *Id.* at 617. **[—18—]**

The Supreme Court applied the substantial-effects test yet again five years later in *Raich* to determine whether the federal Controlled Substances Act ("CSA") was a valid exercise of the interstate commerce clause power as applied to prohibit the purely intrastate growth and use of marijuana for medical purposes in California. 545 U.S. at 15. The Court explained that although the respondents in *Raich* were cultivating the marijuana for local consumption, it was "a fungible commodity for which there is an established, albeit illegal, interstate market." *Id.* at 18. And "a primary purpose of the CSA is to control the supply and demand of controlled substances in both lawful and unlawful drug markets." *Id.* at 19. Thus, "[g]iven the enforcement difficulties that attend distinguishing between marijuana cultivated locally and marijuana grown elsewhere, and concerns about diversion [of the locally grown marijuana] into illicit channels," the Court concluded that Congress had a rational basis for believing that purely intrastate marijuana production would, in the aggregate, have a substantial effect on interstate commerce. *Id.* at 22 (internal citation omitted). Accordingly, the Court upheld the constitutionality of the CSA, as applied to the *Raich* respondents, noting that "case law firmly establishes Congress'[s] power to regulate purely local activities that are part of an economic 'class of activities' that have a substantial effect on interstate commerce," and "the *de minimis* character of individual instances" of regulated conduct did not matter. *Id.* at 17, 22 (quoting *Lopez*, 514 U.S. at 558). **[—19—]**

Notably, in reaching this conclusion, the Court rejected the respondents' argument that the CSA could not "be constitutionally **{-1274-}** applied to their activities because Congress did not make a specific finding that the purely local production of marijuana for medicinal purposes "would substantially affect the larger interstate marijuana market." *Id.* at 21. The Court reiterated that "while we will consider congressional findings in our analysis when they are available, the absence of particularized findings does not call into question Congress'[s] authority to legislate." *Id.* Finally, the Court emphasized that a reviewing court's task under the substantial-effects inquiry is "a modest one. We need not determine whether respondents' activities, taken in the aggregate, substantially affect interstate commerce in fact, but only whether a 'rational basis' exists for so concluding." *Id.* at 22.

2. Application of this framework to the facts of this case

With this framework in mind, we turn to the question of whether the MDLEA as applied to the defendants' conduct in this case is a valid exercise of Congress's authority under the Foreign Commerce Clause to regulate those activities that have a "substantial effect" on the commerce of the United States "with foreign nations." U.S. Const. art. I, § 8, cl. 3. The government maintains the *Baston/Raich* framework requires us to conclude that the application of the **[—20—]** MDLEA to the wholly foreign conduct in this case was a valid exercise of Congress's authority. *Baston*, however, is factually distinguishable.

First, *Baston* involved statutory provisions enacted as part of the TVPA, "a comprehensive regulatory scheme" that included specific congressional findings "that trafficking of persons has an aggregate economic impact on interstate and foreign commerce." *Baston*, 818 F.3d at 668–69 (quoting *United States v. Evans*, 476 F.3d 1176, 1179 (11th Cir. 2007)). Importantly, in applying the substantial-effects test to the extraterritorial conduct at issue in *Baston*, we relied on those congressional findings to determine that "Congress had a 'rational basis' to conclude that such conduct—even when it occurs exclusively overseas—is 'part of an economic "class of activities" that have a substantial effect on . . . commerce' between the United States and other countries." *Id.* at 668 (citing *Raich*, 545 U.S. at 17). Indeed, Congress's findings were the *only* support we cited for this conclusion. *See id.*

Although the government argues that, similar to the TVPA, the MDLEA is a comprehensive regulatory scheme designed to combat a global problem (in this case, drug trafficking), the MDLEA does not contain any congressional findings regarding international drug trafficking's effect on United States commerce "with foreign nations." *See* 46 U.S.C. § 70501. The law mentions only that "trafficking in controlled substances aboard vessels is a serious international problem" and that **[—21—]** it "presents a specific threat to the security and societal well-being of the United States[.]" 46 U.S.C. § 70501. It does not include any findings on the existence or extent of an economic impact, aggregate or otherwise, of the international drug trade on United States commerce with foreign nations. *See id.* Admittedly, such congressional findings are not required nor sufficient to establish substantial effect. *Morrison*, 529 U.S. at 614. Nevertheless, "to the extent that congressional findings would enable us to evaluate the legislative judgment that the [wholly foreign drug trafficking] in question substantially affected [the United States's commerce with foreign nations] . . . they are lacking here." *See Lopez*, 514 U.S. at 563. **{-1275-}**

Second, the statutes at issue in *Baston*, 18 U.S.C. §§ 1591(a) and 1596(a)(2) required both an effect on foreign commerce as an element of the offense and a physical connection to the United States. Specifically, § 1591(a) makes it a crime to, "*in or affecting interstate or foreign commerce*," recruit a person knowing that force, fraud, or coercion "will be used to cause the person to engage in a commercial sex act." 18 U.S.C. § 1591(a) (emphasis added). The MDLEA does not contain a similar "in or affecting interstate or foreign commerce" element. *See* 46 U.S.C. §§ 70502(c), 70503.

Additionally, and more importantly, although not a focal point of the analysis in *Baston* (but certainly a critical factual distinction when compared to the case at hand), under § 1596(a) the United States has jurisdiction over the **[—22—]** extraterritorial sex-trafficking conduct only if the defendant is "a national of the United States," "an alien lawfully admitted for permanent residence," or otherwise "present in the United States, irrespective of the nationality of the alleged offender." *See* 18 U.S.C. § 1596(a). Thus, § 1596 provides a jurisdictional hook that precludes purely foreign activity with no nexus to the United States from being criminalized.[5] In contrast, the MDLEA does not contain a similar jurisdictional hook or nexus to tie wholly foreign extraterritorial conduct to the United States.[6] *See* 46 U.S.C. §§ 70502(c), 70503. In any event, no such jurisdictional hooks are present in this case. **[—23—]**

Furthermore, the facts in *Baston* demonstrated that the defendant's activities were so thoroughly intertwined with the United States's commerce with foreign nations that the issue was not a close call. Baston "resided in Florida, where he rented property,

[5] This distinction means that had the situation in *Baston* in fact been analogous to the facts of this case—if, for example, the defendant had been an Australian who had trafficked women between Australia and New Zealand, and was never present in the United States—the statutes at issue in *Baston*, 18 U.S.C. §§ 1591 and 1596, would not have permitted the defendant's prosecution in the United States.

[6] Our discussion of nexus in the context of the Foreign Commerce Clause does not in any way undercut our holdings that no nexus is necessary where the MDLEA is an exercise of Congress's express authority to define and punish conduct occurring on the high seas pursuant to the Felonies Clause. *See United States v. Campbell*, 743 F.3d 802, 810, 2 Adm. R. 543, 548 (11th Cir. 2014) ("'[W]e have always upheld extraterritorial convictions [for conduct occurring on the high seas] under our drug trafficking laws as an exercise of power under the Felonies Clause.' . . . We also have recognized that the conduct proscribed by the [MDLEA] need not have a nexus to the United States because universal and protective principles support its extraterritorial reach" (first alteration in original) (quoting *Bellaizac-Hurtado*, 700 F.3d at 1257)). Specifically, under the protective principle of international law, Congress "may assert extraterritorial jurisdiction over vessels in the high seas that are engaged in conduct that has a potentially adverse effect and is generally recognized as a crime by nations that have reasonably developed legal systems." *Tinoco*, 304 F.3d at 1108 (quotations omitted). Thus, we have frequently rejected a nexus requirement and upheld the constitutionality of the application of the MDLEA to conduct that occurred on the high seas as a valid exercise of Congress's authority under the Felonies Clause. *See, e.g., Estupinan*, 453 F.3d at 1338–39; *Rendon*, 354 F.3d at 1325.

started businesses, and opened bank accounts," and "portrayed himself as a United States citizen." *Baston*, 818 F.3d at 669. He also "used a Florida driver's license and a United States passport to facilitate his criminal activities." *Id.* at 670. He trafficked a victim "in both the United States and Australia, and when he trafficked her in Australia, he wired the proceeds back to Miami." *Id.* The court described Baston's contacts with the United States as "legion," concluding that he "used this country as a home base and took advantage of its laws; **{-1276-}** he cannot now complain about being subjected to those laws." *Id.* at 669–70. While these facts were discussed in relation to Baston's due-process claim, they nevertheless make clear that Baston could have made no credible argument that his conduct had no effect on United States commerce with foreign nations. In the case at hand, however, the government did not allege that the contraband, the boat, or the defendants had any connection, even a peripheral one, with the United States, when they were seized in the territorial waters of Jamaica. Accordingly, *Baston* is factually distinguishable and is not dispositive of the question of whether the MDLEA as applied to the defendants in this case was a valid exercise of Congress's foreign-commerce power. **[—24—]**

Turning to *Raich*, the government argues that *Raich* reaffirmed that wholly intrastate economic activities could have a substantial effect on interstate commerce and could be regulated by Congress via the Interstate Commerce Clause. Therefore, according to the government, if we logically extend *Raich* to this case, the MDLEA's application to the defendants' extraterritorial conduct is a permissible exercise of Congress's authority under the Foreign Commerce Clause because Congress could rationally conclude that foreign drug trafficking could have a substantial effect on the international drug trade, which has an aggregate economic impact on foreign commerce. However, while *Raich* may serve as a backdrop for our analysis, *Raich* involved Congress's power to regulate commerce "among the states," which undoubtedly presents a different question than Congress's power to regulate commerce "with foreign nations," and, therefore, does not necessarily control our analysis. In other words, the Interstate Commerce Clause jurisprudence must be carefully adapted to fit the "commerce with foreign nations" context.

To be clear, Supreme Court jurisprudence confirms that Congress's power under the Commerce Clause, be it the Interstate, Foreign, or Indian Commerce Clause, "is subject to outer limits." *See Lopez*, 514 U.S. at 556–57; *see also Nat'l Fed'n of Indep. Bus. v. Sebelius*, 567 U.S. 519, 557 (2012) (Congress does not have "a general license to regulate an individual from cradle to grave," even if **[—25—]** "[e]veryone will likely participate in the markets for food, clothing, transportation, shelter, or energy"); *Baston*, 818 F.3d at 668 (noting that the Foreign Commerce Clause has "outer bounds" but declining to demarcate those bounds). Thus, the question in this case, which again presents an as applied challenge, is whether there is a rational basis for concluding that the drug-trafficking conduct here in the territorial waters of a foreign nation, by foreign nationals using a foreign-registered vessel, of drugs not bound for the United States, substantially affects United States commerce with foreign nations. The record contains no evidence to support this conclusion. And the government's attenuated argument that wholly foreign drug trafficking impacts the international drug trade, which could impact United States commerce with foreign nations, requires a chain of inferences like that rejected by the *Lopez* court. *Lopez*, 514 U.S. at 564. As the *Lopez* court noted, "if we were to accept the [g]overnment's arguments, we are hard pressed to posit any activity by an individual that Congress is without power to regulate." *Id.*

Indeed, under the government's reasoning, nothing would prevent Congress from globally policing wholly foreign drug trafficking commerce, potentially intruding on the sovereignty of other Nations, and bringing foreign nationals into the United States for prosecution based **{-1277-}** solely on extra-territorial conduct when the United States was neither a party to, nor a target of, the commerce. *See United States v. Al-Maliki*, 787 F.3d 784, 792–93 (6th Cir. 2015) (cautioning that "an [—26—] unbounded reading of the Foreign Commerce Clause allows the federal government to intrude on the sovereignty of other nations—just as a broad reading of the Interstate Commerce Clause allows it to intrude on the sovereignty of the States"). Moreover, the Constitution withholds "from Congress a plenary police power that would authorize" such regulation. *Lopez,* 514 U.S. at 566. Rather, the Constitution grants Congress the authority to regulate commerce "with foreign nations" not "among and within foreign nations." *cf. Al-Maliki,* 787 F.3d at 792 (noting that "the textualist reading" of the Foreign Commerce Clause "require[s]" "commerce 'with' a foreign Nation").

Accordingly, for the reasons set forth above, as applied to these defendants, the MDLEA is unconstitutional and exceeded Congress's authority under the Foreign Commerce Clause.

B. NECESSARY AND PROPER CLAUSE

The government also argues that the MDLEA's application to this case is a valid exercise of Congress's authority pursuant to Article I's Necessary and Proper Clause to enforce the 1989 Convention Against Illicit Traffic Treaty and the 1997 Jamaica Bilateral Agreement between the United States and Jamaica. We are unpersuaded.

Article II of the Constitution gives the President the "Power, by and with the Advice and Consent of the Senate, to make Treaties . . . ." U.S. Const. art. II, § 2, [—27—] cl. 2. "In determining whether Congress has the authority to enact legislation implementing such a treaty, we look to the Necessary and Proper Clause." *United States v. Belfast,* 611 F.3d 783, 804 (11th Cir. 2010). That clause provides that "Congress shall have Power . . . [t]o make all Laws which shall be necessary and proper for carrying into Execution the foregoing Powers, and all other Powers vested by this Constitution in the Government of the United States, or in any Department or Officer thereof." U.S. Const. art. I, § 8, cl. 18. "Collectively, these clauses empower Congress *to enact* any law that is necessary and proper to effectuate a treaty made pursuant to Article II." *Belfast,* 611 F.3d at 804 (emphasis added).

But the MDLEA was enacted long before the Convention against Illicit Traffic Treaty or the Jamaica Bilateral Agreement; therefore, it was not *enacted* pursuant to the Necessary and Proper Clause *to effectuate* those international agreements. *See id.* And the government has not provided us with any case in which legislation has been upheld as necessary and proper for carrying into execution a treaty which did not yet exist at the time the legislation was enacted. *Cf. United States v. Lara,* 541 U.S. 193, 201 (2004) ("The treaty power does not literally authorize Congress to act legislatively, for it is an Article II power authorizing the President, not Congress, 'to make Treaties.'" (quoting U.S. Const. art. II, § 2, cl. 2)). Moreover, "nothing in the legislative history of MDLEA [—28—] mentions a treaty or intimates that the legislation is in compliance with treaty obligations." *United States v. Cardales-Luna,* 632 F.3d 731, 749 (1st Cir. 2011) (Torruella, J., dissenting). Similarly, "[n]o court decision dealing with [the] MDLEA refers to any treaty obligation as the source of Congress's Article I authority." *Id.* Accordingly, we do not find that, as applied to these defendants, the MDLEA was a valid exercise of Congress's authority under the Necessary and Proper Clause to effectuate the subsequently {-1278-} enacted Illicit Traffic Treaty or the Jamaica Bilateral Agreement.

IV. CONCLUSION

Because as applied to these defendants, the MDLEA exceeded Congress's authority under Article I, we must **VACATE** their convictions.

United States Court of Appeals
for the Eleventh Circuit

No. 19-13883

LACOURSE
vs.
PAE WORLDWIDE INC.

Appeal from the United States District Court for the Northern District of Florida

Decided: November 17, 2020

Citation: 980 F.3d 1350, 8 Adm. R. 523 (11th Cir. 2020).

Before **WILSON**, **NEWSOM**, and **ANDERSON**, Circuit Judges.

[—2—] {–1352–} **NEWSOM**, Circuit Judge:

This appeal requires us to decide whether and to what extent the Death on the High Seas Act, 46 U.S.C. §§ 30301–08, applies to Patricia LaCourse's wrongful-death action, in which she alleges that PAE Worldwide Incorporated failed to properly service and maintain the F-16 that her husband was flying when it crashed into the Gulf of Mexico. We must also determine whether PAE, which was operating under a services contract with the United States Air Force, is shielded from liability by the so-called "government contractor" defense.

For the reasons that follow, we hold that DOHSA governs LaCourse's action, that it provides LaCourse's exclusive remedy and preempts her other claims, and that PAE is entitled to the protection of the government-contractor defense. **{–1353–}**

I

A

The tragic story underlying this appeal began when an Air Force F-16 fighter jet departed Tyndall Air Force Base, east of Panama City, Florida, for a continuation-training sortie. The only person on board was the pilot, Matthew LaCourse, a retired Air Force Lieutenant Colonel employed as a civilian by the Department of Defense. The plan was for Lt. Col. LaCourse to take the jet out **[—3—]** over the Gulf of Mexico, perform a series of training maneuvers, and then return to Tyndall. Unfortunately, he never came back. During the flight—for reasons the parties dispute—the F-16 crashed into the Gulf more than twelve nautical miles offshore. Sadly, Lt. Col. LaCourse was killed.

Five years prior to the accident, PAE's predecessor—Defense Support Services—had been awarded a contract with the Air Force to provide aircraft service and maintenance at Tyndall, including, as it turns out, on the F-16 that Lt. Col. LaCourse was flying when he crashed. In performing under the contract, PAE was required to follow detailed guidelines and adhere to specific standards, including Air Force Instructions (AFIs), Technical Orders (TOs), and Job Guides (JGs), all of which were prepared by or on behalf of the Air Force.

F-16s are equipped with two hydraulic systems: A and B. The systems operate independently of one another and are designed to allow the plane to continue to fly in the event that one of them fails. Beginning two months before the crash, the jet at issue here experienced a succession of problems that implicated one or both of its hydraulic systems. In particular, on separate occasions: (1) hydraulic fluid was discovered in the outboard flight-control accumulator gauge; (2) System B's hydraulically actuated landing gear twice failed to retract during flight; (3) a hydraulic system pressure-line clamp on System A broke; (4) System B's reservoir accumulator was found to be depleted; (5) a pre-flight control check **[—4—]** revealed a hydraulic leak; (6) System A's cockpit indicator showed no pressure and System B's flight-control accumulator pre-charge was low; and (7) both systems failed a "confidence run."[1] The F-16 was serviced and parts were repaired or replaced as these problems were identified.

[1] The district court assumed that each of these problems was related to the hydraulic systems for purposes of deciding LaCourse's claims on summary judgment but noted that this was "far from certain."

On the day of the crash, the F-16 experienced two issues shortly before takeoff. First, the emergency-power unit took longer than expected to activate during the pre-flight check. Second, and more importantly for our purposes, the jet initially failed the "pitch-override check"—in which the pilot applies full pressure to the stick and presses a switch to make the stabilizers at the tail move a few inches or degrees in a nose-down direction. Despite these two "hiccups," as one witness called them, the jet ultimately passed all of its pre-flight checks, which indicated no problem with the hydraulic systems. The PAE mechanics who conducted the pre-flight checks were satisfied that the plane was safe to operate, and they released it for flight.

During the sortie, the F-16 performed a number of aerial maneuvers leading up to a "pitch-back"—an over-the-shoulder tactical maneuver in which the pilot uses the pitch axis to rejoin another aircraft. By all accounts, everything leading up to the pitch-back appeared normal—*i.e.*, no gauge, light, warning, or caution **[—5—]** indicated **{-1354-}** any problem, and there were no reports of any vibrations, shakes, etc. The issue that led to the crash occurred at the end of the pitch-back maneuver—Lt. Col. LaCourse appeared to level off and there followed, as one witness described it, "a period of no data, no inputs, no control or . . . no maneuvers," at which point the jet entered a "pitch-down" from about 12,000 feet. There is no evidence that Lt. Col. LaCourse made any effort to eject or radio for help during his final descent.[2]

B

Lt. Col. LaCourse's widow and personal representative, Patricia LaCourse, filed this wrongful-death action and jury demand in Florida state court alleging state-law claims for negligence, breach of warranty, and breach of contract. PAE removed the case to federal court based on federal-officer jurisdiction, diversity jurisdiction, and jurisdiction under DOHSA—which, in relevant part, confers admiralty jurisdiction "[w]hen the death of an individual is caused by wrongful act, neglect, or default occurring on the high seas." 46 U.S.C. § 30302. Resisting PAE's removal, LaCourse disputed that federal jurisdiction existed on any basis. **[—6—]**

Once in federal court, PAE moved for partial summary judgment, arguing that DOHSA governed LaCourse's suit and, accordingly, that any potential recovery should (per the statute) be limited to pecuniary damages. The district court granted PAE's motion and held that DOHSA applies and "provides the exclusive remedy for death on the high seas, preempts all other forms of wrongful death claims, and only permits recovery for pecuniary damages."

PAE then filed a motion to strike—or, in the alternative, for partial summary judgment—asking the district court to strike LaCourse's state-law breach-of-warranty and breach-of-contract claims, as well as her jury demand. The district court again granted PAE's motion, concluding that because DOHSA preempts all other wrongful-death causes of action, LaCourse's warranty and contract claims had to be stricken. The district court further held that because all that remained was the DOHSA claim, LaCourse was not entitled to a jury trial.

PAE subsequently moved for final summary judgment, contending that it was protected by the "government contractor" defense, which extends the United States' sovereign immunity to a federal-government contractor, thereby shielding it from civil liability, provided that, among other things, the contractor complies with reasonably precise government specifications. The district court once again agreed with PAE and granted it summary judgment on government-contractor grounds. **[—7—]**

[2] Although it has no real bearing on the issues before us, it's worth noting—by way of background—that the parties vigorously dispute the crash's cause. LaCourse and her experts blame the F-16's dual-hydraulic system, as well as PAE's failure to discover, diagnose, and address the problems. PAE and its experts, by contrast, posit that Lt. Col. LaCourse suffered a G-induced loss of consciousness following the pitch-back.

This is LaCourse's appeal.[3] {-1355-}

II

Before us, LaCourse argues that the district court erred in several ways. First, she contends that the court wrongly held that DOHSA governs this case—both (1) because by its plain terms DOHSA applies only when a death is caused by "wrongful act, neglect, or default occurring on the high seas," whereas the alleged negligence here occurred on land, and (2) because, in any event, her husband's plane crash lacked a "maritime nexus." Second, LaCourse argues that the district court erred in striking her breach-of-warranty and breach-of-contract claims because they don't seek a remedy broader than DOHSA and therefore aren't preempted. Finally, she asserts that the district court improperly applied the **[—8—]** government-contractor defense because PAE failed to show that it complied with the Air Force's reasonably precise specifications for maintaining the F-16.[4]

We will examine each contention in turn.[5]

A

The first question we must address is whether DOHSA applies to LaCourse's suit. The district court held that it does; LaCourse insists that it doesn't.

In relevant part, DOHSA's operative provision states that

> [w]hen the death of an individual is caused by wrongful act, neglect, or default occurring on the high seas . . . the personal representative of the decedent may bring a civil action in admiralty against the person or vessel responsible.

46 U.S.C. § 30302. DOHSA's applicability matters, among other reasons, because it limits a plaintiff's recovery to "compensation for the pecuniary loss sustained by the individuals for whose benefit the action is brought" and thereby forecloses recovery for emotional injury and punitive damages. *Id.* § 30303. **[—9—]**

1

LaCourse first argues that the district court erred in holding that DOHSA applies because the "wrongful act, neglect, or default" asserted here—PAE's negligent maintenance of the F-16—did not "occur[] on the high seas," as the Act's plain language requires. Rather, she says, the alleged negligence occurred on land—when the jet was improperly serviced at Tyndall Air Force Base. Accordingly, LaCourse contends, DOHSA doesn't apply to her suit.

---

[3] As PAE points out, LaCourse's notice of appeal identified only two of the district court's three orders—the order striking her non-DOHSA claims and her jury demand (Doc. 90) and the order granting PAE final summary judgment based on the government-contractor defense (Doc. 134). The notice did not specifically state that LaCourse was also appealing the district court's initial order concluding that DOHSA applied and supplied her exclusive remedy (Doc. 74). LaCourse acknowledges the oversight in her reply brief, but as she explains, it is "well settled that an appeal is not lost if a mistake is made in designating the judgment appealed from where it is clear that the overriding intent was effectively to appeal." *KH Outdoor, LLC v. City of Trussville*, 465 F.3d 1256, 1260 (11th Cir. 2006) (citation omitted). LaCourse's intent to appeal all three orders is apparent from the briefing, and PAE addressed all three orders (and constituent issues) in its response. Moreover, and in any event, our review of the latter two orders necessarily requires us to review the district court's determination of DOHSA's applicability. So in short, LaCourse's oversight hasn't prejudiced either party and, based on our case law, it's appropriate to let it slide under the circumstances.

[4] LaCourse also contends that the district court erred in striking her jury demand. But because—for reasons we'll explain—we hold that the district court's grant of summary judgment in PAE's favor is due to be affirmed, we needn't reach the jury-demand issue.

[5] "We review the district court's grants of partial summary judgment and summary judgment *de novo,* reviewing all facts and reasonable inferences in the light most favorable to the nonmoving party, and applying the same standard as the district court." *Allison v. McGhan Med. Corp.*, 184 F.3d 1300, 1306 (11th Cir. 1999).

If we were writing on a clean slate, we would almost certainly agree. LaCourse is **{-1356-}** exactly right that, according to its language, DOHSA applies only when the "death of an individual is caused by wrongful act, neglect, or default occurring on the high seas." And she is also right that the alleged "wrongful act, neglect, or default" here occurred not "on the high seas," but on terra firma. Unfortunately for LaCourse, though, we are bound by controlling precedent to reject her plain-text argument. In *Offshore Logistics, Inc. v. Tallentire*, for instance, the Supreme Court observed that "admiralty jurisdiction is expressly provided under DOHSA *[where] the accidental deaths occurred beyond a marine league from shore*." 477 U.S. 207, 218 (1986) (emphasis added). So too, in *In re Dearborn Marine Service, Inc.*, our predecessor court, whose decisions bind us,[6] recognized that "DOHSA has been construed to confer admiralty jurisdiction over **[—10—]** claims *arising out of airplane crashes on the high seas though the negligence alleged to have caused the crash occurred on land*." 499 F.2d 263, 272 n. 17 (5th Cir. 1974) (emphasis added); *accord, e.g., Smith v. Pan Air Corp.*, 684 F.2d 1102, 1111 (5th Cir. 1982) ("[T]he simple fact that [plaintiff's] death occurred as a result of an aircraft crash into the high seas is alone enough to confer jurisdiction under the DOHSA. . . . [A]dmiralty jurisdiction has repeatedly been extended to cases in which death or injury occurred on navigable waters even though the wrongful act occurred on land. The place where the negligence or wrongful act occurs is not decisive.") (footnote omitted). It's not for the three of us to second-guess the correctness of *Offshore Logistics* or *Dearborn Marine*. Because we are bound by those decisions, we are constrained to agree with the district court that DOHSA applies despite the fact that PAE's alleged negligence occurred on land at Tyndall Air Force Base.

2

LaCourse separately argues that DOHSA doesn't govern here because the plane crash that killed her husband lacked a "maritime nexus," which she insists is required by the Supreme Court's landmark admiralty decision in *Executive Jet Aviation, Inc. v. City of Cleveland*, 409 U.S. 249 (1972).

In that case, a plane flying from Ohio to Maine crashed into Lake Erie after striking a flock of seagulls shortly after takeoff. *Id.* at 250. Although the crew **[—11—]** wasn't injured, the plane was a total loss, so its owners brought an action in admiralty, alleging negligence by several airport employees. *Id.* at 250–51. The Supreme Court held that maritime locality alone—there, Lake Erie's navigable waters—is not a sufficient predicate for admiralty jurisdiction in aviation-tort cases, and that "in the absence of legislation to the contrary," claims arising from airplane crashes are not cognizable in admiralty unless the alleged wrong bears "a significant relationship to traditional maritime activity"—*i.e.*, has a maritime nexus. *Id.* at 268. Because the flight in *Executive Jet* "would have been almost entirely over land . . . within the continental United States" and was "only fortuitously and incidentally connected to navigable waters," the Court determined that it bore "no relationship to traditional maritime activity"—and, accordingly, that admiralty jurisdiction was lacking. *Id.* at 272–73. LaCourse argues that, like the flight in *Executive Jet*, her husband's flight—which was intended to begin and end at Tyndall Air Force Base—was **{-1357-}** also only "fortuitously over water" and thus bore no significant relationship to "traditional maritime activity."

The problem with LaCourse's argument is that *Executive Jet* didn't involve DOHSA—there were no injuries, let alone any fatalities to support a wrongful-death claim. *Id.* at 250. And significantly, the Supreme Court was careful there to include a caveat when announcing its holding—namely, that a maritime nexus is required only "in the absence of legislation to the contrary." *Id.* at 268. And **[—12—]** indeed, the Court in a footnote specifically identified DOHSA as an example of a statute that would constitute "legislation to the contrary." *Id.* at 274 n. 26.

[6] *See Bonner v. City of Prichard*, 661 F.2d 1206, 1209 (11th Cir. 1981) (en banc).

If *Executive Jet* stood alone, LaCourse's maritime-nexus argument might still have a chance. In flagging DOHSA as an example of "legislation to the contrary," the Court suggested that the Act might apply only to flights that *require* traversing the high seas: "Some such flights, e.g., New York City to Miami, Florida, *no doubt* involve passage over 'the high seas beyond a marine league from the shore of any State.' To the extent that the terms of the Death on the High Seas Act become applicable to *such flights*, that Act, of course, is 'legislation to the contrary.'" *Id.* (emphasis added). Because Lt. Col. LaCourse's sortie didn't *require* him to fly over the ocean, the argument would go, it wasn't one of the "such flights" that the *Executive Jet* Court thought DOHSA would cover.

But *Executive Jet* wasn't the Supreme Court's last word on DOHSA's application to aviation-based torts. Rather, as already explained, the Court held in *Offshore Logistics* that DOHSA applies to *all* cases—including aviation-related cases—in which a death occurs on the high-seas. *See* 477 U.S. at 218. In the course of so holding, the Court explained the applicability (or non-applicability, as the case may be) of the maritime-nexus requirement in these terms: "[A]dmiralty jurisdiction is expressly provided under DOHSA [where] the accidental deaths occurred beyond a marine league from shore. *Even without this statutory* **[—13—]** *provision*, admiralty jurisdiction is appropriately invoked here under traditional principles because the accident occurred on the high seas and in furtherance of an activity bearing a significant relationship to a traditional maritime activity." *Id.* at 218–19 (emphasis added). Translation: Where a death occurs on the high seas, DOHSA applies, full stop; separately, in a non-DOHSA case, maritime jurisdiction might still exist, provided that there is a maritime nexus. To the extent that *Executive Jet*'s New-York-to-Miami footnote left any doubt, *Offshore Logistics* clarified that the occurrence of a death on the high seas is a sufficient condition to DOHSA's application—without any further maritime-nexus gloss.[7] **{-1358-}**

In sum, then, we agree with the district court that DOHSA doesn't require a maritime nexus—and therefore, that because (on the Supreme Court's **[—14—]** interpretation) the Act applies whenever a death occurs on the high seas, it governs LaCourse's wrongful-death suit.

B

Having concluded that DOHSA applies to LaCourse's action, we must now determine whether it provides her exclusive remedy, such that it preempts all other claims arising out of her husband's crash.

---

[7] In support of her maritime-nexus argument, LaCourse points to *Miller v. United States*, 725 F.2d 1311 (11th Cir. 1984), in which we assumed (without actually considering or specifically deciding) that a maritime nexus may be required under DOHSA. *See id.* at 1315 (concluding that DOHSA provided jurisdiction over an aviation crash after determining that there *was* a maritime nexus on the facts of that case). We think it a full answer to *Miller* to recognize that it was decided before the Supreme Court clarified in *Offshore Logistics* that DOHSA imposes only a locality requirement, and not a separate maritime-nexus requirement. Other courts have distinguished *Miller* on precisely this basis, and we agree with their assessment. *See, e.g., Ventura Packers, Inc. v. F/V Jeanine Kathleen*, 305 F.3d 913, 918 (9th Cir. 2002) (listing *Miller* as an example of how "several courts initially presumed" that DOHSA required a maritime nexus, but noting that those cases came before *Offshore Logistics* and that now, "the prevailing view holds that DOHSA established independent requirements for the exercise of admiralty jurisdiction"); *see also Palischak v. Allied Signal Aerospace Co.*, 893 F. Supp. 341, 345 & n.5 (D.N.J. 1995) (holding that "the requirement of a traditional maritime nexus is not a prerequisite to the exercise of admiralty jurisdiction pursuant to DOHSA," and (citing *Miller*) noting that "[w]e are unable to locate a single decision after [*Offshore Logistics*] in which a lower court required a maritime nexus before applying DOHSA"); *Bernard v. World Learning Inc.*, 2010 WL 11505188, at *8 n.14 (S.D. Fla. June 4, 2010) (acknowledging the circuit precedent in *Miller* but explaining that it was decided prior to *Offshore Logistics* and holding that a maritime nexus is no longer required in DOHSA cases).

The district court concluded that LaCourse's breach-of-warranty and breach-of-contract claims—both of which she initially brought under Florida's Wrongful Death Act, Fla. Stat. § 768.16—had to be stricken on the ground that where DOHSA applies it "preempts all other forms of wrongful death claims." LaCourse contends that the district court erred because, she says, her state-law claims don't seek a remedy broader than DOHSA and therefore aren't preempted.

Again, while it seems to us that LaCourse might have the plain language on her side—in a section titled "Nonapplication," DOHSA expressly states that it "does not affect the law of a State regulating the right to recover for death," 46 U.S.C. § 30308—the controlling precedent is squarely against her. In particular, the Supreme Court held in *Offshore Logistics* that "in light of the language of the Act as a whole, the legislative history of [§ 30308's predecessor], the congressional purposes underlying the Act, and the importance of uniformity of admiralty law," the provision that is now codified at § 30308 "was intended only to **[—15—]** serve as a jurisdictional saving clause, ensuring that state courts enjoyed the right to entertain causes of action and provide wrongful death remedies both for accidents arising on territorial waters and, under DOHSA, for accidents occurring more than one marine league from shore." 477 U.S. at 221. And, the Court continued, once it is determined that § 30308 (or there, its predecessor) "acts as a jurisdictional saving clause, and not as a guarantee of the applicability of state substantive law to wrongful deaths on the high seas, the conclusion that the state statutes are pre-empted by DOHSA where it applies is inevitable." *Id.* at 232.

Put simply, under *Offshore Logistics*, § 30308 preserves only state-court jurisdiction—*not* state substantive wrongful-death law—and where DOHSA applies, it preempts all other wrongful-death claims under state or general maritime law. Accordingly, we hold that the district court was correct to conclude that DOHSA forecloses LaCourse's breach-of-warranty and breach-of-contract claims.

C

Having concluded that DOHSA governs LaCourse's suit and supplies her exclusive remedy, we must now determine whether LaCourse's claim is barred by **{-1359-}** the so-called "government contractor" defense. Provided that certain conditions are met, that defense—a creation of federal common law—extends the United States' sovereign immunity to a government contractor, thereby protecting it against civil liability. In essence, it allows the contractor to escape liability on the **[—16—]** ground that it was "just following orders." LaCourse asserts that the district court erred in applying the government-contractor defense because PAE failed to establish that it conformed to the government's reasonably specific maintenance procedures.[8]

The Supreme Court fashioned the government-contractor defense in *Boyle v. United Technologies Corporation*, 487 U.S. 500 (1988). There, the Court held, in a suit alleging design defects in military equipment, that a private contractor could partake of the United States' sovereign immunity so long as the following three conditions were satisfied: "(1) the United States approved reasonably precise specifications; (2) the equipment conformed to those specifications; and (3) the supplier warned the United States about the dangers in the use of the equipment that were

[8] LaCourse also argues that PAE shouldn't be entitled to immunity in this case because its maintenance contract with the Air Force specifically stated that PAE "shall be . . . responsible for all injuries to persons or damage to property that occurs as a result of its fault or negligence." But the allocation of liability between PAE and the government has nothing to do with PAE's immunity from liability to a third party. Given the point of the government-contractor defense—to allow the government to hire contractors to perform uniquely governmental duties without subjecting them to the risk of liability to third parties—it would make little sense to interpret the contract language as LaCourse suggests. The far better—and we think obvious—reading is that the quoted text merely allocates liability between PAE and the Air Force, not liability between PAE and a third party.

known to the supplier but not to the United States." *Id.* at 512.

Although *Boyle* dealt specifically with government procurement contracts, we extended its analysis to cover government *service* contracts in *Hudgens v. Bell Helicopters/Textron*, 328 F.3d 1329 (11th Cir. 2003). To account for the **[—17—]** contextual switch from a design-defect case to a negligent-maintenance case, we rejiggered the defense's three elements as follows: "(1) the United States approved reasonably precise maintenance procedures; (2) [the contractor's] performance of maintenance conformed to those procedures; and (3) [the contractor] warned the United States about the dangers in reliance on the procedures that were known to [the contractor] but not to the United States." *Id.* at 1335.

Helpfully, the parties have narrowed the focus here. LaCourse concedes that the Air Force provided reasonably precise maintenance procedures, so there's no question that the first *Boyle/Hudgens* element is satisfied. And the district court held that the third element "does not apply because (as PAE has argued, and as the plaintiff has not disputed) there is no contention that PAE had knowledge that it withheld from the government," and neither party appears to take issue with that conclusion. So all seem to agree that the application of the government-contractor defense here turns on the second *Boyle/Hudgens* element—whether, in servicing the F-16, PAE conformed to the Air Force's reasonably precise maintenance procedures.

In its summary-judgment motion, PAE argued that its maintenance conformed to the government's reasonably precise procedures, and it cited an abundance of supporting evidence, including deposition testimony from multiple employees, an **{-1360-}** Accident Investigation Board maintenance member, and the Safety **[—18—]** Investigation Board investigator. *See* Deposition of Timothy Davis at 7:20–8:11, 117:17–118:18 (testifying that all maintenance performed under the contract, including the service of Lt. Col. LaCourse's F-16, conformed to the Air Force's rules, regulations, and technical orders); *see also* Deposition of Michael Reeves at 106:4–106:18 (similar); Deposition of Michael Bogaert at 7:8–9:20 (similar); Deposition of AIB Investigator, Captain Michelle Chiaravelle at 26:10–26:17 (similar); Deposition of SIB Investigator, Senior Master Sergeant Marquell Fallin at 13:10–13:22, 19:8–19:23 (similar). In light of PAE's extensive evidence of compliance, the district court held that LaCourse failed to present evidence that PAE *violated* government procedures sufficient to create a genuine dispute of material fact.

In the "Statement of Facts" section of her opening brief on appeal, LaCourse identified three Air Force maintenance procedures under the subheading "The Defendant's Lack of Compliance with the Air Force's Specifications and Instructions." First, she stated that under AFI 21-101 ¶ 7.1, when there are system malfunctions of a "chronic nature" the aircraft "should" (her word) be impounded and prevented from flying until there are "'investigative efforts' to uncover the root cause." Second, LaCourse said that under AFI 21-101 ¶ 7.5.4 an airplane "must" be impounded "following an uncommanded flight control movement," which she claims occurred when the stabilizers didn't move as directed during the **[—19—]** final pre-flight check. Finally, she cited TO 1-1-300, which states that a procedure called a "functional flight check" is "normally" conducted following maintenance work and before an airplane is released to fly.

LaCourse's contention that PAE violated reasonably precise maintenance procedures—so as to foreclose its reliance on the government-contractor defense—fails on numerous grounds. As an initial matter, she has almost certainly abandoned her arguments based on the procedures she cites. We have repeatedly held that an appellant abandons an argument on appeal when she fails to "specifically and clearly identif[y]" it or "plainly and prominently" raise it in her opening brief. *Access Now, Inc. v. Southwest Airlines Co.*, 385 F.3d 1324, 1330 (11th Cir. 2004); *Cole v. U.S. Att'y Gen.*, 712 F.3d 517, 530 (11th Cir. 2013). In particular, we will deem an appellant to have abandoned an argument where she makes only "passing references" to it in the background sections of her brief—or, for that matter, even the brief's argument section. *Sapuppo v. Allstate Floridian Ins. Co.*, 739 F.3d 678, 681–82 (11th Cir. 2014). Under our consistent precedent, LaCourse's scattered references to Air Force procedures in the "Statement of the Facts" section of her opening appellate brief—followed by a single (and vague) invocation of "AFI 21-101" on a single page in the "Argument" section—were insufficient to present a legal argument based on PAE's alleged noncompliance with them. **[—20—]**

Moreover, and in any event, LaCourse's arguments fail on the merits. With respect to AFI 21-101 ¶ 7.1 and TO 1-1-300, it is enough to note that they merely permit, rather than require, impoundment and functional check flights, respectively, under specified circumstances. A government contractor doesn't violate reasonably precise maintenance procedures by taking a course of action—repair, replacement, retesting—that those procedures at least implicitly allow.[9] **{-1361-}**

Had LaCourse properly presented it, an argument based on AFI 21-101 ¶ 7.5.4—which, unlike the other two procedures on which she relies, *requires* impoundment following an "uncommanded flight control movement"—might have been somewhat stronger, but for reasons we will explain, even it would fail.

In resisting the application of the government-contractor defense, LaCourse cited testimony from Timothy Davis and Michael Bogaert—PAE employees tasked with the preflight checks on the day of the crash—both of whom testified that Bogaert (1) didn't see the stabilizers move as far as they should have during the initial pitch-override check and (2) instructed Lt. Col. LaCourse to repeat the **[—21—]** sequence until the stabilizers performed properly. LaCourse contends that the jet should have been grounded after the first sequence. PAE counters that Bogaert's description of the check indicates that Lt. Col. LaCourse simply wasn't performing the sequence properly, not that there was any sort of issue with the control.

By way of background, here is the relevant portion of Bogaert's testimony:

> Q: During the pitch override check, did you see the horizontal stabs move at all?
>
> A: After I got on the headset, after when [Mr. Davis] had finished checking brakes, I got on a headset with [Lt. Col. LaCourse] and asked him if he had done it. He said yes. I told him I didn't see it. He said do you want me to do it again. I said yes, if you don't mind. At which point he tried to do it again, and they didn't move. And I asked him, are you holding the stick full forward, and he wasn't. He was just pushing, and they're reaching over and he's releasing his pressure on the stick, is my best guess. But I told him, no, [Lt. Col. LaCourse], that's not it, and asked him, are you holding the stick full forward as you hit that switch. And he did that, and it worked perfect. He released. I said that's what I was looking for, technique.

Even aside from abandonment, there are several problems with LaCourse's AFI 21-101 ¶ 7.5.4 argument. First, whereas that procedure triggers mandatory impoundment only upon the occurrence of an "uncommanded . . . movement," Bogaert's testimony describes (at most) the exact converse—a *commanded non-movement*. In particular, Bogaert recounted that he saw Lt. Col. LaCourse

---

[9] LaCourse also asserted—albeit again only in the "Statement of Facts" section of her opening brief—that Lt. Col. LaCourse's F-16 "should" have been impounded for a "root cause" investigation. When pressed at oral argument about what procedure required such an investigation, LaCourse's counsel pointed to the following language in AFI 21-101 ¶ 7.1: "Impounding aircraft and equipment enables investigative efforts to systematically proceed with minimal risk relative to intentional/unintentional actions and subsequent loss of evidence." Oral Argument at 32:10. But even if LaCourse had developed this assertion into a legal argument outside of the background section of her brief, the cited language says nothing about a root-cause investigation, let alone a mandatory one.

attempt to move the stabilizers by pushing the stick (the command) but explained that they initially "didn't move" (the non-movement). Accordingly, it's not at all clear to us that, by its plain terms, AFI 21-101 ¶ 7.5.4 even applies. **[—22—]**

Second, LaCourse has pointed to no expert testimony or other evidence connecting attorney argument (or, more precisely, attorney factual recitation) to an actual AFI 21-101 ¶ 7.5.4 violation. Rather, she offers only lay testimony describing what happened during the test. She presents no expert (or even lay) testimony explaining *why* what happened constituted an "uncommanded flight control movement" triggering a mandatory impoundment. LaCourse's evidence, we think, is insufficient to **{-1362-}** permit a reasonable jury to find that PAE violated AFI 21-101 ¶ 7.5.4.

Finally, even under the most charitable reading, Bogaert's testimony describes not a breach of procedure, but a likely pilot error—Lt. Col. LaCourse, Bogaert said, simply wasn't performing the check properly. Bogaert explained that Lt. Col. LaCourse wasn't "holding the stick full forward" and that once he performed the check using the proper technique, it "worked perfect[ly]."

For all these reasons, even if LaCourse had properly presented an argument that PAE violated AFI 21-101 ¶ 7.5.4, we would reject it.

* * *

In sum, LaCourse failed to produce evidence sufficient to create a genuine issue of material fact that PAE violated government procedures. LaCourse's real argument seems to be that PAE's mechanics should have dug deeper into the F-16's hydraulic-related problems, because, had they done so, they would have **[—23—]** discovered that the hydraulic systems were compromised. But while what LaCourse and her experts believe PAE should have done differently surely has some bearing on the merits of her DOHSA-based negligence claim, it is irrelevant to the question whether PAE is protected by the government-contractor defense. All that matters on that score is whether PAE violated reasonably precise government procedures, and based on the evidence presented from both parties we conclude that it did not. Accordingly, we affirm the district court's decision that PAE is entitled to summary judgment on government-contractor grounds.

III

For the foregoing reasons, we hold that DOHSA applies to and governs LaCourse's case, that the Act provides her exclusive remedy, and that PAE is shielded from liability by the government-contractor defense. Accordingly, we affirm the district court's grant of summary judgment in favor of PAE.

AFFIRMED.

(Reporter's Note: Concurring Opinion follows on p. 532).

[—24—] {-1362-} **NEWSOM,** Circuit Judge, with whom **WILSON,** Circuit Judge, joins, concurring:

I write separately to explain that, while I agree that we must follow existing precedent to hold that DOHSA applies to (and thereby supplies the exclusive wrongful-death remedy for) any claim arising out of a death occurring on the high seas—even where, as here, the negligence alleged to have caused the death occurred on land—I do so holding my nose, as DOHSA's plain language is squarely to the contrary.

As a refresher, DOHSA's operative provision states in relevant part that "[w]hen the death of an individual is caused by a wrongful act, neglect, or default occurring on the high seas . . . the personal representative of the decedent may bring a civil action in admiralty against the person or vessel responsible." 46 U.S.C. § 30302. LaCourse contends (1) that DOHSA applies only when the *negligence* occurred on the high seas, without respect to where the *death* occurred, and (2) that all here agree that the alleged negligence occurred on land, when the jet was improperly serviced at Tyndall Air Force Base. Accordingly, she insists, DOHSA doesn't govern her case.

LaCourse's logic, it seems to me, is unassailable. By its plain terms, DOHSA limits its application to instances in which the "wrongful act, neglect, or default occur[ed] on the high seas," regardless of where the resulting death occurred. Indeed, there is no reasonable reading of the Act by which the phrase **[—25—]** "occurring on the high seas" modifies the word "death" rather **{-1363-}** than the phrase "wrongful act, neglect, or default." One needn't even resort to the canons to come to that conclusion—the plain, ordinary, and obvious meaning of the words is sufficient. (Having said that, the canons would lead to precisely the same determination. *See Nearest-Reasonable-Referent Canon*, Black's Law Dictionary (11th ed. 2019); Antonin Scalia & Bryan A. Garner, *Reading Law: The Interpretation of Legal Texts* 152 (2012).)

Somehow, though, precedent—mounds of it, some of it binding on us—has whistled past the text's unmistakable focus of the location of the alleged negligence as the decisive factor for determining DOHSA's applicability. For instance—

- *Miles v. Apex Marine Corp.*, 498 U.S. 19, 25 (1990) ("DOHSA . . . create[d] a wrongful death action for *all persons killed on the high seas*.")

- *Offshore Logistics, Inc. v. Tallentire*, 477 U.S. 207, 218 (1986) ("Here, admiralty jurisdiction is expressly provided under DOHSA because the accidental deaths occurred beyond a marine league from shore.")

- *Mobil Oil Corp. v. Higginbotham*, 436 U.S. 618, 620 (1978) (noting that DOHSA creates "a remedy in admiralty for wrongful deaths more than three miles from shore")

- *In re Dearborn Marine Serv., Inc.*, 499 F.2d 263, 272 n. 17 (5th Cir. 1974) ("DOHSA has been construed to confer admiralty jurisdiction over claims arising out of airplane crashes on the high seas though the negligence alleged to have caused the crash occurred on land.") **[—26—]**

- *Bergen v. F/V ST. PATRICK*, 816 F.2d 1345, 1348 (9th Cir. 1987) ("[DOHSA] has been held to refer to the site of an accident on the high seas, not to where . . . the wrongful act causing the accident may have originated.")

- *Smith v. Pan Air Corp.*, 684 F.2d 1102, 1111 (5th Cir. 1982) ("[T]he simple fact that [plaintiff's] death occurred as a result of an aircraft crash into the high seas is alone enough to confer jurisdiction under the DOHSA. ... [A]dmiralty jurisdiction has repeatedly been extended to cases in which death or injury occurred on navigable waters even though the wrongful act occurred on land. The place where

> the negligence or wrongful act occurs is not decisive.") (footnote omitted)

I could go on and on and on—this is but a small sampling of cases holding that DOHSA applies to any claim arising out of a death occurring on the high seas, wholly without regard to where the underlying negligence occurred. But again, that seems obviously wrong to me.

I'm not the first to recognize the textual disconnect. The Fifth Circuit, for instance, once remarked that "[a]t first glance, the plain text of this statutory provision seems to indicate that DOHSA is implicated only when the wrongful act precipitating death occurs on the high seas." *Motts v. M/V Green Wave*, 210 F.3d 565, 569 (5th Cir. 2000). But the court went on: "As subsequent courts have interpreted DOHSA, however, the statute's application is not limited to negligent acts that actually occur on the high seas. The Supreme Court has repeatedly noted that when the death itself occurs on the high seas, DOHSA applies." *Id.* My only disagreement with the Fifth Circuit's assessment is the "[a]t first glance" part. I've **[—27—]** read § 30302 over and over—glanced, peered, gawked, and glared—and I can't make it say anything other than that DOHSA applies when the alleged act of *negligence*—rather **{-1364-}** than the resulting *death*—occurs on the high seas.

So how did we get ourselves into this predicament—reading DOHSA to mean something that it obviously doesn't say? The answer, apparently, traces back to century-old admiralty law premised on a "consummation of the injury" theory. *See e.g., In re Dearborn Marine*, 499 F.2d at 274 ("Historically maritime jurisdiction has been measured by the locality of the wrong with locality defined as where the 'substance and consummation of the injury' took place.") (citing *The Plymouth*, 70 U.S. (3 Wall.) 20, 33 (1886)) (footnote omitted). Put simply, if a claim is premised on a negligence theory, the underlying negligence isn't complete until it is "consummated in an actual injury." *Lasky v. Royal Caribbean Cruises, Ltd.*, 850 F. Supp. 2d 1309, 1312 (S.D. Fla. 2012). So, the argument goes, a DOHSA claim for wrongful death based on negligent service—as we have here—accrues at the time and place where the allegedly wrongful act culminates in an actual injury (the high seas), not when and where the negligence itself allegedly occurred (at Tyndall Air Force Base).

That's fine. It's just not what the statute says. DOHSA doesn't say that the decedent's personal representative may bring an action "when the death of an individual *occurring on the high seas* is caused by wrongful act, neglect, or **[—28—]** default"; rather, it says that the personal representative can sue "[w]hen the death of an individual is caused by wrongful act, neglect, or default *occurring on the high seas*." 46 U.S.C. § 30302. End of story.

Bottom line: As in all cases, we should give effect to DOHSA's unambiguous language. *See, e.g., Estate of Cowart v. Nicklos Drilling Co.*, 505 U.S. 469, 476 (1992) ("The controlling principle in this case is the basic and unexceptional rule that courts must give effect to the clear meaning of statutes as written."). If it were up to me, I would hold that DOHSA doesn't apply here because the alleged negligence—the failure to properly maintain the F-16 that Lt. Col. LaCourse was piloting when he crashed—occurred on land, not on the high seas.

United States Court of Appeals
for the Eleventh Circuit

No. 19-12734

QUINTERO
vs.
GEICO MARINE INS. CO.

Appeal from the United States District Court for the Southern District of Florida

Decided: December 22, 2020

Citation: 983 F.3d 1264, 8 Adm. R. 534 (11th Cir. 2020).

Before **PRYOR,** Chief Judge, **HULL** and **MARCUS,** Circuit Judges.

[—1—] {-1266-} **HULL,** Circuit Judge:

This case involves a marine insurance policy insuring a boat owned by Alfredo Quintero ("Quintero") and the federal maritime doctrine of *uberrimae* **[—2—]** *fidei*. After the boat was stolen, the insurer, Geico Marine Insurance Company ("Geico"), denied coverage based on Quintero's misrepresentation that he was in possession of the boat. Quintero appeals the district court's grant of summary judgment in favor of Geico and denial of his motion for partial summary judgment. The issue is whether Quintero's misrepresentation voided his policy *ab initio*. After careful review, and with the benefit of oral argument, we conclude it did and affirm. **{-1267-}**

I. FACTS

A. Quintero's Policy

Initially, Quintero's 32-foot powerboat was covered by a Geico marine insurance policy that ran from May 5, 2017, to May 5, 2018. On March 13, 2018, Geico sent Quintero a policy renewal package identifying changes to the policy's terms and Quintero's required payment.

Geico's renewal package required a down payment of Quintero's annual premium, or $776 of the premium total of $2580. The package included this urgent reminder: "Your coverage expires on 05/05/2018 at 12:01 AM Local Time. Prevent a lapse in coverage by making your required payment promptly." The annual premium for the upcoming policy period had increased by 25 percent, and Quintero's next payment of $776 was scheduled to be paid through Geico's automatic-payment system. The renewal policy stated that Geico would provide **[—3—]** coverage "during the policy period" on the condition that Quintero pay the premium and comply with all policy terms.

On May 4, 2018, Geico charged Quintero's credit card, but the charge was declined. That same day, Quintero called Geico about the attempted charge and increased premium. Quintero began the call by updating his address information. A customer service representative then explained that (1) Geico ordinarily debited renewal payments from the policyholder's card on file, (2) Quintero's card was declined, (3) he was thus automatically disenrolled from the automatic-payment system, and (4) he could either call in to make payments or put another card back on file.

When the Geico representative explained that rates had increased for everyone and why, Quintero complained that the 25 percent increase was "ludicrous." He stated that if Geico was making a change, he was "making a change too," and that "it's not acceptable, that you're going to increase me 25 percent. It's just not acceptable." The representative said she could not reduce his premium, to which Quintero replied, "So you prefer losing a customer, okay. I guess -- so you're going to lose me as a customer, with all my vehicles, because you want to increase me 25 percent." Quintero asked to speak to a supervisor and was transferred, but the call went to voicemail. Because Quintero had updated his **[—4—]** address information, Geico sent him a new endorsement reflecting the address change.

B. Non-Payment and Expiration

Quintero did not make the required renewal payment prior to the policy expiring on May 5, 2018. On May 10, 2018, Geico sent Quintero a "Notice of Policy Expiration." The Notice stated his policy expired on May 5,

2018, at 12:01 a.m., and that "all liability thereunder terminated on its expiration date."

C. Theft and Policy Reinstatement

On May 25, 2018, at 4:58 a.m.—as detailed in a later police report—a dark pickup truck pulled up to the driveway of Quintero's home, where the boat was stored, and towed the boat away along with its trailer. A neighbor's surveillance camera, a block away, recorded the perpetrator's truck towing the boat away, and the Broward County Sheriff's Office later obtained the footage.

That same morning, at 7:28 a.m., Quintero called Geico to "pay [his] boat policy." A customer service representative observed that "the policy was due the 5th of May," and asked Quintero if he was trying to reinstate it. Quintero said yes and acted as if he was unaware of the lapse:

> [REPRESENTATIVE]: Okay, so it looks like the policy was due the 5th of May. Are you trying to reinstate it? **{–1268–}**
>
> MR. QUINTERO: Yeah. Well, I didn't know it was -- oh, it says here that . . . okay, yeah, I guess I'm -- they told me that I have to pay $700 or something like that, 700 and something dollars. **[—5—]**
>
> [REPRESENTATIVE]: The first payment is $776, that's right.
>
> MR. QUINTERO: Yeah. What are we . . .
>
> [REPRESENTATIVE]: What are we, I'm sorry?
>
> MR. QUINTERO: That I don't know why you guys -- it's only eight months, instead of like the cars are . . . okay. It is what it is. We have to have insurance, so . . . Something -- something happens out there, you know, you want to be insured, so . . .

The representative then asked these questions:

> [REPRESENTATIVE]: I have to ask you some questions, then we can make a payment and reinstate the policy, okay?
>
> MR. QUINTERO: Sure.
>
> [REPRESENTATIVE]: First off, is the boat -- does the boat have any damage or is it -- has it been damaged?
>
> MR. QUINTERO: No. It's beautiful.
>
> [REPRESENTATIVE]: Okay. And is it sound and seaworthy?
>
> MR. QUINTERO: Sound and seaworthy. What it means? It's in good condition?
>
> [REPRESENTATIVE]: Mm-hmm.
>
> MR. QUINTERO: Yeah, yeah, yeah.
>
> [REPRESENTATIVE]: Okay. And when was the last time you physically saw your boat?
>
> MR. QUINTERO: Every day. It's in my house. **[—6—]**

The representative then took Quintero's credit card information and reenrolled him in the automatic-payment system. At one point, Quintero noted the declarations page he had received from Geico showed that his policy expired on May 5. At the end of the call, Quintero asked, "So the policy will be active right away, right? I just want to make sure that I'm not without insurance." The representative confirmed that with the payment, the policy was now reinstated as of May 5, 2018.

That same afternoon, at 2:43 p.m., Quintero reported his boat and trailer stolen to local police. At 6:28 p.m., he called Geico again, this time to make a claim for the stolen boat and trailer. During his call to the claims department, Quintero stated that he stored the boat at his home, "right in front of [his] driveway," and that he had last seen the boat around 11:30 p.m. to 12 a.m. the night before. He told Geico he discovered the boat was missing when his wife came home from work just after noon that day and asked him where the boat was. He had "assumed" the boat was still there when he went to work that morning, having to run to his truck due to heavy rain.

Geico investigated and took statements from Quintero and his wife. In July 2018, Geico informed Quintero it needed further information and was awaiting the final police report. Geico demanded that Quintero submit to an examination under oath. Quintero refused. **[—7—]**

II. PROCEDURAL HISTORY

On July 31, 2018, Quintero filed this action in Florida state court, seeking a declaration that Geico breached the policy by failing to cover his boat loss. Geico removed the case to federal court.

Geico then obtained a final report from the Broward County Sheriff's Office describing the video surveillance obtained from a neighboring residence a block away. According to the report, the surveillance footage captured the boat being towed away just before 5 a.m. on May 25, 2018. It showed two vehicles drive into the community where Quintero resided, and **{-1269-}** one—a dark pickup truck—tow away the boat minutes later.

Then, in a January 30, 2019 letter, Geico informed Quintero that: (1) it had completed its investigation; (2) it had denied coverage and rescinded the policy *ab initio* because Quintero was not in possession of the boat when he called to reinstate his expired marine insurance policy; and (3) Quintero's misrepresentations that the boat was in his possession and in good condition were material to its agreement to insure the vessel after the policy had previously expired and been non-renewed at his request.

Ultimately, the district court granted Geico's motion for summary judgment and denied Quintero's motion for partial summary judgment. The court concluded that Quintero's misrepresentations concerning the status of the boat on May 25, **[—8—]** 2018, voided the policy *ab initio* under the doctrine of *uberrimae fidei* because they were material to Geico's calculation of the risk of insuring the vessel. In addressing Quintero's contention that the policy was never cancelled or non-renewed, the court noted that "the Policy, the Notice of Policy Expiration, and the recorded telephone transcripts indicate that the previous policy's term expired on May 5, 2018." The court concluded that the policy was void *ab initio* under the *uberrimae fidei* doctrine "regardless of whether [it] was renewed, cancelled, or expired."

Later on, the district court denied Quintero's motion for relief under Federal Rules of Civil Procedure 59(e) and 60(b). This appeal followed.

III. STANDARD OF REVIEW

"We review *de novo* a district court's grant of summary judgment, viewing all facts and reasonable inferences in the light most favorable to the nonmoving party." *Jurich v. Compass Marine, Inc.*, 764 F.3d 1302, 1304, 2 Adm. R. 568, 568 (11th Cir. 2014). Summary judgment is appropriate where "there is no genuine dispute as to any material fact and the movant is entitled to judgment as a matter of law." Fed. R. Civ. P. 56(a). "A genuine issue of material fact does not exist unless there is sufficient evidence favoring the nonmoving party for a reasonable jury to return a verdict in its favor." *Haves v. City of Miami*, 52 F.3d 918, 921 (11th Cir. 1995). **[—9—]**

IV. DISCUSSION

Quintero argues the district court erred in applying the doctrine of *uberrimae fidei* because (1) his policy was not cancelled, non-renewed, or expired when he spoke to Geico the morning of May 25, 2018, (2) his coverage continued in full force without a lapse, and (3) his May 25 statements were not material to Geico's decision to insure his boat because Geico reinstated and backdated his policy and did not require a new underwriting process.

A. Expiration of the Policy

First, based on the record, we conclude that Quintero's initial policy, by its terms, expired on May 5, 2018, because Quintero did not pay the required premium for the new policy period. In fact, Quintero's phone call on May 4 with Geico makes clear that Quintero understood that if he did not pay his new premium, Geico would not renew his policy for the May 5, 2018, to May 5, 2019 period.

Notably too, during the May 4 call, Quintero complained that the 25 percent premium increase was "ludicrous" and "not acceptable." After this exchange, Quintero did not pay the installment amount due on May 5, 2018. Accordingly, on May 10, 2018, Geico sent Quintero a Notice of Policy Expiration informing him that the policy had expired as of May 5, 2018, and "all liability thereunder **[—10—]** terminated on its expiration date." Therefore, Quintero's initial **{-1270-}** policy did not cover his boat loss that occurred on May 25, 2018.

Quintero argues that the initial policy was not cancelled or non-renewed, but that is irrelevant. His coverage already expired on May 5, 2018, so he did not have coverage when he called Geico on the morning of May 25, 2018.

Quintero also argues Geico's Jeffrey O'Keefe, an adjuster, inconsistently testified as to whether the policy was ever cancelled or expired. But the district court did not rely on O'Keefe's statements for the proposition that the policy expired. Rather, the district court noted that "the Policy, the Notice of Policy Expiration, and the recorded telephone transcripts indicate that the previous policy's term expired on May 5, 2018 and that Quintero called to reinstate his Policy on May 25, 2018 after the Vessel had been stolen."

Furthermore, O'Keefe clarified any confusion about cancellation and expiration. In his deposition, he repeatedly stated that the policy was not cancelled in May 2018; it expired. And in his supplemental affidavit, he stated that on May 5, 2018, "the subject policy expired and a Notice of Policy Expiration was mailed to Alfredo Quintero on May 10, 2018."

In any event, any initial imprecise statements by O'Keefe do not change the fact that the terms of Geico's policy conditioned renewal of coverage on payment of the premium, Quintero did not pay the premium, and the policy period expired **[—11—]** on May 5, 2018. Indeed, the renewal package informed Quintero that coverage would expire on this date at 12:01 a.m. and included an urgent reminder to "[p]revent a lapse in coverage by making [the] required payment promptly." As a result, when Quintero failed to pay his renewal premium, he received a Notice of Policy Expiration stating his policy had expired on May 5, 2018, at 12:01 a.m., and that "all liability thereunder terminated on its expiration date," making clear that coverage expired along with the policy. Quintero's boat was thus uninsured between May 5, 2018, and when he first called Geico on May 25, 2018. In other words, there was a lapse in coverage, and no policy was in force when Quintero called Geico on May 25.

B. Doctrine of *Uberrimae Fidei*

Even so, Quintero claims that he still had coverage on May 25 because Geico renewed and backdated the policy to run from May 5, 2018, Geico did not treat it as if it was issuing new coverage, and his statements were not material to the issuance of coverage. In response, Geico contends that the renewal policy was void *ab initio* because Quintero made material misrepresentations in his May 25 call before Geico reinstated the policy. Geico relies on the doctrine of *uberrimae fidei*, to which we turn.

Marine insurance contracts are governed by federal maritime law. *Geico Marine Ins. Co. v. Shackleford*, 945 F.3d 1135, 1139, 7 Adm. R. 528, 530 (11th Cir. 2019). In the **[—12—]** absence of an established federal admiralty rule, we rely on state law. *Id.*, 7 Adm. R. at 530.[1] Here, there is controlling federal mari-

[1] Consistent with this rule, the choice-of-law provision in both Quintero's initial policy and renewal policy states that (1) the "policy is to be construed under United States federal admiralty

time law. Specifically, "[i]t is well-settled that the marine insurance doctrine of *uberrimae fidei* is the controlling law of this circuit," *HIH Marine Servs., Inc. v. Fraser*, 211 F.3d 1359, 1362 (11th Cir. 2000), and is "the controlling federal rule even in the face of contrary state authority," **{-1271-}** *Steelmet, Inc. v. Caribe Towing Corp.*, 747 F.2d 689, 695 (11th Cir. 1984), *vacated in part on other grounds*, 779 F.2d 1485 (11th Cir. 1986). We first review the scope of the doctrine and then why it applies here.

As to scope, the *uberrimae fidei* doctrine requires an insured to "fully and voluntarily disclose to the insurer all facts material to a calculation of the insurance risk," and "[t]he duty to disclose extends to those material facts not directly inquired into by the insurer." *HIH Marine*, 211 F.3d at 1362. This disclosure includes all material facts that are "within or ought to be within, the knowledge of one party, and of which the other party has no actual or presumptive knowledge." *Steelmet*, 747 F.2d at 695 (quoting *Gulfstream Cargo, Ltd. v. Reliance Ins. Co.*, 409 F.2d 974, 980 (5th Cir. 1969)); *see also HIH Marine*, 211 F.3d at 1363 ("[T]he **[—13—]** law has placed the burden of good faith disclosure with the person in the best position to know all the facts: the insured.").

This doctrine, which embodies the "highest degree of good faith," applies to marine insurance contracts because the insurance underwriter often cannot ensure the accuracy or sufficiency of the facts supplied by an insured "before the risk is accepted and the premium and conditions set." *Steelmet*, 747 F.2d at 695 (quotation marks omitted). Thus, the doctrine's central principle "is that the *insured* bears the burden of full and voluntary disclosure of facts material to the decision to insure." *HIH Marine*, 211 F.3d at 1363.

Further, under *uberrimae fidei*, an insured's material misrepresentation to an insurer renders a marine insurance policy void *ab initio*. *See AIG Centennial Ins. Co. v. O'Neill*, 782 F.3d 1296, 1303, 3 Adm. R. 643, 647 (11th Cir. 2015). The policy is void even if the insured's misrepresentation was the result of "mistake, accident, or forgetfulness," or the insurer did not inquire about the particular material fact the insured failed to disclose. *HIH Marine*, 211 F.3d at 1362-63 (quotation marks omitted). We examine materiality from a reasonable insurer's perspective, asking whether a particular fact "could possibly influence the mind of a prudent and intelligent insurer in determining whether he would accept the risk." *Kilpatrick Marine Piling v. Fireman's Fund Ins. Co.*, 795 F.2d 940, 942-43 (11th Cir. 1986); *see also AIG Centennial*, 782 F.3d at 1304, 3 Adm. R. at 648 (employing definition from *Kilpatrick*). **[—14—]**

Here, Quintero is correct that the doctrine of *uberrimae fidei* applies only when an insurer issues a policy, not when a policy is already in full force. *See HIH Marine*, 211 F.3d at 1362-63 (requiring the disclosure of "all facts material to a calculation of the insurance risk" and stating that doctrine's central principle is "disclosure of facts material to the decision to insure"); *Kilpatrick*, 795 F.2d at 942-43 (describing material fact as one that could influence insurer "in determining whether he would accept the risk"); *Steelmet*, 747 F.2d at 695 (noting "highest degree of good faith" is required because insurer cannot otherwise ensure the accuracy of facts "before the risk is accepted" (quotation marks omitted)).

But as set forth above, Quintero's policy was not in full force on May 25 because it had expired on May 5, 2018. Although Quintero was not required to go through a new underwriting process, he was required to answer questions about the condition and possession of the boat in order for Geico to issue coverage by renewing the expired policy. Further, Quintero's misrepresentations concerning his possession of the boat during the May 25 phone call were material to Geico's calculation of the insurance risk in reinstating his policy, rendering the renewed policy void *ab initio*.

---

law," and (2) "[i]n the absence of controlling United States federal admiralty law," the policy is to be "construed under the laws of the state" of the insured person, here Florida.

Moreover, when Geico renewed the policy, it issued an amended, new policy, {-1272-} even if it backdated coverage to the original policy's expiration date. Specifically, the cover page of the renewal package sent on March 13, 2018, states, **[—15—]** "GEICO Marine Insurance Company is pleased to announce a new Marine Insurance Policy which will replace your previous policy with this renewal. A copy of the new policy in its entirety is enclosed, along with a Notice of Change in Policy Terms, which details the differences between the new and previous policy." The renewal policy included endorsements that amended the terms of the original policy. To be sure, O'Keefe stated that Geico did not require Quintero to go through the entire underwriting process again when renewing his policy, because "that would be a disservice to Mr. Quintero." However, the facts remain that on May 25, Quintero's policy had expired, his policy was not in full force, and Geico had to decide whether to issue and renew coverage for Quintero's boat. Thus, the doctrine of *uberrimae fidei* applies here.

To avoid the doctrine, Quintero reprises his argument that because his initial policy never expired and Geico renewed and backdated it, his statements on May 25 were thus not material to Geico's decision to issue coverage for his boat. This argument fails for two reasons. First, Quintero's policy did expire on May 5, as explained above.

Second, Quintero's statements were material to Geico's issuance of coverage on May 25, even if by renewal and backdating. Viewed from the perspective of a reasonable insurer, Quintero's misrepresentation that the boat was in his home and possession was material, as no "prudent and intelligent insurer" **[—16—]** would accept the risk of insuring stolen property that is no longer in the insured's possession. *See Kilpatrick*, 795 F.2d at 942-43. When Quintero made the call at 7:28 a.m. on May 25, the boat had already been missing for two and a half hours, and Quintero had a duty to disclose that fact even if Geico did not directly ask him. The call was made several hours after the theft of the boat and after weeks of Quintero not paying his renewal premium.

Even if we assume, dubiously, that Quintero did not know for sure the boat was already gone at the time of his misrepresentation, that has no impact on our analysis. *See HIH Marine*, 211 F.3d at 1363. That the boat was missing from his own home at the time of the 7:28 a.m. reinstatement call is a fact that ought to have been within his knowledge, and one he was obligated to disclose even if Geico had not asked. *See id.* at 1362-63; *Steelmet*, 747 F.2d at 695 (stating that *uberrimae fidei* imposes the burden to disclose material facts that are "within or ought to be within, the knowledge of one party, and of which the other party has no actual or presumptive knowledge" (quotation marks omitted)).

Quintero also argues that O'Keefe's first affidavit should be disregarded as to materiality, but we need not rely on O'Keefe's affidavit to assess materiality. *See Woods v. Indep. Fire Ins. Co.*, 749 F.2d 1493, 1496 (11th Cir. 1985) (noting that materiality "can be decided as a matter of law if reasonable minds could not differ on the question."). An insured's possession of the subject property is clearly **[—17—]** material to the insurer's risk in insuring it, and we agree with the district court's commonsense observation that "insuring a stolen Vessel is akin to insuring a loss." Accordingly, the district court properly applied the doctrine of *uberrimae fidei* and correctly held Quintero's renewal policy was void *ab initio*.[2] **{-1273-}**

V. CONCLUSION

For the reasons above, the district court did not err in granting Geico's motion for summary judgment and denying Quintero's

---

[2] The renewal policy also included a fraud and concealment provision, which stated: "There is no coverage from the beginning of this policy if an **'insured'** has omitted, concealed, misrepresented, sworn falsely, or committed fraud in reference to any material matter relating to this insurance before or after any loss." Because Quintero's renewal policy was void *ab initio* under the doctrine of *uberrimae fidei*, we need not address this provision.

motion for partial summary judgment.[3] Accordingly, we affirm.

AFFIRMED.

---

[3] Quintero's notice of appeal also refers to the district court's denial of his Rule 59(e) and 60(b) motion. To the extent Quintero challenges any aspect of that ruling on appeal, his arguments lack merit.

United States Court of Appeals for the District of Columbia Circuit

United States Court of Appeals
for the District of Columbia Circuit

No. 18-5145

AMERICAN GREAT LAKES PORTS ASS'N
vs.
SCHULTZ

Appeal from the United States District Court for the District of Columbia

Decided: June 16, 2020

Citation: 962 F.3d 510, 8 Adm. R. 542 (D.C. Cir. 2020).

Before **SRINIVASAN,** Chief Judge, and **ROGERS** and **RAO,** Circuit Judges.

[—2—] {–512–} RAO, Circuit Judge:

Ships engaged in foreign trade on the Great Lakes must use pilots registered pursuant to the Great Lakes Pilotage Act of 1960. The Coast Guard administers this licensing monopoly and sets rates for the American pilots, which has resulted in ongoing disputes between the Pilots and the Great Lakes commercial shipping and port interests ("Shippers"). This case requires us to resolve an Administrative Procedure Act challenge by the Shippers to the pilot rates for the 2016 commercial shipping season ("2016 Rule"). The Shippers claim the 2016 Rule set an artificially inflated pilot rate that caused significant harm to the industry. The district court upheld parts of the 2016 Rule setting higher compensation targets for the Pilots, but held several parts of the Rule to be unsupported by the administrative record and remanded to the Coast Guard without vacating the Rule. We affirm the district court's decision in full. Although remand without vacatur is the exception rather than the rule, in these circumstances, the district court acted within its discretion, given the disruption likely to occur from reallocating rates paid several years ago.

I.

The Great Lakes Pilotage Act requires foreign vessels and American vessels participating **{–513–}** in foreign trade to hire an American or Canadian maritime pilot to assist in navigating the **[—3—]** difficult waters of the Great Lakes. *See* 46 U.S.C. §§ 9301–9308. The Act authorizes the Coast Guard to certify pilots, establish conditions of service, and set the rates that pilots must charge for their services. *See* 46 U.S.C. § 9303. Pursuant to this statutory authority, the Coast Guard has certified three pilotage associations to be the exclusive American providers of Great Lakes pilotage services in their assigned regions. *See* 81 Fed. Reg. 11,908, 11,910 (Mar. 7, 2016). When setting rates, the Coast Guard must consider "the public interest and the costs of providing the services." 46 U.S.C. § 9303(f). The Coast Guard must "establish new pilotage rates by March 1 of each year," *id.*,[1] which the agency does through notice and comment rulemaking.

After requests from the Pilots and Shippers, the Coast Guard proposed a new methodology to calculate Great Lakes pilot rates for the 2016 shipping season. The Coast Guard's proposed rule was based largely upon the recommendations of the Great Lakes Pilotage Advisory Committee (GLPAC), an entity created by Congress in 1983 for the purpose of assisting the Coast Guard in formulating rates. *See* 80 Fed. Reg. 54,484, 54,486 (Sept. 10, 2015); 46 U.S.C. § 9307(d)(2) ("The Secretary shall consider the information, advice, and **[—4—]** recommendations of the Committee in formulating policy regarding matters affecting Great Lakes pilotage."). The agency identified two reasons for changing the methodology. First, both the Pilots and the Shippers identified methodological issues that distorted the ratemaking calculation. The Pilots argued that the methodology resulted in artificially low rates that made it difficult to attract and

[1] 46 U.S.C. § 9303(f) reads in full:

> The Secretary shall prescribe by regulation rates and charges for pilotage services, giving consideration to the public interest and the costs of providing the services. The Secretary shall establish new pilotage rates by March 1 of each year. The Secretary shall establish base pilotage rates by a full ratemaking at least once every 5 years and shall conduct annual reviews of such base pilotage rates, and make adjustments to such base rates, in each intervening year.

retain pilots (harming "the public interest") and the Shippers argued that the rates were artificially inflated (ignoring "the costs of providing the services"). *See, e.g.*, 80 Fed. Reg. at 54,486. Second, the Coast Guard previously relied on union compensation data for similarly situated merchant marine masters and mates to help determine target pilot compensation; however, such data was no longer available from the union. *See id.* at 54,484.

After the public comment period, the Coast Guard finalized the 2016 Rule largely along the lines initially proposed and consistent with the GLPAC recommendations. 81 Fed. Reg. at 11,908. In adopting a new methodology, the Coast Guard found that the prior ratesetting undercompensated pilots, which resulted in pilot shortages and threats to vessel safety. The agency concluded rates must be increased to ensure a well qualified pool of pilots. *Id.* at 11,910. The new methodology was designed "to generate sufficient revenue for the pilots to provide the service [the public] require[s]." *See id.* at 11,909. To accomplish this, the Coast Guard, as relevant to this appeal, switched to the Peak Staffing Model, which pegged the number of necessary pilots to peak traffic periods in order to ensure the availability of rested pilots at all times. *See* 80 Fed. Reg. at 54,489; 81 Fed. Reg. at 11,908–909. The agency also employed Canadian pilot compensation as a benchmark for compensation, plus a ten percent cost of living upward adjustment to incentivize American **{-514-}** pilots to remain in the Great Lakes region. 81 Fed. Reg. at 11,914–915. Finally, the **[—5—]** Coast Guard estimated the rule would cost the shipping industry an additional $1.87 million annually, as well as a one-time $1.65 million expense to cover training. *Id.* at 11,937–38.

The Shippers, represented by the American Great Lakes Ports Association, filed a lawsuit challenging the 2016 Rule under the Administrative Procedure Act in the United States District Court for the District of Columbia. The Shippers disputed the overall justification for the new methodology, questioning the agency's conclusion that there was a compensation-driven pilot shortage in the Great Lakes region that could be remedied by increasing pilot rates. They also challenged the Coast Guard's failure to consider "weighting factors"[2] in the methodology; the setting of American pilot rates using Canadian pilot compensation with a ten percent upward adjustment; and the use of the new Peak Staffing Model to calculate rates.

The district court rejected the Shippers' overarching challenge to the Coast Guard's new methodology. *See Am. Great Lakes Ports Ass'n v. Zukunft*, 296 F. Supp. 3d 27, 39–41 (D.D.C. 2017). As an initial matter, the court held the Coast Guard's decision to increase rates was not arbitrary and capricious because it rested on sufficient record evidence "even absent the empirical evidence demanded by Plaintiffs." *Id.* at 39–41. The court also affirmed the Coast Guard's use of the Peak Staffing Model to determine the number of rested pilots **[—6—]** needed throughout the season because one of the agency's rationales—safety—was "amply supported" by the record. *Id.* at 42–43. The court, however, held two aspects of the Coast Guard's new methodology to be unsupported by the record. First, the court held there was no reasoned basis for setting American pilot compensation by reference to a ten percent increase over the base Canadian compensation rate because the figure came from unidentified comments during a GLPAC meeting. *Id.* at 46–48. Second, the court held that the Coast Guard acted arbitrarily by failing to account for increased pilot revenue from vessel weighting factors, resulting in a potential overcharge to the Shippers. *Id.* at 51–52. Noting the difficulty of crafting a remedy, the district court instructed the parties to file

[2] Weighting factors "are multipliers that are used by pilotage associations to calculate the actual pilotage fees that the associations will charge for any given voyage. In essence, the larger the vessel, the higher the weighting factor, and the more the pilotage associations can charge." *Am. Great Lakes Ports Ass'n v. Zukunft*, 296 F. Supp. 3d 27, 35 n.5 (D.D.C. 2017). The Shippers contended that the Coast Guard's failure to account for these factors artificially inflated the pilot rates.

supplemental briefing on the appropriate remedy. *Id.* at 56.

Following additional briefing, the district court determined, in a separate published opinion, that remand without vacatur was the appropriate remedy. *See Am. Great Lakes Ports Ass'n v. Zukunft*, 301 F. Supp. 3d 99, 104–05 (D.D.C. 2018). The Shippers urged the court to vacate the 2016 Rule and order various forms of prospective and retroactive relief to compensate for the unlawfully inflated rates. *Id.* at 102. The district court noted the Shippers' requests demonstrated they "fundamentally misunderstand th[e] Court's prior ruling" because the court had not held that the rates were too high, but instead that the rates were not justified by the administrative record. *Id.* The court found the errors in the 2016 Rule were substantial because the Coast Guard provided no support for pegging compensation to Canadian pilots or for its failure to include **{-515-}** weighting factors (which were included in the 2017 rate review). *Id.* at 103. Although the court determined the Coast Guard's errors to be significant, it remanded without vacatur because the "disruptive consequences" of vacatur outweighed the seriousness of the errors. *Id.* at 103–05. The court noted it was unclear "whether and to what extent the **[—7—]** pilotage associations might be required to issue refunds" in response to vacatur but that "to the extent that they would be required to do so, the disruptive consequences are clear." *Id.* at 104. The court thus remanded to the Coast Guard to "evaluate and justify an appropriate adjustment to benchmark compensation for its ratemaking methodology going forward." *Id.* at 105.

The Shippers appeal, arguing the district court erred in affirming parts of the 2016 Rule and further abused its discretion in declining to vacate the Rule despite finding significant parts of it unsupported by the record.

II.

As an initial matter, this court must assure itself that it has jurisdiction over the Shippers' appeal of the district court's remand order. *See Steel Co. v. Citizens for a Better Env't*, 523 U.S. 83, 94–95 (1998). The courts of appeals have jurisdiction over "all final decisions of the district courts of the United States," 28 U.S.C. § 1291, and "[a] remand order usually is not a final decision," *NAACP v. United States Sugar Corp.*, 84 F.3d 1432, 1436 (D.C. Cir. 1996). We have noted, however, that "[t]he requirement of finality is to be given a practical rather than a technical construction." *Limnia, Inc. v. Dep't of Energy*, 857 F.3d 379, 385 (D.C. Cir. 2017) (internal quotation marks omitted). A remand order "that terminate[s] an action fall[s] within the core of Section 1291's requirement of finality." *Id.* (internal quotation marks omitted).

Here, the district court's remand order effectively terminates the Shippers' action. This appeal presents the only opportunity for the Shippers to challenge the remand order. Although "a remand for significant further proceedings" generally constitutes a nonfinal order, *Pueblo of Sandia v. Babbitt*, 231 F.3d 878, 881 (D.C. Cir. 2000), the remand order **[—8—]** under review does not instruct the Coast Guard to reopen the 2016 rate review and conduct further proceedings. *See Am. Great Lakes Ports Ass'n*, 301 F. Supp. 3d at 105. The order thus finally disposed of the Shippers' APA challenges to the 2016 Rule. *See In re Long-Distance Tel. Serv. Fed. Excise Tax Refund Litig.*, 751 F.3d 629, 633 (D.C. Cir. 2014) ("[T]reating the district court's remand order as unappealable would effectively preclude ... plaintiffs from ever challenging the district court's decisions." (internal quotation marks omitted)). Moreover, it is relevant, although not dispositive, *see Limnia*, 857 F.3d at 386, that the district court characterized its remand order as "a final appealable Order." J.A. 119. In sum, we have jurisdiction over the Shippers' appeal under 28 U.S.C. § 1291.

III.

Turning to the merits, the Shippers challenge the Coast Guard's determination that a compensation-driven pilot retention crisis necessitated increased rates and that the Peak Staffing Model should be used to calculate rates. We review such challenges "*de novo*, evaluating the administrative record directly and invalidating the [agency's] actions only if, based on that record, they are arbitrary, capricious, an abuse of discretion, or otherwise not in accordance with law." **{–516–}** *Stand Up for California! v. Dep't of Interior*, 879 F.3d 1177, 1181 (D.C. Cir. 2018) (internal quotation marks omitted).

A.

The Shippers first challenge the Coast Guard's finding that a compensation-driven pilot shortage was developing on the Great Lakes, endangering both safety and efficient commerce. We agree with the Coast Guard that the record contains ample evidence of a pilot shortage on the Great Lakes and that the shortage was caused by low compensation. **[—9—]**

As to the shortage, the Coast Guard explained that the number of pilots has decreased significantly, with thirty-one pilots leaving the system. The rate of attrition has exceeded the rate of replacement, resulting in a net decrease of twenty-two percent, from forty-four to thirty-six pilots in less than a decade. *See* 81 Fed. Reg. at 11,919. The 2016 Rule includes abundant evidence that this decline has brought pilot numbers below acceptable levels, impairing the safety of Great Lakes navigation. *See, e.g., id.* at 11,918–921.

The agency also cited significant evidence demonstrating that low compensation drove this pilot shortage. For instance, comments from affected individuals and entities supported the Coast Guard's conclusion that compensation was a key factor in the retention and recruitment of pilots. Former pilots and trainees stated they "resigned because of low pay and long hours." 81 Fed. Reg. at 11,919. Hiring agents noted that "low compensation and long hours ... kept many highly qualified mariners from signing on as pilots." *Id.* Finally, one pilot commented that "10 pilots in his association took early retirement to escape the low compensation and long hours." *Id.* The administrative record thus indicated that the Great Lakes have a "retention and attraction problem" because its pilots are "the lowest paid pilots in America" and "have the highest workload in America." J.A. 468 (statement from Pilots' representative at GLPAC meeting).

The Shippers primarily challenge the agency's reliance on public comments, rather than empirical evidence. Appellant Br. 37–40. The APA, however, "imposes no general obligation on agencies to produce empirical evidence." *Stilwell v. Office of Thrift Supervision*, 569 F.3d 514, 519 (D.C. Cir. 2009). The Coast Guard's heavy reliance on comments was legitimate in this proceeding. The Great Lakes pilotage labor market is small—approximately thirty-six pilots—and the agency **[—10—]** received comments from a large segment of current and former pilots, who consistently cited compensation as a leading reason for the pilot shortage. *See* 81 Fed. Reg. at 11,917–920. "A degree of agency reliance on [comments from affected parties] is not only permissible but often unavoidable." *Nat'l Ass'n of Regulatory Util. Comm'rs v. FCC*, 737 F.2d 1095, 1124 (D.C. Cir. 1984). The Shippers provide no contrary evidence, empirical or otherwise, to suggest these firsthand accounts are not representative of pilots at large. "[A]n agency need not—indeed cannot—base its every action upon empirical data; depending upon the nature of the problem." *Chamber of Commerce of U.S. v. SEC*, 412 F.3d 133, 142 (D.C. Cir. 2005). It was entirely reasonable for the agency to rely on reasons provided by the hiring agents, pilots, and former pilots to determine that an increase in compensation would aid retention and recruitment of Great Lakes pilots.

Moreover, the Coast Guard's conclusion that compensation is a major cause of the shortage was supported by the recommendations of the Great Lakes Pilotage Advisory Committee (GLPAC). *See* 80 Fed. Reg. at 54,486; 81 Fed. Reg. at 11,911 (citing GLPAC recommendation). Congress directed that the Coast Guard "shall **{–517–}** consider" GLPAC's recommendations, 46 U.S.C. § 9307(d)(2), and here GLPAC unanimously recommended many aspects of the methodology the agency adopted in the 2016 Rule. *See* 80 Fed. Reg. at 54,486. In addition, the agency relied upon an expert evaluation in the Coast Guard-commissioned Bridge Hour Study, which identified growing concern "regarding the available candidate pool to replace pilots who will soon be retiring" and cited inadequate pay "as a leading issue" alongside "stability of pay," "quality of life," and other issues. J.A. 495; 81 Fed. Reg. at 11,908. **[—11—]**

The administrative record thus included a wealth of evidence supporting the agency's conclusion that if it "fail[ed] to implement this methodology and new rates, ... the pilot associations will not be able to recruit experienced mariners and retain their registered pilots." 81 Fed. Reg. at 11,925; *cf. FCC v. Nat'l Citizens Comm. for Broad.*, 436 U.S. 775, 814 (1978) ("[C]omplete factual support in the record for the [agency's] judgment or prediction is not possible or required; a forecast of the direction in which future public interest lies necessarily involves deductions based on the expert knowledge of the agency." (internal quotation marks omitted)). In sum, the Coast Guard reasonably concluded that "increased pilot rates are the best and quickest way to attract and retain more qualified pilots." 81 Fed. Reg. at 11,921.

B.

The Shippers also challenge the Peak Staffing Model as arbitrary and capricious. Part of the Coast Guard's new ratesetting methodology, the Model seeks to ensure the pilot rate is sufficient to cover the cost of employing "the number of pilots needed to meet each shipping season's peak pilotage demand periods without interruption to service." 80 Fed. Reg. at 54,489. In the 2016 Rule, the Coast Guard predicted the Model would reduce delays caused by insufficient staffing and also increase safe pilotage practices. *See* 81 Fed. Reg. at 11,922. The district court found the delay rationale "inconclusive" but could not "say that the evidence necessarily runs counter to the Coast Guard's conclusion." *Am. Great Lakes Ports Ass'n*, 296 F. Supp. 3d at 42. The court, however, found the record "amply supported the Coast Guard's conclusion that greater staffing levels were needed to improve safe pilotage on the Great Lakes." *Id.* at 43. The Shippers **[—12—]** maintain that the Coast Guard's explanation for its reliance on the Model is inadequate.

We find that the agency adequately supported the Peak Staffing Model on the grounds that it furthered safe pilotage. When setting rates, the Coast Guard must consider "the public interest," 46 U.S.C. § 9303(f), and this court has interpreted the public interest to include safe pilotage. *See Menkes v. DHS*, 637 F.3d 319, 334 (D.C. Cir. 2011); *accord id.* at 351 (Brown, J., dissenting in part) (noting that the text and structure of the Act "promotes maritime safety"). The Coast Guard concluded the Peak Staffing Model is necessary to ensure there are enough pilots on hand throughout the season to cover surge periods. *See* 81 Fed. Reg. at 11,922. Without pegging staffing needs to the peak periods, which may occur anytime during the season, situations will inevitably arise in which pilots will have to forgo the necessary rest periods recommended by the National Transportation Safety Board ("NTSB"). *See id.* ("Setting pilot numbers high enough to accommodate all these peak periods is essential ... to provide the recuperative monthly rest periods recommended by the NTSB in the interests of safety."). Citing multiple reports, commenters, **{-518-}** and the NTSB recommendation, the agency's decision rests on an ample record supporting the conclusion that the shortage of rested pilots endangered safety. *See, e.g.*, 81 Fed. Reg. at 11,918–922. Although the record does not support the reducing delay rationale,[3] the public safety **[—13—]** rationale provides an independent and sufficient reason for the Peak Staffing Model.

---

[3] Like the district court, we find the record inconclusive regarding a correlation between delays and staffing levels. The Coast Guard's support for the delay rationale consists of a series of charts comparing pilot staffing levels and delay hours. 81 Fed. Reg. at 11,920–921. The charts compare only two variables, pilot staffing and delay hours, and fail to demonstrate a correlation between the two. *See id.* The Coast Guard acknowledged that "[o]ther factors contribute to delays," but provided no analysis of the various factors that cause delays. *Id.* at 11,921.

In lieu of the Peak Staffing Model, which required maintaining a greater number of pilots at all times, the Shippers assert that part time contractors could supplement full time Great Lakes pilots during peak periods. Yet the Coast Guard specifically determined this alternative would be unsafe because contract pilots would not have knowledge of local waters and weather conditions in the Great Lakes and could not gain the necessary experience on short notice. *See* 81 Fed. Reg. at 11,922. Moreover, the agency explained that other pilotage systems are not proper comparators because "those systems cover smaller areas in which those pilots more easily can maintain the necessary knowledge without impacting safety." *Id.* With ample record evidence, we decline to second guess the Coast Guard's expertise over maritime safety and uphold the use of the Peak Staffing Model.

IV.

The Shippers prevailed below in their challenges to the failure to consider weighting factors and to the use of an upwardly adjusted Canadian benchmark for target pilot compensation. *See Am. Great Lakes Ports Ass'n*, 301 F. Supp. 3d at 101. Neither the Coast Guard nor the Pilots attempt to defend these aspects of the 2016 Rule on appeal.[4] The Shippers, **[—14—]** however, argue that the district court's decision to remand without vacatur was an abuse of discretion because it effectively precludes the Shippers from obtaining relief from the agency's arbitrary and capricious action.

Although "vacatur is the normal remedy" under the APA, our precedents permit a court to remand without vacating the agency's action in limited circumstances. *Allina Health Servs. v. Sebelius*, 746 F.3d 1102, 1110 (D.C. Cir. 2014). To determine whether to remand without vacatur, this court considers first, "the 'seriousness of the [action's] deficiencies,'" and, second, the "likely 'disruptive consequences' of vacatur." *Id.* (quoting **{–519–}** *Allied-Signal, Inc. v. Nuclear Regulatory Comm'n*, 988 F.2d 146, 150–51 (D.C. Cir. 1993)). The Coast Guard and Pilots do not dispute the seriousness of the errors on appeal, and so we see no need to disturb the district court's finding. *See Am. Great Lakes Ports Ass'n*, 301 F. Supp. 3d at 103 ("[T]he Court cannot conclude that the defects in the Coast Guard's 2016 Rule were not serious."). We focus on the parties' main point of contention, namely the district court's assessment of the disruptive consequences that would flow from vacating the 2016 Rule.

The Shippers contend that the district court could "easily remedy" the error by "ordering a review and repricing of the invoices from the Pilotage Associations to the shipping companies under the rates established under the prior 2015 Rule." Appellant Br. 49. Yet the district court identified **[—15—]** numerous disruptive consequences that would follow from vacating the 2016 Rule. Our review comes nearly four years after rates have been paid in reliance on the 2016 Rule. As the district court found, vacatur would mean that "every payment that was made in the 2016 season was erroneous," *Am. Great Lakes Ports Ass'n*, 301 F. Supp. 3d at 104, and may involve the Coast Guard and the Shippers attempting to recoup and redistribute funds that changed hands years ago in numerous separate transactions. *Cf. Milk Train v. Veneman*, 310 F.3d 747, 756 (D.C. Cir. 2002) (noting disruptive consequences from attempting to retrieve funds erroneously disbursed and likely

---

[4] In subsequent rate adjustments, the Coast Guard addressed both issues by including weighting factors in the calculation and by pegging target compensation to union data (available from earlier years) adjusted for inflation and Great Lakes conditions, rather than the Canadian pilots' compensation. *See* 84 Fed. Reg. 20,551, 20,553 (May 10, 2019) ("In 2017, we added ... new steps that accurately account for the ... weighting factors .... In 2018, we revised the methodology by which we develop the compensation benchmark."). **[—14—]** This controversy remains live, however, because the agency has not attempted to compensate the Shippers for potential overcharges caused by the errors in the 2016 Rule. *Cf. Cape Cod Hosp. v. Sebelius*, 630 F.3d 203, 210 (D.C. Cir. 2011) ("[S]ince the 2008 rule in no way compensated for any underpayments that might have been made in 2007, a live controversy remains regarding the hospitals' objection to the 2007 rule.").

invested by the recipients because "those moneys may not be recoverable three years later"). Further, the precise amount of each refund would be unclear given the lack of an operative 2016 rate. *See Am. Great Lakes Ports Ass'n*, 301 F. Supp. 3d at 104.

Under our precedents, a quintessential disruptive consequence arises when an agency cannot easily unravel a past transaction in order to impose a new outcome. We have rejected approaches similar to the Shippers' proposed reinvoicing as "an invitation to chaos." *Sugar Cane Growers v. Veneman*, 289 F.3d 89, 97 (D.C. Cir. 2002). More generally, although remand without vacatur remains an exceptional remedy, we have held that it is appropriate when vacatur would disrupt settled transactions. *See Milk Train*, 310 F.3d at 756; *Sugar Cane Growers*, 289 F.3d at 97 ("The egg has been scrambled and there is no apparent way to restore the status quo ante."). Because the district court acted within our precedents and its remedial discretion, we affirm its order remanding the 2016 Rule to the agency without vacatur. *Cf. Stand Up for California!*, 879 F.3d at 1190 (holding that "the district court acted well within its discretion in finding vacatur unnecessary to address any harm the defect had caused"). **[—16—]**

We recognize that a remand without vacatur does not provide the Shippers with the complete relief they sought, and agencies often delay or decline to take action in these circumstances. *See In re Core Commc'ns, Inc.*, 531 F.3d 849, 862 (D.C. Cir. 2008) (Griffith, J., concurring) ("[E]xperience suggests that [remand without vacatur] sometimes invites agency indifference."). The limits of a judicial remedy here stem in part from this particular statutory scheme, which requires the Coast Guard to review and adjust pilot rates annually. By the time an appeal winds its way to us, the egg will often be scrambled, leaving us with few options other than telling the Coast Guard, in effect, to "try better next time."[5] In its next annual rate **{–520–}** review, the agency should consider if it has the statutory authority to remedy the harms from the 2016 Rule and if doing so would comport with its mandate to consider "the public interest and the costs of providing the services." 46 U.S.C. § 9303(f).[6] **[—17—]**

* * *

For the foregoing reasons, we affirm the district court's decision in full.

So ordered.

---

[5] Government ratesetting in this regulatory program frequently leaves either the Pilots or Shippers dissatisfied. As one district court recently observed, "each year, it seems, either the shipping companies or the associations that supply the pilots sue the Coast Guard to challenge aspects of the rulemaking. The shippers perennially complain that the rates are too high, while the pilots gripe that they are too low." *Am. Great Lake Ports Ass'n v. Coast Guard*, 18-cv-2650, 2020 WL 1157028, at *1 (D.D.C. Mar. 10, 2020); *see also St. Lawrence Seaway Pilots Ass'n v. Coast Guard*, 357 F. Supp. 3d 30 (D.D.C. 2019); *St. Lawrence Seaway Pilots Ass'n, Inc. v. Coast Guard*, 85 F. Supp. 3d 197 (D.D.C. 2015).

[6] At oral argument, the government suggested the agency could account for potential overcharges to the Shippers in a future rate adjustment. *See* Oral Arg. 27:40–29:35. We take no position on whether the Great Lakes Pilotage Act provides the Coast Guard with the authority to take such an action.

United States Court of Appeals
for the District of Columbia Circuit

No. 19-1101

PACIFIC MARITIME ASS'N
vs.
NATIONAL LABOR RELATIONS BD.

On Petitions for Review and Cross-Applications for Enforcement of an Order of the National Labor Relations Board

Decided: August 4, 2020

Citation: 967 F.3d 878, 8 Adm. R. 549 (D.C. Cir. 2020).

Before **SRINIVASAN,** Chief Judge, and **ROGERS** and **RAO,** Circuit Judges.

[—2—] {-880-} ROGERS, Circuit Judge: **{-881-}**

The National Labor Relations Board determined that Pacific Maritime Association ("Pacific") and Long Beach Container Terminal ("Long Beach") committed two distinct unfair labor practices in violation of the National Labor Relations Act when they applied disciplinary provisions of one employee's collective bargaining agreement for resolving discrimination complaints to an employee represented by a different union under a collective bargaining agreement with different procedures and remedies. Pacific and Long Beach (hereinafter referred to together as "The Employers"), seek to avoid their statutory obligations by contending that they reasonably interpreted their contractual agreement with the disciplined employee to permit the use of procedures and imposition of penalties that were not included in this agreement, and their disciplinary action did not unilaterally change the terms and conditions of the disciplined employee's employment. In view of the plain text of the Employers' agreement that covered the disciplined employee and the record before the Board, we deny their petitions for review and grant the Board's cross-applications for enforcement of its Order.

I.

Pacific Maritime Association ("Pacific") and Long Beach Container Terminal ("Long Beach") are involved in shipping, longshore, and cargo-handling industries at ports on the Pacific coast. Pacific is a mutual benefit corporation that serves as the multi-employer bargaining representative for its employer members, with the primary purpose of negotiating, executing, and administering collective bargaining agreements ("CBAs"). One of its members, Long Beach, operates a marine container **[—3—]** terminal at the Port of Long Beach and employs both watchmen and marine clerks. Each classification of employee is represented by a different union, and Pacific has entered into separate agreements with each union. We begin with a summary of those CBAs.

A.

Watchmen at the Port of Long Beach have long been represented by ILWU, Warehouse, Processing and Distribution Workers Union, Local 26 ("Local 26"). Under the Watchmen's Agreement, Local 26 and Pacific jointly operate a dispatch hall that refers watchmen to work for Pacific's members. Article 18 establishes a procedure for addressing disciplinary issues and other disputes arising under the Agreement. Article 16 of the Agreement broadly prohibits discrimination against "any person" on the basis of "race, color, national origin . . . or political beliefs . . . ." Pursuant to Article 18(C), a Joint Labor Relations Committee of employer and union representatives establishes the rules and penalties governing watchmen's conduct; employers retain an unrestricted right of discipline for five offenses. Otherwise, Article **{-882-}** 18(D)(1) requires the employer to "attempt to notify and discuss the alleged incident with the individuals involved" and Local 26. "Following a good faith discussion with the Union, or inability to contact the designated Union representative within a reasonable time period," the employer may file a formal complaint, Article 18(D)(1), or request a meeting with the Joint Committee, Article 18(E). "If a satisfactory settlement cannot be reached" by the Joint Committee, then "either party may refer the matter" to the contractual Watchmen Arbitrator. *Id.* Rules control the arbitration process, including the parties' selection of arbitrators, and rules also limit appeals. [—4—]

Article 18(H) provides that the "grievance machinery" in the Watchmen's Agreement "shall be the exclusive remedy with respect to any dispute arising under [it] and no other remedies shall be used by the Union, the Employer, or any covered employee until the grievance procedures have been exhausted." Where a disciplinary action affecting a watchman's dispatch right is involved, Article 18(I) specifies that an employer complaint shall only be applicable "to the terminal where the complaint arose." Article 21 states that no provision of the contract "may be amended, modified, changed, altered or waived, except by a written document executed by the parties hereto."

The marine clerks are represented by the International Longshore and Warehouse Union ("the International"). The Pacific Coast Longshore and Clerks' Agreement ("Clerks' Agreement") covers approximately 25,000 longshore workers and marine clerks at Pacific coast ports. This CBA contains its own mechanism for the signatory unions and employers to address disputes regarding covered longshore workers and marine clerks. Notably for present purposes, the Clerks' Agreement includes Section 13.2, which establishes a special grievance procedure for resolving allegations of discrimination or harassment. Under this streamlined procedure, an individual employee may file a complaint, which will be assigned directly to an arbitrator. The arbitrator must promptly schedule an evidentiary hearing to investigate the alleged incident. Within fourteen days after the hearing, the arbitrator shall issue a written decision that includes, as necessary, disciplinary penalties consistent with the guidelines in the Clerks' Agreement. The arbitrator's decision is final, with only limited appeal. In addition to the broad prohibition on discrimination in Section 13.1, side agreements set forth rules of conduct and examples of conduct warranting discipline. In July 2014, Pacific and the International clarified, by letter of [—5—] understanding ("2014 LOU"), that Section 13.2 complaints may be brought against "other employees of [Pacific's] member companies," but those outside employees may not file Section 13.2 complaints.

B.

The events giving rise to the Board's determination that the Employers had violated the Act began on March 28, 2017. Demetrius Pleas, a watchman represented by Local 26, and a marine clerk represented by the International had a work-related argument during which both men allegedly engaged in racial name-calling. At the time, Pleas was working for Long Beach. The two employees resolved the matter informally that day, but on March 30, 2017, the marine clerk filed a grievance against Pleas pursuant to Section 13.2 of the Clerks' Agreement. Long Beach informed Local 26 the next day that it was investigating the incident and intended, if necessary, to pursue discipline against Pleas under Article 18(C) of the Watchmen's Agreement. Long Beach ultimately concluded that there was insufficient evidence {-883-} Pleas engaged in wrongdoing to warrant filing a formal Article 18 complaint, but warned Pleas that future incidents would be dealt with through the Watchmen Joint Committee process.

Meanwhile, the Arbitrator assigned to the Section 13.2 grievance scheduled a hearing for May 3, 2017. Counsel for Local 26 wrote Pacific that Local 26 was not bound by Section 13.2 and neither Local 26 nor Pleas would participate in the hearing, and requested that Pacific not take any adverse action against Local 26 members based on these proceedings. Pacific responded by letter that Long Beach and the other Pacific employer members would implement whatever discipline the Arbitrator determined would be appropriate. Neither Pleas nor a Local 26 representative attended the arbitration hearing, but [—6—] representatives from Pacific and Long Beach did attend and actively participated. At the beginning of the hearing the Arbitrator stated that he did not "really have authority over Mr. Pleas" pursuant to the Clerks' Agreement and that "it would be up to the Employer to enforce any decision if any if action was needed." Arb. Hr'g Tr. 19–20 (May 3, 2017).

Pacific made a statement that the "direct employer" (referring to Long Beach) "is prepared to implement any decision made by the Arbitrator," and that Pleas (the watchman) "is subject to complaints under Section 13.2 of the [Clerks' Agreement] as outlined in the 2014 LOU" between Pacific and the International. Arb. Dec. 3 (June 5, 2017).

The Arbitrator proposed that Pleas be barred from working at Long Beach until a final decision was rendered. In his final decision, the Arbitrator found that Pleas had violated Section 13.2 policies and should be suspended from working at all Pacific employer member terminals for twenty eight days, and also required to undertake an unpaid training video and to sign a statement pledging to abide by Section 13.2 policy before returning to work. *See id.* at 8. Local 26 appealed; the Arbitrator's Order and Decision were sustained, rejecting Local 26's jurisdictional argument. In July 2017, Pacific notified its employer members of Pleas' suspension from working at terminals covered by the Clerks' Agreement.

Local 26 filed unfair labor practice charges against the Employers in May 2017, alleging that they had violated the Act by committing two theoretically distinct unfair labor practices in disciplining watchman Pleas under the Section 13.2 procedure in the Clerks' Agreement: (1) impermissibly modifying the Watchmen's Agreement and (2) unilaterally imposing a new term and condition of employment without bargaining. The Board affirmed the decision of an administrative law judge ("ALJ") that the Employers had **[—7—]** violated Sections 8(a)(5) and (1) of the Act under either of the General Counsel's alternative theories: when they applied Section 13.2 of the Clerks' Agreement, to Pleas, an employee of the watchmen's unit represented by Local 26 and covered by that unit's Watchmen's Agreement, and when they disciplined him pursuant to the Section 13.2 process. *Pac. Mar. Ass'n*, 367 NLRB No. 121, 2019 WL 1977314, at *1, 4–6 (May 2, 2019). The Employers were ordered to cease and desist, to rescind the suspension and make Pleas financially whole, and, among other things, to delete from their records any reference to his suspension. One Member dissented, arguing the Employers did not apply the Section 13.2 procedure since they did not file the complaint, they reasonably believed the Watchmen's Agreement did not preclude imposing Section 13.2 discipline, and they did not unilaterally change the terms and conditions of Pleas' employment because there was no consistent disciplinary practice. Pacific and Long Beach both petitioned for review of the Board's Decision **{-884-}** and Order. The Board filed cross-applications for enforcement of its Order.

II.

The Board determined that the Employers committed two distinct unfair labor practices: contract modification and unilateral change. These alternative grounds for the Board's Decision involve distinct violations of the Act with different governing standards, defenses, and remedies. *Bath Iron Works Corp.*, 345 NLRB 499, 501–03 (2005), *enforced sub nom. Bath Marine Draftsmen's Ass'n v. NLRB*, 475 F.3d 14 (1st Cir. 2007). The Board has concluded that it may find an unlawful unilateral change, in addition or in the alternative, where it has also found an unlawful contract modification. *See, e.g.*, *Comau, Inc.*, 364 NLRB No. 48, 2016 WL 3853834, at *4–6 (July 14, 2016). Its counsel explains that "an employer's actions may modify a provision 'contained in' a [CBA] while **[—8—]** also imposing a change to a mandatory bargaining subject where nothing in the contract 'covers' the employer's right to act unilaterally." Resp'ts' Br. 22 (citations omitted).

The Supreme Court has recognized that "the authority of the Board and the law of contract are overlapping, concurrent regimes," and that "the Board may proscribe conduct which is an unfair labor practice even though it is also a breach of contract remediable as such by arbitration and in the courts." *NLRB v. Strong*, 393 U.S. 357, 360–61 (1969). But neither the Supreme Court nor this court has spoken directly to the question whether the Board has the authority to proceed on different theories of violation based on the same set of facts. Nor need we do so today. The Employers challenge the Board's findings of both statutory violations but they present no challenge to the application of both theories to the same set of facts. Therefore, the court has no occasion to decide whether both unfair labor practices can be properly found in cases of this sort and proceeds on the assumption the Board may do so.

Turning to the Employers' challenges, the scope of the court's review of the Board's decision is limited. As the Supreme Court has long acknowledged, Congress has determined that the Board has "the primary responsibility of marking out the scope . . . of the statutory duty to bargain," *Ford Motor Co. v. NLRB*, 441 U.S. 488, 496 (1979), and "great deference" is due to the Board because determining whether a party has violated this statutory duty is "particularly within" the Board's expertise, *see Crowley Marine Servs., Inc. v. NLRB*, 234 F.3d 1295, 1297 (D.C. Cir. 2000) (quoting *Local 13, Detroit Newspaper Printing & Graphic Commc'ns Union v. NLRB*, 598 F.2d 267, 272 (D.C. Cir. 1979)); *see also Ford Motor*, 441 U.S. at 495. Consequently, this court "must sustain the Board's decision 'unless, reviewing the record as a whole, it appears that the Board's factual findings are not supported by **[—9—]** substantial evidence, or that the Board acted arbitrarily or otherwise erred in applying established law to the facts at issue.'" *S. Nuclear Operating Co. v. NLRB*, 524 F.3d 1350, 1355 (D.C. Cir. 2008) (quoting *Int'l All. of Theatrical & Stage Emps. v. NLRB*, 334 F.3d 27, 31 (D.C. Cir. 2003)); *Universal Camera Corp. v. NLRB*, 340 U.S. 474, 477, 488 (1951); 29 U.S.C. § 160(e). Reviewing courts may not "displace the Board's choice between two fairly conflicting views," even if the court "would justifiably have made a different choice" in the first instance. *Universal Camera*, 340 U.S. at 488.

Where a challenge is made to the Board's interpretation of a contract, however, the court need give "no special deference" **{-885-}** to "ultimate legal conclusions that rest on" the Board's contract interpretations and interprets such contracts *de novo*. *Local Union No. 47, Int'l Bhd. of Elec. Workers v. NLRB*, 927 F.2d 635, 640–41 (D.C. Cir. 1991). The court applies "ordinary principles of contract law." *M&G Polymers USA, LLC v. Tackett*, 574 U.S. 427, 435 (2015). Still, the court's deference to the Board's fact-finding extends to findings necessary to interpret the meaning of the contract, "including evidence of intent from bargaining history, and other factual findings on matters bearing on the intent of the parties," as long as those findings are supported by substantial evidence in the record considered as a whole. *StaffCo of Brooklyn, LLC v. NLRB*, 888 F.3d 1297, 1302 (D.C. Cir. 2018) (citations and internal quotations marks omitted).

A.

An employer violates Sections 8(a)(5) and (1) of the Act by modifying terms and conditions of employment established in a CBA. 29 U.S.C. §§ 158(a)(1), (5), 158(d). Because the unfair labor practice question derives from an employer's statutory duty to bargain, a midterm modification is unlawful **[—10—]** only if it involves a mandatory subject of bargaining for which the employer was required to bargain in the first place. *Allied Chem. & Alkali Workers of Am., Local Union No. 1 v. Pittsburgh Plate Glass Co.*, 404 U.S. 157, 185–88 (1971). Disciplinary procedures are a mandatory subject of bargaining. *See, e.g., El Paso Elec. Co.*, 355 NLRB 428, 453 (2010), *enforced*, 681 F.3d 651, 662–64 (5th Cir. 2012).

The Board has recognized that an employer has not violated Section 8(a)(5) by modifying terms and conditions of employment under a CBA where the employer has a "sound arguable basis" for its interpretation of a contract and it is not motivated by animus or bad faith. *Bath Iron Works*, 345 NLRB at 502. This exception has limits: no "sound arguable basis" in support of an employer's purported interpretation of the contract can exist where, that interpretation runs "counter to the clear intention of the parties," *id.*, or the contract "cannot be colorably interpreted to permit" the employer's interpretation, *MV Transp., Inc.*, 368 NLRB No. 66, 2019 WL 4316958, at *30 (Sept. 10, 2019).

The Employers contend that they reasonably believed enforcing Section 13.2 of the Clerks' Agreement against watchman Pleas was consistent with the Watchmen's Agreement under which Pleas was covered. In their view, they did not modify the Article 18 procedures because no employer had filed the complaint as is contemplated by the Watchmen's Agreement; rather a marine clerk covered by the Clerk's Agreement filed the complaint. So, in their view, it was reasonable to interpret Article 18(D) regarding exhaustion requirements to apply only in cases in which an employer files a complaint. For the same reasons, they contend that there was no modification of Article 18(H), which provides that Article 18's grievance procedures are the exclusive remedy with respect to any dispute arising under the Watchmen's **[—11—]** Agreement, because the dispute was initiated by the marine clerk and arose under the Clerks' Agreement.

But as the Board concluded, Article 18 of the Watchmen's Agreement cannot be colorably interpreted to permit the Employers to unilaterally impose an alternative disciplinary procedure contrary to the exclusive procedure in that CBA, or to affirmatively grant the Employers the right to impose alternative disciplinary procedures unilaterally. First, the Employers' view that Article 18 of the Watchmen's Agreement did not limit their ability as **{-886-}** employers to discipline Pleas for racial harassment is implausible on the face of the plain terms of the CBA. Article 18(H) expressly limits the Employers' ability to discipline employees "with respect to any dispute arising under the [Agreement]" unless the "grievance procedures have been exhausted." Pleas' alleged misconduct arose under the Agreement — specifically, Article 16's anti-discrimination provision, which broadly prohibits discrimination against "any person" on the basis of "race, color, national origin, religious or political beliefs, sex, age, Veteran's status, or disability." Given the plain express terms of the Watchmen's Agreement, an employer who seeks to discipline a covered employee for conduct prohibited by Article 16, must exhaust the grievance procedures in Article 18 before pursuing other disciplinary remedies. *See Pac. Mar. Ass'n*, 367 NLRB No. 121, 2019 WL 1977314, at *5 & n.18, 20. Such procedures include filing a complaint after attempting to informally resolve the dispute with Local 26, Article 18(D)(1), or meeting with the Joint Committee and if a satisfactory settlement cannot be reached, referring the matter to the Watchmen Arbitrator, Article 18(E). The Employers did neither, and Long Beach expressly acknowledged the applicability of Article 18 procedures in declining to file a complaint against Pleas. The employers, therefore, could not reasonably conclude that, without first exhausting these **[—12—]** procedures, enforcing Section 13.2 of the Clerks' Agreement against watchman Pleas was consistent with the Watchmen's Agreement under which he was covered.

The Employers press on, contending that Article 18(C) affirmatively grants employers the right to unilaterally discipline Pleas for racial harassment. This too is facially implausible. The plain text of Article 18(C) limits the employers' unrestricted right of discipline to the specific offenses involving "intoxication, pilferage, assault, incompetency, or failure to perform work as directed." Pleas' misconduct did not fall within these five offenses. Reading Article 18(C) to provide the employers an open-ended right to unilaterally discipline, as the Employers do, would effectively render the enumeration of offenses superfluous and Article 18's established disciplinary procedures largely meaningless.

With Article 18(H) so understood, the Employers lacked a sound arguable basis for interpreting the CBA to permit their disciplinary action. Stark differences between the exclusive Article 18 grievance procedures and the Section 13.2 procedure applied by the Employers compel this conclusion. In a contract modification case, the dispositive issue is whether the Employers "had a 'sound arguable basis' for [their] actions," *Bath Iron Works*, 345 NLRB at 503. Here, the Employers interpreted their CBA with Local 26 to permit a marine clerk, covered by a different CBA, to refer his dispute with Pleas to arbitrators identified under the special Section 13.2 Grievance process and to permit the

Employers to impose the Arbitrator's discipline that exceeded the discipline allowed under the CBA that covered Pleas, and to do so without first exhausting the Article 18 procedures. The Employers' conduct in imposing discipline was inconsistent with the exclusive provisions of Article 18, such as Article 18(E), which provides that the Employers may refer grievances to the "Watchmen Arbitrator," **[—13—]** who is jointly selected and appointed by the Employers and Local 26, if a satisfactory settlement cannot be reached with the Joint Committee. Even if the marine clerk could properly file a complaint against watchman Pleas under Section 13.2, that did not mean the Employers could ignore their CBA with Local 26 that covered Pleas. Therefore, they fail to show that the Board erred in rejecting their attempt to come within the **{-887-}** scope of the sound arguable basis exception for contract interpretation.

Second, the Employers maintain that the basic premise of the Board's Decision, that they applied Section 13.2 against Pleas, is belied by the record. It is true that the Section 13.2 procedures were initially invoked and pursued by the marine clerk, and not initiated by an employer. But the Board's finding that the Employers actively participated before, during, and after the Section 13.2 arbitration hearing is supported by substantial evidence in the record considered as a whole. That evidence effectively rendered the marine clerk's complaint the Employers' complaint. Long Beach suggests it merely observed the arbitration proceeding and did not enforce the Arbitrator's order. But at the hearing, Pacific represented to the Arbitrator, without objection, that Long Beach was Pleas' direct employer and stood ready to carry out any discipline recommended by the Arbitrator, and that Pleas was subject to the Section 13.2 procedures under the 2014 LOU between Pacific and the International. Participating in this Section 13.2 arbitration proceeding was inconsistent with the terms of Pleas' Watchmen's Agreement for addressing discrimination complaints. Furthermore, the Employers "implemented the resulting discipline," Pet'rs' Br. 47, by notifying all member terminals of Pleas' suspension. That action, among others, resulted in penalties beyond those authorized under the Watchmen's Agreement. For example, when Pleas was dispatched in July 2017 for a job at Hanjin Terminal, a covered **[—14—]** terminal under the Watchmen's Agreement, he was ordered to leave.

Third, the parties' bargaining history and past practice further support the Board's conclusion that the plain language of the Watchmen's Agreement does not permit or authorize the Employers to discipline a Local 26 watchman using the special Section 13.2 procedure. In evaluating an employer's sound arguable basis, the Board may examine "both the contract language itself and relevant extrinsic evidence," such as bargaining history or past practice to determine the parties' intent, *Knollwood Country Club*, 365 NLRB No. 22, 2017 WL 1088796, at *1 (Mar. 8, 2017), and the Board has repeatedly relied on extrinsic evidence to support its sound arguable basis analysis, *see, e.g., id.* at *1 & n.8; *see also ADT, LLC*, 369 NLRB No. 31, 2020 WL 996271, at *5 & n.10 (Feb. 27, 2020); *see also Comau*, 364 NLRB No. 48, 2016 WL 3853834, at *5 & n.16. The Board's analysis here is in line with its precedent. The Board first determined that the "clear language" of Article 18 prohibited the Employers' disciplinary action and then explained how the parties' past practice and bargaining history supported this finding. *Pac. Mar. Ass'n*, 367 NLRB No. 121, 2019 WL 1977314, at *5.

There is substantial evidence to support the Board's finding that Local 26 consistently rejected the Employers' proposals to incorporate procedures similar to a Section 13.2 procedure into the Watchmen's Agreement. During negotiations in 2008 and 2014, the Employers proposed that a Section 13.2 procedure be added to the Watchmen's Agreement and Local 26 repeatedly rejected these proposals. The Employers suggest that the Board has mischaracterized the record evidence because the parties never bargained over whether a non-watchman could use Section 13.2 to accuse a watchman of workplace harassment. Yet evidence credited by **[—15—]** the ALJ indicated that in October

2014 Pacific proposed to amend Article 16 to allow "*any* employee" to file a Section 13.2 type grievance, General Counsel Ex. 5 (Employer Proposals: Article 16 (Oct. 8, 2014)) (emphasis added), and Local 26 rejected this proposal. **{-888-}**

There also is substantial evidence to support the Board's finding that the parties have historically used Article 18 procedures to resolve complaints of worker-versus-worker harassment. Sometimes this has been done informally with Local 26; other times it has been done through the formal complaint process. In the instant case, Long Beach notified Local 26 of its investigation into the discrimination allegations, and later issued Pleas an informal warning that future such occurrences would be resolved through the Article 18 disciplinary process. Long Beach's general manager testified that he had had informally resolved at least two dozen similar harassment complaints by issuing warning letters. In 2016, when Long Beach filed a formal Article 18 complaint against a watchman accused of harassing another watchman in violation of Article 16, the matter was resolved by the Joint Committee.

Still, the Employers maintain that the evidence fails to support the Board's position that Article 18 is the exclusive means for addressing these types of complaints. Putting aside the fact that Article 18(H) clearly states as much, the Employers point to no record evidence that the parties intended for the Employers to have a unilateral right to enforce Section 13.2 against covered watchmen accused of discrimination. It is undisputed that the parties have not previously resolved worker-versus-worker harassment allegations in this way. The Board could properly conclude, therefore, that the Employers had no sound arguable basis to believe that their Section 13.2 **[—16—]** disciplinary action was consistent with the Watchmen's Agreement.

Fourth, the Employers maintain that Local 26 is not entitled to override the Employers' agreements with other unions and other workers' rights under these agreements. They misconstrue federal labor law and principles of contract law. The Act establishes a system of exclusive collective-bargaining representation in which employers are statutorily obligated to bargain with their employees' chosen representative over subjects such as employee disciplinary procedures. *See* 29 U.S.C. §§ 158(a)(5), 159(a); *see generally First Nat. Maint. Corp. v. NLRB*, 452 U.S 666, 674–79 (1981). The Employers speculate that if they had refused to enforce Section 13.2, then the Board would have entertained contract modification charges from the marine clerk's union. Even if that were true, which we need not decide, it does not change the Employers' statutory and contractual obligations to Local 26.

"[A] contract cannot bind a nonparty." *EEOC v. Waffle House, Inc.*, 534 U.S. 279, 294 (2002). Local 26, the watchmen employees' union, was not a party to the Clerks' Agreement. Neither was there evidence that Local 26 had acted in a manner as would give the Employers reason to conclude that Local 26 had agreed, albeit informally and not in writing as Article 21 contemplated, to the use of Section 13.2 procedures where a non-watchman files a complaint against a covered watchman, nor any other evidence that the Agreement permitted this departure from Article 18 procedures. Local 26 is apparently the last holdout among unions with which Pacific contracts to use Section 13.2 procedures, most recently in negotiations for the 2014-2019 Watchmen's Agreement. The Employers point to no conduct by Local 26 that provided a basis for them to conclude that the Agreement would permit using Section 13.2 procedures against watchman Pleas. **[—17—]**

In sum, this contractual defense, much like the Employers' others, ignores the plain text of the Watchmen's Agreement, **{-889-}** the parties' bargaining history, and their negotiations for the 2014-2019 contract where Local 26 again rejected the Employers' proposal to import the special Section 13.2 disciplinary procedure in the Clerks' Agreement into the Watchmen's Agreement. The remainder of the Employers' challenges to the contract-modification violation fail because the Board's findings are supported by substantial evidence in the record considered as a whole.

Our dissenting colleague changes the question before the court. To avoid the plain text of the Watchmen's Agreement covering Pleas, the dissent defines the relevant question as whether the Employers had "a sound arguable basis for concluding that employee discipline may occur before or apart from filing an employer grievance under the Watchmen's Agreement." Dis. Op. 13; *see also id.* 2, 16. The answer provided distorts the standard adopted by the Board for the sound arguable basis exception, and it does not meaningfully engage with the Employers' disciplinary action against Pleas nor with Article 18(H)'s exclusivity and exhaustion requirements, much less Article 18's provisions on individual cases of employee discipline. Not only does Article 18(H) provide that the Article 18 procedures are the "exclusive remedy with respect to *any* dispute arising under the [Watchmen's Agreement]," *id.* (emphasis added), but Article 18(D) regarding employer complaints of employee discipline, provides that Employers "may implement the established procedures as outlined in Articles 18 and 19 of Agreement," Article 18(D)(1). Article 18(D)(1) requires the Employers to participate in a good faith discussion with Local 26 prior to implementing the Article 18 procedures, namely referring a matter to the Joint Committee, Article 18(E), or filing a formal complaint, Article 18(D); there is no exception to Article **[—18—]** 18(H)'s exclusivity and exhaustion requirements. To the extent our colleague interprets Article 18(H) to mean that the Pleas disciplinary incident did not "aris[e] under" the Watchmen's Agreement, this interpretation also flounders on the plain text. And in responding to the dissent by pointing to the plain text's statement of what Article 18(H)'s exclusivity entails, the court does not create a rationale for denying the petitions other than the Board's reliance on Article 18.

Authority involving a different context and different contract terms does not advance the dissent's position. *See* Dis. Op. 10–11. For example, in *Nolde Bros., Inc. v. Local No. 358,* 430 U.S. 243 (1977), the Supreme Court considered whether an arbitration clause in a CBA that required the parties to arbitrate "any grievance" arising between the parties applied to a contractual dispute over severance pay that arose after the contract's termination. *Id.* at 244–45, 248–49. Moreover, even applying the reasoning in *Nolde Brothers* to Article 18(H), the Court's interpretation of "arising under" supports the Board's conclusion that the Employers lacked a sound arguable basis for their disciplinary action, which was precluded by the plain text of the Watchmen's Agreement.

Nor does resolution of whether Pleas' conduct violated the no-discrimination provision of Article 16 "hinge[] on the interpretation ultimately given" by the Arbitrator to the Section 13.2 policy of the Clerks' Agreement, *Nolde Bros.*, 430 U.S. at 249, because the present dispute does not cease to arise under the Watchmen's Agreement simply because the Employers chose not to determine whether Pleas violated Article 16 of that Agreement using Article 18 procedures and instead chose to apply the different procedures and penalties in the Clerks' Agreement, enforcing Section 13.2 remedies in the Arbitrator's order. The Employers **{–890–}** did not challenge the Board's internal **[—19—]** operating procedures using three-member panels, *see* Dis. Op. 19, and consequently that issue is not properly before the court, *see* 29 U.S.C. § 160(e).

B.

An employer violates Sections 8(a)(5) and (1) "by unilaterally changing an existing term or condition of employment without first bargaining to impasse." *Regal Cinemas, Inc. v. NLRB*, 317 F.3d 300, 309 & n.5 (D.C. Cir. 2003). The General Counsel must show that "there is an employment practice concerning a mandatory bargaining subject, and that the employer has made a significant change thereto *without bargaining.*" *Bath Iron Works*, 345 NLRB at 501 (emphasis in original). Disciplinary procedures are a mandatory subject of bargaining. *See, e.g., El Paso Elec.*, 355 NLRB at 453.

The Employers contend that the Board's finding that there was a significant change to an established employment practice is not supported by substantial evidence. They assert that allegations of worker-versus-worker discrimination were not previously addressed in any consistent way and were often handled outside of Article 18's process. But the record before the Board shows that the parties had consistently utilized the established Article 18 disciplinary procedure in the Watchmen's Agreement to discipline bargaining unit employees and that this included the informal resolution of disputes prior to the issuance of formal employer complaints. *See, e.g.*, Bill Carson testimony, ALJ Hr'g Tr. 465–66 (Apr. 17, 2018); Letter of March 31, 2017, from Long Beach General Manager Bill Carson to Luisa Gratz, Local 26 President; Letter of April 27, 2017, from Long Beach to Pleas. Indeed, as noted, even in the present case Long Beach acknowledged that if Pleas were to be formally disciplined, it would be pursuant to the **[—20—]** Watchmen's Agreement. Although there is no evidence of an established practice for handling inter-union employee complaints, the Employers acknowledge that a non-Local 26 employee had never filed a harassment complaint against a watchman. Pet'rs' Br. 53. Absent established disciplinary practices to resolve this type of dispute, the Employers' decision to enforce Section 13.2 against a covered watchman was a change in practice and itself a deviation from the *status quo* that supports the Board's determination that there was a unilateral change without bargaining. *See NLRB. v. Katz*, 369 U.S. 736, 744–47 (1962); *Wilkes-Barre Hosp. Co. v. NLRB*, 857 F.3d 364, 375–76 (D.C. Cir. 2017). *Cf. E.I. Du Pont De Nemours & Co. v. NLRB*, 682 F.3d 65, 67–68 (D.C. Cir. 2012).

The Employers' invocation of the contract coverage doctrine fares no better. The court has interpreted the "contract coverage" standard in unilateral-change cases to present the question whether a union has already "exercise[d] its right to bargain" by memorializing in a contract the employer's right to act unilaterally, thereby removing the covered action from the range of further mandatory bargaining. *NLRB v. U.S. Postal Serv.*, 8 F.3d 832, 836 (D.C. Cir. 1993) (quoting *Local Union No. 47*, 927 F.2d at 640). The evidence does not show that Local 26 ever "surrendered the[] right to bargain over the . . . change[] through either waiver or contract." *Wilkes-Barre Hosp.*, 857 F.3d at 376 (quoting *S. Nuclear Operating*, 524 F.3d at 1357).

The Employers maintain that the Board's ruling must be vacated because the Board applied a "clear and unmistakable waiver" standard and the Board recently ruled that the "contract coverage" doctrine is the appropriate mode of analysis, **{-891-}** *MV Transp.*, 368 NLRB No. 66, 2019 WL 4316958, at *1. The Board noted that application of the "contract coverage" standard would not require a different result. *Pac.* **[—21—]** *Mar. Ass'n*, 367 NLRB No. 121, 2019 WL 1977314, at *6 n.21. Even so, the Employers maintain that the Board failed to explain, under the contract coverage doctrine, why procedures related to employee discipline in the Watchmen's Agreement did not encompass the Employers' decision to apply Section 13.2 to Pleas. Yet after reviewing the text of the Watchmen's Agreement, the parties' bargaining history, and the parties' past practice, and concluding that the Employers had no sound arguable basis for their interpretation of the Agreement, the Board also concluded that the Agreement did not cover the Employers' disciplinary action. *Id.* at *5–6 & n.21. Given the overlap between the sound arguable basis and contract coverage analysis, (as conceded by the Employers, *see* Oral Arg. Tape 6:55–8:17 (Jan. 22, 2020)), the Employers fail to demonstrate that the Board's explanation was deficient.

To conclude that a CBA covers the challenged unilateral conduct, the conduct must fall "within the compass or scope of contract language granting the employer the right to act unilaterally." *MV Transp.*, 368 NLRB No. 66, 2019 WL 4316958, at *17; *see also Wilkes-Barre Hosp.*, 857 F.3d at 377. In the Employers' view, their conduct falls "within the compass" of the Watchmen's Agreement even if the Agreement does not specifically authorize discipline pursuant to Section 13.2 because the Agreement grants an "unrestricted unilateral right to impose discipline for a number of broadly stated reasons" and "any dispute over the propriety of Pleas's discipline falls 'within the compass' of the Watchmen's Agreement." Pet'rs' Br. 59–60. As noted, Pleas was not disciplined for any of the exempted offenses in Article 18(C), and disciplinary disputes falling within the terms of Article 16 of the Watchmen's Agreement are governed by Article 18's procedure, which is exclusive and does not encompass Section 13.2. Given the text of the Watchmen's Agreement and the Employers' bargaining history with Local 26, their attempt to **[—22—]** stretch the Agreement to cover the Section 13.2 discipline is implausible at best. Although the contract coverage standard does not require that the parties' Agreement "specifically mention" the disciplinary action at issue, *see Wilkes-Barre Hosp.*, 857 F.3d at 377 (quoting *Enloe Med. Ctr. v. NLRB*, 433 F.3d 834, 839 (D.C. Cir. 2005)), nor does it mean an employer can unilaterally change the terms and conditions of employment without bargaining because they fall within a broad subject area that the parties' Agreement had addressed in other respects, *cf. id.* at 376–77. The Employers' interpretation of the Watchmen's Agreement would render its long-familiar and carefully bargained-for terms meaningless by achieving the modification of the Agreement that Local 26 had repeatedly rejected during bargaining with Pacific. This approach is contrary to the Employers' statutory obligations under Sections 8(a)(5) and (d) of the Act to adhere to the terms of the Agreement and effectively dismisses the Supreme Court's reasoning on the importance of abiding by the parties' Agreement, *see First Nat. Maint. Corp.*, 452 U.S. at 674.

In sum, assuming that both of the theories for violation can be applied, the court sustains the Board's determinations that the Employers made both a midterm contract modification and a unilateral change to the terms and conditions of Pleas' employment. The Board could properly conclude, in view of the plain text of the Watchmen's Agreement, that there was no "sound arguable basis" for the Employers to apply the Clerks' Agreement Section 13.2 procedures and enforce the Arbitrator's order against Pleas, who was covered **{-892-}** under the Watchmen's Agreement. And, by so doing, the Employers unlawfully unilaterally changed the terms and conditions of Pleas' employment. Accordingly, the court denies the petitions for review and grants the Board's cross-applications for enforcement of its Order.

(Reporter's Note: Opinion concurring in part and dissenting in part follows on p. 559).

[—1—] {-892-} **RAO,** Circuit Judge, concurring in part and dissenting in part:

The National Labor Relations Board ("NLRB" or "the Board") found the employers in this case violated federal law by committing two unfair labor practices: first, unlawfully modifying a collective bargaining agreement without union consent; and second, unilaterally imposing new terms and conditions of employment without providing the union notice and an opportunity to bargain. While the majority enforces both unfair labor practices, I would vacate the contract modification finding. The Board may find a contract modification only when an employer violates a specific contractual term that plainly bars the actions taken. Because the relevant collective bargaining agreement is silent or at least ambiguous as to the discipline imposed in this case, the employers had reasonable grounds for their disciplinary actions under the "sound arguable basis" standard. This well-established standard ensures that the Board does not overreach into ordinary labor contractual disputes that Congress placed firmly within the jurisdiction of the federal courts. Because the majority relaxes longstanding standards for contract modification, I respectfully dissent from Part II.A of the court's opinion.

I.

The majority carefully sets out the relevant facts, Maj. Op. 2–7, but I would frame this contractual dispute in a somewhat different way. The Long Beach Container Terminal and the Pacific Maritime Association ("the Employers") entered into a collective bargaining agreement known as the Watchmen's Agreement with ILWU, Warehouse, Processing and Distribution Workers' Union, Local 26 ("the Union"). The Union represents watchmen at the Employers' port facilities. Demetrius Pleas was a member of the Union and thus subject to the Watchmen's Agreement. Marine clerks at the port facilities are represented by a different union operating under a different contract, the Pacific Coast Longshore and Clerks' Agreement ("Clerks' Agreement"). When Pleas made racially [—2—] insensitive comments in the workplace, a marine clerk filed a complaint under Section 13.2 of the Clerks' Agreement, which sends discrimination complaints to an arbitrator to resolve factual disputes and recommend appropriate discipline. The Employers allowed the clerk's complaint against Pleas to proceed under Section 13.2 and imposed the arbitrator's recommended discipline. Both the Board and the majority emphasize that the Employers used the wrong mechanism when disciplining Pleas because they should have filed a grievance under Article 18 of the Watchmen's Agreement rather than use the Section 13.2 process. *Pac. Mar. Ass'n*, 367 NLRB No. 121, at *5–6 (May 2, 2019); *see* Maj. Op. 9–19.

The distinction between Section 13.2 of the Clerks' Agreement and Article 18 of the Watchmen's Agreement, however, is a red herring. The contract modification charge does not turn on whether the Employers disciplined Pleas pursuant to the Section 13.2 process. Rather, the dispositive issue is whether the Watchmen's Agreement allows the Employers to impose discipline at their discretion or instead requires the Employers to discipline Union members exclusively through an Article 18 grievance. Thus, my analysis focuses on whether the Employers justified **{-893-}** disciplining Pleas under a reasonable interpretation of the Watchmen's Agreement—a burden they readily carried here—and whether the Board respected limitations on its jurisdiction by adjudicating this case under the appropriate legal standard.

Understanding the Board's limited authority over contractual matters requires recollecting the distinction between unfair labor practices under the National Labor Relations Act of 1935 ("NLRA") and breaches of contract under the Labor Management Relations Act of 1947 ("LMRA"), a distinction the majority overlooks. The NLRA creates public rights related to collective bargaining and **[—3—]** empowers the Board to adjudicate unfair labor practices infringing those rights. Section 8(a)(5) and (1) of the NLRA make it unlawful for an employer to "refuse to bargain" with employee representatives on wages, hours, and other mandatory subjects of bargaining. 29 U.S.C. § 158(a)(5), (1). Section

8(d) protects the integrity of the collective bargaining process by prohibiting parties from "terminat[ing] or modify[ing]" provisions "contained in" a collectively bargained agreement. *Id.* § 158(d), (d)(4). The Board's authority over matters of contract extends only as far as adjudicating unfair labor practices. Traditional contractual disputes, by contrast, are reserved for the federal courts under Section 301 of the LMRA, which recognizes that collective bargaining agreements are voluntary contracts between employers and unions giving rise to private rights when breached. To vindicate contractual rights, the LMRA grants district courts broad jurisdiction over "[s]uits for violation of contracts between an employer and a labor organization." 29 U.S.C. § 185(a); *see Dist. No. 1 v. Liberty Mar. Corp.*, 933 F.3d 751, 756–58, 7 Adm. R. 536, 537–39 (D.C. Cir. 2019).

The jurisdictional division between the NLRA and the LMRA means the Board interprets contracts only "so far as [is] necessary" to determine whether an unfair labor practice occurred. *Honeywell Int'l, Inc. v. NLRB*, 253 F.3d 119, 124 (D.C. Cir. 2001) (quoting *NLRB v. C&C Plywood Corp.*, 385 U.S. 421, 428 (1967)). "But the federal courts, not the Board, are legislatively empowered to be the primary interpreters of contracts." *Id.* (citing *Litton Fin. Printing Div. v. NLRB*, 501 U.S. 190, 202–03 (1991)). Under prevailing standards for contract-related unfair labor practices and associated defenses, the Board performs a "limited review" of a labor contract's plain language to determine whether to assert jurisdiction. *MV Transp., Inc.*, 368 NLRB No. 66, at *17 (Sept. 10, 2019). Resolving contractual ambiguity by reaching beyond the plain **[—4—]** meaning, however, is a task reserved for the courts. As the agency freely admits, "the Board is not an expert in contract interpretation, nor was it intended to be." *Id.* at *9 (cleaned up). When contractual obligations are in dispute, "[t]he Board is not the proper forum for parties seeking an interpretation of their collective-bargaining agreement." *Vickers, Inc.*, 153 NLRB 561, 570 (1965). That much flows from the bargaining structure of the NLRA, which leaves employers and unions free to set the terms and conditions of employment by mutual consent rather than administrative fiat. Orders of the Board are "ineffective to determine any private rights of the employees and leave[] them free to assert such legal rights as they may have acquired under their contracts." *Nat'l Licorice Co. v. NLRB*, 309 U.S. 350, 366 (1940); *cf. Stern v. Marshall*, 564 U.S. 462, 484 (2011) ("[I]n general, Congress may not 'withdraw from judicial cognizance any matter which, from its nature, is the subject of a suit at the common law, or in **{–894–}** equity, or admiralty.'") (quoting *Murray's Lessee v. Hoboken Land & Improvement Co.*, 59 U.S. (18 How.) 272, 284 (1856)).

Jurisdictional considerations thus operate in the background of the Board's adjudication of contract modification charges under Sections 8(a)(5) and (d). Judicial review of such cases ensures the Board respects limits on its authority and does not decide breach of contract claims that Congress assigned to the courts. Accordingly, we review the Board's contract interpretation de novo while according substantial evidence deference to the agency's findings of fact. *StaffCo of Brooklyn, LLC v. NLRB*, 888 F.3d 1297, 1302 (D.C. Cir. 2018). To determine whether the Board misapplied governing law in an arbitrary and capricious manner, "we must identify the standard at issue, examine its application in prior adjudications, and then determine whether the instant case is a faithful application of existing law or instead a *sub silentio* **[—5—]** revision." *Circus Circus Casinos, Inc. v. NLRB*, 961 F.3d 469, 476 (D.C. Cir. 2020).

II.

As the Board has explained on multiple occasions, contract modification and unilateral change unfair labor practices "are fundamentally different in terms of principle, possible defenses, and remedy." *ADT, LLC*, 369 NLRB No. 31, at *3 (Feb. 27, 2020); *MV Transp.*, 368 NLRB No. 66, at *27–28; *Bath Iron Works Corp.*, 345 NLRB 499, 501 (2005). In this case, the Board found that the Employers both unilaterally changed established practice and modified the

Watchmen's Agreement by imposing terms from Section 13.2 of the Clerks' Agreement. *Pac. Mar.*, 367 NLRB No. 121, at *5–6. In doing so, the Board contradicted precedents that foreclose finding both unilateral change and contract modification based on the same underlying employer conduct.[1] Because the Employers **[—6—]** failed to challenge the joint nature of the findings, however, we cannot vacate the Board's order on this basis. 29 U.S.C. § 160(e); *see* Maj. Op. 8.

On these facts, I join the majority in enforcing the Board's unilateral change finding because the Employers imposed new terms and conditions of employment without giving the Union notice and an opportunity to bargain. *Pac. Mar.*, 367 NLRB No. 121, at *6; *see* Maj. Op. 19–22. Unilateral changes to prior practices violate Sections 8(a)(5) and (1) by circumventing the Section 8(d) procedural protections meant to promote collective bargaining. **{-895-}** *NLRB v. Katz*, 369 U.S. 736, 743 (1962). To prove a unilateral change, the Board must show (1) "an established past practice" and (2) "'a material, substantial, and significant change'" to that practice without bargaining. *ABF Freight Sys., Inc.*, 369 NLRB No. 107, at *2 (June 19, 2020) (quoting *MV Transp.*, 368 NLRB No. 66, at *4). Substantial evidence supports the Board's view that the Employers had established past practices of investigating discrimination allegations against watchmen informally and imposing less severe penalties than those levied against Pleas. By participating in and adopting the results of procedures from Section 13.2 of the Clerks' Agreement, the Employers made material changes to employee discipline, an employment term recognized as a mandatory subject of bargaining. *See El Paso Elec. Co.*, 355 NLRB 428, 453 (2010).

Yet these same facts do not support a contract modification violation, which turns on matters of contract interpretation for which the Board has considerably less prerogative and enjoys **[—7—]** no judicial deference. Contract modification is an unfair labor practice under Sections 8(a)(5) and (d) because failing to adhere to agreed-upon terms undermines collective bargaining and a union's role as the employees' chosen representative. To find contract modification, the Board must (1) identify "a specific term 'contained in' the contract" to which a party failed to adhere without the consent of the counterparty, *United Auto. Workers v. NLRB*, 765 F.2d 175, 179 (D.C. Cir. 1985) (quoting 29 U.S.C. § 158(d)(4)), and (2) assess the four corners of the agreement to determine whether the charged party has a "sound arguable basis" for interpreting the contract to support its actions, *Bath Iron Works*, 345 NLRB at 502. Under the "sound arguable basis" standard, an alleged breach of contract is not an unfair labor practice if the party acted under a "reasonable" interpretation of the contract. *MV Transp.*, 368 NLRB No. 66, at *28. "[W]hen 'an employer has a sound arguable basis for ascribing a particular meaning to his contract and his action is in accordance with the terms of the contract as he construes it,' the Board will not enter the dispute to serve the function of arbitrator in determining which party's interpretation is correct." *NCR Corp.*, 271 NLRB 1212, 1213 (1984) (quoting *Vickers*, 153 NLRB at 570). In

---

[1] Although our court has yet to definitively address the issue, the Board's precedents have long treated contract modification and unilateral change as mutually exclusive. Contract modification charges "require greater proof" because their remedy—specific performance of the contract's terms—is more severe than that assessed for the "lesser allegation" of unilateral change. *ABF Freight Sys., Inc.*, 369 NLRB No. 107, at *4 & n.8 (June 19, 2020) (citing *Bath Iron Works*, 345 NLRB at 502–03). In rare situations, the Board has found both violations when an employer imposed multiple rules at the same time, some of which modified an existing contract and some of which altered established practice. *See, e.g., Comau, Inc.*, 364 NLRB No. 48, at *4–6 (July 14, 2016). Since deciding this case, the Board has reaffirmed that the findings are mutually exclusive: "Unlike an employer that unlawfully modifies a contract, an employer that implements an unlawful unilateral change only needs to restore the status quo ante until the parties reach an impasse in bargaining. Because the remedies are mutually exclusive, an allegedly unlawful employer decision cannot be *both* a unilateral **[—6—]** change *and* a contract modification." *ADT*, 369 NLRB No. 31, at *3 (citing *Bath Iron Works*, 345 NLRB at 503). While the NLRB's general counsel may allege both theories in the alternative, the Board will not find both violations simultaneously. *Id.*

other words, only clear violations of an unambiguous term rise to the level of an unlawful contract modification.

In finding contract modification on these facts, the Board departed from longstanding precedent in three ways. First, the Board failed to identify a specific contract provision "contained in" the Watchmen's Agreement that the Employers modified. Second, the Board misapplied the "sound arguable basis" standard by rejecting the Employers' reasonable interpretation of the Watchmen's Agreement as allowing employee discipline outside the Article 18 grievance process. Third, by relying on extrinsic evidence of bargaining history, the Board transgressed the limitations on its contract interpretation **[—8—]** authority. In my view, any one of these errors requires vacating the contract modification finding. Taken together, they represent a troubling departure from applicable standards and undermine the clarity and predictability of federal labor law.

A.

To determine whether the Employers unlawfully modified the contract, the Board was required first to identify a specific term "contained in" in the Watchmen's Agreement that the Employers ignored without the Union's consent. *United Auto. Workers*, 765 F.2d at 179; *see also St. Vincent Hosp.*, 320 NLRB 42, 42 (1995); *Milwaukee Spring Div.*, 268 NLRB 601, 602 (1984). The Board concluded the **{-896-}** Employers modified Articles 18(D) and (H) by disciplining Pleas after arbitration under Section 13.2 of the Clerks' Agreement rather than filing an employer grievance under Article 18 of the Watchmen's Agreement. *Pac. Mar.*, 367 NLRB No. 121, at *5–6. Although employee arbitration under Section 13.2 was a departure from prior practice and thus an unlawful unilateral change, this does not necessarily mean the Employers modified Article 18 when they adopted the results of arbitration. Instead, the ultimate question is whether the Watchmen's Agreement requires the Employers to discipline Pleas exclusively through Article 18's "Grievance Machinery." Watchmen's Agreement at 33 ("W.A."). For the following reasons, the Watchmen's Agreement provisions identified by the Board do not require the Employers to discipline employees exclusively through an employer grievance under Article 18.

As an initial matter, "grievance" is a term of art in the collective bargaining context that means more than a "complaint" or "dispute." As the Supreme Court has explained, "[t]he processing of disputes through the grievance machinery is actually a vehicle by which meaning and content **[—9—]** are given to the collective bargaining agreement." *United Steelworkers of Am. v. Warrior & Gulf Nav. Co.*, 363 U.S. 574, 581 (1960). The Watchmen's Agreement grievance machinery is a specific type of complaint process that covers some, but not all, disputes arising between employees and the Employers. Article 18(D) requires the Employers to attempt informal resolution with affected parties before submitting a "grievance" to the joint Labor Relations Committee.[2] If the Com-

[2] Article 18(D) reads, in relevant part:

> Prior to a complaint being filed by the Employer or the Union, the following procedures shall apply:
>
> (1.) (A.) The Employer shall notify and discuss the alleged incident with the individuals involved and president and/or a steward of [the Union] and attempt to resolve the matter. Whatever evidence the parties have or have relied upon relating to the discharge and/or grievance shall be provided to the Union at the time of request. ... Following a good faith discussion with the Union, ... the Employers may implement the established procedures as outlined in Articles 18 and 19 of the Agreement.
>
> (B.) The Union shall notify and discuss the alleged incident with management and attempt to resolve the matter. ... Following a good faith discussion with the Employer, ... the Union may implement the established procedures as outlined in Article[s] 18 and 19 of the Agreement.
>
> (2.) In cases of discipline and/or discharge, the Employer shall identify, specifically, and describe in detail the violation committed by the watchman. The Employer shall specify

mittee is unable to negotiate a resolution, the matter may proceed to arbitration between the Employers and the Union. W.A. at 33–34; *see also* Art. 18(E)–(G), W.A. at 34–35. Nothing in Article 18(D) requires or suggests that the **[—10—]** Employers must file a contractual grievance *before* investigating employee misconduct or imposing discipline.

Similarly, Article 18(H) speaks to the scope of the grievance procedure but does not require prior Labor Relations Committee approval of employee discipline: "This grievance machinery shall be the exclusive remedy with respect to any dispute arising under the Collective-Bargaining Agreement and no other remedies shall be used by the Union, the Employer, or any covered employee until the grievance procedures have been exhausted." W.A. at 35. Article 18(H) says nothing about employee discipline. Yet the Board and the majority would insert new language into the Watchmen's Agreement by reading Article 18(H) to "*expressly limit*[] the Employers' ability **{-897-}** to discipline employees 'with respect to any dispute arising under the [Agreement].'" Maj. Op. 11 (emphasis added). There is simply no textual basis for claiming that Article 18(H) makes any provision, express or otherwise, regarding the discipline of employees. *Accord Pac. Mar.*, 367 NLRB No. 121, at *12 (Kaplan dissenting).

The Watchmen's Agreement subjects only those disputes "arising under" its terms exclusively to the Article 18 grievance process. Grievances "aris[e] under" a contract provision when "the resolution of that claim hinges on the interpretation ultimately given the contract clause." *Nolde Bros., Inc. v. Local No. 358*, 430 U.S. 243, 249 (1977). Despite containing detailed rules on many aspects of the employment relationship, the Agreement is generally silent on matters of discipline. The Employers' decision to discipline in this case does not "arise under" the Agreement because no term speaks to Pleas's conduct or the resulting consequences. Grievance procedures like those in Article 18 cannot be read expansively to cover matters outside the contract without undermining the freedom of contract policies embedded in federal labor law. *Cf. Dep't of* **[—11—]** *Navy v. FLRA*, 962 F.2d 48, 57 (D.C. Cir. 1992) ("Because of the fundamental policy of freedom of contract, the parties are generally free to agree to whatever specific rules they like, and in most circumstances it is beyond the competence of the ... National Labor Relations Board or the courts to interfere with the parties' choice."). Without any indication that the parties intended to do so, we have no basis for assuming a contractual grievance process covers individual cases of employee discipline.[3]

In reaching a contrary reading of Articles 18(D) and (H), the Board stated only that "article 18's plain language establishes that the parties intended to prohibit all other mechanisms—including, a fortiori, one set forth in a different contract covering a different bargaining unit—for addressing alleged watchman misconduct." *Pac. Mar.*, 367 NLRB No. 121, at *5. The majority now adopts this finding by relying on an argument the Board did not: that this dispute "arose under" Article 16 of the Watchmen's Agreement, which "broadly prohibits discrimination against 'any person' on the basis of 'race, color, national origin, [and] religious or political beliefs.'" Maj. Op. 11, 18–19. The Board, however, relied exclusively on its reading of Article 18 to find an unlawful contract modification. *See Pac. Mar.*, 367 NLRB No. 121, at **[—12—]** *5–6.[4] We cannot

the company procedure and/or Contract provision violated.

[3] The grievance provision of the Clerks' Agreement, by contrast, explicitly specifies that a joint labor relations committee shall "investigate and adjudicate any complaint against any clerk whose conduct on the job ... causes disruption of normal harmony in the relationship of the parties hereto or the frustration and/or violation of the provisions of the working or dispatching rules or of this Agreement." Clerks' Agreement § 17.125, at 59. The contrast between this language and Article 18(H) demonstrates the Employers and the Union had alternative language readily available but instead left discipline outside the scope of matters subject exclusively to the grievance process in the Watchmen's Agreement.

[4] The Board referred to Article 16 to reject an argument by one of the Employers that the

sustain an agency's decision on a different basis than the one relied upon below. *See SEC v. Chenery Corp.*, 332 U.S. 194, 196–97 (1947); *Point Park Univ. v. NLRB*, 457 F.3d 42, 50 (D.C. Cir. 2006) ("Nor can our Court fill in critical gaps in the Board's reasoning. **{-898-}** We can only look to the Board's stated rationale.").

Because the Board cannot identify a specific term in the Watchmen's Agreement that subjects employee discipline to the grievance procedure, the Employers did not modify specific terms and conditions contained in the Agreement. The Board failed to establish an unlawful contract modification.

B.

Even if Article 18 addressed the question of employee discipline, the Board cannot sustain a contract modification charge if the Employers had a "sound arguable basis" for interpreting the Watchmen's Agreement to permit their disciplinary actions. Reading the Watchmen's Agreement as a whole, the Employers clearly had a "sound arguable basis" for their conduct because the Agreement was at least ambiguous with respect to employee discipline outside the contractual grievance procedures of Article 18.

As discussed above, nothing in the plain terms of Article 18 requires discipline to proceed through an employer grievance. Moreover, despite relying heavily on Article 18(D), the Board and the majority ignore clear references to employee **[—13—]** discipline arising outside the grievance machinery. For instance, Article 18(D)(1) presupposes that a discharge and a grievance are distinct employer actions: "Whatever evidence the parties have or have relied upon relating to the *discharge and/or grievance* shall be provided to the Union at the time of request." W.A. at 33–34 (emphasis added); *see Encino Motorcars, LLC v. Navarro*, 138 S. Ct. 1134, 1141 (2018) ("'[O]r' is 'almost always disjunctive.'") (citation omitted). Moreover, Article 18(D) uses the past tense when referring to employee discipline, suggesting review of discipline under the grievance process could occur post hoc. *See* W.A. at 33–34. These provisions at a minimum support a sound arguable basis for concluding that employee discipline may occur before or apart from filing an employer grievance under the Watchmen's Agreement.

Next, the Board and the majority fail to consider the broader structure of the Labor Relations Committee as reflected in Articles 18(A) and (J). Article 18(A) establishes the Committee "to resolve grievances, secure conformance to the terms of the Agreement, maintain current employee registration rosters, maintain dispatch procedures, and generally administer the Agreement." W.A. at 33. None of these roles for the Committee include employee discipline, and the term "grievance[]" is not naturally read to include allegations of employee misconduct. *Supra* at 8–10. Article 18(J) includes an extensive list of topics the Committee must discuss on at least a monthly basis. W.A. at 35.[5] Yet despite **[—14—]** containing significant detail, the **{-899-}** list does not include matters of employee discipline. If the Committee were

provision, if applicable, would allow the Employers to investigate and discipline based on such complaints. *See Pac. Mar.*, 367 NLRB No. 121, at *6 n.20. But the Board never found the Employers filed a complaint under Article 16 or that the dispute turned on interpreting this provision.

[5] Article 18(J) reads:

There shall be designated monthly [Labor Relations Committee] meetings for the following purposes:

(1.) Two (2) regularly scheduled meetings each month exclusively for general LRC issues **[—14—]**
(2.) One (1) meeting exclusively for Registered Watchmens' complaints (non-dispatch issues)
(3.) One (1) meeting exclusively for Dispatch Violations
(4.) One (1) meeting exclusively for Emergency watchmen complaints
(5.) One (1) Dispatch Committee meeting exclusively for Time Books and Emergency Watchmen Dispatch Audit
(6.) One (1) meeting exclusively to audit Registered guards Dispatch Records and Reports
(7.) One (1) meeting exclusively for Watchmen Safety.

intended as the sole adjudicator of misconduct allegations for hundreds of employees at a large shipping terminal, one would expect this responsibility to be explicit.

Finally, the Employers offer a persuasive interpretation of Article 18(C), which includes the Agreement's only reference to disciplinary rules.[6] This provision instructs the Labor Relations Committee to "establish rules and regulations governing the conduct of watchmen as well as penalties for the breach of these rules and regulations," and provides further that "nothing herein shall restrict the Employer's existing right to discipline or discharge" for five enumerated offenses not implicated in this case. W.A. at 33. According to the **[—15—]** Employers, Article 18(C)'s reference to an "existing right" means they retain the right to discipline for an offense unless the Committee issues rules and penalties applicable to that offense. The five enumerated offenses represent carve-outs for which the Committee cannot preempt the Employers' discretion. Read together, "a reasonable interpretation is that [Article 18(C)] is limited to granting the [Committee] the power to make disciplinary rules, so long as those rules do not restrict the employers' right to discipline for the five enumerated offenses, but does not limit the Employer's ability to discipline employees in the absence of any controlling [Committee] rule." *Pac. Mar.*, 367 NLRB No. 121, at *12 (Kaplan dissenting). The majority says this interpretation renders the enumeration superfluous, Maj. Op. 12, but the Employers' interpretation of Article 18(C) preserves a role for the grievance process to resolve complaints by the Union and the Employers, to channel disputes into binding arbitration, and to allow grievances to be filed after discipline if its imposition conflicts with the Agreement.

The majority's "sound arguable basis" analysis does not square with precedent. Rather than engage de novo with the plain meaning of the contract, the majority seeks to squeeze its interpretation into substantial evidence deference whenever possible. *See* Maj. Op. 13–16. Yet disputed evidence of past practice and bargaining history cannot supplant plain meaning, which, as discussed further below, is the lodestar of the sound arguable basis analysis. At most, the majority demonstrates that Article 18 may be interpreted to cover individual cases of employee discipline. But one plausible interpretation does not foreclose the Employers' interpretation as fundamentally unsound.

To defeat this contract modification charge, the Employers needed only a "sound arguable basis" to argue the Watchmen's **[—16—]** Agreement allowed disciplining Pleas for racial harassment without filing an Article 18 grievance. Because the Agreement is at a minimum ambiguous on employee discipline outside the contractual grievance procedure, the Employers had a "sound arguable basis" for their disciplinary actions.

C.

The Board further erred by supporting its contract modification finding with extrinsic evidence that the Union rejected terms like those in Section 13.2 of the **{-900-}** Clerks' Agreement and that the parties had not previously applied such procedures to discrimination allegations. The Board concluded that "the parties' past practice and bargaining history" meant that the Employers "could not have mistaken or misunderstood [the Union's] intent that no such [Section 13.2] procedure be applicable to watchmen." *Pac. Mar.*, 367 NLRB No. 121, at *5–6, *16. Under the "sound arguable basis" test, however, the Board's authority to interpret contracts ends where ambiguity begins. Rather than dismiss the charge in the face of ambiguity, the Board reached beyond the four

[6] Article 18(C) reads:

> The Labor Relations Committee shall establish rules and regulations governing the conduct of watchmen as well as penalties for the breach of these rules and regulations. However, nothing herein shall restrict the Employer's existing right to discipline or discharge men for intoxication, pilferage, assault, incompetency, or failure to perform work as directed, but any man who considers that he has been improperly disciplined or discharged may appeal to the Labor Relations Committee.

corners of the Watchmen's Agreement by looking to the evidence it used to find a unilateral change violation. Yet as noted earlier, the contract modification analysis does not turn on whether the Employers applied Section 13.2 to Pleas, or whether the Union would have consented to amending Article 18 to include such procedures. Rather, the issue is whether the Employers had a "sound arguable basis" for disciplining Pleas without filing a grievance under the Watchmen's Agreement. Relying on extrinsic evidence caused the Board's decision to run crosswise with longstanding precedent.

To begin with, the Board's use of extrinsic evidence to rebut the Employers' otherwise "sound arguable basis" rests on a misreading of prior cases. For example, the Board cites **[—17—]** *Knollwood Country Club*, 365 NLRB No. 22 (Mar. 8, 2017), for the proposition that plain meaning and extrinsic evidence stand on equal footing when interpreting a contract. In *Knollwood*, however, the Board rejected an employer's interpretation as unreasonable because the employer failed to read the contract as a whole and merely noted that extrinsic evidence "also" was consistent with the plain meaning of the contract. *Id.* at *1 & n.8. This holding is consistent with ordinary principles of contract interpretation embracing the plain meaning approach. Moreover, *Knollwood* relied in relevant part on *Mining Specialists, Inc.*, 314 NLRB 268, 268–69 (1994), a unilateral change case emphasizing that "contractual language … is always paramount." Neither the Board nor the majority cite to a single case in which extrinsic evidence supported a finding of contract modification when the provision in question was ambiguous. In fact, both the agency's precedents and the law of this circuit are clear that plain meaning governs when adjudicating unfair labor practices arising from contract.[7] The Board's limited statutory authority **[—18—]** over contract disputes necessarily means it cannot use extrinsic evidence to refute plain meaning **{-901-}** or resolve ambiguity, which is a role reserved for the courts.

Perhaps the fundamental problem of the Board's approach here is that it sought to revise the contract modification standard *sub silentio*. By deploying extrinsic evidence in a "sound arguable basis" inquiry, the Board failed to adhere to governing law setting out distinct evidentiary standards for contract modification and unilateral change. For example, in *Bath Iron Works*, the Board distinguished between contract modification and unilateral change and rejected arguments to apply the same standard to both charges. *See* 345 NLRB at 501–02. Instead, the Board reaffirmed that the "sound arguable basis" test governs contract modification charges—a policy the Board continues to follow. *See MV Transp.*, 368 NLRB No. 66, at *13–17, *28 (emphasizing the Board's limited authority to interpret contracts and declining to go beyond plain meaning when adjudicating unfair labor practices). Here, rather than assess the Employers' "sound arguable basis" against the plain meaning of the Agreement, the Board held the Employers to a different standard by faulting them for not proving the Union would

---

[7] *See, e.g., Metalcraft of Mayville, Inc.*, 367 NLRB No. 116, at *4–5 (Apr. 17, 2019) (dismissing charge where employer had a "colorable" argument that "conforming to applicable law" provision allowed it to stop deducting union dues pursuant to state law); *MV Transp.*, 368 NLRB No. 66, at *28–34 (dismissing several charges where employer had a "sound arguable basis" for interpreting contract to allow new company policies); *see also Am. Fed'n of Gov't Emps. v. FLRA*, 470 F.3d 375, 381 (D.C. Cir. 2006) ("Interpretation of a contract, like statutory and treaty interpretation, must begin with the plain meaning of the language."). Evidence of prior practice and bargaining history, if mentioned at all, are cited only to note its consistency with plain meaning. *See, e.g., ADT*, 369 NLRB No. 31, at *5 & n.10 (concluding plain language required dismissing modification charge and then noting the parties' past practice "further supports" the interpretation offered by the employer); *Comau*, 364 NLRB No. 48, at *5 & n.16 (in the absence of an applicable contract provision, prior practice demonstrated the **[—18—]** contract applied to employees in question); *Hosp. San Carlos, Inc.*, 355 NLRB 153, 153 & n.5 (2010) (concluding plain meaning foreclosed employer's interpretation before observing that testimony regarding the parties' intent also supported the conclusion).

have accepted procedures like those in Section 13.2 of the Clerks' Agreement.[8] **[—19—]**

This intermingling of legal frameworks for contract modification and unilateral change, however, has never been adopted by the Board as a whole and has been previously advanced only in dissenting opinions.[9] Yet in this case, two members of a three-member panel conflated the evidentiary standard for contract modification with those for unilateral change and waiver. Unlike many multi-member agencies, the NLRB decides cases by delegating to three-member panels as a matter of course. *See* 29 U.S.C. § 153(b); NLRB, Guide to Board Procedures § 3.8(a) (Apr. 2017). As a consequence of this practice, a position held by a two-member minority of the five-member Board may prevail on a panel in a manner inconsistent with the Board's governing precedents.[10] **[—20—]** Although the NLRA authorizes decisions by delegated panels, those panels must follow the Board's announced standards in order to satisfy the reasoned decisionmaking requirement **{-902-}** applicable to all administrative action. *See Allentown Mack Sales & Serv., Inc. v. NLRB*, 522 U.S. 359, 374 (1998). As a reviewing court, we must ensure the Board adheres to its announced standards, not the preferred interpretations of individual members. *See Pub. Citizen, Inc. v. FERC*, 839 F.3d 1165, 1169–70 (D.C. Cir. 2016) (applying the "almost universally accepted common-law rule" that "only a majority of a collective body is empowered to act for the body") (cleaned up).

The majority endorses the Board's use of extrinsic evidence by taking a myopic view of governing law. When reviewing an adjudicatory standard, we must examine its application in prior cases and then determine whether the instant case is a faithful application of existing law. *See Circus Circus*, 961 F.3d at 476. Instead, the majority relies on a selective reading of the Board's decision in *Knollwood*, *see* Maj. Op. 14, and fails to engage with cases like *Bath Iron Works* and *MV Transportation* that set out a clear plain meaning requirement. It is a fundamental principle of administrative law that prior departures from announced standards do not excuse an agency's duty to acknowledge and justify a change in policy. "It is hard to imagine a more violent breach of that requirement than applying a rule of primary conduct or a standard of proof which is in fact different from the rule or standard formally announced. And the consistent repetition of that breach can hardly mend it." *Allentown Mack*, 522 U.S. at 374; *see, e.g.*, *ABM Onsite Servs.-West, Inc. v. NLRB*, 849 F.3d 1137, 1144–46 (D.C. Cir. 2017) (vacating order when the Board improperly applied the applicable standard over the course of four years). Without a reasoned revision by the Board of the "sound arguable basis" standard, **[—21—]** this court must reject individual decisions departing from those standards. The Board in

---

[8] To determine whether an employer unilaterally changed an established prior practice, the Board often looks to evidence of conduct and bargaining history—typically a mix of testimony and non-contractual written records. *See, e.g.*, *ABF Freight*, 369 NLRB No. 107, at *2–3 (discussing evidence of employer's past actions). Similarly, extrinsic evidence is relevant when an employer raises **[—19—]** a waiver defense, which requires showing the union clearly and unmistakably waived its statutory right to bargain on the contested issue. *See, e.g.*, *Provena Hosps.*, 350 NLRB 808, 811 (2007).

[9] Over the years, a persistent minority of the Board has questioned whether *Bath Iron Works* was wrongly decided and advocated for limiting the "sound arguable basis" standard or imposing a different standard that falls within the scope of the Board's substantial evidence deference for factfinding. *See, e.g.*, *Metalcraft*, 367 NLRB No. 116, at *15 (McFerran dissenting); *MV Transp.*, 368 NLRB No. 66, at *41 (McFerran concurring in part and dissenting in part); *Knollwood*, 365 NLRB No. 22, at *1 n.5 (separate footnote by Pearce and McFerran); *Comau*, 364 NLRB No. 48, at *4 n.14 (separate footnote by Pearce and Hirozawa); *Bath Iron Works*, 345 NLRB at 504 (Liebman dissenting); *see also Pac. Mar.*, 367 NLRB No. 121, at *5 n.15 (separate footnote by McFerran) (reserving the question of whether *Bath Iron Works* was wrongly decided).

[10] The question is not whether the procedure is permissible under the NLRA, or whether the Employers challenged its use in this case. *Cf.* Maj. Op. 18–19. Rather, the question is whether this panel of the Board followed the agency's announced standards. Given the unexplained break with precedent evident in this case, I would answer that question in the negative.

this case was wrong to dislodge the employer's reasonable interpretation using extrinsic evidence.

* * *

Contract modifications are breaches of contract that rise to the level of offending public rights by undermining the collective bargaining process. The "sound arguable basis" standard provides a means of separating unfair labor practices from contractual disputes reserved for the courts. *See Honeywell*, 253 F.3d at 123–25; *Int'l Union, United Mine Workers of Am. v. NLRB*, 257 F.2d 211, 215 (D.C. Cir. 1958). By finding a contract modification in these circumstances, the Board departed from precedent in an arbitrary and capricious manner and exceeded its limited jurisdiction over contract disputes. I therefore respectfully dissent from enforcing the Board's contract modification finding.

United States Court of Appeals
for the District of Columbia Circuit

No. 18-1124

INTERNATIONAL LONGSHORE & WAREHOUSE UNION
VS.
NATIONAL LABOR RELATIONS BD.

On Petitions for Review and Cross-Application for Enforcement of Orders of the National Labor Relations Board

Decided: August 21, 2020

Citation: 971 F.3d 356, 8 Adm. R. 569 (D.C. Cir. 2020).

Before **GARLAND** and **KATSAS,** Circuit Judges, and **WILLIAMS,** Senior Circuit Judge.*

* The late Senior Circuit Judge Stephen F. Williams was a member of the panel at the time the case was argued and participated in its consideration before his death on August 7, 2020. Because he died before this opinion's issuance, his vote was not counted. *See Yovino v. Rizo*, 139 S. Ct. 706, 710 (2019). Judges Garland and Katsas have acted as a quorum with respect to this opinion and judgment. *See* 28 U.S.C. § 46(d).

[—2—] {-358-} KATSAS, Circuit Judge:

Under *NLRB v. Burns International Security Services, Inc.*, 406 U.S. 272 (1972), a successor employer inherits the collective-bargaining obligations of its predecessor only if the previously recognized bargaining unit remains appropriate under the successor. In determining whether the unit remains appropriate, the National Labor Relations Board ignores workplace changes caused by unfair labor practices of the successor. Here, the NLRB extended that rule to ignore changes caused by unfair labor practices of the predecessor. We hold that the Board did not adequately explain its decision.

I

This case arises from a longstanding dispute about which of two competing unions represents a group of several dozen **[—3—]** mechanics who maintain and repair shipping equipment in the Port of Oakland, California. The unions are the International Association of Machinists and Aerospace Workers, AFLCIO/ CLC (Machinists) and the International Longshore and Warehouse Union (ILWU). As the mechanics came to work for different companies, two related controversies developed. One, centered around a change in employers that occurred in 2005, has been finally resolved by this Court. Another, centered around a **{-359-}** change in employers that occurred in 2013, is directly at issue here.

A

Before 2005, the mechanics at issue worked for the Pacific Marine Maintenance Company, a contractor providing maintenance and repair services to the shipping company A.P. Moller-Maersk. At that time, the Machinists represented the mechanics under a collective-bargaining agreement covering non-crane mechanics employed by Pacific Marine at the Ports of Oakland and Tacoma, Washington.

In 2005, Maersk ended its contract with Pacific Marine and engaged the Pacific Crane Maintenance Company to provide maintenance and repair services for its Oakland and Tacoma shipping operations. As a result, Pacific Marine shut down and laid off the mechanics. Pacific Crane immediately rehired most of them, but it refused to recognize the Machinists as their bargaining representative. Instead, it recognized ILWU under a collective-bargaining agreement encompassing a much larger unit of some 15,000 employees performing various jobs for various employers at various West Coast ports.

These 2005 changes spawned over a decade of litigation. The Machinists charged that Pacific Crane had committed unfair labor practices by refusing to bargain with it and by **[—4—]** recognizing ILWU as the mechanics' bargaining representative. Likewise, the Machinists charged that ILWU had committed unfair labor practices by accepting the recognition and by applying its collective-bargaining agreement to the mechanics. The NLRB agreed with the Machinists on both points. *PCMC/Pac. Crane Maint. Co.*, 359 N.L.R.B. 1206 (2013) (*Pacific Crane I*). The Board then vacated its decision on procedural grounds, but later reached the same conclusion. *PCMC/Pac. Crane Maint. Co.*, 362 N.L.R.B. 988 (2015) (*Pacific Crane II*). After the Machinists settled their claims against Pacific Crane, we upheld the Board's decision and enforced it against ILWU. *Int'l Longshore & Warehouse Union v. NLRB*, 890 F.3d 1100, 6 Adm. R. 481 (D.C. Cir. 2018) (*Pacific Crane III*). In doing so, we relied "heavily" on a stipulation that Pacific Marine and Pacific Crane, which were affiliated companies, should be treated as a single employer. *Id.* at 1110, 6 Adm. R. at 487.

B

This case involves a third employer—Ports America Outer Harbor—which came into the picture as the *Pacific Crane* litigation unfolded. In 2010, Ports America acquired control of Oakland berths 20–24 from Maersk. As Maersk had done, Ports America used Pacific Crane to provide maintenance and repair services at those berths. Ports America then acquired berths 25–26 from the Transbay Container Terminal. Ports America expanded its service contract with Pacific Crane to cover these berths as well.

In 2013, Ports America decided to bring its maintenance and repair operations in-house. When its contract with Pacific Crane expired, Ports America hired most of the mechanics who previously had been working for Pacific Crane. In doing so, Ports America refused to bargain with the Machinists and **[—5—]** instead recognized ILWU, which continued to apply its collective-bargaining agreement to the mechanics.

The Machinists charged Ports America and ILWU with various unfair labor practices. They alleged that Ports America committed unfair labor practices by failing to bargain with them and by recognizing ILWU as the mechanics' bargaining representative. Further, they alleged that ILWU committed unfair labor practices by accepting the recognition and by applying its collective-bargaining agreement to the mechanics. All these allegations rested on **{-360-}** one central claim—that Ports America had succeeded to Pacific Crane's duty to bargain with the Machinists.

An administrative law judge agreed with the Machinists. She reasoned that from 2005 to 2013, Pacific Crane had a continuing obligation to recognize and bargain with the Machinists. *Ports Am. Outer Harbor, LLC*, 366 N.L.R.B. No. 76, at 10–12 (May 2, 2018) (*Ports America*) (reprinting ALJ recom-mendation). She then concluded that Ports America succeeded to that obligation under *Burns*, in part by refusing to consider any counterarguments "built on unremedied unfair labor practices" committed by Pacific Crane before 2013. *Id.* at 14. In 2018, the Board substantially affirmed the ALJ's decision on similar reasoning. *See id.* at 3–4 & nn. 9–10.

While the proceeding was still pending before the ALJ, Ports America filed for bankruptcy, so the Machinists added new claims against MTC Holdings, another terminal services company, which the Machinists alleged was a single employer with Ports America. The Machinists then reached a partial settlement covering all their claims against MTC Holdings and their non-*Burns* claims against Ports America. Under the settlement, Ports America and MTC Holdings agreed to pay the Machinists $3 million for distribution to the mechanics. In **[—6—]** August 2016, the ALJ approved the settlement and dismissed MTC Holdings from the case. ILWU objected to the settlement and sought reconsideration. In September 2016, the ALJ affirmed her August order. In November 2016, the Board denied ILWU's appeal from the settlement approval.

ILWU now seeks our review of the NLRB's merits order and its order approving the partial settlement. The NLRB seeks enforcement of the merits order. The Machinists have intervened in support of the Board. Ports America, which has ceased operations, did not appear before this Court.

II

We first consider the Board's ruling that ILWU committed unfair labor practices by accepting recognition as the mechanics' bargaining representative in 2013 and by applying its collective-bargaining agreement to them. ILWU argues that the Board arbitrarily refused to consider its arguments that the past bargaining unit was no longer appropriate. We agree.

Our review of NLRB decisions is deferential but not toothless. Among other things, we must consider whether the Board's findings of fact are supported by substantial evidence, 29 U.S.C. § 160(f), and whether its reasoning is arbitrary and capricious, 5 U.S.C. § 706(2)(A). For the latter, the question is whether the agency "examined the relevant considerations and articulated a satisfactory explanation for its action, including a rational connection between the facts found and the choice made." *FERC v. Elec. Power Supply Ass'n*, 136 S. Ct. 760, 782 (2016) (cleaned up). "[A]n agency's unexplained departure from precedent is arbitrary and capricious." *ABM Onsite Servs.—West, Inc. v. NLRB*, 849 F.3d 1137, 1142 (D.C. Cir. 2017). So too is an order resting on "clearly distinguishable precedent." *Exxel/Atmos, Inc. v. NLRB*, 147 F.3d 972, 976 (D.C. Cir. 1998). **[—7—]**

Section 7 of the National Labor Relations Act guarantees the right of employees "to bargain collectively through representatives of their own choosing." 29 U.S.C. § 157. Section 8(a) prohibits employers from engaging in unfair labor practices, which include interfering with collective bargaining, *id.* § 158(a)(1); supporting a union, *id.* § 158(a)(2); and refusing to bargain with a union that enjoys majority support, *id.* § 158(a)(5). Section **{-361-}** 8(b) prohibits unions from engaging in unfair labor practices, which include restraining collective bargaining by employees, *id.* § 158(b)(1)(A), and causing an employer to discriminate against an employee, *id.* § 158(b)(2).

The unfair labor practices at issue follow from a premise that Ports America had a duty to bargain with the Machinists when it insourced the Oakland maintenance and repair work in 2013. If so, then its failure to bargain with the Machinists violated sections 8(a)(1) and (5), and its recognizing ILWU violated sections 8(a)(1) and (2). Likewise, ILWU violated section 8(b)(1)(A) by accepting the recognition, and section 8(b)(2) by applying its collective-bargaining agreement to the mechanics. ILWU does not dispute that these conclusions follow from the premise.

In finding that Ports America had a duty to bargain with the Machinists, the Board reasoned in two steps. First, Pacific Crane had such a duty. We previously held that Pacific Crane had this duty as of 2005, *Pacific Crane III*, 890 F.3d at 1107– 13, 6 Adm. R. at 484–90, and the Board held that it continued through 2013, *Ports America*, 366 N.L.R.B. No. 76, at 2–4. Second, Ports America succeeded to Pacific Crane's bargaining obligation when it hired the mechanics. In reaching this conclusion, the Board summarized the test for successorship as follows:

> An employer is a successor employer obligated to recognize and bargain with the union representing the **[—8—]** predecessor's employees when (1) the successor acquires, and continues in substantially unchanged form, the business of a unionized predecessor (the "substantial continuity" requirement); (2) the successor hires, as a majority of its workforce at the acquired facility, union-represented former employees of the predecessor (the "workforce majority" requirement); and (3) the unit remains appropriate for collective bargaining under the successor's operations.

Id. at 2; *see Burns*, 406 U.S. at 277–81. ILWU accepts this formulation of the governing legal test.

Before the Board, ILWU sought to raise three arguments why the historic bargaining unit was no longer appropriate when Ports America hired the mechanics in 2013. First, the historic bargaining unit had accreted into ILWU's larger, coastwide bargaining unit—in other words, the historic unit had lost its separate identity and acquired an "overwhelming community of interest" with the ILWU unit, *see Dean Transp., Inc. v. NLRB*, 551 F.3d 1055, 1067 (D.C. Cir. 2009) (quotation marks omitted). Second, a majority of mechanics in the historic unit by then supported ILWU, not the Machinists. Third, Ports America had at least a good-faith doubt whether a majority of the unit still supported the Machinists.[1] **[—9—]**

The Board declined to consider ILWU's arguments because they invoked changes that were "a direct result of the *predecessor* employers' unlawful assistance to and recognition of the ILWU." 366 N.L.R.B. No. 76, at 3 (emphasis added); *see also id.* at 3–4 nn. 9–10. In other words, if the historic bargaining unit had become inappropriate by the time Ports America took over, it was only because Pacific Crane had **{-362-}** improperly recognized ILWU, and had failed to recognize the Machinists, during the eight prior years.

To justify its ruling, the Board invoked our decision in *Pacific Crane III*. But that case does not address whether an *incoming* employer may contest successorship obligations by citing workplace changes caused by unfair labor practices of the *outgoing* employer. *Pacific Crane III* involved no successorship issue because the parties there had stipulated that the outgoing Pacific Mutual and the incoming Pacific Crane, which were affiliated companies, should be treated as a single employer. *See* 890 F.3d at 1110, 6 Adm. R. at 487. It was thus undisputed that Pacific Crane, when it took over in 2005, succeeded to the bargaining obligations of Pacific Mutual. Pacific Crane separately argued that the historic Machinists unit had accreted into the larger ILWU unit because of changes that occurred *after* 2005. In response, the Board held that Pacific Crane could not seek to benefit from *its own* unfair labor practices in recognizing ILWU and failing to recognize the Machinists. 359 N.L.R.B. at 1211. Likewise, we explained that "the Board should ignore any impermissible changes made unilaterally by the employer," because "to hold otherwise would allow the **[—10—]** employer to benefit from its own unlawful conduct." 890 F.3d at 1111, 6 Adm. R. at 488 (cleaned up).[2]

We can imagine reasonable arguments either way on the question whether a successor employer should be barred from citing changes caused by the unfair labor practices of a predecessor. Perhaps current employee choices should be given effect, regardless of whether a former employer committed unfair labor practices. Or, perhaps the need to remedy past unfair labor practices is paramount. The Board simply did not engage these questions. Instead, it relied on inapposite precedent, as it virtually conceded at oral argument. Oral Arg. 22:50–56 ("there is no clear case on point"); *id.* 25:22–24 ("there are no cases governing"). That was arbitrary. *See Exxel/Atmos*, 147 F.3d at 976.

Before this Court, the Board presses an alternative theory that Ports America could not have claimed any good-faith doubt that a majority of workers in the unit supported the Machinists. According to the Board, this is so because Ports America knew of Pacific Crane's unremedied unfair labor practices. *See Proxy Commc'ns*, 290 N.L.R.B. 540, 542 (1988), *enforced*, 873 F.2d 552 (2d Cir. 1989); *Bay Diner*, 279 N.L.R.B. 538, 546 (1986); *Silver Spur Casino*, 270 N.L.R.B. 1067, 1074 (1984). But neither the ALJ nor the Board articulated this rationale below, and neither made findings on whether Ports America knew of Pacific Crane's unfair labor **[—11—]** practices in sufficient time. ILWU suggests no, because Ports America had signed its contracts and made its hiring decisions before the Board

[1] As of 2005, the recognized bargaining unit encompassed non-crane mechanics employed by Pacific Marine in Oakland and Tacoma. *See Pacific Crane III*, 890 F.3d at 1103–04 & n.2, 6 Adm. R. at 481 & n.2. In this case, the Board expanded the historic unit to include mechanics at Oakland berths 25 and 26, which Ports America took over in 2010, and contracted it to exclude mechanics in Tacoma, who are not employed by Ports America. *See Ports America*, 366 N.L.R.B. No. **[—9—]** 76, at 3. ILWU contends that the historic unit was absorbed into its unit, but does not otherwise challenge the Board's adjustments to the historic unit.

[2] The Board in this case also cited *Pacific Telephone & Telegraph Co.*, 80 N.L.R.B. 107 (1948), but it too has nothing to do with successorship. There, the Board held that a union could not seek a unit determination reflecting assistance that the employer had unlawfully provided to it. *Id.* at 111–12. The case involved no question of when bargaining obligations flow from a predecessor to a successor.

decided *Pacific Crane I.* The Board suggests yes, because *Pacific Crane I* was decided before Ports America took over the maintenance and repair work. Because the Board did not address these issues below, much less make the findings necessary to resolve them, we cannot uphold its rejection of the good-faith defense on this ground. *See SEC v. Chenery Corp.*, 332 U.S. 194, 196 (1947).

At oral argument, we asked the Board about another possible rationale for upholding **{-363-}** its order: Even if Ports America could seek to benefit from the unfair labor practices of Pacific Crane, ILWU could not seek to benefit from its own past unfair labor practices. The Board wisely declined to press that rationale here. In the proceedings below, the Board pegged ILWU's liability entirely to the proposition that Ports America was a *Burns* successor and had violated its bargaining obligations as such. *See Ports America*, 366 N.L.R.B. No. 76, at 2. Under *Chenery*, we thus cannot uphold the Board's order on the theory that ILWU committed unfair labor practices even if Ports America did not.

As this analysis should make clear, our ruling is narrow. We hold only that the Board did not engage in reasoned decisionmaking in the order under review. On remand, the Board remains free to consider the various open issues and arguments in this case, unencumbered by its invocation of inapposite precedent.[3] **[—12—]**

III

ILWU also seeks review of the Board's order refusing to set aside the partial settlement among the Machinists, Ports America, and MTC Holdings. The Machinists contend that we lack jurisdiction to review that order for two reasons. First, ILWU lacks Article III standing to challenge a settlement of claims made against other parties, which in no way impaired ILWU's ability to defend the claims made against it. Second, the intervening distribution of the settlement funds mooted ILWU's objections to the settlement. We must consider both jurisdictional objections before reaching the merits, *see Steel Co. v. Citizens for a Better Env't*, 523 U.S. 83, 101 (1998), but we may do so in either order, *see Ruhrgas AG v. Marathon Oil Co.*, 526 U.S. 574, 584 (1999). We begin—and end—with the question of mootness.

ILWU does not respond to the Machinists' contention that disbursement of the settlement funds mooted ILWU's challenge. By this silence, ILWU has forfeited any objection to mootness. "Although a party cannot forfeit a claim that we lack jurisdiction, it can forfeit a claim that we possess jurisdiction." *Scenic Am., Inc. v. DOT*, 836 F.3d 42, 53 n.4 (D.C. Cir. 2016). "[T]he ordinary rules of forfeiture apply" to a claim that we have jurisdiction, *Manitoba v. Bernhardt*, 923 F.3d 173, 179 (D.C. Cir. 2019), so ILWU's "failing to respond" to an argument that we lack jurisdiction forfeited any counterargument that we have it, *Perry Capital LLC v. Mnuchin*, 864 F.3d 591, 618 (D.C. Cir. 2017); *see, e.g., Reid v. Hurwitz*, 920 F.3d 828, 833 n.4 (D.C. Cir. 2019). This is consistent with how ordinary forfeiture rules work in other **[—13—]** contexts where one party has raised an argument and the other has "offered nothing in opposition." *Tax Analysts v. IRS*, 117 F.3d 607, 610 (D.C. Cir. 1997); *see Clifton Power Corp. v. FERC*, 88 F.3d 1258, 1267 (D.C. Cir. 1996).

Because ILWU forfeited any argument that this case is not moot, we dismiss its petition to review the Board's order accepting the partial settlement.

IV

We grant the petition for review of the Board's final order, set aside that order, deny the Board's cross-application for enforcement,

[3] The Board ordered Ports America to bargain with the Machinists if it resumed operations, and it ordered ILWU to reimburse fees and dues paid by the mechanics. *Ports America*, 366 N.L.R.B. No. 76, at 6. Because we have set aside the underlying **[—12—]** liability determinations, we need not consider ILWU's challenge to these two remedies. *See Erie Brush & Mfg. Corp. v. NLRB*, 700 F.3d 17, 19 (D.C. Cir. 2012).

and remand for further proceedings **{-364-}** consistent with this opinion. We dismiss as moot the petition for review of the Board's order refusing to set aside the partial settlement.

So ordered.

United States Court of Appeals for the Federal Circuit

United States Court of Appeals
for the Federal Circuit

No. 19-1692

COOPER/PORTS AM., LLC
vs.
SECRETARY OF DEFENSE

Appeal from the Armed Services Board of Contract Appeals

Decided: May 29, 2020

Citation: 959 F.3d 1373, 8 Adm. R. 576 (Fed. Cir. 2020).

Before **DYK, TARANTO,** and **CHEN,** Circuit Judges.

[—2—] {–1374–} DYK, Circuit Judge: **{–1375–}**

Cooper/Ports America LLC ("CPA") provided stevedoring and related terminal services to the government under a contract dated January 28, 2015. CPA submitted a claim that the government failed to provide a timely preliminary written notice of intent to exercise the government's option to extend the parties' contract, and that the subsequent option exercise was ineffective. The claim was denied by a contracting officer, and CPA appealed before the Armed Services Board of Contracts Appeals ("Board"). The Board held that the government satisfied the preliminary written notice requirement. We affirm.

BACKGROUND

In January 2015, CPA's predecessor-in-interest, Shippers Stevedoring Co. ("SSC"), was awarded a contract from the United States Transportation Command, a component of the Department of Defense. The United States Transportation Command supports military transportation to other commands and government organizations. The contract required SSC to provide stevedoring and related terminal services along the Eastern Seaboard of the United States, including Charleston, South Carolina ("the Charleston contract," HTC711-15-D-R036). SSC was separately awarded a contract covering the Gulf region ("the Beaumont contract," HTC711-15-D-R037). Only the Charleston contract is at issue in this appeal.

The original Charleston contract executed by SSC incorporated a Federal Acquisition Regulation ("FAR") provision (section 52.217-9) that gave the government options to extend the term of the agreement for up to four one-year **[—3—]** periods. That provision required that the government give CPA "a preliminary written notice of its intent to extend at least 60 days before the contract expire[d]." J.A. 65; *see also* 48 C.F.R. § 52.217-9 ("Option to Extend the Term of the Contract"). Providing such notice did not obligate the government to actually exercise the option. After the preliminary notice, the government was required to exercise the option itself within 15 days of the contract expiration date. Section 52.217-9 contained no language permitting adjustment of the contract price.

The original contract term expired on June 30, 2016. On April 28, 2016, the government provided a preliminary written notice of its intent to exercise the first-year option to extend the term of the Charleston contract to June 30, 2017. This communication was in a formal letter titled "Contract HTC711-15-D-R036, Preliminary Notice of Intent to Exercise Option" and stated that "[i]n accordance with FAR [§] 52.217-9, Option to Extend the Term of **{–1376–}** the Contract, [SSC is] hereby given preliminary notice of the Government's intent to extend the term of the contract through 30 June 2017." J.A. 107. Thereafter, on June 15, 2016, the government exercised the first-year option, extending the contract period to June 30, 2017. If the government wished to exercise its option for a second-year extension, it had to provide CPA a preliminary written notice of its intent by May 1, 2017, pursuant to the 60-day notice requirement of section 52.217-9.

SSC's business experienced difficulties, and this led to CPA's acquisition of SSC's assets on September 30, 2016.[1] CPA replaced SSC as a party to the Charleston contract through novation and modification agreements that were signed on November 15, 2016, and December 19, 2016, **[—4—]** respectively.

[1] CPA was named "Integrated Marine Services, LLC" when it acquired SSC's assets. CPA changed to its current name in October 2016.

Similar agreements were reached with respect to the Beaumont contract.

After CPA purchased SSC's assets on September 30, 2016, it began urging the government to revise the pricings of the Charleston and Beaumont contracts. CPA then asserted that it might default on the contracts because the contracts' pricings were not profitable. On January 31, 2017, the government's contracting officer, William Seamon, sent an email ("the January 31 email") to CPA's Vice President of Operations, Chris Lewis, stating:

> The Government intends to exercise options at awarded rates on contracts HTC711-15-D-R036 [(i.e., the Charleston contract)] and HTC711-15-D-R037 [(i.e., the Beaumont contract)]. With this, the Government expects [CPA] to continue performing per the terms and conditions of the contract.

J.A. 117. The question here is whether this email constituted a preliminary written notice with respect to the Charleston contract.

No such issue exists with respect to the Beaumont contract, because on February 1, 2017, Mr. Seamon sent a formal letter, stating that "[CPA was] hereby given preliminary notice of the Government's intent to extend the term of the [Beaumont] contract through 2 April 2018." J.A. 111. But it was not until May 3, 2017, that Mr. Seamon sent a formal letter to CPA concerning the Charleston contract, stating that "[CPA was] hereby given preliminary notice of the Government's intent to extend the term of the [Charleston] contract through 30 June 2018." J.A. 109. The May 3 letter would not have been a timely preliminary notice under the contract.

On June 9, 2017, CPA responded to the May 3 letter and stated that the government's preliminary written notice under section 52.217-9 was untimely because the May 3 letter was received after May 1, 2017. On June 13, **[—5—]** 2017, the government pointed to the January 31 email as the preliminary written notice of its intent to exercise the second-year option, and sent a letter exercising that option. On June 15, 2017, CPA responded that it would "be performing the Modification [of the Charleston contract] under protest" because that contract "w[ould] expire by its own terms with the conclusion of the period of performance on June 30, 2017." J.A. 134.

Beginning in July 2017, CPA filed several claims with the government, seeking a declaration that the Charleston contract had expired and requesting compensation for additional money for its performance under protest. A contracting officer denied the claims, and CPA appealed to the Board. The Board granted summary judgment in favor of the government, holding **{–1377–}** that "the January [31] email was a preliminary notice of intent," J.A. 9, and that the "email unambiguously, absolutely, and positively provided preliminary written notice of the government's intent to extend at least 60 days before the contract expired on May 1, 2017," J.A. 6.

CPA appeals, and we have jurisdiction under 41 U.S.C. § 7107(a)(1) and 28 U.S.C. § 1295(a)(10). We review de novo the "the Board's conclusions of law, including grants of summary judgment," *Rex Sys., Inc. v. Cohen*, 224 F.3d 1367, 1371 (Fed. Cir. 2000), and the "interpretation of a government contract," *Lear Siegler Servs., Inc. v. Rumsfeld*, 457 F.3d 1262, 1266 (Fed. Cir. 2006). After oral argument, at our request, the parties supplemented the record on appeal to include additional record documents relating to communications between the parties before and after their January 31 email exchange.

Discussion

The issue in this case is whether the government's January 31 email was a "preliminary written notice" required by section 52.217-9. CPA argues that the January 31 email was ineffective for various reasons. Some of these are **[—6—]** without substance, such as CPA's contentions that the notice was unclear as to whether it referred to the Charleston contract (it did so specifically); that the notice was ambiguous as to whether it was directed to the second option year or a later year (there was no ambiguity); or whether it was ambiguous because in contrast to the earlier notice for the first-year option it was informal (the contract did not re-quire formality). We discuss below CPA's other arguments.

First, CPA asserts that the notice was ambiguous because there was no way to know whether the January 31 email referred to the one-year option under section 52.217-9 or the six-month option under section 52.217-8, which was also provided in the contract. We have recognized that a required notice must be unambiguous. *See McCall Stock Farms, Inc. v. United States*, 14 F.3d 1562, 1569–70 (Fed. Cir. 1993); *see also First Commerce Corp. v. United States*, 335 F.3d 1373, 1379–80 (Fed. Cir. 2003) (holding that a binding agreement requires an unambiguous acceptance); *Holly Corp.*, ASBCA No. 24975, 83-1 BCA ¶ 16,327, 1983 ASBCA LEXIS 272, at *21 ("The acceptance of an option, to be effectual, must be unqualified, absolute, unconditional, unequivocal, unambiguous, positive, without reservation, and according to the terms or conditions of the option."). We think that a similar standard applies to the sufficiency of a preliminary notice of intent to exercise an option in that it must provide clear notice to a reasonable recipient.

The sufficiency of a notice is generally considered in the context of the communication between the parties. *Empire Energy Mgmt. Sys., Inc. v. Roche*, 362 F.3d 1343, 1356 (Fed. Cir. 2004) (considering circumstances outside the notice); *Halifax Engineering, Inc. v. United States*, 915 F.2d 689, 691 (Fed. Cir. 1990) (same); Black's Law Dictionary (11th ed. 2019) (explaining that due notice is "notice that is legally adequate given the particular circumstance"). **[—7—]**

Here, CPA claims that the notice was unclear because there was another option provision in the contract. In addition to the "Option to Extend the Term of the Contract" by one-year extensions (section 52.217-9), the Charleston contract included a separate "Option to Extend Services" provision (section 52.217-8). This latter provision stated that "[t]he Government may require continued performance of any services . . . . The option provision may be exercised more than once, but the total extension of performance hereunder shall **{–1378–}** not exceed 6 months." J.A. 65; *see also* 48 C.F.R. § 52.217-8. In support of its claim, CPA asserts that Mr. Seamon (the contracting officer) testified that the January 31 email "could be interpreted as [referring to] either -9 or -8." J.A. 257. Mr. Seamon, however, was discussing the email's language on its face, and stated that he believed the January 31 email constituted a notice:

> Q: . . . [Do] you think [the January] E-mail constitutes preliminary notice of an intent to exercise an option on the contract?
>
> A: Yes.
>
> Q: Okay. Why is that?
>
> A: Because it specifically states that the government intends to exercise options at award rates on both contracts . . . .

J.A. 4 (alterations in original). In any event, as we discuss below, the subjective and uncommunicated view of the parties as to the notice is of no relevance. Unlike section 52.217-9, the "Option to Extend Services" provision did not require a preliminary written notice. That fact alone makes it unlikely that a reasonable recipient of the notice would think that the January 31 email was related to the "Option to Extend Services" provision. Significantly, the record shows that in late 2016 and early 2017 the parties were discussing pricing for the Charleston contract, **[—8—]** including the next one-year option extension period, and that the subject of the January 31 email was understood to be the option for a one-year extension period under section 52.217-9.

It appears that as early as October 2016 CPA asked for a rate increase under the contract. It is apparent that CPA was concerned about performing the contract at the existing pricing during additional option periods. Only a few months remained in the Charleston contract that was set to expire on

June 30, 2017. On January 21, 2017, Mr. Lewis of CPA emailed Mr. Seamon, stating that "I'd like to discuss next steps for processing the contact [sic] modifications for the labor increase we talked about from Oct. 1st." S.A. 2. On January 24, 2017, Mr. Seamon emailed Mr. Lewis with a subject line "SSC-Charleston," stating that he was "attach[ing] . . . the final schedule of rates from SSC for [the Charleston contract]" in light of their "rate adjustment conversation." S.A. 4–5. In response, on January 24 and 25, 2017, Mr. Lewis communicated that he would "try to back into the numbers so [they could] have an agreed starting point," S.A. 4, and would "start working on the adjustment and w[ould] forward for [Mr. Seamon's] review," S.A. 3.

A few days later, Mr. Seamon sent the January 31 email, stating that "[t]he Government intends to exercise options at awarded rates on [the Charleston and Beaumont contracts]." J.A. 117. At the same time, Mr. Seamon rejected any price adjustments, stating that "the Government expects [CPA] to continue performing per the terms and conditions of the contract." *Id.* After the January 31 email, on February 23, 2017, Mr. Lewis emailed Mr. Seamon, urging an "increase [to be] reflected in *option year two* of the final SSC-Charleston schedule." S.A. 36 (emphasis added). The parties continued to discuss the "O[ption]Y[ear]2 rates." S.A. 57 (March 21, 2017 email); S.A. 60 (showing future adjusted rates for the next one-year period). Under these circumstances, there was no **[—9—]** ambiguity and CPA "had sufficient notice" that the January 31 email was directed to the second-year option of the Charleston contract. *Empire*, 362 F.3d at 1356 (quoting *Halifax*, 915 F.2d at 691).

Second, CPA claims that the January 31 email was not effective because the government did not intend it to be a "preliminary written notice" under **{–1379–}** section 52.217-9, and that CPA did not understand it to be such a notice. This argument lacks merit because the January 31 email expressly stated that "[t]he Government intends to exercise options at awarded rates [of the Charleston and Beaumont contracts]." J.A. 117. It is well established that a notice is judged by objective standards. *See NEC Sols. (Am.), Inc. v. United States*, 411 F.3d 1340, 1346 (Fed. Cir. 2005) (holding that the sender's intent and the recipient's knowledge of that intent were irrelevant to whether an email constituted notice required by a Customs statute and "the relevant inquiry [wa]s whether [the recipient] would or could have reasonably comprehended the e-mail as being unambiguous"); *see also United States v. Locke*, 471 U.S. 84, 88–89, 102 (1985) (holding that the plaintiffs' actual intent was irrelevant to whether they satisfied a federal mining statute's requirement to file a notice of intent to hold a mining claim by a certain date); *Rodash v. AIB Mortg. Co.*, 16 F.3d 1142, 1145–46 (11th Cir. 1994) (holding that the sender's subjective intent and recipient's misunderstanding of the notice required under the Truth in Lending Act ("TILA") was irrelevant to compliance with that requirement), *abrogated on other ground by Veale v. Citibank, F.S.B.*, 85 F.3d 577 (11th Cir. 1996); *Hauk v. JP Morgan Chase Bank USA*, 552 F.3d 1114, 1122 (9th Cir. 2009) (holding that a sender's "undisclosed intent to act inconsistent with its disclosures" required under the TILA was "irrelevant in determining the sufficiency of those disclosures"). The government's purported undisclosed intent and CPA's subjective understanding here did not make an otherwise valid notice ineffective. **[—10—]**

Finally, CPA contends that the January 31 email failed to give notice because it "d[id] not comply with FAR § 17.207(g)'s requirement that any 'written document which notifies the contractor of the exercise of the option shall cite the option clause as authority.'" Appellant's Br. 24 (quoting 48 C.F.R. § 17.207(g)). CPA claims that the January 31 email should have explicitly identified section 52.217-9 in order for it to be an effective notice. We agree with the Board that "by its plain terms, FAR [§] 17.207(g) only applies to '[t]he contract modification or other written document which notifies the contractor of the exercise of the option,' and not to the preliminary notice of the intent." J.A. 8–9 (second alteration in original).

CONCLUSION

For the foregoing reasons, we uphold the Board's decision.

AFFIRMED

COSTS

No costs.

United States Court of Appeals for the Federal Circuit

No. 19-1983

TAYLOR ENERGY CO.
VS.
UNITED STATES

Appeal from the United States Court of Federal Claims

Decided: September 3, 2020

Citation: 975 F.3d 1303, 8 Adm. R. 581 (Fed. Cir. 2020).

Before **LOURIE**, **MOORE**, and **O'MALLEY**, Circuit Judges.

[—2—] {-1305-} O'MALLEY, Circuit Judge:

Under the Outer Continental Shelf Lands Act ("OCSLA" or the "Act"), the Federal Government regulates oil and gas operations on the Outer Continental Shelf ("OCS").[1] 43 U.S.C. § 1301. "[A]ll law on the OCS is federal law, administered by federal officials." *Parker Drilling Mgmt. Servs., Ltd. v. Newton*, 139 S. Ct. 1881, 1886, 7 Adm. R. 36, 36 (2019). The Act grants the federal government complete "jurisdiction, control, and power of disposition" over the OCS, while states have no "interest in or jurisdiction" over it. And, although the Act deems an adjacent state's laws to be federal law on the OCS to the extent they are "applicable and not inconsistent" with other federal laws and regulations, state law cannot be adopted as surrogate federal law if federal law addresses the relevant issue. *Parker Drilling*, 139 S. Ct. at 1889, 7 Adm. R. at 38 (citing 43 U.S.C. § 1333(a)(2)(A)).

The Court of Federal Claims recognized this relationship in the underlying proceedings. It dismissed Taylor's state law breach of contract claims because, *inter alia*, the disputed "contractual" requirements **{-1306-}** addressed in the agreement at issue were already governed by OCSLA regulations. Citing *Rodrigue v. Aetna Casualty & Surety*, 395 U.S. 352 (1969), the Claims Court explained that state law cannot undercut a lessee's regulatory obligations on the OCS. Only two months later, the Supreme Court affirmed the precedent upon which the Claims Court relied in **[—3—]** *Parker Drilling Management Services, Ltd. v. Newton*, holding that "OCSLA makes apparent that federal law is exclusive in its regulation of the OCS." 139 S. Ct. at 1889, 7 Adm. R. at 38 (quotations omitted). "[T]o the extent federal law applies to a particular issue, state law is inapplicable." *Id.*, 7 Adm. R. at 39.

Despite the Court's clear holding in *Parker Drilling*, Taylor argues on appeal that the Claims Court's Rule 12(b)(6) dismissal was erroneous. It contends that the agreement somehow transformed Taylor's regulatory obligations into separate contractual obligations, and that a breach of these independent contractual obligations, under Louisiana contract law, may dissolve the security interest and decommissioning requirements mandated by OCSLA federal regulations. We disagree. The Court's precedent, particularly *Parker Drilling*, establishes that, for OCS-based claims, state law cannot contravene federal law. Despite Taylor's attempt to disguise its regulatory obligations as contractual ones, the Court's precedent applies in these circumstances. Accordingly, we reject Taylor's efforts to circumvent its regulatory duty to address the 14-mile oil slick flowing from its leaking wells by purporting to assert claims under Louisiana state law.

Because OCSLA regulations address the arguments underlying Taylor's contract claims, we conclude that Louisiana state law cannot be adopted as surrogate law and that Taylor's complaint fails to state a claim upon which relief may be granted. We therefore affirm.

[1] The Outer Continental Shelf comprises "all submerged lands lying seaward and outside of the area of lands beneath navigable waters" within the Gulf of Mexico or "any of the Great Lakes as they existed at the time such State became a member of the Union." 43 U.S.C. § 1331(a).

I. BACKGROUND

A. A Lessee's Statutory and Regulatory Obligations on the Outer Continental Shelf

The Department of the Interior ("DOI") and its administering arms, the Bureau of Ocean Energy Management ("BOEM") and the Bureau of Safety and Environmental Enforcement ("BSEE"), promulgate and enforce the regulations necessary to administer oil and gas leases under the **[—4—]** OCSLA. 43 U.S.C. §§ 1334, 1348. Oil and gas producers, moreover, are subject to regulations promulgated under the National Oil and Hazardous Substances Pollution Contingency Plan ("NCP"), which provide the organization and procedures for responding to oil pollution. *See* 40 C.F.R. § 300. Together, these regulations highlight two themes: OCS lessees are (1) held to certain regulatory obligations under federal law; and (2) strictly liable for any pollution generated by their oil and gas operations.

A company holding a lease to oil and gas wells on the OCS accrues certain "pollution prevention" obligations. 30 C.F.R. § 250.300(a). Among these is the obligation to "decommission"—winding down operations on the OCS after the lease ends. 30 C.F.R. §§ 30 C.F.R. § 250.1700(a) (defining decommissioning as "[e]nding oil, gas, or sulphur operations" and "[r]eturning the lease or pipeline right-of-way to a condition that meets the requirements of regulations of BSEE and other agencies that have jurisdiction over decommissioning activities."). To fulfill its decommissioning obligations, an OCS lessee must, among other duties, permanently plug all wells; remove all platforms and other facilities; decommission all pipelines; and clear the seafloor of all obstructions. **{-1307-}** 30 C.F.R. § 250.1703(b)–(e). A lessee must complete its decommissioning obligations within one year after the lease terminates, unless BSEE authorizes alternate procedures or departures.[2] 30 C.F.R. §§ 250.1725, 250.141.

[2] The alternate procedures must provide a level of safety and environmental protection that equals or surpasses the regulatory requirement. 30 C.F.R. § 250.141(a).

To ensure that lessees have the financial means to satisfy their regulatory obligations under the OCSLA, lessees must maintain a bond or other security instrument. 30 C.F.R. § 556.900. For example, BOEM will not issue a new lease or approve the assignment of an existing lease until **[—5—]** the lessee maintains a "lease or area-wide" bond with the Regional Director. 30 C.F.R. § 556.900(a). *See also* 30 C.F.R. § 556.105 ("Regional Director means the BOEM officer with responsibility and authority for a Region within BOEM."). This is not the only type of security interest a lessee might expect to maintain, however. BOEM may determine, for example, that "additional security" is necessary "to ensure [a lessee's] compliance with the obligations under [its] lease," and has broad discretion to determine the supplemental amount. 30 C.F.R. §§ 556.901(d)–(e). In adjusting the amount of additional bond required, the agency may consider "cumulative decommissioning obligations." 30 C.F.R. § 556.901(c) ("[T]he authorized officer may accept a lease surety bond in an amount less than the prescribed amount, but not less than the amount of the cost for decommissioning."); 30 C.F.R. § 556.901(e) ("The Regional Director will consider potential underpayment of royalty and cumulative decommissioning obligations.").

BOEM may alternatively authorize lessees to establish "lease-specific abandonment accounts" to satisfy their decommissioning obligations. 30 C.F.R. § 556.904. Funds deposited into a lease-specific abandonment account must be "pledged to meet [the lessee's] decommissioning obligations" and cover "all decommissioning costs as estimated by BOEM within the timeframe the Regional Director prescribes." 30 C.F.R. § 556.904(a)(1)–(2). Funds may not be withdrawn without the written approval of the Regional Director. 30 C.F.R. § 556.904(a).

An OCS lessee's duties are not limited to preventative and decommissioning measures, moreover. Under the Clean Water Act, facility owners are strictly liable for any discharge of oil in navigable waters unless an exception

[—6—] applies.[3] 33 U.S.C. § 1321 (1982). The Oil Pollution Act further establishes that a lessee whose facilities discharge oil is considered a "responsible party," and is liable for all removal costs. *See* 33 U.S.C. § 2702. A responsible party for an offshore facility is responsible for up to all removal costs plus $75,000,000. 33 U.S.C. § 2704(a)(3).

B. Taylor's OCS Leases and the MC-20 Trust Agreement

In 1994, Taylor became the lessee and operator of three leases covering areas on the OCS. *Taylor Energy Co. v. United States*, 142 Fed. Cl. 601, 605 (Fed. Cl. 2019) ("*Taylor Energy*"); J.A. 37. The leases, which were set to expire on June 28, 2007, incorporated then-present and any later-enacted OCSLA-related regulations. J.A. 193, 199, 205. They also required Taylor to leave the leased area "in a manner satisfactory to the [Regional] Director." J.A. 196, 201, 209. During the lifetime of these leases, Taylor and its predecessor **{-1308-}** drilled twenty-eight wells, each connected to a single oil platform called MC-20. *Taylor Energy*, 142 Fed. Cl. at 605. In 2004, prior to the leases' expiration, Hurricane Ivan toppled Taylor's platform onto the ocean floor, resulting in significant damage to the wells and rendering them inoperable. *Id.* Taylor surveyed the wreckage and discovered oil leaking from the area, but took no actions to stop the leaks at the time. J.A. 290–91.

Approximately three years later, Taylor's MC-20 leases expired. J.A. 39 § 16. Accordingly, DOI's Mineral Management Service ("MMS")—the precursor agency to BSEE and BOEM—ordered Taylor to decommission all the wells at MC-20 within one year. J.A. 39. At that point, twenty-five of the twenty-eight wells at MC-20 needed to be decommissioned. J.A. 38. Due to complications from the hurricane [—7—] damage, Taylor wrote to MMS requesting a departure from the default one-year decommission period. J.A. 825–29. *See also* 30 C.F.R. § 250.1710. It asked for an "indefinite time extension" for the completion of its well-abandonment and structure-removal obligations, insisting that it would keep MMS informed as to its progress. J.A. 826. MMS rejected Taylor's request for an "indefinite term," but it did not require Taylor to complete its MC-20 decommissioning obligations within one year.

By 2008, Taylor had sold and assigned all of its remaining OCS leases. J.A. 40. MMS, which held approval authority over the assignment of OCS leases, allowed the assignment but placed a condition on the sale: Taylor needed to set aside part of the sale proceeds to fund all decommissioning obligations at MC-20. J.A. 40. Accordingly, on March 19, 2008, Taylor as the "Settlor," MMS as the "Beneficiary," and JPMorgan Chase Bank as the "Trustee" executed a trust agreement ("the Trust Agreement"). J.A. 72. The Trust Agreement also incorporates an Agreement to Provide Additional Bond ("the Bond Agreement"), which provides details about the "additional bond" required by MMS. J.A. 93.

As described by the document, the purpose of the agreement is to provide financial security for "certain obligations to plug and abandon wells, remove a portion of the platform and facilities, clear the seafloor of obstructions, and take corrective action associated with wells and facilities on [MC-20]." J.A. 72, 74. Schedule A provides the cost estimates for Taylor's regulatory obligations, including: (1) plugging and abandoning twenty-five wells; (2) removing the platform deck; (3) clearing the seafloor of obstructions; (4) removing pipelines; and (5) removing contaminated soil. J.A. 41 ¶ 25; J.A. 97–98. Notably, the Trust Agreement incorporates OCSLA decommissioning regulations in two areas. First, Schedule A states that Taylor's work "will conform to MMS regulations contained in 30 CFR 250 Subpart Q . . . and Subpart C." J.A. 97. [—8—] Second, the Trust incorporates the terms of the MC-20 leases, which each expressly incorporate OCSLA regulations. J.A. 193, 199, 205. For Taylor to receive reimbursement for completing its decommissioning obligations, the government must confirm the work was conducted "in material compliance with all

[3] 33 U.S.C. § 1321(c)(4)(A) lists the exemptions from liability, which do not apply to the facts underlying this appeal.

applicable federal laws and . . . regulations . . . [and with] the terms and conditions of the Lease(s)." J.A. 86. The Trust Agreement, however, also includes a choice of law provision that it "shall be governed by and construed in accordance with the laws of the State of Louisiana without giving effect to that state's conflict of laws rules." J.A. 94 ¶ 6.9.

Under the Bond Agreement, Taylor deposited $466,280,000 into a trust account based on MMS's "Area-wide Bond Order," and an additional $200,000,000 in compliance with MMS's "Supplemental Bond Order." **{-1309-}** J.A. 2389. The Bond Agreement states that the account was established "in accordance with the requirements of 30 C.F.R. § 256.56 [now 30 § 556.904]"—the regulation governing lease-specific abandonment accounts. J.A. 2392. Notably, it stipulates that "[n]either acceptance of this Agreement by MMS nor fulfillment of this Agreement by Taylor shall limit Taylor's abandonment obligations on the Leases nor MMS's right to require additional bonding to guarantee performance of Taylor's [decommissioning obligations." J.A. 2391.

C. Taylor's Decommissioning Efforts

Following the termination of Taylor's MC-20 leases, Taylor attempted to fulfill its decommissioning obligations. This, however, proved to be difficult. The unique wreckage that resulted from the hurricane hampered "conventional plugging and abandonment techniques." J.A. 39. Thus, the Coast Guard, Taylor, and MMS established a "Unified Command" to direct all response efforts to contain and clean up the spill at MC-20. J.A. 39. Through the Unified Command, the participants performed studies and created **[—9—]** plans to best perform clean-up at MC-20. The government ultimately approved a departure from certain standard decommissioning procedures, allowing Taylor to plug and abandon wells by drilling intervention wells. J.A. 45–46. From April 2008 until March 2011, Taylor drilled intervention wells on nine of the twenty-five wells. J.A. 47–48.

D. The CERA and FRACE Workshops

In 2012, the Unified Command established two working groups to study the risks associated with drilling intervention wells and the conditions of the contaminated soil. J.A. 49, 51. After the working groups completed their assessment, the Unified Command created a workshop to conduct a Consensus Ecological Risk Assessment ("CERA") and evaluate the potential ecological impacts of responses. J.A. 275–76. The CERA workshop released a report in July 2013 (the "CERA Report"), concluding that the risks associated with the planned procedures outweighed any ecological benefits of performing those tasks. J.A. 52, 263–324.

After the CERA workshop, the Unified Command conducted a Final Risk Assessment and Cost Estimate ("FRACE") workshop. J.A. 54. The purpose of the FRACE workshop was to reach a conclusion on the "remaining risk posed by the MC-20 site and the estimated cost to mitigate that risk." *Id.* The FRACE workshop considered expert studies from both Taylor and the government, *id*, and relied on an assumption that only a few gallons a day were leaking from the MC-20 site. At the end of the workshop, the government requested additional time to reach a conclusion but did not take further action. J.A. 55.

E. The "United States Views" Document

In March 2014, Taylor began taking steps to relieve itself of its decommissioning obligations and recover the remaining funds in the trust account. Relying on the FRACE workshop and its supporting documents, Taylor filed two departure requests with BSEE: (1) to grant departures **[—10—]** from further intervention well decommissioning for the remaining sixteen wells; and (2) to grant a departure or alternative procedure authorizing Taylor to leave any contaminated soil at MC-20 in place.[4] J.A. 56–57; J.A. 575. **{-1310-}**

[4] At this point, BSEE and BOEM had replaced MMS via new legislation.

On May 11, 2015, BSEE denied Taylor's requests. J.A. 574–78. The agency first explained that the FRACE workshop's assumptions regarding the daily oil leakage appeared to be incorrect. It observed that "there continues to be an oil sheen on the sea surface" and that "the average reported daily oil volume on the sea surface over the past seven months has been over two barrels [or 84 gallons]." J.A. 575. BSEE also noted that Taylor had not provided clear evidence that "hydrocarbons are coming from decontaminated sediment and not from leaking or unplugged wells." J.A. 576. The agency further explained that Taylor's requests for departure were denied because of the "continuing discharge of oil from the MC-20 site," "Taylor's inability to contain the discharge," and "the possibility that future plugging and abandonment work and/or the removal of contaminated sediments may be required." J.A. 57, 578.

Three days after BSEE denied Taylor's departure request, BSEE, BOEM, the Coast Guard, and the Department of Justice jointly issued a two-page document describing the United States' views on the status of the ongoing oil leaks and Taylor's obligations at MC-20 ("the U.S. Views document"). J.A. 56, 565–66. The U.S. Views document notes that the ongoing oil discharge far exceeds the CERA and FRACE workshops' assumption of an oil discharge comprising a few gallons a day. J.A. 565. The document makes clear that the United States does not agree with the CERA report's conclusions, J.A. 566, and that Taylor's decommissioning efforts up until then had been deficient. J.A. 566 (explaining that even if "proper well **[—11—]** plugging and abandonment is not currently technologically feasible, there is still more that can be done to control and contain the oil that is discharging from the well site"). It acknowledges Taylor's request to recover the remaining $432 million in the trust account but concludes that reduction in funding is unwarranted because the cost of decommissioning the remaining wells likely exceeds the amount held in the Trust. *Id.* Because "[i]t would be contrary to the public interest and inappropriate under applicable law to provide Taylor Energy a release of liability," the document determines that "Taylor Energy must continue to work to permanently stop the ongoing spill." *Id.* at 565–66.[5]

F. Taylor's IBLA Appeal

On July 9, 2015, Taylor filed a notice of appeal of the BSEE denial with the Interior Board of Land Appeals ("IBLA"). J.A. 440–44. This too, was denied. J.A. 3334–53.

With respect to BSEE's refusal to relieve Taylor of its duty to plug and abandon the MC-20 wells, the IBLA explained that the agency was entitled to defer any action on decommissioning while it "consider[ed] additional research studies" for further improvements in decommissioning the remaining wells. J.A. 3348. "To preclude BSEE from awaiting changes in technology and a better understanding **[—12—]** of the undersea environment improperly constrains its statutory and regulatory authority over offshore well decommissioning and unnecessarily limits its overriding responsibility to protect the environment from the adverse consequences of offshore drilling and production." J.A. 3349. The IBLA **{-1311-}** concluded that BSEE had a rational basis, supported by the administrative record, to decline relieving Taylor of its regulatory obligation to permanently plug and abandon the wells at that time.

The IBLA also found that BSEE had a rational basis for denying Taylor's request to leave contaminated sediment in place. J.A. 3351. It explained that BSEE properly denied Taylor's request because, based on the evidence contained in the record, the agency remained convinced that the contaminated sediment posed a continuing threat to the undersea environment. J.A. 3349. "Given

[5] The existence of the U.S. Views document and the opinions and conclusions on which it was based directly refutes Taylor's claim at oral argument that "it is undisputed that Taylor Energy can take no further measures to decommission the MC-20 site without doing more environmental harm than good." *Taylor Energy Co., LLC v. United States*, No. 19-1983, Oral Arg. at 0:33–0:55, *available at* http://oralarguments.cafc.uscourts.gov/default.aspx?fl=19-1983.mp3.

uncertainty regarding the source of the sheen, its continuing presence on the surface, and a potential need for Taylor to remove contaminated sediment in the future," the IBLA concluded that BSEE's denial was supported by the administrative record. J.A. 3351. Notably, the IBLA characterized the trust account as a "lease-specific abandonment account," created "to provide a secure source of funding for decommissioning undertaken by Taylor or by BSEE (in the event of default by Taylor)." J.A. 3337. Taylor did not appeal the IBLA decision.[6] **[—13—]**

II. PROCEDURAL HISTORY

Rather than appeal the IBLA decision to federal district court, Taylor filed suit against the government in the Court of Federal Claims. Taylor's complaint asserts four claims involving Louisiana state law: (1) breach of the Trust Agreement for inserting an indefinite term (Count I); (2) request for dissolution of the trust account based on impossibility of performance (Count II); (3) request for reformation or recission based on mutual error (Count III); and (4) breach of the duty of good faith and fair dealing (Count IV). J.A. 60–70. In response, the United States filed a 12(b)(1) motion to dismiss for lack of jurisdiction based on the six-year statute of limitations. The government also moved to dismiss under Rule 12(b)(6) for failure to state a claim.

The Claims Court denied the United States' 12(b)(1) motion but granted the Rule 12(b)(6) motion and dismissed the case. With respect to the government's 12(b)(6) motion, the court determined that Taylor's indefinite period claim (Count I) failed to state a claim upon which relief could be granted. Applying Louisiana law, the court explained that "no particular language is required to create a trust" and the Trust Agreement "without question established a trust." *Id.* at 610 (citing La. Stat. Ann § 9:1753). The court further noted that, under Louisiana law, a trust without an explicit term has a default expiration of "fifty years from the creation of the trust." *Id.* at 610 (quoting La. Stat. Ann. § 9:1831(4)). Thus, the court reasoned that the Government could not be held liable for inserting an indefinite **[—14—]** term until 2058—fifty years after the creation of the trust.[7] *Id.* The Claims Court then concluded **{-1312-}** that, for the same reason, the government could not be held liable for breaching its implied duty of good faith and fair dealing (Count IV) until fifty years had passed. *Id.* at 610–11.

The court then determined that Taylor's remaining claims of impossibility and mutual mistake (Counts II and III) failed to state a claim because "Taylor's federal obligations under the Trust Agreement are not governed by state law." *Id.* at 611. The court noted that the Trust Agreement "was established to fulfill Taylor's federal regulatory obligations," and that these obligations do not terminate until the Department of Interior says they may. *Id.* The Claims Court explained that a finding of impossibility or mutual mistake would "second guess the IBLA" and independently relieve Taylor of its regulatory obligations. *Id.* at 611 ("[U]ntil Taylor is relieved of its federal decommissioning obligations by Interior, this court cannot find on its own that it is 'impossible' for Taylor to

---

[6] An IBLA decision must be appealed to a United States district court. 5 U.S.C. §§ 701–06 (1976). Neither the Claims Court nor this court is empowered to review IBLA decisions. *See also Underwood Livestock, Inc. v. United States*, 89 Fed. Cl. 287, 290 (2009), *aff'd*, 417 Fed. Appx. 934, 939 (Fed. Cir. 2011) (holding that the Claims Court and the Federal Circuit do not have jurisdiction to review IBLA decisions). In addition, both this court and the Supreme Court have recognized the binding effect of **[—13—]** IBLA decisions on related lawsuits before the Claims Court. *United States v. Utah Constructions and Mining Co.*, 384 U.S. 394, 422–23 (1966); *Aulston v. United States*, 823 F.2d 510, 514–15 (Fed. Cir. 1987).

[7] The parties disputed whether the Claims Court should apply Louisiana law or federal law in interpreting the disputed provisions of the Trust Agreement. *Taylor Energy*, 142 Fed. Cl. at 609. The Claims Court, however, declined to address this issue, explaining that it was "a matter that d[id] not have to be presently resolved." Rather, it concluded that, "to the extent the Trust Agreement regarding the length of performance or term must be construed using Louisiana law . . . Taylor's claim that the Trust Agreement is a contract under Louisiana law is not supported." *Id.* at 610.

comply with its Trust Agreement obligations or that the Trust Agreement was entered based on a mutual mistake."). It then rejected Taylor's argument that the court must "separate Taylor's regulatory obligations under the Trust Agreement from its regulatory obligations under the OCSLA," explaining that **[—15—]** such an argument "ignores the fact that the Trust Agreement was entered into to ensure compliance with Taylor's federal regulatory obligations." *Id.* at 612. The Claims Court dismissed Taylor's complaint in its entirety under Rule 12(b)(6) and denied Taylor's motion for summary judgment as moot.

Taylor appealed the Claims Court's determination. We have jurisdiction pursuant to 28 U.S.C. § 1295(a)(3).

III. Discussion

"This court reviews *de novo* whether the Court of Federal Claims possessed jurisdiction and whether the Court of Federal Claims properly dismissed for failure to state a claim upon which relief can be granted, as both are questions of law." *Turping v. United States*, 913 F.3d 1060, 1064 (Fed. Cir. 2019) (quoting *Wheeler v. United States*, 11 F.3d 156, 158 (Fed. Cir. 1993)).

Taylor argues that the Claims Court erred in dismissing Counts II and III of its complaint because, under Louisiana state law, it plausibly stated a claim for dissolution based on impossibility and reformation based on mutual error. Appellant Br. 37–40. It contends that Counts I and IV properly alleged that the Trust Agreement includes an implicit term requiring performance within a "reasonable time," pursuant to La Civ. Code Art. 1778. And it maintains that the Claims Court's reliance on Louisiana *trust* law was erroneous because Louisiana *contract* law applies. *Id.* at 55.

We need not reach any of those arguments. In the context of OCS-based claims, state law does not apply if federal law addresses the relevant issue. As evident from the **[—16—]** text of the Trust Agreement, the issues underlying Taylor's claims are governed by federal law.[8] **{-1313-}**

A.

"The purpose of the Lands Act was to define a body of law applicable to the seabed, the subsoil, and the fixed structures . . . on the outer Continental Shelf." *Rodrigue v. Aetna Cas. & Sur. Co.*, 395 U.S. 352, 355 (1969). That this law was to be federal law "is made clear by the language of the Act." *Id.* at 355–56. The OCSLA denies states any interest in or jurisdiction over the OCS, and it deems the adjacent state's laws to be federal law only in limited circumstances. *Parker Drilling*, 139 S. Ct. at 1886, 7 Adm. R. at 36. Section 1333(a)(2)(A) provides:

> *To the extent that they are applicable and not inconsistent* with this subchapter or with other Federal laws and regulations of the Secretary now in effect or hereafter adopted, the civil and criminal laws of **[—17—]** each adjacent State, now in effect or hereafter adopted, amended, or repealed are declared to be the law of the United States for that portion of the subsoil and seabed of the outer Continental Shelf, and artificial islands and fixed structures erected thereon, which would be within the area of the State if its boundaries were

---

[8] The government also argues in its responsive brief that the Trust Agreement is a regulatory instrument in its entirety, such that "no contractual remedy can be available for any breach by the government." Appellee Br. 44–45; *id.* at 41–53. *See also* J.A. 3337 (finding that the trust account is a lease-specific abandonment account as defined in the governing OCSLA regulations). Although this argument is compelling, *see, e.g.*, *Anderson v. United States*, 344 F.3d 1343 (Fed. Cir. 2003) (holding that regulatory boilerplate provisions, added by the government as a regulator, are not contracts), the government appeared to concede during oral argument that the Trust Agreement *is* a contract. *See Taylor Energy Co., LLC v. United States*, No. 19-1983, Oral Arg. at 18:55–19:25, *available at* http://oralarguments.cafc.uscourts.gov/default.aspx?fl=19-1983.mp3. Accordingly, although this issue may have been dispositive, we decline to address it.

> extended seaward to the outer margin of the Continental Shelf . . . .

43 U.S.C. § 1333(a)(2)(A) (emphasis added). Section 1333(a)(3) emphasizes that "[t]he provisions of this section for adoption of State law as the law of the United States shall never be interpreted as a basis for claiming any interest in or jurisdiction on behalf of any State for any purpose over the" OCS.

In *Parker Drilling Management Services, Ltd. v. Newton*, the Supreme Court clarified the meaning of the phrase, "to the extent that they are applicable and not inconsistent with other federal law," under § 1333(a)(2)(A). 139 S. Ct. at 1888, 7 Adm. R. at 37. The Court concluded that "state laws can be 'applicable and not inconsistent' with federal law under § 1333(a)(2)(A) only if federal law does not address the relevant issue." *Parker Drilling*, 139 S. Ct. at 1887–89, 7 Adm. R. at 37–38. It rejected the respondent's argument that state law is inconsistent "only if it would be pre-empted under [the Court's] ordinary pre-emption principles." Such an interpretation, explained the Court, is unsupported by the statutory text. *Id.* at 1888, 7 Adm. R. at 38. It noted that OCSLA "extends all federal law to the OCS, and instead of also extending state law writ large, it borrows only certain state laws." *Id.* at 1889, 7 Adm. R. at 38. And, it explained, "[g]iven the primacy of federal law on the OCS and the limited role of state law, it would make little sense to treat the OCS as a mere extension of the adjacent State." *Id.*, 7 Adm. R. at 38.

Taylor asserts that *Parker Drilling* "does not alter the analysis of Taylor Energy's claims." Appellant Br. 35 n.10. It alleges that *Parker Drilling* "adopted the rule of the Fifth **[—18—]** Circuit, which has repeatedly held that state law, as surrogate federal law, governs breach-of-contract claims on the OCS." *Id.* And it argues that, at most, we should remand the case to the Claims Court to consider "the impact of *Parker Drilling*" in the first instance. *Id.*

We disagree. *Parker Drilling* makes clear that its holding accords with **{-1314-}** the standard "long applied by the Fifth Circuit" that "state law only applies to the extent it is necessary to fill a significant void or gap in federal law." 139 S. Ct. at 1886, 7 Adm. R. at 36 (internal quotations omitted); *id.* at 1889, 7 Adm. R. at 39 (citing *Continental Oil Co. v. London Steam-Ship Owners' Mut. Ins. Assn.*, 417 F.2d 1030, 1036 (1969)). In so stating, the Court did not broadly exempt its holding from "breach-of-contract claims on the OCS." This makes sense. "All law on the OCS is federal, and state law serves a supporting role, to be adopted only where there is a gap in federal law's coverage." *Parker Drilling*, 136 S. Ct. at 1892, 7 Adm. R. at 41. Thus, when interpreting an OCS contract, state contract law applies only to the extent it is "applicable and not inconsistent" with federal law.[9]

B.

Against this legal backdrop, it is clear that Louisiana state law applies only where there is a "gap" in federal law. This application of the law, however, dooms Taylor's appeal. All of the issues underlying Taylor's claims—*e.g.*, the duration of Taylor's decommissioning obligations, the **[—19—]** possibility of completing such tasks, and the reimbursement process—are addressed by OCSLA regulations.

For instance, Counts I and IV of Taylor's complaint are premised on the application of La Civ. Code Art. 1778, which requires completion of a party's contracted performance within a "reasonable time" when the agreement is silent as to the term. J.A. 60–63. But federal law already addresses the amount of time available to an OCS lessee for completion of its decommissioning obligations. A lessee generally must complete its decommissioning obligations within a year, but BSEE has the authority to modify the required term at any time. 30 C.F.R. §§

[9] Indeed, we note that the Fifth Circuit case upon which Taylor relies acknowledges that "Louisiana contract law governs the interpretation of the [OCS] contracts at issue, to the extent that law is applicable and not inconsistent with OCSLA or with other Federal laws and regulations." *Total E&P USA, Inc. v. Kerr-McGee Oil & Gas Corp.*, 719 F.3d 424, 434 (5th Cir. 2013) (internal quotations omitted).

250.1725, 250.141. A lessee, moreover, remains liable for decommissioning until all of its wells have been successfully decommissioned to regulatory standards, *or* the lessee has obtained express departures from those requirements. 30 C.F.R. § 250.1701(a). Accordingly, La. Civ. Code Art. 1778, which would effectively limit the duration of a lessee's liability in conflict with the OCSLA, does not provide the rule of decision on the OCS. To the extent Taylor's OCS-based claims rely on that law, they necessarily fail.

Similarly, Counts II and III of Taylor's complaint rely on La. Civ. Code Art. 1876 and 1877, which provide that a contract is dissolved "[w]hen the entire performance owed by one party has become impossible," J.A. 64–68, but the satisfaction and feasibility of a lessee's decommissioning obligations is already addressed by federal law, 30 C.F.R. §§ 250.1703, 250.1753–250.1754. In addition, as discussed above, a lessee's liability does not end until "each obligation is met" or BSEE authorizes an express departure. 30 C.F.R. §§ 250.1701, 250.1725, 585.103. Therefore, Louisiana state law addressing the "impossibility" of a lessee's decommissioning obligations is not adopted as federal law and does not apply.

Finally, to the extent Taylor's OCS-based claims rely on La. Civ. Code Art. 1759 to allege that Taylor is entitled **[—20—]** to recover the remaining trust funds, J.A. 68, federal law already provides guidance **{-1315-}** on the financial security related to a lessee's decommissioning obligations. 30 C.F.R. § 556.900 *et seq.* As provided by 30 C.F.R. § 556.900, lessees must maintain a bond or security instrument to finance their regulatory obligations under the OCSLA. BOEM is authorized to order "additional security" to ensure a lessee's compliance with its decommissioning obligations. 30 C.F.R. 556.901(d)–(e). And with respect to a "lease-specific abandonment account," such as the one formed by the Trust Agreement, funds may not be withdrawn without the written approval of the BOEM regional director. 30 C.F.R. § 556.904. Accordingly, Louisiana state law does not apply to the maintenance of a lessee's OCSLA financial security.

Indeed, the Trust Agreement itself acknowledges the applicability of OCSLA regulations to the terms of the agreement. It incorporates the terms of the MC-20 leases, as well as the "applicable federal regulations related to such Leases." J.A. 74. Schedule A also reaffirms the relevance of federal law, explaining that Taylor's "work plan and obligations under this Trust [A]greement will conform to MMS regulations contained in 30 C.F.R 250 Subpart Q . . . and Subpart C." J.A. 97. The incorporated Bond Agreement, moreover, provides that the trust account was established in accordance with the lease-specific abandonment account requirements of 30 C.F.R. § 256.56 [now 30 C.F.R. § 556.904]. J.A. 2392. The Trust Agreement's repeated references to the OCSLA regulations erase any doubt that federal law governs the issues underlying the agreement.

Taylor presents two arguments to the contrary—both of which are premised on a misreading of precedent and inconsistent with the Court's holding in *Parker Drilling*.

First, Taylor alleges that state law applies because the Trust Agreement formed separate contractual obligations answerable only to state contract law. Appellant Br. 43. **[—21—]** Notably, Taylor does not dispute that federal law addresses the issues underlying these "contractual" duties. Rather, citing to the D.C. Circuit's decisions in *Noble Energy*, Taylor maintains that when the government and a lessee enter into a contract, the government's breach can release the lessee from its contractual obligations, regardless of whether they are otherwise mandated by regulation. Appellant Br. 43; *see Noble Energy, Inc. v. Salazar ("Noble I")*, 671 F.3d 1241 (D.C. Cir. 2012); *Noble Energy, Inc. v. Jewell ("Noble II")*, 650 F. App'x 9 (D.C. Cir. 2016). In other words, Taylor argues that the creation of the trust agreement somehow transformed its regulatory obligations into independent contractual obligations, which are no longer subject to federal law. Appellant Br. 43. And, because the Trust Agreement's choice of law provision refers to "the laws of the State of Louisiana," Taylor reasons that all of its claims are subject to Louisiana state contract law. Appellant Br. 43.

Taylor's reliance on *Noble Energy* is unfounded. There, the lessee, Noble, acquired a lease to drill for oil on roughly six thousand acres of submerged lands off the coast of California. *Noble I,* 671 F.3d at 1242. It drilled one exploratory well, but temporarily plugged and abandoned the well for twenty-seven years. *Id.* During those years, Noble applied for and received several suspensions on its lease.[10] *Id.* In 1999, two years into its last suspension's **{-1316-}** four-year term, a district court set the suspension aside based on new amendments to the Coastal Zone Management Act. *Id.* The new amendments required suspensions to be consistent with state management plans and Noble's suspension had not been assessed for consistency with California's **[—22—]** coastal management plan. *Id.* Accordingly, it was revoked. Reviewing the Court of Claims' judgment in a suit brought by Noble against the government based on these facts, we held the government effectively had repudiated the lease agreements by applying a newly enacted law not foreseen by the original lease. *Id.*; *Amber Res. Co. v. United States,* 538 F.3d 1358 (Fed Cir. 2008). Noble received restitution for the breach of contract and was discharged from all obligations arising from its lease agreements. *Noble I,* 671 F.3d at 1243. Among its discharged contractual duties was the obligation to "remove all devices, works, and structures from the premises no longer subject to the lease." *Id.*

Subsequently, MMS contacted Noble and ordered it to complete its decommissioning obligations. *Id.* at 1243–44. Noble refused. *Id.* at 1344. It argued that the government's breach discharged the lessees from any obligations recited in the contract, including its obligation to "conduct, arrange or pay for the plugging and abandonment of the 320 # 2 exploratory well." *Id.* Noble then sued the Secretary of the Interior and MMS in federal district court, seeking injunctive and declaratory relief. *Id.* The district court determined, however, that the common law doctrine of discharge did not relieve Noble of its regulatory obligation to plug its well permanently because that obligation was not created by the lease, but by federal regulation.

After initially remanding the case to the agency for clarity on the scope of § 250.1700 *et seq.*, the D.C. Circuit affirmed. *Id.* at 1245–46; *Noble II,* 650 F. App'x at 11. It relied on BSEE's explanation that the regulations governing a lessee's decommissioning obligations, 30 C.F.R. § 250.1700 *et seq.*, operate independently from any lease agreement and impose an independent obligation on Noble to permanently plug the well. "Because the regulations impose an obligation to plug Well 320-2 regardless of the government's breach of the lease contract, Noble's argument fail[ed]." *Noble II,* 650 F. App'x at 11. **[—23—]**

Stripped of Taylor's mischaracterized depiction, the *Noble Energy* cases do little for the appellant. The underlying facts are different here (in *Noble Energy,* the government breached a *lease agreement* by subjecting the lessee to *new "court-mandated" rules*); a significant portion of the D.C. Circuit's analysis addresses the meaning and scope of § 250.1700 *et seq.*, (which is not at issue here); and most importantly, Noble was still required to complete its regulatory decommissioning obligations. *Noble Energy* does not suggest that a lessee may be relieved of its regulatory obligations in the event of a breach, just because those obligations were incorporated into the trust agreement. Rather, *Noble Energy* holds that a party must comply with its contractual duties if they are mandated by federal law, even if the contract is ultimately dissolved.

Taylor's second argument—that state contract law principles apply to contracts between the government and a private party, even where the contract incorporates regulatory duties—also mischaracterizes the case upon which it relies. Appellant Br. 41 (citing *Mobil Oil Exploration & Producing Southeast v. United States,* 530 U.S. 604, 607 (2000)). **{-1317-}**

In *Mobil Oil,* two oil companies sought restitution of a $156 million up-front payment

---

[10] A suspension extends the life of a lease, which is generally five years, and defers the lessee's obligation to produce oil. *Noble I,* 671 F.3d at 1242 (citing 43 U.S.C. §§ 1334(a)(1), 1337(b)(2) & 5).

they made to the Government in exchange for ten-year renewable lease contracts. *Mobil Oil*, 530 U.S. at 607. Under the governing agreements, the leases would provide the lessees with rights to explore and develop oil off the North Carolina coast, so long as the companies received certain permissions governed by certain federal statutes. 530 U.S. at 610–612. While the companies attempted to obtain the necessary permissions, the Outer Banks Protection Act ("OBPA") came into effect, prohibiting approval of any exploration plan or drilling permit unless several *new* requirements were met. *Id.* at 612. Because the Secretary could not approve the plans until these new regulations were met, the petitioners' plans were delayed and later denied. Petitioners brought **[—24—]** a breach of contract lawsuit in the Claims Court. The court ruled in favor of the petitioners, we reversed, and the Supreme Court reversed our judgment.

Because the Secretary denied the lessee's plans for failure to comply with the new OBPA regulations, the Court concluded that the government violated the contracts. *Id.* at 618. It explained that the OBPA changed the pre-existing contract-incorporated requirements in several ways, that the changes were of a kind that the contracts did not foresee, and that the government communicated its intent to violate the contracts when it expressed its intent to follow OBPA. *Id.* at 619–621. After concluding that the companies did not receive significant post-repudiation performance, the Court ordered the government to refund certain sums to the companies. *Id.* at 624.

Mobil Oil has little relevance in the present appeal. In *Mobil Oil*, the government repudiated the lease agreement because its denials relied on *newly created* statutory authority, outside of those statutes and provisions incorporated in the original lease agreement, *id.* at 615. In contrast, BSEE's refusal to grant Taylor's departure request is in compliance with the OCSLA, and the Trust Agreement specifically references the OCSLA regulations that govern the parties' contractual duties. *Mobil Oil* says nothing about the application of state law to provisions governed by federal regulation at the time the parties entered into the original lease agreement. To the extent Taylor asserts that *Mobil Oil* stands for the proposition that state law *is* applicable in such circumstances, any such holding was certainly abrogated by *Parker Drilling*.

Because Taylor fails to state a claim to relief that is plausible on its face, its complaint must be dismissed. *Ashcroft v. Iqbal*, 556 U.S. 662, 678 (2009). **[—25—]**

III. Conclusion

For these reasons, the Claims Court's order dismissing Taylor's complaint is affirmed.

AFFIRMED

Costs

Costs to Appellee.

This page intentionally left blank

Tables of Authority

This page intentionally left blank

Table of Cases

This page intentionally left blank

TABLE OF CASES[1]

PAGE

[1] Cases named solely after ships, *see, e.g., The Pennsylvania*, 86 U.S. (19 Wall.) 125 (1873), are alphabetized under the letter "T." Cases where the United States is the plaintiff are alphabetized by defendant under the letter "U."

B

C

D

E

F

G

H

I

J

K

L

M

N

O

P

Q

R

S

T

U

V

W

Y

Z

This page intentionally left blank

Table of Statutes and Rules

This page intentionally left blank

Table of Statutes and Rules[1]

Page

Treaties/International

Federal

Constitution

Miscellaneous

[1] As cited in the opinions reported.

STATUTES

RULES

REGULATIONS

State

This page intentionally left blank

Index

This page intentionally left blank

Index

Page

A

C

D

E

F

G

H

I

J

L

M

N

O

P

R

S

T

U

V

W

This page intentionally left blank

www.ingramcontent.com/pod-product-compliance
Lightning Source LLC
LaVergne TN
LVHW060011210926
848481LV00013B/3685